The College of Law
of England and Wales

LIBRARY & INFORMATION SERVICES

FOR REFERENCE ONLY
Not to be removed from the
Chambers Library

MEDICAL NEGLIGENCE

AUSTRALIA
Law Book Co
Sydney

CANADA AND USA
Carswell
Toronto

HONG KONG
Sweet & Maxwell Asia

NEW ZEALAND
Brookers
Wellington

SINGAPORE AND MALAYSIA
Sweet & Maxwell Asia
Singapore and Kuala Lumpur

MEDICAL NEGLIGENCE

by

Michael A. Jones B.A., LL.M., Ph.D.,
Solicitor of the Supreme Court
Professor of Common Law of the University of Liverpool

London
Sweet & Maxwell
2003

First Edition 1991
Second Edition 1996
Third Edition 2003

Published in 2003 by
Sweet & Maxwell Limited of
100 Avenue Road London NW3 3PF
http://www.sweetandmaxwell.co.uk
Typeset by Servis Filmsetting Ltd, Manchester
Printed and bound in Great Britain by
MPG Books Ltd, Bodmin, Cornwall

No natural forests were destroyed to
make this product: only farmed timber
was used and replanted

ISBN 0421 717 300

A catalogue record for this book is available
from the British Library

ISBN 0421-717-30-0

9 780421 717305

FOR ANNIE

PREFACE

It is now almost eight years since the publication of the second edition of this book, and much has changed in that time. The most important changes, in practical terms, have taken place outside the courtroom. The National Health Service Litigation Authority, which was established in 1995, now has a central role in the handling of claims for clinical negligence in the NHS, and administering the Clinical Negligence Scheme for Trusts and the Existing Liabilities Scheme, which were both in their infancy in 1995. As a result of the annual financial audit of the NHS by the National Audit Office, we now have much more information about the costs of litigation to the NHS, though data on the number of medical accidents is becoming available more slowly. However, the data that is emerging on the numbers of accidental injuries portrays a health service that exacts a huge toll, in terms of injury and death, on the very people it is designed to serve, its patients (see paragraph 1-007). The trend, identified in the last edition, to greater awareness of risk management issues in the NHS has accelerated, though whether ultimately it will stem the apparently rising tide of iatrogenic injury remains to be seen.

One consequence of better information on the costs of clinical negligence litigation is that compensation claims now have a much higher profile, both in the press and in the NHS, than they once had. This in turn led to the review of clinical negligence litigation by the Department of Health, and the Chief Medical Officer's consultation report, *Making Amends*, published in June this year. At one point, there was at least the possibility that no-fault compensation for the victims of medical accidents would re-emerge onto the political agenda. *Making Amends* shied away from that option for reform, while making important recommendations for dealing with claims of relatively small value and for cases involving brain damaged babies. Dealing with the consequences of babies who sustain brain damage at birth takes up some 60 per cent of the total cost of NHS clinical negligence litigation, so the proposal, in effect, to offer a form of no-fault compensation to this category of claimants (but only this category) should have a significant effect on overall litigation costs, if it is accepted. Although this proposal would seem to fall squarely within Professor Atiyah's general criticism of all piecemeal reform of accident compensation mechanisms as selecting yet another group of victims for preferential treatment to the exclusion of others with similar disabilities, this particular group of victims may exert a strong call on our collective sympathies.

The Woolf reforms, still being developed in 1995, have produced a whole new system of civil procedure and appear to have succeeded in establishing much greater openness in the conduct of litigation. The Civil Procedure Rules have also encouraged the parties to litigation to seek alternative methods of resolving their dispute, though "pressure" to mediate rather than litigate claims has not yet produced a major shift to alternative dispute resolution. Clinical negligence is the only area of personal injury litigation for which legal aid is still available, and it remains the case that the vast majority of claimants (over 90 per cent) in medical negligence actions are legally aided. That figure, in itself, tells a story about the number of potential claims that go unlitigated because claimants do not qualify for legal aid and cannot afford the cost of access to the courts (which, like the Ritz, are open to all who have the means to pay).

The Human Rights Act 1998 constitutes the single most important statutory change since the last edition, and the incorporation of the European Convention for the Protection of Human Rights and Fundamental Freedoms (referred to in the text by its shorthand, "European Convention on Human Rights") into domestic law is already having an impact on judicial thinking. Although the "bread and butter" issues of breach of duty and causation are unlikely to be much affected by human rights considerations, its influence is already being felt in relation to the existence and scope of the duty of care in negligence and in the law of consent and confidentiality. Apart from a brief discussion in chapter 1, I have not treated human rights issues separately, but dealt with them as they have arisen in the context of the specific domestic law issues being discussed.

The basic structure of the common law (and of the book) remains intact, but much of the detail has altered or been expanded upon in the cases. The *Bolam* test, though still central to medical negligence litigation, was considered once more by the House of Lords in *Bolitho* v *City and Hackney Health Authority*. Although the claimant lost, the explicit requirement to subject expert evidence to logical scrutiny has established the judicial perception that medical evidence should never be determinative of the outcome. The decision of the House of Lords *McFarlane* v *Tayside Health Board* to deny recovery for the financial costs of raising a healthy child following a negligent sterilisation has spawned a minor industry of litigation, the discussion of which has taken up quite a few paragraphs in chapters 2 and 9.

One thing that has not changed is the title of the book. Despite the change in terminology adopted within the NHS and in the litigation of claims, from "medical negligence" to "clinical negligence" I have resisted the temptation to call the book "Clinical Negligence." The subject matter always extended beyond doctors and hospitals (to include defective products, for example) and beyond the narrow confines of the tort of negligence (to include the law on consent and confidentiality, for example). I have similarly resisted the call to banish the use of all Latin terms. They are rare enough in the law of Tort and most lawyers are comfortable with the shorthand that the Latin tags reflect. Moreover, I would hope that the exposition of the legal principles is as understandable to the lay reader as the legal practitioner, no matter what label is applied to the principle in issue. The one exception to a change in terminology is the demise of the "plaintiff". I have substituted the modern English litigant, the claimant, except where the word "plaintiff" appears in a direct quotation.

The new system of neutral citation is very useful, though it does entail the citation of two references, the neutral citation and, where available, a "hard copy" law report. Wherever law reports are provided with paragraph numbers, as all cases with a neutral citation are, references to paragraph numbers are given in square brackets. Another innovation concerns the citation of Web addresses. So much more material is now available on the Web, and wherever appropriate I have referred readers to the original documentation at the website from which I have taken it.

Medical Negligence remains, I trust, an exposition and analysis of the potential legal liabilities of healthcare professionals and organisations arising out of the provision of medical treatment to patients. Notwithstanding the chapter on Procedure, it is not a manual on "how to sue your doctor." I have retained the references to the more important Commonwealth material, though the sheer volume of English law makes it increasingly difficult to give more than the highlights from other jurisdictions. The Australian decision of *Cattanach* v *Melchior* [2003] H.C.A. 38, 199 A.L.R. 131, in which a bare majority of the High Court of Australia declined an invitation to follow the House of Lords' ruling in *McFarlane* v *Tayside Health Board* came to my attention too late be included, even as a footnote.

As always, thanks are due to the team at Sweet & Maxwell, particularly Samira Mahmood and Julie Clarke for their patience and encouragement, and Ed Farrow for turning round the manuscript so quickly. The law is stated on the basis of the materials available to me at the end of July 2003. I have made some minor amendments after that date at proof stage, though I have not been able to make more than passing footnote reference to the radical decision of the Court of Appeal in *JD* v *East Berkshire Community Health NHS Trust* [2003] EWCA Civ 1151; *The Times*, August 22, 2003, apparently "overruling" the decision of the House of Lords in *X* v *Bedfordshire County Council* on the basis that it could no longer be regarded as compatible with the European Convention on Human Rights. I am also conscious that the decision of the House of Lords in *Rees* v *Darlington Memorial Hospital NHS Trust* (which was heard in June 2003) may significantly alter the rules on recovery of the costs of raising a child following a failed sterilisation where either the child or the parent has a disability (though *Rees* was concerned with parental disability). Moreover, appeals from the decisions of the Court of Appeal in *Gregg* v *Scott* (on loss of chance claims in medical negligence actions) and *Chester* v *Afshar* (on the correct test for causation following the failure to warn of the risks involved in treatment) await determination by their Lordships.

Michael A. Jones
Liverpool
September 2003

PREFACE TO FIRST EDITION

It is now widely accepted that the number of claims for medical negligence has increased markedly over the last 10 years or so, although there is less agreement on the causes of this phenomenon. The impact on the medical profession, particularly in terms of the increase in subscription rates to the defence organisations and allegations about the practice of "defensive medicine," has been widely canvassed. The impact on the legal profession has, perhaps, been less apparent. In the early 1980s there were few lawyers acting for plaintiffs with extensive experience of medical malpractice litigation. Defendants' work, on the other hand, was channelled through the defence organisations and health authorities to a small number of solicitors' firms who had the appropriate expertise. This imbalance between plaintiffs and defendants has, to some extent at least, been redressed, with the emergence of specialist firms acting for plaintiffs, and the establishment of Action for the Victims of Medical Accidents, which provides a support service for plaintiffs' lawyers and undertakes an important educational role.

This book is directed primarily at legal practitioners, though I would hope that it would also make the law of medical negligence accessible to non-lawyers. Medical negligence is an all-encompassing term. The major focus of the text is on the professional liability of doctors and other health care professionals, and on the organisations providing facilities for health care. On the whole, I have not distinguished between the liability of doctors and other health professionals such as dentists, nurses, or pharmacists (for an extensive definition of "health professional" see the Access to Health Records Act 1990, s.2). The legal principles applicable to their liability for negligence are essentially the same. Differences, such as they are, arise from the different roles of the professionals concerned and, where relevant, these are indicated in the text. *Medical Negligence* is principally concerned with the tort of negligence applied in the specific context of the provision of health care, but I have sought to deal with all aspects of professional liability which may arise out of medical treatment, and accordingly I have included discussion of contractual liability, the duty of confidentiality, consent to treatment, product liability, damages for personal injury and death, and some aspects of procedure.

I have concentrated on the law of England and Wales, though I have made frequent reference to Commonwealth caselaw, wherever appropriate, on the basis that as a general rule Commonwealth jurisdictions apply much the same common law principles to the question of medical negligence. The cases provide concrete illustrations of the relevant principles, and where there are differences they are indicated in the text (*e.g.* in relation to the Canadian law on "informed consent"). Canadian caselaw tends to dominate the Commonwealth material, but this is simply due to the fact that there is far more of it. There are also occasional references to American caselaw.

It is inevitable that lawyers specialising in this area of the law will tend to come across some of the worst aspects of medical practice. It is worth pausing, however, to reflect that by far the greater part of medical treatment is provided by highly skilled, competent and dedicated professionals. The lawyer's perspective can become distorted through the filter of aggrieved patients. It is also understandable that, as more patients have sued their doctors, an element of hostility towards the legal profession has become apparent within the ranks of the medical profession. This too may be the product of a particular perspective, which does not take into account the lawyer's corresponding duty to represent the interests and rights of the client/patient with skill, competence and dedication. That the professional skills of doctor and lawyer may sometimes lead to conflict is a matter for regret but it should not diminish the high mutual respect and esteem that the two professions have long shared.

The team at Sweet and Maxwell has been patient and supportive throughout. I am extremely grateful for all their encouragement and hard work. Special thanks are due to my colleague Anne Morris, who kindly read the manuscript, prepared the index, and helped to compile the glossary of medical terms. Her assistance has been invaluable. I would also like to thank Bernadette Walsh, who cheerfully explained the intricacies of the Children Act 1989 to me, in so far as it affects consent to medical treatment of children. Any remaining errors, of course, are my sole responsibility. The task of writing a book puts a strain, not merely on the author, but on family, friends and colleagues. My thanks are due to all who endured the process with such fortitude, tact and charm.

The law is stated as at the end of July 1991.

Michael A. Jones
Liverpool
October 1991

CONTENTS

ABBREVIATIONS

A. = Atlantic Reporter
A.B.P.I. = Association of the British Pharmaceutical Industry
A.C. = Appeal Cases (Law Reports)
A.L.J. = Australian Law Journal
A.L.J.R. = Australian Law Journal Reports
A.L.R. = Australian Law Reports
A.R. = Alberta Reports
A.V.M.A. = Action for the Victims of Medical Accidents
Alberta L. Rev. = Alberta Law Review
All E.R.(D) = All England Reports Direct
All E.R. = All England Law Reports
Alta. Q.B. = Alberta Queen's Bench
Alta. C.A. = Alberta Court of Appeal
Am. J. Comp. Law = American Journal of Comparative Law
Anglo-American L.R. = Anglo-American Law Review
A.P.R. = Atlantic Province Reports

B.C.C.A. = British Columbia Court of Appeal
B.C.L.R. = British Columbia Law Reports
B.H.R.C. = Butterworths Human Rights Cases
B.C.S.C. = British Columbia Supreme Court
B.L.R. = Building Law Reports
B.M.A. = British Medical Association
B.M.J. = British Medical Journal
B.M.L.R. = Butterworths Medico-Legal Reports
B.N.F. = British National Formulary
Build.L.R. = Building Law Reports

C.C.L.T. = Canadian cases on the Law of Torts
C.F.L.Q. = Child and Family Law Quarterly
C.J.Q. = Civil Justice Quarterly
C.L. = Current Law
C.L.B. = Commonwealth Law Bulletin
C.L.J. or Camb.L.J. = Cambridge Law Journal
C.L.P. = Current Legal Problems
C.L.R. = Commonwealth Law Reports

C.L.Y. = Current Law Year Book
C.M.L.R. = Common Market Law Reports
C.P.R. = Civil Procedure Rules
C.P.Rep. = Civil Procedure Reports
C.R.M. = Committee on the Review of Medicines
C.S.M. = Committee on the Safety of Medicines
Cal. L. Rev. = California Law Review
Can. Bar Rev. = Canadian Bar Review
Ch. = Chancery (Law Reports)
Com.Cas = Commercial Cases
Com.L.R. = Commercial Law Reports
Conv.(N.S.) (*or* Conv. *or* Conveyancer) = Conveyancer and Property Lawyer
   (New Series)
Cr.App.R. = Criminal Appeal Reports
Crim.L.J. = Criminal Law Journal
Crim.L.R. = Criminal Law Review
Crim.R. = Criminal Reports

D.C. = Divisional Court
D.L.R. = Dominion Law Reports

E.A.T. = Employment Appeal Tribunal
E.C.H.R. = European Court of Human Rights
E.E.C. = European Economic Community
E.G. = Estates Gazette
EWCA Civ = England and Wales Court of Appeal, Civil
EWCA Crim = England and Wales Court of Appeal, Criminal
EWHC = England and Wales High Court
Eur. J. Health Law = European Journal of Health Law

F.C.R. = Family Court Reporter
F.H.S.A. = Family Health Service Authority
F.L.R. = Family Law Reports
F.Supp. = Federal Supplement
Fam. = Family Division (Law Reports)
Fam.Law = Family Law

G.M.C. = General Medical Council

H.C.A. = High Court of Australia (Law Report)
H.C. of Aus. = High Court of Australia
H.L.R. = Housing Law Reports
Har.L.R. or Harvard L.R. = Harvard Law Review
Harv.J.Leg. = Harvard Journal on Legislation

I.C.L.Q. = International and Comparative Law Quarterly
I.C.R. = Industrial Case Reports

I.L.J. = Industrial Law Journal
I.L.T. *or* Ir.L.T. = Irish Law Times
I.L.T.R. = Irish Law Times Reports
I.R. *or* Ir.R. = Irish Reports (Eire)
I.R.L.R. = Industrial Relations Law Reports
Ir.Jur = Irish Jurist
Ir.Jur.(N.S.) = Irish Jurist (New Series)

J. *and* JJ. = Justice, Justices
J.P. = Justice of the Peace Reports
J.P.I.L. = Journal of Personal Injury Law (formerly Journal of Personal Injury
   Litigation)
J.P.L. = Journal of Planning and Environmental Law
J.P.N. = Justice of the Peace Journal
J.R. = Juridical Review
J.S.P.T.L. = Journal of the Society of Public Teachers of Law
J.S.W.F.L. = Journal of Social Welfare and Family Law
J.S.W.L. = Journal of Social Welfare Law
J. of Child Law = Journal of Child Law
J. Contemp. Health Law and Policy = Journal of Contemporary Health Law
   and Policy
J. Law and Med. = Journal of Law and Medicine
J. of Law and Soc. = Journal of Law and Society
J. of the M.D.U. = Journal of the Medical Defence Union

K.B. = King's Bench (Law Reports)
K.I.L.R. = Knight's Industrial Law Reports
K.I.R. = Knight's Industrial Reports

L.J. = Law Journal Newspaper
L.J.R. = Law Journal Reports
L.Q.R. = Law Quarterly Review
L.R. = Law Reports
L.R.C.P. = Law Reports Common Pleas
L.S. = Legal Studies
L.S.Gaz. = Law Society's Gazette
L.T. = Law Times
L.T.J. = Law Times Journal
L.T.R. = Law Times Reports

Ll.L.Rep. = Lloyd's List Reports (before 1951)
Lit. = Litigation
Lloyd's Rep. = Lloyd's List Reports (1951 onwards)
Lloyd's Rep. Med. = Lloyd's Law Reports Medical (formerly Medical Law
   Reports)
Lloyd's Rep. P.N. = Lloyd's Law Reports Professional Negligence

M.D.U. = Medical Defence Union
M.L.R. = Modern Law Review
M.P.S. = Medical Protection Society
M.R.C. = Medical Research Council
McGill L.J. = McGill Law Journal
Man. C.A. = Manitoba Court of Appeal
Man. Q.B. = Manitoba Queen's Bench
Med. J. Aus. = Medical Journal of Australia
Med. L.R. = Medical Law Reports
Med. Law Int. = Medical Law International
Med. L. Rev. = Medical Law Review
Med.Sci. & Law = Medicine, Science and the Law
Melbourne Univ. L.R. = Melbourne University Law Review
M.I.M. = Monthly Index of Medical Specialists
Monash Univ. L.R. = Monash University Law Review

N.B.C.A. = New Brunswick Court of Appeal
N.B.Q.B. = New Brunswick Queen's Bench
N.B.R. = New Brunswick Reports
N.E. = North Eastern Reporter
N.H.S. = National Health Service
N.I. = Northern Ireland; Northern Ireland Reports
N.I.J.B. = Northern Ireland Judgment Bulletin
N.I.L.Q. = Northern Ireland Legal Quarterly
N.I.L.R. = Northern Ireland Law Reports
N.L.J. = New Law Journal
N.S.S.C. = Nova Scotia Supreme Court
N.S.W.C.A. = New South Wales Court of Appeal
N.S.W.L.R. = New South Wales Law Reports
N.W. = North Western Reporter
N.Y. = New York Reports
N.Z.C.A. = New Zealand Court of Appeal
N.Z.L.R. = New Zealand Law Reports
N.Z.U.L.R. = New Zealand Universities Law Review
New Eng. J. Med. = New England Journal of Medicine
New L.J. = New Law Journal
Newfd. C.A. = Newfoundland Court of Appeal
Newfd. S.C. = Newfoundland Supreme Court

O.J. = Official Journal (European Community)
O.J.L.S. = Oxford Journal of Legal Studies
O.R. = Ontario Reports
Ont. C.A. = Ontario Court of Appeal
Ont. H.C. = Ontario High Court
Osgoode Hall L.J. = Osgoode Hall Law Journal

P. = Pacific Reporter [also Probate, Divorce and Admiralty (Law Reports)]
P.I.Q.R. = Personal Injury and Quantum Reports

P.L. = Public Law
P.M.I.L.L. = Personal and Medical Injuries Law Letter
P.N. = Professional Negligence
P.N.L.R. = Professional Negligence Law Reports

R.P.C. = Reports of Patent, Design and Trade Mark Cases

Q.B. = Queen's Bench (Law Reports)
Q.L.R. = Queensland Law Reporter
Qd.R. = Queensland Reports
Q.S. = Quarter Sessions
Q.S.R. = Queensland State Reports

R.S.C. = Rules of Supreme Court
R.T.R. = Road Traffic Reports

S.A.S.R. = South Australian State Reports
S.C. = Session Cases
S.C.C. Supreme Court of Canada
S.C. of S. Aus. = Supreme Court of South Australia
S.E. = South Eastern Reporter
S.J. = Solicitor's Journal
S.L.T. = Scots Law Times
S.L.T.(Notes) = Scots Law Times Notes of Recent Decisions
S.L.T. (Sh. Ct.) = Scots Law Times Sheriff Court Reports
S.N. = Session Notes
S.W. = South Western Reporter
Sask. C.A. = Saskatchewan Court of Appeal
Sask. K.B. = Saskatchewan King's Bench
Sask. Q.B. = Saskatchewan Queen's Bench
Stat.L.R. = Statute Law Review
Sydney L.R. = Sydney Law Review

Tas.S.R. = Tasmanian State Reports
Tort L. Rev. = Tort Law Review
Torts L.J. = Torts Law Journal
Tulane L.R. = Tulane Law Review

U.B.C.L. Rev. = University of British Columbia Law Review
U.K.H.L. = United Kingdom House of Lords
U.K.P.C. = United Kingdom Privy Council
U.T.L.J. = University of Toronto Law Journal

V.L.R. = Victorian Law Reports
V.R. = Victorian Reports

W.A.L.R. = West Australian Law Reports
W.L.R. = Weekly Law Reports

W.N. = Weekly Notes (Law Reports)
W.W.R. = Western Weekly Reports
Washington L.Q. = Washington Law Quarterly
Web J.C.L.I. = Web Journal of Current Legal Issue

Yale L.J. = Yale Law Journal

TABLE OF CASES

Decisions of the Tribunal of Social Security Commissioners

TABLE OF STATUTES

TABLE OF STATUTORY INSTRUMENTS

TABLE OF CIVIL PROCEDURE RULES

TABLE OF PRACTICE DIRECTIONS

TABLE OF PRE-ACTION PROTOCOLS

TABLE OF NATIONAL LEGISLATION

TABLE OF EUROPEAN AND INTERNATIONAL
CONVENTIONS AND TREATIES

TABLE OF EUROPEAN DIRECTIVES

CHAPTER 1

MEDICAL NEGLIGENCE IN CONTEXT

Medical negligence is an emotive term: emotive for doctors and for patients.   1–001
Lawyers, however, have to take a more dispassionate view about the rights
and wrongs of medical accidents. The tort of negligence applies an objective
standard as a measure of professional conduct, and though it is known as
"fault liability" there is no necessary correlation between a finding that a
doctor was negligent in law and a judgment that his conduct was morally
blameworthy. Mistakes are made in all areas of professional life. Some are
negligent, some are not; some cause harm, most probably do not. When Lord
Denning insisted that in order to reach the conclusion that a doctor was negligent his conduct should be deserving of censure or inexcusable, he clearly
took the view that it should be more difficult to prove negligence against a
doctor.[1] The converse of this proposition, however, is that whenever a doctor
is held liable in negligence his conduct deserves censure. This has probably
made it more difficult to view negligence in the context of medical practice
in terms of the inadvertent slip, the error which almost anyone could have
(and probably has) made, and which though careless does not say anything
about the defendant's general competence in the practice of medicine. On
another occasion Lord Denning sought to characterise such mistakes as
errors of clinical judgment and, accordingly, not negligent. This view was
categorically rejected by the House of Lords on the ground that to state that
the defendant made an error of judgment, whether clinical or otherwise, tells
one nothing about whether the error was negligent or not.[2] One consequence, perhaps, of judicial attitudes such as that of Lord Denning is that a
claim for compensation by an injured patient is often perceived by doctors
to be accompanied by denigration of the defendant's professional competence. This may partly explain why the medical profession, of all the professions, is most sensitive to allegations of negligence.

The process of identifying individual fault through the tort of negligence   1–002
tends to overlook the wider issues involved in dealing with medical accidents. While on the one hand it may be acknowledged that some accidents
are inevitable, and indeed that some accidents through carelessness will

---

[1] *Hucks v Cole* (1968), [1993] 4 Med. L.R. 393, 396; *Hatcher v Black, The Times*, July 2,
1954. See further para. 3–145.
[2] The disagreement occurred in *Whitehouse v Jordan* [1980] 1 All E.R. 650, CA; [1981] 1 All
E.R. 267, HL; see para. 3–067.

always occur, on the other hand the tort action is not well-suited to identifying those accidents attributable to "organisational errors," or methods of delivering health care which equate cost-cutting with efficiency, and result in overworked staff, inadequate safety measures, and an emphasis on the quantity at the expense of the quality of health care provision. An action for medical negligence must focus on the particular accident. One of the strengths of the forensic process is the ability to dissect events in fine detail, although this cannot always achieve that elusive goal "the truth." But by focussing on the particular, tort cannot hope to address the broader question of how accidents might be prevented, apart from the notion that the threat of an action for negligence has some value in deterring careless conduct. There is a growing realisation within the health service that many of the accidents that result in injury to patients are the result of organisational errors or systemic failures in risk management procedures.[3] The emphasis now emerging within the NHS is on dealing with system failures, rather than trying to blame individuals. Although efforts to reduce the number of "adverse events" are to be applauded[4] from the perspective of the individual claimant it is not likely to have much relevance in the legal context, because it is significantly easier to identify the error of the last individual in the chain, and hold the NHS vicariously liable for that, than it is to establish that the whole organisation was at fault in having insufficient risk management techniques to avoid or reduce the incidence of error. However, in so far as risk management processes lead to greater standardisation of procedures through the adoption of protocols, departure from those procedures could more readily be characterised as carelessness.[5]

1–003   To concentrate simply on the general question of medical accidents obscures the significance of medical negligence as an ethical or moral issue. Doctors are familiar with the principle of non-maleficence ("do no harm") as an element of medical ethics. Normally the problem in applying this principle lies in identifying what is harmful and how it should be avoided, but

---

[3] See *An Organisation with a Memory*, Department of Health, 2000 (available at *www.doh.gov.uk/orgmemreport/index.htm*); and *Making Amends*, Department of Health, June 2003 (available at *www.doh.gov.uk/makingamends/cmoreport.htm*). On March 18 2000 the British Medical Journal had an entire issue devoted to medical error: (2000) 320 BMJ (available at *www.bmj.com*). The National Patient Safety Agency is a special health authority with the specific remit of improving the safety for patients in the NHS through reporting, analysing and learning from adverse incidents (see *www.npsa.nhs.uk*). The NHS Litigation Authority also seeks to improve risk management strategies in the NHS through a risk management programme against which NHS Trusts are assessed.

[4] Though some may say that it took fifteen years of rapidly rising medical malpractice litigation, and a the realisation that this represented a significant cost to the health service, before risk management and patient safety rose to the top of the agenda.

[5] Attempts to sue the NHS for a failure to undertake risk management processes are unlikely to be successful. A claim against a regulatory agency for an alleged failure to undertake adequate risk management in instructing members of the profession about the risks associated with certain treatment was rejected in *Rogers v Faught* (2002) 212 D.L.R. (4th) 366. The Ontario Court of Appeal held that no duty of care was owed to a patient by the body with statutory responsibility for regulating the dental profession. The position could be different, however, if the NHS had promulgated national standards for risk management procedures in a particular area of medical practice with which a NHS Trust had failed to comply.

these difficulties do not apply to negligence. Other things being equal, it is always better to be careful than to be careless if the consequences of carelessness are personal injury to a patient. Negligence is also a moral issue in that it is concerned with attributing responsibility and, in some instances, blame. To say that accidents are inevitable and that mistakes will always be made, though perfectly true, misses the significance that an injured patient may attach to having an explanation and apology for his injuries, and the satisfaction of knowing that steps have been taken to prevent a recurrence of the error. The evidence from organisations representing patients' interests, such as Action for the Victims of Medical Accidents, is that the absence of an adequate explanation is frequently the spur to litigation.[6] Information and accountability are seen as central to the needs of medical accident victims, and they are at least as important as compensation.[7] Despite some efforts to reduce the barriers to offering patients an explanation and an apology[8] the problem of communication failures after a medical accident remains a significant factor in patients resorting to litigation.[9] But litigation cannot in itself force an apology or even a full explanation of events from an unwilling defendant, which is one reason that mediation of clinical disputes, still in its infancy, could have a significant role in the future.[10] The modern

---

[6] "... the vast majority of the victims of medical accidents do not initially seek financial compensation but want an explanation for what went wrong, sympathetic treatment and, if appropriate, an apology": Simanowitz, "Medical Accidents: The Problem and the Challenge" in P. Byrne (ed.) *Medicine in Contemporary Society: King's College Studies 1986–7.* See also Vincent, Young and Phillips, "Why do people sue doctors? A study of patients and relatives taking legal action" (1994) 343 *The Lancet* 1609, commenting that "patients taking legal action wanted greater honesty, an appreciation of the severity of trauma they had suffered, and assurances that lessons had been learnt from their experiences." See also *Making Amends*, June 2003, p. 75, reporting that nearly 60% of respondents who had suffered an adverse incident wanted an apology, explanation or inquiry into the cause of the incident.

[7] House of Commons, Committee of Public Accounts, *Handling clinical negligence claims in England*, 37th report of Session 2001–2002, HC Paper No. 280, para. 17. These concerns are also apparent in the New Zealand *Report of the Committee of Inquiry into the Treatment of Cervical Cancer*, 1988: see McGregor Vennell "Medical Misfortune in a No Fault Society" in Mann and Havard, *No Fault Compensation in Medicine*, 1989, p. 40; Takach (1995) 3 J. Law and Med. 60, 72.

[8] See the NHS Litigation Authority, Circular No. 02/02, *Apologies and Explanations*, February 2002 (available at *www.nhsla.com*).

[9] See *Handling Clinical Negligence Claims in England*, May 2001, Part 3 (available at *www.nao.gov.uk/publications/nao_reports/00-01/0001403.pdf*).

[10] On mediation see: Polywka, "Mediation of clinical negligence claims" (1997) 3 Clinical Risk 80; Simanowitz, "Mediation in medical negligence" (1998) 4 Clinical Risk 63; Polywka "Achieving resolution: considering all the options" (2002) 8 Clinical Risk 1; Simanowitz, "A new approach to mediation" (2002) 8 Clinical Risk 14; Rhodes-Kemp "Mediation" (2002) 8 Clinical Risk 16. Mulcahy, Selwood and Netten, *Mediating medical negligence claims: An option for the future?*, University of London, 2000. See also the Clinical Disputes Forum's *User's Guide to Mediation*, (available at *www.clinical-disputes-forum.org.uk/ publications/Appendix2b.pdf*) and the Clinical Disputes Forum's *Guide to Mediating Clinical Negligence Claims* (available at *www.clinical-disputes-forum.org.uk/publications/ 40Appendix2a.pdf* and reproduced in (2002) 8 Clinical Risk 4). The Chief Executive of the NHS Litigation Authority has said that, apart from litigation to a full trial, "mediation remains the most expensive means of dispute resolution. It is hard to see how it will ever be cost-effective or proportionate for low-value claims, but our experience is that it has therapeutic benefits for claimants and possibly clinicians in the larger claims": *National Health*

tort system is very good at identifying the financial costs of medical accidents to patients and their families, but it is simply not equipped to deal with the emotional trauma that "adverse events" entail for real people leading real lives, sometimes compounded by the response of the NHS to the adverse event.[11]

1–004   Since the last edition of this book was published the problems of medical malpractice litigation have achieved a much higher profile. Lord Woolf's review of the civil justice system paid particular attention to clinical negligence litigation,[12] and the Civil Procedure Rules now include specific measures designed to improve the litigation process for clinical negligence actions. The National Audit Office has adopted the practice of highlighting the financial costs associated with clinical negligence claims when reporting on the NHS accounts, and in 2001 published a study on clinical negligence litigation.[13] This has had the effect of focussing the minds of policy-makers on the inefficiencies and costs of the litigation process. At the same time there has been a growing recognition of the weaknesses of litigation from the perspective of injured patients. With this in mind, the *Final Report of the Bristol Royal Infirmary Inquiry*,[14] recommended that:

> "There should be an urgent review of the system for providing compensation to those who suffer harm arising out of medical care. The review should be concerned with the introduction of an administrative system for responding promptly to patients' needs in place of the current system of clinical negligence and should take account of other administrative systems for meeting the financial needs of the public."

Indeed, the Bristol Inquiry recommended that the clinical negligence system should be abolished and replaced by an alternative system for compensating patients who suffer harm arising out of treatment by the NHS.[15] In 1999 the House of Commons Health Committee also recommended that the Department of Health should review the issue of no-fault compensation and publish a consultation document on the possible introduction of a no-fault

---

(n.10 contd.) *Service Litigation Authority, Report and Accounts 2002* (available at *www.nhsla.com*). See also *Making Amends*, June 2003, pp. 95–96.

[11] *Making Amends*, June 2003, pp. 42–44. For discussion of the "human" consequences of medical accidents see Vincent, "Understanding and Responding to Adverse Events" (2003) 348 New Eng. J. Med. 1051.

[12] *Access to Justice*, 1996, Ch. 15 (available at *www.law.warwick.ac.uk/Woolf/report*).

[13] NAO, *Handling Clinical Negligence Claims in England*, May 2001, HC 403, Session 2000–2001. The House of Commons Public Accounts Committee subsequently considered this report in *Handling clinical negligence claims in England*: 37th report of Session 2001–2002, HC Paper No. 280.

[14] See: *www.bristol-inquiry.org.uk*, recommendation 37.

[15] *ibid.* recommendation 119. The government agreed that there was a need for an urgent review and that "the current system of clinical negligence compensation needs to be reformed", but did not go so far as to agree that no-fault compensation would be the solution: *Learning from Bristol: The Department of Health's Response to the Report of the Public Inquiry into children's heart surgery at the Bristol Royal Infirmary 1984–1995*, January 2002, Cm. 5363.

compensation scheme within the NHS.[16] In response to these calls in 2001 the Department of Health initiated a review of the system of handling compensation claims and complaints in the NHS under the chairmanship of the Chief Medical Officer.[17] The possibility of a no-fault compensation scheme for the victims of medical accidents was just one item on a wide agenda of how systems to deal with claims arising from clinical negligence should be amended. Other possibilities include greater use of structured settlements;[18] schemes with fixed tariffs for specific injuries;[19] and greater use of mediation or other alternative dispute resolution mechanisms.[20] The CMO's report of this review, *Making Amends*, was published in June 2003, and makes a number of important recommendations for changes to the methods of compensation for injury sustained by patients in the NHS. Although there is now a greater recognition of the difficulties faced by injured patients in obtaining redress, many of the criticisms of the present system of handling clinical negligence litigation relate to the overall cost to the NHS of dealing with claims for compensation, the relatively high administrative costs of the tort system, and the consequences for the financial management of NHS bodies, principally NHS Trust hospitals which bear the brunt of negligence claims. These concerns are reflected in *Making Amends*.

This book seeks to describe, analyse and, where appropriate, criticise the   **1–005** law of medical negligence in its widest sense. Before embarking on that task, however, it may be helpful to identify the main themes and problems surrounding medical malpractice litigation to enable practitioners, whether lawyers or doctors, to see the wider context within which the law operates. The first section considers the suggestion that there is a "malpractice crisis",

---

[16] Session 1998–99, Sixth Report, *Procedures Related to Adverse Clinical Incidents and Outcomes in Medical Care*, Vol. I, London: The Stationery Office, October 1999, para. 133.

[17] The terms of reference are at: *www.doh.gov.uk/clinicalnegligencereform/index.htm.*

[18] This issue was overtaken by events, since the government announced in November 2002 that the Damages Act 1996 is to be amended to give the courts the power to award damages as periodical payments rather than as a lump sum; see para. 9–012.

[19] This would be similar to the revised Criminal Injuries Compensation Scheme, which has not proved popular, because the awards are substantially lower than those awarded by the courts for comparable injuries. It would be difficult to see how such a limited scheme could exclude an injured patient's right to litigate, without breaching Art. 6 of the European Convention on Human Rights.

[20] See the Civil Procedure Rules, *Pre-Action Protocol for the Resolution of Clinical Disputes*, para. 5. Under the court's case management powers, the court can "encourage" the parties to litigation to use an alternative dispute resolution procedure: CPR r. 1.4(2)(e). But a refusal to participate in mediation would not necessarily result in a penalty in costs: *Societe Internationale de Telecommunications Aeronautiques SC v Wyatt Co (UK) Ltd (Costs)* [2002] EWHC 2401 (Ch D). The Legal Services Commission requires the use of alternative dispute resolution to be considered in clinical negligence disputes at key stages of a claim, and reserves the right to limit a clinical negligence certificate to ensure alternative dispute resolution is pursued if it has been rejected without good reason: *Legal Services Commission Annual Report 2001/02*, para. 2.125. Similarly, since May 2000 the NHS Litigation Authority has required defendants' solicitors to consider every case for mediation, to offer mediation where appropriate, and to report on cases considered unsuitable: *Making Amends*, June 2003, p. 95, para. 20. Approximately 65% of offers of mediation are refused by claimants: *ibid.* para. 22. Recommendation 15 of that report, at p. 126, states that mediation should be seriously considered before litigation for the majority of claims which do not fall within the proposed new NHS Redress Scheme (on which see para. 1–054).

at least in terms of the financial cost of compensating for medical negligence. Data on the numbers and cost of medical malpractice litigation has improved significantly over the last few years, and information on the prevalence of medical accidents has also become more accessible. Putting the two categories together highlights the huge disparity between the number of injuries occurring and the numbers of patients receiving compensation. The next section deals with an argument that has often plagued the debate, namely that doctors practise defensive medicine in response to the perceived litigation crisis. Section 3 addresses another perennial issue, that is whether a system of no-fault compensation specifically for the victims of medical accidents would both solve the malpractice crisis and provide a fairer and more efficient method of compensating injured patients. Section 4 discusses the proposals from the CMO in *Making Amends* for reform of the compensation mechanisms. The chapter concludes with a brief consideration of the implications of the Human Rights Act 1998 for the future development of the law of medical negligence.

(1) A malpractice crisis?

1–006   There has been a widespread perception over the last fifteen years or so, particularly in the medical literature and the popular press, that the UK is in the grip of a medical malpractice "crisis." In the past that sense of crisis came, not from the realisation that large numbers of patients were suffering serious injury in the course of their medical treatment, but from the fact that claims for negligence and the cost of meeting those claims was rapidly increasing. More recently, there has been much greater recognition, certainly within the NHS, if not the general public, that litigation is probably a symptom of the underlying problem of iatrogenic injury attributable to "adverse events" in health care.[21] It makes no sense to talk of a crisis in malpractice litigation, which sometimes leads to criticism of the victims of medical negligence and their lawyers for having the temerity to sue, without addressing the prior question of the size of the problem of accidental injury (whether attributable to fault or not) in health care. In the absence of any reliable information about how many *injuries* occur each year as a result of medical negligence it is impossible to identify what the "appropriate" level of litigation should be. All the evidence suggests that there are far fewer claims than the incidence of negligently inflicted harm would warrant. From the patients' perspective it could be argued that the malpractice "crisis" arises from too few patients being able to litigate, rather than too many doctors becoming defendants. In this arena perceptions are everything.[22]

---

[21] See, in particular, *An Organisation with a Memory*, 2000 (available at *www.doh.gov.uk/org-memreport/index.htm*).

[22] In an unpublished survey carried out in 1994 by the author 20% of doctors replying (total sample 1,559) considered that the number of claims against doctors was at "crisis level." One third of the sample had received a solicitors' letter once or more frequently, but only 12.7% had ever had proceedings for professional negligence issued against them.

(a) How many medical injuries occur?

It is not known with any precision how many accidental injuries attribut-   1–007
able to health care occur each year in the UK. In *An Organisation with a
Memory* the Department of Health estimated that 850,000 adverse events
could occur in NHS hospitals each year, resulting in £2 billion direct cost in
additional hospital days alone (*i.e.* excluding the economic and personal
costs to victims).[23] Around half of these adverse events might be avoidable.
The figure of 850,000 adverse events was an extrapolation from the *Harvard
Medical Practice Study*[24] and the *Quality in Australian Health Care Study*,[25]
on the basis of which it was estimated that there could be between 314,000
and 1,414,000 potential adverse events a year in NHS hospitals alone (based
on 8.5 million inpatient episodes a year), and between 60,000 and 255,000
potential instances of permanent disability or death in cases where an
adverse event has occurred.[26] A small UK study[27] involving a review of 1014
files from two acute hospitals found that 10.8 per cent of patients experienced an adverse event[28] though the overall number of adverse events was
11.7 per cent (some patients suffered multiple adverse events) and almost
half (48 per cent) of the adverse events were judged to be preventable. Of the
adverse events, 66 per cent of patients had minimal impairment or recovered
within a month; 19 per cent had moderate impairment; 6 per cent had suffered permanent impairment; and in 8 per cent of patients the adverse event
contributed to death. Each adverse event led to an average of 8.5 additional

---

[23] *An Organisation with a Memory*, 2000, para. 1.15. This figure was repeated in *Making
Amends*, June 2003, p. 32, para. 6.
[24] Harvard Medical Practice Study to the State of New York, *Patients, Doctors and Lawyers:
Medical Injury, Malpractice Litigation and Patient Compensation in New York*, 1990. This
study found that adverse events constituted 3.7% of admissions to hospital; 69% of injuries
were caused by errors; 1% of hospital patients suffered injury as a result of negligence; and
over 90% of the patients who suffered injury as a result of negligence went uncompensated.
The Report is summarised in three articles in the *New England Journal of Medicine*:
"Incidence of Adverse Events and Negligence in Hospitalized Patients" (1991) 324 New
Eng. J. Med. 370; "The Nature of Adverse Events in Hospitalized Patients" (1991) 324 New
Eng. J. Med. 377; "Relation Between Malpractice Claims and Adverse Events Due to
Negligence" (1991) 325 New Eng. J. Med. 45.
[25] Wilson, Runciman and Gibberd *et al.* (1995) 163 Med. J. Aus. 58–471, (cited in S.N.
Weingart, *et al.*, "Epidemiology of medical error" (2000) 320 B.M.J. 774). This study estimated that adverse events occurred in 16.6% of admissions to hospital, and 51% were considered to be preventable.
[26] *An Organisation with a Memory*, Table 2.2. Not all of these adverse events will necessarily
have caused or contributed to the injury or death in these cases. If the figures from the
Harvard Medical Practice Study are extrapolated to the UK, medical error may contribute
to up to 40,000 deaths a year. This is an astonishing figure, which far exceeds the combined
number of deaths each year in road and work accidents.
[27] Vincent, *et al.*, "Adverse events in British hospitals: preliminary retrospective record review"
(2001) 322 B.M.J. 517.
[28] Defined by Vincent *et al.* as "an unintended injury caused by medical management rather
than by the disease process and which is sufficiently serious to lead to prolongation of hospitalisation or to temporary or permanent impairment or disability to the patient at time of
discharge." Note that different definitions of an adverse event may partially explain the large
differences in estimates between the *Harvard Medical Practice Study* and the *Quality in
Australian Health Care Study*.

days in hospital at a cost of £290,268 to the hospitals concerned. The study estimated that around 5 per cent of the 8.5 million patients admitted to hospitals in England and Wales per annum (*i.e.* 425,000 patients) experience a *preventable* adverse event, resulting in an additional three million bed days, at a cost of around £1 billion to the NHS in bed days alone.[29] *An Organisation with a Memory*[30] also stated that:

- there were over 38,000 complaints about all aspects of Family Health Services in 1998-1999 and nearly 28,000 written complaints are made about aspects of clinical treatment in hospital;[31]

- where were over 6,600 adverse incidents involving medical devices reported to the Medical Devices Agency in 1999, including 87 deaths and 345 serious injuries;

- hospital acquired infections, around 15 per cent of which may be avoidable, are estimated to cost the NHS nearly £1 billion a year;[32]

- nearly 10,000 people are reported to have experienced serious adverse reactions to drugs;[33]

- around 1,150 people who have been in recent contact with mental health services commit suicide.

Not all of these incidents necessarily reflect adverse events, but still the information currently available "must be regarded as a serious underestimate of the size of the problem."[34] That report observed that even less is known about the number of adverse events in primary care settings. Research carried out for the Chief Medical Officer's review of clinical negligence in the NHS, *Making Amends*, found that of 8,000 people interviewed approximately 400 considered that they had suffered injury or other adverse effects as a direct result of medical care.[35] Of these, almost 30 per cent (*i.e.* about 1.5 per cent of the total sample) reported that the event had had a permanent impact on their health. Just over half of the adverse events happened in NHS hospitals and 25 per cent in primary care.

---

[29] *An Organisation with a Memory*, para. 3.15 suggests that, in the healthcare setting, as many as 70% of adverse events may be preventable.
[30] *ibid.* at para. 1.15.
[31] Figures taken from *Handling complaints: monitoring the NHS complaints procedures (England, Financial Year 1998–99)*, Department of Health, 2000. In 2000–2001 written complaints concerning hospital treatment had risen to almost 33,000, and there were 44,442 complaints in primary care: *Making Amends*, June 2003, p. 79, paras 14 and 15.
[32] Figures taken from *The Management and Control of Hospital Acquired Infection in Acute NHS Trusts in England*, National Audit Office, 2000 (available at *www.nao.gov.uk*).
[33] *An Organisation with a Memory*, Table 2.1.
[34] *ibid.*, para. 2.1.
[35] *Making Amends*, p. 33, para. 8.

(b) How many claims are there?

If knowledge about the number of medical accidents that occur each year, **1–008** and the number which result from negligence, is sketchy, knowledge about the number and cost of claims has improved significantly in the last ten years. Until 1989 information on claims was not systematically collected by the NHS, and even after 1989 information was patchy.[36] Knowledge about the number and cost of claims has steadily improved since the creation of the NHS Litigation Authority in 1995. Whatever the inadequacies of claims data in the 1980s, it was possible to identify a clear trend of significant increases in claims. Between 1983 and 1987 alone the number of claims doubled, and this was accompanied by a substantial increase in the value of damages awards.[37] This was reflected in a marked increase in doctors' annual subscription rates to the medical defence organisations.[38] The increase in claims, or, more specifically, the increase in subscription rates that the increased claims produced, provoked an outcry from the medical profession against lawyers, patients, the Legal Aid system, and the courts.[39] It was claimed that there was a "malpractice crisis" and that doctors were practising defensive medicine.[40] There were calls for the introduction of a scheme of no-fault

---

[36] H.C. (89) 34, Annex B, required health authorities to supply annual returns to the Department of Health about the number and cost of claims for medical negligence in NHS hospitals, starting at May 31, 1990. The figures supplied in the first few years were not particularly reliable: see the second edition of this book para. 1–005, n. 5.

[37] Ham, Dingwall, Fenn, Harris *Medical Negligence: Compensation and Accountability* (1988) King's Fund Institute, p. 11. This phenomenon is not new. In the 1950s Lord Nathan commented that the post-war years had seen a very substantial increase in the volume of medical negligence actions: Nathan, *Medical Negligence*, Butterworths, 1957, p. 5. This was attributed to the introduction of the NHS, which had created a subtle change in the relationship between doctor and patient, to the introduction of the Legal Aid system which enabled impecunious patients to litigate, and finally to changes in the law on the liability of hospitals (on which see paras 7–003 to 7–008). For discussion of possible reasons for the increase in medical malpractice litigation see Ham, Dingwall, Fenn and Harris, *Medical Negligence: Compensation and Accountability*, 1988, p. 15.

[38] In 1977 the cost of subscription to a medical defence organisation (the Medical Defence Union or the Medical Protection Society) was £40. By 1988 this had reached £1,080. In 1978 one in 1,000 doctors in Britain had a claim paid, but by 1990–1991 this had risen to 26 in 1,000 doctors: Fenn, Hermans and Dingwall, "Estimating the cost of compensating the victims of medical negligence" (1994) 309 B.M.J. 389. The frequency of claims against British doctors doubled between 1985 and 1988 alone: Hoyte "Medical Negligence Litigation, Claims Handling and Risk Management" (1994) 1 Med. Law Int. 261. For a detailed analysis of claims settled by the Medical Defence Union in 1989 see Hoyte (1995) 3 Med. L. Rev. 53.

[39] See Jones (1987) 3 P.N. 43.

[40] Comparisons with the position in the USA were often drawn, implying that the UK would follow a similar path. The analogy is unhelpful, however, for many reasons: see Quam, Fenn and Dingwall (1987) 294 B.M.J. 1529 and 1597; Ham, Dingwall, Fenn and Harris, *Medical Negligence: Compensation and Accountability*, 1988, pp. 19–20. There is considerable dispute as to the causes of the American medical malpractice "crises": see Terry (1986) 2 P.N. 145; and the evidence suggested that claim rates in the USA fell after 1985: Fenn, Dingwall and Quam (1990) 301 B.M.J. 949. J.R.S. Prichard, "Liability and Compensation in Health Care," *A Report to the Conference of Deputy Ministers of the Federal/Provincial/Territorial Review of Liability and Compensation Issues in Health Care* (1990) found that there was no crisis in Canada arising out of the number of successful malpractice claims. Despite a growth in litigation only a modest percentage of patients

compensation for the victims of medical accidents.[41] The response of government was first to reimburse two-thirds of defence organisation subscription fees for NHS hospital doctors (general practitioners had always been permitted to deduct subscription fees as a practice expense under their terms of service), and then to take over the whole cost of hospital medical accidents under arrangements for NHS indemnity.[42]

1–009   In 1996 the Woolf Report estimated that there were about 20,000 claims outstanding against the NHS, with about 2,500 having a value in excess of £100,000. About 5,000 claims were disposed of each year, a figure matched by the number of claims entering the system.[43] The National Audit Office report, *Handling Clinical Negligence Claims in England*,[44] indicated there were about 23,000 claims against the NHS outstanding. 10,000 new claims were received in 1999-2000, with 9,600 claims cleared, with the rate of new claims per thousand finished consultant episodes having increased by 72 per cent between 1990 and 1998.[45] The NHS Litigation Authority reported an increase in new claims, from 2,411 in 1999-2000 to 4,115 in 2000–2001 for the Clinical Negligence Scheme for Trusts (*i.e.* post-March 31st 1995 incidents),[46] but this figure fell significantly to 2,068 in 2001–2002.[47] For 2002–2003, the first year when the NHS Litigation Authority would have received notification of all claims under both the Existing Liabilities Scheme and the Clinical Negligence Scheme for Trusts (therefore covering both pre-April 1995 and post-March 1995 incidents), a total of 6,797 claims were received.[48] The NHS Litigation Authority reported reductions in claims in 2001–2002 and 2002–2003, which is line with reductions in the number of cases approved for legal aid, as reported by the Legal Services

---

(n.40 contd.) suffering avoidable health care injuries receive compensation. In 1987 fewer than 250 injured patients received compensation of any kind from medical malpractice litigation, whether by way of settlement or a judgment. On the other hand $200 million was spent on liability insurance. Semenuk and Smith (1991) 70 Can. Bar Rev. 557 identify problems with pre-trial procedure as one of the causes of this low success rate. For discussion of these issues in an Australian context see Sappideen (1991) 13 Syd. L. Rev. 523; and for a comparative analysis see Trebilcock, Dewees and Duff (1990) 17 Melbourne Univ. L. Rev. 539.

[41] See Jones (1987) 3 P.N. 83.

[42] See para. 7–052.

[43] *Access to Justice*, 1996, Ch. 15, para. 10; (available at *www.law.warwick.ac.uk/Woolf/report*).

[44] May 2001. This report is available at *www.nao.gov.uk/publications/nao_reports/00-01/0001403.pdf*.

[45] This figure was taken from Fenn, Diacon, Gray, Hodges, and Rickman, "Current cost of medical negligence in NHS hospitals: analysis of claims database" (2000) 320 B.M.J. 1567.

[46] *NHS (England) Summarised Accounts 2000–2001*. All the NHS (England) Summarised Accounts are available from the National Audit Office at *www.nao.gov.uk*.

[47] *NHS (England) Summarised Accounts 2001–2002*, para. 6.9. See also the *Legal Services Commission Annual Report 2001/02*, para. 2.110: "The volume of clinical negligence certificates granted has remained remarkably stable for the last three years (7,309 compared to 7,375 in 1999/00 and 7,329 in 2000/01). Current volumes are 45% down from 1995/96." Of the funding certificates granted in 2001/02, 5,976 were for investigative help and 1,330 were for full representation (Table CLS 8). The report is available at *www.legalservices.gov.uk*.

[48] *Making Amends*, p. 58, para. 32.

Commission.[49] The medical defence organisations (the Medical Defence Union and the Medical Protection Society) settle approximately 700 new claims *per annum* arising from incidents in primary care.[50]

It can be seen that these figures bear no relationship to the estimated   1–010
number of patients who suffer a *preventable* adverse event (425,000 patients) in NHS hospitals each year. Of course, not all preventable adverse events would necessarily be categorised as negligent by the legal system, and most of them would lead to only temporary or minor impairment or disability which may not justify litigation. Nonetheless, and notwithstanding the comparatively poor success rates for claimants in medical malpractice litigation, it seems likely that there are many more patients with a genuine potential claim who do not litigate than there are patients with a spurious claim who do.

(c) How many claims are successful?

The success rate for claims depends upon how they are measured. In 1978   1–011
the Pearson Commission estimated that for all personal injury claims brought the success rate for claimants was about 85 to 90 per cent, but for medical negligence claims it was only 30 to 40 per cent.[51] The Review of Legal Aid expenditure, *Eligibility for Civil Legal Aid*,[52] estimated that for Legally Aided litigation the success rate for medical negligence claims was 42 per cent, whereas for road traffic claims it was 84 per cent, and 79 per cent for work accident claims. Other studies have put the overall success rate for medical negligence claims at around 25 per cent[53] to 30 per cent.[54] If, however, one separates overall claims from claims that proceed after the initial investigation as to whether there may have been negligence, a different figure for success rates is seen. The National Audit Office[55] reported on figures produced by the Legal Aid/Legal Services Commission for clinical negligence claims for 1999-2000:

- Total claims   9,117
- Not pursued beyond initial investigation   60 per cent

---

[49] *ibid.* The report expressed the caveat that it is not yet clear whether this is the start of a downward trend in claims.

[50] *An Organisation with a Memory*, para. 4.39; *cf.* the figures in *Making Amends*, June 2003, pp. 62–63, indicating that the Medical Protection Society *receives* between 400 and 500 claims against general practitioners *per annum*, and the number of claims *received* by the Medical Defence Union ranged between about 1400 and 1800 *per annum* between 1995 and 2000.

[51] *Royal Commission on Civil Liability and Compensation for Personal Injury*, Cmnd. 7054 (1978), Vol. I, paras 78 and 1326.

[52] (1991) HMSO.

[53] Hawkins and Paterson, "Medicolegal audit in the West Midlands: Analysis of 100 Cases" (1987) 295 B.M.J. 1533; Fenn, Hermans and Dingwall, "Estimating the cost of compensating the victims of medical negligence" (1994) 309 B.M.J. 389.

[54] P. Fenn *et al.*, "Current cost of medical negligence in NHS hospitals: analysis of claims database" (2000) 320 B.M.J. 1567.

[55] *Handling Clinical Negligence Claims in England*, May 2001, p. 32.

- Of the 40 per cent (3,645 cases) proceeding   61 per cent were successful

- Of the total number of cases (9,117)   24 per cent were successful[56]

The Woolf Report[57] found that 92 per cent of medical negligence cases were legally aided. Full funding by legal aid is available only to those on income support (or comparable incomes), though partial support is available for just under half the population. There is no evidence that the victims of medical negligence are disproportionately poor. The inference is that many victims of medical negligence do not bring proceedings because of the difficulties of proof and the disproportionate costs of litigating.

(d) The cost of claims

1–012   A truer picture of the overall cost of medical negligence litigation has emerged in recent years in the National Audit Office summarised accounts of the NHS. The accounts distinguish between the actual amounts spent in meeting claims in any one year and provisions in the accounts for the cost of future claims. Estimates of future expenditure include both claims that are known about and those that it is anticipated will be made in the future in respect of incidents that have already occurred, but the patient is either unaware of the damage or has yet to make a claim (incurred but not reported (IBNR) claims).[58] The latter category of provisions is clearly an estimate that involves quite a degree of speculation, both as to the number of successful future claims and their overall value. There is a very marked difference between the sums (including costs) actually paid out in a given financial year, and estimates of the future total cost of all potential claims arising from incidents up to the date of the assessment. Moreover, the sums allowed for potential future claims have increased significantly over the last few years, sometimes simply to reflect different actuarial assumptions, rather than any perceived future increase in litigation.

1–013   Tracing the accounts over a number of years demonstrates the increase in the liability of the NHS, most significantly in terms of the assessment of future claims. At April 1, 1996[59] the estimated actual cost of NHS clinical negligence litigation was put at £200 million *per annum*, with an expectation

---

[56] The overall success rate for legally aided claimants increased to 27% in 2001–2002: *Making Amends*, June 2003, p. 68, para. 51.

[57] *Access to Justice*, 1996, Ch. 15.

[58] The pattern for the percentage of reported incidents in any given year following the year in which the event occurred was set out in the *Membership Prospectus for the Clinical Negligence Scheme for Trusts*, and showed a "long tail" of unreported incidents. For example, at the end of the first year following the year in which incidents occur only 26% of the claims that will ultimately arise from the year's activities will have been reported. By the end of the third year only 53% of incidents will have been reported.

[59] Until 1996, data on NHS claims was not routinely collected. An estimate of the annual cost of medical negligence litigation to the NHS in 1990–1991 was £53.2 million (£74.5 million at 2002 prices): *Making Amends*, June 2003, p. 60, para. 35.

that this would grow by about 25 per cent *per annum* over the next five years.[60]
The estimated *actual* expenditure of the NHS on medical negligence claims in
1997-98 was £223.5 million.[61] At March 31, 1998 NHS Trusts, Health
Authorities and the NHS Litigation Authority had made provision for clinical
negligence of £394 million, with contingent liabilities (where it was estimated
there was a less than 50 per cent chance of a successful claim) of £733 million.
The potential liabilities of the NHS amounted to £1.8 billion (£394 million of
provisions by NHS Trusts, plus £1.4 billion of assistance by the Department
of Health under the Clinical Negligence Scheme for Trusts and the Existing
Liabilities Scheme). This excluded IBNR claims and contingent liabilities. In
1998-1999 the NHS paid out around £400 million in settlement of clinical
negligence claims, and at March 31, 1999 had estimated potential liabilities
of £2.4 billion, plus approximately £0.9 billion for IBNR claims.[62] The following year provisions for the potential liabilities of the NHS amounted to
£3.9 billion (£2.6 billion provisions for reported claims, plus £1.3 billion for
IBNR claims), an increase of £0.7 billion over the previous year.[63]

In 2001 the National Audit Office undertook a particular study of clini-   1–014
cal negligence. Its report, *Handling Clinical Negligence Claims in England*
stated that:

- At March 31, 2000, there were 23,000 outstanding claims with
  provisions for likely settlements of £2.6 billion.[64] A further £1.3
  billion was estimated as required for incidents that have occurred
  but not yet been reported.[65]

- Cerebral palsy and brain damage cases account for 80 per cent of
  outstanding claims by value and 26 per cent of claims by number
  in the largest scheme (the Existing Liabilities Scheme).

- For claims closed in 1999-2000 with settlement costs in excess of
  £10,000 the average time from claim to payment was 5½ years.
  Claims still outstanding were on average 8.3 years old, with 22
  per cent over 10 years old.

---

[60] EL(96)11, n. 2. This estimate was repeated in the *NHS (England) Summarised Accounts
1995–96*, para. 48.
[61] *NHS (England) Summarised Accounts 1997–98*.
[62] *NHS (England) Summarised Accounts 1998–99*.
[63] *NHS (England) Summarised Accounts 1999–2000*.
[64] As at March 31, 2000 provisions for outstanding claims in Scotland were £38 million, for
Wales £111 million, and for Northern Ireland £100 million: NAO, *Handling Clinical
Negligence Claims in England*, para. 2.3.
[65] These are the same figures as appear in the *NHS (England) Summarised Accounts
1999–2000*. Note that these figures of £2.6 billion and £1.3 billion are provisions in the
accounts representing the total cost of all outstanding claims (and possible future claims in
relation to past events) where it is estimated that there is a better than 50% chance of the
claim succeeding. They do not represent an annual cost to the NHS of medical negligence
litigation. *cf.* an earlier study on clinical negligence costs, Fenn *et al.*, "Current cost of
medical negligence in NHS hospitals: analysis of claims database" (2000) 320 B.M.J. 1567:
on the basis of a study of a database of claims in the Oxfordshire Health Authority they estimated that the annual cost of medical negligence claims in England in 1998 was £84 million.

- In 65 per cent of settlements in 1999-2000 below £50,000 the legal and other costs of settling claims exceeded the damages awarded.

- Only 24 per cent of claims funded by the Legal Services Commission were successful.

Some of the figures in this report have been questioned, because the National Audit Office looked at claims closed since April 1, 1995, for events that occurred before April 1, 1995, *i.e.* they were looking at cases from the Existing Liabilities Scheme, which by 2000–2001, by definition, were old cases. It was therefore likely that delays in settlement would be above the average and costs in claims of that age would be likely to be unrepresentative of the costs in claims conducted more recently.[66] This criticism is borne out by figures from the most recent NHS Accounts, which show a marked reduction in the time from claim to settlement. With claims under the Existing Liabilities Scheme the average time for claims to be settled in 2001–2002 was 3.89 years (compared to 5.5 years in 1999-2000), and for claims settled under the Clinical Negligence Scheme for Trusts (*i.e.* post March 31, 1995, incidents) in 2001–2002 the average time was 1.27 years.[67]

1–015   Since *Handling Clinical Negligence Claims in England* was published in May 2001 the estimated net present value of known and anticipated claims has increased from £3.9 billion to £5.25 billion at the end of March 2002.[68] The increase was due to a further reassessment of the assumptions applied by the actuaries in calculating the level of provision required to take account of increased awards of damages to fund the costs of future care.[69] It is apparent that these very large sums do not bear much resemblance to the actual sum paid out by the NHS for clinical negligence claims which in 2001–2002 was £446 million (as at March 31, 2002), up from £415 million in 2000–2001.[70] Although the figures do represent a significant increase (*e.g.* from the estimated £223.5 million in 1997-98), they are closer to the annual growth rate for closed claims arising from events in hospitals suggested by Fenn *et al.* which was put at 11 per cent *per annum* in absolute terms between 1990–1998, and 7 per cent *per annum* when adjusted for the increase in "finished consultant episodes" (*i.e.* relative to the increase in

---

[66] See *Clinical Negligence: What Are the Issues and Options for Reform? Response by the Association of Personal Injury Lawyers*, October 2001, para. 2.5.4.

[67] *NHS (England) Summarised Accounts 2001–2002*, fig. 17. This figure has now fallen to 1.19 years: *Making Amends*, June 2003, p. 92, para. 11.

[68] *NHS (England) Summarised Accounts 2001–2002*. The comparable figure for March 2001 was £4.4 billion: *NHS (England) Summarised Accounts 2000–2001*. See also *Making Amends*, June 2003, p. 72, para. 59.

[69] This was the case in both accounting years: *NHS (England) Summarised Accounts 2000–2001*, para. 6.5 and *NHS (England) Summarised Accounts 2001–2002*, para. 6.9. In 2000–2001, the first year of significant payments under CNST, approximately £157 million was paid to claimants: *ibid.* para. 6.12. Compare settlements under the Existing Liabilities Scheme: 1998–1999 – £107 million; 1999–2000 – £386 million; source: National Audit Office, *Handling Clinical Negligence Claims in England*, May 2001, para. 2.18.

[70] *NHS (England) Summarised Accounts 2001–2002*, para. 6.6.

medical activity).[71] The authors of that research commented that: "We regard estimates of the outstanding liability of the NHS, such as the £2.8 billion quoted earlier, as deeply misleading. We have shown that this represents the aggregate estimated cost of outstanding claims, most of which will never be paid a single penny and some of which will not be paid for many years, if not decades." The Chief Medical Officer has remarked that although an annual cost of compensation claims of approximately £450 million is a large sum in absolute terms, it represents slightly less than 1 per cent of the annual expenditure of the NHS.[72] Moreover, an increase in the total cost of settlements in any given year tells one nothing about whether the number of *claims* is increasing, since the cost of settlement may reflect increases in the awards of damages and increased efficiency in disposing of some of the backlog of cases. Indeed, the most recent evidence on the number of claims is that they are falling.[73]

The distribution of claims by specialty is highly skewed. It is known that cases involving brain damage to babies at birth are particularly expensive to compensate. In 2000, *An Organisation with a Memory* estimated that the average amount of compensation in such cases is around £1.5 million, with some awards as high as £4 million, and that such claims account for 50 per cent of the NHS £400 million litigation bill *per annum*.[74] More recently, *Making Amends* has stated that the average payment of compensation for birth related cerebral palsy claims handled by the NHS Litigation Authority to the end of September 2002 was £670,000 for claims relating to incidents since 1995, and £1,225,000 for older cases, with the highest payment being £5.5 million in February 2003.[75] In only a third of claims did the claimants receive damages. Figures from the NHS Litigation Authority[76] indicate that Obstetrics & Gynaecology gives rise to 26.1 per cent of claims by number, but 61.7 per cent of the total cost:

1–016

Number of Claims by Specialty	%	Percentage of total cost	%
Surgery	37.6	Obstetrics & Gynaecology	61.7
Obstetrics & Gynaecology	26.1	Surgery	14.3
Medicine	14.6	Medicine	13.8
A&E	12.3	A&E	4.8
Anaesthesia	2.9	Anaesthesia	2.0
Psychiatry/Mental	2.0	Psychiatry/Mental	1.3

[71] Fenn *et al.*, "Current cost of medical negligence in NHS hospitals: analysis of claims database" (2000) 320 B.M.J. 1567.
[72] *Making Amends*, June 2003, p. 26, para. 14.
[73] See above para. 1–009 the text at n. 49.
[74] *An Organisation with a Memory*, para. 4.34.
[75] *Making Amends*, p. 50, para. 52.
[76] Data is taken from the *NHSLA Journal*, No. 1, Winter 2001 (based on CNST claims, i.e. incidents post March 31, 1995), available at *www.nhsla.com*. The *National Health Service Litigation Authority, Report and Accounts 2002*, indicates that for CNST, Obstetrics & Gynaecology represents approximately 25.6% of claims and approximately 48% of the value of reported claims [calculated from the data provided in "Facts and Figures"].

Number of Claims by Specialty	%	Percentage of total cost	%
Radiology	1.6	Radiology	0.8
Pathology	1.4	Pathology	0.6
Paramedical Support	0.9	Ambulance	0.5
Ambulance	0.6	Public Health	0.2

The most recent figures, for the financial year 2002/2003, are even more stark. Birth-related brain damage (including cerebral palsy) in the NHS accounted for just over 5 per cent of all cases of medical litigation in which damages were paid, and 60 per cent of all expenditure on medical litigation.[77] The implications for priority setting in developing risk management procedures are self-evident. In primary care failed or delayed diagnosis gives rise to 57 per cent of claims, and medication error 22 per cent of claims.[78]

(2) Defensive medicine

1–017   Defensive medicine has to be viewed in terms of a reaction by doctors to the perceived threat of litigation. In *Whitehouse v Jordan* Lawton L.J. said that defensive medicine consists of "adopting procedures which are not for the benefit of the patient but safeguards against the possibility of the patient making a claim for negligence."[79] This has two aspects: positive defensive medicine, which involves undertaking additional procedures, such as diagnostic tests and X-rays, which, in the doctor's professional judgment, are unnecessary; and negative defensive medicine, which involves avoiding procedures which in the doctor's professional judgment are necessary in the patient's best interests because of the risk of something going wrong. Positive defensive medicine, it is said, is wasteful of time and resources and possibly increases the risk to patients of medical intervention, and negative defensive medicine deprives patients of potentially beneficial treatment. It is important to appreciate that the term "defensive medicine" is used in a pejorative sense, to indicate that the risk of liability induces doctors to adopt practices which are not medically required or justified. The charge is that the law dictates medical practice, indeed, dictates bad medical practice.

1–018   The difficulty with the argument about defensive medicine is that as a legal concept defensive medicine does not make sense. The standard of care required by the *Bolam* test[80] is that of a reasonably competent medical practitioner exercising and professing to have that skill. This is essentially a medical test requiring medical evidence as to proper professional practice.[81]

---

[77] *Making Amends*, June 2003, p. 47, para. 43.
[78] *ibid.*, p. 40, para. 23.
[79] [1980] 1 All E.R. 650, 659.
[80] *Bolam v Friern Hospital Management Committee* [1957] 2 All E.R. 118; see paras 3–007 *et seq.*
[81] This remains the case notwithstanding the decision of the House of Lords in *Bolitho v City and Hackney Health Authority* [1998] A.C. 232 that the courts should subject medical judgments to "logical analysis"; see para. 3–028.

If a defendant's fellow professionals agree that a specific procedure was unnecessary and wasteful a doctor cannot be held negligent for omitting to carry it out. On this basis it is difficult to see how a doctor can *protect* himself from a claim in negligence by carrying out an unnecessary test or procedure. If he could not be held liable for failing to do something, he could not protect himself from liability by doing it. Indeed, to the extent that the procedure carries additional risk to the patient a doctor increases the risk of a claim if something goes wrong precisely *because* the procedure was unnecessary. Moreover, under the *Bolam* test it does not matter that some doctors do regard the procedure as essential provided that there is a responsible body of medical opinion that takes a contrary view. The same argument applies to negative defensive medicine. If the procedure would have been performed by a responsible body of professional opinion the doctor cannot be negligent for performing it (even where a responsible body of opinion would not have undertaken the procedure), and so he cannot "protect" himself by declining to undertake it, and he may increase the risk of a finding of negligence on the basis that he has failed to perform a procedure which responsible medical opinion considers to have been necessary.

Although the existence of defensive medicine as a sociological fact appears to have achieved some acceptance in the English courts,[82] there is very little empirical, as opposed to anecdotal, evidence to support the theory that doctors do practise defensively.[83] Doctors may *say* that they practise defensively, but there is considerable scope for confusion as to what, precisely, "defensive" means and, indeed, whether it is detrimental to patients.[84] Some doctors use the term "defensive" simply to mean treating patients conservatively or even "more carefully." What to one doctor may seem defensive may to another doctor be good practice. Moreover, from the point of view of the individual patient defensive practice, such as over-testing, may be positively beneficial if it discovers something previously unsuspected or even if it simply sets the patient's mind at rest, although it is arguably prejudicial to the NHS because of the extra costs involved. It is unfortunate, to say the least, that such an important document as the Chief Medical Officer's report

1–019

---

[82] See para. 3–110. It was also assumed both to exist and to be detrimental to the consumers of NHS care in the National Health Service (Compensation) Bill 1991, Sch. 2 para. 4.

[83] A commonly cited example of defensive practice is an increased rate of Caesarian section deliveries as a consequence of obstetricians fearing that claims in respect of birth injuries could arise from forceps deliveries or allowing a difficult labour to progress too long. Caesarian section rates have been increasing, however, in many developed countries with very different systems of health care provision and different patterns of litigation, and may be explained by factors which have very little to do with litigation: Ham, Dingwall, Fenn and Harris, *Medical Negligence: Compensation and Accountability*, 1988, p. 14.

[84] Jones and Morris (1989) 5 J. of the M.D.U. 40; Tribe and Korgaonkar (1991) 7 P.N. 2; Summerton (1995) 310 B.M.J. 27. M.J. Powers in R.V. Clements (ed.) *Safe Practice in Obstetrics and Gynaecology*, (1994) Churchill Livingstone, p. 15, comments that: ". . . it should be appreciated that 'defensive medicine' is a figment of the paranoid medical profession's imagination . . . Often what is regarded as 'defensive' medicine is simply the prevailing view of safe and prudent practice." Black (1990) 335 *The Lancet* 35, 37 concluded that litigation does not seem to be damaging the quality of medical care, although "the cost of medical litigation may yet prove to be damaging to the quality of care." For discussion of defensive medicine in Canada see Dickens (1991) 41 Univ. of Toronto L.J. 168.

on the review of the system of handling compensation claims and complaints in the NHS, *Making Amends*, refers uncritically to the existence of "defensive medicine" without citing a single piece of empirical evidence to support its existence in the NHS.[85]

1–020   In any event, defensive medicine can only be relevant to certain types of medical negligence. There is a difference between, on the one hand, the negligence involved in leaving a swab in a patient or removing the wrong kidney or prescribing the wrong dosage of a drug and, on the other hand, the conscious assessment of risk as between alternative procedures or the risk in not doing certain things. Inadvertent errors (which probably constitute the bulk of medical accidents) cannot be the subject of defensive medicine in its pejorative sense, since the doctor has not made a conscious decision to do or avoid something due to of the risk of liability. Indeed, if he had thought about it he would have avoided the error. Moreover, insofar as the threat of litigation may lead to the introduction of procedures which are specifically designed to avoid inadvertent errors the law serves an important function in promoting good practice and preventing accidents.[86] By definition, defensive medicine implies that doctors respond to liability rules, *i.e.*, they modify their behaviour in response to the risk of liability.[87] If the threat of liability were to be removed, as a consequence of, say, the introduction of a scheme of no-fault compensation, would doctors become less careful, or even careless? This is at least one implication of the evidence that was presented to the Pearson Commission by the medical profession.[88]

---

[85] *Making Amends*, June 2003, p. 27, para. 17; p. 76, para. 5; p. 108, para. 61; p. 110, para. 6; p. 118, para. 8, where there is a reference to "the rising tide of defensive medicine." No explanation is offered as to how "potentially hazardous and costly investigations" carried out "not for the benefit of the patient but for the sole purpose of fending off a successful lawsuit" are likely to achieve this particular objective.

[86] For an argument that the way to reduce defensive medicine and the costs of medical malpractice is to shift the burden of liability from the individual doctor to the hospital and to change the standard of liability from negligence to strict liability see: Chapman (1990) 28 Osgoode Hall L.J. 523.

[87] It is arguable that it has been the upsurge in medical malpractice litigation over the last twenty years or so which has produced a greater emphasis on clinical risk management which is designed to identify the factors that can lead to medical accidents and identify ways of reducing accidents. This is clearly in the interests of patients, but there is a strong element of seeking to reduce the cost of accidents to the NHS driving this development. The whole concept of risk management simply reiterates the point that acting in the interests of patients, by reducing the risk of accidental harm, is also in the interests of doctors in that it reduces the risk of being sued, and in the interests of the NHS which has to meet both the cost of claims and the cost of treating those patients who suffer accidental injury even if they do not sue. It is in this context that the comment in *Making Amends*, June 2003, p. 117, para. 2, about the effect of litigation on individual doctors is entirely misplaced: "Few neutral observers would try to argue that quality and safety of health care are improving because health care professionals are behaving more conscientiously clinically as a result of having watched their colleagues being sued." There are two responses to this point: (1) no-one, whether neutral or not, has produced any evidence to show that the quality and safety of health care has deteriorated because health care professionals are aware that they can be sued; (2) there is abundant evidence that one consequence of the growth in litigation, and its rising cost to the NHS, has been to persuade policy-makers in the NHS to appreciate the pressing need for much greater safety in the delivery of health care.

[88] *Royal Commission on Civil Liability and Compensation for Personal Injury*, Cmnd. 7054 (1978), Vol. I, paras 1342–1343; see para. 1–026. "Liability and Compensation in Health

It is sometimes suggested that a sense of public duty is what motivates 1–021
individuals working in the public sector, and that therefore the imposition of
a duty of care on a health professionals would not lead to higher standards
of medical care;[89] whereas the profit motive is what drives individuals in the
private sector. This rather oversimplifies the situation in the real world. It
suggests that somehow professionals working in the public sector always
achieve high levels of competence from motives of altruism, professionalism
or a sense of public duty, whereas private sector defendants (solicitors,
accountants, surveyors, etc.) need a sharp prod from the law of tort in order
to achieve an acceptable level of competence. There may be situations where
the profit motive leads individuals to cut corners and thereby increase the
risk of damage to others, but the risk of cutting corners is not exclusive to
the private sector. Indeed, the need to keep the paying client happy may
produce higher standards of care, whereas the public sector employee has a
"captive market", and clients who, as a general rule, cannot take their business elsewhere, a situation that may lead to complacency rather than high
standards. Moreover, linking the statement that imposing a duty of care in
negligence would not lead to higher standards of care with the statement that
it could lead to defensive practices[90] is logically incoherent. It asserts that,
on the one hand, public sector professionals are not likely to respond to the
threat of liability for carelessness by improving their performance, whereas,
on the other hand, they are likely to respond to the threat of liability by
indulging in defensive practices. Either they do respond as rational individuals to liability rules or they do not, but it seems highly improbable that they
do both at the same time. Of course, the views of the judiciary on this subject
are not necessarily uniform. Indeed, some judges take the view that imposing a duty of care "may have the healthy effect of securing that high standards are sought and secured."[91]

The claim that it is the law that is positively detrimental to the practice of 1–022
medicine in this country cannot be accepted. When the rhetoric is stripped
away, it is the tort of negligence that provides the bottom line: the *minimum*
standard of acceptable professional conduct. In practice, medical negligence
is a failure to live up to proper medical standards, and those standards are
set, not by lawyers, but by doctors.

(n.88 contd.) Care," J.R.S. Prichard, *A Report to the Conference of Deputy Ministers of the Federal/Provincial/Territorial Review of Liability and Compensation Issues in Health Care* (1990) found that malpractice litigation had a net positive effect on the quality of health care in Canada, including systematic risk reduction in areas of recurrent injury, and the introduction of quality assurance, risk management and audit. On the other hand, the threat of potential liability resulted in greater stress and anxiety in the medical profession.

[89] For example, in *Palmer v Tees Health Authority* [1998] Lloyd's Rep. Med. 447, 460 Gage J. said: "As Lord Keith pointed out in *Hill*'s case, on the whole public duty motivates police forces. The same applies to doctors. There is a considerable danger that doctors, to avoid being sued, might lean towards defensive medicine."

[90] As Gage J. did in *Palmer v Tees Health Authority*.

[91] See the comments of Lord Clyde in *Phelps v Hillingdon London Borough Council* [2001] 2 A.C. 619, 672, quoted more fully at para. 3–116. See also *Barrett v Enfield London Borough Council* [1997] 3 All E.R. 171, 181 *per* Evans L.J.; *Capital and Counties plc v Hampshire County Council* [1997] Q.B. 1004, 1043–1044, CA.

(3) No-fault compensation

1–023   Until the Department of Health review of the system of handling compensation claims and complaints in the NHS[92] there had not been a serious consideration of whether to introduce no-fault compensation for the victims of medical accidents. The Pearson Commission considered, and rejected, the idea of no-fault compensation specifically for medical accidents, although it was accepted that a change of circumstances might shift the balance of the arguments in favour of such a proposal.[93] The evidence from the medical profession to the Commission was overwhelmingly in favour of retaining the tort action. It was argued that:

> "Liability was one of the means whereby doctors could show their sense of responsibility and, therefore, justly claim professional freedom. If tortious liability were abolished, there could be some attempt to control doctors' clinical practice to prevent mistakes for which compensation would have to be paid by some central agency. It was said that this could lead to a bureaucratic restriction of medicine and a brake on progress. It was further argued that the traditions of the profession were not sufficient in themselves to prevent all lapses which, though small in number, might have disastrous effects. Some penalty helped to preserve the patient's opportunity to express disapproval and obtain redress."[94]

The Medical Defence Union commented that, although they paid the compensation, their investigation into the circumstances brought home to the doctor the part he had played and encouraged a sense of personal responsibility.[95]

1–024   The growth of medical malpractice litigation in the 1980s led the medical profession to reconsider its position. By 1987 the British Medical Association had come to the view that what was needed was a non-statutory scheme of compensation which "within defined limits would provide compensation without apportionment of blame." The opening paragraph of the BMA Report put the case succinctly:

> "As a caring profession we wish to see adequate arrangements to provide compensation and support to those who suffer personal injury, given according to need and not to cause. It is clear that patients with similar disabilities may receive different benefits under current provisions. A child may remain brain damaged following (a) encephalitis, (b) vaccine inoculation, (c) traumatic birth delivery. The needs of all three children may be similar. There will be great sympathy for all three sets

---

[92] See para. 1–054.
[93] *Royal Commission on Civil Liability and Compensation for Personal Injury*, Cmnd. 7054 (1978), Vol. I, paras 1348–1371.
[94] *ibid*. at para. 1342.
[95] *ibid*. at para. 1343.

of parents. However, the available compensation will range through no compensation at all, through £20,000, to some hundreds of thousands of pounds. This cannot be legal, fair or sensible."[96]

While the moral force of this argument is undeniable, the statement is misleading since a no-fault compensation scheme would probably not have changed the outcome of this particular example. The child with encephalitis would not be compensated under any current no-fault scheme since illness and/or disease and congenital disability are excluded, and even the child with vaccine damage would probably not receive compensation under some no-fault schemes. This highlights a major concern with any no-fault scheme for the victims of medical accidents, namely who would be eligible to claim? The BMA returned to the issue of compensation in its *No Fault Compensation Working Party Report*, 1991, and in that year a private members Bill, the National Health Service (Compensation) Bill 1991, was introduced in Parliament but was opposed by the government.

The problems with the action in tort as a means of compensating for injury   1–025
or disease are well-documented.[97] They include the following:

(i) Delay, which appears to be endemic in the adversarial system.[98] It is not yet clear whether the procedural reforms introduced by the Civil Procedure Rules have had a significant impact on the speed at which disputes are resolved. There is some recent evidence that the NHS Litigation Authority is settling claims for clinical negligence much more quickly.[99]

(ii) The cost of bringing an action, which is notoriously high, at least in relation to the sums recovered in damages.[1] *Handling Clinical*

---

[96] *Report of the BMA No Fault Compensation Working Party*, 1987. The same point was made in the Report of the Royal College of Physicians, *Compensation for Adverse Consequences of Medical Intervention*, 1990, para. 3.3.

[97] See the *Royal Commission on Civil Liability and Compensation for Personal Injury*, Cmnd 7054 (1978); the *Civil Justice Review*, Cmnd. 394, 1988; and *Access to Justice*, 1996.

[98] The *Civil Justice Review*, Cmnd. 394, 1988, para. 421 put the average time from accident to trial at over five years in the High Court and almost three years in the County Court. For a more recent analysis of the relationship between costs and delay see *Access to Justice—Final Report*, Annexe 3, 1996. Delay in medical negligence cases tends to be greater, on average, than in other types of personal injuries action (*Royal Commission on Civil Liability and Compensation for Personal Injury*, Cmnd. 7054 (1978), Vol. II, Table 129 and para. 242), and individual cases of over 10 years duration are not unknown. The National Audit Office report, *Handling Clinical Negligence Claims in England*, found that for claims closed in 1999–2000 where settlement costs were in excess of £10,000 the average time from claim to payment was 5½ years, and claims still outstanding were on average 8.3 years old, with 22% over 10 years old (though this finding was based on data from the Existing Liabilities Scheme, where incidents arose before April 1, 1995—which by definition were "old" cases).

[99] See para. 1–014.

[1] The *Royal Commission on Civil Liability and Compensation for Personal Injury*, Cmnd. 7054 (1978), Vol. I, para. 83 put the administrative costs of the tort system at 85% of the amounts paid in damages, whereas the cost of running the social security system came to 11% of the total paid out (para. 121). The *Civil Justice Review*, Cmnd. 394, 1988, paras 427–432, estimated that legal costs alone amounted to up to 75% of the sums recovered in the High Court and up to 175% of the sums recovered in the County Court.

Negligence Claims in England found that in 65 per cent of settlements in 1999-2000 below £50,000 the legal and other costs of settling claims exceeded the damages awarded. The overriding objective of civil litigation introduced by the Civil Procedure Rules is to deal with cases justly, having regard, amongst other things, to saving expense and dealing with the case in ways which are proportionate to the amount of money involved.[2] Whether this has produced a significant reduction in the cost of litigation remains to be seen.

(iii) Limited access to the courts for injured patients because the cost of bringing an action excludes many people from pursuing otherwise legitimate claims for negligence, and the financial restrictions on eligibility for civil legal aid mean that in practice only the poorest citizens qualify for assistance.[3] The advent of conditional fees for personal injury litigation has not had a major impact in medical negligence litigation because of the relatively high cost of insurance premiums to cover the risk of having to pay the defendants' costs if the claim is lost, and the much greater difficulty of predicting the outcome in medical negligence cases.[4]

(iv) Success depends on proof of both negligence and causation (which can be particularly difficult in cases of medical negligence).

(v) Problems of proof make the outcome of legal proceedings unpredictable, and the effects of this can be quite arbitrary, some cases succeeding and others failing on grounds which may appear to have little connection with the substantive merits of the respective claims.

(vi) Awards of damages in the form of a lump sum mean that if the claimant's circumstances change it is not possible to adjust the award, a situation which can result in either over-compensation or under-compensation.[5]

(vii) There is also evidence that litigation itself tends to have adverse effects on claimants.[6]

---

[2] CPR r. 1.1.

[3] The percentage of claims for medical negligence brought with legal aid has remained remarkably consistent. Hoyte "Medical Negligence Litigation, Claims Handling and Risk Management" (1994) 1 Med. Law Int. 261, 264 commented out that 90% of claims made against doctors are funded by legal aid; and in a study of 100 claims, 95% were legally aided: Neale (1993) 307 B.M.J. 1483. *Access to Justice*, 1996, found that 92% of medical negligence claims were legally aided. *Making Amends*, June 2003, p. 67, para. 48, puts the figure at 90%.

[4] The availability of insurance is also limited, reflecting the much higher risk to insurers: *Making Amends*, June 2003, p. 71, para. 57.

[5] See para. 9–011. The courts will, however, have the power to award damages as periodical payments in due course: see para. 9–012.

[6] In a study of patients who presented with head injuries which at the time of the accident were indistinguishable, it was found that a year after settlement (approximately three years after

The problems with tort as a compensation mechanism apply to all types **1–026** of personal injuries action, whether the claimant's injuries were sustained on the road, at work or in a hospital, although in practice medical negligence claimants often have a more difficult task in proving negligence and/or causation.[7] Moreover, these problems have been present for many years, despite occasional attempts to improve the efficiency of the civil litigation system. What has changed quite dramatically in the last 10 years or so, is not the nature of the problem, nor even the growth in numbers of claims, but the gradual realisation of how much the tort system costs the NHS. It is this, and the acknowledgment that modern health care carries a high risk of injury to patients, that has prompted more recent calls for reform, with no-fault compensation again advocated as a possible solution.[8] Although the Chief Medical Officer's report, *Making Amends*, has ultimately rejected the no-fault option as too expensive, it is worth considering the advantages and disadvantages of no-fault compensation schemes, first, because the CMO's report is not necessarily the last word on the subject, and secondly because it illustrates some of the issues that any scheme of reform would have to address. A useful starting point is briefly to consider the two best-known examples of no-fault compensation schemes, in New Zealand and Sweden, which illustrate some of the complexities involved in defining eligibility criteria. Two American states have enacted no-fault compensation schemes specifically targeted at cases involving brain-damaged babies, and given, the model for reform chosen by the CMO in *Making Amends*, these schemes have a particular significance.

New Zealand

The New Zealand no-fault compensation scheme is a statutory compen- **1–027** sation scheme which applies to all cases of "personal injury by accident." If an individual qualifies for compensation under the no-fault scheme, a claim in tort in respect of the same injuries is barred, although where an individual does not qualify for compensation a common law claim is available, assuming of course that the common law recognises the relevant loss.[9] The scheme is funded by a levy on vehicles for motor accidents, levies on employers, employees and the self-employed for accidents to earners (at differential rates for different occupational risks), a levy on health care providers in respect of personal injury from medical error or medical mishap, and out of

---

(n.6 contd.) the accident) patients participating in litigation in respect of their personal injuries had a symptom rate two to three times that of the general series of patients one year after the accident: see Rutherford and Fee (1988) 297 B.M.J. 1405. This was not simply a case of the more severe injuries leading to litigation, because in the sample, 82% of the claimants had contacted a solicitor within two months of the accident.

[7] See para. 1–011.
[8] See para. 1–004.
[9] See *van Soest v Residual Health Management Unit* [2000] 1 N.Z.L.R. 179; commented on by Mullany at (2001) 117 L.Q.R. 182; Teff at (2001) 9 Tort L. Rev. 109; Todd (2001) 17 P.N. 230.

general taxation for other accidents. Initially funded on a "pay as you go" basis (funds being raised in a given year to cover the cost of claims made in that year), from 1999 the process of switching to a "fully funded" scheme (like private insurance) was started. Private insurers were allowed to participate in the funding arrangements for the first time. The scheme is limited to personal injury by "accident" (which includes occupational disease), but does not cover disease or the consequences of the ageing process. The distinction between accident and disease has caused some problems in practice, and is open to the objection that it is wrong in principle when the underlying rationale of a comprehensive no-fault scheme is that attention should focus on the disability itself, not the cause of the disability.

1–028   An "accident" is defined as any of the following kinds of occurrences:

(a) a specific event, or a series of events, that (i) involves the application of force or resistance external to the human body; and (ii) is not a gradual process;

(b) the inhalation or oral ingestion of any solid, liquid, gas, or foreign object on a specific occasion . . .;

(c) a burn, or exposure to radiation or rays of any kind, on a specific occasion . . .;

(d) the absorption of any chemical through the skin with a defined period of time not exceeding 1 month;

(e) any exposure to the elements, or to extremes of temperature or environment . . . that causes (i) disability lasting for a continuous period exceeding 1 month; or (ii) death.[10]

The scheme has experienced problems in relation to eligibility arising from medical accidents because of the difficulty of identifying what constitutes medical misadventure.[11] These difficulties were clarified in amendments to the scheme introduced in 1992, and there were further amendments to the scheme in 1998. The effect has been to provide a more precise definition of what amounts to medical misadventure, but this has also narrowed entitlement to circumstances where, essentially, there has been negligence. Personal injury caused by medical misadventure is defined as: "personal injury caused by medical error or medical mishap."[12] This definition expressly includes personal injury caused by the claimant's abnormal reaction to treatment or a complication the claimant suffers later because of the treatment given to him/her providing that the medical error/mishap occurs at the time of treatment.[13] Medical error is "the failure of a registered health professional to observe a standard of care and skill reasonably to be

---

[10] Accident Insurance Act 1998, s. 28(2) (*New Zealand*).
[11] See, *e.g.*, *Childs v Hillock* [1994] 2 N.Z.L.R. 65 (N.Z.C.A.).
[12] *ibid.*, s. 35.
[13] *ibid.*, s. 35(2).

expected in the circumstances."[14] This includes a registered health professional's negligent failure to obtain informed consent to treatment, or to diagnose correctly an insured's medical condition; or a negligent failure to give the insured treatment.[15] Medical mishap is very narrowly defined as an adverse consequence of treatment when: (a) the treatment is given to a claimant, is given properly, and is given by or at the direction of a registered health professional; and (b) the adverse consequence is suffered by the claimant; and (c) the adverse consequence is severe; and (d) the likelihood that treatment of the kind that was given would have the adverse consequence is rare.[16] An adverse consequence is "severe" if it results in the claimant dying, being hospitalised as an inpatient for more than 14 days or suffering significant disability lasting more than 28 days in total.[17] An adverse consequence is "rare" if the probability of that adverse consequence occurring is *less than one per cent* of cases in which that treatment is given. But a medical mishap will not be "rare", if the risk was known to the insured before the treatment was commenced.[18]

The New Zealand no-fault scheme is drafted in such a way as to exclude 1–029 from compensation many medical injuries which in the true sense of the word are "accidental." In the specific context of medical injuries it is now little more than a statutory "fault compensation scheme."[19] For those who do meet the statutory criteria compensation is designed to meet pecuniary losses, rather than non-pecuniary losses. Claimants are entitled to medical expenses and loss of earnings of up to 80 per cent of pre-accident earnings, subject to a maximum figure linked to a multiple of national average earnings.

Sweden[20]

The Swedish Patient Insurance Plan was introduced as a non-statutory 1–030 scheme in 1975 and was put on a statutory basis in 1996 by the Patient Damages Act 1996. This scheme is probably more comprehensive in its coverage than the New Zealand scheme, and there is no explicit reference to the claimant having to prove negligence by the health care provider. All persons who conduct any form of health care and medical services are required to take out patient insurance. There is a separate scheme of Pharmaceutical Insurance which is a voluntary agreement largely financed

---

[14] *ibid.*, s. 36(1).

[15] *ibid.*, s. 36(2).

[16] *ibid.*, s. 37.

[17] *ibid.*, s. 37(2).

[18] The chances of a successful claim under this criterion have been said to be about as good as winning the New Zealand national lottery: (1991) 338 *The Lancet* 1583.

[19] For further discussion see Todd and Black (1993) 1 Tort L. Rev. 197, 217–226; and Oliphant, "Defining 'Medical Misadventure': Lessons From New Zealand" (1996) 4 Med. L. Rev. 1, commenting on the scheme as established under the Accident Rehabilitation and Compensation Insurance Act 1992 (*New Zealand*), which in this respect did not differ significantly from the current scheme.

[20] There are similar schemes in Finland, Denmark and Norway, based on the Swedish model.

by the pharmaceutical companies. The 1996 Act applies in respect of personal injuries caused in the course of health care and medical services provided in Sweden. The scheme compensates for injuries independently of whether the health care provider has been seriously negligent or the action was intentional. "Patient injuries" are largely defined in accordance with the principles that applied to the voluntary patient insurance schemes, though the term now also includes purely psychological injuries. As under the previous scheme, there is a threshold requirement in terms of the seriousness of the injury: the patient must have been sick for a minimum of 30 days, or been hospitalised for at least ten days, or have suffered permanent disability or died. Claimants are compensated on a similar basis to that of the tort system, including awards for non-pecuniary loss,[21] but the overall cost of the scheme is relatively low because payments are used to top-up relatively generous social security benefits.[22]

1–031   Patient injuries are divided into six different types of injuries:[23] (1) *treatment injuries* which includes "an examination, care, treatment or similar measure provided that the injury could have been avoided either through a different performance of the chosen procedure or through the choice of another available procedure which, according to an assessment, made retroactively from a medical point of view would have satisfied the need for treatment in a less hazardous manner." Treatment which is unable to halt the progression of a disease or illness is not a basis for compensation. The treatment must have caused an injury separate from the underlying disease or illness for which it was given; (2) *defective equipment*—compensation is payable for injuries caused by "defects in the medical-technical products or hospital equipment used in the performance of an examination, care, treatment or similar measure, or improper use of the same"; (3) *diagnostic errors* —where a diagnostic injury has occurred as the result of an incorrect diagnosis; diagnostic injuries may be the consequence of the underlying illness or disease and can also occur where treatment was delayed or was incorrect either because actual visible symptoms were not observed, or because those observations were incorrectly evaluated; (4) *infection injuries*—compensation is payable for injuries caused as the result of the "transfer of a contagious substance leading to infection in connection with an examination, care, treatment, or similar measure." There is no compensation where the infection is a complication which must be tolerated: *e.g.* the patient has decreased immunity level, the surgery/treatment was performed in a part of the body with reduced vitality, or the treatment itself entailed an increased risk of infection; (5) *accidents*—accidental injuries caused "in connection with an examination, care, treatment or similar measure or during a patient

---

[21] Approximately 12% of the total compensation awarded relates to pain and suffering: Fallberg and Borgenhammar, "The Swedish No-Fault Patient Insurance Scheme" (1997) 4 Eur. J. Health Law 279, 284.

[22] There is also a limit on the maximum award per claim. In 1998 the maximum award was 5 million SEK (approximately £350,000), but this level is rarely reached.

[23] Patient Damages Act 1996, s. 6 (*Sweden*).

transport or in connection with a fire or other damage to health care premises or equipment"; this means bodily injury that a person suffers involuntarily due to a sudden, outer event; (6) *incorrect use of medicines*—injury arising through the use of medicines can be indemnified, but only if the injury has been caused because the medical or pharmaceutical staff have incorrectly used, prescribed or dispensed, or otherwise incorrectly handled pharmaceuticals.

There are a number of specific exceptions to entitlement. Compensation will not be paid to a claimant: "if (1) the damages are a consequence of a necessary procedure for the diagnosis or treatment of an illness or injury which without treatment is directly life threatening or leads to severe disability, or (2) the damages are caused by pharmaceuticals in cases other than those mentioned in section 6."[24] This refers to a situation where a patient's need for medical care is so acute that treatment must be commenced even though it has not been possible to undertake the normal preparations, for example, in an emergency, or where it is necessary, knowingly, to take major risks in order to prevent the development of serious complications in the patient's disease or injury. This exception only applies in cases where the treatment relates to an injury or disease which is directly life threatening or can result in serious disability if treatment is not commenced.

1–032

Brain-damaged babies

Two states in the U.S.A., Virginia and Florida, have schemes of no-fault compensation in respect of birth-related injuries. In Virginia[25] a claim can be made in respect of birth-related neurological injury, namely "injury to the brain or spinal cord of an infant caused by the deprivation of oxygen or mechanical injury occurring in the course of labor, delivery or resuscitation in the immediate post-delivery period in a hospital." The disability must be serious, causing the infant to be permanently in need of assistance in all activities of daily living. Pain and suffering is not compensated. Eligible children qualify for two categories of benefits.[26] First, they are entitled to compensation for "necessary and reasonable costs of [lifetime] care" which in practice have been broadly defined.[27] This includes payment for medical

1–033

---

[24] Patient Damages Act 1996, s. 7 (*Sweden*).

[25] Birth-Related Neurological Injury Compensation Act 1987. For a general overview of the no-fault scheme in Virginia, see D.G. Duff, "Compensation for Neurologically Impaired Infants: Medical No-Fault in Virginia" (1990) 27(2) Harv. J. Leg. 391.

[26] See Gallup, "Can No-Fault Compensation of Impaired Infants Alleviate the Malpractice Crisis in Obstetrics" (1989) 14(4) J. Health Politics, Policy and Law 691 at 692, who asserted that no-fault compensation "may decrease the amount of reimbursement these neurologically damaged children receive". Gallup also suggests that obstetricians are more likely to benefit financially from the Virginia Act than neurologically damaged children: *ibid.* at p. 700.

[27] s. 38.2–5009 of the Virginia Act sets out the benefits authorised by law. See Board of Directors for the Virginia Birth-Related Neurological Injury Compensation Program, *Study to Increase the Scope and Magnitude of the Virginia Birth-Related Neurological Injury Compensation Program*, 1998, at 19.

expenses, rehabilitation costs, special equipment or facilities, and travel and residential expenses, provided that these costs are not reimbursable through any other state or federal governmental programme or private insurance. They can also recover the reasonable expenses incurred in filing a claim, including lawyers' fees.[28] The expenses are paid as they are incurred, not in a lump sum. Secondly, at the age of 18, they become eligible for monetary benefits to replace lost wages payable until age 65. This is conclusively presumed to be "fifty per cent of the average weekly wage in the Commonwealth of workers in the private, non-farm sector." The number of successful claims is small. As of October 16, 1997, applications had been pursued for just 45 children. Thirty one of these claims had been successful, four unsuccessful, five claimants had withdrawn their applications and five claims were still pending.[29] The scheme is funded by levies on health professionals and hospitals in the state, but participation in the scheme is voluntary. If a child is born in a non-participating hospital, or the claim is rejected as not satisfying the eligibility criteria, a tort claim can be made. A successful claim under the scheme precludes a subsequent tort action except for "intentional or wilfully caused harm."

1–034   Florida's Birth Related Injury Compensation Plan differs from Virginia's in several key respects. First, there is a difference in the meaning of "birth-related neurological injury", which is defined as, "injury to the brain or spinal cord of a live infant weighing at least 2,500 grams at birth caused by oxygen deprivation or mechanical injury occurring in the course of labor, delivery, or resuscitation in the immediate post-delivery in a hospital, which renders the infant permanently and substantially mentally and physically impaired. This definition shall apply to live births only and shall not include disability or death caused by genetic or congenital abnormality." The Florida definition is stricter in excluding low birth weight babies, and requiring both substantial impairment *mentally and physically*, but less strict in not requiring the child to be permanently in need of assistance in all activities of daily living. Doctors can choose whether to participate in the scheme, but it is compulsory for hospitals. For qualifying infants, compensation is provided for expenses incurred on medically necessary and reasonable medical and hospital costs, rehabilitation and training, the cost of residential and custodial care and service, for medically necessary drugs, special equipment and facilities, and for related travel. Anything covered by state benefits or benefits arising from private insurance or healthcare plans is excluded. There is

---

[28] See Sloan *et al.*, "No-Fault System of Compensation for Obstetric Injury: Winners and Losers" (1998) 91 Obstet. Gynecol. 437 at 440, who state that legal expenses paid on behalf of no-fault claimants have fallen dramatically. In 1989 legal expenses paid on behalf of a no-fault claimant averaged $24,000. Contrast this to the estimated payment to claimants' attorneys of $151,000 per tort case from 1989–1991.

[29] Board of Directors for the Virginia Birth-Related Neurological Injury Compensation Program, *Study to Increase the Scope and Magnitude of the Virginia Birth-Related Neurological Injury Compensation Program*, 1998, at 6–7. *Making Amends*, June 2003, p. 102, para. 37, indicates that there are between 10 and 15 new claims a year, with 72 children currently receiving payments under the scheme.

no provision for loss of earnings, though the parents of the infant may receive an allowance of up to $100,000. The costs of filing a claim, including reasonable lawyer's fees, are compensatable. Payments for future expenses are made as they arise, not in a lump sum. It would appear that medical expenses are well compensated under the scheme, but that the other losses that a family experiences due to caring for a brain-damaged child are not compensated.[30] As with the Virginia scheme, a successful claim precludes a tort action. Only 282 cases have been through the Florida scheme since it was established in 1989.[31]

The UK

There are currently few examples of no-fault compensation schemes in the UK. The industrial injuries scheme, which has existed in its present form since 1948, provides one example.[32] The scheme offers compensation to employees injured during the course of employment regardless of fault. Claimants have to satisfy two conditions. First, that the person injured or killed is or was an "employed earner" at the time of the accident (and had therefore paid employee national insurance contributions—the self-employed are excluded from the scheme). Secondly, that the injury was caused by an "accident arising out of and in the course of his employment" or resulted from a disease prescribed in relation to that employment. An injured employee must reach a threshold of 14 per cent disablement before benefit becomes payable. In addition, no benefit is payable in respect of the first 90 days disablement. Thus, someone who suffers a fairly serious injury but recovers rapidly may not be entitled to benefit unless there is continuing disablement exceeding 14 per cent. If the claimant satisfies these conditions, he is entitled to compensation in the form of disablement benefit. Disablement benefit is calculated on a formulaic basis, it is not related to any specific financial loss. Indeed, the claimant's financial loss is irrelevant both to entitlement and the amount of benefit. The benefit is payable in the form of a pension with the claimant receiving a weekly sum proportionate to the degree of disablement.

1–035

Certain social security disability benefits such as disability living allowance (awarded for assistance with mobility and personal care needs) are effectively a form of no-fault compensation scheme. Individuals who meet the threshold of disability receive the benefit, irrespective of fault. There are two components of disability living allowance, care component (which addresses the needs of those who need assistance from another person in connection with bodily functions) and mobility component (which provides for assistance in getting around). The care component is payable at three

1–036

---

[30] K. Whetten-Goldstein *et al.*, "Compensation for Birth-Related Injury—No-Fault Programs Compared with Tort System" (1999) 153 Arch. Pediatric Adolesc. Med. 41 at 47.
[31] *Making Amends*, June 2003, p. 103, para. 43.
[32] Social Security Contributions and Benefits Act 1992, Part V, ss. 94–111. See D. Bonner, I. Hooker and R. White, *Social Security Legislation 2002, Volume 1, Non-Means Tested Benefits*, 2002, Sweet & Maxwell, pp. 188–229.

different rates to reflect degrees of disability and need for attention, whereas mobility component is payable at two rates.[33] Although the benefit is not designed to compensate for financial loss, but provides some recognition of the additional costs associated with disability, it is a more comprehensive "no-fault" scheme than, say disablement benefit, since entitlement is based on the existence of applicant's disability not the cause of the disability.

1–037   The Vaccine Damage Payments scheme is a true no-fault scheme, in that payments do not depend on proof of fault, but it is limited in terms of the numbers who receive compensation and the circumstances in which compensation will be awarded.[34] It is also limited to a single one-off payment, which is not directly related to the damage suffered by the individual. The Vaccine Damage Payments Act 1979 currently provides for compensation of £100,000[35] for claims made on or after July 22, 2000 for an individual who is shown to have suffered injury due the administration of a vaccine against a specified list of diseases,[36] and as a result is, or was immediately prior to their death, "severely disabled." This term means at least 60 per cent. disabled,[37] as assessed for the industrial injuries scheme.[38] A compensation payment may also be made where: (1) the disabled person was severely disabled because his or her mother was vaccinated against one of the diseases in the list while she was pregnant; or (2) they have been in close physical contact with someone who has been vaccinated against poliomyelitis with vaccine that was given orally. Children must be two years old or more before they can get a payment. The vaccination must have been before the person's 18th birthday unless it was against poliomyelitis or rubella, or during an outbreak of the disease in the UK (*i.e.* England, Scotland, Wales and Northern Ireland) or the Isle of Man. The claim has to be made: (a) on or before the vaccinated person attained the age of 21 (or if the person has died, the date they would have reached age 21); or (b) within six years of the vaccination

---

[33] Social Security Contributions and Benefits Act 1992, ss. 71–76; see D. Bonner, I. Hooker and R. White, *op. cit.* pp. 127–165. See also ss. 64–67 which provide for attendance allowance.

[34] See Pywell [2000] J.P.I.L. 246.

[35] The amount has been changed several times since the Act came into force on March 22, 1979. For claims made on/after March 22, 1979 the sum was £10,000. For claims made on/after August 16, 1985 — £20,000. For claims made on/after April 15, 1991 — £30,000. For claims made on/after July 1, 1998 — £40,000. For claims made on/after July 22, 2000 — £100,000.

[36] The specified diseases are: diphtheria, tetanus and whooping cough (triple); diphtheria; tetanus; whooping cough; poliomyelitis; measles, mumps, rubella (mmr); meningitis C (meningococcal group C); measles; mumps; rubella; tuberculosis; Hib (Haemophilus Influenzae type b).

[37] Vaccine Damage Payments Act 1979, s. 1(4) as amended by the Regulatory Reform (Vaccine Damage Payments Act 1979) Order 2002 (S.I. 2002 No. 1592). Originally, the claimant had to be 80% disabled.

[38] Social Security Contributions and Benefits Act 1992, s. 103. Within the industrial injuries scheme 100% relates to that level of disablement for which 100% of the benefit is payable, which does not necessarily equate to total disability. In physical terms, 80% disablement equates to, for example, amputation below the hip or below the shoulder, or to deafness so severe that the sufferer cannot hear a shout beyond a distance of one metre (see the Social Security (General Benefit) Regulations 1982 (S.I. 1982 No. 1408), Sch. 2).

to which the claim relates, whichever is the later.[39] Payment under the scheme, which is funded out of general taxation, is not tailored to the financial needs of the individual. The payment is tax free, but it can affect entitlement to means-tested welfare benefits. The burden of proof, on the balance of probabilities, that the disability was caused by vaccination against one of the specified diseases lies with the claimant. Proving causation is the major problem for applicants. There are few successful claims. Over the five years to the end of 1999-2000 an average of 110 claims a year were received and an average of four awards a year were made.[40]

These examples of limited "no-fault" schemes indicate that a scheme of   **1–038** no-fault compensation for medical accidents would not necessarily be a revolutionary step in the UK. Whether it would be a "solution" to the problem of medical accidents, however, depends very much on the detail of such a scheme. The proposals put forward by the BMA in 1991 would have excluded significant categories of accidental medical injury, namely: (a) injuries which are a consequence of the progress of the disease under treatment; (b) diagnostic error which could only have been avoided by hindsight; (c) unavoidable complications, however carefully and competently the procedure was carried out; (d) infections arising under circumstances which made them difficult to avoid; and (e) complications of drug therapy carried out in accordance with the drug manufacturer's instructions.[41] These restrictions on eligibility would have excluded injuries which can truly be said to be accidental, and raised the question of whether such a scheme would compensate for accidental injury or would look for something equivalent to negligence. If "unavoidable complications," for example, are excluded then the test for eligibility is that the complication must have been avoidable, which might well be interpreted to mean avoidable with the exercise of reasonable care. The result would be that:

"... the scheme would do little more than convert the negligence test into a statutory formula, thereby making it easier for the victims of negligence to obtain compensation, but doing nothing for those suffering medical injury from other causes."[42]

Even more fundamental is the problem of proving causation, which is   **1–039** frequently the major hurdle facing a claimant bringing an action for medical negligence. A scheme limited to medical accidents must inevitably

---

[39] Vaccine Damage Payments Act 1979, s. 3(1)(c) as amended by the Regulatory Reform (Vaccine Damage Payments Act 1979) Order 2002 (S.I. 2002 No. 1592).

[40] *Amending the Vaccine Damage Payments Act 1979*, Consultation Paper, Department of Work and Pensions, July 2001, para. 47; *cf.* the figures quoted in *Making Amends*, June 2003, p. 104, para. 48: "Since the scheme began, approximately 5,000 claims have been received and 910 awards made to June 2003."

[41] *No Fault Compensation Working Party Report*, 1991. The Report of the Royal College of Physicians, *Compensation for Adverse Consequences of Medical Intervention*, 1990, did not identify any eligibility criteria.

[42] *Royal Commission on Civil Liability and Compensation for Personal Injury*, Cmnd. 7054 (1978), Vol. I, para. 1366.

distinguish between injuries which are *caused* by a medical accident (however widely or narrowly this may be defined) and those which are not. Unlike road traffic accident or work accident victims, patients are usually receiving treatment because there is already something wrong with them. The process of identifying a medical accident necessarily involves attributing damage to medical treatment (or the lack of it), which necessarily involves separating the consequences of the injury or disease for which the patient was receiving treatment from the consequences of the medical treatment. This, in turn, requires the patient to show that the harm about which she is complaining could have been avoided. How could it have been avoided? By an "appropriate" or "standard" or "normal" medical intervention. But how can one establish what was "appropriate" or "standard" or "normal", except by asking whether what the healthcare professionals did complied with the common practice of the profession or was reasonable in the circumstances? In other words, to some extent, the causation question (the question: what is caused by the treatment and what is caused by the disease?) forces one to ask whether the treatment was reasonable in the circumstances. As the New Zealand accident compensation scheme discovered, for medical accidents it is very difficult to get away from a fault standard. Questions of eligibility, or who would qualify for compensation under a no-fault scheme, are not the only issues that have to be weighed in the balance when considering the potential ramifications of such a radical change to the compensation mechanism. There is the relationship between the medical profession and patients to consider (would a no-fault compensation scheme reduce professional accountability? would it reduce concerns about "defensive medicine"?); crucial issues of detail such as what would be compensated for and at what level; the question of the overall cost of a no-fault scheme (is it affordable?); and despite the inherently practical nature of problem (who should be compensated for what losses) there are also issues of principle in deciding who should be the beneficiaries of a scheme to which all taxpayers contribute in some shape or form.

(a) Accountability and no-fault

1–040   Lack of accountability, and a doctor's sense of individual responsibility, were the principal reasons given by the medical profession for opposing the introduction of a no-fault scheme in its evidence to the Pearson Commission. Although there have been a number of changes to NHS complaints procedures, and to the powers of the Health Service Commissioner[43] and the General Medical Council in the last ten years or so, the question of accountability remains problematic.[44] The General Medical Council, which is the

---

[43] The Health Service Commissioner now has the power to investigate clinical complaints: Health Service Commissioners Act 1993, as amended.

[44] For discussion see Kennedy & Grubb, *Medical Law*, 3rd ed., 2000, pp. 247–268; Longley (1997) 5 Med. L. Rev. 172; Harpwood (1996) 3 Eur. J. Health Law 207. The House of Commons Health Committee, Session 1998–99, Sixth Report, *Procedures Related to*

only body to exercise a disciplinary jurisdiction over all doctors whether in the NHS or private practice, may discipline a registered medical practitioner who has been convicted of a criminal offence or is guilty of "serious professional misconduct."[45] In the past, a persistent criticism of the way in which the GMC exercised its disciplinary powers was that it failed to deal with what by any standard was culpable conduct in the treatment of patients because it could not be categorised as *serious* professional misconduct.[46] That issue was, to some extent, addressed by the Medical (Professional Performance) Act 1995 which conferred the power to investigate "seriously deficient performance"[47] but the question of accountability through the General Medical Council remains problematic.[48]

Despite the evidence given to the Pearson Commission the BMA subsequently questioned whether a system of no-fault compensation "importantly diminishes the accountability of doctors."[49] This was not the view of the Royal College of Physicians, which accepted that a no-fault scheme could remove a source of medical accountability.[50] The Royal College recommended that a no-fault scheme should be accompanied by "a separate mechanism for the scrutiny of each claim in which doctors were involved to ensure that appropriate care had not been transgressed. If transgression is demonstrated, questions of professional discipline should be pursued." Although this recognises that the principle of medical accountability is important, it fails to address the point that the present mechanisms for accountability, although improving, remain less than ideal in all but the most serious of cases. If transgression of "appropriate care" would result in the doctor being referred to the GMC, it would only be the most flagrant

1–041

(n.44 contd.) *Adverse Clinical Incidents and Outcomes in Medical Care*, Vol. I, London: The Stationery Office, October 1999, paras 72 to 106 found that there was extensive criticism of NHS complaints procedures, despite changes to the procedures introduced in 1996. See also *Making Amends*, June 2003, p. 78, para. 12.

[45] Medical Act 1983, s. 36. See also the GMC guide *Good Medical Practice*, 3rd ed., May 2001, and *Maintaining Good Medical Practice*, both available at *www.gmc-uk.org/standards/default.htm*.

[46] See, *e.g.*, Brazier, *Medicine, Patients and the Law*, 2nd ed., 1992, pp. 13–17.

[47] Medical Act 1983, s. 36A. See Sprince and Laing, "Disciplining Doctors: 'Seriously Deficient Performance' under the Medical (Professional Performance) Act 1995" [1997] 4 Web J.C.L.I. (available at *webjcli.ncl.ac.uk/1997/issue4/sprince4.html*). See also Grubb (2001) Med. L. Rev. 70, discussing the reforms to GMC powers and procedures introduced by the Medical Act 1983 (Amendment) Order 2000 (S.I. 2000 No. 1803); Gentleman (2001) 7 Clinical Risk 169, discussing the GMC's new powers to require revalidation of a doctor's registration.

[48] de Prez, "Self-Regulation and Paragons of Virtue: The Case of 'Fitness to Practice'" (2002) 10 Med. L. Rev. 28. For a more general discussion of the regulatory framework in the NHS see Davies (2000) 20 O.J.L.S. 437; and Newdick (2002) 10 Med. L. Rev. 111.

[49] Report of the *BMA Working Party on No Fault Compensation*, 1991. It is argued that the tort action does not produce accountability because the worst cases of negligence never get to court, but are settled in private, with only the marginal claims being fought. The result is that there may be an unfair burden of publicity on doctors who may well have acted perfectly properly. This misses the point about accountability, however, which enables an individual patient to hold a doctor to account for his actions in law, whether this results in a settlement or a trial. The payment of compensation may be completely irrelevant.

[50] Report of the Royal College of Physicians, *Compensation for Adverse Consequences of Medical Intervention*, 1990, p. 21.

instances of negligence that would be subject to accountability. Moreover, it has been claimed that the introduction of a no-fault compensation scheme would remove the deterrent effect of possible litigation, thereby tending to lower rather than raise health care standards.[51]

(b) Defensive medicine and no-fault

1–042   A no-fault compensation scheme would probably not change a doctor's defensive reaction to medical errors. The present tort system has no direct financial effect on a doctor, since damages are paid by the NHS Trust or a defence organisation, and a negligent doctor is not penalised financially. Thus, the deterrent effect of tort must be linked to the perceived consequences of litigation on the doctor's reputation. No-fault compensation seeks to remove the link between proving fault and obtaining compensation,[52] it does not remove "fault" from the practice of medicine. Separating compensation from proof of fault does not reduce the risk to a doctor's reputation if there is to be genuine accountability. If a suitable system of accountability was introduced along with no-fault, in which doctors who have been guilty of blameworthy conduct are held accountable for their actions, some doctors would, presumably, still be inclined to practise "defensively" in order to protect their reputation and avoid disciplinary proceedings. In other words, no-fault compensation has no relevance to a debate about "defensive medicine", and it seems unlikely that a reduction in "defensive" practice could be said to be a potential benefit of introducing a no-fault compensation scheme.

(c) Levels of Compensation

1–043   The levels of compensation for patients under the no-fault schemes in operation in Sweden and New Zealand are very different. The Swedish system opts for broadly the same levels of compensation as tort damages, but payments are comparatively modest because social security benefits are high and the scheme is frequently merely topping up the patient's pecuniary losses. The New Zealand scheme does not attempt to replicate tort damages, but concentrates on compensating economic losses subject to capping the loss of earnings element. The BMA *No Fault Compensation Working Party Report*, 1991, envisaged compensation for loss of income up to a limit of

---

[51] Andrew Morrison, a Royal Society of Medicine Council member of the Medical Defence Union, in Mann and Havard *No Fault Compensation in Medicine*, 1989, p. 156. In New Zealand, where since 1974 the action in tort has been unavailable if the patient receives compensation under the no-fault scheme, complaints to the equivalent of the GMC between 1974 and 1987 increased by 1800%: Dr J.A. Wall in Mann and Havard, *op. cit.*, p. 72. There has been concern in New Zealand about the lack of accountability of doctors in the absence of tort litigation: Ham, Dingwall, Fenn and Harris, *Medical Negligence: Compensation and Accountability*, 1988, p. 23; McGregor Vennell "Medical Misfortune in a No Fault Society" in Mann and Havard, *op. cit.*, 1989, p. 40. See further Brown (1985) 73 Cal. L. Rev. 976.

[52] Although, arguably, this can never be fully achieved: see para. 1–039.

twice the national average wage, but overall aimed at "awards about half the size of those which a court would make in a successful action." From a patient's point of view the value of a no-fault compensation scheme would relate both to the ease with which a claim could be made and the amount of compensation available. If the levels of compensation were comparable with social security benefits, for example, many people might prefer the tort action, with all its vagaries, for the chance of substantial compensation.

(d) Cost

Estimates of the overall cost of a no-fault scheme limited to medical accidents are little more than guesswork. There are three variables: (i) how many successful claimants there will be; (ii) how much the average payment of compensation will be; and, (iii) how much the system will cost to administer. There is virtually no information about either of the first two variables, and thus costings are extremely speculative.[53] Administration costs would certainly be lower, at least in terms of the percentage of compensation paid out, than under the tort system.[54]

The number of successful claimants would depend upon a whole range of variables, some of which depend upon the scope of the scheme and some of which it would be almost impossible to predict (*e.g.* how many more claimants than currently resort to the tort system would be encouraged to claim as a result of the existence of the scheme). The scope of the scheme depends upon what constitutes a compensatable event (would it be limited to, in effect, negligently caused harm?[55]) and what exclusionary criteria are adopted (*e.g.* would certain events fall outside the scheme, perhaps because they are regarded as part of the risk of treatment; how severe must the patient's damage be to qualify?[56]).

The level of compensation is entirely within the control of those establishing the no-fault scheme. The range of options goes from: (1) the full equivalent of current tort damages; (2) limiting claims to financial losses; (3) compensating for a part of the financial losses (*e.g.* New Zealand compensates loss of earnings up to 80 per cent of pre-accident earnings, subject to a maximum figure linked to a multiple of national average earnings); (4) excluding the costs of private medical care, except where that care is not available on the NHS; to (5) adopting a social security approach which

1–044

1–045

1–046

---

[53] Ham, Dingwall, Fenn and Harris, *Medical Negligence: Compensation and Accountability*, 1988, p. 31 estimated between £177 million and £235 million, at 1988 prices. The BMA *No Fault Compensation Working Party Report*, 1991, paras 7.1 and 7.2, estimated a cost of £100.4 million, at 1990 prices, for the whole UK. This was on the basis of awards at half the level of tort damages, following a survey of claims rates in 10% of district health authorities in 1988. The Report did not attempt to quantify the possible increase in claims rates, but conceded that it was probable that there would be an exponential rise in the number of claims during the first decade of operating a no-fault scheme.

[54] See para. 1–025, n. 1 above. The administrative costs of the Swedish system are put at 16% of the premiums.

[55] See paras 1–028 and 1–039.

[56] All no-fault schemes exclude minor injuries. The question would be "how minor?"

awards a specific weekly sum according to degree of disability without direct reference to the claimant's financial loss or needs (*e.g.* as under the industrial injuries scheme). There are numerous intermediate positions or combinations that could be considered. The levels of compensation chosen would clearly have an effect on the success of the scheme, which may also be linked to other issues, such as whether claimants would remain entitled to bring a tort claim. Combining relatively low levels of compensation with retention of the right to sue in tort would do little to address the problems associated with the current litigation system. On the other hand, a denial of tort remedies without reasonable levels of compensation might fall foul of Article 6 of the European Convention on Human Rights.

1–047   The administrative cost of running the system would depend upon precisely how the scheme was run. In any event, it is likely to be significantly lower than the tort system. In New Zealand the cost of running the Medical Misadventure Account comes to 17 per cent of the total expenditure of the Account (though the cost of running the whole New Zealand no-fault scheme was about 9.4 per cent). In 1998 administration costs for the Swedish scheme amounted to approximately 7.8 per cent of the total expenditure for the scheme.

1–048   The Chief Medical Officer has now ruled out a no-fault compensation scheme on the basis that the overall cost would be too high compared to the sums presently spent on the tort system.[57] That conclusion depends, of course, on the assumptions one makes about the number of successful claims and the levels of compensation that would be paid.

(e) Questions of principle

1–049   The deficiencies of the tort system have been apparent for a number of years. Much of the criticism which can be directed at the action in negligence as a means of compensating the victims of medical accidents applies with equal force to claims arising out of other types of accidents. It is not clear why no-fault compensation should be adopted for one, small category of accident victims to the exclusion of others with equally serious injuries sustained in other ways. In theory, the tort of negligence provides a conceptual basis for distinguishing between patients who are entitled to compensation and those who are not, in that negligence "identifies" an individual (or his employer) who is responsible in law for the infliction of the patient's injury, and so in fairness ought to recompense the patient for that loss. This is not how the system works in practice, because it may not be possible to establish fault, and insurance (through NHS indemnity in hospitals and through the medical defence organisations in primary care) removes a large element of individual responsibility. On the other hand, the conceptual underpinning of a scheme of no-fault compensation rests on a theory of social responsibility for the victims of misfortune, namely those who suffer

---

[57] See paras 1–056 and 1–057.

injury by "accident." It is not apparent why the victims of a particular type of accident (medical accidents) should receive compensation on a no-fault basis when other accident victims have to prove fault. This is particularly the case when only certain types of medical accident, those which qualify under the eligibility criteria, would be compensated under such a scheme. These issues become especially important when it is proposed to fund a no-fault scheme from general taxation to which everyone must contribute, whether they fall into the favoured category of accident victim or not.

1–050 The argument that the principle of no-fault compensation selects its beneficiaries on a fairer basis (namely "need" not "fault") than the tort of negligence is questionable. It selects them on a *different* basis but it still draws arbitrary distinctions between those who will be compensated and those who will not. Clearly, the needs of a child with brain damage are no different whether caused by congenital disability or medical intervention at birth. On the one hand, a no-fault compensation scheme would probably provide compensation for more patients (depending upon how strict the eligibility criteria were), more quickly and more efficiently than the present tort system. It could provide readier access to compensation for patients who may not be in a financial position to sue; and it would provide for periodic payments so that the compensation reflects the patient's actual loss. On the other hand, if the problem is that too few patients succeed in recovering compensation because of the difficulties of proving fault, it would be possible to improve claimant success rates under the tort system by introducing strict liability and reversing the burden of proof.[58] This would also separate the question of compensation from the proof of fault. The argument for a no-fault compensation scheme limited to the victims of medical accidents must be based on pragmatic justifications, rather than principle. Under the tort system:

- the victims of medical accidents have much lower success rates in terms of obtaining some compensation than other accident victims;

- the victims of medical accidents, on average, suffer the longest delays of all personal injury victims in obtaining compensation;

- there is highly skewed access to the legal system for the victims of medical accidents, with approximately 90 per cent of all clinical negligence claimants receiving legal aid—even the moderately well-off may be unable to afford to bring a claim;

- there is some evidence that the effect on health professionals of dealing with claims for negligence can be detrimental to their

---

[58] The European Commission did consider a proposal which would have had the effect of reversing the burden of proof in respect of the liability of suppliers of services for personal injuries: O.J. 1991, No. C 12/8, January 18, 1991. It seemed likely that the construction industry and the medical profession would have been excluded from the effect of this Directive (*The Times*, January 6, 1992), but in any event the proposal has not been pursued.

clinical performance (though this is not necessarily the phenomenon of so-called "defensive medicine")[59];

• perhaps most crucially, the high cost of running the tort system is a very inefficient way of transferring money to accident victims, and it would be better to reduce transaction costs and compensate more accident victims or spend any cost savings on the provision of healthcare.[60]

A carefully constructed no-fault compensation scheme would go some way to addressing most of these issues.

1–051   The relationship between a no-fault scheme and the tort system is an issue that would also have a profound effect on the success, or otherwise, of the scheme. Should a tort claim be barred for anyone falling within the terms of the scheme (as in New Zealand), or would a tort claim remain an option (as in Sweden)? Barring the tort remedy might fall foul of Articles 6 and 14 of the European Convention on Human Rights, since it would prevent access to the legal system for a particular category of accident victim. This argument would be stronger if the amount of compensation available under the scheme bore little relationship the accident victim's real loss. On the other hand, certain employment rights (with capped levels of compensation) have to be pursued in an employment tribunal rather than in the courts, and it has not yet been suggested that this constitutes a breach of Article 6. Allowing tort claims to run alongside (or as a backup to) the scheme (as in Sweden or the industrial injuries scheme, which does not prevent an injured employee from suing the employer for negligence), would avoid a possible conflict with Article 6, but would not address the failings of the tort system, in particular the administrative cost. The result could be that there is no reduction in litigation, but that some injured patients whose tort claim currently fails, might receive compensation under the no-fault scheme, thereby significantly increasing the overall cost of paying for accidental injury to patients. Another option would be to require injured patients to "elect" either for the no-fault scheme or for tort. Once having elected for the scheme, any tort claim is barred. The problem with this approach is that if there are comparatively short time limits for bringing a claim for no-fault compensation, it will effectively create a situation where the patient is forced to opt for the scheme.

1–052   Any consideration of the merits of a no-fault compensation scheme should also take into account the potential negative effects of a such a scheme, particularly if the right to sue in tort were removed. If, as rational individuals, health professionals and NHS organisations respond to the threat of negligence claims by modifying their behaviour (and all claims that doctors

---

[59] Genn, "Effects of claims on doctors" (1996) 2 Clinical Risk 181; Hirst, "Supporting staff during litigation—managerial aspects" (1996) 2 Clinical Risk 189; *Making Amends*, June 2003, p. 43.

[60] This argument is not unique to medical accidents, of course.

practise defensive medicine are claims that doctors do respond to the deterrent effect of liability rules, though with "defensive medicine" the claim is that they *overreact* to the risk of liability by doing things that are potentially detrimental to patients[61]) then there is a risk that removing the threat of litigation would have adverse consequences for patient safety. Individuals and organisations might have less of an incentive to adopt measures which improve patient safety by reducing risk. The financial arrangements for CNST include a discount on contributions for NHS Trusts that implement risk management standards. Without litigation, there would be no need for CNST and therefore no direct financial incentive to reduce risk (unless NHS Trusts were required to pay into the no-fault compensation fund). This type of argument is difficult to test empirically. It could be observed that if tort is meant to act as a deterrent to risky conduct it does not have a particularly good record, given what is now emerging about the staggering numbers of adverse clinical incidents that occur in modern hospitals. On the other hand, it could be said that the significant rise in the number and cost of claims over the last 15 to 20 years has finally persuaded the NHS to take the question of patient safety seriously through a number of initiatives linked to quality of service and risk management.

A no-fault compensation scheme cannot stop doctors from acting negligently, nor would it stop patients seeking to hold doctors to account for blameworthy conduct. Indeed, it would be strange if doctors were the only profession to be unaccountable in the courts. The Pearson Commission commented that:

1–053

> ". . . there would have to be a good case for exempting any profession from legal liabilities which apply to others, and we do not regard the special circumstances of medical injury as constituting such a case."[62]

The fact that since the early 1980s patients have sued their doctors in larger numbers than ever before can hardly be considered a "good case," since this is true of every other professional group. Ultimately, the arguments for no-fault compensation have to be grounded in improving the position of patients injured by the healthcare system in which they placed their trust. If no-fault compensation is seen as a solution to defendants' problems (by reducing cost, or reducing the opportunity to "blame" healthcare professionals who are already stressed) it will fail to address the real crisis of medical accidents, which is that there are so many patients injured by their medical treatment and so few who manage to obtain compensation for those injuries.

---

[61] Although no one has yet managed to explain how doing something that is potentially harmful to patients can be a sensible strategy for avoiding litigation.

[62] *Royal Commission on Civil Liability and Compensation for Personal Injury*, Cmnd. 7054 (1978), Vol. I, para. 1344.

(4) Making Amends

1–054   The Chief Medical Officer's report, *Making Amends*, considered many of the issues that have already been touched on in this Chapter. The need to take systematic steps to reduce error and accidental harm is self-evident. A health system that, in attempting to alleviate suffering, and with the best will in the world, kills and injures so many of its patients needs to ask itself some serious questions. That would be true whatever the arrangements adopted for compensating the victims of those errors. Twenty five years ago the Pearson Commission highlighted many of the problems with tort as a means of compensating for personal injury, though shied away from recommending any root and branch reform. Despite attempts to improve the efficiency of the litigation process, it remains a relatively slow, expensive, inefficient and sometimes capricious means of transferring money from a negligent defendant to an injured claimant. Medical malpractice litigation tends to accentuate the flaws in that process. But, though it is easy to criticise the present system, it is not as easy to come up with an alternative that fits within current perceptions of what is affordable. If the steadily growing overall cost to the NHS of litigation is seen as the problem, the criticism that tort is expensive and inefficient, while true, is likely to redound if the solution is to put in place a much more efficient compensation system, when combined with the knowledge that the vast majority of the victims of medical accidents currently go uncompensated by the tort system. In other words, the solution to a problem depends on what the problem is perceived to be. If it is that the overall cost of compensating for medical error is too high, then one will look for ways of cutting the cost. If it is that there is far too much medical error, and far too many injured patients who go uncompensated, then one would look for ways to reduce error and improve the mechanisms for paying compensation to include a wider pool of accident victims. Both outcomes may be desirable, but they are probably incompatible objectives.

1–055   *Making Amends*, while recognising the need to improve risk management in the NHS (reiterating the points made three years earlier in *An Organisation with a Memory*), opts for measures to reduce, or at least attempt to contain the overall cost. *Making Amends* identified four options for reform: (1) continue with reforms to the tort system; (2) introduce no-fault compensation; (3) introduce a system of fixed tariffs for particular types of injury administered by a national tribunal; (4) a composite package of reform. The first three options were rejected. Change based solely on continued tort reform was rejected, because:

- it remains a lottery who can and who cannot prove "negligence" —not least in cerebral palsy cases;

- it does little to support patients making complaints and claims;

- the current legal system provides little or no incentive to report, learn from and reduce errors;

- the adversarial system undermines the relationship between the patient and healthcare profession, reduces trust in the NHS as a whole and diverts staff from clinical care;

- if a litigation culture takes hold, as in the USA, costs will spiral out of control and the practice of defensive medicine will increase; and

- an independent evaluation of a small claims pilot supported by the Department of Health and NHS Litigation Authority found that even patients who receive compensation often remain dissatisfied if they do not also receive the explanations or apologies they seek or reassurance about the action taken to prevent repetition.

Although it is not difficult to be critical of the tort system, some of these particular criticisms are either tendentious or misplaced. It is not the function of the torts system to support patients making complaints. That is the function of the complaints system, which under current arrangements excludes the complaint as soon as the complainant hints that she is considering bringing a claim. Nor is it true that the current legal system provides little or no incentive to learn from and reduce errors. The incentive to the NHS of reducing the costs of claims is enormous. Fewer injured patients should mean fewer claims for compensation. If that is not an incentive it is difficult to know what would be an incentive. It may be that there are certain aspects of litigation which inhibit the reporting of adverse events (the process of disclosure, for example), but that is not the reason that the NHS is only now waking up to the real cost of medical accidents. The adversarial system can contribute to polarising attitudes between the parties, but so can the reaction of healthcare professionals to injured patients. That reaction occurs long before the patient embarks on the long road to litigation. The provision of explanations and apologies is not something that is within the gift of the tort system, but it is something that the NHS could do something about, whatever mechanism for compensating injured patients is in place. Finally, for reasons already addressed,[63] the issue of defensive medicine is a red herring.

No-fault compensation was rejected, principally because it would be too expensive. *Making Amends* summarised the advantages of a comprehensive no fault compensation system: (1) claims are settled more quickly (months rather than years for many no-fault schemes); (2) administrative and legal costs per claim are lower; (3) patients are clearer about the circumstances when they will receive compensation; (4) there is reduced conflict between clinicians and claimants; (5) because of the removal of "blame", clinicians are more willing to report adverse events and repetition can be avoided. The potential disadvantages were said to be: (1) overall costs are far higher than under equivalent tort systems because of a lower threshold for claiming (*i.e.* no need to prove negligence) and increased numbers of claims; (2) for a

1–056

---

[63] See paras 1–017 *et seq.*

no-fault scheme to be affordable compensation would need to be at substantially lower levels than tort awards currently, which would not necessarily meet the needs of the harmed patient; (3) it would be difficult to distinguish harm from the natural progression of a disease. In addition, there was the effect of the Human Rights Act 1998 to take into consideration. If the quid pro quo for a no-fault scheme was to remove the right to litigate in tort, as in New Zealand, claimants would still have to have a right to a fair hearing under Article 6 of the European Convention on Human Rights. This could involve having a public hearing, with equal rights for both sides to present their case, which might mean that the NHS would have to run and fund a hearing mechanism similar to, but in parallel with, the courts.

1–057   The Chief Medical Officer commissioned research to assess the cost of a comprehensive no-fault based compensation scheme, first on the basis of a causation test and secondly on the basis of the concept of "preventability" of the damage (on the Swedish model). It has already been pointed out that the cost of a no-fault compensation depends on three factors: the number of successful claims; the levels of compensation; and the administration costs.[64] The research took the percentage of cases likely to be compensated from the Swedish scheme (47 per cent of claims, which represents 41 paid claims *per annum* per 100,000 population[65]); the number of likely applicants was taken from the survey of adverse events undertaken for the report (which gave an estimate of just over 800,000 preventable adverse events per year); and levels of compensation were estimated from the present level of tort damages. The assumed damages payments were then reduced by 25 per cent and 50 per cent to reflect the restrictions in other no-fault schemes. The conclusion was that with a 25 per cent reduction in the current level of compensation the cost of a true no-fault scheme (*i.e.* one based on causation alone) would vary between £1.6 billion a year (if 19 per cent of eligible claimants claimed) to almost £4 billion a year (if 28 per cent of eligible claimants claimed).[66] It is not surprising then that the Chief Medical Officer rejects as unaffordable a wide ranging no-fault scheme for all types of injury, when the current cost of the litigation system is £450 million.[67] Of course, different assumptions about the numbers of successful claimants and the levels of compensation would have produced different estimates of the overall costs. Excluding non-pecuniary losses entirely, and adopting a fairly high level of impairment as a threshold to entitlement, might have made a scheme more affordable, by cutting out many of the relatively small claims. The Pearson Commission found that non-pecuniary loss accounts for more than half of all tort compensation for personal injury, and for a particularly high proportion of small payments. The Commission recommended that no damages should be

---

[64] See paras 1–044 et seq.

[65] *Making Amends*, June 2003, p. 112, para. 12; and see the table at p. 106.

[66] *ibid.* at para. 13. It is not clear why a less than 50% increase in the number of eligible claimants claiming (from 19% to 28%) produces an increased cost of 150% (from £1.6 billion to £4 billion).

[67] See para. 1–015.

recoverable for non-pecuniary loss suffered during the first three months after the date of the injury.[68] At that time, this would have eliminated many small claims altogether, with a consequent saving of administration costs, and reduced by about 20 per cent the total tort compensation for personal injury.

Making Amends also rejected a system of fixed tariffs administered   1–058 through a national tribunal, as under the Criminal Injuries Compensation scheme. Levels of awards under the Criminal Injuries scheme are significantly lower than the sums awarded in tort damages and bear little relationship to the actual losses of victims. If the goal was to put the patient back in the position they would have been in (as far as that is possible), a fixed tariff scheme, which would have involved the administrative cost of setting up a national tribunal, was never likely to be a serious option.

A composite package of reform?

The CMO's recommendations for reform (which apply to England only)   1–059 constitute what the report calls a composite package. They would provide "redress" for patients harmed as a result of "seriously substandard" NHS hospital care in relatively low value claims, and a compensation package for brain damaged babies who suffer severe neurological impairment related to or resulting from birth, irrespective of the proof of fault. The report states that the process would be based on the concept that the patient should be returned to the condition they would have been in had the injury not occurred.[69] In all cases where harm to a patient has arisen from an adverse event, the response should be: (1) an investigation of the incident which is alleged to have caused harm and of the harm that has resulted; (2) provision of an explanation to the patient of what has happened and why, and the action proposed to prevent repetition; (3) the development and delivery of a package of care, providing remedial treatment, therapy and arrangements for continuing care where needed. In "suitable cases" there would be consideration of whether payment for pain and suffering, for out of pocket expenses and for care or treatment which the NHS could not provide should be made. A decision on the case should be made within six months from the initial approach from the patient. This redress scheme would initially be available only to patients treated in hospital and community health settings. Consideration would be given to whether it should be extended to primary care at a later stage. *Making Amends* recognises that, initially at least, the capacity of the NHS to provide packages of care may be limited and therefore financial recompense may be offered as an alternative. However, the aim would be to develop this capacity over time. The package includes proposals "designed to improve prevention and handling of adverse events at local level; to provide rehabilitation and remedial treatment to reduce the long

---

[68] *Royal Commission on Civil Liability and Compensation for Personal Injury*, Cmnd. 7054 (1978), Vol. I, para. 388.

[69] Which of course is the basis upon which tort damages are assessed: see para. 9–002.

term impact of the harm caused; and to reduce the need to fund private care for those harmed."[70] It would "be beneficial to doctors, the vast majority of whom would have the cloud of clinical negligence litigation removed but who would be free to learn from and improve their practice in a positive way."[71] These proposed reforms were said to be intended to be fair to individual patients and meet their needs, while making care safer for all NHS patients.[72] On the other hand, it is not obvious that there is a need to change the litigation system *in order to* make health care safer. There is no evidence that the litigation process makes health care less safe, but there is plenty of evidence that the less safe health care is, the more litigation there will be (which is not to suggest that this is the only factor at work in the increase in litigation over the last twenty years). Moreover, under the tort system there is nothing to prevent a full investigation of the incident, nor to prevent healthcare professionals from giving patients an explanation of what has happened. This is something that patients' organisations, such as Action for the Victims of Medical Accidents, have been calling for, for the last 20 years.

1-060   Under the proposals there would effectively be three parallel compensation schemes, one providing "NHS Redress" for low value claims and for cases involving brain damaged babies. All other claims would still have to be resolved through the tort system, though *Making Amends* makes recommendations designed to reduce the cost to the NHS of the tort system.

Low value claims

1-061   For claims not involving brain damaged babies, successful claimants would be entitled to a "package of care" from the NHS to deal with the effects of the injury and possible financial compensation. The financial element of the compensation would be limited to: (1) the notional cost of the episode of care or other amount as appropriate, at the discretion of the local NHS Trust; (2) up to £30,000 where authorised by the national body managing the new scheme.[73] Access to the package of care and *possible* financial compensation for an adverse outcome of NHS care would follow: a local investigation of the adverse event or of a complaint; an independent review of a complaint by the Commission for Healthcare Audit and Inspection;[74] a recommendation by the Health Services Commissioner; or an investigation of a claim made directly by a patient or relatives to the NHS Litigation Authority.[75] The criteria for receiving payment would be that: (1) there were serious shortcomings in the standards of care; (2) the harm could have been avoided; (3) the adverse outcome was not the result of the natural progression of the illness.

---

[70] *Making Amends*, June 2003, p. 115, para. 23.
[71] *ibid*. at para. 24.
[72] *ibid*. at p. 117, para. 4.
[73] *Making Amends* recommends that, subject to evaluation, consideration should be given to extending the scheme to a higher monetary threshold (recommendation 4).
[74] A new statutory health inspectorate which will inspect the quality of local NHS services and investigate complaints not resolved at local level.
[75] *Making Amends*, June 2003, p. 119.

There are a number of uncertainties in these proposals, some of which may   1–062
be resolved when further detail is put on the bones of the scheme. It is not
apparent what will constitute "serious shortcomings" in the standards of
care (also referred to in the report as "sub-standard care"), but it would
appear that this is to be judged by the NHS. It would seem to be a negligence
standard by another name. The requirement that the harm could not have
been avoided clearly involves a causation test, which combined with a negligence standard would effectively be little different from the entry criteria
currently set by the tort of negligence, but possibly not including all the situations in which the tort of negligence might grant a remedy. For example,
would the test encompass failing to provide appropriate information to the
patient prior to treatment ("informed consent")? What would be entirely
novel under this system is "the development and delivery of a package of
care, providing remedial treatment, therapy and arrangements for continuing care where needed." Providing compensation in kind, rather than in
cash, would probably be less expensive to the NHS, though since this part
of the scheme is limited to relatively low value claims it would seem to be
aimed at the less serious cases where long-term care may not necessarily be
needed. Also novel, and welcome, would be a requirement to reach a decision within six months from the initial approach of the patient.

The financial part of the package would cover the notional cost of the   1–063
episode of care or other amount as appropriate, at the discretion of the local
NHS Trust; and (or is it "or"—the recommendations do not make this clear)
up to £30,000 where authorised by the national body administering the
scheme. It is not clear what the "notional cost of the episode of care" is
meant to be compensating the patient for. It seems to suggest that the NHS
wants to approach compensation on a contractual basis. The claimant is
then entitled to a refund of the "fees" that he would have paid for the service,
had he been required to purchase his health care. This bears no relationship
to anything. The claimant needs compensation for his losses, not for the
notional cost of the service that he did not have to pay for directly in the first
place. Moreover, since this payment would be *at the discretion* of the body
responsible for causing the damage arising out of that treatment there is no
entitlement to the compensation (whatever it is intended to compensate for)
and no guarantee that any NHS Trust would pay it. Nor is it entirely clear
what the payment of up to £30,000 by the national body would be compensation for. The report refers to payment in "suitable cases" for pain and suffering (measured by tort standards?), for "out of pocket expenses" (which is
presumably meant to refer to things rather more substantial than simply
reimbursement of taxi fares to and from hospital, such as loss of earnings)
and for care or treatment which the NHS could not provide. Would the
family of a patient who dies as a result of treatment be entitled to compensation, and on what basis? If the patient was not offered any financial compensation, but simply a "care package", and refused the offer because he
considered that financial compensation should have been included, what
happens to the care package? Does the NHS then simply refuse to treat the
patient for the injury that it has caused? This would clearly be untenable,

and there is no suggestion in *Making Amends* that this would happen. But if the patient was in any event receiving ongoing treatment in the NHS for the injury sustained, the "NHS Redress" might amount to little more than the patient would have been provided with in the first place. Payment for "care or treatment which the NHS could not provide" is clearly problematic. Who is to say whether the NHS can provide appropriate care? What happens if the NHS considers that it can provide the care, but it subsequently transpires that, for whatever reason (financial constraints, re-organisation, changing priorities, whether political or managerial) it fails to live up to the promise?

Brain damaged babies

1–064   The meat of the new scheme is not in the somewhat limited scope of the initial proposal—a care package plus up to £30,000 in, as yet, unspecified circumstances, for, as yet, unspecified losses. It is in the recommendation that the NHS Redress scheme "should encompass care and compensation for severely neurologically impaired babies, including those with severe cerebral palsy." Given that under the tort system brain damaged babies currently account for about 60 per cent of the total costs, this was always going to be the pivotal issue. In order to qualify for "redress" under the scheme there would have to be: (1) birth under NHS care; (2) severe neurological impairment (including cerebral palsy) related to or resulting from the birth; (3) a claim made to the scheme within eight years of the birth; (4) the care package and compensation would be based on a severity index judged according to the ability to perform the activities of daily living; (5) genetic or chromosomal abnormality would be excluded.[76] Crucially, under this part of the scheme there is no reference to "serious shortcomings in the standards of care" or "sub-standard care" as a qualifying criterion. This would truly be revolutionary. It would constitute a form of no-fault compensation for brain damaged babies. Everything hinges on the meaning of the phrase "severe neurological impairment (including cerebral palsy) related to or resulting from the birth." The implication, however, from the report's introductory comments about one small cohort of claimants receiving compensation under the tort system while another larger group does not, is that this is intended to cover all brain damaged babies, provided the damage is "birth-related." The specific exclusion of genetic or chromosomal abnormality would seem to suggest that the scheme is meant to cover all babies suffering brain damage as a result of their medical management, though it is not clear whether "severe neurological impairment (including cerebral palsy) related to or resulting from the birth" includes something having gone wrong during the management of the pregnancy prior to the onset of labour.[77] Pre-conception errors, such as negligent genetic counseling, and diagnostic errors

---

[76] *ibid*. p. 121.
[77] The scheme envisages a national panel of experts who would "review the severity of impairment and causation (*i.e.* whether the impairment related to or resulted from the birth)."

during pregnancy, would seem to be excluded, since the consequence of such errors is usually the birth of a child with a genetic or chromosomal defect.

Compensation would be provided in both cash and in kind, according to the needs of the child for assistance with the tasks of daily living resulting from the severity of impairment. This would include: (1) a managed care package; (2) a monthly payment for the costs of care which cannot be provided through a care package (in the most severe cases this could be up to £100,000 *per annum*); (3) lump sum payments for home adaptations and equipment at intervals throughout the child's life (up to £50,000); (4) an initial payment in compensation for pain, suffering and loss of amenity capped at £50,000.   **1–065**

The benefits of this scheme, as the report notes, are that compensation and support would be available to a wider range of severely disabled babies and children without the need to establish negligence or fault, although perhaps more importantly for the NHS "it would also control costs to the NHS by meeting the actual care needs as they arose."[78] Crucial to the success of this scheme will be the ability of the NHS to develop and consistently deliver the care packages that these children need. Under the tort system compensation provides the wherewithal to purchase the lifetime care that claimants need to cope with their disabilities. If a provider fails to live up to standards the family has the option of purchasing care from a different provider. If the NHS has undertaken to provide a package of care as part of the settlement, and at some point in the future fails to deliver what options are open to the child's family to enforce the undertaking? This is not an improbable situation, given that the NHS has to respond to so many different, and frequently changing priorities, within a limited budget.   **1–066**

Administration

The scheme would be administered by a national body having eight main functions[79]:   **1–067**

- assessing claims or recommendations for NHS compensation payments from patients or families, NHS service providers, the Commission for Healthcare Audit and Inspection, and the Health Service Commissioner;

- allocating compensation payments based on the merits of the claim or recommendation up to a maximum of £30,000 (except for neurologically impaired babies);

- assessing claims and developing packages of care and compensation under the scheme for severely neurologically impaired babies;

- levying "insurance" payments from NHS service providers to fund the new schemes;

---

[78] *Making Amends*, June 2003, p. 121.
[79] *ibid.* p. 122.

- monitoring the provision of care and rehabilitation packages under the scheme at local level;

- monitoring the local and national compensation payments made and publishing annual listings by NHS providers to act as an incentive to reduce risk and improve patient safety at local level;

- assessing and managing claims for care (other than neurologically impaired babies) where damages of greater than £30,000 are progressing under the tort system;

- continuing to manage older medical negligence claims for care given prior to the date of introduction of the new scheme.

The right to litigate

1–068   The right to litigate under the tort system would remain for patients or families who chose not to apply for packages of care and payment under the NHS Redress scheme, but patients who accepted compensation under the scheme would not subsequently be able to litigate for the same injury. Before accepting an offer under the scheme "a small amount of money would be made available to patients to allow them to seek independent advice on the fairness of the offer." This apparently preserves the right of patients to choose, but exercising that right to litigate would be severely curtailed if recommendation 14 of the report were to be implemented. This suggests that where a claimant was seeking legal aid to pursue a claim for clinical negligence, the Legal Services Commission should take into account whether or not the case had already been pursued through the scheme. Moreover, the report recommends that the results of the investigation undertaken to inform decisions on eligibility and level of award under the NHS Redress scheme would "provide valuable information to the LSC in deciding whether or not to support an application for Legal Aid to someone pursuing a claim for clinical negligence where they had not accepted a package of care and compensation under the scheme."[80] Thus, for the lower value claims (though not cerebral palsy cases) the expectation would be that they would have been pursued through the scheme in order to protect the public purse "from the unnecessary expenditure on legal aid." The implication is that those claimants who exercised their continuing right to sue for negligence would effectively be prevented from doing so by the Legal Services Commission (remember that 90 per cent of medical negligence litigation is legally aided). If the patient had refused an offer of redress, for example because the patient considered that it did not fairly compensate for the loss suffered, then the Legal Services Commission would also take that into account, presumably by refusing legal aid. The further implication, though not expressly stated in the report, is that if the patient has pursued a claim for redress under the scheme and had the claim turned down (*e.g.* because the administrators of

---

[80] *ibid.* p. 126.

the scheme disputed causation), the Legal Services Commission would also take that into account when applying the merits test for legal aid. The net result for most patients whose claim is worth less than £30,000 is that the "right" to litigate would become illusory. On the other hand, given that for claimants who do not qualify for legal aid, the right to litigate a low value claim is already illusory, since most people are not in a position to risk having to pay the costs of losing such an action, the new Redress scheme does open up the possibility of obtaining some form of compensation (whether in kind or in cash) that previously would not have been available to them. It does "equalise" access to a remedy, in that everyone who met the criteria for redress would be compensated, irrespective of income or wealth. However, the tort system would remain the only option for patients whose claim exceeded the compensation limits of the scheme.

The brain damaged baby cases would not be subject to the restrictions on   **1–069** access to legal aid, and so it would remain open to the parents litigate these cases. But the decision as to whether to litigate will now be heavily influenced by the prospects of succeeding on both negligence and causation. The Redress scheme would remove entirely the need to prove fault, though proof of causation would remain a major issue ("severe neurological impairment ... related to or resulting from the birth"). No claimant lawyer could sensibly advise the parents of a brain damaged baby falling with the scheme's criteria to ignore that route to compensation and use the tort system, except in the very clearest of cases of negligence. The risk would be that when, eventually, the tort case was lost because the claimant has not been able to prove negligence, a claim under the scheme would be too late (it must be made within eight years of birth), and the lawyer would then find himself the defendant in a professional negligence action on the basis that his advice caused the child to lose entitlement under the Redress scheme.[81] More difficult issues of judgment may have to be made by claimants' lawyers when an offer of redress under the scheme is made. If the offer is reasonably close to what might have been recoverable as tort damages, it will be easy to recommend acceptance given the risk of a tort claim failing to establish fault. If, however, there is a substantial gap, between what is on offer under the scheme and the potential tort damages, a judgment will have to be made as to whether the difference is worth undertaking the litigation risk. No doubt that is something that the Legal Services Commission would consider when applying the merits test for legal aid.

Other recommendations

Making Amends makes a number of other recommendations, some to the   **1–070** way in which the NHS should respond to patients injured by an adverse event, and some to the legal system.

---

[81] Of course, if the tort case was lost solely on causation, the chances are that a claim under the scheme would also have been rejected on causation, and therefore the negligence of the lawyer, if any, would not have been the cause of the loss of compensation.

- Adverse events and complaints should have a full and objective investigation, commensurate with the severity of the harm, so that patients are given a full explanation, an apology where something has gone wrong, and a specification of the action (local and national) being taken to reduce the risk of a similar event happening to future patients (recommendation 6). NHS Trusts should also offer remedial treatment or rehabilitation measures, to improve after care. This would reduce suffering and the long term effects of any harm, "with obvious benefits to the patient and savings to the NHS."

- The initial response to a local complaint should be an automatic investigation, which may indicate that compensation under the NHS Redress scheme was appropriate. Even if patients decide to pursue litigation, the complaints process should continue to provide the explanations which patients and families seek (recommendation 8).

- Effective rehabilitation services for personal injury, including that caused by medical accidents, should be developed (recommendation 10).

- The Department of Health should consider the scope for providing more accessible high quality but lower cost facilities for severely neurologically impaired and physically disabled children, regardless of cause (recommendation 11).

- A duty of candour should be introduced together with exemption from disciplinary action when reporting incidents with a view to improving patient safety (recommendation 12). This would be a statutory duty requiring all healthcare professionals and managers to inform patients where they become aware of a possible negligent act or omission. This should include exemption from disciplinary action for those reporting adverse events except where the healthcare professional has committed a criminal offence or it would not be safe for the professional to continue to treat patients.

- Documents and information collected for identifying adverse events should be protected from disclosure in court (recommendation 13). This would be so that such documents could not be compelled to be produced in a court so reducing the disincentive to the reporting of errors. But the protection would only apply to reports of adverse events where full information on the event was also included in the medical records.

1-071   Two crucial recommendations are designed to reduce the cost to the NHS of compensating those tort claims that remain outside the system of NHS Redress. The first, is that in paying damages for future care costs and losses in clinical negligence cases the expectation that should be that periodical payments will be used (recommendation 16). This is now far less controversial than it once was, particularly since the courts are to be given the power to order periodical payments in place of lump sum awards where appropriate. But as this recommendation recognises, the legislation will only impact directly on cases decided in the courts. The vast majority of claims are settled out of court, and there is no power to insist on periodical payments when reaching a settlement. But it is always open to the NHS Litigation Authority to refuse to settle on the basis of a lump sum award where it considers that periodical payments would be a more suitable option. That might lead to some cases being litigated on this point alone, but the courts would, no doubt, soon set the parameters for cases where periodical payments were the expected solution.

The second recommendation is far more controversial. This is that the **1–072** costs of future care included in any award for clinical negligence made by the courts should no longer reflect the cost of private treatment (recommendation 17). Section 2(4) of the Law Reform (Personal Injuries) Act 1948 provides that in an action for personal injuries, in determining the reasonableness of any expenses the possibility of avoiding those expenses, or part of them, by taking advantage of facilities available under the NHS is to be disregarded. The claimant can insist on damages to cover the cost of private medical treatment even though that treatment is available free under the NHS. The rule applies to all personal injury claims, including claims against the NHS, with the result that the NHS may have to fund private medical treatment at much higher cost than the NHS could itself provide. *Making Amends* recommends that clinical negligence cases arising from NHS treatment should be exempted from this provision. The NHS defendant would undertake to fund "a specified package of care or treatment to defined timescales." Initially, the report acknowledges, the costs would probably be similar to providing a sum of money to purchase private care, because the NHS would have to fund some elements of the care package privately.

The recommendation that section 2(4) of the Law Reform (Personal **1–073** Injuries) Act 1948 should be abolished was made by the Pearson Commission 25 years ago,[82] but not in the context of a particular type of accident or defendant. The problem with this proposal, which if anything has become more acute with the passage of time, is that there is no guarantee that the care the claimant needs will be provided by the NHS when it is needed. It is all very well stating that "the NHS defendant should undertake to fund a specified package of care or treatment to defined timescales." What happens if the NHS fails to deliver? Does the claimant have to go back to court to enforce the "undertaking"? The report identified the objections of claimant and patient groups to removing a patient's right to the cost of private medical treatment: (1) it would be inequitable to remove them only from those suffering medical injury; (2) there was insufficient capacity in the

---

[82] *Royal Commission on Civil Liability and Compensation for Personal Injury*, Cmnd. 7054 (1978), Vol. I, para. 342.

NHS to provide care for everyone who might need it if provision for private care costs was removed from all personal injury cases; (3) injured patients would not be able to access the full range of treatments and care needed though the NHS; (4) injured patients would not wish to have an ongoing relationship with the organisation which had injured them; (5) rehabilitation services available to the NHS were inadequate to meet the need for either rapid and intensive or long term support.[83] There is much force in these criticisms of the proposal. The response of the report was the assertion that: "it can be argued that the NHS itself should be under an obligation to put right the damage caused. Although money is now the traditional response, a comprehensive care package (*i.e.* 'non-financial compensation'), promptly provided and efficiently delivered, is an obvious alternative."[84] If the care package was comprehensive, and if it was delivered promptly and efficiently, this would be a perfectly reasonable response to the criticisms, but these are two very big "ifs."

1–074   *Making Amends* asserts that the "new NHS Redress Scheme is centred on the needs of NHS patients."[85] This claim is only partly true. It takes out of the tort system the relatively low value claims, which are disproportionately expensive to litigate, and it extends the possibility of some form of compensation in the low value claims for all patients, not just those qualifying for legal aid. The qualifying criteria for compensation appear to remain proof of fault and causation, as under the tort system, and the scope of that compensation remains, at this point, unclear. The scheme for brain damaged babies, by removing proof of fault, is truly revolutionary, although the eligibility criteria still include restrictions that may result in the drawing of invidious distinctions between claimants. But the NHS Redress scheme will do nothing for the patients who have sustained more serious injuries from other causes. Is the NHS concerned only about patients who have suffered less serious injuries? Why are the patients who suffer the greatest harm at the hands of the NHS to be left to the lottery of the tort system (which is rightly criticised in the report), though also having their rights to compensation curtailed in comparison with other accident victims? That does not look particularly patient-centred. Rather it looks as though the primary concern that prompted the CMO's review, the cost of medical negligence litigation, has strongly influenced these recommendations.

(5) Human Rights

1–075   The incorporation of the European Convention for the Protection of Human Rights and Fundamental Freedoms into domestic law through the Human Rights Act 1998 has had some, though limited, impact on the way in which the courts deal with claims for medical negligence. A conventional common law action for medical negligence involves three elements. It must

---

[83] *Making Amends*, June 2003, pp. 83–84.
[84] *ibid.* para. 33.
[85] *ibid.* p. 119.

be shown that: (1) the defendant owed a duty of care to the claimant; (2) that there was breach of that duty; and (3) that this breach caused the claimant's damage. The vast majority of claims involve disputes about the last two elements: breach and causation. It seems unlikely that the Human Rights Act will have a significant effect on these two "bread and butter" issues for medical negligence litigation. But there is some room for human rights jurisprudence to influence judicial perceptions of the scope of the duty of care in negligence, particularly in the context of so-called "immunities." This issue was highlighted by the European Court of Human Rights' understanding of decision of the Court of Appeal in *Osman v Ferguson*[86] which struck out the claimant's action against the police on policy grounds, before a hearing on the facts, effectively granting the police a "blanket immunity" against negligence claims where the police have failed to prevent a third party injuring the claimant. In *Osman v UK*[87] the European Court of Human Rights concluded that the decision *Osman v Ferguson* was in breach of Article 6 of the Convention, which grants a right to a fair trial, because the claimant had not had an opportunity to establish the facts of his case at a trial. This, said the Court, was a breach of the principle of proportionality, since there was no real weighing of the claimant's interests in the decision to confer the immunity (which was essentially concerned with the defendants' interests). Although the European Court of Human Rights has subsequently acknowledged that its decision in *Osman v UK* was based on a misunderstanding of the English tort of negligence and the procedural rules which permit a party to apply to the court to strike out a claim on the basis that it discloses no reasonable cause of action,[88] it is arguable that *Osman v UK* will nonetheless have long-term influence when English courts consider common law rules, particularly rules that confer an apparent immunity from suit.[89] The interplay between the law of torts and human rights principles will continue to shape the courts' understanding of and approach to arguments about the relevant tort rules.

There has already been a tendency for claimants, and more particularly their lawyers, to seek to graft human rights arguments onto more traditional common law thinking on the question of civil obligations, particularly in claims against public bodies, but also extending to claims between private individuals in some cases. The Court of Appeal has had to "advise" lawyers to take a responsible attitude to raising arguments based on the Human Rights Act, and has indicated that judges should be robust in resisting inappropriate attempts to introduce such arguments.[90] The likelihood is that, where it is considered to be necessary, there will be attempts to adapt

1–076

---

[86] [1993] 4 All E.R. 344.

[87] (1998) 5 B.H.R.C. 293.

[88] *Z v UK* [2001] 2 F.L.R. 612 at [94] to [101]; *TP and KM v UK* [2001] 2 F.L.R. 549; see Davies (2001) 117 L.Q.R. 521; and Gearty (2002) 65 M.L.R. 87.

[89] See Newdick (2002) 10 Tort L. Rev. 127, 136, discussing the principle of proportionality after *Osman v UK*.

[90] *Daniels v Walker* [2000] 1 W.L.R. 1382, 1387.

the existing rules of the common law, although that has always occurred as judicial perceptions of the needs of society have changed over time.

1–077   Potentially more significant is the use of Convention Rights effectively to sidestep the limitations of the common law principles of negligence. Thus, the fact that the House of Lords declared, for what it sees as good policy reasons, that a psychiatrist conducting an interview for the purpose of identifying whether a child has been abused, and if so the identity of the abuser, should owe no duty of care in negligence to the child or her mother,[91] did not prevent the European Court of Human Rights from concluding that, on the same facts, there was a breach of the claimants' Convention rights and awarding (modest) damages.[92] The decision that a claimant's human rights have been breached is not directly equivalent to a finding that the defendant is liable in tort.[93] The criteria for breach of a Convention right and breach of a common law duty of care are different, and the rules on awards of damages are also different.[94] Nonetheless, it seems likely that where claimants have established a breach of their Convention rights in circumstances where tort claims have previously failed, the courts may be willing to reconsider the common law position, or at least to weigh the balance more carefully between claimants' rights and defendants' interests.[94a] The common law approach is nothing if not pragmatic, and has always prided itself on its adaptability. Sometimes, the court may consider that it is simpler to alter the common law rule than to leave the rule open to a Human Rights Act challenge. For example, in deciding to abolish the common law immunity from suit of advocates for negligence in the conduct of trials the House of Lords was apparently influenced by the prospect that a "blanket immunity" would not be consistent with Article 6 of the Convention.[95]

1–078   There are some areas where there is a clear overlap between a common law duty of care and a breach of Convention rights. For example, in *Keenan v UK*[96] it was held that the suicide of a prisoner, who was a known suicide risk,

---

[91] See *X (minors) v Bedfordshire County Council*; *M. (a minor) v Newham London Borough Council* [1995] 2 A.C. 633, paras 2–061 *et seq.*

[92] *TP and KM v UK* [2001] 2 F.L.R. 549—the failure of the social services authority properly to involve the child's mother in the decision-making process which, on the facts of the case, would have avoided the authority's error, constituted a breach of Art. 8 of the Convention, the right to respect for family life.

[93] Although there is an argument that the Human Rights Act 1998 creates a new form of tort action for breach of statutory duty: see the Law Commission, *Damages under the Human Rights Act 1998*, Law Com. No. 266, 2000, para. 4.20.

[94] See Fairgrieve [2001] P.L. 695.

[94a] See now *JD v East Berkshire Community Health NHS Trust* [2003] EWCA Civ 1151; *The Times*, August 22, 2003, where the Court of Appeal concluded that the jurisprudence of the European Court of Human Rights meant that the decision of the House of Lords in *X (minors) v Bedfordshire County Council*; *M. (a minor) v Newham London Borough Council* [1995] 2 A.C. 633 could not survive the Human Rights Act 1998. As a consequence it will "no longer be legitimate to rule that, as a matter of law, no common law duty of care is owed to a child in relation to the investigation of suspected child abuse and the initiation and pursuit of care proceedings" at [84], (though the position of the parent, whose interests are in potential conflict with the child's interests was "very different").

[95] See *Arthur J.S. Hall & Co (a firm) v Simons* [2002] 1 A.C. 615.

[96] (2001) 10 B.H.R.C. 319.

in police custody could give rise to a breach of Article 3 ("No one shall be subjected to torture or to inhuman or degrading treatment or punishment"), arising out of a failure to provide adequate medical supervision. But a duty of care would be held to exist at common law in these circumstances, although there might be some debate as to the precise measures necessary to meet that duty.[97] There are also some situations where the existence of a duty of care would be the subject of considerable debate, where Convention rights could influence the balance of the argument. For example, it is not clear that English law would conclude that a doctor owes a duty to a third party to warn that his patient is potentially dangerous to that third party (*e.g.* a psychiatric patient who has made genuine threats to harm others or a patient with a highly infectious condition[98]). It might be argued that the failure to warn someone known to be at risk of a life-threatening condition constitutes a breach of Article 2 ("Everyone's right to life shall be protected by law"). Similarly, in appropriate circumstances Article 3 can impose a positive obligation on a public authority to prevent harm to individuals caused by other private individuals.[99] Thus, Convention rights may be called in aid to point the common law in a particular direction.

Beyond claims based in negligence, it is apparent that some forms of medical treatment without consent may breach human rights principles. Although the European Court of Human Rights has held that the compulsory treatment of a psychiatric patient does not necessarily breach Article 3, because a measure which is a therapeutic necessity is not to be regarded as inhuman or degrading, that medical necessity must be convincingly shown to exist.[1] This has already led the Court of Appeal to modify the traditional approach to challenges by patients to compulsory treatment under the Mental Health Act 1983.[2] It would also be arguable that to enrol a patient into a therapeutic programme of medical research without informing the patient that the treatment was experimental would constitute "inhuman or degrading treatment" contrary to Article 3, no matter how medically necessary the treatment, and even if the patient has expressly consented to the specific procedure. Human rights arguments have been invoked in the context of claims based on breach of confidentiality, though in practice Article 8 (the right to respect for family life) has not proved to be significantly easier for claimants to use than the law of confidentiality.[3]

1–079

In many of the cases where human rights arguments have been raised the court has concluded that the European Convention has added nothing to the existing law, but it would be over-optimistic to think that the common law has nothing to learn from the human rights jurisprudence. Where questions of human rights have been raised they are dealt with in this book in the context of the substantive issues that the cases address.

1–080

---

[97] *cf. Knight v Home Office* [1990] 3 All E.R. 237, para. 4–099.
[98] See paras 2–147 *et seq.* and paras 2–089 *et seq.*
[99] See *Z v UK* [2001] 2 F.L.R. 612.
[1] *Herczegfalvy v Austria* (1992) 15 E.H.R.R. 437.
[2] See para. 6–075.
[3] See paras 2–168, 2–183 to 2–184, 2–192.

CHAPTER 2

THE BASIS OF LIABILITY

2–001 The nature of the relationship between doctors and patients is determined largely by the practice of the medical profession, and shaped by a strong commitment to long-standing principles of medical ethics. The law plays a significant role, however, in providing a structure within which the doctor-patient relationship is conducted. Whether it is the civil law or the criminal law which is invoked, legal rules can only set the outer limits of acceptable conduct—a minimum standard of professional behaviour—leaving the question of "ideal" standards of practice to the profession itself. Some doctors seem to believe that the law sets too high a standard, which does not take account of the realities of medical practice, but the courts apply the same principles, whether they be from the law of tort, contract or equity, that are used for any other section of the community when disputes between individuals arise. Accordingly, the professional liability of medical practitioners is determined by the rules of tort, contract or equity.[1]

2–002 In practice most claims for medical malpractice are brought in tort, and of these the vast majority are for the tort of negligence. This is reflected in the structure of this chapter, the bulk of which deals with the circumstances in which a doctor will be held to owe a duty of care in the tort of negligence. The Chapter begins with a section on contractual liability which, in theory, governs the respective rights and responsibilities of patients and doctors in the private sector. It will be seen, however, that in practical terms there is very little difference between the obligations undertaken by a medical practitioner in private practice and those imposed on his colleagues working in the NHS. All doctors owe a duty to their patients to exercise reasonable care in carrying out their professional skills of diagnosis, advice and treatment,[2] and

---

[1] This book is concerned with civil liability, although there are occasions when a doctor's conduct could give rise to liability under both the civil and the criminal law. Thus, instances of gross negligence could lead to a charge of manslaughter: *R. v Bateman* (1925) 94 L.J.K.B. 791; *R. v Adomako* [1994] 5 Med. L.R. 277; and a surgeon who, knowing that he was a Hepatitis B carrier, but nonetheless continued to practise surgery, infecting 19 patients and putting hundreds of others at risk, was jailed having been convicted of the offence of public nuisance: *The Times*, September 30, 1994; see Mulholland (1995) 11 P.N. 70; see also Bronitt (1994) 1 J. Law and Med. 245 on the liability of donors of HIV-infected blood for the crime of public nuisance. In *R. v Thornton* (1991) 1 O.R. (3d) 480 (Ont. C.A.); affirmed (1993) 13 O.R. (3d) 744 (S.C.C.) the defendant was convicted of the crime of common nuisance for donating blood knowing that he was infected with HIV.

[2] The meaning of "reasonable care" is considered in Chs 3 and 4.

the situations in which a stricter duty will be applied are quite rare. In addition to the contractual or tortious duty to exercise reasonable care, a medical practitioner is subject to a duty of confidence in respect of information about his patients acquired in his capacity as a doctor, and this is dealt with in the final section of this Chapter. With private patients the duty arises under the contract between doctor and patient, whereas in the absence of a contractual relationship the duty of confidence is imposed by equity. This distinction has little relevance to the nature of the *duty* owed by the doctor, but it does have significant consequences for the remedies available, since there is some doubt as to whether there can be an action for damages in respect of a past breach of confidence where the duty is non-contractual.[3]

1. CONTRACT

Most patients treated under the National Health Service do not enter into a 2–003 contractual relationship with their doctor or the hospital where they receive treatment, although it had been suggested that there is a contract between a patient and his general practitioner, since the addition of the patient's name to the general practitioner's list increases the doctor's remuneration under his terms of service and this might constitute consideration by the patient.[4] An argument of this nature was accepted in the Canadian case of *Pittman Estate v Bain*[5] in which a hospital claimed that there was no contractual relationship with a patient because there was no consideration, the payment to the hospital for the patient's care coming not from the patient but from the government through universal health care plans. It was held that patients provide indirect or non-monetary consideration for their hospital care. They contributed indirectly through taxes and health premiums, and they also conferred a benefit on a hospital by providing the hospital with patients, without which the hospital would not operate. A hospital benefited in terms of government financial compensation, and enhancement of its reputation when patients chose it for their care. Lang J. concluded that by agreeing to

---

[3] See para. 9–113. Where the patient has sustained personal injury as a result of the breach of confidence a claim for damages could be based on the tort of negligence: see *Furniss v Fitchett* [1958] N.Z.L.R. 396.

[4] Earlier editions of *Jackson & Powell on Professional Negligence* had argued that this might be a possibility, but in the 5th edition, 2002, paras 12.005—12.007 the editors conclude that it is no longer tenable, particularly in light of *Reynolds v The Health First Medical Group* [2000] Lloyd's Rep. Med. 240, below. See also the *Royal Commission on Civil Liability and Compensation for Personal Injury*, Cmnd. 7054 (1978), Vol. I, para. 1313, stating that there is no contract where treatment is provided under the NHS. Patients who pay a prescription charge for medicinal products supplied on prescription under the NHS do not obtain the products under a contract of sale, but by virtue of the pharmacist's statutory duty to supply them: *Pfizer Corpn v Ministry of Health* [1965] A.C. 512. Presumably, the position of patients who make a partial payment for services under the NHS (*e.g.* for dental treatment) is similar.

[5] (1994) 112 D.L.R. (4th) 257 (Ont. Ct., Gen. Div.).

submit himself for treatment at the hospital, the claimant conferred a benefit
on the hospital, which received funding for its cardiac services as a result of
its overall patient care. This was sufficient consideration to support a contract between the hospital and the patient.[6]

2–004   In theory, the same rationale would apply to patients receiving hospital
treatment in the NHS, but in *Reynolds v The Health First Medical Group*[7]
the argument was rejected. The increased remuneration to a general practitioner arising from the patient permitting her name to be added to the practitioner's list did not constitute consideration for a contract. Rather, the
position was exactly parallel with prescription charges.[8] Moreover, the statutory context in which a general practitioner's services were provided to
patients (including the National Health Service (General Medical Services)
Regulations 1992) left no room for bargaining between doctor and patient,
and negated any suggestion that the parties intended to enter into contractual relations. The claimant in *Reynolds* had sought to put her claim in contract in order to avoid the effect of the House of Lords' decision in
McFarlane v Tayside Health Board[9] that the financial costs of raising a
healthy child were not recoverable in the tort of negligence. In that case Lord
Slynn had suggested that if a client wants to be able to recover such costs "he
or she must do so by an appropriate contract." It is not clear what an appropriate contract would consist of. Even if it could be established that the
doctor had warranted the outcome[10] it would not necessarily follow that the
scope of liability extended to the child-rearing costs, applying the normal
rules of remoteness of damage in contract.

2–005   Patients receiving private medical treatment clearly do have contractual
rights and may sue for breach of a relevant term. Since a doctor providing
private treatment also owes a concurrent duty in tort to the patient, the
patient's claim may be pleaded in both contract and tort, but in practice it is
rare for much to turn on this, because the doctor's contractual obligations
are usually no greater than the duties owed in tort.[11] The courts are understandably reluctant to draw a sharp distinction between the rights of patients
treated privately and under the NHS. For example, in *Hotson v East
Berkshire Area Health Authority* Sir John Donaldson M.R. said that:

> ". . . I am quite unable to detect any rational basis for a state of the law,
> if such it be, whereby in identical circumstances Dr. A who treats a
> patient under the National Health Service, and whose liability thereby

---

[6] *ibid.* at 334.
[7] [2000] Lloyd's Rep. Med. 240 (Hitchin County Court).
[8] Applying *Pfizer Corp v Ministry of Health* [1965] A.C. 512.
[9] [2000] 2 A.C. 59. See paras 2–039 *et seq.*
[10] Which is particularly difficult to prove: see paras 2–010 to 2–011.
[11] See, *e.g.*, *Thake v Maurice* [1986] Q.B. 644 and *Eyre v Measday* [1986] 1 All E.R. 488
(where on appeal the claim in tort had been abandoned). *Edwards v Mallan* [1908] 1 K.B.
1002 provides an early example of concurrent liability in the medical context. In *Henderson
v Merrett* [1995] 2 A.C. 145 the House of Lords held that where a defendant owes concurrent duties in contract and the tort of negligence, the claimant is entitled to pursue the action
which will give him a practical advantage for the purposes of the law of limitation.

falls to be determined in accordance with the law of tort, should be in a different position from Dr. B who treats a patient outside the service, and whose liability therefore falls to be determined in accordance with the law of contract, assuming, of course, that the contract is in terms which impose upon him neither more nor less than the tortious duty."[12]

Where there are differences between contract and tort they tend to be minimised, which may partially explain the courts' attitude to strict contractual warranties in the medical context.[13]

(1) Reasonable care

In the absence of an express term, a term will be implied into a contract   2–006
to provide a service that the service will be performed with reasonable care
and skill.[14] The standard of care required to satisfy this obligation is the
same as in the tort of negligence.[15] The surgeon who contracts to perform

---

[12] [1987] A.C. 750, 760; see also, *per* Croom-Johnson L.J. at 768; and Sir John Donaldson M.R. in *Naylor v Preston Area Health Authority* [1987] 2 All E.R. 353, 360; *Gold v Essex County Council* [1942] 2 K.B. 293, 297, *per* Lord Greene M.R. In *Lee v Taunton and Somerset NHS Trust* [2001] 1 F.L.R. 419, 423 which concerned a negligent failure by a radiologist to identify neural tube defects in a foetus following a scan, thereby depriving the claimant of an opportunity to terminate the pregnancy under the Abortion Act 1967, Toulson J. commented that: "In the present case the relationship between Mrs Lee and the defendants was equivalent to contract. It should not make any difference in a civilised system of law whether Mrs Lee underwent the scan as an NHS patient or a private patient. The radiologist possessed a special skill. He undertook to report on what the scan revealed and, by necessary implication, to exercise a proper degree of professional skill in so doing."

[13] See para. 2–010. Nonetheless some technical differences between actions in contract and tort do remain, *e.g.*, different rules on limitation periods (though special rules apply to actions for personal injuries in both contract and tort: see Ch. 10); different measures of damages; possibly different tests for remoteness of damage; possibly different approaches to claims involving "loss of a chance" following the House of Lords' ruling in *Hotson v East Berkshire Area Health Authority* [1987] A.C. 750, see paras 5–051 *et seq*. Moreover, there may be practical differences between the NHS and private medicine which have legal consequences. See, *e.g.*, the comments of Finlay J. in *Dryden v Surrey County Council* [1936] 2 All E.R. 535, 539 on the different levels of staffing that could legitimately be expected in public and private hospitals.

[14] Supply of Goods and Services Act 1982, s. 13; *Eyre v Measday* [1986] 1 All E.R. 488; *Thake v Maurice* [1986] Q.B. 644; *Greaves & Co (Contractors) Ltd v Baynham Meikle & Partners* [1975] 3 All E.R. 99, 103–104, *per* Lord Denning M.R.: "The law does not usually imply a warranty that [a professional] will achieve the desired result, but only a term that he will use reasonable care and skill. The surgeon does not warrant that he will cure the patient. Nor does the solicitor warrant that he will win the case."

[15] *Roe v Minister of Health* [1954] 1 W.L.R. 128, 131, *per* McNair J. In *Sidaway v Bethlem Royal Hospital Governors* [1985] A.C. 871, 904, Lord Templeman said that: "The relationship between doctor and patient is contractual in origin, the doctor performing services in consideration for fees payable by the patient. The doctor . . . impliedly contracts to act at all times in the best interests of the patient." It is difficult to see how a duty to act in the patient's "best interests" can differ in any substantive way from a doctor's duty to exercise reasonable care in practising the skills of medicine. The Canadian courts have taken the view that the doctor-patient relationship is a fiduciary relationship, which may give rise to obligations on the part of the doctor which are more extensive than would be the case under either contract or tort: see *McInerney v MacDonald* (1992) 93 D.L.R. (4th) 415 (S.C.C.); *Norberg v Wynrib* (1992) 92 D.L.R. (4th) 449 (S.C.C.), particularly the judgment of McLachlin J.;

an operation undertakes to carry out the operation with reasonable care; he does not guarantee that it will prove to be a success. If, however, he agrees to give the case his personal attention this means that he will perform the operation personally and pay such subsequent visits as are necessary for the supervision of the patient until the discharge of the patient.[16] Delegation of the operation to another doctor would constitute a breach of contract. Contractual duties of care are "non-delegable," so the doctor is liable for a failure to exercise reasonable care by the person who performs the service, notwithstanding that reasonable care has been taken in selecting a competent person.[17] Even if the procedure was a success the patient would still be entitled to nominal damages for the breach.

2–007   Within the NHS a doctor is under an obligation to provide personal treatment to his patients, by virtue of the contract of employment in the case of hospital doctors, and under the terms of service in the case general practitioners.[18] A patient would not be entitled to sue on that contract, but it does allow the Health Authority to place reasonable limits on the use of a deputising service.[19] Although it would seem that health authorities owe

---

(n.15 contd.) *Taylor v McGillivray* (1993) 110 D.L.R. (4th) 64 (N.B.Q.B.). In *Sidaway v Bethlem Royal Hospital Governors* [1984] 1 All E.R. 1018, CA, however, both Dunn and Browne-Wilkinson L.JJ., at 1029 and 1032 respectively, said that in English law the relationship of doctor and patient was not fiduciary in character, a view with which Lord Scarman agreed: at [1985] A.C. 871, 884. In *Breen v Williams* (1996) 138 A.L.R. 259 the Australian High Court held that the doctor-patient relationship is not fiduciary in character, but based on the doctor's contractual/tort duty to exercise reasonable care, and a doctor does not owe a general duty to act with the utmost good faith and loyalty. The Court expressly declined to adopt the Supreme Court of Canada's analysis in *McInerney v MacDonald*. Commenting on Lord Templeman's dictum in *Sidaway*, Gaudron and McHugh JJ. said, at 282, that a "doctor does not impliedly promise that he or she will always act in the 'best interests' of the patient. The primary duty that a doctor owes a patient is the duty 'to exercise reasonable care and skill in the provision of professional advice and treatment.'" For further discussion of the doctor as fiduciary see Grubb [1994] C.L.P. 311; Bartlett (1997) 5 Med. L. Rev. 193.

[16] *Morris v Winsbury-White* [1937] 4 All E.R. 494, 500, although Tucker J. doubted whether this obligation depended upon a specific undertaking by the surgeon; rather, it was part of the retainer in the ordinary case. In any event, the consent to treatment given by the patient is consent to surgery by a *specific* doctor (see *Michael v Molesworth* (1950) 2 B.M.J. 171), unless he specifies otherwise. To deal with this problem the standard NHS consent form contains a clause stating that: "I understand that you cannot give me a guarantee that a particular person will perform the procedure. The person will, however, have appropriate experience." See H.S.C. 2001/023, *Good practice in consent*. The forms are available at *www.doh.gov.uk/consent*. See further para. 6–014.

[17] Dugdale and Stanton, *Professional Negligence*, 3rd ed., 1998, para. 16.20.

[18] National Health Service (General Medical Services) Regulations 1992 (S.I. 1992 No. 635), as frequently amended. See Sch. 2, para. 19(1). General practitioners are not under an obligation to provide treatment personally where reasonable steps are taken to ensure the continuity of the patient's treatment, in accordance with para. 19(2).

[19] *R. v Secretary of State for Health, ex parte Spencer* [1990] 1 Med. L.R. 255; see now the National Health Service (General Medical Services) Regulations 1992 (S.I. 1992 No. 635), Sch. 2, paras 18A to 26. In *Roy v Kensington and Chelsea and Westminster Family Practitioner Committee* [1992] 1 A.C. 624 the House of Lords doubted, without deciding, whether the relationship between a general practitioner and the Health Authority was contractual in nature. There were "contractual echoes in the relationship." But, irrespective of whether there is a contract or not the general practitioner has a "bundle of rights" which are individual private law rights against the Health Authority, arising from the statute and

non-delegable duties to their "patients"[20] it is unlikely that a general practitioner would be held to owe a non-delegable duty to ensure that reasonable care has been taken by a deputising doctor if sued in tort. The general
practitioner terms of service provide that a doctor is responsible for all acts
and omissions of any doctor acting as a deputy, any organisation providing
deputising services, and any person employed by or acting on behalf of him
or the deputy or deputising organisation, except where the deputy is responsible.[21] But since the deputy is responsible for his own acts and omissions
and of any person employed by him or acting on his behalf,[22] the circumstances in which the principal can be responsible will be exceptional. In any
event, the rules are expressly imposed in relation to "obligations under these
terms of service," which do not purport to set out the common law position.

The National Health Service and Community Care Act 1990, section 4   **2–008**
permits one health service body to "contract" to provide goods or services
to another health service body as part of the "internal market" of the NHS,
but such "contracts" do not give rise to any contractual rights or liabilities.[23]
Although it is undoubtedly the case that the health service body providing
the treatment will be liable to the patient if the treatment is negligent, it has
been suggested that a purchasing authority could also be liable if it placed a
"contract" which did not provide for an adequate standard of treatment or
there was reason to believe that the providing authority was not reasonably
able to perform the "contract."[24] The liability to the patient would be in tort,
however, not contract.[25] It is unlikely that this argument will ever be tested,
since if the patient can establish negligence against the health service body
providing the treatment, there would be no practical reason for the patient
to claim against the "purchaser." The issue of the liability of a health service
body which provides services by "contracting out" to a non-NHS body
remains important, however, though this situation is covered by the general
rules applicable to the delegation of duties, not section 4.

In most cases of private medical treatment the existence of a contract does   **2–009**
not affect the duties owed by the doctor in practical terms, since the same

---

(n.19 contd.) regulations (the National Health Service Act 1977 and the National Health
Service (General Medical Services) Regulations 1992 (S.I. 1992 No. 635), as frequently
amended); Mulholland (1993) 9 P.N. 154. An "honorary clinical contract" can be a binding
contract of employment, even though the services rendered under it are not in return for pay:
*R. v North Thames Regional Health Authority, Chelsea and Westminster NHS Trust, ex
parte L* [1996] 7 Med. L.R. 385.

[20] *M v Calderdale & Kirklees Health Authority* [1998] Lloyd's Rep. Med. 157 (Huddersfield
County Court). See paras 3–100 to 3–102, 7–026 *et seq.*

[21] National Health Service (General Medical Services) Regulations 1992 (S.I. 1992 No. 635),
Sch. 2, para. 20(1).

[22] *ibid.*, para. 20(2).

[23] National Health Service and Community Care Act 1990, s. 4(3).

[24] Jacob [1991] P.L. 255, 264.

[25] The analogy that Jacob draws is with the liability that used to apply to voluntary hospitals
in employing consultants as independent contractors, where the obligation was to exercise
reasonable care in the selection of competent staff: *ibid.*, citing *Hillyer v Governors of St.
Bartholemews Hospital* [1909] 2 K.B. 820.

duties are owed in tort. There are, however, some circumstances in which the liabilities under the contract do differ from those in tort.

(2) Express and implied warranties

2–010   It is theoretically possible for a doctor to give a contractual warranty that he will achieve a particular result, but the court will be slow to infer such a warranty in the absence of an express term, because medicine is an inexact science and it is unlikely that a responsible doctor would intend to give such a warranty. This point was demonstrated by decisions of the Court of Appeal in two cases involving failed sterilisations. In *Eyre v Measday*[26] the claimant underwent a sterilisation operation performed by the defendant. The defendant had explained the nature of the operation (a laparoscopic sterilisation), emphasising that it was irreversible, but he did not inform the claimant that there was a less than one per cent risk of pregnancy occurring following such a procedure. Both the claimant and her husband believed that the operation would render the claimant completely sterile. The claimant subsequently became pregnant. She issued proceedings claiming that the defendant was in breach of a contractual term that she would be rendered irreversibly sterile and/or a collateral warranty to that effect which induced her to enter the contract. It was common ground that the contract was embodied partly in oral conversations and partly in the written consent form signed by the claimant. It was also common ground that the appropriate test as to the nature and terms of the contract was objective not subjective. This does not depend upon what the claimant or the defendant thought were the terms of the contract, but on what the court objectively considers the words used by the parties must be reasonably taken to have meant. The Court of Appeal held that it was a contract to perform a particular operation, not a contract to render the claimant sterile. Additionally, there was neither an express nor an implied warranty that the procedure would be an unqualified success. Although the claimant could reasonably have concluded from the defendant's emphasis on the irreversible nature of the operation that she would be sterilised, it was not reasonable for her to have concluded that he had given her a guarantee that she would be absolutely sterile.[27]

2–011   In *Thake v Maurice*[28] the Court of Appeal (Kerr L.J. dissenting) reversed the decision of Peter Pain J. that the defendant had contracted to make the

---

[26] [1986] 1 All E.R. 488.

[27] See also *Dendaas v Yackel* (1980) 109 D.L.R. (3d) 455 (B.C.S.C.) where there was similar confusion between doctor and patient, the patient believing that the doctor's emphasis on the "irreversible" and permanent nature of the sterilisation procedure meant that there was no chance of a future pregnancy. Bouck J. held that since there was no clear meeting of minds on this essential term the claim in contract must fail; *Grey v Webster* (1984) 14 D.L.R. (4th) 706, 713; see paras 6–192 *et seq.* on the question of the failure to disclose the risk of future pregnancy.

[28] [1986] Q.B. 644.

male claimant irreversibly sterile following a vasectomy operation. The defendant had given the claimants a graphic demonstration of the nature of the procedure and its effects, but had failed to give his usual warning that there was a slight risk that the male claimant might become fertile again. Both Neill and Nourse L.JJ. concluded that, on an objective interpretation, the defendant had not guaranteed the outcome, relying on the observation that medicine is not an exact science and results are to some extent unpredictable.[29] Nourse L.J. said that a doctor cannot be objectively regarded as guaranteeing the success of any operation or treatment unless he says as much in clear and unequivocal terms.[30]

By contrast, in the Canadian case of *La Fleur v Cornelis*[31] a plastic surgeon contracted to reduce the size of the claimant's nose, and drew a sketch to show the changes that would be made. After the operation the claimant had some scarring and deformity. Barry J. held the defendant strictly liable for breach of contract, stating that whilst there is usually no implied warranty of success, there is no law preventing a doctor from contracting to do that which he is paid to do. The defendant had said to the claimant that there would be "no problem. You will be very happy." This was held to constitute an express warranty of success. **2–012**

Accordingly, while it may be possible to establish that a doctor has guaranteed a particular result,[32] this is likely to be a rare occurrence.[33] Indeed, the converse, a statement by the doctor that he could *not* guarantee the **2–013**

---

[29] "Medicine, though a highly skilled profession, is not, and is not generally regarded as being, an exact science. The reasonable man would have expected the defendant to exercise all the proper skill and care of a surgeon in that speciality; he would not in my view have expected the defendant to give a guarantee of 100% success": *ibid.* at 685, *per* Neill L.J.

[30] *ibid.* at 688. However, the claim that the defendant was liable in negligence for failing to warn about the small risk that the male claimant would become fertile again succeeded. See para. 6–194. In *ter Neuzen v Korn* (1995) 127 D.L.R. (4th) 577, 599 (S.C.C.) an argument that the information sheet about the proposed treatment (artificial insemination) given by a doctor to a patient provided the basis for a finding of an express warranty was rejected. The purpose of the information sheet was to provide information; there was no intention that the statements in it would constitute an express warranty.

[31] (1979) 28 N.B.R. (2d) 569 (N.B.S.C.).

[32] Both Pain J. and Kerr L.J. came to this conclusion in *Thake v Maurice*. Note also that under the Misrepresentation Act 1967, s. 2(1) where a person has entered into a contract after a misrepresentation has been made to him by another party to the contract, and has suffered loss as a result, if the person making the misrepresentation would be liable to damages had the misrepresentation been made fraudulently, that person shall be so liable notwithstanding that the misrepresentation was not made fraudulently, unless he proves that he had reasonable grounds to believe and did believe up to the time the contract was made that the facts represented were true. This action is more advantageous to a claimant than a claim in negligent misrepresentation because there is no question of whether a duty of care was owed and the defendant bears the burden of proof. Moreover, damages are measured under tortious rather than contractual principles, but the measure is that for the tort of deceit rather than for negligence, and so includes unforeseeable losses: *Royscot Trust Ltd v Rogerson* [1991] 2 Q.B. 297.

[33] It may be that with elective procedures such as sterilisation operations and cosmetic surgery the courts will be more willing to find express warranties of a successful outcome. For example, in *La Fleur v Cornelis* (1979) 28 N.B.R. (2d) 569, 577 Barry J. said that a cosmetic surgeon was in a different position from an ordinary physician; he was selling a special service and was more akin to a businessman.

outcome, would seem to be a more likely event in practice.[34] It must be borne in mind, however, that some contractual terms have nothing to do with the exercise of reasonable care. If a defendant contracts to perform a specific act, such as attend upon the patient,[35] or use a particular procedure,[36] then he is liable for failing to carry it out irrespective of whether he exercised reasonable care.

Supply of goods

2–014   Where the contract involves a transfer of goods there will be implied terms as to the quality and fitness for purpose of the goods supplied.[37] For example, in *Samuels v Davis*[38] the defendant dentist agreed to make a set of dentures for the claimant, but the dentures did not fit. It was held that there was an implied term that the dentures would be reasonably fit for their purpose. Similarly, in *Dodd v Wilson*[39] an injection of a vaccine into a herd of cattle by a veterinary surgeon resulted in some of the cattle becoming ill. There was held to be an implied term in the contract between the vet and the farmer that the vaccine would be reasonably fit for its purpose. There is no reason why the same proposition should not apply to injections given to patients.

2–015   This principle could apply to many forms of treatment, such as the supply of drugs, prosthetics, heart pacemakers or artificial heart valves,[40] although in Canada it has been held to be inappropriate to imply a contractual warranty as to fitness for purpose in a contract for artificial insemination where the donated semen was infected with HIV, on the basis that it was a contract for the supply of medical services, not goods, which should be confined to a

---

[34] A person cannot, however, by a contractual term or by notice exclude or restrict liability for death or personal injury resulting from negligence: Unfair Contract Terms Act 1977, s. 2(1). Any attempt to exclude or restrict liability for other forms of loss or damage resulting from negligence is subject to a test of reasonableness: *ibid.*, s. 2(2). These provisions apply to persons who act "in the course of a business" (*ibid.*, s. 1(3)(a)), but that term is broad enough to include health care provided under the NHS.

[35] *Morris v Winsbury-White* [1937] 4 All E.R. 494. See also the comments of Oliver J. in *Midland Bank Trust Co Ltd v Hett, Stubbs & Kemp* [1979] Ch. 384, 434: "A contract gives rise to a complex of rights and duties of which the duty to exercise reasonable care and skill is but one."

[36] A dentist who contracts to employ his painless process of tooth extraction will be strictly liable for breach of contract if he fails to employ his painless process, but an allegation that the tooth was unskilfully extracted is a claim that the defendant failed to exercise reasonable care, which in substance may be treated as an action in tort: *Edwards v Mallan* [1908] 1 K.B. 1002, 1005, CA.

[37] Supply of Goods and Services Act 1982, ss. 4 and 9, as amended by the Sale and Supply of Goods Act 1994. For detailed discussion see Bell (1984) 4 L.S. 175.

[38] [1943] 1 K.B. 526.

[39] [1946] 2 All E.R. 691.

[40] It has been suggested, for example, that the circumstances of *Roe v Minister of Health* [1954] 2 Q.B. 66 (see para. 3–071) might be covered by the proposition: see Nathan, *Medical Negligence*, 1957, pp. 18–19. Pharmacists who supply non-prescription products or who supply products under a private prescription will be liable in contract to the purchaser if the product is not of satisfactory quality or fit for its intended purpose; see paras 8–005 to 8–008.

claim in negligence.[41] Similarly, in *Pittman Estate v Bain*[42] Lang J. concluded that because blood used for transfusions, in the form of cryoprecipitate, is not a manufactured product in the nature of other equipment and supplies it was not reasonable to imply a contractual term that a hospital warranted that the blood would be free from disease.[43] Blood, as a biological product, might be "unavoidably unsafe." Moreover, different considerations applied to the supply of blood, taking it out of the usual chain of commercial manufacture and distribution, because of the nature of the collection and distribution of blood, and society's need for a product for which there is no feasible alternative. The hospital would have no contractual claim against the suppliers, the Canadian Red Cross Society, or against the donor for latently defective blood, since the blood was donated free of charge, and provided by the suppliers to the hospital free of charge. Thus, it would not be possible for the hospital to pass on liability for breach of a contractual warranty up a chain of distribution by suing on the contracts, as would normally be the case with other products and which provided the rationale for the ordinary common law rules on implied warranties.[44] There were additional factors to take into account in the case of blood transfusions:

"... it is not in the best interests of our health care system to impose absolute liability on the hospital in these circumstances. When a patient may be in need of a transfusion, society wants the hospital or physician to make the decision to transfuse or not on the basis of its skilled perception of the patient's best interests, after balancing the risks of transfusion against the risks of the presenting problem. To hold a hospital or physician to strict liability for a product such as blood may operate to discourage those responsible for our health care from exercising their professional judgment, because they are concerned about their own liability."[45]

The same issue arose in the Australian case of *E. v Australian Red Cross Society*[46] where the Federal Court of Appeal held that the trial judge had

---

[41] *ter Neuzen v Korn* (1993) 103 D.L.R. (4th) 473, 517 (B.C.C.A.): "In the face of the American experience, we are unable to identify any policy reason why a physician should face stricter liability for 'goods' which are furnished to a patient in the course of medical service than he or she would be for any lack of professional care and skill which must be brought to every healing or treating engagement," *ibid.* at 517–518. This statement was specifically approved on appeal by the Supreme Court of Canada: (1995) 127 D.L.R. (4th) 577, 609.

[42] (1994) 112 D.L.R. (4th) 257 (Ont. Ct., Gen. Div.).

[43] Not all blood products are used in "unmanufactured" form, and therefore a different approach might apply to products that had undergone some form of "manufacturing process."

[44] This issue was also considered to be an important factor by the Supreme Court of Canada in *ter Neuzen v Korn* (1995) 127 D.L.R. (4th) 577, 607 in declining to imply a warranty in the case of donated semen.

[45] (1994) 112 D.L.R. (4th) 257, 354.

[46] (1991) 105 A.L.R. 53 (Aus. Fed. C.A.); affirming (1991) 99 A.L.R. 601; [1991] 2 Med. L.R. 303.

been correct to find that there was no contract with the hospital for the supply of blood plasma to the claimant when he received a blood transfusion in the course of treatment.[47] It was a contract for services, namely the provision of hospital, medical and nursing services for the purpose of treating the claimant for his medical condition. The blood was intended to be supplied, if necessary, free of charge. Lockhart J. said that:

> "To the extent that goods were provided to him such as food, sleeping tablets, antibiotics, dressings and things of this nature, they were provided as an incident to the contract for the provision of services. There was no contract for the supply of goods. The contract . . . was one for services and is not divisible into a contract for services and for the supply of goods. I leave open, however, the question whether in an appropriate case a contract between a patient and a hospital may be divisible in other circumstances. But the provision on the facts of this case of medicines, drugs and blood cannot be severed into concepts of the provision of services on the one hand and of purchase and sale of goods on the other."[48]

2–016   The distinction between a contract for the sale of goods and a contract for the performance of services, which is often a fine one, was the central issue on the contractual claim in *E. v Australian Red Cross Society*, as indeed it is in the American courts.[49] But, as Lang J. noted in *Pittman Estate v Bain*, the American cases have taken a different route from the English and Canadian cases, since they do "not seem to consider implying common law warranties to material in a hybrid contract that provides both services and material."[50] In *ter Neuzen v Korn*[51] and *Pittman Estate v Bain* the question was whether *at common law* there should be implied into the contract for the supply of services and goods a warranty that the semen and blood, respectively, would be fit for their purpose and free from latent defects. It may be that the Supply of Goods and Services Act 1982, sections 4 and 9, makes this argument redundant by implying a *statutory* term as to the quality and fitness for purpose of the goods where the contract involves "a transfer of goods." Thus, it is arguable that in English law the question of whether there could

---

[47] A finding that the giving of blood to the claimant was a "supply of goods" under a contract for the supply of goods within the meaning of s. 71 of the Trade Practices Act 1974 (which is in similar terms to the English Sale of Goods Act 1979, s. 14) would have resulted in the conclusion that there were implied conditions that the goods were of merchantable quality and fit for their purpose.

[48] (1991) 105 A.L.R. 53, 59. Query whether the distinction here is between consumables, such as food and drugs, and more durable products, such as artificial joints or heart valves.

[49] The leading case is *Perlmutter v Beth David Hospital*, 123 N.E. (2d) 792 (1954) in which the New York Court of Appeals held that the essence of the contractual relationship between a patient and a hospital was a contract for services which was not divisible into a contract for the provision of services and the transfusion of blood. Not all jurisdictions have followed *Perlmutter*, however, see: *Cunningham v MacNeal Memorial Hospital*, 266 N.E. (2d) 897 (S.C. of Illinois) (1970), holding that there was a contract to supply goods to the patient.

[50] (1994) 112 D.L.R. (4th) 257, 351.

[51] (1993) 103 D.L.R. (4th) 473, 517 (B.C.C.A.); affirmed (1995) 127 D.L.R. (4th) 577 (S.C.C.).

be a warranty that bodily products such as blood or semen are fit for their purpose, *i.e.* not contaminated in some potentially harmful manner, would depend upon whether it could be said that there had been a transfer of goods. Do blood or semen constitute "goods"? In *E. v Australian Red Cross Society* the trial judge specifically left open the question of whether blood was "goods" within the meaning of the Trade Practices Act 1974, as did Lockhart J. on appeal.[52] In *PQ v Australian Red Cross Society*,[53] however, McGarvie J. appears to have assumed, without comment, that a "blood product" constituted "goods" for the purpose of the legislation, observing that a blood product contaminated by HIV infection could not be regarded as being of merchantable quality. The issue arose in the context of determining whether the claimant's cause of action in contract was statute-barred, but nonetheless, the judge proceeded on the basis that such a claim was correctly conceived and that blood did constitute "goods." On the other hand, the defendant to the contractual claim was a manufacturer of blood concentrate (such as Factor VIII), not the Red Cross in respect of its supply of cryoprecipitate. The blood had gone through a manufacturing process, and it may be easier to categorise the end result of a manufacturing process as "goods" or a "product."[54] The issue remains unresolved in English law, though in practice it has less significance since the decision in *A v The National Blood Authority*[55] that blood can be treated as a product for the purpose of the regime of strict liability under the Consumer Protection Act 1987, a position that had been recommended by the Pearson Commission.[56] In any event, it is arguable that the difficulty that the courts perceived with implying a warranty in these cases stems from the fact that the "goods" consisted of a biological product. Where the item that is transferred to the patient is in the nature of an artificial medical device which is manufactured, the courts may be more willing to approach the issue in terms of contractual warranties.[57]

It is possible that the contractual obligations as to fitness for purpose and satisfactory quality would apply to the design of an article, so that there may be a warranty that the design is fit for its intended purpose.[58] When it does

2–017

---

[52] (1991) 99 A.L.R. 601; [1991] 2 Med. L.R. 303, 326 and (1991) 105 A.L.R. 53, 58, respectively.

[53] [1992] 1 V.R. 19, 41–42.

[54] See also *Pittman Estate v Bain* (1994) 112 D.L.R. (4th) 257, 318 where Lang J. drew a distinction between cryoprecipitate and fractionated blood products, which do undergo a manufacturing process.

[55] [2001] 3 All E.R. 289. See paras 8–079 *et seq.*

[56] *Royal Commission on Civil Liability and Compensation for Personal Injury*, Cmnd. 7054, (1978), Vol. I, para. 1276.

[57] In *ter Neuzen v Korn* (1993) 103 D.L.R. (4th) 473, 514 the British Columbia Court of Appeal did not rule out the possibility that cases could arise where common law contractual warranties could have a role to play in medical malpractice actions (a view apparently accepted by the Supreme Court of Canada, on appeal: (1995) 127 D.L.R. (4th) 577, though not for biological products such as blood and semen, which carry "inherent risks"), and in *E. v Australian Red Cross Society* (1991) 105 A.L.R. 53, 59 Lockhart J. left this option open.

[58] *Independent Broadcasting Authority v EMI Electronics Ltd and BICC Construction Ltd* (1980) 14 Build. L.R. 1, 47–48, *per* Lord Scarman. This strict design duty only applies where the defendant has supplied or manufactured the article as well as designing it: *George Hawkins v Chrysler (UK) Ltd and Burne Associates* (1986) 38 B.L.R. 36; see Dugdale and

apply the obligation is strict, in that the exercise of reasonable care is not a defence. If the goods are not of satisfactory quality or fit for their purpose there is a breach of contract. This does not mean, however, that the product must be effective in preventing the illness or producing a cure, which would be the equivalent of giving a guarantee of successful treatment. Rather the implied term is that the goods will be fit for their intended purpose, which they may not be if they cause harm. Moreover, a product such as a drug may be of satisfactory quality and fit for its purpose even though it carries an inherent risk of an adverse reaction from known "side-effects."[59]

2. TORT

2–018   The vast majority of claims for medical malpractice are brought in the tort of negligence, where the issue will usually be whether the defendant was in breach of a duty of care and/or whether the breach caused damage to the patient.[60] Normally, there will be no difficulty in finding a duty of care owed by the doctor to his patient, at least where the claim is in respect of personal injuries, and this is true even where there is a contractual relationship.[61] The practitioner may also owe a duty of care to the patient in respect of pure financial loss. In addition, there are a number of circumstances where the doctor may owe a duty of care to a third party arising out of the treatment given to the patient, but the incidence and extent of such duties is more problematic.

2–019   In some instances an action for trespass to the person may be available, particularly in the form of the tort of battery. Battery is an intentional tort which requires "the actual infliction of unlawful force on another person."[62] The action is potentially relevant to any medical treatment or examination which involves a touching of the patient, since, with the exception of certain

---

(n.58 contd.) Stanton, *Professional Negligence*, 3rd ed., 1998, paras 4–008–4–009. The circumstances in which this type of strict design liability might apply in a medical context are somewhat limited, but it could be relevant in appropriate circumstances to claims arising out of cosmetic surgery, for example. An allegation of *negligent* design in the conduct of breast reduction surgery was made in *White v Turner* (1981) 120 D.L.R. (3d) 269, 279, but failed on the facts; see also *La Fleur v Cornelis* (1979) 28 N.B.R. (2d) 569 (N.B.S.C.), para. 2–012, above.

[59] See para. 8–006, n. 17. The rupture of an artificial breast implant, from some unidentified cause, does not establish as a matter of law that it was not reasonably fit for its purpose: *Hollis v Dow Corning Corp.* (1993) 103 D.L.R. (4th) 520, 556 (B.C.C.A.); affirmed (1995) 129 D.L.R. (4th) 609 (S.C.C.).

[60] On this see Chs 3 to 5.

[61] See n. 11, above. In some circumstances the patient may be owed a duty of care by the institution providing the health care, such as a hospital or health authority, in addition to the duties owed by individual health care professionals. This form of "direct" liability is discussed in Ch. 7.

[62] *Collins v Wilcock* [1984] 3 All E.R. 374, 377. It is the act that constitutes the trespass (the touching) that must be intentional; an intention to cause the harm is not necessary: *Wilson v Pringle* [1987] Q.B. 237.

forms of unavoidable or socially accepted contacts (such as jostling in a busy street or engaging someone's attention), any unwanted touching without lawful excuse will constitute a battery. So the surgeon who performs an operation without the patient's consent commits a battery, even though his intention is to benefit the patient.[63] Consent by the patient exculpates the doctor, and thus, invariably, the question turns upon whether the requirements for a valid consent have been satisfied or whether the case falls within the circumstances in which consent may be dispensed with. These issues are considered in Chapter 6.

(1) Duty of care

The tort of negligence consists of a legal duty to take reasonable care, and breach of that duty by the defendant causing damage to the claimant.[64] The duty of care determines as a matter of policy whether the type of loss suffered by the claimant in the particular manner in which it occurred can ever be actionable, whereas breach of duty deals with the standard of care required of a defendant in the circumstances in order to satisfy the duty of care, and whether the defendant's conduct fell below that standard; in other words, whether the defendant was careless/negligent.   2–020

The usual starting point for any discussion of the duty of care in the tort of negligence is the landmark decision of *Donoghue v Stevenson*,[65] and the famous dictum of Lord Atkin.[66] Its significance in the context of medical negligence is somewhat limited, however, at least in the context of the paradigm case of physical injury caused to the patient during the course of treatment, since the duty of care owed by a doctor to his patient long ante-dates *Donoghue v Stevenson*, and the relationship between doctor and patient clearly satisfies any test based upon foreseeability of harm, proximity of the relationship between claimant and defendant, or, indeed, a requirement that it be just and reasonable to impose a duty of care.[67] In addition to the   2–021

---

[63] *Re F. (Mental Patient: Sterilisation)* [1990] 2 A.C. 1, 73, *per* Lord Goff; *T. v T.* [1988] 1 All E.R. 613, 625, *per* Wood J. It is assumed throughout this book that the doctor is acting in good faith, although there are occasional examples to the contrary: see *Appleton v Garrett* [1996] P.I.Q.R. P1, para. 6–041.

[64] *Lochgelly Iron Co v M'Mullan* [1934] A.C. 1, 25, *per* Lord Wright.

[65] [1932] A.C. 562.

[66] "You must take reasonable care to avoid acts or omissions which you can reasonably foresee would be likely to injure your neighbour. Who, then, in law is my neighbour? The answer seems to be—persons who are so closely and directly affected by my act that I ought reasonably to have them in contemplation as being so affected when I am directing my mind to the acts or omissions which are called in question": *ibid.* at 580.

[67] This tripartite test for the existence of a duty of care derives from a series of appellate court decisions in the 1980s: see *Peabody Donation Fund v Sir Lindsay Parkinson & Co Ltd* [1985] A.C. 210; *Yuen Kun-yeu v A.-G. of Hong Kong* [1988] A.C. 175; *Smith v Bush* [1990] 1 A.C. 831, 865, *per* Lord Griffiths; *Caparo Industries plc v Dickman* [1990] 2 A.C. 605. These cases (and others) represented a retreat from what was perceived to be the unacceptable implications of a wide formulation of the test for the duty of care by Lord Wilberforce in *Anns v Merton London Borough Council* [1978] A.C. 728, 751–2, a process that culminated in the overruling of that decision by the House of Lords in *Murphy v*

"tripartite test", a number of other tests for the existence of a duty of care
have emerged in recent years, including "voluntary assumption of responsibility" by the defendant, an "incremental" approach, and whether the
imposition of liability satisfies the "requirements of distributive justice." It
is arguable that these different approaches are simply different ways of
looking at the same issue, and that if they are applied correctly they should
produce the same result.[68] Even if it can be said that the defendant owes a
duty of care to the claimant the defendant is not necessarily responsible for
all the consequences that flow from that negligence. The limits of liability are
often set by the concepts of causation and remoteness of damage, but sometimes the court may restrict a defendant's responsibility by reference to the
scope of the duty.[69] Of course, ultimately, these issues involve policy judgments about the appropriate limits of a defendant's responsibility for the
consequences of his negligence.

2–022   It is rare for the courts expressly to invoke policy as a ground for denying
a patient a right of action against a negligent medical practitioner, although
certain "policy" considerations may have a subtle influence at other points.[70]
Some types of claim have been barred on policy grounds, most of them
arising from congenital injury to unborn children. Thus, "wrongful life"
claims on the part of a child whose congenital disabilities the defendant negligently failed to diagnose are not actionable.[71] On the other hand, the
parents may have an action in these circumstances for being deprived of the
opportunity to have the pregnancy terminated, though generally not where
the child is born healthy.[72] But if the termination of the pregnancy would not
be lawful under the Abortion Act 1967, the action for loss of opportunity to
have an abortion will be denied on policy grounds.[73] The basis for barring
such actions seems to rest on the maxim *ex turpi causa non oritur actio* or
some analogous principle, but a denial of a duty of care simply on the ground
of "policy" is equally effective in practice. Thus, where potential claims arise
out of the negligent performance of procedures which are unlawful the likelihood is that they will be barred on the grounds of policy.[74]

(n. 67 contd.) *Brentwood District Council* [1991] 1 A.C. 398. Although these decisions deal
with the duty of care in general terms, they are virtually exclusively concerned with liability
for pure economic loss and have little relevance in the context of medical malpractice litigation.

[68] See *Clerk & Lindsell on Torts*, 18th ed. (2000), para. 7–95, citing Sir Brian Neill in *Bank of
Credit and Commerce International (Overseas) Ltd v Price Waterhouse (No. 2)* [1998]
P.N.L.R. 564, 583–587. See also the comments of Brooke L.J. in *Parkinson v St. James and
Seacroft University Hospital NHS Trust* [2001] EWCA Civ 530; [2002] Q.B. 266 at [17] to
[27].

[69] See para. 2–031.

[70] In particular, in the form of an unquantifiable reluctance on the part of the courts to make
findings of negligence against doctors, possibly due to fears about defensive medicine or the
effects of such a finding on the defendant's professional reputation: see paras 1–017 to 1–022
and 3–110 to 3–116 and 3–145 to 3–146.

[71] *McKay v Essex Area Health Authority* [1982] Q.B. 1166; see para. 2–084.

[72] See para. 2–039.

[73] *Rance v Mid-Downs Health Authority* [1991] 1 Q.B. 587.

[74] See para. 4–148. The principle of public policy that would preclude the cause of action
applies equally to claims in contract or tort.

A rather different form of public policy was invoked in *A.B. v John Wyeth*   2–023
& Brother Ltd[75] to justify the striking out of multiple claims against doctors
who had prescribed tranquillisers to the claimants. In the course of group
litigation against the manufacturers of the drug benzodiazepine, involving
almost 5,000 actions, some claimants also sought to bring claims in the alternative against the prescribers of the drug. The claimants were Legally Aided,
with the consequence that should the actions fail the defendants would be
unlikely to recover their costs against the claimants or the Legal Aid fund.
The actions against the prescribers were struck out as vexatious and an abuse
of the process of the court, on the basis that the irrecoverable costs which
had been and were likely to be incurred by the prescribers were out of all
proportion to the benefit that the claimants could obtain from the litigation
against them. The costs were described as "astronomical." The court has an
inherent jurisdiction to see that its proceedings are not used in a way which
is oppressive and vexatious to the other party or which involves serious
injustice to him. It was not relevant that the claimants were not guilty of any
unreasonable or blameworthy conduct in bringing the litigation:

> ". . . the prescriber defendants will be put to astronomical expense in
> defending these contingent claims. And to what end? If the plaintiffs
> stood to obtain a substantial benefit, the position might well be differ-
> ent. But here the benefit is at best extremely modest, and in all probabil-
> ity nothing. It is no answer that there are public authorities or insurance
> associations that are footing the bill. The National Health Service has
> better things to spend its money on than lawyers' fees and the cost of
> medical insurance is a matter of public concern."[76]

On the other hand, the few cases which were brought against prescribing
doctors alone, without any claim having been made against the manufacturers, were permitted to proceed outside the group litigation as ordinary
medical negligence actions.

(2) Duty to the patient

From ancient times the medical practitioner has been held accountable for   2–024
a failure to exercise reasonable care in treating his patient, independently of
any contractual relationship with the patient. The surgeon, like the inn
keeper or common carrier, exercised a "common calling" which gave rise to
a duty to exercise proper care and skill.[77] Today the duty arises from the tort
of negligence, but it does not depend upon the doctor's status, qualifications

---

[75] [1994] 5 Med. L.R. 149; [1994] P.I.Q.R. P109, CA.
[76] *ibid.* at 153, *per* Stuart-Smith L.J. Subsequently, the claims against the drug manufacturers
were also struck out as an abuse of process, and for want of prosecution, after the Legal Aid
Board withdrew funding for the group litigation: [1997] 8 Med. L.R. 57, CA.
[77] Holdsworth, *History of English Law*, Vol. III, pp. 385–386; Winfield (1926) 42 L.Q.R. 184,
186–7; *cf.* Fifoot, *History and Sources of the Common Law*, pp. 157–158.

or expertise. Rather it is imposed by law when the doctor undertakes the task of providing advice, diagnosis or treatment. It is irrelevant who called the doctor to the patient or who pays his bill.[78] In *R. v Bateman* Lord Hewart C.J. said:

> "If a person holds himself out as possessing special skill and knowledge and he is consulted, as possessing such skill and knowledge, by or on behalf of a patient, he owes a duty to the patient to use due caution in undertaking the treatment. If he accepts the responsibility and undertakes the treatment and the patient submits to his direction and treatment accordingly, he owes a duty to the patient to use diligence, care, knowledge, skill and caution in administering the treatment. No contractual relation is necessary, nor is it necessary that the service be rendered for reward."[79]

2–025   It follows that, although as a general rule there is no legal obligation upon a doctor to play the "Good Samaritan" and render assistance to a stranger who has been involved in an accident,[80] a doctor who chooses to do so will owe a duty of care to the "patient."[81] The duty arises from the performance of the act. In *Everett v Griffiths*[82] Atkin L.J. said that the duty of the medical practitioner to the person whom he undertakes to treat is not based on contract or implied contract:

> "It would apply to a doctor treating a member of the household of the other party to the contract, as it would, in my judgment, apply to a doctor acting gratuitously in a public institution, or in the case of emergency in a street accident; and its existence is independent of the volition of the patient, for it would apply though the patient were unconscious or incapable of exercising a conscious volition."[83]

---

[78] *Gladwell v Steggal* (1839) 5 Bing. (N.C.) 733: ". . . this is an action *ex delicto*", *per* Tindal C.J.; *Pippin v Sheppard* (1822) 11 Price 400; *Edgar v Lamont*, 1914 S.C. 277, 279.

[79] (1925) 94 L.J.K.B. 791 at 794; *Lindsey County Council v Marshall* [1937] A.C. 97, 121. In *Cassidy v Ministry of Health* [1951] 2 K.B. 348, 359 Denning L.J. said that: "If a man goes to a doctor because he is ill, no one doubts that the doctor must exercise reasonable care and skill in his treatment of him: and that is so whether the doctor is paid for his services or not."

[80] But see *Lowns v Woods* (1996) Aust. Torts Rep. 81–376 (N.S.W.C.A.), and *Kent v Griffiths, Roberts and London Ambulance Service* [2001] Q.B. 36, CA, discussed at paras 2–076 to 2–078 below.

[81] Though in these circumstances the precise scope of that duty remains unresolved. On one view the duty is limited to not to making the victim's condition worse: *Capital and Counties plc v Hampshire County Council* [1997] Q.B. 1004, 1035. See below para. 2–075. Of course, in an emergency less may be expected of the doctor to achieve the *standard* of reasonable care; see paras 3–106 to 3–109.

[82] [1920] 3 K.B. 163, 213; *Banbury v Bank of Montreal* [1918] A.C. 626, 657, *per* Lord Atkinson.

[83] See also *Goode v Nash* (1979) 21 S.A.S.R. 419: doctor liable for negligence in the course of conducting a public screening for the detection of glaucoma, notwithstanding that he "was engaged in a valuable community service, entirely on a voluntary basis."

Moreover, the person who does not possess the relevant qualifications, expertise or skill comes under the same duty of care, since by undertaking the treatment he effectively represents that he does have these attributes.[84] In an emergency, such as a road accident, the position may well be different since a layman does not profess any specialist skill. It is doubtful, however, whether a court would conclude that no duty of care was owed in this situation; rather it may be that the standard required to satisfy the duty would be quite low. For example, a trained volunteer who offers first-aid medical help, such as a St. John's Ambulance volunteer, owes a duty of care to those to whom he renders first-aid.[85] The duty derives from the fact that he holds himself out as someone competent to render first-aid, and he undertakes a legal responsibility to that extent. Thus, the standard of care required of a first-aider is not that of a doctor but the standard of an ordinary skilled first-aider exercising and professing to have the special skill of a first-aider.[86] There must be a distinction, however, between a lay person who embarks upon "treatment," and one who merely gives "advice" (such as "take an aspirin and go to bed") in circumstances where it is clear that no responsibility is undertaken. Only if the circumstances are such as to indicate a genuine undertaking of responsibility for the patient's medical care will a duty arise.[87]

2–026

Although it may be trite to state that a doctor owes a duty of care to his patient, it is not so simple to state precisely when the relationship of doctor and patient begins. This is important because it is equally true to say that a doctor is not normally under a legal obligation (whatever the moral or ethical position) to render assistance by way of examination or treatment to a stranger. This stems from the "mere omissions" rule: one who chooses to act must do so carefully so as to avoid inflicting harm on others; but, as a general rule, the tort of negligence does not compel a person to take positive steps to confer a benefit on others. Generally, there is no legal obligation to rescue someone in danger, even if rescue would involve little or no effort and

2–027

---

[84] *R. v Bateman* (1925) 94 L.J.K.B. 791, 794, *per* Lord Hewart C.J.: "the unqualified practitioner cannot claim to be measured by any lower standard than that which is applied to a qualified man"; *Pippin v Sheppard* (1822) 11 Price 400, 409. See *Ruddock v Lowe* (1865) 4 F. & F. 519 and *Jones v Fay* (1865) 4 F. & F. 525 (which were both cases against alleged quacks) where it was said that it was not necessary that the defendant held himself out as a qualified doctor; the question is whether the defendant undertook the treatment of the claimant and did so negligently. With one or two notable exceptions, such as the Abortion Act 1967, s. 1(1), the Nurses, Midwives and Health Visitors Act 1997, s. 16 (attendance on a woman in childbirth), and the Dentists Act 1984, s. 38 (prohibition on practising dentistry unless a registered dentist or a registered medical practitioner) there is no prohibition on the unregistered practice of medicine, although it is a criminal offence for an unregistered person to represent himself as a registered medical practitioner: Medical Act 1983, s. 49; Nurses, Midwives and Health Visitors Act 1997, s. 13. With regard to nurses and midwives see the Nursing and Midwifery Order 2002, S.I. 2002, No. 253, Arts 45 and 44 respectively which will replace ss. 16 and 13 of the 1997 Act. The Order is not yet fully in force.
[85] *Cattley v St John's Ambulance Brigade* (1988, QBD; unreported).
[86] See para. 3–098.
[87] See Nathan, *Medical Negligence*, 1957, pp. 14–15. There is an analogy here with liability under *Hedley Byrne & Co Ltd v Heller & Partners Ltd* [1964] A.C. 465.

no danger to the rescuer,[88] although there are some signs that this overly-rigid rule may be relaxed in some cases of medical emergency.[89] A "stranger" for these purposes is a person with whom the doctor is not and has never been in a professional doctor-patient relationship. Clearly, if such a relationship does exist a doctor may be liable for failing to attend or treat the patient, just as much as for careless treatment.[90]

2–028   Once a patient is accepted for treatment a duty of care will arise.[91] This, to some extent, begs the question of what is meant by the term "accepted for treatment." A person accepted onto a general practitioner's list is clearly the doctor's patient, even if the practitioner has never seen that person in a professional capacity.[92] Moreover, in an emergency the general practitioner may have an obligation to treat persons who are not on his list.[93] Similarly, where a person presents himself at a hospital casualty department complaining of illness or injury, the staff in the department will owe a duty of care to that person even before he is treated or received into the hospital wards.[94] On the other hand, a "patient" is not entitled to demand that he be given a particular treatment where a doctor has decided that it would be inappropriate,[95] or where a health authority does not have the resources to provide the treatment.[96]

2–029   The position of consultants and doctors engaged in private practice is less clear cut. Within the NHS patients are normally referred to a consultant through their general practitioner. It is uncertain whether the doctor-patient relationship can be said to begin when the consultant "accepts" the patient for treatment, *e.g.* by letter, or whether some contact between doctor and

---

[88] For discussion of the rule see: Linden (1971) 34 M.L.R. 241; Weinrib (1980) 90 Yale L.J. 247; Smith and Burns (1983) 46 M.L.R. 147; Logie [1989] C.L.J. 115.

[89] See para. 2–076 *et seq.*

[90] See paras 4–004 to 4–008.

[91] *Jones v Manchester Corporation* [1952] 2 Q.B. 852, 867, *per* Denning L.J. The duty would, of course, apply to any member of the medical team providing the treatment.

[92] See the National Health Service (General Medical Services) Regulations 1992 (S.I. 1992 No. 635), as amended, Sch. 2, para. 4. See also National Health Service (Choice of Medical Practitioner) Regulations 1998 (S.I. 1998 No. 668).

[93] *ibid.*, Sch. 2, para. 4(1)(h). In *Barnes v Crabtree*, *The Times*, November 1 and 2, 1955 counsel for the defendant general practitioner conceded that the doctor's duty under the NHS was to treat any patient in an emergency, whether his own patient or not.

[94] *Barnett v Chelsea and Kensington Hospital Management Committee* [1968] 1 All E.R. 1068, 1072. See also the comments of O'Halloran J.A. in *Fraser v Vancouver General Hospital* (1951) 3 W.W.R. 337, 340 (B.C.C.A.); affirmed [1952] 3 D.L.R. 785 (S.C.C.), cited in para. 4–005.

[95] *R. v Ethical Committee of St. Mary's Hospital, ex parte Harriott* [1988] 1 F.L.R. 512; *Re J. (a minor)(wardship: medical treatment)* [1992] 4 All E.R. 614, CA, where the Court of Appeal said that the court should not order a medical practitioner to treat a minor contrary to the practitioner's clinical judgment; *cf. Airedale NHS Trust v Bland* [1993] A.C. 789, 858 where Lord Keith said that a doctor may be in breach of duty to his patient if he ceases to provide treatment in circumstances where continuance of it would confer some benefit on the patient.

[96] *R. v Secretary of State for Social Services, ex parte Hincks* (1979) 123 S.J. 436, affirmed (1980) 1 B.M.L.R. 93, CA; *R. v Central Birmingham Health Authority, ex parte Walker* (1987) 3 B.M.L.R. 32, CA; *R. v Central Birmingham Health Authority, ex parte Collier* (1988, CA; unreported); *R. v Cambridge Health Authority, ex parte B.* [1995] 1 W.L.R. 898, CA; Newdick (1993) 1 Med. L. Rev. 53. For consideration of whether a lack of resources can be a defence to an allegation of negligence see paras 4–099 *et seq.*

patient, in the form of a consultation, is necessary. It may also be unclear precisely when the doctor-patient relationship ends. If the treatment has been completed, but problems recur at a later date, is the relationship a continuing one, or is a new relationship entered into when the patient re-presents with his complaint? Moreover, in the case of specialists there must be an implied limitation to the scope of the duty created by the doctor-patient relationship. An orthopaedic surgeon, for example, would not normally be responsible for failing to diagnose a patient's heart condition. On the other hand, there are potential dangers in a doctor construing his brief too narrowly. Thus, the duty of a visiting consultant physician who is asked to conduct a physical examination of a psychiatric patient with a view to identifying a physical cause for the patient's mental condition is not limited to examining the patient predominantly in relation to her cerebral condition. By accepting an invitation to give an opinion the physician entered a doctor-patient relationship and was subject to a continuing duty of care towards the patient, which included carrying out a full examination based on the patient's history, regardless of the remit given by the psychiatrists.[97]

The position of doctors engaged in private practice is even more problematic, because there is no equivalent to the general practitioner's "list" of NHS patients. The extent of the doctor's responsibility would depend upon the terms, whether express or implied, of the contract of retainer.[98]　　2–030

Scope of the duty

The doctor's duty to the patient is not necessarily limited to an obligation not to cause harm to the patient. In the case of patients with a psychiatric condition it can extend to an obligation to exercise reasonable care to prevent the patient from harming himself.[99] Moreover, in some circumstances the duty may encompass an obligation to prevent harm inflicted by others. For example, in the Canadian case of *Brown v University of Alberta Hospital*[1] it was held that the doctors at a hospital owed a duty of care to a child to report the suspicion that its injuries were non-accidental. The child was admitted to hospital by its father who claimed that the injuries were the result of a fall. A radiologist was found to have been negligent in failing to pass on to the doctors treating the child the suspicion that injuries observed on a CT scan of the child's brain could be indicative of non-accidental injury (the result of "shaken baby syndrome"). The baby was discharged from hospital without　　2–031

---

[97] *Panther v Wharton* (2001, QBD; unreported), where the defendant failed to identify a serious vascular problem because he considered that he had been given a "limited brief" to exclude a brain condition or viral infection as a cause of the patient's mental state.

[98] See Nathan, *Medical Negligence*, 1957, pp. 39–40, suggesting that with general practitioners in private practice, at least, the question might turn upon whether according to ordinary usage the person could be regarded as a patient.

[99] See para. 4–109. Though this duty is generally limited to preventing physical or psychiatric harm to the patient. The doctor does not normally owe a duty to protect a patient from the legal consequences of the patient's criminal conduct: see *Clunis v Camden and Islington Health Authority* [1998] Q.B. 978, para. 2–140 below.

[1] (1997) 145 D.L.R. (4th) 63 (Alta. Q.B).

any warning to the mother or notifying the child protection authorities. The child was subsequently shaken again, sustaining severe brain damage. It was held that the hospital was vicariously liable, on the basis that the radiologist owed a duty of care to the child.[2] Similarly, in *C v Cairns*[3] it was assumed that a general practitioner could come under a duty to a child patient to report to the relevant authorities (the police or social services) that the child had been sexually abused by a member of her family.[4] The doctor's duty to the child in this type of situation may preclude a duty of care being owed to the parent, because there is a potential conflict between the two duties.[5]

2–032   There are also limits to the scope of a doctor's duty when providing advice to a patient. The fact that had the doctor's advice been different the claimant could have avoided the loss that he has sustained does not necessarily mean that the doctor will be held liable, even if that advice was negligent. Thus in *South Australia Asset Management Corp. v York Montague Ltd*[6] Lord Hoffmann gave an example of a doctor who negligently advises a mountaineer that his knee is fit. As a result the mountaineer goes on an expedition which he would not have undertaken if he had known the true state of his knee. He suffers an injury which is a foreseeable consequence of mountaineering but has nothing to do with his knee. Although the doctor has been negligent and clearly owed a duty to the mountaineer when advising about his knee and it can be said that the injury would not have occurred but for the negligent advice, Lord Hoffmann considered that the doctor would not be liable in this hypothetical example, because he was asked for information on only one of the considerations which might affect the safety of the mountaineer on the expedition. There was "no reason of policy which requires that the negligence of the doctor should require the transfer to him of all the foreseeable risks of the expedition."

Psychiatric harm

2–033   Where a claimant has sustained physical injury and suffers psychiatric damage as a result of that physical injury there is no question of whether a

---

[2] Although the discussion of the basis for the duty of care and its nature was extremely brief and rather lacking in analysis. See *ibid.* at 106.

[3] [2003] Lloyd's Rep. Med. 90.

[4] The action failed on the basis that the defendant had acted as many other general practitioners would have done at the time (1975), *i.e.* he accepted the child's mother's assurance that the abuse was a "one-off" event, and considered himself bound by an obligation of confidentiality, so that there was no breach of duty. The judge, Stuart Brown Q.C., emphasised that this reflected standards at the time, and not modern standards which reflect a greater knowledge and understanding of child sexual abuse.

[5] See now *JD v East Berkshire Community Health NHS Trust* [2003] EWCA Civ 1151; *The Times*, August 22, 2003, where the Court of Appeal held, at [86] and [87], that where consideration is being given to whether a suspicion of child abuse justifies taking proceedings to remove a child from the parents, no common law duty of care is owed to the parents, because the child's interests are in potential conflict with the interests of the parents. This was a matter of public policy. It was "essential that the professionals should not be inhibited in acting in the best interests of [the child] by concern that they might be held in breach of a duty owed to" the parents: *ibid.* at [96].

[6] [1997] A.C. 191, 213–214.

duty of care in respect of the psychiatric damage is owed. It is then regarded as a matter of causation and remoteness, so that even if the claimant commits suicide as a result of depression brought on by physical injury the death may be actionable, being regarded as caused by the initial injury.[7] Emotional distress or anguish are also compensatable where the claimant has sustained physical injuries, and will be dealt with through the award of non-pecuniary damages for pain and suffering. These principles apply equally to injured patients as to any other accident victim.

The courts have had greater difficulty with claims for "pure psychiatric   2–034
damage", where the claimant has not suffered any physical injury. Although most of the problematic cases have involved claims for psychiatric harm sustained by third parties as a result of witnessing traumatic events to others, some have involved claims by individuals arising out of events in which they were participants. In the medical context this could include, for example, psychiatric damage resulting from medical treatment where the patient has not yet sustained any physical injury or the receipt of distressing news. The issues that such cases raise are so closely linked to the broader question of how the courts react to claims for pure psychiatric damage generally, that these cases are discussed along with those involving claims for psychiatric damage by third parties, below.[8]

Financial loss

Whilst it is clear that a doctor normally owes a duty of care to his patient   2–035
in respect of physical or psychological harm that may result from negligent diagnosis, advice or treatment, the position with respect to purely financial loss sustained by the patient as a result of negligent diagnosis or advice is less clear. In *Stevens v Bermondsey and Southwark Group Hospital Management Committee*[9] the claimant was involved in an accident for which he had a claim against the local authority. He visited hospital and was seen by a casualty officer, who considered that there was nothing much wrong with him. On the strength of this the claimant settled his action against the local authority for a small sum. It was subsequently discovered that he was suffering from spondylolisthesis, a congenital condition activated by the accident. He sued the defendants, alleging that if the doctor's diagnosis had not been negligent he would have claimed and received a larger sum from the local authority. Paull J. held that a doctor's duty was limited to the sphere of medicine and had nothing to do with the sphere of legal liability unless he conducted the examination with an eye to liability. In the absence of special circumstances, a doctor was not required to contemplate any question connected with a third party's liability to his patient.[10]

---

[7] *Pigney v Pointer's Transport Services Ltd* [1957] 1 W.L.R. 1121.
[8] See para. 2–096 *et seq.*
[9] (1963) 107 S.J. 478.
[10] The decision apparently rested on the view that the claim against the council was either a *novus actus interveniens* or severed the chain of causation. See also *Pimm v Roper* (1862) 2

On the other hand, in *Hughes v Lloyds Bank plc*[11] the claimant alleged that her general practitioner had negligently provided misleading information as to her prognosis, following a road traffic accident, as a result of which she had settled her action against the negligent motorist for much less than it was worth. The Court of Appeal took the view that the general practitioner owed the claimant a duty to take reasonable care to describe her condition accurately and make, so far as possible, a reliable prognosis. *Hughes* would appear to differ from *Stevens*, in that in *Hughes* the claimant had asked for a letter from the doctor for the express purpose of settling her claim against the motorist.

2–036   The situation of negligent advice or information about prognosis where the patient or a third party is clearly relying on that advice for the purpose of coming to some financial arrangement would seem to fall directly under the principle of *Hedley Byrne & Co Ltd v Heller & Partners Ltd*.[12] Where the defendant is so placed that others could reasonably rely upon his judgment or his skill or upon his ability to make careful enquiry, and the defendant takes it upon himself to give information or advice to, or allows the information or advice to be passed on to, a person that he knows or should know will place reliance upon it, then a duty of care will arise.[13] In *Hedley Byrne* Lord Devlin considered that if the law were not developed to allow recovery for pure economic loss consequent upon a negligent statement relied upon by the claimant the consequences would be very odd. To illustrate this he gave the example of a doctor who advised the patient wrongly that his medical condition was such that he should give up work, it subsequently being discovered that there was no need for this.[14] It would be absurd, said his Lordship, that the fee-paying patient should have an action in these circumstances if the NHS patient had none. There is no reason in principle why the medical profession alone should be immune from claims under *Hedley Byrne*.[15] It may be that the distinction, if any, between Lord Devlin's example, which surely would be the subject of a *Hedley Byrne* duty, and *Stevens v Bermondsey and Southwark*

(n.10 contd.) F. & F. 783, where the claimant was examined by a surgeon employed by a railway company, following a train collision. The surgeon said that his injuries were slight, and relying on this the claimant accepted £5 in compensation from the railway company. The claimant subsequently claimed that his injuries were much more serious, but his action against the doctor failed on the basis that the examination did not cause any injury to the claimant.

[11] [1998] P.I.Q.R. P98. See further the discussion of this case at para. 2–072.

[12] [1964] A.C. 465.

[13] *ibid.* at 503, *per* Lord Morris. Note that in *Caparo Industries plc v Dickman* [1990] 2 A.C. 605 the House of Lords restated the duty of care that may arise under *Hedley Byrne* in more restricted terms. See in particular the speeches of Lord Bridge and Lord Oliver at 621 and 638 respectively. On the other hand, in *Henderson v Merrett Syndicates Ltd* [1995] 2 A.C. 145 their Lordships took a broader view of liability under *Hedley Byrne*, which was said to rest on the principle of a voluntary undertaking of responsibility; see para. 2–037.

[14] *ibid.* at 517.

[15] In *Allen v Bloomsbury Health Authority* [1993] 1 All E.R. 651 Brooke J. regarded a claim limited to the financial costs associated with the upbringing of the unwanted child to be a straightforward *Hedley Byrne* claim for foreseeable economic loss caused by negligent advice or misstatement. See, however, paras 2–039 *et seq.* for discussion of this type of action.

Group Hospital Management Committee is that a hospital casualty officer does not undertake to give advice to a patient with regard to his financial position, and so it would not be reasonable for the patient to rely on the advice for that purpose.[16] The difficulty with this argument is that it is clearly reasonable for a patient to "rely" on a casualty officer's diagnosis where a negligent diagnosis causes personal injury. Both forms of loss are foreseeable. To take a different view of the proximity of the relationship when the loss is purely financial is to resort to a distinction which the House of Lords considered to be untenable in *Hedley Byrne* itself. Nor, arguably, does it help to speak in terms of what a casualty officer "voluntarily undertakes" to do, since an undertaking of responsibility is in reality the imposition of a duty of care by law where the defendant behaves in a particular manner.[17]

However, in *Henderson v Merrett Syndicates Ltd*[18] and *White v Jones*[19]   2–037 both Lord Goff and Lord Browne-Wilkinson suggested that some of the criticism of the concept of a voluntary assumption of responsibility was misplaced. Lord Browne-Wilkinson said that the criticism had proceeded on the basis that "assumption of responsibility" refers to the defendant having assumed legal responsibility rather than responsibility for the task, but the assumption of responsibility referred to is the defendant's assumption of responsibility for the task, not the assumption of legal liability. Even in cases of *ad hoc* relationships, it is the undertaking to answer the question posed which creates the relationship. If the responsibility for the task is assumed by the defendant he thereby creates a special relationship between himself and the claimant in relation to which the law (not the defendant) attaches a duty to carry out carefully the task so assumed. With respect, this appears to be a matter of semantics. If it is a question of the law attaching legal responsibility to the defendant's conduct it is difficult to see what the concept of assumption of responsibility adds to the notion that the courts simply decide when and in what circumstances a duty of care in respect of financial loss will be owed. This is simply a restatement of the proposition that if the defendant chooses to act, and does so negligently, the law deems him to be liable, just as when someone chooses to drive a motor car and does so carelessly the law holds him liable for the resulting damage. More recently,

---

[16] *cf.* where a medical report is prepared for the purpose of litigation: *McGrath v Kiely and Powell* [1965] I.R. 497.

[17] In *Smith v Bush* [1990] 1 A.C. 831, 862, Lord Griffiths said that in the context of liability under *Hedley Byrne & Co Ltd v Heller & Partners Ltd* [1964] A.C. 465 a voluntary assumption of responsibility "can only have any real meaning if it is understood as referring to the circumstances in which the law will *deem* the maker of the statement to have assumed responsibility to the person who acts upon the advice" (emphasis added). See also *Banbury v Bank of Montreal* [1918] A.C. 626, 657, where Lord Finlay L.C. said that: "There is in point of law no difference between the case of advice given by a physician and advice given by a solicitor or banker in the course of his business. By undertaking to advise he makes himself liable for failing to exercise due care in the discharge of his duty to the person who has entrusted him, and the fact that he undertook it gratuitously is irrelevant."

[18] [1995] 2 A.C. 145.

[19] [1995] 2 A.C. 207. See also Lord Steyn in *Williams v Natural Life Health Foods Ltd* [1998] 1 W.L.R. 830, commenting that: "the general criticism is overstated."

in *Phelps v Hillingdon London Borough Council*[20] Lord Slynn said that assumption of responsibility "means simply that the law recognises that there is a duty of care. It is not so much that responsibility is assumed as that it is recognised or imposed by the law."[21]

Wrongful conception and wrongful birth claims

2–038   There are a number of situations in which, following negligence by medical staff, a child is born who would not otherwise have been born. This may be the result of a failed sterilisation procedure, or a failure to inform the patient(s) about the risks of a sterilisation operation not achieving complete sterility. It may be the result of negligence in the performance of an abortion, where the mother has decided to undergo a termination of pregnancy, or it may be the result of a failure to give appropriate advice about the risks of continuing with a pregnancy (usually the risk of foetal abnormality) thereby depriving the mother of the opportunity of having a termination of the pregnancy as she would be entitled to do under the Abortion Act 1967. Typically, in the latter situation, it will be due to negligence in failing to carry out appropriate tests, carrying out the tests negligently, or negligently failing to report the results of those tests. Whilst the child has no claim in these circumstances, the action being one for "wrongful life",[22] the question arises as to potential claims by the parents. A claim by the parents is compendiously called an action for "wrongful birth" distinguishing it from a "wrongful life" claim by the child. Some commentators distinguish between claims for "wrongful conception" and claims for "wrongful birth", which respectively describe the situation where the negligence precedes conception and those cases where the negligence occurs after conception but before birth. Whilst these distinctions may be descriptively accurate, and the nature of the act of negligence clearly differs,[23] it would appear that the same legal analysis

---

[20] [2001] 2 A.C. 619, 654. See also *Dean v Allin & Watts* [2001] EWCA Civ 758; [2001] 2 Lloyd's Rep 249 at [47] *per* Sedley L.J.

[21] Note that in respect of claims for financial loss the courts now draw a distinction between cases where the defendant's duty is merely a duty to *provide information* to the claimant to enable him to decide upon a course of action, and cases where the scope of the defendant's duty encompasses a duty to *advise* the claimant as to what course of action he should take. In the case of advice the adviser must take reasonable care to consider all the potential consequences of that course of conduct, and if he is negligent he will be responsible for all the foreseeable losses. But if the duty is only to supply information he must take reasonable care to see that the information is correct, and if he is negligent he will be responsible only for the foreseeable consequences of the information being wrong. See *South Australia Asset Management Corp. v York Montague Ltd* [1997] A.C. 191, HL; and *cf. Aneco Reinsurance Underwriting Ltd (In Liquidation) v Johnson & Higgins Ltd* [2001] UKHL 51; [2002] 1 Lloyd's Rep. 157. On the distinction between an "informer" and an "adviser" see Dugdale (1996) 12 P.N. 71, 75, and generally on the *South Australia Asset Management Corp. v York Montague Ltd* litigation, Stapleton (1997) 113 L.Q.R. 1.

[22] See *McKay v Essex Area Health Authority* [1982] Q.B. 1166 and the Congenital Disabilities (Civil Liability) Act 1976, s. 1(2)(b) limiting actions under the Act to occurrences where the child is born with disabilities "which would not otherwise have been present." See para. 2–083.

[23] Wrongful conception encompasses failed sterilisation procedures and claims based on the failure to provide appropriate advice about the risks of a sterilisation operation failing, as

applies to both sets of circumstances, and therefore there is no real advantage in seeking to separate them. In *Parkinson v St. James and Seacroft University Hospital NHS Trust*[24] Brooke L.J. had suggested that cases involving post-conception negligence were different from failed sterilisation cases because the opportunity that is lost to the parents in "wrongful birth" cases was the opportunity to terminate a pregnancy which they would have had if the professional services had not been negligently performed, and "[b]ecause the policy issues in wrongful birth cases are different, I do not think it helpful to dwell any longer on that line of authority."[25] Subsequently, in *Groom v Selby*[26] Brooke L.J. explained that, with the wrongful birth cases, because in the case of a risk of foetal handicap a termination of pregnancy under section 1(1)(d) of the Abortion Act 1967 can take place at any time, "the issues relating to causation and to what is fair, just and reasonable in such circumstances are very much more straightforward." Hale L.J. accepted that "the principles applicable in wrongful birth cases cannot sensibly be distinguished from the principles applicable in wrongful conception cases."[27]

The legal rules applicable to wrongful birth claims have recently undergone significant re-evaluation. After some initial reluctance to award damages for the birth of a healthy child following a failed sterilisation operation for reasons of policy,[28] in *Emeh v Kensington and Chelsea and Westminster Area Health Authority*[29] the Court of Appeal held that damages for the birth of a child following a negligent sterilisation were recoverable, reasoning that since a sterilisation operation is lawful there were no good policy reasons for denying a claimant's action for the financial loss resulting from a negligent failure to perform the operation properly, whether or not the child was healthy (though in fact the child in *Emeh* was disabled). This issue was considered by the House of Lords in the Scottish case of *McFarlane v Tayside Health Board*.[30] Following a sterilisation operation, the male claimant was wrongly and negligently informed that he was no longer fertile. He and his wife stopped taking contraceptive precautions and she became pregnant, giving birth to a healthy baby. Although their Lordships were agreed that the

2–039

(n.23 contd.) well as negligent genetic counselling; whereas a claim arising from negligence following conception would encompass negligent performance of an abortion or negligent advice (including an absence of advice) about an abortion, following, for example, negligent screening procedures for foetal handicap.

[24] [2001] EWCA Civ 530; [2002] Q.B. 266, at [46] to [48].

[25] His Lordship referred to *Rand v East Dorset Health Authority* [2000] Lloyd's Rep. Med. 181; *Hardman v Amin* [2000] Lloyd's Rep. Med. 498; and *Lee v Taunton and Somerset NHS Trust* [2001] 1 F.L.R. 419; [2001] Fam. Law 103, all of which involved negligent failures to detect foetal abnormality following routine testing in pregnancy, resulting in the failure to offer the mother the opportunity of a termination.

[26] [2001] EWCA Civ 1522; [2002] P.I.Q.R. P201; [2002] Lloyd's Rep. Med. 1, at [19].

[27] *ibid.* at [28]. See further A. Whitfield (2002) 18 P.N. 234, 239. In this book, unless the context indicates otherwise, references to "wrongful birth" includes cases of both pre-conception and post-conception negligence.

[28] *Udale v Bloomsbury Area Health Authority* [1983] 2 All E.R. 522, Jupp J.

[29] [1985] Q.B. 1012.

[30] [2000] 2 A.C. 59.

failure of the parents to have a termination of the pregnancy or put the child up for adoption did not break the causal link between the alleged negligence and the child-rearing costs, or constitute a failure to mitigate their loss, the House held that no duty of care was owed to the parents in respect of the financial cost of bringing up a healthy child following negligent advice about, or the negligent performance of, a sterilisation operation. The reasons given by their Lordships for excluding the cost of rearing a healthy child varied significantly: (1) the doctor does not assume responsibility for this economic loss and it is not fair, just or reasonable to impose liability (Lord Slynn); (2) principles of distributive justice do not permit such losses to be recovered (Lord Steyn)[31]; (3) the benefits to the parents of having a healthy child are incalculable and therefore it cannot be established that the costs of rearing the child will exceed the value of the benefits (Lord Hope); (4) the extent of the alleged liability was disproportionate to the duties undertaken by the defendants (Lord Clyde and Lord Hope); (5) it was not reasonable for the pursuers to be relieved of the financial obligations of caring for their child (Lord Clyde); (6) the law must treat the birth of a normal, healthy baby as a blessing, not a detriment (Lord Millett). Indeed, Lord Millett considered that it was "morally offensive to regard a normal, healthy baby as more trouble and expense than it is worth", and given that the advantages and disadvantages of parenthood are inextricably bound together it would be "subversive of the mores of society for parents to enjoy the advantages of parenthood while transferring to others the responsibilities which it entails."[32]

2–040   The different views expressed in *McFarlane* as to the reasons for

---

[31] Lord Steyn acknowledged that from the perspective of "corrective justice", where someone has harmed another without justification he is normally liable to indemnify the other, and on this approach the McFarlanes' case must succeed: "But one may also approach the case from the vantage point of distributive justice. It requires a focus on the just distribution of burdens and losses among members of a society. If the matter is approached in this way, it may become relevant to ask commuters on the Underground the following question: Should the parents of an unwanted but healthy child be able to sue the doctor or hospital for compensation equivalent to the cost of bringing up the child for the years of his or her minority, *i.e.* until about 18 years? My Lords, I am firmly of the view that an overwhelming number of ordinary men and women would answer the question with an emphatic 'No.' And the reason for such a response would be an inarticulate premise as to what is morally acceptable and what is not . . . It is my firm conviction that where courts of law have denied a remedy for the cost of bringing up an unwanted child the real reasons have been grounds of distributive justice": *ibid.* at 82. Of course, Lord Steyn does not identify what particular conception of distributive justice he would favour (and there are many to choose from) and his mechanism for arriving at a conclusion (ask commuters on the Underground) is fundamentally flawed. Even if one could be confident that these commuters could articulate a conception of distributive justice, they will not in fact be asked their opinions. As Hale L.J. observed in *Parkinson v St. James and Seacroft University Hospital NHS Trust* [2001] EWCA Civ 530; [2002] Q.B. 266 at [82]: "The traveller on the Underground is not here being invoked as a hypothetical reasonable man but as a moral arbiter. We all know that London commuters are not a representative sample of public opinion. We also know that the answer will crucially depend upon the question asked and the amount of relevant information and argument given to help answer it. The fact that so many eminent judges all over the world have wrestled with this problem and reached different conclusions might suggest that the considered response would be less emphatic and less unanimous."

[32] [2000] 2 A.C. 59 at 114.

excluding the cost of raising a healthy child are indicative of the subjective value-judgments brought to bear on this issue by their Lordships, who were at pains to suggest that it was not a decision based on "policy." It is difficult, however, to see what else, apart from "policy", underlies the decision, particularly when in the context of a claim against any other professional person, patently foreseeable financial loss arising from the defendant's negligence would be held actionable under the principle of *Hedley Byrne & Co Ltd v Heller & Partners Ltd*.[33] The suspicion remains that the unarticulated policy underlying *McFarlane* is that the NHS should not have to be burdened with the financial cost of such claims when it has other calls on its resources.[34]

A further problem arising from the disparity in the reasoning of their   2–041
Lordships in *McFarlane* has been the difficulty of identifying a clear *ratio* from the case. This has led to considerable confusion and disagreement, both at High Court level and in the Court of Appeal, as to its implications, particularly as to what can be recovered and in what circumstances in wrongful birth cases.[35] This is not simply a question of assessment of the quantum of the loss,[36] but goes to the scope of the defendant's duty of care. In *McFarlane* itself, though, the parents could not claim for the economic costs involved in bringing up a healthy child, it was accepted that the mother did have a claim in respect of her losses, including general damages for the pain, discomfort and inconvenience of the unwanted pregnancy and birth, and special damages, which would encompass any additional medical expenses, clothes for herself during pregnancy, equipment on the birth of the baby and, in principle, compensation for loss of earnings due to the pregnancy and birth.[37] It would also follow that if the mother suffered any additional personal injury as result of the pregnancy, through complications in the pregnancy itself or immediately after the birth (including post-natal depression),

---

[33] [1964] A.C. 465.

[34] Consider, however, the comments of Ward L.J. in *Walters v North Glamorgan NHS Trust* [2002] EWCA Civ 1792; [2003] P.I.Q.R. P232 at [44] in the rather different context of a claim for psychiatric damage following the death of her child: "I understand the concern of the Health Authority, and their insurers if there are any, that the drain on National Health resources having to meet claims for medical negligence is already sufficiently alarming as not to encourage claims being advanced by secondary victims of that clinical negligence. If I had to make the choice between redressing a wrong to an injured claimant and protecting the pocket of negligent defendants for economic reasons, then I would unrepentantly prefer to do justice than to achieve fiscal expediency. Fortunately, however, I am not called upon to make that choice. Policy does not govern findings of fact. The facts are either there or they are not. The judge was right to find the facts in the claimant's favour and having found those facts he was bound to apply the principles of law to them, especially since there was no real dispute that those principles applied. Considerations of policy do not enter this case. If the law needs to be changed, Parliament must do it." For comment on *McFarlane* see Norrie (2000) 16 P.N. 76; Weir [2000] C.L.J. 238; Maclean [2000] 3 Web J.C.L.I. 1; Jones (2000) 9 Tort L. Rev. 14; Radley-Gardner (2002) 118 L.Q.R. 11.

[35] See Hoyano (2002) 62 M.L.R. 883; Whitfield (2002) 18 P.N. 234.

[36] See paras 9–079 *et seq.* for further discussion of quantum issues.

[37] This statement is taken from the speech of Lord Slynn. Their Lordships were not, however, unanimous in their views as to what the mother could claim for. For further discussion see paras 9–082 to 9–088.

she would be entitled to compensation for this harm as an ordinary incident of a claim for personal injuries.[38]

2–042   Where, however, a mother gives up work to look after a healthy child she is not entitled to compensation for loss of earnings. This, said the Court of Appeal in *Greenfield v Irwin*,[39] is equivalent to the costs of raising the child. The Court treated the damage as economic loss, not physical damage (the pregnancy).[40] There was no difference between this case (which involved a failure to detect that the claimant was pregnant before administering a course of contraception by injection) and *McFarlane*. But in any event in *McFarlane* Lord Steyn had refused to treat the distinction between economic loss and physical damage as relevant to the outcome, and Lord Millett had agreed that "it should not matter whether the unwanted pregnancy arises from the negligent supply of incorrect information or from the negligent performance of the operation itself." Buxton L.J. observed that the claim in *McFarlane* was not rejected on the narrow ground that related to the economic nature of the loss, but on grounds of very broad principle—which was why the claim for the mother's loss of earnings in bringing up the child should also fail.[41] It was not a claim for physical damage with contingent economic loss. The loss was not caused by the pregnancy, but by the existence of the child.[42]

The disabled child

2–043   An issue that was left untouched by the House of Lords in *McFarlane* was whether the rejection of the claim for the cost of raising a child also applied where the child happened to have disabilities. Immediately after *McFarlane* a number of decisions at first instance concluded that, though the case prohibited claims for the cost of raising a healthy child, the position was different where the child was disabled.[43] The issue came before the Court of

---

[38] This, of course, is subject to the qualification that she would have to prove a causal link between the defendant's negligence and her damage. Thus, in the case of post-conception negligence in failing to identify foetal handicap and offer the opportunity of a termination of the pregnancy, it would have to be shown that the damage was caused by the *continuation* of pregnancy, rather than the pregnancy itself.

[39] [2001] EWCA Civ 113; [2001] 1 W.L.R. 1279; Grubb (2001) 9 Med. L. Rev. 54.

[40] This was despite the ruling in *Walkin v South Manchester Health Authority* [1995] 4 All E.R. 132 that for the purpose of the law of limitation such damage is physical. See also *McLelland v Greater Glasgow Health Board* 2001 S.L.T. 446 at [28] *per* Lord Prosser, stating that the law to be applied to claims in relation to the cost of raising a (disabled) child was "the law governing claims for pure economic loss." *cf. Hardman v Amin* [2000] Lloyd's Rep. Med. 498 where Henriques J. concluded that for the purposes of the Law Reform (Personal Injuries) Act 1948, s. 2(4) (which, in a personal injuries action, requires the court to disregard the possibility that the claimant can avoid expenses by taking advantage of facilities under the NHS) the claim was an action for personal injuries.

[41] [2001] EWCA Civ 113; [2001] 1 W.L.R. 1279 at [28].

[42] *ibid.* at [29]. See also *per* May L.J. at [42].

[43] *Rand v East Dorset Health Authority* [2000] Lloyd's Rep. Med. 181 (failure to inform the mother that the child she was carrying had Down's Syndrome); *Hardman v Amin* [2000] Lloyd's Rep. Med. 498 (failure to diagnose rubella, and inform the mother of the risks of the child being seriously disabled); *Groom v Selby* [2001] Lloyd's Rep. Med. 39 (failure to conduct a pregnancy test before sterilisation); *Lee v Taunton and Somerset NHS Trust* [2001] 1 F.L.R. 419 (failure to diagnose spina bifida from an ultrasound scan).

Appeal in *Parkinson v St. James and Seacroft University Hospital NHS Trust*[44] where it was held that the parents of a disabled child born following a negligently performed sterilisation operation were entitled to the additional costs of raising that child, *i.e.* the additional costs attributable to the disability itself, over and above the costs of raising a healthy child. Drawing on Lord Steyn's speech in *McFarlane* Brooke L.J. suggested that applying the principles of distributive justice "ordinary people would consider that it would be fair for the law to make an award in such a case, provided that it is limited to the extra expenses associated with the child's disability."[45] Hale L.J. considered that the effect of the decision in *McFarlane* was that in the case of a healthy child the benefits of parenthood were to be treated as cancelling out the burdens.[46] The solution of "deemed equilibrium" had its attractions and was in any event binding on the Court.[47] But this approach only dealt with the ordinary costs of the ordinary child. The disabled child needed extra care and extra expenditure. He may be deemed to bring as much pleasure and as many advantages as a normal healthy child (though in practice this was much less likely) and this treated a disabled child as having exactly the same worth as a non-disabled child. "It simply acknowledges that he costs more."[48]

---

[44] [2001] EWCA Civ 530; [2002] Q.B. 266; see Quick (2002) 10 Tort L. Rev. 5.

[45] *ibid.* at [50]. See also *per* Hale L.J. at [95]. This had also been the approach of Henriques J. in *Hardman v Amin* [2000] Lloyd's Rep. Med. 498, 505: "If the commuters on the underground were asked whether the costs of bringing up Daniel (which are attributable to his disability) should fall on the claimant or the rest of the family, or the state, or the defendant, I am satisfied that the very substantial majority, having regard to the particular circumstances of this case, would say that the expense should fall on the wrongdoer." See also *per* Toulson J. in *Lee v Taunton and Somerset NHS Trust* [2001] 1 F.L.R. 419 at 430: "I do not believe that it would be right for the law to deem the birth of a disabled child to be a blessing, in all circumstances and regardless of the extent of the child's disabilities; or to regard the responsibility for the care of such a child as so enriching in the ordinary nature of things that it would be unjust for a parent to recover the cost from a negligent doctor on whose skill that parent had properly relied to prevent the situation. If the matter were put to an opinion poll among passengers on the Underground, I would be surprised if a majority would support such a view. More importantly, Parliament has provided by s. 1(1)(*d*) of the Abortion Act 1967 (as amended by the Human Fertilisation and Embryology Act 1990) that a pregnancy may be terminated if two registered medical practitioners are of the opinion formed in good faith that 'there is a substantial risk that if the child were born it would suffer from such physical or mental abnormalities as to be seriously handicapped'. Parliament must therefore have considered it to be in the public good that a mother should be able to choose to have a termination in those circumstances. I cannot reconcile that provision with the argument that public mores nevertheless require the courts to regard it as a blessing that Mrs. Lee was not able to exercise her right under the Act, when the purpose of the statutory provision (and of the scan) was to enable her to avoid the unhappy and burdensome situation in which she now finds herself."

[46] Though note that Hale L.J. believed that there were "many who would challenge that assumption. They would argue that the true costs to the primary carer of bringing up a child are so enormous that they easily outstrip any benefits." *ibid.* at [88]. Indeed, the "notion of a child bringing benefit to the parents is itself deeply suspect, smacking of the commodification of the child, regarding the child as an asset to the parents." *ibid.* at [89].

[47] *ibid.* at [90].

[48] *ibid.*

How disabled?

2–044   In *Parkinson* the Court of Appeal touched on the question of how disabled a child must be before account can be taken of the additional costs of the disability. Children vary enormously in their abilities, and some may need additional support due to perceived disabilities (such as additional tuition for public examinations). Brooke L.J. referred to "significant disabilities." Hale L.J. said that:

> "The answer is that the law has for some time distinguished between the ordinary needs of ordinary children and the special needs of a disabled child. Thus, for the purposes of the services to be provided under Part III of the Children Act 1989, a child is taken to be in need if, among other things, he is disabled: see s. 17(10)(*c*). For this purpose, a child is disabled if he is blind, deaf or dumb or suffers from mental disorder of any kind or is substantially and permanently handicapped by illness, injury or congenital deformity or such other disability as may be prescribed: see s. 17(11). This or very similar definitions have been used since the legislation establishing the welfare state in the late 1940s to identify those whose special needs require special services. Local social services authorities are used to operating it, for example when maintaining the register of disabled children required by Sched. 2, para. 2 of the 1989 Act. I see no difficulty in using the same definition here."[49]

In *Lee v Taunton and Somerset NHS Trust*[50] the defendants argued that since disabilities can vary infinitely in degree, it would be offensive for the courts to have to draw a line between children who are sufficiently normal to be deemed a blessing and others who are not. Toulson J. considered, however, that the mother's entitlement to have a termination under the Abortion Act 1967 provided the measure of the relevant disability. Thus: "If a scan showed, or should have showed, evidence of such abnormality that the mother would have been entitled under section 1(1)(*d*) of the Act to have her pregnancy terminated, and if she would have exercised that right, but was deprived of the opportunity to do so as a result of clinical negligence, those facts should provide a sufficient foundation for her claim."[51]

The causal connection

2–045   A further problem in applying the distinction between healthy and disabled children arising from *Parkinson* is the nature of the causal link

---

[49] *ibid.* at [91].
[50] [2001] 1 F.L.R. 419, QBD.
[51] *ibid.* at 431. The ground for a termination of pregnancy under s. 1(1)(*d*) of the Abortion Act 1967 is that "there is a substantial risk that if the child were born it would suffer from such physical or mental abnormalities as to be seriously handicapped." The Act does define "seriously handicapped", which is a matter normally left to the judgment of the medical profession.

between the defendant's negligence and the child's disability.[52] The defendant's negligence results in the birth of the child, not the disabilities themselves, and though the connection between the birth and the disabilities is more obvious where the negligence consists of "negligent screening"[53] it is nonetheless causally relevant where it consists of negligently failing to prevent conception (as, *e.g.* with a failed sterilisation) even where there was no apparent reason to anticipate that the child would be disabled. In the latter case, the fact that the child has disabilities is simply an unfortunate coincidence, but it is this very coincidence which gives rise to the parents' claim for the costs of the disability. In *Parkinson* Brooke L.J. indicated that he was only concerned with losses arising when the child's disabilities flow foreseeably from the unwanted conception. Foreseeable incidents during the mother's pregnancy and the time leading up to the birth which caused the child's disabilities would not ordinarily break the chain of causation. But there could be cases in which a child's disabilities, discernible at birth, were caused by a new intervening cause. Thus:

"A negligent surgeon should not, without more, be held liable for the economic consequences of the birth of a child with significant disabilities if the child's disabilities were brought about between conception and birth by some ultroneous cause (for which see Lord Wright in *The Oropesa* [1943] P. 32, 39). Similarly, the ordinary rules relating to contributory negligence will be applied in an appropriate case to limit recovery."[54]

The point arose in *Groom v Selby*,[55] where the negligence consisted of a failure to perform a pregnancy test before carrying out a sterilisation, with

2–046

---

[52] The House of Lords made it clear in *McFarlane* itself that, in a failed sterilisation case, the failure of the mother to have a termination of the pregnancy or to put the child up for adoption did not break the causal link between the alleged negligence and the child-rearing costs. On the other hand, in the case of post-conception negligent screening for a foetal abnormality it is clear that the mother would have to prove that had she been informed about the risk or the fact of the child's disability she would have had a lawful termination of the pregnancy under the terms of the Abortion Act 1967. If, for personal reasons, she would not have had a termination (or if in the circumstances a termination would have been unlawful: *Rance v Mid-Downs Health Authority* [1991] 1 Q.B. 587), there is no causal link between the negligence and the birth of the disabled child. In Canada, where the negligence relates to non-disclosure of the risk that the child will be handicapped, the causation test is objective (applying *Reibl v Hughes* (1980) 114 D.L.R. (3d) 1; para. 6–117), and therefore the question is not whether the claimant would have had an abortion, but whether a reasonable woman in her circumstances would have an abortion: *Mickle v Salvation Army Grace Hospital* (1998) 166 D.L.R. (4th) 743, 758–761, (Ont. Ct.).

[53] The failure to identify or warn about the risk that the foetus may be disabled—which can arise pre-conception, from negligent genetic counselling, and post-conception, from a negligently conducted scan or test.

[54] [2001] EWCA Civ 530; [2002] Q.B. 266 at [54]. See also *per* Hale L.J. at [92]: "I conclude that any disability arising from genetic causes or foreseeable events during pregnancy (such as rubella, spina bifida, or oxygen deprivation during pregnancy or childbirth) up until the child is born alive, and which are not *novus actus interveniens*, will suffice to found a claim."

[55] [2001] Lloyd's Rep. Med. 39, QBD; affirmed [2001] EWCA Civ 1522; [2002] P.I.Q.R. P201; [2002] Lloyd's Rep. Med. 1.

the result that the claimant was unaware that she was pregnant until she was 15 weeks pregnant. Had she known about the pregnancy sooner she would have opted for a termination. The child was born apparently healthy, but some four weeks later she was found to be suffering from salmonella meningitis, producing long-term disabilities. This was caused by exposure to bacteria from the mother's birth canal and perineal area during the delivery. The defendants argued that the causal proximity between the negligence and the damage was not as close in this case as in cases of failing to detect a foetal abnormality during pregnancy (as, *e.g.*, in *Rand v East Dorset Health Authority* or *Hardman v Amin*). The negligence consisted of allowing the pregnancy to continue when the claimant did not want to be pregnant at all. The risk of giving birth to a disabled child was foreseeable, but it was mere chance that the child happened to have a disability. Moreover, the child was healthy at birth. The Court of Appeal held that this was irrelevant to the defendants' liability. It could not be said that the infection constituted an intervening event. The child's handicap arose from the normal incidents of conception, intra-uterine development and birth: "All the causes of her meningitis were in place when the umbilical cord was severed: all that remained was for the bacterium to penetrate a weak point in the child's skin or mucous membranes and the damage was done."[56] It followed that *Parkinson* applied. However, ". . . the longer the period before the disability is triggered off, the more difficult it may be to establish a right to recover compensation, particularly because new intervening causes are likely to be at work."[57]

2–047 The question remains, therefore, as to what the outcome should be if the child's disability arose from a discrete subsequent event unconnected with her condition at birth, such as accidentally catching meningitis in the hospital. Would this break the causal link? Even the negligent conduct of a subsequent actor does not necessarily break the chain of causation,[58] so accidental harm should not necessarily break the link either. In *Groom v Selby* Hale L.J. suggested that in *Parkinson* she and Brooke L.J. were agreed that the child's disability must be genetic or arise from the processes of intra-uterine development and birth.[59] This would seem to exclude post-natal accidental events, and has led one commentator to suggest that negligently caused damage to the foetus *in utero* would also preclude the parent from recovering in respect of the costs of the disability. Rather, those costs could be claimed by the child under the Congenital Disabilities (Civil Liability) Act 1976.[60] But in a case where a claimant who never wanted to be pregnant at

---

[56] *ibid.* at [23] *per* Brooke L.J.
[57] *ibid.* at [26].
[58] See, e.g., *Webb v Barclays Bank* [2001] EWCA Civ 1141; [2002] P.I.Q.R. P61; [2001] Lloyd's Rep. Med. 500 and *Rahman v Arearose* [2001] Q.B. 351 where the Court of Appeal held that subsequent medical negligence did not break the causal link between a defendant's original negligence and the claimant's loss. See paras 5–081 and 5–082.
[59] [2001] EWCA Civ 1522; [2002] Lloyd's Rep. Med. 1 at [32].
[60] See Whitfield (2002) 18 P.N. 234, at 242. Query whether different rules as to intervening conduct should apply in this category of case from other categories of negligence, given that subsequent medical negligence does not necessarily break the causal link between a defendant's original negligence and the claimant's loss. Of course, overlap between the parents'

all gives birth to a healthy child, can it really be said that the benefits of parenthood must be treated as cancelling out the burdens when it is known that the child has subsequently become disabled? The risk of an otherwise healthy child becoming disabled is perfectly foreseeable, whether it occurs during pregnancy, during birth or during infancy. If the defendant has to bear the burden of that risk during pregnancy, then why not in infancy? It is true that the defendant's negligence did not cause the child's disabilities, but this is equally true of all the cases in which the parents have a successful action in respect of the financial costs of the disability. The point is that the defendant's negligence has exposed the claimants to the foreseeable risk of that financial loss. The fact that the parents cannot recover for the costs of raising a healthy child is an exception to the general rule that a negligent defendant is normally held responsible for the foreseeable consequences of that negligence when he has undertaken a responsibility to the claimant.[61] Although, intuitively, one would expect to see some temporal limitation to the defendants' liability, it is difficult to identify a principled basis for taking the date of birth as the cut-off point beyond which the defendant is no longer responsible for the financial consequences of the disability.

The disabled mother

In *Rees v Darlington Memorial Hospital NHS Trust*[62] the claimant had a   2–048
severe visual impairment due to a genetic condition and decided that she wanted to be sterilised because she considered that her disability would prevent her from properly looking after a child. She informed the surgeon who performed the sterilisation of her reason for wanting the procedure. The operation was conducted negligently and she subsequently gave birth to a child. There was a small risk that the child would inherit the mother's genetic condition, but the case proceeded on the basis that he was healthy. The question was whether the claimant could recover for the additional costs of bringing up a healthy child attributable to the *mother's* disability. By a majority the Court of Appeal concluded that the decision in *McFarlane* precluding a claim in respect of a healthy child did not apply. In principle, where, to the knowledge of the surgeon, a disabled woman sought sterilisation because of her disabilities but subsequently gave birth to a healthy child as a result of negligence in carrying out the procedure, she was entitled to damages for the additional costs of bringing up the child that were attributable to *her* disability (though there was no evidence before the court as to how it was more costly for the claimant to raise a child). Hale L.J. drew upon her own analysis of *McFarlane* in *Parkinson* that in the case of a healthy

---

(n.60 contd.) claim for the financial costs of the disability and the child's claim for the consequences of the disability should be avoided, but it is not immediately apparent that the child's claim would subsume all of the additional costs to the parents.

[61] See *Rees v Darlington Memorial Hospital NHS Trust* [2002] EWCA Civ 88; [2002] 2 All E.R. 177 at [13] *per* Hale L.J.: "It must be remembered that the rule laid down by the House of Lords in *McFarlane* is itself an exception to what would otherwise be the normal rule."

[62] [2002] EWCA Civ 88; [2002] 2 All E.R. 177; Grubb (2002) 10 Med. L. Rev. 206.

child the benefits that a healthy child brings had to be assumed to cancel the costs, whether or not they did so in fact. This was the "deemed equilibrium." In the case of a disabled mother the deemed equilibrium applied so that the benefits of the healthy child negative the claim for the ordinary costs of looking after and bringing him up. "But we do not have to assume that it goes further than that. She is not being over-compensated by being given recompense for the extra costs of child care occasioned by her disability. She is being put in the same position as her able-bodied fellows."[63] There was nothing unfair, unjust or unreasonable, said Hale L.J., in holding that the surgeon had assumed a more extensive responsibility for the consequences of his negligence, at least where he knew of the disability and that this was the reason why the claimant wished to avoid having a child. Robert Walker L.J. agreed that, in principle, the claim was maintainable on the basis that there was nothing unfair, unjust, unreasonable, unacceptable or morally repugnant in permitting recovery of compensation for a limited range of expenses found to have a very close connection with the mother's disability and "nothing to do with the blessings which the birth of her healthy son may have brought her."[64] His Lordship, did not accept Hale L.J.'s deemed equilibrium theory, however, although it was "an attractive and convenient theory in the sense that it enables expenses uniquely referable to disablement (whether of mother or child) to be seen as economic loss unrelieved by any countervailing benefit or advantage. If costs and benefits (in the absence of disablement) are assumed to be equal, costs uniquely referable to disablement are economic loss which ought to be recoverable in full."[65]

2–049   The position of the disabled mother is not entirely analogous to that of the disabled child. Although it is true that the burdens of parenthood may weigh more heavily on the disabled parent, it is arguable that the burdens of parenthood may be greater for some parents than others for a whole variety of reasons, such as poverty, the number of existing children, the fact that an existing child is already disabled, or the risk that the parent's own health may be damaged through an inability to cope with an additional child. Presumably everyone who seeks sterilisation has reasons for not wanting a child or another child. Should the disabled parent's reasons be privileged? What if there are two parents, one of whom is disabled but the other is not? Is that any different from the case of a single parent who is not disabled, who has no claim as a result of *McFarlane*? Waller L.J. dissented in *Rees*, on the basis that, applying distributive justice "ordinary people would think that it was not fair that a disabled person should recover when mothers who may in effect become disabled by ill-health through having a healthy child would not."[66]

2–050   In a case like *Parkinson*, the more serious the child's disabilities the greater will be the measure of the damages to enable the parents to cope

---

[63] *ibid.* at [23].
[64] *ibid.* at [37].
[65] *ibid.* at [35].
[66] *ibid.* at [55]. The defendants in *Rees* have been granted permission to appeal to the House of Lords.

with the consequences of the disability. But where the claim is based on the parent's disability, the more serious the disability the greater the risk that the parent will be totally unable to look after the child at all. In *AD v East Kent Community NHS Trust*[67] the mother suffered from a permanent mental impairment, and was compulsorily detained under the Mental Health Act 1983. She was placed in a mixed psychiatric ward, and became pregnant, giving birth to a healthy child. She sued the defendant NHS Trust on the basis that there had been negligent supervision of the patients on the ward. The mother was incapable, due to her mental disability, of bringing up the child herself. The child was being brought up by claimant's mother, the child's grandmother. Cooke J. held that the mother could not recover the additional costs of raising the child attributable to the her own disability. There was no distinction in principle between a claimant with a physical disability and claimant with a mental disability. Rather, the difference was that because the mother was totally incapable of raising the child due to her mental disability, she would never incur the costs of raising the child associated with her disability. One consequence of this is that a "partially disabled mother, as in *Rees*, can recover for the additional costs of bringing up a child which result from her disability, whereas a totally disabled person cannot."[68] The effect of the mother's disability was to disable her from taking any care of the child at all, and therefore she was not going to incur any cost at all in her upbringing, let alone any additional cost resulting from her own mental disability.[69] Cooke J. distinguished *Hunt v Severs*,[70] which permits a claimant to recover the cost of gratuitous services provided by another which otherwise reduces the claimant's loss, on the basis that caring for the child did not involve providing gratuitous services to the mother. The Court of Appeal held that Cooke J.'s approach was correct. A mother who, as a result of her own disability, would never be able to bring up her healthy child could not recover the costs incurred by someone else in bringing up that child; nor did the claimant's mother have an action in her own right in respect of the cost of gratuitously providing for her granddaughter.[71]

A contractual claim?

In *McFarlane v Tayside Health Board*[72] Lord Slynn commented that the doctor does not assume responsibility for the economic costs of raising a healthy child, and that "if a client wants to be able to recover such costs he

2–051

---

[67] [2003] P.I.Q.R. P34; [2002] Lloyd's Rep. Med. 424, QBD.
[68] *ibid.* at [16].
[69] *ibid.* at [23]. "The child needs childcare, maintenance and education, but the claimant does not need support, as a result of her disability, to provide it. She cannot and will not provide it with or without assistance. Her disability has the effect of ruling her out from incurring any cost at all." *per* Cooke J. at [36].
[70] [1994] 2 A.C. 356; see para. 9–038.
[71] *AD v East Kent Community NHS Trust* [2002] EWCA Civ 1872; [2003] 3 All E.R. 1167.
[72] [2000] 2 A.C. 59, 76.

or she must do so by an appropriate contract." His Lordship did not specify what an "appropriate contract" might consist of. Lord Clyde indicated[73] that special considerations might arise in contract which were not relevant to the tort of negligence, though the only obvious distinction was that between a contractual warranty and an obligation to exercise reasonable care, whether contractual or non-contractual. This leaves open the possibility that the position is different where the parties are in a contractual relationship, at least if the defendant has given a warranty as to the outcome.[74] On the other hand, the factors which led their Lordships to exclude the cost of raising a healthy child would seem to be just as relevant to contractual claims as to tort claims. If, for example, the law must treat the birth of a normal, healthy baby as a blessing, not a detriment (*per* Lord Millett), or the benefits to the parents of having a healthy child are incalculable and therefore it cannot be established that the costs of rearing the child will exceed the value of the benefits (*per* Lord Hope), or distributive justice does not permit such losses to be recovered (*per* Lord Steyn), then the existence of a contractual relationship between the parties would not obviously alter the outcome of such an approach, whether the obligation was to exercise reasonable care or to achieve a specific result. In any event, patients receiving treatment through the NHS do not enter into a contractual relationship with their doctor.[75]

Non-NHS defendants

2–052   Despite the perception that *McFarlane* is concerned with protecting the NHS from claims for the cost of raising healthy children, the rule against recovery of the child-rearing costs applies to other defendants, even to commercial organisations. Thus, it has been said, *obiter*, that there could be no claim against the manufacturer of an allegedly defective condom for the cost of raising a healthy child, applying *McFarlane*.[76]

Human Rights

2–053   By the same token, attempts to argue that *McFarlane* is inconsistent with Article 8 of the European Convention on Human Rights, which provides the

---

[73] *ibid.* at 99.
[74] As had been argued in *Eyre v Measday* [1986] 1 All E.R. 488 and *Thake v Maurice* [1986] Q.B. 644; see paras 2–010 *et seq*. If the claimants were receiving fertility treatment privately and the defendants, contrary to the agreement with the claimants, implanted three embryos in the woman instead of two, could it be argued that this is, in effect, a warranty that a third child will not be born? See Grubb (2001) 9 Med. L. Rev. 170, 173, commenting on *Thompson v Sheffield Fertility Clinic* (2000, QBD; unreported).
[75] See *Reynolds v The Health First Medical Group* [2000] Lloyd's Rep. Med. 240 (County Court) where the claimant's attempt to put a failed sterilisation claim on this basis in order to avoid the effect of *McFarlane* was rejected.
[76] *Richardson v LRC Products Ltd* [2000] P.I.Q.R. P164, 174; [2000] Lloyd's Rep. Med. 280, 286 *per* Ian Kennedy J. The action failed on the ground that the condom was not defective: see para. 8–078.

right to respect for private and family life, have also been rejected.[77] On the other hand, in *Hardman v Amin*[78] Henriques J. considered that it was a matter of some satisfaction that the award of damages to the claimants in respect of the birth of a disabled child would permit the family unit to meet that child's needs independent of the state. This was consistent with Article 8, in that a failure to provide compensation would have deprived the family of its autonomy, vesting all major decisions as to the care of the child in the state.

(3) Duty to third parties

There are various circumstances in which a medical practitioner may owe   2–054
duties to persons other than his patient. In some instances it may be unclear whether a doctor-patient relationship has been created, but nonetheless it is possible to say that the doctor owes a duty of care to the person whom he is examining or advising or reporting upon. The nature or scope of that duty may be more limited, however, than where it is clear that the doctor-patient relationship exists. There are other situations in which the doctor may be found to owe a duty of care to third parties who are clearly not the doctor's patient, but the duty to the third party arises out of the relationship that the doctor has with a patient.

(a) Reports on the claimant for purposes other than treatment

There are a number of situations in which a doctor may be involved in pre-   2–055
paring a report on an individual for use by others, where negligence in carrying out that function may lead to harm to that individual. Broadly, they can be divided into those cases where the doctor is examining an individual, or providing information or advice about an individual to a third party, for private purposes, such as a report for employment purposes, and those cases where a doctor examines an individual in the context of legal proceedings or in connection with statutory functions. There may be some overlap between these situations. As a matter of basic principle, it is self-evident that a doctor carrying out a physical examination should owe a duty of care to the examinee not to cause any additional physical injury to the examinee. The fact that the doctor is carrying out the examination for a purpose other than treatment of the examinee is irrelevant to this issue, and doctors should not be in a better a position with respect to the positive infliction of physical damage to the claimant than any other potential defendant. Thus, in *Re N*[79] Clarke L.J. said, *obiter*, that: "It seems to me that [the forensic medical examiner]

---

[77] *Greenfield v Irwin* [2001] EWCA Civ 113; [2001] 1 W.L.R. 1279 at [37] and [48]. See also *Groom v Selby* [2001] Lloyd's Rep. Med. 39 (QBD) on this point. The issue was not addressed by the Court of Appeal in *Groom v Selby*.

[78] [2000] Lloyd's Rep. Med. 498, 510.

[79] [1999] Lloyd's Rep. Med. 257, at 263; also reported as *N v Agrawal* [1999] P.N.L.R. 939, CA.

must have owed a duty of care to carry out any examination with reasonable care, and thus, for example, not to make matters worse by causing injury to the plaintiff." The problem areas concern: (1) claims in respect of economic loss; and (2) cases involving failure to identify a serious medical condition for which the claimant could have obtained more prompt treatment.

(i) Reports for private purposes

2–056   Where a doctor conducts a medical examination at the request of an employer, prospective employer, or insurance company it is arguable that, in addition to the duty owed to the person making the request, the doctor owes a duty of care to the subject of the examination. There are two aspects to this. First, a negligent statement about the state of the examinee's health may result in the employer or insurance company refusing to enter into a contract with the examinee thereby causing him or her financial loss. Secondly, if the doctor negligently misses a condition which if properly diagnosed and disclosed to the examinee could have enabled him to seek appropriate treatment, the examinee may suffer otherwise avoidable physical harm. The position that the English courts have taken appears to exclude a duty of care in each of these situations, though the cases are fact-dependent and could be challenged.

2–057   In *Baker v Kaye*[80] Robert Owen Q.C. held that a doctor who carried out a pre-employment medical assessment on behalf of a company could owe a duty of care to the prospective employee in respect of the financial loss to the prospective employee arising from a negligent report to the company (although, on the facts, there had been no breach of duty). The duty of care applied because the loss was clearly foreseeable, there was sufficient proximity between the parties (the claimant provided detailed medical information to the defendant, who regarded himself as under a duty of confidentiality and under a duty to advise the claimant to seek further medical advice if his assessment revealed a medical condition which required treatment), and it was just and reasonable to impose the duty because there was no conflict between such a duty and the duty that the defendant owed to the company. Indeed, the duty owed to the claimant could be couched in virtually identical terms to the duty the defendant owed to the company. In *Kapfunde v Abbey National plc*,[81] however, the claimant applied for a job and filled in a medical questionnaire, which was considered by a doctor who took the view that the claimant would have a higher than average level of absence from work. The claimant was not offered the job. The Court of Appeal held that there was no proximity of relationship between the doctor and the claimant because the doctor had never seen the claimant, the loss was purely economic, and the prospective employer did not owe a duty to exercise reasonable care in selecting employees. Clearly, there is a distinction between *Kapfunde* and *Baker v Kaye*, in that the claimant was not physically exam-

[80] [1997] I.R.L.R. 219.
[81] [1999] I.C.R. 1; [1999] Lloyd's Rep. Med. 48.

ined in *Kapfunde*. Nonetheless, the Court of Appeal expressed a firm view that *Baker v Kaye* was wrongly decided on the question of the duty of care.[82]

In *R v Croydon Health Authority*[83] a radiologist examining a chest X-ray   2–058
as part of a pre-employment medical examination failed to spot a significant abnormality. If the abnormality had been identified the claimant would have been referred to a cardiologist who would have diagnosed primary pulmonary hypertension (PPH), an untreatable condition which limits life expectancy and which is particularly dangerous if the patient becomes pregnant. Shortly afterwards the claimant did become pregnant, and gave birth to a healthy child, although there were complications in her own health, some of which could have been avoided if the diagnosis had been made earlier. She claimed damages in respect of the effects on her own health and the cost of the pregnancy and raising the child, on the basis that if she had known about the PPH she would have taken steps to avoid conceiving. The Court of Appeal held that where the mother wanted both the pregnancy and the child there was no loss which could give rise to a claim in respect of the cost of the pregnancy and rearing the child.[84] Moreover, the duty of care owed by the radiologist did not extend to the claimant's private life and her decision to become pregnant, since the examination was conducted in the context of a pre-employment medical. But the claimant was awarded damages for the exacerbation to her ill-health that could have been avoided with an earlier diagnosis of the PPH. This award was based on an admission by the defendants that they owed such a duty of care to the claimant in the circumstances, though it is not clear that the Court of Appeal would have accepted this proposition if the matter had been contested.

Despite these reservations and the decision in *Kapfunde*,[85] it is strongly   2–059
arguable that a doctor examining a patient for life insurance or employment purposes does owe a duty of care in negligence to that individual which extends beyond simply not causing injury to the examinee: if the doctor discovers something seriously wrong with the individual then he should come under a duty at least to alert the individual to the problem. This issue was considered in *Thomsen v Davison*,[86] where it was held that a doctor who, in

---

[82] In the light of comments made by the House of Lords in *X. (minors) v Bedfordshire County Council* [1995] 2 A.C. 633. See below, para. 2–066.

[83] [1998] P.I.Q.R. Q26; [1998] Lloyd's Rep. Med. 44.

[84] The claim in respect of the cost of rearing the healthy child would now be excluded, in any event, on the basis of the decision of the House of Lords in *McFarlane v Tayside Health Board* [2000] 2 A.C. 59.

[85] And the *obiter* comments in the Court of Appeal and House of Lords in *M. (a minor) v Newham London Borough Council*, see below paras 2–062, 2–066.

[86] [1975] Qd R. 93. See also *Betesh v United States* 400 F. Supp. 238 (1974) (D.C. District Ct.) in which a man drafted for military service expected to fail his medical examination because of a disability. The draft board doctors found him unfit for service because they discovered that he had cancer, but they did not inform him or his doctor of their diagnosis. Early treatment could have extended his life. His widow's claim against the government succeeded, notwithstanding that the court accepted that there was no doctor-patient relationship created by the medical examination. The doctors were said to be in a professional relationship, which was fiduciary in nature, which gave rise to a duty to disclose the information they had discovered in the "patient's" interests.

a situation in which the relationship of doctor and patient did *not* exist, undertakes the examination of a person in order to assess his state of health has a duty of care not merely to his employer but also to that person to conduct the examination competently, and not do or omit anything in the course of performing the examination which is likely to cause the latter damage.[87] This included a duty to inform himself of the results of pathological tests and advise the person to undergo investigation and treatment if they were adverse. The Canadian courts have tended to conclude that where a doctor undertakes a medical examination for a third party, such as an employer or insurer, a doctor-patient relationship arises between the doctor and the person being examined. Thus, in *Leonard v Knott*[88] Kirke Smith J. held that where employees underwent annual health checks conducted by a doctor who was engaged by their employer for the purpose, the relationship of doctor-patient existed between the doctor and the examinees; and in *Parslow v Masters*[89] Hunter J. concluded that a doctor-patient relationship was created between a doctor who examined a person for the purpose of providing a medical report on that person to an insurance company and the subject of the report. Although the insurers paid for the report, the subject was required to disclose private and personal information about herself to enable the defendant to prepare the report. This gave rise to a physician-patient relationship, even though the purpose of the consultation was not to enable the doctor to advise the patient and prescribe a course of treatment for her. There was only a difference of degree, not of substance, between the situation where a patient attended a physician for a third party medical rather than for professional services.[90] The defendants argued that the doctor did not assume or undertake responsibility for the claimant's interests as a patient nor did he expressly or impliedly undertake to exercise any power over the claimant for her benefit or assume responsibility for her interests. The assessment was completed for the benefit of the insurer. In response to this argument Hunter J. commented that:

"In my view, this construes the nature of the obligation on the physician who conducts a third party medical too narrowly. Surely, such a physician undertakes the responsibility to complete a proper examination of the patient, draw conclusions from the examination and report the results of the examination and the conclusion. Such examination is for the benefit of the patient as well as the insurance company. The

---

[87] A similar duty is arguably owed to persons whom a doctor certifies to be of unsound mind for the purpose of involuntary admission to hospital under the Mental Health Act 1983: see paras 2–142 to 2–144.

[88] [1978] 5 W.W.R. 511, 513 (B.C.S.C.).

[89] [1993] 6 W.W.R. 273 (Sask. Q.B.).

[90] "In both instances, the patient must disclose personal and private information to allow the physician to make a proper assessment of his/her condition. In addition, the patient may be required to undergo physical examination as well as some tests to assist in such an assessment. In both cases the physician may make certain observations and draw conclusions about the condition of the patient," *ibid.* at 281.

patient is required by the terms of the policy to submit to such an examination at the request of the insurance company. Failure to submit to such an examination may result in a discontinuance of benefits to the insured. The reported conclusion of the physician to the insurance company affects the interests of the insured person. The physician assumes the responsibility to carry out a proper examination and exercises the power over the patient to the extent that the medical report may impact on disability benefits to the patient. In some cases, the physician may even recommend a treatment program which a patient should undertake in an effort to rehabilitate and become re-employable. Accordingly, there is a fiduciary obligation to [the claimant] in respect of the contents of the medical report prepared for [the insurers]."[91]

English law has no difficulty in holding that a doctor who is aware of a   **2-060**
risk of individuals developing a serious medical condition has a duty to take steps to monitor their condition and give an appropriate warning. Thus, in *Stokes v Guest, Keen and Nettlefold (Bolts and Nuts) Ltd*[92] Swanwick J. held that a factory medical officer was under a duty to institute six monthly medical examinations of certain employees, given his knowledge of the risk to those employees of contracting cancer from the work in which they were engaged, and notwithstanding that strictly speaking they were not his patients. This situation is not substantially different from that which occurred in *Thomsen v Davison*. Even if one takes the view that a doctor should owe no duty of care in respect of pure financial loss to the examinee (though it is not clear why a doctor should be in any better position than a person writing a reference, who may owe a duty to the subject of the reference[93]), it by no means follows that the doctor should owe no duty in respect of a negligent failure to identify and report to the examinee a serious medical condition that requires treatment. As a general proposition physical harm is in a different category from pure economic loss, when it comes to the existence of a duty of care. In *Re N*[94] Clarke L.J. considered that it was arguable that if the doctor discovered something seriously wrong with the individual then he should come under a duty at least to alert the individual to the

---

[91] *ibid.* at 282. The fact that the Canadian courts regard the doctor-patient relationship as giving rise to a fiduciary relationship (see para. 2–006, n. 15) does not mean that the criteria for establishing the relationship should be different under English law.

[92] [1968] 1 W.L.R. 1776. In *Spring v Guardian Assurance plc* [1995] 2 A.C. 296 the House of Lords held that where A gives advice to B about C (in this case a reference on a former employee), A owes a duty to C to exercise reasonable care in giving that advice. Although the decision is concerned with the financial consequences for C of A carelessly giving information or advice to B about C, it would be strange if, in the analogous situation where a doctor is advising a third party about the state of the claimant's health, it were to be held that there was no duty of care owed to the claimant at least to inform him of any problems that had been discovered as a result of the medical examination. The courts are usually more willing to protect a claimant's interest in physical well-being than his financial interests.

[93] *Spring v Guardian Assurance plc* [1995] 2 A.C. 296. See also *Cox v Sun Alliance Life Ltd* [2001] EWCA Civ 649; [2001] I.R.L.R. 448; *Legal & General Insurance Ltd v Kirk* [2001] EWCA Civ 1803; [2002] I.R.L.R. 124.

[94] [1999] Lloyd's Rep. Med. 257, 263.

problem. On the facts of *Kapfunde* there was no physical examination of the claimant, so that the question of what the doctor ought to have discovered and reported *to the claimant* about her state of health did not arise. Moreover, it is clear that, in some circumstances, a doctor may owe a duty of care to third parties arising out of treatment or advice given to someone who is undoubtedly a patient,[95] and it might seem strange that a court could conclude that no duty is owed to someone in a "quasi-patient" relationship with an examining doctor.

(ii) Reports for "public" purposes

2–061   Doctors are also asked to prepare reports in connection with legal proceedings or with the exercise of the statutory functions of a public authority, for example the child protection functions of a local authority. In *M. (a minor) v Newham London Borough Council*[96] a child and her mother brought an action for negligence against a psychiatrist and social worker in respect of the manner in which they conducted an interview with the child for the purpose of identifying whether, and if so by whom, the child had been sexually abused. The psychiatrist and social worker were negligent in ascertaining the identity of the abuser, with the result that the child was needlessly removed from her mother's home for a lengthy period. Both mother and child alleged that this had caused them psychiatric harm. A majority of the Court of Appeal held that the psychiatrist and social worker did not owe a duty of care to a child when advising the social services authority. Both Staughton and Peter Gibson L.JJ. had some difficulty with the notion that the psychiatrist could owe the child a duty of care in negligence when the child was not strictly speaking the psychiatrist's "patient." Peter Gibson L.J. said that since the psychiatrist was involved by the local authority in order to advise it in relation to its decision whether or not to intervene, it was inapt to regard the psychiatrist as under the same duty of care as if the child had been referred to the psychiatrist in order that advice or treatment be given for the child or

---

[95] See, *e.g.*, paras 2–089 to 2–092, 2–147 *et seq.*

[96] [1995] 2 A.C. 633; Dugdale (1994) 10 P.N. 82; Jones (1994) 6 J. of Child Law 161. It was also held that the local authority did not owe a duty of care when deciding whether, and if so how, to exercise its powers under the child protection legislation; *cf. T. (a minor) v Surrey County Council* [1994] 4 All E.R. 577, where a local authority was held liable in negligence for negligently advising a parent that there was no reason why a child not should be placed with a particular child-minder, when the authority knew or ought to have known that there was a significant risk, because the child-minder in question could well have previously inflicted a serious non-accidental injury to another child. See also *W v Essex County Council* [1999] Fam. 90 where a local authority placed a 15-year old boy, who was a known sexual abuser, with a foster family without informing the parents of his full history, and despite oral assurances from the local authority that a suspected or known sexual abuser would not be placed with them, with the result that the family's children were sexually abused. The Court of Appeal held that the local authority had "assumed a responsibility" for the accuracy of the statements that they gave about the boy placed with the family, and therefore the claims of the children should not be struck out as disclosing no reasonable cause of action. The authority were not exercising any statutory function in respect of these children. The claims of the parents in respect of psychiatric damage were struck out, but the House of Lords reversed the Court of Appeal on this point: [2001] 2 A.C. 592.

her mother. It was true that the advice related to and foreseeably affected the child and her mother, and therefore for some limited purposes, such as a duty of confidentiality, the child was properly to be regarded as the psychiatrist's patient. But the psychiatrist did not owe the child or the mother a duty of care in relation to the advice given to the local authority, "as it was never intended that the psychiatrist should give that advice to the child or her mother."[97] In principle, however, there is no objection to holding that A can owe a duty to B in respect of advice given to C in circumstances where the advice was never intended to be communicated to B, as both the Court of Appeal and the House of Lords have concluded.[98] Staughton L.J. emphasised that neither the child nor her mother had sought the doctor's services; they had been thrust upon them. With respect, having services thrust upon one gives no indication that the individual is not entitled to have those services performed with reasonable care. For example, the services of a psychiatrist are thrust upon a person who is compulsorily admitted to hospital for treatment under the Mental Health Act 1983, and yet no one would suggest that for this reason the psychiatrist does not owe a duty of care in negligence to that person.

Their Lordships drew an analogy with a medical examination for the purpose of a life insurance proposal where the doctor is advising the proposed insurers. It was said that the doctor would owe no duty to the individual in the advice he gave to the insurers, even though for the purpose of confidentiality he may treat the individual as a patient.[99] Staughton L.J. also compared the child's position to that of an errant motorist who is deprived of a small quantity of blood by a police surgeon, but the significance of this analogy is obscure. If a police surgeon negligently infected the motorist with hepatitis or HIV in the course of extracting blood, no one would suggest that the doctor did not owe a duty of care to avoid such damage to the motorist.[1] His status, patient or not, is entirely irrelevant to the issue. The doctor's duty derives from the fact that he undertook the task in hand and inflicted foreseeable personal injury on the claimant. His Lordship appeared to recognise this point when he said:

2–062

> "In all those cases the medical person without doubt owes *some* duty to the person being examined or treated. We have been asking the wrong

---

[97] *ibid.* at 684.

[98] *Spring v Guardian Assurance* [1995] 2 A.C. 296; *White v Jones* [1993] 3 W.L.R. 730, CA; [1995] 2 A.C. 207, HL; see also *Gorham v British Telecommunications plc* [2000] 1 W.L.R. 2129, CA. These cases concern the somewhat different matter of liability for economic loss, but normally the courts show a greater willingness to protect a claimant from personal injury than economic loss. The analogy of *White v Jones* was specifically rejected, however, by the House of Lords in *M v Newham*: see *X. (minors) v Bedfordshire County Council* [1995] 2 A.C. 633, 752.

[99] On the doctor's duty of confidentiality in these circumstances see the General Medical Council's guidance, *Confidentiality: Protecting and Providing Information*, June 2000, para. 14, (available at *www.gmc-uk.org*) which requires the *patient's* written consent to a medical examination for insurance or employment purposes.

[1] See *Re N* [1999] Lloyd's Rep. Med. 257; also reported as *N v Agrawal* [1999] P.N.L.R. 939, where the Court of Appeal accepted, *obiter*, that the duty of a forensic medical examiner was not to make the examinee's position worse. See para. 2–069 below.

question, whether *any* duty is owed. The right question is, *what* duty? It is a duty to use reasonable skill and care so as not to cause harm in the course of examination or treatment. But the general duty to perform the task allocated with reasonable skill and care—whether it be 'diagnosing' the name of an abuser, or assessing the expectation of life, or producing a blood sample for analysis—is in my opinion owed to the person who engages the doctor to perform that task. That is the health authority or local council in the first case, the insurance company in the second, and the police authority in the third."[2]

With respect, this is puzzling. Clearly, any employee owes to his employer a "general duty to perform the task allocated" and the psychiatrist certainly owed a duty to exercise reasonable care in reporting her findings to the local authority. But this is not in the least inconsistent with owing a duty of care to the child. The local authority and the child were "on the same side," as it were,[3] and both had an interest in the doctor performing her professional duties with reasonable care. It could be said that a doctor employed in a hospital "owes a general duty to his employers to perform the tasks allocated," as indeed she does, but this cannot possibly be taken as a basis for concluding that she therefore owes no duty to the individuals upon whom she exercises her professional skills (whether categorised as patients or not). If it were, no NHS doctor would owe a duty of care to a patient, since a hospital doctor clearly owes a duty to the employing NHS Trust and a general practitioner owes duties to the "employer" under the National Health Service (General Medical Services) Regulations 1992.[4] As Lord Slynn observed in *Phelps v Hillingdon London Borough Council*,[5] a case involving a claim in respect of alleged negligence by an educational psychologist: "The fact that the educational psychologist owes a duty to the authority to exercise skill and care in the performance of his contract of employment does not mean that no duty of care can be or is owed to the child."

2–063   In a dissenting judgment in *M. v Newham* Sir Thomas Bingham M.R. accepted that the relationship between the child and the psychiatrist was not a normal doctor-patient relationship, but it was a very direct and personal relationship, and thus the child was the psychiatrist's patient in the sense that it was for the child alone that she was being invited to exercise her professional skill and judgment. That would ordinarily lead to the conclusion that the psychiatrist owed the child a duty of care, in the absence of any reasons of policy why this should not follow.[6] It is submitted that this simple analysis is entirely in accordance with principle.

---

[2] [1995] 2 A.C. 633, 674 (original emphasis).
[3] See *Ross v Caunters* [1980] Ch. 297; *White v Jones* [1995] 2 A.C. 207.
[4] S.I. 1992 No. 635.
[5] [2001] 2 A.C. 619, 654.
[6] For discussion of the policy factors which the majority considered also supported the conclusion that no duty of care should be owed see paras 3–113 to 3–115. Sir Thomas Bingham M.R. agreed with Staughton and Peter Gibson L.JJ. that the psychiatrist owed no duty of care to the child's mother.

Subsequently, in *E. (a minor) v Dorset County Council*[7] a differently con- **2–064**
stituted Court of Appeal (though including Sir Thomas Bingham M.R.) distinguished *M. (a minor) v Newham London Borough Council* in a case
where claims for damages were brought by children against education
authorities alleging negligence in the assessment of their need for special educational provision. It was held that the actions should not be struck out as
disclosing no reasonable cause of action since it was arguable that a doctor,
educational psychologist or head teacher could owe a duty of care to a child
when assessing the child's educational needs. Evans L.J. observed that:

> "It is uncomfortable to think of the doctor, educational psychologist or
> the head teacher being constrained by an awareness that he could be
> held liable in damages if he was negligent towards his employer but was
> immune if he was negligent towards the child. He might even find it dif-
> ficult to distinguish between a duty owed to the child as well as the
> authority and one owed to authority alone. He would either exercise the
> necessary degree of professional skill and care, or he would not."[8]

The basis for the duty owed to the child was not the contract under which the
professional person was consulted, said his Lordship, nor the statutory requirement that the local authority should consult the professional, but the relationship
which is brought about between them: "Put another way, the consultant owes a
duty in tort to the child as his patient, *or as the person in whose interests his professional advice is sought and given.*"[9] There were significant differences between
the situation of a doctor asked to examine a child in order to report to the local
authority whether there was evidence of sexual abuse, so that the authority can
consider whether or not to exercise its statutory powers to remove the child into
care, and a doctor who was asked to advise whether the child suffered from a
medical, including psychological, disorder which required treatment and what
form that treatment should take. But it was unnecessary to explore these differences, said Evans L.J., because in *M. (a minor) v Newham London Borough
Council* the majority considered that the case was analogous to a doctor acting
for an insurance company who examined an applicant for life insurance. The
facts of *E. (a minor) v Dorset County Council* did not fall into the same category:

> "The insurance company's doctor undertakes by contract to examine
> and report upon the physical condition of the applicant. He does not
> undertake by contract or otherwise to treat the applicant, and it may
> well be the case—I do not know the answer to this—that it would be a
> breach of professional etiquette towards the applicant's own doctor if he
> was to offer or undertake any form of treatment, including professional
> advice. In these circumstances, there clearly is a limited relationship
> between him and the applicant and this is reflected in the limited scope
> of the duty of care which he owes to the applicant in tort."[10]

---

[7] [1995] 2 A.C. 633.
[8] *ibid.* at 714.
[9] *ibid.*, emphasis added.
[10] *ibid.* at 715.

2–065   In *E. (a minor) v Dorset County Council*, on the other hand, the doctor or specialist was engaged not merely to report but to advise on the best interests of the child. The advice was a form of treatment, and the child and its parents as well as the authority were entitled to expect that the advice would be carefully and competently given. With great respect, it is submitted that the similarities between the two cases are much greater than the differences, though it may be that the court in *E. (a minor) v Dorset County Council* felt constrained to distinguish *M. (a minor) v Newham London Borough Council*, which was otherwise a binding authority. As Evans L.J. put it, the doctor owed a duty in tort to the child as his patient, "or as the person in whose interests his professional advice is sought and given." That principle applied equally to the child in *M. v Newham*: the child's interests were essentially the *only* interests at stake in that case, and therefore it is distinctly odd that a doctor could be said to owe a duty to exercise reasonable care in advising the local authority, but not to the child, when the very purpose of the duty owed to the local authority was to enable it to act in the best interests of the child. If, as Evans L.J. noted, the doctor might find it difficult to distinguish between a duty owed to both the authority and the child, on the one hand, and a duty owed to the authority alone, on the other, this is perhaps because there is no valid distinction between them.

2–066   The appeals to the House of Lords in the cases of *M. (a minor) v Newham London Borough Council* and *E. (a minor) v Dorset County Council* were considered together, along with several other actions brought against social services authorities and education authorities.[11] Their Lordships agreed with the majority of the Court of Appeal in *M. (a minor) v Newham London Borough Council* that the psychiatrist and social worker were retained by the local authority to advise the local authority, not the claimants. The fact that the carrying out of the retainer involved contact with and a relationship with the child did not alter the extent of the duty owed by the professionals under the retainer from the local authority. The analogy with the doctor instructed by an insurance company to examine an applicant for life insurance was correct, said their Lordships. The doctor does not, by examining the applicant, come under any general duty of medical care to the applicant: "He is under a duty not to damage the applicant in the course of the examination: but beyond this his duties are owed to the insurance company and not to the applicant."[12] Similarly, the social worker and the psychiatrist did not assume any general professional duty of care to the child.[12a]

---

[11] sub. nom. *X. (minors) v Bedfordshire County Council* [1995] 2 A.C. 633.

[12] *ibid*. at 753.

[12a] But see now *JD v East Berkshire Community Health NHS Trust* [2003] EWCA Civ 1151; *The Times*, August 22, 2003, where the Court of Appeal held that *X (minors) v Bedfordshire County Council; M. (a minor) v Newham London Borough Council* [1995] 2 A.C. 633 could not survive the Human Rights Act 1998. It was no longer "legitimate to rule that, as a matter of law, no common law duty of care is owed to a child in relation to the investigation of suspected child abuse and the initiation and pursuit of care proceedings." Although it was possible that there could be factual situations where it was not fair, just or reasonable to impose a duty of care "each case will fall to be determined on its individual facts": at [84].

With great respect, the situation in *M. (a minor) v Newham London* **2–067**
Borough Council was closer to the case where a doctor examining an
applicant for life insurance causes injury than one where, having diagnosed
a potentially dangerous condition, he fails to inform the applicant, with the
result that the applicant loses an opportunity to have expeditious treatment.
On the pleaded case in *M. (a minor) v Newham London Borough Council*
the psychiatrist *did* cause injury to the child, namely psychiatric injury, as a
direct result of the negligent advice given to the local authority which
resulted in the child being separated from her mother. Nor should it be an
answer that the damage occurred as a result of the decision of the local
authority to institute legal proceedings to remove the child, since this was
the very event that the psychiatrist's advice was likely to produce.[13]
Curiously, their Lordships accepted that in the case of *E. (a minor) v Dorset
County Council* the local authority could be both directly liable in negligence
and vicariously liable for the negligence of an educational psychologist in
assessing a child's special educational needs. The direct duty of care arose
because the authority held itself out as offering a specialist service (psychological advice) to the public: "By opening its doors to others to take advantage of the service offered, it comes under a duty of care to those using the
service to exercise care in its conduct. The position is directly analogous with
a hospital conducted, formerly by a local authority now by a health authority, in exercise of statutory powers."[14] The educational psychologist owed a

---

[13] In considering whether the local authority could owe a direct duty of care to the claimant (as
opposed to vicarious liability for the negligence of individuals) in *X. (minors) v Bedfordshire
County Council* it was accepted that there was the requisite foreseeability and proximity of
relationship, but the House of Lords concluded that no duty should exist because of policy
considerations, applying the third limb of the *Caparo* test, namely that it should be "just and
reasonable" to impose a duty of care: *Caparo Industries plc v Dickman* [1990] 2 A.C. 605.
The same policy factors applied with equal force to the question of whether the psychiatrist
or social worker should owe a duty of care as individuals in *M. (a minor) v Newham London
Borough Council*: see [1995] 2 A.C. 633, 754, *per* Lord Browne-Wilkinson. Lord Nolan, at
772, dissented on the question of whether, public policy apart, the psychiatrist and social
worker should be exempt from a general professional duty of care towards the child. The relationship was not analogous to that arising in the commercial context of an examination by
an insurance company doctor of an applicant for life insurance. However, the policy considerations justified the defendants' immunity. Note that on the facts of *X (minors) v
Bedfordshire County Council*, which involved allegations that a social services authority had
negligently failed to take children who were being physically abused into care, the European
Court of Human Rights subsequently found that the UK was in breach of Art. 3 of the
European Convention on Human Rights, which prohibits torture or inhuman or degrading
treatment, in that the welfare system had failed to protect the children from serious, long-
term neglect and abuse: *Z v United Kingdom* [2001] 2 F.L.R. 612. In so far as the policy
reasons listed by the House of Lords in *X (minors) v Bedfordshire* for denying a duty of care
included the impact of damages claims on the resources of a local authority, breach of
Convention rights could also have an impact on the resources of a social services authority
(although awards of damages for breach of Convention rights are not made on the same basis
as damages in tort, and are typically much more modest: see the Law Commission, *Damages
under the Human Rights Act 1998*, Law Com. No. 266, 2000; Fairgrieve [2001] P.L. 695).
See also *TP and KM v UK* [2001] 2 F.L.R. 549, para. 2–074, below. And see now *JD v East
Berkshire Community Health NHS Trust* [2003] EWCA Civ 1151; *The Times*, August 22,
2003 on the effects of the Human Rights Act 1998 in this situation.

[14] *X. (minors) v Bedfordshire County Council* [1995] 2 A.C. 633, 763, *per* Lord Browne-
Wilkinson.

duty of care because there was no potential conflict of duty between the professional's duties to the claimant and his duty to the education authority. Nor was there any obvious conflict, said Lord Browne-Wilkinson, between the professional being under a duty of care to the claimant and the discharge by the authority of its statutory duties. It remains a puzzle why their Lordships considered that there was such a conflict between the duty owed by the psychiatrist to the local authority and a potential duty of care owed to the child. The psychiatrist could only discharge the duty owed to the local authority by acting with reasonable care in conducting the examination, which was being conducted in the interests and for the benefit of the child. It cannot be in the interests of either the child or the local authority that the authority should act upon negligent advice (whether the careless advice is to the effect that the child has been abused or that it has not been abused). There is simply no conflict between these duties.

2–068   In *Phelps v Hillingdon London Borough Council*[15] the House of Lords had no difficulty in concluding that an educational psychologist could be liable in negligence when making an assessment of a pupil's educational needs for failing to diagnose dyslexia, as a result of which the claimant's education was seriously prejudiced, and that the local authority could be vicariously liable for the psychologist's negligence. The fact that the acts which were claimed to be negligent were carried out within the ambit of a statutory discretion was not a reason why a claim for negligence should not be permitted. Although it was important that those engaged in the provision of educational services under statute should not be hampered by the imposition of liability, it was unlikely that the existence of such duties would lead to that result, because "the recognition of the duty of care does not of itself impose unreasonably high standards."[16] The obligation was merely to exercise reasonable care in the circumstances. As Lord Clyde expressed the point: "in order to get off the ground the claimant must be able to demonstrate that the standard of care fell short of that set by the *Bolam* test . . . That is deliberately and properly a high standard in recognition of the difficult nature of some decisions which those to whom the test applies require to make and of the room for genuine differences of view on the propriety of one course of action as against another."[17] The difference between an educational psychologist providing a report on a child's educational needs and a psychiatrist reporting on a child

[15] [2001] 2 A.C. 619.
[16] *ibid*. at 655 *per* Lord Slynn. See also the comments of Buckley J. in *A and B v Essex County Council* [2002] EWHC 2707 (QB); [2003] 1 F.L.R. 615 at [25] where the local authority was held to have been negligent in failing to provide full information to prospective adopters about a child who was placed with them for adoption: "I cannot see how such a duty would detract from the importance of a child's interests or in any way interfere with the statutory regime. On the contrary, as has been pointed out in some of the cases, it might encourage those involved to perform their tasks better. It is clearly in the public interest that professionals and those with special skills who are paid to offer their services to the public should act to the appropriate standard and, at least in the context of this case, I can see no danger of such a duty encouraging unacceptably defensive behaviour. Indeed such action, if displayed here, might well have avoided the problems."
[17] *ibid*. at 672.

who may have been abused is probably that in the former case, but not the latter, the public authority has taken on the role of providing a quasi-professional service, corresponding to a service that could be provided by the private sector. In these circumstances it is easier to argue that the authority should be liable for negligence in the provision of that service.

Forensic Medical Examinations

In *Re N*[18] the Court of Appeal held that a doctor who carries out a foren-   2–069
sic medical examination does not owe a duty of care to the person examined, other than not to cause further damage during the examination. Thus, where the defendant examined the claimant following a complaint to the police that the claimant had been raped by a third party, there was no duty of care upon the defendant to attend court to give evidence at the prosecution of the third party, even though it was foreseeable that if there was an acquittal the claimant would suffer further psychiatric harm. There is no duty to give evidence, since this would be inconsistent with the immunity of witnesses.[19] Thus, the claim was that there was a duty to take reasonable steps to attend the trial. This, however, missed the point. As Stuart-Smith L.J. pointed out the duty must be a duty to take reasonable care to prevent the claimant from suffering damage of the type in question, *i.e.* psychiatric injury. A failure to attend to give evidence could be a breach of such a duty, but it was not the duty itself. The forensic examination at the request of the police or the Crown Prosecution Service did not create a doctor-patient relationship, and the doctor did not assume responsibility for the claimant's psychiatric welfare. The duty was simply to take reasonable care not to make the patient's condition worse during the examination.[20] The doctor was in the same position as the psychiatrist in *X v Bedfordshire County Council*. Mere attendance at the trial achieved nothing without the defendant also giving evidence consistent with her earlier examination and report—but there could be no duty in relation to any evidence the doctor would give in the witness box.

If, on the other hand, a witness *was* under a duty to attend and give evi-   2–070
dence on the lines of his or her witness statement, the position might be different. There were cases where a claimant in a civil action had issued a witness summons and the witness failed to attend where the claimant would have an action on the case against the witness, though the older cases limited the damages to the costs of the abortive hearing.[21] It might also be arguable that the claimant could have an action against the witness for loss of a chance

---

[18] [1999] Lloyd's Rep. Med. 257, also reported as *N v Agrawal* [1999] P.N.L.R. 939, CA.
[19] See para. 2–071 below.
[20] Though note that Clarke L.J. considered, *obiter*, that it was "at least arguable that where [a forensic medical examiner] carries out an examination and discovers that the person being examined has, say, a serious condition which needs immediate treatment, he or she owes a duty to that person to inform him or her of the position": [1999] Lloyd's Rep. Med. 257 at 263.
[21] See *Couling v Coxe* (1848) 6 Dow & L 399; *Roberts v J. & F. Stone Lighting and Radio Ltd* (1945) 172 L.T. 240, 242.

of succeeding in the litigation,[22] although if a material witness failed to attend upon subpoena a trial judge ought to grant an adjournment.[23] In such a case the recoverable damage would be the costs thrown away by the adjournment. Moreover, "A similar position would arise if the witness was contractually bound to attend."[24] Clarke L.J. also considered that "where a duty to attend court and give evidence is established, as for example by a contract between a party to civil proceedings and an expert" a claimant may be able to "recover substantial damages for any loss which he could establish as a result, no doubt assessed as the loss of a chance of success", though this was "a point which can be considered when it arises for decision."[25] Obviously, a contractual obligation to attend court to give evidence will not arise in the context of criminal law or child protection proceedings, but could be relevant in civil litigation.

Witness immunity

2–071   An issue that is closely related to the question of whether a doctor conducting an examination in the context of the statutory functions of public bodies owes a duty of care to the examinee, is the question of the immunity of witnesses. A witness in legal proceedings (whether civil or criminal) has immunity from suit with respect to evidence given in those proceedings,[26] and this immunity applies to a proof or a report prepared for trial by a witness.[27] The immunity applies to an expert witness who prepares a joint statement with an expert instructed by the opposing party to the litigation for the purpose of identifying what issues are in dispute between the experts, and this is the case notwithstanding that the expert does not give evidence at the trial.[28] The immunity is based on public policy in protecting the proper administration of justice so that witnesses are able to be frank when giving evidence free from the threat of civil proceedings, and to avoid a multiplicity of actions in which the truth of their evidence would be tried over again.[29] In the case of an expert witness the immunity extends only to what can fairly be said to be preliminary to giving evidence in court. Thus, the production of a report for disclosure to the other side is immune, but work done for the principal purpose of advising the client, as to the merits of the claim, for example, is not.[30] In

---

[22] Applying *Allied Maples Group Ltd v Simmons & Simmons* [1995] 4 All E.R. 907; para. 5–060.
[23] [1999] Lloyd's Rep. Med. 257, 259, at [11] *per* Stuart-Smith L.J.
[24] *ibid.* Chadwick L.J. appears to have accepted that the position could be different if there was a contractual relationship: "In the absence of contract, it cannot be said that the defendant owed to the plaintiff a duty to take care to provide evidence or to attend a trial." *ibid.* at 262.
[25] *ibid.* at 263.
[26] *Rondel v Worsley* [1969] 1 A.C. 191, 268.
[27] *Evans v London Hospital Medical College* [1981] 1 W.L.R. 184.
[28] *Stanton v Callaghan* [2000] Q.B. 75, CA.
[29] *Watson v M'Ewan* [1905] A.C. 480; *Saif Ali v Sydney Mitchell & Co* [1980] A.C. 198; *Evans v London Hospital Medical College* [1981] 1 W.L.R. 184.
[30] *Palmer v Durnford Ford* [1992] 1 Q.B. 483, 488.

Landall v Dennis Faulkner & Alsop[31] the claimant was suing, *inter alia*, a
medical expert who had provided a number of reports on the condition and
prognosis of his back for the purpose of a claim being brought by the claimant against a negligent motorist. He alleged that the expert's report and/or
advice was negligent in that the prospects of further successful treatment for
the claimant's back condition were unduly optimistic, with the result that the
claimant settled his action against the negligent motorist for much less than
the claim was worth. The claimant argued that the reports provided by the
expert had a dual role. They were not simply for the purposes of the litigation, but also constituted advice to the claimant as to the potential benefits of
a spinal fusion operation. This argument was rejected by Holland J. The
report constituted "pre-trial work . . . so intimately connected with the
conduct of the case in court that it could fairly be said to be a preliminary
decision affecting the way that the case was to be conducted when it came to
a hearing."[32] Accordingly, the claim was struck out as disclosing no reasonable cause of action.

In *Hughes v Lloyds Bank plc*[33] the claimant sustained injuries in a road   2–072
traffic accident for which she brought a claim against the other motorist. She
telephoned her general practitioner, the defendant, requesting that he
prepare a report on her injuries for service on the motorist's insurers. The
general practitioner wrote two letters, the first stating that the claimant had
been X-rayed, that her back was normal and that her symptoms would settle
down in a few weeks, and the second setting out the history and observing
that though the claimant's back and neck were still causing discomfort, this
would "settle down in time". He also referred to her painful foot and problems sleeping at night. The claimant settled the claim for £600 general
damages three months after the accident. Subsequently she found that her
injuries were more serious than had been indicated, and brought an action
against the general practitioner. She alleged that the defendant's prognosis
had been negligent with the result that she suffered financial loss by settling
her claim for less than she would have done, had she known the true position. The Court of Appeal rejected the defendant's argument that he was
entitled to rely on witness immunity. The proceedings had not been issued
and the evidence from the general practitioner had been supplied in the
context of negotiations:

> "The doctor received a request from the client, not her solicitors, to
> provide a letter. He did not judge it necessary to examine the claimant.
> There was no indication that his report, if supplied, would form part of
> any pleading. He was not asked to prepare a proof or give evidence. It
> seems plain that he provided the letters which he did in order that the
> claimant (his patient, whom he had treated) might negotiate a fair

---

[31] [1994] 5 Med. L.R. 268, QBD.
[32] Applying *Saif Ali v Sydney Mitchell & Co* [1980] A.C. 198, and *Palmer v Durnford Ford*
[1992] 1 Q.B. 483, 488. In any event, on the facts the report was not negligent.
[33] [1998] P.I.Q.R. P98.

settlement of her claim on the basis of an accurate statement of her medical condition since the accident and a sound prognosis of her future recovery. It is clear that he would have appreciated in all probability that if no settlement could be negotiated, proceedings might well follow."[34]

Thus, the letters written by the general practitioner could not be regarded as preliminary to giving evidence as an expert. The documents were not supplied for disclosure to the other side in the context of proceedings but purely in the context of negotiation. The probability was that, had there been a trial on quantum, the general practitioner would not have been the witness relied on by the claimant as her expert medical witness, and it was unlikely that the general practitioner, if giving what was likely to become a proof of evidence, would not have wished to make a further detailed examination of the claimant. Thus, the doctor's letters were not covered by the immunity of a witness.[35]

2–073   In *M. (a minor) v Newham London Borough Council*[36] the defendants claimed that they were protected by witness immunity because when interviewing the child, and advising on future action, the psychiatrist would have known that, if she concluded that there had been abuse and that separation was desirable, there were likely to be proceedings in which she would be a witness. This argument was rejected, however, by Sir Thomas Bingham M.R. and Staughton L.J., on the ground that witness immunity does not apply to those who have never become involved in the administration of justice, even though at the time of the interview the psychiatrist would have appreciated that there might very well be court proceedings in which she would be a witness. The defendants' argument would extend the immunity too far. The House of Lords concluded, however, that witness immunity should apply to the psychiatrist. The policy considerations which applied to witnesses in criminal proceedings were equally applicable to a local authority's investigation, in the performance of a public duty, of whether or not there is evidence on which to bring proceedings for the protection of children from child abuse.[37] The psychiatrist knew that if abuse was discovered, proceedings by the local authority for the protection of the child would ensue and that her findings would be the evidence on which those proceedings would be based. The investigations had an immediate link with possible proceedings in pursuance of a statutory duty, and therefore could not be made the basis of subsequent actions.[38] But in *JD v East*

---

[34] *ibid.* at 104, *per* Lord Bingham C.J.

[35] *ibid.* at 106.

[36] [1995] 2 A.C. 633.

[37] sub. nom. *X. (minors) v Bedfordshire County Council* [1995] 2 A.C. 633, 755. Lord Browne-Wilkinson expressed "no view as to the position in relation to ordinary civil proceedings".

[38] Note that the decision of the House of Lords in *Arthur J.S. Hall & Co (a firm) v Simons* [2002] 1 A.C. 615 to abolish the immunity from suit of advocates may ultimately have an effect on the scope of the immunity of witnesses. The impact of the Human Rights Act 1998 will be to limit such immunities to those that are proportionate (under Art. 6). It also seems likely that there will be more of a focus on the courts' power to strike out claims as an abuse of process where they involve the initiation of proceedings for the purpose of mounting a collateral attack on a final decision against the intending claimant, which has been made by

Berkshire Community Health NHS Trust[38a] the Court of Appeal held that, in light of the decision of the House of Lords in *Darker v Chief Constable of West Midlands Police*,[38b] where the question of witness immunity was given careful consideration, there was a distinction to be drawn between the investigation of offences and the preparation of evidence. Witness immunity did not attach simply to the investigation process. Although it might not be easy in some cases of suspected child abuse to draw the line between investigation and the preparation of evidence, in the *Newham* case "the activities of the social workers probably fell into the category of investigations."[38c]

In *TP and KM v UK*[39] the European Court of Human Rights found that on the facts of *M v Newham London Borough Council* the failure of the social services authority properly to involve the child's mother in the investigation of alleged sexual abuse of her child (with the consequence that the child was unnecessarily taken into local authority care) constituted a breach of Article 8 of the European Convention on Human Rights, the right to respect for family life. The local authority had refused to disclose to the mother a video of an interview with the child. If this had been done it would have been apparent to the mother that the local authority had failed to identify the abuser, and had mistakenly identified her partner as the abuser. The refusal to disclose the video denied the mother adequate involvement in the decision-making process concerning the care of her daughter, and this constituted a breach of Article 8. — 2–074

(b) A duty to rescue?

As a general proposition the tort of negligence does not impose a duty to rescue. The failure to intervene to prevent harm to another (as opposed to causing damage by some positive act) does not give rise to liability. There are quite a few exceptions to this rule, including situations based on particular relationships, such as parent and child, employer and employee, or the doctor-patient relationship. Moreover, where a defendant holds himself out as providing a particular service he may be taken to have undertaken a responsibility for negligence in failing to provide that service which leads to harm to an individual who has relied on that undertaking. It is on this basis that a hospital casualty department can owe a duty of care to a patient who is turned away unseen.[40] But as a general rule, there is no duty to play the "Good Samaritan" where the doctor-patient relationship does not exist.[41] In — 2–075

(n.38 contd.) another court of competent jurisdiction in previous proceedings, in which the intending claimant had a full opportunity of contesting the decision: see *Hunter v Chief Constable of West Midlands* [1982] A.C. 529. For discussion of the implications of *Hall* for the courts' power to strike out claims as an abuse of process on the basis of a collateral attack see Evans (2001) 17 P.N. 218.

[38a] [2003] EWCA Civ 1151; *The Times*, August 22, 2003.

[38b] [2001] 1 A.C. 435.

[38c] [2003] EWCA Civ 1151 at [116].

[40] *Barnett v Chelsea and Kensington Hospital Management Committee* [1968] 1 All E.R. 1068.

[41] So there is generally no legal duty upon a doctor to volunteer his services in an emergency, *e.g.* in reply to the call "is there a doctor in the house?": *In Re F. (Mental Patient: Sterilisation)* [1990] 2 A.C. 1, 77 *per* Lord Goff.

Powell v Boladz[42] the Court of Appeal commented that: "a doctor who goes to the assistance of a stranger injured in an accident . . . does not, as a rule, undertake the patient-doctor relationship so as to make him liable for lack of care, but only a duty not to make the condition of the victim worse." On this basis, a doctor who comes across a man who is bleeding to death, who could easily prevent this but is careless in his attempts, is not liable in negligence for the man's death, unless his intervention prevented other, more effective, aid reaching the deceased. In these circumstances, it is said, there is no practical difference between the negligent doctor and a doctor who simply ignores the deceased and passes by, and imposing liability on the former but not the latter could be seen as deterring medical intervention. This view has been strongly criticised by Kennedy & Grubb, who assert that:

> "There is no basis for stating this as a matter of law and there is no English authority for so limiting the content of the doctor's duty . . . A doctor who allows a road accident victim to die by failing to deal with his injuries does not make the victim's condition 'worse'—even assuming he would not have died with immediate treatment. Yet, there can be no doubt that medical evidence will in many circumstances suggest that the doctor could reasonably have done something to improve, or prevent a deterioration in, the victim's condition. Such a doctor is in breach of his duty to act reasonably in preventing foreseeable injury to the victim and should be liable in negligence."[43]

The basis in law for the Court of Appeal's statement is the "no duty to rescue" principle, which has been applied in a number of contexts. The statement by Kennedy & Grubb that "there is no English authority for so limiting the content of the doctor's duty" assumes that the duty is held to *exist*, as does the assertion that "such a doctor is in breach of his duty to act reasonably in preventing foreseeable injury." It is trite law that in the absence of a duty of care the unreasonableness of the defendant's conduct is irrelevant, no matter how foreseeable or catastrophic the damage. Of course, the assertion that the doctor *should be liable in negligence* is a normative judgment about what the law ought to be, a judgment with which many commentators would agree.[44] Unless it can be said that the doctor rendering Good Samaritan services has undertaken a responsibility to the

---

[42] [1998] Lloyds Rep. Med. 116, 124, citing the statement of the Court of Appeal in *Capital and Counties plc v Hampshire County Council* [1997] Q.B. 1004, 1035: "If he volunteers his assistance, his only duty as a matter of law is not to make the victim's condition worse."

[43] *Medical Law*, 3rd ed., 2000, at pp. 297–298.

[44] See also the comment of Atkin L.J. in *Everett v Griffiths* [1920] 3 K.B. 163, 213, cited above at para. 2–025; and Williams (2001) 21 O.J.L.S. 393. Certainly, the vast majority of both public (98%) and the medical profession (96%) consider that a doctor who comes across a road traffic accident ought to render some assistance: Zwitter *et al.* (1999) 318 B.M.J. 251. For an argument that a doctor should be held responsible for damage caused by a careless rescue, when in the absence of intervention the rescuee would have died, see Stapleton (1997) 113 L.Q.R. 257, 277 *et seq.*; and for criticism of Stapleton's argument see Smith (1997) 113 L.Q.R. 426.

claimant[45] the mere omissions rule provides the logic, if not the moral justification, for limiting the doctor's duty. This is that if the doctor would not be liable for simply walking past the injured victim, it would be irrational to hold him liable for failing to improve the victim's position (as opposed to making it worse), not least because of the risk that this would discourage doctors from volunteering assistance in an emergency.[46] It would seem that in practice, however, there is little evidence that the risk of liability does deter doctors from rendering assistance.[47]

The "no duty to rescue" principle has been applied to most emergency services, including the police,[48] the coastguard,[49] and the fire service,[50] although there have been some cases where an undertaking of responsibility has been found to have occurred on the particular facts.[51] The position of the ambulance service was considered by the Court of Appeal in *Kent v Griffiths, Roberts and London Ambulance Service*,[52] where the issue was whether the ambulance service owed a duty of care to an individual when the service is summoned to render assistance to that individual. A general practitioner telephoned the ambulance service to take his patient, the claimant, to hospital because she was experiencing breathing difficulties. It was clearly an emergency. After 12 minutes the claimant's husband telephoned again, to be told that the ambulance was on its way. After another 16 minutes the doctor telephoned again. The ambulance eventually arrived 38 minutes after the original call, and had taken 34 minutes to travel a distance (six and a half miles) that would normally have taken about nine minutes. No explanation for this was ever given by the defendants.[53] On the way to the hospital the claimant suffered respiratory arrest which resulted in brain damage. If she had been taken to the hospital sooner the brain damage could have been avoided. The defendants argued that, by analogy with the fire service, they were an emergency service and should not owe a duty of care to those whom they were summoned to assist. It was conceded that the risk

2–076

---

[45] It is better not to call the accident victim a patient, since this assumes what one is seeking to prove, namely that the doctor-patient relationship has arisen.

[46] Which is the justification often given for "Good Samaritan" legislation in North America, conferring various degrees of immunity from claims in relation to altruistic medical intervention. See McInnes (1992) 26 U.B.C.L. Rev. 239.

[47] See Williams (2001) 21 O.J.L.S. 393, 405–406.

[48] *Hill v Chief Constable of West Yorkshire* [1989] 1 A.C. 53; *Alexandrou v Oxford* [1993] 4 All E.R. 328.

[49] *Skinner v Secretary of State for Transport, The Times*, 3 January 1995; *OLL Ltd v Secretary of State for Transport* [1997] 3 All E.R. 897.

[50] *Capital and Counties plc v Hampshire County Council* [1997] Q.B. 1004.

[51] Usually involving police officers who have failed to go to the assistance of a fellow officer. See: *Costello v Chief Constable of Northumbria Police* [1999] 1 All E.R. 550; *Mullaney v Chief Constable of West Midlands Police* [2001] EWCA Civ 700, *The Independent*, July 9, 2001; *cf. Cowan v Chief Constable of Avon & Somerset Constabulary* [2001] EWCA Civ 1699; *The Times*, 11 December 2001, where it was held that merely turning up at the scene of a disturbance did not create an assumption of responsibility to a claimant who was being unlawfully evicted from his home.

[52] [2001] Q.B. 36.

[53] Indeed, the ambulance crew tried to falsify the log to suggest that the journey took nine minutes.

of harm was foreseeable, and the defendants did not rely on public policy arguments to exclude a duty of care. Rather it was argued that there was no proximity between the defendants and the claimant: their duty was limited to taking reasonable care not negligently to create an additional danger causing injury to the individual. The Court of Appeal rejected this approach and held that the ambulance service does owe a duty of care to those whom it is summoned to assist. This duty arises once the service "accepts the call" for assistance. The analogy was not with the emergency services, but with the medical services provided by a hospital. A hospital accident and emergency department owes a duty of care to those who seek its assistance, and cannot simply turn patients away without accepting responsibility in the tort of negligence. Thus, the ambulance service is in a different category from other emergency services, and by accepting a call for assistance undertakes a positive obligation to exercise reasonable care. An alternative basis upon which the decision could be justified is that the defendants' negligence did actually worsen the claimant's position, since it was clear on the facts that if the patient's husband or doctor had known that there was going to be such a long delay they would have transported the claimant to hospital in a private vehicle. However, the duty as expressed in *Kent* would seem to apply even where there is no other means of obtaining the medical assistance that the claimant needs.

2–077   Situations could arise in which the ambulance service might have to make a judgment about which of a number of individuals should be given priority. But that was not a reason for saying that no duty should be owed, since the requirement to prove that there had been negligence would provide the ambulance service with protection.[54] The situation might be different if the effect of the negligence action was to challenge the allocation resources, for example by arguing that the damage would not have been sustained but for the failure to provide sufficient ambulances, or sufficient drivers or paramedics:

> "There then could be issues which are not suited for resolution by the courts. However, once they are available, both in the form of an ambulance and in the form of manpower, the resources to provide an ambulance on which there are no alternative demands, the ambulance service would be acting perversely 'in circumstances such as the present,' if it did not make those resources available. Having decided to provide an ambulance an explanation is required to justify a failure to attend within reasonable time."[55]

---

[54] [2001] Q.B. 36 at [46] *per* Lord Woolf M.R.: "The result would depend on the facts. I would be resistant to a suggestion that the ambulance service could be regarded as negligent because by an error of judgment a less seriously injured patient was transported to hospital leaving a more seriously injured patient at the scene who, as a result, suffered further injuries. In such a situation, on the facts, it is most unlikely that there would be conduct which could be properly regarded as negligent."

[55] *ibid.* at [47] *per* Lord Woolf M.R.

In *Lowns v Woods*[56] a majority of the New South Wales Court of Appeal   2–078
held that a general practitioner who had failed to respond to a request to
attend a child who was having an epileptic fit was liable in negligence,
despite the fact that the child was not his patient and there was no prior
professional relationship between the doctor and the child. In reaching the
conclusion that a duty of care was owed to the child, Kirby P. and Cole J.A.
placed considerable emphasis on two matters. First, the relevant statutory
context (the Medical Practitioners Act 1938, section 27(2)) provided that it
was professional misconduct for a doctor to

> "refuse or fail without reasonable cause, to attend, within a reasonable
> time after being requested to do so, upon a person for the purpose of ren-
> dering professional services in his capacity as a registered medical prac-
> titioner in any case where he has reasonable cause to believe that such
> person is in need of urgent attention by a registered medical practitioner
> but shall not be guilty under this paragraph of such conduct if he causes
> another registered medical practitioner to attend as aforesaid."

As Kirby P. acknowledged, the statute did not impose a duty giving rise to a
claim for damages in respect of its breach—it was concerned with professional discipline. But it did reflect the expectations which were accepted as
appropriate and proper amongst medical practitioners in responding to a call
to the aid of a "person . . . in need of urgent attention." This was a high standard, going beyond what was expected of other professions. But it was a
standard expressed by Parliament and accepted by the medical profession.
Secondly, the defendant, Dr Lowns, had himself accepted that he should have
attended the claimant. His case at trial had been that he had never been
requested to attend, and that a conversation which the claimant alleged had
taken place had not taken place (which had been rejected by the trial judge
on the facts). He had conceded that if he had received the alleged request for
assistance, he would and should have gone to the child. It followed that a
relationship of proximity between claimant and defendant was established,
notwithstanding the absence of any previous professional link between
them. The decision raises the question of when it is legitimate to convert an
ethical duty into a legal duty, based on general expectations that the defendant would act when called upon to do so. In the UK the General Medical
Council's guidance to doctors, *Good Medical Practice*, states that: "In an
emergency, wherever it may arise, you must offer anyone at risk the assistance you could reasonably be expected to provide."[57] It remains to be seen

---

[56] (1996) Aust. Torts Rep. 81–376 (N.S.W.C.A.). Discussed by D. Mendelson (1996) 4 Tort L.
Rev. 242; K. Day (1996) 18 Sydney L. Rev. 386; Haberfield (1998) 6 Tort L. Rev. 56; Grubb
(1998) 6 Med. L. Rev. 120; and more generally Williams (2001) 21 O.J.L.S. 393.
[57] *Good Medical Practice*, May 2001, para. 9 (available at the GMC website *www.gmc-
uk.org/standards/default.htm*). Note also the duty of a general practitioner to treat individuals who are not on the general practitioner's list in an emergency under the National Health
Service (General Medical Services) Regulations 1992 (S.I. 1992 No. 635), Sch. 2, para. 4(1).
See para. 2–028.

whether a court could be persuaded that this statement of an appropriate professional standard can be translated into a legal obligation sounding in damages for breach.

(c) Congenital disability

2–079   For many years there was no case in the United Kingdom in which it was decided that a duty of care at common law was owed to an unborn child,[58] although the principle had been accepted in other common law jurisdictions.[59] The assumption that a duty of care would be owed to a foetus was finally confirmed by the Court of Appeal in the consolidated appeals in *Burton v Islington Health Authority* and *De Martell v Merton and Sutton Health Authority*.[60] The claimants, who were born before July 22, 1976, when the Congenital Disabilities (Civil Liability) Act 1976 came into force, claimed damages in respect of injuries inflicted prior to birth. The defendants argued that the damage was suffered while the claimants were still in the womb and therefore while not a person. It is clear that a foetus has no independent legal personality in English law, and cannot, while a foetus, sue or be made a ward of court.[61] Thus, it was argued, the claimants could not sue in respect of negligently inflicted injuries because no duty of care was owed to them at the time that the damage was caused. Nonetheless, the Court of Appeal held that a child born alive can recover damages at common law for a pre-natal injury. Damage to a foetus was within the foreseeable risk of harm that could arise from the defendants' negligence, and the cause of action arose when the foetus was born injured, at which point the claimant acquires

---

[58] The point was conceded by counsel for the defendant in *Williams v Luff*, *The Times*, February 14, 1978, and in *McKay v Essex Area Health Authority* [1982] Q.B. 1166. A duty was assumed to exist in the thalidomide cases: *Distillers Co (Biochemicals) Ltd v Thompson* [1971] A.C. 458, and in *Whitehouse v Jordan* [1981] 1 All E.R. 267.

[59] See *Montreal Tramways v Leveille* [1933] 4 D.L.R. 339 and *Duval v Seguin* (1972) 26 D.L.R. (3d) 418 (Canada); *Watt v Rama* [1972] V.R. 353 and *Pratt v Pratt* [1975] V.R. 378; *X. and Y. v Pal* (1991) 23 N.S.W.L.R. 26; [1992] 3 Med. L.R. 195 (N.S.W.C.A.) (Australia); *Presley v Newport Hospital* (1976) 365 A. 2d 748 (U.S.A.). In *Cherry v Borsman* (1992) 94 D.L.R. (4th) 487 (B.C.C.A.) the defendant was negligent in performing an abortion with the result that the pregnancy was not terminated and the child was subsequently born with injuries inflicted during the attempted abortion. The defendant argued that he should not be liable to the injured child because he owed a clear duty of care to the mother to carry out the abortion, and this duty was in sharp conflict with any alleged duty of care owed to the child. The British Columbia Court of Appeal rejected this contention. The surgeon owed a duty of care to the mother to perform the abortion properly, but at the same time owed a duty of care to the foetus not to harm it if he should fail to meet the duty of care owed to the mother, the cause of action arising on the live birth of the foetus. Had the abortion been effective the cause of action of the foetus would not have arisen.

[60] [1993] Q.B. 204, CA, affirming *B. v Islington Health Authority* [1991] 1 Q.B. 638, and *De Martell v Merton and Sutton Health Authority* [1992] 3 All E.R. 820; [1991] 2 Med. L.R. 209. The statement that "a duty of care is owed to a foetus" is not strictly accurate, but can be taken as shorthand for the statement that a duty of care is owed to a person who is born injured as a result of negligence by a defendant which preceded the claimant's birth and affected the claimant before birth. See the formulation of Mahoney J.A. in *X. and Y. v Pal* (1991) 23 N.S.W.L.R. 26, 30, cited at n. 64, below.

[61] *Paton v British Pregnancy Advisory Service Trustees* [1979] Q.B. 276; *C. v S.* [1988] Q.B. 135; *Re F. (In Utero)* [1988] Fam. 122.

the legal personality to sue.[62] There is nothing in principle which would prevent a relevant duty being owed in respect of negligent conduct which preceded not only the child's birth but also its conception. In *X. and Y. v Pal*[63] the New South Wales Court of Appeal held that an obstetrician who had failed to test a patient for syphilis owed a duty to the child conceived later, and who had contracted syphilis from the mother *in utero*. No sensible distinction could be drawn, said Clarke J.A., between children who were injured as a result, say, of eating baby food which had been negligently contaminated with a harmful substance by the manufacturer, on the basis that some children had been born at the time of the breach of duty, that some were still *in utero*, or that some had not yet been conceived. The same point applied to the builder of a bridge which subsequently collapsed some time after being opened to the public. The rights of a child injured in the accident could not depend upon whether it had been born, or conceived, before the defendant's negligent breach of duty. His Honour commented that the duty of care was owed to a class or category of persons, and there may be within the class persons who are not born or conceived when the careless conduct occurs. Damage which is actionable in law only arises when the child is born.[64]

Burton v Islington Health Authority is important for establishing that a duty of care owed to a foetus exists at common law, but its significance is limited to births that occurred before July 22, 1976 because the Congenital Disabilities (Civil Liability) Act 1976 applies to births occurring on or after that date.[65] The Act confers a right of action on a child who is born alive and disabled in respect of the disability,[66] if it is caused by an occurrence which affected either parent's ability to have a normal healthy child, or affected the mother during pregnancy, or affected the mother or child in the course of its birth, causing disabilities which would not otherwise have been present.[67] A

2–080

---

[62] See also *Hamilton v Fife Health Board* [1993] 4 Med. L.R. 201, 206 (Court of Session, Inner House) where it was held that doctors engaged in the delivery of a foetus owe a duty of care to avoid injuring it, and once the foetus becomes a person on birth there is a concurrence of the wrong and the damage, the child having the right to sue the person whose breach of duty has caused the child's damage; *McWilliams v Lord Advocate*, 1992 S.L.T. 1045. See Whitfield (1993) 1 Med. L. Rev. 28 for discussion of some of the implications of the decision in *Burton v Islington Health Authority*.

[63] (1991) 23 N.S.W.L.R. 26; [1992] 3 Med. L.R. 195 (N.S.W.C.A.).

[64] Mahoney J.A. said that putting the issue in terms of whether a defendant can owe a duty of care to an unborn person was not an entirely accurate statement: "The issue is whether a defendant can or should be held liable *to an existing person* for damage accruing from his negligent act or omission where the act or omission occurred before the person was born and where the detrimental effects in question arose before she was born," *ibid.* at 30 (emphasis added). The answer to that question was yes.

[65] Congenital Disabilities (Civil Liability) Act 1976, s. 4(5), replacing the common law.

[66] Disability means "being born with any deformity, disease or abnormality, including predisposition (whether or not susceptible of immediate prognosis) to physical or mental defect in the future": Congenital Disabilities (Civil Liability) Act 1976, s. 4(1). See Murphy (1994) 10 P.N. 94 who argues that there is a distinction between being injured or damaged and suffering a "disability."

[67] Congenital Disabilities (Civil Liability) Act 1976, s. 1(1), (2). For detailed discussion of the legislation see Pace (1977) 40 M.L.R. 141. The child's mother is specifically excluded by s. 1(1) as a potential defendant, except where the injury is attributable to her negligent driving of a motor vehicle: s. 2. The exclusion of a claim against the mother is for policy reasons.

defendant is liable to the child if he is or would, if sued in time, have been liable in tort to the parent, and it is no answer that the parent has suffered no actionable injury.[68] Thus, the child's action is derivative, in that it depends on a tortious duty owed to the parent, except that it is not necessary to show that the parent suffered any actionable injury. A child damaged by a drug taken by its mother during pregnancy, for example, can sue the manufacturer even though the mother did not suffer any harm, if there was a breach of a duty of care owed to the mother. Section 1A, which was added by the Human Fertilisation and Embryology Act 1990, section 44, effectively extends the provisions of section 1 of the Act to children born disabled as a result of damage to an embryo or to gametes in the course of infertility treatment, by the placing in a woman of an embryo, or of sperm and eggs or of artificial insemination. Where the disability results from an act or omission in the course of the selection, or the keeping or use outside the body, of the embryo carried by the woman or of the gametes used to bring about the creation of the embryo, and a person is answerable under the section to the child in respect of the act or omission, the child's disabilities are to be regarded as damage resulting from the wrongful act of that person. A person is answerable under section 1A if he was, or would if sued in due time have been, liable in tort to one or both of the parents, and it is no answer that the parent suffered no actionable injury.[69]

2–081   The fact that a duty to the child depends upon a duty owed to the parent may create difficulties, however, in some circumstances. Where, for example, there is a conflict between the interests of the mother and those of the child during labour a doctor will owe a duty to the mother to exercise reasonable care for her health and safety. It is irrelevant that what has to be done in the mother's interests involves a risk of harm to the child, since if the doctor has exercised reasonable care there is no tort against the mother (whether damage is caused or not), and so the child can have no claim under the Act.[70] This would also be the position where the mother refused to accept recommended treatment, a Caesarian section for example, since she is entitled to refuse to give her consent to any treatment and the doctor commits no tort by accepting her decision. Indeed, there is no legal mechanism by which the mother's rights could be overridden, and the doctor who attempted to do so

---

(n.67 contd.) A duty owed to the foetus would interfere drastically with the mother's freedom of action when pregnant, not least in respect of medical treatment that she might need but which was also potentially harmful to the foetus. The assumption must also be that, at common law, the mother would not owe a duty of care to the foetus. See further *Dobson v Dobson* (1999) 174 D.L.R. (4th) 1 where the Supreme Court of Canada held that at common law no duty of care was owed by the mother to a foetus injured in a road traffic accident, on grounds of policy; McInnes (2000) 116 L.Q.R. 26. It follows that a defendant sued in respect of damage to the child cannot seek contribution from the mother in respect of her alleged prenatal negligence which may have contributed to the child's damage: *Preston v Chow* (2002) 211 D.L.R. (4th) 758 (Man. C.A.).

[68] *ibid.*, s. 1(3).
[69] For discussion of some of the difficulties that may arise under this section see Lee and Morgan, *Human Fertilisation & Embryology*, 2000, pp. 258–260.
[70] See Eekelaar and Dingwall [1984] J.S.W.L. 258.

would commit the tort of battery.[71] Even where there is no conflict of interest between mother and child there may be circumstances where there is no
breach of a duty owed to the mother, but there has been negligence with
respect to the child.[72]

The derivative nature of the duty is also apparent from the defences avail-   **2–082**
able. The child is bound by a contractual exclusion or limitation clause that
would have applied to the parents' action.[73] Damages may be reduced to take
account of the parent's share of the responsibility for the child being born disabled.[74] Finally, where the disability is the result of an occurrence preceding
the time of conception which affects the parents' ability to have a normal,
healthy child, the defendant is not responsible to the child if either or both of
the parents knew of the risk of disability, except that if the child's father is the
defendant and he knew of the risk but the mother did not he will be answerable to the child.[75] Under this provision the parents' knowledge apparently
defeats the child's claim even where objectively it would be reasonable for
them to attempt to have a normal, healthy child (*e.g.* if the defendant's negligence has created a one per cent chance of them producing a disabled child).

Wrongful life

The Act applies only to children born alive, the claim effectively crystalis-   **2–083**
ing at birth. If the defendant's negligence causes the death of the foetus *in utero*
there can be no claim by the child, though either or both parents may have an
action in appropriate circumstances.[76] Moreover, the action is limited to

---

[71] There is no power to make a foetus a ward of court: *Re F. (in utero)* [1988] Fam. 122. See
    also *St. George's Healthcare NHS Trust v S* [1999] Fam. 26, para. 6–102.

[72] Cane (1977) 51 A.L.J. 704, 708 gives an example of a drug manufacturer who warns the
    mother of adverse side-effects which might cause her injury but negligently fails to warn
    about potential harm to the foetus. If the mother takes the drug and suffers no injury, but the
    child is injured, the child has no claim under the Act because, although the manufacturer owes
    a duty to the mother, there is no breach of duty against her (because a warning may discharge
    the manufacturer's duty: see paras 8–034 *et seq.*). As Cane comments, this is "unfortunate."

[73] Congenital Disabilities (Civil Liability) Act 1976, s. 1(6). However, a contractual exclusion
    clause which sought to exclude liability for death or personal injury caused by negligence
    would be ineffective: Unfair Contract Terms Act 1977, s. 2(1).

[74] *ibid.*, s. 1(7); except where the mother causes the damage in the course of driving a motor
    vehicle: s. 2. If a woman discovers during the course of the pregnancy that the child is likely
    to be born disabled it is not unreasonable for her to refuse to undergo an abortion: *Emeh v
    Kensington and Chelsea and Westminster Area Health Authority* [1985] Q.B. 1012;
    McFarlane v Tayside Health Board [2000] 2 A.C. 59, 74, 81, 104, 113. Moreover, the
    mother's decision to decline an abortion does not contribute to the child's disabilities; rather
    it results in the birth of the child. This is not a ground for saying that the mother "shares
    responsibility" for the child's disabilities.

[75] *ibid.*, s. 1(4). A specific version of this defence applies to actions arising out of errors in the
    course of assisted conception. By s. 1A(3) a defendant is not answerable to the child if at the
    time the embryo, or the sperm and eggs, are placed in the woman, or at the time of her
    insemination, either or both parents knew the risk of their child being born disabled, *i.e.*, the
    particular risk created by the act or omission. See further Lee and Morgan, *Human
    Fertilisation & Embryology*, 2000, at p. 259. The other defences in the Act apply to actions
    under s. 1A: s. 1A(4).

[76] See, *e.g.*, *Kralj v McGrath* [1986] 1 All E.R. 54; *Bagley v North Hertfordshire Health
    Authority* (1986) 136 N.L.J. 1014 where damages were awarded to a mother in respect of

"disabilities which would not otherwise have been present." This wording was intended to exclude so-called "wrongful life" actions in which a child who is born with non-tortiously inflicted disabilities claims that, due to the defendant's negligence in failing to diagnose that the child was likely to be born disabled, the child has been permitted to be born in circumstances where, had the true position been known, the parent(s) would not have had the child either because the mother would have undergone a termination of pregnancy or the child would not have been conceived (hence "wrongful entry into life").

2–084   This issue arose for resolution under the common law in *McKay v Essex Area Health Authority*.[77] Tests conducted on a pregnant woman failed to disclose that she had contracted rubella, and her child was born severely disabled. The Court of Appeal held that a doctor did not owe a duty of care *to the child* to advise the mother of the serious consequences for the child of exposure to rubella and of the desirability of an abortion, although such a duty was owed to the mother.[78] The child's action claimed a right to be aborted (effectively a right not to enter the world with disabilities), and this was contrary to public policy as a violation of the sanctity of human life. This view overstates the nature of the child's claim somewhat, since the doctor could not compel a pregnant woman to have an abortion. At its highest, the child's claim is that through the defendant's negligence the mother has been deprived of the opportunity to make a choice on the child's behalf as to whether it would be in the child's interests either to be born with disabilities or not to be born at all (a point apparently accepted by Griffiths L.J.). This is an interest which is implicitly recognised by the Abortion Act 1967 itself, which permits abortion where there is a substantial risk that the child would have disabilities which would cause it to be seriously handicapped.[79] Moreover, Stephenson L.J. did concede that there might be some "extreme cases" where it could be said that it would be better for the child not to be born.[80] Thus, this policy argument against wrongful life actions is by no means clear-cut.

(n.76 contd.) a stillborn child, although Simon Brown J. held that there can be no claim for damages for bereavement under the Fatal Accidents Act 1976, s. 1A(2), which provides a fixed statutory sum for the parents of an unmarried minor child (a foetus cannot be said to be a "minor child" since it only attains the status of a legal person at birth, not before: *C v S* [1987] 1 All E.R. 1230, 1234, *per* Heilbron J.); *cf. Kerby v Redbridge Health Authority* [1993] 4 Med. L.R. 178; [1994] P.I.Q.R. Q1, where Ognall J. held that there should be no award for the "dashed hopes" of bringing a pregnancy to a successful conclusion, because this was either the same as bereavement, or an award for grief, sorrow or distress attendant on the loss of a loved one, which is not actionable in negligence. See further *McWilliams v Lord Advocate*, 1992 S.L.T. 1045, where the parents of a child that died shortly after birth as a result of the alleged negligence of the defendant were held entitled to maintain a claim for loss of society under the Damages (Scotland) Act 1976, despite the fact that the injuries to the child occurred before he was born, and therefore at a time when he was not a "person" in law. On claims by parents arising out of *in vitro* fertilisation see Hill (1985) 25 Med. Sci. and Law 270.
[77] [1982] Q.B. 1166. The child was born before the Act came into force.
[78] See also *Arndt v Smith* (1997) 148 D.L.R. (4th) 48 (S.C.C.); *B. v P.* (1991) 2 A.V.M.A. *Medical & Legal Journal* (No. 3) p. 8, and *Boon v Hanratty* (1992) 3 A.V.M.A. *Medical & Legal Journal* (No. 4) p. 12, on the duty owed to the mother.
[79] Abortion Act 1967, s. 1(1)(*d*), as amended. This point was acknowledged by Stephenson L.J. in *McKay* at 1179–1180.
[80] His Lordship cited the example of *Croke v Wiseman* [1981] 3 All E.R. 852; see also *Re B. (a minor)(wardship: medical treatment)* [1981] 1 W.L.R. 1421, 1424 where Templeman L.J.

The Court of Appeal also took the view that if the child's action were to be allowed the court would have to engage in the impossible task of assessing damages by comparing the value of non-existence (of which the court has no knowledge) with the value of existence in a disabled state, although it could be said in reply that the courts do not find any particular difficulty in assessing many other imponderable forms of loss. Finally, it was suggested, that allowing the wrongful life action might lead to claims by children born handicapped against their mothers for not having an abortion, an argument which would seem to have more force, although, again, this objection is not insuperable since such claims could be barred on policy grounds.[81] Paradoxically, it was accepted in *McKay* that a doctor would owe a duty of care to the mother in these circumstances to advise her of her right to an abortion under the Abortion Act.[82] Thus, an action on behalf of the parents may provide some redress for families in this situation.[83] 2–085

The Congenital Disabilities (Civil Liability) Act 1976 replaces the common law for births after its commencement, but curiously only in respect of a defendant's potential liability for causing the child's disabilities.[84] Accordingly, although it is not possible to bring a wrongful life action under section 1 of the Act, it is arguable that the legislation did not remove the possibility of bringing an action at common law. Such a claim is not an action in "respect of disabilities with which it might be born," but rather a claim not to have been born at all, which theoretically could be brought by a healthy child. The Court of Appeal in *McKay*, however, took the view that the Act did prevent *all* wrongful life claims for births after its commencement. With respect, this seems to misread the legislation, particularly section 4(5). Of course, even if such an action is not precluded by the Act, a common law claim would have to overturn the decision in *McKay*.[85] Even more 2–086

(n.80 contd.) said that the court, in exercising its wardship jurisdiction, might refuse to authorise life saving medical treatment where the child's life would be demonstrably awful, an exercise that involves weighing the quality of the child's potential life; *Re J. (a minor) (wardship: medical treatment)* [1990] 3 All E.R. 930. For a similar Canadian case see *Re Superintendent of Family & Child Service and Dawson* (1983) 145 D.L.R. (3d) 610.

[81] See the *Royal Commission on Civil Liability and Compensation for Personal Injury*, Cmnd. 7054 (1978), Vol. I, para. 1465; Whitfield (1993) 1 Med. L. Rev. 28, 49–52. See also Teff (1985) 34 I.C.L.Q. 423; Morris and Saintier (2003) 11 Med. L. Rev. 167; Grainger (1994) 2 Tort L. Rev. 164; and Symmons (1987) 50 M.L.R. 269 for discussion of the policy factors raised by "wrongful life" and "wrongful birth" actions.

[82] This assumes that she would be entitled to an abortion under the legislation. If not, the claim against the doctor will fail on the grounds of causation and public policy: see *Rance v Mid-Downs Health Authority* [1991] 1 Q.B. 587. Note, however, that there is now no time limit under the Abortion Act 1967 where there is a substantial risk that the child would be seriously handicapped. The mother would also have to prove that had she been given an appropriate warning she would have had a termination of the pregnancy, otherwise the claim will fail on causation: *Arndt v Smith* (1997) 148 D.L.R. (4th) 48 (S.C.C.).

[83] See paras 2–038 *et seq*. See Robertson (1982) 45 M.L.R. 697; Morris and Saintier (2003) 11 Med. L. Rev. 167.

[84] "... in respect of any such birth it replaces any law in force before its passing, whereby a person could be liable to a child in respect of disabilities with which it might be born ...": Congenital Disabilities (Civil Liability) Act 1976, s. 4(5). The Act came into force on July 22, 1976.

[85] See Fortin [1987] J.S.W.L. 306 and Slade (1982) 132 N.L.J. 874 for the arguments; *cf.* Law Com. No. 60, Cmnd. 5709, 1974.

curious is the provision in section 1A which was inserted to deal with the problem of negligence in the course of fertility treatment involving assisted conception. Liability can arise where the child's disability results from an act or omission in the course of the selection, or the keeping or use outside the body, of the embryo carried by the woman or of the gametes used to bring about the creation of the embryo. It is arguable that negligent *selection* of an embryo for implantation or of the gametes (*e.g.* negligent screening of a sperm donor for HIV[86]) gives rise to a wrongful life claim, since the child's argument is that had the defendant chosen the embryo carefully or properly screened the gametes its existence would not have been brought about, because a different embryo would have been implanted or different sperm would have been used, with the result that this *particular* child would not have been created. This inconsistency in the policy of the Act appears to have gone unnoticed by Parliament.

2–087   Section 1(2)(*a*) of the Act provides that an "occurrence" includes one which "affected either parent of the child in his or her ability to have a normal healthy child," which allows for the possibility of an action by the child in respect of pre-conception negligence. This appears to recognise a form of legal interest in not being conceived.[87] However, this would probably be limited to claims arising from physical harm to one or both of the parents.[88] Negligent genetic counselling, for example, in which parents are wrongly advised that it is safe for them to conceive, because the risk of bearing a child with a genetic disability is minimal, would normally give rise to a wrongful life claim by the child since if the correct advice had been given (and acted upon) the result would have been that the parents would not have conceived, *i.e.* the child would not have been born at all. The correct advice would not have resulted in the child being born without disabilities. Where the negligence concerns not simply the question of whether to conceive or not but the precautions required to conceive a healthy child, the position is more complicated. If precautions would have prevented damage *to that child*

---

[86] *ter Neuzen v Korn* (1993) 103 D.L.R. (4th) 473 (B.C.C.A.); affirmed (1995) 127 D.L.R. (4th) 577 (S.C.C.) involved a claim by the mother in respect of infection with HIV from contaminated sperm; see para. 4–087.

[87] See Pace (1977) 40 M.L.R. 141, 153. See also Whitfield (1993) 1 Med. L. Rev. 28, 42–49.

[88] Examples of this type of injury would include exposure of the mother or father to radiation causing gene mutations; a congenital disease, such as syphilis, caused by a blood transfusion negligently given to the mother before conception or the negligent failure to diagnose syphilis in the mother prior to conception: *X. and Y. v Pal* (1991) 23 N.S.W.L.R. 26; [1992] 3 Med. L.R. 195 (N.S.W.C.A.); or the supply of contaminated sperm for artificial insemination: see Law Com. No. 64, Cmnd. 5709, 1974, para. 77. Brazier, *Medicine, Patients and the Law*, 2nd ed., 1992, p. 243 cites the example of mismanagement of a previous pregnancy with the result that Rhesus incompatibility goes undiscovered and untreated, causing damage to a subsequent foetus. In *Roberts v Johnstone* [1989] Q.B. 878 a mother who was Rhesus negative was given a Rhesus positive blood transfusion, and this created a real risk that any subsequent child would suffer from haemolytic disease without appropriate treatment during pregnancy, which was not given. The defendants, who were aware of these facts throughout, admitted liability; see also *Fairhurst v St. Helens and Knowsley Health Authority* [1994] 5 Med. L.R. 422; *Bagley v North Hertfordshire Health Authority* (1986) 136 N.L.J. 1014; and *Scrimshaw v Harrow Health Authority* (1992) 3 A.V.M.A. Medical & Legal Journal (No. 3) p. 15 on Rhesus incompatibility.

then there could be a claim under the Act, but if the precautions (such as recommending an amniocentesis test) would simply have revealed that the
foetus had an abnormality and the mother would have had an abortion, the
child has no claim because this is a wrongful life claim.[89] There is, of course,
no reason why a parent should not have an action in respect of negligent
genetic counselling, with the damages reflecting the additional cost of raising
a handicapped child over and above the cost of raising a healthy child, or if
an abortion is carried out damages for the disappointment of being unable
to complete the pregnancy, and pain and suffering.[90]

Probably the most difficult aspect of bringing an action under the   **2–088**
Congenital Disabilities (Civil Liability) Act 1976 is the problem of proving
causation. The Pearson Commission, for example, considered that only a
"minute proportion" of children born with congenital defects would succeed
in proving both negligence and causation.[91]

(d) Infectious disease

Where a doctor has negligently permitted a person to come into contact   **2–089**
with a contagious disease there should be no difficulty in establishing a duty
of care, whether that person was the doctor's patient or not. In *Lindsey
County Council v Marshall*[92] the House of Lords held the defendants liable
for negligently failing to warn the claimant of the risk of infection by puerperal fever when she was admitted to their maternity home, following a
recent outbreak of the disease. Similarly, if a doctor negligently discharged
an infectious patient from hospital and, as a result, a third party contracted
the disease, the doctor would probably owe a duty of care to the third party.[93]

---

[89] See Brazier, *Medicine, Patients and the Law*, 2nd ed., 1992, p. 249, who points out that
realistic examples of the former circumstance are difficult to identify.

[90] See *Anderson v Forth Valley Health Board* 1998 S.L.T. 588; (1997) 44 B.M.L.R. 108 (Court of
Session, Outer House). See paras 2–038 *et seq.* for discussion of the nature of the doctors' duty
of care to the parents; and paras 9–079 *et seq.* for consideration of the assessment of damages.

[91] *Royal Commission on Civil Liability and Compensation for Personal Injury*, Cmnd. 7054
(1978), Vol. I, para. 1452, and Annexes 12 and 13; Law Com. No. 60, Cmnd. 5709 (1974),
para. 28. See, *e.g.*, *Reay v British Nuclear Fuels plc* [1994] 5 Med. L.R. 1; [1994] P.I.Q.R.
P171, where the claimants were unable to prove that paternal pre-conception irradiation of
the gonads had caused the claimants' cancer; *X. and Y. v Pal* (1991) 23 N.S.W.L.R. 26;
[1992] 3 Med. L.R. 195 (N.S.W.C.A.), in which the claimant was unable to prove that negligent exposure to congenital syphilis in the womb caused dysmorphia and brain damage;
De Martell v Merton and Sutton Health Authority [1995] 6 Med. L.R. 234, QBD, where
the claimant was unable to prove that negligent mismanagement of his birth was probably
the cause of his disabilities.

[92] [1937] A.C. 97; *Heafield v Crane, The Times*, July 31, 1937. See also *McDaniel v Vancouver
General Hospital* (1934) 152 L.T. 56, where the claimant was a patient being treated for
diphtheria in the defendant hospital, and contracted smallpox by cross-infection from other
patients. The hospital was held not liable because, having conformed to accepted practice,
there was no negligence.

[93] See *Evans v Liverpool Corporation* [1906] 1 K.B. 160, where on essentially similar facts a
claim against the hospital authority failed on the ground that, as the law then stood, the
defendants were not vicariously liable for the acts of the physician. In the United States this
form of liability is commonplace: *Hofmann v Blackmon* 241 So. 2d 752 (1970), where there
was a failure to diagnose tuberculosis in the father and the doctor was held liable to the

In *X. and Y. v Pal*[94] the example was given of a doctor who negligently failed to diagnose a child's illness as German measles (rubella) so that the child attending school passed on the infection to another child whose mother was pregnant, with the result that she gave birth to a child suffering from disabilities as a result of exposure to the rubella *in utero*. Could the disabled child sue the doctor? Without purporting to answer this question Clarke J.A. commented that:

> "Given the undemanding nature of the test of foreseeability it may well be that that chain of events was foreseeable. On the other hand it is clear that there was no element of reliance by either the pregnant mother or her child on the doctor and it would be difficult to suppose that he would have had such persons in contemplation when tending his own patient."[95]

With respect, the question of reliance is not the issue here. Clearly, the child cannot in any meaningful sense have "relied" on anything. The question whether a doctor should be liable to a pregnant *patient* in respect of the failure to diagnose rubella with the result that her child suffers disabilities does not depend upon whether the patient *relied* upon the doctor. Of course, all patients rely in some sense on their doctors to act with reasonable care, just as all road users "rely" in some sense on other motorists to drive carefully, and it might be said that the public "rely" on doctors and hospitals not negligently to permit dangerously infectious people unwittingly to spread disease. But this is not the basis for imposing liability in negligence where that negligence has resulted in physical damage to the claimant. Liability derives from the fact that the defendant has undertaken to perform the act (of driving, or diagnosis) and comes under a corresponding duty to exercise reasonable care, imposed by law.[96] The issue that Clarke J.A.'s example identifies is how extensively the scope of any duty of care owed by the doctor should be drawn. Foreseeability cannot place sensible limits on the potential claims that could arise from the spread of disease by infectious patients. Indeed, the existence of the reporting provisions of the Public Health (Control of Disease) Act 1984[97] makes the foreseeability issue virtually a foregone conclusion in respect of certain diseases. The issue is one of the "proximity" of the relationship between the defendant and the claimant, an

---

[n.93 contd.] daughter infected by the patient; *Fosgate v Corona* 330 A. 2d 355 (1974), where there was liability for the discharge of infectious tuberculosis patients without warnings to persons identifiable as at risk (*i.e.* relatives). See also *Bradshaw v Daniel*, 854 S.W. 2d 865 (1993) where a doctor was held liable for negligently failing to warn the spouse of a patient who had died from Rocky Mountain Spotted Fever of the risk of contracting the disease, despite the fact that it is not a contagious disease, because it tends to occur in clusters arising from infected ticks which transmit the disease to people.
[94] (1991) 23 N.S.W.L.R. 26; [1992] 3 Med. L.R. 195 (N.S.W.C.A.).
[95] *ibid.* at 43.
[96] See para. 2–024.
[97] Public Health (Control of Disease) Act 1984, s. 10; Public Health (Infectious Diseases) Regulations (S.I. 1988 No. 1546).

admittedly artificial device[98] by which the courts, as a matter of judicial policy, exclude from the ambit of compensation claims which do not satisfy the required degree of "directness" or "closeness" of relationship.[99] Possibly claims of this nature would be limited to relatives or close friends who are more foreseeably at risk of contracting an infection.

By analogy it is arguable that a doctor, such as a general practitioner, might be under a duty of care to warn the sexual partner(s) of a patient who has AIDS or who is diagnosed as HIV positive about the patient's condition and the potential risk to their health, if the patient refused to consent to the disclosure. If the sexual partner was also the doctor's patient there would probably be little difficulty in finding a duty of care, since a "duty to inform" could be seen as part and parcel of the doctor's more general duty to exercise reasonable care to safeguard the health of his patient. It would be somewhat arbitrary, however, if the doctor's liability in this situation turned upon whether the sexual partner happened also to be one of his patients. Arguably the duty would arise irrespective of the sexual partner's status, on the basis that serious physical harm was foreseeable as a real risk.[1] In *Pittman Estate v Bain*[2] a general practitioner was held liable in negligence to the wife of a patient who had contracted HIV from a blood transfusion. The doctor was negligent in failing to inform the patient of his HIV status with the result that the patient did not take any precautions to protect his wife from infection with the virus through sexual intercourse. The question of whether there was an independent duty upon the doctor to inform the patient's wife of the risk to her did not arise, since it was found as a question of fact that had the general practitioner informed the patient, the patient would certainly have informed his wife and they would have taken appropriate precautions. Moreover, it was assumed that the doctor owed a duty of care in negligence

2–090

---

[98] In *Caparo Industries plc v Dickman* [1990] 2 A.C. 605, 633, 651 Lord Oliver said that "proximity" was simply a label which described the circumstances from which the courts conclude that a duty of care exists; see also *per* Lord Bridge and Lord Roskill at 618 and 628 respectively.

[99] The same issues arise in relation to whether a psychiatrist can be held liable for injuries inflicted on a third party by a psychiatric patient who is known to be dangerous: see para. 2–147.

[1] This view is not unproblematic, however, since disclosure would be a breach of the doctor's duty of confidence to the patient which would have to be justified by the public interest defence; see Jones (1990) 6 P.N. 16, 22, and para. 2–185; Casswell (1989) 68 Can. Bar Rev. 225. The GMC advises doctors that they may disclose information to a known sexual contact of a patient with HIV where they have reason to think that the patient has not informed that person, and cannot be persuaded to do so: *Serious Communicable Diseases*, October 1997, para. 22 (available at *www.gmc-uk.org/standards*); see para. 2–185, below. The National Health Service (Venereal Diseases) Regulations 1974 (S.I. 1974 No. 29) create a specific statutory duty of confidence with respect to venereal disease, which may apply to AIDS patients: *X. v Y.* [1988] 2 All E.R. 648, 656. AIDS is not a notifiable disease under the Public Health (Control of Disease) Act 1984, s. 10, but see the Public Health (Infectious Diseases) Regulations (S.I. 1988 No. 1546) which extend ss. 35, 37 and 38 (allowing for compulsory medical examination, removal to or detention in a hospital) to persons suffering from AIDS, though not persons diagnosed as infected with HIV. As to whether AIDS should be a notifiable disease see Keown (1989) 5 P.N. 121.

[2] (1994) 112 D.L.R. (4th) 257 (Ont. Ct., Gen. Div.), para. 4–040.

to the patient's wife, the only issues being whether the doctor had been negligent and whether the failure to inform the patient had caused any damage.

2–091   A claimant in this position will normally face considerable difficulty in proving causation, since it would have to be shown that the infection occurred after the time at which the doctor ought reasonably to have disclosed the risk, and, given the substantial interval between an individual becoming HIV positive and developing AIDS, it would be unlikely that the claimant could pinpoint the exact time of infection. In *Pittman Estate v Bain*,[3] however, the claimant did succeed in proving that the fact that she had contracted HIV from her husband was probably caused by the failure of her husband's doctor to warn her husband of his HIV status, because on the facts she probably contracted the infection in the last year of his life.

2–092   There may well be other circumstances in which it is foreseeable that a patient could be a potential hazard to third parties where a doctor would be held to owe a duty of care. If, for example, a patient's medical condition (such as epilepsy) or the side-effects of a drug that the doctor has prescribed render certain conduct (such as driving a motor vehicle) hazardous, the doctor will be under a duty to warn the patient. If he fails to do so and as a result the patient causes an accident injuring others there could be little doubt that the doctor would owe a duty of care, both to the patient and the third parties.[4] In *Spillane v Wasserman*[5] the defendant W suffered an epileptic seizure while driving a heavy goods vehicle, passed through a red light, and killed a cyclist. W had a long history of epileptic seizures and should not have been driving at the time of the accident. He frequently neglected to take the medication prescribed for his condition and misrepresented his medical condition when renewing his driver's licence. Two doctors had been involved in treating W's epilepsy for years, but had failed to conduct periodic tests to monitor and control patient compliance with the medication regime. These tests would have revealed W's lax attitude to taking the medication. Neither doctor had warned W not to drive commercial vehicles, or not to drive at all except in specified circumstances, as the Canadian Medical Association's Guide required them to do. Neither doctor reported W's condition to the Registrar of Motor Vehicles as required by legislation. The doctors were held liable in negligence to the deceased's estate, being found 40 per cent responsible, with W being 60 per cent responsible.

---

[3] *ibid.*

[4] See Giesen, *International Medical Malpractice Law*, 1988, para. 255; *Freese v Lemmon*, 210 N.W. 2d 576 (S.C. of Iowa) (1973). See also the GMC guidance to doctors in *Confidentiality: Protecting and Providing Information*, June 2000 [at *www.gmc-uk.org*] Appendix 2, "Disclosure of information about patients to the Driver and Vehicle Licensing Agency (DVLA)" which states that if a patient is medically unfit to drive the doctor should make this clear to the patient and advise the patient that he or she has a legal duty to inform DVLA about the condition; and that where the doctor has evidence that a patient is continuing to drive contrary to advice, he should disclose relevant medical information immediately, in confidence, to the medical adviser at the DVLA.

[5] (1992) 13 C.C.L.T. (2d) 267 (Ont. H.C.).

(e) The duty owed to rescuers

As a general rule a person is not obliged to undertake a rescue, but the   2–093
courts are likely to be favourably disposed to a claimant who does attempt
to rescue someone endangered by the defendant's negligence and who is
injured in the process.[6] Thus, a duty of care is owed to a person who is foreseeably likely to intervene to assist a person put in danger by the defendant,
provided the rescuer did not act with wanton disregard for his own safety.
Foreseeability of the particular emergency that arose is unnecessary, provided some emergency is foreseeable,[7] or, alternatively, provided the emergency is of the same "kind or class" as that which is foreseeable.[8]

The circumstances in which this principle can be applied in the context of   2–094
medical negligence will probably be rare. The issue did arise, however, in the
Canadian case of *Urbanski v Patel*.[9] The defendant removed an ectopic
kidney from his patient during the course of a sterilisation operation, mistakenly believing it to be an ovarian cyst. It was then discovered that the
patient had only one kidney, and the effect of removing it was much more
serious than would have been the case had she had the normal complement
of two. Her father, Mr Urbanski, donated one of his kidneys for transplant
("as what father would not?" remarked the trial judge, Wilson J.) in what
turned out to be an unsuccessful attempt to alleviate his daughter's condition. In an action by the father for the expenses of and the pain and suffering involved in the operation the doctor was held liable by analogy to the
rescue principle. An argument that the donation was unforeseeable was
rejected, as was the suggestion that the claimant's conduct was voluntary and
intentional, and so broke the chain of causation.[10]

It is probable that an English court would follow the approach adopted in   2–095
Urbanski v Patel, although it may be that claims would be limited to donations
by close family members who are clearly more foreseeable as potential donors,
and who would feel a greater sense of moral obligation to the patient.[11] This

---

[6] "Danger invites rescue. The cry of distress is the summons to relief. The law does not ignore
these reactions of the mind in tracing conduct to its consequences. It recognises them as
normal. It places their effects within the range of the natural and probable. The wrong that
imperils life is a wrong to the imperilled victim; it is a wrong also to his rescuer . . . The risk
of rescue, if only it be not wanton, is born of the occasion. The emergency begets the man.
The wrongdoer may not have foreseen the coming of a deliverer. He is accountable as if he
had," *per* Cardozo J. in *Wagner v International Railway Co*, 232 N.Y. 176, 180 (1921), cited
with approval by Willmer L.J. in *Baker v T.E. Hopkins & Son Ltd* [1959] 3 All E.R. 225,
241, and by Lord Wright in *Bourhill v Young* [1943] A.C. 92, 108–109.

[7] *Videan v British Transport Commission* [1963] 2 Q.B. 650, 669.

[8] *Knightley v Johns* [1982] 1 All E.R. 851, 860.

[9] (1978) 84 D.L.R. (3d) 650 (Manitoba Q.B.).

[10] This type of argument has been consistently rejected in rescue cases: see, *e.g.*, *Haynes v
Harwood* [1935] 1 K.B. 146; *Baker v T.E. Hopkins & Son Ltd* [1959] 3 All E.R. 225.

[11] See Spencer [1979] C.L.J. 45; Robertson (1980) 96 L.Q.R. 19. See also Giesen, *International
Medical Malpractice Law*, 1988, para. 1331, discussing a similar German case in which the
donor succeeded in an action against the doctor. Curiously, in the United States the courts
have denied claims by organ donors against the original tortfeasor: *Sirianni v Anna*, 285
N.Y.S. 2d 709 (1969); *Moore v Shah*, 458 N.Y.S. 2d 33 (1982); *Petersen v Farberman*, 736
S.W. 2d 441 (1987).

view is reinforced by section 2 of the Human Organ Transplants Act 1989, which prohibits the transplantation of an organ from a living donor who is not genetically related to the donee, except where authorised by regulations made by the Secretary of State.[12] Moreover, it is probably the element of moral compulsion that undermines the argument that the claimant was a volunteer or that the decision to donate broke the chain of causation. One issue that might have to be addressed is the possibility that if the first transplantation proved to be unsuccessful further donations could take place. Is the defendant liable to all the donors? Possibly there would come a point at which the damage would be regarded as too remote or the donation would be treated as a *novus actus interveniens*, but there is nothing in either principle or logic which would dictate this, since if the first donation is both a foreseeable and reasonable consequence of the defendant's negligence then subsequent donations merit the same categorisation.

(f) Psychiatric harm[13]

2–096   Claims in respect of "pure" psychiatric harm, that is psychiatric harm which is not linked to physical harm sustained by the claimant, have always been problematic and continue to arouse controversy. In theory different rules apply to cases involving claims by patients from those involving claims by third parties, but the distinctions between categories of claimants can become very blurred at the margins, and at times the general rules appear not to apply in the medical context. Therefore, in this section, the distinction between the duty of care owed to patients and the duty owed to third parties has not been followed. Rather, the exposition considers the courts' general approach (it would be misleading to call them "principles") to claims for "pure" psychiatric harm, and then attempts to put that general approach into the medical context (though some of the cases illustrating the general rules do involve cases of medical negligence).

Psychiatric illness not emotional distress

2–097   There can be no claim for emotional distress, anguish or grief unless this leads to a positive psychiatric illness (such as an anxiety neurosis or reactive

---

[12] See the Human Organ Transplants (Unrelated Persons) Regulations 1989 (S.I. 1989 No. 2480); para. 6–186.
[13] "Nervous shock" was the term that was used in the past by lawyers to describe a medically recognised psychiatric illness, although it has been described as a "misleading and inaccurate expression," *per* Bingham L.J. in *Attia v British Gas* [1988] Q.B. 304, 317. Although in some cases the courts still require a "shocking" event as one of the criteria to establish liability, it is better to refer to the resulting injury as psychiatric harm or psychiatric damage. "Psychiatric damage" encompasses "all relevant forms of mental illness, neurosis and personality change": *ibid.* On post-traumatic stress disorder see Weller (1993) 143 N.L.J. 878; O'Brien [1994] J.P.I.L. 257; Turnbull [1997] J.P.I.L. 234; Lipsedge (1999) 5 Clinical Risk 155. See generally Mullany and Handford, *Tort Liability for Psychiatric Damage*, 1993, and Napier and Wheat, *Recovering Damages for Psychiatric Injury*, 2nd ed., OUP, 2002.

depression) or physical illness (such as a heart attack).[14] In *Vernon v Bosley (No. 1)*[15] the Court of Appeal held that where the claimant has developed a mental illness which has been contributed to partly by the defendant's negligence (the claimant witnessing the death of a loved one caused by the defendant's negligence) and partly by pathological grief attributable to the death itself, the claimant was entitled to damages for the mental illness, with no discount for the consequences of the grief and the consequences of bereavement, even though the mental illness was partly caused by the grief.[16] On the other hand, in *Calascione v Dixon*[17] the Court of Appeal did draw a distinction between post-traumatic stress disorder, which was held to be compensatable since it was attributable to the events the claimant had witnessed, and a pathological grief disorder which could not be causally linked to the immediate aftermath of the accident. In principle, if the courts are going to continue to distinguish between psychiatric harm attributable to the events witnessed by the claimant and psychiatric harm attributable to the consequences of those events (grief at the death of a loved one, which may become pathological grief—itself a recognised psychiatric condition) then the approach adopted in *Calascione v Dixon* would seem to be correct. Moreover, it is arguable that in the light of the Court of Appeal decision *Holtby v Brigham & Cowan (Hull) Ltd*,[18] where it is possible to identify the extent of the contribution made by the defendant's negligence to the claimant's psychiatric damage, then the defendant is only liable to that extent and no more.[19] This would suggest that unless the psychiatric harm was indivisible in *Vernon v Bosley (No. 1)* the outcome in that case was incorrect.

---

[14] *McLoughlin v O'Brian* [1983] 1 A.C. 410, 431, *per* Lord Bridge; *Alcock v Chief Constable of the South Yorkshire Police* [1992] 1 A.C. 310, 409, *per* Lord Oliver; *Hinz v Berry* [1970] 2 Q.B. 40, 42; *Tame v New South Wales*; *Annetts v Australian Stations Pty Ltd* [2002] H.C.A. 35; (2002) 191 A.L.R. 449 at [44] and [193] (High Court of Australia); *van Soest v Residual Health Management Unit* [2000] 1 N.Z.L.R. 179 (N.Z.C.A.); commented on by Mullany (2001) 117 L.Q.R. 182; Teff (2001) 9 Tort L. Rev. 109; Todd (2001) 17 P.N. 230. In *Reilly v Merseyside Regional Health Authority* [1995] 6 Med. L.R. 246 the Court of Appeal held that normal human emotions, together with their normal physical consequences, did not constitute either psychiatric illness or physical injury. If, however, the claimant's mental distress or grief exacerbates other injuries which the claimant sustained in the same incident, preventing the claimant from making a recovery as quickly as would otherwise have occurred, this can be reflected in the award of damages in respect of the other injuries. In *Kralj v McGrath* [1986] 1 All E.R. 54, 62, Woolf J. said: ". . . if the situation is one where the plaintiff's injuries have on her a more drastic effect than they would otherwise because of the grief which she is sustaining at the same time in relation to the death of a child who died in the circumstances in which Daniel died, that is something which the court can take into account." See also *Bagley v North Hertfordshire Health Authority* (1986) 136 N.L.J. 1014. *Kralj v McGrath* was approved by the Court of Appeal in *A.B. v South West Water Services Ltd* [1993] Q.B. 507. For criticism of the law's distinction between psychiatric disorder and "ordinary suffering" from a psychiatrist see Lipsedge (1999) 5 Clinical Risk 155.
[15] [1997] 1 All E.R. 577.
[16] Applying *Bonnington Castings Ltd v Wardlaw* [1956] A.C. 613, see para. 5–020.
[17] (1993) 19 B.M.L.R. 97.
[18] [2000] 3 All E.R. 421, see para. 5–042.
[19] See the discussion of this point in *Hatton v Sutherland* [2002] EWCA Civ 76; [2002] 2 All E.R. 1 at [36] to [41]; and *Rahman v Arearose Ltd* [2001] Q.B. 351.

Distinguish gradual onset of psychiatric harm from "sudden" events

2–098   A distinction is drawn between cases involving the gradual onset of psychiatric harm and psychiatric harm which flows from sudden, traumatic events. As will be seen, in the case of sudden traumatic events, claims based on the gradual onset of symptoms are specifically excluded. Where, however, there is an existing legal relationship between the claimant and defendant (which may be contractual or tortious) then it may be possible to claim in respect of the gradual onset of psychiatric harm. The typical example of this is the employer-employee relationship, where in appropriate circumstances it may be possible for an employee to claim in respect of psychological damage attributable to "occupational stress."[20] The existence of a duty of care in such cases is not problematic because it arises from the existing relationship between the parties, and the legal problems usually centre on breach of duty and causation. This type of claim has recently been extended to the solicitor-client relationship;[21] but it also explains why an action by a patient against a psychiatrist in respect of psychiatric harm negligently inflicted in the course of the psycho-therapeutic relationship does not raise an issue about the duty of care in respect of pure psychiatric damage.[22] Despite the existence of a relationship between the parties which would normally give rise to a duty of care, the courts have still attempted to apply some of the language and legal categories that are applied in the context of claims arising out of sudden events, particularly the so-called "primary" victim or "secondary" victim labels. This tends to confuse, rather than illuminate, the picture.

Sudden events

2–099   It is now well established, medically, that where individuals are exposed to the risk of injury or death, or witness injury to or the death of others, there is a real prospect that they may suffer a psychiatric reaction to the events, even though they have not sustained any physical harm. The issue that the courts have struggled with for over a century now is in what circumstances a defendant who has negligently brought about the events should be held responsible for that psychiatric harm. Scepticism about the nature of psychiatric damage and the danger of fraudulent claims led, initially, to a stark refusal to contemplate any claims for pure psychiatric harm. Then it was held that someone who had been put in fear of losing her own life as a result of the defendant's negligence was entitled to recover for psychiatric harm.[23] A quarter of a century later, the Court of Appeal extended the category of

---

[20] *Walker v Northumberland County Council* [1995] 1 All E.R. 737; *Hatton v Sutherland* [2002] EWCA Civ 76; [2002] 2 All E.R. 1; Teff (2002) 10 Tort L. Rev. 161.
[21] *McLoughlin v Jones* [2001] EWCA Civ 1743; [2002] Q.B. 1312—solicitors liable for psychiatric illness suffered by their client who was wrongly convicted of an offence and sent to prison as a result of their negligent failure to investigate the case.
[22] *Landau v Werner* (1961) 105 S.J. 257, and 1008, CA.
[23] *Dulieu v White & Sons* [1901] 2 K.B. 669.

claimants to those who had not been personally endangered, but had witnessed the events themselves.[24] There was no need for any direct impact to the claimant or fear of immediate personal injury to the claimant.

The potential for opening up liability to a wide range of claimants who happened to witness the events caused by the defendant's negligence led the courts to impose a number of specific requirements, particularly in those cases arising out of witnessing harm to others. Thus, the nature of the relationship between the accident victim and the person who suffered the psychiatric harm was important. A parent or spouse of a victim would more readily be accepted as a person likely to be affected, and accordingly within the range of a duty of care owed by the defendant. A bystander who was a total stranger to the accident victim was treated as an unforeseeable claimant.[25] At one time, a claimant who came to the rescue at an accident was given more favourable consideration than a mere bystander if he subsequently sustained psychiatric harm as a result of what he had witnessed,[26] but this rule has been tightened up and rescuers are no longer treated as belonging to a special category of claimant.[27] A further restriction was that the psychiatric harm must be the product of what the claimant perceived with his own unaided senses. There was no claim in respect of psychiatric harm sustained as a result of what the claimant was told by others.[28] The effect was to limit actions to claimants who were in fairly close physical proximity to the accident, although it was not essential that they had seen the accident itself.[29]

2–100

In *McLoughlin v O'Brian*[30] the House of Lords came close to establishing a principle of liability for psychiatric harm based on foreseeability of psychiatric harm, without formal exclusionary criteria. The claimant's husband and her three children were involved in a road accident caused by the defendant's negligence. One child was killed and her husband and other two children were badly injured. The claimant was informed about the accident two hours after the event, and she was taken to the hospital where she was told about the death of her child and saw the injuries to her family in distressing circumstances. The House of Lords was unanimous in holding that the claimant's action should succeed. Lords Bridge and Scarman preferred a test based upon foreseeability alone, "untrammelled by spatial, physical or temporal limits," which would be largely arbitrary in their application. But Lords Wilberforce and Edmund-Davies considered that foreseeability of psychiatric harm was not the sole requirement. There must be some additional limits based on: (i) the class of person who could sue — the closer the

2–101

---

[24] *Hambrook v Stokes Bros* [1925] 1 K.B. 141.
[25] *Bourhill v Young* [1943] A.C. 92.
[26] *Chadwick v British Railways Board* [1967] 1 W.L.R. 912; *Wigg v British Railways Board* (1986) 136 N.L.J. 446.
[27] *White v Chief Constable of the South Yorkshire Police* [1999] 2 A.C. 455.
[28] *Hambrook v Stokes Bros* [1925] 1 K.B. 141; *cf. Schneider v Eisovitch* [1960] 2 Q.B. 430.
[29] *Boardman v Sanderson* [1964] 1 W.L.R. 1317, where the claimant heard the accident and saw the aftermath; *Chadwick v British Railways Board* [1967] 1 W.L.R. 912, where the claimant saw the aftermath of a major train crash; *Benson v Lee* [1972] V.R. 879.
[30] [1983] 1 A.C. 410; Teff (1983) 99 L.Q.R. 100. See also the very similar Irish case of *Kelly v Hennessy* [1995] 3 I.R. 253 (Supreme Court of Ireland).

emotional tie the greater the claim for consideration; (ii) physical proximity to the accident, which must be close both in time and space, though this could include persons who did not witness the accident but came upon the "aftermath" of events—persons who would normally come to the scene, such as a parent or spouse, would be within the scope of the duty; (iii) the means by which the psychiatric harm was caused—it must come through the claimant's own sight or hearing of the event or its immediate aftermath; communication by a third party would not be sufficient.

2–102   In *Alcock v Chief Constable of the South Yorkshire Police*[31] actions for psychiatric harm were brought against the police arising out of the Hillsborough stadium disaster in April 1989, when 95 people were killed and over 400 injured by crushing when too many people were allowed to crowd into a confined area of the football stadium. The events were shown in a live television broadcast, and some scenes were repeated in news broadcasts. The actions were brought by 16 people, some of whom were at the stadium but not in the area where the disaster occurred, and some of whom identified bodies at the mortuary. All the claimants were relatives, or in one case a fiancée, of people who were in the disaster area, but none were either a spouse or parent of the victims. The police admitted liability for negligence in respect of those who were killed and injured in the disaster, but denied that they owed a duty of care to the claimants. The House of Lords dismissed the claimants' actions. Psychiatric harm arising from the apprehension of physical injury or the risk of physical injury to another person was actionable only if the claimant satisfied *both* the test of reasonable foreseeability that he would be affected by psychiatric illness because of his close relationship of love and affection with the accident victim; *and* the test of proximity of relationship to the tortfeasor in terms of a physical and temporal connection between the claimant and the event (applying Lord Wilberforce's "aftermath test" in *McLoughlin v O'Brian*). Lord Oliver divided pure psychiatric damage cases into two broad categories: (i) cases in which the injured claimant was involved, either mediately or immediately, as a participant; and (ii) those in which the claimant was simply a passive and unwilling witness of injury caused to others.

"Primary" victims

2–103   Lord Oliver's first category has come to be known as "primary" victims and the second category as "secondary" victims. "Primary" victims, said his Lordship, included cases where the claimant was put in fear for her own safety[32] and the "rescue cases".[33] These were cases where the claimant was, to a greater or lesser degree, personally involved in the incident out of which the claim arose, either through the direct threat of bodily injury to the

---

[31] [1992] 1 A.C. 310. See Teff (1992) 12 O.J.L.S. 440; Nasir (1992) 55 M.L.R. 705; Davie (1992) 43 N.I.L.Q. 237; Hedley [1992] C.L.J. 16; Wheat [1994] J.P.I.L. 131 and 207.
[32] *Dulieu v White & Sons* [1901] 2 K.B. 669.
[33] Such as *Chadwick v British Railways Board* [1967] 1 W.L.R. 912.

claimant or in coming to the aid of others injured or threatened. In the same category were cases such as *Dooley v Cammell Laird & Co Ltd*[34] where it could be said that the negligent act of the defendant had put the claimant in the position of being, or thinking that he was about to be or had been, the involuntary cause of another's death or injury, and the psychiatric illness stemmed from the shock to the claimant of the consciousness of this supposed fact.[35] The fact that the defendant's negligence had foreseeably put the claimant in the position of being an unwilling participant in the event was sufficient to establish a proximate relationship between them. The principal question then was simply whether injury of that type to that claimant was reasonably foreseeable.

In *Page v Smith*,[36] by a majority, the House of Lords held that in the case of a "primary" victim if personal injury of some kind to the claimant was foreseeable the defendant was liable for psychiatric injury sustained as a result of the defendant's negligence. The defendant must take the claimant "as he finds him" with respect to any psychiatric damage which results, even if physical injury did not occur. On the facts, which involved a minor road traffic accident, since some form of physical injury was foreseeable (though none in fact occurred) it was irrelevant that the claimant's psychiatric damage was unforeseeable. This treats psychiatric injury as damage of the same type or kind as physical injury.[37]   2–104

Subsequently, in *White v Chief Constable of the South Yorkshire Police*[38] the House of Lords held that not only was an exposure to the risk of foreseeable physical injury a sufficient condition for a claimant to qualify as a "primary" victim, it was also a necessary condition. This means that a rescuer will not succeed for the psychiatric harm he suffers as a result of the scenes he has witnessed unless he was "fortuitously" exposed to a risk of physical harm, or he can satisfy the much more stringent requirements of a   2–105

[34] [1951] 1 Lloyd's Rep. 271; and *Wigg v British Railways Board, The Times*, February 4, 1986.
[35] The claimant's belief that he was responsible for the death of a work colleague has to be a reasonable belief; an irrational, though genuine, feeling of responsibility is not sufficient: *Hunter v British Coal Corp* [1998] 2 All E.R. 97, CA.
[36] [1996] A.C. 155.
[37] Thus Lord Lloyd commented, *ibid.* at 188 that: "In an age when medical knowledge is expanding fast, and psychiatric knowledge with it, it would not be sensible to commit the law to a distinction between physical and psychiatric injury, which may already seem somewhat artificial, and may soon be altogether outmoded. Nothing will be gained by treating them as different 'kinds' of personal injury, so as to require the application of a different test." See also the comments of Lord Browne-Wilkinson at 182–183. For discussion of *Page v Smith* see Sprince (1995) 11 P.N. 124; Trindade (1996) 112 L.Q.R. 22; Handford (1996) 4 Tort L. Rev. 5; Hopkins [1995] C.L.J. 491. Contrast *Tame v New South Wales; Annetts v Australian Stations Pty Ltd* [2002] H.C.A. 35; (2002) 191 A.L.R. 449 where the High Court of Australia held that liability for negligently caused psychiatric harm depends on reasonable foreseeability of psychiatric harm. Foreseeability of personal injury in general was not sufficient. Moreover, the test of what is reasonably foreseeable is ultimately for the court to determine, not expert psychiatric witnesses. For discussion of *Tame* see Trindade (2003) 119 L.Q.R. 204.
[38] [1999] 2 A.C. 455; [1999] 1 All E.R. 1. For discussion of *White* see Todd (1999) 115 L.Q.R. 345; Handford (1999) 7 Tort L. Rev. 126; Mullender and Speirs (2000) 20 O.J.L.S. 645.

"secondary" victim.[39] *White* also left a question mark over the status of cases such as *Dooley v Cammell Laird* where the claimant was not himself exposed to the risk of physical harm but, as a result of the defendant's negligence, thought that he had been the agency of harm to others and suffered psychiatric harm as result of that belief.[40] However, in *W v Essex County Council*[41] the House of Lords held that it was at least arguable that the parents of children abused by a boy placed with a foster family by the local authority might establish that they were "primary" victims, on the basis that they had suffered psychiatric damage as a consequence of feeling that they were indirectly responsible for their children's sexual abuse, having brought the boy into their home. The caselaw did not show conclusively that the parents would be unable to establish that they were "primary" victims. Lord Slynn said that: "the categorisation of those claiming to be included as primary or secondary victims is not as I read the cases finally closed. It is a concept still to be developed in different factual circumstances."[42]

2–106　　　Thus, a "primary" victim is someone who was in the zone of physical danger, and thereby exposed to the foreseeable risk of physical injury, or who reasonably believed that he had been exposed to such a risk,[43] or someone who, as a result of the defendant's negligence, reasonably believes that he has been the cause of injury to another. Claimants suing their employers in respect of occupational stress are also referred to as "primary" victims,[44] although these cases do not typically involve the exposure of the employee to a risk of physical harm.

2–107　　　The identification of a claimant as a "primary" or "secondary" victim has taken on enormous significance because of the different rules now applied to the two categories.[45] A claimant exposed to the risk of foreseeable physical

---

[39] For an illustration of the arbitrary consequences of this see the example of the two Mr. Chadwick's in Lord Goff's dissenting speech, *ibid.* at 487.

[40] Lord Hoffmann commented *ibid.* at 508 that: "there may be grounds for treating such a rare category of case as exceptional and exempt from the *Alcock* control mechanisms. I do not need to express a view . . ."

[41] [2001] 2 A.C. 592. See also *A and B v Essex County Council* [2002] EWHC 2707 (QB); [2003] 1 F.L.R. 615 where Buckley J. held that psychiatric harm to adoptive parents as a result of having a child with severe behavioural problems being placed with them for adoption was recoverable, the local authority having failed to inform the parents in advance about the child's behaviour.

[42] *ibid.* at 601.

[43] That belief must not be irrational: *McFarlane v E.E. Caledonia Ltd* [1994] 2 All E.R. 1 and *Hegarty v E.E. Caledonia Ltd* [1997] 2 Lloyd's Rep. 259.

[44] See *Hatton v Sutherland* [2002] EWCA Civ 76; [2002] 2 All E.R. 1.

[45] It seems likely that Lord Oliver in *Alcock* was merely identifying two descriptive categories of claimant which might help to explain some of the previous cases. The distinction between "primary" and "secondary" victims is not a *justification for* the present legal structure. A "primary" victim has suffered psychiatric illness *as a* consequence of what (s)he has witnessed/experienced, just as the relatives in *Alcock* suffered psychiatric illness as a result of what they had witnessed/experienced. The *mechanism* by which the psychiatric illness was caused is essentially the same in each case. The categorisation merely states a conclusion rather than a basis for the distinction. See Jones [1995] 4 Web J.C.L.I. (available at *http://webjcli.ncl.ac.uk/articles4/jones4.html*) where this argument is developed in more detail. For an extended discussion of why recovery for negligently inflicted psychiatric harm should be put on a more rational basis see Teff [1998] C.L.J. 91.

injury, unlike a "secondary" victim, does not have to prove that psychiatric harm was foreseeable.[46] Thus, the claimant does not have to demonstrate reasonable fortitude (that is that a person of reasonable fortitude would also have succumbed to psychiatric harm—a test designed to exclude claimants who are particularly susceptible to suffering psychiatric harm[47]). For a "primary" victim, the "question of what might be foreseen in a person of ordinary phlegm does not arise. The question of foreseeability must be considered in relation to this particular claimant, and what the defendants knew or ought to have known about him."[48] Moreover, the "primary" victim who is exposed to the risk of physical harm can recover for the resulting psychiatric damage, even if that damage was not produced by the fear of injury to himself, but rather was caused by witnessing the injuries of others.[49] In other words, the risk of physical injury is a "threshold test" for categorising such claimants as "primary" victims, it is not necessary as a *causal* mechanism.

For those claimants who can qualify as a "primary" victim in circumstances where physical injury to the claimant was not foreseeable, it must be demonstrated that the psychiatric damage was foreseeable, but, again, in assessing the foreseeability of the psychiatric reaction the claimant does not have to prove that he was a person of "reasonable fortitude". As a general rule, the question of what is foreseeable is normally assessed *ex post facto*, on the basis of what a hypothetical reasonable man would say it was proper to foresee.[50] This principle works in the case of an action where the claimant and defendant were strangers before the incident giving rise to the claim. Where, however, the parties are in a contractual relationship and the alleged breach of duty is a breach of a contractual term, or a breach of a duty of care arising out of the parties contractual relationship which gives rise to a concurrent claim in tort, the rule does not apply.[51] Most commonly this arises in actions by employees in respect occupational stress claims, but it is not limited to such claims as *McLoughlin v Jones* demonstrates. In such cases, in assessing the question of what is foreseeable, the court will take account of "all those features of [the claimant's] personal life and disposition of which the defendants were aware."[52] It is not yet clear whether this principle applies to those "primary" victims who fall into the category on the basis

2–108

---

[46] *Page v Smith* [1996] A.C. 155; *McLoughlin v Jones* [2001] EWCA Civ 1743; [2002] Q.B. 1312.
[47] *Bourhill v Young* [1943] A.C. 92, 110.
[48] *McLoughlin v Jones* [2001] EWCA Civ 1743 at [56] *per* Hale L.J.
[49] *White v Chief Constable of the South Yorkshire Police* [1999] 2 A.C. 455.
[50] *Bourhill v Young* [1943] A.C. 92, 110.
[51] *McLoughlin v Jones* [2001] EWCA Civ 1743; [2002] Q.B. 1312, at [26] *per* Brooke L.J.
[52] *ibid.* at [46]. Notwithstanding this more relaxed approach to the more vulnerable claimant, the foreseeability requirement (plus the need to prove the causal connection between the claimant's working conditions and the psychiatric harm) has usually resulted in claims by employees in respect of occupational stress failing: see *Hatton v Sutherland* [2002] EWCA Civ 76; [2002] 2 All E.R. 1; *Garrett v London Borough of Camden* [2001] EWCA Civ 395; *Petch v Customs and Excise Commissioners* [1993] I.C.R. 789, CA; *Fraser v State Hospitals Board for Scotland*, 2001 S.L.T. 1051. In the landmark decision of *Walker v Northumberland County Council* [1995] 1 All E.R. 737, the claimant succeeded on the basis of his *second*, and therefore entirely foreseeable, nervous breakdown.

that, as a result of the defendant's negligence, they believed that they were responsible for causing harm to another. The judgment as to what is foreseeable is a matter for the court, not expert psychiatrists, but this should be done on the basis of "informed judicial opinion."[53] In other words, judicial opinion must be "informed" by the expert evidence of psychiatrists.[54]

"Secondary" victims

2–109   The second category of case identified by Lord Oliver in *Alcock v Chief Constable of the South Yorkshire Police*[55] was where the psychiatric injury was attributable simply to witnessing the misfortune of another person in an event by which the claimant was not personally threatened or in which he was not directly involved as an actor. The claimant was a "mere witness" of the event. The potential number of claimants who could fall into this category of "secondary" victim is much larger than those who were in the zone of physical danger or were participants in the event, and therefore there are stricter limits on who can claim. Psychiatric harm to the claimant must be foreseeable, and when applying the test of foreseeability to "secondary" victims it has to be demonstrated that the claimant is a person of reasonable fortitude or "customary phlegm" and is not unduly susceptible to some form of psychiatric reaction.[56] This excludes persons who are abnormally sensitive to psychiatric harm. If, however, a person of ordinary fortitude would have sustained psychiatric harm in the circumstances, the claimant who was particularly sensitive can also recover;[57] and, moreover, he is entitled to damages for the full extent of his injuries, even if they are exacerbated by a predisposition to mental illness or disorder and thus are more severe than an ordinary individual would have experienced.[58] In other words, the "eggshell skull" rule applies to psychiatric damage in the same way as it applies to physical harm.[59]

2–110   In addition to foreseeability, in *Alcock* Lord Oliver identified four factors that had to be considered: (1) the nature of the relationship between the claimant and the accident victim; (2) the proximity of the claimant to the

---

[53] *McLoughlin v O'Brian* [1983] 1 A.C. 410, 432 *per* Lord Bridge.

[54] *Farrell v Avon Health Authority* [2001] Lloyd's Rep. Med. 458, 473 *per* Bursell J. In a case involving a "primary" victim where the parties' relationship stems from contract it is open to the court to accept evidence from expert witnesses "about the statistical incidence of the occasions when people who are not immediately identifiable as vulnerable personalities suffer psychiatric illness of different kinds as a result of being exposed to events comparable to those experienced by the claimant": *McLoughlin v Jones* [2001] EWCA Civ 1743 at [44] *per* Brooke L.J.

[55] [1992] 1 A.C. 310; [1991] 4 All E.R. 907.

[56] *Bourhill v Young* [1943] A.C. 92, 110; *McLoughlin v O'Brian* [1983] 1 A.C. 410, 429; *Tame v New South Wales*; *Annetts v Australian Stations Pty Ltd* [2002] H.C.A. 35; (2002) 191 A.L.R. 449 (High Court of Australia).

[57] *Jaensch v Coffey* (1984) 54 A.L.R 417.

[58] *Brice v Brown* [1984] 1 All E.R. 997; *Benson v Lee* [1972] V.R. 879; *Bechard v Haliburton* (1991) 84 D.L.R. (4th) 668; *Tame v New South Wales*; *Annetts v Australian Stations Pty Ltd* [2002] H.C.A. 35; (2002) 191 A.L.R. 449 at [117] and [279] *per* McHugh and Hayne JJ. respectively.

[59] See para. 5–109.

accident or its immediate aftermath; (3) the means by which the claimant perceived the events or received the information; (4) the manner in which the psychiatric illness was caused.

(i) The nature of the relationship between the claimant and the accident victim

There must be a close relationship between the accident victim and the clai-   2–111
mant. The class of persons to whom a duty could be owed was not limited by reference to a particular relationship, such as husband and wife or parent and child, but it must be within the defendant's contemplation as foreseeable. The crucial factor was the existence of a relationship between the accident victim and the claimant which involved close ties of love and affection, a tie that would have to be proved by the claimant. There was a rebuttable presumption that such ties would exist between spouses and in the parent-child relationship, though they could be present in other family relationships or those of close friendship, and may be stronger in the case of engaged couples than in that of persons who have been married to each other for many years.[60] Psychiatric injury to a bystander unconnected with the accident victim is not ordinarily reasonably foreseeable, although Lords Keith, Ackner and Oliver contemplated the possibility that a bystander who suffered psychiatric harm after witnessing a particularly horrific catastrophe close to him might be entitled to claim damages from the person whose negligence caused the catastrophe, if a reasonably strong-nerved person would have been so affected, but the circumstances in which this exception could apply would have to be extreme.[61]

(ii) The proximity of the claimant to the accident or its immediate aftermath

The claimant has to be in close physical proximity to the accident. In   2–112
McLoughlin v O'Brian the requirement that the claimant be at the scene of the accident was extended to the "immediate aftermath," which was held to

---

[60] [1992] 1 A.C. 310, 397, *per* Lord Keith. In *Attia v British Gas* [1988] Q.B. 304 the Court of Appeal held that where a claimant sustained psychiatric harm as a result of witnessing a fire which caused extensive damage to her home, the shock could not be regarded as unforeseeable *as a matter of law*, although there were no personal injuries to anyone else and the claimant had not been at risk of physical injury to herself. Rather it was a question of fact on the medical evidence whether psychiatric damage was reasonably foreseeable. The status of this decision is unclear after *Alcock*, since although it was cited in argument their Lordships did not refer to it in their speeches. Clearly, the claimant did not satisfy the "relationship" requirement of *Alcock*. The Court of Appeal in *Attia* treated the issue as a matter of remoteness of damage rather than duty of care, since the defendants undoubtedly owed the claimant a duty of care not to inflict physical damage to her house.

[61] See *McFarlane v E.E. Caledonia Ltd* [1994] 2 All E.R. 1, CA, where it was held that no duty was owed to a person of ordinary fortitude who witnessed at close range the "horrific catastrophe" of the "Piper Alpha" oil rig disaster; *a fortiori* where the claimant was not a person of ordinary fortitude, though the same result was reached in *Hegarty v E.E. Caledonia Ltd* [1997] 2 Lloyd's Rep. 259, where the claimant, who was on the same support vessel as Mr. McFarlane and witnessed similar events, was found to be a person of ordinary fortitude. For comment on *McFarlane* see Tan Keng Feng (1995) 111 L.Q.R. 48; Oughton and Lowry (1995) 46 N.I.L.Q. 18. Note that no duty of care is owed by the negligent victim of self-inflicted injuries towards a claimant who suffers psychiatric injury as a result of witnessing the event which caused the injury or its aftermath: *Greatorex v Greatorex* [2000] 1 W.L.R. 1970.

include seeing the victims at the hospital two hours later before they had been properly attended to by medical staff. In *Jaensch v Coffey*[62] Deane J. said that the "aftermath" extended to the hospital to which the injured person was taken, and persisted for so long as he remained in the state produced by the accident up to and including immediate post-accident treatment. In *Alcock* their Lordships refused to extend the meaning of "immediate aftermath" to include the identification of a victim's body at a mortuary some eight or nine hours after death. This failed the test on the ground that even if the identification could be described as part of the "aftermath," it could not be described as part of the "immediate aftermath."[63] Lord Jauncey said that to attempt a comprehensive definition of the "immediate aftermath" would be a fruitless exercise. His Lordship emphasised that in *McLoughlin v O'Brian* the victims were waiting to be attended to, and were in very much the same condition as they would have been had the claimant found them at the scene of the accident.[64] Moreover, the visits to the mortuary were not made for the purpose of rescuing or giving comfort to the victim but purely for the purpose of identification.

(iii) The means by which the claimant perceived the events or received the information

2–113   *Alcock* confirmed that a claimant must either see or hear the event or its immediate aftermath. Psychiatric harm induced by communication of events by a third party was outside the ambit of liability. The scenes broadcast on television did not depict the suffering of recognisable individuals (this being excluded by the broadcasting code of ethics, a fact known to the defendant), and therefore the viewing of these scenes could not be equated with the claimant being within sight or hearing of the event or its immediate aftermath. Although the television pictures certainly gave rise to feelings of the deepest anxiety and distress, this was equivalent to being told about the events by a third party.[65] The correctness of the decisions in both *Hevican v Ruane*[66] and *Ravenscroft v Rederiaktiebolaget Transatlantic*[67] was doubted in *Alcock*,

---

[62] (1984) 54 A.L.R. 417, 462–3 (H.C. of Aus.).

[63] [1992] 1 A.C. 310, 405, *per* Lord Ackner. *McLoughlin v O'Brian* was a case "upon the margin" of what was acceptable as the aftermath. But as Teff (1992) 12 O.J.L.S. 440, 446 comments: "Invidious distinctions are inevitable when the 'immediate aftermath' is treated in isolation, as a crude notion of temporal proximity."

[64] Arguably, the emphasis on the fact that in *McLoughlin v O'Brian* the victims had not been cleaned up or attended to by medical staff when the claimant saw them makes too much hang on an entirely arbitrary circumstance. Should liability for psychiatric harm depend upon a race between the claimant and the ambulance? See the comment of Brennan J. in *Jaensch v Coffey* (1984) 54 A.L.R. 417, 439.

[65] Both Lord Ackner and Lord Oliver agreed that simultaneous broadcasts of a disaster could not always be ruled out as providing the equivalent of the actual sight or hearing of the event or its immediate aftermath.

[66] [1991] 3 All E.R. 65, where Mantell J. held that a claimant who had identified his son's body at the mortuary was entitled to succeed for psychological trauma following the death, although he was not present at the scene of the accident or the aftermath.

[67] [1991] 3 All E.R. 73, where Ward J. held that a mother who had been called to the hospital and on arrival was informed by her husband that her son was dead, was entitled to succeed for a reactive depression, not having even seen her son's body. This case was subsequently

"since in both of these cases the effective cause of the psychiatric illness would appear to have been the fact of a son's death and the news of it."[68]

(iv) The manner in which the psychiatric illness was caused

The older cases on liability for psychiatric harm referred to claims for   **2–114**
"nervous shock". The term nervous shock itself tends to suggest that the claimant's psychiatric illness must be caused by a single event, which in colloquial terms can be regarded as "shocking," notwithstanding that medical understanding of the mechanisms by which psychiatric injury may occur does not correspond with this approach. In *Alcock* Lord Keith said that the scenes witnessed on television could not reasonably be regarded as giving rise to shock, in the sense of a sudden assault on the nervous system. Lord Ackner agreed that:

"Even though the risk of psychiatric illness is reasonably foreseeable, the law gives no damages if the psychiatric injury was not induced by shock. Psychiatric illnesses caused in other ways, such as from the experience of having to cope with the deprivation consequent upon the death of a loved one, attracts no damages. Brennan J. in *Jaensch*'s case (1984) 54 A.L.R. 417 at 429 gave as examples: the spouse who has been worn down by caring for a tortiously injured husband or wife and who suffers psychiatric illness as a result, but who, nevertheless, goes without compensation; a parent made distraught by the wayward conduct of a brain-damaged child and who suffers psychiatric illness as a result also has no claim against the tortfeasor liable to the child."[69]

(n.67 contd.) reversed on appeal, on the ground that the claimant's illness had not come about through sight or hearing of the relevant event or its immediate aftermath, applying *Alcock*: see [1992] 2 All E.R. 470n; Steele (1993) 56 M.L.R. 244. In *Petrie v Dowling* [1992] 1 Qd R. 284 (Qd S.C.) a claimant succeeded in a claim for psychiatric harm in circumstances that were virtually identical to *Ravenscroft*, the judge acknowledging that this was a step further than the High Court of Australia had gone in *Jaensch v Coffey* (1984) 54 A.L.R. 417. But see now *Galli-Atkinson v Seghal* [2003] EWCA Civ 697; [2003] All E.R.(D) 341 (March) where the aftermath of a road traffic accident extended from the accident itself until the claimant left the mortuary, this being treated as an uninterrupted sequence of events.

[68] [1992] 1 A.C. 310, 398, *per* Lord Keith; see also *per* Lords Ackner and Oliver at 401 and 418 respectively. The requirement that the claimant perceive the event with his own unaided senses appears to have been dropped by the High Court of Australia: *Tame v New South Wales*; *Annetts v Australian Stations Pty Ltd* [2002] H.C.A. 35; (2002) 191 A.L.R. 449, where the claimants in *Annetts* recovered for psychiatric harm essentially in respect of what they had been told about the disappearance and death of their son. The New Zealand Court of Appeal has reserved its position on whether this requirement ought to apply in such cases: *van Soest v Residual Health Management Unit* [2000] 1 N.Z.L.R. 179; Mullany (2001) 117 L.Q.R. 182; Teff at (2001) 9 Tort L. Rev. 109; Todd (2001) 17 P.N. 230.

[69] [1992] 1 A.C. 310, 400. Thus, psychiatric damage, clinical depression for example, which is simply attributable to the claimant having to live with the fact that a loved one is permanently disabled as a result of the defendant's negligence will not be actionable following *Alcock*; *cf. Beecham v Hughes* (1988) 52 D.L.R. (4th) 625, where the British Columbia Court of Appeal contemplated such a claim. The claimant suffered from reactive depression which commenced some time after a motoring accident which had rendered his common law wife permanently brain damaged. The claimant failed to prove a causal connection between the events and his depression, but the majority took the view that if the claimant's depression had resulted from the stress of seeing his wife, day after day, in a condition utterly unlike her condition before the accident, the damage would have been foreseeable.

Accordingly, "secondary" victims must suffer psychiatric harm as a result of a "shocking" event, involving the sudden appreciation by sight or sound of a horrifying event, which violently agitates the mind. Psychiatric illness caused by the accumulation over a period of time of more gradual assaults on the nervous system is excluded.[70] The requirement that a "secondary" victim's psychiatric harm be "shock-induced" is based on an outmoded scientific view about the causal mechanism for suffering psychiatric harm and, given that the legal expression "nervous shock" has been described as inaccurate and misleading, it is artificial to re-introduce the notion of "shock" as an element in the chain of causation.[71] It certainly leads to apparently arbitrary outcomes.[72]

Human Rights

2–115   In *Walters v North Glamorgan NHS Trust*[73] an argument that the restrictions on recovery for psychiatric damage in English law constituted an immunity which could not be justified in pursuit of a legitimate aim and was not proportionate for the purpose of Article 6 of the European Convention on Human Rights was rejected. In the light of *Z v United Kingdom*,[74] there was no breach of Article 6 where the court was dealing with substantive, as opposed to procedural, rights.[75]

Reform

2–116   The Law Commission has recommended legislative reform of liability for the negligent infliction of psychiatric harm.[76] The Commission considered that the problematic issues concerned "secondary victims," and did not see a need for legislation in relation to recovery by rescuers, involuntary

---

[70] [1992] 1 A.C. 310, 401; see also *Rhodes v Canadian National Railway* (1990) 75 D.L.R. (4th) 248, 298 (B.C.C.A.); *Campbelltown City Council v Mackay* (1989) 15 N.S.W.L.R. 501, 503 (N.S.W.C.A.); *Spence v Percy* [1992] 2 Qd R. 299 (Qd C.A.). On the other hand, it has been said that this requirement is based on an "outmoded scientific view" about the causal mechanism for suffering psychiatric harm: *Campbelltown City Council v Mackay* (1989) 15 N.S.W.L.R. 501, 503, *per* Kirby P. It would seem that the High Court of Australia has now abandoned the "sudden shock" requirement: see *Tame v New South Wales; Annetts v Australian Stations Pty Ltd* [2002] H.C.A. 35; (2002) 191 A.L.R. 449 at [18] *per* Gleeson C.J., [66] *per* Gaudron J. and [206], [213] *per* Gummow and Kirby JJ.

[71] See Teff (1996) 4 Tort L. Rev. 44 for cogent criticism of the "sudden shock" requirement. See also Teff (1992) 12 O.J.L.S. 440, 442 who points out that generally speaking it is the closeness of the *actual* bond between claimant and accident victim which is the key indicator of whether psychiatric illness will ensue. Focusing on precisely how the shock is experienced is "artificial."

[72] Contrast, *e.g.*, *Taylorson v Shieldness Produce Ltd* [1994] P.I.Q.R. P329, CA with *Calascione v Dixon* (1993) 19 B.M.L.R. 97, CA, both cases arising out of the parents' reaction to the consequences of road traffic accidents involving their children.

[73] [2002] EWHC 321 (QB); [2002] Lloyd's Rep. Med. 227; [2003] P.I.Q.R. P15.

[74] [2001] 2 F.L.R. 612.

[75] This ruling was not appealed when the case reached the Court of Appeal: [2002] EWCA Civ 1792; [2003] P.I.Q.R. P232 at [18].

[76] *Liability for Psychiatric Illness*, Law Com No. 249, 1998. For discussion of the Report see Teff (1998) 61 M.L.R. 849; Tan Keng Feng (1999) 7 Tort L. Rev. 165.

participants, employees, bystanders, in respect of occupational stress, for psychiatric illness suffered as a result of damage or danger to property, or for psychiatric illness suffered as a result of the negligent communication of distressing news.[77] In order to improve the position of "secondary" victims the Commission proposed that there should be a new statutory duty of care in the tort of negligence, leaving the common law to supply the remaining features such as the necessary requirements for breach of that duty, remoteness of damage, and any defences. Under the proposed statutory duty of care, a claimant who suffered a reasonably foreseeable psychiatric illness as a result of the death, injury or imperilment of a person with whom he had a close tie of love and affection would be entitled to recover damages from the negligent defendant, regardless of the claimant's closeness in time and space to the accident, or its aftermath, or the means by which the claimant learned of it. Thus, it would no longer be a requirement that the claimant be close to the accident in time and space and directly perceive the event. There would be a fixed list of relationships covered by the statutory duty of care, creating an irrebuttable presumption that there was a close tie of love and affection. It would be open to a claimant outside the list to prove that a close tie of love and affection did in fact exist between himself and the immediate victim. The one recommendation that would cover all types of claimant was that the proposed legislation should remove the requirement that psychiatric illness be induced by "shock". This would apply to both cases governed by the new statutory duty of care and those continuing to be covered by the common law duty of care (*i.e.* the there would no longer be any need to demonstrate a "sudden assault on the nervous system", whether the claimant was a "primary" victim or a "secondary" victim).

Psychiatric harm in the context of medical negligence

The general rules on the recovery of pure psychiatric harm provide the framework for considering cases arising in the medical context. One difficulty has been that the distinctions between "primary" and "secondary" victims do not always readily fit the circumstances in which psychiatric harm arises from medical negligence.[78] It might be thought that patients are "primary" victims, but they sometimes suffer psychiatric harm in circumstances where

2–117

---

[77] However, the law has moved on since the Law Commission reported its views. The ability of rescuers to claim as "primary" victims has been significantly narrowed as a result of *White v Chief Constable of the South Yorkshire Police* [1999] 2 A.C. 455, which has arguably also limited claims by "involuntary participants" in the event to those exposed to the risk of physical injury (though *cf. W v Essex County Council* [2001] 2 A.C. 592). On the other hand, liability for the negligent communication of distressing news would appear to have broadened.

[78] See Handford, P. "Psychiatric Injury Resulting from Medical Negligence" (2002) 10 Tort L. Rev. 38, who argues that the rules on recovery of damages for psychiatric harm have developed principally for cases where the parties were strangers (as in a road traffic accident) and are not necessarily appropriate to cases where the claim arises out of the provision of a service where the parties were in a pre-existing relationship of care, such as that between doctor and patient.

they have not been exposed to a risk of physical harm (*e.g.* where they have been given negligent information). Relatives will rarely be in a position to witness events as they occur, and therefore will often have difficulty in qualifying as a "secondary" victim.

2–118   In *Kralj v McGrath*[79] the claimant suffered physical injuries as a result of "horrific treatment" by the defendant in the course of delivering a baby. She also suffered shock on being told about the baby's injuries and seeing the child for the eight weeks that it survived. Woolf J. held that she was entitled to be compensated for this "nervous shock," although no specific psychiatric illness was identified. This would seem to fall into the first of Lord Oliver's two categories in *Alcock*, namely a case in which the injured claimant was involved, either mediately or immediately, as a participant: the claimant was undoubtedly owed a duty of care, as the doctor's patient, and she also suffered physical injury, and therefore could be regarded as a "primary" victim of the defendant's negligence.[80]

2–119   Similarly, in *Farrell v Merton, Sutton and Wandsworth Health Authority*,[81] where a mother did not see her severely disabled child for more

---

[79] [1986] 1 All E.R. 54. In the American case of *Molien v Kaiser Foundation Hospitals* 616 P. 2d 813 (1980) a doctor was held liable for a negligent diagnosis which led to the break up of the claimant's marriage. See also Norrie (1985) 34 I.C.L.Q. 442, 463 discussing the possibility of claims for psychiatric harm following unauthorised post-mortems, and, by extension, following the unauthorised removal of organs for transplantation contrary to the Human Tissue Act 1961. As to whether the retention of organs and tissue from a deceased person without the consent of the relatives can give rise to an action for any resulting distress and psychological damage to the relatives see: Ellis [2001] J.P.I.L. 264; Austin (2002) 8 Clinical Risk 185. This issue was given particular emphasis by the "retained organs" scandal, which focused initially on Alder Hey Children's Hospital in Liverpool, but was subsequently found to be a widespread practice. The report of the Inquiry at Alder Hey can be found at *www.rlcinquiry.org.uk*. For a general discussion of proprietary rights in bodies and body parts in the context of the Alder Hey Inquiry and the Bristol Royal Infirmary Inquiry see Skene (2002) 22 L.S. 102. There is no duty of care owed to the relatives of a deceased person to store organs or tissue removed in a post mortem examination on the basis that it might be evidence in civil litigation in the future: *Dobson v North Tyneside Health Authority* [1997] 1 W.L.R. 596.

[80] The case thus resembles *Schneider v Eisovitch* [1960] 2 Q.B. 430 where the claimant was told that her husband had been killed, but she herself was directly involved as a victim suffering physical injuries in the accident in which her husband was killed. In *M. (a minor) v Newham London Borough Council* [1995] 2 A.C. 633, para. 2–061, the defendants argued that the psychiatric disorder suffered by the child and the mother as a result of their separation was not actionable in law, since it was not the product of some sudden, shocking event, relying on Lord Ackner's speech in *Alcock*. This argument was misplaced, however, since both claimants were "primary" victims of the defendants' negligence. They were not claiming on the basis of witnessing an event, rather it was for the enforced separation which had been inflicted as a result of the defendants' alleged negligence. They fell into Lord Oliver's first category as persons directly involved as participants in the events (a point acknowledged by Staughton L.J. in *Sion v Hampstead Health Authority* [1994] 5 Med. L.R. 170, 173). Accordingly, the test should have been simply whether their psychiatric injury was a foreseeable consequence of the defendants' negligence. As Sir Thomas Bingham M.R. observed, at 664: "It would be little short of absurd if the child were held to be disentitled to claim damages for injury of the very type which the psychiatrist should have been exercising her skill to try and prevent." Neither Staughton nor Peter Gibson L.JJ. expressed an opinion on this issue in *M. v Newham*, and it was not dealt with by the House of Lords: sub. nom. *X. (minors) v Bedfordshire County Council* [1995] 2 A.C. 633.

[81] (2000) 57 B.M.L.R. 158.

than 24 hours after the birth, Steel J. considered that, since the delay in the mother seeing her child was wholly attributable to the defendants' conduct in not taking her to see the child (who had been moved to another hospital) and choosing not to tell her about her baby's condition, the sight of her child on the following day constituted the "immediate aftermath" of the birth. The trauma of the birth included not only the events in the operating theatre, but also the situation up to and including the first sight of her baby and the realisation that he was severely disabled. But in any event, the mother was held to be a "primary" victim, though she had also suffered separate physical injury and therefore it might be thought that she readily fell within the "primary" victim category as someone who was not only exposed to the risk of physical harm but who actually sustained physical harm. A claimant who satisfies the threshold test of being exposed to the risk of foreseeable physical harm qualifies as a "primary" victim and does not have to prove that the psychiatric harm was caused by the physical injury. Indeed, a "primary" victim who was exposed to the risk of physical injury does not even have to prove that psychiatric harm was foreseeable,[82] although there must be some temporal connection between the events.[83]

The fact that fathers are often present in the delivery room means that   **2–120** when something goes wrong with the delivery of a child there is a realistic prospect of the father qualifying as a "secondary" victim. Two contrasting county court decisions illustrate the point. *Tredget v Bexley Health Authority*[84] involved negligence by medical staff at a delivery, with the result that the child died two days later. There came a point in the labour where the mother should have been strongly advised to undergo a Caesarian section, but this was not done. This was admittedly negligent. The parents claimed for psychiatric illness, which it was alleged was the result of their involvement in or proximity to the traumas of the birth. H.H. Judge White held that they were entitled to recover for psychiatric harm. The defendants disputed that the parents' psychiatric illness was the result of shock, as opposed to stress, strain, grief, or sorrow from either a gradual or a retrospective realisation of events. The death did not take place until two days after the birth, and during this time there would have been a gradual realisation by the parents of the child's situation. The judge found that the actual birth, with its "chaos" or "pandemonium", the difficulties that the mother had had during the delivery, the sense in the room that something was wrong, and the arrival of the child in a distressed condition requiring immediate resuscitation, was frightening and horrifying for the parents. Both parents were directly involved in and with the event of the delivery. They were participants in the events rather than passive witnesses. On this basis both parents established liability, even though a full appreciation of the gravity of the child's condition only came during the following 48 hours. It

---

[82] *Page v Smith* [1996] A.C. 155.
[83] In *Page v Smith* the event giving rise to the psychiatric injury was contemporaneous with the claimant's exposure to the risk of physical harm.
[84] [1994] 5 Med. L.R. 178 (Central London County Court).

was unrealistic to isolate the delivery as an event from the other sequence of happenings from the onset of labour to the child's death two days later. Although lasting for over 48 hours from the onset of labour to the death, "this effectively was one event."[85]

2–121   On the other hand, in *Tan v East London and the City Health Authority*[86] the negligence of the hospital resulted in the death *in utero* of a child. The father was informed about this, and he attended the hospital and comforted his wife while a Caesarian section was carried out to deliver the child, some four hours after it had died. He held the dead child briefly, kept vigil overnight and saw her being placed in a metal box. It was held that the death *in utero* of the child was an accident/event at which the claimant was required to have been present. The death, stillbirth, overnight vigil and removal of the baby were not all one event. The event did not give rise to "shock" because there was foreknowledge, and planning of the stillbirth, and the subsequent stillbirth was not part of the immediate aftermath.[87]

2–122   Two of the *Alcock* criteria create particular problems for the relatives of patients seeking to recover in respect of psychiatric harm. The first is the extent to which the requirement of proximity in time and space to the events can be stretched by the concept of the "aftermath" — does a relative who sees the injured patient in hospital after the events which caused the patient's injuries fall within the "immediate aftermath"? Where the claimant is present at the hospital and witnesses the traumatic events (such as the father in the delivery room) there should be less difficulty in recovering for resulting psychiatric illness,[88] although the claimant will still have to establish the causal link between the events witnessed and the resulting psychiatric harm.[89] The second is the requirement that there be a sudden, shocking event. Sometimes claimants fail on both grounds.

---

[85] Distinguishing *Sion v Hampstead Health Authority* [1994] 5 Med. L.R. 170, para. 2–124 below, by the degree of involvement in and the immediacy of the parents to the birth of the child in *Tredget*. See also *Armatage v North Tees Health Authority* (1993) 4 A.V.M.A. *Medical & Legal Journal* (No. 1) 17, a case in which £5,000 was paid in respect of "psychiatric damage" to a father who was present at the birth of his child and witnessed the mismanagement of the birth, resulting in asphyxial brain damage to the child who died 12 days later. Liability was admitted. In *X. and Y. v Pal* (1991) 23 N.S.W.L.R. 26; [1992] 3 Med. L.R. 195 the New South Wales Court of Appeal awarded $15,000 damages for the psychiatric harm suffered by a mother on discovering that her three month old child was suffering from congenital syphilis. Query, however, whether under English law this would be considered to be a sufficiently "shocking" event, given that the reaction was to an oral communication.

[86] [1999] Lloyd's Rep. Med. 389 (Chelmsford County Court).

[87] In addition, the claimant's depression did not amount to a recognised psychiatric illness, because it was not categorised as clinical depression; *cf. Farrell v Avon Health Authority* [2001] Lloyd's Rep. Med. 458 discussed at para. 2–130 below.

[88] For example, *Hobbs v Bexley Health Authority* (1992) 3 A.V.M.A. *Medical & Legal Journal* (No. 1) p. 14, involved a settlement in which the claimant received £8,250 for post-traumatic stress disorder, having waited outside the operating theatre, heard alarm bells sounding and observed much "toing and froing" as medical staff treated her husband. She realised that something had gone seriously wrong, and at one point believed that her husband was dead. After a prolonged period of uncertainty she was allowed to see him with two drains in his chest and looking extremely ill.

[89] In *Dube (Litigation Guardian of) v Penlon Ltd* (1994) 21 C.C.L.T. (2d) 268 (Ont. Court of Justice) the parents of a 3–year-old child claimed damages for psychiatric harm having seen

In *McLoughlin v O'Brian* some emphasis was placed on the fact that the   **2–123**
claimant saw her family at the hospital in a distressed state, before they had
been fully attended to by the medical staff. This is unlikely to be the case in
most instances of medical negligence, at least where the injuries occur in the
hospital itself. In *Taylor v Somerset Health Authority*[90] the claimant's
husband suffered a fatal heart attack at work. He was taken to hospital and,
at about 3.00 p.m., found to be dead. Having been informed that her
husband had been taken to hospital, the claimant arrived at about 3.20 p.m.
Fifteen minutes or so later she was informed that her husband was dead.
Shortly afterwards she identified his body in the mortuary, partly because she
was requested to do so but mainly because she could not believe that he had
died. The sight of his body caused further shock and distress, and the claimant suffered a psychiatric illness. It was admitted that there had been negligence on the part of the health authority (in the form of an earlier failure to
diagnose and treat the deceased's serious heart condition) and that this
caused the death. Auld J. held that the claimant did not witness the "immediate aftermath" of the events resulting in the death of her husband. The
doctor's communication to the claimant of her husband's death did not fall
within the "aftermath" principle, and the purpose of the visit to the mortuary was to confirm the information that her husband was dead, and settle
her disbelief.[91] It was concerned with the fact of death rather than the
circumstances in which death came about.

In *Sion v Hampstead Health Authority*[92] the claimant was alleged to have   **2–124**
suffered psychiatric illness as a result of negligence by the hospital caring for
his son, aged 23, who had been injured in a road traffic accident. The claimant stayed by his bedside for 14 days, as his son gradually deteriorated and
eventually died. It was alleged that there was a negligent failure to diagnose
internal bleeding from the son's left kidney. The Court of Appeal held that
there was no sudden "shocking" event, in the sense of a "sudden appreciation by sight or sound of a horrifying event, which violently agitates the
mind," and accordingly there was no cause of action, applying *Alcock*.
There was a process which continued for some time, from first arrival in the
hospital to the appreciation, after the inquest, that there may have been
medical negligence. The son's death, when it occurred, was not surprising
but expected, and therefore the claimant suffered no sudden and unexpected

---

(n.89 contd.) the aftermath of a catastrophic overdose of anaesthetic administered during
the course of minor surgery. The child suffered serious and permanent brain damage.
Although the parents had undoubtedly suffered psychiatric damage, their claims were
rejected on the basis that there was no evidence that their illnesses were caused by a reaction
to the shock of witnessing the immediate aftermath as opposed to being worn down by the
depression, grief and constant demands of caring for their disabled child. See above para.
2–114.

[90] [1993] 4 Med. L.R. 34; [1993] P.I.Q.R. P262, QBD.

[91] *cf. Galli-Atkinson v Seghal*; [2003] EWCA Civ 697; [2003] All E.R. (D) 341 (March) where
the Court of Appeal held that the immediate aftermath of the claimant's daughter's death
had extended from the moment of the accident (a road traffic accident) until the moment the
claimant left the mortuary. That had been an uninterrupted sequence of events.

[92] [1994] 5 Med. L.R. 170.

shock to his nervous system. His psychiatric problems were due to an abnormal grief reaction to the son's death. Peter Gibson L.J. commented that in such a claim it was the sudden awareness, violently agitating the mind, of what is occurring or what has occurred that was the crucial ingredient of shock. It was not the violence or suddenness of the incident causing injury to the accident victim that mattered. Accordingly:

> "I see no reason in logic why a breach of duty causing an incident involving no violence or suddenness, such as where the wrong medicine is negligently given to a hospital patient, could not lead to a claim for damages for nervous shock, for example where the negligence has fatal results and a visiting close relative, wholly unprepared for what has occurred, finds the body and thereby sustains a sudden and unexpected shock to the nervous system."[93]

2-125   In *Palmer v Tees Health Authority*[94] a mother's claim for severe post-traumatic stress disorder and pathological grief reaction following the abduction and murder of her four-year old daughter by a psychiatric patient failed. She alleged that the defendants had been negligent in failing to diagnose that the patient posed a serious risk to children. Within 15 minutes of discovering that her daughter was missing she believed that she had been abducted, and she said that this produced an immediate shock to her nervous system. The child's body was discovered three days later, and the claimant was in the vicinity at the time of the discovery although she was not allowed to see the body at that time. She claimed that the psychiatric illness was caused by her presence at the scene and the immediate aftermath of her daughter's abduction, and the search for and discovery of the body, which she later identified. The Court of Appeal held that she had not witnessed the events herself (*i.e.* the abduction and murder) and the events which she had witnessed did not constitute a "sudden shocking event." Mrs. Palmer was in the same position as the relatives in *Alcock* who, on learning about the unfolding tragedy at the Hillsborough football ground, underwent a period of grave worry and anxiety before, some hours later, having their worst fears confirmed. They did not satisfy the "immediate aftermath" test. Moreover, her imagination of what had happened, subsequently confirmed by events, did not constitute "the sudden appreciation by sight or sound of the horrifying event."

2-126   More recent cases have taken a slightly more relaxed approach to the question of what constitutes a single, shocking event. In *Walters v North Glamorgan NHS Trust*[95] a mother attending her baby son in hospital where his acute hepatitis was negligently misdiagnosed, leading to his death, was held to be entitled to claim for psychiatric harm. She was sleeping in her son's room in hospital when she was awoken in the night by the sound of him

---

[93] *ibid.* at 176.
[94] [1999] Lloyd's Rep. Med. 351.
[95] [2002] EWHC 321 (QB); [2002] Lloyd's Rep. Med. 227; [2003] P.I.Q.R. P15.

choking. His body was stiff and she found blood. She was told that he was having a fit and it was unlikely that he would have any serious damage, but in fact he had suffered a major epileptic seizure causing a coma and brain damage. He was transferred to a London hospital to undergo a liver transplant, where she was told that he had suffered severe brain damage and was on life support. His brain was so seriously damaged that he would not have had any quality of life, so she agreed to the withdrawal of life support and he died in her arms, 36 hours after the initial fit. Thomas J. held that she was not a "primary" victim. There was no risk of physical injury to her and she had not played any causative role in her son's death, so she was not a "participant" in the events. Rather, the claimant was a "secondary" victim. The only issue was whether her psychiatric illness (pathological grief reaction) was caused by shock as a result of a sudden appreciation of a horrifying event or its immediate aftermath. Thomas J. held that the period of 36 hours from the time of the epileptic fit to the time of the child's death was a horrifying event, the sudden appreciation of which had caused her psychiatric illness. The waking to see the child's fit was not on its own a horrifying event, but the court should look realistically at what happened, and an event extending over a period of 48 hours could be treated as a single shocking event. On the psychiatric evidence it was impossible to isolate the causative effect of each incident over the 36 hours.[96] Everything that happened in that period had contributed to cause the psychiatric illness. The period of 36 hours from the moment of the epileptic fit, the misdiagnosis by the hospital, the correct diagnosis by the London hospital, and the decision to turn off the life support machine could be looked on in law as a horrifying event. The claimant's appreciation of the horrifying event was sudden within that temporal context, in contradistinction to more gradual assaults on her mind, and it was that sudden appreciation of the event that caused the pathological grief reaction. The Court of Appeal affirmed the ruling of Thomas J.[97] Ward L.J. said that the court should take a realistic view of what constitutes the necessary "event." The word should not be construed is if it were in a statute, but could be given a wide meaning to refer to a "series of events which make up the entire event beginning with the negligent infliction of damage through to the conclusion of the immediate aftermath whenever that may be."[98] This would depend on the facts and circumstance of each case. In this case: "there was an inexorable progression from the moment when the fit occurred as a result of the failure of the hospital properly to diagnose and then to treat the baby, the fit causing the brain damage which shortly thereafter made termination of this child's life inevitable and the dreadful climax when the child died in her arms. It is a seamless tale with an obvious beginning and an equally obvious end. It was played out over a period of 36

---

[96] Note that the medical evidence was to the effect that the psychiatric impact of the extended period over which the claimant was exposed to the event was more severe than if the child had died suddenly.

[97] *Walters v North Glamorgan NHS Trust* [2002] EWCA Civ 1792; [2003] P.I.Q.R. P232.

[98] *ibid.* at [34].

hours, which for her both at the time and as subsequently recollected was undoubtedly one drawn-out experience."[99] Ward L.J. also rejected the defendant's argument that the court could not take account of what the claimant was told about her son's condition from time to time. There was a distinction between a case where the claim was founded upon *merely* being informed of, or reading, or hearing about the accident and directly perceiving by sight or sound the relevant event: "Information given as the events unfold before one's eyes is part of the circumstances of the case to which the court is entitled to have regard."[1] Clarke L.J. commented that the *Alcock* control mechanisms should not be applied too rigidly or mechanistically.[2]

2–127   A more flexible approach to what constitutes the immediate aftermath is also apparent in the comments of Lord Slynn in *W v Essex County Council*.[3] His Lordship indicated that the concept of the immediate aftermath of an incident has to be assessed in the particular factual situation. The parents were claiming that they suffered a psychiatric reaction to the realisation that, due to the defendants' negligence, they felt responsible for the fact that their children had been sexually abused by a foster-child placed with the family by the defendants. His Lordship did not rule out the possibility that the parents could establish that they fell within the immediate aftermath:

> "I am not persuaded that in a situation like the present the parents must come across the abuser or the abused "immediately" after the sexual incident has terminated. All the incidents here happened in the period of four weeks before the parents learned of them. It might be that if the matter were investigated in depth a judge would think that the temporal and spatial limitations were not satisfied. On the other hand he might find that the flexibility to which Lord Scarman referred [in *McLoughlin v O'Brian*] indicated that they were."

2–128   In *Froggatt v Chesterfield and North Derbyshire Royal Hospital NHS Trust*[4] Forbes J. held that the spouse and child of a woman who underwent a mastectomy following a negligent misdiagnosis of cancer were entitled to recover for their psychiatric injury as "secondary" victims. In the case of the husband he had had a sudden appreciation of the trauma suffered by his wife as a result of the defendant's negligence when he saw her undressed for the first time after the mastectomy. "He was quite unprepared for what he saw and he was profoundly and lastingly shocked by it."[5] In the child's case, the sudden appreciation came as a result of overhearing a telephone conversation that his mother was having, "and his immediate belief, based on the negligent advice that had been given to his mother and that she felt obliged to

---

[99] *ibid.*
[1] *ibid.* at [35].
[2] *ibid.* at [48].
[3] [2001] 2 A.C. 592, 601.
[4] [2002] All E.R. (D) 218 (Dec). QBD, December 13, 2002.
[5] *ibid.* at [79].

repeat to him, that she had cancer and was likely to die. He was completely unprepared for such a shock and, as a result, he suffered a moderate Post Traumatic Stress Disorder".[6] These "shocking" events, though clearly foreseeable consequences of the defendants' negligence, would seem to be at some temporal remove from the defendant's negligence, and it is not clear how this decision can be reconciled with, for example, *Sion v Hampstead Health Authority*, even allowing for the comments of Lord Slynn in *W v Essex County Council* and the flexibility applied in *Walters v North Glamorgan NHS Trust*. When the patient's husband saw his wife undressed for the first time after the surgery, it could hardly be said that he was unaware that she had undergone a mastectomy. The "event" (seeing his wife without a breast) was just as expected as the son's death in *Sion*. It was simply that the husband in *Froggatt* reacted badly to the sight. Does this mean that a husband who reacts badly to the first sight of a wife's scars following a road traffic accident would recover for psychiatric harm against the negligent motorist, even though that event was days or even weeks after the accident? This would seem to stretch the "immediate aftermath" of an event far beyond what was contemplated in *McLoughlin v O'Brian*, and certainly beyond the point drawn by the House of Lords in *Alcock*.

Communicating bad news

A further question concerns the potential liability of the person who communicates information to the claimant, as a result of which the claimant sustains psychiatric harm. It has been said that if the statement is true there is no obligation to break bad news gently, even if it is foreseeable that the person will be shocked by it.[7] This proposition had been questioned, however, at least where the circumstances are such that the impact of the news is needlessly exacerbated.[8] Of course, doctors frequently have to give bad news, both to patients and relatives. It is at least arguable that in some cases the claimant who develops psychiatric harm as a result of what she is told will be a "primary" victim of a negligent statement, where in theory the test is simply foreseeability of psychiatric damage. In *AB v Tameside & Glossop Health Authority*[9] the defendants conceded that they owed a duty of care to break distressing, though truthful, news to patients in a manner which reduced the risk of patients developing psychiatric illness in response to the news, though the defendants were held not to have been negligent in choosing to inform patients that there was a small risk that they might have contracted HIV from a doctor by letter rather than face-to-face. It is not clear on what basis the defendants' concession was made, given the traditional

2–129

---

[6] *ibid.* at [80].
[7] *Mount Isa Mines Ltd v Pusey* (1970) C.L.R. 383, 407.
[8] *Winfield & Jolowicz on Tort*, 16th ed., 2002, p. 188. In *Furness v Fitchett* [1958] N.Z.L.R. 396 it was accepted that a doctor may be under a duty of care to his *patient* not to inform her about her medical condition. The defendant was held liable for harm to the claimant's psychiatric health even though the information was true.
[9] [1997] 8 Med. L.R. 91.

view that a duty does not arise simply from the manner in which accurate information is given.[10] In *Allin v City & Hackney Health Authority*,[11] as a result of the defendants' negligence, the distressing information was *inaccurate* and the claimant alleged that she had suffered psychiatric harm from this distressing "news", subsequently corrected, although the incorrect information was imparted in a sensitive and appropriate manner (*i.e.* if it had been correct). The claimant had undergone a very difficult labour and was told by the medical staff that her baby was dead when in fact it had not died. She only began to appreciate that the child was alive the following day when a doctor spoke to her about the baby's condition. Again, counsel for the defendants conceded the existence of a duty of care, but in this case the defendants were held liable on the facts. Again, the basis of this concession of a duty of care is not clear,[12] but if it is correct the somewhat odd consequence would be that a claimant who is correctly informed about the death of a loved one killed by the defendant's negligence has no claim against the person who killed that loved one for the psychiatric damage which results (applying *Alcock*), whereas a person who is incorrectly, and negligently, informed that a loved one has died may have a claim for psychiatric harm against the careless informant, even though no one has died and there was no negligence in respect of the loved one. On the other hand, Mullany comments that: "It is unquestionably right for the common law to insist that those who communicate objectively distressing (indeed, potentially life-shattering) news take all reasonable precautions to ensure that such news is accurate."[13] While there is much force in this statement as a matter of principle, given the present structure of English law (and particularly the restrictions imposed by *Alcock*), as matter of consistency between claimants *Allin* looks distinctly out of line.[14]

2–130   In *Farrell v Avon Health Authority*,[15] without reference to *Allin*, Bursell J. held that the father of a newborn baby who was wrongly told that his baby had died, and was then given the body of a dead baby to hold, was owed a duty of care as a "primary" victim. He was informed twenty minutes later

---

[10] See Dziobon and Tettenborn (1997) 13 P.N. 70; *cf.* Mullany (1998) 114 L.Q.R. 380. In *Anderson v Wilson* (1999) 175 D.L.R. (4th) 409 (Ont. C.A.) a group of patients had been exposed to the risk of contracting hepatitis B, but had been tested and found to be negative. The Ontario Court of Appeal held that it was at least arguable that the notice to patients would produce psychiatric harm, and given the uncertain state of the law on liability for psychiatric harm, it could not be said to be unarguable that a claim in respect of mental distress alone, without a recognised psychiatric illness, would fail.

[11] [1996] 7 Med. L.R. 167.

[12] See Jones (1997) 13 P.N. 111. See also *Guay v Sun Publishing Co* [1953] 4 D.L.R. 577 where a newspaper was held not liable for the psychiatric harm suffered by the claimant on reading a false report of her family's death published negligently by a newspaper.

[13] (1998) 114 L.Q.R. 380, 385.

[14] Consistency between different categories of claimant was an important factor in the decision of the House of Lords in *White v Chief Constable of the South Yorkshire Police* [1999] 2 A.C. 455 to deny the claims for psychiatric damage brought by police officers at the Hillsborough disaster. The objection was to allowing the police officers' claims to succeed simply because they fell into the category of "rescuer", having denied the relatives' claims in *Alcock*.

[15] [2001] Lloyd's Rep. Med. 458; see Case (2002) 18 P.N. 248.

that there had been a mistake, and that his baby was still alive. He visited the baby, but stayed only a few minutes. Although he had not had contact with the mother before the birth and did not see the child again, the claimant alleged that the experience had caused a psychiatric reaction. Bursell J. held that he was a "primary" victim on the basis that he was physically involved in the incident, and the only victim of the incident was the claimant himself: "How can there be a secondary victim if there is no other person who was physically involved as a potential victim?"[16] The significance of finding that the claimant was a "primary" victim was that he merely had to prove that psychiatric damage was foreseeable—and if it was foreseeable it mattered not that the claimant had a vulnerable personality because the defendants had to take the claimant as they found him. This looks odd when compared with the position of an employee suing his employer in respect of occupational stress, where it is clear that if the employee has a vulnerable personality which is unknown to the employer the employee's action will fail for want of foreseeability.[17] However, in applying the foreseeability test the judge held that foreseeability had to be judged by reference to the circumstances at the time of the negligence, including the defendants' knowledge at that time. On the facts, the defendants were unaware of the claimant's lack of contact with the mother, and therefore of the lack of pre-natal bonding with the child, and so foreseeability of the risk of psychiatric harm had to be assessed on the basis of an ordinary parental relationship with the unborn child. Since, the judge concluded, it was foreseeable that an ordinary father could suffer a psychiatric reaction in such circumstances, it was irrelevant that the claimant was not an ordinary father or had a vulnerable personality. Of course, this does not address the more general issue of why a claimant should succeed in such circumstances. It is true that the claimant was the only "victim", but that was because he was told, erroneously as it turned out, that there was an accident victim, his "dead" son. His psychiatric reaction was the result of what he thought had happened to his son, and what he perceived, wrongly, as the consequences of that, namely the baby's dead body. Is there any difference (other than the length of time that elapsed) between this situation and seeing a dead body to identify it at the mortuary (as occurred to some of the claimants in *Alcock*)? If the claimant's baby had in fact been killed by the defendants' negligence, and the father had simply been told about this some hours later, he would probably not have recovered because he would have been treated as a "secondary" victim.

The position is clearly different where the claimant is informed that as a result of the defendant's negligence there is a risk that at some point in the future *he* will suffer physical damage and death. In *CJD Litigation: Group B Plaintiffs v Medical Research Council*[18] the claimants had been injected with human growth hormone (HGH) which can carry the agent that causes

2–131

---

[16] *ibid.* at 471.
[17] See *Hatton v Sutherland* [2002] EWCA Civ 76; [2002] 2 All E.R. 1.
[18] (1997), [2000] Lloyd's Rep. Med. 161; (1997) 41 B.M.L.R. 157. See J. O'Sullivan, "Liability for Fear of the onset of future Medical Conditions" (1999) 15 P.N. 96.

Creutzfeldt-Jakob Disease (CJD), an extremely unpleasant and invariably fatal condition. None of the claimants had developed CJD by the time of the claim but they were aware that they were at risk of developing the disease in the future. The risk of the claimants developing a psychiatric condition as a result of receiving information about the risk of developing CJD, and its effects, was reasonably foreseeable and was actually foreseen by the defendants. Morland J. held that any claimant who could prove that he developed a genuine psychiatric illness caused by awareness of the risk of developing CJD was entitled to compensation for the psychiatric damage "whether of normal phlegm and ordinary fortitude or having a vulnerable personality."[19] The psychiatric injury was not triggered by a physical event which involved some physical impact on the claimants (injections of potentially contaminated human growth hormone), but from the subsequent knowledge that that event created a risk of developing the disease in the future.

2–132   Morland J. held that the claimants were not "primary" victims, because of the ramifications of such a ruling in other cases (and they were clearly not "secondary" victims). If the claimants were "primary" victims, then so would individuals exposed to asbestos or radiation who subsequently learned of the exposure and developed a psychiatric reaction in response to knowledge of the risk of developing cancer in the future. The potentially huge number of claims in similar situations would make insurance difficult or impossible to obtain. It could involve all manner of products and a huge range of potential tortfeasors. It could inhibit the producers, prescribers and suppliers of a product from warning the public of the danger of a product. For example, if a potentially lethal substance had been introduced into a production batch of canned food, "it would be disastrous if a supplier or producer were inhibited from warning the public of danger for fear that some who of those who had already eaten the canned food might bring a claim as a 'primary' victim for psychiatric injury triggered by the warning. Against such a claim the producer could not raise defences either that the psychiatric injury was unforeseeable to a person of normal fortitude or that the law insists upon certain control mechanisms to limit the number of potential claimants."[20] The relationship between the defendants and the recipients of the injection was akin to that of doctor and patient, said his Lordship, one of close proximity. That, combined with the fact that the cohort of potential victims of psychiatric damage was small, and the very serious nature of the potential disease which causes terrible suffering for the victim and cannot be treated or ameliorated by medical treatment, was sufficient to establish a duty of care.

> "Although it may not be reasonably foreseeable that the man of ordinary fortitude would develop psychiatric illness if the information that he was at slight theoretical risk of CJD was given to him by a doctor or

---

[19] *ibid.* at 168.
[20] [2000] Lloyd's Rep. Med. 161 at 165.

counsellor who would no doubt give the information with optimistic stress, in the case of a special therapeutic trial or programme as the HGH programme, it should have been reasonably foreseeable to the defendants by 1 July 1977 that, when news of the potential risk of CJD broke to those who were or had been children when treated, the news would reach Group B plaintiffs not only from considerate and skilled clinicians and counsellors but also from the media which foreseeably would tend to highlight or sensationalise the risk of the potential terrible outcome and from anxious and perhaps angry relations and friends who would be ignorant of scientific knowledge and likely to use unhelpful language."[21]

The defendants had actually foreseen this risk. It was irrelevant, said Morland J., whether the news of the risk of developing CJD produced a sudden shock or the news was received over a period of time from various sources. There was no logical reason to limit the foreseeability to an area of time contemporaneous or almost contemporaneous to the negligent physical event, i.e. the injection. Nor should the delay between the shock of the news of the first cases of CJD and the onset of psychiatric injury defeat the claims. "A psychiatric injury can be readily induced by an accumulative awareness or drip-feed of information over a prolonged period of time although the court will scrutinise rigorously a claim so based."[22]

Similarly, in *A.P.Q. v Commonwealth Serum Laboratories Ltd*[23] Harper   2–133
J. refused to strike out as disclosing no reasonable cause of action a claim in respect of psychiatric harm arising from the knowledge that the claimant had been exposed to the risk of developing CJD, following treatment with human pituitary gonadtrophins manufactured by the defendants: "a person who suffers psychiatric illness when informed that medical treatment undergone by her may leave her with a horrible and terminal disease probably has a good cause of action against the manufacturer of a drug used in the [claimant's] treatment where its manufacture (and its subsequent distribution) was conducted negligently and where that negligence exposed the [claimant] to that risk."[24] The defendant's argument that no duty of care arose because the claimant's psychiatric condition did not arise from the sudden perception of a shocking event was rejected. The claimant was a "primary" victim, with her psychiatric illness resulting from her awareness of the possibility of her own death following an unpleasant disease:

"The shock suffered by someone who is informed without any prior warning that she (or he) might contract a particularly undesirable disease could seldom if ever be said to arise from a 'sudden sensory perception of a person, thing or event.' Yet it might well be so distressing

---

[21] *ibid.* at 166.
[22] *ibid.* at 168.
[23] [1999] 3 V.R. 633 (Vict. S.C.).
[24] *ibid.* per Harper J. at 635.

that it affronts or insults the mind and thereby causes a recognisable psychiatric illness. This being so, it is difficult to understand why the absence of the sudden sensory perception of a person, thing or event should make the difference between a cause of action on the one hand and no cause of action on the other, where in each instance psychiatric harm has been caused. Unless I have sadly mistaken the present [claimant's] claim, this case is not analogous to that of the worn-out spouse or the parent of the brain-damaged child."[25]

2–134   In both of these cases the judges were anxious to sidestep the normal requirement that the claimant sustained the psychiatric harm as a result of a sudden shocking event. This can be done simply by categorising the claimants as "primary" victims. It is arguable that *Page v Smith* renders any individual who has been exposed to the risk of foreseeable physical injury a "primary" victim, even if they have not suffered physical injury and the psychiatric injury was unforeseeable. For example, a patient who as a result of negligence received inappropriate treatment and thereby might expect in due course to suffer physical injury (*e.g.* an overdose of radiation therapy), and, being aware of the error, developed a psychiatric illness as a reaction to the events, would appear to fall within the principle of *Page v Smith* even if ultimately the physical injury did not materialise. Since the physical injury was foreseeable, so was the psychiatric injury.

2–135   It is clear that Morland J. wanted to avoid the conclusion that patients given HGH were "primary" victims, because his Lordship was anxious to distinguish the CJD claimants (involving an extremely unpleasant and invariably fatal disease) from other cases where a claimant has been exposed to the risk of future disease (such as cancer arising from exposure to radiation or asbestos). It is not obvious, however, that this distinction will hold.[26] The seriousness of the consequences is, after all, only a matter of degree. For example, workers who contract mesothelioma as a result of having been exposed to asbestos at work will almost invariably die within two years of diagnosis. The disease is extremely unpleasant and painful. It may be a nice question whether, given the option, one would choose to die from mesothelioma or CJD. Why should those who have been exposed to the risk of developing CJD as a result of a defendant's negligence have a claim for psychiatric damage arising out of their fear of the future, when those who have been exposed to the risk of mesothelioma due to inhaling asbestos particles do

---

[25] *ibid.* at 639.

[26] *cf. Bryan v Phillips New Zealand Ltd* [1995] 1 N.Z.L.R. 632 where an action for psychiatric harm induced by "cancer phobia" by a claimant who had been exposed to asbestos dust was not struck out as disclosing no reasonable cause of action. Note that the risk or chance of developing a physical condition in the future (such as cancer) as a result of the defendants' negligence in exposing the claimant to the risk of harm (*e.g.* exposure to asbestos dust) is not damage giving rise to an action for damages: *Gregg v Scott* [2002] EWCA Civ 1471; [2003] Lloyd's Rep. Med. 105 at [80] *per* Mance L.J.; see also *per* Latham L.J. at [39]. Of course, this is not the same situation as a claimant who has developed a psychiatric condition as a result of the knowledge that he may develop a serious condition in the future, where the psychiatric harm itself constitutes the relevant damage.

not? The fact that there are potentially far more claimants, a point of concern to Morland J., hardly provides a principled justification. Indeed, it might suggest that such claimants should have a stronger case in that the risk of developing mesothelioma may be higher,[27] and therefore the psychiatric reaction to the risk correspondingly more foreseeable and reasonable. Moreover, *Page v Smith* is authority for the proposition that a claimant has an action for his unforeseeable psychiatric illness provided he was exposed to the risk of foreseeable physical injury, even though the physical injury did not occur *and never will occur*. Mr Page was never going to develop a physical injury from the minor traffic accident in which he was involved. But his exposure to the risk of such injury was a threshold test, which was *sufficient* to establish the defendant's duty of care with respect to the psychiatric harm.[28]

Where there is *no* risk that the claimants will develop a serious condition   **2–136** in the future, the claimants should not be entitled to claim in respect of a genuine psychiatric illness which is an irrational response. In *The Creutzfeldt-Jakob Disease Litigation*[29] a different group of claimants who had received HGH that had been processed by a different method, which the judge considered carried no risk of CJD, argued that they should be entitled to claim for psychological injury from the news that they were at risk of CJD. Morland J. held that this claim was bound to fail, commenting:

> "Every man and woman will receive bad news about himself or herself or a loved one, bad news of death, fatal illness or disabling injury or accident or other disaster. It is the inevitable experience of life. Naturally, such bad news will cause grief, stress, worry, concern, unhappiness, a feeling of being depressed. Such reactions are normal. Their severity will vary from person to person. Every man and woman is expected to face such situations with such fortitude as he or she can muster. In my judgment, it would be an unhealthy society that thought it was entitled to monetary compensation in such situations. Indeed, the existence of the belief to such entitlement might well create the psychological injury which otherwise would not have occurred. . . . Unless such bad news comes into the public domain, advances in medicine and public health will be inhibited. Scientific advance will inevitably lead from time to time to the discovery of new risks and side-effects, both from well-tried and experimental drugs. Full, well-informed and frank

---

[27] There are about 1,500 cases of mesothelioma as a result of exposure to asbestos diagnosed each year (see the figures quoted in *Fairchild v Glenhaven Funeral Services Ltd* [2002] UKHL 22; [2003] 1 A.C. 32, para. 5–027). By 1998 there were 27 confirmed cases of CJD due to human growth hormone since 1985: see para. 3–057, n. 29. It is impossible to compare the relative risk, however, since the population of individuals given human growth hormone is clearly far lower than the population exposed to asbestos fibres.

[28] Subsequently, the House of Lords held that exposure to the risk of foreseeable physical injury was also a *necessary* condition: *White v Chief Constable of the South Yorkshire Police* [1999] 2 A.C. 455.

[29] (1996) 54 B.M.L.R. 79.

debate about the problem is required for further progress. Once a new risk is known, the recipient of the drug should be informed in a sensitive and balanced manner, preferably before lurid scare stories appear in the media. The recipient of the news of the risk should then be expected foreseeably to be able to cope and live with that news."[30]

Thus, it was not in the public interest that the ambit of the litigation be extended to this category of claimants.

Deliberately misleading information

2-137   If a doctor can be liable for negligently providing false information then arguably there is an even stronger case where the defendant tells deliberate lies. In *Jinks v Cardwell*[31] a doctor who falsely told a wife that her husband had committed suicide by drowning in a bath because it would look better for the hospital was held liable for her "physical and emotional distress." At best he was negligent, said the judge, at worst callous and unfeeling. In *Powell v Boladz*[32] the defendants admitted liability in respect of the death of a child following a failure to diagnose the child's condition. The parents alleged that a general practitioner had removed or falsified medical records concerning the child's death as part of a "cover-up", and brought an action in respect of psychiatric damage allegedly caused as a result of the cover-up. The Court of Appeal held that, though the parents of a child might be on a general practitioner's list of patients, nonetheless when the general practitioner is treating a child, the only patient seeking medical advice and treatment is the child, and it is to the child that the general practitioner owes a duty of care. The discharge of that duty in the case of a young child would usually involve giving advice and instructions to the parents, so that they can administer the appropriate medication, observe relevant symptoms and seek further medical assistance if need be, and in giving such advice, the doctor obviously owed a duty be careful. "But the duty is owed to the child, not to the parents."[33] Any duty owed by the doctor to the parents would depend upon whether he was called upon to undertake treatment of the parents as patients. But a doctor who has been treating a patient who has died, who tells relatives what has happened, does not thereby undertake a doctor-patient relationship with the relatives. The mere fact that the person communicating the bad news is a doctor, does not, without more, mean that he

---

[30] *ibid.* at 83.
[31] (1987) 39 C.C.L.T. 168 (Ont. H.C.).
[32] [1998] Lloyds Rep. Med. 116, CA.
[33] *ibid.* at 123, *per* Stuart-Smith L.J. His Lordship drew an analogy with the duty said to be owed by the psychiatrist in *X. (minors) v Bedfordshire County Council* [1995] 2 A.C. 633 when examining a child and interviewing a parent for the purposes of discharging the local authority's care responsibilities, and an examination of a claimant by a doctor on behalf of an insurance company. "In neither of these cases does the doctor undertake to treat the person as a patient and his only duty is not to damage him in the course of the examination." *ibid.* at 123–124. See the discussion of these issues at paras 2–056 *et seq.*

undertakes the doctor-patient relationship. The doctor might realise, on passing on bad news, that the shock was so great that some immediate treatment was necessary, but that situation was more akin to the doctor giving emergency treatment to an accident victim.[34] The fact that the relatives happened to be on the doctor's register as patients would make no difference, except to the extent that the doctor ought to have realised that they needed counselling or medical treatment in their own right as patients.[35] In that situation the doctor-patient relationship would exist in relation to the advice and treatment given and so a duty of care would arise. But on the alleged facts no duty of care was owed to the parents. Psychiatric harm was not foreseeable as a consequence of the claimants discovering the alleged "cover-up" by alteration of the medical records following the death of their son.

An alternative approach is to argue that a deliberate lie which causes psychiatric damage could be actionable under the principle of *Wilkinson v Downton*,[36] but in *Powell v Boladz* a claim based on the intentional infliction of psychological harm, relying on *Wilkinson v Downton*, was also rejected. Stuart-Smith L.J. suggested that *Wilkinson v Downton* was authority for two propositions: 2–138

> "first, that making a statement known to be false with the intention that it should be believed and with the intention of causing injury, which in fact results, is actionable; and, secondly, that where the defendant's act is plainly calculated to produce some effect of the kind which was produced, an intention to produce it ought to be imputed to the defendant, regard being had to the fact that the effect was produced on a person in an ordinary state of health and mind. Another way of putting the second proposition is to say that a man, who foresees the consequences of his act, is to be taken to intend those consequences, even if he does not desire them."[37]

On this analysis, the facts of *Powell v Boladz* did not support the necessary degree of foresight for the imputed intent required under *Wilkinson v Downton*.

(g) Psychiatric patients

There can be no doubt that a doctor, such as a psychiatrist or clinical psychologist, will owe a duty of care to his psychiatric patients,[38] and that   2–139

---

[34] *ibid.* at 124.

[35] *ibid.*

[36] [1897] 2 Q.B. 57.

[37] [1998] Lloyds Rep. Med. 116, 125. The scope of liability for psychiatric damage under the principle in *Wilkinson v Downton* has been considered in two recent decisions of the Court of Appeal: *Wong v Parkside Health NHS Trust* [2001] EWCA Civ 1721; ([2003] 3 All E.R. 932, and *W v Home Office* [2001] EWCA Civ 2081; [2002] Q.B. 1334. See the discussion in *Clerk & Lindsell on Torts*, 18th ed. (2000), *Second Supplement* (2002), para. 13–16.

[38] Although a psychiatrist does not owe a duty of care to child who is being examined for the purpose of determining whether she has been the victim of abuse and identifying the abuser: *M. (a minor) v Newham London Borough Council* [1995] 2 A.C. 633, CA; affirmed sub. nom. *X. (minors) v Bedfordshire County Council* [1995] 2 A.C. 633, HL, paras 2–061 to 2–066.

this duty may require the doctor to take reasonable steps to protect the patient from harming himself, including, in some instances, the prevention of suicide attempts.[39] A hospital authority may also be responsible for injuries inflicted on a patient by a fellow patient where the injuries are the result of a failure to provide adequate control and supervision.[40]

2–140   But this duty does not encompass protecting a patient from the consequences of his own criminal actions, at least where he is found to bear some degree of responsibility for his actions. In *Clunis v Camden & Islington Health Authority*[41] the claimant was a man with a history of mental disorder and seriously violent behaviour. He had been detained under the Mental Health Act 1983 and following his discharge from hospital the defendants came under a duty, by virtue of section 117 of that Act, to provide after-care services, but he did not receive any after-care. Three months after his discharge from hospital the claimant killed a stranger in a sudden and completely unprovoked attack. He was charged with murder, but a plea of manslaughter on the ground of diminished responsibility was accepted by the prosecution and he was ordered to be detained in a special hospital. He brought an action against the defendants alleging that they were in breach of a common law duty of care to treat him with reasonable professional care and skill, arguing that if he had received an appropriate assessment he would not have gone on to commit the crime because he would either have consented to become a voluntary patient or would have been detained under the Act. As a result of the alleged negligence he would now be detained for much longer than he would otherwise have been. The Court of Appeal struck out the claim as disclosing no reasonable cause of action, on the grounds that: (1) the action was based the claimant's own illegal act, and therefore the maxim *ex turpi causa non oritur actio* applied; and (2) the statutory obligation to provide after-care created by section 117 of the Mental Health Act 1983 did not give rise to a duty of care at common law. The fact that the claimant was found guilty of manslaughter is most obviously relevant to the defence of *ex turpi causa*, but it appears also to have influenced the Court's view of the duty of care—it was not fair or reasonable to hold the health authority responsible for the consequences of the claimant's criminal act. Although it was accepted that the claimant's mental responsibility

---

[39] See paras 4–110 *et seq.*

[40] *Wellesley Hospital v Lawson* (1977) 76 D.L.R. (3d) 688 in which the Supreme Court of Canada proceeded on the basis that such a common law duty existed, though the case was concerned with the interpretation of a provision in the Ontario Mental Health Act 1970; *Stewart v Extendicare Ltd* [1986] 4 W.W.R. 559 (Sask. Q.B.), where a nursing home was held liable for injuries caused by a patient to another patient; *Wenden v Trikha* (1991) 8 C.C.L.T. (2d) 138, 155–156 (Alta. Q.B.); affirmed (1993) 14 C.C.L.T. (2d) 225 (Alta. C.A.), where Murray J. pointed out that the duty owed by a hospital to exercise control and supervision over mentally ill patients to see that they do not harm other patients is "confined to reasonable and foreseeable dangers." An analogous case is *Ellis v Home Office* [1953] 2 All E.R. 149 in which the prison authorities were held to owe a duty of care to a prisoner assaulted by another prisoner. On the facts the defendants were not found negligent since the attack was unforeseeable. See also *Stenning v Home Office* [2002] EWCA Civ 793.

[41] [1998] Q.B. 978.

was substantially impaired, nonetheless a plea of diminished responsibility did not remove liability for his criminal act. He had to be taken to have known what he was doing and that it was wrong: "public policy would . . . preclude the court from entertaining the plaintiff's claim unless it could be said that he did not know the nature and quality of his act or that what he was doing was wrong."[42]

There are, however, two other situations in which a duty of care may arise which is owed to someone other than the doctor's patient. First, where a doctor certifies that a person is "insane" for the purpose of compulsory admission to hospital under the mental health legislation, and secondly, possibly, where a psychiatric patient has injured a third party in circumstances in which the damage was foreseeable.   **2–141**

(i) Certificates of "insanity"

Applications to commit individuals compulsorily to hospital under Part II of the Mental Health Act 1983 must be supported by the recommendations of (normally) two doctors, one of whom must be an approved specialist in mental disorder, although an approved specialist will not necessarily be a qualified psychiatrist.[43] Under section 2 of that Act a person may be detained for 28 days for assessment, during which time he may receive some treatment without his consent. The doctors must certify that the patient is suffering from a mental disorder of a nature or degree which warrants detention for assessment, and that he ought to be detained in the interests of his own health or safety or for the protection of other persons.[44] In an emergency the application for admission for assessment needs the support of only one doctor, who does not have to be an approved specialist.[45] Under section 3 a person may be compulsorily detained for treatment, initially for up to six months. The doctors must certify: **2–142**

(i)   that the person is suffering from mental illness, severe mental impairment, psychopathic disorder or mental impairment and his condition is of a nature or degree which makes medical treatment in hospital appropriate;

(ii) that, in the case of psychopathic disorder or mental impairment, the treatment is likely to alleviate or prevent a deterioration of his condition; and

(iii) it is necessary for the health or safety of the patient or for the protection of other persons that he should receive such treatment which cannot be provided unless he is detained.[46]

---

[42] *ibid.* at 989.
[43] Hoggett, *Mental Health Law*, 4th ed., 1996, pp. 69–70.
[44] Mental Health Act 1983, s. 2(2).
[45] *ibid.*, s. 4.
[46] See also s. 7 of the Mental Health Act 1983 on reception into guardianship; the National Assistance Act 1948, s. 47 and the National Assistance (Amendment) Act 1951 which require medical evidence in support of compulsory removal procedures.

2–143   These procedures clearly contemplate that the person detained will not necessarily be a patient of the doctor(s) supporting admission, since the Act specifies that one of the doctors must, *if practicable*, have "previous acquaintance" with the person.[47] It is strongly arguable, however, that the doctors owe a duty of care to that person in giving the certificate and may be liable in an action for negligence.[48] In *De Freville v Dill*[49] McCardie J. was apparently opposed to the existence of such a duty but felt compelled to hold that a duty of care did exist on the balance of authority, particularly the majority decision of the Court of Appeal in *Everett v Griffiths*.[50] On the other hand, in *Everett v Griffiths*[51] the House of Lords held that the defendant doctor was not liable on the facts, without expressing a concluded view on the decision of Crompton J. in *Hall v Semple*[52] in which a duty had been held to exist. In *X (minors) v Bedfordshire County Council*[53] Lord Browne-Wilkinson pointed out that the question whether a doctor owes a duty of care to a patient when certifying that a patient is fit to be detained under the Mental Health Acts was left undecided in *Everett v Griffiths* and remains open for decision in an appropriate case.

2–144   If a doctor owes a duty not to issue a certificate negligently, it would also follow that there may be liability for negligently *failing* to issue a certificate if the person is in fact of unsound mind and through the absence of certification and restraint he inflicts injury on himself. This point was acknowledged by McCardie J., *obiter*, in *De Freville v Dill*.[54]

2–145   On the other hand, in *X. v A., B. and C. and the Mental Health Act Commission*[55] Morland J. held that where a registered medical practitioner and two laypersons consider whether to grant or withhold a certificate that a detained patient is competent to, and has in fact, consented to treatment under the provisions of section 57 of the Mental Health Act 1983,[56] they are performing quasi-judicial, public law duties, and accordingly they do not owe a private law duty of care in negligence to the patient, even if the decision could legitimately be challenged on public law principles. His Lordship distinguished the situation where a doctor is acting as a doctor and giving medical opinions, for example for the purpose of compulsory admission under section 3 or for the purpose of giving electro-convulsive therapy under section 58(3)(*b*) of the Mental Health Act 1983. In those circumstances it

---

[47] ss. 12(2), 4(3).

[48] *Hall v Semple* (1862) 3 F. & F. 337; *De Freville v Dill* (1927) 96 L.J.K.B. 1056; *Everett v Griffiths* [1920] 3 K.B. 163, CA; [1921] 1 A.C. 631, HL; *Harnett v Fisher* [1927] A.C. 573; *Buxton v Jayne* [1960] 1 W.L.R. 783; [1962] C.L.Y. 1167. On the procedural restrictions to bringing such an action see Mental Health Act 1983, s. 139, paras 4–127 *et seq*.

[49] (1927) 96 L.J.K.B. 1056.

[50] [1920] 3 K.B. 163.

[51] [1921] 1 A.C. 631.

[52] (1862) 3 F. & F. 337.

[53] [1995] 2 A.C. 633, 753.

[54] (1927) 96 L.J.K.B. 1056, 1060–1061. In *Everett v Griffiths* [1920] 3 K.B. 163, 196 Scrutton L.J., in a dissenting judgment, considered that the prospect of such a duty being owed was a reason for *not* imposing a duty generally in the granting of certificates.

[55] (1991) 9 B.M.L.R. 91, QBD.

[56] See para. 6–070.

was possible that a doctor could be in breach of a common law duty in private law, because the doctor, *qua* doctor, is giving a medical opinion about a patient, albeit not his patient.

Breach of the duty imposed by section 117 of the Mental Health Act 1983 **2–146** to provide after-care services for a psychiatric patient who has been detained under the Act and then released, does not give rise to a common law action for breach of statutory duty. In *Clunis v Camden and Islington Health Authority*[57] the Court of Appeal held that the primary means of enforcing section 117 was by way of complaint to the Secretary of State. Nor did a common law duty of care in the tort of negligence arise because the statutory context in which section 117 functioned was inconsistent with a duty of care owed to the patient where there had been a negligent failure to provide after-care.[58]

(ii) Injury to third parties

Is a doctor, who is aware or ought reasonably to be aware that a psychi- **2–147** atric patient constitutes a serious risk of harm to others, under a duty of care to the third parties to take steps to prevent the harm or minimise the risk? If, for example, a patient has threatened to kill someone does the doctor have a duty to warn either that person or the police, or to initiate the compulsory detention procedures under the Mental Health Act 1983.[59] If so, the doctor could be liable in damages to a victim of the patient if he negligently failed to take the appropriate steps.

In *Tarasoff v Regents of the University of California*[60] the Supreme Court **2–148** of California held that a psychologist owed a duty of care to a woman murdered by the psychologist's patient. The patient had expressed an intention to kill the woman, who was a former girlfriend. The court accepted that there was a balance to be drawn between the public interest in effective treatment of mental illness and the consequent requirement of protecting confidentiality, and the public interest in safety from violent assault. Nonetheless, the protection of confidentiality must end where the public peril begins.[61]

This duty of care is not as wide as might at first appear. First, in *Tarasoff*, **2–149**

---

[57] [1998] Q.B. 978.

[58] Applying the view expressed by Lord Browne-Wilkinson in *X (minors) v Bedfordshire County Council* [1995] 2 A.C. 633, 739 that a common law duty of care cannot be superimposed on a statutory duty if the observance of the common law duty of care would be inconsistent with or have a tendency to discourage the due performance by the public authority of its statutory duties.

[59] Note that there is a difference between saying that the statutory grounds for compulsory detention are satisfied, and that the doctor owes a common law duty of care to a third party to detain the patient.

[60] 551 P. 2d 334; Sup., 131 Cal. Rptr. 14 (1976); see de Haan (1986) 2 P.N. 86.

[61] "In this risk-infected society we can hardly tolerate the further exposure to danger that would result from a concealed knowledge of the therapist that his patient was lethal. If the exercise of reasonable care to protect the threatened victim requires the therapist to warn the endangered party or those who can reasonably be expected to notify him, we see no sufficient societal interest that would protect and justify concealment. The containment of such risks lies in the public interest," *ibid.* at 347, *per* Tobriner J.

it was recognised that the nature of the "psychotherapeutic dialogue" may lead patients to express threats of violence, few of which are ever executed, and a therapist should not be encouraged routinely to reveal such threats. Secondly, the California Supreme Court has subsequently distinguished *Tarasoff* in a case where a patient made general threats of violence against children, on the basis that *Tarasoff* involved a known and specifically foreseeable and identifiable victim.[62]

2-150   It remains debatable whether *Tarasoff* would be followed in this country. In *Holgate v Lancashire Mental Hospitals Board*[63] a hospital was held liable for negligently releasing on licence a dangerous patient who had been compulsorily detained following convictions for violent offences. The patient entered the claimant's home and assaulted her. The trial judge seemed to assume that a duty of care existed and the report deals largely with the question of whether there had been negligence. The case could have been justified on the basis of the degree of control exercised by the defendants over the dangerous patient, a control analogous to the relationship between gaoler and prisoner which may give rise to a duty of care.[64] This is the basis upon which a hospital authority may be held liable for injuries to a patient inflicted by a fellow patient as a result of negligent supervision, and there is no obvious reason why this duty should be owed only to patients, and not, for example, to visitors to the hospital.[65] However, in *Home Office v Dorset Yacht Co Ltd*[66] Lord Diplock specifically reserved his opinion on *Holgate v Lancashire Mental Hospitals Board*, and it has been pointed out that the discretion to admit or release a patient under the Mental Health legislation constitutes the exercise of a statutory power for which there can be civil liability only where the exercise of the power is unlawful, applying public law principles.[67] On the other hand, in *Home Office v Dorset Yacht Co Ltd* Lord Morris considered that in a situation comparable to *Holgate v Lancashire*

---

[62] *Thompson v County of Alameda*, 614 P. 2d 728 (1980); see also *Brady v Hopper*, 751 F. 2d 329 (1984); *cf. Jablonski v U.S.*, 712 F. 2d 391 (1983). *See also Peterson v State of Washington* 671 P. 2d 230 (1983) and *Taggart v State of Washington* 822 P. 2d 243 (1992), both in the Supreme Court of Washington, where the requirement of an identifiable victim was rejected.

[63] [1937] 4 All E.R. 19.

[64] See *Home Office v Dorset Yacht Co Ltd* [1970] A.C. 1004; *Ellis v Home Office* [1953] 2 All E.R. 149; *Stenning v Home Office* [2002] EWCA Civ 793; *S.(J.) v Clement* (1995) 122 D.L.R. (4th) 449 (Ont. Ct (Gen. Div)).

[65] See *Wellesley Hospital v Lawson* (1977) 76 D.L.R. (3d) 688 (S.C.C.) where the duty was said to be owed to "third persons," not simply patients. See also *Partington v Wandsworth London Borough Council, The Independent*, November 8, 1989.

[66] [1970] A.C. 1004, 1062–1063.

[67] Hoggett, *Mental Health Law*, 4th ed., 1996, p. 168, citing *Anns v Merton London Borough Council* [1978] A.C. 728. Presumably where the release was *ultra vires* an action could lie, particularly if there were negligence at what Lord Wilberforce termed the "operational level": see *Anns v Merton London Borough Council* [1978] A.C. 728, 754 and the speech of Lord Diplock in *Home Office v Dorset Yacht Co Ltd* [1970] A.C. 1004. This aspect of Lord Wilberforce's speech in *Anns* is, presumably, still applicable following the overruling of that decision in *Murphy v Brentwood District Council* [1991] 1 A.C. 398: see *X. (minors) v Bedfordshire County Council* [1995] 2 A.C. 633, 736–737, although Lord Browne-Wilkinson preferred not to express the point in terms of the public law concept of *ultra vires*; rather, the question was whether the decision was outside the ambit of the public authority's discretion.

Mental Hospitals Board "a duty of reasonable care would be owed to those whose safety, as reasonable foresight would show, might be in jeopardy."[68] More recently in *Palmer v Tees Health Authority*[69] the Court of Appeal dismissed *Holgate* as a case of unsatisfactory authority where little attention was paid to the question of the defendants' duty of care. The case could not be reconciled with *Hill v Chief Constable of West Yorkshire*[70] on the question of proximity.[71]

In *Palmer* itself, a patient who was diagnosed as suffering from a personality disorder or psychopathic personality abducted, sexually assaulted and murdered a young child. It was alleged that the defendant health authority had negligently failed to identify that the patient constituted a serious risk to children. He had expressed sexual feelings towards children and said that a child would be murdered after his discharge from hospital. It was argued that there was a real, substantial and foreseeable risk of serious offences being committed against children, and that the authority had been negligent in failing to provide treatment that would have substantially reduced the risk of the patient committing such an offence and/or ensured that he was contained during periods of risk. The Court of Appeal held that no duty of care was owed by the defendants to either the child or the child's mother.[72] In *Hill v Chief Constable of West Yorkshire*[73] the House of Lords held that the police do not owe a duty of care to a victim of crime in respect of their alleged negligence in failing to identify and arrest the perpetrator before he committed the offence against the claimant, partly because the victim "was one of a vast number of the female general public who might be at risk from his activities but was at no special distinctive risk." Relying on *Hill*, the Court of Appeal in *Palmer* concluded that there was no proximity of relationship between the child and the defendants. She was not specifically identified as being at risk of attack, but was merely one of a large unascertained class of potential victims who were at risk of harm.[74] This conclusion, that there was no proximity in the absence of a threat to a specific individual, is broadly in line with the position reached by the American courts. In *Tarasoff* the victim was named, and readily identifiable by the psychologist. Where

2–151

---

68 [1970] A.C. 1004, 1041. Lord Reid said that *Holgate* "could only be supported if it could be said that the release was authorised so carelessly that there had been no real exercise of discretion," *ibid.* at 1031–1032.
69 [1999] Lloyd's Rep. Med. 351.
70 [1989] 1 A.C. 53.
71 [1999] Lloyd's Rep. Med. 351 at 358–359, *per* Stuart-Smith L.J.
72 The mother sought damages in respect of her psychiatric illness arising out of the events: see para. 2–125.
73 [1989] 1 A.C. 53; *cf. Doe v Toronto Commissioners of Police* (1990) 72 D.L.R. (4th) 580 (Ont. H.C., Div. Ct.).
74 Though note the comment of Pill L.J. in *Palmer v Tees Health Authority* [1999] Lloyd's Rep. Med. 351 at 363, that there was: "force in the submission that the question whether the identity of a victim is known ought not to determine whether the proximity test is passed. It is forcefully argued that the difference between the threat 'I will kill X' and the threat 'I will kill the first bald-headed man I meet' ought not to determine whether a duty is placed upon a defendant, though it would obviously go to the extent of the duty and the measures necessary to discharge it."

there have been more general threats the courts have tended to deny a duty of care.[75]

2–152   There was also an issue, which will always arise where there is a general threat as opposed to a specific threat to an individual, as to what the defendants could have done to have reduced the risk. If the threat is to a specific individual, as in *Tarasoff*, then there should be little difficulty in providing a warning to that individual, but if the patient has not made threats against specific individuals the warning can only realistically go to the police or those with responsibility for instituting the compulsory detention procedure. Stuart-Smith L.J. commented that:

> "it seems to me to be a relevant consideration to ask what the defendant could have done to avoid the danger, if the suggested precautions, *i.e.* committal under s. 3 of the Mental Health Act or treatment are likely to be of doubtful effectiveness, and the most effective precaution cannot be taken because the defendant does not know who to warn."[76]

On the other hand, there is provision in the Mental Health Act 1983 compulsorily to detain a psychiatric patient where it is necessary for the health or safety of the patient or for the protection of others. Thus, there is a mechanism available in law, and it is clearly contemplated that this may be invoked for the protection of third parties. Moreover, it is arguable that the question of what the defendant ought to have done is a matter which goes to whether there was a breach of duty, rather than whether the duty of care exists or should exist.

2–153   The issue that the decision in *Palmer* leaves unresolved is whether the outcome on the duty of care would have been different if there had been a specific threat to an identified child, rather than a general threat to children. In other words, would an English court follow *Tarasoff*?[77] At first instance, Gage J. at least contemplated the possibility of a duty arising in these circumstances, subject to arguments about policy.[78] In the Court of Appeal Stuart-Smith L.J. specifically reserved his opinion as to whether a duty of care could arise if the victim was identified or identifiable, "as for example a child in

---

[75] See also *K v Secretary of State for the Home Department* [2002] EWCA Civ 775; (2002) 152 N.L.J. 917 where the claimant was raped by an individual, M, who had previously committed a serious sexual offence and burglary, and had been recommended for deportation. A deportation order had been made, but the Secretary of State subsequently released M from detention. The Court of Appeal held that no duty of care was owed by the Home Office. Laws L.J. rejected, at [29], the argument that a defendant could owe a duty to prevent damage to the claimant by a third party where the defendant knows that the risk the third party poses is especially grave: "A defendant does not become the world's insurer against the grave danger (where the danger is general) posed by a third agency, which he might control but does not, by virtue only of the fact that he appreciates that the danger exists." Arden L.J. said, at [35], that proximity of relationship cannot be established simply by showing knowledge on the part of the defendant of a glaring danger to the public as a result of the release. Thus, the case could not be distinguished from *Palmer*.

[76] [1999] Lloyd's Rep. Med. 351, 359.

[77] For an earlier discussion of this issue see Jones (1990) 6 P.N. 16, 21.

[78] [1998] Lloyd's Rep. Med. 447, 461.

the household of the abuser." The example of a child in the household of the abuser arose in *W v Essex County Council*[79] where a local authority had placed a 15–year old boy, who was a known sexual abuser, with a foster family without informing the parents of his full history, with the result that the family's children were sexually abused. A majority of the Court of Appeal held that the claims for negligence by the children abused by the 15–year old foster child should not be struck out as disclosing no reasonable cause of action. The parents had relied on oral assurances from the local authority that a suspected or known sexual abuser would not be placed with them, and in answer to a specific question about the boy were told, wrongly, that he was not known or suspected of being a sexual abuser. Thus, the local authority had assumed a responsibility for the accuracy of the statements that they gave about the boy placed with the family.[80] There are clearly differences between the factual situation in *W v Essex County Council* and *Palmer* in that there was an element of misrepresentation in the former case. Another distinction is that in *W v Essex County Council* the defendants were active in placing the perpetrator in a situation where he was able to inflict the harm on the children, whereas in *Palmer* the defendants merely failed to prevent him from causing harm in general. Nonetheless, it is arguable that *W v Essex County Council* goes some way to supporting the proposition that a duty of care could arise where there is a known, identifiable victim.

In the Canadian case of *Wenden v Trikha*[81] Murray J. considered the circumstances in which a duty of care might be imposed upon a hospital or psychiatrist, taking into account both the decision in *Tarasoff* and the English cases, particularly *Home Office v Dorset Yacht Co Ltd*. A voluntary psychiatric patient left the hospital in which he was receiving treatment and drove a vehicle in a trance state, causing an accident in which the claimant was injured. Murray J. accepted that a hospital treating mentally ill patients did owe a duty of care to a person or class of persons other than its staff or patients if it could be said that it was foreseeable that harm would be likely to occur to such a person or persons as a result of the behaviour of a mentally ill patient, provided that there was some further ingredient which established a relationship between the hospital and that third party. That "further ingredient" consisted of exposing the claimant to a particular risk of danger due to "the nature of the patient" which was different in its incidence from the general risk shared with all members of the public.[82] The learned judge acknowledged that:

2–154

> "A psychiatrist treating an out-patient or a voluntary admittee to a hospital may not have the degree of control which one encounters in a prison-like setting or in those cases where the patient has been certified

---

[79] [1999] Fam. 90.

[80] The case reached the House of Lords on the question of whether the parents could claim in respect of psychiatric harm. See paras 2–105.

[81] (1991) 8 C.C.L.T. (2d) 138 (Alta. Q.B.); affirmed (1993) 14 C.C.L.T. (2d) 225 (Alta. C.A.).

[82] *ibid.* at 156–7, citing Lord Diplock in *Home Office v Dorset Yacht Co Ltd* [1970] A.C. 1004.

or confined. It depends upon the evidence whether or not one can say that the future pattern of behaviour of the patient would or would not be more or less accurate than predicting the behaviour of an escaped prisoner . . . However, as Tobriner J. pointed out [in *Tarasoff*], the psychiatrist does have the necessary special relationship involving at least the care of the patient and as such may become privy to information by which he or she knows that the patient poses a serious danger of causing damage to a third person or to a class of third parties. The psychiatrist is also highly trained in assessing mentally ill people, at least to the degree possible given today's technology, which, by its very nature, is at best an imprecise and problematic science."[83]

It was not correct, said the judge, that only one of the two special relationships identified in *Tarasoff* need exist to except the psychiatrist/patient relationship from the general rule that one person does not owe a duty to control the conduct of another nor to warn those endangered by such conduct. In any given case there must be such a relationship between the psychiatrist and his patient that there is imposed upon the psychiatrist a duty to control the conduct of his patient, but in addition, when deciding whether or not a third party should be given a warning of the danger or whether steps should be taken to confine or restrain the patient, one must decide whether or not the requisite proximity of relationship exists between the psychiatrist and the third party:

"... it is a logical application of the reasoning in the *Dorset Yacht* decision that it is only fair and reasonable that both a hospital and a psychiatrist who becomes aware that a patient presents a serious danger to the well-being of a third party or parties owe a duty to take reasonable steps to protect such a person or persons if the requisite proximity of relationship exists between them . . . However, as pointed out by Lord Diplock, whether or not a person or persons fall within the necessary category will depend upon the particular nature of the risk posed by the patient, the predictability of future behaviour giving rise to the risk, and the ability to identify the person or class of persons at risk."[84]

On the facts of the case there had been no negligence by the hospital, and therefore Murray J. did not decide whether a duty of care was owed by the hospital to the particular claimant. Nonetheless, it is submitted that on the stated test it would have been difficult to conclude that a duty of care was owed in the circumstances of this case, since there was nothing to indicate that the harm which the claimant sustained was the product of a risk which was different in its incidence from the general risk shared with all members of the public using public roads. The "further ingredient" required to

---

[83] *ibid.* at 160.
[84] *ibid.* at 161.

establish the relationship of proximity between the hospital and the claimant was missing.

The difficulty that the English courts would have in following *Tarasoff* is   2–155
that, ultimately the basis of such a duty of care must be the foreseeability of
harm to the victim. But foreseeability alone is not sufficient to impose a duty
of care. There must also be a proximate relationship between claimant and
defendant, and it must be just and reasonable in the circumstances to impose
a duty.[85] The more foreseeable the harm the more likely it is that a court will
find the relationship between the parties to be proximate.[86] Nonetheless, the
duty, if any, arises from the defendant's knowledge of the foreseeable danger
of serious physical harm to the third party.[87] The problem is that, as a general
rule, there is no obligation in the tort of negligence to take positive steps to
confer a benefit on others by preventing harm befalling them. The "mere
omissions" rule states that there is no obligation to rescue someone in
danger, even if rescue would involve little or no effort and involves no danger
to the rescuer.[88] In the absence of a special relationship giving the defendant
some degree of control over the patient, there is nothing upon which to base
a duty to intervene, other than foreseeability of the harm, which in the case
of damage caused by a third party (here the patient) is not normally sufficient to impose a duty of care.[89] If the courts were to accept that, in certain
circumstances, doctors do have a duty to rescue,[90] then this issue would carry
less weight in the context of harm caused by a psychiatric patient known to
be potentially dangerous to others.

A second objection might be that imposing a duty of care could create a con-   2–156
flict of duties for the doctor, between the duty of confidence owed to the patient
and the duty of care owed to a third party. It is true that where the imposition
of a duty of care might lead to a defendant being subject to conflicting duties
the courts may be reluctant to find a duty of care, but where the public interest defence to an action for breach of confidence applies there is no duty to
maintain confidentiality and so no conflict with a possible duty of care.[91] The

---

[85] *Caparo Industries plc v Dickman* [1990] 2 A.C. 605, 617–618, *per* Lord Bridge; *Smith v Bush* [1990] 1 A.C. 831, 865, *per* Lord Griffiths.

[86] *Caparo Industries plc v Dickman* [1989] 1 All E.R. 798, 803, *per* Bingham L.J.

[87] There is an analogy with the infection cases here, since it is the doctor's failure to warn the third party or the failure to isolate the patient which leads to the spread of the infection, and the duty must be based on foreseeability of the risk; see paras 2–089 to 2–092. In *De Freville v Dill* (1927) 96 L.J.K.B. 1056, 1060–1061 McCardie J., discussing the liability of a doctor who negligently certifies that a person is of unsound mind, raised the prospect of liability for negligently failing to issue a certificate where the person is in fact of unsound mind, and as a result the person inflicts injury on himself that could have been avoided by treatment or restraint. Such a duty, owed to someone who is not the doctor's patient, is not so far removed from the situation in *Tarasoff*.

[88] See above para. 2–075.

[89] See Norrie (1984) 24 Med. Sci. & Law 26, 30, who argues that *Tarasoff* would not be followed in this in country because of the objection to imposing an affirmative duty to act;
Brazier, *Medicine, Patients and the Law*, 2nd ed., 1992, p. 58; see also Giesen, *International Medical Malpractice Law*, 1988, pp. 160–1; *cf.* de Haan (1986) 2 P.N. 86, 88.

[90] See paras 2–076 to 2–078.

[91] Though *cf.* Brazier, *Medicine, Patients and the Law*, 2nd ed., 1992, p. 58: "The doctor is
faced with a stark conflict of duty." The doctor's problem is, arguably, not the conflict of

public interest defence recognises that in some circumstances other, more valued, social considerations outweigh the confidentiality of the doctor-patient relationship, and it is arguable that the public interest in safety from individuals known to be lethal falls into this category. It was this point which the court considered to be persuasive in *Tarasoff*. A third factor which a court might consider relevant in determining whether there should be a duty of care is the possibility of an alternative remedy for the victim under the Criminal Injuries Compensation Scheme.[92]

(h) Financial loss to third parties

2–157   There is, in theory, no reason why a doctor should not owe a duty of care to a third party in respect of purely financial loss when giving advice to that third party as to a person's medical condition, under the principle in *Hedley Byrne & Co Ltd v Heller & Partners Ltd*.[93] For example, a doctor who prepared a medical report on a patient for the purpose of an insurance company that was contemplating issuing a life policy on the patient would clearly owe a duty of care to the insurance company under this principle, whether or not the doctor was paid for the service.[94] The position would be similar where the report was for an employer or prospective employer of the patient as to his medical fitness to perform his job.[95] Whatever the position of the person about whom the report is made,[96] it is difficult to see how the insurance company or prospective employer does not fall squarely within the *Hedley Byrne* principle, subject to any exclusion of liability.[97]

2–158   There is also an issue arising out of failed sterilisations where the person who has to bear the cost of raising the child is not the person who was sterilised or negligently advised about a sterilisation. Of course, the effect of *McFarlane v Tayside Health Board*[98] is that, in any event, there can be no

---

(n.91 contd.) duties but the difficulty of deciding where, on the facts of the case before him, his duty lies. For a graphic illustration of the problem see Langton and Torpy (1988) 28 Med. Sci. & Law 195. See further Abadee (1995) 3 J. Law and Med. 75 on the relationship between a duty of disclosure and the duty of confidentiality. On the public interest defence see paras 2–185 *et seq.*

[92] See *Hill v Chief Constable of West Yorkshire* [1989] 1 A.C. 53; the lack of a conviction, *e.g.* for want of *mens rea*, does not prevent a claim under the scheme.

[93] [1964] A.C. 465; see para. 2–036.

[94] See the discussion of *M. (a minor) v Newham London Borough Council; X. (minors) v Bedfordshire County Council* [1995] 2 A.C. 633, above paras 2–061 to 2–067. Although, since a contract of insurance is a contract *uberrimae fidei*, the insurers would have a right to avoid the contract if the patient/insured had failed to disclose a material fact about his medical history, and in these circumstances would suffer no loss. The action against the doctor would only be relevant if the patient was unaware of his medical condition.

[95] See *Spring v Guardian Assurance plc* [1995] 2 A.C. 296, HL, where it was held that an employer owes a duty of care to an employee or former employee when providing a reference about the individual to a prospective employer, and it would seem to follow from this that he also owes a duty to the prospective employer.

[96] See para. 2–057, above.

[97] See the comments of Millett L.J. in *Kapfunde v Abbey National plc* [1999] I.C.R. 1; [1999] Lloyd's Rep. Med. 48, at [44]: "The doctor is taken to assume responsibility for his advice, but only to the employer or insurer who commissioned [the report] and not to the 'patient' who is the subject of the advice."

[98] [2000] 2 A.C. 59. See paras 2–039 *et seq.*

claim in respect of the financial cost of raising a healthy child following negligent advice about, or the negligent performance of, a sterilisation operation. But there remains the question of the mother's losses arising out of an
unwanted pregnancy and the entitlement to the financial costs of raising a
disabled child. In the case of a husband and wife, the courts (or defendants)
have not taken the point that the parent who did not undergo the surgery
was not the doctor's patient and therefore was seeking to recover for pure
economic loss in a situation where the doctor-patient relationship did not
arise. The claim of the *parents* for the financial losses involved in raising the
disabled child is treated as a single loss.

In *Goodwill v British Pregnancy Advisory Service*[99] the Court of Appeal   **2–159**
held that a woman who knew and relied on the fact that her sexual partner
had undergone a vasectomy did not have a cause of action in negligence
against the person who performed the surgery or advised her partner about
the effects of the surgery, if she became pregnant as a result of the failure of
the vasectomy to achieve complete sterility. The man (M) had been assured
that the vasectomy had been successful and that he did not need to use
contraception in the future. Four years later the claimant began a sexual relationship with M and he told her that he had been sterilised. The claimant
also consulted her doctor who assured her that the chances of becoming
pregnant by M were minute. Following this neither the claimant nor M used
any form of contraception. The claimant became pregnant and subsequently
gave birth to a daughter. She claimed damages from the defendants for the
expenses of the birth, the cost of bringing up the child and loss of earnings.
The Court of Appeal held that there was no duty of care owed to the claimant because the defendants could not have known that their advice to M
would be communicated to the claimant and acted on by her as a warranty
of M's sterility without independent inquiry. They could know nothing
about the likely conduct of M's future sexual partners, and had not voluntarily assumed any responsibility to the claimant. It would have been different if the claimant had been M's current sexual partner at the time of the
advice, and that advice had been given directly to both of them.[1] It is arguable that *Goodwill* was based on unexpressed policy concerns about compensating for the costs of raising a healthy child, although Gibson L.J. sought
to base his judgment on arguments about the proximity of relationship
between the defendant doctor and the woman:

> "The doctor who performs a vasectomy on a man on his instructions
> cannot realistically be described as employed to confer a benefit on the
> man's sexual partners in the form of avoiding pregnancy. Still less can
> he be so described when he is giving advice on tests after the operation.
> The doctor is concerned only with the man, his patient, and possibly
> that man's wife or partner if the doctor intends her to receive and she

---

[99] [1996] 2 All E.R. 161; see Davies (1996) 12 P.N. 54.
[1] *ibid.* at 168 *per* Peter Gibson L.J.

receives advice from the doctor in relation to the vasectomy and the subsequent tests. Whether the avoidance of pregnancy is a benefit or a disadvantage to a sexual partner of the man will depend on her circumstances. If the existence of that partner is known to the doctor and the doctor is aware that she wishes not to become pregnant by the man and vasectomy is carried out to meet her wish as well as the man's wish, it may be said that the doctor is employed to confer a benefit on her. But that is not this case."[2]

With all respect to Gibson L.J., if a vasectomy is not intended to confer "a benefit on the man's sexual partners in the form of avoiding pregnancy" then what benefit is it intended to confer? Of course, the man may very well desire to avoid the consequences of pregnancy in his sexual partner, for both financial and other reasons. But those consequences can be avoided only by avoiding the pregnancy, which the woman may equally wish to avoid, and she may have relied on the fact that the man had been sterilised just as much, if not more than the man (given that pregnancy generally has more serious consequences for women than men, and that sterilisation is regarded as the most effective means of contraception). Such reliance is patently foreseeable by the defendant, and the potential range of claimants is limited to an ascertainable class (the man's present and future female sexual partners—generally limited to the first to become pregnant, since thereafter the man should normally be aware that he was not sterile). Thus, excluding such claimants looks very much like a policy decision.

3. THE DUTY OF CONFIDENCE

2–160   A doctor owes a duty of confidence in respect of information concerning his patient which he acquires in his capacity as a doctor, whether from the patient himself or from others.[3] This obligation is widely regarded as one of

---

[2] *ibid.* at 167.

[3] English law has not yet reached the position of recognising a discrete right to privacy, of which a law of confidentiality might be regarded as merely a subsidiary element. The impetus of Art. 8 of the European Convention for the Protection of Human Rights and Fundamental Freedoms, which provides that "Everyone has the right to respect for his . . . family life . . .", may ultimately lead to a distinct law of privacy, though Art. 8.2 provides for various exceptions, including "the interests of national security, public safety or the economic well-being of the country, for the prevention of disorder or crime, for the protection of health or morals, or for the protection of the rights and freedoms of others." One of the most important "rights and freedoms of others" is contained in Art. 10 providing for the right to freedom of expression, though it too is subject to similar exceptions. The Human Rights Act 1998, s. 12(4) provides that if a court is considering whether to grant any relief which, if granted, might affect the exercise of the Convention right to freedom of expression the court "must have particular regard to the importance of the Convention right to freedom of expression." For consideration of how the balance between these competing rights should be drawn see: *Douglas v Hello! Ltd* [2001] Q.B. 967, CA; *Venables v News Group Newspapers Ltd* [2001] Fam. 430, CA; *Campbell v MGN Ltd* [2002] EWCA Civ 1373; [2003] 2 W.L.R. 80; discussed by Arnold (2003) 119 L.Q.R. 193.

the cornerstones of the doctor-patient relationship, and this is reflected in a number of international ethical codes.[4] The most important statement of the medical profession's ethical duty is contained in the General Medical Council's guidance *Confidentiality: Protecting and Providing Information*[5] which states that:

> "Patients have a right to expect that information about them will be held in confidence by their doctors. Confidentiality is central to trust between doctors and patients. Without assurances about confidentiality, patients may be reluctant to give doctors the information they need in order to provide good care. If you are asked to provide information about patients you should: (a) Seek patients' consent to disclosure of information wherever possible, whether or not you judge that patients can be identified from the disclosure; (b) Anonymise data where unidentifiable data will serve the purpose; (c) Keep disclosures to the minimum necessary."[6]

The confidentiality of the doctor-patient relationship is protected in law, although information that an individual is receiving therapy from a self-help group (Narcotics Anonymous) is not to be equated with disclosure of the clinical details of medical treatment, and so is not confidential.[7] There is little caselaw where the issue of medical confidentiality has had to be decided, although there are numerous *dicta* which simply assume that medical information is confidential.[8] In *W. v Egdell* Scott J. said of a psychiatrist who had prepared a medical report on the claimant for use at a Mental Health Review

2–161

---

[4] See, *e.g.*, the *Hippocratic Oath*: "All that may come to my knowledge in the exercise of my profession or outside of my profession or in daily commerce with men, which ought not to be spread abroad, I will keep secret and will never reveal"; *Declaration of Geneva*: "I will respect the secrets which are confided in me, even after the patient has died"; *International Code of Medical Ethics*: "A doctor shall preserve absolute secrecy on all he knows about his patients because of the confidence entrusted in him."

[5] June 2000, available at *www.gmc-uk.org*. See also the Department of Health, *Confidentiality: NHS Code of Practice*, July 2003, available at *www.doh.gov.uk/ipu/confiden* (replacing the previous guidance on confidentiality, *The Protection and Use of Patient Information*, HSG (96) 18/LASSL (96)5); the BMA guidance, *Confidentiality & disclosure of health information*, October 1999, available at *web.bma.org.uk*; and the Royal College of General Practitioners, *Confidentiality*, November 2000, available at *www.rcgp.org.uk*.

[6] *ibid.* para. 1. In *W. v Egdell* [1990] Ch. 359, 390 an earlier version of the GMC guidelines was described by Scott J. as "valuable" in showing the approach of the GMC to the breadth of the doctor's duty of confidence; see also *per* Bingham L.J. *ibid.* at 420.

[7] *Campbell v MGN Ltd* [2002] EWCA Civ 1373; [2003] 2 W.L.R. 80 at [48]; commented on by Arnold (2003) 119 L.Q.R. 192.

[8] "The law has long recognised that an obligation of confidence can arise out of particular relationships. Examples are the relationships of doctor and patient, priest and penitent, solicitor and client, banker and customer," *per* Lord Keith in *A.-G. v Guardian Newspapers (No. 2)* [1990] 1 A.C. 109, 255; see also *Goddard v Nationwide Building Society* [1986] 3 All E.R. 264, 271, *per* Nourse L.J.: "The equitable jurisdiction is well able to extend, for example, to the grant of an injunction to restrain an unauthorised disclosure of confidential communications between priest and penitent or doctor and patient"; see also *Hunter v Mann* [1974] Q.B. 767, 772, *per* Boreham J.: ". . . the doctor is under a duty not to disclose [voluntarily], without the consent of his patient, information which he, the doctor, has gained in his professional capacity."

Tribunal: "The question in the present case is not whether Dr Egdell was under a duty of confidence; *he plainly was*. The question is as to the breadth of that duty."[9] In *Cornelius v De Taranto*[10] it was held that a medico-legal report which contained information about an individual's medical history and private life obtained from an interview and from her medical records, was confidential to the person commissioning the report.

2–162   A duty of confidence frequently arises from the relationship between a professional person (such as a lawyer or accountant) and the client. Usually, the duty will derive from the contract, as either an express or implied term. Patients within the NHS do not normally enter into a contractual relationship with their doctor. But, apart from a duty in contract, equity will intervene to protect confidences where three requirements are satisfied, namely: (i) the information must have the necessary quality of confidence about it; (ii) it must have been imparted in circumstances importing an obligation of confidence; and (iii) there must be unauthorised use of that information to the detriment of the person who communicated it.[11] If these requirements are satisfied, the burden lies upon the defendant to establish some justification for disclosure of the confidential information.[12]

2–163   Medical information imparted in the context of the doctor-patient relationship clearly satisfies the first two requirements. The question of what amounts to "detriment" to a patient is more problematic and has not been fully addressed. Does a patient who does not base his claim for breach of confidence on a contractual relationship have to establish that the breach has, or is likely to, cause financial or physical/psychological harm, or is the disclosure of the information sufficient in itself to constitute a detriment?

2–164   In *A.-G. v Guardian Newspapers Ltd (No. 2)*[13] there was a division of opinion in the House of Lords on this issue, with Lord Griffiths in favour of a requirement of some detriment, whereas Lord Keith considered that it was a sufficient detriment to the confider that the information given in confidence is to be disclosed to persons whom he would prefer not to know of it, even though the disclosure would not be harmful to him in any positive way. As

---

[9] [1990] Ch. 359, 389, emphasis added. In the Court of Appeal Bingham L.J. said, *ibid.* at 419, that: "It has never been doubted that the circumstances here were such as to impose on Dr. Egdell a duty of confidence owed to W . . . It is not in issue here that a duty of confidence existed." In *R. v Department of Health, ex parte Source Informatics* [2001] Q.B. 424 at [19] Simon Brown L.J. commented on Bingham L.J.'s observation that "a dictum from that source is worth many a *ratio decidendi* from another." See also *X. v Y.* [1988] 2 All E.R. 648, although the breach of confidence at issue in this case was the duty owed by a hospital employee to his employers under a contract of employment, not the duty owed by a doctor to his patient.

[10] [2001] EWCA Civ 1511; (2001) 68 B.M.L.R. 62.

[11] *Coco v A. N. Clark (Engineers) Ltd* [1969] R.P.C. 41, 47, *per* Megarry J.; *Stephens v Avery* [1988] 2 All E.R. 477, 479; *A.-G. v Guardian Newspapers (No. 2)* [1990] 1 A.C. 109, 268.

[12] *A.-G. v Guardian Newspapers (No. 2)* [1990] 1 A.C. 109, 269 *per* Lord Griffiths. The public interest in the freedom of the press may, in some circumstances, be sufficient justification. See the discussion by the Court of Appeal in *A v B plc* [2002] EWCA Civ 337; [2003] Q.B. 195 on how the courts should approach the balancing exercise (though this case was somewhat removed from issues of medical confidentiality, since it involved publication of details about the extra-marital affairs of a well-known footballer).

[13] [1990] 1 A.C. 109.

a general rule, said his Lordship, it is in the public interest that confidences should be respected, and the encouragement of such respect may in itself constitute a sufficient ground for recognising and enforcing the obligation of confidence, even in the absence of specific detriment. Although Lord Griffiths insisted on some detriment, he did accept that the court would protect a marital confidence from disclosure on the ground that this might involve the loss of a friend, "and friends can be precious."[14] For Lord Keith the invasion of personal privacy in such a case was a sufficient reason for intervening. The disclosure of confidential medical information may, of course, result in the loss of a friend, or in extreme cases (as possibly with HIV and AIDS) substantial financial loss.[15]

The legal protection afforded to medical confidences should not, however, depend upon this fortuitous and arbitrary circumstance or the artificial identification of hypothetical or notional losses, and for this reason Lord Keith's view is to be preferred. In *Cornelius v De Taranto*[16] Morland J. held that the claimant had suffered a detriment because the defendant transmitted a medico-legal report to a psychiatrist and a NHS hospital in breach of contract and in breach of confidence. It mattered not that "no use detrimental to the claimant was made of this report."[17] There is clearly a public interest in the preservation of medical confidences, since full disclosure by a patient to his doctor of information about his medical condition is an essential requirement for diagnosis and treatment. Patients should not be afraid to speak frankly about embarrassing matters, or be deterred from obtaining necessary medical assistance by the fear of unauthorised disclosure.[18] This problem is likely to be most acute with illnesses such as venereal disease and AIDS (or HIV infection),[19] and psychiatric disorders.[20]

2–165

---

[14] See *Argyll v Argyll* [1965] 1 All E.R. 611.

[15] See, *e.g.*, Napier (1989) 18 I.L.J. 84; Wacks (1988) 138 N.L.J. 254, 255.

[16] [2001] EWCA Civ 1511; (2001) 68 B.M.L.R. 62.

[17] *ibid.* at [72], citing *X. v Y.* [1988] 2 All E.R. 648, 657 where Rose J. said that detriment in the use of information about two patients' medical history was not a necessary precondition to injunctive relief: "I respectfully agree with Megarry V.-C. [in *Coco v A. N. Clark (Engineers) Ltd* [1969] R.P.C. 41, 48] that an injunction may be appropriate for breach of confidence where the plaintiff may not suffer from the use of the information and that is borne out by more recent observations in the Court of Appeal and the House of Lords . . . which contain no reference to the necessity for detriment in use, and indeed point away from any such principle." His Lordship referred to *Lion Laboratories Ltd v Evans* [1984] 2 All E.R. 417; *Schering Chemicals Ltd v Falkman Ltd* [1981] 2 All E.R. 321; and *British Steel Corporation v Granada Television Ltd* [1981] 1 All E.R. 417.

[18] *X. v Y.* [1988] 2 All E.R. 648, 656, *per* Rose J.

[19] Venereal disease is the subject of a specific statutory duty of confidence: see the National Health Service (Venereal Diseases) Regulations 1974, (S.I. 1974 No. 29). In *X. v Y.* [1988] 2 All E.R. 648, 656 Rose J. seemed to assume that this statutory duty applied to AIDS patients. In *H (a health care worker) v Associated Newspapers Ltd* [2002] EWCA Civ 195; [2002] Lloyd's Rep. Med. 210 Lord Phillips M.R. said, at [27], that: "there is an obvious public interest in preserving the confidentiality of victims of the AIDS epidemic and, in particular, of healthcare workers who report the fact that they are HIV positive." See also *Z. v Finland* (1997) 25 E.H.R.R. 371; (1997) 45 B.M.L.R. 107 at [96] (E.C.H.R.).

[20] *cf.*, however, Scott J. in *W. v Egdell* [1990] Ch. 359, 393, responding to the suggestion that if patients could not suppress unfavourable psychiatric reports they would not be wholly

2–166   It is unlikely that a court would refuse to grant an injunction to restrain a threatened breach of medical confidence on the ground that a patient has suffered no detriment. Given that the doctor-patient relationship is widely cited as the paradigm example of a confidential relationship, the court would either strain to find something detrimental to the claimant on the facts or would simply accept that the disclosure itself is a detriment. If the patient's complaint concerns a past breach of confidence, however, the position may be different since there is considerable uncertainty about the availability of damages as a remedy for breach of a confidence which is not based on breach of contract, and even here, where the claim is for distress or invasion of privacy, damages may be nominal.[21] For this reason the disciplinary powers of the General Medical Council and the profession's ethical standards may be more effective in maintaining patient confidentiality.

2–167   The duty of confidence binds not only the first recipient of the information, but also anyone else to whom that information is communicated who knows or ought to know that the information which he has received is confidential in character.[22] In exceptional circumstances, the law of confidentiality can extend to cover information as to the identity or whereabouts of individuals, where disclosure would place them at risk of serious injury or death, and an injunction may be granted against the whole world.[23]

2–168   In addition to domestic law on confidentiality it is clear that the confidentiality of medical records is considered to be a central aspect of the requirement of Article 8 of the European Convention on Human Rights, providing the right to respect for private and family life. In *Z. v Finland*[24] the European Court of Human Rights stated that:

> ". . . the protection of personal data, not least medical data, is of fundamental importance to a person's enjoyment of his or her right to respect for private and family life as guaranteed by Article 8 of the Convention. Respecting the confidentiality of health data is a vital principle in the legal systems of all the Contracting Parties to the Convention. It is crucial not only to respect the sense of privacy of a patient but also to preserve his or her confidence in the medical profession and in the health services in general.

(n.20 contd.) frank: "I do not think that this answer has much weight. The possibility of a lack of frankness must always be present when a psychiatric examination takes place. An experienced psychiatrist would, I think, expect to be able to detect it. And the lack of frankness itself would constitute material of interest to the psychiatrist."

[21] See paras 9–112 to 9–115. This discrepancy may mark a difference between private patients and patients treated under the NHS.

[22] Though the breadth and nature of the duty of confidence must be considered separately against each defendant, because "the third party recipient may be subject to some additional and conflicting duty which does not affect the primary confidant or may not be subject to some special duty which does affect the confidant. In such situations the equation is not the same in the case of the confidant and that of the third party and accordingly the result may be different," *per* Sir John Donaldson M.R. in *A.-G. v Guardian Newspapers Ltd (No. 2)* [1990] 1 A.C. 109, 183, cited by Scott J. in *W. v Egdell* [1990] Ch. 359, 388.

[23] *Venables v News Group Newspapers Ltd* [2001] Fam. 430, CA.

[24] (1997) 25 E.H.R.R. 371; (1997) 45 B.M.L.R. 107 at [95].

Without such protection, those in need of medical assistance may be deterred from revealing such information of a personal and intimate nature as may be necessary in order to receive appropriate treatment and, even, from seeking such assistance, thereby endangering their own health and, in the case of transmissible diseases, that of the community."[25]

But as with the law of confidentiality, this right is not absolute. The interests of a patient and the community in protecting the confidentiality of medical information may be outweighed by other interests, such as the prosecution of criminal offences or the publicity of court proceedings.[26] Any interference with the claimant's Article 8 rights must be necessary in a democratic society and proportionate to the legitimate aims pursued.

(1) Scope of the duty of confidence

The duty of confidentiality only applies to information relating to identifiable individuals. Thus, if data is anonymised before being released there is no breach. In *R v Department of Health, ex parte Source Informatics*[27] the Court of Appeal held that pharmacists were entitled to pass on anonymised information concerning drug prescriptions to a commercial organisation which proposed to sell information about doctors' prescribing habits to pharmaceutical companies for marketing purposes. Simon Brown L.J. commented that:

2-169

". . . the confidant is placed under a duty of good faith to the confider and the touchstone by which to judge the scope of his duty and whether or not it has been fulfilled or breached is his own conscience, no more and no less. One asks, therefore, on the facts of this case: would a reasonable pharmacist's conscience be troubled by the proposed use to be made of patients' prescriptions? Would he think that by entering Source's scheme he was breaking his customers' confidence, making unconscientious use of the information they provide?"[28]

The concern of the law was to protect the confider's personal privacy. The patient had no property in the information and no right to control its use, provided that his privacy was not put at risk, and therefore "the confidence is not breached where the confider's identity is protected."[29] It followed that the "pharmacists' consciences ought not reasonably to be troubled by co-operation with Source's proposed scheme. The patient's privacy will have

---

[25] See also *MS v Sweden* (1997) 28 E.H.R.R. 313; (1997) 3 B.H.R.C. 248 at [41].
[26] (1997) 25 E.H.R.R. 371; (1997) 45 B.M.L.R. 107 at [97]. See also *MS v Sweden* (1997) 28 E.H.R.R. 313; (1997) 3 B.H.R.C. 248, para. 2–183, n. 59 below.
[27] [2001] Q.B. 424.
[28] *ibid.* at [31].
[29] *ibid.* at [34].

been safeguarded, not invaded. The pharmacist's duty of confidence will not have been breached."[30]

2–170   Even where the disclosure of the information would affect the privacy of an identifiable individual, the duty of confidence is not absolute, and it is only by looking at the circumstances in which a breach of confidence can be justified in law that the scope of the duty can be appreciated. The General Medical Council, while emphasising the importance of maintaining confidentiality, sets out a number of circumstances in which information about a patient may be disclosed.[31] Some of these circumstances correspond to exceptions to the duty of confidentiality in law, and most of them do not give rise to difficulty.

(a) Consent by the patient[32]

2–171   Consent does not have to be in writing to be valid and may be express or implied.[33] Thus, the right to confidentiality is the patient's not the doctor's.

---

[30] *ibid.* at [35]. For criticism see D. Beyleveld and E. Histed, "Betrayal of Confidence in the Court of Appeal" (2000) 4 Med. Law Int. 276.

[31] *Confidentiality: Protecting and Providing Information*, June 2000.

[32] *ibid.* at paras 13–14. Where a doctor has contractual obligations to third parties, such as employers or insurance companies, as well as obligations to patients, the disclosure of information to that third party requires the patient's consent, unless disclosure is "necessary to protect others from risk of death or serious harm": *ibid.* at paras 34–35.

[33] *Hunter v Mann* [1974] Q.B. 767, 772. Though in cases where it is sought to argue that patients in general may be taken to have impliedly consented to the use of information for a particular purpose, it may be better to deal with the situation as part of the wider public interest defence: *R. v Department of Health, ex parte Source Informatics* [2001] Q.B. 424 at [51]. This avoids the problem of seeking to rely on the implied consent of those individuals who may expressly *refuse* consent. The GMC guidance states that where the patient may be personally affected by the disclosure the doctor must obtain express consent. As to the patient's right of access to his medical records see paras 10–105 *et seq.* Where medical records have been compiled by servants or agents of the defendant himself, the claimant is still entitled to claim that as between himself and the doctor they are confidential, and the defendant must obtain either the claimant's waiver of confidentiality or an order of the court for their disclosure: *Dunn v British Coal Corporation* [1993] P.I.Q.R. P275, CA; *Nicholson v Halton General Hospital NHS Trust* [1999] P.I.Q.R. P310, CA—where a claimant brings an action for personal injuries the court will not compel the claimant to waive the right of confidentiality of medical records, but in an appropriate case it can order that the action be stayed until he consents to waive the right; *cf. Shaw v Skeet* [1996] 7 Med. L.R. 371, QBD, where it was suggested that in bringing a personal injury action the claimant waives his right to confidentiality. This was also the view in *Hay v University of Alberta Hospital* (1990) 69 D.L.R. (4th) 755; [1991] 2 Med. L.R. 204 (Alta. Q.B.) where it was held that a patient puts his health in issue by bringing proceedings for damages against a doctor or health authority, so he impliedly consents to the defendants' lawyers having access to his medical records and discussing his medical condition with the physicians who treated him; *cf.* however *St. Louis v Feleki* (1990) 75 D.L.R. (4th) 758 (Ont. H.C.) where Craig J. held that it was not the case that simply by commencing an action for damages resulting from personal injuries a litigant-patient waives the right to confidentiality, or that there is an implied consent to a doctor releasing information to the defendant. The Rules of Civil Procedure as to discovery and the defendant's right to have the claimant medically examined were sufficient protection for defendants.

(b) Sharing information with others providing care[34]

Doctors working in hospital and general practice are usually working in   2–172
a health care team, some of whose members may need access to confidential
information about the patient in order to perform their duties. The General
Medical Council states that express consent is not usually needed before relevant personal information is shared to enable the treatment to be provided.
Doctors must make it clear to members of the team who receive the information that it is given to them in confidence. Clearly, all the members of the
health care team come under a corresponding duty of confidentiality with
regard to the information communicated to them about the patient.
Similarly, public bodies, such as health authorities, have a responsibility to
take appropriate steps to preserve the confidentiality of medical records
when transmitting them to another public body.[35]

The sharing of medical information for the purpose of treatment would   2–173
probably be regarded by a court as an instance of implied consent by the
patient, although in *W. v Egdell*[36] Scott J. considered that the disclosure of
an independent psychiatrist's report to the hospital where the claimant was
detained was justified under this provision, even though the patient had
expressly refused his consent. The Court of Appeal doubted whether this
exception applied,[37] however, because the psychiatrist did not have a continuing professional relationship with the claimant, although the circumstances
of the disclosure fell within the letter of the exception. If Scott J.'s view were
correct then implied consent could not be the basis for the exception. The
GMC guidance states that the doctor has a responsibility to ensure that
arrangements exist to inform patients about the circumstances in which
information about them is likely to be shared and to give patients the opportunity to state any objection to this.

(c) Medical emergency

The GMC Guidance provides for situations, such as a medical emergency,   2–174
where a patient cannot be informed about the sharing of information. In
these cases the doctor should pass relevant information promptly to those
providing the patient's care.[38]

(d) Children and other patients who may lack competence to consent

Where a patient who is incapable of giving consent to treatment or disclo-   2–175
sure because of immaturity, illness or mental incapacity asks a doctor not to

---

[34] GMC, *Confidentiality: Protecting and Providing Information*, June 2000 at paras 7–9.
[35] *A Health Authority v X* [2001] 2 F.L.R. 673; [2001] Lloyd's Rep. Med. 349 at [57] *per* Munby J.; affirmed [2001] EWCA Civ 2014; [2002] 2 All E.R. 780.
[36] [1990] Ch. 359, 392; see paras 2–187 to 2–188 for the facts of this case.
[37] *ibid.* at 420–421, *per* Bingham L.J.
[38] *Confidentiality: Protecting and Providing Information*, June 2000, para. 10.

disclose information to a third party, the GMC guidance indicates that the doctor should try to persuade the patient to allow an appropriate person to be involved in the consultation. If the patient refuses and the doctor judges that it is essential, in their medical interests, she may disclose relevant information to an appropriate person or authority.[39] The doctor should tell the patient before disclosing any information.[40]

(e) Abuse or neglect

2–176   Where a doctor believes that a patient may be the victim of abuse or neglect, and the patient is not capable of giving or withholding consent to disclosure, the doctor should disclose information promptly to an appropriate responsible person or statutory agency, where disclosure is in the patient's best interests.[41] In law, this exception would probably be justified under the "public interest" defence.

(f) Statutory obligations

2–177   A doctor "must disclose information to satisfy a specific statutory requirement, such as notification of a known or suspected communicable disease."[42] There are a number of statutes under which the disclosure of information is compulsory, and doctors are not exempt from these requirements.[43]

---

[39] *ibid*. para. 38. This modified guidance is derived from the decision of the House of Lords in *Gillick v West Norfolk and Wisbech Area Health Authority* [1986] A.C. 112, on which see paras 6–046 to 6–051. Clearly, where a child does have sufficient maturity and understanding the doctor must respect the confidentiality of the doctor-patient relationship.

[40] *ibid*. Note that there may be rare circumstances in which there could be a duty of care not to reveal facts about the patient's condition to the patient. *Furniss v Fitchett* [1958] N.Z.L.R. 396 provides an unusual example. The Data Protection Act 1998, s. 30 and the Data Protection (Subject Access Modification) (Health) Order 2000 (S.I. 2000 No. 413) exempts from the general right of access to information conferred by that Act information as to the physical or mental health of a data subject, where, *inter alia*, access would be likely to cause serious harm to the physical or mental health of the data subject. The circumstances in which these exceptions apply have yet to be considered by the courts. See also Supreme Court Act 1981 ss. 33 and 34 under which disclosure of medical records can be limited to the applicant's legal advisers and/or any medical or other professional adviser of the applicant; see further paras 10–112, 10–117, 10–130.

[41] *ibid*., para. 39. See also *Brown v University of Alberta Hospital* (1997) 145 D.L.R. (4th) 63 (Alta. Q.B), where a radiologist was held to owe a duty of care to a child to pass on information to the doctors treating the child which raised a suspicion that the child's injuries were non-accidental.

[42] *ibid*. para. 43.

[43] See, *e.g.*, Public Health (Control of Disease) Act 1984, s. 11; Abortion Act 1967, s. 2 and the Abortion Regulations 1991 (S.I. 1991 No. 499) as amended by the Abortion (Amendment) (England) Regulations 2002 (S.I. 2002 No. 887); Road Traffic Act 1988, s. 172(2) [on which see *Hunter v Mann* [1974] 1 Q.B. 767]; Police and Criminal Evidence Act 1984, ss. 9–12; Misuse of Drugs Act 1971, s. 23; Prevention of Terrorism (Temporary Provisions) Act 1989, s. 18; National Health Service Act 1977, s. 124 and the National Health Service (Notification of Births and Deaths) Regulations 1982 (S.I. 1982 No. 286). For consideration of the extent to which it is possible to prevent publication of the name and address of a person against whom an order for the compulsory removal to hospital of a

(g) Monitoring public health, medical teaching, clinical audit and medical research

These activities may involve disclosure of information about individuals   **2–178**
for purposes other than the patient's health care. If the information is in a
form which does not enable individuals to be identified, there is no question
of a breach of confidence.[44] In the case of public health monitoring (which
would include, *e.g.*, reporting on the safety of medicines or medical devices),
the GMC advises that if disclosure of the information would enable individuals to be identified, the doctor should seek express consent, wherever practical, but does allow for the possibility that if obtaining consent is not
practical disclosure may be justified in the public interest.[45] For the purpose
of clinical audit and education the GMC considers that anonymised data will
usually be sufficient, but in any event non-anonymised data should not be
disclosed without the patient's consent.[46]

Some of the earlier versions of the General Medical Council's advice on   **2–179**
confidentiality and medical research made no reference to the patient's
consent, and it was at least arguable that a legal justification for the exception could derive from the public interest defence, in that it is in the public
interest that properly regulated medical research should be conducted and
that the results should be available to the scientific community.[47] On the
other hand, research should not normally be conducted without the patients'
consent, and if the doctor can reasonably practicably obtain consent to conducting the research there would seem to be no reason for not obtaining
consent to disclosure of the results at the same time. The GMC suggest that
where a research project depends on using identifiable information, and it is
not practical to contact patients to seek their consent, this should be drawn
to the attention of a research ethics committee so that it can consider

---

(n.43 contd.) person with a notifiable disease has been made under the Public Health
(Control of Disease) Act 1984, s. 37, see: *Birmingham Post & Mail Ltd v Birmingham City
Council* (1993) 17 B.M.L.R. 116.

[44] See *R. v Department of Health, ex parte Source Informatics* [2001] Q.B. 424.

[45] *Confidentiality: Protecting and Providing Information*, June 2000, paras 23–26.

[46] *ibid.* para. 28. However, in *R. v Department of Health, ex parte Source Informatics* [2001]
Q.B. 424 at [53] it was suggested that the use of identifiable data for the purpose of audit,
provided the use is "very strictly controlled", would be acceptable, either because it falls
within the public interest defence or because the scope of the duty of confidentiality is
circumscribed to accommodate it.

[47] Researchers may not be able to maintain the confidentiality of their data, even where it is
supplied to them on a confidential basis. In the litigation concerning claims that some children have sustained brain damage as a reaction to pertussis vaccine, the defendants sought
access to the data contained in the National Childhood Encephalopathy Study, which had
been provided to the researchers on a confidential basis by doctors and hospitals. Stuart-
Smith J. held that the interests of justice outweighed both the interests of patients in maintaining confidentiality of their records and the public interest in conducting research, which
could be damaged if doctors and patients who co-operated in research projects believed that
the information they supplied would not be kept confidential. It was ordered that the data
be produced, with patient anonymity preserved by referring to patients by number: *Kinnear
v Wellcome Foundation Ltd*; *Loveday v Renton*, both unreported on this point. On the relationship between research, access to records and confidentiality see Thomson (1993) 1 J.
Law and Med. 95.

whether the likely benefits of the research outweigh the loss of confidentiality. But as the GMC acknowledges, although the views of a research ethics committee would, no doubt, be taken into account by a court if a claim for breach of confidentiality were made, the court would make its own assessment of whether the public interest was served in determining whether the breach of confidentiality was justified.[48]

2–180   There is now statutory provision covering situations where the consent of the patient to the use of health records cannot practically be obtained, and anonymised information is insufficient. Research projects may involve tens of thousands of patients where contact would be impracticable, but it may be judged that the essential nature of the research is such that the public interest outweighs issues of privacy. Some patients are not capable of giving consent, but the health service may still need to know about them and their medical conditions. Moreover, sometimes excluding those who refuse consent could bias data collection to the extent that it loses all value. In order to deal with the potential problem that these situations create, section 60 of the Health and Social Care Act 2001 allows the Secretary of State to make regulations to permit the processing of prescribed patient information for medical purposes where it is considered necessary or expedient (a) in the interests of improving patient care, or (b) in the public interest.[49] Section 60(3) provides that regulations may not authorise the processing of confidential patient information for any purpose if it would be reasonably practicable to achieve that purpose otherwise than pursuant to such regulations, having regard to the cost of and the technology available for achieving that purpose, in other words if it would be reasonably practicable to obtain the patient's consent or anonymise the information. Nor may regulations permit the processing of prescribed patient information in a manner inconsistent with the Data Protection Act 1998. The Health Service (Control of Patient Information) Regulations 2002 cover essentially: (1) the information held by and activities of cancer registries (medical purposes related to the diagnosis or treatment of neoplasia); (2) the diagnosis and control of communicable diseases and other risks to public health (including monitoring and managing the delivery, efficacy and safety of immunisation programmes, adverse reactions to vaccines and medicines, and risks of infection acquired from food or the environment); (3) medical research; and (4) the audit, monitoring and analysing of the provision made by the health service for patient care and treatment. The processing of confidential patient information in accordance with the regulations is not unlawful, despite any obligation of confidence owed by that person in respect of it.[50]

---

[48] Confidentiality: Protecting and Providing Information, June 2000, para. 31.
[49] See the Health Service (Control of Patient Information) Regulations 2002, S.I. 2002 No. 1438.
[50] Health and Social Care Act 2001, s. 60(2)(c); and Health Service (Control of Patient Information) Regulations 2002, S.I. 2002 No. 1438, reg. 4. For the definition of "patient information" and "confidential patient information" see ss. 60(8) and (9). s. 61 of the Act establishes a Patient Information Advisory Group whose function is to advise the Secretary of State about applications made under the regulations to use confidential patient information for the specified purposes.

(h) Where a doctor is directed to disclose information by virtue of an order of the court[51]

Examples include the direction of a judge that a doctor must give evidence in court either orally or by producing documents, and an order under sections 33 or 34 of the Supreme Court Act 1981,[52] though in most cases the applicant seeking disclosure under these provisions will be the patient, who will effectively have consented to the disclosure. The GMC cautions that where litigation is in prospect, unless the patient has consented to disclosure or a formal court order has been made for disclosure, information should not be disclosed merely in response to demands from other persons such as another party's solicitor or an official of the court. On the other hand, in *Walker v Eli Lilly & Co*[53] Hirst J. commented that health authorities and doctors who are not likely to be defendants should respond readily and promptly to requests for disclosure to avoid unnecessary expense and delay.

2–181

A judge has a discretion to allow a doctor to decline to answer a question when giving evidence in court. In *Hunter v Mann*[54] Widgery C.J. said that:

2–182

". . . if a doctor, giving evidence in court, is asked a question which he finds embarrassing because it involves him talking about things which he would normally regard as confidential, he can seek the protection of the judge and ask the judge if it is necessary for him to answer."

The judge's exercise of this discretion clearly depends on the importance of the potential answer to the issues being tried.

(i) Disciplinary proceedings

Similarly, it is expected that a doctor will comply with an official request to disclose personal information from a statutory regulatory body for any of the health care professions, where it is necessary in the interests of justice and for the safety of other patients.[55] The public interest in the proper regulation of the health care professions will justify the disclosure of otherwise

2–183

---

[51] *Confidentiality: Protecting and Providing Information*, June 2000, para. 44. Doctors do not enjoy a privilege equivalent to legal professional privilege: *A.-G. v Mulholland and Foster* [1963] 1 All E.R. 767, 771. See also Matthews (1984) 1 L.S. 77.

[52] See paras 10–125 to 10–130, 10–141. See, *e.g.*, *Australian Red Cross Society v B.C.* [1992] 3 Med. L.R. 273 (S.C. of Vict., App. Div.); *P.D. v Australian Red Cross Society (New South Wales Division)* (1993) 30 N.S.W.L.R. 376 (N.S.W.C.A.); *Sharpe Estate v Northwestern General Hospital* (1991) 76 D.L.R. (4th) 535 (Ont. Ct. Gen Div.), affirming (1990) 74 D.L.R. (4th) 43, in which courts have ordered the defendants to disclose the identity of blood donors to the claimant, because the public interest in the administration of justice outweighed the public interest in preserving the privacy and confidentiality of blood donors; *cf. A.B. v Glasgow and West of Scotland Blood Transfusion Service* (1989), 1993 S.L.T. 36; 15 B.M.L.R. 91. See further paras 10–140 to 10–156.

[53] *The Times*, May 1, 1986.

[54] [1974] 1 Q.B. 767, 775.

[55] *Confidentiality: Protecting and Providing Information*, June 2000, para. 46.

confidential information to a professional regulatory agency. In *Woolgar v Chief Constable of Sussex Police*[56] the Court of Appeal held that the disclosure of information about a nurse by the police to the United Kingdom Central Council for Nursing, Midwifery and Health Visiting (the UKCC[57]) was justified both under the law of confidentiality and Article 8 of the European Convention on Human Rights:

"... where a regulatory body such as the UKCC, operating in the field of public health and safety, seeks access to confidential material in the possession of the police, being material which the police are reasonably persuaded is of some relevance to the subject matter of an inquiry being conducted by the regulatory body, then a countervailing public interest is shown to exist which, as in this case, entitles the police to release the material to the regulatory body on the basis that save in so far as it may be used by the regulatory body for the purposes of its own inquiry, the confidentiality which already attaches to the material will be maintained."[58]

Although Article 8(1) of the Convention provides that every one has the right to respect for his family life, Article 8(2) allows for exceptions in the interests of national security, public safety or the economic well-being of the country, for the prevention of disorder or crime, for the protection of health or morals, or for the protection of the rights and freedoms of others, provided it can be said that the interference was also "necessary in a democratic society". The police were justified in reporting information to the UKCC "in the interests of ... public safety ... or for the protection of health or morals, or for the protection of the rights and freedoms of others." Indeed, the police were free to pass on confidential information even if there was no request from the regulatory body, which in their reasonable view, in the interests of public health or safety, should be considered by a professional or regulatory body.[59]

2–184   Similarly, in *A Health Authority v X*[60] the Court of Appeal held that disclosure by a local authority, following a public law case in the Family Division, of general practitioner records to a health authority for the purpose

---

[56] [2000] 1 W.L.R. 25; [1999] 3 All E.R. 604.
[57] Now the Nursing and Midwifery Council: Nursing and Midwifery Order 2001, S.I. 2002, No. 253.
[58] [2000] 1 W.L.R. 25 at 36.
[59] *ibid.* See also *MS v Sweden* (1997) 28 E.H.R.R. 313; (1997) 3 B.H.R.C. 248 in which the applicant sustained a back injury and objected to the disclosure of medical records to the Social Insurance Office for the purpose of assessing her compensation claim. The European Court of Human Rights held that there were relevant and sufficient reasons for the communication of the medical records and this was not disproportionate to the legitimate aim pursued. This justified what would otherwise have been a breach of the applicant's rights under Art. 8.1 of the European Convention on Human Rights.
[60] [2001] EWCA Civ 2014; [2002] 2 All E.R. 780. *A Health Authority v X* (No. 2) [2002] EWHC 26; [2002] 1 F.L.R. 383; [2002] Lloyd's Rep. Med. 145 concerned an unopposed application to vary an order granting permission to disclose documents from care proceedings to certain official and professional bodies, including the General Medical Council.

of the authority carrying out its regulatory function, was justified provided that there were effective safeguards of the patients' confidentiality and anonymity. There was, said the Court, a high public interest, analogous to the public interest in the administration of justice, in the proper administration of professional disciplinary hearings, particularly in the field of medicine. The question was whether the public interest in effective disciplinary procedures for the investigation and eradication of medical malpractice outweighed the confidentiality of the records, but as Thorpe L.J. observed: "The balance came down in favour of production *as it invariably does*, save in exceptional cases."[61]

(j) Disclosure in the public interest

The GMC Guidance indicates that medical information may be disclosed   **2–185** without the patient's consent "in the public interest where the benefits to an individual or to society of the disclosure outweigh the public and the patient's interest in keeping the information confidential."[62] This includes situations where third parties are exposed to a risk so serious that it outweighs the patient's privacy interest,[63] such as: (a) where a doctor, who is also a patient, is placing patients at risk as a result of illness or other medical condition; (b) where a patient continues to drive, against medical advice, when unfit to do so; and (c) where a disclosure may assist in the prevention or detection of a serious crime.[64] This is supplemented by the advice given in the GMC's guidance, *Serious Communicable Diseases*[65]:

> "You may disclose information about a patient, whether living or dead, in order to protect a person from risk of death or serious harm. For example, you may disclose information to a known sexual contact of a patient with HIV where you have reason to think that the patient has not informed that person, and cannot be persuaded to do so. In such circumstances you should tell the patient before you make the disclosure, and you must be prepared to justify a decision to disclose information."

The law has long-recognised that disclosures of confidential information   **2–186** may be justified in the public interest, and it seems likely that the specific examples given by the GMC would meet the criteria for the public interest test in law. It has been said that "there is no confidence as to the disclosure

---

[61] *ibid.* at [20] (emphasis added). See also *Re A (a minor) (disclosure of medical records to the General Medical Council)* (1998) 47 B.M.L.R. 84; [1999] 1 F.C.R. 30—the court has the power to attach conditions protecting the confidentiality of patients to an order directing the release of case papers in Children Act proceedings to a third party.

[62] *Confidentiality: Protecting and Providing Information*, June 2000, paras 18–20.

[63] *ibid.* at para. 36.

[64] *ibid.* at para. 37. "Serious crime" is said to be an offence that puts someone at risk of death or serious harm, such as abuse of children.

[65] October 1997, para. 22 (available at *www.gmc-uk.org/standards*). See also para. 19.

of iniquity,"[66] though the iniquity rule is itself only part of the wider principle of public interest which may justify disclosure. This inevitably involves the weighing of competing interests, as Lord Goff observed in *A.-G. v Guardian Newspapers (No. 2)*:

> ". . . although the basis of the law's protection of confidence is that there is a public interest that confidences should be preserved and protected by the law, nevertheless that public interest may be outweighed by some other countervailing public interest which favours disclosure . . . It is this limiting principle which may require a court to carry out a balancing operation, weighing the public interest in maintaining confidence against a countervailing public interest favouring disclosure."[67]

2–187   The scope of the public interest defence in the specific context of the doctor-patient relationship was considered in *W. v Egdell*,[68] where the question was whether a psychiatrist who had prepared a medical report on a patient was entitled to disclose the contents of the report both to the hospital where the patient was detained and to the Home Secretary. W was detained as a patient in a secure hospital without limit of time following a conviction for manslaughter of five neighbours on the grounds of diminished responsibility. He was diagnosed as suffering from paranoid schizophrenia. Ten years after his detention he applied to a Mental Health Review Tribunal for a transfer to a regional secure unit with a view, ultimately, to obtaining a conditional discharge. W's solicitors instructed Dr Egdell, a consultant psychiatrist, to produce an independent psychiatric report for the purpose of the Tribunal hearing. Dr Egdell referred to the possibility that W was suffering from a paranoid psychosis rather than paranoid schizophrenia, which meant that medication would be less effective in protecting against a relapse. Moreover, there was a possibility that W might have a psychopathic deviant personality.

2–188   In view of the report W's solicitors withdrew the application to the Tribunal. Dr Egdell then sent the report to the hospital, also urging the hospital to forward a copy to the Home Secretary. Subsequently the Home Secretary referred W's case to the Mental Health Review Tribunal under section 71(2) of the Mental Health Act 1983, and sent a copy of the report to the Tribunal. W sought an injunction restraining the defendants from using or disclosing the contents of the report, and damages (including aggravated damages) against the hospital board and the Home Secretary. Scott J. held that Dr Egdell's duty to W was not his only duty, since W was not an ordinary member of the public. He was a detained patient in a secure hospital subject to a regime whereby decisions concerning his future were to be taken by public authorities. In taking those decisions W's interests would not

---

[66] *Fraser v Evans* [1969] 1 All E.R. 8, 11, *per* Lord Denning M.R. citing Page Wood V.-C. in *Gartside v Outram* (1856) 26 L.J. Ch. 113, 114.
[67] [1990] 1 A.C. 109, 282.
[68] [1990] Ch. 359.

be the only or even the main criterion. The safety of the public would be the main criterion. In those circumstances Dr Egdell had a duty to the public to place the result of his examination before the proper authorities, if, in his opinion, the public interest so required. The public interest in disclosure outweighed W's private interest.[69]

The Court of Appeal agreed that Scott J. had struck the correct balance   **2–189** between the public interest in patients being able to make full and frank disclosure to their doctors in reliance on the doctors' obligation of confidence, and the public interest in the safety of members of the public who might be at risk if W were released:

> "Where a man has committed multiple killings under the disability of serious mental illness, decisions which may lead directly or indirectly to his release from hospital should not be made unless the responsible authority is properly able to make an informed judgment that the risk of repetition is so small as to be acceptable. A consultant psychiatrist who becomes aware, even in the course of a confidential relationship, of information which leads him, in the exercise of what the court considers a sound professional judgment, to fear that such decisions may be made on inadequate information and with a real risk of consequent danger to the public is entitled to take such steps as are reasonable in all the circumstances to communicate the grounds of his concern to the responsible authorities."[70]

In *Re C (A Minor) (Evidence: Confidential Information)*[71] a mother, who   **2–190** had looked after her child for only four days after its birth, refused consent to the child being adopted. The mother's general practitioner voluntarily

---

[69] The actions against the other defendants also failed, though Scott J. considered that even if the case against Dr Egdell had succeeded the other defendants would have had a valid public interest defence in view of the nature of the statutory scheme created by the Mental Health Act 1983. The claims against the other defendants were not pursued on appeal. An argument that Dr Egdell's report was the subject of legal professional privilege was rejected by Scott J., and dismissed almost peremptorily by the Court of Appeal.

[70] [1990] Ch. 359, 424. See also *R. v Crozier* (1990) 8 B.M.L.R. 128, CA, where a psychiatrist instructed by the appellant acted reasonably and responsibly in showing his report on the appellant to prosecuting counsel, since he believed that the appellant suffered from a psychopathic disorder which made him a danger to the public. The public interest in disclosure outweighed the duty of confidence owed to the appellant. In *Smith v Jones* (1999) 169 D.L.R. (4th) 385 a psychiatrist instructed by the defence to provide a forensic assessment on an individual accused of aggravated sexual assault on a prostitute formed the view that the accused was dangerous and likely to commit further offences involving the kidnap and murder of prostitutes. When he discovered that his concerns would not be brought to the attention of the sentencing judge, he issued an application for a declaration that he was entitled to disclose his opinion, and the statements made to him by the accused, in the interests of public safety. The Supreme Court of Canada held that the safety of the public may justify the disclosure of information even though the solicitor-client privilege, which attaches to communications between clients and experts retained by their lawyer for the purpose of preparing a defence, would normally apply (*i.e.* legal professional privilege, see para. 10–145). Disclosure would be justified where there was a clear, imminent risk of serious bodily harm or death to an identifiable person or group.

[71] [1991] 2 F.L.R. 478.

provided to the applicants information about the mother's medical condition which the applicants sought to introduce as evidence in the adoption proceedings. The mother sought to exclude the evidence on the basis that it had been provided by her general practitioner in breach of confidence. The Court of Appeal had some doubts as to whether a breach of confidence had actually occurred, but nonetheless held that, if it had, the breach was justified. The public interest in the court dealing with the adoption proceedings in the child's best interests in full possession of the relevant information outweighed the public interest in preserving confidentiality between doctor and patient. Moreover, the doctor had not disclosed the information to the world at large, but only for the restricted purpose of the adoption proceedings.

Limits to the public interest

2–191   The public interest defence to a breach of confidence is potentially very wide in its scope, but it is possible to identify certain limitations on the application of the defence. First, it is well-settled that there is a distinction between what is interesting to the public and what is in the public interest. It does not follow that simply because information would be of interest to the public it is in the public interest to disclose it.[72]

2–192   Secondly, the public interest defence justifies disclosure to the "proper authorities" not necessarily to the world at large.[73] If, for example, Dr Egdell had sold his report to the newspapers he would undoubtedly have been in breach of his duty of confidence.[74] By the same token, in order to satisfy the requirements of Article 8 of the European Convention on Human Rights, any disclosure which the defendant seeks to justify under Article 8.2 must be the minimum necessary to meet the defendant's legitimate objective, *i.e.* it must be proportionate.[75] So a disclosure which goes beyond what is necessary for the proper protection of individuals will not be justified. For example, in *Peters-Brown v Regina District Health Board*[76] the claimant had infectious hepatitis B, but recovered after two months, and thereafter tested negative. For the protection of its staff, the defendant hospital made a list of patients who had infectious blood or bodily fluids. The list was circulated in its laboratories and taped to a computer in a private room in its emergency department. The claimant subsequently found a copy of the list posted in the staff room at her place of work. The Saskatchewan Court of Appeal held

---

[72] *X. v Y.* [1988] 2 All E.R. 648. See further *H (a health care worker) v Associated Newspapers Ltd* [2002] EWCA Civ 195; [2002] Lloyd's Rep. Med. 210 where the Court of Appeal acknowledged that a public debate about the procedures to be adopted by a health authority when a health care worker was diagnosed as HIV positive would raise some issues of public interest.

[73] *W. v Egdell* [1990] Ch. 359, 392; *A.-G. v Guardian Newspapers (No. 2)* [1990] 1 A.C. 109, 282 *per* Lord Goff; *Re C (A Minor) (Evidence: Confidential Information)* [1991] 2 F.L.R. 478; *Furniss v Fitchett* [1958] N.Z.L.R. 396, 406.

[74] *ibid.* at 389 and 419 *per* Scott J. and Bingham L.J. respectively.

[75] *Z. v Finland* (1997) 25 E.H.R.R. 371; (1997) 45 B.M.L.R. 107 at [105]; *MS v Sweden* (1997) 28 E.H.R.R. 313; (1997) 3 B.H.R.C. 248 at [44].

[76] [1996] 1 W.W.R. 337; affirmed [1997] 1 W.W.R. 638 (Sask. C.A.).

that, although the defendant was entitled to notify its staff, who were also subject to a duty of confidentiality, it had been negligent in the manner of posting the information, which should have been loaded on the computer rather than being taped to the computer. It was entirely foreseeable that ambulance crew, police and other unauthorised persons would see the list, even in the private room, causing the claimant mental distress.

Thirdly, the risk of danger to the public must be a "real risk".[77] It is not clear what constitutes a real risk, though on the facts of *W. v Egdell* a possibility of danger rather than a probability appears to be sufficient. It is for the court to determine whether the doctor's assessment of the risk is sound.[78]   **2–193**

A further issue concerns the meaning of the word "public." In *W. v Egdell* both Scott J. and the Court of Appeal spoke of the danger *to the public* as the criterion which justified disclosure. Although it might be argued that danger to a single individual does not constitute danger to the public, the public interest is broader in conception than simply "danger to the public." It is submitted that, on principle, even where the danger is merely to a single individual the public interest in protecting that individual from physical harm would justify disclosure.[79]   **2–194**

This could be relevant not only in the case of psychiatric patients who constitute a danger to others, but also HIV positive patients who, despite counselling, refuse either to tell their sexual partner(s) about their condition or to change their sexual behaviour so as to minimise the risk of infecting their partner(s). It is arguable that there may be rare cases where a strict ethic of confidentiality may be broken to protect the interests of others from a potentially fatal disease.[80] Few would doubt that the disclosure in these circumstances would be justified in law, in the public interest.   **2–195**

---

[77] *W. v Egdell* [1990] Ch. 359 at 424, *per* Bingham L.J.

[78] "Where, as here, the relationship between doctor and patient is contractual, the question is whether the doctor's disclosure is or is not a breach of contract. The answer to that question must turn not on what the doctor thinks but on what the court rules. But it does not follow that the doctor's conclusion is irrelevant. In making its ruling the court will give such weight to the considered judgment of a professional man as seems in all the circumstances to be appropriate": *ibid.* at 422, *per* Bingham L.J.

[79] For example, in *Schering Chemicals Ltd v Falkman Ltd* [1981] 2 All E.R. 321, 327 Shaw L.J. said that: "If the subject matter is something which is inimical to the public interest or *threatens individual safety*, a person in possession of knowledge of that subject matter cannot be obliged to conceal it . . ." (emphasis added). See also Barrowclough C.J. in *Furniss v Fitchett* [1958] N.Z.L.R. 396, 405–6: "Take the case of a doctor who discovers that his patient entertains delusions in respect of another, and in his disordered state of mind is liable at any moment to cause death or grievous bodily harm to that other. Can it be doubted for one moment that the public interest requires him to report that finding to someone?"

[80] Gillon (1987) 294 B.M.J. 1675, 1676; Wacks (1988) 138 N.L.J. 283; *cf.* Caswell (1989) 68 Can. Bar Rev. 225. Note that Gillon considers that this is "particularly clearly justified" if the sexual partner is also a patient of the doctor concerned. The GMC accepts that disclosure may be made in exceptional circumstances, where the failure to disclose would put the health of any of the health care team or other patients at serious risk, or where it is necessary to safeguard sexual partners of the patient from a possibly fatal infection. This would apply where there is a serious risk of death or serious harm. See the GMC guidance *Serious Communicable Diseases*, October 1997, paras 19 and 22. See also Mulholland (1993) 9 P.N. 79 for consideration of the position where it is the health care worker who is infected with HIV.

2–196   A final question concerning the limits of the public interest defence, which arises from *W. v Egdell*, is whether different considerations apply to patients who are compulsorily detained under the provisions of the Mental Health Act 1983.[81] Scott J. expressly based his decision on the circumstances in which the psychiatric report had been commissioned, including the fact that W was subject to a restriction order under the Act. This, his Lordship concluded, placed W and persons like him "in a position in which the duty of confidence owed by their psychiatrists is less extensive than the duty that would be owed by psychiatrists to ordinary members of the public."[82] The limitation on W's rights was justified by the need that the hospital, the Home Secretary and the Tribunal should be fully informed about W when considering his clinical management and possible discharge. However, Bingham L.J. said that restricted patients under the Mental Health Act 1983 should not enjoy different rights from any other patient with respect to the duty of confidence, except in so far as a breach of confidence could be justified in the public interest. In W's circumstances decisions about his release from hospital should not be made unless the responsible authority was able to make an informed judgment that the risk was so small as to be acceptable. That consideration weighed the balance of public interest decisively in favour of disclosure.[83]

2–197   The problem for a doctor with a patient who is not subject to a restriction order lies in the difficulty of assessing the risk. With a patient in W's position then, arguably, the evidence of the potential danger is more readily apparent, and those to whom disclosure should be made are more readily identified, namely persons who have some degree of control over W's future conduct. It does not necessarily follow that the duty of confidence owed by psychiatrists varies with different types of patient, except to the extent that each patient is different and accordingly the psychiatrist's professional judgment as to the risk presented to the public varies.

Discretion or duty?

2–198   In *W. v Egdell* Scott J.'s judgment was ambiguous about whether a doctor who forms the view that his patient constitutes a potential risk to others merely has a discretion to breach the confidentiality of the doctor-patient relationship (which would give him a defence to a claim for breach of confidence by the patient) or whether he comes under a duty to disclose the information. At one point Scott J. said that a doctor in Dr Egdell's position "owes a duty not only to his patient but also a duty to the public. His duty to the public would require him, in my opinion, to place before the

---

[81]   ss. 37 and 41; formerly Mental Health Act 1959, ss. 60 and 65.
[82]   [1990] Ch. 359, 393.
[83]   The hospital, the Secretary of State and the tribunal were all engaged in public law functions in the exercise of statutory powers which placed a strong emphasis on public safety and, bearing in mind W's history, his status as a detained patient was, almost inevitably, a significant factor to be weighed in assessing the public interest.

proper authorities the result of his examination if, in his opinion, the public interest so required."[84] The Court of Appeal indicated that the defendant was justified in disclosing the report, but the decision does not suggest that he was under a duty to disclose it. This would seem to be the better view.[85]

---

[84] [1990] Ch. 359, 392.

[85] It is unlikely that it would be a criminal offence to withhold such information, in the absence of a specific statutory requirement for disclosure (as, *e.g.*, in *Hunter v Mann* [1974] Q.B. 767). Similarly, it is difficult to see how such a duty could arise in equity or by whom it would be enforced. Possibly Scott J. considered that Dr Egdell was under some "quasi public law duty" to disclose the report to the relevant authorities, in view of the particular circumstances under which the report was prepared. In this sense it might be argued that Dr Egdell was engaged in a "public" function, even though the report had been prepared at W's request and for the purpose of supporting his application to the tribunal. Possibly Scott J. had a duty of care in negligence in mind when he referred to Dr Egdell's duty, but this is also doubtful given the context in which the words were used, particularly the reference to a duty owed to the public. Duties of care are normally expressed in much more restricted terms than this, being owed to persons who are foreseeable as likely to be directly affected by the defendant's failure to exercise reasonable care.

Chapter 3

STANDARD OF CARE—GENERAL PRINCIPLES

3–001   The standard of care, and whether the defendant has failed to meet that standard, are normally the central issues in an action for medical negligence. Essentially, the question is: was the defendant careless? In law, the test for breach of duty in the tort of negligence is whether the defendant's conduct was reasonable in all the circumstances of the case. If it was reasonable he was not negligent; if it was unreasonable he was. At this level of abstraction the test is almost meaningless, since it begs all the important questions, namely what *is* reasonable and which circumstances of the case have to be considered. It is only when the general is applied to the particular that the term "reasonable care in all the circumstances" acquires any significance.

3–002   Within the blanket term "reasonable care" it is possible to identify some general principles which the courts have employed in the decision-making process about what constitutes negligence. They are, however, in practical terms, no more than guidelines, and as often as not competing principles point to different outcomes. The question of where the balance between negligence and due care is to be drawn can only be appreciated by developing a common-sense "feel" for the way in which the courts use these guidelines. This Chapter deals with the general principles applied to the issue of breach of duty, and Chapter 4 looks at specific types of medical negligence. There is, inevitably, some overlap between these two chapters, because they seek to provide different perspectives on the caselaw.

3–003   Medical evidence is invariably a vital element in an action for medical negligence, but the importance attached to expert opinion should not obscure the underlying basis for a finding that the defendant has been negligent, or not (as the case may be). This is that, in the light of the expert evidence, the defendant has taken an unjustified risk, for example, or has failed to keep up to date, or has undertaken a task beyond his competence, or conversely that the risk was justified by the potential benefit to the patient, or the harm was unforeseeable, and so on. In other words, expert opinion about the defendant's conduct (whether favourable or unfavourable) should itself be measured against the general principles applied to the question of breach of duty. This point was emphasised by the House of Lords in *Bolitho v City and Hackney Health Authority*[1] where Lord Browne-Wilkinson made it clear

---

[1] [1998] A.C. 232, 241–242.

that the court has to weigh expert evidence in a form of risk-benefit analysis:

> "the court has to be satisfied that the exponents of the body of opinion relied upon can demonstrate that such opinion has a logical basis. In particular in cases involving, as they so often do, the weighing of risks against benefits, the judge before accepting a body of opinion as being responsible, reasonable or respectable, will need to be satisfied that, in forming their views, the experts have directed their minds to the question of comparative risks and benefits and have reached a defensible conclusion on the matter."

(1) The Basic Principle

When jury trials were the norm in civil litigation the issue of whether the defendant had been negligent was for the jury to decide, and so it was treated as a question of fact. There are two stages, however, in this process. First, there must be an assessment by the court of how, in the circumstances, the defendant *ought* to have behaved—what standard of care should he have exercised? This enquiry necessarily involves a value judgment which should be made by the court. That judgment may be conditioned, but should not necessarily be determined, by the evidence. It is here that the hypothetical "reasonable man" is employed, partly as a measure of careless conduct and partly as a device to obscure the policy element of a judicial decision.[2] In a famous dictum Alderson B. said: "Negligence is the omission to do something which a reasonable man, guided upon those considerations which ordinarily regulate the conduct of human affairs, would do, or doing something which a prudent and reasonable man would not do."[3] This judicial abstraction has also been described as the ordinary man, the average man, or the man on the Clapham omnibus.[4] The standard of care expected of the reasonable man is objective. It does not take account of the subjective attributes of the particular defendant.[5] Nor, despite references to the average man, is it necessarily determined by the average conduct of people in general if that conduct is routinely careless. Similarly, there is no concept of an "average" standard of care by which a defendant might argue that he has provided an adequate service on average and should not be held liable for the occasions when his performance fell below the norm. No matter how skilled the defendant's conduct was, he will be responsible for even a single occasion when he fell below the standard of reasonable care.[6]

3–004

---

[2] See, *e.g.*, P. Cane, *Atiyah's Accidents, Compensation and the Law*, 6th ed., Butterworths, 1999, pp. 29–31.
[3] *Blyth v Birmingham Waterworks Co* (1856) 11 Exch. 781, 784.
[4] *Hall v Brooklands Auto Racing Club* [1933] 1 K.B 205, 217.
[5] *Glasgow Corporation v Muir* [1943] A.C. 448, 457.
[6] *Wilsher v Essex Area Health Authority* [1987] Q.B. 730, 747, *per* Mustill L.J. The courts have not accepted a distinction between "ordinary" negligence and "gross" negligence

3–005   The second stage requires a decision about whether on the facts of the case (as determined from the evidence) the defendant's conduct fell below the appropriate standard. This is truly a question of fact. Although these two stages are logically discrete, in practice it may be difficult to separate findings of "fact" and value judgments about the defendant's conduct.

(a) The reasonable doctor

3–006   Since the ordinary or average man would be ill-equipped to judge the competence of a professional, a person who professes a special skill is judged, not by the standard of the man on the Clapham omnibus, but by the standards of his peers. Thus, for the "reasonable man" is substituted the "reasonable professional", be it doctor, lawyer, accountant, architect, etc.[7]

3–007   The classic statement of the test of professional negligence is the direction to the jury of McNair J. in *Bolam v Friern Hospital Management Committee.*[8] Now widely known as the "*Bolam* test", this statement of the law has been approved by the House of Lords on no fewer than four occasions in recent years as the touchstone of liability for medical negligence.[9] Moreover, the Court of Appeal has confirmed that the test is not restricted to doctors, but is of general application to any profession or calling which requires special skill, knowledge or experience.[10]

3–008   McNair J. explained the law in these terms:

> "But where you get a situation which involves the use of some special skill or competence, then the test whether there has been negligence or not is not the test of the man on the Clapham omnibus, because he has not got this special skill. The test is the standard of the ordinary skilled man exercising and professing to have that special skill. A man need not possess the highest expert skill at the risk of being found negligent . . .

(n.6 contd.) (despite the efforts of Lord Denning: see para. 3–145). In *Wilson v Brett* (1843) 11 M. & W. 113 Rolfe B. said that there was no difference: "it was the same thing with the addition of a vituperative epithet." Thus, any failure to meet the standard of reasonable care constitutes a breach of duty: Dugdale and Stanton, *Professional Negligence*, 3rd ed., 1998, para. 15.03.

[7] "The public profession of an art is a representation and undertaking to all the world that the professor possesses the requisite ability and skill. An express promise or express representation in the particular case is not necessary," *per* Willes J. in *Harmer v Cornelius* (1858) 5 C.B. (N.S.) 236, 246.

[8] [1957] 2 All E.R. 118.

[9] *Whitehouse v Jordan* [1981] 1 All E.R. 267: treatment; *Maynard v West Midlands Regional Health Authority* [1984] 1 W.L.R. 634: diagnosis; *Sidaway v Bethlem Royal Hospital Governors* [1985] A.C. 871: information disclosure; *Bolitho v City and Hackney Health Authority* [1998] A.C. 232: failure to attend. See also *Chin Keow v Government of Malaysia* [1967] 1 W.L.R. 813, Privy Council.

[10] *Gold v Haringey Health Authority* [1988] Q.B. 481, 489: "I can see no possible ground for distinguishing between doctors and any other profession or calling which requires special skill, knowledge or experience," *per* Lloyd L.J. In *Whitehouse v Jordan* [1981] 1 All E.R. 267, 276j Lord Edmund-Davies prefaced his restatement of the *Bolam* test with the comment that "doctors and surgeons fall into no special category."

it is sufficient if he exercises the ordinary skill of an ordinary competent man exercising that particular art."[11]

His Lordship agreed that counsel's statement that "negligence means failure to act in accordance with the standards of reasonably competent medical men at the time" was a perfectly accurate statement of the law, provided that it was remembered that there may be one or more perfectly proper standards:

> "A doctor is not guilty of negligence if he has acted in accordance with a practice accepted as proper by a responsible body of medical men skilled in that particular art . . . Putting it the other way round, a doctor is not negligent, if he is acting in accordance with such a practice, merely because there is a body of opinion that takes a contrary view."[12]

In *Hunter v Hanley* Lord President Clyde dealt with the question of different professional practices in these terms: 3–009

> "In the realm of diagnosis and treatment there is ample scope for genuine difference of opinion and one man clearly is not negligent merely because his conclusion differs from that of other professional men, nor because he has displayed less skill or knowledge than others would have shown. The true test for establishing negligence in diagnosis or treatment on the part of a doctor is whether he has been proved to be guilty of such failure as no doctor of ordinary skill would be guilty of if acting with ordinary care."[13]

This statement of the law has also been approved by the House of Lords,[14] although it has been argued that there is a difference between this formulation and the *Bolam* test.[15] There is, moreover, a distinction between a test of negligence based on the standards of the ordinary skilled man and one based on the reasonably competent man. The former places considerable emphasis on the standards which are in fact adopted by the profession, whereas the latter makes it clear that negligence is concerned with departures from what *ought* to have been done in the circumstances, which is measured by reference to the hypothetical "reasonable doctor."[16] The point here is that it is for the court to determine what the reasonable doctor would have done, not the profession. Of course, what the profession does in a given situation will

---

[11] [1957] 2 All E.R. 118, 121.
[12] *ibid.* at p. 122.
[13] 1955 S.C. 200, 204–5; *Dunne v National Maternity Hospital* [1989] I.R. 91, 109 (Supreme Court of Ireland); Symmons (1990) 6 P.N. 201.
[14] *Maynard v West Midlands Regional Health Authority* [1984] 1 W.L.R. 634, 638; *Sidaway v Bethlem Royal Hospital Governors* [1985] A.C. 871, 897, *per* Lord Bridge.
[15] See Howie [1983] J.R. 193; *cf.* Norrie [1985] J.R. 145.
[16] For critical discussion of *Bolam* see Montrose "Is Negligence an Ethical or a Sociological Concept?" (1958) 21 M.L.R. 259.

be an important indicator of what ought to have been done, but it should not necessarily be determinative. In other words, in the final analysis the court sets the standard of care in negligence, drawing, of course, upon the evidence presented. The *Bolam* test fails to make this important distinction between the ordinary skilled doctor and the reasonably competent doctor, and this has produced some confusion in the cases.[17] In the vast majority of cases the distinction is irrelevant, indeed it passes largely unnoticed in the courts. It does become significant, however, when the question arises whether compliance with common professional practice can be negligent.

3–010   Similar formulations of the standard of care required of the medical profession can be found in other Commonwealth jurisdictions. In Canada one of the most widely cited statements is that of Schroeder J.A. in *Crits v Sylvester*:

> "Every medical practitioner must bring to his task a reasonable degree of skill and knowledge and must exercise a reasonable degree of care. He is bound to exercise that degree of care and skill which could reasonably be expected of a normal, prudent practitioner of the same experience and standing and, if he holds himself out as a specialist, a higher degree of skill is required of him than of one who does not profess to be so qualified by special training and ability."[18]

Again, in Australia King C.J. has said that:

> "The standard of care is that to be expected of an ordinarily careful and competent practitioner of the class to which the practitioner belongs"[19]

3–011   Here, too, there is no clear demarcation between the ordinary doctor and the reasonable doctor. The assumption is that the terms express essentially the same standard. These epithets—the "reasonable" man, the "average" man, or the "ordinary" man—were introduced at a time when judges had to give juries guidance as to the appropriate standard to apply in deciding whether conduct was negligent. In many respects they do little more than give a "flavour" of a suitable test, which it was left to the good sense of the jury to apply. On the whole, they serve their purpose even where actions are tried by judge alone.

---

[17] *Jackson & Powell on Professional Negligence*, 5th ed., 2002, para. 2.116.
[18] (1956) 1 D.L.R. (2d) 502, 508; affirmed (1956) 5 D.L.R. (2d) 601 (S.C.C.). This standard also allows for differences of view within the medical profession: see *Lapointe v Hôpital Le Gardeur* (1992) 90 D.L.R. (4th) 7, 15 (S.C.C.). Note that Schroeder J.A.'s reference to the standard which could reasonably be expected of a "normal, prudent practitioner of the same *experience* and standing" is potentially misleading since inexperience is not a defence. Commenting on Schroeder J.A.'s statement, Holland J., in *Dale v Munthali* (1977) 78 D.L.R. (3d) 588, 594; affirmed (1978) 90 D.L.R. (3d) 763, said that the reference to a practitioner "of the same experience" was not supported by the authorities. The standard "should not be lower by reason of [the defendant's] inexperience." See further para. 3–090 *et seq.*
[19] *F. v R.* (1982) 33 S.A.S.R. 189, 190.

(b) What is reasonable care?

Reasonable care can only be measured by reference to the defendant's   3–012
conduct in the circumstances. In one sense it is meaningless to say that the
standard required is reasonable care, without knowing the particular situation with which the defendant was confronted. Nonetheless, the term is frequently used to emphasise that doctors do not guarantee a favourable
outcome to their efforts. The medical practitioner is not an insurer, and so
cannot be blamed every time something goes wrong. Indeed, it is widely
acknowledged that in medicine, in particular, things can go wrong in the
treatment of a patient even with the very best available care. This has long
been reflected in judicial statements of the law:

> "A surgeon does not become an actual insurer; he is only bound to
> display sufficient skill and knowledge of his profession. If from some
> accident, or some variation in the frame of a particular individual, an
> injury happens, it is not a fault in the medical man . . . The plaintiff must
> show that the injury was attributable to want of skill; you are not to
> infer it."[20]

> ". . . the standard of care which the law requires is not insurance against
> accidental slips. It is such a degree of care as a normally skilful member
> of the profession may reasonably be expected to exercise in the actual
> circumstances of the case in question. It is not every slip or mistake
> which imports negligence and, in applying the duty of care to the case of
> a surgeon, it is peculiarly necessary to have regard to the different kinds
> of circumstances that may present themselves for urgent attention."[21]

The practitioner is not judged by the standards of the most experienced,   3–013
most skilful, or most highly qualified member of the profession, but by reference to the standards of the ordinarily competent practitioner in that particular field.

> "Every person who enters into a learned profession undertakes to bring
> to the exercise of it a reasonable degree of care and skill. He does not
> undertake, if he is an attorney, that at all events you shall gain your case,
> nor does a surgeon undertake that he will perform a cure; nor does he
> undertake to use the highest possible degree of skill. There may be
> persons who have higher education and greater advantages than he has,
> but he undertakes to bring a fair, reasonable and competent degree of
> skill . . ."[22]

---

[20] *Hancke v Hooper* (1835) 7 C. & P. 81, 84, *per* Tindal C.J.
[21] *Mahon v Osborne* [1939] 2 K.B. 14, 31, *per* Scott L.J.; "To fall short of perfection is not the
same thing as to be negligent": *Daniels v Heskin* [1954] I.R. 73, 84.
[22] *Lanphier v Phipos* (1838) 8 C. & P. 475, 479, *per* Tindal C.J. See also *Greaves & Co
(Contractors) Ltd v Baynham Meikle and Partners* [1975] 3 All E.R. 99 at 103–104, *per*
Lord Denning M.R., cited at para. 2–006, n. 14.

"The doctor 'owes a duty to the patient to use diligence, care, knowledge, skill and caution in administering the treatment . . . The jury should not exact the highest, or a very high, standard, nor should they be content with a very low standard. The law requires a fair and reasonable standard of care and competence.'"[23]

3–014   Nor is the doctor to be judged by the standards of the least qualified or least experienced.[24] It is not a defence that he acted in good faith, to the best of his ability if he has failed to reach the objective standard of the ordinarily competent and careful doctor. In *Eckersley v Binnie & Partners*[25] Bingham L.J. summarised the responsibility of the professional person:

"a professional man should command the corpus of knowledge which forms part of the professional equipment of the ordinary member of his profession. He should not lag behind other ordinarily assiduous and intelligent members of his profession in knowledge of new advances, discoveries and developments in his field. He should have such awareness as an ordinarily competent practitioner would have of the deficiencies in his knowledge and the limitations on his skills. He should be alert to the hazards and risks inherent in any professional task he undertakes to the extent that other ordinarily competent members of the profession would be alert. He must bring to any professional task he undertakes no less expertise, skill and care than other ordinarily competent members of his profession would bring, but need bring no more. The standard is that of the reasonably average. The law does not require of a professional man that he be a paragon, combining the qualities of polymath and prophet."

(2) Common professional practice

3–015   As a general rule within the tort of negligence, where the defendant has acted in accordance with the common practice of others in a similar situation this will be strong evidence that he has not been negligent.[26] People do not normally adopt systematic practices that pay careless disregard for the safety of others. Following a common practice is only *evidence*, however, it is not conclusive, since the court may find that the practice is itself negligent.[27] There may be many reasons, such as convenience, cost, or habit, why

---

[23] *R. v Bateman* (1925) 94 L.J.K.B. 791, 794, *per* Lord Hewart C.J., approved in *Gent v Wilson* (1956) 2 D.L.R. (2d) 160 (Ont. C.A.) and *Parkin v Kobrinsky* (1963) 46 W.W.R. 193 (Man. C.A.).

[24] See paras 3–090 *et seq.*

[25] (1988) 18 Con. L.R. 1, 80.

[26] *Morton v William Dixon Ltd* 1909 S.C. 807, 809; *Morris v West Hartlepool Steam Navigation Co Ltd* [1956] A.C. 552, 579.

[27] See, *e.g., Lloyds Bank Ltd v E.B. Savory & Co* [1933] A.C. 201; *Cavanagh v Ulster Weaving Co Ltd* [1960] A.C. 145; *General Cleaning Contractors v Christmas* [1953] A.C. 180, 193, *per* Lord Reid; *Roberge v Bolduc* (1991) 78 D.L.R. (4th) 666, 710 (S.C.C.).

a particular practice is commonly followed, which have nothing to do with reasonable prudence against potential harm to others. In the graphic words of Lord Tomlin: "Neglect of duty does not cease by repetition to be neglect of duty."[28]

A central feature of medical negligence claims is the importance that is attached to compliance with common or accepted practice. It will be recalled that in *Bolam v Friern Hospital Management Committee* McNair J. directed the jury that: **3–016**

> "A doctor is not guilty of negligence if he has acted in accordance with a practice accepted as proper by a *responsible* body of medical men skilled in that particular art . . . Putting it the other way round, a doctor is not negligent, if he is acting in accordance with such a practice, merely because there is a body of opinion that takes a contrary view."[29]

There is no reason in theory why the general approach taken by the courts to accepted practice should not also apply to actions for medical negligence. Within the *Bolam* test attention would then focus on whether the practice which the defendant had followed was accepted by *responsible* medical opinion, with the court deciding whether on the evidence before it the body of opinion which approved of the defendant's conduct could be said to be responsible. There are, however, some judicial statements which appear to take the view that the practice of the medical profession is determinative of the issue, and that it is not open to the court to condemn as negligence a commonly adopted practice. It may be that such statements reflected the inherent ambiguity in the *Bolam* test itself, the conflation of the normative judgment of what *ought* to have happened with the factual judgment of what usually *does* happen. But as the House of Lords has made clear in *Bolitho v City and Hackney Health Authority*[30] the courts must now be much more careful to distinguish these elements of the test. What usually happens is evidence of what ought to have happened, but it is not conclusive.

(a) Complying with professional practice

In *Vancouver General Hospital v McDaniel*[31] Lord Alness said that a defendant charged with negligence can "clear his feet" if he shows that he has acted in accordance with general and approved practice. This view was repeated by Maugham L.J. in *Marshall v Lindsey County Council*:   **3–017**

---

[28] *Bank of Montreal v Dominion Gresham Guarantee and Casualty Co* [1930] A.C. 659, 666; *Carpenters' Co v British Mutual Banking Co Ltd* [1937] 3 All E.R. 811, 820, *per* Slesser L.J.

[29] [1957] 2 All E.R. 118, 122, emphasis added; *Holmes v Board of Hospital Trustees of the City of London* (1977) 81 D.L.R. (3d) 67, 91, *per* Robins J. (Ont. H.C.): "Where in the exercise of his judgment a physician selects one of two alternatives, either of which might have been chosen by a reasonable and competent physician, he will not be held negligent"; *Darley v Shale* [1993] 4 Med. L.R. 161 (N.S.W.S.C.).

[30] [1998] A.C. 232, 241–242; see para. 3–028.

[31] (1934) 152 L.T. 56, 57–8.

"An act cannot, in my opinion, be held to be due to a want of reasonable care if it is in accordance with the general practice of mankind. What is reasonable in a world not wholly composed of wise men and women must depend on what people presumed to be reasonable constantly do."[32]

3–018   There are many cases in which actions for medical negligence have been dismissed on the basis that the doctor conformed to an accepted practice of the profession.[33] Where there is more than one common practice, as the *Bolam* test contemplates, compliance with one of the practices will normally excuse the defendant. In *Maynard v West Midlands Regional Health Authority*[34] Lord Scarman, delivering the judgment of the House of Lords, expressed the position in the following terms:

"A case which is based on an allegation that a fully considered decision of two consultants in the field of their special skill was negligent clearly presents certain difficulties of proof. It is not enough to show that there is a body of competent professional opinion which considers that theirs was a wrong decision, if there also exists a body of professional opinion, equally competent, which supports the decision as reasonable in the circumstances . . . Differences of opinion and practice exist, and will always exist, in the medical as in other professions. There is seldom any one answer exclusive of all others to problems of professional judgment. A court may prefer one body of opinion to the other: but that is no basis for a conclusion of negligence."[35]

3–019   This statement is unexceptional. In a later passage, however, Lord Scarman appears to take the view that compliance with accepted practice will, without more, absolve a doctor from liability:

". . . a judge's 'preference' for one body of distinguished professional opinion to another also professionally distinguished is not sufficient to establish negligence in a practitioner whose actions have received the

---

[32] [1935] 1 K.B. 516, 540.

[33] *Vancouver General Hospital v McDaniel* (1934) 152 L.T. 56; *Whiteford v Hunter* [1950] W.N. 553; *Bolam v Friern Hospital Management Committee* [1957] 2 All E.R. 118; *Gold v Haringey Health Authority* [1988] Q.B. 481.

[34] [1984] 1 W.L.R. 634; *Belknap v Meakes* (1989) 64 D.L.R. (4th) 452, 473–475 (B.C.C.A.); *Neilson v Basildon of Thurrock Health Authority* (1991, QBD; unreported).

[35] *ibid.* at p. 638; *Ratty v Haringey Health Authority* [1994] 5 Med. L.R. 413, 416, CA, where Kennedy L.J. said that it was important "once it was accepted that [the defendants' expert witnesses] represented a responsible and respectable body of colo-rectal opinion, to accept without qualification their [evidence] when evaluating the conduct of the second defendant"; *Dunne v National Maternity Hospital* [1989] I.R. 91, 109 (Supreme Court of Ireland); *Kaban v Sett* [1994] 1 W.W.R. 476, 479–480 (Man. Q.B.); affirmed [1994] 10 W.W.R. 620 (Man. C.A.). On the other hand, where there has been not been a considered clinical judgment, but rather "a catalogue of errors", the approach in *Maynard* to competing bodies of professional opinion is not relevant: *Le Page v Kingston and Richmond Health Authority* [1997] 8 Med. L.R. 229, 240, QBD.

seal of approval of those whose opinions, truthfully expressed, honestly held, were not preferred. If this was the real reason for the judge's finding he erred in law even though elsewhere in his judgment he stated the law correctly. For in the realm of diagnosis and treatment negligence is not established by preferring one respectable body of professional opinion to another. Failure to exercise the ordinary skill of a doctor (in the appropriate specialty, if he be a specialist) is necessary."[36]

Here, the "seal of approval" of a distinguished body of professional opinion, held in good faith, acquits the defendant of negligence. Lord Scarman seems to equate a *competent* (or "responsible") body of professional opinion with "distinguished" or "respectable" in fact. He thus conflates accepted practice with the absence of negligence. This interpretation is supported by Lord Scarman's speech in *Sidaway v Bethlem Royal Hospital Governors* where he said:

> "The *Bolam* principle may be formulated as a rule that a doctor is not negligent if he acts in accordance with a practice accepted at the time as proper by a responsible body of medical opinion even though other doctors adopt a different practice. *In short, the law imposes the duty of care; but the standard of care is a matter of medical judgment.*"[37]

3–020

It is also apparent from earlier passages in his Lordship's speech in *Sidaway* that he considered the *Bolam* test required the determination of whether there has been a breach of a doctor's duty of care to be conducted "exclusively by reference to the current state of responsible and competent professional opinion and practice at the time."[38] As Lord Scarman himself recognised "the implications of this view of the law are disturbing. It leaves the determination of a legal duty to the judgment of doctors." It was this point which led Lord Scarman to dissent in *Sidaway* on the question of the standard to be applied to the disclosure of information to patients about the risks of treatment, but he was apparently content to apply the standard of "responsible medical judgment" (as his Lordship had identified it) to diagnosis and treatment.[39]

3–021

This was an interpretation of the *Bolam* test that was not accepted by Lord Bridge in *Sidaway* who said:

3–022

> "... the issue whether non-disclosure in a particular case should be condemned as a breach of the doctor's duty of care is an issue to be decided

---

[36] *ibid.* at p. 639.
[37] [1985] A.C. 871, 881, emphasis added; *cf.* Sir John Donaldson M.R. in the Court of Appeal, [1984] 1 All E.R. 1018, 1028: "The definition of the duty of care is a matter for the law and the courts. They cannot stand idly by if the profession, by an excess of paternalism, denies its patients a real choice. In a word, the law will not permit the medical profession to play God."
[38] *ibid.* at p. 876.
[39] *ibid.* at p. 882.

primarily on the basis of expert medical evidence, applying the *Bolam* test . . . Of course, if there is a conflict of evidence whether a responsible body of medical opinion approves of non-disclosure in a particular case, the judge will have to resolve that conflict. But, even in a case where, as here, no expert witness in the relevant medical field condemns the non-disclosure as being in conflict with accepted and responsible medical practice, I am of opinion that the judge might in certain circumstances come to the conclusion that disclosure of a particular risk was so obviously necessary to an informed choice on the part of the patient that no reasonably prudent medical man would fail to make it."[40]

In other words, the court may condemn even a universally followed practice as to risk disclosure as negligent on the basis that the hypothetical reasonable doctor would not have adopted it.[41] There, is, of course, no reason to confine this approach to risk disclosure since the majority of their Lordships in *Sidaway v Bethlem Royal Hospital Governors* said that the *Bolam* test applied to all aspects of the doctor's duty of care: diagnosis, advice and treatment.[42]

3–023   It is clear that outside the context of medical negligence the courts have had no difficulty with the notion that commonly adopted practices may themselves be negligent. This has been most apparent in cases of employers' liability,[43] but it is also evident in some cases involving professional liability. In *Lloyds Bank v Savory & Co*,[44] for example, Lord Wright rejected the proposition that a bank is not negligent if it takes all the precautions usually taken by bankers "in cases where the ordinary practice of bankers fails in making due provision for a risk fully known to those experienced in the business of banking." More recently, in *Edward Wong Finance-Co Ltd v*

---

[40] *ibid.* at p. 900. See also Sir John Donaldson M.R. in *Sidaway v Bethlem Royal Hospital Governors* [1984] 1 All E.R. 1018, 1028: ". . . in an appropriate case, a judge would be entitled to reject a unanimous medical view if he were satisfied that it was manifestly wrong and that the doctors must have been misdirecting themselves as to their duty in law." Thus, a practice must be "rightly" accepted as proper by the profession. His Lordship drew a specific analogy with the cases in which the courts had held the common practice of employers to be negligent: see n. 43, below. See further the comment of Farquharson L.J. in *Bolitho v City and Hackney Health Authority* [1993] 4 Med. L.R. 381, 386, cited below, para. 3–034, n. 74.

[41] In *Neilson v Basildon of Thurrock Health Authority* (1991, QBD; unreported) Garland J., referring to the speech of Lord Bridge in *Sidaway*, said that a judge might substitute his own assessment of risk for that of medical opinion: ". . . in an extreme case or where it can be demonstrated that the profession as a whole or a *supposedly* responsible body of opinion within it have failed to take into account some relevant factor or that some underlying of public policy requires them to change their standards." (emphasis added)

[42] See, however, *Gordon v Wilson* [1992] 3 Med. L.R. 401, 426 (Court of Session) where Lord Penrose appeared to suggest that Lord Bridge's comments were confined to the disclosure of information to patients, and that "nothing in the speech of Lord Bridge was intended to qualify the *Bolam* test." With respect, though this last observation is accurate, it is clear that the *Bolam* test applies to all aspects of a doctor's duty of care to a patient.

[43] As, *e.g.*, in *Cavanagh v Ulster Weaving Co Ltd* [1960] A.C. 145; *Morris v West Hartlepool Steam Navigation Co Ltd* [1956] A.C. 552; *Stokes v Guest, Keen & Nettlefold (Bolts & Nuts) Ltd* [1968] 1 W.L.R. 1776, 1783.

[44] [1933] A.C. 201, 203.

Johnson, Stokes and Masters[45] the Privy Council held that a particular conveyancing practice widely followed in Hong Kong was negligent because the practice had an inherent risk which would have been foreseen by a person of reasonable prudence, and there was no need to take this risk. The fact that virtually all other solicitors adopted the same practice was not conclusive evidence that it was prudent, nor did it make the risk less apparent or unreal.

It might be added that condemning accepted practice does not depend   3–024
upon the risks being "fully known to those experienced" in the profession, but may extend to those risks which ought reasonably to have been known, but were simply not addressed by the profession as a whole. This point may be illustrated by *Re The Herald of Free Enterprise: Appeal by Captain Lewry*[46] which concerned an appeal by the captain of the *Herald of Free Enterprise* against the revocation of his master's certificate following the disaster at Zeebrugge harbour. The ferry had set sail with both the inner and outer doors to the main deck open, and capsized soon after leaving the harbour with a substantial loss of life. The Divisional Court found that the practice of failing to check that the doors had been closed was prevalent in respect of most, if not all, of the masters who commanded ferries of that class. The court concluded, however, that this was not evidence of the required standard of care, but rather of a general and culpable complacency, born perhaps of repetitive routine, and fostered by the shortcomings of the ships' owners and managers. There had been a failure to apply common sense in respect of elementary precautions required for the safety of the ship.

In other common law jurisdictions the courts have been careful to ensure   3–025
that, ultimately, decisions as to what constitutes negligence remain for the court to determine. In *Anderson v Chasney*[47] Coyne J.A. commented that if following general practice was a conclusive defence "a group of operators by adopting some practice could legislate themselves out of liability for negligence to the public by adopting or continuing what was an obviously negligent practice, even though a simple precaution, plainly capable of obviating danger which sometimes might result in death, was well known." Thus, expert evidence from doctors as to a general or approved practice could not be accepted as conclusive on the issue of negligence, especially where the conduct in question did not involve a matter of technical skill and experience. Similarly, in *Crits v Sylvester*[48] Schroeder J.A. commented that:

---

[45] [1984] A.C. 296. See also *Nye Saunders & Partners v Bristow* (1987) 37 Build. L.R. 92, CA, where it was held that no responsible body of architects would have failed to warn clients about the risks of inflation when undertaking a building project; *Roberge v Bolduc* (1991) 78 D.L.R. (4th) 666 (S.C.C.), where a notary was held liable in negligence despite following a general notarial practice because the practice was simply not reasonable.

[46] *The Independent*, December 18, 1987, D. Ct.

[47] [1949] 4 D.L.R. 71, 85 (Man. C.A.); affirmed [1950] 4 D.L.R. 223 (S.C.C.). See also *Hajgato v London Health Association* (1982) 36 O.R. (2d) 669, 693, *per* Callaghan J.: the courts have "a right to strike down substandard approved practice when commonsense dictates such a result. No profession is above the law and the courts on behalf of the public have a critical role to play in monitoring and precipitating changes where required in professional standards."

[48] (1956) 1 D.L.R. (2d) 502; affirmed (1956) 5 D.L.R. (2d) 601.

"Even if it had been established that what was done by the anaesthetist was in accordance with 'standard practice', such evidence is not necessarily to be taken as conclusive on an issue of negligence, particularly where the so-called standard practice related to something which was not essentially conduct requiring medical skill and training either for its performance or a proper understanding of it . . . If it was standard practice, it was not a safe practice and should not have been followed."[49]

3–026   King C.J. explained the justification for this in the Australian case of *F v R*:

". . . professions may adopt unreasonable practices. Practices may develop in professions, particularly as to disclosure, not because they serve the interests of the clients, but because they protect the interests or convenience of members of the profession. The court has an obligation to scrutinise professional practices to ensure that they accord with the standard of reasonableness imposed by the law. A practice as to disclosure approved and adopted by a profession or a section of it may be in many cases the determining consideration as to what is reasonable . . . The ultimate question, however, is not whether the defendant's conduct accords with the practices of his profession or some part of it, but whether it conforms to the standard of reasonable care demanded by the law. That is a question for the court and the duty of deciding it cannot be delegated to any profession or group in the community."[50]

---

[49] *ibid.* at p. 514; *Reynard v Carr* (1983) 30 C.C.L.T. 42, 68 (B.C.S.C.): "If that was the standard practice at the time, it was not good enough because it was 'inconsistent with provident precautions against a known risk'. Simply because it was 'usual and long established' is not a sufficient justification," *per* Bouck J.; *Winrob v Street* (1959) 28 W.W.R. 118, 122 (B.C.S.C.); *Hajgato v London Health Association* (1982) 36 O.R. (2d) 669, 693; *Goode v Nash* (1979) 21 S.A.S.R. 419, 422 (S.C. of S. Aus.); see also *O'Donovan v Cork County Council* [1967] I.R. 173, 193, *per* Walsh J.: "If there is a common practice which has inherent defects, which ought to be obvious to any person giving the matter due consideration, the fact that it is shown to have been widely and generally adopted over a period of time does not make the practice any the less negligent. Neglect of duty does not cease by repetition to be neglect of duty"; *Albrighton v Royal Prince Alfred Hospital* [1980] 2 N.S.W.L.R. 542, 562–563, *per* Reynolds J.A. (N.S.W.C.A.): ". . . it is not the law that, if all or most of the medical practitioners in Sydney habitually fail to take an available precaution to avoid foreseeable risk of injury to their patients, then none can be found guilty of negligence"; *Roberge v Bolduc* (1991) 78 D.L.R. (4th) 666, 710 (S.C.C.), *per* L'Heureux-Dubé J.: "The fact that a professional has followed the practice of his or her peers may be strong evidence of reasonable and diligent conduct, *but it is not determinative*. If the practice is not in accordance with the general standards of liability, *i.e.*, that one must act in a reasonable manner, then the professional who adheres to such a practice can be found liable, depending on the facts of each case" (original emphasis); *ter Neuzen v Korn* (1995) 127 D.L.R. (4th) 577, 591 (S.C.C.).

[50] (1982) 33 S.A.S.R. 189, 194 (S.C. of S.Aus.), approved by Zelling J. in *Battersby v Tottman* (1985) 37 S.A.S.R. 524, 537; and Lockhart, Sheppard and Pincus JJ. in *E. v Australian Red Cross Society* (1991) 105 A.L.R. 53, 68, 82–83, 87 (Aus. Fed. C.A.). In *F. v R.* Bollen J. commented, at p. 201, that: "I respectfully think that some of the cases in England have concentrated rather too heavily on the practice of the medical profession." Professor Giesen (1993) 9 J. of Contemp. Health Law and Policy 273, 291 observed that the law of England and Scotland was "singularly deferential to the interests of the medical profession and

This approach was approved by the High Court of Australia in *Rogers v Whitaker*,[51] where it was accepted that, while evidence of acceptable medical practice might be regarded as a useful guide, it was for the court to determine whether the defendant's conduct conformed to the standard of reasonable care demanded by the law. The duty of deciding on this standard could not be delegated to the medical profession. This view was reiterated by the High Court of Australia in *Naxakis v Western General Hospital*[52] where it was said that the test for medical negligence is not what other doctors say they would or would not have done in the same or similar circumstances. To treat what other doctors do or do not do as decisive was to adopt a variant of the *Bolam* test, but the *Bolam* test had been rejected in *Rogers v Whitaker*.[53] In *Dunne v National Maternity Hospital*[54] the Supreme Court of Ireland said that although a medical practitioner may rely on a general and approved practice of the profession, this will not exculpate him if the claimant establishes that the practice has "inherent defects which ought to be obvious to any person giving the matter due consideration."[55]

On some occasions the English courts have found that compliance with common practice was negligent. In *Clarke v Adams*[56] the claimant was being treated for a fibrositic condition of the heel and he was warned by the physiotherapist to say if he felt anything more than a "comfortable warmth." He suffered a burning injury resulting in the leg being amputated below the knee. Slade J. held the defendant liable for giving an inadequate warning to enable the claimant to be safe, although it was the very warning that the defendant had been taught to give. In *Hucks v Cole* Sachs L.J. said that:

3–027

(n.50 contd.) correspondingly weak in the protection it affords to patients who have been carelessly injured in the course of undergoing treatment or diagnosis." This is not an inevitable consequence of the *Bolam* test, but of the reluctance of English courts to set a truly objective standard of care: "The determination of whether a particular mode of professional conduct is responsible or not involves a process of critical evaluation, quite distinct from any mere summary of widespread practices," *ibid*.

[51] (1992) 109 A.L.R. 625; [1993] 4 Med. L.R. 79; Trindade (1993) 109 L.Q.R. 352; McDonald and Swanton (1993) 67 A.L.J. 145; Malcolm (1994) 2 Tort L. Rev. 81.

[52] [1999] H.C.A. 22; (1999) 162 A.L.R. 540 at [18].

[53] *ibid.* at [19] *per* Gaudron J.

[54] [1989] I.R. 91, 109.

[55] See also *Collins v Mid-Western Health Board* [2000] 2 I.R. 154 (Supreme Court of Ireland): ". . . a lay tribunal will be reluctant to condemn as unsafe a practice which has been universally approved in a particular profession. The defects in a practice universally followed by specialists in the field are unlikely to be as obvious as the test requires: if they were, it is a reasonable assumption that it would not be so followed. But the principle, which was first stated by the court in *O'Donovan v Cork County Council* [1967] I.R. 173, is an important reminder that, ultimately, the courts must reserve the power to find as unsafe practices which have been generally followed in a profession." *per* Keane J. at 156.

[56] (1950) 94 S.J. 599; see also *Jones v Manchester Corpn* [1952] Q.B. 852, 863–864, *per* Singleton L.J. citing Oliver J., the trial judge. Some commentators consider *Clarke v Adams* to be of questionable authority on the basis that it predates *Bolam v Friern Hospital Management Committee* [1957] 2 All E.R. 118: see Montgomery (1989) 16 J. of Law and Soc. 319, 323; Dugdale and Stanton, *Professional Negligence*, 3rd ed., 1998, para. 15.26, n. 6. The *Bolam* test, however, was not new, it simply encapsulated earlier statements of the law. This, at least, was Lord Diplock's interpretation: *Sidaway v Bethlem Royal Hospital Governors* [1985] A.C. 871, 892.

"When the evidence shows that a lacuna in professional practice exists by which risks of grave danger are knowingly taken, then, however small the risks, the courts must anxiously examine that lacuna—particularly if the risks can be easily and inexpensively avoided. If the court finds, on an analysis of the reasons given for not taking those precautions that, in the light of current professional knowledge, there is no proper basis for the lacuna, and that it is definitely not reasonable that those risks should have been taken, its function is to state that fact and where necessary to state that it constitutes negligence. In such a case the practice will no doubt thereafter be altered to the benefit of patients."[57]

His Lordship added that the fact that other practitioners would have done the same thing as the defendant was a weighty factor to be put in the scales on his behalf, but it was not conclusive. The court had to be vigilant to see whether the reasons given for putting a patient at risk were valid in the light of any well-known advance in medical knowledge, or whether they stemmed from a residual adherence to out of date ideas. Commenting on *Hucks v Cole* in *Bolitho v City and Hackney Health Authority*[58] Dillon L.J. said that the court could only adopt the approach of Sachs L.J. and reject medical opinion on the ground that the reasons of one group of doctors does not really stand up to analysis "if the court, fully conscious of its own lack of medical and clinical experience, was nonetheless clearly satisfied that the views of that group of doctors were *Wednesbury* unreasonable, *i.e.* views such as no reasonable body of doctors could have held." With respect, it is not clear why there is any need to import the restrictive public law principles applied on applications for judicial review into the private law concept of negligence.[59] On applications for judicial review the courts are anxious not to undermine the principle of Parliamentary sovereignty by substituting their own view as to how a public body charged by Parliament with exercising a discretion should have exercised that discretion. The position of doctors and other health care workers is not analogous to that of public bodies, except in so far as they have to exercise professional judgment, which on occasions may involve competing views or the exercise of discretion as to what is the appropriate course of action. But this is no different from any other person exercising a professional judgment and is just as amenable to analysis under the ordinary private law principles of negligence.

---

[57] (1968), [1993] 4 Med. L.R. 393, 397.

[58] [1993] 4 Med. L.R. 381, 392; [1993] P.I.Q.R. P334.

[59] In *Joyce v Merton, Sutton and Wandsworth Health Authority* [1996] P.I.Q.R. P121, 153; [1996] 7 Med. L.R. 1, 20, however, Hobhouse L.J. took a different view: "In my judgment (*pace* Dillon L.J. [1993] 4 Med. L.R. at p. 392), it does not assist to introduce concepts from administrative law such as the *Wednesbury* test; such tests are directed to very different problems and their use, even by analogy, in negligence cases can, in my judgment, only serve to confuse". In *X. (minors) v Bedfordshire County Council* [1995] 2 A.C. 633, 736, in a slightly different context, Lord Browne-Wilkinson commented that: "I do not believe that it is either helpful or necessary to introduce public law concepts as to the validity of a decision into the question of liability at common law for negligence."

In *Bolitho v City and Hackney Health Authority*[60] a two-year-old boy suf-   **3–028**
fered brain damage as a result of cardiac arrest caused by an obstruction of
the bronchial air passages. The claimant was in hospital at the time for the
treatment of croup. The defendants admitted that there had been negligence,
in that a doctor who had been summoned for assistance on more than one
occasion had failed to attend. It was also common ground that had the
claimant been seen by a doctor and intubated, clearing the obstruction, the
brain damage could have been avoided. There were two schools of thought,
however, as to whether in the circumstances it was appropriate to intubate.
The doctor who failed to attend said that had she attended the claimant she
would not have intubated, and therefore the cardiac arrest and subsequent
brain damage would have occurred in any event. There was evidence from
one expert for the defendants, which the trial judge and the Court of Appeal
chose to characterise as a responsible body of professional opinion, that he
would not have intubated in the circumstances, although five medical
experts for the claimant said that the child should have been intubated, and
it was agreed that this was the only course of action that would have prevented the damage in this case. In the House of Lords the claimant submitted that the judge had been wrong in law to treat the *Bolam* test as requiring
him to accept the views of one truthful body of expert professional advice,
even though he was unpersuaded of its logical force, and that ultimately it
was for the court, not for medical opinion, to decide what was the standard
of care required of a professional in the circumstances of each particular
case.

Delivering the judgment of the House, Lord Browne-Wilkinson agreed   **3–029**
that the court was not bound to conclude that a doctor can escape liability
for negligent treatment or diagnosis just because he leads evidence from a
number of medical experts who are genuinely of the opinion that the defendant's treatment or diagnosis accorded with sound medical practice. The
court had to be satisfied that the opinion had a logical basis, which would
involve the weighing of risks against benefits, in order to reach a defensible
conclusion. His Lordship referred to the judgment of Sachs L.J. in *Hucks v
Cole* and the decision of the Privy Council in *Edward Wong Finance Co Ltd
v Johnson Stokes & Master*[61] and commented:

> "These decisions demonstrate that in cases of diagnosis and treatment
> there are cases where, despite a body of professional opinion sanction-
> ing the defendant's conduct, the defendant can properly be held liable
> for negligence (I am not here considering questions of disclosure of risk).
> In my judgment that is because, in some cases, it cannot be demonstrated
> to the judge's satisfaction that the body of opinion relied upon is reason-
> able or responsible. In the vast majority of cases the fact that distin-
> guished experts in the field are of a particular opinion will demonstrate

---

[60] [1998] A.C. 232.
[61] [1984] 1 A.C. 296.

the reasonableness of that opinion. In particular, where there are questions of assessment of the relative risks and benefits of adopting a particular medical practice, a reasonable view necessarily presupposes that the relative risks and benefits have been weighed by the experts in forming their opinions. But if, in a rare case, it can be demonstrated that the professional opinion is not capable of withstanding logical analysis, the judge is entitled to hold that the body of opinion is not reasonable or responsible."[62]

3–030   It will be rare for the courts to condemn as negligence a commonly accepted practice. Only where the risk was, or should have been, obvious to the defendant so that it would be folly to disregard it will the courts take this step.[63] The point was stressed by Lord Browne-Wilkinson in *Bolitho v City and Hackney Health Authority*.[64] It would very seldom be right, said his Lordship, for a judge to reach the conclusion that views genuinely held by a competent medical expert were unreasonable. It would be wrong to allow the assessment of medical risks and benefits, which was a matter of clinical judgment, to deteriorate into seeking to persuade the judge to prefer one of two views both of which are capable of being logically supported: "It is only where a judge can be satisfied that the body of expert opinion cannot be logically supported at all that such opinion will not provide the bench mark by reference to which the defendant's conduct falls to be assessed."

3–031   In *Marriott v West Midlands Health Authority*[65] the claimant sustained a head injury in a fall and was unconscious for about half an hour. He was admitted to hospital, and, after X-rays and neurological observations he was discharged the next day. At home he was lethargic, had headaches and no

---

[62] [1998] A.C. 232, 243. For a more detailed discussion of *Bolitho*, see Teff (1998) 18 O.J.L.S. 473; Jones (1999) 7 Tort L. Rev. 226; Brazier and Miola (2000) 8 Med. L. Rev. 85; Maclean (2002) 5 Med. Law Int. 205.

[63] *Paris v Stepney Borough Council* [1951] A.C. 367, 382, *per* Lord Normand: "obvious folly"; *General Cleaning Contractors v Christmas* [1953] A.C. 180, 193, *per* Lord Reid: "obvious danger"; *Morris v West Hartlepool Steam Navigation Co Ltd* [1956] A.C. 552, 579, *per* Lord Cohen: "obvious risk"; *Stokes v Guest, Keen & Nettlefold (Bolts & Nuts) Ltd* [1968] 1 W.L.R. 1776, 1783; see also *O'Donovan v Cork County Council* [1967] I.R. 173, 193, *per* Walsh J.; *ter Neuzen v Korn* (1995) 127 D.L.R. (4th) 577, 591 (S.C.C.): the standard practice may be found to be negligent only "where the standard practice is 'fraught with obvious risks' such that anyone is capable of finding it negligent, without the necessity of judging matters requiring diagnostic or clinical expertise"; *Webster v Chapman* (1997) 155 D.L.R. (4th) 82, 88, *per* Twaddle J.A. (Man. C.A.): the usual reliance placed on the opinions of medical experts is not an invariable requirement, and it is "open to a judge to find negligence without proof of a general standard and despite expert evidence which exonerates the defending doctor." Although such cases were infrequent, *Webster v Chapman* was one of them.

[64] [1998] A.C. 232, 243. In *Gent v Wilson* (1956) 2 D.L.R. (2d) 160, 165 (Ont. C.A.) Schroeder J.A. said that: "If a physician has rendered treatment in a manner which is in conformity with the standard and recognised practice followed by the members of his profession, unless that practice is *demonstrably unsafe or dangerous*, that fact affords cogent evidence that he has exercised that reasonable degree of care and skill which may be required of him." (emphasis added.)

[65] [1999] Lloyd's Rep. Med. 23; Jones (1999) 15 P.N. 117.

appetite. He did not improve. Eight days after the fall his general practitioner visited the claimant at home, but the neurological tests he carried out showed no abnormality. The general practitioner advised the claimant's wife to telephone him if the claimant deteriorated and suggested analgesics for the headaches. Four days later the claimant's condition suddenly deteriorated, and following emergency surgery on a skull fracture he was left paralysed and with a speech disorder. At the trial, the defendant's expert considered that whilst other general practitioners might have referred the claimant back to hospital, nonetheless it was reasonable in the circumstances to leave the claimant at home with the guidance the defendant had given. The claimant's expert said that, in the circumstances, a general practitioner ought to have referred the patient to hospital for a comprehensive neurological examination. The trial judge held that if there was a body of professional opinion which supported the course of leaving a patient at home in these circumstances, then it was not a reasonable body of opinion. The risk might be small, but the consequences if something went wrong would be disastrous for the patient:

> "In such circumstances, it is my view that the only reasonably prudent course in any case where a general practitioner remains of the view that there is a risk of an intracranial lesion such as to warrant the carrying out of neurological testing and the giving of further head injury instructions, then the only prudent course judged from the point of view of the patient is to re-admit for further testing and observation."[66]

The Court of Appeal held that the trial judge was entitled reject the defendant's expert evidence. She had subjected the body of opinion to analysis to see whether it was properly regarded as reasonable, applying *Bolitho*. She had considered the small risk of something going wrong, but had weighed that against the seriousness of the consequences for the claimant if the risk did materialise, and the fact that the facilities available in modern hospitals for carrying out scans and other diagnostic procedures were readily available.[67]

---

[66] *ibid.* at pp. 26–27, cited by Beldam LJ.

[67] An expert's views which are based on a mistaken diagnosis are likely to be condemned as illogical: *Drake v Pontefract Health Authority; Wakefield and Pontefract Community NHS Trust* [1998] Lloyd's Rep. Med. 425, 445, QBD. See also *Hunt v NHS Litigation Authority* (2000, QBD; unreported) where the defendant's expert's view that the circumstances for the administration of the drug syntocinon to a mother in the course of labour (in order to speed up contractions) had not changed in a 47 minute period during which there were signs of foetal distress on the CTG trace was rejected as "without logical support", not least because it was inconsistent with other answers that the witness had given in evidence. See further *Reynolds v North Tyneside Health Authority* [2002] Lloyd's Rep. Med. 459, discussed at para. 3–081, where the defendants' argument that it was reasonable to ignore a small risk of catastrophic consequences, when the burden of precautions was minimal, was rejected as indefensible; *Hutchinson v Leeds Health Authority*, (2000) unreported, at [78], where Bennett J. held an expert's evidence to be "less than helpful (putting it tactfully) and illogical."

When is evidence of common practice relevant?

3–032　　Where the case does not involve difficult or uncertain questions of medical or surgical treatment, or abstruse or highly technical scientific issues, but is concerned with whether obvious and simple precautions could have been taken, the question of the practice of experts should be largely irrelevant. The courts do not rely on expert rally drivers, for example, to say whether a motorist was negligent.[68] On the other hand, in a case where there are difficult, uncertain, highly technical scientific questions requiring information not ordinarily expected of a practitioner, and where the state of medical knowledge was highly variable between scientists, public health authorities and different medical communities, it is not appropriate for the court to find a practice which conformed to what other similarly situated practitioners were following was negligent.[69] In these circumstances the court should confine itself to the prevailing standards of practice.

What evidence counts?

3–033　　Before any question of complying with accepted practice can arise the court must be satisfied on the evidence presented to it that there is a responsible body of professional opinion which supports the practice. Evidence which amounts simply to an expression of opinion by an expert witness of what he thinks he would have done had he been placed, hypothetically and without the benefit of hindsight, in the position of the defendant, is of little assistance in determining whether there was a responsible practice.[70] Moreover, it is always open to the court to reject expert evidence applying the ordinary principles of credibility that would be applied in any courtroom, for example, that the evidence is internally contradictory, or that the

---

[68] "Ordinary common sense dictates that when simple methods to avoid danger have been devised, are known, and are available, non-user, with fatal results, cannot be justified by saying that others also have been following the same old, less-careful practice; and that when such methods are readily comprehensible by the ordinary person, by whom, also, the need to use them or not is easily apprehended, it is quite within the competence of Court or jury, quite as much as of experts to deal with the issues; and that the existence of a practice which neglects them, even if the practice were general, cannot protect the defendant surgeon," *per* Coyne J.A. in *Anderson v Chasney* [1949] 4 D.L.R. 71, 86–87 (Man. C.A.); affirmed [1950] 4 D.L.R. 223 (S.C.C.). Similarly, in *Chapman v Rix* (1959) 103 S.J. 940 Morris L.J., in a dissenting judgment, said that: "The question whether the omission was negligent was one on which expert technical guidance was not needed. Medical witnesses had . . . stated that if similarly placed their conduct would have been no different from that under review. But the duty still remained with the court to decide whether such conduct amounted in law to negligence." See further para. 3–049 below.

[69] *ter Neuzen v Korn* (1993) 103 D.L.R. (4th) 473, 506 (B.C.C.A.); affirmed (1995) 127 D.L.R. (4th) 577, 595 (S.C.C.).

[70] *J.D. Williams & Co Ltd v Michael Hyde & Associates Ltd* [2000] Lloyd's Rep. P.N. 823, 831, *per* Ward L.J., citing Oliver J. in *Midland Bank Trust Co Ltd v Hett Stubbs & Kemp* [1979] Ch. 384, 402. In *Chapman v Rix* (1960), [1994] 5 Med. L.R. 239, 247 Lord Goddard said that a doctor cannot avoid a finding of negligence merely by finding two doctors to say that they would have acted as he did, provided there was evidence the other way.

witness was acting as an advocate rather than an impartial and objective expert.[71]

How many experts?

In *Hills v Potter* Hirst J. denied that the *Bolam* test allows the medical profession to set the standard of care: "In every case the court must be satisfied that the standard contended for . . . accords with that upheld by a substantial body of medical opinion, and that this body of medical opinion is both respectable and responsible, and experienced in this particular field of medicine."[72] In *De Freitas v O'Brien*[73] the claimant argued that Hirst J.'s reference to a "substantial body of medical opinion" meant that the defendant could not simply rely on a small number of experts in the field as supporting a particular practice. The Court of Appeal rejected this argument. The test was whether there was a "responsible body" of opinion, which could not be measured in purely quantitative terms. On the facts, a body of 11 doctors who specialised in spinal surgery, out of a total of well over 1,000 orthopaedic and neurosurgeons in the country, could represent a responsible body of opinion. Thus, the question of what constitutes a responsible body of professional opinion is not a "numbers game". The issue is whether the evidence supporting the defendant's conduct is reasonable and logically defensible.[74]   3–034

Accordingly, following accepted practice, or one of several such practices, is strong evidence of the exercise of reasonable care, but ultimately it is for the court to determine what constitutes negligence.[75] Although it is rare for the court to conclude that a common practice was negligent, when this does happen it will be through a finding that the practice was not "responsible." Once the practice followed by the defendant is acknowledged to be a "responsible" practice it is not open to the court to hold that it was negligent,   3–035

---

[71] See para. 3–153. In *Dowdie v Camberwell Health Authority* [1997] 8 Med. L.R. 368, 375, Kay J. observed that: "The mere fact that two distinguished expert witnesses have testified that it was within the range of acceptable practice to proceed in that way does not oblige me to accept their evidence and, on this issue, I accept the evidence of the plaintiff's experts . . ."

[72] [1983] 3 All E.R. 716, 728. See also *per* Lord Diplock in *Sidaway v Bethlem Royal Hospital Governors* [1985] A.C. 871, 895, stating that the court must be satisfied by the expert evidence that a body of opinion qualifies as a "responsible" body of medical opinion. In *Gascoine v Ian Sheridan & Co* [1994] 5 Med. L.R. 437, 444 Mitchell J. said that "as a matter of common sense . . . simply because a number of doctors gave evidence to the same effect, that does not automatically constitute an established and alternative 'school of thought' if, for example, the reasons given to substantiate the views expressed do not stand up to sensible analysis: see *Hucks v Cole* above (*per* Sachs L.J.)."

[73] [1995] P.I.Q.R. P281; [1995] 6 Med. L.R. 108.

[74] In *Bolitho v City and Hackney Health Authority* [1993] 4 Med. L.R. 381, 386, Farquharson L.J. commented that: "There is of course no inconsistency between the decisions in *Hucks v Cole* and *Maynard's* case. It is not enough for a defendant to call a number of doctors to say what he had done or not done was in accord with accepted clinical practice. It is necessary for the judge to consider that evidence and decide whether that clinical practice puts the patient unnecessarily at risk."

[75] See *Jackson & Powell on Professional Negligence*, 5th ed., 2002, para. 2.117; Dugdale and Stanton, *Professional Negligence*, 3rd ed., 1998, paras 15.25–15.26; Norrie [1985] J.R. 145.

even where another body of "responsible" professional opinion is critical of the practice.

3–036   The inherent danger in the *Bolam* test is that if the courts defer too readily to expert evidence medical standards could decline, since where there are competing views within the medical profession *Bolam* opts for the lowest common denominator. Thus, Dr Scott has cogently argued that the *Bolam* test should be restricted to those cases where an adverse result follows a course of treatment which has been intentional and has been shown to benefit other patients previously. It should not be extended to certain kinds of medical accident merely on the basis of how common they are: "To do this would set us on the slippery slope of excusing carelessness when it happens often enough."[76]

(b) Departing from professional practice

3–037   Just as compliance with accepted practice is good evidence that the defendant has acted with reasonable care, a departure from accepted practice may be evidence of negligence,[77] but in neither case is the evidence conclusive.[78] If deviation from a common professional practice was considered proof of negligence then no doctor could introduce a new technique or method of treatment without facing the risk of a negligence action if something went wrong. As Lord President Clyde commented in *Hunter v Hanley* this "would be disastrous . . . for all inducement to progress in medical science would then be destroyed."[79] His Lordship suggested that there were three requirements to establish liability where deviation from normal practice is alleged:

---

[76] Scott (1991) 2 *AVMA Medical & Legal Journal* (No. 3) p. 16. For example, the fact that posterior dislocation of the shoulder is a rare condition in which the diagnosis is very often missed, does not necessarily mean that it is reasonable or competent to miss the diagnosis. See also the comment of Harris, *ibid.*, describing the missed diagnosis in such cases as "inexcusable" because the classical signs are always present: "the problem arises because the examining doctor fails to think of the possibility and does not look for the signs."

[77] *Robinson v Post Office* [1974] 2 All E.R. 737, 745. In *Thake v Maurice* [1986] Q.B. 644 the defendant surgeon carelessly forgot to give his own usual warning that there was a slight risk that the claimant might become fertile again after a sterilisation operation. In the absence of any other expert evidence the Court of Appeal held that the defendant's usual practice was evidence of what constituted "responsible" practice, and held him negligent for failing to comply with it.

[78] *Holland v The Devitt & Moore Nautical College, The Times*, March 4, 1960, QBD, where a slight departure from the standard textbook treatment was held not negligent, since the doctor had to treat a particular patient, whereas the textbooks deal with a subject generally; *Dunne v National Maternity Hospital* [1989] I.R. 91, 109, where it was said that deviation from general and approved practice does not establish negligence unless the course of conduct was one which no medical practitioner would have followed had he been taking ordinary care.

[79] 1955 S.C. 200, 206. This proposition also receives statutory recognition in the Congenital Disabilities (Civil Liability) Act 1976, s. 1(5) which provides that: "The defendant is not answerable to the child, for anything he did or omitted to do when responsible in a professional capacity for treating or advising the parent, if he took reasonable care having due regard to then received professional opinion applicable to the particular class of case; *but this does not mean that he is answerable only because he departed from received opinion*" (emphasis added).

first, it must be proved that there is a usual and normal practice; secondly, it must be proved that the doctor has not adopted that practice; and thirdly, it must be established that the course which he adopted is one which no professional man of ordinary skill would have taken if he had been acting with ordinary care. In other words, the fundamental test remains whether the defendant acted with reasonable care in all the circumstances, and the significance of compliance with or deviation from common professional practice lies in its evidential value.

One consequence of the *Bolam* test is that where there are two competing   3–038
responsible bodies of professional opinion and the defendant adheres to one view, but carelessly fails to follow his own normal practice with the result that he complies with the alternative approach, he will not be held negligent because he will have conformed to a practice accepted as proper by a responsible body of professional opinion. Thus, where the doctor fails to give a warning about the risks of treatment which he would usually give, but there is a responsible body of medical opinion which, as a matter of deliberate policy, would not warn the patient of the particular risks, the defendant will not be liable since, though he has departed from his own clinical practices, he has conformed to a practice accepted as proper by a responsible body of professional opinion, albeit by accident.[80] As Mitchell J. observed in *Gascoine v Ian Sheridan & Co*,[81] a case of alleged negligent overtreatment: "If on some hit-and-miss basis [the defendants] treated correctly (or correctly in the opinion of a respected reasonably competent body of thinking in 1978) then liability in negligence could not be established."

Sometimes, a departure from accepted practice may provide overwhelm-   3–039
ing evidence of a breach of duty, particularly where the practice is specifically designed as a precaution against a known risk and the defendant has no good reason for not following the normal procedure. If the risk should materialise the defendant will have great difficulty in avoiding a finding of negligence. In *Clark v MacLennan*,[82] for example, the claimant developed stress incontinence soon after the birth of her first child. Conservative treatment failed to improve the claimant's condition, and so a month after the birth the defendant gynaecologist performed an anterior colporrhaphy operation. The normal practice of gynaecologists was not to perform such an operation until at least three months after the birth, because the condition may in any event improve with the passage of time, and if it is clear that the operation is required there is a much greater chance of success after three months, since the risk of haemorrhage is smaller. This was not an absolute rule since there might be exceptional cases, but it was not a case where there were two schools of thought amongst gynaecologists. None of the witnesses could point to any instance where the operation had been performed at less than three months. The operation was not a success because a haemorrhage caused the repair to break down. Two further operations were necessary,

---

[80] *Moyes v Lothian Health Board* [1990] 1 Med. L.R. 463, 470.
[81] [1994] 5 Med. L.R. 437, 458.
[82] [1983] 1 All E.R. 416.

neither of which were successful with the result that the claimant's condition became permanent. The defendant was held liable. Peter Pain J. said that a doctor owes a duty to his patient to observe the precautions which are normal in the course of the treatment that he gives. Where "there is but one orthodox course of treatment and he chooses to depart from that . . . [o]ne has to inquire whether he took all proper factors into account which he knew or should have known, and whether his departure from the orthodox course can be justified on the basis of these factors."[83]

3–040   His Lordship went further, however, suggesting that where there is a general practice to take a particular precaution against a specific risk but the defendant fails to take that precaution, and the very damage occurs against which the precaution is designed to be a protection, then the *burden of proof* lies with the defendant to show both that he was not negligent and that the negligence did not cause the damage.[84] This view, that negligence can be established merely by showing that some step which is designed to avert or minimise a risk has not been taken, was disapproved by Mustill L.J. in *Wilsher v Essex Area Health Authority*,[85] though the decision in *Clark v MacLennan* was described as, on its facts, "unimpeachable." Thus, although the burden of proving negligence remains with the claimant, in a case where the defendant has departed from the single orthodox procedure he will probably be found liable, unless there is evidence before the court which would justify the departure.[86]

3–041   Some instances of departure from accepted practice are quite clearly negligent even where they are performed consciously and routinely. For example, in *Chin Keow v Government of Malaysia*[87] a doctor gave a patient an injection of penicillin without making any enquiry about the patient's medical history. Had he done so he would have discovered that she was allergic to penicillin. The patient died due to an allergic reaction to the drug. The doctor was aware of the remote possibility of this risk arising but he carried on with his routine practice of not making any enquiry because he had had no mishaps before. All the medical evidence was to the effect that enquiries, which would have taken no more than five minutes, were necessary. The Privy Council held the doctor liable.

3–042   In *Landau v Werner*[88] a psychiatrist engaged in social contact with a female patient who had developed a strong and obsessive emotional attachment to him. This was a departure from recognised standards in the practice of psychiatry and led to a serious deterioration in the patient's mental health. Barry J. said that although the defendant had acted from the best of intentions he had made a tragic mistake; there was no body of professional

---

[83] *ibid.* at p. 425.
[84] *ibid.* at p. 427, relying on *McGhee v National Coal Board* [1972] 3 All E.R. 1008.
[85] [1987] Q.B. 730, 752, 753. The House of Lords also disapproved this approach to the proof of causation in *Wilsher v Essex Area Health Authority* [1988] A.C. 1074; see para. 5–025 *et seq.*
[86] For discussion of the burden of proof and the evidential burden, see paras 3–117 *et seq.*
[87] [1967] 1 W.L.R. 813.
[88] (1961) 105 S.J. 257 and 1008, CA.

opinion which would have adopted this course of conduct with a patient in these circumstances, indeed, the medical evidence was all one way in condemning social contacts. Accordingly the defendant was liable. This was upheld on appeal. Sellers L.J. said that:

> ". . . a doctor might not be negligent if he tried a new technique but if he did he must justify it before the court. If his novel or exceptional treatment had failed disastrously he could not complain if it was held that he went beyond the bounds of due care and skill as recognised generally. Success was the best justification for unusual and unestablished treatment."

In *Coughlin v Kuntz*[89] the defendant adopted a method of performing an operation which was experimental, unsupported by clinical study, and favoured by no other orthopaedic surgeon. The procedure was under investigation by the College of Physicians and Surgeons, which had urged the defendant to undertake a moratorium on the procedure. The defendant was held to have been negligent. Similarly, in *Cryderman v Ringrose*[90] the defendant took of a biopsy at a time when there was a "presumptive pregnancy." The normal practice would have been to alert the claimant to the possibility of pregnancy and wait until a more certain diagnosis could be made. In the circumstances the biopsy was not medically justified since it could cause an abortion, and the defendant was liable.

3–043

(c) Codes of Practice

Codified standards of professional conduct may constitute significant evidence of what constitutes reasonable care. In *Lloyd Cheynham & Co Ltd v Littlejohn & Co.*[91] Woolf J. said of accounting and audit standards that:

3–044

> "While they are not conclusive, so that a departure from their terms necessarily involves a breach of a duty of care, and they are not . . . rigid rules, they are very strong evidence as to what is the proper standard which should be adopted and unless there is some justification, a departure from this will be regarded as constituting a breach of duty."[92]

---

[89] (1987) 42 C.C.L.T. 142 (B.C.S.C.); affirmed [1990] 2 W.W.R. 737 (B.C.C.A.).

[90] [1977] 3 W.W.R. 109; affirmed [1978] 3 W.W.R. 481 (Alta. S.C. Appellate Division). See also *Zimmer v Ringrose* (1981) 124 D.L.R. (3d) 215, 223 on a doctor's duty to inform the patient that a new procedure or technique had not been approved by the medical profession. A reasonable practitioner would have disclosed this since he would realise that the information would be likely to influence the patient's decision whether to undergo the procedure.

[91] (1985) 2 P.N. 154.

[92] See Gwilliam (1986) 2 P.N. 175. See also *Bevan Investments Ltd v Blackhall and Struthers (No. 2)* [1973] 2 N.Z.L.R. 45, 66 on engineering codes of practice; *Ward v The Ritz Hotel (London) Ltd* [1992] P.I.Q.R. P315, CA—failure to comply with the British Standards Institution's recommendation as to the height of a balustrade on a balcony was strong evidence of negligence.

Such standards are not, however, determinative of negligence. Thus, in *Johnson v Bingley*[93] it was held that breach of the *Guide to Professional Conduct of Solicitors* published by the Law Society was not *per se* proof of negligence. The *Guide* was proper and accepted practice for solicitors, but negligence was a legal concept, and neither the Law Society nor any other professional body could, by issuing rules or codes of conduct, alter the law.[94]

3-045   In the context of health care, the introduction of medical audit and NHS clinical governance could lead to the development of treatment protocols and practice guidelines, providing a consensus view of experts in the field as to the proper standards.[95] It might then become increasingly difficult for a doctor to argue that the protocol was rejected in favour of some alternative method, even if there are some doctors prepared to state that they disagree with the protocol produced by the experts.[96] There is already evidence that the courts are prepared to consider, and accept as highly persuasive, guidelines produced by the medical profession on appropriate standards of conduct.[97] In *Pierre v*

---

[93] [1997] P.N.L.R. 392, QBD.

[94] See also *Green v Building Scene Ltd* [1994] P.I.Q.R. P259, where the Court of Appeal held that although a failure to comply with Building Regulations or the British Standards Institution's recommendations about the safety of a staircase was evidence which the court should take into account, because it represented current professional opinion as to what was desirable to avoid accidents, it was not conclusive. There was a difference between laying down standards and defining what is reasonably safe in all the circumstances of the case. In *Caldwell v Maguire and Fitzgerald* [2001] EWCA Civ 1054; [2002] P.I.Q.R. P45 it was held that the fact that the defendants had been found guilty of "careless riding" under Jockey Club rules by the stewards after a horserace did not establish that an error of judgment or a momentary lapse of skill in the stress of a competitive race constituted a breach of duty owed to a fellow rider.

[95] One consequence of the introduction of clinical governance has been a proliferation of agencies of the Department of Health issuing guidance, some of which is directly relevant to patient safety. See, *e.g.*, the National Patient Safety Agency (*www.npsa.org.uk*), the National Institute for Clinical Excellence (*www.nice.org.uk*), and the Commission for Health Improvement (*www.chi.nhs.uk*).

[96] Harpwood (1994) 1 Med. Law Int. 241, 250, 251. Instructive here are the C.E.P.O.D. Reports into perioperative deaths which have identified certain systematic errors which can occur during surgery: see Buck, Devlin and Lunn, *Report of a Confidential Enquiry into Perioperative Deaths*, Nuffield Provincial Hospitals Trust and the King's Fund, 1987; Campling, Devlin, Lunn *Report of the National Confidential Enquiry into Perioperative Deaths* (1989), National Confidential Enquiry into Perioperative Deaths, London; Campling, Devlin, Hoile and Lunn, *Report of the National Confidential Enquiry into Perioperative Deaths* (1990); Campling, Devlin, Hoile, Lunn *Report of the National Confidential Enquiry into Perioperative Deaths* (1993). The 1990 Report on surgery on children under 10 years of age produced recommendations which have been embodied in guidelines published by the Royal College of Surgeons. As one of the authors comments on the effects of the C.E.P.O.D. Reports: "Guidelines or standards generated by competent professional and academic bodies will be included into clinical contracts and become benchmarks for the outcome expected," Devlin (1993) 4 *AVMA Medical & Legal Journal* (No. 2) p. 8, 11. Moreover, the techniques for measuring clinical activity "challenge the individual autonomy of consultants and probably render the traditional *Bolam* definition of negligence obsolete," *ibid.* at p. 9. See also Devlin (1995) 1 Clinical Risk 97. On the other hand, rigid adherence to guidelines can be inappropriate. Guidelines and protocols vary in their validity, and attempts to reach professional "consensus" can result in inadequate and biased guidelines: Hurwitz (1995) 1 Clinical Risk 142; Hurwitz (1999) 318 B.M.J. 661.

[97] See *W. v Egdell* [1990] Ch. 359 in the context of confidentiality; and *Airedale NHS Trust v Bland* [1993] A.C. 789 in the context of the treatment for patients in a persistent vegetative state. The General Medical Council publishes extensive Codes of Practice for doctors,

Marshall,[98] for example, the defendant was held to have been negligent for failing to follow the recommendations of the Alberta Medical Association and the Society of Obstetricians and Gynaecologists of Canada that there should be universal screening of pregnant women for gestational diabetes, notwithstanding that there was still controversy about the cost-effectiveness of universal screening. Even some experts who believed that universal screening was not cost-effective considered that doctors should heed the guidelines until the controversy was settled.

(d) When the *Bolam* test does not apply

(i) When the dispute between expert witnesses concerns a question of fact

The *Bolam* test encompasses two limbs. The first is the requirement of a professional person to exercise reasonable care in undertaking the tasks associated with the particular professional calling. The second, and more commonly invoked, is the assertion that a defendant will not be liable under the first limb if he has complied with a responsible professional practice, allowing always for the possibility that there may be more than one such practice. This is essentially a question of proof, since battle is usually joined between expert witnesses as to whether the defendant has followed a professional practice and, if so, whether it was a "responsible" practice. At this point, the requirement to subject the evidence of expert witnesses to logical scrutiny, applying the approach in *Bolitho v City and Hackney Health Authority*,[99] can be invoked. If, having undertaken that scrutiny, the court concludes that there is more than one *responsible* practice, it cannot then choose between them and find the defendant negligent on the basis that though his practice was responsible there was another practice that was better or more responsible. Thus, at this stage the court is precluded from choosing between expert evidence.

It is important, however, to keep this limitation in its proper perspective. Where there is a difference of opinion between expert witnesses about a question of fact, the court has a duty to resolve that dispute and reach a finding about the facts. In *Penney, Palmer and Cannon v East Kent Health Authority*[1] the claimants alleged that there had been negligence in the screening of cervical smear tests, in that some of the smears were falsely reported as negative, resulting in delay in obtaining treatment for cervical cancer. Screening was carried out by biomedical scientists or by qualified cytology screeners. They did not diagnose, they merely reported what they saw on the slides. If there was an abnormality or if there was doubt as to what was seen,

3–046

3–047

(n.97 contd.) ranging from general statements of good practice (e.g. *Good Medical Practice*, May 2001) to specific advice on how to proceed in particular circumstances. These codes are available from the GMC website *www.gmc-uk.org/standards/default.htm*.

[98] [1994] 8 W.W.R. 478 (Alta. Q.B.).

[99] [1998] A.C. 232.

[1] [2000] Lloyd's Rep. Med. 41; Faulks (2000) 6 Clinical Risk 153.

the slide was passed on to a senior screener (a checker). If the checker agreed with the categorisation it was passed on to a pathologist. If the pathologist confirmed the abnormality the patient was referred to a gynaecologist for a colposcopy or a biopsy. The expert witnesses (five pathologists) agreed that if a screener was in doubt about what was seen on the slide, he should not classify it as negative. In each case the claimants' smears were reported as normal or negative, but they all developed cervical cancer. The trial judge had held that the *Bolam* test did not apply, and found the defendants to have been negligent. The Court of Appeal held that the *Bolam* test did apply, subject to the *Bolitho* proviso that expert evidence as to the defendants' conduct had to stand up to logical analysis. The *Bolam* test did not apply, however, to questions of fact, including the question of what could be seen on the individual slides. Thus, the questions that had to be asked were: (i) what could be seen on each slide; (ii) could a reasonably competent cytoscreener have failed to see what was on the slide; (iii) could a reasonably competent cytoscreener, bearing in mind what he or she should have observed, have treated the slide as negative? The answer to the first question required expert evidence, but if there was a dispute amongst the experts as to what was visible on the slides the judge had to make his own finding of fact, on the balance of probabilities, a finding which might inevitably involve the rejection of some of the expert evidence. Once the judge had made that finding of fact, he then had to consider the second and third questions in determining whether there had been a breach of duty. Those issues involved an assessment of the expert evidence. All the experts were agreed, however, that an "absolute confidence" standard should have applied, whereby if there was any doubt in the cytoscreener's mind as to whether the slide was normal it should not have been classified as negative. To the extent that the defendants' experts were saying that it was acceptable to classify a slide as negative when the cytoscreener could not say whether the features of the slide were or were not pre-cancerous, their opinion did not withstand logical analysis.

3–048   Similarly, if the question is which of two possible explanations for an event having occurred is to be accepted, and there are competing theories from the expert witnesses, the court has to resolve that dispute in determining factual causation. In *Fallows v Randle*[2] there were competing theories as to how an operation to sterilise the claimant could have failed, one of which involved negligence by the defendant whereas the other did not. The trial judge preferred the claimant's explanation. Stuart-Smith L.J. said that the *Bolam* principle:

> "has really no application where what the judge has to decide is, on balance, which of two explanations—for something which has undoubtedly occurred which shows that the operation has been unsuccessful—is to be preferred. That is a question of fact which the judge

2 [1997] 8 Med. L.R. 160.

has to determine on the ordinary basis on a balance of probability. It is not a question of saying whether there was a respectable body of medical opinion here which says that this can happen by chance without any negligence, it is a question for the judge to weigh up the evidence on both sides, and he is, in my judgment, entitled in a situation like this, to prefer the evidence of one expert witness to that of the other."[3]

(ii) Where no special skill is required in determining whether there has been negligence

In *J.D. Williams & Co Ltd v Michael Hyde & Associates Ltd*[4] the Court of Appeal held that the *Bolam* test does not apply where no special skill is required in determining whether there has been negligence (in which case the test would be the usual "reasonable man" standard of reasonable care in all the circumstances). On the facts of the case (which involved a judgment as to whether further investigation of the risk of discolouration of garments by a particular type of heating system was required or not) it was held that the exercise of judgment required did not involve any architectural skills, and therefore the judge was entitled to conclude that the failure to investigate the risk by the defendant architects was negligent, without reference to the *Bolam* test. The fact that other architects would also have ignored the risk was irrelevant. Sedley L.J. commented that: "the *Bolam* test is typically appropriate where the neglect is said to lie in a conscious choice of available courses made by a trained professional, and that it is typically inappropriate where it is in an oversight that the neglect is said to lie. This is not least because it is likely to be much easier to characterise the former than the latter as errors of judgment."[5] In many, but not all, cases where a profession embraced more than one tenable view of acceptable practice, competence should not be measured by a single forensically determined standard, so that where there is more than one acceptable standard, competence has to be gauged by the lower or lowest of them: "But to extend the *Bolam* principle to all allegations of professional negligence would be to make the professions, to an extent large enough to accommodate much harm to the public, judges in their own cause."[6]

It is clear that in Sedley L.J.'s view the *Bolam* test should have a much more restricted ambit, so that it could not be invoked by a professional person where he has not in fact exercised a professional judgment. In *Adams v Rhymney Valley District Council*[7] a majority of the Court of Appeal held that the *Bolam* test applied even where the particular defendant did not have the qualifications of a professional in the relevant field, and even though he

3–049

3–050

---

[3] *ibid.* at 165. See also *St.-Jean v Mercier* (2002) 209 D.L.R. (4th) 513 (S.C.C.) at [55]: "It is not enough to say that there are opposing medical theories on causation and that it is not up to the court to decide between them."

[4] [2000] Lloyd's Rep. P.N. 823.

[5] *ibid.* at 835.

[6] *ibid.*

[7] [2000] Lloyd's Rep. P.N. 777. See de Prez (2001) 17 P.N. 75.

did not go through the process of reasoning which a qualified professional would undertake before choosing a particular course of action. Thus, if the defendant had in fact adopted a course of conduct which a responsible body of opinion would have supported, even by accident, then he is not to be held negligent. In a dissenting judgment, Sedley L.J. said[8] that the purpose of the *Bolam* test was to enable the court to determine whether a person professing and purporting to exercise a particular skill has exercised it with sufficient competence to escape a charge of negligence. A defendant who had failed to set about exercising a professional skill could not expect to be judged by the court as if he had exercised it: the court could not proceed as if an educated choice had been made when it knew that it was not. It was a "requirement of the *Bolam* test that the defendant should have considered and reflected upon the alternative courses available and made a conscious choice between them". The question then, was whether the defendant's eventual choice of a course of conduct made any difference to the outcome, but that was a question of causation, not professional competence. Thus, if on the balance of probabilities, the professional who should have been consulted would have acted as the defendant did, the negligence did not have any causal effect. But if the professional would probably have done something different which would have affected the outcome, the defendant could not rely on the argument that other responsible professionals might have acted in a way which would not have avoided the damage.

3–051   The approach of Sedley L.J. would seem to be somewhat out of step with the traditional analysis of negligence. Clearly, it is appropriate for the courts to remind themselves that the purpose of the *Bolam* test is to stop judges from attempting to resolve genuine differences of view as to an appropriate practice within a profession, where lawyers may be ill-equipped to address the fine technical detail of a well-balanced argument, while not allowing incompetent professionals to escape responsibility by setting their own low standards. Nonetheless, it remains the case that negligence measures an objective standard of conduct rather than a subjective process of reasoning. Thus, if a motorist is driving his vehicle in a manner which, to an external observer, is reasonably safe in the circumstances, it matters not that subjectively the motorist is being inadvertent, for example in thinking about some other matter. It is well-known that many of the tasks involved in driving a motor car can be done "automatically", in the sense that the motorist may not be consciously adverting to every movement or weighing every risk of each manoeuvre. Thus, a motorist may be "careless" in the sense of being inadvertent to a risk, but nonetheless his conduct may objectively conform to a standard of reasonable care. There is no reason why the same reasoning should not apply to the conduct of professionals. Thus, it is respectfully submitted that the analysis of the majority of the Court of Appeal in *Adams v Rhymney Valley District Council* is correct. If, objectively, the defendant conformed to a standard

---

[8] *ibid.* at [16] to [19].

of care that would have been adopted by a *responsible* body of professional opinion, the fact that he did so as a result of a flawed process of reasoning, or indeed without any reasoning, is simply nothing to the point.[9] An analysis of the reasoning process, the weighing of foreseeable risks and benefits against the burden of precautions, clearly *is* important when considering whether a particular professional practice constitutes a responsible practice. That, however, is part and parcel of subjecting professional practice to the logical scrutiny required by *Bolitho*.

(3) Experimental or novel techniques

The practitioner who departs from the accepted methods of treatment will   3–052 normally have to provide some justification for doing so if, as a consequence, the patient suffers injury.[10] This could have an inhibiting effect on doctors who seek to employ novel or experimental methods in the interests of their patients where traditional techniques have failed. Moreover, there is also an obligation to keep up to date with new methods,[11] but, inevitably, someone has to be the first to try the innovation. On the other hand, patients should not be recklessly subjected to untried and potentially dangerous experimentation. The law has to reach a delicate balance between these competing considerations. One response has been to say that in such circumstances the courts should be careful not to make a finding of negligence simply because the patient has sustained injury. In *Wilsher v Essex Area Health Authority*[12] Mustill L.J. said that where the doctor embarks on a form of treatment which is still comparatively untried, with techniques and safeguards which are still in the course of development, then "if the decision to embark on the treatment at all was justifiable and was taken with the informed consent of the patient, the court should . . . be particularly careful not to impute negligence simply because something has gone wrong." It is debatable whether this adds much to the usual caveat that the courts give against findings of negligence merely because an error has occurred. It simply begs the question whether the decision to proceed was indeed justifiable.

Lord Diplock has also touched upon this problem in *Sidaway v Bethlem*   3–053 *Royal Hospital Governors*:

---

[9] Commenting on the decisions in *Adams v Rhymney Valley District Council* and *J.D. Williams & Co v Michael Hyde & Associates* in *Green v Hancocks (A Firm)* [2001] Lloyd's Rep. P.N. 212 at [60] Chadwick L.J. observed: "I do not think it necessary, in the context of this case, to consider whether it could ever be right to look at the advice given in isolation from the thought process which led to that advice. If the advice is correct, it may well be irrelevant whether the adviser hit upon it as the result of careful and detailed thought, or as the result of experience which overrode the need for a detailed analysis of the reasoning process, or purely by luck. I would not endorse the view that, in every case, a professional adviser will be held negligent because he does not spell out in detail the reasons which lead him to the advice which he gives."

[10] *Clark v MacLennan* [1983] 1 All E.R. 416; *Landau v Werner* (1961) 105 S.J. 1008, CA.

[11] See para. 3–062.

[12] [1987] Q.B. 730, 749.

"Those members of the public who seek medical or surgical aid would be badly served by the adoption of any legal principle that would confine the doctor to some long-established, well-tried method of treatment only, although its past record of success might be small, if he wanted to be confident that he would not run the risk of being held liable in negligence simply because he tried some more modern treatment, and by some unavoidable mischance it failed to heal but did some harm to the patient. This would encourage 'defensive medicine' with a vengeance."[13]

This statement clearly reflects the public interest in allowing the medical profession to develop new, and more effective methods of health care, without the fear that they may be sued for negligence simply for trying something different from established practice. The passage also indicates one factor that would be relevant to the question of whether embarking on the new procedure would be justified, namely where the past record of success of the established treatment is small. However, his Lordship also appeared to suggest that the *Bolam* test protects the doctor in this situation by acknowledging that there may be a number of different accepted practices at any particular time. This view is open to question. There is likely to be a time-lag between the development of new methods and their acceptance by the profession.[14] Where the new treatment is not yet established as a practice accepted as proper by a responsible body of medical opinion a defendant will have to justify his decision simply by reference to the "reasonable doctor." This will depend to a large extent on the relative risk of the treatment in comparison to the alternative treatments and the nature of the illness for which it is prescribed. Where the patient's condition is very serious and the standard treatment is ineffective, a doctor will be justified in taking greater risks in an attempt to provide some effective treatment. On the other hand, the patient should not be exposed to excessive risk and there should be some attempt to provide scientific validation for a new technique. In *Hepworth v Kerr*[15] the defendant anaesthetist adopted a new hypotensive anaesthetic technique which he knew had never been attempted routinely before, in order to provide a blood-free field for the operating surgeon. He knew that he was experimenting, but did not embark upon any proper scientific validation of his technique in some 1,500 patients by the time of the claimant's operation. It was not a minor adjustment to well-established techniques, but a step completely outside conventional wisdom which was right at the margins of safety and effectively took patients "to the very edge of existence." McKinnon J. held the defendant liable for the condition of anterior spinal artery syndrome (spinal stroke) which the claimant was subsequently found to have developed, despite the fact that this amounted to a condemnation of the defendant's "life-time work".

[13] [1985] A.C. 871, 893. See also the comments of Butler-Sloss P. in *Simms v Simms* [2002] EWHC 2734 (Fam); [2003] 1 All E.R. 669 at [48], cited at para. 6–173 at n. 76.
[14] As, *e.g.*, in *Crawford v Charing Cross Hospital*, *The Times*, December 8, 1953.
[15] [1995] 6 Med. L.R. 139; discussed at (1996) 2 Clinical Risk 73–87.

The question of experimental procedures has been considered by the   3–054
Canadian courts. The use of an innovative technique will not be treated as
negligence *per se*. In *Zimmer v Ringrose* Prowse J.A. said that:

> "A physician is entitled to decide that the situation dictates the adop-
> tion of an innovative course of treatment. As long as he discharges his
> duty of disclosure, and is not otherwise in breach of his duties of skill
> and care, *e.g.*, has not negligently adopted the procedure given the
> circumstances, the doctor will not be held liable for implementing such
> a course of treatment."[16]

The defendant's method of sterilisation was "experimental and quite
unsupported by clinical study as a method acceptable for human beings."[17]
He was held to have been negligent in failing to inform the claimant that
the technique had not been approved by the medical profession, although
this aspect of the claim failed on the grounds of causation (the claimant
would have undergone the procedure in any event). In *Cryderman v
Ringrose*[18] the claimant agreed to be sterilised by the same defendant by
the same experimental procedure, which involved introducing silver nitrate
into the fallopian tubes through the uterus. The claimant was not informed
that the procedure was unreliable or that it might damage the uterus. The
claimant believed that she was sterile, although the defendant knew that
the procedure had not been successful and he did not inform her. She
became pregnant and later underwent an abortion. The trial judge rejected
the claimant's argument that the defendant was negligent because there
was a usual and normal practice which had not been followed, on the
ground that it would impede medical progress. He also distinguished
Halushka v University of Saskatchewan[19] on the basis that that was a case
of "pure medical experimentation," where different considerations would
apply:

> "When an experimental procedure is employed the common law
> requires a high degree of care and also disclosure to the patient of the
> fact that the treatment is new and risky."[20]

---

[16] (1981) 124 D.L.R. (3d) 215, 223–224 (Alta. C.A.); affirming in part (1978) 89 D.L.R. (3d)
646. See also *Waters v West Sussex Health Authority* [1995] 6 Med. L.R. 362 where the
novel surgical technique of a neurosurgeon was found to accord with the standards of
responsible medical opinion.

[17] (1978) 89 D.L.R. (3d) 646, 652, *per* MacDonald J.; see also pp. 655–656; see also *Coughlin
v Kuntz* (1987) 42 C.C.L.T. 142 (B.C.S.C.); affirmed [1990] 2 W.W.R. 737 (B.C.C.A.), above
para. 3–043.

[18] [1977] 3 W.W.R. 109; affirmed [1978] 3 W.W.R. 481 (Alta. S.C. Appellate Division).

[19] (1965) 53 D.L.R. (2d) 436; see further para. 6–177.

[20] [1977] 3 W.W.R. 109, 118; *Crossman v Stewart* (1977) 82 D.L.R. (3d) 677, 686; *Poole v
Morgan* [1987] 3 W.W.R. 217, 254, *per* Cawsey J. (Alta. Q.B.) stating that ". . . where the
risks involved in the treatment are great, or the treatment is a new one, the standard of care
increases." It is submitted that the standard of care does not change, rather the precautions
required to satisfy the standard of "reasonable care in all the circumstances" are greater.

The standard of care was, nonetheless, that of a reasonable doctor considering all the circumstances, including the seriousness of the condition, the risks, the patient's capacity to comprehend and decide the question involved and the likely effect on her of the knowledge of the risks involved. Moreover, the court should be alert to the risk of a conflict of interest between the patient's welfare and the interests of the doctor, particularly when the doctor is prescribing *his* new process (as distinct from the objectivity that was to be presumed in the use of someone else's new process).

3–055   A similar approach would probably be taken in this country. A degree of care is expected which is commensurate with the risk involved, and innovative treatment would be regarded as inherently "risky" until it has become tried and tested. In *Independent Broadcasting Authority v EMI Electronics Ltd and BICC Construction Ltd*[21] the House of Lords held that a defendant employed to design an experimental television mast had to demonstrate that he had exercised a high degree of care both in assessing the risks of the venture and the possible alternatives. He could not justify his actions simply by saying "we were taking a step into the unknown and so the risks were unforeseeable." There was an obligation to think things through and to assess the dimensions of the "venture into the unknown."[22]

3–056   This proposition would also apply to claims arising out of a systematic research project, whether therapeutic or non-therapeutic.[23] An allegation of negligence in conducting research would involve proving that the design, the performance or the follow-up of the experimental procedure was negligent, or that the disclosure of information concerning risks was inadequate.[24] A researcher has a duty fully to investigate the possible consequences of the research using existing published literature and animal experiments where appropriate, prior to conducting research on human subjects.[25] The research should be well-designed, and should seek to minimise the risks to the research subjects. This would include: the provision of a "stopping rule" by

---

[21] (1980) 14 B.L.R. 1.

[22] *ibid.* at p. 31, *per* Lord Edmund-Davies. Dugdale and Stanton, *Professional Negligence*, 3rd ed., 1998, para. 16.07 comment that: "In law the burden of proving lack of reasonable care in such circumstances remains on the plaintiff, but, in practice, once the plaintiff has shown that the work has proved to be faulty and that it diverged from the accepted professional approach to such issues, it will be for the defence to justify their actions."

[23] Therapeutic research is an activity which has a therapeutic intention, as well as a research intention, towards the subjects of the research; the subjects are also patients. Non-therapeutic research is an activity which does not have a therapeutic intention. This is normally carried out on healthy volunteers, who are not patients. See further paras 6–163 *et seq.* The Royal College of Physicians, *Guidelines on the Practice of Ethics Committees in Medical Research Involving Human Subjects*, 2nd ed., 1990 and *Research Involving Patients*, 1990 distinguish *research*, which is designed to develop or contribute to generalisable knowledge, from *innovative therapy*, where a clinician departs significantly from standard practice entirely for the benefit of a particular patient. The latter may not constitute research, although it may be described as experimental in the sense that it is novel and unvalidated.

[24] See generally Giesen (1995) 3 Med. L. Rev. 22. On the disclosure of information to research subjects see paras 6–165 to 6–172, 6–177 to 6–178.

[25] *Vacwell Engineering Co Ltd v BDH Chemicals* [1971] 1 Q.B. 88, where the defendant was negligent in failing to check all relevant publications dealing with a little known chemical prior to marketing it.

which the project would be halted if a serious risk of harm became apparent; provision for emergencies; and careful periodic observation of the subjects.[26] It is also arguable that a research project which failed to comply with national or international ethical codes on medical experimentation could be found to have been conducted negligently, on the basis that the codes constitute evidence of what is reasonable care, by reference to the accepted practice of the profession.[27]

The one English case which has involved a finding of negligence against a **3–057** major clinical trial is *The Creutzfeldt-Jakob Disease Litigation, Plaintiffs v United Kingdom Medical Research Council*,[28] which concerned the transmission of the "slow virus" which causes Creutzfeldt-Jakob Disease (CJD) from human growth hormone (HGH) extracted from the pituitaries of cadavers. Between 1959 and 1985 almost 2,000 children were treated with HGH. The claimants had all been treated with HGH when they were children. Since 1985, 16 of the recipients had died of CJD and a further three were expected to do so.[29] Eleven claimants (the group A claimants) had developed CJD as a consequence of receiving HGH contaminated with the CJD virus. There were a further 87 claimants in Group B who had received HGH who had not, as yet, been diagnosed with CJD. Until July 1, 1977 responsibility for the collection and processing of pituitaries and the allocation of HGH to nominated recipients was that of the Medical Research Council (MRC). Thereafter, it was the responsibility of the Secretary of State for Health (the Department). Treatment of those children who received HGH was under the auspices of the MRC. Under the MRC, the HGH programme had been a clinical trial but by 1976, because of the numbers receiving HGH, it had effectively become a therapeutic programme. Until 1980, the safety of HGH had remained the responsibility of the MRC, while the Department prepared for the programme's takeover. In June 1977 the Department of Health Services Human Growth Hormone Committee (HSHGHC) was responsible for the safety of HGH, but the committee believed that it was not concerned with slow viruses, a belief which had permeated the Department's staff and, through them, the professional staff at the MRC and then upwards to the chair of the committee. Morland J. found that information about the risk of slow virus infection was conveyed in a

---

[26] *Zimmer v Ringrose* (1978) 89 D.L.R. (3d) 646, 656.

[27] See para. 3–044. See also Dugdale and Stanton, *Professional Negligence*, 3rd ed., 1998, para. 15.23. Both therapeutic and non-therapeutic medical research are governed by the guidelines of the *Declaration of Helsinki*, extracted in Kennedy & Grubb, *Medical Law*, 3rd ed., 2000, p. 1678. See further the Royal College of Physicians, *Guidelines on the Practice of Ethics Committees in Medical Research Involving Human Subjects*, 2nd ed., 1990 and Royal College of Physicians *Research Involving Patients*, 1990. On the potential liability of Research Ethics Committees see Brazier (1990) 6 P.N. 186. The decisions of ethics committees may, in some circumstances, be subject to judicial review: *R. v Ethical Committee of St. Mary's Hospital, ex parte Harriott* [1988] 1 F.L.R. 512, 518–519.

[28] (1996) 54 B.M.L.R. 8; [1996] 7 Med. L.R. 309.

[29] Two years later there were 27 confirmed cases of CJD: see *The Creutzfeldt-Jakob Disease Litigation, Andrews and others v Secretary of State for Health (Damages Assessments)* (1998) 54 B.M.L.R. 111, 113.

cursory manner. HSHGHC had not had the appropriate expertise to make an informed decision of the risk of slow virus infection. From 1976 to 1980, the collection of pituitaries and the production of HGH had continued in the same way, despite evidence pointing to the potential risks which emerged in 1976. The HSHGHC had been deliberately kept in the dark about the details of slow viruses, despite its responsibility for the safety of the treatment.

3–058   Morland J. held that the defendants had been negligent in permitting the programme to continue. From July 1, 1977 the treatment programme should have been partially suspended. New patients should not have been started on the programme after that date, unless they were suffering from hypocalcaemia and would otherwise have suffered serious ill health. However, it would not have been negligent to continue treatment for patients who had already started the treatment, since the risk was considered to be low, the cessation of treatment for ongoing recipients would have had psychological and physical disadvantages, and a synthetic product was still a few years off. Prior to October 1976, although knowledge of transmissibility of the CJD agent and slow viruses was growing, it was not established that the defendants had been guilty of negligence in failing to undertake a thorough re-appraisal of the HGH programme or in failing to have imposed more stringent criteria with regard to the collection of pituitaries. Prior to 1976 CJD had been mistakenly assumed to be much rarer than it was. The claimants had not established that, before 1976, the method used to process pituitaries was negligent, although a purer HGH could have been produced by a different method. Nowhere in the world in which HGH was in production was CJD regarded as a risk through contaminated HGH. However, there was no good reason why the changes in production methods of HGH which were made in 1980 should not have been made in early 1977 if proper advice had been sought. It was not a defence that no greater action was being taken outside the UK because only in the UK had specific warning of the risk of CJD being transmitted through HGH been given. The delays in making appropriate inquiry had been negligent.[30]

3–059   In the initial trial of the group action Morland J. held that only those claimants whose treatment had started after July 1, 1977 could claim. However, the Court of Appeal held that the "straddlers", *i.e.* those who had received injections both before and after July 1, 1977, should also be permitted to claim, on the basis that their actions were not bound to fail simply because Morland J. had concluded that it would not have been negligent for the HSHGHC to have recommended that treatment for existing patients should have continued.[31] This was because they might be able to prove that

---

[30] Subsequently, in *CJD Litigation: Group B Plaintiffs v Medical Research Council* (1997) 41 B.M.L.R. 157; (1997), [2000] Lloyd's Rep. Med. 161 it was held that the Group B claimants, none of whom had developed CJD but all of whom were aware that they were at risk of developing the disease, were entitled to compensation in respect of a genuine psychiatric illness caused by their awareness of the risk that they may develop CJD in the future. See para. 2–131.

[31] *The Creutzfeldt-Jakob Disease Litigation, Newman and others v Secretary of State for Health* (1997) 54 B.M.L.R. 85, CA.

had they been aware of the risk, those patients would have discontinued the treatment after July 1, 1977 and thereby avoided the injection which carried the fatally contaminated HGH. As the Court of Appeal pointed out, the dangers in the use of HGH did not suddenly increase after July 1, 1977. What happened was greater knowledge and awareness of the risks. Following the hypothetical meeting of the HSHGHC which should have taken place, at which the recommendation of a partial suspension of the programme would have been made, these risks would have been of urgent concern to every clinician responsible for administering HGH to an existing patient. The "community" involved in the programme would have become aware of the existence of the perceived risk in the use of HGH. The same duty of care was owed by the defendants to all patients involved in the programme (not simply to new patients), and once the risk associated with HGH was properly appreciated there was, at least arguably, a breach of duty owed to existing patients if their treatment proceeded without those responsible for their care informing them of the risks, so that they (usually through their parents) could decide whether or not to continue with the treatment. The fact that the hypothetical meeting would not have recommended suspending HGH treatment for ongoing recipients did not mean that it was bound to continue for each of them, once the treating clinicians became aware of the risks. "The treatment was not compulsory."[32] The claims of the straddlers were not bound to fail on the basis of the finding that the result of the meeting would have been a recommendation that treatment for existing patients should continue. Thus, the claimants should be entitled to adduce evidence and legal argument about the effect of the decision at the hypothetical meeting on the patients whose treatment straddled July 1, 1977. The question was whether in their individual cases treatment with HGH would have continued or been brought to a halt, and whether on the balance of probabilities the infecting dose or doses were received before or after July 1, 1977. Subsequently, in *The Creutzfeldt-Jakob Disease Litigation, Straddlers Group A and C v Secretary of State for Health*[33] Morland J. accepted evidence on behalf of the straddler claimants that the clinicians treating existing patients would probably have stopped the treatment, in the light of the risks which should have been made known to them by the defendants. That issue was to be determined on the balance of probabilities, not on the basis of the loss of a chance.[34]

In concluding that the Department had been negligent on the basis of its lethargy in carrying out inquiries and research into the risk of slow virus transmission, once it had been alerted to that risk, Morland J. stated a number of general principles. First, and axiomatically, the question of negligence has   **3–060**

---

[32] *ibid.* at 90.
[33] (1998) 54 B.M.L.R. 104.
[34] For consideration of how Morland J. approached the determination of the causation question of whether the infecting dose or doses were received before or after July 1, 1977 see: *The Creutzfeldt-Jakob Disease Litigation, Groups A and C Plaintiffs* (1998) 54 B.M.L.R. 100, para. 5–040.

to be assessed on the basis of the standards and knowledge which could reasonably have been expected at the time of the alleged negligence. Secondly, the risks of the programme had to be weighed against the benefits:

> "Many advances in medicine carry with them risk. A risk may be, from a scientific point of view, theoretical and may never become a reality. A risk may be a real risk, but, weighed against the benefit of a drug or treatment, a risk upon careful consideration worth taking, but the risks of a drug or a treatment need constant review in the light of expanding knowledge and experience."[35]

In assessing that risk the courts had to balance the dangers of too readily condemning novel procedures which went wrong as negligent, against the potential progress that research could produce:

> "The courts must be very cautious in condemning a clinical trial or therapeutic programme. Too ready a labelling of an act or omission as negligent by the courts could stultify progress in medical and scientific research and render eminent experts reluctant to serve on committees voluntarily. However, during the clinical trial of a new drug or form of treatment, and especially when the clinical trial is becoming a general therapeutic programme, all reasonably practicable steps should be taken to minimise dangers and side-effects. To discharge this duty, constant alert and inquiring evaluation of the trial or programme is required."[36]

Thirdly, the standard of care applied to publicly funded or sponsored research should not be lower than that applied to commercial organisations:

> "I do not accept that a government department or a quasi-governmental agency such as the MRC can discharge this duty by a lower standard of care than a commercial pharmaceutical company. In my judgment, shortage and limitation of funding and the fact that the collection of pituitaries, the production of HGH and the allocation of HGH to selected approved patients were under the responsibility and supervision of committees manned by unpaid volunteers are irrelevant. In my judgment, the same duty with the same standard of care is owed to all patients who are the subjects of clinical trials or new therapeutic programmes, whether the responsibility of a pharmaceutical company, government department or other agency."[37]

Finally, in respect of the standard of care that could be expected of an advisory committee Morland J. concluded that:

---

[35] (1996) 54 B.M.L.R. 8 at 14.
[36] *ibid.* at 23.
[37] *ibid.*

"The standard of care . . . to be imposed in respect of a committee is that of a reasonably competent and carefully inquiring group of professionals in the relevant disciplines, of sufficient standing to be entrusted with the membership of that committee, bearing in mind it is a committee which is not merely advisory but is carrying out executive and administrative functions."[38]

This applied as much to the scientific and technical staff advising the committee. While a committee which was not properly briefed could not reasonably be faulted for not requesting scientific material from its staff, those staff could be. The medical and scientific staff of both the MRC and the Department had a dual role, one administrative, the other in the use of their professional skills. In servicing the HGH committees, they were under a duty to alert the members to current medical and scientific knowledge. Committee members, though experts within their own fields, could not have been expected to have had all current knowledge about CJD and transmissible slow viruses. It was the failure of the committees to be provided with that information and their failure to seek it which gave rise to negligence.

The Pearson Commission recommended that a volunteer for medical   3–061
research or a clinical trial who suffers severe damage as a result should have a cause of action on the basis of strict liability.[39] This proposal has not been implemented, although *ex gratia* compensation may be available to a volunteer injured in a study sponsored by the Medical Research Council, or during drug trials.[40] In an appropriate case a research subject might have an action against a drug manufacturer under Part I of the Consumer Protection Act 1987, but the chances of such a claim succeeding are small given the difficulty that the claimant would have in proving that the drug was defective, and the fact that the manufacturer could rely on the development risks defence.[41]

(4) Keeping up to date

Professional practice may change over time so that what was once   3–062
accepted as the correct procedure is no longer considered to be respectable or responsible. In *Bolam v Friern Hospital Management Committee* McNair J. pointed out that a medical practitioner cannot "obstinately and pig-headedly carry on with some old technique if it has been proved to be contrary

---

[38] *ibid.* at 24.
[39] *Royal Commission on Civil Liability and Compensation for Personal Injury*, Cmnd 7054 (1978), paras 1339–1441.
[40] See the Association of the British Pharmaceutical Industry, *Guidelines for Medical Experiments in Non-Patient Human Volunteers*, and the ABPI *Guidelines: Clinical Trials— Compensation for Medicine-Induced Injury*, considered in Kennedy & Grubb *Medical Law*, 3rd ed., 2000, p. 1737. See also Department of Health, HSG (96)48, *Arrangements for Handling Clinical Negligence Claims Against NHS Staff*, Annex B (in Appendix 1 to this book).
[41] See paras 8–075, 8–102.

to what is really substantially the whole of informed medical opinion."[42] Thus, there is an obligation on doctors to keep up to date with new developments in their particular field. This principle is easy enough to state, but it is more difficult to determine precisely when a new development will render adherence to the old method negligent. In the same passage McNair J. illustrated his point in this way: "Otherwise you might get men today saying: 'I don't believe in anaesthetics. I don't believe in antiseptics. I am going to continue to do my surgery in the way it was done in the eighteenth century'. That would clearly be wrong." No doubt patients will be relieved to know that they should not be subjected to the surgical methods of the eighteenth century, but this still leaves considerable scope for debate about when practices become outdated.

3–063   In *Crawford v Charing Cross Hospital*[43] the claimant developed brachial palsy in an arm following a blood transfusion. At first instance the defendants were held liable on the basis that the anaesthetist had failed to read an article published in *The Lancet* six months earlier, concerning the best position of the arm when using a drip. The Court of Appeal reversed this decision, taking the view that it would be too great a burden on a doctor to say that he has to read every article appearing in the current medical press.[44] Moreover, it was wrong to suggest that a practitioner was negligent simply because he did not immediately put into operation the suggestions made by a contributor to a medical journal, although the time might come when a recommendation was so well proved and so well accepted that it should be adopted. In *Gascoine v Ian Sheridan & Co.*[45] Mitchell J. commented that a "shop floor gynaecologist" had a responsibility to keep himself generally informed on mainstream changes in diagnosis, treatment and practice through the mainstream literature, such as the leading textbooks and the *Journal of Obstetrics and Gynaecology*. Equally, it was unreasonable to suppose that he had an opportunity to acquaint himself with the content of the more obscure journals.

3–064   Once the risks associated with the old procedure become generally known,

---

[42] [1957] 2 All E.R. 118, 122.

[43] *The Times*, December 8, 1953.

[44] See also *Dwan v Farquhar* [1988] 1 Qd R. 234, where an article in a journal concerning the risks of contracting the AIDS virus from blood transfusions was published in March 1983, and a patient contracted HIV from a blood transfusion performed in May 1983; it was held that there was no negligence. On the transmission of HIV through blood transfusions see: *H. v Royal Alexandra Hospital for Children* [1990] 1 Med. L.R. 297 (N.S.W.S.C.); *E. v Australian Red Cross Society* (1991) 99 A.L.R. 601; [1991] 2 Med. L.R. 303; (1991) 105 A.L.R. 53 (Aus. Fed. C.A.); *Walker Estate v York-Finch General Hospital* (2001) 198 D.L.R. (4th) 193 (S.C.C.); and *Pittman Estate v Bain* (1994) 112 D.L.R. (4th) 257 (Ont. Ct., Gen. Div.); paras 4–040, 4–084. For consideration of transmission of HIV through infected semen see *ter Neuzen v Korn* (1993) 103 D.L.R. (4th) 473 (B.C.C.A.); (1995) 127 D.L.R. (4th) 577 (S.C.C.), para. 4–087. For discussion of the possibility of strict liability under the Consumer Protection Act 1987 in respect of contaminated or defective donated gametes see Stern (1994) 2 Med. L. Rev. 261. This argument has been significantly strengthened by the decision in *A v The National Blood Authority* [2001] 3 All E.R. 289 applying the Act to blood products. See para. 8–079.

[45] [1994] 5 Med. L.R. 437, 447.

so that it can be said that an ordinary and reasonably competent practitioner would have changed his practice, it will be negligent to continue with that procedure.[46] But as Ebsworth J. commented in *Newbury v Bath District Health Authority*,[47] changes in technique or the use of particular instruments may sometimes simply be a matter of fashion:

"[T]he fact that new methods become available does not make the continued use of the old negligent unless and until they are shown to be wrong or to carry an unacceptably higher risk to the patient than the new. A competent consultant surgeon will keep abreast of his field and in the light of the information he acquires thereby adjust his procedures as appropriate but he remains entitled to keep the old tried method in his armoury for use where properly judged to be suitable. The fact that other surgeons, however distinguished, may use other methods with success does not render the use of a well tried method negligent. The very extent to which a surgeon is skilled in a technique is a factor to be weighed in the balance."[48]

The problem is to identify precisely when it can be said that an unacceptable risk has become generally known. For example, there may be a difference of knowledge and understanding between research scientists and clinicians, since research scientists are usually better informed about new discoveries in discrete areas of their discipline than practitioners, who have to rely on researchers and professional publications to keep them informed.[49] The obligation is to make a reasonable effort to keep up to date. A doctor cannot realistically be expected to read every article in every learned medical journal,[50] but where a particular risk has been highlighted on a number of occasions the practitioner will ignore it at his peril.

---

[46] See, *e.g.*, *Roe v Minister of Health* [1954] 2 Q.B. 66; *McLean v Weir* [1977] 5 W.W.R. 609; affirmed [1980] 4 W.W.R. 330, below, para. 3–071; *McCormick v Marcotte* (1971) 20 D.L.R. (3d) 345 (S.C.C.), where a surgeon was held liable for using an obsolete method of treating a broken bone (plate and screw) notwithstanding a specialist orthopaedic surgeon recommended a different procedure (the insertion of an intramedullary nail); *Reynard v Carr* (1983) 30 C.C.L.T. 42, 67–68; reversed in part on other grounds (1986) 38 C.C.L.T. 217, where the defendant was ignorant about the serious side-effects of a drug he was prescribing, although this was general knowledge within the profession.

[47] (1998) 47 B.M.L.R. 138, QBD.

[48] *ibid.* at 162.

[49] *ter Neuzen v Korn* (1993) 103 D.L.R. (4th) 473, 497–498 (B.C.C.A.). Moreover, there may be a lack of effective communication between public health officials and practitioners, again producing a "time lag" in the knowledge of the profession.

[50] Although it is acknowledged that "where there is developing knowledge, [the defendant] must keep reasonably abreast of it and not be too slow to apply it": *Stokes v Guest, Keen & Nettlefold (Bolts & Nuts) Ltd* [1968] 1 W.L.R. 1776, 1783, *per* Swanwick J.; on the other hand, where the defendant's omission involves an absence of initiative in seeking out knowledge of facts which are not in themselves obvious "the court must be slow to blame him for not ploughing a lone furrow": *Thompson v Smith Shiprepairers (North Shields) Ltd* [1984] 1 All E.R. 881, 894, *per* Mustill J. In the context of developing knowledge of the risks to employees' hearing within the industry, a reasonable employer should demonstrate "proper but not extraordinary solicitude for the welfare of his workers." See also *Heyes v Pilkington Glass Ltd* [1998] P.I.Q.R. P303, CA.

3–065   Practices adopted in other countries are not necessarily evidence of the appropriate standard here. In *Whiteford v Hunter*[51] the defendant mistakenly diagnosed prostate cancer without performing a biopsy or using a cystoscope, procedures which were both standard practice in the United States. The instrument was rare in England at the time and the defendant did not have one. Moreover, the evidence indicated that it was against approved practice in England to use a cystoscope where, as with the claimant, there was acute urinary retention. The House of Lords held that the defendant was not negligent.[52]

3–066   There is an inevitable tension between the doctor's obligation to keep up to date, and the trite observation that doctors should not adopt any and every new idea until it has been proved to be both effective and safe. Doctors should not subject patients to untried methods of treatment unless the traditional approach has proved ineffective and the anticipated benefits are justified by the risks. On the other hand, despite the emphasis within many malpractice actions on complying with common practice, the courts are careful to avoid the suggestion that findings of negligence may stifle innovation.[53] A new technique may carry an unforeseen danger, notwithstanding the reasonable efforts of the profession to identify risks in advance, and this will not be held negligent.[54]

(5) Errors of Judgment

3–067   The view was sometimes expressed that there was a difference between negligence and an "error of professional judgment" or a "mere" error of

---

[51] [1950] W.N. 553; *ter Neuzen v Korn* (1993) 103 D.L.R. (4th) 473 (B.C.C.A.); affirmed (1995) 127 D.L.R. (4th) 577 (S.C.C.), where knowledge of the risk of transmission of HIV by artificial insemination was available in Australia in late 1984, but not generally known in British Columbia until mid-1985. The claimant contracted HIV from an artificial insemination procedure carried out in January 1985. The Supreme Court of Canada upheld the decision of the British Columbia Court of Appeal that it was not open to a jury to find the common practice of Canadian practitioners to be negligent; the issue was whether the defendant acted as reasonable doctor by reference to the prevailing standards. Note, however, that the Court of Appeal considered, at p. 501, that published guidelines in a specialised field of medicine in the United States would be admissible evidence, because it was reasonable for Canadian physicians practising within that specialty to be aware of them.

[52] In *Ritchie v Chichester Health Authority* [1994] 5 Med. L.R. 187, QBD, an article in the medical literature submitted as part of the evidence ("The wrong drug Problem in Anaesthesia—An Analysis of 2,000 incident reports") found that of 2000 incidents reported anonymously to the Australian Incident Monitoring Study 7.2% involved cases of the wrong drug being administered. The American experience was approximately 6%. No UK figures were available, but as the judge said, at pp. 208–209, "it would be wholly unrealistic to assume that it could not and does not happen here." This was important because it assisted the finding that the accident should not simply be attributed to "medical mystery" (an argument advanced by the defendants) and supported the conclusion that the anaesthetist had injected a neurotoxic substance into the claimant when administering an epidural anaesthetic, despite the fact that for this to have happened there would have to have been a series of errors.

[53] See paras 3–052 to 3–053.

[54] "Doctors, like the rest of us, have to learn by experience; and experience often teaches in a hard way. Something goes wrong and shows up a weakness and then it is put right," *per* Lord Denning M.R. in *Roe v Minister of Health* [1954] 2 Q.B. 66, 83.

judgment. In *Whitehouse v Jordan*, for example, Lord Denning M.R., having commented on malpractice litigation in the United States and its consequences, said: "We must say, and say firmly, that, in a professional man, an error of judgment is not negligent."[55] In the House of Lords this statement was strongly criticised. Lord Edmund-Davies said that:

> "To say that a surgeon committed an error of judgment is wholly ambiguous, for while some such errors may be completely consistent with the due exercise of professional skill, other acts or omissions in the course of exercising 'clinical judgment' may be so glaringly below proper standards as to make a finding of negligence inevitable."[56]

Referring to the *Bolam* test, his Lordship added that if a surgeon fails to measure up to the standard of the ordinary skilled man exercising and professing to have that skill in *any* respect ("clinical judgment" or otherwise), he has been negligent.

Lord Fraser adopted a similarly forthright approach, commenting that merely to describe something as an error of judgment says nothing about whether it is negligent or not. Rather, whether an error of judgment is negligent or not depends on the nature of the error. If it is one that would not have been made by a reasonably competent professional man professing to have the standard and type of skill that the defendant held himself out as having, and acting with ordinary care, then it is negligent. If, on the other hand, it is an error that a man, acting with ordinary care, might have made, then it is not negligence.[57]   **3–068**

Subsequently, Lord Denning M.R. returned to this issue in *Hyde v Tameside Area Health Authority*,[58] repeating his comment that, in a professional man, an error of judgment is not negligent: **3–069**

> "Not every error of judgment, of course, but only those errors which a reasonably competent professional man, acting with ordinary care, might commit. So explained I stand by every word I used in *Whitehouse v Jordan*. It is of the first importance so that 'medical malpractice' cases

---

[55] [1980] 1 All E.R. 650, 658. His Lordship took this approach for policy reasons: "Take heed of what has happened in the United States. 'Medical malpractice' cases there are very worrying, especially as they are tried by juries who have sympathy for the patient and none for the doctor who is insured. The damages are colossal. The doctors insure but the premiums become very high: and these have to be passed on in fees to the patients. Experienced practitioners are known to have refused to treat patients for fear of being accused of negligence. Young men are even deterred from entering the profession because of the risks involved. In the interests of all, we must avoid such consequences in England." See also *per* Lawton L.J. at p. 659 referring to defensive medicine; *cf.* Donaldson L.J. at p. 662.

[56] [1981] 1 All E.R. 267, 276.

[57] *ibid.* at p. 281. See also *per* Lord Diplock in *Saif Ali v Sydney Mitchell & Co* [1980] A.C. 198 at 220 referring to the liability of barristers: "No matter what profession it may be, the common law does not impose on those who practise it any liability for damage resulting from what in the result turned out to have been errors of judgment, unless the error was such as no reasonably well informed and competent member of that profession could have made."

[58] (1981), reported at (1986) 2 P.N. 26, 29.

should not get out of hand here as they have done in the United States of America."

So explained, the term "error of judgment" is redundant as a guide to what constitutes negligence. It merely represents the conclusion that, applying the *Bolam* test, the defendant has not been negligent.

3–070   The Canadian courts have apparently accepted that an "error of judgment" may excuse the defendant. In *Wilson v Swanson*[59] Rand J. said that: "An error of judgment has long been distinguished from an act of unskilfulness or carelessness or due to lack of knowledge . . . [T]he honest and intelligent exercise of judgment has long been recognised as satisfying the professional obligation." It has been treated as a specific defence,[60] although it may be that the term is used as a *post hoc* explanation of a finding that the doctor exercised reasonable care notwithstanding the occurrence of injury to the patient.[61] On this basis it stands in the same category as statements that doctors cannot guarantee results, that they are not insurers, and so on.

(6) Unforeseeable harm

3–071   It is axiomatic within the concept of negligence that if a particular danger could not reasonably have been anticipated, the defendant has not acted negligently, because a reasonable man does not take precautions against unforeseeable consequences. This is measured by reference to knowledge at the date of the alleged negligence, not with hindsight. The principle is illustrated by the decision of the Court of Appeal in *Roe v Minister of Health*.[62] Anaesthetic was kept in glass ampoules which were stored in disinfectant. The anaesthetic had become contaminated by the disinfectant which had seeped through cracks in the glass that were invisible to the naked eye.[63] The claimant suffered permanent paralysis due to the administration of the contaminated anaesthetic during the course of an operation. The risk of contaminating anaesthetic in this way was not known at the time of the accident in 1947. It was held that there was no negligence because the danger was not reasonably foreseeable. The court "must not look at the 1947 accident with 1954 spectacles," but it would have been negligence to adopt the same

---

[59] (1956) 5 D.L.R. (2d) 113, 120 (S.C.C.); approved by Ritchie J. in *Vail v MacDonald* (1976) 66 D.L.R. (3d) 530, 535 (S.C.C.); *Lapointe v Hôpital Le Gardeur* (1992) 90 D.L.R. (4th) 7, 14 (S.C.C.).

[60] Picard, *Legal Liability of Doctors and Hospitals in Canada*, 3rd ed., 1996, pp. 280–283.

[61] Thus, where the defendant has made a "judgment call" he is not necessarily negligent simply because damage has occurred: *Pilon v Bouaziz* [1994] 1 W.W.R. 700 (B.C.C.A.).

[62] [1954] 2 Q.B. 66.

[63] There is some doubt as to whether this was the true cause of the contamination. A more likely explanation is that there was an error in the process of sterilising the needle used to administer the anaesthetic: see Hutter (1990) 45 *Anaesthesia* 859. Of course, this does not affect the principle of law for which *Roe v Minister of Health* stands, although different findings of fact may well have changed the outcome of the trial.

practice in 1954 when the risk was more widely known.[64] In *McLean v Weir*[65] a similar approach was taken in circumstances where the claimant sustained paralysis in the course of an angiogram, when too much contrast medium was introduced into the spinal cord. This specific risk was not appreciated within the profession at the time. Subsequently, it became known that a different procedure would have avoided the mishap. Accordingly the defendant had not been negligent, although it would have been negligent to adopt exactly the same procedure after the risk had been identified.

This principle applies not merely to questions of factual knowledge but also to the relevant standards of reasonable care, which will be judged by reference to professional practices at the time of the treatment, not those applicable at the time when the action is tried.[66] It should be noted, however, that if damage of the same "type" was foreseeable it does not matter that the particular damage which occurred was unforeseeable, and, similarly, it is not necessary that the precise manner in which the injury occurred be foreseeable if it is of a type which was foreseeable in a general way.[67]   3–072

(7) Degrees of Risk

A defendant is not negligent if the damage was not a foreseeable consequence of his conduct. It does not follow, however, that a defendant is negligent if the damage was foreseeable. A reasonable man may "foresee the   3–073

---

[64] [1954] 2 Q.B. 66, 86. Denning L.J. commented, at p. 83, that: "It is so easy to be wise after the event and to condemn as negligence that which was only misadventure. We ought always to be on our guard against it, especially in cases against hospitals and doctors"; *Knight v West Kent Health Authority* [1998] Lloyd's Rep. Med. 18, 23 *per* Kennedy L.J. warning against the dangers of hindsight. See also *C v Cairns* [2003] Lloyd's Rep. Med. 90 where what by modern standards was undoubtedly a very naïve response by a general practitioner to information that a child patient had been sexually abused was found not to have been negligent by reference to standards at the time of the alleged negligence (1975).

[65] [1977] 5 W.W.R. 609; affirmed [1980] 4 W.W.R. 330 (B.C.C.A.). On complications resulting from an aortagram see *O'Malley-Williams v Board of Governors of the National Hospital for Nervous Diseases* (1975) 1 B.M.J. 635; *Ferguson v Hamilton Civic Hospitals* (1983) 144 D.L.R. (3d) 214. In *ter Neuzen v Korn* (1993) 103 D.L.R. (4th) 473 (B.C.C.A.); affirmed (1995) 127 D.L.R. (4th) 577 (S.C.C.), the defendants were not negligent where the claimant contracted HIV from artificial insemination in January 1985, but the risk of infection from artificial insemination was not widely known in North America until mid-1985. [A new trial was ordered on the question of whether the doctor had been negligent in failing properly to screen donors for sexually transmitted diseases]. Similarly, in *Pittman Estate v Bain* (1994) 112 D.L.R. (4th) 257 (Ont. Ct., Gen. Div.) Lang J., in holding that the Canadian Red Cross Society was not negligent in the manner that it collected blood in 1984, commented that: "It is imperative to avoid the temptation of evaluating measures taken or not taken in 1984 according to our knowledge today"; *cf. Walker Estate v York-Finch General Hospital* (2001) 198 D.L.R. (4th) 193 (S.C.C.) where the Canadian Red Cross Society was held to have been negligent in the method of screening blood donors for HIV, in that it had asked potential donors about their general health instead of asking about symptom specific conditions (as the American Red Cross had done in its screening procedures).

[66] See, *e.g.*, *Gold v Haringey Health Authority* [1988] Q.B. 481 where the issue was the appropriate standard of disclosure prior to a sterilisation operation in 1979.

[67] See paras 5–098 to 5–106.

possibility of many risks, but life would be almost impossible if he were to attempt to take precautions against every risk which he can foresee. He takes precautions against risks which are reasonably likely to happen."[68] In determining the level of acceptable risk the courts engage in a balancing exercise in which the magnitude of the risk, the purpose of the defendant's conduct, and the cost or practicability of taking precautions is evaluated. In some circumstances it may be reasonable simply to ignore a small risk, because the chance of it materialising is remote and the cost of precautions high.[69] On the other hand, if the cost of avoiding the risk is minimal it may be negligent to ignore a remote risk.[70] It is now clear that medical experts, in giving an expert opinion about the defendant's conduct, have to be able to demonstrate that they have addressed the question of assessing the relative risks and benefits of adopting a particular medical practice, and that their opinion stands up to logical analysis.[71]

3-074   The law requires a degree of care commensurate with the risk created by the defendant's conduct.[72] The greater the risk of harm the greater the precautions that must be taken. This principle applies just as much to professional liability as it does to any other category of negligence. In *Battersby v Tottman* Jacobs J. expressed the point in this way:

> ". . . there is a clear relationship between the magnitude of the risk and the duty of care, in particular the standard of care. The greater the risks involved in any proposed course of treatment, the more carefully and anxiously must the medical practitioner weigh and consider the possible alternatives before deciding to resort to the proposed treatment."[73]

3-075   For example, when an anaesthetist was handling a dangerous substance which was known to be highly inflammable and he knew of the hazard arising from electrostatic sparks in an operating room, the degree of care required from him was proportionately high and he was bound to take special precautions to prevent injury to his patient.[74] In *Darley v Shale*[75] the

---

[68] *Bolton v Stone* [1951] A.C. 850, 863, *per* Lord Oaksey.
[69] As in *Bolton v Stone* [1951] A.C. 850 itself.
[70] *Overseas Tankship (U.K.) Ltd v Miller Steamship Co Pty Ltd, The Wagon Mound (No. 2)* [1967] 1 A.C. 617, 642.
[71] *Bolitho v City and Hackney Health Authority* [1998] A.C. 232, 243.
[72] *Read v J. Lyons & Co Ltd* [1947] A.C. 156, 173, *per* Lord Macmillan.
[73] (1985) 37 S.A.S.R. 524, 542; *Glasgow Corporation v Muir* [1943] A.C. 448, 456, *per* Lord Macmillan: "Those who engage in operations inherently dangerous must take precautions which are not required of persons engaged in the ordinary routine of daily life"; *McAllister v Lewisham and North Southwark Health Authority* [1994] 5 Med. L.R. 343, 347, QBD, where Rougier J. commented that: "The decision whether or not to operate is the product of a tripartite equation: 1. The risks of operating. 2. The benefits of operating. 3. The risks of not operating;" see also *O'Donovan v Cork County Council* [1967] I.R. 173, 190, *per* Walsh J.; *Buchan v Ortho Pharmaceuticals (Canada) Ltd* (1986) 25 D.L.R. (4th) 658, 678–679, *per* Robins J.A. (Ont. C.A.).
[74] *Crits v Sylvester* (1956) 1 D.L.R. (2d) 502, 511 (Ont. C.A.); affirmed (1956) 5 D.L.R. (2d) 601 (S.C.C.).
[75] [1993] 4 Med. L.R. 161 (N.S.W.S.C.).

issue was whether the defendant gynaecologist had been negligent to perform a laparoscopy rather than a laparotomy on a patient with a history of gynaecological problems. Woods J. explained the nature of the issues to be addressed by the court in the following terms:

> "The inquiry thus called for involves a balancing of the known complications in general of laparotomy and laparoscopy respectively, and of the practical consequences each procedure has for a patient in terms of hospitalisation and recuperation, as well as any implications for abdominal surgery in the future. Further, and importantly for the present case, it involves a consideration of whether because of the plaintiff's history of earlier abdominal surgery, there were special, *i.e.* increased risks applicable for either diagnostic approach. It is necessary to weigh the magnitude of those risks and specifically that concerning the presence of an organ such as the bowel adherent to the abdominal wall in the vicinity of the point of entry, the probability of their occurrence, and the potential consequences for the patient depending on which approach was taken, in order to determine whether the defendant's response was negligent."[76]

The magnitude of the risk involves two elements. First, the likelihood that the harm will occur. The more remote the chance that any damage to the claimant will arise the more reasonable it will be to take fewer, or even no, precautions against the eventuality.[77] On the other hand, the degree of risk also takes into account the severity of the potential consequences. If the harm is likely to be serious, should it occur, then greater precautions must be taken. Thus, a risk that a patient may be accidentally infected with HIV from a contaminated blood transfusion will impose a high standard of care upon the supplier of the blood, given the seriousness of the consequences.[78] This principle applies to the individual claimant, so that if it is foreseeable that the damage *to this claimant* is likely to be severe, greater precautions will be required than for the average individual. In *Paris v Stepney Borough*

3–076

---

[76] *ibid.* at p. 168.
[77] As, *e.g.*, in *Warren v Greig* (1935) *The Lancet* vol. 1, 330, where a patient died from excessive bleeding following an operation to remove his teeth. He was suffering from acute myeloid leukaemia which was a rare disease. It was held that a blood test was not necessary against such a remote possibility.
[78] *E. v Australian Red Cross Society* (1991) 105 A.L.R. 53, 77 (Aus. Fed. C.A.) *per* Sheppard J. The assumption is that infection with HIV almost invariably leads to the individual developing AIDS, which in the current state of medical knowledge is a fatal condition. Despite the high duty, the defendants were found not to have been negligent in this case because of the very limited options for reasonable precautions against infection with HIV at the time (October 1984). A test specifically for HIV did not become available until March 1985. See also *Pittman Estate v Bain* (1994) 112 D.L.R. (4th) 257, 319 *per* Lang J. (Ont. Ct., Gen. Div.): "If the [Canadian Red Cross Society] knew of a potential risk to the consumer, then it had a duty commensurate with the degree of risk, and with the gravity of the potential harm to the recipient, to protect that consumer." Note, however, that the importance of the blood supply in saving lives may justify the taking of greater risk than would otherwise be acceptable.

Council,[79] for example, the defendant employers knew that the claimant was blind in one eye. In the course of the claimant's work a chip of metal entered his good eye, rendering him totally blind. The House of Lords held the employers liable in negligence for failing to provide goggles, although it was not usual to do so for that type of work. The duty of care was owed to each particular employee and in determining the requisite degree of care the defendants ought to have taken into account the gravity of the consequences for each individual employee—an injury to the claimant's good eye was a much more serious consequence than a similar injury to a fully sighted man, and a reasonable man would take account of the risk of greater injury as well as the greater risk of injury. Thus, where a doctor has formed an opinion as to the appropriate diagnosis of a patient's condition, he should take into account the possibility that an alternative diagnosis would explain the symptoms, especially where the consequences of the alternative diagnosis, if correct, would be very serious.[80]

3–077   A similar principle applies where the claimant's peculiar susceptibility makes the risk of harm occurring greater than would be the case with a normal individual. For example, a person who digs a hole in the pavement must take reasonable precautions to avoid the risk that a blind person might fall into the hole. Precautions that would protect the fully sighted will not necessarily protect the blind.[81] Accordingly, "a measure of care appropriate to the inability or disability of those who are immature or feeble in mind or body is due from others, who know of or ought to anticipate the presence of such persons within the scope and hazard of their own operations."[82]

3–078   The purpose of the defendant's conduct will also be taken into account in assessing what is reasonable. If sufficiently important, it will justify the assumption of abnormal risk.[83] In *Watt v Hertfordshire County Council*[84] it was held that it was not negligent to transport a heavy lifting jack on a vehicle that was not designed to carry it to an emergency where a woman

---

[79] [1951] A.C. 367.

[80] *Lankenau v Dutton* (1986) 37 C.C.L.T. 213, 232 (B.C.S.C.); affirmed (1991) 79 D.L.R. (4th) 707 (B.C.C.A.), where a doctor failed to reassess his initial diagnosis of the cause of the patient's paralysis following major surgery, with the result that it became permanent; *Bergen v Sturgeon General Hospital* (1984) 28 C.C.L.T. 155 (Alta. Q.B.); *Law Estate v Simice* (1994) 21 C.C.L.T. (2d) 228, 236 (B.C.S.C.); affirmed [1996] 4 W.W.R. 672 (B.C.C.A.), where it was said that once cerebral aneurism was included in a differential diagnosis there was a duty to rule it out or treat it as soon as possible because of its potentially life-threatening consequences. See further paras 4–022 to 4–023.

[81] *Haley v London Electricity Board* [1965] A.C. 778.

[82] *Glasgow Corporation v Taylor* [1922] 1 A.C. 44, 67, *per* Lord Sumner, approved by Lord Reid in *Haley v London Electricity Board* [1965] A.C. 778, 793.

[83] *Daborn v Bath Tramways Motor Co Ltd* [1946] 2 All E.R. 333, 336, *per* Asquith L.J., where the need for ambulances during wartime justified the use of a left-hand-drive vehicle, although it created greater risk of road accidents due to inadequate hand signals. See also the comments of Lang J. in *Pittman Estate v Bain* (1994) 112 D.L.R. (4th) 257, 313 (Ont. Ct., Gen. Div.): "In the case of blood, the societal need for the component produces different considerations. This is not a product that should be removed from the market if inherently dangerous. Blood is an essential source of life to many. Although biologic, and, therefore, dangerous, the need for the product outweighs the risk."

[84] [1954] 1 W.L.R. 835.

was trapped under a lorry. A fireman was injured when the jack slipped. The risk had to be balanced against the end to be achieved and, said Denning L.J., the saving of life and limb justifies taking considerable risk. This proposition is of obvious importance to the medical profession, who, when entering upon a treatment will invariably be seeking to improve the patient's health, even if life or limb are not at stake. This does not mean, however, that the purpose of saving life and limb can justify taking any risk. It is a matter of balancing the risk against the consequences of not taking the risk. If, for example, the patient's condition is such that he will almost certainly die without some form of medical intervention, then treatment with a high degree of risk will be justified, unless, of course, there is an equally effective alternative treatment that carries less risk. Difficulty in assessing the reasonableness of the defendant's conduct may arise where the alternative treatment is less risky or has less debilitating consequences, but is possibly a less effective form of treatment.

A further factor to be considered in assessing whether the taking of a foreseeable risk was justified is the practicability (or cost) of taking precautions. The practicability of taking precautions should be measured on an objective basis: the defendant's impecuniosity is not a defence if objectively a precaution was reasonably required.[85] If the risk can be avoided at small cost or with a trivial expenditure of time and effort it will be unreasonable to run the risk. Conversely, some risks can only be eliminated or reduced at great expense. A reasonable man would only neglect a risk if he had a valid reason for doing so, for example, "that it would involve considerable expense to eliminate the risk. He would weigh the risk against the difficulty of eliminating it." But a reasonable man would not ignore even a small risk "if action to eliminate it presented no difficulty, involved no disadvantage and required no expense."[86]

3–079

This principle has been applied in cases of medical negligence. For example, in *Hucks v Cole*[87] Sachs L.J. said that when risks of great danger

3–080

---

[85] In *P.Q. v Australian Red Cross Society* [1992] 1 V.R. 19 (Vict.S.C.) the claimant, who was a haemophiliac, alleged negligence against the Red Cross in failing to protect him from HIV infection from a transfusion of blood products. McGarvie J. held that the actual resources of the defendants was not an issue that was relevant to the practicability of any precautions required. Whether the Red Cross "fell short of the required standard of care is to be tested, not by reference to a reasonable person with the defendant's actual resources of staff facilities and finance, but by reference to a reasonable person with adequate resources available to conduct the enterprise in which the Red Cross was engaged," *ibid.*, at p. 33. In *Pittman Estate v Bain* (1994) 112 D.L.R. (4th) 257 (Ont. Ct., Gen. Div.), on the other hand, Lang J. held that when assessing the conduct of a blood bank it should be measured against that of other blood banks, not by reference to commercial organisations, on the basis that it was a "professional service" not a commercial service. It would follow from this, that if other "responsible" blood banks were unable or unwilling through lack of resources to take such precautions, the defendant would probably not be liable for failing to take the same precautions.

[86] *Overseas Tankship (U.K.) Ltd v Miller Steamship Co Pty Ltd, The Wagon Mound (No. 2)* [1967] 1 A.C. 617, 642; and in the medical context see *Chin Keow v Government of Malaysia* [1967] 1 W.L.R. 813, P.C., para. 3–041; *Leonard v Knott* [1978] 5 W.W.R. 511, 516 (B.C.S.C.).

[87] (1968), [1993] 4 Med. L.R. 393, 397.

are knowingly taken as a matter of professional practice then, however small the risks, the court must carefully examine the practice, particularly where the risks can be easily and inexpensively avoided. In *Coles v Reading and District Management Committee*[88] it was held to be negligent not to have given the patient an anti-tetanus injection, since it was a simple precaution, and the consequences of the infection are serious.[89] Again, in *Anderson v Chasney* McPherson C.J.M. commented that:

> "It is not sufficient for the surgeon to say: 'I never adopted the use of either of such precautions in operations of this nature.' By doing so he took an unnecessary risk, as both were available for his use on that occasion and he assumed full responsibility for the lack of use of the same, and I would hold that he was negligent in so doing."[90]

3–081   In *Reynolds v North Tyneside Health Authority*[91] a mother was admitted to hospital for the birth her child, having had a spontaneous rupture of the membranes and with the baby's head ⅗ palpable. In these circumstances there was a foreseeable risk of a cord prolapse, which was put at between 1 in 250 and 1 in 500. This was described as low risk, but the potential consequences from foetal hypoxia extended to death or brain damage. The alleged negligence of the defendants consisted of an omission by the midwife to carry out an immediate vaginal examination given the foreseeable risk of a cord prolapse. A vaginal examination was neither difficult nor costly. The defendants argued that the risk of cord prolapse was so slight that it could be ignored. Gross J. held that the defendants were not entitled simply to ignore the risk. Although the risk was low, it was not far-fetched or fanciful. It was not a case where a nice clinical balance had to be struck. The relevant considerations pointed overwhelmingly to the conduct of an immediate vaginal examination. "Set against the low risk of cord prolapse were (i) the gravity of the consequences should the risk materialise and (ii) the ease and economy of undertaking an immediate [vaginal examination]."[92] The argument against an immediate vaginal examination was that it created a risk of infection. But, a vaginal examination was likely to be conducted at some point during labour and the risks of infection would have been the same whenever it was performed; and in any event, the risk of infection was heavily outweighed by the risk of cord prolapse. In terms of the gravity of the consequences they were not "in the same league". Following this analysis of the

---

[88] (1963) 107 S.J 115.

[89] The patient died. See also *Robinson v Post Office* [1974] 2 All E.R. 737, 745, *per* Orr L.J.: "It was, in our judgment, a very relevant consideration that, although the risks of tetanus having developed in the wound did not amount to any high probability, they could not be dismissed as unreal, and the consequence, if they had materialised, would be likely to be fatal unless ATS were administered."

[90] [1949] 4 D.L.R. 71, 75, affirmed [1950] 4 D.L.R. 223 S.C.C.; see further para. 4–074; *Crits v Sylvester* (1956) 1 D.L.R. (2d) 502, 511; affirmed (1956) 5 D.L.R. (2d) 601.

[91] [2002] Lloyd's Rep. Med. 459.

[92] *ibid.* at [43].

respective risks, the question remained whether the defendants' omission could be supported on the basis that there was a responsible body of professional opinion supporting the view that an immediate vaginal examination was not called for in the circumstances. Gross J. was not convinced, on the evidence before the court, that there was a body of professional opinion which supported the view that the risk was so slight that it could be ignored. But, in any event:

> "even if there was any such contrary practice, or body of opinion, then the only reason articulated in its support for not conducting an immediate [vaginal examination], namely the risk of infection, does not withstand scrutiny. Where the sole reason relied upon in support of a practice is untenable, it follows (at least absent very special circumstances) that the practice itself is not defensible and lacks a logical basis. That is the case here. The suggested contrary practice (or body of opinion) is neither defensible nor logical. Having carefully examined the evidence, this is one of those rare cases where it is appropriate to conclude that there is a lacuna in the practice for which there is no proper basis. Put another way, insofar as any such contrary practice turns on the risk of infection, I would be unable to accept that its proponents had (i) properly directed their minds to the comparative risks and benefits and (ii) reached a defensible conclusion."[93]

Moreover, since the conclusion that the defendants were negligent was also supported by medical and midwifery evidence, the decision did not impose unrealistic standards on the relevant professionals.

Some risks are unavoidable. In this situation the risks of proceeding have to be weighed against the disadvantages of not proceeding, also taking into account the expected benefits to the patient's health. Where the consequences of not treating the patient are potentially very serious then the doctor will normally be justified in taking greater risks.[94] Conversely, where the treatment is for a minor ailment even small risks should not be disregarded;[95] *a fortiori*, where a diagnostic test which carries a real risk of an

3–082

---

[93] *ibid.* at [47].

[94] *Davidson v Connaught Laboratories* (1980) 14 C.C.L.T. 251, where the patient suffered an allergic reaction to a rabies vaccine, having come into contact with a rabid animal. Rabies is almost invariably fatal. Linden J. said, at p. 270, that: "Although the risk was only slight that the plaintiff might contract the disease as a result of that contact, the doctor was not negligent in advising caution when the consequences of not doing so were potentially so severe." See also *H. v Royal Alexandra Hospital for Children* [1990] 1 Med. L.R. 297 (N.S.W.S.C.) where it was held that even when the risk of transmitting AIDS through contaminated blood products became known it would not have been a practical or reasonable measure to recall or withdraw the products, given the level of risk and the need for the products.

[95] The obvious example would be cosmetic surgery, although there may well be room for disagreement as to the importance to the individual patient of removing certain cosmetic defects. In *La Fleur v Cornelis* (1979) 28 N.B.R. (2d) 569, 573 (N.B.S.C.) Barry J. commented that cosmetic surgeons do not treat illnesses in the ordinary sense, and accordingly a "doctor who undertakes to operate on the nose of a healthy person for cosmetic purposes

adverse reaction is conducted when there are no clinical indications for per-forming such a test.[96]

3–083   This balancing exercise must take account of the individual patient. So, for example, the risks of a general anaesthetic are greater for an elderly patient than for a young, and otherwise fit, patient, and a surgeon or anaesthetist would have to take this into account in making a decision as to whether the risks involved in an operation outweighed the potential advantages. In *Battersby v Tottman*[97] a doctor prescribed a very high dose of a particular drug to his patient who was suffering from a mental illness. He was aware that there was a risk of the drug causing serious and permanent eye damage, but he took the view that the benefits of the drug outweighed the risk from the side-effects, since without treatment the patient was "dangerously suicidal," and other methods of treatment had failed. It was held that in these circumstances the decision to prescribe a dosage that was far in excess of the recommended dosages was not negligent.[98] Similarly, in *Whiteford v Hunter*[99] the defendant doctor did not perform a biopsy to confirm his diagnosis of prostate cancer, since he considered there was a risk of perforating the bladder wall, and that if the condition were cancerous, an unhealing ulcer would supervene. It was held that he was not negligent.

(8) Specialists

3–084   A specialist is expected to achieve the standard of care of a reasonably competent specialist in that field. He must "exercise the ordinary skill of his specialty."[1] This is inherent in the *Bolam* test itself, as Lord Bridge recognised in *Sidaway v Bethlem Royal Hospital Governors*:

> "The language of the *Bolam* test clearly requires a different degree of skill from a specialist in his own special field than from a general practitioner. In the field of neuro-surgery it would be necessary to substitute for the . . . phrase 'no doctor of ordinary skill', the phrase 'no neuro-surgeon of ordinary skill'. All this is elementary, and . . . firmly established law."[2]

(n.95 contd.) has a very high duty indeed." On the performance of breast reduction surgery see *MacDonald v Ross* (1983) 24 C.C.L.T. 242 (N.S.S.C.); *White v Turner* (1981) 120 D.L.R. (3d) 269; (1982) 12 D.L.R. (4th) 319; and on cosmetic surgery that resulted in the death of a seven-year-old boy, see Dyer (1986) 293 B.M.J. 686.

[96] *Leonard v Knott* [1978] 5 W.W.R. 511 (B.C.S.C.), see para. 4–010.

[97] (1985) 37 S.A.S.R. 524; see also Scott L.J. in *Mahon v Osborne* [1939] 2 K.B. 14, 31 on the surgeon's problem of balancing competing risks and objectives when performing an operation.

[98] See also *Vernon v Bloomsbury Health Authority* (1986), [1995] 6 Med. L.R. 297 where the doctors were treating a life-threatening condition, and were aware of the risk of side-effects from the high dosage of drug used. See, however, the comments on the evidence in this case at [1995] 6 Med. L.R. 434.

[99] [1950] W.N. 553.

[1] *Maynard v West Midlands Regional Health Authority* [1984] 1 W.L.R. 634, 638, *per* Lord Scarman.

[2] [1985] A.C. 871, 897. See also *per* Lord Fraser in *Whitehouse v Jordan* [1981] 1 All E.R. 267, 280: negligence meant "a failure . . . to exercise the standard of skill expected from the

References to "a doctor" in the *Bolam* test are simply shorthand for "a   3–085
doctor undertaking this type of act or procedure." Thus, while a general
practitioner must be judged by the standards of general practitioners and not
specialists,[3] if a general practitioner were to undertake something that was
considered a specialist task he would be judged by the standards of the
specialty. If he is unable meet those standards then he will be held negligent
for undertaking work beyond his competence.[4]

The standard of care within a specialist field is that of the ordinary com-   3–086
petent specialist, not the most experienced or most highly qualified within
the specialty:

> "A medical practitioner who holds himself out as being a specialist in a
> particular field is required to attain the ordinary level of skill amongst
> those who specialise in the same field. He is not required to attain the
> highest degree of skill and competence in that particular field."[5]

If the defendant has knowledge of some fact that makes harm to the   3–087
claimant more likely than would otherwise be the case, then as a reasonable
man he must take account of that fact. A greater than average knowledge of
the risks will entail more than the average or standard precautions.[6] This
appears to require that the specialist must take greater precautions than the
average doctor when undertaking the same task, if the specialist's actual
knowledge and experience gives him a greater knowledge of risks that ought
to be guarded against.[7] His conduct should not be judged by reference to
lesser knowledge than in fact he had. On the other hand, he does not have to
use a higher degree of skill than comparable specialists. There may come a

---

(n.2 contd.) ordinary competent specialist having regard to the experience and expertise that
the specialist holds himself out as possessing." See also *McCaffrey v Hague* [1949] 4 D.L.R.
291; *Holmes v Board of Hospital Trustees of City of London* (1977) 81 D.L.R. (3d) 67, 78
(Ont. H.C.); *Rietze v Bruser (No. 2)* [1979] 1 W.W.R. 31; *Crits v Sylvester* (1956) 1 D.L.R.
(2d) 502, 508; affirmed (1956) 5 D.L.R. (2d) 601 (S.C.C.); *Wilson v Swanson* (1956) 5
D.L.R. (2d) 113, 119, *per* Rand J. (S.C.C.): "What the surgeon by his ordinary engagement
undertakes with the patient is that he possesses the skill, knowledge and judgment of the generality or average of the special group or class of technicians to which he belongs and will
faithfully exercise them."

[3] *Langley v Campbell, The Times*, November 5, 1975; *Sa'd v Robinson* [1989] 1 Med. L.R.
41; *Thornton v Nicol* [1992] 3 Med. L.R. 41; *Gordon v Wilson* [1992] 3 Med. L.R. 401
(Court of Session); *Stockdale v Nicholls* [1993] 4 Med. L.R. 190; *Durrant v Burke* [1993] 4
Med. L.R. 258; *Stacey v Chiddy* [1993] 4 Med. L.R. 216 (N.S.W.S.C.); affirmed [1993] 4
Med. L.R. 345 (N.S.W.C.A.). See further para. 4–020.

[4] See para. 3–097. This has important implications for the question of expert testimony on the
appropriate standard of care to be expected of a specialist practitioner: see para. 3–151.

[5] *O'Donovan v Cork County Council* [1967] I.R. 173, 190, *per* Walsh J. (Supreme Court of
Ireland); *Giurelli v Girgis* (1980) 24 S.A.S.R. 264, 277, *per* White J.; *F. v R.* (1983) 33
S.A.S.R. 189, 205, *per* Bollen J.

[6] *Stokes v Guest, Keen & Nettlefold (Nuts & Bolts) Ltd* [1968] 1 W.L.R. 1776, 1783, *per*
Swanwick J.; *Wilson v Brett* (1843) 11 M. & W. 113, 115, *per* Rolfe B.: "If a person more
skilled knows that to be dangerous which another not so skilled as he does not, surely that
makes a difference in the liability."

[7] A point accepted as correct by Webster J. in *Wimpey Construction U.K. Ltd v Poole* [1984]
2 Lloyd's Rep. 499, 506–507.

point, of course, where a sub-discipline develops within a specialty such that it can be said that a practitioner undertaking that form of work must achieve the standards of the new "specialty."[8] Conversely, where it can be said that a new specialty has developed the question of whether the defendant has conformed to the practice of a responsible body of professional opinion will be judged by reference to the standards of that specialty rather than the standards of doctors engaged in a more generalised practice. This may make it reasonable, for example, for a specialist surgeon to undertake intricate exploratory surgery, on the basis that this conforms to a practice accepted as proper by a responsible body of surgeons in the specialty, in circumstances where surgeons in other fields might consider the procedure to be too risky.[9]

3-088   In *Duchess of Argyll v Beuselinck*[10] Megarry J. questioned the proposition that a uniform standard of care would always apply to specialists:

> "But if the client employs a solicitor of high standing and great experience, will an action for negligence fail if it appears that the solicitor did not exercise the care and skill to be expected of him, though he did not fall below the standard of a reasonably competent solicitor? If the client engages an expert, and doubtless expects to pay commensurate fees, is he not entitled to expect something more than the standard of the reasonably competent? I am speaking not merely of those expert in a particular branch of the law, as contrasted with a general practitioner, but also of those of long experience and great skill as contrasted with those practising in the same field of the law but being of a more ordinary calibre and having less experience."[11]

3-089   This higher standard would be based on an implied term in the contract of retainer to the effect that the solicitor will use the care and skill that he actually possesses rather than the care and skill of the average solicitor specialising in that field of law. There is no reason in principle why a client should not be able to purchase a higher standard of care, though this justification would confine the higher duties to actions in contract. Megarry J. distinguished contractual duties from the tort of negligence, where "the unusually careful and highly skilled are not held liable for falling below their own high standards if they nevertheless do all that a reasonable man would have done." Clearly, if this distinction was accepted, and applied to the medical profession, it could lead to differential duties being owed to patients in contract and tort, a position that the courts have been reluctant to countenance.[12] In *Wimpey Construction U.K. Ltd v Poole*,[13] however, Webster J.

---

[8] See, *e.g.*, *Poole v Morgan* [1987] 3 W.W.R. 217.
[9] *De Freitas v O'Brien* [1993] 4 Med. L.R. 281, 296; affirmed [1995] P.I.Q.R. P281; [1995] 6 Med. L.R. 108, identifying a separate specialism of spinal surgeons, comprising both orthopaedic and neurosurgeons engaged wholly or mainly in spinal surgery.
[10] [1972] 2 Lloyd's Rep. 172.
[11] *ibid.* at p. 183.
[12] See para. 2–005.
[13] [1984] 2 Lloyd's Rep. 499, 506.

considered Megarry J.'s dictum and concluded that the *Bolam* test had been approved by the House of Lords and the Privy Council without qualification, and so should be applied without this gloss. More recently, in *Matrix-Securities Ltd v Theodore Goddard*[14] Lloyd J. held that the mere fact that the defendants were an established firm of City solicitors who professed very high levels of skill and experience did not increase their duty or lead to an inference that a higher duty had been undertaken by them. Their obligation, in advising on a complex tax avoidance scheme, was to exercise that standard of care which could be expected from a reasonably competent firm of solicitors with a specialist tax department. In other words, a solicitor advising in tax matters must exercise the standard of care appropriate to that sector of the profession specialising in tax matters. This is clearly the same test as that applied to specialist doctors.

(9) Inexperience

(a) The Doctor

It is axiomatic that the standard of care expected of the reasonable man is objective, not subjective. It eliminates the personal equation and takes no account of the particular idiosyncrasies or weaknesses of the defendant.[15] Thus, the defendant who is inexperienced or who is just learning a particular task or skill must come up to the standards of the reasonably competent and experienced person. His "incompetent best" is not good enough.[16] This principle applies with as much force to an inexperienced doctor as it does to an inexperienced motorist. In *Jones v Manchester Corporation*[17] a patient died from an excessive dose of anaesthetic administered by a doctor who had been qualified for five months. In an action which was concerned with the respective responsibilities of the junior doctor and the hospital authority, the Court of Appeal made it clear that it was no defence to an action by a patient to say that she did not have sufficient experience to undertake the task, or to say that the surgeon in charge was also to blame:

3–090

> "The patient was entitled to receive all the care and skill which a fully qualified and well-experienced anaesthetist would possess and use. If Dr Wilkes failed to exercise that care and skill, she would be liable to the patient or his widow for the consequences, no matter that the hospital authorities knew that she had not sufficient experience for the task and

---

[14] [1998] P.N.L.R. 290.
[15] *Glasgow Corporation v Muir* [1943] A.C. 448, 457, *per* Lord Macmillan. There remains, however, a subjective element in that it is left to the individual judge to decide what is reasonable and what could have been foreseen: "What to one judge may seem far-fetched may seem to another both natural and probable." *ibid.*
[16] *Nettleship v Weston* [1971] 2 Q.B. 691, 698, 710.
[17] [1952] Q.B. 852.

were much to blame for asking her to do it without proper supervision."[18]

3-091   This issue arose in the more recent case of *Wilsher v Essex Area Health Authority*.[19] A premature baby in a special care baby unit received excess oxygen due to an error in monitoring its supply of oxygen. A junior and inexperienced doctor inserted a catheter (by which the blood oxygen pressure was to be measured) into a vein rather than an artery. This in itself was not negligent, since it was the sort of mistake that any reasonably competent doctor might have made in the circumstances. The position of the catheter in the body can be checked, however, by means of an X-ray. This was done and the doctor failed to spot that the catheter was mispositioned, though he did ask a senior registrar in the unit to check the X-ray. The registrar failed to notice the mistake. The baby was subsequently discovered suffering from retrolental fibroplasia[20] which causes blindness, possibly as a result of the exposure to excess oxygen.[21] In the Court of Appeal there was a division of opinion as to the appropriate standard of care to be applied to the junior doctor.

3-092   Sir Nicolas Browne-Wilkinson V.-C., dissenting, said that the general standard of care required of a doctor is that he should exercise the skill of a skilled doctor in the treatment which he has taken on himself to offer. This being the general standard, it is normally no answer to say that the treatment was of a specialist or technical nature in which he was inexperienced: "In such a case, the fault of the doctor lies in embarking on giving treatment which he could not skilfully offer: he should not have undertaken the treatment but should have referred the patient to someone possessing the necessary skills."[22] The position was different, said his Lordship, in the case of a junior houseman in his first year after qualifying or of someone who has just started in a specialist field in order to gain the necessary skill in that field. Such doctors cannot in fairness be said to be at fault if, at the start of their time, they lack the very skills which they are seeking to acquire:

"Of course, such a doctor would be negligent if he undertook treatment for which he knows he lacks the necessary experience and skill. But one of the chief hazards of inexperience is that one does not always know the risks which exist. In my judgment, so long as the English law rests liability on personal fault, a doctor who has properly accepted a post in

---

[18] *ibid.* at p. 868, *per* Denning L.J. See also at p. 871: "Errors due to inexperience or lack of supervision are no defence as against the injured person . . ."

[19] [1987] Q.B. 730.

[20] This term is somewhat dated. The condition is now known as retinopathy of prematurity. For discussion of the appropriate medical management of the condition see (1997) 3 Clinical Risk 35–51; Clements (1995) 1 *AVMA Medical & Legal Journal* 215.

[21] The decision of the Court of Appeal on the causation issue was reversed by the House of Lords: [1988] A.C. 1074; see paras 5–025 *et seq.* There was no appeal on the question of the standard of care.

[22] [1987] Q.B. 730, 777.

a hospital in order to gain necessary experience should only be held liable for acts or omissions which a careful doctor with his qualifications and experience would not have done or omitted."[23]

With great respect, this view appears to confuse the concept of "fault" in the tort of negligence with moral blameworthiness. A finding of negligence in a court of law does not necessarily mean that the defendant was morally blameworthy, since negligence is treated as an objective measure of a standard of conduct without any inquiry into why the defendant failed to achieve that standard, as might occur in a court of morals.[24] The majority of the Court of Appeal (Mustill and Glidewell L.JJ.) adhered to the objective standard. Mustill L.J. said that the notion of a duty tailored to the actor, rather than to the act which he elects to perform, has no place in the law of tort. The consequence of applying a subjective test would be that the standard of care that a patient would be entitled to expect would depend upon the level of experience of the particular doctor who, by chance, happened to treat him. However, having said that if a professional person assumes to perform a task, he must bring to it the appropriate care and skill,[25] his Lordship added that the standard of care should be related, not to the individual, but to the post which he occupies, though distinguishing "post" from "rank" or "status". It followed that: **3–093**

> "In such a case as the present, the standard is not just that of the averagely competent and well-informed junior houseman (or whatever the position of the doctor) but of such a person who fills a post in a unit offering a highly specialised service. But, even so, it must be recognised that different posts make different demands. If it is borne in mind that the structure of hospital medicine envisages that the lower ranks will be occupied by those of whom it would be wrong to expect too much, the risk of abuse by litigious patients can be mitigated, if not entirely eliminated."[26]

---

[23] *ibid.* This statement seems to echo the comment of the Lord Chancellor in *Junor v McNicol, The Times,* March 26, 1959 that a house surgeon had a duty to "display the care and skill of a prudent qualified house surgeon, it being remembered that such a position was held by a comparative beginner." At what point, it might be asked, would the inexperienced doctor be deemed to have sufficient experience to be judged by the ordinary objective standard?

[24] "There are very few professional men who will assert that they have never fallen below the high standards rightly expected of them. That they have never been negligent. If they do, it is unlikely that they should be believed. And this is as true of lawyers as it is of medical men. If the judge's conclusion is right, what distinguishes Mr. Jordan from his professional colleagues is not that on one isolated occasion his skill deserted him, but that damage resulted. Whether or not damage results from a negligent act is almost always a matter of chance and it ill becomes anyone to adopt an attitude of superiority," *per* Donaldson L.J. in *Whitehouse v Jordan* [1980] 1 All E.R. 650, 666. See also *Clark v MacLennan* [1983] 1 All E.R. 416, 433, and 422, *per* Pain J.: "Counsel for the defendant has referred to Professor Turnbull's Olympian reputation. I hope Professor Turnbull will take comfort in the thought that even Apollo, the god of healing, and the father of Aesculapius, had his moments of weakness"; "My recollection of classical mythology is that the gods on Olympus were no strangers to error"; and *Thake v Maurice* [1986] Q.B. 644, 663, *per* Peter Pain J.

[25] [1987] Q.B. 730, 747.

[26] *ibid.* at p. 751.

3–094   This statement is puzzling, since, having rejected a subjective test of negligence, his Lordship seems to reintroduce variable standards of care by reference to the "posts" occupied by different doctors. Glidewell L.J. simply applied the *Bolam* test, commenting that this was the standard by which to weigh the conduct of all the doctors in *Wilsher*: "In my view, the law requires the trainee or learner to be judged by the same standard as his more experienced colleagues. If it did not, inexperience would frequently be urged as a defence to an action for professional negligence."[27] With respect, it is submitted that this is the correct and long-established approach.[28] In *Djemal v Bexley Health Authority*[29] Tudor Evans J. held that the standard of care required of a senior houseman in an Accident and Emergency department is that of "a reasonably competent senior houseman acting as a casualty officer without any reference to the length of experience," which his Lordship said represented the test applied by the majority in *Wilsher*.

3–095   A single standard of care for patients can only be achieved by relating the reasonableness of the defendant's conduct to the task that is undertaken, and what is objectively reasonable does not change with the experience of the defendant, or, for that matter, the post he holds.[30] This is at its most obvious if a doctor in a specialist "post" were to undertake some procedure which was completely outside the sphere of that specialty. He would be required to achieve the standard of the reasonably competent doctor in performing that procedure, and if it were a specialised procedure he would have to achieve the standards of the specialty. This has nothing to do with his post. The duty arises by virtue of the fact that he has undertaken to perform the act, and by doing so professes that he has the competence to perform it with skill and care, just as an unqualified person would be held to the standard of a reasonably competent surgeon if he undertook surgery.[31] Thus, undertaking work which is beyond one's competence will constitute negligence. As a matter of practice and common sense the inexperienced doctor will normally undertake less complex tasks than his experienced colleagues, but if he does perform tasks beyond the level of his competence the fault lies not so much

---

[27] *ibid.* at p. 774; *Dale v Munthali* (1977) 78 D.L.R. (3d) 588, 594; affirmed (1978) 90 D.L.R. (3d) 763. In *Wills v Saunders* [1989] 2 W.W.R. 715 (Alta. Q.B.) a junior doctor took it upon himself to insert a central feeding line into the patient's subclavian vein, without supervision, resulting in loss of consciousness and permanent damage to the patient's vision. Power J., holding the defendant negligent, stated that the standard of care to be applied "should not be lower by reason of his inexperience."

[28] Note that only Mustill L.J. was in favour of linking the standard to the post occupied by the defendant.

[29] [1995] 6 Med. L.R. 269 at 271.

[30] See Dugdale and Stanton, *Professional Negligence*, 3rd ed., 1998, para. 15.11; and para. 15.12 making the same point in relation to the standard to be applied to specialists.

[31] ". . . the unqualified practitioner cannot claim to be measured by any lower standard than that which is applied to a qualified man . . . It is, no doubt, conceivable that a qualified man may be held liable for recklessly undertaking a case which he knew, or should have known, to be beyond his powers, or for making his patient the subject of reckless experiment," *per* Lord Hewart C.J. in *R. v Bateman* (1925) 94 L.J.K.B. 791, 794; *Freeman v Marshall & Co* (1966) 200 E.G. 777, where Lawton J. observed of an estate agent who was not a qualified surveyor that "if he held himself out in practice as a surveyor he must be deemed to have the skills of a surveyor and be adjudged upon them."

in not having the skills, which by definition he does not possess, but in undertaking the task at all.

It has been suggested that it is "unrealistic" to demand identical standards   3–096
of competence from persons who come from different ranks of the same profession, and, accordingly, that the appropriate standard of care for a professional person should be a combination of objective and subjective considerations, namely the "skill and care which is ordinarily exercised by reasonably competent members of the profession, who have the same rank and profess the same specialisation (if any) as the defendant."[32] What is not clear, however, is why a patient's claim to legal redress should differ where he receives the identical treatment from Dr A (a consultant, say) and from Dr B (a senior house officer), a situation which could arise if the standard of care varied with the "rank" of the defendant. It is submitted that it would be unrealistic to apply different standards to the performance of the same task: if the defendant cannot exercise reasonable care he should not undertake the task at all.[33]

It must be emphasised that this principle is not limited to actions against   3–097
newly qualified doctors. It can apply at any stage where a doctor gets in above his head. The doctor who holds himself out as a specialist will be held to the standards of a reasonably competent specialist, "even if he is a novice specialist,"[34] and even where he is performing the procedure for the first time.[35] A doctor must recognise his limitations and where necessary seek the advice or supervision of more experienced colleagues, or refer the patient to a specialist.[36] The inexperienced doctor will discharge his duty of care by seeking the assistance of his superiors to check his work, even though he may himself have made a mistake. It was on this basis that the junior doctor was found not to have been negligent in *Wilsher v Essex Area Health Authority*,

---

[32] *Jackson & Powell on Professional Negligence*, 5th ed., 2002, para. 2.120. The editors concede that the term "rank" is not entirely satisfactory, but it is meant to describe different levels within hierarchical professions such as medicine. It is not, presumably, the same as "post."

[33] In *Bova v Spring* [1994] 5 Med. L.R. 120, 122, QBD it was common ground that the minimum standard of care to be expected of a trainee general practitioner was no lower than that to be expected of an experienced one.

[34] *Poole v Morgan* [1987] 3 W.W.R. 217, 254 (Alta. Q.B.). The defendant ophthalmologist was held to be inadequately qualified to use laser treatment, a procedure normally performed by a retina vitreous specialist, even though ophthalmologists were permitted to use laser treatment by their governing body.

[35] *McKeachie v Alvarez* (1970) 17 D.L.R. (3d) 87 (B.C.S.C.), where a surgeon was held liable for severing a nerve which could have been seen and avoided, and of whose existence he should have been aware, even though this was the first occasion on which he had done this type of operation.

[36] See the comment of Browne-Wilkinson V.-C. in *Wilsher v Essex Area Health Authority* [1987] Q.B. 730, 777, quoted at para. 3–092; *Fraser v Vancouver General Hospital* (1951) 3 W.W.R. 337 (B.C.C.A.); affirmed [1952] 3 D.L.R. 785 (S.C.C.); *Payne v St Helier Group Hospital Management Committee, The Times*, July 12, 1952, where a casualty officer was held to be negligent in failing to detain a patient for examination by a doctor of consultant rank. See para. 4–029. In *Dillon v Le Roux* [1994] 6 W.W.R. 280 (B.C.C.A.) a family physician, who was working as a relief doctor in a hospital emergency room but had no training as an emergency room physician, was held liable for failing to call an experienced hospital doctor to assist with the diagnosis of a patient's medical condition.

although the registrar was held negligent.[37] In *Drake v Pontefract Health Authority; Wakefield and Pontefract Community NHS Trust* a consultant psychiatrist was found to have been negligent in allowing an inexperienced Senior House Officer to interview and treat the claimant without immediate supervision from a more experienced psychiatrist, when the patient had been expressly referred as a suicide risk.[38]

3–098   In an emergency it may well be reasonable for a practitioner inexperienced in a particular treatment to intervene, or indeed for someone lacking medical qualifications to undertake some forms of treatment. For example, a bystander who renders assistance at a road accident does not necessarily hold himself out as qualified to do so. He would be expected to achieve only the standard that could reasonably be expected in the circumstances, which would probably be very low.[39] This approach is clearly born of the emergency since if there was no urgency, the unqualified person who undertook treatment which was beyond his competence would be held to the standard to be expected of the reasonably competent and experienced practitioner. A person who holds himself out as trained in first-aid must conform to the standards of "the ordinary skilled first-aider exercising and professing to have that special skill of a first-aider."[40] This will obviously be greater than the standard of a layman performing first-aid, and would be relevant, for example, in a claim against paramedically trained ambulance crew.

3–099   The rule that inexperience is not a defence is a consequence of the objective nature of the standard of care in negligence, and applies to other factors as well as inexperience. If the defendant is unable to measure up to the objectively required standard for any reason, be it stress, overwork, tiredness, or

---

[37] See also *Junor v McNicol*, *The Times*, March 26, 1959 where the House of Lords held that a house surgeon who had acted on the instructions of a consultant orthopaedic surgeon was not liable; *Tanswell v Nelson*, *The Times*, February 11, 1959, where McNair J. said that a dentist was entitled to rely on a doctor's opinion about a patient's response to antibiotics, unless that opinion was clearly inconsistent with the observed facts; *Leonard v Knott* [1978] 5 W.W.R. 511 (B.C.S.C.), where it was held that a radiologist is entitled to rely on the judgment of the referring physician as to whether a radiological investigation is required, unless there is some obvious problem; *Weir v Graham* [2002] EWHC 2291 (Q.B.) at [55]—a general practitioner who has referred a patient to hospital for diagnostic tests is entitled to assume that the hospital is taking reasonable care of the patient and it is not for a general practitioner to go through hospital notes to check that the hospital has done what it should have done (held to be reasonable for a general practitioner to assume that the hospital doctors were aware of the test results and were taking them into consideration in their diagnostic investigations); *cf. Davy-Chiesman v Davy-Chiesman* [1984] 1 All E.R. 321, 332, 335, stating that solicitors should not rely blindly on the advice of counsel, although in this case the solicitor had failed to detect an "obvious error"; *Matrix-Securities Ltd v Theodore Goddard* [1998] P.N.L.R. 290—a solicitor is entitled to rely on counsel's advice, and would be negligent for failing to do so unless that advice was obviously wrong; *FirstCity Insurance Group Ltd v Orchard* [2002] Lloyd's Rep. P.N. 543 at [82].

[38] [1998] Lloyd's Rep. Med. 425.

[39] On the difficulties of laymen diagnosing mental illness see *Ali v Furness Withy* [1988] 2 Lloyd's Rep. 379, where the question was the standard applicable to a ship's master diagnosing insanity in a crewman.

[40] *Cattley v St John's Ambulance Brigade* (1988, QBD; unreported) *per* Judge Prosser Q.C.: ". . . the true test for establishing negligence in a first-aider is whether he has been proved to be guilty of such failure as no first-aider of ordinary skill would be guilty of, if acting with ordinary care . . ."

ill-health he will nonetheless be found negligent.[41] In *Barnett v Chelsea and Kensington Hospital Management Committee*[42] a casualty officer, who was himself unwell, refused to see three nightwatchmen who had presented themselves in the casualty department of a hospital, telling them to go home and call in their own doctors. One of the men subsequently died. Nield J. held that the doctor's failure to see and examine the deceased was negligent: "It is unfortunate that Dr Banerjee was himself at the time a tired and unwell doctor, but there was no-one else to do that which it was his duty to do."[43]

(b) The hospital authorities

Whatever the position of the inexperienced doctor, it is possible that a health authority could be in breach of a primary duty of care to the patient if they allow inexperienced staff to practise without adequate supervision. In *Jones v Manchester Corporation*[44] a majority of the Court of Appeal held that the hospital board was liable to make a contribution to the inexperienced doctor whose negligence caused the patient's death. Indeed, the board bore the brunt of the blame (80 per cent), even though counsel for the doctor admitted that she had been negligent to a degree which was inexcusable even in an inexperienced person. The hospital board should not leave patients in inexperienced hands without proper supervision, said Denning L.J.:

> "It would be in the highest degree unjust that the hospital board, by getting inexperienced doctors to perform their duties for them, without

3–100

---

[41] Old age or infirmity is not a defence for a negligent driver of a motor vehicle: *Roberts v Ramsbottom* [1980] 1 All E.R. 7, 15; *cf. Mansfield v Weetabix Ltd* [1999] 1 W.L.R. 1263 where the Court of Appeal held that a driver who becomes unable to control a vehicle will not be liable for damage caused by his loss of control if he is unaware of the disabling condition from which he is suffering, whether the disabling event is sudden or gradual. On this point, *Roberts v Ramsbottom* had been wrongly decided, though the decision could be supported on the alternative ground that the defendant continued to drive when he was unfit to do so, and when he should have been aware of his unfitness. To apply an objective standard in a way which did not take account of the defendant's condition (of which he was unaware) would be to impose strict liability (*per* Leggatt L.J. in *Mansfield*). A defendant who knows that he is susceptible to such attacks will be liable for harm resulting from a loss of control: *Hill v Baxter* [1958]1 Q.B. 277; and similarly if he ought to have known that he was subject to a condition rendering him unfit: *Waugh v James K. Allan Ltd* [1964] 2 Lloyd's Rep. 1. In *Nickolls v Ministry of Health, The Times*, February 4, 1955 the surgeon who operated on the claimant was suffering from cancer. The question was whether he was in a fit condition to have undertaken the operation. It was held that, on the facts, he was and therefore he was not negligent. Clearly, if the conclusion had been that he was unfit, it would have been negligent to operate.
[42] [1968] 1 All E.R. 1068.
[43] *ibid.* at p. 1073. It is common for junior hospital doctors to have to work excessively long hours. If this was a factor in an error made by the doctor the health authority may also be responsible: see para. 3–101. It is doubtful that overwork or the fact that resources are stretched would fall within the notion of "battle conditions" which Mustill L.J. has suggested could influence the court's assessment of negligence: see *Wilsher v Essex Area Health Authority* [1987] Q.B. 730, 749, para. 3–106. The term seems to indicate something in the nature of an emergency, rather than the everyday circumstances in which doctors have to work, even if they themselves feel "embattled."
[44] [1952] Q.B. 852.

adequate supervision, should be able to throw all the responsibility on to those doctors as if they were fully experienced practitioners."[45]

3–101   This point was reiterated in *Wilsher v Essex Area Health Authority*.[46] Sir Nicolas Browne-Wilkinson V.-C. recognised that applying a subjective standard of care to inexperienced junior doctors might mean that the rights of a patient would depend on the experience of the doctor who treats him. This would not be the case, said his Lordship, because the health authority could be directly liable: "In my judgment, a health authority which so conducts its hospital that it fails to provide doctors of sufficient skill and experience to give the treatment offered at the hospital may be directly liable in negligence to the patient."[47] There was no reason why, in principle, the health authority should not be directly liable if its organisation was at fault. Arguably, this proposition would apply with equal, if not greater, force to other organisational failures which expose patients to serious risk of injury, such as requiring junior hospital doctors to work excessive hours, with the result that they become so fatigued that their judgment or competence becomes impaired. Whilst a claim that the doctor was overworked would not provide a defence for the doctor in an action by the patient, it is a good reason to place the burden of responsibility upon the health authority.[48]

3–102   There is, however, a problem with this line of argument. The standard of

---

[45] *ibid.* at p. 871; *Murphy v St. Catharines General Hospital* (1963) 41 D.L.R. (2d) 697 (Ont. H.C.), where a hospital was held to have been negligent in failing to give instruction to and supervision of junior doctors in the use of a new method of inserting an intravenous catheter. In *Hinfey v Salford Health Authority* [1993] 4 Med. L.R. 143 an allegation that the health authority was negligent in allowing an inexperienced obstetrician to deliver a baby unsupervised was rejected on the evidence.

[46] [1987] Q.B. 730.

[47] *ibid.* at p. 778; see also *per* Glidewell L.J. at p. 775. See further the comments of Lord Browne-Wilkinson in *X. (minors) v Bedfordshire County Council* [1995] 2 A.C. 633, 740. In, *Dryden v Surrey County Council* [1936] 2 All E.R. 535, 539 Finlay J. commented that it could not possibly be held that the mere presence of probationary nurses was evidence of negligence. Although, as it stands the statement is clearly correct, this must, presumably, be a matter of degree.

[48] Employers owe a non-delegable duty to their employees to provide competent staff, a safe system of work, proper plant and equipment, and a safe place of work: *Wilsons & Clyde Coal Co Ltd v English* [1938] A.C. 57; *McDermid v Nash Dredging and Reclamation Co Ltd* [1987] A.C. 906. There is no obvious reason why a similar duty should not be owed to patients, otherwise health authority employees would be in a better position than patients with regard to questions of safety. In *Denton v South West Thames Regional Health Authority* (1980, QBD; unreported), for example, a health authority was held liable to a nurse for a back injury sustained when a bed tipped over. There was no system for checking the safety of beds, and Park J. held that, given the risk of injury to patients, there should have been. It may be that the advent of NHS indemnity has removed much of the practical force of the distinction between primary and vicarious liability, since the health authority will be fully responsible for the financial consequences of a doctor's error, and will not seek to shift some of the loss to the doctor's defence organisation. This still leaves Browne-Wilkinson V.-C.'s point, that doctor's should not be blamed for the organisational faults of the health authority, unanswered. See further paras 7–016 to 7–038. Note that a health authority which requires a doctor to work an excessive number of hours, so damaging the doctor's health, may be liable to the doctor in its capacity as an employer: see *Johnstone v Bloomsbury Health Authority* [1992] Q.B. 333; Dolding and Fawlk (1992) 55 M.L.R. 562; Weir [1991] C.L.J. 397. This action was subsequently settled: (1995) 310 B.M.J. 1155.

care applicable to a health authority or a NHS Trust in determining whether it had been at fault in failing to provide either sufficient numbers of staff or staff with sufficient experience would be whether the authority had acted reasonably in the circumstances, and the circumstances may include the resources at the authority's disposal. This could make such an action difficult to sustain,[49] although NHS indemnity makes the issue of less significance, at least to claimants, since the health authority or NHS Trust will be vicariously liable and therefore financially responsible for a doctor's culpable errors attributable to overwork.

In *Collins v Mid-Western Health Board*[50] the hospital authority was held to have been negligent in the system it had adopted for decisions about admitting patients to the hospital. A general practitioner made arrangements for a patient's immediate admission to hospital. When he attended the hospital, a junior doctor took the view that the patient needed further examination by a specialist and sent the patient home. A day later the patient suffered a brain haemorrhage and subsequently died. Barron J. commented that: "It seems to me that any system which gives absolute authority to a junior doctor is inadvisable. By its very nature the position of a senior house officer is one where the holder is learning his profession. He must meet from time to time cases with which he is not familiar and in which he would welcome the opinion of a senior. If he is given absolute authority there is a danger that he may miss things which his seniors would not."[51] This was not to question the importance of having a filtering system, operated by junior doctors, to ensure that the limited time and resources of the hospital were not overtaxed by the admission of relatively minor cases.[52] But the system operated by the defendants allowed a junior hospital doctor effectively to disregard the opinion of an experienced general practitioner that his patient required further investigation as a matter of urgency, without obtaining an opinion from a more senior doctor. This "clearly suffered from an inherent defect which should have been obvious to any person giving it due consideration. It cannot be equated to a medical practice followed by specialists in a particular field."[53] Keane J. took the view that the court was not concerned with "a medical practice as such." Thus: "The claim that the [hospital] was negligent and in breach of its duty to the deceased in operating such a system cannot be refuted, in my view, simply by demonstrating that it is a system in use in at least some other hospitals in these islands."[54]

3–103

In *Wilsher v Essex Area Health Authority*[55] the Court of Appeal rejected the concept of "team negligence" whereby each of the persons who formed

3–104

---

[49] See paras 4–099 *et seq*.
[50] [2000] 2 I.R. 154 (Supreme Court of Ireland).
[51] *ibid*. at 166.
[52] *ibid*. at 159 *per* Keane J.
[53] *ibid*. at 158 *per* Keane J.
[54] *ibid*. at 156–157.
[55] [1987] Q.B. 730, 749–750, and 775, *per* Mustill and Glidewell L.JJ. respectively. For criticism of the insistence on setting the legal standard by reference to individual professional responsibility, when the reality of modern health care is co-operative care by interdisciplinary teams: see Montgomery (1989) 16 J. of Law and Soc. 319, 333.

the staff of the unit held themselves out as capable of undertaking the specialised procedures which the unit set out to perform. It would not be right, said Mustill L.J., to attribute to each individual member of the team a duty to live up to the standards demanded of the unit as a whole, because that would expose a student nurse to an action in negligence for a failure to possess the skill and experience of a consultant. On the other hand, if "team negligence" sought to fix a standard for the performance of the unit as a whole, this was simply a reformulation of the direct liability theory.

(10) Alternative medical practice

3–105   It is axiomatic that a person who holds himself out as having a specialist skill will be judged by the objective standards of a reasonably competent man exercising that skill, even though he does not in fact possess the requisite skill. Care must be taken, however, in determining just what the defendant has held himself out as capable of performing. In the case of practitioners of "alternative medicine" they will be judged by reference to the standards of fellow practitioners, not by the standards of conventional medicine. Thus, a practitioner of traditional Chinese herbal medicine must conform to the standards of a reasonably competent practitioner of that art. He is not to be held to the standards of orthodox medicine, unless the claimant can prove that the prevailing standard of skill in that art was deficient in the UK having regard to the risks which were not, but should have been taken into account. In *Shakoor v Situ (t/a Eternal Health Co)*[56] the defendant was a practitioner of traditional Chinese herbal medicine who was consulted by a patient about a skin condition for which the only orthodox medical treatment was surgery. The defendant prescribed a herbal remedy, but after taking nine doses the patient suffered acute liver failure and died. The evidence indicated that this was probably due to a very rare and unpredictable idiosyncratic reaction. Papers published in orthodox medical journals suggested that taking such herbal remedies gave rise to a risk of liver damage. The defendant did not read orthodox medical journals, but believed the remedy to be completely safe in the light of Chinese medical textbooks. The judge, Bernard Livesey Q.C., held that the defendant should not be judged by the standards of orthodox medicine, since he did not hold himself out as practising orthodox medicine, and his patient had rejected the orthodox approach. But in assessing the standard of care to be applied, the court should also have regard to the fact that he was practising his art alongside orthodox medicine, and he had to take account of the implications of that fact. The fact the defendant believed the medication not to be harmful was irrelevant. He had a duty to ensure that it was not actually or potentially harmful. He also had an obligation to check that there had not been any adverse report on the remedy in an orthodox medical journal.[57] In

---

[56] [2001] 1 W.L.R. 410.
[57] The alternative practitioner is not thereby required to subscribe to a range of orthodox medical journals. It was sufficient if he subscribed to an association which arranged to search the relevant literature and promptly report any material publication to him.

assessing this the judge considered that an appropriate benchmark was that of a general practitioner of orthodox medicine. On the facts, a general practitioner would not have been negligent if he had not noticed the letters and warnings in the orthodox medical literature; and even if he had seen them, the reasonably competent general practitioner would not have been put on notice that the remedy was too hazardous to prescribe since the warnings were equivocal and did not paint a consistent picture of serious risk. If a general practitioner would not have been negligent in failing to identify the risk, then the defendant had conformed to the standard of care appropriate to traditional Chinese herbal medicine, practised in accordance with standards required in the UK.[58]

(11) Emergencies

In determining what was reasonable care the court will take account of the particular situation as it presented itself to the defendant, as part and parcel of "all the circumstances of the case." The defendant faced with a dilemma or an emergency, having to act on the spur of the moment will not be judged too critically simply because with hindsight a different course of action might have avoided the harm.[59] This clearly may apply to medical practitioners. In *Wilsher v Essex Area Health Authority* Mustill L.J. said that:

3–106

> "full allowance must be made for the fact that certain aspects of treatment may have to be carried out in what one witness . . . called 'battle conditions'. An emergency may overburden the available resources, and, if an individual is forced by circumstances to do too many things at once, the fact that he does one of them incorrectly should not lightly be taken as negligence."[60]

This does not mean that a different standard of care is applied in an emergency situation, simply that reasonable care takes into account the circumstances in which a doctor has to operate. If the error is one which a reasonably competent doctor could have made in the circumstances the defendant is not negligent. Conversely, if a reasonably competent doctor

3–107

---

[58] See further the Department of Health Press Release 2001/0448, September 27, 2001, "Concern over Quality and Safety Standards of Traditional Chinese Medicines." The Medicines Control Agency has found a number of dangerous and illegal ingredients in traditional Chinese medicines, including mercury, arsenic and Aristolochia (which can cause kidney failure and cancer). The Agency has produced guidance *"Traditional ethnic medicines, public health and compliance with medicines law"* which can be found on the MCA web site: *www.mca.gov.uk.*

[59] *Parkinson v Liverpool Corporation* [1950] 1 All E.R. 367; *Ng Chun Pui v Lee Chuen Tat* [1988] R.T.R. 298, 302 (both non-medical cases); *Knight v West Kent Health Authority* [1998] Lloyd's Rep. Med. 18, 23, CA.

[60] [1987] Q.B. 730, 749; *Rodych v Krasey* [1971] 4 W.W.R. 358, where a doctor who examined a drunken accident victim at night, with no more than a flashlight and streetlamp to see by, and then referred the patient to hospital, was held not to have been negligent in the manner of conducting the examination.

would not have made that error the defendant will be liable, notwithstanding the fact that it occurred in the course of an emergency.[61]

3–108   In *Wilson v Swanson*[62] there was uncertainty as to the correct diagnosis of the patient's condition, which could have been either cancer or a gastric ulcer. The defendant surgeon recommended an operation, which revealed a large gastric ulcer. He was unsure whether this was cancerous, and he requested an immediate pathological investigation, which took ten or twenty minutes. The pathologist thought that cancer was probably present, but could not make a conclusive diagnosis at that stage. The defendant had to make an instant decision whether to bring the operation to a close and wait for a more accurate pathological diagnosis, or whether to proceed on the basis that there was cancer present. He decided to continue and removed a large section of the patient's stomach. Subsequently it was discovered that there was no cancer. The Supreme Court of Canada held that in the circumstances the defendant was not negligent.

3–109   On the other hand, where an emergency is foreseeable it may be negligence to have an inadequate system for dealing with the known risks that the emergency is likely to create,[63] or in failing to have an essential piece of equipment readily available.[64]

(12) Policy and defensive medicine

3–110   The increase in medical malpractice litigation in recent years has been accompanied by claims that, in response to the threat of litigation, doctors now practise defensively. This involves undertaking procedures which are not medically justified for the patient's benefit but are designed to protect the doctor from a claim for negligence. The most commonly cited examples are unnecessary diagnostic tests, such as X-rays, and unnecessary Caesarian section deliveries. Given the nature of the *Bolam* test, however, these claims do not make a great deal of sense, because a reasonable doctor would not undertake an *unnecessary* procedure and so a doctor cannot avoid a finding of negligence by performing one; to the extent that the procedure carries some inherent risk the practitioner acting in this way may increase the chances of being sued. Moreover, there is little clear understanding within the medical profession of what "defensive medicine" means.[65] Nonetheless,

---

[61] *Cattley v St John's Ambulance Brigade* (1988, QBD; unreported): "An objective standard must still be applied and a person's own judgment or impulse is still not the sole criterion. He may still be found negligent if, notwithstanding the emergency, his acts are found to be unreasonable," *per* Judge Prosser Q.C.

[62] (1956) 5 D.L.R. (2d) 113 (S.C.C.).

[63] *Bull v Devon Area Health Authority* (1989), [1993] 4 Med. L.R. 117, CA.

[64] *Meyer v Gordon* (1981) 17 C.C.L.T. 1 (B.C.S.C.); or in failing to have a system to check the safety of equipment: *Denton v South West Thames Regional Health Authority* (1980, QBD; unreported) (not a case involving an emergency).

[65] See Jones and Morris (1989) 5 J. of the M.D.U. 40; *cf.* Tribe and Korgaonkar (1991) 7 P.N. 2; Summerton (1995) 310 B.M.J. 27. "Defensive" may mean simply treating patients conservatively or even "more carefully," and this begs the question whether that treatment option is medically justified in the patient's interests.

the courts have apparently acknowledged the existence of the phenomenon of defensive medicine, despite the fact that there is virtually no empirical, as opposed to anecdotal, evidence of such practices in this country. In *Wilsher v Essex Area Health Authority*,[66] for example, Mustill L.J. said that: "The risks which actions for professional negligence bring to the public as a whole, in the shape of an instinct on the part of a professional man to play for safety, are serious and are now well recognised," and in *Sidaway v Bethlem Royal Hospital Governors*[67] Lord Scarman commented that "the danger of defensive medicine developing in this country clearly exists." Lord Denning, in particular, has been most vocal in his warnings about defensive medicine.[68]

What impact does this have on individual cases of medical negligence? In non-medical cases the courts have occasionally relied on the prospect of unduly defensive practices developing in response to a potential liability in order to deny the existence of a duty of care.[69] This essentially involves a judgment that imposing liability for negligence will tend to "over-deter" potential defendants, damaging the service in question, rather than contributing to an improvement in standards of conduct, though this is an intuitive judgment rather than being based on empirical evidence.[70] Logically, the same argument would apply to any defendant who is held accountable in the tort of negligence, but no one suggests that imposing a duty of care on, say, motorists makes them drive *too* carefully. Clearly, the option of denying the existence of a duty of care is not available in the vast majority of medical negligence cases, since the doctor undoubtedly owes a duty of care to his patient.[71] In *Barker v Nugent*[72] counsel for the defendant doctor argued that as a matter of public policy, to avoid an escalation of defensive medicine, the

3–111

---

[66] [1987] Q.B. 730, 747. See also *Royal Commission on Civil Liability and Compensation for Personal Injury*, Cmnd. 7054 (1978), paras 1318–1324.

[67] [1985] A.C. 871, 887.

[68] "We should be doing a disservice to the community at large if we were to impose liability on hospitals and doctors for everything that happens to go wrong. Doctors would be led to think more of their own safety than of the good of their patients. Initiative would be stifled and confidence shaken": *Roe v Minister of Health* [1954] 2 Q.B. 66, 86–7; *Lim v Camden and Islington Area Health Authority* [1979] 1 Q.B. 196, 217; *Whitehouse v Jordan* [1980] 1 All ER 650, 658; *Hyde v Tameside Area Health Authority* (1981) reported at (1986) 2 P.N. 26 (see the quotation in para. 4–119); in *Hatcher v Black, The Times*, July 2, 1954 Lord Denning compared an action for negligence against a doctor to having a dagger plunged into his back (see the extract in his *The Discipline of Law*, 1979, p. 243). See also *per* Lawton L.J. in *Whitehouse v Jordan* [1980] 1 All ER 650, 659; *Sidaway v Bethlem Royal Hospital Governors* [1984] 1 All E.R. 1018, 1031, 1035, *per* Dunne and Browne-Wilkinson L.JJ.; *Robinson v Post Office* [1974] 2 All E.R. 737, 745; *Fletcher v Bench* (1973) 4 B.M.J. 117, 118, *per* Megaw L.J.; *De Freville v Dill* (1927) 96 L.J.K.B. 1056, 1062.

[69] *Hill v Chief Constable of West Yorkshire* [1989] A.C. 53; *Rowling v Takaro Properties Ltd* [1988] A.C. 473, 502; *Yuen Kun-yeu v A.-G. of Hong Kong* [1988] A.C. 175; *Saif Ali v Sydney Mitchell & Co* [1980] A.C. 198; *Elguzouli-Daf v Commissioner of Police of the Metropolis* [1995] 1 All E.R. 833; *Marc Rich & Co v Bishop Rock Marine Co Ltd* [1996] A.C. 211.

[70] See Hartshorne, Smith and Everton (2000) 63 M.L.R. 502 pointing out that the courts rarely have any empirical evidence to justify assertions about "defensive" practices.

[71] Though see *M. (a minor) v Newham London Borough Council*; affirmed sub. nom. *X. (minors) v Bedfordshire County Council* [1995] 2 A.C. 633, HL, para. 3–113.

[72] (1987, QBD; unreported).

courts should be slower to impute negligence to the medical profession than to others. Rougier J. rejected the argument, pointing out that comparisons with the position in the United States of America are not entirely sound. Moreover, his Lordship added:

> "I can think of only one thing more disastrous than the escalation of defensive medicine and that is the engendering of a belief in the medical profession that certain acts or omissions which would otherwise be classed as negligence can, in a sense, be exonerated."

3–112   Similarly, in *Wilsher v Essex Area Health Authority* Mustill L.J. responded to his own acknowledgement of the risks of defensive practice with the comment that "the proper response cannot be to temper the wind to the professional man. If he assumes to perform a task, he must bring to it the appropriate care and skill." This was immediately followed, however, by the statement that the courts must constantly bear in mind the fact that whilst, in retrospect, the choice actually made can be shown to have turned out badly it is not in itself proof of negligence, and that conterminously the duty of care is not a warranty of a perfect result. Whilst this is perfectly accurate as a statement of the law, the linking of comments about defensive medicine, however vague and imprecise that notion may be, to the frequent reminders that the courts feel constrained to give themselves regarding the inherent risks of medical treatment suggests that "defensive medicine" does sometimes play a role in medical litigation, as part of the judicial "mind set" which creates an additional, though unquantifiable, hurdle that claimants have to overcome. This may be reflected in the standard of proof that claimants have to achieve in practice, although the formal standard of proof remains the same. But as Kilner Brown J. observed in *Ashcroft v Mersey Regional Health Authority*[73]: "the medical and social consequences of medical men being found guilty of negligence on insufficient evidence may be appropriate as a statement of probable consequences, but beg the question which has to be decided." In other words, the question remains as to what constitutes "sufficient" evidence.

3–113   In *M. (a minor) v Newham London Borough Council*[74] a majority of the Court of Appeal was strongly influenced by arguments about defensive practice in holding that a psychiatrist and a social worker did not owe a duty of care to a child or its parents when advising a social services authority as to whether the child had been physically or sexually abused, and as to the identity of the abuser. The child had been needlessly removed from its home into local authority care, and both the child and her mother claimed that they had suffered psychiatric harm as result. The defendants argued that imposing a duty of care in these circumstances would have serious adverse consequences, particularly in terms of: (a) the financial implications for local

---

[73] [1983] 2 All E.R. 245, 247.
[74] [1995] 2 A.C. 633.

STANDARD OF CARE — GENERAL PRINCIPLES

authorities; and (b) the reaction of social workers and doctors working the field of child protection to the risk of liability.

Both Peter Gibson and Staughton L.JJ. took the view that if a new duty of care was established many claims would be brought and a major diversion of resources to defending actions would occur, placing further strain on an already overstretched system of child protection. Time, trouble and expense would be required for the investigation of claims, to the prejudice of the defendants' budget for their proper functions.[75] In his dissenting judgment Sir Thomas Bingham M.R. accepted that, to a greater or lesser extent, the overstretched resources of local authorities would be diverted from the function of looking after children and wasted on litigation:

> "But this is an argument frequently (and not implausibly) advanced on behalf of doctors: it has not prevailed. Other professions resist liability on the ground that it will in the end increase the cost to the paying customer; that resistance has not on the whole been effective either. Save in clear cases, it is not for the courts to decide how public money is best spent nor to balance the risk that money will be wasted on litigation against the hope that the possibility of suit may contribute towards the maintenance of higher standards."[76]

The assumption that investigating and defending actions will involve the expenditure of time and resources, and that awards of damages will eat into limited budgets is not unreasonable, but it begs the fundamental question of whether the expenditure of these resources would be detrimental. If the imposition of a duty of care were to result in social services authorities exercising greater care in carrying out their functions and this resulted in fewer children wrongly being taken into care and more children rightly being taken into care then on balance it may be that resources are being more efficiently deployed than at present. The point is that, as Sir Thomas Bingham notes, it is impossible to speculate about this. The expenditure may have an impact on the defendants' budget, but it is no part of the proper functions of a social services authority to conduct investigations into allegations of abuse negligently. Moreover, when considering the potential adverse consequences it is strongly arguable that the *only* factors which it is legitimate to take into account are those which impinge on the interests of those children who it is the local authority's statutory responsibility to protect. It should be no concern of a court that imposing liability would create additional costs, in

3–114

---

[75] Staughton L.J. even went so far as to suggest that many claims with little or no prospect of success would be financed by the legal aid fund; and that many cases would be decided in favour of a claimant whose misfortunes attract sympathy, although there has been no more than an error of judgment: *ibid.* at p. 675. It is remarkable that his Lordship should think it appropriate to deny the existence of a duty of care partly on the basis that otherwise the legal aid fund would, in breach of its statutory duty, finance actions which have *no* prospects of success, or that judges would, out of sympathy, decide cases in favour of claimants where negligence has not been proved.

[76] *ibid.* at p. 667.

damages and legal costs, because precisely the same argument would justify granting a local authority immunity from liability attributable to the negligence, say, of its employees who injure people through careless driving on public roads. By definition any decision to impose liability creates additional costs, either in the form of damages, awards or in the costs of preventing the losses that might otherwise lead to damages claims, and there would be little point in holding the defendants liable if it did not. Appeals to the cost of damages to the public purse, in order to justify denying liability, miss the point.[77] If the claimants' claim to redress for injuries which are recognised as a compensable form of damage is in accordance with legal principle there should be no distinction on purely financial grounds between their claims and those of injured road users.

3–115   The defendants also argued that imposing a duty of care would lead to defensive practices by social workers and doctors engaged in child protection work. Essentially the question is whether imposing liability in negligence would improve standards of conduct or contribute to a deterioration in standards. It was said that the decisions that have to be taken in the context of child protection are difficult and delicate, involving an exercise of professional judgment. Imposing liability could lead to such decisions being taken in a "detrimentally defensive frame of mind." Staughton L.J. very much doubted whether the imposition of a duty of care encouraged people not to be negligent, though it might encourage defensive practices. This appears to be inconsistent, for as Sir Thomas Bingham observed: "The common belief that the imposition of such a duty may lead to overkill is not easily reconciled with the suggestion that it has no effect."[78] Staughton L.J.'s view assumes that people on the one hand do not respond to liability rules by acting more carefully, while on the other it assumes that they do respond to liability rules by being over-careful. Sir Thomas Bingham M.R. did not accept, as a general proposition, that the imposition of a duty of care makes no contribution to the maintenance of high standards. His Lordship gave a full and clear rebuttal of the arguments about "defensive practice." It was true that the task was very difficult, delicate and judgmental in nature, but this meant that it would be very difficult for a claimant prove negligence. It was not enough that a doctor or social worker had made an error. The test of professional negligence is whether the conduct failed to conform to the standards of *any* responsible body of professional opinion. It was not enough that other well-qualified professionals would have taken a different view. As a result few cases would succeed. There was no reason why, in a

---

[77] See also the arguments on this issue in *Capital and Counties plc v Hampshire County Council* [1997] Q.B. 1004, 1043–1044 concerning the cost to the public purse of imposing a duty of care on the fire service. As the Court of Appeal acknowledged, ultimately, this is an argument for the immunity from suit of government departments and all public authorities. Judicial concern at the cost of litigation to the NHS was expressed by Stuart-Smith L.J. in *A.B. v John Wyeth & Brother Ltd* [1994] 5 Med. L.R. 149, 153: "The National Health Service has better things to spend its money on than lawyers' fees and the cost of medical insurance is a matter of public concern."

[78] [1995] 2 A.C. 633, 662.

case such as *M. (a minor) v Newham London Borough Council*, a doctor's performance of a duty to form the best judgment that he could and give the soundest advice that he could would be inhibited by the knowledge that he might be held liable to the child:

> "He might no doubt be anxious to be as sure as possible before expressing any opinion, and would be careful to express no opinion stronger than the facts in his judgment warranted, but both these results are to be encouraged. I do not think he would be deterred from prompt action where the facts appeared to warrant it, since he would be as vulnerable to criticism for failing to advise urgent action when the facts appeared to call for it as for acting precipitately when the facts did not. The doctor's only certain protection would be sound performance of his professional duty, and that is how it should be."[79]

This is a refreshing judicial response to the stock argument about so-called defensive practices.

In the House of Lords, however, it was accepted that there was a risk of **3–116** defensive practices developing and that local authorities would adopt a more cautious approach to their duties. In circumstances where a speedy decision to remove a child may be vital there would be a substantial temptation to postpone making the decision until further inquiries had been made in the hope of getting more concrete facts: "Not only would the child in fact being abused be prejudiced by such delay: the increased workload inherent in making such investigations would reduce the time available to deal with other cases and other children."[80] This was a factor in persuading their Lordships that a duty of care should not be imposed for reasons of policy.[81] With respect, this argument carries weight when the assumption is made that "the child in fact is being abused." It looks less persuasive if the premise is that the child may or may not be being abused, and the local authority has a responsibility to carry out reasonable investigation of the facts to determine

---

[79] *ibid.* It might be added that the "frame of mind" with which any professional person approaches the tasks to be carried out is so subjective to the individual as to be almost meaningless. What is "defensive" for one may well be regarded as good practice by another. What counts is whether *objectively* the professional is exercising reasonable standards of professional conduct; and, moreover, questions of immunity aside, this is the only way in which the professional can be sure of being found not negligent.

[80] sub. nom. *X. (minors) v Bedfordshire County Council* [1995] 2 A.C. 633, 750, *per* Lord Browne-Wilkinson.

[81] There were several other matters that contributed to this policy judgment: a common law duty would cut across the statutory system for the protection of children at risk; the task of dealing with these issues was "extraordinarily delicate"; the conflict between social workers and parents was fertile ground in which to breed ill-feeling and vexatious litigation, the cost of which would be diverted from child protection services; regulatory agencies charged with the task of protecting society from the wrongdoings of others should not normally be held liable in negligence. See *ibid.* at pp. 749–751. See also the comments of Lord Hoffmann in *Stovin v Wise* [1996] A.C. 923, 958: "I think that it is important, before extending the duty of care owed by public authorities, to consider the cost to the community of the defensive measures which they are likely to take in order to avoid liability."

the truth of the matter. It is not in the interests of children that they be wrongly taken into local authority care as a result of negligence, any more than it is in the interests of children that they be negligently left at risk of abuse. In other words, the exercise of reasonable care by all those engaged in child protection, including doctors, is in the interests of all children, whether they are the victims of abuse or not. As long as it is remembered that the obligation in negligence is only to exercise reasonable care, not to achieve perfection, and that difficult decisions taken in circumstances of some urgency will not lightly be condemned as careless, a duty to exercise reasonable care should hold no terrors for the professional person. Negligence sets a minimum standard of conduct below which individuals should not be permitted to fall without being called to account. Thus, in *Phelps v Hillingdon London Borough Council*,[82] a case involving allegations of negligence against an educational psychologist in failing to diagnose dyslexia when making an assessment of a pupil's educational needs, Lord Clyde, observed:

> "I am not persuaded that the recognition of a liability upon employees of the education authority for damages for negligence in education would lead to a flood of claims, or even vexatious claims, which would overwhelm the school authorities, nor that it would add burdens and distractions to the already intensive life of teachers. Nor should it inspire some peculiarly defensive attitude in the performance of their professional responsibilities. On the contrary it may have the healthy effect of securing that high standards are sought and secured."

(13) Proof of Breach

(a) Burden of proof

3–117   The burden of proof, on the balance of probabilities, that the defendant has been negligent and that the negligence caused damage to the claimant lies with the claimant.[83] It is not for the defendant to show that he was not negligent. If there are two equally possible explanations for an accident, one of which indicates that the accident occurred without negligence by the defendant, the claimant's action will fail.[84] On the other hand, the claimant does

---

[82] [2001] 2 A.C. 619, 672. See also *Reynolds v North Tyneside Health Authority* [2002] Lloyd's Rep. Med. 459, where Gross J. commented, at [43], that "in a fault based system, it is indeed necessary both (i) to exclude hindsight and (ii) to recognise the social costs of inadvertently encouraging 'defensive' medicine by setting unrealistic standards." His Lordship concluded, however, that a finding that it was negligent to ignore a small risk of catastrophic consequences (death or brain damage) was neither unfair nor unrealistic.

[83] On the proof of causation see paras 5–015 *et seq.* The Civil Evidence Act 1968, s. 11, provides that proof that a person has been convicted of an offence shall be taken as proof that he committed the offence unless the contrary is proved. Provided the conviction is relevant to the facts in issue this means that the defendant will have to disprove negligence. This provision will rarely be of any assistance in a medical negligence claim.

[84] *Jones v Great Western Railway Co* (1930) 47 T.L.R. 39, 45, *per* Lord Macmillan; *The Kite* [1933] P. 154; *Harrington v Essex Area Health Authority, The Times*, November 14, 1984

not have to adduce positive evidence to disprove every theoretical explanation, however unlikely, that the defendant might devise to explain what happened in a way which would absolve him of fault.[85] Cases should not normally be decided on the burden of proof, since a tribunal of fact should make findings of fact in relation to the matters before it, even where this might be difficult. Only in an exceptional case would a judge be obliged in conscience to say that he did not know where the truth lay, and decide the issue on the basis of the burden of proof.[86] But a judge is not required to choose between two theories, both of which he regards as extremely improbable, or one of which he regards as extremely improbable and the other of which he regards as virtually impossible. The third option is to conclude that the evidence left him in doubt as to the cause of the damage, and that, in these circumstances, the claimant has failed to discharge the burden of proof.[87]

Where two people are simultaneously negligent, and only one of them   **3–118**
caused the damage but it is not possible to identify which of them, then in theory the claimant's action would fail because he would not be able to attribute responsibility to either of them on the balance of probabilities. This problem arose in *Cook v Lewis*[88] when two people on a hunting trip simultaneously discharged their guns, and the claimant was hit by one of them, but he was unable to prove which one. The Supreme Court of Canada held that in these circumstances the burden of proof was reversed, and it was for the defendants to prove that they did not cause the damage. If neither could do so then both would be liable. This might be hard on the "innocent" defendant, but the alternative rule, putting the burden of proof on the claimant would be just as harsh on the innocent and injured claimant. It is not clear whether *Cook v Lewis* would be followed in this country,[89] although the logic of the decision of the House of Lords in *Fairchild v Glenhaven Funeral Services Ltd*[90] now suggests that it would. In any event, where a defendant health authority is vicariously liable for the negligence of all the potential defendants (surgeon, anaesthetist, nurses, etc.) the claimant does not have to prove which particular defendant caused the harm.[91]

In *Clark v MacLennan*[92] Peter Pain J. had suggested that where there is a   **3–119**

(n.84 contd.) QBD, where Beldam J. felt unable to select either one of two possible explanations for the claimant's necrosis of the skin, and the claimant's action failed on the burden of proof; see also *Ashcroft v Mersey Regional Health Authority* [1983] 2 All E.R. 245; affirmed [1985] 2 All E.R. 96, a case formally decided on the balance of probabilities, but seemingly resting on the burden of proof.

[85] *Bull v Devon Area Health Authority* (1989), [1993] 4 Med. L.R. 117, 138, C.A., *per* Dillon L.J.

[86] *Morris v London Iron & Steel Co Ltd* [1987] I.R.L.R. 182, CA (a non-medical case).

[87] *The Popi M.* [1985] 2 Lloyd's Rep. 1, 6, HL.

[88] [1952] 1 D.L.R. 1.

[89] *cf. Baker v Market Harborough Co-operative Society Ltd* [1953] 1 W.L.R. 1472, 1475, *per* Somerville L.J. suggesting that it would not, and *Roe v Minister of Health* [1954] 2 Q.B. 66, 82, *per* Denning L.J. implying that it would and citing *Baker* in support; *Bray v Palmer* [1953] 1 W.L.R. 1455.

[90] [2002] UKHL 22; [2003] 1 A.C. 32. See paras 5–027 *et seq.*

[91] *Cassidy v Ministry of Health* [1951] 2 K.B. 343.

[92] [1983] 1 All E.R. 416.

general practice to take a particular precaution against a specific risk but the defendant fails to take that precaution, and the very damage against which it is designed to be a protection occurs, the burden of proof lies with the defendant to show both that he was not in breach of duty and that the breach did not cause the damage. The justification for this was that where a defendant has deliberately chosen to omit the usual precautions and has thereby significantly increased the risk of injury, it is unfair for the claimant to be defeated solely by the burden of proof.[93] This approach to the proof of negligence, as opposed to causation, was criticised by Mustill L.J. in *Wilsher v Essex Area Health Authority*,[94] although his Lordship accepted that in some instances breach and causation may be so closely linked that in practice it may be difficult maintain a different rule for proof of breach of duty when proof of causation was governed by *McGhee v National Coal Board*.[95] When *Wilsher v Essex Area Health Authority*[96] reached the House of Lords, their Lordships made it clear that the burden of proving *causation* remains with the claimant throughout. Nonetheless, despite the fact that, technically, the burden of proving causation remains with the claimant, it is now clear that there are some circumstances where it is legitimate for the court to conclude that a claimant who cannot show that the defendant's breach of duty has probably caused the damage of which he complains can nonetheless succeed.[97] However, whether this could be extended to proof of breach of duty in the circumstances outlined by Peter Pain J. remains doubtful.

3–120   Of course, to say that the claimant has the burden of proof does not necessarily mean that he must provide direct evidence that the defendant has fallen below the requisite standard of care. He may rely upon any legitimate inferences that can be drawn from the proved facts, and in the absence of evidence to the contrary the inference may well be that the defendant has been negligent. Indeed, although the discussion of *McGhee v National Coal Board* in *Wilsher v Essex Area Health Authority* centred upon the issue of the location of the burden of proving causation, it may be that the crucial, and largely unanswered, question is in what circumstances the court will draw inferences of fact which support the claimant's version of events in the absence of direct evidence. An inference is a deduction from the evidence, which, if it is a reasonable deduction, may have the validity of legal proof, as opposed to conjecture which, even though plausible, has no value, "for its essence is that it is a mere guess."[98]

Res ipsa loquitur

3–121   The principle of *res ipsa loquitur* is, in essence, an evidential principle, which, in certain instances, allows the court to draw an inference of

---

[93] His Lordship relied on *McGhee v National Coal Board* [1972] 3 All E.R. 1008.
[94] [1987] Q.B. 730, 752.
[95] [1972] 3 All E.R. 1008.
[96] [1988] A.C. 1074.
[97] See *Fairchild v Glenhaven Funeral Services Ltd* [2002] UKHL 22; [2003] 1 A.C. 32, paras 5–027 et seq.
[98] *Jones v Great Western Railway Co* (1930) 47 T.L.R. 39, 45, *per* Lord Macmillan.

negligence. Although in some cases it has been suggested that the principle has the effect of reversing the burden of proof, the better view would seem to be that this is incorrect. The burden of proof remains with the claimant, but the defendant must adduce evidence to rebut the inference of negligence, in order to avoid a finding of liability.[99]

The maxim applies where an accident occurs in circumstances in which accidents do not normally happen unless there has been negligence by someone. The fact of the accident itself may give rise to an inference of negligence by the defendant which, in the absence of evidence in rebuttal, would be sufficient to impose liability. There is no magic in the phrase *res ipsa loquitur*— "the thing speaks for itself." It is simply a submission that the facts establish a *prima facie* case against the defendant.[1] The value of this principle is that it enables a claimant who has no knowledge, or insufficient knowledge, about how the accident occurred to rely on the accident itself and the surrounding circumstances as evidence of negligence, and prevents a defendant who does know what happened from avoiding responsibility simply by choosing not to give any evidence.[2]

(i) When does res ipsa loquitur *apply?*

Res ipsa loquitur is intended to assist a claimant who, through no fault of his own, is unable to adduce evidence as to how the accident occurred. If all the facts about the cause of the accident are known the maxim does not apply. Rather, the question then is whether, on the known facts, negligence by the defendant can be inferred.[3]

The principle derives from the case of *Scott v London & St. Katherine Docks Co*[4] in which several bags of sugar fell from a hoist onto the claimant below. Erle C.J. said that:

> "... where the thing is shown to be under the management of the defendant or his servants, and the accident is such as in the ordinary course

3–122

3–123

3–124

---

[99] See para. 3–138 below.

[1] *Roe v Minister of Health* [1954] 2 Q.B. 66, 87–88, *per* Morris L.J.; *Ballard v North British Railway Co* 1923 S.C. 43, 56, *per* Lord Shaw: "If that phrase had not been in Latin, nobody would have called it a principle."

[2] For example, patients under a general anaesthetic are not aware of what is going on about them, and the facts are peculiarly within the knowledge of the anaesthetist and others attending them: *Crits v Sylvester* (1956) 1 D.L.R. (2d) 502, 510, *per* Schroeder J.A. (Ont. C.A.); see also *Mahon v Osborne* [1939] 2 K.B. 14, 50, *per* Goddard L.J.: "The surgeon is in command of the operation, it is for him to decide what instruments, swabs and the like are to be used, and it is he who uses them. The patient, or if he dies, his representatives, can know nothing about this matter ... If, therefore, a swab is left in the patient's body, it seems to me clear that the surgeon is called on for an explanation ..." Note that the court has the power at any time to require a party to give additional information in relation to any matter which is in dispute in the proceedings which may assist a claimant to ascertain facts within the defendant's knowledge: see CPR r. 18.

[3] *Barkway v South Wales Transport Co Ltd* [1950] 1 All E.R. 392; *Johnston v Wellesley Hospital* (1970) 17 D.L.R. (3d) 139, 146 (Ont. H.C.).

[4] (1865) 3 H. & C. 596.

of things does not happen if those who have the management use proper care, it affords reasonable evidence, in the absence of explanation by the defendants, that the accident arose from want of care."[5]

There are two main elements to this; first, the defendant, or someone for whom he is responsible, must have been in "control" of the thing or circumstances that caused the damage; and secondly, the accident must be such as "in the ordinary course of things" does not happen without negligence.

"Control"

3–125   In order to impute negligence to the defendant the circumstances must speak of negligence *by the defendant*, which they will not do if the defendant is not in control. Thus, in *Morris v Winsbury-White*,[6] where the patient's post-operative treatment was under the control of several people (nurses, and resident medical officers) as well as the defendant surgeon, it was held that *res ipsa loquitur* did not apply. On the other hand, where the defendant is responsible in law for all the staff who played some role in the claimant's treatment, this is sufficient control.[7] The test is whether outside interference was likely. If it is unlikely that some unauthorised person could have interfered with the thing that caused the damage, the defendant has sufficient control.[8] Where the events were under the control of two or more independent persons, but the claimant cannot say which, then possibly he is entitled to call on each of them for an explanation.[9] This could be important where a patient receives private treatment but is unable to identify which member of the medical team was negligent, because the hospital may not be vicariously liable for all the staff, *e.g.* where the patient engaged the surgeon himself. Unless the patient can call on each defendant for an explanation of events the action will fail, because he cannot prove which of two or more defendants was responsible.

"Ordinary course of things"

3–126   The circumstances must be such that in the ordinary course of things accidents do not happen unless someone has been negligent. This is largely a "common sense" judgment based on the common experience of life. Common experience indicates that barrels of flour do not normally fall from warehouse windows into the street in the absence of negligence.[10] On the

---

[5] *ibid.* at p. 601; cited with approval by Singleton L.J. in *Cassidy v Ministry of Health* [1951] 2 K.B. 343, 353–354.

[6] [1937] 4 All E.R. 494, 499; see also *McFadyen v Harvie* [1942] 4 D.L.R. 647.

[7] *Cassidy v Ministry of Health* [1951] 2 K.B. 343.

[8] *Lloyde v West Midlands Gas Board* [1971] 1 W.L.R. 749; *Easson v London & North Eastern Railway Co* [1944] K.B. 421.

[9] *Roe v Minister of Health* [1954] 2 Q.B. 66, 82, *per* Denning L.J.

[10] *Byrne v Boadle* (1863) 2 H. & C. 722; *Scott v London & St. Katherine Docks Co* (1865) 3 H. & C. 596; *Chaproniere v Mason* (1905) 21 T.L.R. 633, where stones were found in buns; *Skinner v London, Brighton & South Coast Railway Co* (1850) 5 Exch. 787, colliding trains.

other hand, financial losses on the commodity market are not, without more, evidence of negligence by brokers.[11]

It might be thought that, given that much of medical practice is outside the common experience of life and given the courts' frequent reference to the inherent risks of medical treatment, *res ipsa loquitur* could not be invoked in the context of a medical negligence action.[12] This, however, is not the position. The principle may be relied upon in an appropriate case, but the courts are cautious about drawing inferences of negligence simply because something has gone wrong with the treatment. In *Hucks v Cole*,[13] for example, Lord Denning M.R. said that it was not right to invoke *res ipsa loquitur* against a doctor "save in an extreme case."

3–127

When does res ipsa loquitur *apply in a medical context?*

In *Cassidy v Ministry of Health*[14] the claimant was suffering from Dupuytren's contraction of the third and fourth fingers of his left hand. The hand was operated on and following the operation the hand and arm had to be kept in a rigid splint for eight to fourteen days. When the hand was released from the splint it was found to be virtually useless. The two fingers which had been operated on were completely stiff and the trouble had spread to the other two good fingers as well. The Court of Appeal held that, on the basis that the hospital was responsible for all those who treated the claimant, the facts raised a case of *res ipsa loquitur*. It was impossible to come to any clear conclusion as to why the injury occurred, and the defendants, having chosen not to call any independent expert evidence, failed to rebut the *prima facie* inference of negligence. Singleton L.J. said that it was unnecessary for the claimant to identify the particular employee who was at fault. As Denning L.J. commented:

3–128

"If the plaintiff had to prove that some particular doctor or nurse was negligent, he would not be able to do it. But he was not put to that

[11] *Stafford v Conti Commodity Services Ltd* [1981] 1 All E.R. 691.
[12] See, *e.g.*, Scott L.J. in *Mahon v Osborne* [1939] 2 K.B. 14, 23: "How can the ordinary judge have sufficient knowledge of surgical operations to draw such an inference, or . . . what does he know of the 'ordinary course of things' in a complicated abdominal operation?" Note, however, that on the question of applying *res ipsa loquitur* this was a dissenting judgment. In *Ritchie v Chichester Health Authority* [1994] 5 Med. L.R. 187, 205, QBD, the defendants argued that there was no place for the maxim *res ipsa loquitur* in a medical negligence case, relying on a comment by Stuart-Smith L.J. in *Delaney v Southmead Health Authority* (1992), [1995] 6 Med. L.R. 355, 359 doubting whether the maxim was of much assistance "in a case of medical negligence, at any rate when all the evidence in the case has been adduced." H.H. Judge Thompson Q.C. did not understand Stuart-Smith L.J. to be saying that *res ipsa loquitur* could not apply in cases of medical negligence, or that medical negligence was in a special category which put it outside the ordinary English law of negligence. Rather, the maxim may not be of much help where there has been a lot of medical evidence. In Canada the view that *res ipsa loquitur* had no application to malpractice cases was expressly rejected by the Supreme Court in *Nesbitt v Holt* [1953] 1 D.L.R. 671.
[13] (1968), [1993] 4 Med. L.R. 393, 396.
[14] [1951] 2 K.B. 343.

impossible task: he says, 'I went into the hospital to be cured of two stiff fingers. I have come out with four stiff fingers, and my hand is useless. That should not have happened if due care had been used. Explain it, if you can'. I am quite clearly of opinion that that raises a *prima facie* case against the hospital authorities."[15]

3–129   This statement cannot be taken to suggest that the fact that a patient comes out of hospital in a worse condition than he went in constitutes proof of negligence by the hospital staff. It is widely accepted that medical treatment carries risks, and that the occurrence of injury is not necessarily evidence of a lack of reasonable care.[16] Thus, in *O'Malley-Williams v Board of Governors of the National Hospital for Nervous Diseases*[17] the claimant went into hospital for an X-ray of his arteries and came out with a serious neurological injury. His argument that this indicated negligence was rejected by Bridge J. There is a distinction, however, between saying that "things can go wrong in medicine," or "it is not an exact science and an untoward occurrence is not evidence of negligence," on the one hand, and, on the other hand, saying that this particular procedure carries a specific risk of a particular complication and that complication has occurred. The former statement makes a vague appeal to "risk" in general to deny the applicability of *res ipsa loquitur*. Such a claim would not necessarily be confined to medical treatment, and seeks in effect to deny the validity of the principle entirely. The latter approach identifies a particular feature of the circumstances, an inherent and specific risk, which provides a reasonable explanation of how the injury could have occurred without negligence.

3–130   On occasions the courts are tempted to accept an explanation of events which relies on the occurrence of extremely remote risks. In *Howard v Wessex Regional Health Authority*[18] the claimant sustained tetraplegia

---

[15] *ibid.* at p. 365–6, citing Goddard L.J. in *Mahon v Osborne* [1939] 2 K.B. 14, 50; see also *Fraser v Vancouver General Hospital* (1951) 3 W.W.R. 337, 343, *per* O'Halloran J.A. (B.C.C.A.): ". . . the evidence is clear a man died who should not have died and it is a legitimate inference therefrom that the man died because of negligence of some kind by the hospital. There was no duty upon respondent plaintiff to attempt to isolate the specific act or omission which started and continued the chain of events which led directly to the man's death". In *Moore v Worthing District Health Authority* [1992] 3 Med. L.R. 431, 434, QBD it was said that where a claimant goes into hospital with no impediment to the use of his upper limbs and no obvious risk to them, but comes out crippled, this creates a *prima facie* case of negligence; though on the facts the injury was found to be attributable to the claimant's abnormal susceptibility.

[16] For similar comments in the context of *res ipsa loquitur* see: *Roe v Minister of Health* [1954] 2 Q.B. 66, 80; *Holmes v Board of Hospital Trustees of the City of London* (1977) 81 D.L.R. (3d) 67, 78; *Girard v Royal Columbian Hospital* (1976) 66 D.L.R. (3d) 676, 691 (B.C.S.C.).

[17] (1975) 1 B.M.J. 635; see also *Fletcher v Bench* (1973) 4 B.M.J. 17 CA, a case of alleged negligence by a dentist where Megaw L.J. said that it would be facile to say "something plainly went wrong and what went wrong is unexplained. Therefore the dentist must have been negligent." In *Delaney v Southmead Health Authority* (1992), [1995] 6 Med. L.R. 355, 360, Dillon L.J. said that: "I cannot for my part accept that medical science is such a precise science that there cannot in any particular field be any room for the wholly unexpected result occurring in the human body from the carrying out of a well-recognised procedure."

[18] [1994] 5 Med. L.R. 57, QBD.

following maxillo-facial surgery (a saggital split osteostomy). The issue was whether this was caused by trauma during surgery or by a very rare event. It was accepted by the defendants that over-extension of the claimant's neck during the course of the operation carried a serious risk of causing the problems from which the claimant suffered, and it was admitted that if this had occurred it would have been negligent. The claimant relied on *res ipsa loquitur*. The defendants' explanation for the claimant's injuries (which was not advanced until 10 years after the operation) was that the claimant had, by coincidence, suffered a fibro-cartilaginous embolism (FCE). This was an extremely rare occurrence, with 29 documented cases in the world over the last 30 years.[19] Nonetheless, the defendants were held not liable, the judge concluding that there had not been any over-extension of the claimant's neck because no-one in the operating theatre had noticed anything untoward during the operation.[20]

In *Ratcliffe v Plymouth and Torbay Health Authority*[21] the Court of Appeal made it clear that *res ipsa loquitur* will rarely be relevant in medical negligence cases because in practice the parties will have obtained relevant evidence from the medical records, and have expert medical opinion available. The issue then is simply what weight should be given to the evidence and whether an inference of negligence is appropriate. Following surgery on his ankle the claimant was left with a serious neurological deficit on the right side from the waist down. The cause of this neurological deficit was a mystery. Almost six years after the operation, an MRI scan showed a lesion in the spinal cord. This did not solve the mystery since the site of the lesion was at a different point in the spine from that at which the defendants maintained the claimant had received a spinal injection. The trial judge held that the claimant's symptoms were attributable to the spinal injection, and that by some mechanism, as to which he was not able to make any positive findings, the injection had caused nerve damage, but he also concluded that the anaesthetist had acted with reasonable care. Even though the defendant's hypothesis as to the aetiology of the claimant's condition only emerged three days into the trial, and was of a very rare and unexplained complication of surgery, the Court of Appeal held that the trial judge was entitled to reach the conclusion that this was the causal mechanism. Brooke L.J. commented that the medical witnesses:

3–131

---

[19] *cf. Ritchie v Chichester Health Authority* [1994] 5 Med. L.R. 187, QBD, where, although advanced by the defendants, FCE was ruled out as a cause of the claimant's injury.

[20] It is perhaps worth remembering that the claimant does not have to rebut every theoretical possibility put forward by the defendants in explanation: para. 3–117. The defendants' explanation in *Howard v Wessex Regional Health Authority* seemed implausible, but the judge simply did not believe that there could have been negligence in the light of the evidence of the surgical team; *cf. Betts v Berkshire Health Authority* [1997] 8 Med. L.R. 87 where the fact that the risk of damage to a testicle occurring during the course of an operation to repair an inguinal hernia was very small (possibly less than 0.03%) was taken as an indication that, *on the balance of probabilities*, the damage to the claimant's testicle was caused by the surgeon's negligence.

[21] [1998] P.I.Q.R. P170; [1998] Lloyd's Rep. Med. 162.

"were doing their best to explain an untoward event which was on the frontiers of medical understanding. The human body is not a man-made engine. It is possible that a man's body contains weaknesses, particularly after nearly fifty years of life, which there has been no previous reason to identify. Medical science is not all-knowing. The Greek tragedian Aeschylus addressed the unforeseen predicaments of human frailty in terms of the sport of the gods. In a modern scientific age, the wisest of experts will sometimes have to say: 'I simply do not know what happened.' The courts would be doing the practice of medicine a considerable disservice if in such a case, because a patient has suffered a grievous and unexpected outturn from a visit to hospital, a careful doctor is ordered to pay him compensation as if he had been negligent in the care he afforded to his patient."[22]

All the anaesthetic expert witnesses agreed that for the defendant to have injected the spinal anaesthetic at the point in the patient's back where the spinal lesion was identified in the MRI scan would have been a "staggering mistake". The trial judge was impressed by the demeanour of the defendant, whom he described as a "meticulous and conscientious man", and this made it "highly unlikely" that he could have made such a mistake. This was supported by the evidence of a junior anaesthetist who had not noticed any blood at the site of the injection. Given that positive finding, said the Court of Appeal, the inference of negligence "fell away."[23] This left the explanation for the claimant's injury as either the "remote possibility" of the surgery having triggered a previously asymptomatic constitutional condition or as a complete mystery. But as Hobhouse L.J. commented: "There is no rule that a defendant must be liable for any accident for which he cannot give a complete explanation."[24]

3–132   In *Ratcliffe* Brooke L.J. summarised[25] the application of the maxim to medical negligence actions:

"(1) In its purest form the maxim applies where the [claimant] relies on the *res* (the thing itself) to raise the inference of negligence, which is supported by ordinary human experience, with no need for expert evidence. (2) In principle, the maxim can be applied in that form in simple situations in the medical negligence field (surgeon cuts off right foot instead of left; swab left in operation site; patient wakes up in the course of surgical operation despite general anaesthetic). (3) In practice, in contested medical negligence cases the evidence of the [claimant], which establishes the *res*, is likely to be buttressed by expert

---

[22] *ibid.* at 176.
[23] Note, however, that a judge's finding that the defendant was a careful and competent doctor does not in itself justify the conclusion that there was no negligence: *Connelly v Wigan Area Health Authority* (1994, CA; unreported) *per* Glidewell L.J.
[24] [1998] P.I.Q.R. P170 at 187. For comment on *Ratcliffe* see Jones (1998) 14 P.N. 174.
[25] *ibid.* at 184.

evidence to the effect that the matter complained of does not ordinarily occur in the absence of negligence.

(4) The position may then be reached at the close of the [claimant's] case that the judge would be entitled to infer negligence on the defendant's part unless the defendant adduces evidence which discharges this inference.

(5) This evidence may be to the effect that there is a plausible explanation of what may have happened which does not connote any negligence on the defendant's part. The explanation must be a plausible one and not a theoretically or remotely possible one, but the defendant certainly does not have to prove that his explanation is more likely to be correct than any other. If the [claimant] has no other evidence of negligence to rely on his claim will then fail.

(6) Alternatively, the defendant's evidence may satisfy the judge, on the balance of probabilities, that he did exercise proper care. If the untoward outcome is extremely rare, or is impossible to explain in the light of the current state of medical knowledge, the judge will be bound to exercise great care in evaluating the evidence before making such a finding, but if he does so, the *prima facie* inference of negligence is rebutted and the [claimant's] claim will fail. The reason why the courts are willing to adopt this approach, particularly in very complex cases, is to be found in the judgments of Stuart-Smith and Dillon L.JJ. in *Delaney*.[26]

(7) It follows from all this that although in very simple situations the *res* may speak for itself at the end of the lay evidence adduced on behalf of the [claimant], in practice the evidence is then buttressed by expert evidence adduced on his behalf, and if the defendant were to call no evidence, the judge would be deciding the case on inferences he was entitled to draw from the whole of the evidence (including the expert evidence), and not on the application of the maxim in its purest form."

Even within medicine, there are some circumstances where harm to the patient does not normally occur in the absence the negligence and the maxim *res ipsa loquitur* can apply. As Brooke L.J. suggested in *Ratcliffe*, leaving swabs or surgical instruments inside the patient after an operation will normally speak of negligence.[27] In *Mahon v Osborne* Goddard L.J. said that:

3–133

"There can be no possible question but that neither swabs nor instruments are ordinarily left in the patient's body, and no one would venture to say that it is proper, although in particular circumstances it may be excusable, so to leave them. If, therefore, a swab is left in the patient's body, it seems to me clear that the surgeon is called on for an explanation, that is, he is called on to show not necessarily why he missed it but

---

[26] *Delaney v Southmead Health Authority* [1995] 6 Med. L.R. 355; see para. 3–137 below.
[27] *Garner v Morrell, The Times*, October 31, 1953, CA; *Nesbitt v Holt* [1953] 1 D.L.R. 671 (S.C.C.).

that he exercised due care to prevent it being left there . . . [I]f a patient on whom had befallen such a misfortune as we are now considering were not entitled to call on the surgeon for an explanation, I cannot but feel that an unwarranted protection would be given to carelessness, such as I do not believe the profession itself would either expect or desire."[28]

3-134   In *Saunders v Leeds Western Health Authority*[29] a child suffered cardiac arrest lasting 30 to 40 minutes while undergoing an operation, suffering quadriplegia. The evidence was that the heart of a fit child does not arrest under anaesthesia if proper care is taken in the anaesthetic and surgical processes. The defendants accepted that *prima facie* this was correct, but sought to explain the accident by suggesting that the child's normal pulse had suddenly stopped. This evidence was rejected as mistaken, and the inevitable inference was that proper monitoring of the pulse would have given a fore-warning of the arrest, and that in those circumstances the anaesthetic procedure, or the system for monitoring it or the execution of it was performed negligently. Similarly, in *Holmes v Board of Hospital Trustees of the City of London*[30] an anaesthetist who administered an anaesthetic requiring a method of artificial ventilation which involved injecting jets of high pressure oxygen through a needle into the trachea produced massive tissue emphysema in the patient. This was a known danger of the procedure if the needle was not in the trachea but it did not normally happen with the exercise of due care. The anaesthetist was held liable on the basis of *res ipsa loquitur*.

3-135   The maxim has been held to apply in the following cases:

- where a patient sustained a burn from a high frequency electrical current used for "electric coagulation" of the blood;[31]

- where gangrene developed in the claimant's arm following an intramuscular injection;[32]

- when a patient underwent a radical mastoidectomy and suffered partial facial paralysis;[33]

---

[28] [1939] 2 K.B. 14, 50 (approved by Denning L.J. in *Cassidy v Ministry of Health* [1951] 2 K.B. 343, 365–366). This was a dissenting judgment, but not on this point. MacKinnon L.J. apparently agreed (at p. 38, though the point is not entirely free from doubt: Brazier and Murphy, *Street on Torts*, 10th ed., 1999, p. 259, n. 7) that *res ipsa loquitur* was applicable, although he agreed with Scott L.J. that the verdict against the defendant must be set aside. Scott L.J. was opposed (at pp. 21–24) to applying *res ipsa loquitur*.

[29] (1984), [1993] 4 Med. L.R. 355. See also *Glass v Cambridge Health Authority* [1995] 6 Med. L.R. 91, where it was held that *res ipsa loquitur* applied to a case where the heart of a healthy man went into cardiac arrest while under general anaesthesia.

[30] (1977) 81 D.L.R. (3d) 67 (Ont. H.C.).

[31] *Clarke v Warboys, The Times*, March 18, 1952, CA.

[32] *Cavan v Wilcox* (1973) 44 D.L.R. (3d) 42 (N.B.C.A.); rev'd on the facts (1974) 50 D.L.R. (3d) 687 (S.C.C.); *Cox v Saskatoon* [1942] 1 D.L.R. 74 (Sask. K.B.), in which the claimant's arm was badly damaged during the course donating blood for an operation. The procedure took up to three quarters of an hour when normally it took ten minutes, and the hospital had 100 similar operations that week without such a disastrous result. Held that *res ipsa loquitur*.

[33] *Eady v Tenderenda* (1974) 51 D.L.R. (3d) 79 (S.C.C.).

- where the defendant failed to diagnose a known complication of surgery on the patient's hand for Paget's disease;[34]

- where there was a delay of 50 minutes in obtaining expert obstetric assistance at the birth of twins when the medical evidence was that at the most no more than 20 minutes should elapse between the birth of the first and the second twin;[35]

- where, following an operation under general anaesthetic, a patient in the recovery ward sustained brain damage caused by hypoxia for a period of four to five minutes;[36]

- where, following a routine appendisectomy under general anaesthetic, an otherwise fit and healthy girl suffered a fit and went into a permanent coma;[37]

- when a needle broke in the patient's buttock while he was being given an injection;[38]

- where a spinal anaesthetic became contaminated with disinfectant as a result of the manner in which it was stored causing paralysis to the patient;[39]

- where an infection following surgery in a "well-staffed and modern hospital" remained undiagnosed until the patient sustained crippling injury;[40] and

- where an explosion occurred during the course of administering anaesthetic to the patient when the technique had frequently been used without any mishap.[41]

---

[34] *Rietze v Bruser (No. 2)* [1979] 1 W.W.R. 31 (Man. Q.B.).

[35] *Bull v Devon Area Health Authority* (1989), [1993] 4 Med. L.R. 117, 131, CA, *per* Slade L.J. However, Mustill L.J. doubted, at p. 142, whether *res ipsa loquitur* would assist because "all the facts that are ever going to be known are before the court," but in the absence of a proved explanation for the "inordinate delay," the judge had no choice, said his Lordship, but to find the defendants liable.

[36] *Coyne v Wigan Health Authority* [1991] 2 Med. L.R. 301, QBD.

[37] *Lindsay v Mid-Western Health Board* [1993] 2 I.R. 147, 181 (Supreme Court of Ireland) *per* O'Flaherty J.: ". . . it seems to me that if a person goes in for a routine medical procedure, is subject to an anaesthetic without any special features, and there is a failure to return the patient to consciousness, to say that that does not call for an explanation from defendants would be in defiance of reason and justice."

[38] *Brazier v Ministry of Defence* [1965] 1 Ll. Law Rep. 26, 30.

[39] *Roe v Minister of Health* [1954] 2 Q.B. 66. See also *Brown v Merton, Sutton and Wandsworth Area Health Authority* [1982] 1 All E.R. 650 where the claimant developed quadriplegia following the administration of an epidural anaesthetic, in the course of preparation for giving birth. The defendants, in their stock defence, initially denied that *res ipsa loquitur* was applicable, but on a request for further and better particulars of the facts that they would rely on to show that "this type of accident happens in the ordinary course of epidural anaesthesia when proper care is used" the defendants conceded that the maxim did apply.

[40] *Hajgato v London Health Association* (1982) 36 O.R. (2d) 669, 682; affirmed (1983) 44 O.R. (2d) 264 (Ont. C.A.), although the mere occurrence of infection did not give rise to an inference of negligence.

[41] *Crits v Sylvester* (1956) 1 D.L.R. (2d) 502 (Ont. C.A.); affirmed (1956) 5 D.L.R. (2d) 601 (S.C.C.); *cf. McFadyen v Harvie* [1942] 4 D.L.R. 647 (S.C.C.); affirming [1941] 2 D.L.R. 663 (Ont. C.A.).

3-136   Conversely, *res ipsa loquitur* has been held not to apply in the following circumstances:

- when a dentist left part of the root of a tooth behind during an extraction and broke the claimant's jaw;[42]

- when a dental drill broke and was left embedded in the jaw resulting in a fracture;[43]

- where the claimant became incontinent following a prostate operation;[44]

- where a patient suffered permanent partial paralysis of the legs following anaesthesia;[45]

- when the patient suffered neurological complications leading to partial paralysis of his hand following the performance of an aortagram;[46]

- where a patient died from haemorrhage during the course of spinal disc surgery when the surgeon pierced an artery with a surgical instrument;[47]

- where paralysis occurred following a cervical laminectomy,[48]

- or following arteriography;[49]

- where a baby suffered cerebral palsy following a forceps delivery;[50]

- where a sterilisation operation failed to render the claimant sterile;[51]

---

[42] *Fish v Kapur* [1948] 2 All E.R. 176; *Carter v Higashi* [1994] 3 W.W.R. 319 (Alta. Q.B.); *cf. Lock v Scantlebury, The Times,* July 25, 1963 where the dentist was found negligent for failing to discover that he had dislocated the patient's jaw during an extraction.

[43] *Fletcher v Bench* (1973) 4 B.M.J. 17 CA; *Keuper v McMullin* (1987) 30 D.L.R. (4th) 408.

[44] *Considine v Camp Hill Hospital* (1982) 133 D.L.R. (3d) 11 (Nova Scotia S.C.). For discussion of the complications that can arise from prostate surgery see Moore (1995) 1 *AVMA Medical & Legal Journal* 121

[45] *Girard v Royal Columbian Hospital* (1976) 66 D.L.R. (3d) 676 (B.C.S.C.): ". . . medical science has not yet reached the stage where the law ought to presume that a patient must come out of an operation as well or better than he went into it," *per* Andrews J. at p. 691; *Lindsay v Mid-Western Health Board* [1993] 2 I.R. 147, 182 (Supreme Court of Ireland).

[46] *O'Malley-Williams v Board of Governors of the National Hospital for Nervous Diseases* (1975) 1 B.M.J. 635.

[47] *Kapur v Marshall* (1978) 85 D.L.R. (3d) 566 (Ont. H.C.).

[48] *Rocha v Harris* (1987) 36 D.L.R. 410 (B.C.C.A.).

[49] *Ferguson v Hamilton Civic Hospitals* (1983) 144 D.L.R. (3d) 214.

[50] *Whitehouse v Jordan* [1980] 1 All E.R. 650, 658, 661; *Goguen v Crowe* (1987) 40 C.C.L.T. 212 (Nova Scotia S.C.).

[51] *Grey v Webster* (1984) 14 D.L.R. (4th) 706; nor where the patient's ureter was damaged in the course of a tubal ligation operation: *Hobson v Munkley* (1976) 74 D.L.R. (3d) 408; *Videto v Kennedy* (1980) 107 D.L.R. (3d) 612; rev'd on other grounds (1981) 125 D.L.R. (3d) 127 (Ont. C.A.), perforation of the bowel during the course of a laparoscopic sterilisation held not to be a case of *res ipsa loquitur.*

- where a patient was infected with HIV from a blood transfusion at a time when the virus had not been identified and there was no test available to show whether a particular blood product was contaminated;[52]

- where perforation of the globe of the eye occurred in the course of administering a local anaesthetic prior to cataract surgery;[53] and

- where the treatment is under the control of several people.[54]

As a general rule, the maxim will not apply where the injury sustained by the claimant is of a kind recognised as an inherent risk of the treatment, since such accidents can occur without negligence.[55] In *Kapur v Marshall*[56] Robins J. said that *res ipsa loquitur* only comes into play when common experience or the evidence in the case indicates that the happening of the injury itself may be considered as evidence that reasonable care had not been used, and this will not be the case where the complication is a recognised, even if rare, risk is inherent in the operation.[57]

It does not follow that simply because the claimant is in a position to   3–137 invoke *res ipsa loquitur* that his action will necessarily succeed. The inference of negligence may be rebutted by evidence adduced by the defendant which explains how the accident occurred without negligence on his part.[58]

---

[52] *Dwan v Farquhar* [1988] 1 Qd R. 234.

[53] *Fischer v Waller* [1994] 1 W.W.R. 83 (Alta. Q.B.).

[54] *Morris v Winsbury-White* [1937] 4 All E.R. 494, 499; *cf. Cassidy v Ministry of Health* [1951] 2 K.B. 343.

[55] *O'Malley-Williams v Board of Governors of the National Hospital for Nervous Diseases* (1975) 1 B.M.J. 635; *Guertin v Kester* (1981) 20 C.C.L.T. 225, on complications following plastic surgery on the patient's eyelids; *Considine v Camp Hill Hospital* (1982) 133 D.L.R. (3d) 11 (Nova Scotia S.C.), where the medical evidence indicated that the operation could produce incontinence in 1% to 4% of cases; *Videto v Kennedy* (1980) 107 D.L.R. (3d) 612, 618; rev'd on other grounds (1981) 125 D.L.R. (3d) 127—statistics demonstrated that perforation injuries are an inherent risk of a laparoscopic sterilisation. Statistical evidence of this kind does not show, of course, how many of the cases in which complications ensue are the result of a lack of reasonable care (see, *e.g.*, *Dendaas v Yackel* (1980) 109 D.L.R. (3d) 455, 463, *per* Bouck J.). On the other hand, where the risk is known but does not normally occur in the absence of negligence *res ipsa loquitur* will apply: *Holmes v Board of Hospital Trustees of the City of London* (1977) 81 D.L.R. (3d) 67 (Ont. H.C.).

[56] (1978) 85 D.L.R. (3d) 566, 574 (Ont. H.C.).

[57] In *Chubey v Ahsan* (1977) 71 D.L.R. (3d) 550, 552 Freedman C.J.M. (in a dissenting judgment) took a robust approach to the occurrence of remote risks: "If in 7,000 operations of this kind, 6,999 are performed without damage to the aorta one may safely conclude that the surgeons attained this happy result by the exercise of due care. What can successfully be done in 6,999 cases ought to have been also done in the 7,000th. That it was not done in the 7,000th case must be ascribed to lack of due care." A majority of the Manitoba Court of Appeal took the view that the injury was simply the result of an inherent risk of the operation for which the surgeon was not liable. In *Fischer v Waller* [1994] 1 W.W.R. 83, 86 (Alta. Q.B.) the majority approach was applied: "The rarity of the occurrence does not change the fact that this unfortunate result may occur without negligence," *per* Deyell J.

[58] See, *e.g.*, *Roe v Minister of Health* [1954] 2 Q.B. 66, where an anaesthetic was contaminated by the passage of phenol through invisible cracks in the glass ampoules in which the anaesthetic was stored, and this risk was unknown at the time; *Brazier v Minister of Defence* [1965] 1 Ll. Law Rep. 26, where a needle broke in the patient due to a latent defect in the needle rather than negligence in administering the injection; *Moore v Worthing District*

Indeed, it is not incumbent on the defendant to explain how the accident happened at all, provided there is evidence to show that he exercised reasonable care. In *Delaney v Southmead Health Authority*,[59] following otherwise successful surgery, the claimant sustained a lesion of the brachial plexus which she alleged was due to her left arm having been hyper-abducted and externally rotated by the anaesthetist. The claimant argued that *res ipsa loquitur* should have been applied by the judge, because it was found as a fact that the claimant had suffered an injury to the brachial plexus, the injury had occurred during the course of the operation, and that there was no explanation for the claimant's injury other than that the arm had been hyper-abducted and/or externally rotated. There was no direct evidence as to what the defendant had actually done on this particular occasion, but the trial judge accepted his evidence that he had probably acted in accordance with his usual practice, which did not involve hyper-abduction or external rotation of the arm. This depended on the judge's assessment of the defendant in the witness box as a careful and conscientious professional, from which he inferred that, on the balance of probabilities, it was unlikely that the defendant had departed from his normal practice. The Court of Appeal held that a defendant was entitled to rely on evidence as to his normal practice to rebut an inference of negligence. The defendant had not succeeded in giving an explanation of what had happened to the claimant which was inconsistent with negligence, but he had proved to the judge that he had exercised reasonable care. The result was that, as far as the court was concerned there was no explanation as to how the claimant's injury was sustained, notwithstanding that there was evidence in the medical literature from 1942 onwards, backed up by expert evidence for the claimant, which, it was argued, demonstrated that there were effectively only two possible explanations for brachial plexus palsy, namely a narrowing of the thoracic outlet (which the trial judge found had not occurred) and hyper-abduction and external rotation of the arm.[60]

(ii) What is the effect of invoking res ipsa loquitur?

3–138   There are two possible views as to the consequences in law of a successful plea of *res ipsa loquitur*. The first is that it raises a *prima facie* inference of negligence which requires the defendant to offer some reasonable explanation as to how the accident could have occurred without negligence by

---

(n.58 contd.) *Health Authority* [1992] 3 Med. L.R. 431, QBD, where bilateral ulnar nerve lesions during the course of a mastoidectomy were found to be attributable to the claimant's abnormal susceptibility to this type of injury; *Lindsay v Mid-Western Health Board* [1993] 2 I.R. 147 (Supreme Court of Ireland), where the patient failed to regain consciousness from a general anaesthetic administered in the course of a routine operation, but the defendants were able to show that they had exercised reasonable care and were not negligent. They were not required to take the further step of proving how the claimant had sustained brain damage; *Wilcox v Cavan* (1974) 50 D.L.R. (3d) 687 (S.C.C.); *Hajgato v London Health Association* (1982) 36 O.R. (2d) 669; affirmed (1983) 44 O.R. (2d) 264 (Ont. C.A.).

[59] [1995] 6 Med. L.R. 355.
[60] For further comment on *Delaney*, see Jones (1998) 14 P.N. 174.

him. In the absence of such evidence the *prima facie* case is established, and he will be found liable. If the defendant does adduce evidence that is consistent with the absence of negligence on his part, then the inference of negligence is rebutted, and the claimant has to produce positive evidence that the defendant has acted without reasonable care.[61] In practice, it is unlikely that the claimant will be able to do this, since he would not have relied on *res ipsa loquitur* if he had positive evidence of the defendant's carelessness. On this basis, the burden of proof does not shift to the defendant. If the probabilities are equally balanced that the defendant was or was not negligent, the claimant's action fails. So, for example, in *Colevilles Ltd v Devine*[62] it was said that the defendants had to show that the accident was just as consistent with their having exercised reasonable care as with negligence. It was not suggested that their explanation had to be more likely than the inference of negligence raised by applying the maxim, which would be the position if the burden of proof was reversed. This interpretation treats *res ipsa loquitur* as "no more than an exotic, although convenient, phrase to describe what is in essence no more than a common sense approach, not limited by technical rules, to the assessment of the effect of the evidence."[63]

The alternative view is that when *res ipsa loquitur* applies it has the effect of   3–139
reversing the burden of proof, so requiring the defendant to show that the harm was not the product of his carelessness. The case which provides the strongest support for this proposition is the decision of the House of Lords in *Henderson v Henry E. Jenkins & Sons*[64] in which both Lord Reid and Lord Donovan specifically stated that the burden of proof lay with the defendants, and the effect of the majority finding that the defendants were liable was clearly that they had failed to discharge the burden of proof which lay upon them. A similar result was achieved in *Ward v Tesco Stores Ltd*[65] where the only evidence before the court was that the claimant had slipped on some yoghurt in the defendants' store. There was no evidence as to how long the spillage had been there or as to whether the defendants had been careless in failing to clean it up. As Ormrod L.J. pointed out, in a dissenting judgment, the accident might have occurred no matter how careful the defendants had been.

In *Ng Chun Pui v Lee Chuen Tat*[66] the Privy Council explicitly stated that   3–140
the burden of proof does not shift to the defendant, but rests throughout the

---

[61] *Ballard v North British Railway Co* 1923 S.C. 43, 54, *per* Lord Dunedin.
[62] [1969] 1 W.L.R. 475, 479, *per* Lord Donovan.
[63] *Lloyde v West Midlands Gas Board* [1971] 1 W.L.R. 749, 755, *per* Megaw L.J., approved by the Privy Council in *Ng Chun Pui v Lee Chuen Tat* [1988] R.T.R. 298, 301; see also the same judge in *Ward v Tesco Stores Ltd* [1976] 1 W.L.R. 810, 816. In *Bergin v David Wickes Television* [1994] P.I.Q.R. P167, 168, CA, Steyn L.J. observed that: "It is in truth not a doctrine, nor a principle, nor a rule. It is simply a convenient label for a group of situations in which an unexplained accident is, as a matter of common sense, the basis for an inference of negligence."
[64] [1970] A.C. 282.
[65] [1976] 1 W.L.R. 810; *Moore v R. Fox & Sons* [1956] 1 Q.B. 596; Atiyah (1972) 35 M.L.R. 337; see also *per* Goddard L.J. in *Mahon v Osborne* [1939] 2 K.B. 14, 50 stating that the defendant is required to show that he exercised due care.
[66] [1988] R.T.R. 298.

case with the claimant. Lord Griffiths, delivering the opinion of the Board, said that in an appropriate case the claimant can establish a *prima facie* case by relying upon the fact of the accident. However, the "so-called doctrine of *res ipsa loquitur* . . . is no more than the use of a Latin maxim to describe the state of the evidence from which it is proper to draw an inference of negligence."[67] If the defendant adduces no evidence there is nothing to rebut the inference of negligence and the claimant will have proved his case. But if the defendant does adduce evidence, that evidence must be evaluated by the court:

> "Loosely speaking this may be referred to as a burden on the defendant to show he was not negligent, but that only means that faced with a *prima facie* case of negligence the defendant will be found negligent unless he produces evidence that is capable of rebutting the *prima facie* case."[68]

The duty of the court is to examine all the evidence and decide whether on the proved facts and legitimate inferences negligence has been established. Thus, the defendant's position is no different from that which arises when he is faced with positive evidence from the claimant raising an inference of negligence.

3–141   Certainly, this is the view that has been taken by the Canadian courts on the effect of *res ipsa loquitur* in medical malpractice cases. In *Holmes v Board of Hospital Trustees of the City of London* Robins J. explained the position in these terms:

> "The fact of the happening is, as I view *res ipsa loquitur*, simply a piece of circumstantial evidence justifying an inference of the defendant's negligence. The weight to be given that inference, like that to be given any other circumstantial evidence, will depend on the particular factual circumstances of the case. The strength of the inference may vary: it may be very strong or it may be sufficiently potent only to present a *prima facie* case and prevent the plaintiff from being non-suited . . . What evidence, if any, the defendant need adduce will depend on the strength of the inference raised against him. The burden of proof remains with the plaintiff throughout; *res ipsa loquitur* does not shift the onus to the defendant or create a legal presumption in favour of the plaintiff which the defendant must disprove before he can escape liability."[69]

---

[67] *ibid.* at p. 300. See also *Lindsay v Mid-Western Health Board* [1993] 2 I.R. 147, 183–184 (Supreme Court of Ireland).

[68] *ibid.* at p. 301. This is sometimes referred to as the defendant's "evidential burden," meaning that faced with a *prima facie* case of negligence he has a burden to give an explanation of the accident which is consistent with the absence of negligence.

[69] (1977) 81 D.L.R. (3d) 67, 79 (Ont. H.C.); *Crits v Sylvester* (1956) 1 D.L.R. (2d) 502, 510 (Ont. C.A.); *Kapur v Marshall* (1978) 85 D.L.R. (3d) 566, 574 (Ont. H.C.); *Girard v Royal Columbian Hospital* (1976) 66 D.L.R. (3d) 676, 691 (B.C.S.C.); *MacDonald v York County Hospital* (1972) 28 D.L.R. (3d) 521, 542; rev'd in part 41 D.L.R. (3d) 321 (Ont. C.A.);

But an explanation of how the events could have occurred without negli- 3–142
gence will not necessarily rebut the inference of negligence, particularly
where the explanation is a remote or unusual eventuality.[70] The claimant
does not have to disprove every theoretical explanation, however unlikely,
that might be devised to explain what happened in a way which absolves the
defendant.[71] Just as the claimant is not entitled to rely on conjecture or speculation to establish his case on the balance of probabilities, so the defendant
cannot resort to this when he is called upon for an explanation of events.
Where an inference of negligence does arise from the circumstances of the
accident, a general denial by way of defence will not be sufficient to rebut
the inference of negligence.[72]

The differences between the two views of the effect of *res ipsa loquitur* 3–143
have probably been exaggerated. It is a fine line between the probabilities
being equally balanced and tipping the scale one way or the other. The issue
turns upon the cogency that the court attributes to particular pieces of evidence, and this is necessarily a subjective judgment which it is virtually
impossible to quantify.[73]

(b) Standard of proof

The standard of proof in cases of medical negligence is, in theory, the same 3–144
as for any other case of negligence, *i.e.* the general standard applicable in
civil cases, namely "on the balance of probabilities." This standard tends to
conceal the fact that the cogency of the evidence that the courts require in
order to satisfy the test can vary with the issues at stake.[74] It is more difficult, for example, to establish that the defendant has behaved fraudulently

---

(n.69 contd.) affirmed sub. nom. *Vail v MacDonald* (1976) 66 D.L.R. (3d) 530 (S.C.C.). In
Wilcox v Cavan (1974) 50 D.L.R. (3d) 687, 695 the Supreme Court of Canada said that:
". . . in medical cases where differences of expert opinion are not unusual and the sequence
of events often appears to have brought about a result which has never occurred in exactly
the same way before to the knowledge of the most experienced doctors, great caution should
be exercised to ensure that the rule embodied in the maxim *res ipsa loquitur* is not construed
so as to place too heavy a burden on the defendant."

[70] *Holmes v Board of Hospital Trustees of the City of London* (1977) 81 D.L.R. (3d) 67, 82;
Glass v Cambridge Health Authority [1995] 6 Med. L.R. 91, where the defendant's explanation for the claimant's cardiac arrest under general anaesthetic, namely that he had suffered from gas embolism caused by oxygen entering the blood stream as a result of the use
of hydrogen peroxide in the cleansing and irrigation track of the claimant's wound, was
rejected as "at best a highly unlikely possibility."

[71] *Bull v Devon Area Health Authority* (1989), [1993] 4 Med. L.R. 117, 138, CA, *per* Dillon
L.J.; *Ballard v North British Railway Co* 1923 S.C. 43, 54, *per* Lord Dunedin, that the defendant's explanation must be a reasonable one; *cf. Lindsay v Mid-Western Health Board*
[1993] 2 I.R. 147, 185 (Supreme Court of Ireland) where it was said that "it was legitimate
. . . for the defendant to adduce evidence of possibilities, remote though they might be, as an
explanation; in contradistinction to saying that it could not offer *any* explanation of any
description whatsoever" (original emphasis).

[72] *Bergin v David Wickes Television* [1994] P.I.Q.R. P167, 168, CA.

[73] In *Levinkind v Churchill-Davidson* (1983; unreported) Kenneth Jones J., denying the applicability of the maxim to a medical negligence action, remarked that he should not allow
himself to be "trammelled by the logical intricacies associated with *res ipsa loquitur*."

[74] See Pattenden (1988) 7 C.J.Q. 220.

than to prove that he was negligent.[75] It has been suggested that cases of professional negligence create particular problems for the courts and, in practice, this may result in what is effectively a higher standard of proof than for "ordinary" cases of negligence. In *Dwyer v Roderick* May L.J. said that:

> "Professional men . . . are entitled to no special preference before the law, to no rule requiring a higher standard of proof on the balance of probabilities than any other. But it is to shut one's eyes to the obvious if one denies that the burden of achieving something more than that mere balance of probabilities is greater when one is investigating the complicated and sophisticated actions of a qualified and experienced lawyer, doctor, accountant, builder or motor engineer than when one is enquiring into the momentary inattention of the driver of a motor car in a simple running-down action."[76]

3–145   The disclaimer that professionals are entitled to no special treatment clearly belies what follows in this passage. There is, however, a suspicion that this judicial attitude is largely confined to the medical profession.[77] Most prominent amongst the judges taking this approach to the medical profession was Lord Denning, who was concerned both for the effect that findings of negligence might have on the reputation of individual defendants, and with the more general consequences of medical malpractice litigation for the conduct of medicine.[78] In *Hucks v Cole* these concerns were reflected in his view of the standard of proof:

> "A charge of negligence against a medical man, a solicitor or any other professional man, stands on a very different footing from a charge of

---

[75] *Hornal v Neuberger Products Ltd* [1957] 1 Q.B. 247; and an allegation of murder made in civil proceedings requires the criminal standard of proof: *Halford v Brookes* [1992] P.I.Q.R. P175.

[76] *The Times*, November 12, 1983; (1983) 127 S.J. 806.

[77] *Jackson & Powell on Professional Negligence*, 5th ed., 2002, para. 12.086: "In England, the medical profession seems to fare better before the courts than most other professions. The defence of 'non-negligent mistake' succeeds more often." The editors attribute this to the *Bolam* test as it has been applied to the medical profession, and the greater degree of deference which the courts show to expert witnesses in medical negligence actions. See also Robertson (1981) 44 M.L.R. 457, 459 commenting on the "strong pro-defendant policy" evident in many medical negligence cases; and Montgomery (1989) 16 J. of Law and Soc. 319 for an insight into why this happens. Giesen (1993) 1 Med. Law Int. 3, 5 observed that "decisions in England and Scotland betray an unusual deference to doctors' interests" in contrast to the standards expected of doctors in all other member states of the European Community and all the major common law jurisdictions. See also Giesen (1993) 9 J. of Contemp. Health Law and Policy 273. The long-term effect of *Bolitho v City and Hackney Health Authority* [1998] A.C. 232 on these judicial attitudes to expert medical witnesses remains to be seen: see paras 3–028 *et seq.* See Maclean (2002) 5 Med. Law Int. 205 who argues that judges are now more willing to question the views of experts on issues of fact, but that this does not extend to the question normative standard-setting. Lord Woolf has suggested that courts' excessive deference to the medical profession is in the process of changing: (2001) 9 Med. L. Rev. 1.

[78] See *Roe v Minister of Health* [1954] 2 Q.B. 66, 86–7; *Hatcher v Black, The Times*, July 2, 1954; *Whitehouse v Jordan* [1980] 1 All ER 650, 658; *Hyde v Tameside Area Health Authority* (1981) reported at (1986) 2 P.N. 26.

negligence against a motorist or employer. The reason is because the consequences for the professional man are far more grave. A finding of negligence affects his standing and reputation. It impairs the confidence which his clients have in him. The burden of proof is correspondingly greater. The principle applies that: 'In proportion as the charge is grave, so ought the proof to be clear': see *Hornal v Neuberger Products Ltd* [1957] 1 Q.B. 247 . . . A doctor is not to be held negligent simply because something goes wrong . . . He is not liable for mischance, or misadventure. Nor is he liable for an error of judgment . . . He is only liable if he falls below the standard of a reasonably competent practitioner in his field—so much so that his conduct may fairly be held to be —I will not say deserving of censure, but, at any rate, inexcusable."[79]

This approach to allegations of negligence against doctors is also appar- **3–146** ent in the frequent reiteration of the point that medical procedures often carry unavoidable risks, not all errors connote negligence, there is no liability for mere "errors of judgment," judgment with hindsight should be avoided, doctors are not insurers of a favourable result, and so on. The law reports are replete with such comments. It may be that the difference between motorists and doctors is that in a medical negligence action the doctor's professional reputation is perceived to be in issue, and the courts hesitate before impugning the conduct of a member of a highly respected profession. On the other hand, some judges have taken a more robust attitude to this issue. In *Ashcroft v Mersey Regional Health Authority* Kilner Brown J. doubted the validity of such an approach:

"Furthermore, the suggestion that a greater burden rests on a plaintiff alleging negligence against a doctor is plainly open to question . . . If there is an added burden, such burden does not rest on the person alleging negligence; on the contrary, it could be said that the more skilled a person is the more care that is expected of him."[80]

The question for consideration, said his Lordship, was whether on a **3–147** balance of probabilities it has been established that a professional man has failed to exercise the care required of a man possessing and professing special skill in circumstances which require the exercise of that special skill. Similarly, in *Whitehouse v Jordan*,[81] Donaldson L.J. pointed out that very few professionals can claim never to have been negligent, and that often the

---

[79] (1968), [1993] 4 Med. L.R. 393, 396. This virtually repeats his Lordship's direction to the jury in *Hatcher v Black, The Times*, July 2, 1954, where he said that a doctor should not be found negligent unless his conduct was deserving of censure. Similarly, in *Whitehouse v Jordan* [1980] 1 All E.R. 650, 659 Lawton L.J. commented that: "The more serious the allegation the higher the degree of probability that is required. In my opinion allegations of negligence against medical practitioners should be considered as serious."
[80] [1983] 2 All E.R. 245, 247.
[81] [1980] 1 All E.R. 650, 666 (see para. 3–093, n. 24); see also *Clark v MacLennan* [1983] 1 All E.R. 416, 433; *Thake v Maurice* [1986] Q.B. 644, 663.

only difference between those who are sued and their colleagues is that the error happens to have caused harm to the claimant.

3–148   Some instances of negligence are so glaring that they do warrant censure, but many departures from the standard of reasonable care can be attributed to understandable human error. The fact that errors are understandable does not mean, however, that they should be condoned, nor that patients should face a higher standard of proof in order to preserve the chimera of professional reputation.

3–149   It is not permissible to adopt a different standard of proof to allow for the prejudice to the defendant of a long delay by the claimant in bringing proceedings within the limitation period. In *Bull v Devon Area Health Authority*[82] an action was brought on behalf of a child which suffered brain damage at birth. The consequence of section 28 of the Limitation Act 1980 in these circumstances is that effectively there is no limitation period. The defendants argued that in a case involving long delay there should be a variation in the standard of proof, so that allegations of "ancient negligence" should be more strictly proved than allegations of negligence a few years ago, and where ordinarily the judge would approach the matter on the footing that the defendants have something to explain, the burden of proof should be reversed so as to rest on the claimant. While Mustill L.J. expressed sympathy for this argument, he could not see how it could be sustained either in theory or in practice. The doctrine of *res ipsa loquitur* was just a summary of the obvious:

> "A barrel does not fall out of a first floor opening on the head of a passer-by without something having gone wrong: and that something, according to the ordinary rules of life, is liable to be connected with the conduct of those who have control of the barrel and the warehouse. By what intellectual process can it be said that the plain inference of fault in such a case is to be displaced just because the event occurred fifteen rather than two years ago? I can see none. So also where the burden is acknowledged to be upon the plaintiff. If the balance of probabilities will suffice in a recent case, why should some other standards be required if the case is old; though not so old that the court will not allow it to be pursued at all? Again, I can see no answer."[83]

The defendant's argument was also unworkable in practice, said his Lordship, since it would require a standard of proof that varied with the length of the delay and this could not be operated fairly in practice. Slade L.J. commented that if the law permitted the claimant, who was himself without fault, to bring the claim after a long lapse of time, his case could not be treated as prejudiced by the delay, save only in so far as the lapse of time might render more difficult the task of proving, on the available evidence and

---

[82] (1989), [1993] 4 Med. L.R. 117, CA.
[83] *ibid.* at p. 139.

on the balance of probabilities, those facts in respect of which the onus fell on the claimant at the trial.[84]

(c) Expert evidence and the role of the court[85]

Expert witnesses have a vital function in medical negligence actions, but   3–150
the emphasis that is sometimes placed on accepted professional practice can obscure their true role, which is to provide the evidence upon which the court decides whether there has been negligence or not. This is not for the witnesses to determine. This was forcefully expressed by Bollen J. in the Australian case of *F v R*:

> "Expert evidence will assist the court. But in the end it is the court which must say whether there was a duty owed and a breach of it. The court will have been guided and assisted by the expert evidence. It will not produce an answer merely at the dictation of the expert evidence. It will afford great weight to the expert evidence. Sometimes its decision will be the same as it would have been had it accepted dictation. But the court does not merely follow expert evidence slavishly to a decision. The court considers and weighs up all admissible evidence which it has received. If the court did merely follow the path apparently pointed by expert evidence with no critical consideration of it and the other evidence, it would abdicate its duty to decide, on the evidence, whether in law a duty existed and had not been discharged."[86]

In *Sidaway v Bethlem Royal Hospital Governors*[87] Lord Diplock said that   3–151
in matters of diagnosis and treatment the court has to rely on and evaluate expert evidence (remembering, however, that it is no part of its task of evaluation to give effect to any preference it may have for one responsible body of professional opinion over another), provided it is satisfied by the expert evidence that both qualify as responsible bodies of medical opinion. This is a consequence of the *Bolam* test, a point which was made abundantly clear in *Maynard v West Midlands Regional Health Authority*.[88] Lord Diplock's proviso, however, is crucial. The court must be satisfied that the experts' view constitutes a "responsible" body of professional opinion, experienced in the particular field of medicine concerned.[89] Thus, on questions of liability it is important to obtain expert opinion in the appropriate specialty, and conversely the evidence of a specialist may be of little assistance in an action

---

[84] *ibid*. at p. 126.
[85] See also paras 10–157 *et seq*.
[86] (1982) 33 S.A.S.R. 189, 201; see also *Anderson v Chasney* [1949] 4 D.L.R. 71, 81–82; affirmed [1950] 4 D.L.R. 223 (S.C.C.); *Goode v Nash* (1979) 21 S.A.S.R. 419, 422 (S.C. of S. Aus.).
[87] [1985] A.C. 871, 895.
[88] [1984] 1 W.L.R. 634; see para. 3–018.
[89] *Hills v Potter* [1983] 3 All E.R. 716, 728; *Bolitho v City and Hackney Health Authority* [1993] 4 Med. L.R. 381, 386, *per* Farquharson L.J., cited at para. 3–034, n. 74.

against a general practitioner.[90] Where conflicting bodies of opinion are not "equally competent" or responsible the court is entitled to prefer the evidence of one body of professional opinion over another.[91]

3–152   The court may accept or reject in whole or in part the evidence of any witness on the grounds of credibility or plausibility. On the other hand, on complicated technical matters, where acquaintance with and experience of matters such as anatomy and physiology are essential, the court may not be justified in disregarding expert testimony or reaching conclusions contrary to those of the experts.[92] Conversely, where the case does not involve such considerations it will be easier for the court to form its own view of the circumstances. Where the medical evidence is equivocal, or where, for example, there is a conflict of evidence whether a responsible body of medical opinion supports a particular practice, the judge has to resolve that conflict.[93] In resolving the conflict the judge should not invent his own version of the facts which is not based on the evidence.[94] Of course, all expert evidence must be tested by reference to the criteria laid down in *Bolitho v City and Hackney Health Authority*.[95] It must be demonstrated that it has a logical basis, and where the issue depends upon whether a risk taken by the defendant was reasonable, the experts must have directed their minds to the question of comparative risks and benefits and have reached a defensible conclusion.[96]

3–153   The cogency of the expert evidence can be affected by a number of factors such as the unimpressive demeanour of the witness or the defective logic of an argument advanced by the witness.[97] In *Caldeira v*

---

[90] For example, in *Wilson v Swanson* (1956) 5 D.L.R. (2d) 113, 119, the claimant's expert's evidence was described as "a collection of elementary views on the diagnosis of cancer by one who is a virtual stranger to the exercise of such a medical and surgical judgment." See the comments of Brooke J. in *Scott v Bloomsbury Health Authority* [1990] 1 Med. L.R. 214 on the use of expert witnesses who have retired from practice; and on this question see also (1990) 6 J. of the M.D.U. 25, 33–34; (1990) 1 *AVMA Medical & Legal Journal* (No. 3) p. 10. Solicitors who have difficulty in finding an expert in the relevant specialty should contact Action for the Victims of Medical Accidents.

[91] *Poole v Morgan* [1987] 3 W.W.R. 217, 253.

[92] *Anderson v Chasney* [1949] 4 D.L.R. 71, 81–82, *per* Coyne J.A.; *McLean v Weir* [1977] 5 W.W.R. 609, 620, *per* Gould J. (B.C.S.C.); affirmed [1980] 4 W.W.R. 330; *ter Neuzen v Korn* (1993) 103 D.L.R. (4th) 473, 506 (B.C.C.A.); affirmed (1995) 127 D.L.R. (4th) 577 (S.C.C.).

[93] *Sidaway v Bethlem Royal Hospital Governors* [1985] A.C. 871, 900, *per* Lord Bridge; *Fincham v Anchor Insulation Co Ltd, The Times,* June 16, 1989, QBD, stating that the judge has a duty to make a legal diagnosis where the medical experts were unable to agree on whether the claimant was suffering from asbestosis.

[94] *McLean v Weir* [1977] 5 W.W.R. 609, 620, *per* Gould J. (B.C.S.C.); affirmed [1980] 4 W.W.R. 330; *Hajgato v London Health Association* (1982) 36 O.R. (2d) 669, 683; *cf. Hotson v Fitzgerald* [1985] 3 All E.R. 167 where Simon Brown J. appeared to adopt a compromise theory about causation.

[95] [1998] A.C. 232.

[96] *ibid.* at 241–242.

[97] *Maynard v West Midlands Regional Health Authority* (1981, CA; unreported) *per* Sir Stanley Rees. See, *e.g., Hotson v Fitzgerald* [1985] 3 All E.R. 167, 173; *Hucks v Cole* (1968), [1993] 4 Med. L.R. 393, 398, where Sachs L.J. commented that the reasons given by the *four* experts for the defence for failing to take the simple precaution of prescribing penicillin did "not stand up to analysis"; *McAllister v Lewisham and North Southwark Health Authority* [1994] 5 Med. L.R. 343, where Rougier J. rejected the evidence of one defence expert witness concerning the appropriate level of risk disclosure as inherently contradictory.

Gray[98] the Privy Council had no doubt that in assessing the value of the testimony of expert witnesses their demeanour, their personality, and the impression they make upon the trial judge, *e.g.* whether they confined themselves to giving evidence or acted as advocates, may powerfully and properly influence the mind of the judge who sees and hears them in deciding between them. Again, in *Joyce v Yeomans*, speaking of the advantage that a trial judge has over an appellate court in seeing a witness, even an expert witness, give evidence, Brandon L.J. observed that:

> "Sometimes expert witnesses display signs of partisanship in a witness box or a lack of objectivity. This may or may not be obvious from the transcript, yet it may be quite plain to the trial judge. Sometimes an expert witness may refuse to make what a more wise witness would make, namely, proper concessions to the viewpoint of the other side. Here again this may or may not be apparent from the transcript."[99]

On the other hand, where the crucial issue of negligence turns upon an inference drawn from the primary facts which depends on the evidentiary value that the trial judge gave to the witnesses evidence and not on their credibility or demeanour, an appellate court is in just as good a position as the judge to determine the proper inference to be drawn and is entitled to form its own view.[1]   3–154

There is a, not unnatural, tendency for defendants to rely not on their recollection of what they actually did or said in the case, because with the passage of time they are unable to remember, but on what was their usual practice in similar cases. In some instances the court will be willing to accept this as cogent evidence, drawing an inference (since there is no direct evidence) that the defendant did what he normally does.[2] The Supreme Court   3–155

---

[98] [1936] 1 All E.R. 540, 542.
[99] [1981] 1 W.L.R. 549, 556, cited with approval in *Maynard v West Midlands Regional Health Authority* [1984] 1 W.L.R. 634, 637.
[1] *Whitehouse v Jordan* [1981] 1 All E.R. 267, HL. For criticism of the manner in which this principle was applied to the facts of *Whitehouse v Jordan* see Robertson (1981) 44 M.L.R. 457. See also *per* Lord Bridge in *Wilsher v Essex Area Health Authority* [1988] A.C. 1074, 1091, speaking of a conflict of expert evidence on the question of causation: "Where expert witnesses are radically at issue about complex technical questions within their own field and are examined and cross-examined at length about their conflicting theories, I believe that the judge's advantage in seeing them and hearing them is scarcely less important than when he has to resolve some conflict of primary fact between lay witnesses in purely mundane matters." See further *Lapointe v Hôpital Le Gardeur* (1992) 90 D.L.R. (4th) 7 for the view of the Supreme Court of Canada on the role of an appellate court. See also *Hay v O'Grady* [1992] 1 I.R. 210, 217 (Supreme Court of Ireland) *per* McCarthy J.: "It may be that the demeanour of a witness in giving evidence will, itself, lead to an appropriate inference which an appellate court would not draw. In my judgment, an appellate court should be slow to substitute its own inference of fact where such depends upon oral evidence or recollection of fact and a different inference has been drawn by the trial judge. In the drawing of inferences from circumstantial evidence, an appellate tribunal is in as good a position as the trial judge."
[2] See, *e.g.*, *Sidaway v Bethlem Royal Hospital Governors* [1985] A.C. 871; *Chatterton v Gerson* [1981] Q.B. 432; *Hills v Potter* [1983] 3 All E.R. 716; *Belknap v Meakes* (1989) 64 D.L.R. (4th) 452, 465–466 (B.C.C.A.). For an alternative inference to be drawn from the defendant's failure to recall events see *Holmes v Board of Hospital Trustees of the City of*

of Canada, however, has taken a more sceptical approach to this form of evidence. In *Martel v Hotel-Dieu St.-Vallier*[3] Pigeon J. took the view that the defendant's testimony was not convincing "because he did not have an exact recollection of this particular case. It was not because he remembered exactly what he had done that he swore that he had not committed an error, but it was only because he was convinced that he did what he always does." Conversely, the claimant, for whom the incident is unique and therefore far more memorable, may have a better recollection of events.[4] Against this has to be set the fact that the claimant may not recall the details because he was distressed at the time, lacked the necessary technical knowledge, or may simply have no knowledge of the crucial facts because, for example, he was under anaesthetic at the time.

3–156   In *National Justice Compania Naviera SA v Prudential Assurance Company Ltd, "The Ikarian Reefer"*[5] Cresswell J. set out the duties and responsibilities of expert witnesses in civil cases:

(i)   Expert evidence presented to the court should be, and should be seen to be, the independent product of the expert uninfluenced as to form or content by the exigencies of litigation;

(ii)   An expert witness should provide independent assistance to the court by way of objective unbiased opinion in relation to matters within his expertise. An expert witness should never assume the role of an advocate;[6]

(n.2 contd.) *London* (1977) 81 D.L.R. (3d) 67, 92 (Ont. H.C.), where it was said that in an unusual case where almost immediately the possibility of litigation was recognised and proceedings were commenced within six months, the details of the treatment given to the particular patient should be more memorable. The failure to testify, and to remember, left the impression that "the whole story has not been told and requires that more inferences be drawn than should be necessary in a case involving professional standards of care."

[3] (1969) 14 D.L.R. (3d) 445, 449 (S.C.C.); *cf. Wilcox v Cavan* (1974) 50 D.L.R. (3d) 687, 694; rev'g (1973) 44 D.L.R. (3d) 42, 54 (N.B.C.A.).

[4] In *Rhodes v Spokes and Farbridge* [1996] 7 Med. L.R. 135, 139, Smith J. criticised a general practitioner's medical notes as "scanty in the extreme", then commented: "The failure to take a proper note is not evidence of a doctor's negligence or of the inadequacy of treatment. But a doctor who fails to keep an adequate note of a consultation lays himself open to a finding that his recollection is faulty and someone else's is correct. After all, a patient has only to remember his or her own case, whereas the doctor has to remember one case out of hundreds which occupied his mind at the material time." See also *Skelton v Lewisham and North Southwark HA* [1998] Lloyd's Rep. Med. 324, 329 where Kay J. commented of poor medical notes that "the significance of the poor notetaking is not that it was negligent in the legal sense but that it is indicative of an unexplained carelessness, whether in breach of a duty of care or not." In *Gray v Southampton and South West Hampshire Health Authority* [2001] EWCA Civ 855; (2001) 67 B.M.L.R. 1, at [29], the Court of Appeal refused to draw an inference from the defendants' poor record keeping that the claimant's brain damage had been caused by negligence.

[5] [1993] 2 Lloyd's Rep. 68, 81–82, QBD; affirmed [1995] 1 Lloyd's Rep. 496.

[6] See the comments of Sir Nicolas Browne-Wilkinson V.-C. in *Cemp Properties (UK) Ltd v Dentsply Research & Development Corporation* [1991] 34 E.G. 62, 67 lamenting the "sad feature of modern litigation" that expert witnesses enter into the arena as advocates: "If experts do this, they must not be surprised if their views carry little weight with the judge." Expert medical evidence may be specifically rejected on this ground: see, *e.g.*, *Early v Newham Health Authority* [1994] 5 Med. L.R. 214, 216; *Parry v North West Surrey Health*

CHAPTER 4

STANDARD OF CARE—SPECIFIC INSTANCES AND DEFENCES

4-001   The circumstances which can give rise to a claim for medical negligence are as diverse as the practice of medicine itself. It is possible for any diagnosis or treatment to be performed in a careless fashion, or for some essential step to be negligently omitted. Some situations seem to recur, however, on a regular basis and it may be helpful to discuss the law in terms of these "types" of error. This Chapter attempts to translate into legal categories the wide variety of forms of negligence that may arise in practice. It must be remembered, however, that these specific instances of error must always be measured against the general test for negligence embodied in the *Bolam* test. It does not follow that simply because in one case a doctor has been held negligent for omitting to take a particular precaution, that it will always be negligent to omit that precaution. The test is whether the defendant has acted as a reasonably competent doctor in all the circumstances of the case, and this is essentially a question of fact.[1] There must be some precedential value in previous cases, however, and where a particular practice has been found to be negligent in the past a defendant who has adopted that practice should at least be required to indicate how the circumstances of this case differ from that of the earlier case. In addition, practices change over time and what was once accepted and proper practice may now be negligent in the light of new knowledge.[2]

4-002   The doctor's duty to his patient encompasses diagnosis, advice and treatment, but these components can be further divided.[3] Thus, diagnosis should be preceded by the taking of a full history from the patient, a physical examination, and, where necessary, diagnostic tests. It is obvious that this may be difficult if the doctor fails to attend the patient—"remote" diagnosis is a potentially risky exercise. Diagnosis should also be kept under review if the

---

[1] See *Qualcast (Wolverhampton) Ltd v Haynes* [1959] A.C. 743, where the House of Lords cautioned against relying too heavily on previous cases as precedents for what constitutes negligence.

[2] *Roe v Minister of Health* [1954] 2 Q.B. 66.

[3] See *Sidaway v Bethlem Royal Hospital Governors* [1985] A.C. 871, 896, *per* Lord Bridge. This division is for the purpose of exposition; it is not to imply that different criteria apply to the different components: see *ibid*. at p. 893, *per* Lord Diplock. However, note that a doctor's single duty of care owed to a patient can give rise to separate causes of action: *Golski v Kirk* (1987) 72 A.L.R. 443 (Fed. Court of Aust.) where it was held that a failure to give appropriate information to a patient before surgery is a different cause of action from an allegation of negligence in performing the surgery.

emergency will not be negligent where the seriousness of the patient's condition is not made clear to the general practitioner.[7] Where a doctor is opposed in principle, on ethical grounds, to a particular form of treatment such as the termination of a pregnancy, then a patient who is considering that option should be referred to a colleague at once.[8] The doctor should not simply refuse to offer that treatment to the patient.

4–005   A hospital casualty department that opens its doors to the public undertakes the task of providing an emergency service and will be liable for negligently failing to do so. In *Fraser v Vancouver General Hospital*[9] O'Halloran J.A. said that:

> "The operation of a public hospital is for the public good; the carrying on of an emergency ward therein is a general invitation to the public without unreasonable limitations or reservations, and thus it is bound to the utmost extent to serve the public with that skill and professional knowledge the hospital holds out to the public that it possesses, and without negligence."[10]

This is illustrated by *Barnett v Chelsea and Kensington Hospital Management Committee*[11] in which three nightwatchmen had become ill after drinking some tea. They attended hospital, clearly appearing ill, and a nurse was informed that they had been vomiting. The nurse telephoned the casualty officer, who did not see the men, but said that they should go home and see their own doctors. They left, and about five hours later one of the men died from arsenic poisoning. Nield J. held that in these circumstances the casualty officer should have seen and examined the deceased, and was negligent in failing to do so.[12] The deceased should have been admitted for

---

[7] *Morrison v Forsyth* [1995] 6 Med. L.R. 6, Court of Session; *Cavan v Wilcox* (1973) 44 D.L.R. (3d) 42, 53 (N.B.C.A.), where the information the doctor received over the telephone was not sufficiently serious to alert him to the emergency; *Lobley v Nunn* (1985, CA; unreported) where it was alleged that a general practitioner's receptionist was negligent in not having a small child, who had been brought into the surgery, seen immediately by the doctor as an emergency. The action failed because the parents had not, initially at least, brought home to the receptionist the urgency of the situation; *cf. Ball v Howard*, *The Lancet*, February 2, 1924, p. 253 QBD, where a doctor was held negligent for "not attending at once to the patient's call" when the patient had appendicitis.

[8] *Barr v Matthews* (1999) 52 B.M.L.R. 217, where the question of whether the defendant general practitioner's view that the patient did not fall within the terms of the Abortion Act 1967 for a lawful termination of pregnancy, though contrary to the views of four expert witnesses, was reasonable in the context of the *Bolam* test, did not have to be resolved on the facts. See also GMC *Good Medical Practice*, May 2001, para. 6: "If you feel that your beliefs might affect the advice or treatment you provide, you must explain this to patients, and tell them of their right to see another doctor" (available at the GMC website *www.gmc-uk.org/standards/default.htm*).

[9] (1951) 3 W.W.R. 337 (B.C.C.A.); affirmed [1952] 3 D.L.R. 785 (S.C.C.).

[10] *ibid.* at p. 340. If, on the other hand, the hospital simply closes the doors of the casualty department there is no longer an undertaking of responsibility and there will be no liability for failing to treat (provided that the hospital has given appropriate notice of the closure).

[11] [1968] 1 All E.R. 1068.

[12] The action failed, however, on the ground that the negligence did not cause the death, since there was no effective treatment that could have been given in time to prevent it: see para. 5–004.

case the duty arose out of the relationship between the employer and employee, and the fact that the doctor's function was partially to discharge the employer's duty to the employees. It might be more difficult, however, to establish a general duty to engage in preventive medicine, on the part of general practitioners for example, giving rise to a claim in negligence. If it became standard practice for general practitioners to conduct screening exercises for a particular disease, such as cervical cancer, then it would be easier to argue that the failure to do so constituted negligence.[18] Moreover, where a doctor is aware that the patient's lifestyle may be putting his health at serious risk there will be a duty to advise the patient to take appropriate steps to reduce that risk.[19]

2. ERRORS IN DIAGNOSIS

4–009   Diagnostic errors can arise for various reasons, such as: an inadequate medical history; errors in examining the patient; errors of judgment in interpreting the patient's symptoms; a failure to spot something "serious"; the failure to conduct tests or refer the patient for specialist consultation; or a failure to monitor treatment and revise the diagnosis where the treatment is proving ineffective.

(1) Failure to take a full medical history

4–010   The necessity for taking a full medical history before embarking upon treatment ought to be obvious, and the failure to do so can have tragic consequences. In *Chin Keow v Government of Malaysia*[20] a doctor did not make

---

[18] The terms of service of general practitioners include an element of "preventive medicine": see the National Health Service (General Medical Services) Regulations 1992 (S.I. 1992 No. 635), as amended. On liability in respect of the failure to identify patients at risk of developing cervical cancer through a screening programme see *Penney, Palmer and Cannon v East Kent Health Authority* [2000] Lloyd's Rep. Med. 41, C.A.; para. 3–047; Faulks (2000) 6 Clinical Risk 153. More generally on cervical screening see (2000) 6 Clinical Risk 177–198; Coleman "Limitations of the cervical smear test as a method of detecting women at risk of cervical cancer" (2001) 7 *AVMA Medical & Legal Journal* 235. For discussion of the consequences of errors in screening for breast cancer see: (2001) 7 Clinical Risk 211–223. See also para. 4–027, n. 87 below.

[19] *Hutchinson v Epson & St. Helier NHS Trust* [2002] EWHC 2363 (QB)—defendants held to have been negligent to fail to advise a patient who was a heavy drinker, and at serious risk of developing fatal cirrhosis of the liver, to stop drinking alcohol. Query whether a failure to advise a patient to stop smoking would be negligent?

[20] [1967] 1 W.L.R. 813. See also *Hollingsworth v Dartford and Gravesham Health Authority* (1993) 4 *AVMA Medical & Legal Journal* (No. 3) p. 13, where, prior to a Caesarian section operation under general anaesthetic, the anaesthetist failed to take a pre-operative history which would have identified a history of allergies and asthma. The claimant suffered an allergic reaction to the drug suxamethonium. The anaesthetist failed to diagnose the allergic reaction and gave her a further dose, as a result of which the claimant developed disseminated intravascular coagulation. Negligence was admitted.

any inquiry into the patient's medical history before giving an injection of penicillin, and the patient died from an allergic reaction to the drug. The defendant was aware of the remote possibility of danger, but nevertheless carried on with his normal practice of not making any inquiry because he had not had any mishaps before. The Privy Council considered that this was a clear case of negligence, given that the precautions required to avoid the risk could easily have been taken. In *Leonard v Knott*[21] the defendant physician, who conducted annual "executive health examinations" for client corporations, referred a patient for a radiological examination of the kidneys and urinary tract by means of an intravenous pyelogram (IVP). This was simply part of the "package" included in the annual check-up, and at that stage the defendant had never even met the patient, let alone examined him, taken a medical history, done any routine tests, such as urine analysis, or sought any information from the family doctor. The patient died from an allergic reaction to the contrast medium used in the IVP, a risk which was known and foreseeable to the medical profession. The defendant was held liable for exposing the deceased to such a risk without taking a history, examining him, or consulting the family doctor. The medical evidence indicated that 99 per cent of problems can be determined from a comprehensive history and a proper physical examination, and the deceased had never had any signs or symptoms relating to the kidneys or urinary tract.

The patient's medical history may include not only the signs and symptoms   **4–011** of the illness or injury for which the patient is seeking treatment, but also details of any previous treatment either for the same condition or, in appropriate circumstances, a previous injury or disease. For example, in *Coles v Reading and District Hospital Management Committee*[22] a patient who had sustained a crushing injury to his finger subsequently died of toxaemia due to tetanus infection. He had attended a cottage hospital where he was given first aid treatment by a nurse but he was not given an anti-tetanus injection. He was instructed to go to Battle hospital for further treatment but he did not go to the hospital, either because it was not clearly explained to him or because he was suffering from shock. Later he saw his own doctor, who made no inquiries as to what had happened at the hospital but simply redressed the wound. If the patient had been given an anti-tetanus injection he would probably not have died. Sachs J. held both the cottage hospital and the general practitioner liable. The general practitioner probably assumed that the hospital had done everything that was necessary, but he should have made inquiries of the hospital or the deceased. If he had decided against giving the anti-tetanus injection on the basis that it was unnecessary he would have been negligent for neglecting an elementary precaution. Similarly, in *Meyer v Gordon*[23] it

---

[21] [1978] 5 W.W.R. 511 (B.C.S.C.).
[22] (1963) 107 S.J. 115. See also *Chute Farms v Curtis*, The Times, October 10, 1961 in which a veterinary surgeon was held negligent for failing to give a yearling colt an anti-tetanus injection after it went lame.
[23] (1981) 17 C.C.L.T. 1; *Schanczi v Singh* [1988] 2 W.W.R. 465 (Alta. Q.B.), in which a surgeon was held liable for performing spinal disc surgery without first trying conservative management, having failed to take a full history, either from the patient or the referring doctor.

was held that the failure of hospital staff to take details of the patient's obstetric history, which would have revealed that her previous labour had been a rapid one and put the staff on notice that the labour must be closely monitored, contributed to hypoxia suffered by the baby, which led to brain damage.

4–012   The duty to take a full history obviously requires the doctor to *listen* to what the patient is saying. Sometimes, particularly if the patient is considered to be "difficult," a doctor may disregard or discount what the patient is telling him and this can colour the diagnosis. A failure to listen to a patient who is describing symptoms which would affect diagnosis and treatment will amount to negligence, where harm results.[24] The Australian case of *Giurelli v Girgis*[25] provides a vivid illustration. The claimant sustained a broken leg which was operated on by the defendant orthopaedic surgeon, who fixed a steel plate to the front outer surface of the tibia. The claimant complained on a number of occasions about serious pain in the leg and an inability to put any weight on the leg. The surgeon took the view that the claimant was a difficult patient, with a propensity for histrionics, who exaggerated his complaints. When the steel plate was removed and the claimant attempted to put weight on the leg, it gave way. A further operation was required to repair the fracture. White J. held that the surgeon was liable, because he had failed to take into account the possibility that the fracture was not uniting satisfactorily and had dismissed the claimant's complaints without making any proper investigation. The claimant was not believed or given sufficient time or opportunity to describe his symptoms, or the defendant did not ask sufficient questions. He had allowed only five to ten minutes for consultations, but "pressure of time did not justify the risks of not listening and inquiring."[26] Complaint of serious pain is a significant indicator of movement at the fracture site and the possibility of non-union, and the full facts were vital to a correct diagnosis. As White J. observed:

> "I do not think that it was disputed that listening to the patient's history is as much a part of the art of medicine as clinical examination. Modern aids to diagnosis no doubt assist the medical practitioner in varying degrees depending upon the circumstances, but they can hardly take the place of listening to the patient's history."[27]

---

[24] In some cases a judgment that the patient's description of physical symptoms is probably attributable to a psychiatric condition may mislead a doctor into failing to spot a genuine physical problem. See, e.g., *Panther v Wharton* (2001, QBD; unreported), where both a general practitioner and a consultant physician fell into this trap.

[25] (1980) 24 S.A.S.R. 264.

[26] *ibid*. at p. 270.

[27] *ibid*. at pp. 276–7; see also *Cassidy v Ministry of Health* [1951] 2 K.B. 343, 349 on the question of medical staff ignoring the claimant's complaints of intense and excessive pain; *Saumarez v Medway and Gravesend Hospital Management Committee* (1953) 2 B.M.J. 1109; *Rietze v Bruser (No. 2)* [1979] 1 W.W.R. 31, where it was held that a doctor should not attribute the claimant's complaints of pain to "anxiety" until all the possible causes of the symptoms have been explored.

Of course, the patient also bears some responsibility to give truthful and **4–013** frank replies when questioned by a doctor. If the information given by the patient is misleading the doctor will not be held accountable for acting upon it, at least where it is reasonable to rely upon the information.[28] It may not be reasonable where what the patient says is clearly contradicted by the symptoms, or where it is contradicted by information provided by others, such as a spouse or family member.[29] It is self-evident that relying on the patient's description of his symptoms without seeking any necessary clarification by appropriate questions may give rise to an incomplete history. In *Collins v Mid-Western Health Board*[30] Barron J. commented:

> "In the present case, a question arises as to whether [a general practitioner] was entitled to rely on upon what he was told by the deceased. Obviously yes, but that did not absolve him from asking questions to establish that his patient had left nothing out that he as a doctor would have considered material to a proper diagnosis. Here, the information was given in reply to 'tell me all about it'. While that must be a good starting point, it should not be the finishing point also. He has to be satisfied that the patient has left out nothing which might be of significance to the doctor. Simple questions would probably be all that was necessary to satisfy the doctor that what he has been told does not mask anything else."

Moreover, there is a tendency on the part of patients to "rationalise their problem" *i.e.* they may tend to ascribe their problem to something which they themselves can identify. There may be a danger in the doctor being too ready to put symptoms down to the cause suggested by the patient,[31] and a psychiatrist should not always take at face value what he is told by a patient about how the patient feels.[32]

---

[28] See, *e.g.*, *Venner v North East Essex Area Health Authority*, *The Times*, February 21, 1987, where the claimant assured the defendant gynaecologist immediately before a sterilisation operation that she could not be pregnant. The defendant did not perform a dilatation and curettage (D and C) which probably would have terminated any pregnancy. The claimant was in fact pregnant at the time of the sterilisation operation, and subsequently gave birth to a healthy child. Tucker J. held that the defendant was not negligent in not performing a D and C as a matter of course.

[29] *Collins v Mid-Western Health Board* [2000] 2 I.R. 154, 165 (Supreme Court of Ireland) *per* Barron J.: "Where, as here, information is supplied by someone other than the patient whether in arranging the consultation or before or after a visit, it should be taken into account and, if necessary, further questions asked. This is particularly so when, as here, there is a discrepancy between what is said by the patient on the on hand and the family member on the other." It was held that a severe headache of sudden onset did not justify a diagnosis of upper respiratory tract infection, at least not without eliciting further information from the patient.

[30] *ibid.* at 164.

[31] *Bova v Spring* [1994] 5 Med. L.R. 120, 127, QBD; *Djemal v Bexley Health Authority* [1995] 6 Med. L.R. 269, 277, QBD.

[32] *Drake v Pontefract Health Authority; Wakefield and Pontefract Community NHS Trust* [1998] Lloyd's Rep. Med. 425, 443, QBD.

(2) Wrong diagnosis

4–014   As with any form of medical error, an error of diagnosis will not necessarily be negligent. Ultimately, this is determined by the requirements of the *Bolam* test and whether the defendant acted as a reasonable doctor in the circumstances. It will depend to a large extent upon the difficulty of making the diagnosis given the symptoms presented, the diagnostic techniques available such as tests or instruments, and the dangers associated with the alternative diagnoses. This last point is well illustrated by *Maynard v West Midlands Regional Health Authority*[33] in which the claimant alleged that two consultants were negligent in failing to diagnose tuberculosis, and subjected her to an unnecessary operation. They recognised that tuberculosis was the most likely diagnosis, but there was a possibility that the claimant was suffering from Hodgkin's disease, which at the time was likely to be fatal unless the patient received early treatment. They decided that a diagnostic operation, a mediastinoscopy, should be performed. This operation carried certain inherent risks even when performed correctly, and one of these risks, damage to the claimant's left laryngeal recurrent nerve, did materialise. The claimant's case was that the evidence of tuberculosis was so strong that it was negligent to defer the diagnosis and subject her to the operation. The House of Lords held that a responsible body of professional opinion approved of what the defendants had done and accordingly they were not negligent, applying the *Bolam* test. Clearly, a factor that weighed heavily in this assessment was the seriousness of the consequence if the condition proved to be Hodgkin's disease.[34]

4–015   The difficulty of making a diagnosis will often excuse a defendant, and *a fortiori* where other doctors have in fact made the same mistake with the patient.[35] The diagnosis must be judged in the light of the pertinent facts at the time the practitioner rendered his professional opinion; he cannot be expected to possess the sharper vision and higher wisdom of hindsight.[36] In

---

[33] [1984] 1 W.L.R. 634.

[34] See also *Dillon v Le Roux* [1994] 6 W.W.R. 280 (B.C.C.A.), where a doctor was held negligent having made a working differential diagnosis of reflux esophagitis rather than myocardial infarction, despite the fact that myocardial infarction is a very serious, life-threatening condition whereas reflux esophagitis is not life-threatening.

[35] In *Pudney v Union-Castle Mail S.S. Ltd* [1953] 1 Lloyd's Rep. 73 rheumatoid arthritis was found to be very difficult to diagnose in its early stages; *Crivon v Barnet Group Hospital Management Committee, The Times*, November 18, 1958, CA, where an expert in the field of breast cancer said that he would have made the same diagnosis as the defendant in the circumstances; *Walker v Semple* (1993, CA; unreported): "[The judge] was plainly entitled to find (as he did) that the defendant was mistaken, but he was likewise plainly entitled to find in my judgment that however grave the error in diagnosis, it did not amount to negligence for it was reached upon information which might well have misled the ordinary, competent doctor into the mistaken diagnosis which the judge found to be the case here," *per* Russell L.J.; *Pilon v Bouaziz* [1994] 1 W.W.R. 700 (B.C.C.A.).

[36] *Holmes v Board of Hospital Trustees of the City of London* (1977) 81 D.L.R. (3d) 67, 91 (Ont. H.C.); *Wilkinson Estate (Rogin) v Shannon* (1986) 37 C.C.L.T. 181 (Ont. H.C.); *Roe v Minister of Health* [1954] 2 Q.B. 66, 83, *per* Denning L.J.: "It is so easy to be wise after the event and to condemn as negligence that which was only misadventure. We ought always to be on our guard against it, especially in cases against hospitals and doctors."

Hulse v Wilson[37] it was held that the failure to diagnose cancer of the penis was not negligent, given that in a young man it was extremely rare. Finnemore J. commented that: "The dangers of making a diagnosis too quickly are just as great as making a diagnosis too slowly." On the other hand, it is not necessarily negligent mistakenly to diagnose cancer.[38] In *Whiteford v Hunter*[39] the House of Lords held that the defendant, who had diagnosed the claimant to be suffering from terminal cancer, was not liable for omitting to use a diagnostic instrument that was rare in England at the time; nor was it negligent to fail to take a biopsy when that involved a serious risk of perforating the bladder wall, which would have caused an unhealing ulcer if the condition was cancerous.

When making a diagnosis much depends on the symptoms observed: 4–016 obviously, where symptoms do not indicate the illness from which the patient is in fact suffering the doctor cannot be blamed for failing to identify the specific illness.[40] On the other hand, even where the particular condition cannot be diagnosed the symptoms may be such as to indicate that the claimant is suffering from something serious which needs further investigation,[41] or indeed the difficulty of making a diagnosis may in itself suggest that the doctor take additional precautions such as admitting the patient for observation, or conducting further testing.[42] In *Bova v*

---

[37] (1953) 2 B.M.J. 890; *Phillips v Grampian Health Board* [1991] 3 Med. L.R. 16, where a failure to diagnose cancer of the testes was held not negligent; *cf. Sutton v Population Services Family Planning Programme Ltd, The Times*, November 7, 1981 on the diagnosis of cancer; *Judge v Huntingdon Health Authority* [1995] 6 Med. L.R. 223; *Stacey v Chiddy* [1993] 4 Med. L.R. 216 (N.S.W.S.C.); affirmed [1993] 4 Med. L.R. 345 (N.S.W.C.A.); *Lindores v Barnet Health Authority* (1992) 3 AVMA Medical & Legal Journal (No. 1) p. 12; *Taylor v West Kent Health Authority* [1997] 8 Med. L.R. 251 where there was a negligent failure to interpret a cytology report correctly. It was held that the doctors should have sought clarification of the report, and should have been alerted to the need for further investigations.

[38] *Crivon v Barnet Group Hospital Management Committee, The Times*, November 18, 1958, CA; *Graham v Persyko* (1986) 27 D.L.R. (4th) 699, 703–704, where a doctor who mistakenly diagnosed Crohn's disease was held not to have been negligent; *cf. M.W. v Bolton Health Authority* (1993) 4 AVMA Medical & Legal Journal (No. 2) p. 12, where an elderly patient who had been incorrectly diagnosed as suffering from terminal cancer recovered £30,000, having given up her own home and spent over two years in a nursing home.

[39] [1950] W.N. 553.

[40] *Sadler v Henry* (1954) 1 B.M.J. 1331, where in the absence of symptoms of meningitis a general practitioner was not negligent in diagnosing hysteria; *Barker v Nugent* (1987, QBD; unreported) where a general practitioner was not negligent, on the facts, in failing to diagnose meningitis in a baby; *Thornton v Nicol* [1992] 3 Med. L.R. 41 and *B (A Child) v Kingston and Richmond Health Authority* (1999, QBD; unreported) are to the same effect; but on the diagnosis of meningitis see *Dale v Munthali* (1976) 78 D.L.R. (3d) 588; affirmed (1978) 90 D.L.R. (3d) 763, para. 4–020 below; *Serre v de Tilly* (1975) 8 O.R. (2d) 490, where a patient died from a brain haemorrhage; the defendant's diagnosis of hysteria was a reasonable mistake given the symptoms. For consideration of the medical aspects of diagnosing meningitis see (1996) 2 Clinical Risk 1–9; Burton (2000) 6 AVMA Medical & Legal Journal 161.

[41] See para. 4–020.

[42] *Barnett v Chelsea and Kensington Hospital Management Committee* [1968] 1 All E.R. 1068, 1073. In *Seyfert v Burnaby Hospital Society* (1986) 27 D.L.R. (4th) 96 a casualty officer who discharged a patient who had presented with a stab wound in the abdomen after 1½ hours was held to have been negligent; observation of patients with stab wounds was normally for a minimum of 24 hours due to the risk of penetration of the peritoneum, which could result in the very dangerous condition of peritonitis.

Spring[43] a general practitioner diagnosed a muscle strain in the patient's chest, but the patient died two days later from pneumonia. The defendant was held to have been negligent in "failing to recognise the uncertainties attending his diagnosis." If the natural history of pneumonia had been present in his mind the defendant would have arranged a follow-up visit to the patient, or at the very least have told the patient to call for a further domiciliary visit the following day if his condition had not improved.

4-017   A number of cases in which doctors have been held responsible for negligent diagnosis concern missed fractures. In *McCormack v Redpath Brown & Co Ltd*[44] a casualty officer who failed to discover a depressed fracture of the skull and penetration of the bone into the brain tissue was found negligent. Head injuries were common at the hospital and the casualty officer had assumed, without checking, that this was just another cut head. Similarly, in *Wood v Thurston*[45] a casualty officer examined a patient who was in an intoxicated condition and had been involved in an accident. The patient was allowed to go home, but he died the next day. The post-mortem showed a fractured collar bone, 18 fractured ribs and congested lungs, which the defendant had failed to diagnose. He claimed that the deceased's state of intoxication had dulled his sensation to pain and prevented him from giving an accurate account of events. Pritchard J. held the casualty officer liable, because although the patient's intoxication might have deceived a doctor as to the patient's true condition, the examination should have been more thorough in the circumstances. The use of a stethoscope, for example, would have revealed the deceased's condition. Whilst it may not be negligent to fracture a patient's jaw when extracting a tooth,[46] a dentist who failed to notice that he had dislocated the patient's jaw, either at the time of the extraction or at one of the patient's subsequent visits, was held to be negligent.[47]

4-018   The failure of a hospital casualty officer to diagnose appendicitis in a child who presented with pain on the right side of the abdomen and vomiting has been held to be negligent,[48] as has a failure to diagnose the early stages of

---

[43] [1994] 5 Med. L.R. 120, QBD.

[44] *The Times*, March 24, 1961; see also *Newton v Newton's Model Laundry, The Times* November 3, 1959, on a failure to diagnose a compound fracture of the patella of the left knee after the claimant had fallen twelve feet onto a concrete floor; the defendant was held to be negligent; *Saumarez v Medway and Gravesend Hospital Management Committee* (1953) 2 B.M.J. 1109, on a fracture of the distal phalanx of the left middle finger. The defendant, who ignored the patient's complaints about pain in the finger, was held to be negligent; *Fraser v Vancouver General Hospital* (1951) 3 W.W.R. 337 (B.C.C.A.); affirmed [1952] 3 D.L.R. 785 (S.C.C.), on the failure to identify a dislocated fracture of the neck apparent on the X-rays; *Hotson v East Berkshire Area Health Authority* [1987] A.C. 750, on a failure to identify an acute traumatic fracture of the femoral epiphysis; *Walker v Huntingdon Health Authority* [1994] 5 Med. L.R. 356, where a casualty officer failed to diagnose ruptured ligaments and a damaged lateral popliteal nerve in the claimant's knee. For discussion of the types of error, principally misdiagnosis, which commonly occur in accident and emergency departments see Guly (1993) 9 J. of the M.D.U. 36.

[45] *The Times* May 5, 1951. See also Medical Defence Union, *Annual Report 1988*, p. 43 on intoxicated patients presenting in a casualty department.

[46] *Fish v Kapur* [1948] 2 All E.R. 176; *Carter v Higashi* [1994] 3 W.W.R. 319 (Alta. Q.B.).

[47] *Lock v Scantlebury, The Times*, July 25, 1963.

[48] *Edler v Greenwich & Deptford Hospital Management Committee, The Times*, March 7,

pneumonia in a baby on the basis that the defendant general practitioner had not examined the baby closely enough.[49] In *Wipfli v Britten*[50] it was said that the failure of a general practitioner to diagnose twins was not necessarily negligent, but on the facts there were sufficient indications of a possible multiple gestation to have aroused the defendant's suspicions, and he should have investigated the possibility more carefully.

Where a practitioner has diagnostic aids available it may be negligence not to use them.[51] In *Holmes v Board of Hospital Trustees of the City of London*[52] the doctors responsible for the claimant's treatment ordered X-rays to be carried out but then delayed for five days before examining them. They were held negligent for failing to inform themselves of the factual data (which included X-rays and nursing notes) which they had themselves identified as pertinent and necessary to the claimant's diagnosis, and which they knew or ought to have known was available. Robins J. said that in a complex medical situation a physician would be expected to conduct more frequent and more extensive examinations, and would be expected in making his assessment to seek all ancillary assistance (*e.g.* by means of tests). In *Hutton v East Dyfed Health Authority*[53] a doctor was held to have been negligent when he did not carry out a chest X-ray on a patient with chest pain because she was pregnant and he wrongly thought that it would involve danger to the foetus. On the other hand, it has been held that, when monitoring the growth of a tumour, the practice of comparing the latest X-ray with the immediately preceding X-ray, instead of comparing it to the first X-ray, was not negligent.[54]

4–019

(n.48 contd.) 1953; on a failure to diagnose appendicitis see also *Bergen v Sturgeon General Hospital* (1984) 28 C.C.L.T. 155, para. 4–023; *Reeves v Carthy* [1984] I.R. 348 (Supreme Court of Ireland), where there was an alleged failure to diagnose an abdominal perforation as a result of an inadequate medical examination.

[49] *Riddett v D'Arcy* (1960) 2 B.M.J. 1607. See also *Bova v Spring* [1994] 5 Med. L.R. 120, QBD, on the diagnosis of pneumonia; *Duggan v Tameside and Glossop Health Authority* (1987, QBD; unreported) where a failure to diagnose infection in the claimant's foot due to an inadequate examination was held to be negligent; *Moffatt v Witelson* (1980) 111 D.L.R. (3d) 712 (Ont. H.C.), where an ophthalmologist who failed to recognise the serious danger of a penetrating wound of the cornea causing an infection of the anterior chamber of the eye was held to be negligent; *Wintle v Piper* [1994] 9 W.W.R. 390 (B.C.C.A.), where a failure to diagnose osteomyelitis was held to be negligent. On a failure to diagnose diabetes see Medical Defence Union, *Annual Report*, 1990 p. 26, and *Yepremian v Scarborough General Hospital* (1980) 110 D.L.R. (3d) 341 (Ont. C.A.).

[50] (1982) 28 C.C.L.T. 104; affirmed (1984) 13 D.L.R. (4th) 169 (B.C.C.A.).

[51] The simplest diagnostic tool may be a physical examination of the patient. See *Stacey v Chiddy* [1993] 4 Med. L.R. 216, 224–225 (N.S.W.S.C.); affirmed [1993] 4 Med. L.R. 345 (N.S.W.C.A.), where a general practitioner was held to be negligent for failing to examine the patient's breast for lumps following an inconclusive ultrasound scan, thus missing an opportunity to confirm or revise his provisional diagnosis (although the action failed on causation).

[52] (1977) 81 D.L.R. (3d) 67 (Ont. H.C.).

[53] [1998] Lloyd's Rep. Med. 335 at 345, QBD.

[54] *Sharpe v Southend Health Authority* [1997] 8 Med. L.R. 299, although Cresswell J. expressed "considerable reservations", he was not prepared to condemn the practice as negligent in 1987 and 1988.

(3) Failure to spot something "serious"

4–020   In some cases, although the practitioner cannot be faulted for failing to
identify the specific illness or disease from which the patient is suffering, the
patient's condition is so serious that he ought to have realised that either
further tests were required for a more accurate diagnosis, or the patient
should have been referred on to a specialist who was capable of making the
diagnosis. In *Dale v Munthali*,[55] for example, the defendant diagnosed the
patient as suffering from influenza, when in fact he had meningitis. It was
held that there was no negligence in failing to diagnose meningitis, but the
patient was so extremely ill that the defendant should have realised that it
was more than gastro-intestinal 'flu. The defendant's examination should
have been more thorough, and the severity of the symptoms demanded that
the patient should have been admitted to hospital for further tests.[56]
Similarly, in *Langley v Campbell*[57] the patient presented with symptoms of
fever, headache and alternate sweating and shivering. His general practitioner diagnosed influenza, but the patient subsequently died from malaria,
having recently returned from Uganda. The medical evidence was that, in the
absence of complications, a patient with ordinary influenza began to feel
better after three or four days. A patient who had no complications yet deteriorated should be the cause of special concern. General practitioners did
not normally come across malaria, but in these circumstances it should have
entered the defendant's head that it might be a tropical disease of some kind
(particularly since the patient's family had told him that the patient had suf-

---

[55] (1976) 78 D.L.R. (3d) 588; affirmed (1978) 90 D.L.R. (3d) 763 (Ont. C.A.); *Rhodes v Spokes and Farbridge* [1996] 7 Med. L.R. 135—a general practitioner was held to have been negligent for failing promptly to refer a patient to a neurosurgeon for further investigation, when he knew that she had had an intracranial shunt and had developed symptoms of visual disturbance, vomiting and headaches; *cf. Thornton v Nicol* [1992] 3 Med. L.R. 41 where an allegation that a general practitioner had failed to diagnose "something serious" and there-fore had failed to refer the patient to hospital, where meningitis would have been diagnosed when it developed, was rejected on the evidence.

[56] See also *Barnett v Chelsea and Kensington Hospital Management Committee* [1968] 1 All E.R. 1068, 1073. In *Collins v Mid-Western Health Board* [2000] 2 I.R. 154, 164 (Supreme Court of Ireland) Barron J. commented: "The second defendant [a general practitioner] was not expected to make the correct diagnosis. But he was expected to be in a position to know when his patient should be referred to a specialist. Undoubtedly, on both examinations there were negative findings which would have suggested that there was nothing seriously wrong. Nevertheless, history was said to be 80% of diagnosis. So that if no proper history in the sense of correct questions is taken the chance of an accurate diagnosis or decision to refer is seriously restricted."

[57] *The Times*, November 5, 1975; see also *Sa'd v Robinson* [1989] 1 Med. L.R. 41, where a general practitioner was negligent in failing immediately to refer to hospital a child who had sucked hot tea from the spout of a teapot; *Panther v Wharton* (2001, QBD; unreported)—a general practitioner was not negligent in failing to diagnose vasculitis, but should have diagnosed severe ischaemia; *cf. Stockdale v Nicholls* [1993] 4 Med. L.R. 190, where a general practitioner was not negligent in failing to refer a baby that was subsequently found to be suffering from septicaemia to hospital earlier than he did. Nor was it negligent for a general practitioner to send a practice nurse in response to a first telephone call instead of attending at the patient's home himself. On a general practitioner's "duty to visit" see also *Durrant v Burke* [1993] 4 Med. L.R. 258; *Morrison v Forsyth* [1995] 6 Med. L.R. 6, Court of Session.

fered from malaria during the war, and had suggested blood tests). He might not be capable of diagnosing malaria, but he should have been alerted to the possibility that it might not be an indigenous disease.

(4) Failure to revise initial diagnosis

A doctor should always keep the diagnosis under review as the treatment **4–021** progresses, and keep an open mind about the causes of the patient's condition if it does not respond to treatment. The dangers of acquiring "tunnel vision" are well demonstrated in the Canadian case of *Layden v Cope*.[58] The claimant, who had a history of gout, saw his general practitioner complaining of a sore foot. The doctor made a tentative diagnosis of gout, arranged for some tests and prescribed medication. After some improvement the condition deteriorated and the claimant was admitted to a local hospital and seen by another general practitioner, who confirmed the diagnosis of gout. The foot continued to deteriorate and the claimant experienced fever, but the doctors continued with the treatment for gout. Eventually the claimant was transferred to another hospital and seen by a specialist who diagnosed a staphylococcal and/or streptococcal infection. The infection was so serious that a few days later the claimant's leg had to be amputated below the knee. Rowbotham J. held that the general practitioners were negligent on the basis that they had failed to reconsider their diagnosis or treatment, or both, and had failed to consult with or refer the patient to a specialist. In the light of the patient's prolonged period of hospitalisation and the obviously rapid deterioration of his overall medical condition, they should have been willing to revise their diagnosis. The need to explore all the alternative diagnoses was especially important when it became increasingly evident that the original diagnosis may have been incomplete or erroneous.[59]

The need to consider alternatives was stressed by Hewak J. in *Rietze v* **4–022** *Bruser (No. 2)*:

"It is not sufficient in my view for a medical practitioner to say 'of the two or three probable diagnoses I have chosen diagnosis (A) or diagnosis (B) or (C)'. It must be expected that the practitioner would choose diagnosis (A) over (B) or (C) because *all* of the facts available to that practitioner and *all* of the methods available to check the accuracy of those facts and that diagnosis had been exercised with the result that diagnosis (A) remains as the most *probable* of all. For example, if there were symptoms of persistent pain and puffiness associated with a limb

---

[58] (1984) 28 C.C.L.T. 140 (Alta. Q.B.).
[59] Tunnel vision was also in evidence in *Panther v Wharton* (2001, QBD; unreported) where a general practitioner had formed the view that the patient's symptoms were largely psychiatric in origin, and referred her for a psychiatric assessment, and a consultant physician at the hospital, asked to advise the psychiatric team, failed to approach his physical examination of the patient with an open mind, and so failed to identify a serious vascular problem. Both the general practitioner and the consultant were held to have been negligent.

encased in a cast and if that cast was split in an attempt to eliminate the cast as the source and cause of the pain and puffiness then if the symptoms of pain and puffiness still persisted an alternative procedure or check would be indicated to determine an alternative cause."[60]

This point becomes even more important where the consequences of the alternative diagnosis, if it turns out to be the correct diagnosis, are likely to be serious.[61] In *Lankenau v Dutton*[62] the medical evidence was that a surgeon confronted with a patient with paralysis after major surgery should not only attempt to diagnose the cause but also "should make a differential diagnosis, that is to say that he should consider other likely causes of her condition and test them against her symptoms and be ready with an alternative theory to direct her treatment if his first diagnosis and treatment should fail to produce an improvement in her condition."[63] The defendant had diagnosed an aortic dissection occurring during surgery, which initially was a reasonable diagnosis. As the patient's symptoms progressed, however, he failed to reassess the diagnosis, which resulted in the paralysis becoming permanent. He clung to the original diagnosis although the symptoms should have made him question it; he failed to test his theory by X-ray, and he failed to seek the assistance of neurological experts quickly enough. The surgeon was held negligent.

4–023   Similarly, in *Bergen v Sturgeon General Hospital*[64] a female patient was admitted to hospital complaining of pains in her abdomen. The provisional diagnosis was acute gastroenteritis, with appendicitis to be checked out. A general surgeon made a tentative diagnosis of pelvic inflammatory disease and referred the patient to a gynaecologist, who confirmed this diagnosis. The patient did not respond to treatment, and indeed deteriorated. She died from a ruptured appendix, following an emergency operation which was too late to save her. The defendants were held to have been negligent, not for the wrong diagnosis itself "for everyone will make mistakes," but for failing take account of the fact that there was no improvement in the patient's condition after 48 hours of massive doses of penicillin (for the pelvic inflammation), and for failing to take any steps to rule out appendicitis when it explained all the symptoms and they had the facilities to do so by means of an exploratory laparotomy, bearing in mind that appendicitis is life-threatening. Indeed the

---

[60] [1979] 1 W.W.R. 31, 47 (original emphasis).

[61] In *Bova v Spring* [1994] 5 Med. L.R. 120, 129, QBD, a general practitioner was held negligent not for the initial diagnosis, but in being "unjustifiably sanguine about it and failing to take proper professional care to verify or falsify it in time to protect the patient if . . . the diagnosis should prove faulty." In *Rhodes v Spokes and Farbridge* [1996] 7 Med. L.R. 135, 145 a consultant neurologist was too concerned with questions about the patient's psychiatric state, and failed to explore the possibility of organic explanations for her symptoms. In *Hutton v East Dyfed Health Authority* [1998] Lloyd's Rep. Med. 335, QBD, a consultant physician was held negligent in failing to revise an initial diagnosis of myopericarditis in a patient with chest pain, having received normal test results for that condition, and in failing to include in his differential diagnosis the risk of pulmonary embolus, despite the real risk of disastrous consequences if a further pulmonary embolus occurred.

[62] (1986) 37 C.C.L.T. 213 (B.C.S.C.); affirmed (1991) 79 D.L.R. (4th) 707 (B.C.C.A.).

[63] *ibid*. at p. 231, *per* Spencer J.

[64] (1984) 28 C.C.L.T. 155 (Alta. Q.B.).

evidence was that where there is doubt as to whether or not a person has appendicitis, it is such a dangerous condition that an appendectomy will be performed, and hospitals themselves expect 15 per cent to 20 per cent of appendectomies to yield healthy appendixes. As Hope J. observed:

> "Ordinary common sense must dictate that when you are dealing with a life-threatening malady that has been brought to your attention for the purpose of ruling it out, you do not ignore these precautions in the face of such signs, symptoms and information."[65]

(5) Failure to arrange for tests for diagnosis

Where diagnostic aids would assist a doctor in reaching an accurate diag- **4-024**
nosis it may well be negligent to fail to use them, if available,[66] although, again, this is not necessarily the case.[67] Where a gynaecologist was aware of the possibility that his patient could be pregnant he should have conducted tests before subjecting the uterus to X-rays.[68] In some instances the patient's

---

[65] *ibid.* at p. 174. In *Law Estate v Simice* (1994) 21 C.C.L.T. (2d) 228, 236 (B.C.S.C.); affirmed [1996] 4 W.W.R. 672 (B.C.C.A.), Spencer J. observed that: "Where a potentially life-threatening condition is included in a differential diagnosis, there is a duty on the physician to take prompt steps to confirm it or rule it out with reasonable dispatch . . . I accept that once a possible intracranial lesion is included in a differential diagnosis, it becomes an urgent matter either to confirm it or rule it out because of its potentially life-threatening consequences.."

[66] *Bergen v Sturgeon General Hospital* (1984) 28 C.C.L.T. 155; *Lankenau v Dutton* (1986) 37 C.C.L.T. 213; (1991) 79 D.L.R. (4th) 707 (B.C.C.A.); *Smith v Salford Health Authority* [1994] 5 Med. L.R. 321, QBD, where it was held that the defendant should have undertaken a CT scan prior to performing a spinal fusion operation, because this would have been a far more sophisticated and informative piece of radiology than the X-rays upon which he relied in assessing the need for the operation and the technique that would be required. In *McEwan v James* (1992) 3 *AVMA Medical & Legal Journal* (No. 3) p. 12 the claimant recovered substantial damages from a general practitioner who had failed to diagnose subacute endocarditis, a condition which could have been identified with a full blood count and a proper check of the patient's heart and blood pressure.

[67] *Whiteford v Hunter* [1950] W.N. 553, see para. 4-015. Writing over forty years ago Lord Nathan, *Medical Negligence*, 1957, p. 45 suggested that X-rays were now so commonplace that there would be a grave danger of a finding of negligence if they are not used in a case where there was a real possibility of fractures or dislocations. This may be questioned, however, since the test is whether a reasonable doctor would have ordered an X-ray in the circumstances. They are unnecessary, for example, where the doctor is able to make a diagnosis on the basis of his clinical examination of the patient, or where the result of the X-ray would not normally affect the treatment given (*e.g.* as is often the case with a broken nose). See *Lakey v Merton, Sutton and Wandsworth Health Authority* (1999) 48 B.M.L.R. 18, CA —casualty officer not negligent in failing to X-ray a patient who presented with pain in the hip following a fall, when there were no clinical signs of a fracture.

[68] *Zimmer v Ringrose* (1981) 125 D.L.R. (3d) 215, (Alta. C.A.); affirming (1978) 89 D.L.R. 646, 656–657, where the defendant had diagnosed the patient's pelvic pain as constipation; *Gardiner v Mounfield* [1990] 1 Med. L.R. 205, where the defendant dismissed the possibility that the claimant, who was overweight and had a history of amenorrhoea, was pregnant; *Tucker v Tees Health Authority* [1995] 6 Med. L.R. 54, where the defendant was held negligent for performing a laparotomy to remove a presumed ovarian cyst without first conducting an ultrasound scan to check whether the claimant was pregnant; *Bagley v North Hertfordshire Health Authority* (1986) 136 N.L.J. 1014, on the failure to perform blood tests during pregnancy when it was known that the claimant suffered from blood incompatibility.

condition may be such that he should be admitted to hospital for observation and tests.[69] In *Pierre v Marshall*[70] a general practitioner who failed to screen a pregnant woman for gestational diabetes, contrary to the recommendations of the Alberta Medical Association and the Society of Obstetricians and Gynaecologists of Canada, was held to have been negligent. Moreover, the defendant also failed to do an ultrasound scan to confirm the expected size of the baby, despite his suspicion that the foetus was slightly larger than it should have been at 36 weeks. Screening for gestational diabetes is not routine practice in the UK, however, and a doctor is not necessarily negligent for failing to undertake the standard test for that condition (a glucose tolerance test). The question of whether a pregnant woman should be tested for gestational diabetes is a matter of clinical judgment involving a number of factors.[71] In *X. and Y. v Pal*[72] it was accepted that an obstetrician who failed to test a patient for syphilis during her pregnancy was negligent. On the other hand, a doctor should not be criticised for a refusal to offer a CT scan, or any other diagnostic procedure, which he considered inappropriate just because the patient was willing to pay and wanted reassurance.[73]

4–025   Where tests are required there may be negligence in carrying out the tests,[74] in failing to interpret the results properly,[75] or in mislaying or mixing up the samples, or where the pathologist fails to inform the doctor properly or at all of the test results,[76] or where the doctor fails to read the report.[77] In some circumstances a consultant physician may have a responsibility actively to seek out the results of blood tests, rather than leaving a general instruction to junior staff to inform him if any of the results are

---

[69] *Dale v Munthali* (1976) 78 D.L.R. (3d) 588; affirmed (1978) 90 D.L.R. (3d) 763 (Ont. C.A.); *Barnett v Chelsea and Kensington Hospital Management Committee* [1968] 1 All E.R. 1068, 1073.

[70] [1994] 8 W.W.R. 478 (Alta. Q.B.).

[71] *Hallatt v North West Anglia Health Authority* [1998] Lloyd's Rep. Med. 197, CA.

[72] (1991) 23 N.S.W.L.R. 26; [1992] 3 Med. L.R. 195 (N.S.W.C.A.).

[73] *Rhodes v Spokes and Farbridge* [1996] 7 Med. L.R. 135, 146.

[74] *Robertson v Nottingham Health Authority* [1997] 8 Med. L.R. 1, CA—the failure of midwives to check cardiotacograph scans of fetal heart rate at regular 15–30 minute intervals resulted in poor quality traces, making interpretation of the results difficult, and caused culpable delay in proceeding to a Caesarian section delivery.

[75] See, *e.g.*, *Fraser v Vancouver General Hospital* (1951) 3 W.W.R. 337 (B.C.C.A.); [1952] 3 D.L.R. 785 (S.C.C.), and *R. v Croydon Health Authority* [1998] P.I.Q.R. Q26; [1998] Lloyd's Rep. Med. 44 on the negligent interpretation of X-rays; *Rance v Mid-Downs Health Authority* [1991] 1 Q.B. 587, on an allegedly negligent failure to interpret an ultrasound scan of a foetus, which was subsequently discovered to be suffering from spina bifida; *B. v P.* (1991) 2 *AVMA Medical & Legal Journal* (No. 3) p. 8, on a general practitioner's failure to interpret a positive test for Rubella in a pregnant woman; *Penney, Palmer and Cannon v East Kent Health Authority* [2000] Lloyd's Rep. Med. 41, CA—failure to interpret smear tests for cervical cancer accurately.

[76] Allegations to this effect were made in *McKay v Essex Area Health Authority* [1982] Q.B. 1166; see also *Thomsen v Davison* [1975] Qd. R. 93, on the pathologist's duty to communicate the results of testing to the doctor; *Gregory v Pembrokeshire Health Authority* [1989] 1 Med. L.R. 81, CA, on the doctor's duty to communicate results to the patient (see para. 4–038 n. 14).

[77] *Fredette v Wiebe* [1986] 5 W.W.R. 222 (B.C.S.C.).

abnormal.[78] On the other hand, a misleading pathology report may result in a finding that a surgeon was not negligent in embarking on radical surgery in a case of suspected cancer.[79] Where a hospital sends the results of blood tests to a general practitioner it is a reasonable assumption that the hospital doctors are aware of the information that has been sent, and that in sending the information the hospital is sharing information and not indicating that the responsibility for acting upon it is being passed to the general practitioner. In these circumstances, it is reasonable for the general practitioner to assume that the hospital doctors will take the test results into consideration in conducting their diagnostic investigations.[80]

In addition to diagnostic tests, the nature of the treatment or medication being given to the patient may require that the patient be tested in advance for an allergic reaction or that the patient be carefully monitored for an adverse drug reaction. In *Robinson v Post Office*,[81] for example, a doctor who departed from standard practice at the time by giving the claimant an anti-tetanus injection without first administering a test dose for an allergic reaction was held to have been negligent, although the action failed on the issue of causation. Similarly, in *Male v Hopmans*[82] the claimant became deaf due to a side-effect of a drug administered to treat an infection in his knee. The manufacturer's instructions warned the doctor that the drug was particularly dangerous in the presence of impaired renal function, and the claimant exhibited some evidence of kidney dysfunction which, it was held, should have been investigated further by testing. The manufacturer also suggested that audiometric tests of hearing should be made prior to and during the course of therapy, because evidence of impairment to hearing can be detected by the audiometer before clinical signs develop. This precaution was particularly important when excessive doses were being given. The doctor was found negligent in failing to prescribe such tests either before or during the course of treatment, even though facilities for conducting them were readily available at the hospital.[83] On the other hand, where a risk associated with

4–026

---

[78] *Panther v Wharton* (2001, QBD; unreported): "In the abstract, the proposition that a consultant is entitled to rely on junior staff fulfilling his instructions may be unobjectionable. However, in my judgment, the instruction in this case has to be considered in the context of what should have been in Dr Wharton's mind at the conclusion of his examination ... Given my finding that he should have at least suspected severe vascular compromise, the cause of which was unknown, his investigation was, without the outstanding test results, incomplete. The test results were important ... The decision as to whether the results or any of them were abnormal was his decision as consultant, not that of junior colleagues", *per* Peter Heppel QC (sitting as judge of the High Court).

[79] *Abbas v Kenney* [1996] 7 Med. L.R. 47.

[80] *Weir v Graham* [2002] EWHC 2291 (Q.B.).

[81] [1974] 2 All E.R. 737. For a discussion of allergic reactions associated with anaesthesia see Fisher (1990) 6 J. of the M.D.U. 4, stating that test dosing in this context is inherently invalid, though the availability of resuscitation facilities and drugs may affect the patient's chance of survival to such a reaction.

[82] (1967) 64 D.L.R. (2d) 105, 113–115 (Ont. C.A.).

[83] See also *Marshall v Rogers* [1943] 4 D.L.R. 68 (B.C.C.A.), para. 4–045; *cf. Battersby v Tottman* (1985) 37 S.A.S.R. 524, where following a failure to monitor the known side-effects of a drug (a risk of serious and permanent eye damage) the defendant was held not negligent in the circumstances.

the treatment is remote it will probably not be negligent to omit to test for the condition.[84]

(6) Failure to consult or refer patient to a specialist

4–027   Where a doctor is unable to diagnose or treat the patient he will be under a duty either to seek advice from an appropriate specialist or refer the patient on to a specialist. If he attempts to diagnose or treat the patient himself he is, in effect, undertaking work beyond his competence, for which he will be held liable if harm results.[85] For example, in *Poole v Morgan*[86] the defendant ophthalmologist was inadequately trained in the use of a laser, although he had often used it in his practice. The treatment that he gave to the claimant was usually performed by a retina vitreous specialist. The defendant had to come up to the standard of that specialty, and since he was unable to do so he had a duty to refer the claimant to such a specialist. It has also been said that where a doctor suspects cancer he should immediately refer the patient to a specialist or arrange for an immediate biopsy. A failure to do so was held to be negligent.[87] Even a consultant in a specialist field may come across a problem that he has never previously encountered and accordingly may have a responsibility to seek advice.[88]

---

[84] *Warren v Greig* (1935) *The Lancet*, vol. 1, 330, where a patient who was suffering from acute myeloid leukaemia, which was a rare disease, died from excessive bleeding following an operation to remove his teeth. The defendants were not liable for not testing the patient's blood prior to the operation.

[85] See para. 3–077. It may well be a nice question whether a doctor does have sufficient experience in the relevant field: see, *e.g.*, *Mose v North West Hertfordshire Health Authority* (1987, CA; unreported).

[86] [1987] 3 W.W.R. 217; *Layden v Cope* (1984) 28 C.C.L.T. 140, 148, para. 4–021 above, *per* Rowbotham J.: "Their most critical error in judgment was their failure, when faced with a medical problem they were unable to resolve, to consult with or refer the patient to a medical specialist until it was too late to save the patient's foot"; *Lankenau v Dutton* (1986) 37 C.C.L.T. 213; (1991) 79 D.L.R. (4th) 707 (B.C.C.A.).

[87] *Wilson v Vancouver Hockey Club* (1983) 5 D.L.R. (4th) 282, 288; affirmed (1985) 22 D.L.R. (4th) 516 (B.C.C.A.). On the failure to diagnose cancer see *Sutton v Population Services Family Planning Programme Ltd*, *The Times*, November 7, 1981; *Judge v Huntingdon Health Authority* [1995] 6 Med. L.R. 223; *Taylor v West Kent Health Authority* [1997] 8 Med. L.R. 251—negligent failure to interpret a cytology report correctly; doctors should have sought clarification of the report, and should have been alerted to the need for further investigations; *Penney, Palmer and Cannon v East Kent Health Authority* [2000] Lloyd's Rep. Med. 41, CA; *Lindores v Barnet Health Authority* (1992) 3 AVMA Medical & Legal Journal (No. 1) p. 12; Baum (1991) 2 AVMA Medical & Legal Journal (No. 4) p. 10, on delay in diagnosing breast cancer; *Stacey v Chiddy* [1993] 4 Med. L.R. 216 (N.S.W.S.C.); affirmed [1993] 4 Med. L.R. 345 (N.S.W.C.A.); *Gordon v Wilson* [1992] 3 Med. L.R. 401 (Court of Session), where an allegation that a general practitioner, having noted and recorded certain clinical symptoms, failed to recognise the need for urgent specialist investigation which would have revealed that the patient needed surgery to remove a benign brain tumour, was rejected on the facts. For cases in which the defendants were responsible for failing to diagnose brain tumours see: *Mitchell v Tunbridge Wells and Eastbourne Health Authorities* (1990) 1 AVMA Medical & Legal Journal (No. 4) p. 7 and *Guyer v Cassidy* (1990) 1 AVMA Medical & Legal Journal (No. 4) p. 9.

[88] *Gascoine v Ian Sheridan & Co* [1994] 5 Med. L.R. 437, 447, *per* Mitchell J., where a consultant gynaecologist was faced with an unexpected finding of an invasive carcinoma following the performance of a simple hysterectomy. His obligation was to seek specialist advice

In *MacDonald v York County Hospital*[89] the claimant sustained a severe   4–028
fracture of the ankle in a road traffic accident. The defendant, a general
surgeon, performed a closed reduction of the fracture and put the leg in a cast
as a temporary measure, intending to perform an open reduction at a later
stage. At the time of the emergency treatment there was no pulse in the ankle,
and this was put down to a spasm of the artery resulting from the trauma
which was expected to clear up in a few hours. The next day the condition of
the claimant's foot and toes caused concern to the nurses, which they
expressed to the defendant when he visited the claimant on two occasions.
The defendant did nothing about the condition of the foot, which ultimately
had to be amputated because it became gangrenous as a result of circulatory
impairment. The conclusion was that the defendant knew that he did not
know the cause of the impairment and he should have taken the advice of a
cardiovascular specialist or had the claimant attended by a specialist:

> ". . . when he found himself unable to diagnose the cause of the symp-
> toms displayed in the plaintiff's foot, I consider that he failed in his duty
> to the plaintiff in not seeking the advice or collaboration of such a
> specialist, or at least in failing to recommend the desirability of such a
> course of action . . ."[90]

The difficulty for inexperienced practitioners is that their very lack of   4–029
experience may prevent them from knowing when they are out of their
depth.[91] Nonetheless they will be held responsible for negligently failing to
refer patients to more senior or experienced colleagues. In *Payne v St. Helier
Group Hospital Management Committee*[92] a casualty officer allowed a

---

(n.88 contd.) because he had no specific postgraduate specialist training in the field of
gynaecological cancer, and none of the other consultants at the hospital had any particular
interest in gynaecological cancer; *Robinson v Jacklin* [1996] 7 Med. L.R. 83, QBD—consultant paediatrician failed to refer a child to another hospital with a specialist neurosurgi-
cal team who would have been better placed to make a diagnosis.

[89] (1973) 41 D.L.R. (3d) 321 (Ont. C.A.); affirmed sub nom. *Vail v MacDonald* (1976) 66
D.L.R. (3d) 530 (S.C.C.).

[90] *ibid.* at pp. 349–350, *per* Dubin J.A. See *Ares v Venner* (1970) 14 D.L.R. (3d) 4 (S.C.C.)
which also involved the amputation of the claimant's leg as a result of the defendant negligently ignoring the classic symptoms of circulatory impairment. The normal practice of the
profession in such cases was to split the cast, and if no relief is obtained refer to a specialist
or, if equipped to do so, explore further to ascertain the cause of the problem; *Badger v
Surkan* (1970) 16 D.L.R. (3d) 146 (Sask. Q.B.); *Bayliss v Blagg* (1954) 1 B.M.J. 709.

[91] See the comments of Browne-Wilkinson V.-C. in *Wilsher v Essex Area Health Authority*
[1987] Q.B. 730, 777.

[92] *The Times*, November 12, 1952; *cf. Parkinson v West Cumberland Hospital Management
Committee* (1955) 1 B.M.J. 977, where a newly qualified casualty officer discharged a
patient who had complained of chest pains, and the patient died of a coronary thrombosis
fifteen minutes later. The casualty officer was held not to have been negligent, either to discharge the patient or by refraining from seeking a more experienced view; *Richardson v
Kitching* [1995] 6 Med. L.R. 257, QBD—a general practitioner was not negligent, on the
facts, in failing to refer a patient who presented with long-standing deafness for specialist
treatment sooner than he did; but in *Marriott v West Midlands Health Authority* [1999]
Lloyd's Rep. Med. 23 a general practitioner was found negligent in failing to refer a patient
with a serious head injury to hospital for neurological tests (discussed at para. 3–031).

patient who had been kicked in the stomach by a horse to leave the casualty department and go home. The patient subsequently died from peritonitis, and the casualty officer was found to have been negligent in not admitting the patient for examination by a consultant. Similarly, in *Fraser v Vancouver General Hospital*[93] a patient who attended the casualty department of a hospital following a road accident presented with cuts on his forehead and pain and stiffness in the back of his neck. He was examined by the junior doctors in charge, X-rays were taken and examined by the doctors. The patient was then discharged from the hospital, but later he died as a result of a dislocated fracture of the neck which was apparent on the X-rays but went unnoticed by the doctors at the hospital. The defendants were held liable. The patient should not have been discharged. In view of their limited knowledge and experience it was negligence to attempt to read the X-rays at all. If the doctors were not competent to read the X-rays then they ought to have called in one of the specialist radiologists who were available for such an eventuality.

4–030   Not all errors in failing to refer the patient to a specialist stem from the doctor's inexperience. In *Webster v Chapman*[94] the patient became pregnant while she was taking a drug which was potentially harmful to the foetus if taken during the first trimester of pregnancy. She consulted her general practitioner who, believing that she was approximately 11 weeks pregnant, advised her to keep taking the drug because it was too late in the pregnancy to make any difference to the foetus. Subsequently, on the basis of an ultrasound scan, an obstetrician estimated she was 11½ weeks pregnant, not the 14 weeks that she would have been had the general practitioner's estimate been correct. He advised her to stop taking the drug immediately, but the delay had caused the mother to take the drug for a further three weeks. The child was born with serious physical and mental disabilities. The Manitoba Court of Appeal held that the general practitioner had been negligent in failing to consult with a specialist immediately to obtain advice as to the patient continuing on the drug once he knew she was pregnant, because the general practitioner was uncertain as to foetal age and was aware of the risk of foetal abnormalities if a mother took the drug during the first trimester of the pregnancy. He was also aware of the risk to the mother of sudden withdrawal of the drug and the need for consultation with a specialist. This should have alerted any prudent and diligent general practitioner to the need for the consultation to be immediate and for disclosure to the mother of both the risks involved and the treatment options available.[95]

---

[93] (1951) 3 W.W.R. 337 (B.C.C.A.); affirmed [1952] 3 D.L.R. 785 (S.C.C.).
[94] (1997) 155 D.L.R. (4th) 82 (Man. C.A.).
[95] See also *Hutchinson v Leeds Health Authority*, (2000) unreported, QBD, where an expert haematological team treating a teenager for leukaemia were held to have been negligent in failing to call in a surgical team to investigate the patient's highly abnormal bowel function.

(7) Overtesting

Claims that are sometimes made about defensive medicine suggest that **4–031** defensive practices tend to be manifested in the form of unnecessary diagnostic tests. If a diagnostic test or procedure is unnecessary by reference to the standards of the medical profession, *i.e.* according to the standards of the reasonably competent doctor exercising and professing to have that skill, it will be negligence to perform it, and it will be actionable if the patient suffers injury as a consequence.[96] This was the essence of the claimant's action in *Maynard v West Midlands Regional Health Authority*,[97] namely that the defendants had undertaken an unnecessary diagnostic operation during which an inherent risk of the procedure materialised, causing her injuries. The action failed because on the evidence a responsible body of professional opinion agreed that the operation was justified in the circumstances. It was not suggested in *Maynard* that the doctors were acting "defensively," but ultimately the issue of "defensive medicine" is merely a question of the doctor's motive for performing the procedure, and motives may be mixed.[98] It matters not whether the doctor was misguidedly seeking to protect himself from litigation or whether he simply misjudged the nature of the patient's symptoms; if no doctor of ordinary skill and acting with ordinary care would have considered the procedure to be called for it is negligence to perform it. This would apply with as much force to unnecessary diagnostic tests, such as X-rays, as it would to unnecessary operations, such as Caesarian sections.[99]

---

[96] *Leonard v Knott* [1978] 5 W.W.R. 511 (B.C.S.C.); see para. 4–010.

[97] [1984] 1 W.L.R. 634.

[98] See, *e.g.*, *Robinson v Post Office* [1974] 2 All E.R. 737, 743–744. Orr L.J. said, at p. 745, that it would be "asking too much of human nature" that the doctor should have excluded the possibility of being sued from his mind when he decided to give the patient an anti-tetanus injection, but he also weighed up the competing medical considerations in reaching his decision. In *Schanczi v Singh* [1988] 2 W.W.R. 465 (Alta. Q.B.) the defendant was held negligent for failing to attempt conservative treatment before resorting to spinal surgery. The operation was "unnecessary" in the circumstances, but this was not attributed to defensive practice.

[99] The Royal College of Radiologists and the National Radiological Protection Board have estimated that unnecessary X-rays cause between 100 and 250 deaths a year: see *Patient dose reduction in diagnostic radiology*, H.M.S.O., 1990; Gifford (1990) 301 B.M.J. 451. Poor management, excessive dosages and unnecessary repeat X-rays are blamed. See further the Royal College of Radiologists Working Party, *Influence of the Royal College of Radiologists' guidelines on hospital practice* (1992) 304 B.M.J. 740, which concluded that at least a fifth of radiological examinations carried out in NHS hospitals are clinically unhelpful, at a cost of some £50m to £60m *per annum*. Hoyte (1994) 1 Med. Law Int. 261, 266 comments that: "it can only be a matter of time before 'unnecessary' exposure to investigative radiation becomes a cause for claim in its own right." Of course, the fact that a fifth of radiological investigations are clinically unhelpful does not necessarily mean that they were undertaken for the purpose of avoiding litigation. Spurgeon (2001) 323 B.M.J. 185 reported that radiation doses in CT scans could be halved. For discussion of the "10 commandments of accident and emergency radiology" see Touquet, Driscoll and Nicholson (1995) 310 B.M.J. 642. For an updated report on the exposure of patients to diagnostic radiation see the National Radiological Protection Board, *Radiation Exposure of the UK Population from Medical and Dental X-ray Examinations*, 2002 (available at *www.nrpb.org/publications/w_series_reports*). See further National Radiological Protection Board, *Principles for the Protection of Patients and Volunteers During Clinical Magnetic Resonance Diagnostic Procedures*, 1991, (available at *www.nrpb.org/publications/documents_of_nrpb*).

3. FAILURES OF ADVICE AND COMMUNICATION

4–032   A lack of communication is often said to be at the heart of many medical negligence actions. This comment is usually directed to the fact that a patient who has suffered a medical accident may initiate proceedings because following the incident health care professionals have refused to discuss the circumstances frankly with the patient or his family. This results in a breakdown of the doctor/patient relationship, and the patient is left with the feeling that the only way to find out what happened is to resort to the courts.[1] Failures of communication, however, whether between doctor and patient or between practitioners, may frequently be the source of the initial injury.

(1) Failure to warn about risks

4–033   It is axiomatic that a patient will normally need some information about the nature of his medical condition and the form of treatment that the doctor proposes in order to decide whether to accept the treatment. This is required both for the purpose of the patient giving a valid consent to treatment and as part of the doctor's duty of care to advise of the inherent risks of the proposed treatment, so that the patient can make an informed decision. The legal consequences of this type of communication failure are considered in chapter 6. In some circumstances, the nature of the "treatment" is such that it simply involves advice to the patient for the purpose of enabling the patient to make certain decisions, such as whether it is safe to become pregnant or whether to terminate a pregnancy.[2]

4–034   In addition, however, to the doctor's duty of care to warn patients in advance of the risks of treatment, it is possible that in some circumstances the practitioner will come under a duty to inform the patient that something has gone wrong with the treatment.[3] In *Gerber v Pines*[4] Du Parcq J. said that as a general rule a patient was entitled to be told at once if the doctor had

---

[1] For example, in *Stamos v Davies* (1985) 21 D.L.R. (4th) 507, 519 Krever J. commented that: ". . . the underlying cause of both the misadventure and of the litigation is a less than satisfactory physician-patient relationship arising out of the failure on the part of the physician to take the patient into his confidence . . ." See further, Simanowitz, "Medical Accidents: The Problem and the Challenge" in Byrne (ed.), *Medicine in Contemporary Society: King's College Studies* 1986–87, p. 117.

[2] See *Anderson v Forth Valley Health Board* 1998 S.L.T. 588; (1997) 44 B.M.L.R. 108 (Court of Session, Outer House) where the allegation of negligence was that the doctors had failed to give advice and information about genetic risks and had failed to refer the pursuers to genetic counselling. See also *Enright v Kwun and Blackpool Victoria Hospital NHS Trust* [2003] EWHC 1000 (Q.B.); *The Times*, May 20, 2003 – negligent omission to counsel a pregnant woman of 37 to undergo an amniocentisis test.

[3] In some circumstances solicitors have a duty to advise their client that they have been negligent and that the client should seek independent legal advice: *The Guide to the Professional Conduct of Solicitors*, 1999, Chapter 29.09 (available in updated form at *www.guide-online.lawsociety.org.uk*). This professional duty may also translate into a duty of care in negligence: see, e.g., *Gold v Mincoff Science & Gold (A Firm)* [2001] Lloyd's Rep P.N. 423 at [98] to [102].

[4] (1934) 79 S.J. 13.

left some foreign object in his body. This view was disapproved, however, in the Irish case of *Daniels v Heskin*[5] where it was said that there was no abstract duty to tell patients what is wrong with them, or in particular to say that a needle had been left in their body. Everything depended upon the circumstances—the character of the patient, her health, her social position, her intelligence, the nature of the tissue in which the needle is embedded, the possibility of subsequent infection, the arrangements made for future observation and care, and so on.[6] The disclosure of such information was, accordingly, a matter within the discretion of the doctor's professional judgment.

It may be that this approach reflects the attitudes of an earlier age, when medical paternalism was more widely accepted than it is today.[7] The more recent trend is for the courts to insist that patients do have a right to know what has been done to them, particularly where something has gone wrong, just as they have the right to know what is going to be done to them prior to treatment. For example, in *Lee v South West Thames Regional Health Authority*[8] Sir John Donaldson M.R. pointed out that following *Sidaway v Bethlem Royal Hospital Governors*[9] a doctor has a duty to answer a patient's questions about proposed treatment, and he could see no reason why the position should be any different where the patient asks what treatment he has in fact had. Why, asked his Lordship, is the duty different before the treatment from what it is afterwards?[10] Subsequently, in *Naylor v Preston Area Health Authority*[11] his Lordship said that:

4–035

> "I personally think that in professional negligence cases, and in particular in medical negligence cases, there is a duty of candour resting on the professional man . . . In my judgment, still admittedly and regretfully *obiter*, it is but one aspect of the general duty of care, arising out of the patient/medical practitioner or hospital authority relationship and gives rise to rights both in contract and in tort."

In Canada the courts have treated this issue as part and parcel of the doctor's duty of care to the patient. In *Stamos v Davies*[12] the defendant, while performing a lung biopsy, punctured the claimant's spleen. The claimant asked what the defendant had obtained from the biopsy, and the defendant said simply that he had not obtained what he wanted, but he did not inform the claimant of the ruptured spleen. The claimant was discharged

4–036

---

5 [1954] I.R. 73, Supreme Court.
6 *ibid.* at p. 87, *per* Kingsmill Moore J.
7 In *Walsh v Family Planning Services Ltd* [1992] 1 I.R. 496, 520 (Supreme Court of Ireland) McCarthy J. commented that the observations of Kingsmill Moore J. on matters such as the social position of the patient or the class and standard of education of the patient and her husband were difficult to understand as relevant criteria: "The learned judge may well have been offending against the very principle that he was seeking to uphold."
8 [1985] 2 All E.R. 385.
9 [1985] A.C. 871; see para. 6–108.
10 [1985] 2 All E.R. 385, 389; see the quotation in para. 10–135.
11 [1987] 2 All E.R. 353, 360.
12 (1986) 21 D.L.R. (4th) 507 (Ont. H.C.); Robertson (1987) 25 Alberta L. Rev. 215.

from hospital but had to be admitted as an emergency three days later, due to the bleeding into his abdominal cavity. The spleen was removed surgically, and the claimant recovered uneventfully. Krever J. said that he found the reasoning of Sir John Donaldson M.R. in *Lee* compelling, and held that the defendant was under a duty to inform the claimant that the spleen had been punctured. The defendant's failure to be candid was a breach of that duty.

4–037   The General Medical Council now gives explicit guidance to doctors on the issue of informing patients or relatives when something has gone wrong with the treatment. Paragraph 22 of *Good Medical Practice*,[13] states that:

> "You must explain fully and promptly to the patient what has happened and the likely long- and short-term effects. When appropriate you should offer an apology. If the patient is an adult who lacks capacity, the explanation should be given to a person with responsibility for the patient, or the patient's partner, close relative or a friend who has been involved in the care of the patient, unless you have reason to believe the patient would have objected to the disclosure. In the case of children the situation should be explained honestly to those with parental responsibility and to the child, if the child has the maturity to understand the issues."

Of course, the GMC's guidance does not create an entitlement to damages for its breach, though a doctor might be found guilty of professional misconduct if he failed to comply.

4–038   Even in the context of a legal duty to disclose that something has gone wrong with the treatment, the difficulty is in proving that the breach of duty caused the claimant damage.[14] The claimant's ignorance that something untoward has occurred will rarely contribute to any further loss, and since the damage has already occurred the failure to be candid is not a cause of the harm.[15] This was the position in *Stamos v Davies*, where it was held that there was no causal connection: informing the patient of the damage to his

---

[13] GMC *Good Medical Practice*, May 2001. See also para. 23 dealing with the death of a patient.

[14] Although a negligent omission to inform the patient that diagnostic tests have failed to produce any results clearly could cause damage, since the patient may make the erroneous assumption that everything is normal. In *Gregory v Pembrokeshire Health Authority* [1989] 1 Med. L.R. 81, CA, a patient who was never informed that an amniocentesis test had failed to produce a result subsequently gave birth to a Down's Syndrome baby. She alleged that if she had been informed she would have insisted on a second test being performed, and, had it proved positive, would have had an abortion. The omission to inform, the result of an administrative mix-up, was held negligent, but the action failed on the ground of causation. On the evidence, she would have accepted the doctor's advice not to have the test repeated at a late stage in her pregnancy. See also *Fredette v Wiebe* [1986] 5 W.W.R. 222 (B.C.S.C.), where the failure to inform the patient stemmed from the doctor's negligence in not reading the pathologist's report; *Arndt v Smith* (1997) 148 D.L.R. (4th) 48 (S.C.C.), where the failure to inform the patient was the product of "classic medical paternalism," but the action failed on causation since the mother would not have had a termination of the pregnancy.

[15] *Daniels v Heskin* [1954] I.R. 73, 81, 88. Even in *Gerber v Pines* (1934) 79 S.J. 13 the claimant was awarded only £5 damages.

spleen in the course of the biopsy would not have saved the spleen, which was doomed from the moment it was injured.[16]

In an appropriate case, however, the failure to inform may cause further injury if, for example, the patient takes a risk that he would otherwise have avoided, or if the patient's ignorance leads to delay in diagnosis (resulting in additional harm) if an emergency should subsequently arise as a result of the injury of which he is unaware. This point was accepted in *Daniels v Heskin* where Kingsmill Moore J. said that a doctor would not always be justified in keeping such knowledge to himself, since he has a duty to take precautions against further injury to the patient. The nature of the precautions will vary with the circumstances of the case, but might include informing the patient to enable him to avoid unnecessary risks.[17] In *Kiley-Nikkel v Danais*[18] the claimant's breast was removed following a mistaken diagnosis of cancer, but she was not informed of the error, with the result that she sought follow-up treatment for cancer in another locality and had to live with the belief that she had cancer for a considerable time. Part of the award of damages was for the psychiatric harm resulting from non-disclosure of the error, since the consequences of the error in diagnosis would have been much less serious had she known immediately that she was not suffering from cancer.

4–039

In *Pittman Estate v Bain*[19] a patient, Mr Pittman, received a blood transfusion contaminated with HIV during the course of heart surgery in December 1984. In November 1985 the Canadian Red Cross Society, which had collected the donated blood, discovered that the donor was HIV positive, but it was not until June 1987 that the Red Cross Society traced the donor's potentially infected 1984 donation to the hospital where Mr Pittman had had his surgery. The hospital did not trace the blood to the transfusion given to Mr Pittman until February 1989, and informed his general practitioner in April 1989. The general practitioner decided not to inform Mr Pittman of the chance (put at about 37 per cent) that he had contracted HIV from the blood transfusion, because he was concerned about Mr Pittman's cardiac condition and his mental health, and assumed, wrongly, that his patient was not having sexual intercourse with his wife. Mr Pittman died of an AIDS related condition in March 1990, and in April the general practitioner learned that his patient had been HIV positive. In September 1990

4–040

---

[16] The defendant was found liable on a different ground; see para. 4–044, below. See also *Keuper v McMullin* (1987) 30 D.L.R. (4th) 408, where a dentist left a small piece of a drill bit in the patient's tooth without informing her and without discussing with her the various alternatives open. The tooth remained asymptomatic for eighteen months. The New Brunswick Court of Appeal held that the defendant was under a duty to disclose the incident to the patient since she was alert and able to be consulted about the alternatives, but the action failed on the grounds of causation; see further *Fletcher v Bench* (1973) 4 B.M.J. 17, CA, on broken drill bits.

[17] [1954] I.R. 73, 88; see also *Stamos v Davies* (1985) 21 D.L.R. (4th) 507, 523: "There is no suggestion in the evidence that anything the plaintiff did at home caused the spleen to rebleed and thus cause its removal." Clearly, if there was evidence to this effect the result would have been different.

[18] (1992) 16 C.C.L.T. (2d) 290 (Qué.S.C.).

[19] (1994) 112 D.L.R. (4th) 257 (Ont. Ct., Gen. Div.).

Mrs Pittman learned that she was HIV positive, having contracted the virus from her husband in the last year of his life. It was held that the general practitioner was negligent for failing to inform a patient that he had received a blood transfusion that was potentially contaminated with HIV. If Mr Pittman had known about his HIV status there were steps that he could have taken which would have extended his life expectancy by two years, and he would have told his wife and taken appropriate precautions to avoid infecting her. In addition, both the Canadian Red Cross Society and the hospital at which Mr Pittman had received the transfusion were held to have been negligent in the design and implementation of a "lookback" program, which sought to identify individuals who had received blood donated before there was an HIV antibody test by a donor who on a subsequent donation was found to be HIV positive.[20]

4–041   Cases in which, due to the defendant's negligence, the claimant is unaware that she is or might become pregnant, do not present causation difficulties. For example, in *Scuriaga v Powell*[21] the defendant performed a lawful abortion on the claimant, but failed to terminate the pregnancy. She subsequently gave birth to a healthy child. After the abortion operation the defendant assured the claimant that all was well, although he had found no evidence of foetal parts and believed that she had a potentially dangerous disorder. When the claimant became aware that she was still pregnant the defendant told her that the operation had failed because she had a structural defect. "In fact," said Watkins J. "the doctor botched the operation, then seized on a speculative and dangerous explanation for his failure. He should have placed the matter before a consultant without delay." If he had told the claimant the true position within two or three weeks she would have agreed to a second operation, but the delay had increased the risk to her health. She refused a second termination and gave birth to a healthy child.[22] The defendant was held liable for the claimant's loss of earnings, loss of marriage prospects and pain and suffering.[23]

---

[20] The negligence of the Canadian Red Cross Society consisted of: not responding promptly to the serious risks to recipients of potentially infected blood; delaying the introduction of a requirement that hospitals maintain suitable transfusion records (by unit number); failing to bring home to the hospital the urgency of the lookback program and the potential risk to recipients by monitoring the hospital's progress in implementing lookback and the eventual outcome of the warning to be given to the recipient; and failing to write to general practitioners, cardiologists or other specialists, or hospital cardiac patients to give them information about the risks of transfusion associated AIDS and counselling about the ramifications. See *ibid*. at p. 377. The negligence of the hospital consisted of: failing to consider alternative methods to the lengthy and cumbersome lookback procedure that they adopted; failing to follow up in writing a telephone conversation with the patient's general practitioner informing him of the patient's possible HIV status; and failing to ensure that the general practitioner had sufficient information to give an adequate warning to the patient. See *ibid*. at pp. 381–383.

[21] (1979) 123 S.J. 406; affirmed (1980, CA; unreported).

[22] Note that following *McFarlane v Tayside Health Board* [2000] 2 A.C. 59 damages will not be awarded for the costs associated with bringing up a healthy child. See paras 2–039 *et seq*.

[23] *Fredette v Wiebe* [1986] 5 W.W.R. 222 (B.C.S.C.) is another example, where the claimant was unaware that an abortion operation had failed to terminate her pregnancy, and subsequently decided to continue with the pregnancy. The defendant doctor was also unaware

Similarly, in *Cryderman v Ringrose*[24] the defendant doctor failed to **4–042** inform the claimant that a sterilisation operation had not succeeded, and she believed she was sterile. She subsequently became pregnant and underwent an abortion by hysterectomy. If the claimant had been aware of the unreliability of the procedure used by the defendant, and had been told that the treatment had not rendered her sterile (as the defendant knew) she could have tried other methods of contraception or sterilisation. The defendant was held liable for this omission.

(2) Failure to give proper instructions to the patient

A doctor will frequently need the patient's co-operation, in performing an **4–043** examination, for example, or administering the treatment. This may be as simple as requiring the patient to keep still or instructing the patient about taking medication in the right quantity and at the right times of day. It may also be necessary to give the patient a warning as to any danger signs that he should look out for (*e.g.* as to the side-effects of a drug or the symptoms that indicate that his condition is deteriorating) with instructions as to what should be done if they occur, such as stopping the medication or seeking medical assistance immediately.[25] Sometimes this will be absolutely vital. In these circumstances the doctor will be under a duty to take special care in giving the patient instructions in comprehensible terms, and making sure that the patient understands both the instructions and the importance of strictly adhering to them.[26] This obligation is not limited to advice about treatment, but can extend to advice about the risks that the patient's lifestyle poses to his health. Thus, it can be negligent to fail to advise a patient who is a heavy drinker and at serious risk of developing fatal cirrhosis of the liver, to stop drinking alcohol,[27] or to fail to advise an epileptic patient not to drive a motor vehicle.[28]

(n.23 contd.) that the abortion had not succeeded because she negligently failed to examine a post-operative pathologist's report. In *Cherry v Borsman* (1991) 75 D.L.R. (4th) 668; affirmed (1992) 94 D.L.R. (4th) 487 (B.C.C.A.) the defendant performed an abortion operation but negligently failed to terminate the claimant's pregnancy. He also negligently failed to identify the fact that the claimant was still pregnant, and by the time this was discovered it was too late for a legal therapeutic abortion. The defendant was held liable both to the mother in respect of the pain and suffering and the costs of raising an "unwanted" child, and to the child for the injuries inflicted upon it during the course of the failed termination.

[24] [1977] 3 W.W.R. 109; affirmed [1978] 3 W.W.R. 481 (Alta. S.C. Appellate Div.); *cf. McLennan v Newcastle Health Authority* [1992] 3 Med. L.R. 215, QBD, where it was held not to be negligent to let the claimant leave hospital with the impression that she had undergone a successful sterilisation.

[25] See, *e.g.*, *Crossman v Stewart* (1977) 82 D.L.R. (3d) 677 where the defendant doctor was held negligent for failing to identify the indications of side-effects. For the position where the risk of further injury is the result of something having gone wrong with the patient's treatment see para. 4–034.

[26] See Karp (1993) 9 J. of the M.D.U. 26.

[27] *Hutchinson v Epson & St. Helier NHS Trust* [2002] EWHC 2363 (QB). It has to be demonstrated, of course, that the deceased would probably have heeded the warning, which in an appropriate case may have to be in rather stark terms, such as: "If you do not stop drinking you will be dead in 12 months."

[28] *Spillane v Wasserman* (1992) 13 C.C.L.T. (2d) 267 (Ont. H.C.).

4-044   A failure to inform the patient how to avoid the potential dangers involved in the treatment will be negligence. In *Stamos v Davies*[29] the defendant was performing a lung biopsy, a procedure which required complete co-operation by the patient, in effect, to keep still while it was carried out. The defendant punctured the patient's spleen because, the judge held, the patient moved. The defendant was held negligent because he had failed to take the patient into his confidence by more, and effective, communication with him about what was required of him in this situation. Again, in *Clarke v Adams*[30] the claimant was being treated for a fibrositic condition of the heel. He sustained a burning injury resulting in the leg being amputated below the knee. The defendant physiotherapist had given a warning to the claimant before administering the treatment in these terms: "When I turn on the machine I want you to experience a comfortable warmth and nothing more; if you do I want you to tell me." Slade J. held the defendant liable on the basis that the warning, although the very warning that he had been taught to give, was inadequate to enable the claimant to be safe, because the words used would not indicate to a reasonable person that his safety depended on his informing the defendant as soon as he felt more than a comfortable warmth: "The warning must be couched in terms which made it abundantly clear that it was a warning of danger." Similarly, where it is unwise for a patient to engage in certain types of activity following the treatment, he must be warned of the danger.[31]

4-045   A number of cases concern the failure of doctors to warn patients about the significance of the side-effects of drugs, and what they should do if the symptoms appear.[32] In *Crichton v Hastings*[33] the claimant was prescribed an anti-coagulant drug, but she was given no warning about the dangerous side-effects (haemorrhage), nor any instructions as to the importance of immediately reporting the appearance of these side-effects to her doctor. This was held to be negligent. Similarly, in *Sheridan v Boots Co Ltd*[34] a doctor who prescribed a potent anti-inflammatory drug, but failed to give the patient a warning that if he experienced any stomach trouble he should stop taking the drug and consult a doctor immediately was said to have been negligent.[35] In some instances the risk associated with the treatment may be so great that

---

[29] (1986) 21 D.L.R. (4th) 507.

[30] (1950) 94 S.J. 599.

[31] *Brushett v Cowan* (1987) 40 D.L.R. (4th) 488; affirmed (1990) 69 D.L.R. (4th) 743 (Newfd CA), where the claimant was given crutches to use following a biopsy on her leg, but she was not warned that she should not bear weight on the leg. While engaging in ordinary activity without the crutches the leg broke at the site of the biopsy. The doctor was held negligent.

[32] "The physician cannot always be in constant attendance upon his patient, who may have to be left to his own devices; and if the former knows of some specific danger and the possibility of its occurring, it may well be part of his duty to his patient to advise him of the proper action in such emergency," *per* Winter J. in *Murrin v Janes* [1949] 4 D.L.R. 403, 405–406 (Newfd S.C.).

[33] (1972) 29 D.L.R. (3d) 692 (Ont. C.A.).

[34] (1980, QBD; unreported).

[35] The claim failed because the omission did not cause the injury. The claimant contracted Stevens-Johnson syndrome, causing blindness. He did not suffer any symptoms of stomach disorder, and so even if he had been given the warning about stomach trouble he would not have gone back to the doctor earlier than he did.

it will be negligence for the doctor to rely on the patient accurately reporting his symptoms. In *Marshall v Rogers*[36] a diabetic patient wanted to reduce his dependence on insulin, so the defendant put him on a strict diet, and reduced the insulin dosage. The defendant told the patient to report any symptoms of the changed diet. The new treatment failed and the patient became ill. The defendant claimed that the damage was caused by the patient's negligence in failing to report his symptoms. The British Columbia Court of Appeal held that the defendant was negligent. He had admitted that the method he adopted was dangerous, and thus it was negligent not to perform daily tests on the patient and watch over the patient very carefully. Fisher J.A. said that:

". . . in a case such as this, where admittedly a dangerous remedy was being tried . . . the appellant was negligent in delegating to the patient himself the duty of deciding what his real condition was from time to time from what might be called only his subjective symptoms without having daily tests made."[37]

In *Webster v Chapman*[38] the patient was taking a drug to treat pelvic thrombosis which was potentially harmful to the foetus if she became pregnant. She was advised by her general practitioner not to become pregnant in her medical condition, but was not informed that the drug could damage a foetus. She had indicated that she would take care of contraception, but subsequently became pregnant. It was held that the general practitioner was negligent in failing to inform the mother of the risks to the unborn child if she remained on the drug. She was not aware that she should seek immediate medical advice if she became pregnant or of the significance of failing to do so.

4–046

If the patient's treatment has not been completed he should be told of this and advised to return for further treatment or to seek treatment elsewhere. The doctor has a responsibility to bring home to the patient the importance of obtaining further treatment and the dangers involved in failing to do so.[39] Where there is a risk that a patient who has been discharged from hospital following an operation may start bleeding again, or that some other emergency may arise, the surgeon should make suitable arrangements for the claimant to contact him.[40] In *Joyce v Merton, Sutton and Wandsworth Health Authority*[41] the claimant underwent a surgical procedure which

4–047

---

[36] [1943] 4 D.L.R. 68 (B.C.C.A.).
[37] *ibid.* at p. 77; *cf. Battersby v Tottman* (1985) 37 S.A.S.R. 524 where, in the circumstances, a failure to monitor the known and serious side-effects of a drug was held not negligent.
[38] (1997) 155 D.L.R. (4th) 82 (Man. C.A.).
[39] *Coles v Reading and District Hospital Management Committee* (1963) 107 S.J. 115, where the patient should have been warned of the importance of having an anti-tetanus injection.
[40] *Corder v Banks*, *The Times*, April 9, 1960; *Videto v Kennedy* (1980) 107 D.L.R. (3d) 612, 616–617; rev'd on other grounds (1981) 125 D.L.R. (3d) 127 (Ont. C.A.); *cf. Murrin v Janes* [1949] 4 D.L.R. 403 where the claimant's delay in seeing a doctor to deal with excessive bleeding following the extraction of some teeth was held to be the sole cause of his problems.
[41] [1996] P.I.Q.R. P121; [1996] 7 Med. L.R. 1.

resulted in a partially occluded artery, leading three months later to an upper brain stem infarction causing almost total paralysis. The Court of Appeal found that the defendants were negligent in discharging the claimant too soon after surgery and without appropriate instructions and advice as to what to do if he experienced further problems, though the action failed on causation.

(3) The manner in which information is communicated to the patient

4–048   It has been suggested that there is an obligation to break distressing, though truthful, news to patients in a manner which reduces the risk of patients developing psychiatric illness in response to the news. In *AB v Tameside & Glossop Health Authority*[42] the defendant health authority discovered that there was a small risk that some patients might have contracted HIV from a doctor. They wrote to the patients informing them of this risk.[43] Some of the patients brought an action alleging that the manner in which they were informed, namely by letter rather than face-to-face, created a foreseeable risk that the patients would suffer psychiatric harm. The defendants conceded that they owed a duty of care to break distressing, though truthful, news to patients in a manner which reduced the risk of patients developing psychiatric illness in response to the news, though, on the facts, the defendants were held not to have been negligent in choosing to inform patients by letter rather than in an individual meeting. It is not entirely clear that the defendants' concession of a duty of care was correct.[44] But in any event, where, as a result of the defendants' negligence, the distressing information was *inaccurate* and the claimant suffers psychiatric harm as a result of hearing this distressing "news", there may be an action, even though the incorrect information was imparted in a sensitive and appropriate manner.[45]

(4) Failure to communicate with other health professionals

4–049   A breakdown in essential communication between health care professionals with responsibility for the patient can have dangerous consequences for the patient. These errors may be the result of isolated acts of carelessness[46]

---

[42] [1997] 8 Med. L.R. 91.

[43] For consideration of when it will be appropriate to undertake patient notification see *HIV Infected Health Care Workers: A Consultation Paper on Management and Patient Notification* (June 2002) (available at *www.doh.gov.uk/aids.htm*).

[44] See Dziobon and Tettenborn "When the truth hurts: the incompetent transmission of distressing news" (1997) 13 P.N. 70; *cf.* Mullany (1998) 114 L.Q.R. 380.

[45] *Allin v City & Hackney Health Authority* [1996] 7 Med. L.R. 167. Note, however, that the existence of duty of care was also conceded in this case; see Jones (1997) 13 P.N. 111; Mullany (1998) 114 L.Q.R. 380.

[46] As, *e.g.*, in *Law Estate v Simice* (1994) 21 C.C.L.T. (2d) 228 (B.C.S.C.); affirmed [1996] 4 W.W.R. 672 (B.C.C.A.) where, in referring the patient to an ophthalmologist, a doctor failed to pass on significant findings that she had identified in the course of a physical examination,

or they may be the product of some organisational failure. The system of communication may be so poor that mistakes are almost inevitable, or the methods adopted may fail to take into account the risks of human error by providing some mechanism for checking.

A hospital authority must have an adequate system for summoning 4–050 specialist assistance when needed,[47] and there must be a system for dealing with a surgeon's patients when the surgeon goes away for a week-end.[48] The General Medical Council emphasises the individual responsibility of doctors to make appropriate arrangements for patients' care when they are off duty.[49] It is also to be expected that there will be a system for communication between hospitals or between a hospital and general practitioners about the treatment that a patient has received. In *Coles v Reading and District Hospital Management Committee*[50] a patient died of toxaemia due to tetanus infection because he had not received an anti-tetanus injection. The cottage hospital where he received his initial treatment told the patient to go to Battle hospital for further treatment, but he did not do so. He subsequently saw his own doctor, who made no inquiries as to what had happened at the hospital but simply redressed the wound. Sachs J. held the cottage hospital and the general practitioner negligent on the basis that they had omitted an elementary precaution of giving the anti-tetanus injection, and on the ground that the system of communication was inadequate. The patient should have been given a document to take to Battle hospital saying what

---

(n.46 contd.) which would have pointed to the possibility of an intracranial lesion. In *Starcevic v West Hertfordshire Health Authority* [2001] EWCA Civ 192; (2001) 60 B.M.L.R. 221 the claimant's husband died from a pulmonary embolism due to a deep vein thrombosis (DVT) during the course of minor surgery on his leg. It was held that the failure of an occupational therapist and a nurse to pass on information they had been given by the patient and the claimant about the condition of the patient's leg to the surgeon, which would have alerted the doctor to the risk of DVT, constituted negligence.

[47] *Bull v Devon Area Health Authority* (1989), [1993] 4 Med. L.R. 117, CA where Slade L.J. described the system of summoning expert obstetric assistance as "operating on a knife edge." The length of the delay pointed strongly either to inefficiency in the system or to negligence by some individual in working the system; *Denton v South West Thames Regional Health Authority* (1980, QBD; unreported) where the lack of a system to check the safety of equipment was held to be negligent. Of course, even the best systems may not be foolproof. In *Bolitho v City and Hackney Health Authority* [1998] A.C. 232 one doctor failed to attend an emergency call from a nurse because the battery in her bleeper was flat.

[48] *Cassidy v Ministry of Health* [1951] 2 K.B. 343, 359, *per* Singleton L.J.; *Crichton v Hastings* (1972) 29 D.L.R. (3d) 692, 700 (Ont. C.A.), held that a doctor who is going away and relinquishing to others the care of his patient should arrange for the patient to be given adequate warning of the dangers of developing side-effects from the prescribed medication; *Ball v Howard, The Lancet*, February 2, 1924, p. 253 QBD.

[49] See the GMC *Guidance, Good Medical Practice*, May 2001, para. 39: "You must be satisfied that, when you are off duty, suitable arrangements are made for your patients' medical care. These arrangements should include effective hand-over procedures and clear communication between doctors"; and para. 40: "If you arrange cover for your own practice, you must satisfy yourself that doctors who stand in for you have the qualifications, experience, knowledge and skills to perform the duties for which they will be responsible. Deputising doctors and locums are directly accountable to the GMC for the care of patients while on duty."

[50] (1963) 107 S.J. 115; see also *Schanczi v Singh* [1988] 2 W.W.R. 465 (Alta. Q.B.) on a specialist's failure to obtain adequate information about a patient from the referring doctor before proceeding to surgery.

treatment he had received. The responsibility for ensuring that there was a proper system of communication between hospitals rested on the hospital authorities not on individual nurses.[51]

4–051   This case can be contrasted with *Chapman v Rix*[52] in which a patient who had suffered a knife wound in the stomach visited a cottage hospital, where the defendant general practitioner diagnosed wrongly that the wound had not penetrated the peritoneum. He sent the patient home, telling him to see his own doctor that evening and tell him what had happened. When the patient saw his own doctor he had symptoms of pain and nausea. He told the doctor that he had been told at the hospital that the wound was "superficial". The general practitioner, thinking that the patient had attended a general hospital, accepted this statement and treated the patient for dyspepsia. Five days later the patient died of peritonitis, the wound having penetrated the small intestine. It was common ground that prompt surgery would have saved his life. The trial judge had found the defendant liable on the basis that he had failed to communicate directly with the patient's own general practitioner. This was reversed on appeal. With hindsight it would have been better if the defendant had sent a letter to the patient's doctor, but that was not the kind of precaution which in practice was regularly adopted between general practitioners, and the expert witnesses approved of the defendant's conduct.[53]

4–052   Breakdowns in communication between doctors, or doctors and nurses can also occur within hospitals if there is an inadequate system of consultation between them. A doctor who fails to read the nursing notes will probably be found negligent.[54] Similarly, the failure of nurses to read the medical notes, particularly on a change of staff at the start of a new shift, can also constitute negligence. In *Robertson v Nottingham Health Authority*[55] the Court of Appeal held that there had been a negligent breakdown in the communication of instructions between a hospital's medical staff and its nursing and midwifery staff. A senior house officer gave oral instructions to the midwives about the use of a stethoscope when carrying out a cardiotacograph

---

[51] "The NHS had been developed on the basis that a patient might well be transferred for treatment from one person to another so that the responsibility for the patient shifted . . . Any system which failed to provide for adequate communication was wrong and negligently wrong." *ibid. per* Sachs J.

[52] (1959) 103 S.J. 940, CA; (1960), [1994] 5 Med. L.R. 239, HL; see also *Seyfert v Burnaby Hospital Society* (1986) 27 D.L.R. (4th) 96 on the diagnosis of penetrating stab wounds.

[53] In the House of Lords both Lord Keith and Lord Denning dissented. Lord Keith commented that the patient had fallen between two stools, due chiefly to a failure of communication: ". . . a doctor who is expected to look after a patient with an abdominal wound which has already been diagnosed and treated by another doctor who decides that the injury does not require operative, or observational, treatment in a hospital, should be put in possession of information on what has been observed and done by the first doctor. Otherwise the patient is being deprived of the full skill, knowledge and aid in diagnosis that the second doctor could otherwise apply to his case," *per* Lord Keith at [1994] 5 Med. L.R. 239, 245. Lord Denning said that: "Misleading information is a very dangerous thing to throw about. There is no telling where it will finish up": *ibid.* p. 248.

[54] *Holmes v Board of Hospital Trustees of the City of London* (1977) 81 D.L.R. (3d) 67, 94 (Ont. H.C.).

[55] [1997] 8 Med. L.R. 1.

(CTG) trace, to monitor fetal heart rate in conjunction with the timing of the mother's contractions. This had become necessary because previous scans had not produced reliable information. The doctor also recorded these instructions in the medical notes which were kept beside the nursing station so that the midwives would have access to both sets of notes, nursing and medical. The process of hand over from one nursing shift to the next involved using the nursing cardex, but not the doctors' notes. The stethoscope was not used, with the result that the information obtained from the CTG trace was difficult to interpret, and this resulted in "culpable delay" in proceeding to a Caesarian section delivery of the child. There was no evidence as to the systems in place at the hospital for ensuring that there was not such a breakdown in communication between the medical staff and the nursing staff. The Court of Appeal held that the paucity of evidence on this issue was irrelevant. If an effective system was in place to see that such breakdowns in communication did not occur, then the health authority would be vicariously liable for the negligence of any employee who did not take reasonable care to ensure that the system worked efficiently. If, on the other hand, there were no effective systems in place, the authority would be directly liable on the basis of a breach of a non-delegable duty to establish a proper system of care. Thus, "if a patient is injured by reason of a negligent breakdown in the systems for communicating material information to the clinicians responsible for her care, she is not to be denied redress merely because no identifiable person or persons are to blame for deficiencies in setting up and monitoring the effectiveness of the relevant communication systems."[56]

Relying too heavily on casual exchanges can also cause problems, and this was criticised in the Canadian case of *Bergen v Sturgeon General Hospital*: **4–053**

"There appears to be an accepted practice of what is referred to as 'Curbstone Consultations'. This appears to happen when doctors casually meet in such places as hospital corridors and discuss a patient. In my opinion, this is bad practice and to be discouraged. It seems to me that when an attending physician calls in a specialist for a 'consultation' the least that might be expected is for those physicians to have a meaningful discussion between them, or among them, as the case may require, whereby each advises the other of what they did, when they did it, and what should be done. In this way each would be fully aware of the procedure of the other, the findings of the other and the reasons for the diagnosis arrived at by the other. In this case, such a consultation did not take place which, in my opinion, contributed to the bad result."[57]

Communication errors can occur from simply mishearing or misreading an instruction, sometimes with catastrophic consequences. This may be **4–054**

---

[56] *ibid.* at 13 *per* Brooke L.J., applying *Bull v Devon Area Health Authority* (1989), [1993] 4 Med. L.R. 117. The claimant failed on causation.
[57] (1984) 28 C.C.L.T. 155, 175, *per* Hope J.

attributable to a single lapse of concentration by a doctor or nurse, but the further question may then arise as to whether there was any system for checking for such errors given that it is known that mistakes do sometimes happen. In *Collins v Hertfordshire County Council*[58] a patient died after being injected with cocaine instead of procaine as a local anaesthetic. The surgeon had told a junior, unqualified medical officer over the telephone his requirements for the operation the next day, and the word "procaine" was misheard for "cocaine". The pharmacist dispensing the drug at the hospital pharmacy did not question the order for an "unheard of dosage" of a dangerous drug, and the surgeon did not check prior to injecting the solution that he was in fact injecting what he had ordered. It was held that both the surgeon and the medical officer were liable, as was the hospital authority for having an unsafe system for dispensing.[59]

4–055   A doctor who prepares a report or medical notes which he is aware may be relied upon by others for the treatment of the patient has a duty to exercise reasonable care in writing the report.[60] This also applies to the writing of a prescription which should be reasonably legible. For example, in *Prendergast v Sam and Dee Ltd*[61] the defendant general practitioner wrote a prescription for Amoxil for the claimant's chest infection. The pharmacist misread the doctor's writing, taking the word Amoxil for Daonil, a drug used to control diabetes. The claimant suffered symptoms of hypoglycaemia as a result of taking Daonil, since he was not a diabetic, and he was left with permanent brain damage. It was held that both the doctor and the pharmacist were negligent. A doctor has a duty to his patients to write a prescription clearly, and must allow for some mistakes or carelessness on the part of a busy pharmacist. Standing on its own the prescription could reasonably have been read incorrectly, and thus the doctor was liable, notwithstanding that there were other factors which should have alerted the pharmacist to the pos-

---

[58] [1947] 1 K.B. 598; see also *Strangeways-Lesmere v Clayton* [1936] 2 K.B. 11, where a nurse who misread her instructions and gave an excess dose was held to be negligent.

[59] *cf. Fussell v Beddard* (1942) 2 B.M.J. 411 in which a patient received a fatal overdose of anaesthetic because the nurse misheard the anaesthetist's instructions about the strength of the dose. The patient received a 1% solution of decicaine instead of 0.1%. Lewis J. said that when the nurse is inexperienced the surgeon and the anaesthetist should take care to see that she is carrying out or is competent to carry out the duties assigned to her, but when the nurse is experienced they are entitled to rely on her to carry out their instructions. His Lordship held that neither the anaesthetist nor the nurse had been negligent, but that an unfortunate mistake had been made. It would be difficult to support such a remarkable conclusion on negligence today.

[60] *Everett v Griffiths* [1920] 3 K.B. 163, 213. See the observations of Sir Thomas Bingham M.R. on *Everett v Griffiths* in *X (minors) v Bedfordshire County Council* [1995] 2 A.C. 633, at 664–665; though see also the comments of Lord Browne-Wilkinson, *ibid.* at 753, on these observations, when *X (minors)* reached the House of Lords. In *Trustees of London Clinic v Edgar* (2000, QBD; unreported) a surgeon who failed to record that the results of his post-operative tests for the patient's limb movement, following spinal surgery, were normal was held to have been negligent, because the nursing staff with responsibility for the patient's post-operative care then assumed (also negligently) that the surgeon was aware that the patient's response was not normal. The consequence was that the surgeon was not called to deal with the patient's deteriorating condition until it was too late.

[61] [1989] 1 Med. L.R. 36, CA.

sibility of error. The pharmacist has a duty to give some thought to the prescriptions he is dispensing and should not dispense them mechanically; if there is doubt he should contact the doctor for clarification. If he had been paying attention he would have realised that there was something wrong with the prescription, since the dosage and the small number of tablets were unusual for Daonil; moreover, the claimant paid for the prescription whereas drugs for diabetes were free under the NHS.[62]

A pathologist who has been given specimens for testing or analysis owes   **4–056**
a duty to the patient not only to conduct the tests in a proper manner but also to take reasonable steps to communicate the results to the referring doctor, and it is irrelevant that the doctor also has a corresponding duty to find out the results.[63] On the other hand, a general practitioner who is sent the results of a blood test by the hospital is entitled to assume that the hospital doctors are aware of those results and are taking them into account in their investigation of the patient's symptoms; it is not for the general practitioner to go through hospital notes to check that the hospital has done what it should have done.[64] Similarly, it was not negligent for a general practitioner to fail to advise parents that there was an alternative means of providing immunisation of a child against measles, when immunisation was not imminent and the general practitioner was aware that the parents would be being advised by another doctor at another practice in 12 to 18 months about the options for immunisation.[65] The general practitioner was entitled to assume that appropriate advice would be given at the relevant time.

(5) Medico-legal reports

Doctors who prepare medical reports for use in legal proceedings clearly   **4–057**
come under a duty to exercise reasonable care in preparing those reports, although where the doctor will also be a witness in those proceedings the scope of that duty may be limited by the immunity from suit that attaches to witnesses.[66] In many instances the doctor's medical skills, as to diagnosis, causation of symptoms and prognosis will be called into play, to which the *Bolam* test would be applicable. In other cases, however, the negligence may be of a more mundane nature and judgments about whether the defendant exercised appropriate professional skill by reference to the standards of his

---

[62] For similar cases of negligence by a pharmacist failing to spot prescription errors see *Collins v Hertfordshire County Council* [1947] 1 K.B. 598 and *Dwyer v Roderick, The Times,* November 12, 1983; McKevitt (1988) 4 P.N. 185. See generally on the pharmacist's liability: Crawford (1995) 2 J. Law and Med. 293.

[63] *Thomsen v Davison* [1975] Qd R. 93; see also *McKay v Essex Area Health Authority* [1982] Q.B. 1166 on an alleged omission to communicate test results; *Gregory v Pembrokeshire Health Authority* [1989] 1 Med. L.R. 81 CA; *Fredette v Wiebe* [1986] 5 W.W.R. 222.

[64] *Weir v Graham* [2002] EWHC 2291 (Q.B.).

[65] *Thompson v Blake-James* [1998] P.I.Q.R. P286; [1998] Lloyd's Rep. Med. 187, CA. The action also failed on causation because the claimant's mother was fully aware of the options for immunisation after subsequent discussions with other doctors.

[66] See para. 2–071.

peers are irrelevant. This was the view of the Alberta Court of Appeal in *Kelly v Lundgard*[67] where it was held that the standard of care required of doctors expressing opinions in medico-legal reports was to exercise such care as the circumstances required to ensure that the representations made in the report are accurate and not misleading. It was not simply a matter of asking what the doctor should have disclosed, because the doctor may go further than required and make positive, but misleading statements, *i.e.* a negligent misrepresentation. Two doctors (including the claimant's general practitioner) provided medico-legal reports for the purpose of the claimant's action against a negligent motorist, advising that she would make a full recovery from her injuries. In fact, she was rendered sterile. The settlement with the motorist did not include compensation for infertility. When the claimant subsequently discovered the infertility she sued the doctors, on the basis that their negligent reports had led to her settling her claim for less than it was worth. The general practitioner was held to have been negligent in that she had failed to obtain a report on the surgery undertaken by the surgeon before writing her report. She had also failed to disclose in her report that she had not seen the surgery report. Had she seen the report she should have been alerted to the real risk of infertility developing as a result of the injuries sustained in the road traffic accident (though if the risk had been merely "speculative" there would have been no liability for failing to report it).

4–058   Conrad J.A. said that the standard of care in writing medico-legal reports did not require expert evidence. It was a question of common sense and fairness on which the court was competent to rule.[68] The preparation of a medico-legal report involved ordinary communication skills. A doctor may fail to exercise reasonable care in different ways. A statement may be a negligent misrepresentation because the doctor did not exercise proper care in diagnosing the subject's condition. The lack of care is the improper diagnosis, which is a technical issue requiring expert evidence: "At the other extreme, a misrepresentation may occur where a fully informed physician, apprised of all risks known and accepted by a skilled physician, carelessly fails to communicate information properly, or fails to disclose information that reasonably should have been disclosed in the circumstances."[69] An example would be where the doctor knew that the patient had a risk of paralysis, but inadvertently wrote that there was no risk of paralysis. The document was not proof-read and the error was not spotted. That carelessness was not connected to the doctor's expertise, and yet clearly showed a lack of care. No expert evidence would be required for the court to conclude that a lack of care in proof-reading was unreasonable. Thus, diagnostic and clinical skills were not engaged because the case turned on whether the known risk should have been communicated.[70]

---

[67] (2001) 202 D.L.R. (4th) 385 (Alta. C.A.).
[68] *ibid.* at [115].
[69] *ibid.* at [117].
[70] *ibid.* at [128] *per* Conrad J.A. See also *Hughes v Lloyds Bank plc* [1998] P.I.Q.R. P98, CA, discussed at para. 2–072.

4. ERRORS IN TREATMENT

Errors in treatment can take a multitude of forms. They may arise from the defendant's lack of knowledge (*e.g.* as to the generally known adverse reactions of a drug[71]), a lack of skill in performing a particular procedure (*e.g.* where the doctor is inexperienced[72]), a momentary, inadvertent slip (*e.g.* with a surgical instrument during the course of an operation[73]) or a conscious decision by the doctor to depart from the standard procedure normally employed in the circumstances.[74] Categorising the defendant's conduct as an error or a mistake does not, however, determine the issue of negligence. The question remains whether the error was such as no reasonably competent doctor exercising ordinary care would have made, applying the *Bolam* test. Thus, even where it is proved that the defendant made a mistake and that the claimant's injury was caused by that mistake, the claimant must still show that it was an unreasonable mistake.

4-059

Where the doctor has made a conscious decision to depart from the standard treatment, this may be evidence of negligence, but it is not necessarily conclusive.[75] The decision may well be justified by the particular circumstances of the patient, it being remembered that doctors have to treat the individual patient and not the "standard" patient found in the textbooks.[76] On the other hand, a substantial departure from accepted practice, even undertaken consciously and in full knowledge of the potential risks, will place a heavy onus on the defendant to justify his decision. If he cannot do so he will be found liable.[77]

4-060

If the defendant has taken a conscious decision about the balance of risks and benefits attached to a proposed treatment, then he has exercised a "professional judgment." To describe a mistake as an "error of professional judgment" is unhelpful, however, in determining the question of negligence because some such errors "may be so glaringly below proper standards as to make a finding of negligence inevitable."[78] But, in the nature of things, if a doctor has taken a considered decision it may be more difficult to conclude that there has been negligence[79] than where he has made an unintentional or

4-061

---

[71] See *Reynard v Carr* (1983) 30 C.C.L.T. 42 (B.C.S.C.).

[72] *Jones v Manchester Corporation* [1952] Q.B. 852.

[73] *Gonda v Kerbel* (1982) 24 C.C.L.T. 222.

[74] *Clark v MacLennan* [1983] 1 All E.R. 416.

[75] See paras 3–037 to 3–043. Remember also that there may be more than one accepted practice. Adopting one rather than another is not negligence.

[76] *Holland v The Devitt & Moore Nautical College*, *The Times*, March 4, 1960 in which Streatfield J. held that a doctor whose treatment had departed from the recommendations of the textbooks was not negligent. A doctor was entitled to use his experience and common sense, and a slight departure from the textbook was not necessarily a mistake let alone negligence.

[77] *Clark v MacLennan* [1983] 1 All E.R. 416; see para. 3–039.

[78] *Whitehouse v Jordan* [1981] 1 All E.R. 267, 276, *per* Lord Edmund-Davies; see para. 3–067.

[79] See, *e.g.*, *Darley v Shale* [1993] 4 Med. L.R. 161 (N.S.W.S.C.), where the defendant gynaecologist was found not liable for perforating the transverse colon during a laparoscopy, having weighed up the respective risks of performing a laparoscopy and a laparotomy. For discussion of the implications and risks of "minimal access surgery" see (1995) 1 Clinical Risk, No. 1 and No. 3.

inadvertent "error," since in the latter situation there has been no balancing of risks and benefits. For example, in *Goode v Nash*[80] the Supreme Court of South Australia declined to characterise the defendant's conduct as a "mere error of professional judgment," because:

> "There was indeed no exercise of a decision-making process at all, nor the taking of a calculated risk. There was simply a failure, however unintentional and inadvertent, to observe the obvious but critical precaution of ensuring that the instrument was not too hot to place upon the patient's eye."

4–062   On the other hand, it is not negligence if the decision which is probably the wisest one in the circumstances is reached by accident rather than by design, even where the accident was created by faulty management procedures.[81]

4–063   Most instances of negligence probably arise from simple, inadvertent errors that even the defendant would concede should not have been made (although he might not concede that the error amounted to negligence). This includes, for example, damage caused by surgical instruments;[82] or during post-operative treatment;[83] unnecessary and gross cosmetic distortion following breast reduction surgery;[84] administering the wrong anaes-

---

[80] (1979) 21 S.A.S.R. 419, 423.

[81] *Lachambre v Nair* [1989] 2 W.W.R. 749 (Sask. Q.B.).

[82] *Leckie v Brent & Harrow Area Health Authority* (1982, QBD; unreported), where a scalpel cut to a baby's face during the performance of a Caesarian section was held to be negligent; *Gonda v Kerbel* (1982) 24 C.C.L.T. 222, where the perforation of the claimant's bowel during a bowel examination by sigmoidoscope raised an inference of negligence; *Bentley v Bristol and Weston Health Authority (No. 2)* [1991] 3 Med. L.R. 1, QBD, where the claimant sustained sciatic nerve paralysis in the course of a total hip replacement operation, and although there were other possible causes of the damage, the strong probability was that it was caused by stretching or traction of the nerve during the operation, and stretching to the extent necessary to cause such an injury would not have occurred with the exercise of reasonable care; *Heath v West Berkshire Health Authority* [1992] 3 Med. L.R. 57, QBD, where damage to the patient's lingual nerve during the course of an operation to remove wisdom teeth was held to be negligent, on the ground that although it was possible to cause unavoidable damage to the nerve, on a balance of probabilities the injury occurred as a result of the retractor being incorrectly positioned in front of the nerve, or incorrectly adjusted to the drill in front of the nerve, or through inadvertent mis-application of the drill. On negligently inflicted damage to the lingual nerve during removal of wisdom teeth see also: *Christie v Somerset Health Authority* [1992] 3 Med. L.R. 75 and *Tomkins v Bexley Health Authority* [1993] 4 Med. L.R. 235. In *Smith v Salford Health Authority* [1994] 5 Med. L.R. 321, QBD, it was held that the defendant's technique in using an aneurism needle in performing a particular type of spinal fusion was inappropriate for the site of the spine at which he was operating, because it was inherently likely to intrude too far into the spinal canal.

[83] *Powell v Streatham Manor Nursing Home* [1935] A.C. 243, where a patient's bladder was punctured by a catheter inserted by a nurse; see also *Cassidy v Ministry of Health* [1951] 2 K.B. 343, 355 on post-operative care.

[84] *MacDonald v Ross* (1983) 24 C.C.L.T. 242 (N.S.S.C.); see also *White v Turner* (1981) 120 D.L.R. (3d) 269; (1982) 12 D.L.R. (4th) 319 on breast reduction surgery; *Flanagan v Bloomsbury Health Authority* (1992) 3 AVMA Medical & Legal Journal (No. 4) p. 14; and Medical Defence Union, *Annual Report 1989*, p. 43. See Ward (1992) 3 AVMA Medical & Legal Journal (No. 1) p. 2, for discussion of the possible complications arising from breast

thetic;[85] or too much anaesthetic;[86] prescribing the wrong dosage of a drug;[87] or injecting the wrong dosage by mistake;[88] damaging a nerve while administering an injection;[89] allowing an elderly patient to fall off a trolley;[90] or failing to check the position of a catheter monitoring the blood oxygen level of a premature baby.[91]

(1) Operations

Difficulties may arise in assessing negligence in performing operations because of the number of people involved (surgeon(s), anaesthetist, nurses) each with their own duties and responsibilities. In the case of operations under the NHS, from the patient's point of view it does not matter if he cannot identify the particular person at fault, provided he can prove fault on the part of someone for whom the hospital authorities will be vicariously liable.[92] With private treatment, where the patient has contracted with a specific surgeon for whom the hospital is not vicariously responsible, it may be more important for the patient to be able to identify the person at fault. Moreover, from the defendants' perspective it will always be relevant to determine who was to blame.   4–064

Normally, a doctor will not be responsible for the negligence of others, such as nurses, in carrying out the instructions that have been given with regard to the patient's treatment.[93] Nursing staff remain the employees of the hospital: 4–065

"... the true ground on which the hospital escapes liability for the act of a nurse who, whether in the operating theatre or elsewhere, is acting under the instructions of the surgeon or doctor is, not that *pro hac vice* she ceases to be the servant of the hospital, but that she is not guilty of negligence if she carries out the orders of the surgeon, however negligent those orders may be."[94]

(n.84 contd.) augmentation surgery; and Balen (2002) 8 Clinical Risk 177. See also *La Fleur v Cornelis* (1979) 28 N.B.R. (2d) 569, 573 (N.B.S.C.) on a negligently performed rhinoplasty.

[85] *Collins v Hertfordshire County Council* [1947] 1 K.B. 598; *Ritchie v Chichester Health Authority* [1994] 5 Med. L.R. 187, QBD.

[86] *Jones v Manchester Corporation* [1952] Q.B. 852.

[87] *Dwyer v Roderick, The Times*, November 12, 1983. On drug errors generally see (1998) 4 Clinical Risk 103–109, 173–183; Rolfe and Harper (1995) 310 B.M.J. 1173. See further para. 4–089.

[88] *Strangeways-Lesmere v Clayton* [1936] 2 K.B. 11.

[89] *Caldeira v Gray* [1936] 1 All E.R. 540; *Hammond v North West Hertfordshire Health Authority* (1991) 2 AVMA Medical & Legal Journal (No. 1) p. 12.

[90] *Smith v Lewisham Group Hospital Management Committee* (1955) 2 B.M.J. 65; *cf. Robertson v Smyth* (1979) 20 S.A.S.R. 184, where it was held that there is no duty to assist a patient descending from an examination table.

[91] *Wilsher v Essex Area Health Authority* [1987] Q.B. 730.

[92] *Cassidy v Ministry of Health* [1951] 2 K.B. 343.

[93] *Perionowsky v Freeman* (1866) 4 F. & F. 977; *Morris v Winsbury-White* [1937] 4 All E.R. 494, 498. In *Wilsher v Essex Area Health Authority* [1987] Q.B. 730, 749–750, Mustill L.J. said that the law does not recognise the concept of "team negligence," (although this comment was directed at the standard of care to be expected from individual members of the team).

[94] *Gold v Essex County Council* [1942] 2 K.B. 293, 299, *per* Lord Greene M.R.

The fact that a nurse acts under the instructions of a doctor, however, does not mean that he is excused from making any professional judgment. There may be circumstances where a nurse could be negligent even though following a doctor's instructions. For example, if a doctor ordered an obviously incorrect and dangerous dosage of a drug a nurse who administered it without obtaining confirmation from the doctor or higher authority might well be found negligent.[95] Similarly, a pharmacist has been held to be negligent for failing to check a request for an "unheard of dosage" of cocaine.[96]

4–066   Conversely, the doctor may be negligent if he knows or ought reasonably to have known that another person in the team, whether it be the anaesthetist or a nurse, has done something which puts the patient at risk but fails to take any steps to remedy the error.[97] He will also have a responsibility to take into account the possibility of error by another, for example, by making some check of what he is about to inject into a patient.[98] Moreover, it is negligent for a doctor to rely on information provided by a nurse whom he knows or ought to know is overconfident in her own abilities and not qualified to make the clinical judgment in question.[99]

4–067   The courts have long-recognised that the mere fact that something has gone wrong during the course of an operation is not *per se* indicative of negligence. Thus, where a surgeon accidentally cut the patient's retina in the course of an operation on his eye this was held not to be negligent, because the surgeon was working within an extremely small margin of error.[1] Similarly, the fact that a patient sustained damage to a facial nerve does not

---

[95] *ibid.* at p. 313, *per* Goddard L.J., although his Lordship added that: "In the stress of an operation, however, I should suppose that the first thing required of a nurse would be an unhesitating obedience to the orders of the surgeon." See also the analogous case of *Davy-Chiesman v Davy-Chiesman* [1984] 1 All E.R. 321, 332, 335, stating that solicitors should not rely blindly on the advice of counsel; though a solicitor will normally be entitled to rely on counsel's advice unless the advice was obviously wrong: *Matrix-Securities Ltd v Theodore Goddard* [1998] P.N.L.R. 290.

[96] *Collins v Hertfordshire County Council* [1947] 1 K.B. 598.

[97] *Perionowsky v Freeman* (1866) 4 F. & F. 977, 982; *Wilsher v Essex Area Health Authority* [1987] Q.B. 730, where the registrar was held to have been negligent in failing to spot the senior house officer's error. In *Jones v Manchester Corporation* [1952] Q.B. 852 the Court of Appeal took the view that the inexperienced doctor who administered the fatal injection was not as culpable as the experienced doctor who supervised her: "She administered the pentothal under his very eyes and to his entire approval. In these circumstances it seems to me that her share in the responsibility is much less than his," *per* Denning L.J. at p. 871.

[98] *Collins v Hertfordshire County Council* [1947] 1 K.B. 598; see para. 4–054.

[99] *Wiszniewski v Central Manchester Health Authority* [1996] 7 Med. L.R. 248, 256, a finding that was not challenged on appeal: [1998] P.I.Q.R. P324; [1998] Lloyd's Rep. Med. 223, 229 CA.

[1] *White v Westminster Hospital Board of Governors*, The Times, October 26, 1961; see also *Chubey v Ahsan* (1977) 71 D.L.R. (3d) 550 (Man. C.A.), where an orthopaedic surgeon who inadvertently pierced the aorta and vena cava during spinal surgery was held not to be negligent because this was recognised as an inherent risk of the procedure, albeit a remote risk; *Kapur v Marshall* (1978) 85 D.L.R. (3d) 567, 573, *per* Robins J. (Ont. H.C.): "That the accident happened in this case, when it so rarely does happen, does not compel, as in effect was argued, a finding of negligence. An unfavourable result is not synonymous with negligence. A surgeon is not an insurer"; *cf.* the comments of Freedman C.J.M. (dissenting) in *Chubey v Ahsan* (1977) 71 D.L.R. (3d) 550, 552, cited at para. 3–136, n. 57.

indicate that the surgeon used excessive force in removing granulated tissue from the eardrum.[2] On the other hand, a surgeon who accidentally knocked out four of patient's teeth during a tonsillectomy had fallen below a proper standard of care.[3] Perforation of the uterus during the course of performing a Dilatation and Curettage is relatively common, and not in itself indicative of negligence, but damage to the small bowel during the operation is so rare as to be outside the range of normal practice and is indicative of negligence.[4] In *Hendy v Milton Keynes Health Authority (No. 2),*[5] during the course of an abdominal hysterectomy, a suture was unintentionally passed around the right ureter, ultimately causing the occluded ureter to burst from a build up of pressure. The evidence indicated that it is possible for ureteric damage to occur despite the use of a competent surgical technique, but these rare instances of non-culpable ureteric damage were attributable to anatomical variations that were outside the normal range. Most cases of ureteric damage where the anatomy was normal were due to poor technique. Thus, the likeliest explanation of ureteric damage in such cases, in the absence of evidence of an abnormal position of the ureter, was that the bladder was not sufficiently pushed down at the sides during surgery, and in the absence of pathology or other abnormality a competent surgeon should make a sound visual assessment of the position of the bladder to see that the ureters are in a position of safety. Jowitt J. held that the failure to do so amounted to a negligent misjudgment.[6]

Obstetric errors are frequently the subject of litigation, partly because the consequences for the child can be extremely serious, and partly because the parents' expectation is to have a normal, healthy child. Obstetrics is widely regarded as a high risk specialty for doctors; indeed it was the prospect of the Medical Protection Society introducing differential subscriptions for membership, with obstetricians paying several thousand pounds *per annum,* which led the government to introduce NHS indemnity.[7] In *Whitehouse v Jordan*[8] an allegation that the defendant had pulled too long

4–068

---

[2] *Ashcroft v Merseyside Regional Health Authority* [1983] 2 All E.R. 245; affirmed [1985] 2 All E.R. 96.

[3] *Munro v United Oxford Hospitals* (1958) 1 B.M.J. 167; *Gagnon v Stortini* (1974) 4 O.R. (2d) 270, where a dentist who removed a wrong tooth was held liable in negligence.

[4] *Bovenzi v Kettering Health Authority* [1991] 2 Med. L.R. 293, QBD.

[5] [1992] 3 Med. L.R. 119, QBD. For discussion of ureteric damage during gynaecological surgery see Simanowitz (1991) 2 *AVMA Medical & Legal Journal* (No. 1) p. 2.

[6] In *Ratty v Haringey Health Authority* [1994] 5 Med. L.R. 413 the Court of Appeal upheld a finding of negligence where there was damage to the claimant's ureters during the course of colo-rectal surgery (an abdomino-perineal resection). The negligence consisted, not in the initial damage to the ureters, which could occur even with the exercise of reasonable care, but in failing to discover and correct the damage before the end of the operation. See also *Bouchta v Swindon Health Authority* [1996] 7 Med. L.R. 62—damage to the ureter during the course of an hysterectomy found to be negligent; *cf. Hooper v Young* [1998] Lloyd's Rep. Med. 61, CA where there was an explanation for the damage to a ureter which did not involve negligence, and the claimant failed to prove that the explanation which involved negligence by the defendant was the correct one.

[7] See para. 7–052.

[8] [1981] 1 All E.R. 267. For discussion of the "obstetric nemesis" which it is claimed that *Whitehouse v Jordan* has precipitated see Symonds (1989) 5 J. of the M.D.U. 52.

and too hard in the course of a forceps delivery, and thus was negligent in failing to proceed to a Caesarian section delivery, was ultimately rejected on the facts.[9] In *Parry v North West Surrey Health Authority*,[10] on the other hand, the defendant was held liable for attempting to deliver a child by forceps when it was too high in the mother's pelvis, and thus for failing to undertake a Caesarian section delivery.[11] Human error is frequently implicated in obstetric accidents, many of which are avoidable,[12] but the causal

---

[9] See also *Knight v West Kent Health Authority* [1998] Lloyd's Rep. Med. 18; *Corley v North West Herefordshire Health Authority* [1997] 8 Med. L.R. 45; *Hinfey v Salford Health Authority* [1993] 4 Med. L.R. 143, where an allegation that the failure to undertake a Caesarian section delivery constituted negligence was rejected on the evidence; *James v Camberwell Health Authority* [1994] 5 Med. L.R. 253, where a delay in proceeding to a Caesarian section was held not negligent on the facts; *Goguen v Crowe* (1987) 40 C.C.L.T. 212 (Nova Scotia S.C.); *Hallatt v North West Anglia Health Authority* [1998] Lloyd's Rep. Med. 197, CA—failure to undertake a glucose tolerance test for gestational diabetes (which is an indication for a Caesarian section delivery) not negligent on the facts. For consideration of the potential problems arising from a breech delivery see *W (A Child) v North Durham Acute Hospital NHS Trust* (2001, QBD; unreported); and for discussion of the appropriate management of breech presentations see Thorpe-Beeston (2002) 8 Clinical Risk 99.

[10] [1994] 5 Med. L.R. 259. See also *Bowers v Harrow Health Authority* [1995] 6 Med. L.R. 16; *De Martell v Merton and Sutton Health Authority* [1995] 6 Med. L.R. 234; *Townsend v Worcester and District Health Authority* (1994, QBD; unreported), where the defendant was held to have been negligent in pulling too hard with a ventouse, causing traumatic injuries to the child's brain; *Gentleman v North Essex Health Authority* (2001, QBD; unreported), where the obstetrician was held to have been negligent in attempting a forceps delivery in the delivery room rather than in the operating theatre, resulting in a delay in proceeding to a Caesarian section delivery; *Murphy v Wirral Health Authority* [1996] 7 Med. L.R. 99, on the duty of a midwife to monitor the progress of labour by conducting regular vaginal examinations; *Reynolds v North Tyneside Health Authority* [2002] Lloyd's Rep. Med. 459, QBD—midwife failed to undertake a vaginal examination despite the existence of circumstances in which the risk of cord prolapse was foreseeable, see para. 3–081; *Robertson v Nottingham Health Authority* [1997] 8 Med. L.R. 1, para. 4–052 above; *Hill v West Lancashire Health Authority* [1997] 8 Med. L.R. 196; *Wisniewski v Central Manchester Health Authority* [1998] P.I.Q.R. P324; [1998] Lloyd's Rep. Med. 223, where a SHO failed to attend a patient in labour despite having been informed of signs of fetal distress; *Briody v St Helen's & Knowsley Health Authority* [1999] Lloyd's Rep. Med. 185; *Simms v Birmingham Health Authority* (2000) 58 B.M.L.R. 66—SHO failed to report the presence of undiluted meconium to the registrar, and left the midwife to interpret the CTG trace in a high-risk situation; *Hunt v NHS Litigation Authority* (2000, QBD; unreported)—obstetric registrar failed to respond soon enough to signs of foetal distress from the CTG trace; *Dowdie v Camberwell Health Authority* [1997] 8 Med. L.R. 368 where the defendant was held to have been negligent in failing to proceed to a Caesarian section in a case of shoulder dystocia; *Gaughan v Bedfordshire Health Authority* [1997] 8 Med. L.R. 182, QBD—midwife used force for longer than was acceptable in a case of shoulder dystocia; *Sutcliffe v Countess of Chester Hospital NHS Trust* [2002] Lloyd's Rep. Med. 449—injury to the brachial plexus held to be negligent in a case of undiagnosed shoulder dystocia (*cf. Lobb v Hartlepool and East Durham NHS Trust* [2002] Lloyd's Rep. Med. 442 and *Jackson v Bro Taf Health Authority* [2002] EWHC 2344 (QB) where the development Erb's palsy, which arises from damage to the brachial plexus, was found not to have been the result of negligence); *KF (A Child) v Mayday Healthcare NHS Trust* (2001, QBD; unreported)—obstetrician applied excessive traction in a case of shoulder dystocia, causing damage to the brachial plexus; and on obstetric brachial plexus injury generally, see (1995) 1 Clinical Risk 49–73, and (2002) 8 Clinical Risk 215–231.

[11] It is usually said that Caesarian delivery is safer for the foetus than natural delivery, although the risks of harm to the mother are greater. It should not be assumed, however, that Caesarian section operations carry no risk for the foetus: see Roberts (1993) 9 J. of the M.D.U. 76.

[12] Ennis and Vincent (1990) 300 B.M.J. 1365. This reflects a number of general problems,

link between any negligence and the child's injuries may be more difficult to establish.[13]

A doctor may be liable for proceeding to an operation too quickly without considering the alternative treatments available. In *Schanczi v Singh*[14] the defendant surgeon was held negligent for failing to attempt conservative treatment before resorting to spinal surgery:

4–069

> "For a specialist to plunge ahead and operate in the circumstances was exercising entirely undue haste . . . [A] surgeon is retained to perform surgery, but also to avoid performing surgery in the appropriate circumstances."[15]

In *Doughty v North Staffordshire Health Authority*[16] the claimant was born with an extensive birth mark on her face. She underwent a series of 11 to 13 operations between the age of five and 17, performed by a plastic surgeon. Ultimately, she was left with a considerable area of scarring, and the birth mark remained and could not be concealed by make-up. Henry J. held the defendants liable because in 1963 there was no body of competent, professional opinion which would have accepted surgical procedures spanning the claimant's life from five to 17 as proper treatment for the birth mark, and the surgeon was negligent to embark on that course of surgery. On the other hand, in *Defreitas v O'Brian*[17] the defendant's decision to resort to spinal surgery, despite the absence of definite clinical and radiological evidence of nerve compression, was held not to have been negligent. Judge Byrt observed that:

> "To say that every operation in spinal surgery for nerve root compression must always, to be reasonable, supported by clear and unequivocal

---

(n.12 contd.) including inadequate training and supervision of junior and middle ranking staff in the labour ward: *ibid*. See further the Department of Health's *Report on confidential enquiries into maternal deaths in England and Wales*, (1989) H.M.S.O. For discussion of the general practitioner's responsibility in shared obstetric care see Burton (1995) 1 Clinical Risk 148.

[13] *De Martell v Merton and Sutton Health Authority* [1995] 6 Med. L.R. 234; *Robertson v Nottingham Health Authority* [1997] 8 Med. L.R. 1, CA; *Corley v North West Herefordshire Health Authority* [1997] 8 Med. L.R. 45. For discussion of the connection between cerebral palsy and events during labour see Moore (1993) 4 *AVMA Medical & Legal Journal* (No. 3) p. 3; Campbell (1995) 1 Clinical Risk 28. The general view amongst clinicians is that "no more than 15% of children born at term, subsequently demonstrated to have one of the cerebral palsy syndromes, can have this attributed to perinatal asphyxial damage": Rosenbloom (1996) 2 Clinical Risk 43. The so-called "international consensus statement" on the causal relationship between acute intrapartum events and cerebral palsy (published in the *British Medical Journal*: (1999) 319 B.M.J. 1054) has been strongly criticised both in terms of scientific and legal causation: see (2000) 6 Clinical Risk 135–144.

[14] [1988] 2 W.W.R. 465 (Alta. Q.B.).

[15] *ibid*. at p. 472, *per* Marshall J.; see also *Coughlin v Kuntz* (1987) 42 C.C.L.T. 142 (B.C.S.C.); affirmed [1990] 2 W.W.R. 737, 744 (B.C.C.A.) on a failure to try conservative treatment before surgery; *Haughian v Paine* (1987) 37 D.L.R. (4th) 625, 629–635 (Sask. C.A.); *Mann v Judgeo* [1993] 4 W.W.R. 760 (Sask. Q.B.), on the performance of aggressive surgery when "first treatment surgery" was appropriate; *Cherewayko v Grafton* [1993] 3 W.W.R. 604, 619 (Man. Q.B.), on an "unnecessary" operation.

[16] [1992] 3 Med. L.R. 81, QBD.

[17] [1993] 4 Med. L.R. 281; affirmed [1995] P.I.Q.R. P281; [1995] 6 Med. L.R. 108, CA.

clinical and/or radiological evidence is in my judgment a counsel of caution which if applied across the board to those specialising in spinal surgery, too, would deprive many a patient of help when they had been given up as a lost cause by everyone else."[18]

4–070   Conversely, a delay in recommending surgery may also be negligent. In *Powell v Guttman*[19] the claimant developed a condition of avascular necrosis following an operation on her leg performed by the defendant orthopaedic surgeon. The defendant failed to advise the claimant to undergo an arthoplasty operation to correct this. A year after the first operation another surgeon performed the operation, and during the course of that operation the claimant sustained a rotary fracture of the femur. Due to the delay, the condition of the bone had deteriorated as a result of osteoporosis, and this was a "significant cause" of the fracture that occurred. The defendant was held liable on the basis that the delay in the second operation was attributable to his negligence, and this had caused an increase in the osteoporosis which rendered the femur more susceptible to the fracture. This "materially increased the risk of the very fracture which did occur."[20]

(a) Burns

4–071   Where a patient sustains burns in an operating theatre this is usually indicative of negligence. Thus, anaesthetists have been held liable for an explosion caused by a spark igniting a mixture of ether and oxygen,[21] and for knocking a bottle of ether over onto an electric fire.[22] It is negligence to allow a patient's arm to hang over the side of the operating table and come into contact with a hot water can,[23] and where alcohol used to sterilise the patient's body is ignited on the application of a diathermy electrode.[24] In

---

[18] *ibid.* at p. 297. In *Goguen v Crowe* (1987) 40 C.C.L.T. 212 (Nova Scotia S.C.) it was alleged that the defendant obstetrician had intervened prematurely with the use of forceps to deliver a baby who sustained cerebral palsy; this was found, with hindsight, to have been an "error of judgment" but not, on the facts, negligent; *Knight v West Kent Health Authority* [1998] Lloyd's Rep. Med. 18, 23—an obstetrician who elects to use forceps does not know that it will involve "a long and difficult pull" of a baby with an "enormous head" until it becomes difficult.

[19] (1978) 89 D.L.R. (3d) 180 (Man. C.A.).

[20] *ibid.* at p. 188; see further para. 5–046 on the causation aspects of this decision.

[21] *Crits v Sylvester* (1956) 1 D.L.R. (2d) 502; affirmed (1956) 5 D.L.R. (2d) 601 (S.C.C.).

[22] *Paton v Parker* (1942) 65 C.L.R. 187. For discussion of anaesthetic practice in the course of a difficult intubation see *Chambers v Southern Health and Social Services Board* [1990] 1 Med. L.R. 231; *Early v Newham Health Authority* [1994] 5 Med. L.R. 214; and (1995) 1 Clinical Risk, No. 4.

[23] *Hillyer v Governors of St. Bartholomew's Hospital* [1909] 2 K.B. 820, although the case turned on the question of the hospital authority's liability for the negligence of its professional staff. A similar case is *Hall v Lees* [1904] 2 K.B. 602 where a nurse negligently placed a hot water bottle against a patient still under the influence of anaesthetic. The report deals with the question of the liability of the nursing association who employed the nurse.

[24] *Crysler v Pearse* [1943] 4 D.L.R. 738, where the excess alcohol should have been swabbed off or allowed to evaporate; *cf. McFadyen v Harvie* [1941] 2 D.L.R. 663; affirmed [1942] 4 D.L.R. 647 where, in the process of cauterising an ulcer on the claimant's body, there was a

Clarke v Warboys[25] the claimant was undergoing an operation in which extensive bleeding was anticipated, and so electric coagulation was applied. This involved passing a high frequency electrical current through her body, and for this purpose a pad was placed on her buttock. She sustained a severe burn at the site of the pad. The Court of Appeal held the defendants liable, applying *res ipsa loquitur*. Such an accident did not normally happen if reasonable care was exercised. A patient who sustained burns on her face from the use of Grenz rays succeeded in an action against the radiotherapist who had omitted to cover the face with a protective cloth.[26]

(b) "Swab" cases

The danger of swabs or surgical instruments being left inside the patient   4–072
at the end of an operation is clearly something which must be guarded against. But, even in this type of case where the risk of harm to the patient is obvious, the doctor does not give a guarantee that this cannot happen. He is not absolutely liable for leaving a swab behind, but must exercise reasonable care to see that it does not happen. The consequences can be very serious and accordingly the degree of care required in order to satisfy the requirement of reasonableness may be very high indeed. The precautions which can be adopted with swabs include using swabs with tapes to flag their position, a count by nurses, and a search by the surgeon at the conclusion of the operation.

It is not negligence for a surgeon to delegate the task of counting swabs to   4–073
a nurse, but the question remains as to the extent of his responsibility. A surgeon will not necessarily avoid liability by relying on the count by the nurse:

> "As it is the task of the surgeon to put swabs in, so it is his task to take them out, and in that task he must use that degree of care which is reasonable in the circumstances and that must depend on the evidence. If, on the whole of the evidence, it is shown that he did not use that standard of care, he cannot absolve himself if a mistake be made, by saying 'I relied on the nurse.'"[27]

(n.24 contd.) flash. Alcohol had been applied to the site to sterilise it. A jury held that there was no evidence of how the accident occurred.

[25] *The Times*, March 18, 1952. Burns to the buttocks following surgery are, apparently, a common type of claim: Medical Defence Union, *Annual Report 1990*, p. 45; (1993) 9 J. of the M.D.U. 95. The Department of Health has issued specific warning to hospitals about the danger of inflammable liquids igniting during surgery: H.C. (Hazard) (90) 25.

[26] *Gold v Essex County Council* [1942] 2 K.B. 293; *McCaffrey v Hague* [1949] 4 D.L.R. 291, where burns were caused by an excessive dose of X-rays; *Goode v Nash* (1979) 21 S.A.S.R. 419, where a patient's eye was burned by an instrument placed on the eye before it had cooled sufficiently after being sterilised.

[27] *Mahon v Osborne* [1939] 2 K.B. 14, 47, *per* Goddard L.J. (dissenting). See also the extract from *James v Dunlop* (1931) 1 B.M.J. 730, cited by Goddard L.J. at pp. 47–8; and MacKinnon L.J. at pp. 42–43.

He must, at the very least, make some check by asking for confirmation that all the swabs are accounted for; he cannot assume this.[28] In some circumstances the surgeon may have to take additional precautions. In *Urry v Bierer*[29] a surgeon conducting a Caesarian section relied almost exclusively on the count. He did not use swabs with tapes. Pearson J. held that in a routine operation it was negligent not to take any additional precautions, although different considerations might apply in an emergency. The nurses' count might be fallible, and was itself meant to be a secondary check on the procedure adopted by the surgeon for removing the swabs. This decision was affirmed by the Court of Appeal. There was no reason, it was said, why the surgeon should not make some mental effort to remember where he had placed the swabs, particularly since he had chosen not to use tapes.

4–074   In *Anderson v Chasney*[30] the child patient died following an operation to remove his tonsils because a sponge was left in the base of the child's nostrils causing suffocation. It was not the surgeon's practice to use sponges with tapes attached nor to have a nurse present to keep a count of the sponges used, although sponges with tapes were available and the hospital would supply a nurse, on request, to keep a count. The surgeon asked his assistant at the operation whether all the sponges were removed, and the assistant had replied, no. He felt for any remaining sponges and found none. When, after the operation, it was noticed that the child was not breathing a nurse managed to remove the sponge. The Manitoba Court of Appeal, holding the defendant liable, rejected the contention that since he had complied with the accepted practice at the hospital he was not negligent:

> "While the method in which the operation was performed may be purely a matter of technical evidence, the fact that a sponge was left in a position where it was or was not dangerous is one which the ordinary man is competent to consider in arriving at a decision as to whether or not there was negligence."[31]

4–075   On the other hand, although leaving a swab in the patient will be strong evidence of negligence it is not necessarily conclusive. This point is emphasised in the judgment of Scott L.J. in *Mahon v Osborne*,[32] where his Lordship identified some of the factors that might have to be taken into account:

> "It is not every slip or mistake which imports negligence and, in applying the duty of care to the case of a surgeon, it is peculiarly necessary to have regard to the different kinds of circumstances that may present themselves

---

[28] *Mahon v Osborne* [1939] 2 K.B. 14; *James v Dunlop* (1931) 1 B.M.J. 730, CA, discussed in *Mahon v Osborne.*

[29] *The Times,* July 15, 1955, CA.

[30] [1949] 4 D.L.R. 71 (Man. C.A.); affirmed sub nom. *Chasney v Anderson* [1950] 4 D.L.R. 223 (S.C.C.).

[31] *ibid.* at p. 74, *per* McPherson C.J.M.

[32] [1939] 2 K.B. 14. Note, however, that Scott L.J. dissented on the question of whether *res ipsa loquitur* applied to a swab case.

for urgent attention. I will mention a few applicable to a major abdominal operation: (1) The multiform difficulties presented by the particular circumstances of the operation, (2) the condition of the patient and the whole set of problems arising out of the risks to which he is being exposed, (3) the difficulty of the surgeon's choice between risks, (4) the paramount need of his discretion being unfettered if he thinks it right to take one risk to avoid a greater, (5) at the penultimate stage (swab removal) he may, particularly where the patient has been taking the anaesthetic badly and is suffering from shock, be so anxious on surgical grounds to bring the operation to an end as rapidly as possible that, in the exercise of his discretion, perhaps unconsciously exercised, as soon as he has completed the removal of all swabs of which he is at that moment aware he asks the sister for the count and forthwith starts to close the wound."[33]

In *Anderson v Chasney*[34] Coyne J.A. regarded *Mahon v Osborne* as an unsatisfactory case which turned ultimately on a misdirection of the jury. There is, however, a significant difference between the two cases. In *Mahon v Osborne* it was an emergency operation for a perforated duodenal ulcer which the surgeon performed alone. It was a complicated and urgent operation and there was a system for counting the swabs. But in *Anderson v Chasney* it was a routine operation in which there was no system for counting. These circumstances may justify a different conclusion on negligence, although *Mahon v Osborne* probably makes the position in swab cases seem more complicated than it is. In practice such cases are usually settled as indefensible, and most of the cases that are litigated end in a finding of negligence.[35] Even if, on the facts, the conclusion is that the surgeon was not negligent in leaving the swab inside the patient, the result will almost invariably be that the nurse conducting the count was negligent.[36] The position

4–076

---

[33] *ibid.* at pp. 31–32. See also *per* Adamson J.A. in *Anderson v Chasney* [1949] 4 D.L.R. 71, 94: "If a surgeon places a foreign article or substance such as a sponge or instrument in the body of a patient and fails to remove it and the patient is thereby injured, it is evidence of lack of care. Whether it should be held to be negligence depends on the circumstances in each particular case." In *Elliott v Bickerstaff* [1999] N.S.W.C.A. 453; (1999) 48 N.S.W.L.R. 214 it was held that the claimant could not rely on *res ipsa loquitur* in a swab case in which he sued the surgeon, but not the hospital. The surgeon had acted in accordance with responsible practice by conducting a manual search for swabs in the abdominal cavity and seeking confirmation from the theatre sister that all sponges were accounted for.

[34] [1949] 4 D.L.R. 71 (Man. C.A.); affirmed *sub nom. Chasney v Anderson* [1950] 4 D.L.R. 223 (S.C.C.).

[35] See, *e.g., James v Dunlop* (1931) 1 B.M.J. 730 which is considered in *Mahon v Osborne* [1939] 2 K.B. 14; *Dryden v Surrey County Council* [1936] 2 All E.R. 535; *Holt v Nesbitt* [1951] 4 D.L.R. 478, where a dental patient died of asphyxia when a swab lodged in his windpipe; the dentist, who had made no count of swabs used and assumed that they had all been removed when he could see no swabs in the patient's mouth, was held liable; *Garner v Morrell, The Times,* October 31, 1953, where on similar facts the Court of Appeal held the defendant liable on the basis of *res ipsa loquitur; Urry v Bierer, The Times,* July 15, 1955; *Fox v Glasgow South Western Hospitals* 1955 S.L.T. 337; *Cooper v Nevill, The Times,* March 10, 1961 (P.C.).

[36] In *Frandle v MacKenzie* (1990) 5 C.C.L.T. (2d) 113 (B.C.C.A.) liability for not keeping a proper count of the swabs was ascribed 80% to the surgeon and 20% to the nurses.

will usually be the same in the case of a surgical instrument inadvertently left inside the patient's body.[37]

(c) Failed sterilisation

4–077   There have been a number of cases arising from an unwanted pregnancy following a sterilisation operation. The cases tend to fall into two (not mutually exclusive) categories: (i) where the claimant alleges that the sterilisation operation itself was performed negligently;[38] and (ii) where, although the operation was performed with reasonable care, the defendant failed adequately to inform the claimant about the risks of the procedure failing to achieve the desired result of rendering the claimant sterile.[39] Whatever the nature of the negligent error, English law has followed Scottish law in ruling that the parents cannot recover the costs of raising an unplanned child where the child is healthy, but a claim in respect of the child-rearing costs can be maintained where the child is disabled or where the parent is disabled (limited to the costs associated with the disability).[40] On the other hand, where the child is born healthy, the mother may have a claim in respect of her own losses, including general damages for the pain, discomfort and inconvenience of an unwanted pregnancy and birth, and medical expenses and loss of earnings due to the pregnancy and birth (though not loss of earnings attributable to having to give up work to look after the child[41]).

---

[37] *Hocking v Bell* [1948] W.N. 21 (P.C.), where part of a drainage tube was left *in situ*, following a thyroidectomy operation; the defendant was held negligent; *Gloning v Miller* [1954] 1 D.L.R. 372, where a surgeon who left pair of forceps inside a patient was held negligent. No count was made, and no other precautions were taken at the time of the operation; *cf. McDonald v Pottinger* [1953] N.Z.L.R. 196, another forceps case, where a jury found that the surgeon was not guilty of negligence.

[38] *Udale v Bloomsbury Area Health Authority* [1983] 2 All E.R. 522; *Emeh v Kensington and Chelsea Area Health Authority* [1985] Q.B. 1012; *Fallows v Randle* [1997] 8 Med. L.R. 160; *Taylor v Shropshire Health Authority* [1998] Lloyd's Rep. Med. 395; *Dendaas v Yackel* (1980) 109 D.L.R. (3d) 455. For unusual examples of failed sterilisation, where the procedure was experimental see: *Cryderman v Ringrose* [1978] 3 W.W.R. 481 (Alta. C.A.), and *Zimmer v Ringrose* (1981) 125 D.L.R. (3d) 215 (Alta. C.A.). On the negligent performance of an abortion see *Scuriaga v Powell* (1979) 123 S.J. 406; affirmed (1980, CA; unreported), para. 4–041 above; *Fredette v Wiebe* [1986] 5 W.W.R. 222 (B.C.S.C.); *Cherry v Borsman* (1991) 75 D.L.R. (4th) 668 (B.C.S.C.); affirmed (1992) 94 D.L.R. (4th) 487 (B.C.C.A.).

[39] *Eyre v Measday* [1986] 1 All E.R. 488; *Thake v Maurice* [1986] Q.B. 644; *Gold v Haringey Health Authority* [1988] Q.B. 481; *Gowton v Wolverhampton Health Authority* [1994] 5 Med. L.R. 432; *Stobie v Central Birmingham Health Authority* (1994) 22 B.M.L.R. 135; *Lybert v Warrington Health Authority* [1996] 7 Med. L.R. 71, CA; *Dendaas v Yackel* (1980) 109 D.L.R. (3d) 455; *Grey v Webster* (1984) 14 D.L.R. (4th) 706; *Videto v Kennedy* (1981) 125 D.L.R. (3d) 127 (Ont. C.A.—risk of bowel perforation). On the non-disclosure of the risk of the sterilisation failing to achieve complete sterility see para. 6–192.

[40] See *McFarlane v Tayside Health Board* [2000] 2 A.C. 59; *Parkinson v St. James and Seacroft University Hospital NHS Trust* [2001] EWCA Civ 530; [2002] Q.B. 266; *Rees v Darlington Memorial Hospital NHS Trust* [2002] EWCA Civ 88; [2002] 2 All E.R. 177. The cases are discussed at paras 2–038 *et seq.*, and for the assessment of damages in such cases see para. 9–079 *et seq.*

[41] *Greenfield v Irwin* [2001] EWCA Civ 113; [2001] 1 W.L.R. 1279.

It is well-known, at least within the medical profession, that there is a risk   4–078
that a sterilisation operation will prove to be unsuccessful, and the risk varies
with the type of operation and the time at which it is carried out.[42] The fact
that these procedures carry a small, but quantifiable, failure rate can make
it difficult to prove that there has been negligence in the performance of the
operation itself.[43] Thus, in *Grey v Webster*[44] the claimant's claim was unsuccessful because the evidence showed that a failed sterilisation can occur
without negligence and the procedure adopted by the defendant was
approved by expert evidence. But as Bouck J. commented in *Dendaas v
Yackel*,[45] referring to failure rates of 3 to 17 per 1,000 for tubal ligation
"there was of course no indication as to how many of these resulted from
improper or negligent technique and how many came about because of
matters beyond the control of the surgeon." In that case the defendant was
held liable for the negligent performance of the operation itself, because in
a subsequent tubal ligation performed on the claimant the surgeon found
inadequate cauterisation of the fallopian tubes, and the judge was able to
conclude that, on the balance of probabilities, for reasons unknown, the
defendant did not properly cauterise the tubes. In *McLennan v Newcastle
Health Authority*[46] it was held that the defendants were not negligent in
failing to offer the claimant an HSG (hysterosalpingogram) to check that a
sterilisation by tubal ligation had been successful. Such procedures were not
performed routinely, they were uncomfortable, carried a risk of infection,
and there was a possibility of re-opening an occluded tube. Nor was the test
foolproof.

(2) Causing or failing to prevent infection

The commonest type of case falling into this category is that of a patient   4–079
who acquires an infection during a stay in hospital. More rarely a patient
may be discharged from hospital in an infectious condition and infect
someone else with whom he comes into contact. About nine per cent of
patients pick up infections while they are in hospital, and this costs the NHS

---

[42] See, *e.g.*, *Eyre v Measday* [1986] 1 All E.R. 488, 490–491; *Gold v Haringey Health
Authority* [1988] Q.B. 481, 484; *Videto v Kennedy* (1980) 107 D.L.R. (3d) 612, 618 (Ont.
H.C.). The guidance of the Royal College of Obstetricians and Gynaecologists now puts the
risk of pregnancy following sterilisation at a 1 in 200 lifetime risk after female sterilisation
and a 1 in 2000 risk for male sterilisation: see RCOG, *Male and Female Sterilisation*, 1999,
available at *www.rcog.org.uk* (good practice; guidelines).
[43] In *Fallows v Randle* [1997] 8 Med. L.R. 160, CA there were competing theories as to how
the sterilisation operation could have failed, one of which involved negligence by the defendant whereas the other did not. The Court of Appeal held that the trial judge was entitled
to prefer the explanation put forward on behalf of the claimant, thereby finding the defendant negligent.
[44] (1984) 14 D.L.R. (4th) 706 (N.B.Q.B.); *Videto v Kennedy* (1980) 107 D.L.R. (3d) 612, 618
(Ont. H.C.). Similarly, an allegation that the sterilisation had been negligently performed was
rejected by the trial judge in *Gold v Haringey Health Authority* [1988] Q.B. 481, and abandoned by the claimant in *Eyre v Measday* [1986] 1 All E.R. 488.
[45] (1980) 109 D.L.R. (3d) 455 (B.C.S.C.).
[46] [1992] 3 Med. L.R. 215, QBD.

up to £1 billion a year in additional treatment.[47] Cases may arise from cross-infection, with patients acquiring a disease from another patient, or they may result from surgical intervention, or poor hygiene techniques by staff.

4–080   In *Lindsey County Council v Marshall*[48] the claimant was admitted to the defendants' maternity home notwithstanding an outbreak of puerperal fever in the home a week earlier. Neither the claimant nor her doctor was informed of the outbreak. The House of Lords held the defendants liable on the basis of a breach of the general duty owed by occupiers of premises to entrants to ensure that premises are reasonably safe. Lord Wright said that he did "not put the obligation as high as that of a warranty; but the gravity of the risk must emphasise the gravity of the precautions proper to be taken to guard against it."[49] Similarly, in *Heafield v Crane*[50] the claimant was admitted to a cottage hospital for her confinement. After the birth she was moved from the maternity ward to a general ward where a patient was suffering from puerperal fever, and the claimant caught the infection from this patient. Singleton J. held that the hospital authorities were negligent in placing the claimant in a ward where there was a gravely suspicious case of infection, and in failing to warn the claimant. The claimant's doctor was negligent because he ought to have isolated the other patient (he was her doctor too) and when he found that the claimant had been placed in the same ward he should have had her moved to prevent her becoming infected.

4–081   In *Vancouver General Hospital v McDaniel*[51] the claimant went into a hospital for infectious diseases for the treatment of diphtheria, and contracted smallpox. She claimed that the defendants were negligent in the system that they adopted, which involved the juxtaposition of smallpox patients to the claimant, and the attendance on the claimant by nurses who also nursed smallpox patients. On appeal to the Privy Council it was held that the defendants had not been negligent to adopt a new system for managing infectious patients by sterilisation rather than isolation, because they had conformed to a practice accepted as proper by a responsible body of professional opinion. At the time of this decision the claimant would have been unable to proceed against the hospital on the basis that it was vicariously liable for the negligence of the staff in implementing the system of sterilisation that had been adopted.[52] Today, however, such a claim could be made

---

[47] National Audit Office, *The Management and Control of Hospital Acquired Infection in Acute NHS Trusts in England*, 2000, HC 230 Session 1999–2000 (available at *www.nao.gov.uk*). An earlier report, *Hospital Acquired Infections*, Office of Health Economics, 1997, (reported in *The Independent*, September 16, 1997) estimated that hospital acquired infections cause 5,000 deaths a year and contribute to a further 15,000 (more deaths a year in the UK than road deaths or suicides). This report suggested that up to a third of hospital acquired infections could be prevented, whereas the NAO report on managing hospital acquired infections estimated that up to 15% were avoidable. The problem of hospital acquired infection has been recognised for many years. See: *The Times*, September 4, 1990; Cooke (1989) 5 J. of the M.D.U. 62. See further, Ormonde-Walsh and Newham, "Proving hospital-acquired infection" (2003) 9 Clinical Risk 61.
[48] [1937] A.C. 97.
[49] *ibid.* at p. 121.
[50] *The Times*, July 31, 1937.
[51] (1934) 152 L.T. 56.
[52] Applying *Hillyer v Governors of St. Bartholemews Hospital* [1909] 2 K.B. 820; see para. 7–003.

and it would be irrelevant that the claimant was unable to identify which employee was at fault.[53] Moreover, the stronger the evidence that the defendants' system was foolproof, the easier it is to infer that if cross-infection occurred it must have been caused by the negligence of one of the hospital staff in applying the system.[54] This point is illustrated by *Voller v Portsmouth Corporation*[55] in which the claimant developed meningitis after the administration of a spinal anaesthetic. It was admitted that the illness must have been caused either by contamination of the anaesthetic or by an infection occurring during its administration. The court found that the anaesthetic was not contaminated, and the staff had taken the usual precautions to disinfect themselves prior to the operation, but nonetheless held the hospital liable. It could not be said precisely how the accident occurred but there must have been some failure to follow the appropriate sterilisation procedure resulting in contamination from the equipment used.

In the case of post-operative infection, the infection itself cannot be treated   4–082
as evidence of negligence, because no-one can guarantee that post-operative infection will not occur.[56] On the other hand, it is not unreasonable to expect that specialists should be quick to recognise the development of complications following surgery, such as infection, at the earliest possible moment and to treat them accordingly.[57] Discharging an infectious patient from hospital prematurely, with the result that others who come into contact with the patient contract the disease is negligent.[58]

Some cases of infection arise from the transplantation of human organs or   4–083
the transfusion of bodily fluids from a donor who carried the infection.[59]

---

[53] *Cassidy v Ministry of Health* [1951] 2 K.B. 343.

[54] There is an analogy here with the inference that may be drawn as to negligence by an employee where a product has a construction defect and the manufacturer claims that the manufacturing or quality control system is designed to be foolproof: see para. 8–057.

[55] (1947) 203 L.T.J. 264.

[56] *Hajgato v London Health Association* (1982) 36 O.R. (2d) 669, 681 (Ont. H.C.). See further Eykyn (1991) 2 *AVMA Medical & Legal Journal* (No. 4) p. 6; Mann (1993) 1 J. Law and Med. 91, discussing the difference between cases where the claimant is unlikely to succeed and cases where the claimant has some prospect of succeeding; and Sanderson (1995) 310 B.M.J. 1452 on hospital acquired urinary and respiratory infection.

[57] *Rietze v Bruser (No. 2)* [1979] 1 W.W.R. 31, 49–50, *per* Hewak J. (Man. Q.B.): "The fault lies not with the risk or development of infection but with the failure to recognise that it is present as quickly as possible and to take steps to treat it"; *Hajgato v London Health Association* (1982) 36 O.R. (2d) 669, 682, where failure to detect and treat a post-operative infection before crippling injury resulted, in a well-staffed and modern hospital, was held to be evidence of negligence, but on the facts the defendants' evidence rebutted the inference of negligence; see also *Hucks v Cole* (1968), [1993] 4 Med. L.R. 393, CA, where the claimant developed fulminating septicaemia following the normal delivery of a child, and the defendant general practitioner was held negligent in failing to prescribe penicillin when he was aware that, in the circumstances, there was a risk of this potentially fatal infection developing. The fact that the risk was small was irrelevant given the very serious consequences of the infection.

[58] *Evans v Liverpool Corporation* [1906] 1 K.B. 160. The hospital authority was held not liable for the doctor's negligence on the basis that, as the law then stood, it was not vicariously liable for his negligence.

[59] See Norrie (1985) 34 I.C.L.Q. 442 for discussion of both the principles of liability in negligence and the question of consent. As to whether the doctor who performs a blood transfusion can rely on the blood having been screened by the blood bank see *ibid*. at p. 446. See further Giesen (1994) 10 P.N. 2.

One case has been commenced in this country by a patient who developed cancer following the transplantation of a cancerous kidney.[60] This involves allegations of negligence in failing to ensure that the kidney was healthy, failing to communicate the cause of the donor's death to the hospital where the transplant was performed, and failing to remove the kidney when it was discovered that the donor had suffered from cancer. Another potential source of infection stems from the transfusion of bodily fluids, such as blood.[61] In *Re HIV Haemophiliac Litigation*[62] haemophiliacs treated with imported HIV infected blood products commenced proceedings against the Department of Health, the Blood Products Laboratory and the National Blood Transfusion Service, alleging *inter alia* negligence in screening donors, failing to treat the blood products to minimise the risk of infection, failing to warn donors, and failing to achieve a self-sufficiency in blood products within the NHS. Although the litigation was subsequently settled, the Court of Appeal accepted that the claimants had made out at least an arguable case for the existence of a duty of care. Similarly, in *Brown v Alberta*[63] the claimants alleged that the government had negligently failed to pass regulations and adopt policies relating to the safe collection and distribution of blood products, and had negligently failed to provide funding for the implementation of a system of testing for HIV contamination in donated blood. The government sought to have the actions struck out as disclosing no reasonable cause of action, but it was held that the pleadings raised difficult and important issues which needed to be tried, since it could not be said that the actions were doomed to fail. If the proximity of relationship was sufficiently close then it could very well raise a duty of care.[64]

4–084 A number of cases have arisen in Australia and Canada concerning the liability of a blood bank for the infection of patients with HIV from blood transfusions, at a time before a test for HIV had been developed, in 1985. The allegations of negligence consist essentially of the failure to adopt ade-

---

[60] *Sumners v Mid-Downs Health Authority and South East Thames Health Authority*, see (1989) 298 B.M.J. 1544.

[61] The Law Commission identified an example of a successful claim in the German Supreme Court in respect of pre-natal injury for congenital syphilis caused by a negligent blood transfusion given to the mother before conception: Law Com. No. 60 Cmnd. 5709, 1974, para. 77. In *Morgan v Gwent Health Authority*, The Independent, December 14, 1987, CA, a young unmarried woman was negligently given a transfusion of Rhesus positive blood instead of Rhesus negative blood following an operation, which raised the level of antibodies in her blood and put at risk any future pregnancy. She was awarded £20,000 in damages. For a case involving a negligent failure to carry out blood tests during pregnancy when it was known that the patient suffered from blood incompatibility see *Bagley v North Hertfordshire Health Authority* (1986) 136 N.L.J. 1014; see also *Fairhurst v St. Helens and Knowsley Health Authority* [1994] 5 Med. L.R. 422; and *Scrimshaw v Harrow Health Authority* (1992) 3 AVMA Medical & Legal Journal (No. 3) p. 15 on known Rhesus incompatibility.

[62] (1990), [1996] P.I.Q.R. P220.

[63] [1994] 2 W.W.R. 283 (Alta. Q.B.).

[64] "A question that must be answered, based on evidence that can only be assessed at trial, is whether or not the defendants were entitled to rely on the [Canadian Blood Committee] and the Crown as a member of the CBC to ensure the safety of the public in relation to the blood supply in Alberta," *ibid.* at p. 289 *per* Moore C.J.Q.B.

quate screening methods to exclude as donors those from groups known to be at high risk of being infected with HIV, and the failure to introduce "surrogate testing."[65] In addition, there may be allegations that the blood bank or the hospital where the transfusion took place failed to warn doctors and/or patients of the risk of contracting HIV from blood transfusions.[66] Clearly, where the risk of infection was unknown or unforeseeable it will not be negligent to fail to take precautions against the risk.[67] Once the risk of transmission of HIV through blood products became recognised the question of negligence becomes a matter of whether reasonably practicable steps could have been taken to eliminate or reduce the risk. Negligence actions based on the failure to adopt adequate screening or surrogate testing have not been successful, bearing in mind the fact that negligence must be judged, not with the benefit of hindsight, but by reference to the state of knowledge at the time, which between 1982 and 1984 was in constant flux as scientists and health authorities sought to discover the causes of the newly identified condition of AIDS.[68] Surrogate testing, for example, namely testing blood for Hepatitis B core antibodies (the anti-HBc test) on the basis that there was an association between those who tested positive and those in high risk groups for AIDS, was highly controversial. It was not particularly effective as a surrogate test,[69] and there were fears that introducing surrogate testing could lead to a reduction in the blood supply by three to five per cent, because a positive test would result in the discarding of blood that might be

---

[65] *H. v Royal Alexandra Hospital for Children* [1990] 1 Med. L.R. 297 (N.S.W.S.C.); *E. v Australian Red Cross Society* (1991) 105 A.L.R. 53 (Aus. Fed. C.A.); affirming (1991) 99 A.L.R. 601; [1991] 2 Med. L.R. 303; *P.Q. v Australian Red Cross Society* [1992] 1 V.R. 19 (Vict.S.C.); *Pittman Estate v Bain* (1994) 112 D.L.R. (4th) 257 (Ont. Ct., Gen. Div.). On infection with Hepatitis from blood products see: *Kitchen v McMullen* (1989) 62 D.L.R. (4th) 481 (N.B.C.A.). On the question of whether the identity of blood donors should be revealed for the purpose of litigation see paras 10–154 to 10–156.

[66] *H. v Royal Alexandra Hospital for Children* [1990] 1 Med. L.R. 297 (N.S.W.S.C.); *P.Q. v Australian Red Cross Society* [1992] 1 V.R. 19 (Vict.S.C.).

[67] Thus, in *H. v Royal Alexandra Hospital for Children* [1990] 1 Med. L.R. 297 it was not negligent to fail to give a warning of the risk to doctors or patients in 1982, though by 1983 the situation had changed.

[68] See, *e.g.*, the comments of Sheppard J. in *E. v Australian Red Cross Society* (1991) 105 A.L.R. 53, 82 (Aus. Fed. C.A.): "In cases such as this, where the facts involve a question at the cutting edge of medical and scientific knowledge concerning the development, the identification and the effects of a horrendous disease and the precautions necessary to safeguard the community against its consequences, the law will not lightly reach the conclusion, high though the duty of care may be, that institutions such as the Society here were required to do something about which there is disagreement amongst experienced persons in medical science and which may or may not have obviated the risk. Where, as here, the suggested course which the defendant should have followed runs counter to a body of medical and scientific opinion genuinely held by highly qualified and experienced persons with front line responsibility for combating the grave problem which AIDS has posed for the community, the court will not easily find that another course, advocated by other medical and scientific experts though it may be, should have been followed." See also *per* Pincus J. at p. 87.

[69] A positive anti-HBc test does not establish that the donor is HIV positive, and a negative test does not negative HIV. A positive surrogate test had about a 50% coincidence with HIV infection, according to the evidence in *E. v Australian Red Cross Society* (1991) 105 A.L.R. 53. In *Pittman Estate v Bain* (1994) 112 D.L.R. (4th) 257 this figure was put at 80%.

perfectly safe to use.[70] There was also the possibility of a "magnet effect" whereby those who were at risk of having contracted the "AIDS virus" donated blood for the specific purpose of having the surrogate test performed on them. Given that a positive surrogate test had at best a 50 per cent coincidence with HIV infection, this could have had the effect of increasing the number of undetected donations of HIV-infected blood in the blood supply, rather than reducing it. The fact that the defendants decided against surrogate testing could not be considered negligent when no more than 10 of the 2000 blood banks in the United States ever adopted surrogate testing, and no blood banking or government organisation ever recommended the adoption of surrogate testing. Moreover, the standard of care to be expected of a blood bank should reflect the fact that it was neither a commercial organisation operating for a profit nor a public health organisation, with a duty to monitor, investigate and control the spread of disease.[71]

4–085   On the other hand, in *Walker Estate v York-Finch General Hospital*[72] the Canadian Red Cross Society was held to have been negligent in the method of screening blood donors for HIV, in that it had asked potential donors about their general health instead of asking about symptom specific conditions. The Supreme Court of Canada held that the trial judge was entitled to reject expert evidence that the screening procedures were reasonable, because he was not asked to assess complex scientific or highly technical matters. The issue was simply whether the general health question was sufficient to deter an HIV infected donor from donating blood. The issue was not how an expert would respond to the donor screening questions, but how a lay person would respond.[73]

4–086   In this country the question of whether any NHS body could owe a duty of care in negligence to patients in respect of infected blood has been rendered largely redundant by the ruling of Burton J. in *A v The National Blood Authority*[74] that contaminated blood is a defective product to which the strict liability rules of Part 1 of the Consumer Protection Act 1987 apply.[75] Liability under the Act is strict, in that it does not depend on the proof of

---

[70] A positive anti-HBc test did not mean that the blood was infectious for Hepatitis, merely that the donor had previously had the infection.

[71] *Pittman Estate v Bain* (1994) 112 D.L.R. (4th) 257, 313, 318–319. Lang J. commented that the social need for a continued supply of blood created different considerations. It was not a product that could simply be removed from the market if inherently dangerous because it is an essential source of life to many. The need for the product outweighs the risk. This did not mean that the collector of the blood did not have a duty to exercise reasonable care, but it did suggest that the calculation of what was reasonable had to be approached with some sensitivity to these issues. Note, however, the claimants' actions in this case succeeded on the basis that there had been negligence both by the Canadian Red Cross Society and the hospital where the patient had received his transfusion in implementing a suitable "lookback" program to identify those patients whom it was subsequently discovered had received HIV-infected blood, see para. 4–040.

[72] (2001) 198 D.L.R. (4th) 193 (S.C.C.).

[73] *ibid.* at [82] *per* Major J.

[74] [2001] 3 All E.R. 289.

[75] Burton J. actually applied the European Community Directive on Liability for Defective Products (85/374/EEC) which has direct effect in English Law. The Consumer Protection Act 1987 was enacted in order to comply with the Directive.

fault. The fact that the risk of infection (with Hepatitis C) was unavoidable, the impracticability and the cost of identifying the potentially harmful virus and taking appropriate precautions, and the fact that blood was supplied by the defendants as a service to society, were all irrelevant to the defendants' liability.[76]

Similar issues arise from the possibility of transmitting infection through the donor insemination of semen.[77] In *ter Neuzen v Korn*[78] the claimant contracted HIV from artificial insemination in January 1985. The risk of infection from artificial insemination was not widely known in North America until mid-1985, although in Australia it was known by November or December 1984 that HIV could be transmitted through blood transfusion, and there was a decision to impose a moratorium on all bodily fluid and tissue transfers, because it was known that the Elisa test for HIV was being developed in the United States, was already being used in a research setting, and would soon be available for clinical use. The defendant and North American experts did not learn of the Australian moratorium until after September 1985. It was held that this was not a case in which the jury, acting judicially, could find the common practice of competent Canadian doctors to be negligent. The proper test was whether the defendant conducted himself as a reasonable doctor, and this required the jury to confine itself to prevailing standards of practice.[79]

4–087

Surgeons who are infected with HIV or Hepatitis B or C and who knowingly continue to practise surgery expose their patients to a foreseeable and unacceptable risk of infection, given the seriousness of the consequences, notwithstanding that the risk of passing on infection is comparatively small. This would almost certainly be deemed to be negligent if a patient were infected in this way. The General Medical Council guidance, *Serious Communicable Disease*,[80] advises doctors who have any reason to believe that they have been exposed to a serious communicable disease to seek and follow professional advice on whether they should undergo testing, and whether, and in what ways, they should modify their practice to protect their

4–088

---

[76] For a more detailed discussion see paras 8–079 *et seq.*

[77] For discussion of the risks of sexually transmitted disease and HIV infection associated with donor insemination see Barratt and Cooke (1989) 299 B.M.J. 1178, and 1531. Stern (1994) 2 Med. L. Rev. 261 discussed the possibility of strict liability under the Consumer Protection Act 1987 in respect of donated gametes. In the light of *A v The National Blood Authority* [2001] 3 All E.R. 289 it seems likely that infected gametes would fall within the Act. The analogy between donated blood and donated gametes is very close.

[78] (1993) 103 D.L.R. (4th) 473 (B.C.C.A.); affirmed (1995) 127 D.L.R. (4th) 577 (S.C.C.).

[79] A new trial was ordered to consider the question of whether the defendant had exercised reasonable care in selecting and screening the semen donors for sexually transmitted diseases. It was accepted that HIV was within the same class of injury as other sexually transmitted diseases, so that the defendant could be liable for the damage caused notwithstanding that he did not foresee that a failure to undertake appropriate screening could result in HIV infection.

[80] October 1997 (available at *www.gmc-uk.org/standards*). See also Mulholland (1993) 9 P.N. 79 for discussion of the position of health care workers who are HIV positive; Department of Health, *HIV Infected Health Care Workers: A Consultation Paper on Management and Patient Notification* (June 2002) (available at *www.doh.gov.uk/aids.htm*).

patients. Doctors should not rely on their own assessment of the risks they pose to patients. One surgeon, a Hepatitis B carrier who had infected 19 patients and put hundreds of others at risk, was convicted of the offence of public nuisance and jailed.[81]

(3) Miscalculating drug reactions

4–089   Doctors must take account of manufacturers' instructions and known side-effects when prescribing drugs, although they should not necessarily rely on the manufacturers' information unthinkingly, since it is known that manufacturers are not always entirely frank about the contra-indications or risks associated with their product.[82] But a decision to exceed manufacturers' guidelines or the dosages indicated in MIMMS in prescribing a drug is not necessarily negligent.[83] Where a doctor ignores the manufacturer's instructions and warnings, it is the doctor who is responsible for any adverse reactions;[84] the manufacturer will not be liable since a warning addressed to the doctor will normally discharge the manufacturer's duty of care to the patient in the case of prescription drugs.[85]

4–090   Three types of case will tend to arise. First, where the doctor is simply unaware of the known side-effects. If he ought reasonably to have known then he is negligent.[86] Secondly, where the doctor is generally aware of the dangers but makes an isolated error and gives an overdose or prescribes the wrong drug.[87] Thirdly, there may be cases where the doctor is aware of the risk from

---

[81] *The Times*, September 30, 1994 (news report); see Mulholland (1995) 11 P.N. 70. See also *R. v Thornton* (1991) 1 O.R. (3d) 480 (Ont. C.A.); affirmed (1993) 13 O.R. (3d) 744 (S.C.C.), and Bronitt (1994) 1 J. Law and Med. 245 on liability for the crime of public nuisance of persons who knowingly donate HIV-infected blood.

[82] See, *e.g.*, *Buchan v Ortho Pharmaceuticals (Canada) Ltd* (1986) 25 D.L.R. (4th) 658 (Ont. C.A.), paras 8–036 and 8–039.

[83] *Vernon v Bloomsbury Health Authority* (1986), [1995] 6 Med. L.R. 297, where the doctors were treating a life-threatening condition. See, however, the comments on the evidence in this case at [1995] 6 Med. L.R. 434.

[84] For a case in which it was alleged that a general practitioner had ignored the manufacturer's statement of contra-indications for giving a combined vaccination against cholera and typhoid see *King v King* (1987, CA; unreported). The action was successful at first instance, but reversed on appeal. See also *Newman v Hounslow & Spelthorne Health Authority* (1985, QBD; unreported), where the claimant suffered chronic adhesive arachnoiditis, a known reaction to myodil, a contrast agent used in myelography. The defendants negligently failed to spot this complication, and so failed to take the remedial measures indicated in the manufacturer's warning of adverse reactions; Herxheimer and Young (1990) 140 N.L.J. 859 on the adverse effects of minoxidil, including excessive hair growth and skin pigmentation.

[85] See para. 8–035.

[86] In *Reynard v Carr* (1983) 30 C.C.L.T. 42 (B.C.S.C.) the defendant was ignorant of the risks of avascular necrosis associated with prolonged use of prednisone, and apparently indifferent even to its other well-known side-effects. For a case of osteoporosis resulting from long term use of prednisolone see (1990) 1 *AVMA Medical & Legal Journal* (No. 3) p. 10. "Side-effects" can include the risk of the patient becoming dependent upon the drug, as occurred with some patients taking benzodiazepines: (1988) 4 J. of the M.D.U. 46. See *Rowan or Kennedy v Steinberg* [1997] 8 Med. L.R. 30 (Court of Session, OH) where general practitioners were held not to have been negligent in failing to withdraw the tranquiliser Equanil from the claimant, who was addicted to the drug.

[87] See, *e.g.*, *Dwyer v Roderick*, (1983) 127 S.J. 806; *The Times*, November 12, 1983 where a

side-effects, but calculates that it is a reasonable risk to run in the circumstances, given the condition for which the drug is prescribed. If the calculation is correct by reference to the standards of the profession he is not negligent, but if the risk was unreasonable in the circumstances he will be liable.

For example, in *Battersby v Tottman*[88] a doctor prescribed a very high dose of melleril to a patient who was suffering from a mental illness. He knew that there was a danger that the drug could cause serious and permanent eye damage, but he took the view that the benefits of the drug outweighed the risk from the side-effects, since without treatment the patient was suicidal, and other methods of treatment had failed. The risk materialised, the patient suffering permanent eye damage. It was held that the decision to prescribe a dosage that was far in excess of the recommended dosages was not negligent; the risk was justified by the potential consequences of not using the drug.[89] By way of contrast, in *Graham v Persyko*[90] the defendant gastroenterologist wrongly, but not negligently, diagnosed that the claimant had Crohn's disease, and prescribed prednisone which caused avascular necrosis of the femoral heads. This is a rare but known complication of the drug. Prednisone is a very potent drug with a multitude of serious adverse effects, and, it was said, a low safety margin. When the defendant prescribed the drug the patient was asymptomatic, although the drug is only used to treat symptoms, since there is no cure for Crohn's disease. The defendant was found negligent; the risk from side-effects was disproportionate to the anticipated benefit to the patient. **4–091**

It is also possible that the correct dosage of a drug may be undercalculated. A number of cases have arisen in which patients undergoing surgery have been awake and conscious of pain during the operation but unable to communicate with medical staff due to being paralysed by muscle relaxant drugs. This may or may not be due to a fault in the administration of the anaesthetic.[91] **4–092**

(n.87 contd.) general practitioner negligently directed the patient to take an overdose in the prescription, and a pharmacist failed to spot the error; *McCaffrey v Hague* [1949] 4 D.L.R. 291, where a doctor miscalculated the dosage of X-rays. See further (1990) 1 *AVMA Medical & Legal Journal* (No. 1) p. 11, reporting on the overdoses of radiation given to over 200 patients over a six month period at the Royal Devon and Exeter Hospital, due to the miscalibration of a mobaltron cobalt radiotherapy machine. The miscalculation of drug doses through arithmetic error is apparently not uncommon: see Rolfe and Harper (1995) 310 B.M.J. 1173; (1998) 4 Clinical Risk 103–109, 173–183. Taxis and Barber (2003) 326 B.M.J. 684 found that errors occurred in about half of the intravenous drug doses observed in a hospital setting.

[88] (1985) 37 S.A.S.R. 524 (S.C. of S.Aus.).

[89] "It was a considered professional judgment made after consideration of all aspects and was supported by a body of medical evidence called by the respondent": *ibid.*, p. 526, *per* King C.J.

[90] (1986) 27 D.L.R. (4th) 699 (Ont.C.A.); (1986) 34 D.L.R. (4th) 160 (S.C.C.) leave to appeal refused.

[91] See *Ludlow v Swindon Health Authority* [1989] 1 Med. L.R. 104; *Taylor v Worcester and District Health Authority* [1991] 2 Med. L.R. 215; *Ackers v Wigan Health Authority* [1991] 2 Med. L.R. 232; *Jacobs v Great Yarmouth and Waveney Health Authority* [1995] 6 Med. L.R. 192. See further (1990) 1 *AVMA Medical & Legal Journal* (No. 1) pp. 13 and 16; *ibid.*, (No. 2), p. 15; Medical Defence Union, *Annual Report 1990*, p. 18. This problem appears to have arisen most frequently in the case of women undergoing Caesarian section deliveries, but not all cases have involved "two patients": see *Phelan v East Cumbria Health Authority* [1991] 2 Med. L.R. 419; Medical Defence Union, *Annual Report 1989*, p. 21. In

(4) Injections

4-093   Injections may be a source of problems because they are given in the wrong place, or the hypodermic may contain the wrong substance, or an excessive dose, or the needle may break. Not all errors, however, will give rise to a claim for negligence. In *Caldeira v Gray*[92] damage to the sciatic nerve following an injection in the buttocks was found to have been caused by negligence, but in *Wilcox v Cavan*[93] the Supreme Court of Canada held that where gangrene had developed in the claimant's arm following an intramuscular injection, the nurse who administered the injection was not liable under the principle of *res ipsa loquitur*. Although there was no explanation as to how the injection had found its way into the claimant's circumflex artery, the defendant's version of events was consistent with the absence of negligence. It has been held that an injection into the patient's surrounding tissues instead of a vein is not necessarily negligent if the vein is difficult to find.[94] On the other hand, administering an excessive dose of a drug having misread the instructions is clearly negligent,[95] as is an excessive dose of anaesthetic given through misjudgment attributable to inexperience.[96]

4-094   In *Collins v Hertfordshire County Council*[97] a patient died following an injection of cocaine instead of procaine as a local anaesthetic, due to a misunderstanding between the surgeon and the inexperienced doctor who had been requested to prepare the anaesthetic. Hilbery J. said that every surgeon must take responsibility for what he injects into a patient as an infiltration or injection for a local anaesthetic, and this requires reasonable steps to make sure that he is injecting that which he ordered. Even allowing for the

(n.91 contd.) *Early v Newham Health Authority* [1994] 5 Med. L.R. 214 the claimant recovered consciousness when she was still under the effect of paralysing drugs, producing panic and distress. It was held that on the facts there had been no negligence. For discussion see (1995) 1 Clinical Risk, No. 4. For consideration of the psychiatric consequences of anaesthetic awareness see Hay (1996) 2 Clinical Risk 172.

[92] [1936] 1 All E.R. 540; see also *Hammond v North West Hertfordshire Health Authority* (1991) 2 *AVMA Medical & Legal Journal* (No. 1) p. 12, where, in the course of injecting hydrocortisone into the claimant's wrist as treatment for carpal tunnel syndrome, the defendant negligently injected the median nerve, rendering the claimant's hand virtually useless; *Feist v Gordon* (1990) 74 D.L.R. (4th) 140 (Alta. C.A.), where an ophthalmologist was held liable for piercing the claimant's eyeball when administering an injection, having omitted a standard precaution.

[93] (1974) 50 D.L.R. (3d) 687 (S.C.C.); rev'g (1973) 44 D.L.R. (3d) 42 (N.B.C.A.); *Fischer v Waller* [1994] 1 W.W.R. 83 (Alta. Q.B.), where it was held that perforation of the globe of the eye during the course of administering a local anaesthetic prior to cataract surgery was a rare but recognised risk of the procedure which could occur in the absence of negligence.

[94] *Williams v North Liverpool Hospital Management Committee*, *The Times*, January 17, 1959; *Prout v Crowley* (1956) 1 B.M.J. 580; *Gent v Wilson* (1956) 2 D.L.R. (2d) 160, where an allegation of negligence in selecting a site for vaccination of a child failed on the evidence.

[95] *Strangeways-Lesmere v Clayton* [1936] 2 K.B. 11; *Smith v Brighton and Lewes Hospital Management Committee*, *The Times*, May 2, 1958; *Sellers v Cooke* [1990] 2 Med. L.R. 16, 19, where a "virtually barbaric" dosage of an intravenous drip was used in the performance of an abortion. For discussion of some of the problems that can arise from the use of intravenous drips see Marcovitch (1991) 2 *AVMA Medical & Legal Journal* (No. 3) p. 14.

[96] As, *e.g.*, in *Jones v Manchester Corporation* [1952] Q.B. 852; *Skelton v Lewisham and North Southwark Health Authority* [1998] Lloyd's Rep. Med. 324, 332, QBD.

[97] [1947] 1 K.B. 598.

fact that the person to whom the request was given was skilled in such things and that the solution was made up in a hospital pharmacy:

". . . still there remains in him a residuum of obligation and duty as the surgeon who will make the injection . . . to make an efficient check to see that he is getting what he ordered, whoever has mixed it or however it has been mixed."[98]

In *Ritchie v Chichester Health Authority*[99] the treatment protocol for the administration of an epidural anaesthetic to a woman in the course labour required both the midwife and the anaesthetist to check that the correct drug had been selected for injection by reading the name on the ampoule. Despite the fact that there would have to have been a series of errors on the part of the medical staff involved, the defendants were held liable on the basis that the anaesthetist had injected a neurotoxic substance into the claimant when administering the epidural anaesthetic. This type of error is not uncommon. An article referred to in evidence in *Ritchie* suggested that administering the wrong drug can occur in over seven per cent of adverse anaesthetic incidents. The article commented that: 4–095

"All anaesthetists should be aware that errors are common, and that they occur both with ampoules and with syringes. It may help if they are also aware that slips are usually caused by failure to monitor a highly routine action, and that this failure is much more likely when limited cognitive resources are compromised by haste, inattention, distraction or fatigue."[1]

It is not uncommon for needles to break in the course of giving an injection, but this is not necessarily an indication of negligence. In *Brazier v Ministry of* 4–096

---

[98] *ibid.* at p. 607; see also Medical Defence Union, *Annual Report 1990*, p. 19 on a mix up with an unlabelled syringe; Hill (1990) 6 J. of the M.D.U. 10; *cf. Fussell v Beddard* (1942) 2 B.M.J. 411, above, para. 4–054, n. 59; and *Bugden v Harbour View Hospital* [1947] 2 D.L.R. 338 where, in the course of an operation, a doctor asked for novocaine, was handed a bottle by a nurse, and without examining the label he injected it into the patient. The solution was adrenalin and the patient died. It was held that the doctor was not negligent in failing to look at the label since it was a routine matter and there was nothing about the circumstances to put him on inquiry, and he was entitled to rely on experienced nurses. The nurse was negligent. This decision is difficult to reconcile with *Collins*.
[99] [1994] 5 Med. L.R. 187, QBD.
[1] *ibid.* at p. 210. See also Dr. J. Lunn, "The Role of the Anaesthetist," in Action for the Victims of Medical Accidents, *Risk Areas in Medical Practice*, 1993, pp. 128–136; and Dr. Hannington-Kiff, "Overview of Obstetric Lumbar Epidural Blocks" (1993) 4 *AVMA Medical & Legal Journal* (No. 1) p. 2. See *Hepworth v Kerr* [1995] 6 Med. L.R. 139; (1996) 2 Clinical Risk 73–87 for a case where the anaesthetist was held negligent for adopting a novel, and unvalidated, method of hypotensive anaesthesia; *Glass v Cambridge Health Authority* [1995] 6 Med. L.R. 91, where the anaesthetist failed adequately to monitor the patient's transition from automatic to spontaneous ventilation at the end of an operation under general anaesthetic; *Muzio v North West Herts Health Authority* [1995] 6 Med. L.R. 184, where an anaesthetist was found not negligent when, in the course of inserting a needle for a spinal anaesthetic, she penetrated the dura, leading the claimant to develop severe spinal headaches.

Defence[2] the court accepted that a needle which broke in a patient's buttock was caused by a latent defect in the needle for which the defendant was not responsible.[3] By contrast, in *Cardin v City of Montreal*[4] a doctor administered a vaccine by hypodermic needle to a child who was struggling against his mother's efforts to keep him still. The doctor insisted on proceeding with the injection despite the mother's protestations and her offer to return another day when the child was calmer, and the needle broke in the child's arm with serious consequences. The Supreme Court of Canada held that the doctor was negligent in not postponing the injection until the child was in a less agitated state, since complete immobilisation of the arm was an essential precaution.

4-097   The fact that an instrument, such as a needle, has broken may indicate that the instrument itself was defective in which case there may be an action against the manufacturer either in negligence or under the Consumer Protection Act 1987. In *G. v Fry Surgical International Ltd*[5] the blade of a pair of arthroscopy scissors fractured during the course of an operation and a fragment was lost in the claimant's knee. An action under the Consumer Protection Act 1987 against the importers of the scissors, on the basis that the scissors were defective, was settled by the defendants.[6]

(5) Failure to monitor treatment

4-098   A doctor has a duty to monitor the treatment given to the patient, particularly where the treatment carries a high risk of an adverse reaction.[7] This duty obviously extends to post-operative conditions which the patient may develop. In *Bayliss v Blagg*[8] the defendants were held negligent for

---

[2] [1965] 1 Lloyd's Rep. 26.

[3] See also *Gerber v Pines* (1935) 79 S.J. 13; *Galloway v Hanley* (1956) 1 B.M.J. 580; *Daniels v Heskin* [1954] I.R. 73: "It is certainly not open to a jury . . . to hold that the breaking was caused by imperfection of technique on the ground that say in 60% of cases of broken needles it is so caused . . ." *per* Lavery J. at p. 79.

[4] (1961) 29 D.L.R. (2d) 492 (S.C.C.). See also *Murphy v St. Catharines General Hospital* (1963) 41 D.L.R. (2d) 697 (Ont. H.C.), where a junior doctor's negligence in inserting an intravenous catheter resulted in severing the catheter which was left in the patient's vein.

[5] (1992) 3 *AVMA Medical & Legal Journal* (No. 4) p. 12.

[6] For definition of an importer see the Consumer Protection Act 1987, s. 2(2)(c); and for definition of when a product is defective see *ibid.*, s. 3(1). See further paras 8–071, 8–075.

[7] *Marshall v Rogers* [1943] 4 D.L.R. 68, where a doctor who changed a diabetic's diet and reduced his insulin dosage should have conducted daily urine tests on the patient and have watched the patient very carefully; *Male v Hopmans* (1967) 64 D.L.R. (2d) 105, 113–115 (Ont. C.A.), where a doctor was held negligent in failing to prescribe audiometric tests during the course of treating a patient with a drug for which the manufacturers recommended such testing; *Wilsher v Essex Area Health Authority* [1987] Q.B. 730, on negligence in monitoring the blood oxygen levels of a premature baby in a special care baby unit.

[8] (1954) 1 B.M.J. 709; see also *Ares v Venner* (1970) 14 D.L.R. (3d) 4 (S.C.C.) and *Harrington v Essex Area Health Authority, The Times*, November 14, 1984 QBD, on plaster casts; and on post-operative infection see *Rietze v Bruser (No. 2)* [1979] 1 W.W.R. 31, 49–50. In *Lee v O'Farrell* (1988) 43 C.C.L.T. 269 (B.C.S.C.) the defendant was negligent in relying on an inadequate post-operative X-ray of the patient's femur. During the course of the operation the femur had been inadvertently broken at the base of the femoral neck. This could easily have been repaired at the time, but because the X-ray did not show the head and neck of the femur it was not spotted and, left untreated for several weeks, avascular necrosis set in.

failing to do anything about a marked deterioration in the condition of the patient's leg following the application of a plaster cast, and in *Poole v Morgan*[9] it was held that a patient who had received laser treatment on his eye should be examined as soon as possible after the treatment. A delay of one month was too long, and negligent. Where a defendant had performed an "innovative" sterilisation procedure he was found negligent for failing to follow the patient's progress by conducting regular medical examinations.[10] A patient recovering from a general anaesthetic will require careful monitoring. In *Coyne v Wigan Health Authority*[11] the claimant sustained brain damage caused by hypoxia for a period of four to five minutes when she was in the recovery ward following an operation under general anaesthetic. The defendants accepted that the principle of *res ipsa loquitur* applied, seeking to explain the incident on the basis that the hypoxia was the result of silent regurgitation of gastric content. Rose J. held that the evidence did not support the defendants' explanation, which was implausible because there was no recorded instance of silent aspiration leading to brain damage and only one such case was referred to in evidence. Accordingly, the appropriate inference was that there had been negligence in monitoring the patient. In *Newbury v Bath District Health Authority*[12] the claimant developed cauda equina syndrome following spinal surgery. The defendants were held to have been negligent in failing to carry out tests for neurological deficit in the immediate post-operative period in light of the patient's symptoms.

(6) Lack of resources

Although there is no case in this country in which a hospital authority   4–099
has been held liable in negligence for failing to provide adequate resources for the treatment of a patient, the possibility of such a claim has been canvassed in two Court of Appeal decisions. As a general rule, the defendant's resources, or lack of them, is not relevant to the question of liability in the tort of negligence. The burden, or cost, of taking precautions against a foreseeable risk is a factor to be taken into account in determining whether the defendant acted reasonably, but if on an objective assessment he ought reasonably to have taken precautions his impecuniosity is not a

---

[9] [1987] 3 W.W.R. 217; *Cavanagh v Bristol and Weston Health Authority* [1992] 3 Med. L.R. 49, QBD, where the defendants were held negligent for failing to follow up and monitor the patient's condition, which deteriorated following an operation on his eye; *Chaunt v Hertfordshire Area Health Authority* (1982, QBD; unreported), where there was a negligent failure to keep adequate records of the patient's progress, with the result that there was a failure to detect intra-peritoneal bleeding leading to peritonitis. On the duty of a midwife to conduct regular vaginal examinations during the course of labour, see *Murphy v Wirral Health Authority* [1996] 7 Med. L.R. 99.

[10] *Zimmer v Ringrose* (1981) 125 D.L.R. (3d) 215, 225–226 (Alta. C.A.), affirming (1978) 89 D.L.R. (3d) 646.

[11] [1991] 2 Med. L.R. 301, QBD.

[12] (1998) 47 B.M.L.R. 138, QBD.

defence.[13] In *Knight v Home Office*[14] Pill J. held that prison authorities were not negligent in failing to provide the same level of staffing for prisoners suffering from a psychiatric illness that would be found in a psychiatric hospital outside prison. Thus, the standard of reasonable care "in all the circumstances" allows for different standards of medical care in a prison compared to a hospital. The lack of resources to provide a better staff/patient ratio, however, was not necessarily a complete defence. If, his Lordship observed, it was said that there were no funds to provide any medical facilities for prisoners there would be a breach of the duty of care, just as lack of funds would not excuse a public body which operated its vehicles on public roads without any system of maintenance, if an accident occurred due to lack of maintenance. Subsequently, in *Brooks v Home Office*[15] Garland J. held that a pregnant prisoner on remand was entitled to the same standard of antenatal care as if she were at liberty, subject to the practical constraints of having to be escorted to hospital. *Knight* was distinguished on the basis that it was concerned with the level of supervision for convicted prisoners with psychiatric problems and a propensity to self-harm.

4–100   The example given by Pill J. in *Knight* is, of course, extreme, but in *Wilsher v Essex Area Health Authority*[16] Browne-Wilkinson V.-C. suggested that "a health authority which so conducts its hospital that it fails to provide doctors of sufficient skill and experience to give the treatment offered at the hospital may be directly liable in negligence to the patient."[17] Given the structure of hospital medicine within the NHS, in which very junior and overworked doctors are often stretched to the limit of their endurance and professional capacity, this is not in the least a far-fetched example. Such a claim, however, as his Lordship recognised, would raise "awkward" questions:

> "To what extent should the authority be held liable if (*e.g.* in the use of junior housemen) it is only adopting a practice hallowed by tradition?

---

13 In *P.Q. v Australian Red Cross Society* [1992] 1 V.R. 19, 33 (Vict.S.C.) McGarvie J. held that, in assessing the conduct of a blood bank in an action alleging that the defendants had been negligent in failing to take reasonable precautions to protect the claimant from infection with HIV from a transfusion of blood products, the question of whether the blood bank had fallen short of the required standard of care was to be measured, not by reference to a reasonable person with the defendant's actual resources in terms of staff, facilities and finance, but by reference to a reasonable person with adequate resources available to conduct the enterprise in which the Red Cross was engaged. The defendant's compliance with its duty of care should not be tested "by reference to the standard which might be expected of a partly voluntary charitable or benevolent organisation with limited resources of finance or staff," *ibid.* at p. 34; *cf. Pittman Estate v Bain* (1994) 112 D.L.R. (4th) 257, holding that blood banks should be judged by the standards of other blood bank, not by reference to commercial organisations, and thus if other "responsible" blood banks were unable, through lack of resources, to take such precautions the defendant will not be liable for failing to take the same precautions.

14 [1990] 3 All E.R. 237.

15 [1999] 2 F.L.R. 33.

16 [1987] Q.B. 730, 778.

17 See also the comments of Lord Browne-Wilkinson in *X. (minors) v Bedfordshire County Council* [1995] 2 A.C. 633, 740. See, *e.g., Jinks v Cardwell* (1987) 39 C.C.L.T. 168 (Ont. H.C.) where the hospital was held negligent for providing insufficient nursing staff for adequate supervision of a psychiatric patient.

Should the authority be liable if it demonstrates that, due to the financial stringency under which it operates, it cannot afford to fill the posts with those possessing the necessary experience?"[18]

Both of these questions were touched upon in *Bull v Devon Area Health*   **4–101**
Authority[19] in which the health authority were held liable for implementing an unsatisfactory and unreliable system for calling expert assistance to an obstetric emergency. Either there was negligence in the operation of the system, or it was inadequate to cope with even minor hitches which fell short of the kind of major breakdown against which no system could be invulnerable. Counsel for the claimant did not argue that the levels of staffing were inadequate in terms of obstetric cover because the response would have been that the levels of staffing should be judged according to professional standards at the time, and the medical evidence was that the standards did not compare unfavourably with those that existed at other split-site hospitals in the provinces at the time. Mustill L.J. was disturbed by the implications of this reply which at one and the same time put the foetus at risk and claimed to be good enough to be "par for the course."[20] It was not a question of highly specialist techniques or advanced equipment which it might be unrealistic to expect in provincial hospitals,[21] but simply a matter of getting the

---

[18] [1987] Q.B. 730, 778.

[19] (1989), [1993] 4 Med. L.R. 117, CA.

[20] See further the decision of the Supreme Court of Ireland in *Collins v Mid-Western Health Board* [2000] 2 I.R. 154 where a hospital was held to have been negligent in adopting an admissions system whereby a comparatively inexperienced junior doctor was allowed to substitute his own judgment as to whether the patient required admission and investigation as an emergency for the judgment arrived at by an experienced general practitioner. Keane J. stated, at 156–157, that the court was not concerned with "a medical practice as such" and therefore the claim that the hospital was negligent in operating such a system could not be refuted "simply by demonstrating that it is a system in use in at least some other hospitals in these islands."

[21] It is obvious that in some situations facilities for specialist treatment which are available at a large teaching or specialist hospital may not be available in a district hospital, and that could not, in itself, form the basis of an allegation of negligence where the patient has suffered harm as a result of the lack of specialist treatment: *Ball v Wirral Health Authority* [2003] Lloyd's Rep. Med. 165, QBD. The issue of negligence will turn on whether there was any fault in not referring the patient to the specialist centre. See further *Koerber v Kitchener-Waterloo Hospital* (1987) 62 O.R. (2d) 613 (Ont. H.C.) on the question of the different standards that might be expected in community hospitals as compared with a teaching hospital or a specialist hospital. In *Bateman v Doiron* (1991) 8 C.C.L.T. (2d) 284 (N.B.Q.B.); affirmed (1993) 18 C.C.L.T. (2d) 1 (N.B.C.A.) a patient died having been admitted to an emergency department of a hospital that was staffed only by a part-time general practitioner (with specialist doctors on call). Despite the defendant doctor doing all that could be reasonably expected of a general practitioner in the circumstances, the evidence indicated that if the patient had been attended to by a specialist in emergency medicine he would not have died. It was held that it was not negligent for the hospital to staff its emergency facility with part-time general practitioners, given that it was a small urban community in a Maritime Province. Creaghan J. said that a hospital has an obligation to meet standards reasonably expected by the community it serves in the provision of competent personnel and adequate facilities and equipment and with respect to the competence of physicians to whom it grants privileges to provide medical treatment: "However, to suggest that the defendant Moncton Hospital might be reasonably expected by the community to staff its emergency department with physicians qualified as expert in the management of critically ill patients does not meet

right people together in the right place at the right time. Mustill L.J was also unhappy about the (hypothetical) argument that the hospital was doing the best that could be expected with its limited resources:

> "I have some reservations about this contention, which are not allayed by the submission that hospital medicine is a public service. So it is, but there are other public services in respect of which it is not necessarily an answer to allegations of unsafety that there were insufficient resources to enable the administrators to do everything which they would like to do. I do not for a moment suggest that public medicine is precisely analogous to other public services, but there is perhaps a danger in assuming that it is completely *sui generis*, and that it is necessarily a complete answer to say that even if the system in any hospital was unsatisfactory, it was no more unsatisfactory than those in force elsewhere."

His Lordship acknowledged that these matters "raise important issues of social policy, which the courts may one day have to address." Dillon L.J. was content to observe that the level of staffing should be "reasonably sufficient for the foreseeable requirements of the patient." This leaves open the possibility of arguing that the provision of inadequate resources for a particular service constitutes negligence in itself.

4–102   There would be formidable obstacles, however, in mounting such a claim. From the perspective of the common law, there is a distinction to be drawn between undertaking a task with inadequate resources and being found negligent for failing to perform the task properly (which would be the form of an action in a situation analogous to *Bull v Devon Area Health Authority*), and, on the other hand, not having the resources to perform the task at all, where the claimant claims that the failure to provide the service constitutes negligence. In the former circumstances a finding of negligence on the basis of inadequate resources would create the risk that, in response, a service might be withdrawn altogether, and the courts would hesitate long and hard before taking such a step.[22] The latter situation would almost certainly fall foul of the "mere omissions" rule, since there could be no common law duty

---

(n.21 contd.) the test of reality, nor is it a reasonably expected community standard. The non-availability of trained and experienced personnel, to say nothing of the problems of collateral resource allocation, simply makes this unrealistic, albeit desirable," *ibid*. at p. 292. The hospital had to be judged by the standards reasonably expected by the community it served, "not communities served by large teaching facilities." There is an element, here, of applying a "locality rule" which permits different standards of care to prevail in different localities. Although still found in some U.S. jurisdictions, it was thought that the locality rule had effectively disappeared in Canada following *McCormick v Marcotte* (1971) 20 D.L.R. (3d) 345 (S.C.C.), where the defendant was held liable, despite practising in a rural community, because he was within easy reach of large centres of population. The objection to the locality rule is that inferior standards of heath care are deemed to be acceptable.

[22] In *Dryden v Surrey County Council* [1936] 2 All E.R. 535, 539, Finlay J. said that it would be "most dangerous to hold that, because an increase of staff was recommended, therefore negligence by understaffing was established." His Lordship commented that it was impossible to receive in a public hospital the attention which a person will receive who is fortunate enough to be able to pay for the undivided attention of one or even two nurses. This remark predates the foundation of the NHS, but nonetheless it may still be accurate in practical terms.

to provide medical services, as opposed to acting carefully if one chooses to provide such services.[23] Moreover, decisions about the allocation of resources to a public service are normally taken in pursuance of statutory powers which confer a discretion on the decision-making body. An allegation that such a decision has been taken negligently must first establish that the discretion was exercised *ultra vires* the statutory power, applying public law principles.[24] The courts have demonstrated an extreme reluctance to become directly involved in resource allocation issues in the health service, and they are likely to take a highly sympathetic view of the health authority's or NHS Trust's position.[25] In *Hardaker v Newcastle Health Authority & the Chief Constable of Northumbria*[26] Burnton J. accepted that a Health Authority's duty of care to the claimant was qualified by the resources available to them. It was not negligent to fail to devote the resources to deal with the claimant's comparatively rare condition (decompression illness). Moreover, the claimant had not suggested any specific alternative procedure that could have been adopted by the Health Authority: "In my view, it is not sufficient for a claimant to criticise a system as negligent without identifying what would have been an adequate system. I am not satisfied that a better system was available that did not involve significant additional resources;

---

[23] So, *e.g.*, a casualty department of a hospital that opens its doors to the public "undertakes" the task of providing an emergency service and will be liable for negligently failing to do so: *Barnett v Chelsea and Kensington Hospital Management Committee* [1968] 1 All E.R. 1068, 1073. If, on the other hand, it simply shuts down, there would be no liability.

[24] See *Anns v Merton London Borough Council* [1978] A.C. 728, 754; *Dorset Yacht Co Ltd v Home Office* [1970] A.C. 1004, 1067; *X. (minors) v Bedfordshire County Council* [1995] 2 A.C. 633, 736–737, though for Lord Browne-Wilkinson it was not a question of whether the decision was *ultra vires*, but whether it was outside the ambit of the public authority's discretion.

[25] See, *e.g.*, *R. v Secretary of State for Social Services, ex parte Hincks* (1979) 123 S.J. 436, affirmed (1980), 1 B.M.L.R. 93, CA; *R. v Central Birmingham Health Authority, ex parte Walker* (1987), 3 B.M.L.R. 32, CA; *R. v Central Birmingham Health Authority, ex parte Collier* (1988, CA; unreported); *R. v Cambridge Health Authority, ex parte B.* [1995] 1 W.L.R. 898; [1995] 2 All E.R. 129, CA. See, however, *Re HIV Haemophiliac Litigation* (1990), [1996] P.I.Q.R. P220, which involved allegations about the negligent allocation of resources, including a failure to achieve self-sufficiency in the supply of blood products within the NHS. This report of the case deals with disclosure of documents, not the substantive issue of negligence. Cases in which the applicant establishes that a health authority or NHS Trust has failed to establish a policy for the allocation of resources, contrary to Department of Health recommendations, or where the health authority has fettered its discretion as to the implementation of a policy may be successfully challenged on judicial review: see *R. v North Derbyshire Health Authority, ex parte Fisher* [1997] 8 Med. L.R. 327; *North West Lancashire Health Authority v A, D and G* [2000] 1 W.L.R. 977. This is not to say, however, that such decisions will necessarily give rise to private law actions for negligence. See generally Newdick (1993) 1 Med. L. Rev. 53; Schwehr [1994] J.P.I.L. 192.

[26] [2001] Lloyd's Rep. Med. 512 at [54]. In *Ball v Wirral Health Authority* [2003] Lloyd's Rep. Med. 165 at [32] Simon J. commented that: "In the field of medicine where resources are limited and the demands on those resources are many, it may be necessary to make difficult decisions as to how resources are to be allocated. In general, English public and private law leaves such decisions to those who have the legal responsibility for making such decisions. The fact that an area of medicine may be underfunded (for example, neonatal care in the 1970s) or that a particular hospital may not have the facilities that another hospital has, may give rise to a concern among the general public and the experts in the field; but it does not necessarily provide the basis of a claim in negligence by a patient who may suffer from the effects of the underfunding or the lack of facilities . . ."

and I am in no position to criticise the Authority's allocation of its doubt-lessly limited resources."[27]

4–103   What, it might be asked, is the responsibility of the doctor faced with having to treat patients in circumstances of resource constraints? It is argu-able that when engaged in diagnosis or treatment the doctor's legal duty is to act in the best interests of *this* patient, without reference to the interests of other patients or potential patients. For example, in *Law Estate v Simice*,[28] a case where the patient died because of a delay in diagnosing an intracranial aneurism, Spencer J. commented that:

> ". . . throughout this case there were a number of times when doctors testified that they feel constrained by the British Columbia Medical Insurance Plan and by the British Columbia Medical Association stan-dards to restrict their requests for CT scans as diagnostic tools. No doubt such sophisticated equipment is limited and costly to use. No doubt there are budgetary restraints on them. But this is a case where, in my opinion, those constraints worked against the patient's interest by inhibiting the doctors in their judgment of what should be done for him. That is to be deplored. I understand that there are budgetary problems confronting the health care system. I raise it in passing only to point out that there were a number of references to the effect of financial restraint on the treatment of this patient. I respectfully say it is something to be carefully considered by those who are responsible for the provision of medical care and those who are responsible for financing it. I also say

---

[27] *ibid.* at [57]. It has been argued that the acknowledged under-funding of the NHS should lead the courts to adopt a lower standard of care so as to "ensure that hospitals and their staff are less vulnerable to findings of negligence for systematic failures in care which cannot reason-ably be attributed to them": Witting (2001) 21 O.J.L.S. 443, 444. The logic of this argument is that the worse the service provided the less likely it is that a claim for negligence will succeed when a patient is injured by that service. It seems doubtful that such an approach would be considered tolerable in any other sphere of service provision, whether public or private. Even if it is acknowledged that many errors are due to "systems failures" (as it is by the Department of Health: *An organisation with a memory* (2000), available at *www.doh.gov.uk/orgmemre-port/index.htm*), some of which may be associated with a scarcity of resources, there will almost invariably be an individual at the end of a "chain of error" who makes the final mistake. It will probably rarely be possible to demonstrate that the claimant's damage was attributable *exclusively* to under-funding, as opposed to avoidable human error. On the other hand, as *Hardaker* demonstrates, the *Bolam* test takes account of what is reasonable in the circumstances, including whether, objectively, precautions against a small risk are reasonably required given the cost of taking those precautions and the degree of risk.

[28] (1994) 21 C.C.L.T. (2d) 228, 240 (B.C.S.C.); affirmed [1996] 4 W.W.R. 672 (B.C.C.A.). See also *McLean v Carr Estate* (1994) 363 A.P.R. 271 (Newfd.S.C.), where the issue of negligence turned upon whether the defendant doctor should have carried out a CT scan on a patient with a serious head injury who died from an epidermal haematoma while "under observation." It was claimed that it was too expensive to perform a CT scan on all patients who had suffered a head injury. There was no evidence, however, that the cost of scans for those patients who had suffered serious head injuries resulting in a skull fracture would have been prohibitive. Barry J. commented, at p. 289, that: "Where the consequence of missing the epidermal haematoma would probably be serious injury or death, I believe this court need not, when evidence of pro-hibitive cost is lacking, defer to any body of medical opinion which would not, in the circum-stances, have scanned in 1987." This leaves open, of course, what the court's response might have been had the cost been prohibitive, and indeed what the term "prohibitive" means.

that if it comes to a choice between a physician's responsibility to his or her individual patient and his or her responsibility to the medicare system overall, the former must take precedence in a case such as this. The severity of the harm that may occur to the patient who is permitted to go undiagnosed is far greater than the financial harm that will occur to the medicare system if one more CT scan procedure only shows the patient is not suffering from a serious medical condition."

A similar view was expressed in the American case of *Wickline v State of California*[29] in which the claimant was admitted to hospital for surgery. Medi-Cal, which was paying for the treatment, authorised the surgery and a stay of ten days in hospital. There were complications and two more operations were required. The doctor treating the claimant wanted her to remain in hospital for a further eight days. He submitted the request for additional time to Medi-Cal which authorised only a further four days, but the doctor made no complaint and did not try to have the decision overturned. The claimant was discharged after the four days, and due to further complications her leg had to be amputated above the knee. She sued the State, alleging that Medi-Cal had negligently discontinued her eligibility for benefits causing her to be discharged prematurely. The California Court of Appeal held that on the facts the discharge after four days had not been negligent because a responsible body of professional opinion would have supported the decision. Nonetheless, the doctor had a duty to make an effort to obtain the necessary resources, and should have stood by his clinical judgment:

> "The court appreciates that what is at issue here is the effect of cost containment programs upon the professional judgment of physicians to prescribe hospital treatment for patients requiring the same. While we recognize, realistically, that cost consciousness has become a permanent feature of the health care system, it is essential that cost limitation programs not be permitted to corrupt medical judgment."[30]

It must be recognised that the methods of funding and delivering health care are different in the UK from those that are employed in the United States and even Canada. Nonetheless, the National Health Service is not immune from cost-containment pressures. In *Airedale NHS Trust v Bland*[31] there are clear statements that in English law the doctor's duty is to act in the patient's   **4–104**

---

[29] 228 Cal. Rptr. 661 (1986) (Cal. C.A.).
[30] *ibid.* at p. 672. "... the physician who complies without protest with the limitations imposed by a third party payer, when his medical judgment dictates otherwise, cannot avoid his ultimate responsibility for his patient's care. He cannot point to the health care payer as the liability scapegoat when the consequences of his own determinative medical decisions go sour," *ibid.* at p. 671. In *Wilson v Blue Cross of California* 271 Cal. Rptr. 876, 880 (1990) (Cal. C.A.), however, it was said that this broadly stated language was unnecessary to the decision in *Wickline*, and did not correctly state the law in all contexts. The suggestion that civil liability for a discharge decision rests solely with the treating physician in all contexts was merely dicta.
[31] [1993] A.C. 789.

best interests. Thus, Lord Keith commented that in general it would not be lawful for a medical practitioner who assumed responsibility for the care of an unconscious patient simply to give up treatment in circumstances where continuance of it would confer some benefit on the patient, although there was no duty to continue to treat such a patient where a large body of informed and responsible medical opinion was of the view that no benefit would be conferred by continued treatment.[32] The implication here appears to be that where a patient could benefit, it would not be lawful to discontinue treatment simply on the basis that the resources are needed for the treatment of other patients or future patients who might derive greater benefit from treatment. Lord Browne-Wilkinson was quite explicit about this:

> "Moreover, it is not legitimate for a judge in reaching a view as to what is for the benefit of the one individual whose life is in issue to take into account the wider practical issues as to allocation of limited financial resources . . ."[33]

On the other hand, in *Re J. (a minor) (wardship: medical treatment)*[34] the Court of Appeal overturned an order that a doctor and health authority should continue to treat a seriously handicapped child in a particular way, since it would be an abuse of the power of the court directly or indirectly to require a doctor to act contrary to the doctor's fundamental duty to the patient, which was to treat the patient in accordance with the doctor's best clinical judgment. Moreover, the order, to the effect that the health authority were required to use intensive therapeutic measures for so long as they were capable of prolonging the child's life, did not adequately take account of the fact that health authorities may find that they have too few resources to treat all the patients whom they would like to treat in the way in which they would like to treat them. It was the health authority's duty to make choices, and the court had no knowledge of competing claims to a health authority's resources and was in no position to express any view as to how it should elect to deploy them.[35] Admittedly, these cases are at some remove from the question of whether a doctor has been negligent in consciously implementing a cost-containment procedure which has adversely affected a patient's treatment, but to the extent that they identify the nature of the doctor's duty to the individual

---

[32] *ibid.* at p. 858–859.

[33] *ibid.* at p. 880. Lord Mustill commenting on the point that the resources expended in keeping a patient in a "persistent vegetative state" alive might more usefully be devoted to improving the condition of other patients, who with treatment might have useful, healthy and enjoyable lives for many years, said: "This argument was never squarely put, although hinted at from time to time. In social terms it has great force, and it will have to be faced in the end. But this is not a task which the courts can possibly undertake. A social cost-benefit analysis of this kind, which would have to embrace 'mercy killing', to which exactly the same considerations apply, must be for Parliament alone, and the outcome of it is at present quite impossible to foresee," *ibid.* at p. 896.

[34] [1993] Fam. 15.

[35] *ibid.* at p. 28, *per* Lord Donaldson M.R.

patient they are instructive.[36] The comments in *Bland* suggest that failing to provide resources for treatment simply because other patients might benefit from those resources is a breach of the doctor's duty to act in the patient's best interests; whereas *Re J.* suggests that this is a matter within the discretion of the doctor's "clinical judgment" (which, presumably, may well be constrained by the health authority's allocation of resources). The effect of the *Bolam* test is that provided a responsible body of professional opinion would support the doctor's decision to use more "cost-effective" (*i.e.* resource-constrained) methods the doctor cannot be held negligent, notwithstanding that a responsible body of professional opinion would disagree. In this sense the medical profession acts as the "gatekeeper" for access to health care resources, and the *Bolam* test means that the patient is only ever entitled to the lowest common denominator. If pressure on resources pushes standards down *in fact*, the minimum acceptable standard *in law* will also decline.[37]

The central issue that the case of *Wickline v State of California* raised was the potential liability of a third-party that made a decision about the allocation of resources which caused the patient harm that would not otherwise have occurred. The Court took the view that a third party decision-maker could be held liable for an allocation decision:

    4–105

> "The patient who requires treatment and who is harmed when care which should have been provided is not provided should recover for the injuries suffered from all those responsible for the deprivation of such care, including, when appropriate, health care payers. Third party payers of health care services can be held legally accountable when medically inappropriate decisions result from defects in the design or implementation of cost containment mechanisms as, for example, when appeals made on a patient's behalf for medical or hospital care are arbitrarily ignored or unreasonably disregarded or overridden."[38]

---

[36] *Kangas v Parker* [1976] 5 W.W.R. 25, 43; affirmed [1978] 5 W.W.R. 667 (Sask. C.A.), in which the patient died from inhaling blood while under general anaesthetic in the defendant's office, demonstrates a slightly different point. In deciding not to refer the patient to hospital for the removal of his teeth, where there would have been better facilities in an emergency, the defendant dentist put his own financial interests over the best interests of the patient. The defendant was held negligent on this and numerous other grounds. Thus, in choosing a facility for the patient the doctor must do so with the best interests of the patient in mind.

[37] The comments by Spencer J. in *Law Estate v Simice* (1994) 21 C.C.L.T. (2d) 228, 240 (B.C.S.C.); affirmed [1996] 4 W.W.R. 672 (B.C.C.A.), cited above, para. 4–103, can be seen as an attempt to place limits in law on the extent to which standards may decline due to resource constraints. It seems likely, however, that such an attempt is bound to fail under the present test for medical negligence. On the other hand, it must be recognised that as new medical techniques develop patients may be entitled to the benefit of a higher standard of care if the new technique is regarded by the profession as the minimum standard. Thus, in *Pierre v Marshall* [1994] 8 W.W.R. 478 (Alta. Q.B.). the Alberta Medical Association and the Society of Obstetricians and Gynaecologists of Canada recommended screening pregnant women for gestational diabetes, despite the fact that there was controversy as to whether universal screening was cost-effective. The defendant was held negligent for failing to comply with these recommendations.

[38] 228 Cal. Rptr. 661, 670–671 (1986) (Cal. C.A.).

Thus, *Wickline* recognises that decisions about funding for medical treatment may attract the same liability as medical decisions themselves. Indeed, for patients with limited economic resources a funding decision *is* a medical decision. It also acknowledges that economic pressure by third parties can influence doctors' medical decisions to the point of amounting to negligence.[39] If resources are explicitly rationed by a third party then the doctor may simply have no control over the use of a facility (*e.g.* if it has been withdrawn). But *Wickline* also accepts that more subtle economic pressure may be enough to "persuade" doctors to do something that would be against their clinical judgment, and this may also be enough to establish liability against the third party. The circumstances in which this type of argument could be employed in the UK are probably limited, given the courts' general reluctance to get involved in resource allocation issues.[40]

4–106   In any event, an action based on an allegation that the defendant failed to provide the "best" available treatment or diagnostic procedure (*i.e.*, the more expensive drug or test or surgical technique) on the ground of resource constraints, as opposed to allegations that the resource or facility had been completely withdrawn, may well run into problems in proving causation. Given that medical advances tend to come in comparatively small increments, rather than in great leaps, the use of, say, a new, more expensive, drug might produce a better result in 10 or even 20 per cent of cases. Even if the claimant can prove that it was negligent for a doctor to prescribe the cheaper, standard medication, the claimant still has to prove that the negligence caused the injury, or, rather, failed to prevent a deterioration in his condition. The claimant would have to prove, on a balance of probabilities, that he would have been one of the 10 or 20 per cent of patients who would have had an improved result, and that this improvement would have avoided the harm. He cannot argue simply that he lost the chance of a better outcome, and on the balance of probabilities the statistics are against him.[41]

4–107   The one situation in which a claim apparently based on a lack of resources would succeed is where a vital piece of equipment, which is normally available and should have been available, is absent or has gone missing with the result that the patient sustains avoidable harm. An instrument which is essential for resuscitation in an emergency, for example, may have been negligently mislaid.[42] This is not a true example of a shortage of resources, rather it is mismanagement of the available resources.

---

[39] Caulfield (1994) Alberta L. Rev. 685, 715. See also Kryworuk, Butler and Otten, "Liability in the Allocation of Scarce Health Care Resources" (1996) 16 Health Law in Canada 65.

[40] See paras 7–022 to 7–025. For an argument that distributing healthcare resources on the basis of ageism (effectively withholding treatment from the elderly because of lack of resources) could constitute a breach of the European Convention on Human Rights see Sayers and Nesbitt (2002) 9 Eur. J. Health Law 5.

[41] See Irvine (1994) 21 C.C.L.T. (2d) 259, 260; and paras 5–050 *et seq.*

[42] As, *e.g.*, in *Meyer v Gordon* (1981) 17 C.C.L.T. 1, 15; *cf. Koerber v Kitchener-Waterloo Hospital* (1987) 62 O.R. (2d) 613 (Ont. H.C.), where the doctor had to leave the patient in order to check on the availability of a piece of equipment in the main operating room and the claimant's injury occurred while the doctor was absent. The defendants were held not to have been negligent.

5. MENTAL HEALTH

A psychiatrist or clinical psychologist clearly owes a duty of care to his   **4–108**
psychiatric patients, which, as with any doctor/patient relationship covers
diagnosis, advice and treatment in all its forms.[43] Generally, there are no
special rules applicable to psychiatric patients and the *Bolam* test will
apply.[44] Thus, a psychiatrist was held negligent where he engaged in social
contact with a female patient who had developed a strong and obsessive
emotional attachment to him, leading to a serious deterioration in the
patient's mental health.[45] This was a departure from recognised standards in
the practice of psychiatry which no body of professional opinion would have
supported. In some instances, however, the nature of the patient's illness
makes him dangerous, either to himself or to others, and claims can arise out
of an alleged failure to exercise control over the patient.

(1) Failing to control the patient

A doctor undoubtedly has a duty to take reasonable steps to protect a   **4–109**
psychiatric patient from harming himself, and in an institutional setting a hospital authority may be responsible for injuries inflicted on a patient by
himself,[46] or by a fellow patient where the injuries are the result of a failure to
provide adequate control and supervision.[47] But there will normally be no

---

[43] In *X. (minors) v Bedfordshire County Council* [1995] 2 A.C. 633 the House of Lords held
that a psychiatrist does not owe a duty of care either to a child or its parents when advising
a social services authority whether the child has been the victim of physical or sexual abuse,
with the result that the child is removed from the parents' home. See paras 2–061 to 2–067,
3–113 to 3–116. See further *C v Cairns* [2003] Lloyd's Rep. Med. 90 where it was assumed
that a general practitioner would owe a duty of care to a child patient who was reported to
the general practitioner to have been sexually abused by a member of her family, although
the claim failed on breach of duty because the defendant had acted as most other general
practitioners would have done at the time.

[44] The claimant in *Bolam v Friern Hospital Management Committee* [1957] 2 All E.R. 118
itself was a psychiatric patient who sustained serious physical injuries in the course of
electro-convulsive therapy administered to treat depression. The defendant did not use relaxant drugs or strap the claimant down before administering the treatment. There were,
however, two schools of thought about the use of relaxant drugs, which reduced the danger
from fractures but carried a small risk of death. There were also two schools of thought
about the degree of physical restraint that should be used, one taking the view that it reduced
the risk of fractures the other taking the view that it increased the risk. A jury acquitted the
defendant of negligence, following the direction of McNair J.; see para. 3–008.

[45] *Landau v Werner* (1961) 105 S.J. 257, and 1008, CA.

[46] *Jinks v Cardwell* (1987) 39 C.C.L.T. 168 (Ont. H.C.), where there was negligent supervision
of a schizophrenic patient who was known to be prone to fainting spells as a reaction to his
medication; the patient drowned accidentally in a bath; *Kelly v Board of Governors of St.
Laurence's Hospital* [1988] I.R. 402 (Supreme Court of Ireland), where the claimant was in
hospital specifically for observation, for the purpose of which he had been taken off all medication, but was permitted to leave the ward unobserved and fell out of a window.

[47] *Wellesley Hospital v Lawson* (1977) 76 D.L.R. (3d) 688 where the Supreme Court of
Canada assumed that such a common law duty existed. In *Ellis v Home Office* [1953] 2 All
E.R. 149 prison authorities were held to owe a duty of care to a prisoner assaulted by another
prisoner, although on the facts the defendants were held not to have been negligent. See also
Stenning v Home Office [2002] EWCA Civ 793.

duty to protect a psychiatric patient from the legal consequences of his own actions in causing injury to others, at least where the patient continues to have some degree of responsibility for his actions. In *Clunis v Camden & Islington Health Authority*[48] the Court of Appeal rejected a claim in negligence by a patient who had attacked and killed an innocent bystander. He alleged that had he received proper psychiatric treatment he would not have committed the offence and therefore he would not have been convicted of a criminal offence and sent to prison. The claim was struck out as contrary to public policy, because his plea of manslaughter by reason of diminished responsibility still required some degree of personal responsibility, even though it was accepted that his mental responsibility was substantially impaired. The Court of Appeal did, however, contemplate that there could be liability in negligence in such a case if it could be proved that the claimant did not know the nature and quality of his act or that what he had done was wrong.

4–110   The duty owed to the psychiatric patient can include an obligation to make reasonable efforts to prevent suicide attempts.[49] The risk of suicide must be foreseeable for the duty of care to exist, though with certain categories of claimant, such as prisoners in custody, it is known that there is an increased risk of suicide which will give rise to a specific obligation to assess whether or not a prisoner presents a suicide risk. But a duty to exercise reasonable care to prevent a prisoner from committing suicide arises only where the defendant knew (following an appropriate assessment), or ought to have known, that the individual prisoner presented such a risk.[50] In the medical context there will generally be two types of case: (i) where the patient is a known suicide risk; and (ii) where it is alleged that the medical staff ought to have realised that he was a suicide risk, but failed to do so.

(a) The known suicide risk

4–111   Here, the issue may turn upon how much supervision the patient should have been given, and this may in turn depend upon the degree of risk—how serious is the threat, and so, in legal terms, how foreseeable was the patient's behaviour?

4–112   In *Thorne v Northern Group Hospital Management Committee*[51] the nursing staff on a medical ward of a general hospital were aware that a patient, who was a suspected depressive, had threatened suicide. The patient walked out of the hospital, went home and committed suicide while mentally ill but not legally insane. Her husband sued the hospital alleging that a

---

[48] [1998] Q.B. 978.
[49] Jones (1990) 6 P.N. 107. See also Hill, "Suicide risk and its management" (1997) 3 Clinical Risk 178.
[50] *Orange v Chief Constable of West Yorkshire Police* [2001] EWCA Civ 611; [2002] Q.B. 347 at [41] to [43]. See also *Keenan v UK* (2001) 10 B.H.R.C. 319, where the European Court of Human Rights held that inadequate medical treatment and a lack of effective monitoring of a prisoner who was known to be mentally ill and an identified suicide risk could constitute a breach of Art. 3 of the European Convention for the Protection of Human Rights, which provides that "No one shall be subjected to torture or to inhuman or degrading treatment or punishment."
[51] (1964) 108 S.J. 484.

failure to provide adequate supervision of his wife was negligent. Edmund-Davies J. held that there had been no negligence since in the circumstances constant supervision was not appropriate. His Lordship did comment, however, that the degree of care and supervision required of hospital staff in relation to a patient with known or, perhaps, even suspected suicidal tendencies was greater than that called for in relation to patients generally.

By contrast, in *Selfe v Ilford and District Hospital Management Committee*[52] it was accepted that reasonable care demanded reasonable supervision of a patient at risk of committing suicide, which included continuous observation by a nurse on duty in the ward. The claimant, when aged 17, was admitted to hospital following an attempted suicide by overdose of sleeping tablets. The staff knew that he was a serious suicide risk, and he was put in a ground floor ward with 27 patients, four of whom were suicide risks. The expert evidence was that with four such patients a minimum of three nurses was required. There were three nurses on duty, but two of them were briefly absent from the ward, and the third was assisting a patient at the far end of the ward. The claimant climbed out of a window and jumped off a roof, causing serious injuries. Hinchcliffe J. held the defendants liable. The degree of care required was proportionate to the degree of risk, and in this case there had been a breakdown in proper nursing supervision, which had caused the accident.   **4–113**

In *Villemure v L'Hôpital Notre Dame*[53] a patient was admitted on an emergency basis to the psychiatric section of a hospital (where the windows were barred) following an attempted suicide, but was subsequently moved to a semi-private room in the medical section (where the windows were not barred). The patient's pleas to be allowed to return to the psychiatric ward were ignored and no supervision or other precautions were taken to prevent a recurrence. The patient leapt to his death from the window of his room. The Supreme Court of Canada concluded that the defendants had been negligent. On the other hand, where the suicide attempt is unforeseeable there will be no liability.[54]   **4–114**

Another factor which may have to be considered in the case of a known suicide risk is the degree of restraint or supervision appropriate in the light of   **4–115**

---

[52] (1970) 114 S.J. 935; *Hay v Grampian Health Board* [1995] 6 Med. L.R. 128, Court of Session, where the regime for supervising a known suicide risk broke down; *Mahmood v Siggins* [1996] 7 Med. L.R. 76, QBD, where a general practitioner was held liable for failing to refer a known manic depressive to a community mental health team for assessment, treatment and supervision; *Drake v Pontefract Health Authority; Wakefield and Pontefract Community NHS Trust* [1998] Lloyd's Rep. Med. 425, QBD, where an inexperienced psychiatrist was held negligent in failing to diagnose the claimant's condition correctly, failing to assess the risk of suicide, and failing to provide appropriate treatment, though the patient had been referred by the general practitioner as a suicide risk.

[53] (1972) 31 D.L.R. (3d) 454.

[54] *Orange v Chief Constable of West Yorkshire Police* [2001] EWCA Civ 611; [2002] Q.B. 347; *Lepine v University Hospital Board* (1966) 57 D.L.R. (2d) 701 (S.C.C), where a leap out of a hospital window by a patient suffering from post-epileptic automatism was found to be unforeseeable, and reasonable care did not demand that the claimant be either physically restrained or kept at ground level; *Stadel v Albertson* [1954] 2 D.L.R. 328 (Sask. C.A.) where the defendant was not liable for the suicide of a patient whose symptoms did not suggest that he was a danger either to himself or anyone else.

the patient's mental condition. A psychiatrist, for example, may take the view that imposing restraint on a patient may exacerbate the patient's condition, or at least inhibit effective treatment. If it is against the patient's wishes it might undermine the trust between doctor and patient. This judgment has to balance competing risks to the patient's health, including the risk of suicide. In *Haines v Bellissimo*,[55] Griffiths J. said that a the therapist must weigh the advantages and disadvantages of hospitalisation against the advantages of continuing out-patient treatment. If there is a real risk of suicide or if the therapist is in doubt about this, said the judge, he should opt for hospitalisation. On the other hand, close observation, restrictions, and restraint of the patient may be anti-therapeutic and aggravate the patient's sense of worthlessness, which in itself can increase the risk of suicide. On the facts, the defendants had not been negligent because hospitalisation, whether voluntary or involuntary, would have been a blow to the patient's self-esteem and pride, interfered with his long term rehabilitation, and, most significantly, would have destroyed the strong therapeutic bond which had developed.

(b) The undiagnosed suicide risk

4–116   Where it is claimed that the medical staff negligently failed to appreciate that the patient was a suicide risk the question will usually be cast in terms of whether non-specialist (*i.e.* non-psychiatric) staff (whether doctors or nurses) ought to have realised that the patient's mental condition was such that there was a genuine risk of a suicide attempt. This will not be judged by reference to whether a psychiatrist could have made this diagnosis, unless the patient is receiving psychiatric treatment, but whether in the defendant's position a reasonable doctor or nurse would have identified the risk.

4–117   In *Hyde v Tameside Area Health Authority*[56] the claimant was admitted to hospital with a painful shoulder. Twelve days later he jumped from a third floor window in an attempt to kill himself having convinced himself, erroneously, that he had cancer. The attempt failed, but he suffered catastrophic injuries. The alleged negligence consisted of a failure by the medical staff to identify the claimant's mental distress, and a failure to realise "that the hospital had a serious psychiatric case on its hands which called for psychiatric treatment". At first instance the defendants were held liable. The Court of Appeal reversed this decision, finding that on the particular facts of the case there was no negligence, merely, in the words of Watkins L.J., a "forgivable failure to achieve a standard approaching perfection."

4–118   The court will make allowance for the fact that a decision to introduce psychiatric treatment for patients who are not being treated for a psychiatric illness or disorder is one that involves competing considerations. In *Hyde v Tameside Area Health Authority* Watkins L.J. pointed out that many patients in hospital suffer from anxiety, and worry about their medical condition.

---

[55] (1977) 82 D.L.R. (3d) 215 (Ont.H.C.).
[56] (1981), reported at (1986) 2 P.N. 26.

They may need reassurance; sometimes they need drugs to ease pain or stress, but to tell a patient who requires surgery that he also needs psychiatric help may be counter-productive. As Watkins L.J. put it: "A decision to use psychiatry may do more harm than good. An over eager resort to, and an excessive use of, this branch of medicine in hospitals other than those where the mentally ill are treated could have unfortunate and unsettling consequences."[57]

In *Hyde v Tameside Area Health Authority* Lord Denning M.R. was **4–119** hostile to actions based on suicide or attempted suicide:

> "I feel it is most unfitting that the personal representatives of a suicide should be able to claim damages in respect of his death. At any rate, when he succeeds in killing himself. And I do not see why he should be in any better position when he does not succeed. By this act—in self-inflicting this grievous injury—he has made himself a burden on the whole community. Our hospital services and our social welfare services have done, and will do, all they can to help him and his family—in the grievous injury that he has inflicted on himself and them. But I see no justification whatever in his being awarded, in addition, the huge sum of £200,000 because he failed in his attempt. Such a sum will have to be raised, in the long run, by society itself—a sum which it cannot well afford. The policy of the law should be to discourage these actions. I would disallow them altogether—at the outset—rather than burden the community with them."[58]

This view was clearly based on considerations of policy, and in particular Lord Denning's belief that "'medical malpractice' cases should not get out of hand here as they have done in the United States of America." In *Kirkham v Chief Constable of Greater Manchester Police*[59] Lloyd L.J. said that he did not share this view, noting that neither Watkins nor O'Connor L.JJ. expressed agreement with Lord Denning's comments.

It has been argued that, quite apart from the question of breach of duty, claims **4–120** for negligence based on suicide or attempted suicide should not be permitted, on the grounds of causation, *volenti non fit injuria, ex turpi causa non oritur actio.* The causation argument states that the defendant's negligence merely provided the opportunity for the deceased's act of suicide, which amounted, in effect, to a *novus actus interveniens*, so breaking the chain of causation. In *Kirkham v Chief Constable of Greater Manchester Police*[60] Tudor Evans J. rejected the causation argument on the basis that the suicide was the very thing that the defendants had a duty to take precautions against,[61] and concluded that

---

[57] *ibid.* at p. 30.
[58] (1981), reported at (1986) 2 P.N. 26, 29–30.
[59] [1990] 2 Q.B. 283, 292.
[60] [1989] 3 All E.R. 882; affirmed [1990] 2 Q.B. 283.
[61] Where the intervening conduct is the very thing that the defendant was under a duty to guard against, he cannot avoid liability by arguing that the conduct constituted an intervening act: *Haynes v Harwood* [1935] 1 K.B. 146, 156; *Perl (Exporters) Ltd v Camden London Borough Council* [1984] Q.B. 342, 353. See also *per* Farquharson L.J. in *Kirkham v Chief Constable of Greater Manchester Police* [1990] 2 Q.B. 283, 295 in relation to the defence of *volenti non fit injuria.*

on the evidence the suicide would probably have been prevented.[62] His Lordship seemed to regard the deceased's state of mind as relevant to the question of causation: "Although the act of suicide was in a sense a conscious and deliberate act, the deceased's mental balance was, I am satisfied, affected at the time."[63] This left open the question whether, if the deceased's mind was not "affected", the suicide could be regarded as a *novus actus interveniens*.[64]

4–121   In *Reeves v Commissioner of Police for the Metropolis*[65] a case which also involved the suicide of prisoner who was a known suicide risk, though not found to be mentally ill, the House of Lords held that the suicide did not constitute a *novus actus*. The damage arose from breach of a duty to prevent just such an act and thus did not obliterate the defendants' wrongdoing. It was not a new act, but the very harm that the defendants were under a duty to try to prevent. Lord Hoffmann commented that in cases where the law imposes a duty to guard against loss caused by the free, deliberate and informed act of a human being, "it would make nonsense of the existence of such a duty if the law were to hold that the occurrence of the very act which ought to have been prevented negatived causal connection between the breach of duty and the loss."[66] Though a duty to protect a person of full understanding from causing harm to himself was very rare, once it was accepted that such a duty was owed, it was self-contradictory to say that the breach could not have been a cause of the harm because the victim caused it to himself.[67] Moreover, the deceased's mental state was irrelevant, since the defendant's duty arose out of the fact that the deceased was a known suicide risk, not from any particular mental state.

4–122   The same reasoning was used in *Reeves* to reject the defence of *volenti non fit injuria*. In *Kirkham* Lloyd L.J. had suggested that there was no reason why *volenti* should not provide a complete defence where a man "of sound mind" committed suicide or injured himself in an unsuccessful attempt, though it was unclear precisely what the term "of sound mind" meant. In *Kirkham*, although the deceased was legally sane and his suicide was a deliberate and conscious act, nonetheless he "was suffering from clinical depression. His judgment was impaired . . . [H]e was not truly *volens*."[68] Thus, insanity was not essential in order to defeat the *volenti* defence; some impairment of judgment sufficed,[69] but that left open the possibility that suicides who could not

---

[62] See also *Funk Estate v Clapp* (1986), reported at 68 D.L.R. (4th) 229, and (1988) 54 D.L.R. (4th) 512 (B.C.C.A.), where it was held that *novus actus interveniens* was not a defence to a claim following the suicide of a prisoner.

[63] [1989] 3 All E.R. 882, 889.

[64] Thus, in *Wright Estate v Davidson* (1992) 88 D.L.R. (4th) 698 (B.C.C.A.) the deceased's suicide was held to constitute a *novus actus interveniens* where there was no evidence of disabling mental illness; *cf. Costello v Blakeson* [1993] 2 W.W.R. 562 (B.C.S.C.).

[65] [2000] 1 A.C. 360.

[66] *ibid.* at 367–368.

[67] *ibid.* at 368.

[68] [1990] 2 Q.B. 283, 290, *per* Lloyd L.J. Farquharson L.J. said, at 295, that it was "quite unrealistic" to suggest that Mr. Kirkham was truly *volens*: "His state of mind was such that, through disease, he was incapable of coming to a balanced decision even if his act of suicide was deliberate."

[69] *cf. Robson v Ashworth* (1987) 40 C.C.L.T. 164, (Ont. C.A.)., where the fact that the deceased took his life "knowingly and deliberately while he was sane" barred the action by his widow.

be categorised as suffering from some form of mental illness would be met with the *volenti* defence. However, in *Reeves* the House of Lords held that *volenti* did not apply where the claimant's act was the very thing that the defendant was under a duty to take reasonable care to prevent, irrespective of the suicide's mental state. Once it was accepted that the defendant owed a duty to take reasonable care to prevent a suicide attempt he could not be permitted to argue that the very act which he was under a duty to prevent gave rise to the defence of *volenti*. The argument would undermine the purpose of imposing the duty in the first place. Since the duty arose because the deceased was a known suicide risk, not because of his mental state, it would be wrong to distinguish between different mental states when applying *volenti*.

The defendant in *Kirkham* also relied on the principle *ex turpi causa non* **4–123** *oritur actio*. The Court of Appeal accepted that the *ex turpi causa* defence was not confined to criminal conduct, but could apply to illegal or immoral conduct by the claimant "if in all the circumstances it would be an affront to the public conscience to grant the plaintiff the relief which he seeks because the court would thereby appear to assist or encourage the plaintiff in his illegal conduct or to encourage others in similar acts."[70] The question, then, was whether awarding damages following a suicide would "affront the public conscience, or, as I would prefer to say, shock the ordinary citizen."[71] Their Lordships concluded that the answer should be "No." Thus, said Lloyd L.J., the defence of *ex turpi causa* is not available in suicide cases "at any rate where, as here, there is medical evidence that the suicide is not in full possession of his mind."[72] Farquharson L.J. said that an action could hardly be said to be grounded in immorality where "grave mental instability" on the part of the victim has been proved, although "the position may well be different where the victim is wholly sane." However, in *Reeves v Commissioner of Police of the Metropolis*[73] the Court of Appeal held that the defence of *ex turpi causa* should not apply in a case where the claimant's conduct was the very act that the defendant was under a duty of care to prevent, whether or not the claimant was of sound mind.[74] There was no distinction between persons suffering from a mental illness and persons who were not, since the claimant recovered damages, not because of his mental state, but because he was a suicide risk and had not received the care that he should have. In the House of Lords, the deceased was held to have been 50 per cent contributorily negligent, however, on the basis that where the deceased was of sound mind at the time he killed himself he bore at least partial responsibility for his death.

---

[70] *Euro-Diam Ltd v Bathurst* [1990] 1 Q.B. 1, 35, *per* Kerr L.J., cited by Lloyd L.J. in *Kirkham*. See para. 4–146.

[71] [1990] 2 Q.B. 283, 291, *per* Lloyd L.J.

[72] *ibid.*; see also *Funk Estate v Clapp* (1986), reported at 68 D.L.R. (4th) 229, and (1988) 54 D.L.R. (4th) 512 where it was held that *ex turpi causa* was not a defence to an action by the widow of a prisoner who committed suicide, although there was no negligence on the facts.

[73] [1999] Q.B. 169.

[74] *per* Buxton L.J., *ibid.* at 185. There was no appeal on the issue of *ex turpi causa* in the House of Lords. *cf. Clunis v Camden & Islington Health Authority* [1998] Q.B. 978 where the Court of Appeal held that the defence of illegality would only be inappropriate if it could be said that the claimant did not know the nature or quality of his act or that it was wrong.

(c) Harm to third parties

4-124   It remains uncertain whether, in this country, a psychiatrist could be held responsible for foreseeable harm inflicted by a patient on a third party. Even if it were possible to identify reasonably practicable steps that a doctor could have taken (such as requesting compulsory admission for assessment or treatment under the Mental Health Act 1983) it is not clear that a duty of care would be held to exist.[75] On one view, where the patient is compulsorily detained the greater degree of control exercised over the patient may be sufficient to tip the balance in favour of a duty of care.[76] On the other hand, most psychiatric patients admitted to hospital or not compulsorily detained but are voluntary patients, and might seem strange that hospital's responsibility in tort should rest upon the technical issue of whether the patient had been formally detained under the Mental Health Act 1983.

4-125   In *Palmer v Tees Health Authority*[77] a young child was abducted and killed by a mental patient who had previously stated, while a hospital in-patient, that he had sexual feelings towards children and that a child would be murdered after his discharge. The Court of Appeal held that no duty of care was owed by the defendant health authority either to the child herself or the child's mother, in respect of an alleged negligent failure to diagnose that the patient constituted a serious risk to children. The threats made by the patient in *Palmer* were of a general nature. It would at least be arguable that, if a psychiatric patient were to make threats against a specific individual or individuals, where there was a real risk of such threats being carried out, then a duty of care on the part of a psychiatrist or psychologist might arise.[78]

(2) Negligent certification

4-126   A doctor who provides a written recommendation supporting the compulsory admission of a patient into hospital under Part II of the Mental Health Act 1983 must exercise reasonable care.[79] This necessarily requires that the

---

[75] See para. 2–150.

[76] By analogy with the position of a prisoner who is negligently allowed to escape and causes harm during the course of the escape: see *Home Office v Dorset Yacht Co Ltd* [1970] A.C. 1004, although in this case the House of Lords was careful to limit the potential duty to damage caused during the escape. There would be no liability for the escapee's subsequent criminal activity.

[77] [2000] P.I.Q.R. P1; [1999] Lloyd's Rep. Med. 351; para. 2–151. See further Jones (2000) 16 P.N. 3.

[78] As in *Tarasoff v Regents of the University of California* 551 P. 2d 334; Sup., 131 Cal. Rptr. 14 (1976); para. 2–148.

[79] *Hall v Semple* (1862) 3 F. & F. 337; *De Freville v Dill* (1927) 96 L.J.K.B. 1056; *Everett v Griffiths* [1921] 1 A.C. 631; *Harnett v Fisher* [1927] A.C. 573; *Buxton v Jayne* [1960] 1 W.L.R. 783; [1962] C.L.Y. 1167. See para. 2–143. Differing views were expressed in the Court of Appeal in *Everett v Griffiths* as to whether a duty of care was owed. In X *(minors) v Bedfordshire County Council* [1995] 2 A.C. 633, at 664–665 Sir Thomas Bingham M.R. found the judgment of Atkin L.J. in the Court of Appeal in favour of imposing a duty of care

doctor examine the patient,[80] and that he should make such further enquiries as are necessary.[81] On the one hand, the court must make due allowance for the difficulty in making an accurate diagnosis in some cases of mental illness, and on the other hand, they should require "very considerable care" where a person is being deprived of his liberty.[82]

(3) Procedural bars

Section 139(1) of the Mental Health Act 1983 provides that no person 4–127
shall be liable to any civil or criminal proceedings in respect of any act purporting to be done under the mental health legislation unless the act was done in bad faith or without reasonable care.[83] The section does not apply to an application for judicial review, so that proceedings for judicial review of a decision purportedly taken in the exercise of powers conferred by the Mental Health Act 1983 can be brought even though the applicant does not allege that the decision was made negligently or in bad faith.[84] Nor does section 139 refer to omissions, so that a negligent failure compulsorily to detain someone would not fall within section 139.[85] It is, however, arguable that a private law action brought under section 7 of the Human Rights Act 1998 would require leave under section 139(2) of the Mental Health Act 1983.[86]

In addition, section 139(2) provides that civil proceedings may not be 4–128
instituted in respect of such an act without leave of the High Court. Proceedings issued without leave are a nullity,[87] although the requirement for leave applies only to patients who are formally detained under the Act; voluntary patients need not seek leave to bring an action.[88]

(n.79 contd.) persuasive. However, Lord Browne-Wilkinson in X *(minors), ibid.* at 753, pointed out that though there were dicta in the House of Lords in *Everett v Griffiths* in favour of a duty of care, the issue had not been finally decided by their Lordships.

[80] Mental Health Act, 1983, s. 12(1).

[81] *Hall v Semple* (1862) 3 F. & F. 337, 354, *per* Crompton J.

[82] *ibid.* at pp. 355–356.

[83] See Jaconelli [1998] J.S.W.F.L. 151.

[84] *Re Waldron* [1986] Q.B. 824 (also reported as *R. v Hallstrom, ex parte* W [1985] 3 All E.R. 775). It was conceded in this case that s. 139 would not apply to a writ of habeas corpus. On judicial review of a decision involving the forcible treatment of a detained patient there must be an assessment of the substantive merits of the decision, involving the finding of primary facts following oral evidence, if necessary: *R. (on the application of W) v Broadmoor Hospital* [2001] EWCA Civ 1545; [2002] 1 W.L.R. 419.

[85] Since the claimant would in any event still have to prove lack of reasonable care the practical consequence of this is simply that the requirement to obtain leave of the High Court under s. 139(2) would not apply. Claimants would nonetheless face formidable hurdles in establishing a duty of care. See paras 2–147 *et seq.*

[86] *R. (on the application of W) v Broadmoor Hospital* [2001] EWCA Civ 1545; [2002] 1 W.L.R. 419 *per* Brooke L.J. at [54] and Hale L.J. at [61].

[87] *Pountney v Griffiths* [1976] A.C. 314.

[88] *R. v Runighian* [1977] Crim. L.R. 361 where it was held that acts done to an informal patient are not done in pursuance of the Mental Health Act. This case is concerned with the earlier provision requiring leave, s. 141 of the Mental Health Act 1959, but the differences in the wording of the section do not affect the point. On the other hand, it is clear that s. 139(1) covers acts "*purporting* to be done in pursuance of this Act" so that if a doctor *bona fide* and reasonably believed that an informal patient was in fact detained, it would seem that

4–129   The requirement to obtain leave does not apply to actions against the Secretary of State, a health authority or a NHS Trust.[89] But in *C v South London and Maudsley Hospital NHS Trust*[90] McCombe J. held that, having refused to grant leave under section 139(2) to bring proceedings against the individual doctors, the proceedings against the defendant NHS Trust would be bound to fail if begun, for the same reasons as given under section 139(2), and therefore it was inevitable that they would either be struck out under the court's case management powers (Civil Procedure Rules 1998, Part 3) or judgment would be given in favour of the defendants on the basis that the claim had no real prospect of succeeding. In practice this would seem to undermine the effect of section 139(4), if whenever leave is refused under section 139(2) it is probable that other procedural rules will be applied to strike out the claim.

4–130   Moreover, it had been thought that one consequence of section 139(4) was that, irrespective of the substantive defence provided to an individual doctor by section 139(1), the hospital employing that doctor would be vicariously liable for his actions (*e.g.* in the tort of battery) even if the doctor was held not liable because he acted in good faith and with reasonable care.[91] But in *R. (on the application of W) v Broadmoor Hospital*[92] Hale L.J. suggested that a health authority or NHS Trust could only be held vicariously liable for the actions for which the individual doctors would themselves be liable, which would indirectly confer the benefit of section 139(1) on the employers. Brooke L.J.[93] even suggested, provisionally, that a hospital may not be vicariously liable at all for the actions a responsible medical officer (RMO) in making treatment decisions under sections 57 or 58 of the Mental Health Act, on the basis that the Act vests the duty to carry out the specified functions in the RMO personally.[94] It was not the hospital, through the agency of one of its medical staff, in whom was vested the power to direct treatment without consent, but the RMO himself.

4–131   The rationale for a provision protecting individuals who have to make decisions under the mental health legislation has been said to be that "patients under the Mental Health Act may generally be inherently likely to harass those concerned with them by groundless charges and litigation, and may therefore have to suffer modification of the general right of free access to the courts."[95]

(n.88 contd.) s. 139(1) would apply. It is not apparent, then, why s. 139(2) would not also apply to the informal patient since that subsection requires leave of the High Court for any civil proceedings "in respect of any such act", i.e. the act purporting to be done referred to in s. 139(1).

[89] Mental Health Act 1983, s. 139(4). Accordingly, it does not apply to the Mental Health Act Commission, which is a special health authority: *X. v A., B. and C. and the Mental Health Act Commission* (1991) 9 B.M.L.R. 91, 97, QBD.

[90] (2001, QBD; unreported).

[91] See *R. (on the application of W) v Broadmoor Hospital* [2001] EWCA Civ 1545; [2002] 1 W.L.R. 419 at [24] *per* Simon Brown L.J. and [58] *per* Hale L.J.

[92] *ibid. per* Hale L.J.

[93] *ibid.* at [42] and [43].

[94] For consideration of ss. 57 and 58 see paras 6–070 to 6–071.

[95] *Pountney v Griffiths* [1976] A.C. 314, 329, *per* Lord Simon. See also *per* Scrutton L.J. in

This justification has been strongly criticised on the grounds that very few patients, even of those compulsorily detained, are suffering from disorders which make it likely that they will harass others, and rather more of them are suffering from disorders which makes it likely that they will not complain at all, even where complaint would be justified.[96] Patients with a mental disorder are often in a "peculiarly powerless position which merits, if anything, extra safeguards rather than the removal of those available to everyone else."[97]

Under section 141 of the Mental Health Act 1959 the court could not grant leave unless it was "satisfied that there is a substantial ground for the contention that the person to be proceeded against has acted in bad faith or without reasonable care."[98] The requirement that there be a "substantial ground" was omitted from section 139 of the Mental Health Act 1983.[99] In *Winch v Jones*[1] the Court of Appeal accepted that this was intended to be a change of substance, reducing the protection given to persons purporting to act under the legislation. Otton J. had held that although the claimant's application was neither frivolous nor vexatious, nor an abuse of the process of the court, he should not grant leave under section 139 unless there was a *prima facie* case of negligence against the defendant. The Court of Appeal, allowing the claimant's appeal, rejected this approach because it would lead to a full dress-rehearsal of the action which is inappropriate to an application for leave to commence proceedings, and at that stage an applicant who has a reasonable suspicion that there has been negligence may be quite unable to put forward a *prima facie* case before disclosure. Sir John Donaldson M.R. said that section 139 is *sui generis* and the question that has to be resolved is whether on the materials immediately available to the court "the applicant's complaint appears to be such that it deserves the

4–132

(n.95 contd.) *Everett v Griffiths* [1920] 3 K.B. 163 at pp. 197–198: "Very few lunatics think they are properly incarcerated, and most of them would enjoy an action in which the individual has always a better chance of getting the sympathy of the jury than the officers of the state who are performing the unpleasant duty of incarcerating him. . . . To leave the person who has to decide this difficult question as to the exact degree of unsoundness of mind which justifies immediate restraint, when he has acted honestly in forming his judgment, exposed to the threat of an action by the person restrained, to be decided by persons who did not see the alleged lunatic at the time he was incarcerated, but do see him when his condition may be different, by persons who may be struck by his cleverness without appreciating how near it may be to deranged intellect, seems to me calculated to hinder his properly executing the duty he owes to the community. This exemption is not giving him a licence to be negligent; it is removing from him the threat of harassing actions."

[96] Hoggett, *Mental Health Law*, 4th ed., 1996, p. 250.
[97] *ibid.*
[98] "Hesitancy in accepting medical opinions, particularly in the difficult discipline of psychiatry and in relation to the controversial subject of psychopathy, provides no evidence of bad faith", *per* Lawton L.J. in *Kynaston v Secretary of State for Home Affairs* (1981) 73 Cr. App. R. 281at 285 (a decision on s. 141(2) of the Mental Health Act 1959).
[99] s. 141(2) of the Mental Health Act 1959 having been repealed and replaced by the Mental Health (Amendment) Act 1982, s. 60, now consolidated in the Mental Health Act 1983, s. 139. The draft Mental Health Bill 2002 (available at *www.doh.gov.uk/mentalhealth/draftbill2002*) would reverse the burden of proof in the s. 139 defence, i.e. it would be a defence for the defendant to demonstrate that he acted in good faith and with reasonable care.
[1] [1985] 3 All E.R. 97.

fuller investigation which will be possible if the intended applicant is allowed to proceed."[2] Parker L.J. took the view that if an action is neither frivolous nor vexatious it is *prima facie* fit to be tried, and if it is fit to be tried leave ought to be given. The purpose of the section, said his Lordship, was to prevent harassment by clearly hopeless actions, it was not to see that only those actions which could be seen to be likely to succeed should go ahead. Defendants would still have some protection under the section, however, in comparison to the procedure for striking out frivolous and vexatious claims, because the claimant has to take the initiative by obtaining leave.[3]

4–133   In *James v London Borough of Havering*,[4] however, Farquharson L.J. distinguished *Winch v Jones* and refused the applicant leave under section 139(2) because it was "virtually unarguable" to say that the doctor and the social worker concerned in an emergency compulsory admission for assessment could have acted without reasonable care. On the facts, there were ample grounds for them to take the course that they did, and even if they were wrong an action by the applicant would be bound to fail. His Lordship commented that:

> "What one has to look at in deciding whether they are entitled to the protection of section 139 is what appeared to the social worker and the doctor at the time and how they reacted to it. When one discovers that, to the extent which it is agreed, one decides whether there is a *prima facie* case of their acting without reasonable care."[5]

4–134   This would appear to be inconsistent with the views expressed by the Court of Appeal in *Winch v Jones*, in that it requires the claimant to establish a *prima facie* case on the application for leave. Indeed, Farquharson L.J. disagreed with the approach of Sir John Donaldson M.R., on the ground that the object of section 139 was to protect a social worker or doctor from the consequences of a wrong decision made in purported compliance with the Mental Health Act, particularly in circumstances where decisions have to be made quickly for the safety of the patient or others:

> "Section 139 . . . is designed to protect a witness making that decision, provided they act in good faith and with reasonable care. To that extent it seems to me that the section goes beyond the effect referred to by Sir

---

[2] *ibid.* at p. 102. It is arguably inappropriate to invoke the *Bolam* test when considering whether to grant leave to proceed, because this could involve adjudicating on the merits in advance, before all the evidence has been considered and before matters which arguably require investigation have been resolved: *O'Neill v Morrison* (1993, CA; unreported) *per* Hirst L.J.

[3] The fact that an application for leave under s. 139(2) has been successful does not preclude a judge from subsequently concluding, following further investigation, that the action should be struck out as disclosing no reasonable cause of action: *X. v A., B. and C. and the Mental Health Act Commission* (1991) 9 B.M.L.R. 91, QBD.

[4] (1992) 15 B.M.L.R. 1.

[5] *ibid.* at p. 4.

John Donaldson M.R. in *Winch v Jones* . . . It is not only protection against frivolous claims; it is also a protection from error in the circumstances set out in the subsection."[6]

With great respect, it is not clear why social workers or doctors need this particular "protection from error" when it is well-established that the tort of negligence does not condemn reasonable errors, particularly those made in an emergency, as carelessness for which a defendant should be held liable. Requiring a claimant to establish a *prima facie* case, before discovery, and in circumstances where facts are in dispute (which was the case in *James v London Borough of Havering*) arguably sets the procedural hurdle for claimants too high, a point that had been accepted in *Winch v Jones*.[7]

In *C v South London and Maudsley Hospital NHS Trust*[8] McCombe J.   **4–135** refused leave under section 139(2) where the claimant argued that the doctors had used the procedure for compulsory admission for assessment (under section 2) in order to avoid the statutory requirements associated with compulsory admission for treatment (under section 3) because it was known that the claimant's mother objected. There was no reason why a doctor could not reasonably and in good faith take the view that the grounds for admission under section 2 were met, even if he thought that in the end a section 3 admission for a longer period would almost inevitably follow. The decision to admit under section 2 was taken on the day the claimant was admitted, on the basis of his condition on that day. His Lordship added that, when considering the question of granting leave under 139(2), the question of the overriding objective under the Civil Procedure Rules has no application. That concept directs how decisions to be taken under the Rules are to be approached, but the Civil Procedure Rules did not direct how a discretion arising under an entirely different statute was to be exercised.

6. DEFENCES

Where a claimant fails to establish the necessary elements of the tort of   **4–136** negligence (duty of care, breach of that duty, and the causal link to the damage), his action will fail, and in a sense the defendant's "defence" has succeeded. The claimant loses because he has failed to establish that a tort was committed. But even where he succeeds in proving the required elements of the tort of negligence, he will still lose if the defendant can rely on a general defence (though in the case of contributory negligence the effect is

---

[6] *ibid.*
[7] Since the decision in *James v London Borough of Havering* was of a single judge of the Court of Appeal, on an application for leave to appeal, and the decision in *Winch v Jones* was of a two judge Court on a full appeal, it is the latter which should be preferred.
[8] (2001, QBD; unreported).

that the damages are reduced).[9] It is comparatively rare for such general defences to be raised in the context of medical negligence actions, principally because the circumstances in which medical treatment occurs is unlikely to create much scope for the type of "misbehaviour" by claimants which typically gives rise to a specific defence.

(1) Contributory negligence

4–137   In many instances a doctor needs the patient's co-operation to enable him to make an accurate diagnosis or for the purpose of administering the treatment. Sometimes this will be absolutely vital. For example, the doctor will need reasonably accurate information regarding the patient's symptoms, and/or medical history (*e.g.* the patient may forget to mention that he is allergic to penicillin). Similarly, the co-operation of the patient may be essential in implementing a treatment regime, for example, with regard to taking medication in the right quantity and at the right times of day, or returning for further treatment or tests. If the patient fails to follow proper instructions and this is a cause of his injuries then it will be possible to argue that the patient has been contributorily negligent, or in an extreme case that his conduct is the sole cause of the damage.[10] Alternatively, where a patient has failed to communicate the nature of the symptoms from which she is suffering the conclusion may simply be that the doctor was not negligent in failing to make the correct diagnosis on the basis of the available information.[11]

4–138   Where damage is attributable partly to the fault of the defendant and partly to the fault of the claimant then the award of damages may be reduced

---

[9] Note that, in addition to general defences, there are sometimes specific immunities available to particular categories of defendant. s. 10 of the Crown Proceedings Act 1947 conferred immunity on the Crown in respect of death or injury to a member of the armed forces who "at the time when that thing was suffered" was on duty or who, though not on duty, was on any service property. This immunity has been repealed but only in respect of causes of action accruing from May 15, 1987. In *Derry v Ministry of Defence* [1999] P.I.Q.R. P204 a soldier alleged that a military doctor had been negligent in failing to diagnose cancer. He argued that the defendants could not rely on s. 10 where there was a negligent failure to diagnose a pre-existing medical condition, but the Court of Appeal held that the immunity applied. The "thing suffered" was the misdiagnosis, which occurred on each occasion he was examined at the military hospital, and therefore fell within that subsection. The House of Lords has also held that s. 10 was not incompatible with Art. 6 of the European Convention on Human Rights: *Matthews v Ministry of Defence* [2003] UKHL 4; [2003] 1 All E.R. 689.

[10] *Venner v North East Essex Area Health Authority, The Times,* February 21, 1987; *Murrin v Janes* [1949] 4 D.L.R. 403, 406 (Newfd. S.C.) where a claimant's delay in seeing a doctor to deal with excessive bleeding following extraction of his teeth was held to be the sole cause of his misfortune.

[11] *Gordon v Wilson* [1992] 3 Med. L.R. 401, Court of Session (Outer House); *Morrison v Forsyth* [1995] 6 Med. L.R. 6, Court of Session, where a general practitioner was found not liable for failing to visit a patient because the seriousness of the patient's condition was not made clear in the course of a telephone conversation; *Friedsam v Ng* [1994] 3 W.W.R. 294 (B.C.C.A.), where the patient's omission to inform a general practitioner of isolated instances of chest pains and incontinence meant that the defendant had not been negligent in failing to embark upon a more detailed inquiry.

by reason of the claimant's contributory negligence.[12] The reduction will be to such extent as the court thinks just and equitable having regard to the claimant's share in responsibility for the damage.

Fault means "negligence, breach of statutory duty or other act or omission which gives rise to a liability in tort or would, apart from this Act, give rise to the defence of contributory negligence."[13] The legislation clearly applies to the tort of negligence, although there has been uncertainty as to whether it also applies to actions for battery. The balance of authority is now in favour of the view that it can apply to actions in trespass to the person.[14] Similarly, there has been some controversy about the extent to which the legislation applies to actions in contract. The Act is open to different interpretations and this has produced conflicting authorities.[15] It has now been held that where the defendant's negligent breach of contract would have given rise to liability in the tort of negligence independently of the existence of the contract, damages may be apportioned for the claimant's contributory negligence.[16] This means that the defence will be available in virtually all actions arising out of private medical treatment, since the obligations imposed by the contract are normally the same as the duty to exercise reasonable care in the tort of negligence.[17] On the other hand, where (a) liability does not depend on negligence but arises from breach of a strict contractual duty; or (b) liability arises from breach of a contractual obligation which is expressed in terms of exercising reasonable care, but does not correspond to a common law duty of care which would exist independently of the contract; apportionment under the Act is not available.[18] Thus, if a patient was able to establish that the doctor had given a contractual warranty to achieve a particular result, this would fall into category (a) and the damages could not be apportioned for contributory negligence.[19] In the context of the relationship

4–139

---

[12] Law Reform (Contributory Negligence) Act 1945, s. 1. The defence must be specifically pleaded: *Fookes v Slaytor* [1979] 1 All E.R. 137; see also CPR r. 16.5. In *Brown v Merton, Sutton and Wandsworth Area Health Authority* [1982] 1 All E.R. 650, 652 counsel for the defendants intimated that he would rely on the defence of inevitable accident. This defence is generally regarded as limited to actions in trespass, and in any event it is confined to accidents that could not have been avoided by the exercise of reasonable care. Thus, in an action for negligence a plea of inevitable accident is, in effect, a denial of negligence.

[13] *ibid.*, s. 4.

[14] *Barnes v Nayer, The Times*, December 19, 1986, CA; *Wasson v Chief Constable of the Royal Ulster Constabulary* [1987] 8 N.I.J.B. 34; *Murphy v Culhane* [1977] Q.B. 94; cf. *Lane v Holloway* [1968] 1 Q.B. 379; Hudson (1984) 4 L.S. 332.

[15] See Burrows, *Remedies for Torts and Breach of Contract*, 2nd ed., Butterworths, 1994, pp. 80–87.

[16] *Forsikringsaktieselskapet Vesta v Butcher* [1988] 3 W.L.R. 565; [1988] 2 All E.R. 43, CA, approving the analysis of Hobhouse J. at [1986] 2 All E.R. 488, 508.

[17] The concurrent duty of care in tort to exercise reasonable skill and care owed by a professional to a client under the contract of retainer will normally fall into this category, so that the negligent professional can rely on contributory negligence as a defence: *UCB Bank plc v Hepherd Winstanley & Pugh (a Firm)* [1999] Lloyd's Rep. P.N. 963, CA; *Platform Home Loans Ltd v Oyston Shipways Ltd* [2000] 2 A.C. 190; see also *Barclays Bank plc v Fairclough Building Ltd (No. 2)* [1995] P.I.Q.R. P152; (1995) 76 B.L.R. 1.

[18] *Forsikringsaktieselskapet Vesta v Butcher* [1988] 3 W.L.R. 565; [1988] 2 All E.R. 43; *Barclays Bank plc. v Fairclough Building Ltd (No. 1)* [1995] Q.B. 214, CA.

[19] For the difficulties of proving this see para. 2–010. If, in the case of a strict contractual

between doctor and patient, it is difficult to imagine contractual duties expressed in terms of exercising reasonable care which would not correspond to duties in the tort of negligence (category (b)), particularly since the courts have stressed that patients who receive treatment under the NHS should not be placed at a disadvantage, in terms of their legal rights, in comparison with patients who receive treatment privately.[20]

4–140   Although, in theory, there is no reason why contributory negligence should not apply in a claim for medical negligence, as with any other type of action for negligence, in practice the defence is rarely invoked successfully, and this is reflected in a comparative dearth of cases.[21] It may be that, as a general rule, the plea is considered to be inappropriate in an action for medical negligence, given the inequality between the respective positions of doctor and patient. Patients do not usually question the advice or conduct of their doctors, at least initially, even when they are aware that their condition is deteriorating or not improving. Contributory negligence is measured by the standard of the reasonable, prudent man, which is meant to be the same standard of care as that applied to defendants.[22] In practice the courts tend to require less from claimants in the way of prudence for their own safety than from defendants, and this is likely to be even more apparent with patients, who rely heavily on the skills and knowledge of medical practitioners. If the patient has ignored his doctor's advice (for example, by discharging himself from hospital or failing to return for further treatment) it may be easier to establish contributory negligence. It would have to be shown that a reasonable person would have been aware of the significance of the advice, which could depend upon the nature of the advice given by the doctor and whether the advice was clear to the patient. Moreover, in some circumstances there may well be a responsibility upon the doctor to adopt a system for following-up patients who do not comply with advice to re-attend for further treatment or tests.[23]

4–141   The one English reported case in which the claimant's conduct was held to have been negligent is *Pidgeon v Doncaster Health Authority*[24] where a claimant who developed cervical cancer, having been told that the results of smear test were negative, was held to have been two-thirds contributorily negligent in failing to have a further smear test despite frequent reminders. It would also be possible for a plea of contributory negligence to apply in cases where the claimant attempts suicide and a claim is brought against medical staff on the basis of a negligent failure to prevent the suicide attempt. In *Reeves v Commissioner of Police for the Metropolis*,[25] a similar type of

---

(n.19 contd.) warranty, the claimant has been guilty of "contributory" fault there is a risk that the court will conclude that the defendant's breach was not a *cause* of the loss, in which case the claim fails entirely: see, *e.g.*, *Lambert v Lewis* [1982] A.C. 225.
[20] See para. 2–005.
[21] See Giesen, *International Medical Malpractice Law*, 1988 para. 236; Picard & Robertson, *Legal Liability of Doctors and Hospitals in Canada*, 3rd ed. 1996, pp. 284–286.
[22] *Jones v Livox Quarries Ltd* [1952] 2 Q.B. 608, 615.
[23] Scott (1993) 4 *AVMA Medical & Legal Journal* (No. 3) p. 7.
[24] [2002] Lloyd's Rep. Med. 130 (Doncaster County Court).
[25] [2000] 1 A.C. 360.

claim brought against the police, the deceased was held 50 per cent contributorily negligent because he was partially responsible for his death, which was the result of the combination of the failure of the police to protect a prisoner who was a known suicide risk from harming himself and his own deliberate decision to end his life. Possibly, where the deceased was of unsound mind his suicide would not give rise the defence of contributory negligence, by analogy with the position of young children who are not of full understanding.[26] In this situation the court is comparing the negligence of the defendant against the intentional conduct of the claimant, but it is not simply a matter of assessing relative blameworthiness, but the parties' respective "responsibility for the damage". Thus, the Act requires the court to apportion "not merely degrees of carelessness but 'responsibility' and . . . an assessment of responsibility must take into account the policy of the rule, such as the Factories Acts, by which liability is imposed. A person may be responsible although he has not been careless at all, as in the case of breach of an absolute statutory duty. And he may have been careless without being responsible, as in the case of 'acts of inattention' by workmen."[27]

4–142 By raising the plea of contributory negligence the defendant may highlight the extent of the doctor's duty to take special care in giving the patient instructions, and making sure that the patient understands both the instructions and the importance of strictly adhering to them.[28] In *Marshall v Rogers*,[29] for example, the defendant alleged that the claimant's injury was caused by his own negligence in failing to follow the instructions that he had been given and to report his symptoms. It was held, however, that where a dangerous remedy was being attempted the doctor was negligent in delegating his own professional duty of deciding the true meaning of the patient's progressive symptoms to the patient himself, especially given that the patient had to make a subjective assessment of his symptoms. The defendant should have conducted daily tests.

4–143 Some Canadian courts have made findings of contributory negligence against careless patients. In *Brushett v Cowan*[30] the claimant was contributorily negligent in engaging in ordinary activities without crutches following a bone biopsy on her leg, because she had failed to ask for clear instructions regarding the use of the crutches. A failure to have a post-operative check-up, as suggested by the doctor, has been held to be negligent,[31] and in *Crossman v*

---

[26] *ibid.* at 372 *per* Lord Hoffmann.
[27] *ibid.* at 371.
[28] See paras 4–043 to 4–047. See Karp (1993) 9 J. of the M.D.U. 26, who points out that educating patients results in fewer injuries, and better compliance with medical advice.
[29] [1943] 4 D.L.R. 68, 77.
[30] (1987) 40 D.L.R. (4th) 488; affirmed (1990) 69 D.L.R. (4th) 743 (Newfd. C.A.). In *Vancouver General Hospital v McDaniel* (1934) 152 L.T.R. 56 it was suggested that the failure to be vaccinated against smallpox might constitute contributory negligence in a claim for infecting the patient with the disease, but this allegation was not pursued.
[31] *Fredette v Wiebe* [1986] 5 W.W.R. 222 (B.C.S.C.). See also *Locher v Turner* (1995) Aust. Torts Rep. 81–336 (Qd C.A.) where a patient reported rectal bleeding to her doctor, who examined her and concluded that the source of the bleeding was piles. The claimant did not report further episodes of bleeding to her doctor when she saw him, because she thought that

Stewart[32] a patient who obtained prescription drugs from an unorthodox source, and continued to use the drugs on a prolonged basis without obtaining prescription renewals and without consulting the "prescribing" physician, was described as "foolhardy in the extreme." She was held to be responsible for two thirds of the damage to her eyesight caused by the side-effects of the drug.

(2) *Volenti non fit injuria*

4–144   *Volenti non fit injuria* consists of a voluntary agreement by the claimant to absolve the defendant from the legal consequences of an unreasonable risk of harm created by the defendant, where the claimant has full knowledge of both the nature and extent of the risk. This should not be confused with *consent* to medical treatment which provides a defence to what would otherwise be the tort of battery. The patient who consents to medical treatment does not thereby agree to run the risk of negligence by the doctor.[33]

4–145   The one situation where the *volenti* defence could plausibly apply to a medical negligence action is in the case of suicide by a patient in circumstances where the doctor was under a duty a to take reasonable precautions to prevent a suicide attempt. The point had been touched upon by the Court of Appeal in *Kirkham v Chief Constable of Greater Manchester Police*,[34] though it was said that the defence would only arise where the person was "of sound mind." But in *Reeves v Commissioner of Police for the Metropolis*[35] the House of Lords held that *volenti* does not apply where the claimant's act was the very thing that the defendant was under a duty to take reasonable care to prevent, irrespective of the suicide's mental state. If the defendant owed a duty of care to prevent a suicide attempt he cannot argue that the act which he was under a duty to prevent gave rise to the defence of *volenti*, because that would undermine the point of imposing a duty of care.

(3) Illegality

4–146   The fact that the claimant was involved in committing a criminal offence at the time of sustaining damage may, in some instances, constitute a defence. This is usually expressed in the Latin maxim *ex turpi causa non oritur actio*

(n.31 contd.) this was also attributable to her piles, but it turned out to be caused by colon cancer. The doctor was found negligent in failing to review the initial diagnosis, but the claimant was held 20% contributorily negligent for failing to report the further episodes of rectal bleeding.

[32] (1977) 82 D.L.R. (3d) 677, 686 (B.C.S.C.). It is also possible that unreasonable behaviour by a patient after the defendant's negligent conduct could be characterised as a failure to mitigate his loss: see para. 9–027. In *Brain v Mador* (1985) 32 C.C.L.T. 157 (Ont. C.A.) a patient who failed to take steps to seek further medical advice following a vasectomy which had developed complications was held to have acted unreasonably, and his damages were reduced by 50% for failing to mitigate the loss.

[33] See *Freeman v Home Office* [1984] Q.B. 524, 557, *per* Sir John Donaldson M.R.

[34] [1990] 2 Q.B. 283.

[35] [2000] 1 A.C. 360.

(an action cannot be founded on a base cause). Of course, it will be extremely rare for a claimant in a medical negligence action to be involved in illegality which is directly linked to the treatment, although in *Kirkham v Chief Constable of Greater Manchester Police* the Court of Appeal accepted that the *ex turpi causa* defence is not confined to criminal conduct, but could apply to illegal or immoral conduct by the claimant if in all the circumstances an award of damages would be an affront to the public conscience.[36] Awarding damages following a suicide would not affront the public conscience, at least where there was medical evidence that the suicide was "not in full possession of his mind."[37] Farquharson L.J. said that an action could hardly be said to be grounded in immorality where "grave mental instability" on the part of the victim has been proved, although "the position may well be different where the victim is wholly sane."[38] In the context of a claim following a suicide attempt it would appear that there is considerable overlap between the *ex turpi causa* defence and the *volenti* defence.[39] But in *Reeves v Commissioner of Police of the Metropolis*[40] the Court of Appeal held that *ex turpi causa* does not apply in a case where the claimant's conduct was the very act that the defendant was under a duty of care to prevent, whether or not the claimant was of sound mind.[41]

In *Clunis v Camden & Islington Health Authority*[42] the claimant was a mental   **4–147** patient, with a history of seriously violent behaviour, who had been compulsorily detained under the Mental Health Act 1983. Three months after his discharge from hospital the claimant killed a stranger in an unprovoked attack, and he was subsequently convicted of manslaughter on the ground of diminished responsibility. The claimant brought an action against the health authority claiming that if he had received appropriate after-care he would not have committed the crime and would not therefore have been detained in a special hospital, or at

---

[36] [1990] 2 Q.B. 283, 291, *per* Lloyd L.J. Note, however, that there is significant controversy about the conceptual basis of the *ex turpi causa* defence. For some judges it rests on the affront to the "public conscience" involved if the court is effectively seen to be assisting a criminal, thereby bringing the law into disrepute. For others it depends on whether the claimant has to *rely* on his own criminal act as the basis of the claim. For an extended discussion see *Clerk & Lindsell on Torts*, 18th ed., 2000, paras 3–02 to 3–19.

[37] *ibid.* at 291, *per* Lloyd L.J.; see also *Funk Estate v Clapp* (1986), reported at 68 D.L.R. (4th) 229, and (1988) 54 D.L.R. (4th) 512.

[38] The meaning of the phrases "grave mental instability" and "wholly sane" is a matter of some conjecture. Query whether a person who is not insane, but whose judgment is impaired by an emotional, as opposed to a psychological, disturbance falls into the category of "not wholly sane."

[39] In *Hyde v Tameside Area Health Authority* (1981), reported at (1986) 2 P.N. 26, 29–30 Lord Denning M.R. was opposed to allowing actions based on suicide or attempted suicide, a view that was clearly based on considerations of policy, and in particular his Lordship's belief that "'medical malpractice' cases should not get out of hand here as they have done in the United States of America." In *Kirkham v Chief Constable of Greater Manchester Police* [1990] 2 Q.B. 283, 292–293 Lloyd L.J. did not share this view.

[40] [1999] Q.B. 169.

[41] *ibid.* at 185, *per* Buxton L.J. There was no appeal on the issue of *ex turpi causa* in the House of Lords, but the reasoning of their Lordships in relation to the argument that the deceased's suicide constituted a *novus actus interveniens* or that the deceased was *volenti* is entirely consistent with the Court of Appeal's approach to *ex turpi causa*.

[42] [1998] Q.B. 978.

least would not have been detained for as long (if the after-care had involved compulsory admission to hospital under the Mental Health Act). The Court of Appeal struck out the claim, *inter alia*, on the ground that the action was based the claimant's own illegal act, and therefore the maxim *ex turpi causa non oritur actio* applied. Although the claimant's mental responsibility was impaired, a plea of diminished responsibility did not remove liability for his criminal act. He must have known what he was doing and that it was wrong, and therefore the claim was contrary to public policy. The court would not aid a litigant who relied on his own criminal or immoral act.[43] On the other hand, it would seem that where a claimant "did not know the nature and quality of his act or that what he was doing was wrong"[44] public policy would not necessarily preclude a claim against a health authority in these circumstances (provided that the claimant can establish that the defendants owed him a duty of care).

4–148   In some cases the medical treatment which the claimant alleges she should have received is unlawful because there is a statutory prohibition. In *Rance v Mid-Downs Health Authority*[45] a mother had negligently been denied the opportunity to have an abortion, but the period of gestation was such that, as the law then stood,[46] a termination of the pregnancy would probably not have satisfied the requirements of Abortion Act 1967 and therefore would not have been lawful. Her claim for damages was denied on policy grounds, since the claimant could not have taken advantage of the lost opportunity to terminate the pregnancy without breaking the law. Similarly, a claim for damages in respect of rendering the claimant infertile cannot include the cost of procedures connected with surrogate motherhood if those procedures would be in breach of the Surrogacy Arrangements Act 1985.[47] Thus, claims arising out of the negligent performance of procedures which are unlawful are likely to be barred on the grounds of policy.[48]

---

[43] See also *Wilson v Coulson* [2002] P.I.Q.R. P300, QBD where a claimant suffered brain damage in an accident caused by the defendant's negligence. He alleged that this had produced a personality change which led him to start using heroin. Harrison J., applying *Clunis*, held that there was no action in respect of further brain damage caused by an overdose of heroin, because the claimant's decision to use heroin was voluntary, deliberate and informed, and he had not lost the capacity or the power to say no. His action was both unreasonable and illegal and he should not be allowed to profit from his own actions.

[44] [1998] Q.B. 978 at 989.

[45] [1991] 1 Q.B. 587.

[46] Following amendment of the Abortion Act 1967 by the Human Fertilisation and Embryology Act 1990, s. 37, there is now no time limit where the termination is necessary to prevent grave permanent injury to the health of the woman, where the pregnancy involves risk to her life, or where there is a substantial risk that the foetus would be seriously handicapped. Where any of these grounds applied the causation issue in *Rance* would be irrelevant. The time limit under s. 1(1)(a) of the Abortion Act 1967 is 24 weeks.

[47] See *Briody v St Helens and Knowsley Area Health Authority* [2001] EWCA Civ 1010; [2002] Q.B. 856, para. 9–099.

[48] Another example would be a claim arising out of an unlawful organ transplant operation contrary to the Human Organ Transplants Act 1989. In *Norberg v Wynrib* (1992) 92 D.L.R. (4th) 449 the Supreme Court of Canada held that *ex turpi causa* did not apply to an action where the defendant doctor had supplied drugs to a patient who was addicted to pain-killers and tranquillisers in exchange for sexual contact. The patient had also been obtaining drugs from other doctors, and was convicted of the offence of "double-doctoring." The illegality was not causally linked to the harm suffered by the claimant.

CHAPTER 5

CAUSATION AND REMOTENESS OF DAMAGE

In the tort of negligence damage is the gist of the action. If the claimant cannot show that he sustained injury as a result of the defendant's breach of duty, there is no tort and the action fails. In contract a claimant who proves that the defendant was in breach of contract is entitled to nominal damages, but, again, he will not be awarded substantial damages unless he establishes a causal link between the breach and his loss. A similar principle applies to a claim in battery, which, as an action in trespass to the person, is actionable *per se*.[1]

5–001

Causation is concerned with the physical connection between the defendant's negligence and the claimant's damage. No matter how gross the defendant's negligence he is not liable if, as a question of fact, his conduct did not cause the damage. Thus, there must be a causal link between the defendant's breach of duty and the damage sustained by the claimant.[2] This is essentially an explanatory inquiry: how, in fact, did the damage occur? In medical malpractice litigation this issue is largely a matter of medical and scientific evidence, for example, about the pathology of a particular disease and the prospects for successful treatment with proper care. The question is normally dealt with by the "but for" test. In some instances there may be several causal factors involved and the precise aetiology may be unknown. This can leave a claimant with virtually insuperable difficulties of proof. Even if the "but for" test is satisfied, so that it is clear that the defendant's negligence is *a* cause, there may be other sufficient causes or the negligence may form part of a sequence of events which led to the claimant's injury. Here the question is whether the defendant's conduct is to be regarded as the cause in law of the loss. The court may allocate causal responsibility to another cause, which is treated as a supervening event or an intervening act which "breaks the chain of causation."

5–002

Remoteness of damage is concerned with those situations where the defendant has undoubtedly caused the claimant's loss, but the damage is not of the same type as would normally be anticipated in similar circumstances, or the damage occurred in an unusual manner. There has to be some limit, it is said, to a defendant's responsibility and it is considered to be unfair to hold

5–003

---

[1] *Allan v New Mount Sinai Hospital* (1980) 109 D.L.R. (3d) 634, 643 (Ont. H.C.). For discussion of causation in the context of battery see para. 6–146.

[2] See, generally, Hart and Honoré, *Causation in the Law*, 2nd ed., 1985.

a person liable for all the consequences of his negligence, however bizarre or freakish they might be.[3] In practice, while proof of factual causation can be a very real problem, questions of remoteness of damage are comparatively rare in medical negligence actions.

1. CAUSATION IN FACT

(1) The "but for" test

5–004   If damage to the claimant would not have occurred "but for" the defendant's negligence then the negligence is *a* cause of the damage. It is not necessarily *the* cause because there may well be other events which are causally relevant. Putting this another way, if the loss would have occurred in any event, the defendant's conduct is not a cause. Two cases, both involving medical negligence, illustrate this point. In *Barnett v Chelsea and Kensington Hospital Management Committee*[4] three nightwatchmen attended hospital, clearly appearing ill, and they informed a nurse that they had been vomiting. The nurse telephoned the casualty officer, who did not see the men, but said that they should go home and see their own doctors. They left, and about five hours later one of the men died from arsenic poisoning. Nield J. held that in these circumstances the casualty officer was negligent in failing to have seen and examined the deceased. It could not be said, however, that but for the doctor's negligence the deceased would have lived, because the medical evidence indicated that even if the patient had received prompt treat-

---

[3] The term "remoteness" is also sometimes used to describe a causation problem, rather than being confined to setting the limits of actionability for damage which was clearly caused by the defendant's negligence. Where there has been an intervening event, and the question is whether the defendant's negligence can still be treated as a cause of the claimant's loss, the damage may be described as "too remote." This is simply a way of saying that the defendant's conduct was not a cause in law of the damage.

[4] [1968] 1 All E.R. 1068. In *Kerry v England* [1898] A.C. 742, P.C., the defendants' negligence accelerated the death of the patient, "but not to any appreciable extent." It was held, in effect, that there was no causal connection because it was within the principle *de minimis non curat lex*; *Stamos v Davies* (1985) 21 D.L.R. (4th) 507 (Ont. H.C.), where the defendant failed to tell the claimant that during the course of performing a lung biopsy the claimant's spleen had been punctured. The failure to be candid was held to be a breach of duty, but there was no causal connection between the breach and the damage, namely the loss of the spleen, because the spleen "was doomed from the moment it was injured." See also *Serre v de Tilley* (1975) 58 D.L.R. (3d) 362, 365 (Ont. H.C.), where Stark J. commented that it was "only conjectural that the treatment could have been sufficiently speedy and effective to prevent" the brain haemorrhage which resulted in the patient's death; *Wilson v Vancouver Hockey Club* (1983) 5 D.L.R. (4th) 282; affirmed (1985) 22 D.L.R. (4th) 516 (B.C.C.A.); *Stockdale v Nicholls* [1993] 4 Med. L.R. 190, where the admission of a baby to hospital three hours earlier than she was in fact admitted would not have changed the observation or treatment that she received, or resulted in a diagnosis of septicaemia any earlier; *Stacey v Chiddy* [1993] 4 Med. L.R. 216 (N.S.W.S.C.); affirmed [1993] 4 Med. L.R. 345 (N.S.W.C.A.), where the negligent failure to examine the patient did not cause her diminished life expectancy from contracting breast cancer, since on the balance of probabilities the abnormalities in the claimant's breast were not at that time malignant.

ment it would not have been possible to diagnose the condition and administer an antidote in time to save him. Thus, the negligence did not cause the death.

Similarly, in *Robinson v Post Office*[5] a doctor was found to have been negligent in the manner in which he administered a test dose to test for an allergic reaction to an anti-tetanus vaccination. He waited only a minute after giving the test before giving the patient the injection, although the standard procedure at the time was to wait half an hour. Nine days after being injected with the vaccine the claimant suffered a serious allergic reaction to the vaccine, which caused encephalitis and brain damage. The Court of Appeal held that the failure to administer a proper test was not causally related to the claimant's damage, because the test was not, in any event, a complete guarantee against a subsequent reaction, and the circumstances of the claimant's reaction were such that a test involving a delay of half an hour would probably not have produced a reaction in time to alert the doctor to the danger.

5–005

Where the defendant has made an error in diagnosis, but the correct diagnosis would not have produced any difference in the treatment or management of the patient, the error has not caused any damage for which the defendant is responsible, even if he was negligent.[6]

5–006

In many cases, though not all, it may be easier to determine what would have happened in the absence of negligence by the defendant where events depend upon physical reactions which are amenable to objective scientific proof. Where the question depends upon how a person would have behaved the issue is to some extent more speculative, but this will not prevent the court from drawing an inference of fact. In *McWilliams v Sir William Arroll & Co Ltd*,[7] for example, a steel erector who was not wearing a safety belt fell to his death. His employers were in breach of a duty to supply a safety belt for his use, but the deceased had rarely, if ever, used a belt in the past, and the natural inference, said the House of Lords, was that he would not have used one on this occasion if it had been available. Thus, the breach of duty did not cause the death which would have occurred in any event.

5–007

This type of causation problem arises in a medical context whenever a claimant alleges that but for the doctor's negligence he would have opted for an alternative course of treatment. Where, for example, the claimant alleges that he was not properly informed about the risks of the treatment he has received and/or of the alternatives, he still has to show that had he been given the information he would not have accepted the treatment which he received. This may be difficult for the claimant to establish because the courts are wary of disappointed patients forming judgments about what they would have done

5–008

---

[5] [1974] 2 All E.R. 737.
[6] *Fish v Kapur* [1948] 2 All E.R. 176, 178, where a dentist who failed to diagnose a patient's broken jaw was not liable because there was no treatment that could have been given in the circumstances, and thus the claimant did not suffer any additional pain or discomfort as a result of the failure to diagnose the fracture.
[7] [1962] 1 W.L.R. 295.

with the benefit of hindsight.[8] Similarly, where the claimant alleges that the defendants negligently failed to communicate to her the test results following an amniocentisis test during her pregnancy, she must prove to the satisfaction of the court that, had she been informed that the test indicated that the foetus would be handicapped, she would have undergone an abortion.[9]

5–009   This issue is not limited to circumstances where the question is what the claimant would have done, but for the breach of duty. In the case of a negligent omission the outcome may turn upon the answer to the hypothetical question of what the defendant would have done or what a third party would have done, but for the breach of duty. Where the issue turns upon what the defendant would have done the approach to causation is the same: the claimant must still prove that but for the negligence the damage would not have occurred. Where, however, the outcome depends upon what a third party would have done in hypothetical circumstances the correct approach is to assess the value of the chance of benefit (or avoiding a detriment) that the claimant has lost.[10] In *Bolitho v City and Hackney Health Authority*[11] a two-year-old boy suffered brain damage as a result of cardiac arrest caused by an obstruction of the bronchial air passages. The claimant was in hospital at the time for the treatment of croup. The defendants admitted that there had been negligence, in that a doctor had not attended to the claimant in response to calls for assistance by nursing staff following two earlier episodes of respiratory failure. It was common ground that had the claimant been seen by a doctor and intubated, thus clearing the obstruction, the tragedy could have been avoided. There were two schools of thought, however, as to whether in the claimant's circumstances it was appropriate to intubate. The doctor who failed to attend said that had she attended the claimant she would not have intubated, and therefore the cardiac arrest and subsequent brain damage would have occurred in any event.[12] There was

---

[8] *Chatterton v Gerson* [1981] Q.B. 432, 445; *Hills v Potter* [1983] 3 All E.R. 716; see further para. 6–146.

[9] See *Gregory v Pembrokeshire Health Authority* [1989] 1 Med. L.R. 81, CA, where the claimant's action failed on this ground. The test had failed to produce a result, and so the claimant had to show both that if she had known about this she would have insisted on a further test, and that if that test were positive she would have had the abortion. The difficulties inherent in this exercise in speculation about hypothetical events were highlighted by Nicholls L.J., who commented that: "this unhappy case turns on Mrs. Gregory's hypothetical response to Mr. Davies's hypothetical advice given at a hypothetical consultation." See also *Arndt v Smith* [1994] 8 W.W.R. 568 (B.C.S.C.); affirmed (1997) 148 D.L.R. (4th) 48 (S.C.C.), where the mother was not warned about the most serious, though most remote, risks to the foetus of exposure to chickenpox, but the fact that the parents did not want an ultrasound scan of the developing foetus indicated "less concern with risks in foresight than in hindsight"; Honoré (1998) 114 L.Q.R. 52.

[10] See *Allied Maples Group Ltd v Simmons & Simmons* [1995] 1 W.L.R. 1602, discussed below at para. 5–060.

[11] [1993] 4 Med. L.R. 381; [1993] P.I.Q.R. P334, CA; [1998] A.C. 232, HL.

[12] Although as Simon Brown L.J. pointed out in his dissenting judgment in the Court of Appeal, *ibid.* at p. 388: ". . . it would seem to me unsatisfactory to place much reliance upon any doctor's evidence in these circumstances as to what he or she would have done had they complied with their duty to attend (or arranged for someone else to attend) a patient. Inevitably, if unconsciously, any doctor would in that situation tend to believe and suggest that their attendance could and would have made no difference."

evidence that a responsible body of professional opinion would have supported a decision not to intubate, although five medical experts for the claimant said that he should have been intubated, and it was agreed that this was the only course of action that would have prevented the damage. A majority of the Court of Appeal held that the action failed on the ground of causation. In a case of breach of duty by omission it was necessary to decide what course of events would have followed had the defendant's duty been discharged. Whether the doctor's failure to appear would have made any difference in the event depended upon what she would have done had she been present. The claimant had to prove that she would probably have intubated, and that if she did not do so her failure to do so was contrary to accepted medical practice.[13] Simon Brown L.J. expressed a strong dissenting judgment, however, arguing that in determining matters of causation the question that should be asked is what probably would have happened, not whether a responsible body of professional opinion agrees with what the defendant says she would have done.

On appeal to the House of Lords[14] it was argued on behalf of the claimant   5–010
that the *Bolam* test had no relevance in determining questions of causation. Lord Browne-Wilkinson agreed that, as a general proposition, that was correct. In all cases the primary question is one of fact: did the wrongful act cause the injury? But in cases where the breach of duty consists of an omission to do an act which ought to have been done (such as the failure of a doctor to attend the patient) the factual enquiry is necessarily hypothetical. The question is what would have happened if an event, which by definition did not occur, had occurred? The first question is: what would have happened—either the doctor would have intubated, had she attended, or she would not. The *Bolam* test was not, and could not, be relevant to that question. The defendant doctor said that she would not have intubated, and therefore the claimant would in any event have sustained the brain damage. But she could not escape liability by proving that she would have failed to act as any reasonably competent doctor would have acted in the circumstances: "A defendant cannot escape liability by saying that the damage would have occurred in any event because he would have committed some other breach of duty thereafter."[15]

Lord Browne-Wilkinson adopted the reasoning of Hobhouse L.J. in *Joyce*   5–011
v Merton, Sutton and Wandsworth Health Authority[16] in explaining the majority decision of the Court of Appeal in *Bolitho*. In *Joyce* the claimant underwent an operative procedure which resulted in a partially occluded artery, leading three months later to an upper brain stem infarction causing almost total paralysis. Although the procedure was not necessarily negligent, the Court of Appeal considered that the immediate follow-up care that the claimant had received was negligent, in that he was discharged from hospital

---

[13] *ibid.* at p. 386, *per* Farquharson L.J.
[14] [1998] A.C. 232.
[15] *ibid.* at 240.
[16] [1996] P.I.Q.R. P121; [1996] 7 Med. L.R. 1.

without proper instructions and advice. It was accepted that the only thing that could have prevented the damage was if within the first 48 hours the claimant had been seen by a vascular surgeon and the surgeon had decided to operate to deal with the occlusion. The Court of Appeal held that to succeed on causation the claimant had to prove either that had the vascular surgeon at the hospital been summoned he would in fact have re-operated or that it would have been negligent for him not to do so. Hobhouse L.J. said that where the negligence consisted of an act which is alleged to have had physical consequences, the question to be asked is straightforward even though its answer may not be: was the act a cause of the injury? Where the negligence consists of an omission, or an act which does not in itself have physical consequences, identifying the correct question is less easy. These cases could be further subdivided into cases where the question is what steps would have been taken if proper care had been taken and cases where the question is what would have been the outcome of any further steps that ought to have been taken. In *Joyce* the facts fell into the first of these categories, which was the same type of question that *Bolitho* raised. Hobhouse L.J. summarised the position in the following terms:

> "Thus a plaintiff can discharge the burden of proof on causation by satisfying the court *either* that the relevant person would in fact have taken the requisite action (although she would not have been at fault if she had not) *or* that the proper discharge of the relevant person's duty towards the plaintiff required that she take that action. The former alternative calls for no explanation since it is simply the factual proof of the causative effect of the original fault. The latter is slightly more sophisticated: it involves the factual situation that the original fault did not itself cause the injury but that this was because there would have been some further fault on the part of the defendants; the plaintiff proves his case by proving that his injuries would have been avoided if proper care had continued to be taken . . . Properly viewed, therefore, this rule is favourable to a plaintiff because it gives him two routes by which he may prove his case—either proof that the exercise of proper care would have necessitated the relevant result, or proof that if proper care had been exercised it would in fact have led to the relevant result."[17]

5-012   In *Bolitho* Lord Browne-Wilkinson, having cited Hobhouse L.J., concluded that there were two questions for the judge to decide on causation: (1) what would the doctor have done, or authorised to be done, if she had attended the claimant? and (2) if she would not have intubated, would that have been negligent? The *Bolam* test had no relevance to first question but

---

[17] *ibid.* at 152, original emphasis. See also *S (A Minor) v North Birmingham Health Authority* (1998) 40 B.M.L.R. 103, CA, where it was held that a senior house officer was negligent in failing to consult a senior registrar about a patient's deteriorating condition, but that even if the senior registrar been notified about the deterioration sooner he would not have arranged a transfer to the intensive therapy unit at that time, and this would not have been negligent.

was central to the second. Another way of putting this is to say that causation is about *what in fact happened*, which in turn depends upon the hypothetical question of what would have happened had there been no negligence ("but for" the negligence would the damage have occurred?). In *Bolitho* the claimant was claiming that had the doctor not been negligent and attended he would not have suffered brain damage, because the doctor would have intervened to prevent it. The doctor denied that she would have intervened, so that the damage would have occurred in any event (no "but for" causation). The claimant alleged that a hypothetical failure to intervene would itself have been negligent, and a defendant cannot avoid a finding of causation by arguing that, in the hypothetical situation being considered, she would have acted negligently. The defendant then replies that a failure to intervene would not have been negligent because it was supported by a responsible body of professional opinion. Thus, in these circumstances the causation issue *appears* to turn on a question of negligence and the *Bolam* test. In reality *Bolitho* is about whether the failure to intubate, for whatever reason (non-attendance or conscious professional judgment), was negligent. The defendant's evidence that she would not have intubated simply moved the focus of the argument about negligence, *i.e.* breach of duty, from the non-attendance to the non-intubation.

In *Wiszniewski v Central Manchester Health Authority*[18] a doctor failed to attend a patient in labour, either because the midwife did not properly explain that the foetus was showing signs of distress, or because he ignored what he was told. The foetus subsequently sustained brain damage caused by hypoxia as a result of strangulation because the umbilical cord was looped round his neck. The issue was whether, had the doctor attended, the child would have been delivered by Caesarian section, thus avoiding the hypoxia. On the question of what *should* have happened had the doctor attended, there was evidence from experts for the claimant that had he attended the doctor *ought* to have intervened by conducting a vaginal examination and rupturing the membrane, which in the circumstances would have led to a Caesarian section. This was a standard procedure given the signs of foetal distress that were present: "It was not very complicated obstetrics: it was simple stuff." This evidence went to the second of the two questions identified in *Bolitho*, namely if, hypothetically, the doctor had not acted to prevent the damage would this have been negligent? The trial judge rejected evidence from experts for the defendants that it would have been reasonable to continue observation for the time being, while seeking to ascertain the cause of the suspicious signs.[19] This decision was overturned, however, on

5–013

---

[18] [1996] 7 Med. L.R. 248; affirmed at [1998] P.I.Q.R. P324; [1998] Lloyd's Rep. Med. 223, CA. Note that the claimant's name is cited as Wisniewski in the report of the Court of Appeal decision.

[19] This was on the basis that where analysis of the expert evidence "shows that a decision made by a doctor and supported by experts cannot be justified as one that a responsible medical practitioner would have taken, then a judge should not preclude himself from reaching that conclusion simply because clinical judgment is involved": *Wiszniewski v Central Manchester Health Authority* [1996] 7 Med. L.R. 248, 261 *per* Thomas J.

appeal, on the basis that it could not be said that the views expressed by the defendants' experts could not be logically supported and held by responsible doctors.[20] There remained, however, the first question identified in *Bolitho*, namely what would the doctor have done, or authorised to be done, if he had attended the claimant? The judge found as a fact that, had he attended, the doctor *would* have intervened as the experts for the claimant suggested he should. The doctor concerned did not give evidence, because he was in Australia, but the defendants had made no attempt to bring him back to the UK for the trial or to have him give evidence by video-link. The trial judge drew an adverse inference from his failure to give evidence, that had he attended the patient he would probably have intervened. The Court of Appeal held that the judge was entitled to draw this adverse inference from the silence or absence of a witness who could have given material evidence on an issue in the action, provided there was some evidence, however weak, adduced by the party seeking to rely on the adverse inference on the matter in question. In other words there must be a case to answer on that issue. If the reason for the witness's absence or silence satisfies the court then no such adverse inference can be drawn. Given the evidence from the claimant's experts that it was standard practice to conduct a vaginal examination and rupture the membrane in the circumstances that arose, the claimant had adduced sufficient evidence to establish that the doctor would probably have intervened, which in the absence of evidence to the contrary from the doctor himself was sufficient to establish causation.[21]

5–014   The "but for" test operates as a preliminary filter to exclude events which did not affect the outcome. It cannot, however, resolve all the problems of factual causation. In the case of two simultaneous wrongs to the claimant, each of which would have been sufficient to cause the damage, the test produces the ludicrous conclusion that neither wrong caused the harm.[22] The only sensible solution here is to say that both caused the damage, but it should be recognised that this decision involves a policy judgment. Similarly, the "but for" test may be inapplicable in the case of successive sufficient causes, although this depends upon the nature of the respective causes.[23] Policy issues are also apparent in the courts' attitude to the proof of causation. In *Cook v Lewis*,[24] for example, two people on a hunting trip simultaneously discharged their guns and the claimant was hit by one of them, but he was unable to prove which one. The Supreme Court of Canada held that

---

[20] [1998] Lloyd's Rep. Med. 223, 237.

[21] See also *Hunt v NHS Litigation Authority* (2000, QBD; unreported) at [17] where Potts J. commented: "It seems to me, however, that I must not speculate as to the reasons for Dr Walker's non-attendance. I proceed on the basis that where inferences adverse to Dr Walker can properly be drawn from the contemporaneous material, evidence has not been forthcoming from her to rebut those inferences, despite her having had notice of the general allegations made against her. Where inferences can be drawn from the written material adverse to the midwives, I proceed on the basis that I have heard no evidence of rebuttal from them."

[22] See Strachan (1970) 33 M.L.R. 386, 391.

[23] See *Baker v Willoughby* [1970] A.C. 467, and *cf. Jobling v Associated Dairies Ltd* [1982] A.C. 794, below paras 5–074 to 5–075.

[24] [1952] 1 D.L.R. 1.

in these circumstances the burden of proof was reversed, and it was for the defendants to prove that they did not cause the damage. If neither could do so then both would be liable. The defendants' combined negligence had removed the claimant's opportunity to prove which of them had shot him, and it would be unjust to deprive him of a remedy through the operation of the burden of proof.

(2) Proof of causation

It is for the claimant to prove, on the balance of probabilities, that the defendant's breach of duty caused the damage. So where there are conflicting explanations for the claimant's condition, neither of which are wholly satisfactory, the defendant does not have to prove that his explanation is the correct one, though failure to prove it may be a factor in deciding whether the claimant's explanation of the cause should be accepted.[25] In some instances the precise cause of the damage may be unknown, and this tends to be a particular problem with some types of medical injury, where the pathology of the patient's condition may be surrounded in mystery or be the subject of intense scientific dispute. The Pearson Commission reported that:

5–015

> "The Medical Research Council said that while future research was likely to establish more causal relationships it would also reveal increasingly complex interactions which would heighten the problems of proving causation in the individual case."[26]

Faced with this kind of factual uncertainty the claimant may have an impossible burden of proving causation on the balance of probabilities, although it should be remembered that the claimant does not have to achieve scientific standards of proof.[27] In *Kay v Ayrshire and Arran Health*

5–016

---

[25] *Pickford v Imperial Chemical Industries plc* [1998] 1 W.L.R. 1189, where the claimant, a secretary, alleged that cramp in her hand was a work-induced "repetitive strain injury." It was agreed that her symptoms were genuine (*i.e.* she was not malingering) but there was a dispute about their cause. The claimant alleged an organic, physical cause, whereas the defendant alleged that it was psychogenic, due to conversion hysteria. The House of Lords held that where a claimant alleges that her condition has a physical cause she must go on to prove, on the balance of probabilities, that her injury could be attributed to the physical origin that she alleged, which she had failed to do on the somewhat equivocal medical evidence. It was not for the defendant to prove that his explanation was the correct one; *cf. Alexander v Midland Bank plc* [1999] I.R.L.R. 723, CA.

[26] *Royal Commission on Civil Liability and Compensation for Personal Injury*, Cmnd. 7054 (1978), Vol. I, para. 1364; see also para. 1449: "As the boundary of knowledge increases, so does the area of uncertainty."

[27] This is something that should be borne in mind when instructing scientific and medical experts, who may feel uncomfortable with the notion of a standard of "proof" which depends upon the event having been "more likely than not," rather than the more rigorous standards of proof required in scientific inquiry. See the comments of the Supreme Court of Canada on this point in *Snell v Farrell* (1990) 72 D.L.R. (4th) 289, 301–302 and *Laferrière v Lawson* (1991) 78 D.L.R. (4th) 609, 656–657: ". . . a judge will be influenced by expert scientific opinions which are expressed in terms of statistical probabilities or test samplings, but he or she is not bound by such evidence. Scientific findings are not identical to legal

Board,[28] for example, the claimant was unable to prove that an overdose of penicillin could ever cause deafness. The claimant was a child suffering from meningitis who was negligently injected with 30 times the correct dose of penicillin. He recovered from the short term toxic effects of the overdose but was subsequently found to be deaf. One consequence of meningitis can be deafness, and the overwhelming weight of medical opinion was to the effect that penicillin did not cause deafness.[29] Similarly, in *Loveday v Renton*[30] the claimant failed to show, on a balance of probabilities, that pertussis vaccine could cause brain damage in young children, although it was "possible" that it did because the contrary could not be proved either. Medical and expert opinion was deeply divided on this issue. The evidence from the National Childhood Encephalopathy Study supported the conclusion that the vaccine sometimes caused febrile convulsions, but did not provide evidence that such convulsions following the vaccine caused permanent brain damage. Stuart-Smith L.J. identified several factors that might explain a close temporal association between administration of the vaccine and subsequent neurological damage, without establishing a causal link.[31]

(n.27 contd.) findings." It should also be remembered that the medical literature upon which expert witnesses may rely will take a scientific approach to questions of proof. In *Fairhurst v St. Helens and Knowsley Health Authority* [1994] 5 Med. L.R. 422 the judge was faced with a stark conflict of expert evidence as to whether the particular disabilities of which the claimant complained had been caused by kernicterus (bilirubin encephalopathy) as a result of Rhesus incompatibility. In accepting the evidence of the claimant's expert, Judge Clark Q.C. commented that the approach of the defendant's expert "was more akin to that of the scientist seeking scientific certainty." On the other hand, in *Vadera v Shaw* (1998) 45 B.M.L.R. 162, 174 the Court of Appeal accepted that the trial judge had been right to accept the findings of a statistical study which had failed to establish a statistical causal link between the oral contraceptive Logynon and strokes: "Such evidence cannot be ignored by a judge. It is as common sense a conclusion as one could wish to say that if the connection between A and B cannot be shown with confidence to be other than coincidence, then it cannot be held on a balance of probabilities that A caused B. This is not to allow scientists or statisticians to usurp the judge's function, but rather to permit him to use their skills to discern a connection, or a lack of connection, between two phenomena." For criticism of this approach see Goldberg (2000) 8 Med. L. Rev. 316.

[28] [1987] 2 All E.R. 417. See also *Dingley v Chief Constable of Strathclyde Police* (2000) 55 B.M.L.R. 1, HL, where there was insufficient evidence to establish whether as a general proposition multiple sclerosis can ever be triggered by trauma, and therefore the claimant was unable to establish the specific issue that there was a connection between his injury in an accident and the subsequent onset of multiple sclerosis.

[29] For criticism of the approach of the House of Lords to the medical evidence in *Kay* see Logie 1988 S.L.T. 25. In *Marsden v Bateman* [1993] 4 Med. L.R. 181 it was alleged that a general practitioner had failed to diagnose the symptoms of hypoglycaemia, but it was held that the claimant's brain damage probably occurred during gestation. There was no evidence that, in the absence of coma, convulsions or apnoea, significant brain damage is capable of resulting from hypoglycaemia; *X. and Y. v Pal* (1991) 23 N.S.W.L.R. 26; [1992] 3 Med. L.R. 195 (N.S.W.C.A.), where the claimant was unable to prove that dysmorphia and brain damage were probably caused by congenital syphilis to which she had been exposed *in utero*; *De Martell v Merton and Sutton Health Authority* [1995] 6 Med. L.R. 240, QBD, where the claimant was unable to prove that negligent mismanagement of his birth was probably the cause of his disabilities.

[30] [1990] 1 Med. L.R. 117. The Ontario High Court came to the same conclusion on pertussis vaccine in *Rothwell v Raes* (1988) 54 D.L.R. (4th) 193; affirmed (1990) 76 D.L.R. (4th) 280 (Ont. C.A.).

[31] *cf. Best v Wellcome Foundation Ltd* [1993] 3 I.R. 421; [1994] 5 Med. L.R. 81; (1992) 17

Even where it is possible in principle to establish a connection between the   5–017
type of harm suffered by the claimant and a specific hazard, it may be very
difficult to show that the individual claimant's condition was *caused* by
exposure to that hazard rather than some other factor for which the defendant was not responsible. An obvious example is the problem of proving that
an individual contracted cancer as a result of exposure to radiation, rather
than other causes, although it is well known that radiation can cause
cancer.[32]

In such circumstances, where the scientific evidence is equivocal, the   5–018
crucial issue from the claimant's point of view is whether the court will be
prepared to draw an appropriate inference that there must have been some
causal connection, since proof of causation in the medical sphere rests inevitably on the drawing of an inference of fact. In *Jones v Great Western
Railway Co* Lord Macmillan put the matter in this way:

> "The dividing line between conjecture and inference is often a very dif-
> ficult one to draw. A conjecture may be plausible, but it is of no legal
> value, for its essence is that it is a mere guess. An inference in the legal
> sense, on the other hand, is a deduction from the evidence, and if it is a
> reasonable deduction it may have the validity of legal proof. The attri-
> bution of an occurrence to a cause is, I take it, always a matter of infer-
> ence. The cogency of a legal inference of causation may vary in degree
> between practical certainty and reasonable probability. Where the co-
> incidence of cause and effect is not a matter of actual observation there
> is necessarily a hiatus in the direct evidence, but this may be legitimately
> bridged by an inference from the facts actually observed and proved."[33]

The burden of proof, is, ultimately, a burden of persuading the court to
attribute legal responsibility for the claimant's injuries to the defendant. This
is patent in the case of causation in law, where the court must select from a
number of causative factors the event or events that it considers to have been
decisive. This is also the position, although maybe less obviously so, with the
proof of causation in fact. The readiness of the court to draw an inference
of fact, assisted where appropriate by principles of law, depends to some

---

(n.31 contd.) B.M.L.R 11 (Supreme Court of Ireland), where the defendants were held to
have been negligent in distributing a faulty batch of pertussis vaccine, and an inference of
causation was drawn from the temporal connection between the administration of the
vaccine and the claimant's brain damage. It was accepted that there was a possibility that
pertussis vaccine could, in rare cases, cause brain damage.

[32] See Brahams (1988) 138 N.L.J. 570; and Gifford (1990) 301 B.M.J. 451 on reducing the
exposure of patients to radiation during diagnostic radiology. In *Reay v British Nuclear Fuels
plc* [1994] 5 Med. L.R. 1; [1994] P.I.Q.R. P171 the claimants were unable to prove, on the
balance of probabilities, that paternal pre-conception irradiation (radiation injury to the
gonads resulting in mutation of spermatagonia causing a predisposition to either acute lymphatic leukaemia or non-Hodgkin's lymphoma) had caused the claimants' cancer. On the
problems of establishing causation in cases of man-made, usually industrial, disease see
Stapleton, *Disease and the Compensation Debate*, 1986, O.U.P., Ch. 3.

[33] (1930) 47 T.L.R. 39, 45.

extent on the court's subjective assessment of the evidence, which in turn may be influenced by the underlying policy objectives of the law.

5–019   Where the issue is whether the claimant's medical condition would or would not have deteriorated with appropriate treatment, it is not simply a question of opting for the view of the majority of experts or of a reasonable body of medical opinion, since "that would be to import the well-known *Bolam* test into the issue of causation, where it has no proper place."[34] Thus, where what the judge is required to do is to make findings of fact, the *Bolam* test does not apply. This is so, even where those findings of fact are subject to conflicting expert evidence. Accordingly, if there is a dispute amongst the experts about a question of fact (such as what was visible on a laboratory slide) the judge is entitled to prefer one group of experts over the other.[35] On the other hand, in a case of breach of duty by omission where the question of what would have happened had the defendant's duty been discharged arises, the claimant has to prove either that what the doctor would have done would have prevented the damage (which is a pure question of fact to which the *Bolam* test does not apply) or that the failure to adopt such a course of action was negligent, applying the *Bolam* test.[36] So, if a responsible body of professional opinion supports the defendant's version of what she would have done (and this would not have avoided the damage) the claimant will fail to prove causation, notwithstanding that another responsible body of professional opinion would have taken action that would have avoided the damage.

(a) Material contribution to the damage

5–020   The courts have gone some way to relieving a claimant from the rigours of the "but for" test where the difficulty of establishing causation has been a product of scientific uncertainty. In *Bonnington Castings Ltd v Wardlaw*[37] the House of Lords held that the claimant does not have to establish that the defendant's breach of duty was the main cause of the damage provided that it materially contributed to the damage. The claimant contracted pneumoconiosis from inhaling air which contained silica dust at his workplace. The main source of the dust was from pneumatic hammers for which the employers were not in breach of duty (the "innocent dust"). Some of the dust (the "guilty dust") came from swing grinders for which they were responsible by failing to maintain the dust-extraction equipment. There was no evidence as to the proportions of innocent dust and guilty dust inhaled by the claimant. Indeed, such evidence as there was indicated that much the greater proportion came from the innocent source. On the evidence the claimant could not

---

[34] *Cavanagh v Bristol and Weston Health Authority* [1992] 3 Med. L.R. 49, 56, *per* Macpherson J.
[35] *Penney, Palmer and Cannon v East Kent Health Authority* [2000] Lloyd's Rep. Med. 41, 46, CA. See also *St.-Jean v Mercier* (2002) 209 D.L.R. (4th) 513 (S.C.C.) at [55].
[36] *Bolitho v City and Hackney Health Authority* [1998] A.C. 232, 240; para. 5–009.
[37] [1956] A.C. 613.

prove "but for" causation, in the sense that it was more probable than not that had the dust-extraction equipment worked efficiently he would not have contracted the disease. Nonetheless, the House of Lords drew an inference of fact that the guilty dust was a contributory cause, holding the employers liable for the full extent of the loss. The claimant did not have to prove that the guilty dust was the sole or even the most substantial cause if he could show, on a balance of probabilities, the burden of proof remaining with the claimant, that the guilty dust had materially contributed to the disease. Anything which did not fall within the principle *de minimis non curat lex* would constitute a material contribution. Subsequently, in *Nicholson v Atlas Steel Foundry & Engineering Co Ltd*,[38] on virtually identical facts, the House of Lords held the defendants liable for an employee's pneumoconiosis, even though, in the words of Viscount Simonds, it was "impossible even approximately to quantify" the respective contributions of guilty and innocent dust.

These cases were significant in easing the claimant's burden of proof for two reasons. First, they were a departure from "but for" causation—the claimant did not have to prove that he would not have suffered the "damage" (*i.e.* the injury or illness) but for the breach of duty. What had to be proved was redefined as a "material contribution" to the injury or illness, and, notwithstanding this redefinition of the "damage" to which the claimant must establish a causal link in more limited terms than the outcome, the claimant still recovered *damages* for the whole loss, *i.e.* the outcome, having proved causation in respect of a part only of that loss.[39] Secondly, the courts were willing to draw an *inference* of fact that there had been a material contribution when it was in reality impossible to say whether there had been any such contribution, or even to make a statistical guess.

5–021

(b) Material contribution to the risk

Subsequently, the House of Lords appeared to take *Bonnington Castings Ltd v Wardlaw*[40] one step further. In *McGhee v National Coal Board*[41] the claimant, who worked at the defendants' brick kilns, contracted dermatitis as a result of exposure to brick dust. The employers were not at fault for the exposure during working hours, but they were in breach of duty by failing to provide adequate washing facilities. This increased the period of time during which the claimant was exposed to contact with the brick dust while

5–022

---

[38] [1957] 1 All E.R. 776. See also *Clarkson v Modern Foundries Ltd* [1958] 1 All E.R. 33, applying *Bonnington Castings Ltd v Wardlaw* [1956] A.C. 613. "As long as a defendant is *part* of the cause of an injury, the defendant is liable, even though his act alone was not enough to create the injury. There is no basis for a reduction of liability because of the existence of other preconditions: defendants remain liable for all injuries caused or contributed to by their negligence": *Athey v Leonati* [1997] 1 W.W.R. 97, 103 (S.C.C.) (original emphasis).

[39] See Stapleton (1988) 104 L.Q.R. 389, 404–405. See, now, however *Holtby v Brigham & Cowan (Hull) Ltd* [2000] 3 All E.R. 421, para. 5–042.

[40] [1956] A.C. 613.

[41] [1972] 3 All E.R. 1008; [1973] 1 W.L.R. 1.

he bicycled home. It was agreed that the brick dust had caused the dermatitis, but the current state of medical knowledge could not say whether it was probable that the claimant would not have contracted the disease if he had been able to take a shower after work. Thus, he could not establish "but for" causation in respect of the "guilty" exposure. At best it could be said that the failure to provide washing facilities materially increased the risk of the claimant contracting dermatitis. The House of Lords held the defendants liable on the basis that it was sufficient for a claimant to show that the defendants' breach of duty made the risk of injury more probable even though it was uncertain whether it was the actual cause.

5–023   A majority of their Lordships treated a "material increase in the risk" as equivalent to a "material contribution to the damage." Lord Simon, for example, said that "a failure to take steps which would bring about a material reduction of the risk involves, in this type of case, a substantial contribution to the injury."[42] Lord Wilberforce explicitly recognised that this process involves overcoming an "evidential gap" by drawing an inference of fact which, strictly speaking, the evidence does not support (as was done in *Bonnington Castings*), and, moreover, that this "fictional" inference is drawn for policy reasons. Why, his Lordship asked, should a man who is able to show that his employer should have taken certain precautions, because without them there is a risk or an added risk of injury or disease, and who in fact sustains exactly that injury or disease, have to assume the burden of proving more? In many cases it is impossible to prove causation because medical opinion cannot segregate the causes of an illness between compound causes:

> "And if one asks which of the parties, the workman or the employers should suffer from this inherent evidential difficulty, the answer as a matter of policy or justice should be that it is the creator of the risk who, ex hypothesi, must be taken to have foreseen the possibility of damage, who should bear its consequences."[43]

5–024   The potential in this line of reasoning for reversing the burden of proof of causation was enormous—the claimant does not have to show that the defendant's breach of duty caused his injury, merely that it increased the risk of injury.[44] Indeed, Lord Wilberforce appeared to suggest that the burden of disproving causation would shift to the defendant in such cases. The implications of *McGhee* became apparent in *Clark v MacLennan*,[45] a case of medical negligence, where the principle was extended to proof of breach of duty. Pain J. held that where there is a general practice to take a particular precaution against a specific, known risk but the defendant fails to take that precaution, and the very damage against which it is designed to be a protection occurs, then the burden of proof lies with the defendant to show both

---

[42] *ibid.* at p. 1014; see also *per* Lords Reid and Salmon at pp. 1011, 1017.
[43] *ibid.* at p. 1012.
[44] See Weinrib (1975) 38 M.L.R. 518.
[45] [1983] 1 All E.R. 416.

that he was not in breach of duty and that the breach did not cause the damage. This approach to the question of proving negligence, as opposed to causation, was criticised by Mustill L.J. in *Wilsher v Essex Area Health Authority*,[46] although his Lordship accepted that in some instances breach and causation are so closely linked that in practice it may be difficult to maintain a different rule for proof of breach of duty when the *McGhee* rule is applicable to proof of causation.

In *Wilsher* itself the question was whether *McGhee* could be applied to a   5-025
case where there were up to five discrete causes of the claimant's injury any one of which might have caused the damage. The claimant was a premature baby who, through the defendants' negligence, received an excessive concentration of oxygen. It is known that excessive oxygen can damage the retina of a premature baby leading to a condition called retrolental fibroplasia (RLF) which results in blindness.[47] The claimant contracted RLF. However, RLF can occur in premature babies who have not been given additional oxygen and there is evidence of some correlation between RLF and several other conditions from which premature babies can suffer (apnoea, hypercarbia, intraventricular haemorrhage, patent ductus arteriosus), all of which afflicted the claimant. As Mustill L.J. put it: "What the defendants did was not to enhance the risk that the known factor would lead to injury, but to add to the list of factors which might do so."[48] The majority of the Court of Appeal held that *McGhee* could apply in these circumstances, recognising that this represented an extension of that case. Mustill L.J. expressed the principle in the following terms:

> "If it is an established fact that conduct of a particular kind creates a risk that injury will be caused to another or increases an existing risk that injury will ensue; and if the two parties stand in such a relationship that the one party owes a duty not to conduct himself in that way; and if the first party does conduct himself in that way; and if the other party does suffer injury of the kind to which the risk related; then the first party is taken to have caused the injury by his breach of duty, even though the existence and extent of the contribution made by the breach cannot be ascertained."[49]

Browne-Wilkinson V.-C., dissenting, took the view that the position was wholly different from that in *McGhee*:

> "A failure to take preventive measures against one out of five possible causes is no evidence as to which of those five caused the injury."[50]

---

[46] [1987] Q.B. 730, 752.
[47] Retrolental fibroplasia is now known as retinopathy of prematurity. For discussion of medical understanding of its aetiology see Fielder (1997) 3 Clinical Risk 47; Clements (1995) 1 *AVMA Medical & Legal Journal* 215.
[48] [1987] Q.B. 730, 771.
[49] *ibid.* at pp. 771–772; see also *per* Glidewell L.J. at p. 776.
[50] *ibid.* at p. 779.

5–026   The House of Lords reversed the decision of the Court of Appeal on this issue, approving the judgment of the Vice-Chancellor.[51] It was held that *McGhee* did not establish any new principle of law and did not have the effect of reversing the burden of proof. The burden of proof remains with the claimant throughout, and he must establish that the breach of duty was at least a material contributory cause of the harm, applying *Bonnington Castings v Wardlaw*. What the House of Lords did in *McGhee*, said Lord Bridge, was to adopt a robust and pragmatic approach to the undisputed primary facts of the case and draw a legitimate, common sense, inference of fact that the additional period of exposure to brick dust had probably materially contributed to the claimant's dermatitis.[52]

5–027   This interpretation of *McGhee*, however, was not accepted by the House of Lords in *Fairchild v Glenhaven Funeral Services Ltd*[53] which involved three consolidated appeals where workers had developed mesothelioma following negligent exposure to asbestos fibres at work. Mesothelioma is an invariably fatal form of cancer which can be latent for up to 40 years. The precise mechanics of the disease are unknown, but the vast majority of cases result from exposure to asbestos (about 1,500 a year in the UK, with only 50 or 60 cases each year where there has been no history of exposure to asbestos dust). Thus, the overwhelming probability was that the employees' mesothelioma was caused by their occupation. The problem in demonstrating causation was that all of the employees had worked for a number of employers where they had been negligently exposed to asbestos, and with the current level of scientific knowledge about the disease the claimants could not identify which employer was responsible because, unlike asbestosis (and pneumoconiosis) which is also caused by exposure to asbestos dust, mesothelioma is not a "cumulative disease." In the case of a cumulative disease, where the severity of the condition is related to the period of exposure, each negligent employer can be held responsible for a proportionate part of the damage.[54] The *risk* that mesothelioma will occur increases in relation to the total dose of asbestos received, but the severity of the condition and the resulting disability do not vary with the dose. It may be caused by a single fibre, a few fibres, or many fibres. Thus, if there has been more than one employment involving asbestos exposure, there is no means of identifying in which employment the fibre or fibres which caused the disease was inhaled.

---

[51] *Wilsher v Essex Area Health Authority* [1988] A.C. 1074. Martin Wilsher's case was subsequently settled: see Kerry (1991) 2 *A.V.M.A. Medical & Legal Journal* (No. 4) p. 12. See also *Murray v Kensington and Chelsea and Westminster Area Health Authority* (1981, CA; unreported), where the claimant failed to establish a causal link between the excess oxygen he had received and RLF.

[52] *ibid.* at p. 1090. See Fleming (1989) 68 Can. Bar Rev. 661 and (1991) 70 Can. Bar Rev. 136, discussing the various approaches that have been taken to the problem of "probabilistic causation."

[53] [2002] UKHL 22; [2003] 1 A.C. 32. See Stapleton (2002) 10 Torts L.J. 276; and Morgan (2003) 66 M.L.R. 277.

[54] See *Holtby v Brigham & Cowan (Hull) Ltd* [2000] 3 All E.R. 421, CA, para. 5–042 below.

The Court of Appeal[55] had held that the claimants failed to establish   5–028
causation, because they could not prove on a balance of probabilities that
the "guilty" fibres were the result of any particular defendant's breach of
duty. There was an "evidential gap." *McGhee* did not assist because in that
case there was only one causative agent (brick dust) and only one possible
tortfeasor, and therefore in the light of *Wilsher* (which held that an inference of causation could not be drawn where there was more than one causative agent), it was not possible to rely on *McGhee* where there was more
than one tortfeasor in the case of a single, as opposed to a cumulative,
cause. The injustice to the claimants in these circumstances was self-
evident. Unlike *Bonnington Castings* or *McGhee*, none of the exposure was
"innocent"—all the defendants were breach in duty. It was simply that the
claimants could not identify which breach of duty had produced the fatal
fibre.

The House of Lords reversed the decision of the Court of Appeal, on the   5–029
basis that in the special circumstances of this type of case, there should be a
relaxation of the normal rule that a claimant must prove that but for the
defendant's breach of duty he would not have suffered the damage. The possible injustice of imposing liability on a defendant who has not been proved
to have caused the claimants' damage had to be weighed against the injustice to claimants. Lord Bingham observed that:

> ". . . there is a strong policy argument in favour of compensating those
> who have suffered grave harm, at the expense of their employers who
> owed them a duty to protect them against that very harm and failed to
> do so, when the harm can only have been caused by breach of that duty
> and when science does not permit the victim accurately to attribute, as
> between several employers, the precise responsibility for the harm he
> has suffered . . . such injustice as may be involved in imposing liability
> on a duty-breaking employer in these circumstances is heavily out-
> weighed by the injustice of denying redress to a victim."[56]

Despite the views expressed by Lord Bridge in *Wilsher*, the decision of the   5–030
House of Lords in *McGhee* did not rest upon a "robust and pragmatic"
approach to the drawing of an inference of fact. Rather, said their Lordships
in *Fairchild*, *McGhee* decided a question of law which was: "whether, on the
facts of the case as found, a pursuer who could not show that the defender's
breach had probably caused the damage of which he complained could
nonetheless succeed."[57] The *ratio* of *McGhee*, said Lord Bingham, was "that
in the circumstances no distinction was to be drawn between making a
material contribution to causing the disease and materially increasing the

---

[55] [2001] EWCA Civ 1881; [2002] 1 W.L.R. 1052.
[56] [2002] UKHL 22 at [33]. See also Lord Nicholls at [36]: "these appeals should be allowed.
Any other outcome would be deeply offensive to instinctive notions of what justice requires
and fairness demands"; and Lord Hoffmann at [63].
[57] *ibid.* at [21] *per* Lord Bingham.

risk of the pursuer contracting it." This was not, said Lord Hoffmann, because the burden of proof was reversed. It would be artificial to treat the employer as having a burden of proof in a case in which *ex hypothesi* the state of medical knowledge is such that the burden cannot be discharged. Nor was materially increasing the risk equivalent to materially contributing to the damage, because that was precisely what the expert witnesses were not prepared to say in *McGhee*. Thus, what their Lordships meant in *McGhee* was that, "in the particular circumstances, a breach of duty which materially increased the risk should be treated *as if* it had materially contributed to the disease."[58]

5–031   *Wilsher*, however, was also correctly decided on its facts.[59] It was one thing, said Lord Bingham, to treat an increase of risk as equivalent to the making of a material contribution where a single noxious agent was involved, but another where any one of a number of noxious agents may equally probably have caused the damage. It must be questioned, however, whether the distinction between *Wilsher* and *Fairchild* (or *McGhee*) is that there was only one type of noxious agent in *Fairchild* but several in *Wilsher*. For example, what if the claimant in *Fairchild* had been exposed to asbestos dust by employer A, but to a different cancer-producing agent by employer B? If both agents are capable of producing mesothelioma, would the claimant's case fall within *Wilsher* or *Fairchild*? If the relaxation of the causal test is limited to exposure to asbestos dust, then the claim fails, applying *Wilsher*. The injustice that *Fairchild* seeks to address is not, however, limited to a specific noxious agent. It is clear from cases arising in other jurisdictions that similar conceptual problems can arise in very different factual circumstances, the most obvious being the "hunting cases" where a claimant is simultaneously shot by two or more negligent hunters but cannot identify which one shot him.[60] The unfairness to claimants of requiring them to prove the impossible in circumstances where the defendant is in breach of duty is what usually leads the court to relax the normal requirements of proof. Indeed, in *Fairchild* Lord Hoffmann recognised that the distinction between

---

[58] *ibid.* at [65], original emphasis.

[59] See also *Temple v South Manchester Health Authority* [2002] EWCA Civ 1406 where the claimant was unable to prove the causal mechanism for his cerebral oedema produced as a result of developing diabetic ketoacidosis. One theory was that cerebral oedema can be produced if the patient is infused with a below normal concentration of saline solution, and it was on this basis that the defendants were found to have been negligent. But, as in *Wilsher*, the causal mechanism was shrouded in scientific uncertainty, and there were several potential causes which might operate independently or cumulatively. The Court of Appeal upheld the trial judge's conclusion that the claimant had failed to establish the causal link on the balance of probabilities. As Schiemann L.J. pointed out, at [64], the layman might be puzzled by a finding that the defendant was in breach of duty for taking a course of action which might cause the very damage which in the event happened, but was held not liable because causation had not been proved. But the state of scientific knowledge was such that it could not be said that giving a low saline solution was ever the cause of cerebral oedema (although, in the circumstances, giving a low saline solution might cause harm and had no significant advantages, and therefore could be characterised as negligent).

[60] Here, courts have usually reversed the burden of proof: see *Summers v Tice* 199 P. 2d 1 (1948), Supreme Court of California; *Cook v Lewis* [1952] 1 D.L.R. 1, Supreme Court of Canada.

a case involving a single agent and number of different agents was not a principled distinction.[61]

The scope of Fairchild

Fairchild applies where there are multiple defendants in breach of a similar   5–032
duty because it is unfair or unjust as a matter of policy to deprive a claimant of compensation because he is unable to prove the impossible. But in *Wilsher* the claimant was also faced with having to prove the impossible. It is not clear why the injustice in *Wilsher* was any less than that in *Fairchild*. The only obvious difference between these cases is that in *Wilsher* the other potential causes of the damage were "innocent" causes. If the only other defendants were found not to be in breach of duty, despite having exposed the claimant to asbestos, would the principle in *Fairchild* apply? According to Lord Bingham the answer would appear to be "no" (since his Lordship required that both employers, A and B, were in breach of duty). Lord Rodger, however, reserved his opinion on the question of what the position would be if defendant A was in breach of duty but defendant B was held to be "innocent."[62]

A defendant is usually held to be in breach of duty precisely because his   5–033
conduct has created an unreasonable risk of harm. Without caution, the decision in *Fairchild* could be interpreted as creating a general principle that whenever the claimant has difficulty establishing causation, but it can be shown that the defendant's breach of duty increased the risk of harm to the claimant, the rules of causation should be relaxed. In order to avoid this problem their Lordships sought to limit the situations in which the normal requirements of the "but for" test could be dispensed with. Lord Bingham listed six conditions:

> "(1) C was employed at different times and for differing periods by both A and B, and (2) A and B were both subject to a duty to take reasonable care or to take all practicable measures to prevent C inhaling asbestos dust because of the known risk that asbestos dust (if inhaled) might cause a mesothelioma, and (3) both A and B were in breach of that duty in relation to C during the periods of C's employment by each of them with the result that during both periods C inhaled excessive quantities of asbestos dust, and (4) C is found to be suffering from a mesothelioma, and (5) any cause of C's mesothelioma other than the inhalation of asbestos dust at work can be effectively discounted, but (6) C cannot (because of the current limits of human science) prove, on the balance of probabilities, that his mesothelioma was the result of his inhaling

---

[61] See [2002] UKHL 22 at [71]-[72]: "What if [the claimant] had been exposed to two different agents—asbestos dust and some other dust—both of which created a material risk of the same cancer and it was equally impossible to say which had caused the fatal cell mutation? I cannot see why this should make a difference."

[62] *ibid.* at [170].

asbestos dust during his employment by A or during his employment by B or during his employment by A and B taken together."[63]

If each of these conditions was satisfied, and in "no other case", then his Lordship considered that it was "just and in accordance with common sense" to treat the conduct of A and B in exposing C to a risk to which he should not have been exposed as making a material contribution to the contracting by C of a condition against which it was the duty of A and B to protect him.[64] This conclusion followed even if either A or B was not before the court. Lord Hoffmann also limited the principle to circumstances in which there was a duty specifically intended to protect *employees* against being unnecessarily exposed to the risk of (among other things) a particular disease and it is proved that the greater the exposure *to asbestos*, the greater the risk of contracting that disease.[65] In these circumstances, where medical science could not prove whose asbestos was more likely than not to have produced the cell mutation which caused the disease, "a rule requiring proof of a link between the defendant's asbestos and the claimant's disease would, with the arbitrary exception of single-employer cases, empty the duty of content" with the result that the duty could not effectively exist.[66] In such circumstances, said his Lordship "it would be both inconsistent with the policy of the law imposing the duty and morally wrong for your Lordships to impose causal requirements which exclude liability."[67]

5–034   Lord Rodger suggested that certain conditions were necessary, but may not always be sufficient, for applying the *Fairchild* principle:

> "(1) the principle is designed to resolve the difficulty that arises where it is inherently impossible for the claimant to prove exactly how his injury was caused. It applies, therefore, where the claimant has proved all that he possibly can, but the causal link could only ever be established by scientific investigation and the current state of the relevant science leaves it uncertain exactly how the injury was caused and, so, who caused it. *McGhee* and the present cases are examples.
>
> (2) part of the underlying rationale of the principle is that the defendant's wrongdoing has materially increased the risk that the claimant will suffer injury. It is therefore essential not just that the defendant's conduct created a material risk of injury to a class of persons but that it actually created a material risk of injury to the claimant himself.

---

[63] *ibid.* at [2].

[64] *ibid.* at [34].

[65] *ibid.* at [61].

[66] *ibid.* at [62]. Though see the comments of Stapleton (2002) 10 Torts L.J. 276 at 296 on this, who points out that the duty of employers or occupiers to take reasonable steps not to expose employees or visitors to asbestos would still apply to cases of asbestosis, so that the fact that some claimants (those who developed mesothelioma) could not prove causation would hardly "empty the duty of content." See also Morgan (2003) 66 M.L.R. 277, 282 making a similar point.

[67] *ibid.* at [63].

(3) it follows that the defendant's conduct must have been capable of causing the claimant's injury.

(4) the claimant must prove that his injury was caused by the eventuation of the kind of risk created by the defendant's wrongdoing. In *McGhee*, for instance, the risk created by the defenders' failure was that the pursuer would develop dermatitis due to brick dust on his skin and he proved that he had developed dermatitis due to brick dust on his skin. By contrast, the principle does not apply where the claimant has merely proved that his injury could have been caused by a number of different events, only one of which is the eventuation of the risk created by the defendant's wrongful act or omission. *Wilsher* is an example.

(5) this will usually mean that the claimant must prove that his injury was caused, if not by exactly the same agency as was involved in the defendant's wrongdoing, at least by an agency that operated in substantially the same way. A possible example would be where a workman suffered injury from exposure to dusts coming from two sources, the dusts being particles of different substances each of which, however, could have caused his injury in the same way . . .

(6) the principle applies where the other possible source of the claimant's injury is a similar wrongful act or omission of another person, but it can also apply where, as in *McGhee*, the other possible source of the injury is a similar, but lawful, act or omission of the same defendant. I reserve my opinion as to whether the principle applies where the other possible source of injury is a similar but lawful act or omission of someone else or a natural occurrence."[68]

These conditions are clearly at a higher level of generality than those identified by Lord Bingham or Lord Hoffmann. All of their Lordships were clear that in applying *Fairchild* to future cases caution will be essential. There are dangers in over-generalising the principle, which does not apply merely because the claimant has difficulty in discharging the burden of proof.[69] With the greatest respect, it is difficult to see how, or indeed why, the *Fairchild* principle relaxing the need to establish "but for" causation should be restricted to the relationship between employer and employee, still less to the specifics of mesothelioma caused by exposure to asbestos dust. In this respect Lord Rodger's conditions probably reflect a more principled approach. In any event, both Lord Bingham and Lord Hoffmann acknowledged that the principle could be developed to apply in new situations. Given this, conditions seeking to limit it to specific types of relationship or specific types of damage (industrial diseases) are unlikely to be regarded as crucial. Indeed, it is not apparent why the principle should be confined to *scientific* uncertainty about causation. For example, in *Fitzgerald v Lane*[70] the Court of Appeal applied *McGhee* to a case involving three discrete possible causes of injury,

5–035

---

[68] *ibid.* at [169] to [170].
[69] *ibid.* at [43] *per* Lord Nicholls.
[70] [1987] Q.B. 781.

namely three distinct impacts in a road traffic accident involving a pedestrian and two vehicles. This case suggests that *McGhee* is not limited to factual uncertainties due to gaps in medical knowledge about the cause of injuries or diseases, but could apply to other types of factual uncertainty.[71]

5–036   Professor Stapleton[72] has identified a number of factors that *cannot* be freestanding requirements of the *McGhee/Fairchild* principle:

- that the defendant was solely responsible for all the sources of risk to the victim (true in *McGhee*, but not *Fairchild*)

- that all tortfeasors are before the court (all three claimants in *Fairchild* had been exposed to asbestos by parties not before the court)

- that the defendant was the claimant's employer (the claims in *Fairchild* also involved actions against occupiers)

- that the defendant was solely responsible for all the tortious sources of risk to the victim (true in *McGhee*, but not *Fairchild*)

- that there was more than one tortfeasor responsible for tortious exposures (true in *Fairchild*, but not in *McGhee*)

- that the defendant's tortious conduct consisted of a failure to ameliorate a situation that the defendant had earlier created innocently (true in *McGhee*, but not *Fairchild*)

It is difficult to state with precision, however, when the principle *does* apply. Clearly, where there are multiple tortfeasors and they all add to the risk of damage caused by the *same* noxious agent then the principle applies (since that was the decision in *Fairchild* itself); and in the light of their Lordships' approval of *Wilsher* it would seem that where there are four "innocent" possible causes of the claimant's damage, and the defendant adds a fifth "guilty" possible cause, the increase in overall risk cannot be equated with a material contribution to the damage, or as Lord Bingham expressed the *Fairchild* principle, cannot be "treated *as if* it had materially contributed to the disease."[73] It is unclear, however, whether the principle applies where there are multiple tortfeasors and they add to the risk of damage caused by *different* noxious agents, but by the same, or broadly the same, mechanism.[74] It is also uncertain whether the principle applies where there is a single tortfeasor and he adds to the risk of damage caused by the *same* noxious agent, where there is another party who also contributes to the risk by the same mechanism, but that party

---

[71] In *Fairchild* [2002] UKHL 22 at [170] Lord Rodger, without deciding the issue, was inclined to the view that the Court of Appeal had been correct to apply *McGhee* in *Fitzgerald v Lane*.

[72] (2002) 10 Torts L.J. 276, 292.

[73] See further *Temple v South Manchester Health Authority* [2002] EWCA Civ 1406, above n. 59.

[74] According to Lord Bingham, no, but according to Lord Hoffmann and Lord Rodger, possibly yes. For further discussion see Stapleton (2002) 10 Torts L.J. 276, 294–298.

is "innocent", *i.e.* not in breach of duty, though logically this would seem to fall within *McGhee*.[75] The exposure to the risk of harm must be "not insignificant",[76] or the breach of duty must have "contributed substantially to the risk" that the claimant would contract the disease.[77] Their Lordships did not indicate what a *substantial* contribution meant, perhaps not surprisingly given that on any view of the facts in *Fairchild* the defendants' contribution clearly was substantial. Other cases may arise, however, where the only solvent or traceable defendant exposed the claimant to the risk for a relatively short period, where the issue will be important. It will be recalled that in *Bonnington Castings Ltd v Wardlaw* the House of Lords held that anything that did not fall within the principle *de minimis non curat lex* would constitute a material contribution to the claimant's damage, and it would seem that a similar test is appropriate where the breach of duty contributes to the *risk of* damage.[78]

What, then, is the distinction between *Wilsher* and *McGhee/Fairchild*? On one approach the *McGhee/Fairchild* principle will apply where the *specific risk* which has materialised, for which there is some *prima facie* evidence, has been enhanced by the defendant's breach of duty, but not where the negligence enhanced a general risk to the claimant, applying a narrow interpretation of the word "risk." So, for example, in *Wilsher* the risk created by the defendants was "RLF caused *by excess oxygen*," not simply an enhancement of an existing risk of RLF from other causes.[79] Until it could be shown that the RLF was caused by excess oxygen the injury cannot be said to fall squarely within the risk created by the defendants.[80] Of course, if it is possible to say that the

5–037

---

[75] If, for example, in *McGhee* the claimant's exposure to brick dust during the working day was due to the "innocent" conduct of the occupier, it would surely have made no difference to the outcome when the employer was sued in respect of his breach of duty in failing to provide washing facilities.

[76] [2002] UKHL 22 at [42] *per* Lord Nicholls.

[77] *ibid.* at [47] *per* Lord Hoffmann.

[78] In *Athey v Leonati* [1997] 1 W.W.R. 97 the Supreme Court of Canada held that the defendant's negligence, which the trial judge had concluded was no more than a 25% contributory factor to the claimant's injury, constituted a material contribution to the damage and held the defendant liable for the full loss.

[79] In *Kay v Ayrshire and Arran Health Board* [1987] 2 All E.R. 417 the House of Lords made it clear that an overall contribution to "the risk of damage" was insufficient to invoke *McGhee* where the negligence created a risk of a different kind of damage from that which occurred. Lord Mackay (at p. 425) said that: "In my opinion, it is not right to ask whether [the overdose] materially increased the risk of neurological damage when the evidence available distinguishes between different kinds of neurological damage . . . I cannot accept that it is correct to say that because evidence shows that an overdose of penicillin increases the risk of particular types of neurological damage found in these cases that an overdose of penicillin materially increases the risk of a different type of neurological damage, namely that which causes deafness when no such deafness has been shown to have resulted from such overdose"; see also *per* Lord Griffiths at p. 422.

[80] *Wilsher v Essex Area Health Authority* [1987] Q.B. 730, 780, *per* Browne-Wilkinson V.-C. Note, however, the comment of Stapleton (2002) 10 Torts L.J. 276, 297–298: ". . . where the issue of historical connection cannot be established on orthodox principles because of an evidentiary gap, the notion of the sphere of the risk is sufficiently vague to allow manipulation to fit the result desired . . . the claimant in *Wilsher* could have argued that the defendant had created a risk of RLF, and that the injury suffered by the claimant fell squarely within that risk." Of course, the defendant would argue for a narrow formulation of the risk in order to demonstrate that the circumstances of the claimant's injury fell outside that risk.

defendant's negligence enhanced the specific risk which, on the balance of probabilities, has materialised, it is irrelevant that there were other discrete risk factors (as there were in *Wilsher*). In practice, however, the presence of other risk factors will probably make it impossible for the claimant to prove exactly which risk has materialised, and he will be unable to overcome the causation hurdle. The claimants in *Fairchild* were in a much better position in being able to argue that the risk which had materialised (the risk of mesothelioma from exposure to asbestos) had probably been increased by the defendants' breach of duty.

5–038　　　It is not entirely clear why the courts should want to make such fine distinctions when dealing with different types of factual uncertainty. It may be pure chance whether a defendant's negligence enhances an existing risk or adds a new risk factor, even if it is possible to distinguish between such risks. In some cases it may simply be unknown whether an illness is the result of a cumulative effect or of a single event the risk of which has been enhanced by the defendant. In the face of such uncertainty it seems strange to attach such significance to the distinction between cumulative and discrete causes,[81] or "single agent" and "multi-agent" causes. There may be practical reasons for concluding that the *McGhee/Fairchild* principle should be limited to cases involving a single agent, in that it provides a clear boundary and may reduce the problems associated with contribution between tortfeasors or apportionment of responsibility,[82] but it is certainly not a principled way in which to resolve issues of causal uncertainty arising out of gaps in scientific knowledge.[83]

An evidential base

5–039　　　Even before their Lordships in *Fairchild* had explained that *McGhee* was authority for a proposition of law, rather than an example of the drawing of an evidential inference, the Court of Appeal had been careful to stress that there must be evidence supporting the specific inference that the claimant sought to persuade the court to draw. A claimant cannot rely on the simple assertion that the defendant's conduct has increased the risk of harm—there must be specific evidence to link the defendant's breach of duty to the claimant's harm before an inference that it has made a material contribution can be drawn (or as expressed by Lord Bingham in *Fairchild*, "treated *as if* it had materially con-

---

[81] See Stapleton (1988) 104 L.Q.R. 389, 402 and 406 n. 40.
[82] Stapleton (2002) 10 Torts L.J. 276, 295.
[83] The suggestion, hinted at by Lord Hoffmann in *Fairchild v Glenhaven Funeral Services Ltd* [2002] UKHL 22; [2003] 1 A.C. 32 at [69], that *Wilsher* turned upon the identity of the defendants (the NHS rather than an employer sued by an employee) and that "the massive increase in the liability of the National Health Service which would have been a consequence of the broad rule favoured by the Court of Appeal in *Wilsher's* case" might justify a different causation rule surely cannot be correct. Of course, the policy issues that medical negligence litigation raises are important and are the subject of much political debate. Whatever the practical solution to these problems, it cannot be right to distort legal principle simply to protect one public sector defendant. See Morgan (2003) 66 M.L.R. 277, 282 making the point that the decision in *Fairchild* had massive financial implications for insurance companies, but that this was not mentioned in any of the speeches.

tributed" to the claimant's damage). In *Tahir v Haringey Health Authority*[84] the claimant alleged that the delay in providing medical treatment rendered his condition worse than it would otherwise have been, on the basis that, in general terms, delay in operating in his type of case increases the neurological deficit and impairs the prospect of recovery. The Court of Appeal held that where there has been negligence resulting in delayed medical treatment it was not sufficient for the claimant to show simply that there was a material increase in the risk or that delay *can* cause damage. He has to go further and prove that damage was *actually* caused by the delay. In the absence of findings of fact that identify or quantify the additional harm, it was not appropriate for a judge to adopt a proportionate approach by quantifying the total disability and then asking what proportion of that disability is attributable to the delay.[85]

A mathematical approach to discrete causes?

In a case where there is only one defendant and the damage is not cumula-   5–040
tive but is attributable to a single event, but there are multiple events some of which are in breach of duty but others are "innocent" and it is not possible to identify which event caused the claimant's damage, then it may be possible to use a mathematical approach, applying the balance of probabilities. In *The Creutzfeldt-Jakob Disease Litigation, Groups A and C Plaintiffs*[86] the claimants had all developed Creutzfeldt-Jakob Disease (CJD) as a consequence of receiving human growth hormone (HGH) treatment contaminated with the CJD virus. The treatment, consisting of an injection, was given on a regular basis over a period of time. Although there was some uncertainty, the accepted scientific view was that the CJD was caused by a single injection or dose containing a sufficient titre of the CJD agent. There was no issue of a cumulative cause nor that some individuals were more susceptible to developing CJD. The defendants were found to have been in breach of duty from July 1, 1977 by failing to give appropriate information to clinicians treating the claimants about the risks of transmitting CJD. The claimants had received injections of HGH both before and after July 1, 1977, but it was not scientifically possible to identify whether they had received a contaminated dose before or after that date. The defendants would only be liable if it could be proved that the claimants received the contaminated dose after that date. The claimants argued that if a victim received more doses after the cut-off date than before it then it was more likely than not that the contaminated dose was received after the cut-off date. For example, if a pack of cards was divided

---

[84] [1998] Lloyd's Rep. Med. 104.
[85] Similarly, in *Brown v Lewisham and North Southwark Health Authority* [1999] Lloyd's Rep. Med. 110 the Court of Appeal held that it is reasonable to draw a common sense inference that an increased risk of harm must have made a material contribution to the damage where there is some evidence which supports such an inference. But where there were no objective signs or symptoms of any aggravation or worsening of the claimant's condition following an allegedly negligently undertaken journey (between two hospitals) it was not reasonable to draw an inference that the journey contributed to a deterioration.
[86] (1998) 54 B.M.L.R. 100.

into two piles containing 27 and 25 cards respectively there is a higher probability that the pile of 27 cards contains the ace of spades. The defendants argued that this was a simplistic, mechanistic approach. There was a likelihood or possibility that a victim received a number of contaminated doses, although only one would prove fatal. If there were a number of potential aces of spades in the pack then the analogy of the pack of cards was inappropriate. Morland J. rejected the defendants' argument that causation was only established if the preponderance of doses were given after the cut-off date, and that a preponderance should be substantial (possibly three-quarters or two-thirds). That argument, said his Lordship, would alter the civil standard of proof from the balance of probabilities to a standard of substantially probable or very probable. Thus, any "straddler victim" (someone who received doses both before and after July 1, 1977) would succeed on causation if it was proved that he received the majority of doses after the cut-off date.

5–041   The logic of Morland J. would seem to be impeccable, and in theory would also apply in the case of multiple defendants, except that in any case where the claimant's exposure to the risk by any one defendant was less than 50 per cent the claim would fail on causation for the reasons given by the Court of Appeal in *Fairchild*. Since the Court of Appeal's decision in *Fairchild* was overruled by the House of Lords for reasons of policy, it is unclear whether Morland J.'s approach remains relevant after the decision in *Fairchild*. If, due to scientific uncertainty, the claimant was unable to prove on the balance of probabilities which injection resulted in the infection with CJD, one before or one after the cut-off date, it would be at least arguable that the policy which underlies *Fairchild* was just as relevant to the case.

Apportioning causation

5–042   On the facts of *Fairchild* the claimant was entitled to full compensation from the negligent defendant. There was no question of apportioning the loss proportionately to each potential defendant, with the claimant being entitled to damages from each defendant in proportion to his exposure to the noxious agent by that defendant. Each defendant is jointly and severally liable for the full loss (though having a right of contribution against the other defendants liable in respect of the same damage under the Civil Liability (Contribution) Act 1978). This stems from the very factual uncertainty which called into play the *Fairchild* principle, *i.e.* if the extent of the defendant's contribution is unknown, he is liable in full. On the other hand, where the extent of the defendant's contribution is known, the defendant is liable to that extent and no more.[87] In *Holtby v Brigham & Cowan (Hull)*

---

[87] See *Thompson v Smiths Shiprepairers (North Shields) Ltd* [1984] Q.B. 405, where the claimant suffered progressive hearing impairment due to industrial noise. The defendants were held liable only for that part of the deafness occurring after the exposure to noise became a breach of duty; *Dillon v Le Roux* [1994] 6 W.W.R. 280, 300 (B.C.C.A.), where the claimant had a pre-existing condition that was active and disabling prior to his admission to hospital, and the defendant doctor's negligence increased the damage to the claimant's heart.

Ltd[88] the Court of Appeal took the view that where the claimant's case is based on proving a material contribution to the damage the defendant is only responsible for that part of the damage to which his negligence has contributed. The claimant was exposed to asbestos dust over a period of almost 40 years, working for the defendants for about half of that time. For the remainder he worked for other employers doing the same sort of work in similar conditions, in some cases for years and in others for months. He developed asbestosis and sued the defendants, who were held to have been negligent and in breach of statutory duty. The judge held that the defendants were only liable for the damage they had caused, the evidence indicating that if the claimant had only been exposed to asbestos whilst working for the defendants his condition would probably have been less severe. General damages were reduced by 25 per cent. The claimant appealed on the basis that once he established that the defendant's breach of duty materially contributed to his damage he was entitled to recover for the full extent of his loss, applying *Bonnington Castings Ltd v Wardlaw*. Alternatively, he argued that once a claimant has proved that the defendant's conduct had made a material contribution to the damage the onus shifted to the defendant to prove that someone else was responsible for a specific part of the damage. The Court of Appeal rejected both arguments, upholding the judge's deduction of 25 per cent.[89] Stuart-Smith L.J. said that in both *Bonnington Castings* and *McGhee* the House of Lords had not considered the extent of the defendants' liability because it had not been argued that the defendants' were only liable to the extent of their material contribution —their case had been that they were not liable at all. The onus of proof remained with the claimant to show that the defendant's tortious conduct made a material contribution to the loss, but strictly speaking the defendants were liable only to the extent of that contribution. If the point was never raised or argued by the defendant the claimant would succeed in full, as in *Bonnington Castings* and *McGhee*. But once it became an issue the burden of proof was the claimant's.

It had generally been assumed that once the claimant established a "material contribution to the damage" the defendant was liable for the full loss. After all, it is open to the defendant to seek contribution under the Civil Liability (Contribution) Act 1978 from the third parties whom he alleges are also responsible for the claimant's damage, thereby allocating financial responsibility appropriately. One effect of *Holtby* is that the claimant is left to seek a remedy against each individual tortfeasor who may have contributed to his condition over a working life, placing the risk that one or more defendant employers are untraceable or uninsured on the claimant rather than the defendant. It was, perhaps easier in *Holtby* than in many industrial

5–043

---

[88] [2000] 3 All E.R. 421.
[89] Logically, the defendants in *Holtby* should have been liable for only 50% of the loss, rather than the 75% assessed by the judge, given the period of time the claimant had worked for the defendants. Stuart-Smith L.J. explained this as the judge "erring on the side of generosity" to the claimant.

disease cases to identify the defendant's contribution to the damage since the evidence was that there was a linear progression of the disease depending on the amount of dust inhaled, and so it could be said that all the dust contributed to the final disability (which marks the important difference from the situation in *Fairchild*). There could be cases where the medical evidence cannot identify such a linear effect, of which *Fairchild* is clearly one, but the causal mechanism may be even more complex. For example, the defendant's breach may create a "trigger" effect, sparking off an illness that might not otherwise have occurred, and this might be combined with a cumulative effect, *e.g.* exposure to a toxic agent up to a certain point may be "safe" in that it is unlikely to produce the disease, but after that point the probability of the disease occurring rises significantly. In such a case can D1 who contributes a level of exposure below the trigger level argue that he has not contributed to the disease at all, since the exposure to that point was 'safe', whereas D2, who adds to the exposure (possibly adding far less than D1) and thereby takes the claimant over the threshold for the onset of the disease, has materially contributed to the damage? What is the position where it is simply unknown whether the disease is caused by a cumulative effect or a trigger effect or some combination of both? Moreover, does the claimant have the burden of proof, which may be virtually impossible to discharge, as to which defendant contributed what percentage to his loss? This is precisely the sort of problem that their Lordships in *Bonnington Castings* and *McGhee* considered that a claimant should not have to surmount.

5–044   When assessing the extent of the defendant's contribution a judge is entitled to take a "broad brush" approach. The difficulty of undertaking that assessment is not a basis for saying that it should not occur.[90] Thus, the court should not be astute to deny the claimant relief on the basis that he could not establish with demonstrable accuracy precisely what proportion of his injury was attributable to the defendant's tortious conduct.[91] It is arguable, however, that it would only be appropriate to adopt a broad brush approach where the causal mechanism is known to be cumulative in nature, and the court's difficulty stems from the factual uncertainty of how much *this* defendant's breach of duty actually contributed to the overall damage. It could not apply to a case involving the *Fairchild* causal mechanism, since that would be to disregard their Lordships' reasoning and conclusions in that case. Thus, the greater the scientific uncertainty surrounding the causal mechanism the better the chances of the claimant recovering in full from a single defendant, provided that the court can be persuaded to apply the *Fairchild* principle.

---

[90] *Allen v British Rail Engineering* [2001] EWCA Civ 242; [2001] I.C.R. 942, a case concerning vibration white finger.
[91] *ibid.* at [20].

Contributing to psychiatric harm

It would also seem that the principle in *Bonnington Castings* can apply to 5–045 psychiatric harm. In *Page v Smith (No. 2)*[92] the claimant developed a recrudescence of chronic fatigue syndrome (also known as myalgic encephalomyelitis) following a road traffic accident of "moderate severity" in which he suffered no physical injuries. The Court of Appeal accepted that on the evidence there were other possible causes which had contributed to an exacerbation of the claimant's symptoms, but nonetheless considered that the trial judge was entitled to conclude that the accident had materially contributed to the claimant's symptoms, converting his illness from a mild and sporadic state to one of chronic intensity and permanence. This was the position notwithstanding that the claimant's nervous reaction to the accident was "not necessarily proportional to the trauma." The claimant recovered damages for the whole of the consequences of his psychiatric condition. It would now seem that, in the light of *Holtby*, a defendant is entitled to argue that he is only responsible for that part of the psychiatric condition caused by his breach of duty, so that where it is possible to identify the extent of the contribution made by the defendant's negligence to the claimant's psychiatric damage, the court should make an appropriate apportionment of the damage.[93]

Other jurisdictions

In Canada the principle in *McGhee* has had a mixed reception. In *Powell* 5–046 *v Guttman*[94] the claimant developed a condition of avascular necrosis following an operation on her leg performed by the defendant orthopaedic surgeon. The defendant negligently failed to advise the claimant to undergo an arthoplasty operation to correct this. When another surgeon performed the operation the claimant sustained a rotary fracture of the femur because the delay had caused the condition of the bone to deteriorate as result of osteoporosis. The question was whether the negligence was a cause of the fracture. The defendant was held liable because his negligence had caused an increase in the osteoporosis which rendered the femur more susceptible to the fracture. This materially increased the risk of the very fracture which did occur. O'Sullivan J.A. applied the principle of *McGhee*:

"However, I think the law in Canada is that where a tortfeasor creates or materially contributes to a significant risk of injury occurring and injury does occur which is squarely within the risk thus created or materially increased, then unless the risk is spent, the tortfeasor is liable for injury which follows from the risk, even though there are other

---

[92] [1996] 3 All E.R. 272. See also *Vernon v Bosley (No. 1)* [1997] 1 All E.R. 577 applying *Bonnington Castings* to psychiatric damage.
[93] See *Hatton v Sutherland* [2002] EWCA Civ 76; [2002] 2 All E.R. 1 at [36] to [41].
[94] (1978) 89 D.L.R. (3d) 180 (Man. C.A.).

subsequent causes which also cause or materially contribute to that injury."[95]

5–047   The Saskatchewan Court of Appeal has also applied this principle.[96] On the other hand, in *Wilkinson Estate (Rogin) v Shannon*[97] Anderson J. was not convinced that *McGhee* represented the law of Ontario, and in *Wilson v Vancouver Hockey Club*[98] Murray J. declined to apply *McGhee* in a case of alleged medical negligence. In *Snell v Farrell*[99] the trial judge concluded that *McGhee* did shift the onus of proof to the defendant. The defendant had been "asking for trouble" by operating on the claimant's eye when he knew that his patient had a retrobulbar bleed. The increased risk was followed by injury in the same area of risk, and this was sufficient to establish causation. On appeal to the Supreme Court of Canada,[1] however, it was held that the burden of proof remained with the claimant throughout, applying the interpretation of *McGhee* adopted by the House of Lords in *Wilsher*. Nonetheless, though the burden of proof does not change, the court was entitled to draw an inference to establish causation, notwithstanding that causation was not proved by positive evidence:

> "In many malpractice cases, the facts lie particularly within the knowledge of the defendant. In these circumstances, very little affirmative evidence on the part of the plaintiff will justify the drawing of an inference of causation in the absence of evidence to the contrary."[2]

Moreover, the court was entitled to draw such an inference even where there was no firm expert opinion supporting the claimant's theory of causation, since medical experts normally determine causation in terms of certainties whereas the courts deal with the matter on the balance of probabilities.[3]

---

[95]   *ibid*. at p. 192.

[96]   *Nowsco Well Service Ltd v Canadian Propane Gas & Oil Ltd* (1981) 122 D.L.R. (3d) 228, a non-medical case. See also *Meyer v Gordon* (1981) 17 C.C.L.T. 1, 41–42 (B.C.S.C.) where *McGhee* was relied upon as an "additional ground" since the judge had already found that the negligence probably caused the damage. The negligence had "materially increased the risk of injury to the child and materially increased the risk of foetal distress and the resulting hypoxia." In *Wipfli v Britten* (1982) 145 D.L.R. (3d) 80 (B.C.S.C.); affirmed (1984) 13 D.L.R. (4th) 169 (B.C.C.A.) the trial judge had relied on *McGhee* to establish causation, but the British Columbia Court of Appeal considered that this was unnecessary, since causation had been established on a balance of probabilities from the evidence. It was a reasonable inference that had the physicians attending the labour known that there were twins the labour would not have been allowed to continue for so long, and this would have avoided or materially lessened the effects of the prolonged labour on the second twin.

[97]   (1986) 37 C.C.L.T. 181 (Ont. H.C.).

[98]   (1983) 5 D.L.R. (4th) 282, 288; affirmed (1985) 22 D.L.R. (4th) 516 (B.C.C.A.), citing *Murray v Shaughnessy Hospital* (1982) 15 A.C.W.S. (2d) 389 where Esson J. said that he doubted whether *McGhee* applied in British Columbia.

[99]   (1986) 40 C.C.L.T. 298, 312–313 (N.B.Q.B.).

[1]   (1990) 72 D.L.R. (4th) 289.

[2]   *ibid*. at p. 300.

[3]   See *Lankenau v Dutton* (1991) 79 D.L.R. (4th) 705 (B.C.C.A.) where the cause of the claimant's paralysis was known, *i.e.* compression of the spinal cord during an operation. What was not certain was whether the defendant's negligent failure to make a timely diagnosis made

In *Webster v Chapman*[4] a patient had negligently been permitted to con-   5–048
tinue taking a drug to treat pelvic thrombosis which was potentially harmful
to the foetus if she became pregnant. The failure of the defendant general
practitioner to refer the patient to a specialist increased the period during
which the foetus was exposed to the risk of damage by three weeks. The scientific evidence was to the effect that the first trimester of the pregnancy was
the "critical period" but it could not be said whether the damage to child's
nervous system had occurred in the first eight weeks of the pregnancy or
whether the additional three weeks' exposure attributable to the defendant's
negligence had caused the damage. The Manitoba Court of Appeal held that
the claimant would succeed if she could prove that the failure to advise her
to stop taking the drug materially contributed to the damage. There was no
evidence that the damage resulted from a single event. If the taking of the drug
during the critical period was the cause of the damage, as the present state of
scientific knowledge indicated that it was, then the negligent administration
of the drug during part of that period must, at a practical level, be seen as a
materially contributing factor (applying *McGhee*). The scientific uncertainty
as to when the damage was caused prevented the claimant from proving causation, but equally it prevented the defendant from disproving it. The court
then took the view that the negligence must have been a contributory cause.

In *Naxakis v Western General Hospital*,[5] in the High Court of Australia,   5–049
Gaudron J. said that for the purposes of allocating legal responsibility, if a
wrongful act or omission results in an increased risk of injury to the claimant
and that risk eventuates, the defendant's conduct has materially contributed
to the injury that the claimant has sustained whether or not other factors also
contributed to that injury.[6] In that situation, the trier of fact was entitled to
conclude that the act or omission caused the injury in question, unless the
defendant could establish that the conduct had no effect at all or that the risk
would have eventuated and resulted in the damage in question in any event.[7]

(3) Loss of a chance

The claimant's complaint in a medical negligence action is frequently, not   5–050
that the doctor has inflicted "additional" injury, but that as a result of the
defendant's negligence his medical condition has not been improved or has

---

(n.3 contd.) even a partial recovery impossible. In the circumstances of the case, requiring the
claimant to prove this was "importing into the concept of the legal burden of proof a requirement that a plaintiff demonstrate scientifically that which is incapable of scientific proof," *per*
Southin J.A. at p. 717. Accordingly, this was a case for "a robust and pragmatic approach to
the facts." There was sufficient evidence to find that but for the defendant's breach of duty the
claimant would not have been in such a hopeless condition. See also *Pierre v Marshall* [1994]
8 W.W.R. 478, 506 (Alta. Q.B.); *Arndt v Smith* [1994] 8 W.W.R. 568, 579–580 (B.C.S.C.);
affirmed (1997) 148 D.L.R. (4th) 48 (S.C.C.); *Wintle v Piper* [1994] 9 W.W.R. 390, 396
(B.C.C.A.); *Levitt v Carr* (1992) 12 C.C.L.T. (2d) 195 (B.C.C.A.).
[4] (1997) 155 D.L.R. (4th) 82 (Man. C.A.).
[5] [1999] H.C.A. 22; (1999) 162 A.L.R. 540.
[6] Citing *Chappel v Hart* (1998) 156 A.L.R. 517 at 525 *per* McHugh J.
[7] [1999] H.C.A. 22; (1999) 162 A.L.R. 540 at [31].

been allowed to deteriorate. Accordingly, the claimant has been deprived of the opportunity of making a full or proper recovery from the illness or injury for which he first sought treatment. Applying the "but for" test of causation, if on the balance of probabilities competent treatment would have prevented the deterioration which has occurred, or produced an improvement, the negligence is causally linked to the damage and the defendant is responsible. Where, however, the patient's prospects of a successful outcome to the treatment were estimated to be less than 50 per cent, the patient cannot satisfy the "but for" test, because even with proper treatment the damage would probably (*i.e.* more likely than not) have occurred in any event.

5–051   An alternative approach to cases involving this type of factual uncertainty is to deal with them in terms of the measure of damages by reference to the chance of loss, rather than determining liability on an all or nothing basis (using the "but for" test). In *Hotson v East Berkshire Area Health Authority*[8] the claimant suffered an accidental injury to his hip in a fall which created a 75 per cent risk that he would develop a permanent disability through avascular necrosis of the femoral epiphysis. Due to negligent medical diagnosis the hip was not treated for five days, and the delay made the disability inevitable. The claimant contended that the doctor's negligence had deprived him of a 25 per cent chance of making a good recovery, whereas the defendant argued that the claimant had failed to prove, on the balance of probabilities, that the negligence caused the disability. The trial judge, Simon Brown J., held that where a "substantial chance" of a better medical result had been lost it was not necessary to prove that the adverse medical result was directly attributable to the breach of duty because the issue was the proper quantum of damage rather than causation. The claimant could prove causation of the lost chance and accordingly he was entitled to damages on the basis of 25 per cent of the value of the claim for the full disability.[9] This approach was upheld by the Court of Appeal, where Sir John Donaldson M.R. characterised the claim as the loss of the *benefit* of timely treatment, rather than the *chance* of successful treatment. The use of the word "chance" complicated the issue, because it imported probabilities, and opened the way for the defendant's argument. It was also inaccurate, said his Lordship, because it elides the identification of the loss with the valuation of the loss, which are distinct processes. Just as the categories of negligence are never closed, there was no reason why the categories of loss should be closed either.[10]

5–052   It is clear that there was a strong element of policy in the Court of Appeal's decision. Sir John Donaldson M.R. commented that:

"As a matter of common sense, it is unjust that there should be no liability for failure to treat a patient, simply because the chances of a success-

---

[8] [1987] A.C. 750, CA and HL.
[9] *Hotson v Fitzgerald* [1985] 1 All E.R. 167.
[10] [1987] A.C. 750, 761.

ful cure by that treatment were less than 50 per cent. Nor, by the same token, can it be just that, if the chances of a successful cure only marginally exceed 50 per cent, the doctor or his employer should be liable to the same extent as if the treatment could be guaranteed to cure. If this is the law, it is high time that it was changed . . ."[11]

The House of Lords reversed the Court of Appeal, however, on the basis that the judge's finding that there was a high probability, put at 75 per cent, that even with correct diagnosis and treatment the claimant's disability would have occurred, amounted to a finding of fact that the accidental injury was the sole cause of the disability.[12] In other words this was not a "lost chance" case, it was an all or nothing case—either the fall or the misdiagnosis caused the disability, and on the balance of probabilities it was the fall. The valuation of a "lost chance" would only arise once causation had been established. As has been pointed out, however, this decision fails to address the essence of the claimant's argument, which was whether a claim formulated as a loss of a chance was acceptable.[13] If the nature of the damage could be redefined as the loss of a *chance* of a successful outcome, rather than the outcome itself (the disability), then on a traditional causation test the defendants' negligence clearly did cause the damage (*i.e.* the lost chance). Logically, the question of whether the defendant's negligence caused damage is an issue that can only be dealt with *after* the nature of the damage has been defined.

The decision of the House of Lords in *Hotson* had been anticipated in the Scottish case of *Kenyon v Bell*,[14] where an infant sustained an accidental injury to her eye. It was alleged that due to negligent treatment of the eye by a casualty officer the eye was lost, or alternatively that proper treatment would have given the child a "materially greater chance of the eye being saved." The pursuer argued that the loss of a chance of saving the eye was in itself damage, and that the only difficulty was in the assessment of appropriate damages. This argument was rejected by Lord Guthrie as "extravagant and contrary to principle" because the pursuer would be entitled to damages "although on the evidence the balance of probability was that the loss of the eye was not caused by the defender." The pursuer had to show that but for the negligence the eye would have been saved.[15]

5–053

---

[11] *ibid.* at pp. 759–760. Dillon L.J. observed, at p. 764, that: "If [counsel] is right, and the chance is lost through a negligent failure of the doctor to examine the patient properly or to diagnose correctly, with the result that the treatment which alone might have saved the patient is not undertaken, the patient will have no remedy unless he can show that the chance of the treatment, if undertaken, proving successful was more than 50%. That to my mind is contrary to common sense."
[12] [1987] A.C. 750.
[13] Stapleton (1988) 104 L.Q.R. 389, 393. This point was not lost on Sir John Donaldson M.R. in the Court of Appeal.
[14] 1953 S.C. 125.
[15] This he subsequently failed to do: see *Hotson v East Berkshire Area Health Authority* [1987] A.C. 750, 784, *per* Lord Mackay.

5–054   In some jurisdictions of the United States claims for loss of a chance have been accepted. In *Herskovits v Group Health Co-operative of Puget Sound*[16] H died from cancer. When he was first seen, the defendants failed to diagnose his tumour. At that stage, if the tumour had been detected, H had a 39 per cent chance of survival for more than five years. By the time his tumour was discovered and treated his chance of surviving for more than five years was only 25 per cent. The court allowed the case to go to the jury on the question of proximate cause, although the "loss" constituted the 14 per cent reduction in the chance of survival, and any damages would be limited to the loss attributable to the premature death, not the death itself. As Dore J. pointed out:

> "To decide otherwise would be a blanket release from liability for doctors and hospitals any time there was less than a 50 per cent chance of survival, regardless of how flagrant the negligence."[17]

5–055   This comment was echoed in the observations of the Court of Appeal in *Hotson* that applying the all or nothing approach to a patient whose chances of a successful outcome to his treatment were less than 50 per cent means that the patient has no action against the doctor no matter how negligent he has been. This creates what is, in effect, an unenforceable duty to exercise reasonable care, a factor which had influenced both Lord Simon and Lord Salmon to impose liability *McGhee*.

5–056   One of the problems confronting a claimant in this type of case is the courts' attitude to statistical evidence. In *Hotson v East Berkshire Area Health Authority* Croom-Johnson L.J. explained the difficulty:

> "If it is proved statistically that 25 per cent of the population has a chance of recovery from a certain injury and 75 per cent do not, it does not mean that someone who suffers that injury and who does not recover from it has lost a 25 per cent chance. He may have lost nothing at all. What he has to do is prove that he was one of the 25 per cent and that his loss was caused by the defendant's negligence. To be a figure in a statistic does not by itself give him a cause of action. If the plaintiff succeeds in proving that he was one of the 25 per cent and that the defendant took away that chance, the logical result would be to award him 100 per cent of his damages and not only a quarter . . ."[18]

---

[16] 664 P. 2d 474 (1983) (Washington S.C.). This decision was discussed by Lord Mackay in *Hotson v East Berkshire Area Health Authority* [1987] A.C. 750, 786–789. See also *Hicks v United States*, 368 F. 2d 626 (4th Cir.) (1966); *Jeanes v Milner*, 428 F. 2d 598 (U.S.C.A. 8th Cir.) (1970); *Hamil v Bashline*, 481 Pa. 256 (Pennsylvania S.C.) (1978); Price (1989) 38 I.C.L.Q. 735.

[17] *ibid.* at p. 477.

[18] [1987] A.C. 750, 769; see also Lord Mackay's discussion of statistics *ibid.* at 789; see further Hill (1991) 54 M.L.R. 511 arguing that there is a distinction between the loss of a statistical chance and the loss of a chance that was personal to the claimant; *cf.* Stapleton (1988) 104 L.Q.R. 389, 399 n. 23; Scott (1992) 55 M.L.R. 521. In *Taylor v West Kent Health Authority* [1997] 8 Med. L.R. 251, 257 Kay J. drew a clear distinction between the statistical evidence

The claimant's problem, of course, is that by definition he cannot prove that he would have been one of the 25 per cent because if he could, he would be able to show that on a balance of probabilities the defendant did indeed cause the damage. Moreover, he cannot prove this because *as a result of the defendant's negligence* it will never be known whether he would have made a full recovery. It is the defendant's negligence which prevents the claimant from establishing "but for" causation.[19] This in itself might be thought a good policy reason for permitting an action for a lost chance.[20] Lord Bridge acknowledged that in some cases, "perhaps particularly medical negligence cases, causation may be so shrouded in mystery that the court can only measure statistical chances," although "that was not so here."[21] In *Laferrière v Lawson*[22] the Supreme Court of Canada took a robust view of statistical evidence, pointing out that the court is not bound to accept statistical evidence at face value but must look to the claimant's particular circumstances to determine whether an inference of causation can be drawn:

> "If one takes, for example, a case in which a doctor neglects to employ a recommended procedure which is said to have a 50 per cent chance of complete cure, a judge would not necessarily be bound by expert opinion which declined to conclude that application of the procedure to the patient would have avoided the patient's present worsened condition. The judge might well be justified in finding that the procedure in question would probably have benefited the patient, if other factors particular to that plaintiff support that conclusion. The judge's duty is to assess the damage suffered by a particular patient, not to remain paralysed by statistical abstraction.
>
> If one moves then to a procedure which is recommended despite a mere 25 per cent chance of success according to expert evidence, it is still not a foregone conclusion that the doctor's fault in not using this procedure must be said to have had no causal role in the patient's death or sickness. If the experts are examined properly, a judge might well find

---

(n.18 contd.) of average survival rates for patients with breast cancer and evidence particular to the claimant, which indicated that the cancer was particularly aggressive. Although the average patient would have had a greater than 50% prospect of long-term survival, the probability was that even with prompt diagnosis and treatment Mrs. Taylor would probably have died at around the time that she did. For discussion of the medical aspects of proving causation in cases of delayed diagnosis of breast cancer see Weisbrod (1997) 3 *AVMA Medical & Legal Journal* 189.

[19] This was one compelling reason for the Victoria Court of Appeal's decision in *Gavalas v Singh* [2001] V.S.C.A. 23; (2001) 3 V.R. 404 that the claimant was entitled to claim for loss of a chance where there had been a delayed diagnosis of a brain tumour: "It may also be said to be unjust and contrary to the underlying policy objectives for a plaintiff to be denied compensation because critical evidence is unavailable as a result of the negligence of the defendant. The present case is such a case. It was the negligence of the defendant that prevented the parties knowing what the size of the tumour was as at October 25, 1990," *per* Smith A.J.A. at 417.

[20] *cf. Cook v Lewis* [1952] 1 D.L.R. 1, above, para. 5–014 where the Supreme Court of Canada considered that this was a good reason for reversing the burden of proof.

[21] *Hotson v East Berkshire Area Health Authority* [1987] A.C. 750, 782.

[22] (1991) 78 D.L.R. (4th) 609 (S.C.C.).

that he or she is justified in concluding that the omission of that procedure did not cause the death or sickness, but that it caused other lesser
but clearly negative results (*e.g.*, slightly shorter life, greater pain). The
doctor's fault could then be judged causal to the extent of the aggravation of what was otherwise an inevitably terminal or morbid condition."[23]

5-057   The question of whether it would ever be possible to claim for loss of a
chance in tort was specifically left open by their Lordships in *Hotson*.[24] Lord
Mackay took the view that while *McGhee v National Coal Board*[25] was still
good law it would be unwise to lay down as a rule of law that a claimant could
never succeed by proving a loss of a chance in a medical negligence case. A
material increase of the risk of a particular result was "equivalent to material
decrease in the chance of escaping" the result.[26] Unfortunately, the relationship between *McGhee* and potential lost chance claims remains unclear. Could
it be argued that *McGhee* applies where it is impossible to determine the
extent of the increased risk,[27] but the lost chance approach when the risk was
quantifiable, with the result that the less that was known about the risk the
greater the potential award of damages, since under *McGhee* the damages are
not discounted?[28] This apparent anomaly now arises in any event when applying the material contribution to the damage test, because where the court is in
a position to estimate the degree of the defendant's material contribution he
is liable only to that extent,[29] but if the defendant's contribution is shrouded
in scientific uncertainty the claimant recovers in full.[30] Another possibility is
that in cases similar to *Hotson* the facts could be reformulated in terms of a
"material contribution to the damage," treating the disability as having two
causes, the fall and the negligent delay in treatment.[31]

---

[23] *ibid*. at p. 657.
[24] The Supreme Court of Canada has expressly rejected the loss of chance theory: *Laferrière v
Lawson* (1991) 78 D.L.R. (4th) 609 (S.C.C.).
[25] [1972] 3 All E.R. 1008. Of course, the House of Lords has subsequently confirmed that
McGhee is still correct: *Fairchild v Glenhaven Funeral Services Ltd* [2002] UKHL 22; [2003]
1 A.C. 32.
[26] [1987] A.C. 750, 786. See further the discussion of the decision of the Court of Appeal in
Gregg v Scott [2002] EWCA Civ 1471; [2003] Lloyd's Rep. Med. 105, below para. 5–063.
[27] Provided, of course, that the circumstances were such that the *McGhee/Fairchild* principle
of causation could be invoked: see para. 5–030 *et seq.*
[28] In *Seyfert v Burnaby Hospital Society* (1986) 27 D.L.R. (4th) 96 (B.C.S.C.) McEachern
C.J.S.C. adopted a lost chance approach (referring specifically to *Hotson v Fitzgerald*) for
this very reason, namely that *McGhee* would place the whole loss upon the defendant. The
defendant was negligent in failing to diagnose that the patient had a stab wound which had
penetrated the peritoneum, causing a wound to the transverse colon. There were three possible ways of treating this type of injury if diagnosed quickly enough, one of which did not
involve a colostomy and delayed recovery. McEachern C.J. held that the claimant was: "entitled to recover damages representing the loss of the chance he had of avoiding the risk of a
colostomy, a second operation and an extended period of convalescence . . . I would fix that
chance at 25%, making it necessary that the plaintiff's damages be reduced by 75%," *ibid*.
at p. 102.
[29] *Holtby v Brigham & Cowan (Hull) Ltd* [2000] 3 All E.R. 421, para. 5–042.
[30] As in *Fairchild v Glenhaven Funeral Services Ltd* [2002] UKHL 22; [2003] 1 A.C. 32.
[31] See *per* Lord Bridge at [1987] A.C. 750, 782. The case was not argued on this basis.

It is long established that a lost chance may be actionable in contract.[32]   5–058
Where, for example, through a solicitor's negligence a client has lost the
opportunity to bring proceedings (*e.g.* because the limitation period has been
allowed to expire), the client in an action against the solicitor does not have
to prove that he would have won the other case, merely that he has lost
"some right of value, some chose in action of reality and substance."[33]
Damages are then discounted to reflect his chances of success in the original
action. It scarcely seems arguable that the basis of a distinction between
Kitchen and *Hotson* is that one was a claim in contract and the other in tort,
when the duties in each instance are the same, namely a duty to exercise
reasonable skill and care. It would lead to the untenable result that, in identical circumstances, a patient who had received treatment privately might
have a claim but a patient who received treatment under the National Health
Service would not.[34]

In the House of Lords the analogy of *Kitchen* was dismissed as irrelevant,   5–059
though it is not entirely clear why it was irrelevant, particularly as their
Lordships did not give reasons for this assertion. Lord Bridge thought that
the analogy with *Kitchen* was "superficially attractive," but considered that
there were "formidable difficulties in the way of accepting the analogy."[35]
The trial judge, on the other hand, was unable to see any sensible distinction
between the solicitor/client relationship and the doctor/patient relationship
in these circumstances.[36]

An alternative categorisation was suggested by the Court of Appeal in   5–060
Allied Maples Group Ltd v Simmons & Simmons.[37] After the purchase of
business property by the claimants, it became apparent that the property
carried a contingent liability for which the claimants were responsible. They

---

[32] *Chaplin v Hicks* [1911] 2 K.B. 786, on loss of a chance to compete for a prize amongst a limited number of contestants.

[33] *Kitchen v Royal Air Force Association* [1958] 1 W.L.R. 563; *Corfield v D.S. Bosher & Co* [1992] 1 E.G.L.R. 163, where damages were awarded on the basis that the claimant had a one third chance of success.

[34] See *Hotson v East Berkshire Area Health Authority* [1987] A.C. 750, at 760, 764 and 768, *per* Sir John Donaldson M.R., Dillon L.J. and Croom-Johnson L.J. respectively. See also the comments of Mance L.J. in *Gregg v Scott* [2002] EWCA Civ 1471; [2003] Lloyd's Rep. Med. 105 at [65]: "It cannot make all the difference whether such a claim is put in contract or tort, or is against a claim is put in contract or tort, or is against a part of the National Health Service or against a private, contracting hospi-tal." But see *de la Giroday v Brough* [1997] 6 W.W.R. 585 (B.C.C.A.) where a majority of the British Columbia Court of Appeal accepted that the loss of a chance approach was not available in tort but could apply to breach of a contractual obligation to exercise reasonable care and skill: "Why should a solicitor who misses a limitation period be liable in contract for depriving a client of the opportunity to pursue a cause of action even if the client cannot establish that he would have won his case and a physician who has committed a breach of his contractual obligation by, for instance, not sending his patient to a specialist, not be liable for depriving the patient of the opportunity of prompt, appropriate treatment? In such cases, assessing the damages is not easy but liability is one thing and the measure of damages another", *per* Southin J.A. at 599. *de la Giroday* was neither pleaded nor tried as an action for breach of contract. The case was referred for a re-trial.

[35] [1987] A.C. 750, 782.

[36] [1985] 1 All E.R. 167, 176; *cf.* Hill (1991) 54 M.L.R. 511, 519 arguing that *Kitchen* was not a lost chance case.

[37] [1995] 4 All E.R. 907; [1995] 1 W.L.R. 1602.

were unable to reclaim this loss from the vendor under the terms of the sale. They sued the solicitors who had advised them on deal, arguing that if, as it should have been, the risk of the loss had been pointed out to them by the defendants, they would have taken steps to obtain a warranty from the vendor or protect themselves from the loss in some other way. The trial judge found that, on the balance of probability, if asked, the vendor would have agreed to different terms in the contract of sale, giving some form of warranty or protection from the potential liability, and that if the relevant property had not been included in the sale, the whole deal would not have proceeded. In the Court of Appeal Stuart-Smith L.J. said[38] that the classification of the causation issue into "all or nothing" on the balance of probabilities or the quantification of the loss of a chance depends upon whether the negligence consists in some positive act or misfeasance, or an omission or nonfeasance:

(1) In the case of a positive act of misfeasance the question of causation is one of historical fact, which once established on the balance of probability is taken as true. The claimant recovers damages in full.[39] Quantifying the claimant's loss, however, may depend upon uncertain future events, such as the degree to which his medical condition will deteriorate or improve, whether he would have continued to earn at the same rate, etc. These issues are dealt with on the basis of an assessment of the risk, often expressed in percentage terms, that the event will or will not occur.

(2) Where the defendant's negligence consists of an omission, *e.g.* to provide proper equipment, or to give proper instructions or advice, causation depends, not upon a question of historical fact, but on the answer to the hypothetical question, what would the claimant have done if the equipment had been provided or the instruction or advice given? This will be a matter of inference to be determined from all the circumstances. The claimant's own evidence that he would have acted to obtain the benefit or avoid the risk, while important, may not be believed by the judge, especially if there is compelling evidence that he would not.[40] Although the question is a hypothetical one, the claimant must prove on the

---

[38] *ibid.* at pp. 914–916.
[39] *Mallett v McMonagle* [1970] A.C. 166, 176, *per* Lord Diplock, cited by both Lord Mackay and Lord Ackner in *Hotson* [1987] A.C. 750 at pp. 785 and 792 respectively. See also *per* Lord Reid in *Davies v Taylor* [1974] A.C. 207, 212–213. In *Malec v J.C. Hutton Proprietary Ltd* (1990) C.L.R. 638 the High Court of Australia held that the ordinary standard of proof, on the balance of probabilities, applied to the proof of historical facts, whereas for the proof of past hypothetical situations and future possibilities the court should assess the degree of probability that an event would have occurred or might occur and adjust the award of damages to reflect the degree of probability. See also *Poseidon Ltd v Adelaide Petroleum N.L.* (1994) 68 A.L.J.R. 313 (H.C. of Australia), on which see Lunney (1995) 15 L.S. 1.
[40] As, e.g., in *McWilliams v Sir William Arrol & Co Ltd* [1962] 1 W.L.R. 295; above para. 5–007.

balance of probability that he would have taken action to obtain the benefit or avoid the risk, and as with positive acts of misfeasance, if he does establish that, there is no discount of the damages simply because the balance is only just tipped in his favour.[41]

(3) Where, as in *Allied Maples* itself, the claimant's loss depends on the hypothetical action of an independent third party, either in addition to action by the claimant, or independently of it, the claimant does not have to prove on the balance of probability that the third party would have acted so as confer the benefit or avoid the risk to the claimant. The claimant succeeds if he shows that he had a substantial chance, as opposed to a speculative one, that he would have been successful in negotiating total or partial protection, the evaluation of the substantial chance being a question of quantification of damages. There was "no difference in principle between the chance of gaining a benefit and the chance of avoiding a liability." Nor does it depend upon the claimant proving that the chance of success was over 50 per cent. Provided the chance is substantial it may be less than 50 per cent. This is a two-stage process. First the court must be satisfied that the claimant has lost something of value. An action which was bound to fail or had no substantial prospect of success and was merely speculative was not something of value. It was only if the claim passed that test that the court should evaluate in percentage terms the full value of the lost claim.[42]

The effect of the Court of Appeal's approach in *Allied Maples* is that where causation depends upon what the claimant himself would have done in a "past" hypothetical situation the claimant has to establish this on the

5–061

---

[41] In *Bagley v North Hertfordshire Health Authority* (1986) 136 N.L.J. 1014 Simon Brown J. awarded damages for negligence which resulted in a stillbirth, and deducted 5% because even without negligence there was a 5% chance that the child would not have survived. This approach was disapproved by Lord Ackner in *Hotson* at [1987] A.C. 750, 793. See also *Cabral v Gupta* [1993] 1 W.W.R. 648; (1992) 13 C.C.L.T. (2d) 323 where the Manitoba Court of Appeal reversed the trial judge's deduction of 30% of the award of damages which had been made on the ground that there was a 30% risk that even if a foreign body had been detected and removed from the claimant's eye by the defendant ophthalmologist the claimant would nonetheless have had no useful vision in the eye. There was "simply no basis in law for such a deduction."

[42] *Hatswell v Goldbergs (A Firm)* [2001] EWCA Civ 2084; [2002] Lloyd's Rep. P.N. 359 at [48] *per* Sir Murray Stuart-Smith—where the claimant's action in negligence against a firm of solicitors in respect of allowing a claim for medical negligence to become statute barred under the Limitation Act 1980 was held to have no value, because the medical negligence claim was bound to fail. This rather begs the question, of course, of what the defendant solicitors were doing running a medical negligence claim that was bound to fail. On which see: *Mount v Barker Austin (A Firm)* [1998] P.N.L.R. 493, CA. For discussion of how the court should assess the lost chance of successful litigation see *Pearson v Sanders Witherspoon* [2000] P.N.L.R. 110 at 126–135, CA. And for consideration of how to approach the assessment where there are multiple contingencies, each with its own probability, see *Langford v Hebran* [2001] EWCA Civ 361; [2001] P.I.Q.R. Q160, applying *Doyle v Wallace* [1998] P.I.Q.R. Q146, CA.

balance of probabilities. This most commonly arises in the medical negligence context where the claimant states that if he had been informed about the risks of treatment, he would not have consented to undergo the treatment and would therefore have avoided the inherent risk that has materialised.[43] This is also the position where the question turns upon what the defendant would have done in a "past hypothetical situation." The claimant must prove that had the defendant not omitted to act, his hypothetical action would have avoided the damage of which the claimant complains, or that the defendant's hypothetical action would itself have been negligent.[44] But where proof of causation depends upon the independent act of a third party the claimant need only establish that there was a chance.[45] This could mean that in some cases causation depends upon proof of *both* what the claimant or defendant would have done in a hypothetical situation (on the balance of probabilities) and what an independent third party would have done (was there a substantial chance?). *Allied Maples*, of course, was a claim involving concurrent liability to a client in contract and tort, but it is now well-established that this approach should also be applied to cases based exclusively in tort.[46]

5–062   In *Smith v National Health Service Litigation Authority*[47] the defendants argued that *Allied Maples* did not apply to actions for medical negligence but, rejecting the argument, Andrew Smith J. said that *Allied Maples* laid down general principles, and there was no reason to adopt a different approach because the case involved a different category of professional negligence. His Lordship said that when considering the hypothetical actions of the defendant, it is assumed that he would have acted in accordance with his obligations to the claimant, but it is also assumed that he would not have gone beyond his duty. Thus, in *Smith* itself (which concerned allegations that the defendants had failed to examine the claimant at an appropriate time,

---

[43] See paras 6–146 *et seq.*

[44] See *Bolitho v City and Hackney Health Authority* [1998] A.C. 232; para. 5–009.

[45] *cf.* the approach of the Supreme Court of Canada in *Walker Estate v York-Finch General Hospital* (2001) 198 D.L.R. (4th) 193 where the defendants' negligence in screening blood for HIV consisted of asking potential blood donors general questions about their health rather than asking about symptom specific conditions and risks. The causation issue depended upon how the potential donors would have responded to these different questions. The Supreme Court held that the claimants did not have to prove "but for" causation; nor was the issue analysed as one of a loss of chance; rather the test was whether the negligence constituted a material contribution to the damage. See further para. 8–047.

[46] *Stovold v Barlows* [1996] 1 P.N.L.R. 91, CA; *First Interstate Bank of California v Cohen Arnold & Co* [1996] 1 P.N.L.R. 17, CA; *Doyle v Wallace* [1998] P.I.Q.R. Q146, CA—prospects of claimant qualifying and obtaining a job as a drama teacher fell within the third limb of *Allied Maples*, and therefore had to be assessed on the basis of the chance of her doing so, rather than the probability of her being successful. See also *Spring v Guardian Assurance plc* [1995] 2 A.C. 296, 327, a case involving a negligent employment reference about a former employee, where Lord Lowry said: "Once the duty of care is held to exist and the defendants' negligence is proved, the plaintiff only has to show that by reason of that negligence he has lost a reasonable chance of employment (which would have to be evaluated) and has thereby sustained loss . . . He does not have to prove that, but for the negligent reference, [the third party] *would* have employed him." (original emphasis). See further Stauch (1997) 17 O.J.L.S. 205, 217–224.

[47] [2001] Lloyd's Rep. Med. 90, 101.

and thereby had failed to diagnose a congenital problem with her hip which was amenable to treatment), the proper approach to the question of what damage would have resulted from an alleged omission to examine the patient "would be to assume a properly competent, but not an unusually thorough or able, examination and then to assess the chance that this would have resulted in the claimant not suffering the damage which in the event she has suffered."[48] In *Hardaker v Newcastle Health Authority & the Chief Constable of Northumbria*[49] Burnton J., commenting on *Smith*, made it clear that the loss of chance approach could only apply in the medical negligence context where causation depended upon the actions of a third party. Where causation does not depend on the actions of third parties then: "the claimant must establish what injury has been caused, or what aggravation to his injuries has been caused, on the balance of probabilities, by the defendants' negligence. If he succeeds on a probability of 51 per cent, he recovers 100 per cent of the appropriate compensation for his injury (or aggravation of his injuries); if he establishes only a 49 per cent probability, he recovers nothing."[50]

In *Gregg v Scott*[51] the Court of Appeal had to address the question of whether the decision of the House of Lords in *Fairchild v Glenhaven Funeral Services Ltd*[52] had undermined the reasoning in *Hotson*. The claimant developed non-Hodgkin's lymphoma which presented as a lump under his left arm. His general practitioner diagnosed a lipoma, a benign collection of fatty tissue, and negligently failed to refer him for specialist investigation. As a result of this, the claimant's treatment was delayed by about nine months, and this significantly reduced the claimant's chances of survival from 42 per cent to 25 per cent.[53] The trial judge, applying *Hotson*, dismissed the claim on the basis that for a person with his condition the chances of a cure were in any event less than 50 per cent, so that as a matter of past fact it was more probable than not that the claimant would have been in his present position even if treatment had started promptly. In other words, the evidence established, as a matter of past fact, that the probability was that the appellant would not have been cured. There were three issues in the Court of Appeal. First, could the claimant argue that, as a result of the delayed diagnosis, he had suffered physical damage so that causation had been established and the

5–063

---

[48] *ibid.* at 102.
[49] [2001] Lloyd's Rep. Med. 512.
[50] *ibid.* at [70]. "A chance of a better recovery, unless greater than 50%, and of a specified improvement, is not damage for these purposes", *ibid.* at [69].
[51] [2002] EWCA Civ 1471; [2003] Lloyd's Rep. Med. 105.
[52] [2002] UKHL 22; [2003] 1 A.C. 32; para. 5–027 *et seq.*
[53] The statistical evidence was problematic. Nonetheless, the Court of Appeal proceeded on the basis of a worked example provided by one of the expert witnesses. Taking a cohort of 100 patients receiving treatment at the stage at which the claimant should have been treated: "Of the 100, 55 would achieve complete remission as a result of chemotherapy. To these must be added four who could have achieved complete remission by some other route. Of the 59 who had achieved by whatever means complete remission, 40% would relapse, leaving 35 who would survive. Of those who relapsed and went on to high dose chemotherapy, six would survive. Of the remainder, only one would survive a further relapse. Thus, out of the cohort of 100, only 42 would be cured." *per* Latham L.J. [2002] EWCA Civ 1471 at [14].

assessment of his reduced life expectation was a matter of quantum rather than causation? Secondly, was the case covered by *Hotson*? Thirdly, if *Hotson* applied, did *Fairchild* permit the Court of Appeal to depart from it?

5–064   The first issue, as Latham L.J. acknowledged, was "an undisguised attempt to side step the decision of the House of Lords in *Hotson*." The claimant argued that the consequence of the delayed diagnosis and treatment was that the tumour had increased in size, causing pain and suffering, and the treatment was more drastic with greater side-effects than would have been the case if it had occurred sooner. This constituted physical damage which the defendant's negligence had clearly caused. His reduced life expectancy was a result of the increase in the size of the tumour, and therefore this was a case where causation was established. The issue for the judge was merely one of assessment of the loss, where it was accepted that the court could take into account lost chances (as where, for example, the court takes account of the claimant's future employment prospects when assessing future loss of earnings). Thus, the issue was one of quantification, not causation, and in assessing quantum the court could take into account the risk of a relapse in the claimant's cancer. This involved an assessment of the effect of the negligence on the claimant's expectation of life. Just as the court could take into account the risk or chance of epilepsy or osteoarthritis developing in the future when assessing damages arising out of physical injury, so the court should take account of the chance of a reduced life expectancy arising out of the physical damage caused by the growth of the tumour. This argument was expressly rejected by Mance L.J. (and implicitly rejected by Simon Brown L.J.). The diminution of the claimant's life expectancy was a distinct head of loss, *i.e.* a substantive head of claim, for which he could recover if he could show, as a matter of probability, that the defendants' negligence had caused it:

> "If damages cannot be recovered for that as such, it is because the appellant cannot show (as I have concluded that he would have to) that he was not already going to suffer that head of loss, independently of the negligence. It is not possible to change the starting point to the enlarged tumour and to ask the court to assess the prospects that this made any difference to the claimant's life expectancy."[54]

5–065   Latham L.J. considered the claimant's argument in the context of his discussion of the relevance of *Hotson*. His Lordship suggested that in *Hotson* the crucial issue was the "all or nothing nature of avascular necrosis." On the balance of probabilities either the claimant's fall had caused the avascular necrosis or it had not by the time he was seen at the hospital. On the judge's findings of fact the probability (75:25) was that the avascular necrosis had already set in and the hip was "doomed." The lymphoma in *Gregg v Scott* was different because it was agreed that it was "undoubtedly suscep-

---

[54] [2002] EWCA Civ 1471 at [89].

tible to treatment." The question was the extent to which the chances of treating it successfully had been reduced:

> "The evidence which the judge used in order to come to his conclusion was that chemotherapy would have given the appellant, but for the negligence, a better than even chance of complete remission with a less than 40% risk of relapse thereafter. Although statistically it may be shown that less than 50% of the cohort with such a tumour would be cured, a result which failed to reflect the fact that on one analysis of the statistics, it could be said that he would probably have been cured, does not seem just. Nor does it seem just when the only real certainty is that the negligence has reduced the appellant's chances of a cure."[55]

Thus, *Hotson* was not analogous because the avascular necrosis in that case was inevitable, whereas the tumour was treatable. That led Latham L.J. to consider whether the effect of the House of Lords' ruling in *Hotson* had been to rule out loss of chance claims in actions for medical negligence. Although Otton L.J. had stated in *Tahir v Haringey Health Authority*[56] that a claimant "cannot recover damages for the loss of a chance of a complete or better recovery", relying on *Hotson*, Latham L.J. said that this proposition should be approached with some care. Both Lord Bridge and Lord Mackay had expressly reserved the point in *Hotson*[57] and in the light of more recent authority it could not be said that *Hotson* ruled out claims based on the loss of a chance in medical negligence cases.[58] His Lordship placed some emphasis on the view that questions of causation are inevitably tied up with the nature of the defendant's duty.[59] Thus, the "just answer" to the question of whether claims for loss of a chance should be available was to consider the nature of the duty of care in question:

> "For it is in the context of that duty that the limits to the recoverable damages can most sensibly be defined. In the present case, the respondent's duty was to exercise such care as would reduce the risk of an undiagnosed cancer spreading and becoming less amenable to treatment. The spread of the cancer and the reduced chances of successful

---

55 *ibid.* at [25].
56 [1998] Lloyd's Rep. Med. 104, 108.
57 [1987] A.C. 750 at 782 and 786 respectively.
58 [2002] EWCA Civ 1471 at [39]. His Lordship appears to have been particularly persuaded by the judgment of Kirby J. in *Chappell v Hart* [1998] H.C.A. 55; (1998) 156 A.L.R. 517, a decision of the High Court of Australia on causation where a patient had not been informed about the risks of surgery, which was applied by the Court of Appeal in *Chester v Afshar* [2002] EWCA Civ 724; [2003] Q.B. 356; see para. 6–156.
59 Thus, in *Environment Agency v Empress Car Co (Abertillery) Ltd* [1999] 2 A.C. 22 at 31, Lord Hoffmann commented that: ". . . one cannot give a commonsense answer to a question of causation for the purpose of attributing responsibility under some rule without knowing the purpose and scope of the rule." See also *Chester v Afshar* [2002] EWCA Civ 724 where the Court of Appeal applied similar reasoning in the context of the doctor's duty concerning disclosure risks; and *Rahman v Arearose Ltd* [2001] Q.B. 351 at [33], all of which were cited by Latham L.J.

treatment were inextricably intertwined, unlike the plaintiffs pain and the avascular necrosis in *Hotson*. It follows that the appellant can only obtain a proper remedy for the breach of the duty in question if the law is prepared to recognise the lost chance as part of the damages to be awarded for the injury which he has undoubtedly sustained."[60]

The consequence, for Latham L.J., was that it was not necessary to consider whether loss of a chance could, of itself, constitute a head of damage. The cancer had spread as a result of the defendant's negligence, and that was all that was necessary to found his claim in negligence. At that point, the question for the court was simply a matter of quantifying the loss, including the loss attributable to the claimant's reduced prospects of successful treatment.[61]

5–066   The judgment of Latham L.J. in *Gregg v Scott* was a dissenting judgment. Simon Brown L.J., who coincidentally had been the trial judge in *Hotson* itself, could not see a relevant distinction between the two cases. There was no difference in principle, said his Lordship, between the physical effects of the delay in diagnosing the patient's condition in each of the two cases. In *Gregg v Scott* the delay caused the tumour to spread and become less treatable, giving rise to pain and the need for more intensive treatment. In *Hotson* it allowed the pressure caused by the bleeding of ruptured blood vessels into the joint to block whatever blood vessels had remained intact after the claimant's fall (thereby denying him the 25 per cent chance he had of avoiding avascular necrosis) and caused five days of pain for which he was entitled to compensation.[62] For Simon Brown L.J. that left the question of whether *Fairchild v Glenhaven Funeral Services Ltd* had changed the position. Although in *Hotson* the House of Lords had left open the theoretical possibility of a lost chance claim, the effect of the decision was to rule them out.[63] The more relaxed approach to proof of causation confirmed in *Fairchild* only applied in narrowly defined circumstances, and there was nothing in the speeches to suggest a more relaxed approach generally to proof of causation nor to invite any fresh attempt to advance the *Hotson* argument.[64] Thus, the claim in respect of the diminution of life expectancy in *Gregg v Scott* must fail. Despite reaching this conclusion it is clear that Simon Brown L.J. had reservations about the present state of the law. It was:

---

[60] [2002] EWCA Civ 1471 at [40].

[61] Latham L.J. recognised that there was a danger that permitting claims based on the loss of chance, if carried to extremes, might open the door to actions by individuals who had suffered no injury except for the statistical possibility of future damage, for example because they had been exposed to asbestos dust in the vicinity of an asbestos factory, without there being any evidence of adverse effects at the time of the claim. Accordingly, there were "good policy reasons for declining to extend the scope of the tort of negligence to speculative actions such as those, based on the loss of a chance simpliciter." *ibid.* at [39]. See also *per* Mance L.J. at [80] on this point.

[62] *ibid.* at [93].

[63] "It is surely implicit from the speeches as a whole that their Lordships would have rejected the loss of a chance argument had they confronted it squarely", *ibid.* at [97].

[64] *ibid.* at [100].

"less than wholly satisfactory to leave the House of Lords speeches in *Hotson* as the final word on the loss of a chance argument. If I consult a doctor about a specific condition and, through the doctor's negligence in diagnosis or treatment, reduce from 49 per cent to 5 per cent my chance of averting an adverse outcome, not everyone would think it 'just and reasonable' that my claim must inevitably fail on the issue of causation. Particularly that may be thought unfair given that in cases where the claimant can prove on the balance of probabilities that, but for the negligence, he would have escaped the adverse consequence of his condition, his damages will nevertheless be discounted to reflect the possibility that this was not so."[65]

Mance L.J. took yet a different approach. In his Lordship's view *Gregg v Scott* was "not directly covered by *Hotson*" because the outcome in the claimant's case (*i.e.* whether he was one of the patients who fell into the category of the 42 per cent who would have made a recovery with prompt treatment or one of the 58 per cent who would not) did not depend exclusively on past fact(s), nor did it depend entirely on hypothetical or future conduct. There were a range of factors which could influence the outcome, including the characteristics of the cancer, the claimant's own physical makeup and resistance, the medical treatment received, the patient's subsequent lifestyle, and his or others' reaction to the stress of the illness. So, although the case was closer to *Hotson* than to any of the categories (all addressing purely hypothetical or future conduct) identified in *Allied Maples Group Ltd v Simmons & Simmons*,[66] it could not be said to be covered by "any previously identified category." Moreover, for Mance L.J. it may be that there is a distinction between matters which are capable of being the subject of particular evidence (as occurred in *Hotson*) and matters which can only be addressed statistically. Thus, *Gregg v Scott* raised a question that was not directly covered by authority. In his Lordship's view, *Fairchild* did not assist the claimant. *Bonnington*, *McGhee* and *Fairchild* demonstrated that in some circumstances it is just to allow a claimant to recover in full, even though he cannot establish "but for" causation, and an important feature of these cases was the existence of an "evidential gap" caused by scientific uncertainty. This was one factor which distinguished the cases from *Gregg v Scott*, because the claimant's case was not that there was an evidential gap, but rather that it was possible to prove the relevant injury on the balance of probability, and that the risk of curtailed life expectancy could be measured in percentage terms as a consequence of that injury. They were all cases where there was an indisputable and already sustained injury or illness, and the defendant was held 100 per cent liable for the illness. Moreover, a doctor's negligent failure to diagnose a pre-existing disease differed significantly from the fault of an employer who negligently brought about conditions in which an employee

5–067

---

[65] *ibid.* at [101], citing *Smith v Leech Brain and Co Ltd* [1962] 2 Q.B. 405; *Judge v Huntingdon Health Authority* [1995] 6 Med. L.R. 223.
[66] [1995] 4 All E.R. 907; [1995] 1 W.L.R. 1602; para. 5–060.

was exposed to a noxious agent to which either the employer himself without negligence or some other employer by negligence had exposed the employee. The defendants in *Bonnington*, *McGhee* and *Fairchild* were, either individually or together with other negligent employers, the original source of the noxious agents which caused the claimants' injuries in those cases. This was not the case in *Gregg v Scott*.

5–068   Ultimately, Mance L.J. regarded the question of whether the claimant should recover for the diminution in life expectancy as one of policy. His Lordship noted that if the claimant in *Gregg v Scott* could claim for loss of a chance then a claimant in a case such as *Wilsher v Essex Area Health Authority*[67] ought to be able to recover damages apportioned to reflect the percentage prospect that the negligence played a part in causing the damage, rather than nothing at all. There was "no suggestion of this, even in argument, in any prior authority put before us, and it would represent a considerable increase in exposure."[68] For Mance L.J. the claimant's argument would open the gates to claims based on percentages, and create a new category of case which would be difficult to distinguish in practice from other common cases of medical negligence involving an omission. Therefore, as a matter of policy, in this type of case, the courts should stick to an approach based on proof on the balance of probabilities.[69]

5–069   One issue that was not addressed by the judgments in *Gregg v Scott* is precisely what it is that the claimant has to show "as a matter of probability" in a case involving reduced life expectancy. Does he have to demonstrate that the defendant's negligence caused him to lose more than 50 per cent of his chance of a cure, so that if, for example, his prospects of a cure were 80 per cent, but due to the delay they are now only 25 per cent he has lost 55 per cent overall? Or does he merely have to prove that as a result of the defendant's negligence he has moved from the category of patients who would probably have survived (*e.g.* he had, say, a 60 per cent chance of survival with prompt treatment) into the category of patients who will probably not survive (say, he now has only a 40 per cent chance of survival)? Given that the law treats questions of past fact as proved as a certainty once the claim-

---

[67] [1988] A.C. 1074; para. 5–026.

[68] [2002] EWCA Civ 1471 at [81]. It is worth bearing in mind, however, that the fact that the parties in previous cases have not sought to argue their case in a particular way does not, in itself, demonstrate that an argument is wrong. In all the cases concerned with "material contribution to the damage" that had followed *Bonnington Castings Ltd v Wardlaw* [1956] A.C. 613 it had not been argued that the defendant was only responsible for that proportion of the damage to which he had materially contributed, until the decision of the Court of Appeal in *Holtby v Brigham & Cowan (Hull) Ltd* [2000] 3 All E.R. 421, para. 5–042.

[69] *ibid.* at [85]. Contrast *Gavalas v Singh* [2001] V.S.C.A. 23; (2001) 3 V.R. 404, where the Victoria Court of Appeal held that a claimant who had lost the chance of making a full recovery because of a negligent delay in diagnosing a brain tumour was entitled to damages for future loss of earnings and the additional cost future of medical treatment attributable to that lost chance. Callaway J.A. said, at p. 409, that: "No advanced system of law could now deny recovery where late diagnosis, in breach of duty to the patient, appreciably reduces the prospects of success of an operation." Similarly, Smith A.J.A. said, at p. 417, that: "It is difficult to see any reason in principle why a plaintiff should not be compensated in appropriate circumstances for a lost opportunity if it flows from the alleged negligence."

ant establishes that they were more probable than not,[70] in the second situation it is probable, and therefore treated as a certainty, that the patient would have survived. The negligence has caused him to move into the category of patients who will probably not survive, and therefore as a matter of past fact it has caused a diminution in his life expectancy, not as a matter of lost chances but as a matter of probability. Of course, in assessing the value of that diminution in life expectancy as a matter of quantum, account will be taken of the fact that it was already an impaired life expectancy (there was a 40 per cent chance that he would have died in any event). But this does not affect the question of whether the claimant has proved causation. Although this example is based on a reduction of the claimant's chances by 20 per cent (60 per cent down to 40 per cent), there is no logical reason why much smaller reductions could not be treated in the same way, even as little as two per cent (51 per cent down to 49 per cent). This example illustrates the arbitrary effects of the rule excluding claims based on loss of chance. On the medical evidence, the claimant in *Gregg v Scott* had his chances of survival reduced by 17 per cent and yet he recovered nothing for that loss, whereas a claimant who, fortuitously, starts out with a marginally better than 50 per cent chance of successful treatment may recover damages, applying the balance of probabilities approach, for a significantly smaller reduction in chances. Moreover, the contrast with the claimants in *Fairchild*, who could not prove that the particular defendants' negligence had caused them any injury whatsoever, but who recovered for the full extent of their harm, is stark.[71]

A claim based on loss of a chance is not appropriate in the context of an action in respect of a defective product under section 3 of the Consumer Protection Act 1987. In *A v The National Blood Authority*[72] Burton J. held that the Act, and the European Union Product Liability Directive 1985 (Council Directive (EEC) 85/374) upon which the Act is based, imposes strict liability. The question is whether the product was defective, and if so what damage was caused by that defect. It is not what damage was caused by any conduct, whether wrongful or otherwise, or breach of duty. Questions of what would or might have happened in hypothetical circumstances were simply not relevant.

5–070

Where it is possible to identify something specific that the claimant has lost as a result of a diagnostic error, rather than a "mere" statistical chance, then the claimant is entitled to compensation for that loss. Thus, in *Sutton v Population Services Family Planning Programme Ltd*[73] McCowan J.

5–071

---

[70] *Mallett v McMonagle* [1970] A.C. 166, 176, *per* Lord Diplock; *Davies v Taylor* [1974] A.C. 207, 212–213, *per* Lord Reid.

[71] Stapleton (2002) 10 Torts L.J. 276, 286 suggests that the claimants in *McGhee* and *Fairchild* recovered for their full loss by default, because the litigants (and the courts) ignored the associated possibility of apportionment. In *Gregg v Scott* the Court of Appeal granted the claimant permission, unusually, to appeal to the House of Lords.

[72] [2001] 3 All E.R. 289 at [176]-[180].

[73] *The Times*, November 7, 1981. See also *Judge v Huntingdon Health Authority* [1995] 6 Med. L.R. 223 and *Taylor v West Kent Health Authority* [1997] 8 Med. L.R. 251 on the loss attributable to delay in diagnosing breast cancer.

awarded damages for the premature onset of menopause and four "lost years" to a patient whose cancer was not detected early enough because of the negligence of a nurse. Early detection would not have prevented a recurrence of the cancer because it was of high grade malignancy, but it would have delayed the recurrence by four years, and the claimant would have led a normal life for four more years. There was no award for pain and suffering or for the medical treatment required since the claimant would have had to face the same operations and treatment in any event, but four years later.[74] Similarly, in *Laferrière v Lawson*,[75] although the claimant was unable to claim for loss of a chance of a better outcome when the defendant negligently failed to inform her that she had breast cancer or to make any arrangements for appropriate follow-up, she was entitled to compensation for the psychological suffering attributable to her subsequent belief that things might have been different if she had known about her illness earlier and had been treated sooner, which would have exacerbated the pain she experienced as a result of the advance of the disease. She was also entitled to compensation for the fact that earlier treatment would have improved her quality of life in the period during which she survived, although it would not have prevented her death.[76]

2. CAUSATION IN LAW

5–072   The "but for" test excludes those factors which cannot be said to have been *a* cause of the damage, but there may be more than one causal element that satisfies the "but for" test, in which case the court may have to choose which of two or more operative causes are to be treated as the cause *in law* of the claimant's damage. The question is whether the defendant's breach of duty was *the* cause, for the purpose of attributing legal responsibility. The court is not required to find that a single event was the sole legal cause, although there is a tendency for the courts to seek to identify a single cause, at least where the claimant has not been at fault (in which case responsibility will be apportioned under the Law Reform (Contributory Negligence) Act 1945). In practice this can be something of a fiction, and it is important to appre-

---

[74] See also *Gregg v Scott* [2002] EWCA Civ 1471; [2003] Lloyd's Rep. Med. 105 at [60] *per* Mance L.J.: "quite apart from the respondent's negligence, the appellant had cancer, which at least as a matter of statistical probability meant that he was anyway going to suffer a curtailed life, so that there cannot be a simple attribution, to the respondent's negligence, of all the devastating effects on him of his cancer. The extra pain, suffering and distress resulting from the negligence should however be recoverable in damages."

[75] (1991) 78 D.L.R. (4th) 609 (S.C.C.).

[76] See also *Pittman Estate v Bain* (1994) 112 D.L.R. (4th) 257 (Ont. Ct., Gen. Div.), para. 4–040, where the deceased was not informed that a blood transfusion that he had received some years previously had been contaminated with HIV. The transfusion had not been given negligently, but the failure to inform him of his HIV status was negligent. Had he known of his HIV status his death from AIDS could have been delayed. The damage was held to consist of the pain and suffering from his three week terminal illness, and the loss of two years life expectancy.

ciate that there is an element of judicial policy at work in attributing causal connections.

"Common sense" is usually said to be the starting point in this process,[77] and judicial common sense is often filtered through a string of metaphors: was the "chain of causation" broken; was the causal link too remote; was the tort a "proximate" or "direct" or "substantial" or "effective" cause, the *causa causans* not merely the *causa sine qua non*? The use of such phrases should not obscure the fact that the court must make a choice, which may be conditioned by common usages of speech and may have only a tenuous connection with scientific notions of logic. As Lord Wright commented in *Liesbosch Dredger v S.S. Edison*: "In the varied web of affairs, the law must extract some consequences as relevant, not perhaps on grounds of pure logic but simply for practical reasons."[78] In *Rahman v Arearose Ltd*[79] Laws L.J. commented that:

5–073

> "Once it is recognised that the first principle is that every tortfeasor should compensate the injured claimant in respect of that loss and damage for which he should justly be held responsible, the metaphysics of causation can be kept in their proper place: of themselves they offered in any event no hope of a solution of the problems which confront the courts in this and other areas. The law has dug no deeper in the philosophical thickets of causation than to distinguish between a *causa sine qua non* and a *causa causans*. The latter is an empty tautology. The former proves everything, and therefore nothing: if A kills B by stabbing him, the birth of either of them 30 years before is as much a *causa sine qua non* of the death as is the wielding of the knife. So the law makes appeal to the notion of a proximate cause; but how proximate does it have to be? As a concept, it tells one nothing. So in all these cases the real question is, what is the damage for which the defendant under consideration should be held responsible."

(1) Successive sufficient causes

Where there are two independent events, each of which were sufficient to have caused the damage sustained by the claimant, the determination of causal responsibility depends on the nature of the events and the order in which they occurred. Thus, where both events are tortious responsibility will be attributed to the tort which occurred first in time.[80] In *Baker v*

5–074

---

[77] *Cork v Kirby MacLean Ltd* [1952] 2 All E.R. 402, 407; *Yorkshire Dale Steamship Co Ltd v Minister of War Transport* [1942] A.C. 691, 706.

[78] [1933] A.C. 449, 460. See also *Abbott v Kasza and Ace Construction Co* [1976] 4 W.W.R. 20, 28 (Alta. C.A.).

[79] [2001] Q.B. 351 at [32]-[33].

[80] *Performance Cars Ltd v Abraham* [1962] 1 Q.B. 33—defendant negligently damaged a motor vehicle which had previously been damaged by the negligence of another motorist; defendant held not liable for the cost of a respray because, having damaged an already damaged car, his negligence was not the cause of the loss.

Willoughby,[81] for example, the claimant sustained an injury to his leg as a result of the defendant's negligence. The claimant was subsequently shot in the same leg during an armed robbery at his place of work, resulting in the amputation of the leg. The defendant argued that the supervening amputation had submerged or obliterated the original injury, and that he should only have to compensate the claimant for the losses up to the date of the shooting. The House of Lords held that the defendant remained responsible for the initial disability even after the amputation. The person who shot the claimant would only have been liable for the *additional* loss that had been inflicted by the shooting, not the whole disability, and so the defendant's argument would have resulted in the claimant being undercompensated because he would have received no compensation at all for the initial disability caused by the defendant after the date of the amputation. It was wrong, said their Lordships, that the claimant should fall between two tortfeasors, receiving less in damages than he would have received had there been no interval between the torts.[82]

5–075   On the other hand, where the supervening event is not tortious the defendant's responsibility for the injury ends when the event occurs. In *Jobling v Associated Dairies Ltd*[83] the claimant suffered a back injury as a result of his employers' negligence, reducing his earning capacity by 50 per cent. Three years later he developed a disease, unconnected with the accident, which rendered him wholly unfit for work. The House of Lords held that the employers were liable for the claimant's reduced earning capacity only for the three year period. The supervening disease was treated as the sole cause of the claimant's inability to work, although the result was justified, not on the basis of causation, but on the ground of "vicissitudes." When assessing damages for future loss of earnings the award will be discounted for the possibility that other events might have reduced the claimant's earning capacity or working life, even if the tort had not occurred. A subsequent illness is one

---

[81] [1970] A.C. 467.

[82] An argument accepted as correct by the High Court of Australia in *Wynn v NSW Insurance Ministerial Corporation* (1995) 133 A.L.R. 154, 163; *cf. Griffiths v Commonwealth* (1985) 72 F.L.R. 260, 273 applying the preferred solution of the Court of appeal in *Baker v Willoughby* [1969] 2 W.L.R. 489 that the second tortfeasor is liable for the whole loss, having caused the claimant to "lose" his right of action against the original wrongdoer; Hudson (1987) 38 N.I.L.Q. 190–193. See further *Singh v Aitken* [1998] P.I.Q.R. Q37 (County Court) where S died of a heart attack, and it was accepted that he would have survived but for the defendants' negligent misdiagnosis of his heart condition. At the time of his death, S had an unanswerable claim for £120,000 against the Motor Insurer's Bureau in respect a previous accident, but following his death that claim was properly compromised for £20,000. S's dependants brought an action against the defendants under the Fatal Accidents Act 1976 claiming their loss of dependency (on the basis of a 75% dependency claim) in respect of the difference between the original value of the claim against the MIB and the compromise sum. The case was dealt with on the basis that it involved only the assessment of quantum, not a question of causation. It was held that the dependants were entitled to the £75,000 which represented their dependency from the sum that would have been obtained from the MIB by S, but for his death. The defendants had to take S as they found him, namely a man with an unanswerable claim to a large sum of money which was forfeit as a result of their negligence.

[83] [1982] A.C. 794.

of these "vicissitudes of life," and, applying the principle that the court will not speculate about future events when the facts are known, the illness must be taken into account. Their Lordships were critical of the decision in *Baker v Willoughby*, while recognising that a different approach could apply where the supervening event consisted of a tort.[84] Lord Keith rationalised the distinction by suggesting that a supervening tort might not be regarded as one of the ordinary vicissitudes of life, and so would not be taken into account, although Lord Wilberforce conceded that there was no logical justification.

Baker v Willoughby only applies where there are actually two tortious   5–076
events. In *Heil v Rankin*[85] the Court of Appeal held that when assessing damages for future loss of earnings, where there was a risk that the claimant might have become the victim of a tort in the future which would have caused him to give up work, that risk should be taken into account, thereby reducing the loss of future earnings claim, as would occur with the risk of non-tortious events. The claimant relied on *Baker v Willoughby* on the basis that if an actual second tort did not have the effect of removing the first tortfeasor's liability to compensate the claimant, then *a fortiori* an hypothetical second tortious event that had not actually occurred should not reduce the level of compensation. If there was no discount for the reality there should be no discount for a chance. The Court of Appeal rejected this argument, applying the vicissitudes approach, on the ground that otherwise the claimant was likely to be overcompensated. If the claimant had to be compensated on the basis that he would have continued in employment to retirement, but it was likely that future tortious acts would have caused him to give up his employment, then it was "self-evident" that he was being overcompensated.

(2) Intervening Acts

Where the act of another person, without which the damage would not   5–077
have occurred, intervenes between the defendant's negligence and the claimant's damage, the court must decide whether the defendant is responsible or whether the intervening act constituted a *novus actus interveniens*. If the latter, then the act is regarded as having broken the causal connection between the negligence and the damage. This too is treated as a matter of common sense in which metaphor abounds.[86]

There are two broad approaches to this problem. The first asks whether   5–078
the act was reasonable in the circumstances, which refers to the voluntariness

---

[84] See also *Carslogie Steamship Co Ltd v Royal Norwegian Government* [1952] A.C. 292 attributing the loss caused by a ship being laid up for repairs following a collision to the need to repair damage caused by a subsequent storm. This principle also applies to claims brought in contract: *Beoco Ltd v Alfa Laval Co Ltd* [1995] Q.B. 137, 151, CA.

[85] [2001] P.I.Q.R. Q16.

[86] So the question may be whether the intervening event was such as to "isolate" or "insulate" or "eclipse" the defendant's negligence, or whether it was merely a "conduit pipe" or "part of a transmission gear set in motion by" the defendant: *Weld-Blundell v Stephens* [1920] A.C. 956, 986, *per* Lord Sumner; see also *The Oropesa* [1943] P. 32, 39, *per* Lord Wright.

of the act, not whether it was careless. The more voluntary the act the less reasonable it is, and therefore the more likely to be regarded as a *novus actus*, but even deliberate conduct may be "involuntary" in this sense, where, for example, a person is forced to make some conscious response to a situation brought about by the defendant's negligence.[87] The second approach looks to the foreseeability of the intervention. On this view, even where the intervening act is unreasonable it will not necessarily be treated as breaking the chain of causation. Accordingly, a negligent intervention, negligent medical treatment for example, will not automatically exculpate the original tortfeasor if it is a foreseeable consequence of the defendant's initial negligence.

(a) By third parties

5–079   Where there are two successive acts of medical negligence it may be a nice question whether the second incidence of negligence breaks the chain of causation between the first error and the patient's injury. As a general rule, a subsequent act of negligence will normally constitute an intervening act.[88] In *Hogan v Bentinck West Hartley Collieries Ltd*[89] the House of Lords held that an operation which had been unreasonably recommended by a doctor broke the chain of causation between the claimant's initial injury sustained at work and the amputation of his thumb. Lord Normand said that:

> "I start from the proposition, which seems to me to be axiomatic, that if a surgeon, by lack of skill or failure in reasonable care, causes additional injury or aggravates an existing injury and so renders himself liable in damages, the reasonable conclusion must be that his intervention is a new cause and that the additional injury or the aggravation of the existing injury should be attributed to it and not to the original accident. On the other hand, an operation prudently advised and skilfully and carefully carried out should not be treated as a new cause, whatever its consequences may be."[90]

5–080   The latter part of Lord Normand's statement makes it clear that where appropriate medical treatment has been properly carried out, the original tortfeasor will be responsible for any complications arising out of the treatment.[91]

---

[87] *The Oropesa* [1943] P. 32; *Emeh v Kensington and Chelsea Area Health Authority* [1985] Q.B. 1012, below, para. 5–090.

[88] Although this will not always be the case: see *Rouse v Squires* [1973] 1 Q.B. 889; and the discussion of this problem in *Knightley v Johns* [1982] 1 All E.R. 851, below, para. 5–083. Neither of these cases involved medical negligence.

[89] [1949] 1 All E.R. 588.

[90] *ibid.* at p. 596.

[91] See *Robinson v Post Office* [1974] 2 All E.R. 737, para. 5–112, below; *cf.* the South African case of *Alston v Marine & Trade Insurance Co Ltd* 1964 (4) S.A. 112—claimant suffered a stroke as a result of an interaction between the drug he was prescribed for injuries caused by the defendant's negligence and cheese which he ate. In the light of the medical knowledge at the time it was not unreasonable to eat cheese. Nonetheless, it was held that eating the cheese constituted a *novus actus interveniens*, even though the claimant acted reasonably.

This result can be justified, if justification were considered necessary, on the basis that: (i) the intervention was reasonable, arising in the ordinary course of events, and so did not break the chain of causation; or (ii) the unforeseeable consequences of a foreseeable and reasonable intervention are within the risk created by the defendant's negligence; or (iii) some complication from medical treatment is foreseeable and it is not necessary to foresee the precise complication which occurred.

The first part of Lord Normand's statement, on the other hand, suggests that negligence in the performance of corrective treatment will always break the chain of causation. This was never an absolute rule,[92] and in any event can no longer be regarded as correct. Where the intervening event consists of negligent medical treatment it will require a gross act of negligence by the medical staff, amounting to a completely inappropriate response to the patient's condition, to break the causal link.[93] In *Webb v Barclays Bank plc*[94] the Court of Appeal held that there is no rule that where a claimant suffers personal injury due to a defendant's negligence that the defendant's liability ends as a result of negligence by a doctor who treats the original injury but whose negligence makes the claimant's condition worse. Mrs Webb injured an already vulnerable knee in a fall at work for which her employers were found responsible. Subsequently, the surgeon treating her advised Mrs Webb to have an above the knee amputation of her leg, advice which she accepted. That advice was negligent. Her employers settled her claim in full and then brought contribution proceedings against the hospital. The issue was whether the employers' liability in respect of the injuries to the leg included some part of the loss after the amputation, or whether the surgeon's negligent advice broke the causal link between the employers' negligence and the amputation. The Court of Appeal held that the subsequent negligence of a surgeon "did not eclipse the original wrongdoing." The employers were held liable for all the damage attributable to the fall, and 25 per cent of the damage attributable to the amputation. Thus, if the claimant acts reasonably in seeking or accepting treatment, negligence in carrying out the treatment is not necessarily a *novus actus interveniens* relieving the first tortfeasor from liability for the claimant's subsequent condition. The original injury can be regarded as carrying some risk that medical treatment might be negligently given.[95]

5–081

---

[92] See, *e.g.*, the comments of Lord du Parcq in *Grant v Sun Shipping Co Ltd* [1948] A.C. 549, 563: "If the negligence or breach of duty of one person is the cause of injury to another, the wrongdoer cannot in all circumstances escape liability by proving that, though he was to blame, yet but for the negligence of a third person the injured man would not have suffered the damage of which he complains. There is abundant authority for the proposition that the mere fact that a subsequent act of negligence has been the immediate cause of disaster does not exonerate the original offender."

[93] *Webb v Barclays Bank plc and Portsmouth Hospitals NHS Trust* [2001] EWCA Civ 1141; [2002] P.I.Q.R. P61; [2001] Lloyd's Rep. Med. 500 at [55], citing *Clerk & Lindsell on Torts*, 18th ed., 2000, para. 2–55.

[94] *ibid.*

[95] Applying a dictum from *Mahoney v Kruschick (Demolitions) Pty Ltd* (1985) 156 C.L.R. 522, High Court of Australia. In *Price v Milawski* (1977) 82 D.L.R. (3d) 130 (Ont. C.A.) a doctor who negligently failed to identify a fracture of the patient's ankle was held liable for

5–082   In *Rahman v Arearose Ltd*[96] the claimant was seriously assaulted by two black youths, causing an injury to his right eye. His employers were negligent in failing to take reasonable care to reduce the risk of such assaults. Subsequently, as a result of the negligence of a surgeon, he was rendered blind in the right eye. In addition to the physical injuries, the claimant developed severe psychiatric consequences, including post traumatic stress disorder, a severe depressive disorder, a specific phobia of Afro-Caribbean people, and enduring personality change. The evidence indicated that the psychiatric reaction was partly due to the assault and partly due to the loss of his eye: (i) the post traumatic stress disorder was due to the loss of the eye; (ii) the phobia was due to the assault and subsequent events; and (iii) the personality change was due to the synergistic interaction between the depression and the post traumatic stress disorder. The Court of Appeal held that a second act of negligence did not necessarily break the causal link between an initial act of negligence and the subsequent damage. Laws L.J. commented that:

> "it does not seem to me to be established as a rule of law that later negligence always extinguishes the causative potency of an earlier tort. Nor should it be. The law is that every tortfeasor should compensate the injured claimant in respect of that loss and damage for which he should justly be held responsible. To make that principle good, it is important that the elusive conception of causation should not be frozen into constricting rules." [97]

(n.95 contd.) the subsequent negligence of another doctor in the treatment of the patient's condition. It was reasonably foreseeable that once the information generated by the defendant's negligent error got into the hospital records, other doctors subsequently treating the claimant might well rely on the accuracy of that information, *i.e.* that the X-ray showed no fracture of the ankle. It was also foreseeable that some doctor might do so without checking, even though to do so in the circumstances might itself be a negligent act. It was held that on the particular facts this was a risk that a reasonable doctor would not have brushed aside as far-fetched. See also *Reeves v Carthy* [1984] I.R. 348 (Supreme Court of Ireland). Where the defendant's wrongful conduct has generated the very risk of injury resulting from the negligence of another person (whether the claimant or a third party) and that injury occurred in the ordinary course of things, the negligence of the claimant or a third party should not be regarded as a superseding cause: *March v E. & M.H. Stramare Pty Ltd* (1991) 99 A.L.R. 423 (H.C. of Australia); Mullany (1992) 12 O.J.L.S. 431. See also the comment of McHugh J. in *Bennett v Minister of Community Welfare* (1991) 107 A.L.R. 617, 632 (H.C. of Australia) (not a medical negligence case): "If a doctor has negligently omitted to diagnose a condition which leads to a patient's death, it is no answer to a claim of actionable negligence that subsequently another doctor negligently failed to diagnose the condition at a time when its ultimate consequence could have been avoided. Each negligent omission was a separate and independent cause of the patient's death." *cf. Mitchell v Rahman* (2002) 209 D.L.R. (4th) 621 (Man. C.A.) where it was held that negligent misdiagnosis of a dislocated shoulder following a road traffic accident broke the causal link between the accident and the permanent disability which the claimant developed, applying Lord Normand's dictum in *Hogan v Bentinck West Hartley Collieries Ltd* [1949] 1 All E.R. 588, 596, cited above at para. 5–079.

[96] [2001] Q.B. 351.
[97] *ibid.* at [29].

The sensible conclusion was that, "while the second defendants obviously (and exclusively) caused the right-eye blindness, thereafter each tort had its part to play in the claimant's suffering."[98]

In *Knightley v Johns*[99] the Court of Appeal said that the question was   5–083
whether the whole sequence of events was a natural and probable consequence of the defendant's negligence, and whether it was reasonably foreseeable, not foreseeable as a mere possibility.[1] In answering this question it was helpful, but not decisive, to consider which events were deliberate choices to do positive acts and which were mere omissions, which acts and omissions were innocent mistakes or miscalculations and which were negligent. Thus:

> "Negligent conduct is more likely to break the chain of causation than conduct which is not; positive acts will more easily constitute new causes than inaction. Mistakes and mischances are to be expected when human beings, however well trained, have to cope with a crisis; What exactly they will be cannot be predicted, but if those which occur are natural the wrongdoer cannot, I think, escape responsibility for them and their consequences simply by calling them improbable or unforeseeable. He must accept the risk of some unexpected mischances."[2]

In deciding which mischances amount to intervening events the court should apply "common sense rather than logic on the facts and circumstances of each case." In *Prendergast v Sam & Dee Ltd*,[3] for example, the Court of Appeal concluded that a pharmacist's negligence in misreading a doctor's prescription, and consequently supplying a patient with the wrong drug, did not break the chain of causation from the doctor's initial negligence in writing an illegible prescription. It was reasonably foreseeable that the prescription could be misread.

---

[98] *ibid.* at [34]. But for criticism of the court's approach in *Rahman v Arearose Ltd* see Weir [2001] C.L.J. 237.

[99] [1982] 1 All E.R. 851, 865.

[1] See also *per* Lord Reid in *Home Office v Dorset Yacht Co Ltd* [1970] A.C. 1004, 1030: "Where human action forms one of the links between the original wrongdoing of the defendant and the loss suffered by the plaintiff, that action must at least have been something very likely to happen if it is not to be regarded as *novus actus interveniens* breaking the chain of causation."

[2] [1982] 1 All E.R. 851, 865, *per* Stephenson L.J. The difficulty in making categorical statements about the effect of intervening negligence is illustrated by the different results reached by the Court of Appeal in *Knightley v Johns* and *Rouse v Squires* [1973] 1 Q.B. 889, on essentially similar facts. On the other hand, where the intervening conduct can be characterised as reckless, as opposed to merely negligent, it is far more likely to be treated as a *novus actus interveniens*: *Wright v Lodge* [1993] 4 All E.R. 299; [1993] P.I.Q.R. P31, CA; Jones (1994) 2 Tort L. Rev. 133. See further the comments of Lord Hobhouse in *Reeves v Commissioner of Police for the Metropolis* [2000] 1 A.C. 360, 392: "Human conduct, which is not entirely reasonable, for example, where it is itself careless, but is within the range of human conduct that is foreseeable and normally contemplated as not unlikely, may add a further cause of the relevant subsequent event but would not normally mean that an earlier relevant event ceased also to be a cause of that later event. Careless conduct may ordinarily be regarded as being within the range of normal human conduct when reckless conduct ordinarily would not."

[3] [1989] 1 Med. L.R. 36, para. 4–055.

5–084   Where the subsequent negligence results in damage that cannot be said to be causally linked to the initial negligence, the first tortfeasor is not responsible, not because the later conduct intervened, but because the damage fails to satisfy the "but for" test. In *Yepremian v Scarborough General Hospital*,[4] for example, doctor G was negligent in failing to diagnose the patient's diabetes. The claimant's subsequent cardiac arrest was caused by the negligent treatment given to the patient by another doctor, R, after the diabetes had been diagnosed. Thus, G's negligence was not a cause in fact of the cardiac arrest. If, however, said the Ontario Court of Appeal, the cardiac arrest had been part of the natural consequences of untreated diabetes, or even of ineffectively treated diabetes, then the subsequent negligence of R would not have prevented G's negligence from being regarded as a cause of the damage. G could not rely on R's failure to rescue the claimant from the consequences of G's negligence.

5–085   This latter point was the basis of the decision in *Thompson v Toorenburgh*[5] where it was held that the failure of a doctor to provide an *actus interveniens* which would have saved the accident victim's life is not the same as committing an *actus interveniens* that caused her death. The defendant motorist who caused the deceased's initial injuries was liable, notwithstanding medical "mistreatment."[6] Robertson J.A. said that:

> "Mrs. Thompson would almost certainly have recovered if proper treatment had been applied speedily; the doctors failed to apply that treatment and so failed to save her life, but they did not cause her death. They failed to provide an *actus interveniens* that would have saved her life, but that is not the same as committing an *actus interveniens* that caused her death."[7]

5–086   This approach to negligent omissions might be followed in this country.[8] In *Muirhead v Industrial Tank Specialities Ltd*[9] Goff L.J. suggested that a negligent failure by a third party to prevent damage caused by the negligence of the defendant would not exonerate the defendant. The defendant could escape responsibility "only where the act or omission of another was of such a nature that it constituted a wholly independent cause of the damage, *i.e.* a *novus actus interveniens*."[10] On this view it might be argued that a patient's

---

[4] (1980) 110 D.L.R. (3d) 513 (Ont. C.A.); the action was settled prior to the appeal hearing before the Supreme Court of Canada: (1981) D.L.R. (3d) 341.

[5] (1973) 50 D.L.R. (3d) 717 (B.C.C.A.).

[6] The court carefully avoided calling the medical treatment "negligent," although on the facts it is difficult to see how the treatment could not have been negligent.

[7] (1973) 50 D.L.R. (3d) 717, 721.

[8] In *Panther v Wharton* (2001, QBD; unreported) Peter Heppel Q.C. specifically agreed with the statement of Robertson J.A. in *Thompson v Toorenburgh*, holding that the subsequent negligence of a consultant physician (in failing to diagnose the claimant's vascular problem) did not break the causal link between the negligence of a general practitioner in failing to refer to the claimant for investigation of her physical symptoms and the resulting damage to her limbs.

[9] [1986] Q.B. 507, 533.

[10] *ibid.* This rather begs the question of which acts or omissions are of such a nature that they constitute a wholly independent cause.

refusal to accept medical treatment on, say, religious grounds does not break the chain of causation either, since, at worst, it represents an "unreasonable" (negligent) failure to intervene to prevent the damage caused by the defendant.[11]

On the other hand, it seems strange to attach significance to the fact that the doctor's negligence consists of an omission to give life-saving treatment, and so amounts to a failure to provide an *actus interveniens* rather than constituting a *novus actus interveniens*, when it is patently clear that if the doctor were sued for negligence he would be held responsible for the death, at least where, on the balance of probabilities the evidence indicates that the patient's life would have been saved by prompt treatment.[12] Where the doctor has a duty of care to treat the patient the courts have no difficulty in regarding an omission to treat as having causative effect. It is submitted that the better approach in this type of case is to treat both the first tort and the subsequent negligently performed medical treatment as causative of the patient's death, and to apportion liability accordingly. Thus, in *Commonwealth of Australia v Martin*[13] M received injuries in a road traffic accident which were such that death was inevitable without proper corrective surgery. The medical treatment was performed negligently and he died four days later. It was held that both the negligent motorist and the negligent doctor had caused the death, and it was not necessary to show that the doctor's negligence constituted a *novus actus interveniens* before he could be held responsible.

5–087

Where a doctor's negligence has increased the susceptibility of the patient to sustaining further injury, he cannot avoid responsibility for a subsequent injury within the risk created by his negligence, even though there are other later causes which also caused or materially contributed to that injury.[14]

5–088

(b) By the claimant

Medical treatment often depends upon the co-operation of the patient. Where the patient fails to co-operate this may amount to contributory negligence.[15] In an extreme case the patient's conduct may be sufficient to break the chain of causation.[16] The test for an intervening act by the claimant is

5–089

---

[11] See para. 5–094, below.

[12] *cf. Barnett v Chelsea and Kensington Hospital Management Committee* [1968] 1 All E.R. 1068, para. 5–004, above.

[13] (1985) 59 A.L.R. 439 (Fed. Ct. of Australia).

[14] *Powell v Guttman* (1978) 89 D.L.R. (3d) 180 (Man. C.A), para. 5–046, above, where the defendant was held liable for a fracture of the patient's leg which occurred in the course of a later operation performed by another doctor. The second doctor was found not to have been negligent.

[15] See para. 4–137 *et seq.*

[16] *Venner v North East Essex Area Health Authority*, The Times, February 21, 1987; *Murrin v Janes* [1949] 4 D.L.R. 403, 406 (Newfoundland S.C.)—claimant who delayed seeing a doctor to deal with excessive bleeding following extraction of his teeth held to be the sole cause of his misfortune. In *Stevens v Bermondsey and Southwark Group Hospital Management Committee* (1963) 107 S.J. 478 the claimant claimed that a doctor's failure to diagnose the seriousness of his condition following a road traffic accident led to him settling

normally whether he acted reasonably,[17] although it would be open to the court to conclude that a claimant who acted unreasonably was guilty of contributory negligence, and apportion responsibility between the claimant and the defendant.[18] "Unreasonableness" is also used to indicate an element of voluntary conduct by the claimant, and so where the claimant's capacity for rational judgment has been affected this may remove the necessary voluntary element for an *actus interveniens*. It is on this basis that even suicide, which objectively would normally be regarded as an unreasonable act, will not necessarily amount to a *novus actus interveniens*.[19] At one time it was arguable that the issue turned upon whether at the time of the suicide the deceased was suffering from a disabling mental illness as a result of the injuries inflicted by the defendant.[20] But where the defendant was under a duty to exercise reasonable care to prevent the very event that occurred he cannot complain that the intervention broke the causal link, since that would render the duty ineffective. Thus, in the rare case where the defendant has a duty to protect a person of full understanding from causing harm to himself, it is self-contradictory to say that the breach could not have been a cause of the harm because the victim caused it to himself. In *Reeves v Commissioner of Police for the Metropolis*[21] the deceased hanged himself in a police cell. The defendants were aware that the prisoner was a suicide risk although he had not been diagnosed as suffering from any specific mental disorder. It was conceded that the defendants owed a duty of care, but they denied liability on the basis that the act of suicide constituted a *novus actus*, breaking the causal link. The House of Lords held that the suicide did not constitute a *novus actus*. It was not a new act, but the very harm that the defendants were under a duty to try to prevent. Lord Hoffmann said that "it would make nonsense of the existence of such a duty if the law were to hold that the occurrence of the very act which ought to have been prevented negatived

---

(n.16 contd.) his claim against the third party for a small sum. Paull J. dismissed the action against the doctor, partly on the ground that the action against the third party was a *novus actus interveniens*. This seems doubtful, however, and the decision may be better regarded as a case where there was no duty of care with respect to that particular damage; see paras 2–035 to 2–036.

[17] *McKew v Holland & Hannen & Cubitts (Scotland) Ltd* [1969] 3 All E.R. 1621; *cf. Weiland v Cyril Lord Carpets Ltd* [1969] 3 All E.R. 1006.

[18] As, *e.g.*, in *Sayers v Harlow Urban District Council* [1958] 1 W.L.R. 623, or *The Calliope* [1970] P. 172. See also Millner (1971) 22 N.I.L.Q. 168, 176–179 criticising *McKew v Holland & Hannen & Cubitts (Scotland) Ltd* [1969] 3 All E.R. 1621 for not taking this approach. Once it is accepted that the defendant owed a duty of care to take reasonable care against negligent conduct by others (including the claimant) he cannot assert that the circumstances which gave rise to a breach of that duty constitute a *novus actus interveniens*: *March v E. & M.H. Stramare Pty Ltd* (1991) 99 A.L.R. 423 (H.C. of Australia); Mullany (1992) 12 O.J.L.S. 431.

[19] *Pigney v Pointer's Transport Services Ltd* [1957] 1 W.L.R. 1121; *Cotic v Gray* (1981) 124 D.L.R. (3d) 641 (Ont. C.A.); see para. 4–120 to 4–121; Jones (1990) 6 P.N. 107, 110–112.

[20] In *Wright Estate v Davidson* (1992) 88 D.L.R. (4th) 698 (B.C.C.A.) the deceased's suicide was held to constitute a *novus actus interveniens* where there was no evidence of disabling mental illness; *cf. Costello v Blakeson* [1993] 2 W.W.R. 562 (B.C.S.C.), where the claimant suffered from depression amounting to a mental illness, distinguishing it from *Wright Estate v Davidson*.

[21] [2000] 1 A.C. 360.

causal connection between the breach of duty and the loss."[22] Moreover, in *Reeves* the defendant's precise mental state was irrelevant. The duty was owed because the deceased was a known suicide risk, not because of any particular mental state.[23]

In *Emeh v Kensington and Chelsea Area Health Authority*[24] the claimant brought an action in respect of the birth of a handicapped child following a negligently performed sterilisation operation. She was about 20 weeks pregnant when she discovered the pregnancy. The trial judge had taken the view that the claimant's decision not to undergo an abortion was so unreasonable as to eclipse the defendants' wrongdoing, and amounted to a *novus actus interveniens*, and accordingly she was not entitled to damages for the events after she discovered that she was pregnant, except for the expense and pain and suffering of a further sterilisation operation. The Court of Appeal reversed this finding. Purchas L.J. said that it was unacceptable that the court should be invited to consider critically the decision of a mother whether to terminate a pregnancy which has been caused by the defendants' negligence. As Slade L.J. put it: "By their own negligence, they faced her with the very dilemma which she had sought to avoid by having herself sterilised."[25] The fact that she had exercised this particular option in this way did not show that it was an option which she wished to have. His Lordship doubted whether such a decision could ever constitute a *novus actus interveniens*:

5–090

> "Save in the most exceptional circumstances, I cannot think it right that the court should ever declare it unreasonable for a woman to decline to have an abortion, in a case where there is no evidence that there were any medical or psychiatric grounds for terminating the particular pregnancy."[26]

It might be added that if there are no medical or psychiatric grounds for an abortion within the terms of section 1 of the Abortion Act 1967, the abortion would be unlawful, and it could not possibly be unreasonable for a woman to refuse to undergo an unlawful operation. It is unclear, then, what "exceptional circumstances" Slade L.J. had in mind which might justify the conclusion that such a refusal was unreasonable. Purchas L.J. appeared to

5–091

---

[22] *ibid.* at p. 367–368.
[23] See also paras 4–122 and 4–145 on the question of the defences of *volenti non fit injuria* and *ex turpi causa* in relation to suicide. On the other hand, a defendant is not responsible for a claimant's voluntary, deliberate and informed decision to use heroin. In *Wilson v Coulson* [2002] P.I.Q.R. P300, QBD the claimant sustained brain damage in a road traffic accident for which the defendant was responsible. Shortly after the accident he started to use heroin, having previously been an occasional user of other drugs, and subsequently sustained additional brain damage following a heroin overdose. He claimed that the original accident had produced a personality change, which led to him becoming addicted to heroin. Harrison J. held that the claimant had not lost the capacity or the power to say no. His action was both unreasonable and illegal: "He was the author of his own misfortune and what followed was caused by his own conduct."
[24] [1985] Q.B. 1012.
[25] *ibid.* at p. 1024.
[26] *ibid.*

suggest that where the sole motivation for the refusal to terminate the pregnancy was "commercial," in that the claimant continued the pregnancy merely in order to increase the damages that would be awarded in the action for the failed sterilisation, that would be a factor to be considered in deciding whether the chain of causation had been broken. Given the multiplicity of medical, social, emotional, moral, and economic factors which women take into account when making such a decision, it is highly unlikely that the financial prospects of promoting a civil action for damages could be shown to have been the sole motivation of any woman who decides to continue her pregnancy. Moreover, even in such extreme circumstances a decision that the claimant has acted unreasonably effectively stipulates that she was under a duty to abort in order to reduce the loss otherwise payable by the negligent doctor. The Abortion Act 1967 gives a woman the right to have an abortion in certain circumstances, if she chooses, but there is no law which imposes a duty to abort, and such a duty would appear to violate a principle of public policy upholding the sanctity of human life.[27] Thus, on principle it is submitted that a mother's decision not to undergo an abortion should never be held to constitute to a *novus actus interveniens*, irrespective of her motives.

5–092 In *McFarlane v Tayside Health Board*[28] the House of Lords confirmed that the failure to undergo a termination of pregnancy or the failure to give the child up for adoption following birth did not break the chain of causation between a negligently performed sterilisation operation or negligent advice as to the success of the sterilisation procedure and the birth.[29] On the other hand, where following a failed sterilisation operation, a claimant knew that she was not sterile, and decided nonetheless to proceed to have sexual intercourse without taking contraceptive measures, this does break the chain of causation between the negligent performance of the surgery and the subsequent birth of a child.[30]

5–093 In *Pidgeon v Doncaster Health Authority*[31] the claimant was negligently advised in 1988 that a smear test for cervical cancer was normal, when it showed pre-cancerous abnormalities. A further test in 1997 resulted in a diagnosis of cervical cancer. In the intervening period the claimant had been spoken to on no less than seven occasions about the need to have smear test, and had received four letters from the defendants' cervical cancer screening programme about the need to have a smear test. The claimant had not undergone the test because she found it painful and embarrassing, although she was aware that she could develop cervical cancer. The judge held that the claimant's failure to

---

[27] *McKay v Essex Area Health Authority* [1982] Q.B. 1166, see para. 2–084.

[28] [2000] 2 A.C. 59 at 74, 104 and 113.

[29] Their Lordships limited the potential damages awarded in such actions on other grounds. See paras 2–039 *et seq.*; 9–079 *et seq.*

[30] *Sabri-Tabrizi v Lothian Health Board*, 1998 S.C. 373. See also *Richardson v LRC Products Ltd* [2000] P.I.Q.R. P164, 173; [2000] Lloyd's Rep. Med. 280, 286 where Ian Kennedy J. suggested that a claimant's failure to seek advice about the "morning after pill" to avoid conception following the discovery that a condom had "failed" during sexual intercourse could amount to a failure to mitigate the damage or an intervening cause (the judgment is unclear on this point).

[31] [2002] Lloyd's Rep. Med. 130 (County Court).

undergo a smear test did not break the causal link between the original negligence and the fact that she had developed cancer, because the claimant did not know of her condition, and had been reassured by the reported result of the 1988 test. Thus, there was "an important difference between a claimant indulging in behaviour against a background of known vulnerability, whether it be weakness of the leg or ability to conceive, and a claimant failing to take steps which may well reveal a condition, if in fact present, having previously been reassured that it was not present."[32] However, the claimant's conduct constituted contributory negligence, assessed at two-thirds.

Another situation which could result in a finding that the claimant acted so   5–094
unreasonably as to break the chain of causation is where the patient refuses further medical treatment which would alleviate his condition or prevent it from deteriorating. It is clear that a claimant has an obligation to mitigate the damages, which may include seeking suitable medical treatment except where there is a substantial risk of further injury or the outcome is uncertain.[33] Mitigation is a principle applied to the assessment of damages, but this stage will not be reached if the refusal of recommended treatment is categorised as an intervening act. In *R. v Blaue*[34] the Court of Appeal held that a patient's refusal to undergo a blood transfusion on religious grounds did not break the chain of causation between a criminal assault and the patient's death, resulting in a charge of manslaughter.[35] It is clear, however, that this decision was based on policy considerations appropriate to the criminal law. Lawton L.J. suggested that where the victim brought a civil claim the concept of foreseeability could operate in the wrongdoer's favour, presumably by breaking the chain of causation; and, moreover, the wrongdoer was entitled to expect his victim to mitigate the damage by accepting treatment of a normal kind. It may be argued, however, that a refusal of medical treatment on religious grounds constitutes a failure to provide an *actus interveniens* that would have avoided the claimant's loss, which is not the same as committing a *novus actus interveniens* that caused the loss, an argument that has been accepted where a third party fails to intervene.[36] Moreover, the decision to refuse treatment would

---

[32] *ibid.* at [23], distinguishing both *McKew v Holland and Hannen and Cubitts (Scotland) Ltd* [1969] 3 All E.R. 1621 and *Sabri-Tabrizi v Lothian Health Board* 1998 S.C. 373; (1998) 43 B.M.L.R. 190 on the basis that in those cases the claimants knew about their particular condition (weakness in the leg and not being sterile, respectively).

[33] See para. 9–027.

[34] [1975] 1 W.L.R. 1411.

[35] "It does not lie in the mouth of the assailant to say that his victim's religious beliefs which inhibited him from accepting certain kinds of treatment were unreasonable. The question for decision is what caused her death. The answer is the stab wound. The fact that the victim refused to stop this end coming about did not break the causal connection between the act and the death." *ibid.* at p. 1415, *per* Lawton L.J. See also *R. v Malcherek* [1981] 1 W.L.R. 690; *R. v Cheshire* (1991) 93 Cr. App. R. 251; *R. v Dear* [1996] Crim. L.R. 595.

[36] See above paras 5–085 to 5–086. The distinction between the duty to mitigate and the claimant's intervening act may be the difference between the claimant's unreasonable inaction (his failure to minimise loss) and the claimant's unreasonable action (his augmenting of the loss), respectively, although the principles are based on the same policy grounds and are sometimes used interchangeably: see Burrows, *Remedies for Torts and Breach of Contract*, 2nd ed., Butterworths, 1994, p. 38.

not necessarily be categorised as "unreasonable," even under the civil law. In *R. v Blaue* Lawton L.J. responded to the suggestion that a Jehovah's Witness's decision not to have a blood transfusion was unreasonable:

> "At once the question arises—reasonable by whose standards? Those of Jehovah's Witnesses? Humanists? Roman Catholics? Protestants of Anglo-Saxon descent? The man on the Clapham omnibus?"[37]

5–095   A decision based on religious beliefs may well be regarded as reasonable because it is considered to be reasonable to conduct one's life according to a religious faith, even though those specific beliefs are not widely accepted within society. This view could be applied both to the question of whether the claimant's conduct amounts to a *novus actus interveniens* and to whether he has complied with his obligation to mitigate the damage, which requires the claimant only to take reasonable steps in mitigation. It might also be argued that a claimant's refusal of treatment on religious grounds is foreseeable and so did not break the chain of causation, particularly in an action for medical negligence where it could be expected that the doctor would have discussed with the patient in advance what medical treatment would be acceptable. Ultimately, this issue turns upon the courts' assessment of who should bear the burden of the claimant's religious beliefs.

3. REMOTENESS OF DAMAGE

5–096   Rules on remoteness of damage, at least in the tort of negligence, deal with harm which occurs in some freakish or unpredictable fashion. In a system of fault liability, which depends upon foreseeability of the damage as a test of the defendant's breach of duty, it may seem unfair to hold the defendant responsible for all the damage that his negligence has caused, even where the damage is of a different type or occurred in a different manner from that which would normally be expected. There are two broad approaches to the problem of remoteness. The first takes the view that a defendant is liable for all the direct consequences of his negligence, no matter how unusual or unexpected. This treats remoteness as essentially a question of causation. At one time this was thought to be the appropriate rule in the tort of negligence,[38] and it remains the test in actions for trespass to the person.[39] The second

---

[37] [1975] 1 W.L.R. 1411, 1415. See also *Malette v Shulman* (1987) 47 D.L.R. (4th) 18; affirmed (1990) 67 D.L.R. (4th) 321 (Ont. C.A.), para. 6–099, where a doctor who administered a blood transfusion contrary to the patient's instructions was held liable in battery.

[38] *Re Polemis and Furness, Withy & Co Ltd* [1921] 3 K.B. 560.

[39] The defendant is liable for all the consequences which are a direct result of the tortious act whether they are foreseeable or not: "In battery, however, any and all damage is recoverable, if it results from the wrongful act, whether it is foreseeable or not. The limitation devices of foresight and remoteness are not applicable to intentional torts, as they are in negligence law," *per* Linden J. in *Allan v New Mount Sinai Hospital* (1980) 109 D.L.R. (3d) 634, 643.

approach holds that a person is only responsible for consequences that could reasonably have been anticipated, even where he has undoubtedly caused the damage in question. In theory, the test of remoteness in the tort of negligence is now foreseeability of the harm; if the damage was unforeseeable it is too remote.[40] This statement is deceptive, however, because in practice the issue is not that simple. The court must determine precisely what it is that has to be foreseen, and decisions about what falls within the realms of the foreseeable and what may legitimately be ignored in the sequence of events have a vital bearing upon the application of the rules on remoteness. Moreover, the courts have not abandoned the general principle that a tortfeasor must "take his victim as he finds him," which in practice means ignoring certain unforeseeable idiosyncrasies in the claimant which may have contributed to the damage. The result is that the limits of actionability set by the rules on remoteness of damage lie somewhere between the two approaches embodied in directness and foreseeability.

Once it is established that the damage sustained by the claimant was foreseeable, the likelihood that it would occur is irrelevant. In *The Heron II*[41] Lord Upjohn said that: "the tortfeasor is liable for any damage which he can reasonably foresee may happen as a result of the breach however unlikely it may be, unless it can be brushed aside as far-fetched." The likelihood of the occurrence or the degree of foreseeability relates to the question of whether the defendant acted carelessly in the face of the risk.[42] To some extent this makes the test of remoteness of damage as close to a test based on causation as to one based on foreseeability, because many things which could be regarded as unlikely are foreseeable and yet are not necessarily far-fetched.[43] It is not sufficient, therefore, to say that the test of remoteness of damage is foreseeability. The court has scope to determine the outcome of a case through the definition of what, precisely, must be foreseen. The narrower the range of events or damage that must be anticipated the more difficult it will be for the claimant to overcome the remoteness hurdle. Following *The*

5–097

---

[40] *Overseas Tankship (UK) Ltd v Morts Dock & Engineering Co., The Wagon Mound* [1961] A.C. 388, P.C. It is a matter of some uncertainty whether, and if so how, the test for remoteness of damage differs in the tort of negligence from that applied to actions in contract. It may be that the tests are in effect the same, at least for physical damage, following the decision of the Court of Appeal in *Parsons (Livestock) Ltd v Uttley Ingham & Co Ltd* [1978] Q.B. 791; see the excellent discussion in Burrows, *Remedies for Torts and Breach of Contract*, 2nd ed., Butterworths, 1994, pp. 45–56. If there is a difference, the test in negligence is more generous to claimants than that in contract (see *The Heron II* [1969] 1 A.C. 350), but this is probably of little or no practical significance in actions for medical negligence since the claimant with a contractual claim will also have a right of action in tort: see para. 2–003.

[41] [1969] 1 A.C. 350, 422.

[42] Although degrees of foreseeability are used in considering whether the chain of causation has been broken by an intervening act: see para. 5–083.

[43] In *Emeh v Kensington and Chelsea Area Health Authority* [1985] Q.B. 1012, 1019 Waller L.J. concluded that a risk of between 1 in 200 and 1 in 400 of a pregnant woman giving birth to a child with congenital abnormalities was "clearly one that is foreseeable, as the law of negligence understands it. There are many cases where even more remote risks have been taken to be 'foreseeable'." On variable degrees of foresight applied to both the duty of care in negligence and remoteness see Kidner (1989) 9 L.S. 1.

Wagon Mound the courts soon came to the view that provided that the type or kind of damage could have been foreseen, it did not matter that its extent or the precise manner of its occurrence could not have been foreseen, and the eggshell skull rule,[44] which was retained after *The Wagon Mound*, is quite explicitly not based on foreseeability.

(1) Manner of the occurrence

5-098　　The fact that the damage occurred in an unforeseeable way does not necessarily mean that it was not foreseeable. The precise concatenation of events need not be anticipated if the damage is within the general range of what is reasonably foreseeable.[45] In *Hughes v Lord Advocate*[46] some workmen negligently left a manhole open in the street, surrounded by paraffin lamps. Two young boys approached the manhole, out of curiosity, and one of the lamps was knocked into the hole. There was a violent explosion in which one of the boys suffered severe burns. Expert evidence indicated that in these circumstances an explosion was unforeseeable, although burns from a conflagration if the lamp was knocked over could have been anticipated. The House of Lords held that the damage was not too remote. Lord Pearce considered that the accident was simply a "variant of the foreseeable," while Lord Reid took the view that having been caused by a known source of danger, it was no defence that it was caused in an unforeseeable way. Lord Guest concluded that the precise details leading up to the accident do not have to be foreseen; it was sufficient if the accident was "of a type which should have been foreseeable by a reasonably careful person."

5-099　　To a large extent this issue turns upon how the court frames the question of what has to be foreseen. In *Hughes v Lord Advocate* the question was: "was injury by burning foreseeable?" to which the answer was "yes." If the question had been: "was injury by explosion foreseeable?" the answer would have been "no" and the damage would have been considered to be too remote. This is illustrated by the decision of the Court of Appeal in *Doughty v Turner Manufacturing Co Ltd*[47] in which an asbestos cover was knocked into a bath of molten liquid. Shortly after, due to a chemical reaction between the asbestos and the liquid which was unforeseeable at the time, there was an eruption of the liquid which burned the claimant who was standing nearby. It was held that burning by an unforeseeable chemical eruption was not a variant of burning by splashing, which was within the foreseeable risk created by knocking the cover into the liquid, distinguishing *Hughes v Lord Advocate*. If the question had been: "was injury by burning foreseeable?" as a consequence of knocking the cover into the liquid then the

---

[44] See para. 5-109.
[45] *Stewart v West African Terminals Ltd* [1964] 2 Lloyd's Rep. 371, 375; *Wieland v Cyril Lord Carpets Ltd* [1969] 3 All E.R. 1006, 1009; *Sullivan v South Glamorgan County Council* (1985) 84 L.G.R. 415.
[46] [1963] A.C. 837.
[47] [1964] 1 Q.B. 518.

answer must have been "yes," and the court could have taken the view that the precise manner in which the injury occurred was irrelevant.[48]

It is not necessary that the precise events be foreseeable provided that they   5–100
fall within the scope of the risk created by the defendant's breach of duty. In *Wiszniewski v Central Manchester Health Authority*[49] the defendants were held liable in respect of hypoxia suffered by the claimant infant during the course of his birth when the defendants' negligence created a risk of oxygen starvation in the womb, though the actual mechanism by which the claimant sustained the hypoxia was by strangulation because the umbilical cord was looped round his neck and had a knot in it which gradually tightened. The evidence was that a "true knot" in the umbilical cord is very rare, and could not have been foreseen, although a cord being looped around the neck is much more common. The Court of Appeal held that as the damage was of a foreseeable kind, it was irrelevant that the precise mechanism by which the hypoxia occurred was unforeseeable.[50]

(2) Type of harm

The damage will be too remote if it is not of the same type or kind as the   5–101
harm that could have been foreseen. The problem is in defining the "type" of damage that must be foreseen. It would be possible to take a broad view of the classification of harm, dividing it into personal injury, damage to property and financial loss. Thus, if any personal injury were foreseeable the defendant would be liable for any type of personal injuries that occurred. The courts have not done this, although the eggshell skull rule as applied to personal injuries comes close to this result.[51] In practice a compromise position seems to have been adopted in which the courts insist that the damage

---

[48] See also *Tremain v Pike* [1969] 3 All E.R. 1303 and *Crossley v Rawlinson* [1981] 3 All E.R. 674 for examples of how narrowing the scope of the question produces the result that the harm was unforeseeable.
[49] [1998] Lloyd's Rep. Med. 223, CA.
[50] "... it would in my judgment be regarded as an affront to common sense, and the law would look an ass, if we reached any different conclusion," *per* Brooke L.J. *ibid.* at 245. See also *Hutchinson v Leeds Health Authority*, (2000) unreported, where, relying on *Wiszniewski*, Bennett J. held, at [82], that it would also be an affront to common sense if, having established that the defendants were in breach of duty in failing to call in the surgical team to investigate a highly abnormal bowel function in a patient who was very ill, the claimant's action failed because it was not foreseeable that bowel perforation might occur in the posterior rectal wall rather than in some other part of the bowel.
[51] See paras 5–112 to 5–113. In *Page v Smith* [1996] A.C. 155 the House of Lords held that if physical injury to the claimant was foreseeable the defendant was liable for any psychiatric damage which the claimant sustained as a result of the defendant's negligence, even though physical injury did not in the event occur and the psychiatric damage was itself unforeseeable. This effectively treats psychiatric injury as damage of the same "type" as physical injury. If there is to be no distinction between *physical* injury and *psychiatric* injury, there is little obvious justification for distinguishing between different types of physical injury, at least in the case of personal injuries. In *R v Croydon Health Authority* [1998] P.I.Q.R. Q26, 32–33 Kennedy L.J. rejected the suggestion that *Page v Smith* had removed the distinction between physical injury and psychiatric injury in this way, though his Lordship did not analyse the speeches in *Page v Smith* and did not give any reasons for his view.

must be of a foreseeable type or kind, whilst giving this term a comparatively wide meaning. In *Draper v Hodder*,[52] for example, Edmund-Davies L.J. said that:

"... the proper test in negligence is not whether the particular type of physical harm actually suffered ought reasonably to have been anticipated, but whether broadly speaking it was within the range of likely consequence."

5–102   This is illustrated in *Bradford v Robinson Rentals Ltd*[53] in which the claimant sustained frostbite, having been sent on a journey by his employers in a vehicle without a heater at a time of severe winter weather. Rees J. held that frostbite was damage of the same kind as that which was a foreseeable consequence of exposure to extreme cold. On the other hand, in *Tremain v Pike*[54] a farm employee contracted a rare disease transmitted by contact with rats' urine, following an infestation of rats on the farm. Payne J. considered that the disease was damage of a different type from the foreseeable damage which could have occurred from rat bites or contamination of food. This decision, it is submitted, takes an unduly myopic view of what may be foreseeable. If the question had been whether illness from some rat-transmitted disease was a foreseeable consequence of an infestation of rats, the answer must surely have been that it was. Very few people would be capable of identifying in advance the specific disease that would be caused.

5–103   In *Sheridan v Boots Co Ltd*[55] the claimant contracted Stevens-Johnson syndrome, causing blindness, as a side-effect of an anti-inflammatory drug, Butazolidin, which was known to have a number of side-effects ranging from gastro-intestinal disturbance, gastric ulcers and, in rare cases, blood dyscrazia which could take the form of aplastic anaemia, a very dangerous condition. Stevens-Johnson syndrome was known to be a possible side-effect, but this was not widely known. The manufacturer's literature published in the United States mentioned this possibility, but made no mention of it in the literature published in this country. Kenneth Jones J. held that the claimant's injury was too remote, because Stevens-Johnson syndrome was not damage of the same type as gastric disturbance. Stevens-Johnson syndrome involved ulceration over a widespread area of the body, which could affect the eyes. Gastric disturbance, on the other hand, involved localised ulceration in the stomach and does not affect the eyes:

"It would seem contrary to commonsense to say that a condition involving blindness is of the same kind as one causing gastric ulcer. When examined fully, the two conditions in their symptoms are wholly dissimilar."

[52] [1972] 2 Q.B. 556, 573.
[53] [1967] 1 All E.R. 267.
[54] [1969] 3 All E.R. 1303.
[55] (1980, QBD; unreported).

Nor could it be said, his Lordship continued, that they arose through the   5–104
same mechanism. This case can be contrasted with the decision of the
Ontario Court of Appeal in *Graham v Persyko*[56] in which a gastroenterologist was held to have been negligent in prescribing the drug prednisone
for the patient's condition. The drug caused avascular necrosis of the
femoral heads, which was a rare but known complication. Holland J. said
that:

> "The complication of necrosis of femoral heads with a short dose of
> prednisone is known but unusual. There are a number of serious,
> known and more common side-effects. It may be that the particular
> side-effect that Mr Graham suffered was not reasonably foreseeable
> but damage to Mr Graham's health was foreseeable and liability
> results."[57]

Clearly, treating the type of damage that must be foreseen as "damage to   5–105
health" takes a very broad view of what must be foreseen, and would be difficult to reconcile with *Sheridan v Boots Co Ltd*. Given the wide range of
adverse effects which were foreseeable in *Graham v Persyko* it would probably not have been difficult to categorise avascular necrosis as simply a
variant of one of the foreseeable types of injury. Moreover, necrosis was a
known complication "but unusual." It is arguable that this finding made the
necrosis foreseeable, since it is well-established that for the purpose of
remoteness the type of damage need only be foreseeable as a possible risk, it
does not have to be likely or reasonably foreseeable.[58] Thus, in *Smith v
Brighton and Lewes Hospital Management Committee*[59] a patient who was
negligently given 34 instead of 30 injections of streptomycin lost her sense
of balance as a result. It was held that the defendant should have appreciated
that some injury could be caused by giving an overdose, and she did not have
to foresee the quality or extent of the damage. In *Hepworth v Kerr*[60]
McKinnon J. held that anterior spinal artery syndrome (spinal stroke) was
within the range of foreseeable consequences from an experimental hypotensive anaesthetic technique, when the known complications from this procedure included cerebral or cardiac thrombosis. The technique created a

---

[56] (1986) 27 D.L.R. (4th) 699 (Ont. C.A.); (1986) 34 D.L.R. (4th) 160 (S.C.C.) leave to appeal
refused; see para. 4–091.
[57] *ibid.* at p. 708, citing *Hughes v Lord Advocate* [1963] A.C. 837. The known complications
of the drug included: altering the patient's mental state, making some patients suicidal;
effects on the cardiovascular system, and retention of salt and water; hypertension; cataracts
and glaucoma; peptic ulcer; skin complaints; osteoporosis; reduction of the body's response
to infection; diabetes; and, uncommonly, aseptic necrosis of hip joints and other joints.
[58] See para. 5–097.
[59] *The Times*, May 2, 1958. In *Reeves v Carthy* [1984] I.R. 348 (Supreme Court of Ireland) it
was held that since it was foreseeable that, left untreated, peritonitis leads to circulatory
weakness and hypotension, it was also foreseeable that as a consequence of prolonged hypotension the claimant could suffer a stroke. Alternatively, even if the stroke was unforeseeable, it was damage of the same type as the foreseeable harm (circulatory damage and shock)
notwithstanding its unforeseeable extent.
[60] [1995] 6 Med. L.R. 139, 170–171.

foreseeable risk of damage by under-perfusion of major organs of the body, and the injury that occurred was but "a variant of the foreseeable."[61] It was not necessary for the claimant to prove that the defendant must have foreseen that the very mechanism for which the defendant was responsible and which the defendant would have expected to cause a cerebral thrombosis, would be likely to cause a thrombosis in another part of the body closely associated with the brain (the spine).

5–106   In *Kralj v McGrath*[62] an unusual type of loss was said to have been foreseeable. Due to the defendant's negligence one child of twins was born with severe disabilities, and died eight weeks later. The claimant, the child's mother, said that she had always intended to have a family of three children, and as a result of the death she would have to undergo a further pregnancy, which would involve the discomforts involved in the pregnancy (including the fact that it would now have to be delivered by Caesarian section) and additional financial loss. The defendant argued that this was too remote because it was not reasonably foreseeable by the defendant. Woolf J. held that it was foreseeable that the claimant might want to have further children following the death of her child, and it was irrelevant that she had not specifically informed the defendant about this.

(3) Extent of the harm

5–107   If the type of harm and the manner of its occurrence were foreseeable it is irrelevant that the physical extent of the damage was unforeseeable.[63] In *Hughes v Lord Advocate* Lord Reid said that:

> "No doubt it was not to be expected that the injuries would be as serious as those which the appellant in fact sustained. But a defender is liable, although the damage may be a good deal greater in extent than was foreseeable. He can only escape liability if the damage can be regarded as differing in kind from what was foreseeable."[64]

This principle applies to all forms of personal injury, including psychiatric harm,[65] and also to property damage.[66]

---

[61] Applying *Hughes v Lord Advocate* [1963] A.C. 837.
[62] [1986] 1 All E.R. 54, 62.
[63] *Smith v Leech Brain & Co Ltd* [1962] 2 Q.B. 405, 414, *per* Lord Parker C.J., stating that this proposition had not been changed by *The Wagon Mound* [1961] A.C. 388.
[64] [1963] A.C. 837, 845. *Craig v Soeurs de Charité de la Providence* [1940] 3 W.W.R. 336 (Sask. C.A.), where the patient suffered more extensive injuries than otherwise foreseeable from a burn by a hot water bottle because he was diabetic; the defendants were held liable for full loss.
[65] *Brice v Brown* [1984] 1 All E.R. 997. It is irrelevant that the claimant has a predisposition to psychiatric harm which, unknown to the defendant, increases the likelihood of more extensive harm than the ordinary individual would have experienced, provided that it was foreseeable that a person of ordinary fortitude would have sustained psychiatric harm: see para. 2–109. See also *Page v Smith* [1996] A.C. 155, HL.
[66] *Vacwell Engineering Co Ltd v B.D.H. Chemicals Ltd* [1971] 1 Q.B. 88.

Liability for the unforeseeable physical extent of otherwise foreseeable   5–108
physical harm should be distinguished from the measure of damages
required to compensate the claimant's loss. If the defendant injures someone
with a high income, or damages a particularly valuable item of property, he
must compensate the claimant to the full extent of his loss, and he cannot
complain that the damages would have been less if the claimant had a low
income or the property was of little value.[67]

(4) The "eggshell skull" rule

Where the claimant suffers from a latent physical or psychological predis-   5–109
position to a particular injury or illness which has been activated by the
damage inflicted by the defendant, then the defendant is responsible for the
additional, unforeseeable damage that his negligence has produced. This is
usually referred to as the "thin skull" or the "eggshell skull" rule. If the claimant has an unusually thin skull the defendant cannot complain if the injury
is much more serious than would have been the case with a normal person.[68]
Provided that some harm was foreseeable, so that it can be said that the
defendant was in breach of duty, the defendant is responsible.[69] The same
principle has been applied where the claimant had an unusually weak
heart,[70] a weak back,[71] where he was a haemophiliac,[72] and even where he
had an "eggshell personality."[73] The defendant does not, however, have to
take the claimant's family as he finds them.[74]

---

[67] *Smith v London & South Western Railway Co* (1870) L.R. 6 C.P. 14, 22–23; *The Arpad*
[1934] P. 189, 202. As Fleming, *The Law of Torts*, 8th ed., 1992, p. 206 puts it, this is
responsibility, not for unexpected consequences, but for the unexpectable cost of expected
consequences.

[68] *Owens v Liverpool Corporation* [1939] 1 K.B. 394, 401; *Dulieu v White & Sons* [1901] 2
K.B. 669, 679, *per* Kennedy J.: ". . . it is no answer to the [plaintiff's] claim for damages that
he would have suffered less injury, or no injury at all, if he had not had an unusually thin
skull or an unusually weak heart." Distinguish the so-called "crumbling skull" rule—the
defendant is not responsible for the debilitating effects of the claimant's pre-existing condition which he would have experienced in any event. The defendant is liable for any additional damage, but not the pre-existing damage: *Athey v Leonati* [1997] 1 W.W.R. 97, 107
(S.C.C.). Similarly, if there is a risk that the pre-existing condition would have affected the
claimant in the future, irrespective of the defendant's negligence, this is taken into account
in the assessment of damages.

[69] *Bourhill v Young* [1943] A.C. 92, 109, *per* Lord Wright. See *Hewett v Alf Brown's Transport
Ltd* [1992] I.C.R. 530; [1992] P.I.Q.R. P199 where the claimant's injury by lead poisoning
was due to her special susceptibility. The damage was held to be unforeseeable; *Moore v
Worthing District Health Authority* [1992] 3 Med. L.R. 431, QBD, where bilateral ulnar
nerve lesions during the course of a mastoidectomy were attributable, on the facts, to the
claimant's abnormal susceptibility to this type of injury.

[70] *Love v Port of London* [1959] 2 Lloyd's Rep. 541.

[71] *Athey v Leonati* [1997] 1 W.W.R. 97, 110 (S.C.C.).

[72] *Bishop v Arts & Letters Club of Toronto* (1978) 83 D.L.R. (3d) 107.

[73] *Malcolm v Broadhurst* [1970] 3 All E.R. 508, where the injury aggravated a pre-existing
nervous condition; *Page v Smith* [1996] A.C. 155 where the defendant's negligence caused
an accident which produced a recrudescence of the claimant's myalgic encephalomyelitis,
although the claimant did not sustain any physical injury.

[74] *McLaren v Bradstreet* (1969) 119 N.L.J. 484—claimants could not recover for "family

5–110   The eggshell skull rule overlaps with the general principle that the extent of the damage need not be foreseeable. Where the claimant's predisposition exacerbates the otherwise foreseeable type of harm then it provides the mechanism by which that principle comes into effect. It is arguable, however, that the eggshell skull rule goes beyond this by allowing recovery for harm of a different type from that which is foreseeable. In *Smith v Leech Brain & Co Ltd*[75] an employee was burned on the lip by a piece of molten metal. The burn was treated and healed, but due to a premalignant condition the burn promoted a cancerous growth which ultimately led to his death. Lord Parker C.J. held the defendants liable for the death:

> "The test is not whether these [defendants] could reasonably have foreseen that a burn would cause cancer and that [Mr Smith] would die. The question is whether these [defendants] could reasonably foresee the type of injury he suffered, namely, the burn. What, in the particular case, is the amount of the damage which he suffers as a result of that burn, depends upon the characteristics and constitution of the victim."[76]

5–111   Lord Parker's reference to the "amount of the damage" suggests that he regarded cancer and death as simply more extensive harm of the same type as the foreseeable harm, the burn. It is difficult, however, to see how these types of damage can be put into the same category. It is respectfully submitted that only if the harm is classified very broadly as "personal injury" could the death be regarded as merely more extensive damage of the same type as the foreseeable injury.

5–112   The eggshell skull rule predates the move to a test of remoteness based on foreseeability, and the reality is that it is extremely difficult to provide a theoretical reconciliation of the two principles. Nonetheless, it has been confirmed on more than one occasion that the eggshell skull rule was not affected by *The Wagon Mound*.[77] In *Robinson v Post Office*[78] the claimant suffered a minor injury as a result of the defendants' negligence, but he suffered a serious allergic reaction to an anti-tetanus injection given by a doctor, causing brain damage. The Court of Appeal held the defendants responsible for the brain damage:

> ". . . the principle that a defendant must take the plaintiff as he finds him involves that if a wrongdoer ought reasonably to foresee that as a result of his wrongful act the victim may require medical treatment he is, subject to the principle of *novus actus interveniens*, liable for the con-

---

(n.74 contd.) hysteria" resulting from the mother's neurotic reaction to minor injuries to her children caused by the defendant's negligence; *cf. Nader v Urban Transit Authority of New South Wales* [1985] 2 N.S.W.L.R. 501.

[75] [1962] 2 Q.B. 405.

[76] *ibid.* at p. 415.

[77] [1961] A.C. 388. See *Oman v McIntyre* 1962 S.L.T. 168; *Warren v Scruttons Ltd* [1962] 1 Lloyd's Rep. 497; *Winteringham v Rae* (1965) 55 D.L.R. (2d) 108, 112 (Ont. H.C.).

[78] [1974] 1 W.L.R. 1176; [1974] 2 All E.R. 737.

sequences of the treatment applied although he could not reasonably foresee those consequences or that they could be serious."[79]

There was no suggestion that the *type* of consequences had to be foreseeable, provided that the need for treatment was foreseeable. It may be that the Court regarded "the consequences of medical treatment" as a specific "type" of damage, but since this would cover almost any form of personal injury (provided it is a potential consequence of medical treatment) it is difficult to see how different types of personal injury can be identified as being either foreseeable or unforeseeable consequences of otherwise foreseeable harm. In other words, *Robinson v Post Office* appears to support a very wide categorisation of the type of damage that must be foreseen, an approach that clearly favours claimants. This may be justified by the observation that the eggshell skull rule contains a strong element of policy, particularly in the realm of personal injuries, for as Professor Fleming has commented: "Human bodies are too fragile and life too precarious to permit a defendant nicely to calculate how much injury he might inflict."[80]

5–113

It may be arguable that a medical practitioner should be more able to foresee unusual complications arising from negligent medical treatment than other defendants. How many people would appreciate, for example, that if a doctor negligently removed a patient's ectopic kidney believing it to be an ovarian cyst, that this might turn out to be the patient's only kidney, with the result that she would need an organ transplant?[81] The doctor's liability for the consequences of this error can be justified on several grounds: that, as a doctor, this remote risk was foreseeable to him; that the damage was of the same type as the foreseeable harm, although the extent of the damage was unforeseeable; or, that the claimant came within the eggshell skull rule.

5–114

Where the defendant's negligence increases the claimant's susceptibility to further injury, and thus effectively renders the claimant thin-skulled, he may be held responsible when further injury is sustained by the claimant.[82]

5–115

On the other hand, the thin skull rule does not require a defendant doctor to be held responsible for unforeseeable harm which is unconnected with his breach of duty. In *Brown v Lewisham and North Southwark Health Authority*[83] the defendants admitted that there had been negligence in discharging the claimant from hospital with a chest infection, following a quadruple coronary artery bypass operation. This did not mean, however, that they were to be held liable to the claimant when he developed deep vein thrombosis, resulting ultimately in the loss of his leg, when even if he had

5–116

---

[79] See also *Winteringham v Rae* (1965) 55 D.L.R. (2d) 108 (Ont. H.C.) where on similar facts a tortfeasor was held liable for the claimant's rare reaction to anti-tetanus serum. Negligent medical treatment would normally constitute a *novus actus interveniens*, though in *Robinson* the doctor had been negligent but his negligence was not a cause of the harm: see para. 5–005; *cf. Price v Milawski* (1977) 82 D.L.R. (3d) 130.
[80] Fleming, *The Law of Torts*, 8th ed., 1992, p. 206.
[81] *Urbanski v Patel* (1978) 84 D.L.R. (3d) 650 (Man. Q.B.), see para. 2–094.
[82] *Powell v Guttman* (1978) 89 D.L.R. (3d) 180, 190 (Man. C.A), para. 5–046.
[83] [1999] Lloyd's Rep. Med. 110, CA.

stayed in hospital the diagnosis would not have been made any sooner, and the subsequent ambulance journey did not contribute to his developing deep vein thrombosis. Beldam L.J. said:

> "I do not see on what policy ground it would be fair or just to hold a doctor to be in breach of duty who failed to diagnose an asymptomatic and undetectable illness merely because he was at fault in the management of a correctly diagnosed but unrelated condition. In short it must be shown that the injury suffered by the patient is within the risk from which it was the doctor's duty to protect him."[84]

(5) Claimant's impecuniosity

5–117   The defendant is not responsible for losses which are attributable solely to the claimant's impecuniosity.[85] This rule is widely regarded as anomalous, and has been distinguished on a number of occasions.[86] Moreover, the claimant's impecuniosity will be taken into account in deciding whether the claimant has fulfilled his duty to mitigate the loss.[87] In practice this rule will rarely be relevant in an action for medical negligence, since it is limited to claims in respect of damage to property or pure economic loss. It might on occasion be suggested that the claimant's personal injuries could have been reduced by early medical treatment, which would have been available if the claimant had sought private treatment but the claimant was unable to afford the cost of private treatment. In theory the additional damage attributable to the delay is the product of the claimant's impecuniosity, but in practice it is thought that the court would approach this as a question of mitigation of damage. The claimant has a duty to take reasonable steps to mitigate his loss, but the court will take account of his financial position in determining what constitutes "reasonable steps."[88]

---

[84] *ibid.* at 118.
[85] *Liesbosch Dredger v S.S. Edison* [1933] A.C. 449.
[86] *Martindale v Duncan* [1973] 1 W.L.R. 574; *Jarvis v T. Richards & Co* (1980) 124 S.J. 793, holding that the rule was inapplicable where the impecuniosity was caused by the defendant's tort; *Dodd Properties (Kent) Ltd v Canterbury City Council* [1980] 1 All E.R. 928, rule inapplicable where a decision not to effect early repairs to property, because it would lead to financial stringency, was based on commercial prudence rather than lack of resources; *Mattocks v Mann* [1993] R.T.R. 13, CA; *Alcoa Minerals of Jamaica Inc v Broderick* [2002] 1 A.C. 371, P.C. See further Coote [2001] C.L.J. 511.
[87] *Dodd Properties (Kent) Ltd v Canterbury City Council* [1980] 1 All E.R. 928, 935, 941.
[88] See further para. 9–029.

CHAPTER 6

CONSENT TO TREATMENT

Consent to medical treatment is widely regarded as the cornerstone of the   6–001
doctor-patient relationship. As a general rule, patients cannot be required to
accept treatment that they do not want no matter how painless, beneficial
and risk-free the treatment may be and no matter how dire the consequences
of a refusal of treatment. This proposition is recognised as both an ethical
principle and a legal rule, and is founded, ultimately, on the principle of
respect for the patient's autonomy, or, expressed in more compelling terms,
on the patient's "right" to self-determination.[1] Thus, the legal requirement
for consent expresses respect for the patient's autonomy. In the famous
words of Cardozo J.:

> "Every human being of adult years and sound mind has a right to deter-
> mine what shall be done with his own body; and a surgeon who performs
> an operation without his patient's consent commits an assault . . ."[2]

Patient autonomy is not the only value, however, that the requirement of
consent protects. With patients who are unable to exercise autonomous
choices, such as children and adults who do not have the relevant capacity
to give a valid consent, it serves as a reminder that there must be some lawful
justification for a medical procedure which would otherwise constitute the
tort of battery. This affirms the ethical principle of respect for persons by
giving legal protection to a patient's bodily integrity, irrespective of their
mental capacity. There is also some evidence that obtaining the patient's

---

[1] "Even when his or her own life depends on receiving medical treatment, an adult of sound
mind is entitled to refuse it. This reflects the autonomy of each individual and the right of
self-determination": *St. George's Healthcare NHS Trust v S; R v Collins and Others, ex parte
S* [1999] Fam. 26, 43, CA. "At issue here is the freedom of the patient as an individual to
exercise her right to refuse treatment and accept the consequences of her own decision.
Competent adults . . . are generally at liberty to refuse medical treatment even at the risk of
death. The right to determine what shall be done with one's body is a fundamental right in
our society. The concepts inherent in this right are the bedrock upon which the principles of
self-determination and individual autonomy are based. Free individual choice in matters
affecting this right should, in my opinion, be accorded very high priority," *per* Robins J.A.
in *Malette v Shulman* (1990) 67 D.L.R. (4th) 321, 336 (Ont. C.A.). See also *Fleming v Reid*
(1991) 82 D.L.R. (4th) 298, 309–310 (Ont. C.A.).
[2] *Schloendorff v Society of New York Hospital* (1914) 211 N.Y. 125, 126; *Airedale NHS Trust
v Bland* [1993] A.C. 789, 857, 864, 882, 891.

consent may assist in the therapeutic process, by involving the patient in the treatment as an active participant.[3] Moreover, educating patients about their medical care and its limitations results in fewer injuries caused by patients' failure to follow medical advice and a reduction in malpractice litigation.[4]

6–002   This Chapter deals with the requirements for consent as a defence to the action for battery, and the distinct issue of the doctor's duty of care in negligence to supply the patient with information about any proposed treatment or diagnostic procedure. The patient's consent must be a "valid" consent, which means that it must be voluntary, the patient must have the mental capacity to understand the nature of the procedure to which he is consenting, and he must also have a certain minimal amount of information about the nature of the procedure. Where the patient lacks the relevant capacity to give a valid consent the doctor needs some form of proxy consent, or a court order, or some other lawful justification, which may be either statutory or under the common law. There are three major problem areas: children; patients with mental disorder; and emergencies, where patients are temporarily incapacitated. The section on the duty of disclosure in negligence includes discussion of material from several Commonwealth jurisdictions, which may contribute to an understanding of English law. Australian and Canadian law differs in some marked respects from English law, although the position in New Zealand is very similar to that in this country. A section on causation covers both battery and negligence, and serves as a reminder that even where claimants succeed in establishing culpable non-disclosure they may face considerable difficulty in proving that this was a cause of their damage. The final section deals with three special cases, where either the legal requirements for consent and information disclosure may be more extensive (research and transplantation of organs) or the subject has given rise to particular problems in practice (failed sterilisation).

1. BATTERY

6–003   The tort of battery has generally been regarded as unsuitable as a method of providing compensation for the victims of medical accidents, partly because of its technical limitations, but principally because it is an intentional tort (which can overlap with the criminal offence of assault), and this is considered to be inappropriate in the context of the doctor-patient relationship. Nonetheless the tort is relevant because of the nature of medical practice which often involves physical contact with the patient's body. The courts have been anxious to restrict its application, particularly in the area of information disclosure, and in the interpretation given to the defence of necessity.

---

[3] Teff (1985) 101 L.Q.R. 432; Brazier (1987) 7 L.S. 169, 176.
[4] Karp (1993) 9 J. of the M.D.U. 26.

Battery is a form of trespass to the person, and as such it is actionable *per*   6–004
se. Damage is not an essential requirement of the tort, although if a claimant
seeks more than nominal damages he will have to establish that he has suffered loss. A battery consists of the infliction of unlawful force on another
person.[5] It is an intentional tort, in the sense that the defendant must intend
the act which inflicts the force, but an intention to cause injury is not necessary,[6] and the exercise of reasonable care is not a defence. Any direct[7] contact
with the claimant, no matter how trivial, is sufficient force,[8] and thus the tort
protects a person not only from physical injury but also his personal dignity
from any form of physical molestation.[9] An exception to this principle
applies to unavoidable contacts which are generally accepted as a consequence of social life, such as casual jostling in a busy street or touching
someone on the shoulder to engage his attention.[10] In *Wilson v Pringle*[11] the
Court of Appeal said that a touching must be "hostile" in order to constitute a battery. Hostility was said to be a question of fact, but would not be
limited to acts of ill-will or malevolence nor "the obvious intention shown
in acts like punching, stabbing or shooting." The Court did not indicate,
however, what would be considered hostile, except to say that the police
officer who, in *Collins v Wilcock*,[12] touched the claimant without any more
hostile an intention than to restrain her temporarily was acting in a hostile
manner, and therefore unlawfully, because the officer had no power to
restrain her.

This issue is important in the medical context because it would probably   6–005
be rare that the contact of doctor and patient in the course of an examination or treatment could be regarded as hostile. If hostility is a requirement
of the tort, then battery would be largely irrelevant to a medical practitioner's civil liability. It is respectfully submitted that "hostility" is not, and
has never been, an element of the tort of battery. In *Re F. (Mental Patient:*

---

[5] *Collins v Wilcock* [1984] 3 All E.R. 374, 377 CA.

[6] *Wilson v Pringle* [1987] Q.B. 237, 249.

[7] Note that the requirement of a "touching" (a direct application of force) makes battery
unsuitable as a remedy for certain types of treatment where the patient alleges a lack of
consent, *e.g.* drug injuries, where the patient alleges that his consent was invalid because he
was given insufficient information, and the drug was taken orally rather than by injection:
see *Malloy v Shanahan* 421 A. 2d 803 (1980). The deliberate infliction of harm by indirect
means would result in liability under the principle in *Wilkinson v Downton* [1897] 2 Q.B.
57; on which see also *Wong v Parkside Health NHS Trust* [2001] EWCA Civ 1721; [2003]
3 All E.R. 932; *Wainwright v Home Office* [2001] EWCA Civ 2081; [2002] Q.B. 1334. For
the requirements as to information disclosure for the purposes of battery see paras 6–034 to
6–044.

[8] "The least touching of another in anger is a battery": *Cole v Turner* (1704) 6 Mod. 149, *per*
Holt C.J.

[9] *Collins v Wilcock* [1984] 3 All E.R. 374, 378, *per* Goff L.J.: "It has long been established
that any touching of another person, however slight, may amount to a battery." Thus,
battery may take the form of snatching something from the claimant's grasp: *Green v
Goddard* (1702) 2 Salk. 641; throwing water at him: *Pursell v Horn* (1838) 8 A. & E. 602;
or applying a tone rinse to his hair: *Nash v Sheen* [1953] C.L.Y. 3726.

[10] *Collins v Wilcock* [1984] 3 All E.R. 374, 378.

[11] [1987] Q.B. 237.

[12] [1984] 3 All E.R. 374.

Sterilisation) Lord Goff addressed the point, doubting the suggestion that a touching must be hostile for the purpose of battery:

> "A prank that gets out of hand, an over-friendly slap on the back, surgical treatment by a surgeon who mistakenly thinks that the patient has consented to it, all these things may transcend the bounds of lawfulness, without being characterised as hostile. Indeed, the suggested qualification is difficult to reconcile with the principle that any touching of another's body is, in the absence of lawful excuse, capable of amounting to a battery and a trespass."[13]

6–006   In the Court of Appeal Lord Donaldson M.R. had observed that *prima facie* all, or almost all, medical treatment and all surgical treatment of an adult is unlawful, in the absence of consent, however beneficial that treatment might be.[14] Similarly, in *T. v T.*[15] Wood J. commented that the incision of the surgeon's scalpel need not be and is most unlikely to be hostile, but unless a defence or justification is established it falls within the definition of a trespass to the person. This view is consistent with the law in other common law jurisdictions, and provides the whole basis of the proposition that a patient's consent to medical treatment is an essential requirement in law. In *Allan v New Mount Sinai Hospital*, for example, Linden J. said that:

> "Battery is the intentional application of offensive or harmful physical contact to a person. Any surgical operation is a battery, unless the patient consents to it."[16]

The requirement for consent means that the patient has the right to make a choice about whether or not to accept medical treatment, and this right of choice necessarily means that the patient has the right to refuse treatment. The right to decline treatment exists "even where there are overwhelming medical reasons in favour of the treatment and probably even where if the treatment is not carried out the patient's life will be at risk."[17] In *Airedale NHS Trust v Bland* Lord Mustill commented that:

---

[13] [1990] 2 A.C. 1, 73.

[14] "This is incontestable": *Re F. (Mental Patient: Sterilisation)* [1990] 2 A.C. 1, 12.

[15] [1988] Fam. 52, 67.

[16] (1980) 109 D.L.R. (3d) 634, 641 (Ont. H.C.); see also Cardozo J. in *Schloendorff v Society of New York Hospital* (1914) 211 N.Y. 125, 126, cited above, para. 6–001; *Schweizer v Central Hospital* (1974) 53 D.L.R. (3d) 494, 507 (Ont. H.C.); *Parmley v Parmley and Yule* [1945] 4 D.L.R. 81, 88 (S.C.C.); *Marshall v Curry* [1933] 3 D.L.R. 260, 274.

[17] *Re F. (Mental Patient: Sterilisation)* [1990] 2 A.C. 1, 29, *per* Neill L.J. Lord Donaldson M.R., at 19, said that: "The ability of the ordinary adult patient to exercise a free choice in deciding whether to accept or to refuse medical treatment and to choose between treatments is not to be dismissed as desirable but inessential. It is a crucial factor in relation to all medical treatment." See also *Malette v Shulman* (1990) 67 D.L.R. (4th) 321, 328 (Ont. C.A.). But this principle does not apply to minors. See paras 6–052 to 6–056 on the question of overriding a competent minor's refusal of medical treatment.

"If the patient is capable of making a decision on whether to permit treatment and decides not to permit it his choice must be obeyed, even if on any objective view it is contrary to his best interests. A doctor has no right to proceed in the face of objection, even if it is plain to all, including the patient, that adverse consequences and even death will or may ensue."[18]

In *St. George's Healthcare NHS Trust v S*[19] the Court of Appeal emphasised the importance of maintaining this principle in the face of perfectly understandable efforts to save life:

6–007

"When human life is at stake the pressure to provide an affirmative answer authorising unwanted medical intervention is very powerful. Nevertheless the autonomy of each individual requires continuing protection even, perhaps particularly, when the motive for interfering with it is readily understandable, and indeed to many would appear commendable . . ."

Thus, a competent pregnant woman is entitled to refuse non-consensual intervention by way of a Caesarian section delivery of the foetus, even if without the intervention she is likely to die or suffer serious injury, or the foetus is likely to die.[20]

Advance statements

The ability to give or withhold consent extends to the future, so that an individual may give instructions as to the forms of medical treatment that he will or will not accept in anticipation of the prospect that circumstances may arise in which it will not be possible either to give a valid consent or to refuse consent, because, for example, of incapacity.[21] A competent

6–008

---

[18] [1993] A.C. 789, 891. See also Lord Keith at 857; Lord Goff at 864; Lord Browne-Wilkinson at 882. Similarly, in *Re T. (Adult: Refusal of Treatment)* [1993] Fam. 95, 102, Lord Donaldson M.R. said that a competent adult has an absolute right to choose whether to consent to medical treatment or to refuse it "notwithstanding that the reasons for making the choice are rational, irrational, unknown or even non-existent." See also *per* Butler-Sloss L.J. at 116 and Staughton L.J. at 120–121; and *Re MB (Medical Treatment)* [1997] 8 Med. L.R. 217; [1997] 2 F.L.R. 426 at 432.

[19] [1999] Fam. 26, 46–47.

[20] *St. George's Healthcare NHS Trust v S; R v Collins and Others, ex parte S* [1999] Fam. 26; *Re MB (Medical Treatment)* [1997] 8 Med. L.R. 217; [1997] 2 F.L.R. 426. See paras 6–100 to 6–103.

[21] [1993] A.C. 789 at 857, *per* Lord Keith, and 864, *per* Lord Goff, who added that: "in such circumstances especial care may be necessary to ensure that the prior refusal of consent is still properly to be regarded as applicable in the circumstances which have subsequently occurred." See also *Malette v Shulman* (1990) 67 D.L.R. (4th) 321, 330 (Ont. C.A.); *Fleming v Reid* (1991) 82 D.L.R. (4th) 298, 310 (Ont. C.A.). For discussion of "advance directives" see: Morgan (1994) 14 L.S. 411; Law Commission report, *Mental Incapacity*, Law Com. No. 231, (1995) Part V. The Draft Mental Incapacity Bill, June 2003, will, in due course, enact many of the Law Commission's recommendations. See also the BMA Code of Practice on *Advance Statements about Medical Treatment*, April 2000, available at web.bma.org.uk/ap.nsf/Content/codeofpractice; and the GMC guidance, *Seeking patients' consent: the ethical considerations*, February 1999, para. 22, available at *www.gmc-uk.org*.

patient may even obtain an injunction restraining anyone from performing treatment to which he objects.[22] Moreover, there is nothing in the European Convention on Human Rights which alters the right of a competent patient to make a statement refusing life-sustaining medical treatment in the future.[23] But care must be taken to ensure that any advance directive made by the patient covers the circumstances that have arisen. In *Re T. (Adult: Refusal of Treatment)*[24] Lord Donaldson M.R. said that an anticipatory choice made by the patient would bind the doctor "if clearly established and applicable in the circumstances—two major 'ifs'"; and in *St. George's Healthcare NHS Trust v S*[25] the Court of Appeal commented that "if there is reason to doubt the reliability of the advance directive (for example it may sensibly be thought not to apply to the circumstances which have arisen), then an application for a declaration may be made." The Mental Incapacity Bill will give statutory form to an "advance decision", which is defined as a decision made by an adult when he has capacity to do so that if, at a later time, and in such circumstances as he may specify, a specified treatment is proposed to be carried out or continued by a person providing health care for him, and at that time he lacks capacity to consent, the specified treatment is not to be carried out or continued.[26] The advance decision will not apply to treatment if at the relevant time the patient has capacity to give or refuse consent to it; if the treatment is not the treatment specified in the advance decision; if any circumstances specified in the advance decision are absent; or if circumstances exist which were not anticipated at the time of the advance decision and which would have affected the patient's decision had he anticipated them.[27] The Bill provides protection from liability for persons who carry out or continue treatment in ignorance of the fact that a valid advance decision applies to the treatment.[28] Similarly, a person who withholds or withdraws treatment in the reasonable belief that a valid advance decision applies to the treatment is not liable for the consequences.[29] Where a court is asked to rule on whether a valid advance decision applies in the circumstances, then a person will be able to provide life-sustaining treatment or do anything reasonably believed to be necessary to prevent a serious deterioration in the patient's

---

[22] *Re C. (adult: refusal of treatment)* [1994] 1 W.L.R. 290; para. 6–029—where Thorpe J. granted an injunction restraining the amputation of the patient's gangrene-infected foot without express consent.

[23] *Re AK (Adult Patient) (Medical Treatment: Consent)* [2001] 1 F.L.R. 129; *Re B (adult: refusal of medical treatment)* [2002] EWHC 429 (Fam); [2002] 2 All E.R. 449.

[24] [1993] Fam. 95, 103.

[25] [1999] Fam. 26 at 63.

[26] Draft Mental Incapacity Bill, cl. 23(1) (June 2003). The treatment or circumstances may be expressed in broad terms or non-scientific language: cl. 23(2). A person who, with intent to deceive, conceals or destroys another person's written advance decision to refuse treatment commits a criminal offence: cl. 32.

[27] *ibid.* cl. 24(3) and (4). An advance decision will not apply to life-sustaining treatment unless the patient specified that it was to apply to such treatment: cl. 24(5).

[28] *ibid.* cl. 25(2).

[29] *ibid.* cl. 25(3).

condition while the ruling is sought, notwithstanding the apparently valid advance decision.[30]

(1) Consent as a defence to battery

The patient's consent to medical treatment, or indeed any procedure which involves a touching of the patient's body, is essential because it renders lawful what would otherwise constitute the tort of battery, and, indeed, a serious invasion of the person's bodily integrity.[31] Although battery is said to be an intentional tort, it must be emphasised that there is no need for the defendant to have intended to commit a tort. If, through some oversight, a doctor fails to obtain the patient's consent to the procedure in question he will be liable in battery. So, if he performs the wrong operation,[32] or operates on the wrong limb,[33] or the wrong patient, he commits a battery. This is the position even where the doctor acts in all good faith, and is as much the victim of some administrative error as the patient. In *Schweizer v Central Hospital*[34] the claimant consented to an operation on his toe, but due to a mix up a spinal fusion operation was performed. The surgeon was held liable in battery.

6–009

Clearly, the patient's consent must relate to the procedure that the doctor performs. Just as a complete lack of consent will give rise to an action for battery, a doctor who exceeds the consent given by the patient will also be liable. Thus, a patient who consents to the administration of a particular type of anaesthetic does not necessarily consent to the administration of a

6–010

---

[30] *ibid.* cl. 25(5). Some care will be needed in interpreting this provision. Where a "one-off" medical intervention will resolve the issue, there might be a temptation to apply to the court for a ruling in order to rely on the protection of cl. 25(5). For example, in the circumstances of a case such as *Malette v Shulman* (1990) 67 D.L.R. (4th) 321, where an unconscious patient in a casualty department of a hospital was found to be carrying a card stating that, as a Jehovah's Witness, she did not wish to have a blood transfusion, the administration of blood was certainly necessary to prevent a deterioration in her condition. She was given a blood transfusion, and survived, thus being presented with a fait accompli. The Ontario Court of Appeal subsequently ruled that the treatment was unlawful, contrary to a valid advance statement on the card. See para. 6–099. Cl. 25(5) would seem to confer protection upon the doctor, provided an application to the court for a ruling was being sought.

[31] Note that it is not merely the fact of the patient's consent which legitimates the doctor's act, but the fact that it is given within the context of a doctor-patient relationship: *R. v Brown* [1994] 1 A.C. 212, 258–259, *per* Lord Mustill. Consent to battery is not the same as the defence of *volenti non fit injuria*, which is a voluntary agreement by the claimant to absolve the defendant from the legal consequences of an unreasonable risk of harm created by the defendant, where the claimant has full knowledge of both the nature and extent of the risk. The patient who consents to medical treatment does not consent to run the risk of negligence by the doctor: see *Freeman v Home Office* [1984] Q.B. 524, 557, *per* Sir John Donaldson M.R.

[32] For example, a circumcision instead of a tonsillectomy: see *Chatterton v Gerson* [1981] Q.B. 432, 443.

[33] *Shaw v Wright* (1993) 4 *AVMA Medical & Legal Journal* (No. 2) p. 17, where an operation to remove a cataract was performed on the wrong the eye. The action was settled for a modest sum, since coincidentally the operation did produce some improvement in the sight of that eye.

[34] (1974) 53 D.L.R. (3d) 494.

different type of anaesthetic,[35] although it will be a question of fact whether, looking at the matter in broad terms, the consent which the claimant gave was sufficient to encompass a procedure about which she was not informed.[36] A patient who consents to a procedure being performed on one limb does not consent to the same procedure on another limb, especially where the patient has specifically objected. In *Allan v New Mount Sinai Hospital*[37] the claimant gave an anaesthetist specific directions that he should not touch her left arm because he would "have nothing but trouble there." In the past she had had some difficulty with attempts to find a vein in her left arm. The defendant replied that he knew what he was doing, and did administer the anaesthetic by needle in the claimant's left arm. During the operation the needle slipped out of the arm causing the anaesthetic to leak into the tissues interstitially, instead of through the vein. The normal consequence of this is that the patient has a sore arm for a few days, but the claimant suffered a severe reaction which was entirely unexpected. In the High Court of Ontario Linden J. held that although the defendant was not negligent in the way he administered and monitored the anaesthetic, he was liable in battery. The claimant had expressly refused her consent to having the needle inserted into her left arm:

> "Without a consent, either written or oral, no surgery may be performed. This is not a mere formality; it is an important individual right to have control over one's body, even where medical treatment is involved. It is the patient, not the doctor, who decides whether surgery will be performed, where it will be done, when it will be done and by whom it will be done."[38]

If the defendant had thought that the claimant's view was inadvisable, it was his duty to discuss the matter with her and try to convince her to change her mind. Similarly, in *Mulloy v Hop Sang*[39] a patient asked a doctor to repair his injured hand, but not to amputate it, as he preferred to have it looked at in his home town. When the doctor looked at the hand following adminis-

---

[35] *Beausoleil v La Communauté des Soeurs de la Charité de la Providence* (1964) 53 D.L.R. (2d) 65 (Qué.Q.B. Appeal Side).

[36] See *Davis v Barking, Havering and Brentwood Health Authority* [1993] 4 Med. L.R. 85; para. 6–044, where the patient consented to the administration of a general anaesthetic, and was held to have also consented to a caudal block (a type of epidural anaesthetic) administered by the anaesthetist during the course of the operation. See also *Abbas v Kenney* [1996] 7 Med. L.R. 47, QBD, where the defendant surgeon performed a total pelvic clearance, but the mass which the surgeon believed to be cancer turned out to be endometriosis. The claimant's allegation that she had consented to a laparotomy and oophorectomy but not a total pelvic clearance was rejected on the facts.

[37] (1980) 109 D.L.R. (3d) 634; rev'd on a pleading point (1982) 125 D.L.R. (3d) 276.

[38] *ibid.* at 642. In *White v Turner* (1981) 120 D.L.R. (3d) 269, 282–283 (Ont. H.C.), affirmed (1982) 12 D.L.R. (4th) 319 (Ont. C.A.) Linden J. said that the law of battery remains available where there is no consent to the operation, where the treatment given goes beyond the consent, or where the consent is obtained by fraud or misrepresentation (citing *Reibl v Hughes* (1980) 114 D.L.R. (3d) 1 (S.C.C.)).

[39] [1935] 1 W.W.R. 714 (Alta. C.A.).

tration of an anaesthetic he decided that it ought to be amputated, and proceeded to do so. He was held liable in battery because the amputation was contrary to the express objection of the patient.

Just as a patient may place limits on a consent, so she may also withdraw a consent even though a medical procedure is under way. In *Ciarlariello v Schacter*[40] a patient became agitated during the course of a an angiogram, and asked for the test to be stopped. After 10 or 15 minutes the test was resumed and the patient suffered a severe and rare reaction to the procedure. The Supreme Court of Canada stated that where, during the course of a medical procedure, a patient withdraws consent to that procedure, the doctors must halt the process:

6–011

> "An individual's right to determine what medical procedures will be accepted must include the right to stop a procedure. It is not beyond the realm of possibility that the patient is better able to gauge the level of pain or discomfort that can be accepted or that the patient's premonitions of tragedy or mortality may have a basis in reality. In any event, the patient's right to bodily integrity provides the basis for the withdrawal of a consent to a medical procedure even while it is underway. Thus, if it is found that the consent is effectively withdrawn during the course of the proceeding, then it must be terminated. This must be the result except in those circumstances where the medical evidence suggests that to terminate the process would be either life-threatening or pose immediate and serious problems to the health of the patient."[41]

The determination of whether or not consent has been withdrawn is a question of fact. The patient may be under the influence of sedatives or other medication which have affected her competence to withdraw consent, or the words used may be interpreted as a cry of pain rather than a withdrawal of consent.[42] On the facts, the patient had withdrawn her consent but had then renewed her consent to the resumption of the test.[43]

Where a patient consents to the administration of an injection, the consent relates both to the act of inserting the needle and the contents of the syringe. If what is injected is not the substance to which the patient has given consent it is a battery. Thus, in *Potts v North West Regional Health Authority*[44] the claimant agreed to be vaccinated against rubella, but unknown to the claimant the syringe also contained the contraceptive drug Depo-Provera. The defendants were held liable in battery. Consent to the vaccination injection did not amount to consent to anything that the doctors considered to be appropriate being injected into the patient.

6–012

---

[40] (1993) 100 D.L.R. (4th) 609 (S.C.C.).
[41] *ibid.* at 619, *per* Cory J. delivering the judgment of the court.
[42] See, *e.g.*, *Mitchell v McDonald* (1987) 40 C.C.L.T. 266.
[43] See para. 6–122 for consideration of the information that the patient must be given before a resumption of the procedure.
[44] (1983; unreported), see *The Guardian*, July 23, 1983.

6–013   In a number of cases women have been sterilised without their consent in the course of other operative procedures, such as Caesarian sections. This may be because the surgeon has taken the view that it would be better for the woman not to have any more children, or it could be that there has been an administrative mix-up. In *Cull v Royal Surrey County Hospital*,[45] for example, an epileptic patient who was pregnant went into hospital for a termination by curettage, but the surgeon performed the major operation of hysterectomy with a view to sterilising her. The patient had specifically refused consent to the sterilisation, and her general practitioner had written to the hospital to make this clear. The letter was mislaid by the hospital staff, although the hospital admission book indicated for "curettage." The jury awarded damages of £120 against the hospital for negligence, and nominal damages for trespass against the surgeon. In *Devi v West Midlands Regional Health Authority*[46] a surgeon performed a sterilisation operation on the claimant in the course of an operation to repair a perforation of the uterus which had been caused during an earlier dilation and curettage. There had been no prior discussion with the claimant about the possibility of sterilisation, the surgeon had simply taken the view that it was in the patient's interests. The defendants admitted liability for battery.[47] Similarly, in *Murray v McMurchy*,[48] a doctor, during the course of a Caesarean section, discovered fibroid tumours in the patient's uterus which he believed would be a danger if the patient were to become pregnant again, and so he performed a sterilisation operation. He was held liable in battery. The sterilisation could not be justified under the principle of necessity because there was no immediate threat to the patient's health and it would not have been unreasonable to postpone the operation. It was merely convenient to perform the operation without consent as the patient was already under general anaesthetic.[49]

---

[45] [1932] 1 B.M.J. 1195.

[46] (1981, CA; unreported).

[47] Ormrod L.J. questioned whether battery was the appropriate cause of action rather than a claim "on the basis of failure to give proper advice," and said that the case should not be treated as authority on the question of battery, because it had not been discussed in argument. Whatever the status of the case as an authority, it is respectfully submitted that the sterilisation of a competent adult without her consent is undoubtedly a battery, and there is no basis for treating it as simply an instance of negligence.

[48] [1949] 2 D.L.R. 442; *Winn v Alexander* [1940] 3 D.L.R. 778; see also *Hamilton v Birmingham Regional Health Board* [1969] 2 B.M.J. 456 in which the claimant was sterilised without her consent during a Caesarian delivery, which was her third Caesarian. She was never asked whether she wanted to be sterilised. Liability was admitted; *Grayson-Crowe v Ministry of Defence* (1992) 3 AVMA Medical & Legal Journal (No. 3) p. 14, where the claimant believed that she was undergoing minor exploratory surgery, but the surgeon performed a hysterectomy because he discovered fibroids. The defendants admitted liability.

[49] See also *Wells v Surrey Area Health Authority, The Times,* July 29, 1978 (news report) in which a Roman Catholic woman was sterilised in the course of a Caesarian operation. She signed the consent form just before she went into the operating theatre. Croom-Johnson J. held that she had understood the nature of the operation and therefore consented to the sterilisation, but she had been inadequately counselled as to the implications of the operation. In particular the patient should have been told that there was no medical need for sterilisation, and that there was no urgency about the matter because it could be done at a later stage. The defendants were liable in negligence.

Prima facie the patient's consent will be limited to procedures to be per-   **6–014**
formed by a particular doctor. Thus, in *Michael v Molesworth*[50] a patient
recovered nominal damages for breach of contract when an operation was
performed by a doctor other than the doctor whom the patient had anticipated. Older NHS consent forms contained a clause stating that "No assurance has been given to me that the operation/treatment will be performed
or administered by any particular practitioner," a provision which was specifically intended to cover the circumstances of *Michael v Molesworth*.
However, such a clause could not be taken as an invitation to the whole
world to perform surgery upon the patient. For example, if a patient were
to consent to surgery being performed by a person whom the patient mistakenly believed to be a registered medical practitioner, but who was in fact
unqualified, the consent would be invalid because the qualifications of the
person wielding the scalpel go to the *nature* of the transaction.[51] By extension of this argument, it might be said that a patient's consent is not given
simply to "a doctor" (any old doctor?) but a doctor whom the patient
believes to be qualified and competent to perform the procedure in question. Newly qualified junior doctors, for example, do not, and are not
expected to, perform open heart surgery. A patient's signature on a standard consent form could not be taken as consent to such a step. Perhaps to
deal with this point, the current NHS model consent form states that: "I
understand that you cannot give me a guarantee that a particular person
will perform the procedure. The person will, however, have appropriate
experience."

Burden of Proof

It is unclear whether consent is a true defence to an action for battery, or   **6–015**
whether the absence of consent is part and parcel of the tort itself. Must the
claimant prove that he did not consent in order to establish the cause of
action, or is it sufficient to prove the direct interference, leaving the defendant to justify the act by asserting and proving that the claimant consented?
This issue turns, essentially, upon who has the burden of proof. The traditional view has been that consent operates as a defence, and accordingly it
is for the defendant to prove that the claimant consented. In *Freeman v
Home Office*,[52] however, McCowan J. held that the claimant has the burden
of proof, a view which effectively redefines battery to mean an "unconsented
to interference with another's bodily integrity." On the other hand, in *Collins
v Wilcock* Goff L.J. appeared to regard consent as a defence,[53] as did Neill

---

[50] [1950] 2 B.M.J. 171.
[51] Though see *R v Richardson* [1999] Q.B. 444 and *R v Tabassum* [2000] Lloyd's Rep. Med.
404, CA, para. 6–040 below.
[52] [1984] Q.B. 524.
[53] [1984] 3 All E.R. 374, 378: "Generally speaking, consent is defence to battery"; see also *R.
v Brown* [1994] 1 A.C. 212, 246–247 *per* Lord Jauncey; *T. v T.* [1988] Fam. 52, 66–67;
Croom-Johnson L.J. in *Wilson v Pringle* [1987] Q.B. 237, 252 considered that consent was
an example of "so-called 'defences'."

L.J. in *Re F. (Mental Patient: Sterilisation).*[54] In Canada[55] and Australia[56] this is undoubtedly the case.

(2) Forms of consent

6–016   Consent may be either express or implied from the claimant's conduct. If a doctor tells a patient that he wants to give him an injection and the patient silently bares his arm and holds it out for the needle he will be taken to have consented.[57] If the doctor reasonably believes that the patient has consented the patient cannot complain afterwards that there was no consent. Silence by a patient, however, is not necessarily consent; it will depend on the circumstances of the case, and whether the doctor's inference of consent was reasonable.[58]

6–017   Prior to most major surgical procedures the patient will be asked to sign a written consent form. Standard consent forms usually state that the nature and purpose of the operation or treatment have been explained to the patient.[59] But such forms are not conclusive against the patient, they are

---

[54] [1990] 2 A.C. 1, 29: "It is apparent therefore that the defence of consent is not a complete answer . . ." *Clerk & Lindsell on Torts*, 18th ed., 2000, para. 13–07 states that the burden of proving absence of consent lies with the claimant, citing *Freeman v Home Office* [1984] Q.B. 524; *cf.* Dugdale and Stanton, *Professional Negligence*, 3rd ed., 1998, para. 11.57 placing the onus of proving that the patient has given a valid consent on the doctor; and Trindade (1982) 2 O.J.L.S. 211, 229 to the same effect.

[55] *Beausoleil v La Communauté des Soeurs de la Charité de la Providence* (1964) 53 D.L.R. (2d) 65, 69; *Hambly v Shepley* (1967) 63 D.L.R. (2d) 94, 95 (Ont. C.A.); *Kelly v Hazlett* (1976) 75 D.L.R. (3d) 536, 563 (Ont. H.C.); *Schweizer v Central Hospital* (1974) 53 D.L.R. (3d) 494, 510; *Reibl v Hughes* (1980) 114 D.L.R. (3d) 1, 9 (S.C.C.); *Allan v New Mount Sinai Hospital* (1980) 109 D.L.R. (3d) 634, 641. See the discussion by Blay (1987) 61 A.L.J. 25.

[56] *Secretary, Department of Health and Community Services v J.W.B.* (1992) 106 A.L.R. 385, 453 (H.C. of Aus.), *per* McHugh J. His Honour observed that lack of consent is not an essential element of the tort of trespass to the person: "The essential element of the tort is an intentional or reckless, direct act of the defendant which makes or has the effect of causing contact with the body of the claimant. Consent may make the act lawful, but, if there is no evidence on the issue, the tort is made out. The contrary view is inconsistent with a person's right of bodily integrity. Other persons do not have the right to interfere with an individual's body unless he or she proves lack of consent to the interference."

[57] *Allan v New Mount Sinai Hospital* (1980) 109 D.L.R. (3d) 634, 641. Provided, of course, that the syringe contains what the patient believed it to contain: *Potts v North West Regional Health Authority* (1983; unreported), para. 6–012.

[58] *ibid.* See also *Schweizer v Central Hospital* (1974) 53 D.L.R. (3d) 494, 508, *per* Thompson J.: "Consent may be implied where circumstances dictate that it is clearly indicated and it is manifest that the will of the patient accompanies such consent." A lack of objection may not be sufficient for the doctor to infer consent by the patient, a point that becomes significant in the context of the treatment of patients with mental handicap: see Gunn (1987) 16 Anglo-American L.R. 242, 246.

[59] The current NHS model consent form 1 includes a statement by the health professional concerned that: "I have explained the procedure to the patient." The form then asks the health professional to confirm that the patient has been told about the intended benefits, serious or frequently occurring risks, any extra procedures which may become necessary, what the procedure is likely to involve, the benefits and risks of any available alternative treatments (including no treatment) and any particular concerns of the patient. The model NHS consent forms are available at *www.doh.gov.uk/consent*. Where the patient receives treatment privately the contract between doctor and patient may be embodied partly in the written

merely evidence that the patient consented to the procedure in question. In *Chatterton v Gerson* Bristow J. said that:

> "... getting the patient to sign a *pro forma* expressing consent to undergo the operation 'the effect and nature of which have been explained to me' ... should be a valuable reminder to everyone of the need for explanation and consent. But it would be no defence to an action based on trespass to the person if no explanation had in fact been given. The consent would have been expressed in form only, not in reality."[60]

Thus, in *Coughlin v Kuntz*[61] the patient signed consent forms but it was held that he did not understand and appreciate the nature of the procedure and therefore there was no valid consent. The defendant had not informed the patient that the procedure was novel, unique to the defendant, and under investigation by the College of Physicians and Surgeons, who had urged him to undertake a moratorium on the procedure. Conversely, an ineffective signature on the consent form does not necessarily indicate that the patient has not given a valid consent. In *Taylor v Shropshire Health Authority*[62] Popplewell J. commented: "For my part I regard the consent form immediately before operation as pure window dressing in this case and designed simply to avoid the suggestion that a patient has not been told." Nonetheless, on the facts, it was held that the patient had in fact been told about the risks involved in a sterilisation operation, and that she had consented.[63]

Similar principles apply to standard forms used to record a patient's refusal of consent, *e.g.* where a patient refuses to accept a blood transfusion. In *Re T. (Adult: Refusal of Treatment)* Lord Donaldson M.R., commenting on the forms used in that case, said that:

6–018

> "It is clear that such forms are designed primarily to protect the hospital from legal action. They will be wholly ineffective for this purpose if the patient is incapable of understanding them, they are not explained

---

(n.59 contd.) consent form and partly in the oral conversations between doctor and patient prior to the procedure, at which time the nature and effect of the operation should have been explained to the patient: *Eyre v Measday* [1986] 1 All E.R. 488, 492.

[60] [1981] Q.B. 432, 443; *Hajgato v London Health Association* (1982) 36 O.R. (2d) 669, 679; affirmed 40 O.R. (2d) 264 (Ont. C.A.): "While the plaintiff signed a standard form of authorisation and consent prior to the operation in which she acknowledged the nature of the operation had been explained to her satisfaction, the existence of that consent does not protect a doctor from liability unless the patient has been informed to the satisfaction of the court." See also *Bickford v Stiles* (1981) 128 D.L.R. (3d) 516, 520; *Brushett v Cowan* (1987) 40 D.L.R. (4th) 488; rev'd on the facts (1990) 69 D.L.R. (4th) 743 (Newfd. C.A.).

[61] (1987) 42 C.C.L.T. 142 (B.C.S.C.); affirmed [1990] 2 W.W.R. 737, 745 (B.C.C.A.).

[62] [1998] Lloyd's Rep. Med. 395, 398.

[63] See also *Newbury v Bath District Health Authority* (1998) 47 B.M.L.R. 138 where pre-operative consent to complex spinal surgery was obtained by a house officer with less than six months experience of surgery, but Ebsworth J. concluded that the obtaining of the consent had, in any event, to be looked at in the light of the consultations between the surgeon and the patient before the consent form was signed, and before the patient was admitted to hospital. On that basis, the surgeon had informed the patient about the nature of the procedure.

to him and there is no good evidence (apart form the patient's signature) that he had that understanding and fully appreciated the significance of signing it."[64]

6–019   It is not good practice to get patients to sign consent forms just before they have the operation when they have already been sedated. The drug may impair the patient's ability to comprehend, and render an apparent consent invalid. For example, in *Beausoleil v La Communaute des Soeurs de la Charité de la Providence*[65] the claimant went into hospital for a back operation, and told the surgeon that she wanted a general anaesthetic, not a spinal anaesthetic. On the day of the operation she was sedated and taken to the operating theatre where she told the anaesthetist that she did not want a spinal anaesthetic. The anaesthetist then talked the claimant into accepting the spinal anaesthetic, without examining her or consulting the surgeon. This was administered with reasonable care, but after the operation the claimant was paralysed from the waist down, probably as a result of the spinal anaesthetic. It was held that the claimant had not given a valid consent. Due to the sedation the exchange between claimant and defendant "no longer had any real significance for the plaintiff and . . . [was] of no legal consequence."[66] Similarly, in *Kelly v Hazlett*[67] the claimant consented to an osteotomy to correct a deformity in her elbow after the administration of a sedative. Morden J. commented that the giving of a consent in such circumstances, at the very least, leaves the validity of the consent open to question, although he concluded that, on the facts, the claimant had a sufficient understanding of the basic nature and character of the operation for the consent to be effective.[68]

6–020   Just as a signature on a consent form is merely evidence, and not proof, that the patient has consented, the absence of a signature does not necessarily prove the lack of consent. The absence of a signature may, however, when considered with other evidence, indicate that there was no consent or no consent to the extent of the procedure actually carried out. In *Williamson v East London & City Health Authority*[69] the claimant, who had previously

---

[64] [1993] Fam. 95, 114. In *St. George's Healthcare NHS Trust v S* [1999] Fam. 26, 63 the Court of Appeal said that where a competent patient refuses consent to treatment the advice given to the patient should be recorded: "For their own protection hospital authorities should seek unequivocal assurances from the patient (to be recorded in writing) that the refusal represents an informed decision, that is, that she understands the nature of and reasons for the proposed treatment, and the risks and likely prognosis involved in the decision to refuse or accept it. If the patient is unwilling to sign a written indication of this refusal, this too should be noted in writing. Such a written indication is merely a record for evidential purposes. It should not be confused with or regarded as a disclaimer."

[65] (1964) 53 D.L.R. (2d) 65 (Qué.Q.B. Appeal Side).

[66] *ibid.* at 76, *per* Rinfret J. See also *Wells v Surrey Area Health Authority, The Times*, July 29, 1978 (news report) n. 49, above.

[67] (1976) 75 D.L.R. (3d) 536 (Ont. H.C.).

[68] *ibid.* at 563. The defendant was held liable in negligence for failing to inform the claimant about the risk of stiffness associated with the operation; see also *Ferguson v Hamilton Civic Hospitals* (1983) 144 D.L.R. (3d) 214, 237, *per* Krever J., affirmed (1985) 18 D.L.R. (4th) 638 (Ont. C.A.).

[69] [1998] Lloyd's Rep. Med. 6; (1998) 41 B.M.L.R. 85, QBD.

had bilateral breast implants, had signed a consent form in January 1994 for a replacement breast prosthesis and right open capsulotomy. Her condition deteriorated between January and April when she was admitted to hospital. She was examined pre-operatively by the surgeon who discovered lumps in the armpit running down the right arm. The evidence of the surgeon was that she told the claimant that she would now have to remove most of her right breast. The claimant said that she understood that a small portion of breast tissue would have to be removed, and that if she had been told that a mastectomy would be performed she would not have agreed to the procedure, but would have left the hospital and sought a second opinion. The consent form signed in January was amended to reflect the procedure that was actually performed in April, but the amendments were not signed by the claimant. The judge found that, given that the appearance of her breasts was clearly important to the claimant, and the fact that the consent form was not signed by her when it was amended, it was probable that she had not been told about the prospect of a mastectomy. She would have reacted very differently from the way in which the nursing notes had recorded. She would not have been reassured, she would have been horrified and would have expressed that concern. The absence of her signature on the consent form pointed very strongly to the fact that she had not been present when it had been altered. Thus, the claimant had not consented to undergo such an extensive operation.

Some older consent forms included a clause to the effect that the patient consents to "such further or alternative operative measures or treatment as may be found necessary during the course of the operation or treatment."[70] The effect of such a clause was highly questionable, since if the "further or alternative" treatment was not justified in law under the principle of necessity,[71] it is unlikely that such a blanket consent would protect the doctor because the patient would probably be unaware of the nature of the treatment.[72] The

6–021

---

[70] M.P.S. General Consent Form, 1988.

[71] See paras 6–089 to 6–095.

[72] cf. Dugdale and Stanton, *Professional Negligence*, 3rd ed., 1998, para. 11.61, suggesting that such a consent might justify more extensive intervention than would be lawful under the principle of necessity. In *Brushett v Cowan* (1990) 69 D.L.R. (4th) 743 (Newfd. C.A.) the claimant signed a consent form authorising a muscle biopsy, and also consented to "such further or alternative measures as may be found to be necessary during the course of the operation." The defendant performed a muscle biopsy and a bone biopsy, and at first instance was held liable in battery in respect of the bone biopsy (see (1987) 40 D.L.R. (4th) 488, 492). On appeal the decision was reversed, on the basis that the extent of the consent must be judged by looking at all the circumstances, not merely the consent form. The claimant had consented to a diagnostic procedure to determine the cause of her medical problem, and in the circumstances this was a sufficient consent to the bone biopsy. See further *Pridham v Nash* (1986) 33 D.L.R. (4th) 304 (Ont. H.C.) where the patient signed a consent form for an investigative laparoscopy, which included a consent to such "additional procedures as may be necessary or medically advisable during the course of" the procedure. It was held that this consent was sufficient to cover the performance of minor surgery during the course of the examination, such as moving and clearing away obstructions, but it would not have justified major surgery; *O'Bonswain v Paradis* (1993) 15 C.C.L.T. (2d) 188 (Ont. H.C.). Consent to a breast biopsy is not, however, consent to a mastectomy: *Re P.* (1993) 4 *AVMA Medical & Legal Journal* (No. 2) p. 18, where the claimant had her right breast removed, having consented only to re-excision of a scar on the right breast with lymph node sampling. The action, which appears to have been brought in negligence rather than trespass, was settled.

consent form constitutes evidence of consent, but if in fact the patient does not understand the nature of the treatment the consent is invalid. The current NHS model consent forms do not include such a clause but state that the patient understands "that any procedure in addition to those described on this form will only be carried out if it is necessary to save my life or to prevent serious harm to my health."[73] At best, this probably amounts to little more than providing information to the patient, since a procedure that was not necessary to save life or to prevent serious harm to the patient's health would not be justified under the common law principle of necessity, and unless there was express consent would exceed the scope of the patient's consent. The model consent form also states that: "I have been told about the additional procedures which may become necessary during my treatment. I have listed below any procedures which I do not wish to be carried out without further discussion."[74] This wording is an improvement on the previous model consent form since it does at least purport to identify (and thereby place some limit on) the procedures which the patient has to indicate she does not wish to undergo. Nonetheless, there is no obligation in law for a patient to specify what she does not want to have done to her and the failure of the patient to indicate what she does not want to happen is irrelevant. In the absence of a valid justification, such as the patient's consent to the specific procedure that is contemplated, or necessity, all other procedures which involve physical contact with the person are unlawful, as battery. To suggest otherwise, even by implication, as the model consent form appears to do, misrepresents the true position in law. The solution is simple. If, as the model consent form states, the patient has been told about the additional procedures which may become necessary during the treatment, those procedures should be listed on the form and the patient can then give an express consent to them. Those procedures which she does not wish to be carried out can simply be omitted from the form. It may be that listing the procedures which the patient would not want to be carried out is a useful reminder to the medical staff of the limits to the scope of the patient's consent. But the omission of the patient to complete this section of the form does not in itself constitute a consent to those procedures.

(3) Consent must be valid

6–022   In order to be effective as a defence to a claim in battery the patient's consent must be a valid consent. For this purpose the consent must be "real."[75] There are three elements to this. First, it must be voluntary and uncoerced. Secondly, the patient must be capable of understanding the nature of the procedure, *i.e.* he must have the capacity (or competence) to consent. Thirdly, he must have a certain minimum level of information concerning the "nature" of the procedure so that he knows what he is consenting to.

---

[73] See NHS model consent form 1 (available at *www.doh.gov.uk/consent*).
[74] *ibid.*
[75] *Chatterton v Gerson* [1981] Q.B. 432, 442.

(a) Voluntary consent

A person's consent must be voluntary.[76] Consent obtained by coercion or   6–023
duress is invalid. In *Latter v Braddell*[77] it was held that a housemaid, who,
at the insistence of her employer, submitted to a medical examination pro-
testing and sobbing throughout, had consented, even though she mistakenly
believed that she was obliged to comply. The majority of the court took the
view that the consent would be involuntary only where the claimant submitted through fear of violence. This decision was questionable at the time,[78]
and would probably not be followed if the facts were to recur today. Thus,
a mistaken belief as to the authority of the defendant may destroy in substance the claimant's freedom to choose.[79]

In *Freeman v Home Office*[80] it was accepted that in some circumstances a   6–024
person's apparent consent could be vitiated by the defendant's exercise of
authority over him, without any threat of physical violence. The claimant,
who was serving a term of life imprisonment, claimed that in the prison
context it was impossible for there to be a free and voluntary consent by a
prisoner to treatment by a prison medical officer, who was not merely a
doctor but a prison officer within the meaning of the Prison Rules who could
influence the prisoner's life and his prospects of release on licence. This
created an atmosphere of constraint upon an inmate. McCowan J. rejected
this contention as a proposition of law, taking the view that it is a question
of fact in any particular case whether the patient's consent is voluntary. His
Lordship added that where, in a prison setting, a doctor has the power to
influence a prisoner's situation and prospects a court must be alive to the risk
that what may appear, on the face of it, to be a real consent is not in fact so.[81]

A patient's apparent consent or refusal of consent may be vitiated by the   6–025
undue influence of a third party, provided it can be demonstrated that the
patient's will has been overborne. In *Re T. (Adult: Refusal of Treatment)*[82]

---

[76] *Bowater v Rowley Regis Corporation* [1944] K.B. 476, 479, *per* Scott L.J.: "A man cannot
be said to be truly 'willing' unless he is in a position to choose freely, and freedom of choice
predicates, not only full knowledge of the circumstances on which the exercise of choice is
conditioned, so that he may be able to choose wisely, but the absence from his mind of any
feeling of constraint so that nothing shall interfere with the freedom of his will." This remark
was made in the context of the defence of *volenti non fit injuria*, but it has much force in
relation to the defence of consent to battery: see *Freeman v Home Office* [1984] Q.B. 524,
535–536, 556–557

[77] (1881) 50 L.J.Q.B. 448, CA.

[78] See the dissent of Lopes J. at (1880) 50 L.J.C.P. 166.

[79] *Clerk & Lindsell on Torts*, 18th ed., 2000, para. 13–11, citing *T. v T.* [1964] P. 85, 99, 102;
cf. Dugdale and Stanton, *Professional Negligence*, 3rd ed., 1998, para. 11.60, citing *Latter
v Braddell* (1881) 50 L.J.Q.B. 448.

[80] [1984] Q.B. 524.

[81] *ibid.* at 542–543; affirmed by the Court of Appeal *ibid.* at 557. See also *Kaimowitz v
Michegan Department of Mental Health* 42 U.S.L.W. 2063 (1973) where it was said that the
capacity of an involuntarily detained mental patient to consent to psychosurgery was diminished by the very nature of his incarceration, which through the phenomenon of institutionalisation may strip the individual of the support which enables him to maintain his sense of
self-worth.

[82] [1993] Fam. 95.

T was injured in a car accident when she was 34 weeks pregnant. She had been brought up by her mother who was a Jehovah's Witness, although T herself was not a member of the sect. The possibility of a blood transfusion arose. On two occasions, following private conversations with her mother, T told the medical staff that she did not want a blood transfusion. She was informed that there were other options, and that blood transfusions were not normally necessary after a Caesarian section, which was being contemplated. T signed a form of refusal of consent to blood transfusions. Following the operation her condition deteriorated, and she was transferred to intensive care. She remained sedated and in a critical condition until, following an emergency hearing, Ward J. granted a declaration that it would not be unlawful for the hospital to administer the blood transfusion. At a second hearing Ward J. held that T had neither consented to nor refused consent to a transfusion, and in the emergency situation it was lawful for the doctors to do what they considered to be in T's best interests. The Court of Appeal held that T had not been fit to make a genuine decision due to her debilitated medical condition, and the fact that she had been subjected to the undue influence of her mother, which vitiated her decision to refuse a blood transfusion. In the absence of either a valid consent or a valid refusal of consent the doctors had acted lawfully in giving the transfusion, applying the principle of necessity.[83] Lord Donaldson M.R. observed that it was wholly acceptable that a patient should receive advice and assistance from others, particularly members of the family, in reaching a decision about whether to accept or reject treatment, and it matters not how strong the persuasion is, as long as it does not overbear the independence of the patient's decision:

> "The real question in each such case is: does the patient really mean what he says or is he merely saying it for a quiet life, to satisfy someone else or because the advice and persuasion to which he has been subjected is such that he can no longer think and decide for himself? In other words, is it a decision expressed in form only, not in reality? When considering the effects of outside influences, two aspects can be of crucial importance. First, the strength of the will of the patient. One who is very tired, in pain or depressed will be much less able to resist having his will overborne than one who is rested, free from pain and cheerful. Second, the relationship of the 'persuader' to the patient may be of crucial importance. The influence of parents on their children or of one spouse on the other can be, but is by no means necessarily, much stronger than would be the case in other relationships. Persuasion based on religious beliefs can also be much more compelling and the fact that arguments based on religious beliefs are being deployed by someone in a very close relationship with the patient will give them added force and should alert the doctor to the possibility—no more

---

[83] See paras 6–078 et seq.

—that the patient's capacity or will to decide has been overborne. In
other words the patient may not mean what he says."[84]

Thus, a doctor has an obligation to consider whether the decision is really
that of the patient, though in practice this is more likely to be an issue where
the patient is refusing consent since if the patient is agreeing to medically justified treatment recommended by the doctor the normal presumption in
favour of an adult patient's competence will apply.

(b) Capacity to consent

As a general rule, a person's capacity in law to enter into a transaction   6–026
depends upon the nature of the transaction, so a person may, at one and
the same time, be competent in law for some purposes but not for others.[85]
In the context of the doctor-patient relationship, capacity to consent to
treatment depends upon the patient's ability to understand the nature of
the treatment, it does not depend on an assessment of whether the
patient's choice is "correct" or "appropriate".[86] This will be regarded as
a question of fact in each case. The starting point is that adult patients are
presumed to be competent to give a valid consent, unless the contrary is

---

[84] [1993] Fam. 95, 113–114, *per* Lord Donaldson M.R. In *Mrs. U v Centre for Reproductive
Medicine* [2002] EWCA Civ 565; [2002] Lloyd's Rep. Med. 259 a nurse at an IVF clinic
"pressured" the male patient into changing a consent form (to the storage and use of sperm
after his death) by suggesting that, if he did not do so, the IVF treatment that he and his wife
were undergoing would be delayed or halted. The Court of Appeal held that, on the facts,
the patient's withdrawal of consent to the posthumous use and storage of his gametes had
not been vitiated by undue influence. See also *Norberg v Wynrib* (1992) 92 D.L.R. (4th) 449,
457 (S.C.C.), where it was said that the normal presumption that an individual has freedom
to consent may be untenable: "A position of relative weakness can, in some circumstances,
interfere with the freedom of a person's will. Our notion of consent must, therefore, be modified to appreciate the power relationship between the parties," *per* La Forest J. Thus, a
consent given under the influence of an addiction to drugs may not be valid, where there is
an element of exploitation of the doctor-patient relationship by the doctor; *cf. Taylor v
McGillivray* (1993) 110 D.L.R. (4th) 64 (N.B.Q.B.), where the consent of a 16-year-old
patient to a sexual relationship with a physician was held to be valid, despite the inequality
of power between the parties, but the doctor was nonetheless held liable on the basis of a
breach of fiduciary duty owed to his patient, applying *Norberg v Wynrib*.

[85] *Masterman-Lister v Brutton & Co and Jewell and Home Counties Dairies* [2002] EWCA
Civ 1889; [2003] 3 All E.R. 162 at [27] and [58]. For example, a person may have sufficient
understanding to enter into a contract of marriage but not to make a will: *Re Park's Estate*
[1954] P. 89; see also *Re Beaney* [1978] 2 All E.R. 595. See generally *Assessment of Mental
Capacity—Guidance for Doctors and Lawyers*, 2nd ed., 2003, Law Society and BMA;
Grisso and Applebaum, *Assessing Competence to Consent to Treatment*, OUP, 1998.

[86] "Legal capacity depends on understanding rather than wisdom; the quality of the decision
is irrelevant as long as the person understands what he is deciding": *Masterman-Lister v
Jewell and Home Counties Dairies* [2002] EWHC 417 QBD; [2002] Lloyd's Rep. Med. 239
at [19] *per* Wright J. In the Court of Appeal Chadwick L.J. said that "what is required is the
capacity to understand the nature of that transaction when it is explained": [2002] EWCA
Civ 1889; [2003] 3 All E.R. 162 at [58]. See also the Draft Mental Incapacity Bill, June 2003,
cl. 2(3): "A person is not to be treated as unable to make a decision unless all practicable
steps to help him do so have been taken without success." Cl. 2(2) provides that "a person
is not to be treated as unable to make a decision merely because he makes an unwise decision."

established,[87] and the burden of proof rests on those asserting incapacity.[88] The important corollary of this presumption is that the vast majority of adult patients are presumed to be competent to *refuse* treatment if they so choose, which is the context in which disputed questions of competence usually arise.

6–027   In the past questions of capacity were generally left to the good sense of the medical profession. There are several possible tests that could be employed: was the patient's decision about whether to accept or reject treatment rational; was the outcome of the choice reasonable; did the patient have "full" understanding; was the patient's decision-making process rational/reasonable irrespective of the outcome?[89] The difficulty with most, if not all, of these tests is that there is a danger of categorising patients as incompetent simply because they have not chosen the medical option that some other person (whether it be the doctor, a relative or the court) would have chosen in the circumstances, and allowing that person to substitute their own paternalistic view of what is in the patient's best interests.[90] Respect for autonomy and self-determination, which are said to be the foundations of the requirement for consent, must allow for patients to make unreasonable, irrational, or even silly decisions about their health care without the patient immediately being categorised as incompetent. In *Sidaway v Bethlem Royal Hospital Governors*, for example, Lord Templeman said that if a doctor advises a patient to submit to an operation "the patient is entitled to reject that advice for reasons which are rational, or irrational, or for no reason."[91]

---

[87] "Every person is presumed to have the capacity to consent to or to refuse medical treatment unless and until that presumption is rebutted": *Re MB (Medical Treatment)* [1997] 2 FLR 426, 436, *per* Butler-Sloss L.J.; *Re B (adult: refusal of medical treatment)* [2002] EWHC 429 (Fam); [2002] 2 All E.R. 449, at [28] *per* Butler-Sloss P. See also the Law Commission report, *Mental Incapacity*, Law Com. No. 231, (1995) para. 3.2; and the Draft Mental Incapacity Bill, June 2003, cl. 3(1): "For the purposes of this Act, a person must be assumed to have capacity unless it is established that he lacks capacity."

[88] *Masterman-Lister v Brutton & Co and Jewell and Home Counties Dairies* [2002] EWCA Civ 1889; [2003] 3 All E.R. 162 at [17] *per* Kennedy L.J.

[89] For more detailed discussion of this issue see Kennedy & Grubb, *Medical Law*, 3rd ed., 2000, pp. 617 *et seq.*

[90] There is thus a bias in favour of decisions to accept treatment: Gunn (1987) 16 Anglo-American L.R. 242, 251, citing Roth, Meisel and Lidz (1977) Am. J. of Psych. 279, 281. On the assessment of competence see further: Gunn (1994) 2 Med. L. Rev. 8, commenting on the Law Commission Consultation Paper No. 129, *Mentally Incapacitated Adults and Decision-Making: Medical Treatment and Research*, 1993; Jones and Keywood (1996) 2 Med. Law Int. 107; R. McClelland and G. Szmukler (2000) 7 E.J.H.L. 47.

[91] [1985] A.C. 871, 904. See also *Re T. (Adult: Refusal of Treatment)* [1993] Fam. 95, 102, *per* Lord Donaldson M.R., cited above at n. 18; and *Masterman-Lister v Brutton & Co and Jewell and Home Counties Dairies* [2002] EWCA Civ 1889; [2003] 3 All E.R. 162 at [79] where Chadwick L.J. said that a person "should not be regarded as unable to make a rational decision merely because the decision which he does, in fact, make is a decision which would not be made by a person of ordinary prudence." See further *Smith v Auckland Hospital Board* [1965] N.Z.L.R. 191, 219 where T.A. Gresson J. said: "An individual patient must, in my view, always retain the right to decline operative investigation or treatment however unreasonable or foolish this may appear in the eyes of his medical advisers"; and *Lepp v Hopp* (1979) 98 D.L.R. (3d) 464, 470; affirmed (1980) 112 D.L.R. (3d) 67 (S.C.C.), where Prowse J.A. commented that: "Each patient is entitled to make his own decision even though it may not accord with the decision knowledgeable members of the profession would make. The patient has a right to be wrong"; Brazier (1987) 7 L.S. 169, 175.

A test based on the outcome of the individual's decision has never been adopted in English law.[92]

The first guidance from an English court as to the test for capacity in the context of medical treatment came in *Chatterton v Gerson*,[93] where Bristow J. was confronted with the question of how much information a patient must be given before the consent can be regarded as valid. His Lordship said that:

6–028

> "In my judgment once the patient is informed in broad terms of the nature of the procedure which is intended, and gives her consent, that consent is real, and the cause of action on which to base a claim for failure to go into risks and implications is negligence, not trespass."[94]

Although the case was concerned with the scope of the doctor's duty to provide information to the patient, the ruling had clear implications for the assessment of capacity. If the patient need only be given information in broad terms as to the nature of the intended procedure, it must follow that the patient need only understand "in broad terms" the nature of the procedure in order to have sufficient understanding to be considered fully competent to give or withhold consent. This would appear to be quite a low level of understanding.[95]

The issue of the appropriate test for capacity was tangential in *Chatterton v Gerson*, determined only by inference, but in *Re C. (adult: refusal of treatment)*[96] it was central. The patient was a 68 year-old man in Broadmoor who was a paranoid schizophrenic. He was diagnosed as having gangrene in the right foot, and it was believed that his chances of survival with conservative treatment were no more than 15 per cent. C refused to consent to a below-the-knee amputation, but did consent to conservative treatment, which was successful. The hospital refused to give an undertaking that it would not amputate in any future circumstances. C sought an injunction restraining the hospital from amputating his leg now or in the future without his express written consent. The medical evidence suggested that the condition of C's foot was such that it would threaten his life again in the future, and that a below-the-knee amputation itself carried a 15 per cent mortality risk. Thorpe J. said that the question that had to be addressed was whether it had been established that C's capacity was so reduced by his

6–029

---

[92] It follows, of course, that where the outcome of a decision by a patient is apparently rational and reasonable that is not a basis for saying that the patient is competent. So in *Masterman-Lister v Brutton & Co and Jewell and Home Counties Dairies* [2002] EWCA Civ 1889; [2003] 3 All E.R. 162 at [82] Chadwick L.J. commented that a person is not to be regarded as having capacity merely because the decision appears rational. Nonetheless, "to my mind, outcomes are likely to be important (although not conclusive) indicators of the existence, or lack, of understanding."

[93] [1981] Q.B. 432.

[94] *ibid.* at 443.

[95] *cf.* the rule applied to children, which apparently requires a greater level of understanding than with adult patients: see paras 6–047 to 6–049.

[96] [1994] 1 W.L.R. 290. For comment on *Re C* see Stern (1994) 110 L.Q.R. 541; Gordon and Barlow (1993) 143 N.L.J. 1719; Roberts (1994) 10 P.N. 98.

chronic mental illness that he did not sufficiently understand the nature, purpose and effects of the proffered amputation. The decision-making process could be analysed in three stages: first, comprehending and retaining treatment information; second, believing it; and, third, weighing it in the balance to arrive at a choice. Applying that test, the presumption that C had the right to self-determination had not been displaced. Although his general capacity was impaired by schizophrenia, it had not been established that he did not sufficiently understand the nature, purpose and effects of the treatment he refused.[97] There was no direct link between C's refusal of amputation and his persecutory delusions. Moreover, he was content to follow medical advice and to co-operate in treatment appropriately as a patient, as long as his rejection of amputation was respected. Despite the fact that C's capacity was reduced by his mental illness, he had understood and had arrived at a clear choice. In the circumstances it was appropriate to grant the injunction restraining any future amputation without C's express consent.[98]

6–030   The test established by Thorpe J. in *Re C. (adult: refusal of treatment)* was adopted and expanded upon in the important decision of the Court of Appeal in *Re MB (Medical Treatment).*[99] A mother was 40 weeks pregnant when she attended an ante-natal class and it was found that the foetus was in the breech position. The risk of serious injury to the child from a natural birth was assessed as 50 per cent though the risk of physical harm to the mother was small. The mother initially agreed to a proposed Caesarian section, but due to an extreme needle phobia she was unable to accept the needles necessary for an anaesthetic and withdrew her consent to the operation. The hospital was granted a declaration that it would be lawful to carry out such treatment as might be necessary and to use reasonable force in the course of such treatment. The Court of Appeal dismissed the mother's appeal on the basis that her needle phobia rendered her temporarily incompetent, so that the principle of necessity applicable to incompetent patients governed

---

[97] In *Masterman-Lister v Brutton & Co and Jewell and Home Counties Dairies* [2002] EWCA Civ 1889; [2003] 3 All E.R. 162 at [79] Chadwick L.J. said that "a person should not be held unable to understand the information relevant to a decision if he can understand an explanation of that information in broad terms and simple language." His Lordship cited the Law Commission report *Mental Incapacity*, Law Com. No. 231, (1995) which, at paras 3.16 and 3.17, effectively adopted Thorpe J.'s approach. Thus, to be considered competent a person "should be able both (i) to understand and retain the information relevant to the decision which has to be made (including information about the reasonably foreseeable consequences of deciding one way or another or of failing to make any decision) and (ii) to use that information in the decision making process."

[98] See also *Re AK (Adult Patient) (Medical Treatment: Consent)* [2001] 1 F.L.R. 129, and *Re B (adult: refusal of medical treatment)* [2002] EWHC 429 (Fam); [2002] 2 All E.R. 449 where patients found to be competent were held entitled to refuse life-sustaining treatment. See also Wicks, E., "The right to refuse medical treatment under the European Convention on Human Rights" (2001) 9 Med. L. Rev. 17. *Re C. (adult: refusal of treatment)* confirms the, perhaps trite, proposition that simply because an individual is compulsorily detained in a psychiatric hospital it does not necessarily follow that he is incompetent to make decisions about medical treatment. See also *Fleming v Reid* (1991) 82 D.L.R. (4th) 298, 310 (Ont. C.A.).

[99] [1997] 8 Med. L.R. 217; [1997] 2 F.L.R. 426.

her situation.[1] Her needle phobia created a state of panic about the surgery so that she was incapable of making a decision and this amounted to such an impairment of her mental functioning as rendered her temporarily incompetent. The Court of Appeal set out a list of factors that have to be taken into account when considering whether a patient is competent to make a decision about medical treatment, though they were not intended to be determinative in every case, because the decision inevitably depends on the particular facts. Nonetheless, it is probably useful to set them out in full:

"(1) Every person is presumed to have the capacity to consent to or to refuse medical treatment unless and until that presumption is rebutted.
(2) A competent woman who has the capacity to decide may, for religious reasons, other reasons, for rational or irrational reasons or for no reason at all, choose not to have medical intervention, even though the consequence may be the death or serious handicap of the child she bears, or her own death. In that event the courts do not have the jurisdiction to declare medical intervention lawful and the question of her own best interests objectively considered, does not arise.
(3) Irrationality is here used to connote a decision which is so outrageous in its defiance of logic or of accepted moral standards that no sensible person who had applied his mind to the question to be decided it [sic.] could have arrived at it. As Kennedy and Grubb *Medical Law* (Butterworths, 2nd edn, 1994) point out, it might be otherwise if a decision is based on a misperception of reality (*e.g.* the blood is poisoned because it is red). Such a misperception will be more readily accepted to be a disorder of the mind. Although it might be thought that irrationality sits uneasily with competence to decide, panic, indecisiveness and irrationality in themselves do not as such amount to incompetence, but they may be symptoms or evidence of incompetence. The graver the consequences of the decision, the commensurately greater the level of competence is required to take the decision . . .
(4) A person lacks capacity if some impairment or disturbance of mental functioning renders the person unable to make a decision whether to consent to or to refuse treatment. That inability to make a decision will occur when:
    (a) the patient is unable to comprehend and retain the information which is material to the decision, especially as to the likely consequences of having or not having the treatment in question;

---

[1] For discussion of the treatment of incompetent adult patients see paras 6–076 *et seq.* On the particular facts, it was held to be in the mother's best interests to have the surgery, given that she wanted the child to be born alive and healthy (she was not opposed in principle to the surgery, it was only the needle phobia that prevented her from consenting) and there was psychiatric evidence that she was likely to suffer significant long-term damage if there was no operation and the child was born handicapped or died. Where an order declaring that it would be lawful to administer treatment to which the patient objects is granted the necessary corollary is that it would also be lawful to use reasonable force in the course of that treatment: [1997] 8 Med. L.R. 217, 225; [1997] 2 F.L.R. 426, 439.

(b) the patient is unable to use the information and weigh it in the balance as part of the process of arriving at the decision. If, as Thorpe J. observed in *Re C* (above), a compulsive disorder or phobia from which the patient suffers stifles belief in the information presented to her, then the decision may not be a true one. . .

(5) The 'temporary factors' mentioned by Lord Donaldson M.R. in *Re T* (above) (confusion, shock, fatigue, pain or drugs) may completely erode capacity but those concerned must be satisfied that such factors are operating to such a degree that the ability to decide is absent.

(6) Another such influence may be panic induced by fear. Again, careful scrutiny of the evidence is necessary because fear of an operation may be a rational reason for refusal to undergo it. Fear may also, however, paralyse the will and thus destroy the capacity to make a decision."[2]

6–031   In some cases, of which *Re MB (Medical Treatment)* is an example, the condition from which the patient is suffering may affect his or her competence to make decisions about treatment of that condition, even though in other respects the individual is oriented in time and space and appears to be relating to the world in a meaningful way. This is more likely to be the case with the treatment of certain mental illnesses or disorders. In *Re W. (A Minor) (Medical Treatment: Court's Jurisdiction)*[3] the Court of Appeal doubted whether a 16-year-old girl suffering from anorexia nervosa has sufficient understanding to make an informed decision to refuse treatment, because it is a feature of anorexia nervosa that it is capable of destroying the ability to make an informed choice. Similarly, in *Re KB. (adult) (mental patient: medical treatment)*[4] an 18½-year-old patient who was suffering from anorexia nervosa had been detained under section 3 of the Mental Health

---

[2] [1997] 8 Med. L.R. 217, 224; [1997] 2 F.L.R. 426, 436–437. See also the comments of Butler-Sloss P. in *Re B (adult: refusal of medical treatment)* [2002] EWHC 429 (Fam); [2002] 2 All E.R. 449 at [35]. The Law Commission report, *Mental Incapacity*, Law Com. No. 231, (1995) paras 3.14 to 3.21 made a number of recommendations for legislation on the subject of what constitutes a lack of capacity, which are broadly consistent with the Court of Appeal's approach in *Re MB (Medical Treatment)*. For comment on the Law Commission report see Wilson (1996) 4 Med. L. Rev. 227. The Government has agreed that the Law Commission's definitions are helpful, and has indicated that they will be incorporated in legislation: see *Making Decisions* (Cm. 4465) (1999) para. 1.6 [available at *www.lcd.gov.uk/family/mdecisions/indexfr.htm*]. The Draft Mental Incapacity Bill, June 2003, will provide for the first time a statutory definition of what constitutes incapacity. Cl. 1(1) states that a person lacks capacity in relation to a matter if at the material time he is unable to make a decision for himself in relation to the matter because of an impairment of or a disturbance in the functioning of the mind or brain. It does not matter whether the impairment or disturbance is permanent or temporary. Cl. 2(1) provides that a person is unable to make a decision for himself if (a) he is unable to understand the information relevant to the decision; (b) he is unable to retain the information relevant to the decision; (c) he is unable to use the information relevant to the decision as part of the process of making the decision; or (d) he is unable to communicate the decision (whether by talking, using sign language or any other means). The "information relevant to a decision" includes "information about the reasonably foreseeable consequences of (a) deciding one way or another, or (b) failing to make the decision": cl. 2(5).

[3] [1993] Fam. 64.

[4] (1994) 19 B.M.L.R. 144.

Act 1983. The health authority sought a declaration that naso-gastric feeding was medical treatment for mental disorder within the meaning of section 63, which provides that the consent of a patient is not required for any medical treatment given to him for a mental disorder from which he is suffering if the treatment is given by or under the direction of the responsible medical officer. Ewbank J. held that in the circumstances naso-gastric feeding was treatment envisaged by section 63, and does not require the consent of the patient. Moreover, K was not competent to refuse consent. Her condition was such that without food she would die within the next 14 to 21 days. K did not understand the true situation; she saw the prospect of death as a long-term or theoretical prospect, and she was aware that when she got close to death she was likely to be resuscitated under the emergency provisions of the Act. She suffered from a severe mental illness, and the treatment she was refusing was related to the mental illness, not to some unconnected physical condition, as in *Re C.*, where "his mental illness was wholly dissociated from the physical problem that he had and *therefore* despite his mental illness he had the capacity to refuse treatment."[5] Accordingly, K did not have the capacity to refuse consent to treatment.

Competence is not necessarily a question of all or nothing. The patient's capacity may be reduced in certain respects, for example because of the effects of drugs or the patient's physical condition. In these circumstances the patient's competence can vary with gravity of the decision that has to be made.[6] Similarly, the patient may be ambivalent about whether or not to accept treatment. Of course, ambivalence may simply be a sign of careful deliberation by a competent individual about a difficult decision. In *Re B (adult: refusal of medical treatment)*[7] a 43-year-old woman, who was completely paralysed from the neck down, had been put on a ventilator after experiencing respiratory problems. She gave instructions to the hospital that she wanted the ventilator removed, even though she knew that it would almost certainly result in her death. It was suggested on behalf of the hospital that the fact that she had previously agreed to a procedure which involved weaning her from the ventilator over a period of time, although there was a less than one per cent chance of independent breathing being achieved, indicated a degree of ambivalence about her decision which undermined her capacity. Butler-Sloss P. rejected the proposition, in the face of clear medical evidence that B was competent. The question of ambivalence might be relevant "if, and only if, the ambivalence genuinely strikes at the root of the mental capacity of the patient."[8]

6–032

---

[5] *ibid.* at 146 *per* Ewbank J. See also *B. v Croydon Health Authority* [1995] Fam. 133, where on facts similar to *Re KB.* the Court of Appeal agreed with Ewbank J.'s assessment that *Re C.* was distinguishable, because "the gangrene was entirely unconnected with the mental disorder."

[6] *Re T. (Adult: Refusal of Treatment)* [1993] Fam. 95; see para. 6–096.

[7] [2002] EWHC 429 (Fam); [2002] 2 All E.R. 449.

[8] *ibid.* at [35] *per* Butler-Sloss P. In *Re R. (A Minor) (Wardship: Consent to Treatment)* [1992] Fam. 11, a case concerning a 15-year-old girl, it was suggested that the fact that the patient's understanding fluctuated meant that she lacked the relevant capacity to consent. *Re R* was

6-033   In *St. George's Healthcare NHS Trust v S*[9] the Court of Appeal laid down procedural guidelines for any case involving the question of a patient's capacity when surgical treatment or invasive treatment may be needed by a patient. The Court emphasised that the guidelines do not apply where the patient is competent to accept or refuse treatment, and that an application to the court for a declaration where a competent adult patient refuses treatment would be pointless.

(c) Information

6-034   In order to be capable of understanding the nature of the procedure to which he is consenting the patient must have some information about the procedure itself.[10] In *Chatterton v Gerson*[11] the claimant suffered from chronic and intractable pain in the area surrounding an operation scar, following a hernia operation. The defendant was a specialist in the treatment of pain, and he administered an intrathecal injection of a solution of phenol and glycerine near the spinal cord with the object of destroying the pain-conducting nerves near the hernia operation site. The operation only relieved the pain temporarily, and the claimant had a second spinal injection given by the same surgeon. This was also unsuccessful in relieving the pain but the claimant's right leg was rendered completely numb, which impaired her mobility. The defendant's practice was to explain to patients that the treatment involved numbness at the site of the pain and a larger surrounding area, and might involve temporary loss of muscle power. The claimant argued that because she had not been informed about the inherent risk of side-effects materialising from her treatment, her consent was vitiated and the doctor was liable in battery for all the adverse consequences of her treatment. Bristow J. said that in order to vitiate the reality of consent there must be a greater failure of communication between doctor and patient than that involved in a breach of duty if the claim is based on negligence. Accordingly, once the patient was "informed in broad terms of the nature of the procedure which is intended, and gives her consent, that consent is real," and the cause of action on which to base a claim for failure to discuss the risks and implications of a procedure was negligence, not trespass.[12] Miss Chatterton was under no illusion as to the general nature of the proposed procedure, and therefore her consent was not unreal.

(n.8 contd.) a very different case from *Re B*, with the teenager's mental state fluctuating quite frequently depending upon whether she took the prescribed medication for her mental health problem. See further the Draft Mental Incapacity Bill, June 2003, cl. 2(4), which provides that the "fact that a person is able to retain information relevant to a decision for a short period only does not prevent him from being regarded as able to make the decision."

[9] [1999] Fam. 26 at 63–64.

[10] See the quotation from *Bowater v Rowley Regis Corporation* [1944] K.B. 476, 479 cited above, n. 76. A patient may be estopped from denying that he had the relevant information if he so acts as to lead the defendant reasonably to assume that the information was known to him: *Sidaway v Bethlem Royal Hospital Governors* [1985] A.C. 871, 894, *per* Lord Diplock.

[11] [1981] Q.B. 432.

[12] *ibid.* at 443.

Chatterton v Gerson was the first attempt to introduce into this country 6–035
the doctrine of informed consent through the action for battery. From the
claimant's point of view battery was perceived as having distinct advantages
over a claim in negligence (with corresponding disadvantages for defendants). Battery, as a form of trespass, is actionable *per se* and so does not
require proof of damage, although if the claimant seeks more than nominal
damages he will have to establish that the loss was a direct result of the
unlawful force. In the absence of consent it is clear that the medical procedure and any complications arising from it are the direct result of the battery.
Secondly, once it is established that the patient's consent was invalid, it does
not have to be proved that the patient would not have accepted the treatment had he been informed about the inherent risks of the procedure, which
is an essential element of a claim based in negligence.[13] Thirdly, medical evidence as to the profession's usual disclosure practice is considered to be irrelevant to a claim based in battery, again because once the consent is vitiated
the tort is committed. A final factor, which was clearly influential in the
courts' hostility to actions in battery, is the perception of trespass as an intentional tort. It was considered inappropriate that doctors, acting in good
faith, should be held liable for an intentional tort.

The view that failure to discuss or explain the risks of the proposed treat- 6–036
ment, or alternatives to that treatment, goes to the doctor's duty of care in
negligence, not trespass to the person, was adopted in *Hills v Potter*[14] where
it was held that the claimant's undoubted consent to the operation which
was in fact performed negatived liability in battery.[15] This approach has been
affirmed by the Court of Appeal. In *Sidaway v Bethlem Royal Hospital
Governors* Sir John Donaldson M.R. said that: "I am wholly satisfied that
as a matter of English law a consent is not vitiated by a failure on the part
of the doctor to give the patient sufficient information before the consent is
given."[16] Once the patient has been informed in broad terms of the nature
of the treatment, consent in fact amounts to consent in law.[17] A similar attitude to battery is apparent in the Canadian[18] and Irish[19] courts.

---

[13] See para. 6–146.
[14] [1983] 3 All E.R. 716, 728; *Freeman v Home Office* [1984] Q.B. 524, 537, *per* McCowan
J.
[15] Hirst J. said that he deplored reliance on trespass to the person in medical cases of this kind,
a dictum that was approved by Lord Scarman in *Sidaway v Bethlem Royal Hospital
Governors* [1985] A.C. 871, 883. See also *The Creutzfeldt-Jakob Disease Litigation* (1995)
54 B.M.L.R. 1, *per* May J.
[16] [1984] Q.B. 493, 511; see also *per* Dunn L.J. at 515, and Browne-Wilkinson L.J. at 519.
[17] *Freeman v Home Office* [1984] Q.B. 524, 556, *per* Sir John Donaldson M.R.
[18] *Reibl v Hughes* (1980) 114 D.L.R. (3d) 1, 10–11 (S.C.C.), *per* Laskin C.J.C.: "I can appreciate the temptation to say that the genuineness of consent to medical treatment depends on
proper disclosure of the risks which it entails, but in my view, unless there has been misrepresentation or fraud to secure consent to the treatment, a failure to disclose the attendant
risks, however serious, should go to negligence rather than battery." *White v Turner* (1981)
120 D.L.R. (3d) 269, 283 (Ont. H.C.), *per* Linden J.; affirmed (1982) 12 D.L.R. (4th) 319
(Ont. C.A.): "The future use of battery is, therefore, limited to cases involving a real lack of
consent. Where there has been a basic consent to the treatment, there is no place left for discussions of battery."
[19] *Walsh v Family Planning Services Ltd* [1992] 1 I.R. 496, 512, 531 (Supreme Court of Ireland).

6-037   Thus, the courts have drawn a distinction between a lack of information which concerns the *nature* of the procedure (which gives rise to an action in battery) and a lack of information about the risks associated with the procedure (where the action must be based in negligence). It has been forcefully argued that this distinction is untenable: it assumes an inherent difference in terminology and substance between the nature of the treatment and the risks inherent in the treatment.[20] Some risks may be so significant that they relate to the *nature* of the operation itself, so that non-disclosure of the risk would vitiate the consent and lead to liability in battery. It is not self-evidently apparent what the "nature" of any particular medical treatment consists of, nor that, for example, a high risk of serious consequences is not part and parcel of the "nature" of the procedure.[21] It depends, ultimately, on how one chooses to characterise the nature of any particular activity and the level of abstraction that is adopted.

Fraud and misrepresentation

6-038   It is said that if the patient's consent has been obtained by fraud or misrepresentation then it is not a valid consent.[22] Thus, in *Sidaway v Bethlem Royal Hospital Governors* Sir John Donaldson M.R. said that:

> "It is only if the consent is obtained by fraud or by misrepresentation of the nature of what is to be done that it can be said that an apparent consent is not a true consent. This is the position in the criminal law . . . and the cause of action based on trespass to the person is closely analogous."[23]

---

[20] Tan (1987) 7 L.S. 149; see also Somerville (1981) 26 McGill L.J. 740, 742–52. Note that cl. 2(5) of the Draft Mental Incapacity Bill, June 2003, provides that: "The information relevant to a decision includes information about the reasonably foreseeable consequences of— (a) deciding one way or another, or (b) failing to make the decision." This is information that a patient is required to understand, retain and use, in order to be found to have the capacity to make a decision for himself (cl. 2(1)). If the patient is not given this information, it will be impossible to say that he can understand and use it to make a decision for the purpose of assessing competence. Thus, the practical consequence of the Draft Bill is that the patient will have to be given this information, and it is certainly arguable that the reasonably foreseeable consequences of deciding one way or another or failing to make a decision includes some consideration of the risks associated with the treatment options. It is not limited to information in broad terms about the nature of the procedure.

[21] "In some cases it may be difficult to distinguish, and separate out, the matter of consequential or collateral risks from the basic nature and character of the operation or procedure to be performed . . . The more probable the risk the more it could be said to be an integral feature of the nature and character of the operation," *per* Morden J. in *Kelly v Hazlett* (1976) 75 D.L.R. (3d) 536, 559; *cf.* the comments of Laskin C.J.C. in *Reibl v Hughes* (1980) 114 D.L.R. (3d) 1, 9.

[22] "Of course, if information is withheld in bad faith, the consent will be vitiated by fraud," *per* Bristow J. in *Chatterton v Gerson* [1981] Q.B. 432, 443.

[23] [1984] Q.B. 493, 511, citing *R. v Clarence* (1888) 22 QBD 23, 43; see also *Freeman v Home Office* [1984] Q.B. 524, 537, *per* McCowan J., and the comment of Sir John Donaldson M.R., *ibid.* at 556: "Consent would not be real if procured by fraud or misrepresentation . . ."

It is not clear what would constitute fraud or misrepresentation. Must it relate to the nature of the procedure to vitiate consent or will fraud as to the consequences or risks suffice? Sir John Donaldson M.R. appears to require misrepresentation as to the nature of the procedure: "only if the consent is obtained by fraud or by misrepresentation of the nature of what is to be done." But if the claimant does not consent to the *nature* of what is done the consent is not real, *irrespective of the reason why*.[24] The defendant's motive, whether "fraudulent" or in good faith, is irrelevant. This might suggest that if the exception is to have any meaning it should also include fraud or misrepresentation as to consequences or risks. This certainly appears to have been the view of Laskin C.J.C. delivering the judgment of the Supreme Court of Canada in *Reibl v Hughes*: "unless there has been misrepresentation or fraud to secure consent to the treatment, *a failure to disclose the attendant risks*, however serious, should go to negligence rather than battery."[25] On this approach misrepresentation as to risks would vitiate the reality of the patient's consent.

In the criminal law fraud vitiates consent only where the claimant's mistake concerns the real nature of the transaction.[26] There is no obvious justification, however, for applying the criminal law rule in tort, since it is unduly favourable to the defendant.[27] The consequences of an act are often the crucial factor in the granting of a genuine consent. Except in a dire emergency, no one would consent to major surgery by someone who was not trained to perform it. If the defendant obtained the claimant's consent to an operation by misrepresenting his ability to carry it out, it is difficult to see why the claimant's consent should not be regarded as vitiated by the misrepresentation, even though there is no mistake as to the nature of the act (surgery).[28]

6–039

---

[24] Tan (1987) 7 L.S. 149, 156 makes this point: "There is no magic in the character of the conduct concealing or distorting medical advice for [the] purpose of the defence of consent. The misconduct only gives occasion to the concealment. What is material is the content of the medical advice that is concealed, not the mode of concealment."

[25] (1980) 114 D.L.R. (3d) 1, 10–11, emphasis added.

[26] For example, persuading a girl to have sexual intercourse by representing to her that it is a surgical operation: *R. v Flattery* (1877) 2 QBD 410; *R. v Williams* [1923] 1 K.B. 340; *cf. R. v Clarence* (1888) 22 QBD 23, where there was no offence when the defendant infected his wife with venereal disease; her consent was still valid. See also *R. v Linekar* [1995] Q.B. 250. In Canada this approach has been applied to defendants who deliberately engaged in unsafe sexual intercourse knowing that they were infected with HIV. Prosecutions for aggravated sexual assault have failed on the basis that the freely given consent to the act of intercourse was not invalidated by ignorance of the defendant's HIV status: *R. v Lee* (1991) 3 O.R. (3d) 726; *R. v Ssenyonga* (1993) 21 C.R. (4th) 128 (Ont. Ct. (Gen. Div.)).

[27] In *Hegarty v Shine* (1878) 14 Cox C.C. 124 and 145 the claimant's action against her former lover for infecting her with venereal disease failed because she had consented to the sexual intercourse. The court also applied the maxim *ex turpi causa non oritur actio*, and was heavily influenced by the view that the claimant's conduct was unlawful and immoral, a view that would not be persuasive today: see, *e.g.*, the comment of Sopinka J. in *Norberg v Wynrib* (1992) 92 D.L.R. (4th) 449, 483 (S.C.C.).

[28] This example is not hypothetical. Persons masquerading as doctors have been convicted of various criminal offences: see Eekelaar and Dingwall [1984] J.S.W.L. 258, 259, n. 5. Individuals posing as doctors have been convicted of stealing from hospitals: *The Times*, July 8, 1994; and one individual who posed as a locum was known to have put stitches in a head wound, attended a man with a collapsed lung and arranged X-rays. He once tried to help with heart bypass surgery: *The Times*, October 5, 1994; B. Mahandra, "Deception and Self-deception" (2001) 151 N.L.J. 210.

6–040   In *R v Richardson*[29] the Court of Appeal held that the offence of assault,
under section 47 of the Offences Against the Person Act 1861 was not committed when a dentist gave treatment to patients while suspended from practice by the General Dental Council. Consent for the purpose of the criminal
law was vitiated only where there was a mistake as to the *nature or quality
of the act* or the *identity of the person performing it*, not their qualifications
or attributes, such as being authorised to provide dental treatment. The prosecution did not argue the case on the basis that the nature or quality of the
act was different because the defendant was suspended from practice, but on
the ground that the identity of the defendant was different. The assumption
was that if the treatment had been given by a person impersonating a dentist
it would have been assault, and there was no difference between an unqualified dentist and a dentist suspended from practice. The Crown contended
that the concept of the identity of the person should be extended to cover the
qualifications or attributes of the dentist on the basis that the patients consented to treatment by a qualified dentist and not a suspended one. This submission was rejected. The patients were fully aware of the identity of the
defendant:

> "The common law is not concerned with the question whether the mis-
> taken consent has been induced by fraud on the part of the accused or
> has been self-induced. It is the nature of the mistake that is relevant, and
> not the reason why the mistake has been made. In summary, either there
> is consent to actions on the part of a person in the mistaken belief that
> he was other than he truly is, in which case it is assault or, short of this,
> there is no assault."[30]

By way of contrast, in *R v Tabassum*[31] the defendant had told three women
that he was conducting a survey into breast cancer for the purpose of establishing a database software package, and persuaded the women to allow him
to examine their breasts. The women mistakenly believed that he was medically qualified. He was found guilty of indecent assault and the Court of
Appeal upheld the conviction on the basis that there was no valid consent.
The consent to the touching was given for *medical purposes* and not for any
other reason, thus there was consent to the nature of the act but not its
quality.

6–041   In *Appleton v Garrett*[32] a dentist was held liable in trespass to the person
for carrying out unnecessary dental treatment, on a large-scale, for profit. In
bad faith, he deliberately withheld the information that the treatment was
unnecessary because he knew that the claimants would not have consented
had they known the true position. Dyson J. did not specify the nature of the
procedure to which the claimants had "consented", but appears to have

---

[29] [1999] Q.B. 444.
[30] *ibid.* at 450.
[31] [2000] Lloyd's Rep. Med. 404, CA.
[32] [1996] P.I.Q.R. P1; [1997] 8 Med. L.R. 75.

taken the view that the consent was invalid because the claimants would not have proceeded had they known the true position (though this is usually also true of cases where the claimant objects to the consequences, as opposed to the nature of the procedure). The implication to be taken from *Appleton v Garrett* is that where medical treatment is not necessary the "nature" of the treatment is different. Indeed, it is arguable that it ceases to be "medical treatment", but this means that the patient's consent must go, not simply to the defendant's act (*e.g.* the drilling of a tooth), but also to the context in which the act takes place, *i.e.* that the performance of the act is part and parcel of a *bona fide* decision to provide appropriate medical treatment. Thus, *R v Tabassum* and *Appleton v Garrett* indicate that it is the context which gives the act both its nature and its quality. On this basis, if in *R v Tabassum* the defendant had actually been carrying out a genuine survey into breast cancer and the procedures to which the women consented were entirely appropriate to that survey, it is arguable that the fact that he was not medically qualified would have been irrelevant to the nature and quality of the act to which consent was given, unless a medical qualification could be said to be crucial to the *bona fides* of the survey.

It is arguable that a deliberate lie in response to a specific question from the patient as to risks could be taken as evidence of bad faith which might vitiate the patient's consent. In *Re T. (Adult: Refusal of Treatment)*[33] Lord Donaldson M.R. said that: "misinforming a patient, whether or not innocently, and the withholding of information which is expressly or impliedly sought by the patient may well vitiate either a consent or a refusal." This dictum appears to support the view that deliberate lies might vitiate consent, but it would also seem to contradict his Lordship's narrow interpretation of the "fraud or misrepresentation" exception expressed in *Sidaway v Bethlem Royal Hospital Governors*,[34] as being limited to misinformation about the *nature* of the procedure. It seems likely that the courts would seek deal with deliberate lying as an aspect of the doctor's duty of care in negligence in order to take account of the "therapeutic privilege" argument that disclosure of the information would have been harmful to the patient and, accordingly, the lie was in the patient's "best interests."[35]

6–042

---

[33] [1993] Fam. 95, 115.

[34] [1984] Q.B. 493, 511, para. 6–038, above. See further *Halushka v University of Saskatchewan* (1965) 53 D.L.R. (2d) 436 (Sask. C.A.), para. 6–177. Note that there is a distinction between fraud, which implies bad faith, and misrepresentation, which does not. A misrepresentation may simply be negligent. In *Ferguson v Hamilton Civic Hospitals* (1983) 144 D.L.R. (3d) 214, 243–244, affirmed (1985) 18 D.L.R. (4th) 638 (Ont. C.A.) it was argued that the non-disclosure of the risks of surgical treatment prior to conducting a diagnostic procedure (which might indicate a need for the treatment) constituted a misrepresentation of the nature of the diagnostic procedure. This argument was rejected, but it was not suggested that the defendant must have acted in bad faith for the "misrepresentation" exception to apply.

[35] See para. 6–131. For consideration of the lawfulness of testing patients for HIV antibodies without their knowledge or consent see Sherrard and Gatt (1987) 295 B.M.J. 911; Keown (1989) 52 M.L.R. 790. See also the GMC guidance, *Serious Communicable Diseases*, October 1997, para. 4 (available at *www.gmc-uk.org/standards*). Minors may be tested for HIV on the direction of the court where the court makes an interim care order or an interim

6–043   The fact that the material used for the treatment of the claimant has been obtained unlawfully does not in itself vitiate the claimant's consent to an otherwise lawful procedure. Thus, an allegation that the pituitary glands from which was extracted the human growth hormone (HGH) which had been administered to the claimants had been unlawfully removed from the bodies of people who had died did not vitiate the claimants' consent to the injection of the HGH.[36] A tort committed against A cannot be linked to a loss suffered by B so as to give rise to a claim in tort by B where the tort against A did not cause B's loss.[37]

Consent to a different procedure

6–044   Where the patient has been told about and given her consent to one procedure it may not be entirely clear whether that consent applies to a slightly different procedure. Ultimately, this will be treated as a question of fact in any given case. In *Davis v Barking, Havering and Brentwood Health Authority*[38] the claimant underwent a minor operation for marsupialisation of a cyst. She signed a general consent form authorising the performance of the operation and the administration of a general anaesthetic, but during the operation the anaesthetist administered a caudal block (a type of epidural anaesthetic). After the operation the claimant discovered that she could not move her legs or control her bladder. She eventually made a substantial recovery from this condition but was left with a slight disability. She alleged that since she had not been informed about the possibility of a caudal block being performed she had not consented to the procedure. McCullough J. concluded that, looking compendiously at what the claimant had been told about the proposed operation, including the requirement for a general anaesthetic, she had been informed in sufficient detail to have consented to the caudal block. It was inappropriate to divide into sections the information required to be given about the general anaesthetic and information about the caudal block. A sectionalised approach would encourage the "deplorable" prospect of actions being brought in trespass rather than negligence:

> "Clearly if it is proposed that a patient should undergo two separate operations it is the duty of the doctors to give the patient appropriately full information about each of them. This is so whether they are to be

---

(n.35 contd.) supervision order under s.38(6) of the Children Act 1989: *Re O. (Minors) (Medical Examination)* (1992) 15 B.M.L.R. 54; [1993] 1 F.L.R. 860; *Note: Re HIV Tests* [1994] 2 F.L.R. 116. See also *Re C (A Child) (HIV Testing)* [2000] Fam. 48 where the court ordered an HIV test for a new born baby, despite the parents' opposition, because the medical arguments in favour of testing were "overwhelming." The need for an application to the court is likely to be rare: *President's Direction: HIV Testing of Children* [2003] 1 F.L.R. 1299.

[36] *The Creutzfeldt-Jakob Disease Litigation* (1995) 54 B.M.L.R. 1, *per* May J. Another example might be a case where an organ was obtained for transplant contrary to the terms of the Human Organ Transplants Act 1989. The fact that the donation was unlawful would not in itself vitiate consent to the surgery by the recipient.

[37] *ibid.*

[38] [1993] 4 Med. L.R. 85.

performed on two occasions or one. Equally clearly there is no obligation to explain every detail of what is proposed. That would be no more in the interests of the patient than to inform her of every risk, however remote. The extent of the particularity required, whether by way of detail or by way of explanation of risk, must be for the clinical judgment of the doctor, and in the event of a dispute about either the court will apply the *Bolam* test. Each case must depend on its own facts. Whether a particular aspect of what is proposed is a matter of detail or is in reality a matter sufficiently separate to call for separate mention is a question of fact and degree."[39]

There was no realistic distinction, said his Lordship, between omitting to tell a patient that while she is under general anaesthetic a tube will be put into her trachea and omitting to tell her that while she is under a general anaesthetic a needle will be put into her caudal region to provide post-operative analgesia.[40]

(4) Children

For the purpose of the law of consent children fall into two categories: 6–045
either they have the capacity to make their own decisions about medical
treatment, and can give a valid consent on their own behalf in the same way
as an adult; or they do not have capacity, in which case parental consent will
normally be required. English law takes a different approach, however, when
it comes to the decision of a competent minor to refuse consent. The Court
of Appeal has held that parental consent can be sufficient to protect a doctor
from an action in battery where a competent minor is refusing medical treatment (though a parent cannot veto the decision of competent minor to accept
treatment), and that the court has the power both to authorise and refuse to
authorise treatment, notwithstanding the views of a competent minor, in the
best interests of the child.

---

[39] *ibid.* at 90.
[40] See also *Brushett v Cowan* (1990) 69 D.L.R. (4th) 743 (Newfd. C.A.) where a consent to a muscle biopsy was held to cover a bone biopsy on the basis that the claimant had consented to a diagnostic procedure, and in the circumstances this was a sufficient consent to the bone biopsy; *Pridham v Nash* (1986) 33 D.L.R. (4th) 304 (Ont. H.C.), where the patient signed a consent form for an investigative laparoscopy, which was held sufficient to cover the performance of minor surgery during the course of the examination; *O'Bonswain v Paradis* (1993) 15 C.C.L.T. (2d) 188 (Ont. H.C.), where the claimant consented to a gortex graft for the purpose of providing access for renal dialysis, having been informed that a medically preferable procedure (an arteriovenous fistula [AVF]), with lower risk, would not be feasible because her arteries and veins were too small. When the patient was under general anaesthetic it became apparent that an AVF was possible, and the defendant proceeded to perform that procedure rather than the gortex graft. It was held that the claimant's consent covered the AVF. Both procedures were designed to accomplish the same thing, namely access for dialysis, and the consent for the gortex graft included consent to such "additional or alternative treatment or operative procedure as in the opinion of [the defendant] are immediately necessary."

(a) Children with capacity

6–046   By section 8(1) of the Family Law Reform Act 1969 children of sixteen
years or more are presumed to have the same capacity as an adult to consent
to medical treatment.[41] This does not mean that children under the age of
sixteen do not have the relevant capacity. Section 8(3) of the same Act states
that: "Nothing in this section shall be construed as making ineffective any
consent which would have been effective if this section had not been
enacted." It was always assumed that this subsection was intended to make
it clear that the legislation was without prejudice to the position at common
law: if a child below the age of sixteen did have the capacity to consent to
medical treatment, section 8 did not change that. This interpretation was
challenged in *Gillick v West Norfolk and Wisbech Area Health Authority*,[42]
where the claimant argued that no child under sixteen could consent to
medical treatment, and that section 8(3) merely preserved the parental right
to consent for children of sixteen or seventeen years. Although accepted in
the Court of Appeal, this argument was rejected by a majority in the House
of Lords. Lord Fraser said that it was "verging on the absurd" to suggest
that a girl or boy aged 15 could not effectively consent, for example, to have
a medical examination of some trivial injury or even to have a broken arm
set. Provided the patient is capable of understanding what is proposed, and
of expressing his or her own wishes, there was no good reason for holding
that he or she lacks the capacity to express them validly and effectively and
to authorise the doctor to perform an examination or give treatment.[43]

6–047   Lord Scarman said that as a matter of law a minor child below the age of
sixteen will have the capacity to consent to medical treatment "when the
child achieves a sufficient understanding and intelligence to enable him or
her to understand fully what is proposed." This is a question of fact.[44] Lord
Templeman agreed that a doctor may lawfully carry out some forms of treatment with the consent of an infant patient, even against the opposition of a
parent based on religious or any other grounds.[45] The child must also be
capable of understanding the consequences of a failure to treat.[46]

---

[41] S.8(1) provides that: "The consent of a minor who has attained the age of sixteen years to
any surgical, medical or dental treatment which, in the absence of consent, would constitute
a trespass to his person, shall be as effective as it would be if he were of full age; and where
a minor has by virtue of this section given an effective consent to any treatment it shall not
be necessary to obtain any consent for it from his parent or guardian . . ." See also Mental
Health Act 1983, s.131(2); Skegg (1973) 36 M.L.R. 370.

[42] [1986] A.C. 112.

[43] *ibid.* at 169; see also *Johnston v Wellesley Hospital* (1970) 17 D.L.R. (3d) 139 (Ont. H.C.);
Ney v A.-G. of Canada (1993) 102 D.L.R. (4th) 136 (B.C.S.C.); *Walker v Region 2 Hospital
Corp.* (1994) 110 D.L.R. (4th) 477 (N.B.C.A.); *Van Mol (Guardian ad Litem of) v Ashmore*
(1999) 168 D.L.R. (4th) 637 (B.C.C.A.); *Secretary, Department of Health and Community
Services v J.W.B.* (1992) 106 A.L.R. 385 (H.C. of Aus.).

[44] *ibid.* at 189.

[45] "The effect of the consent of the infant depends on the nature of the treatment and the age and
understanding of the infant. For example, a doctor with the consent of an intelligent boy or
girl of 15 could in my opinion safely remove tonsils or a troublesome appendix," *ibid.* at 201.

[46] *Re R. (A Minor) (Wardship: Consent to Treatment)* [1992] Fam. 11, 26, *per* Lord Donaldson

As with adults the question arises as to how much the patient must under-   **6–048**
stand in order to have the relevant capacity. In *Gillick* their Lordships
appeared to require a much greater level of understanding from a child under
sixteen than from an adult, at least with regard to contraceptive advice or
treatment.[47] Lord Scarman commented:

> "When applying these conclusions to contraceptive advice and treat-
> ment it has to borne in mind that there is much that has to be under-
> stood by a girl under the age of 16 if she is to have legal capacity to
> consent to such treatment. It is not enough that she should understand
> the nature of the advice which is being given: she must also have a suf-
> ficient maturity to understand what is involved. There are moral and
> family questions, especially her relationship with her parents; long-term
> problems associated with the emotional impact of pregnancy and its ter-
> mination; and there are the risks to health of sexual intercourse at her
> age, risks which contraception may diminish but cannot eliminate. It
> follows that a doctor will have to satisfy himself that she is able to
> appraise these factors before he can safely proceed on the basis that she
> has at law capacity to consent to contraceptive treatment."[48]

Since, on this approach, the patient has to be able to appraise these   **6–049**
complex issues before "she has at law capacity to consent to contraceptive
treatment" this clearly requires a greater degree of understanding than
simply the nature of the procedure "in broad terms." It would seem to follow
from this that when treating children a doctor has a greater duty to disclose
information about the nature of the treatment and, indeed, the risks or consequences of the procedure, at the risk of being held liable in battery for non-
disclosure, than is required when treating adults. Speaking specifically about
contraceptive advice and treatment, Lord Fraser specified five factors that a
doctor would have to consider:

> ". . . the doctor will, in my opinion, be justified in proceeding without
> the parents' consent or even knowledge provided he is satisfied on the
> following matters: (1) that the girl (although under 16 years of age) will
> understand his advice; (2) that he cannot persuade her to inform her
> parents or to allow him to inform the parents that she is seeking contra-
> ceptive advice; (3) that she is very likely to begin or to continue having
> sexual intercourse with or without contraceptive treatment; (4) that
> unless she receives contraceptive advice or treatment her physical or
> mental health or both are likely to suffer; (5) that her best interests

---

(n.46 contd.) M.R. See, *e.g.*, *Re E. (a minor)(wardship: medical treatment)* [1993] 1 F.L.R.
386, and *Re S. (A Minor) (Consent to Medical Treatment)* [1994] 2 F.L.R. 1065; para.
6–050.

[47] The test for capacity in adults has, admittedly, become a little more sophisticated than it was
at the time of *Gillick*: see paras 6–026 *et seq.*

[48] *Gillick v West Norfolk & Wisbech Area Health Authority* [1986] A.C. 112, 189.

require him to give her contraceptive advice, treatment or both without the parental consent."[49]

Only the first point relates to the girl's *capacity* to consent, the remaining matters being more relevant to the doctor's assessment of whether providing the treatment is in her best interests in the circumstances. Lord Scarman clearly required a higher level of understanding for the purpose of capacity to consent than Lord Fraser,[50] whereas Lord Templeman took the view that a child under the age of sixteen, although capable of consenting to some forms of treatment, could never have sufficient understanding to have the capacity to consent to contraceptive advice or treatment.[51]

6–050   The effect of *Gillick* is that there is no fixed age at which a child can be said to have the capacity to consent. It is a variable approach which depends upon the maturity of the child and the complexity or seriousness of the procedure required.[52] Even a very young child may have sufficient understanding to have capacity to consent to the dressing of a wound, but, conversely, an older child may possibly not be regarded as having sufficient understanding to decline, for example, life-saving treatment. Thus, in *Re E. (a minor) (wardship: medical treatment)*[53] Ward J. held that a 15-year-old Jehovah's Witness who was refusing consent to a potentially life-saving blood transfusion was not competent because, although he had some concept of the fact that he would die, he had no realisation of the full implications of the process of dying. His Lordship commented that the court "should be very slow to allow an infant to martyr himself." Johnson J. adopted a very similar approach in *Re S. (A Minor) (Consent to Medical Treatment)*[54] where a 15½-year-old girl who had suffered from thalassaemia virtually from birth needed monthly

---

[49] *ibid.* at 174. On the doctor's duty of confidentiality owed to patients under the age of sixteen see the General Medical Council, *Confidentiality: Protecting and Providing Information,* June 2000, para. 38, available at *www.gmc-uk.org.*

[50] See further Jones (1986) 2 P.N. 41.

[51] [1986] A.C. 112, 204. "I doubt whether a girl under the age of 16 is capable of a balanced judgment to embark on frequent, regular or casual sexual intercourse fortified by the illusion that medical science can protect her in mind and body and ignoring the danger of leaping from childhood to adulthood without the difficult formative transitional experiences of adolescence. There are many things which a girl under 16 needs to practise but sex is not one of them," *per* Lord Templeman at 201. It is apparent that Lord Scarman's views were also strongly influenced by the fact that the case was concerned with the controversial issue of contraception for girls under sixteen.

[52] See also the Children Act 1989, s.44(7) which provides that if a child is of sufficient understanding to make an informed decision he may refuse to submit to a medical or psychiatric examination ordered by the court when making an emergency protection order. Similarly, a supervision order may require a supervised child to submit to a medical or psychiatric examination or treatment, but again the child can refuse consent where he has sufficient understanding to make an informed decision: Children Act 1989, Sch 3 paras 4 and 5; *cf.,* however, *South Glamorgan County Council v B. and W.* [1993] 1 F.L.R. 574; (1992) 11 B.M.L.R. 162; para. 6–055. See further *C. v Wren* (1986) 35 D.L.R. (4th) 419, where the Alberta Court of Appeal concluded that a 16-year-old girl had the capacity to consent to an abortion, and the fact that she was in disagreement with her parents on the issue did not mean that she lacked sufficient intelligence and understanding to make up her own mind.

[53] [1993] 1 F.L.R. 386.

[54] [1994] 2 F.L.R. 1065.

blood transfusions and daily injections. In 1989 her mother joined the Jehovah's Witnesses, and in May 1994 the girl did not attend for her usual transfusion. Both mother and daughter made it clear that they did not want any more transfusions, and the local authority sought an order authorising transfusions. Johnson J. granted the order, taking the view that the girl was not competent, relying on Lord Donaldson's comments in *Re R. (A Minor) (Wardship: Consent to Treatment)*[55] that to be "*Gillick* competent" a minor requires not merely a full understanding and appreciation of the consequences of the treatment, in terms of intended and possible side-effects and, but equally importantly, understanding of the anticipated consequences of a failure to treat. On this basis S had only a very general understanding of some vital matters relating to her treatment and to the consequences for her of that treatment ceasing. She was confused over many details. She did not know how her death would occur. She thought that there might be a miracle and that "God might save me." She did not believe that a refusal to have further transfusions would certainly lead to her death. She was disillusioned with treatment, "fed up with it," and was susceptible to influence from outside:

> "She does not understand the full implications of what will happen. It does not seem to me that her capacity is commensurate with the gravity of the decision which she has made. It seems to me that an understanding that she will die is not enough. For her decision to carry weight she should have a greater understanding of the manner of the death and the pain and the distress."[56]

"*Gillick* competence" is a developmental concept which does not fluctuate on a day-to-day or week-to-week basis. It involves an assessment of mental and emotional age, as contrasted with chronological age, but the test may not be appropriate where, as a result of mental illness, the child's understanding and capacity varies from day-to-day.[57] Moreover, the illness itself may reduce the child's capacity to make a competent decision.[58]

6–051

---

[55] [1992] Fam. 11, 26.

[56] [1994] 2 F.L.R. 1065, 1075–1076. Johnson J. observed, at 1075, that in 2½ years' time the girl would be able to make up her own mind (when she reached 18). The young man in *Re E. (a minor) (wardship: medical treatment)* had done precisely that and had died. See also *Re L (Medical Treatment: Gillick competency)* [1998] 2 F.L.R. 810; [1999] 2 F.C.R. 524, in which a 14-year-old Jehovah's Witness refused consent to life-saving medical treatment because it would involve blood transfusions. It was held that she was not *Gillick* competent, because her sincerely held beliefs had not been developed through a broad and informed adult experience, but through a sheltered religious upbringing; she knew that she could die without the treatment, but had not been told about unpleasant manner of her death.

[57] *Re R. (A Minor) (Wardship: Consent to Treatment)* [1992] Fam. 11, 25–26, 32, *per* Lord Donaldson M.R. and Farquharson L.J. respectively. The fact that the minor's mental state was fluctuating meant that she was not competent, since it would be dangerous to the ward if her competence were to be judged purely on her state of mind during a period when her mental illness was in recession. For comment on this case see Bainham (1992) 108 L.Q.R. 194; Douglas (1992) 55 M.L.R. 569; Murphy (1992) 43 N.I.L.Q. 60; Urwin (1992) 8 P.N. 69.

[58] See *Re W. (A Minor) (Medical Treatment: Court's Jurisdiction)* [1993] Fam. 64; para. 6–031.

The effect of reaching "Gillick competence"

6–052   At one time the assumption was that a minor who was *Gillick* competent could both give a valid consent to treatment and refuse recommended treatment, just as a competent adult is entitled to decline treatment. In *Gillick v West Norfolk & Wisbech Area Health Authority*[59] it was said that the parental power to consent on the child's behalf is a diminishing one, as the child's understanding and intelligence develops to the stage at which she is capable of making up her own mind and thus acquires the capacity to consent herself. This suggested that as the child developed the capacity to give a valid consent, the power of the parent to consent disappeared, and therefore the competent child effectively had the capacity also to decline proposed treatment. This view was challenged by Lord Donaldson M.R. in *Re R. (A Minor) (Wardship: Consent to Treatment)*,[60] where his Lordship suggested that even where a child is competent, the child's parents have a concurrent power to consent notwithstanding that the child has refused treatment. In his Lordship's view consent was "merely a key which unlocks a door" and there was no difficulty in conceiving of two keyholders, the *"Gillick"* competent' child, whose consent to treatment could not be vetoed by the parents (the situation considered in *Gillick* itself), and the parents whose consent could not be vetoed by the competent child. Thus, parental consent would still protect a doctor from an action in battery despite the child's objection to treatment.

6–053   Although this approach appeared to be inconsistent with *Gillick* (Lord Scarman's speech in particular)[61] it has been confirmed by the Court of Appeal in *Re W. (A Minor) (Medical Treatment: Court's Jurisdiction)*,[62] where it was held that although a competent minor can give a valid consent to medical treatment this does not entail an absolute right to refuse treatment where a parent or person exercising parental responsibility has given a valid consent to treatment.[63] However, Nolan L.J. considered that it was axi-

---

[59] [1986] A.C. 112, 172–173 and 188–189, *per* Lord Fraser and Lord Scarman respectively.
[60] [1992] Fam. 11, 23.
[61] See *ibid.* at 27–28, *per* Staughton L.J. Indeed, it appeared to be inconsistent with some provisions of the Children Act 1989: see para. 6–050, n. 52; but *cf. South Glamorgan County Council v B. and W.* [1993] 1 F.L.R. 574; (1992) 11 B.M.L.R. 162.
[62] [1993] Fam. 64. See Bridgeman (1993) 13 L.S. 69; Eekelaar (1993) 109 L.Q.R. 182; Houghton-James [1992] Fam. Law 550; Lowe and Juss (1993) 56 M.L.R. 865; Mulholland (1993) 9 P.N. 21.
[63] *cf. Walker v Region 2 Hospital Corp.* (1994) 110 D.L.R. (4th) 477 (N.B.C.A.) where it was held that a 15-year-old who was sufficiently mature to be competent was entitled to refuse medical treatment. The right to consent included the right to refuse treatment. Similarly, in *Van Mol (Guardian ad Litem of) v Ashmore* (1999) 168 D.L.R. (4th) 637 the British Columbia Court of Appeal held that once the child (in that case a 16-year old) was found to be competent the parents had no right either to consent or to withhold consent: "But once the required capacity to consent has been achieved by the young person reaching sufficient maturity, intelligence and capability of understanding, the discussions about the nature of the treatment, its gravity, the material risks and any special or unusual risks, and the decisions about undergoing treatment, and about the form of the treatment, must all take place with and be made by the young person whose bodily integrity is to be invaded and whose life and health will be affected by the outcome. At that stage, the parent or guardian will no

omatic that where major surgical or other procedures (such as an abortion) were proposed, and the parents were prepared to give consent but the child (having sufficient understanding to make an informed decision) was not, the jurisdiction of the court should always be invoked. On the other hand, the parents have no right to veto treatment to which a competent minor has consented, since this is a clear consequence of *Gillick*.[64] Lord Donaldson M.R. retreated from his suggestion that consent was the key that unlocked the door, because keys could lock as well as unlock. Rather consent was analogous to a "legal 'flak jacket' which protects the doctor from claims by the litigious." Anyone who gives the doctor a flak jacket (*i.e.* consent) may take it back, but the doctor only needs one jacket to protect himself, whether it be given by the child, the parent,[65] or the court.[66]

Whatever the position of a parent or someone exercising parental responsibility, it would appear that under the wardship or inherent jurisdiction the court has the power to authorise medical treatment of a "*Gillick* competent" minor who is refusing treatment.[67] This is the position whether or not the minor is over 16 years of age. In *Re W. (A Minor) (Medical Treatment: Court's Jurisdiction)*[68] W was a 16-year-old girl who was suffering from anorexia nervosa. Her condition was deteriorating and it was proposed that she be moved to a hospital specialising in the treatment of eating disorders, but she refused to move. On the local authority's application for an order that W be placed in the hospital for treatment and that she be given treatment without her consent if necessary, the judge held that although W had sufficient understanding to make an informed decision, he had the jurisdiction to make such an order and authorised her removal to and treatment at the

6–054

(n.63 contd.) longer have any overriding right to give or withhold treatment. . . . The role of the parent or guardian is as advisor and friend. There is no room for conflicting decisions between a young person who has achieved consenting capacity, on the one hand, and a parent or guardian, on the other" *per* Lambert J.A. at 665.

[64] *cf.* the position of the court, para. 6–054; see also *Ney v A.-G. of Canada* (1993) 102 D.L.R. (4th) 136 (B.C.S.C.).

[65] Some procedures, such as ritual circumcision, require either the consent of *both* parents or a declaration by the court that it is in the child's best interests: *Re J. (Specific Issue Orders: Child's Religious Upbringing and Circumcision)* [2000] 1 F.L.R. 571; [2000] 1 F.C.R. 307, CA.

[66] More remarkable, perhaps, than even this narrow view of the role of consent in the context of medical treatment was Lord Donaldson's comment that in the case of a competent *adult* a refusal to give consent would be fully effective as a veto, "but only *because no one else would be in a position to consent*": [1993] Fam. 64, 77, emphasis added. With respect, this rather puts the cart before the horse. The fundamental proposition is that consent operates as a *defence* to what would otherwise constitute trespass to the person. No one has any claim to invade the bodily integrity of a competent adult without lawful excuse, because the law rightly places such high regard upon the individual's claim to bodily integrity. It is submitted that the notion that the *only* reason that an adult is entitled to reject treatment is because of the happenstance that no one else is in a position to consent is inconsistent with basic principle.

[67] *Re R. (A Minor) (Wardship: Consent to Treatment)* [1992] Fam. 11, CA; *cf. Walker v Region 2 Hospital Corp.* (1994) 110 D.L.R. (4th) 477, 488 where a majority of the New Brunswick Court of Appeal held that if a minor is found to be mature, *i.e.* competent, there was no room for the operation of the court's *parens patriae* jurisdiction.

[68] [1993] Fam. 64.

hospital. The Court of Appeal upheld this decision, on the basis that, in the exercise of its inherent jurisdiction to protect the welfare of minors, the court can, in the child's own best interests, override the wishes of a mentally competent child who is refusing medical treatment in circumstances where there is a probability of death or severe permanent injury.[69] In reaching a decision as to the minor's best interests, the court will ascertain the wishes of the child and should approach its decision with a strong predilection to give effect to the child's wishes. The same principle must also apply where a competent minor has decided to accept medical treatment—the court has the power to refuse to authorise the treatment, although it is difficult to imagine circumstances where this is likely to arise if the treatment is medically justified.

6–055   In *South Glamorgan County Council v B. and W.*[70] Douglas Brown J. held that the Children Act 1989 had not abrogated the powers of the court to override the decisions of even a competent minor, under the court's inherent jurisdiction to safeguard the welfare of minors, applying *Re R. (A Minor) (Wardship: Consent to Treatment)* and *Re W. (A Minor) (Medical Treatment: Court's Jurisdiction)*. The court's jurisdiction is unlimited.

6–056   It remains to be seen whether the approach of the English courts to overriding the refusals of consent of competent minors will withstand a challenge under the European Convention on Human Rights. It is certainly arguable that the non-consensual treatment of competent patients could amount to breach of both Article 3 (protection against torture or inhuman or degrading treatment) and Article 8 (the right to respect for private and family life) of the Convention. Article 8 is a qualified right, and therefore the court could take into account the provisions of Article 8(2),[71] and in particular the qualification "for the protection of health or morals." Article 3 is an absolute right, but in *Herczegfalvy v Austria*[72] it was held that "as a general rule, a method which is a therapeutic necessity cannot be regarded as inhuman or degrading. The court must nevertheless satisfy itself that the medical necessity has been convincingly shown to exist." In that case the patient lacked the capacity to consent. It is not clear that the same approach would be applied to a competent patient refusing consent, though the Mental Health Act 1983 clearly contemplates the compulsory treatment of competent

---

[69] The effect of s.8(1) of the Family Law Reform Act 1969 (see para. 6–046, n. 41) was said to be that it enabled the minor to give a valid *consent* to surgical, medical or dental treatment, but this did not entail a right to refuse treatment when parental consent was forthcoming or the court authorised treatment (or, putting it more accurately, the doctor who proceeded to treat in the face of the minor's objections would not be liable in battery). The court also has the power to direct that a 16-year-old girl can be detained in a specialist clinic until completion of her treatment for anorexia nervosa, where her presence in the clinic is an essential part of her treatment and she would otherwise leave if free to do so: *Re C (detention: medical treatment)* [1997] 2 F.L.R. 180; [1997] 3 F.C.R. 49.

[70] [1993] 1 F.L.R. 574; (1992) 11 B.M.L.R. 162.

[71] Art 8(2) provides that: "There shall be no interference by a public authority with the exercise of this right except such as is in accordance with the law and is necessary in a democratic society in the interests of national security, public safety or the economic well-being of the country, for the prevention of disorder or crime, for the protection of health or morals, or for the protection of the rights and freedoms of others."

[72] (1992) E.H.R.R. 437 at [82].

patients for their psychiatric illness or disorder, and that would not necessarily involve a breach of Convention rights.[73] On the other hand, no one suggests that competent adults should be treated against their wishes for their physical illnesses, no matter how convincingly the medical necessity has been shown to exist and no matter how serious the consequences for the patient. The right to refuse even life-saving treatment is regarded as fundamental. A distinction based on age (17 years, 364 days as opposed to 18 years?), rather than competence to decide, looks arbitrary and disproportionate to the otherwise legitimate objective of protecting the welfare of minors (the justification for which is, in any event, that minors are often not in a position to exercise an informed decision about their best interests—if this justification is absent on the facts of the case, because the minor is judged to be competent, then the argument for "protecting" the minor's welfare dissolves).

(b) Children lacking capacity

Where a child lacks the relevant capacity to consent to treatment, parental consent will be required unless there is an emergency.[74] There must be some limits, however, to the parent's power to give or withhold consent. *Gillick* makes it clear that parental rights to control a child do not exist for the benefit of the parent. They exist for the benefit of the child, and they are justified only in so far as they enable the parent to perform his duties towards the child, and towards other children in the family.[75] Accordingly, the parental power to consent to treatment must be exercised in the best interests of

6–057

---

[73] See *R. (on the application of W) v Broadmoor Hospital* [2001] EWCA Civ 1545; [2002] 1 W.L.R. 419, para. 6–075 below. Hale L.J. commented, at [80]: "I do not take the view that detained patients who have the capacity to decide for themselves can never be treated against their will. Our threshold of capacity is rightly a low one. It is better to keep it that way and allow some non-consensual treatment of those who have capacity than to set such a high threshold for capacity that many would never qualify. Whether the criteria for non-consensual treatment of the capacitated should be limited to treatment which is for their own safety (as opposed to their health) is a difficult and complex question. [Counsel for the applicant] tried to persuade us that there was a developing consensus to that effect. There are indeed indications that the issue of capacity is assuming greater importance in the context of psychiatric treatment. But we have not yet reached the point where it is an accepted norm that detained patients who fulfil the *Re MB* criteria for capacity can only be treated against their will for the protection of others or for their own safety."

[74] *Gillick v West Norfolk & Wisbech Area Health Authority* [1986] A.C. 112, 173, *per* Lord Fraser, and 184 and 188 *per* Lord Scarman; *Ney v A.-G. of Canada* (1993) 102 D.L.R. (4th) 136 (B.C.S.C.). A local authority may exercise the power of consent to treatment when the child is in care and the authority has acquired parental responsibility: Children Act 1989, s.33(3). Parents do not lose parental responsibility (and therefore the power to consent to treatment) by virtue of the making of a care order (*ibid.*, s.2), but where there is a conflict between the views of the parents and the local authority, the authority may restrict the extent to which the parents may exercise parental responsibility: Children Act 1989, s.33(3)(*b*). A person who does not have parental responsibility but has the care of the child may do what is reasonable for the purpose of safeguarding or promoting the child's welfare, which in appropriate circumstances would include giving a valid consent to medical treatment: *ibid.*, s.3(5).

[75] *ibid.* at 410, *per* Lord Fraser.

the child.[76] Arguably, this means that a parent may only authorise procedures which are demonstrably for the benefit of the child, indeed parents
may owe a *duty* to the child to give or withhold consent in the best interests
of the child.[77] In *S. v S.*,[78] however, the House of Lords considered that a
parent would be entitled to require a young child to submit to a blood test
for the purpose of determining who was the child's father in a paternity suit,
even though the blood test could not be said to be in the child's medical interests and carried some, albeit extremely remote, risk of harm. Lord Reid considered that a parent could take into account the general public interest in
the administration of justice and so "would not refuse a blood test unless he
thought that would clearly be against the interests of the child."[79] An
approach which permits parental consent to procedures which are "not
against the child's interests" is clearly wider in its ambit than a test based
solely on the child's "best interests," in that it reverses the assessment of the
balance of interests, and curiously shifts from *best* interests to simply "interests." The change in emphasis may be significant, however, when considering the question of medical research on children or the transplantation of
organs or bodily fluids.[80]

6–058   In *Re B. (a minor)(wardship: sterilisation)*[81] Lord Templeman suggested
that parental consent would not be sufficient to authorise a doctor to
perform a sterilisation operation on a girl under 18 years of age, and that a
doctor who relied on parental consent might still be liable in criminal, civil
or professional proceedings: a court exercising the wardship jurisdiction was
the only authority empowered to authorise such a drastic step after a full and
informed investigation.[82] Although this view was not concurred in by the

---

[76] *ibid.* at 432, *per* Lord Templeman. Note also that some procedures may be unlawful even
with parental consent: see the Prohibition of Female Circumcision Act 1985; and also Lord
Templeman's comments on sterilisation in *Re B. (a minor)(wardship: sterilisation)* [1988]
A.C. 199, 205–206, para. 6–058. It would seem that ritual male circumcision remains lawful
(*R v Brown* [1994] 1 A.C. 212, 231 *per* Lord Templeman), despite being an irreversible oper-
ation which is not medically necessary and which carries physical and psychological risks.
But it is a procedure which requires the consent of both parents: *Re J. (Specific Issue Orders:
Child's Religious Upbringing and Circumcision)* [2000] 1 F.L.R. 571; [2000] 1 F.C.R. 307,
CA. See also the GMC *Guidance for doctors who are asked to circumcise male children*,
September 1997 [at *www.gmc-uk.org/global_sections/search_frameset.htm*], and the BMA
Guidance, *Circumcision of Male Infants*, September 1996, [at web.bma.org.uk/ap.nsf/
Content/circumcismaleinfant]. For consideration of the extreme, and probably unique,
circumstances in which the criminal law will permit the defence of necessity to justify the
taking of positive steps to end life see: *Re A (children) (conjoined twins: surgical separation)*
[2001] Fam 147, CA; commented on by Bainham [2001] C.L.J. 49; Burnet (2001) 13
C.F.L.Q. 91; Tausz & Smith [2001] Crim. L.R. 400; Rogers [2001] Crim. L.R. 515. The
issues are considered in an earlier article by Sheldon and Wilkinson, "Conjoined twins: the
legality and ethics of sacrifice" (1997) 5 Med. L. Rev. 149.

[77] *Re J. (a minor)(wardship: medical treatment)* [1991] Fam. 33, 41, *per* Lord Donaldson M.R.

[78] [1972] A.C. 24.

[79] *ibid.* at 44.

[80] See paras 6–182 and 6–188 to 6–189. Note, however, that in *S. v S.* [1972] A.C. 24 it could
be said to be in the child's interests to have the question of paternity determined.

[81] [1988] A.C. 199, 205–206.

[82] See also *per* Neill L.J. in *Re F. (Mental Patient: Sterilisation)* [1990] 2 A.C. 1, 33, para. 6–189
extending this to organ donation by children; and the dissenting speech of Lord Griffiths in

other members the House, it is now the practice to seek the leave of the High Court in such cases.[83] The approval of the court is not necessary, however, where an operation, such as hysterectomy, is to be performed for therapeutic reasons even though sterilisation would be an incidental result.[84] In these circumstances the parents can give a valid consent. In *R v Portsmouth Hospitals NHS Trust, ex parte Glass*[85] the Court of Appeal indicated that where doctors and parents cannot agree on the course to be taken in relation to the treatment of a child, and the conflict is of a grave nature, the matter should be brought before the court.

Under the wardship or the inherent jurisdiction the High Court has the power to authorise or withhold permission for medical treatment of a minor.[86] Previously the Official Solicitor took the view that the procedural and administrative difficulties attaching to applications for a specific issue order under section 8 of the Children Act 1989 were such that the preferred course was to apply using the court's inherent jurisdiction.[87] Nonetheless, it is clear that the concept of "parental responsibility" includes the responsibility to bring

6–059

(n.82 contd.) *Re F. (Mental Patient: Sterilisation)* [1990] 2 A.C. 1, 70 taking the view that the sterilisation of mentally handicapped adults would only be lawful with the approval of the court.

[83] Either under the Children Act 1989 or the court's inherent jurisdiction. See *Practice Note (Official Solicitor: Appointment in Family Proceedings)* [2001] 2 F.L.R. 155 and *Practice Note (Officers of CAFCASS Legal Services and Special Casework: Appointment in Family Proceedings)* [2001] 2 F.L.R. 151. The House of Lords has held that the court may authorise the sterilisation of a mentally handicapped minor, in her "best interests": *Re B. (a minor)(wardship: sterilisation)* [1988] A.C. 199; *Re M. (a minor)(wardship: sterilisation)* [1988] 2 F.L.R. 497; *cf.* the approach of the Supreme Court of Canada in *Re Eve* (1986) 31 D.L.R. (4th) 1 taking the view that non-therapeutic sterilisation of a minor could never be authorised. See further Lee and Morgan (1988) 15 J. of Law and Soc. 229; Brazier (1990) 6 P.N. 25, 26 suggesting that the courts have paid too little attention to the question of whether girls with a mental handicap were competent to refuse consent, before authorising sterilisation under the wardship jurisdiction. In *Secretary, Department of Health and Community Services v J.W.B.* (1992) 106 A.L.R. 385 the High Court of Australia considered that sterilisation which was not an incidental result of surgery performed to cure a disease or correct some malfunction could not be authorised by a parent, although the procedure could be authorised by the court when it was in the best interests of the minor; *P. v P.* (1994) 68 A.L.J.R. 449 (H.C. of Aus.); Blackwood (1994) 1 J. Law and Med. 252.

[84] *Re E. (a minor)(medical treatment)* [1991] 2 F.L.R. 585; (1991) 7 B.M.L.R. 117. See also *Re G.F. (medical treatment)* [1992] 1 F.L.R. 293; [1993] 4 Med. L.R. 77 for the position in the case of an incompetent adult.

[85] [1999] Lloyd's Rep. Med. 367, 376; [1999] 2 F.L.R. 905, CA. See also *Re J. (Specific Issue Orders: Child's Religious Upbringing and Circumcision)* [2000] 1 F.L.R. 571; [2000] 1 F.C.R. 307, CA, which concerned a dispute between the parents about circumcision; *Re C and F (Children)(Immunisation: Parental Rights)* [2003] EWHC 1376 (Fam); *The Times,* June 26, 2003, where there was a dispute between the parents as to whether their children should be immunised. Sumner J. authorised the immunisation on the basis that, on the medical evidence, it was in the children's best interests.

[86] Wardship is available only where the child is not in the care of the local authority: Children Act 1989, s.9. The court's inherent jurisdiction with respect to children is wider than the wardship jurisdiction, and although the use of wardship by local authorities has been curtailed by the Children Act 1989 this residual jurisdiction is still available: see *S. v McC.* [1972] A.C. 24, 47–50, *per* Lord MacDermott; *Re L. (An Infant)* [1968] P. 119, 156–157, *per* Lord Denning M.R. Indeed, this is the assumption made by s.100(4) of the Children Act 1989; see para. 6–060.

[87] *Practice Note (sterilisation: minors and mental health patients)* [1993] 3 All E.R. 222, para. 2.

before a High Court judge the question whether a child should be sterilised, and accordingly section 8 can be used where there is a proposal to sterilise a child.[88] But, in any event, an application under section 8 is unnecessary where parental consent to treatment has been given, even where the minor is competent and has refused consent.[89]

6–060   A local authority cannot invoke the wardship jurisdiction of the High Court where a child is the subject of a care order,[90] nor can an authority apply for a specific issue order under section 8 of the Children Act 1989 with respect to a child who is in care.[91] This will not normally cause any difficulties in relation to consent to treatment because the authority will have acquired parental responsibility and so will be able to give a valid consent. Where, however, a child is in care but the local authority needs a court order to sanction a controversial medical procedure, such as sterilisation, the authority cannot rely on the wardship jurisdiction. In this situation the local authority may apply to the High Court (with the leave of the court) to exercise its inherent jurisdiction over the welfare of children for the purpose of authorising medical treatment provided that the result could not be achieved through an alternative procedure that the authority is entitled to use, and there is reasonable cause to believe that if the inherent jurisdiction is not exercised the child is likely to suffer significant harm.[92]

6–061   In exercising the wardship or the inherent jurisdiction the welfare of the child is the paramount consideration. This welfare principle is also expressed as "the best interests of the child."[93] In *Re J. (a minor)(wardship: medical treatment)*[94] Balcombe L.J. said that in determining the child's best interests the court should adopt the standpoint of the reasonable and responsible parent who has his or her child's best interests at heart. Both Lord Donaldson M.R. and Taylor L.J. appeared to endorse a form of "substituted judgment" test which requires the decision about whether to authorise medical treatment to be taken "from the assumed point of view of the patient."[95] The court may

---

[88] *Re H.G. (Specific Issue Order: Sterilisation)* [1993] 1 F.L.R. 587. See also *Re R. (A Minor)* (1993) 15 B.M.L.R. 72 where it was held that a specific issue order was appropriate where a local authority sought the court's authorisation for the use of blood products on a child, contrary to the parents' objections; *cf. Re O. (A Minor)(Medical Treatment)* [1993] 4 Med. L.R. 272; (1993) 19 B.M.L.R. 148, suggesting that the appropriate procedure in such a case was to invoke the court's inherent jurisdiction, at least on an *ex parte* application; *Re S. (A Minor) (Medical Treatment)* [1993] 1 F.L.R. 376; (1992) 11 B.M.L.R 105.

[89] *Re K., W. and H. (Minors) (Medical Treatment)* (1992) 15 B.M.L.R. 60, applying *Re R. (A Minor) (Wardship: Consent to Treatment)* [1992] Fam. 11, CA; para. 6–052.

[90] Children Act 1989, s.100(2)(*c*).

[91] *ibid.*, s.9(1) and (5).

[92] *ibid.*, s.100(4).

[93] On the interpretation of the child's "best interests" see: *Re B. (a minor)(wardship: medical treatment)* [1981] 1 W.L.R. 1421; *Re C. (a minor)(wardship: medical treatment)* [1990] Fam. 26, on the appropriate treatment for a terminally ill infant; Roberts (1990) 106 L.Q.R. 218.

[94] [1991] Fam. 33; Wells, Aldridge and Morgan (1990) 140 N.L.J. 1544.

[95] *ibid.* at 46, *per* Lord Donaldson M.R. Taylor L.J. said, at 55, that: "The test must be whether the child in question, if capable of exercising sound judgment, would consider the life tolerable"; *Airedale NHS Trust v Bland* [1993] A.C. 789, 833, *per* Hoffmann L.J.: "The patient's best interests would normally also include having respect paid to what seems most likely to

authorise medical treatment of a ward notwithstanding an express refusal of consent by the parents, and may refuse to authorise treatment to which parents have given consent.[96] Moreover, under the wardship or inherent jurisdiction the court may authorise medical treatment even where the child is competent to refuse treatment and has done so.[97] On the other hand, the court will not exercise its inherent jurisdiction over minors by ordering a medical practitioner to treat the minor in a manner contrary to the practitioner's clinical judgment, since this would require the doctor to act contrary to the fundamental duty owed to the patient, which, subject to obtaining consent, is to treat the patient in accordance with his own best clinical judgment, notwithstanding that other practitioners who were not called upon to treat the patient might have formed quite a different judgment or that the court, acting on expert evidence, might disagree with him.[98] It is not entirely

---

(n.96 contd.) have been his own views on the subject. To this extent I think that what the American courts have called 'substituted judgment' may be subsumed within the English concept of best interests." See also *per* Lord Goff at 872, commenting that the substituted judgment test does not form part of English law, although the best interests test should take account of the patient's personality and preferences; and *ibid.*, at 895, *per* Lord Mustill. In *Re Y (Mental Patient: Bone Marrow Donation)* [1997] Fam. 110, 113 Connell J. said that a substituted judgment test was not relevant in this jurisdiction, in the light of Lord Goff's and Lord Mustill's comments in *Bland*.

[96] *Re P. (a minor)* (1982) 80 L.G.R. 301, where it was held that a termination of pregnancy was in the child's best interests, contrary to the wishes of the parents; *Re B. (wardship: abortion)* [1991] 2 F.L.R. 426, to the same effect; *Re L. (a minor)* [1992] 3 Med. L.R. 78; *Re B. (a minor)(wardship: medical treatment)* [1981] 1 W.L.R. 1421 life-saving medical treatment of newborn baby with Down's Syndrome in child's best interests, notwithstanding parents' refusal of consent; *Re D. (a minor)(wardship: sterilisation)* [1976] Fam. 185, where sterilisation of an 11-year-old girl with Soto's syndrome was held not to be in child's best interests, despite the parent's consent; *Re E. (a minor)(wardship: medical treatment)* [1993] 1 F.L.R. 386, where a potentially life-saving blood transfusion to a 15-year-old Jehovah's Witness was held to be in the ward's best interests despite the objections of both the ward and his parents. The courts consistently authorise the administration of blood products to incompetent minors over the religious objections of Jehovah's Witness parents: see *Re R. (A Minor)* (1993) 15 B.M.L.R. 72; *Re O. (a minor) (medical treatment)* [1993] 4 Med. L.R. 272; (1993) 19 B.M.L.R 148; *Re S. (a minor) (medical treatment)* [1993] 1 F.L.R. 376; (1992) 11 B.M.L.R. 105; *Re S. (A Minor) (Consent to Medical Treatment)* [1994] 2 F.L.R. 1065; see also *B.(R.) v Children's Aid Society of Metropolitan Toronto* (1995) 122 D.L.R. (4th) 1 (S.C.C.); *cf.*, however, *Walker v Region 2 Hospital Corp.* (1994) 110 D.L.R. (4th) 477 (N.B.C.A.) where a 15-year-old Jehovah's Witness was held to be competent and entitled to reject a blood transfusion.

[97] *Re R. (A Minor) (Wardship: Consent to Treatment)* [1992] Fam. 11, CA; *Re W. (A Minor) (Medical Treatment: Court's Jurisdiction)* [1993] Fam. 64; para. 6–054.

[98] *Re J. (a minor)(wardship: medical treatment)* [1993] Fam. 15, CA, the consultant paediatrician in charge of a 16-month old child who was profoundly handicapped took the view that it would not be medically appropriate to intervene with intensive therapeutic measures, such as artificial ventilation, if J suffered a life threatening event, and that although ordinary resuscitation with suction, physiotherapy and antibiotics were appropriate, the more intensive measures that would be required if he was unable to breath spontaneously were not. On an application to the court by the local authority, the judge made an order requiring the health authority to use intensive therapeutic measures, including artificial ventilation, for as long as they were capable of prolonging J's life. The Court of Appeal held that this was wrong in law because the court could not order a doctor to treat a patient in a manner which was contrary to the doctor's view of the patient's best interests. It was also erroneous because of the lack of certainty as to what was required of the health authority, and it did not adequately take into account whether the authority would have sufficient resources to treat the patient, or whether there were other patients who would be much more likely to benefit from the use

clear how this principle is to be reconciled with the view expressed in *Airedale NHS Trust v Bland* that it could be unlawful for a medical practitioner to cease treating an incompetent patient in circumstances where treatment could confer *some* benefit.[99] On this approach, if the treatment could confer "some benefit," in the sense of not being completely futile, the practitioner's clinical judgment as to whether treatment should continue is arguably irrelevant (although, no doubt, it would be a factor in the assessment of whether there was any benefit to be gained from continuing treatment).

6–062   Since *Re J. (a minor) (wardship: medical treatment)*,[1] however, the courts have consistently refused to dictate to doctors what treatment should be provided for a child, even in cases involving the withdrawal of treatment over the objections of the child's parents.[2] This "is subject to the power which the courts always have to take decisions in relation to the child's best interests. In doing so, the court takes fully into account the attitude of medical practitioners."[3] In *A NHS Trust v D*[4] it was held that a declaration that it was not in the child's best interests that he receive mechanical ventilation, but should receive palliative care, was not inconsistent with the European Convention on Human Rights. There was no breach of Article 2, because the declaration was in the child's best interests, and there was no breach of Article 3 because in *D v United Kingdom*[5] it was held that Article 3 includes the right to die with dignity, and that was what the declaration being granted was seeking to protect. On the other hand, where the doctors are in favour of treating the child, the courts are likely to place great significance on the doctors' views in coming to a conclusion about the child's best interests, even to the extent of concluding that heart transplant surgery should be authorised for a 15-year-old girl.[6]

(n.98 contd.) of limited resources. The medical staff were free, subject to the appropriate parental consent, to treat J in accordance with their best clinical judgment. See also *Ney v A.-G. of Canada* (1993) 102 D.L.R. (4th) 136, 145 (B.C.S.C.), where it was held that there is no *obligation* to treat even if the patient is capable of consenting.

[99] [1993] A.C. 789, 858–859, *per* Lord Keith: ". . . in general it would not be lawful for a medical practitioner who assumed responsibility for the care of an unconscious patient simply to give up treatment in circumstances where continuance of it would confer some benefit on the patient. On the other hand a medical practitioner is under no duty to continue to treat such a patient where a large body of informed and responsible medical opinion is to the effect that no benefit at all would be conferred by continuance." Possibly, the distinction between *Re J.* and *Bland* is that while the court will not *order* a doctor to treat, he will be liable for failing to treat if harm results.

[1] [1993] Fam. 15.

[2] *Re C (A Minor) (Medical Treatment)* [1998] Lloyd's Rep. Med. 1; [1998] 1 F.L.R. 384; *R v Portsmouth Hospitals NHS Trust, ex parte Glass* [1999] 2 F.L.R. 905; [1999] Lloyd's Rep. Med. 367, CA; *Royal Wolverhampton Hospitals NHS Trust v B* [2000] 1 F.L.R. 953; [2000] 2 F.C.R. 76 where Bodey J. granted a declaration authorising the removal of a ventilator from a five month old child, on the basis that it was in the child's best interests, though the parents believed that there was a possibility of recovery.

[3] *R v Portsmouth Hospitals NHS Trust, ex parte Glass* [1999] Lloyd's Rep. Med. 367 at 374 *per* Lord Woolf M.R.

[4] [2000] 2 F.L.R. 677; [2000] Lloyd's Rep. Med. 411.

[5] [1997] 24 E.H.R.R. 423.

[6] *Re M (A Child) (Refusal of Medical Treatment)* [1999] 2 F.L.R. 1097; [1999] 2 F.C.R. 577, where it was said that the risks posed by the operation and by her possible future resentment at her wishes being overridden were both outweighed by the need to preserve her life.

The one instance where the parents' views have prevailed over those of the   6–063
medical profession was the decision of the Court of Appeal in *Re T. (a minor)*
(wardship: medical treatment).[7] The doctors treating an 18-month-old child
wanted to perform a liver transplant. It was estimated that he would not
survive beyond 2½ years without the transplant. The parents were opposed,
because the baby had already undergone unsuccessful surgery, which had
caused the child pain and distress. The Court of Appeal held that the paramount consideration was the welfare of the child, and not the unreasonableness or otherwise of the parents' refusal to consent. In assessing the child's best
interests it was legitimate to take into account the mother's concerns as to the
benefits to her son of major invasive surgery and the post-operative treatment,
the dangers of failure long-term and short-term, the possibility of the need for
further transplants, the likely length of life, and the effect on the child of all of
these concerns. It would not be appropriate to coerce the mother into playing
the crucial and irreplaceable part in the aftermath of such major surgery, not
just during the post-operative treatment, but also throughout her son's childhood. The total commitment of the caring parent was essential to the success
of the treatment, and without that commitment it was not in the child's interests to have the surgery: "This mother and this child are one for the purpose
of this unusual case . . . The welfare of this child depends on his mother."[8]

(c) Emergency

In an emergency a doctor will be justified in providing medical treatment   6–064
to a child who lacks the capacity to consent, without parental consent or the
authorisation of the court. The justification is analogous to that which
applies to patients who are temporarily incapacitated, for example patients
who are unconscious following an accident,[9] and is based on the principle
of necessity. It may be, however, that in the case of children the concept of
emergency is wider than that which would be applied to temporarily incapacitated adults. Thus in *Gillick v West Norfolk and Wisbech Area Health
Authority* Lord Scarman commented that:

> "Emergency, parental neglect, abandonment of the child, or inability to
> find the parent are examples of exceptional situations justifying the
> doctor proceeding to treat the child without parental knowledge and
> consent; but there will arise, no doubt, other exceptional situations in
> which it will be reasonable for the doctor to proceed without the
> parent's consent."[10]

If, for example, the parents were available but were refusing consent to life-
saving treatment, perhaps on religious grounds, a doctor would be justified

---

[7] [1997] 1 All E.R. 906; Michalowski (1997) 9 C.F.L.Q. 179.
[8] *ibid.* at 914–915 *per* Butler-Sloss L.J.
[9] See para. 6–092.
[10] [1986] A.C. 112, 189.

in performing the treatment, even in the face of an express parental prohibition. In *Gillick* Lord Templeman seemed to have such a situation in mind when he said:

> "I accept that if there is no time to obtain a decision from the court, a doctor may safely carry out treatment in an emergency if the doctor believes the treatment to be vital to the survival or health of an infant and notwithstanding the opposition of a parent or the impossibility of alerting the parent before the treatment is carried out. In such a case the doctor must have the courage of his convictions that the treatment is necessary and urgent in the interests of the patient and the court will, if necessary, approve after the event treatment which the court would have authorised in advance, even if the treatment proves to be unsuccessful."[11]

6–065   Under the Children Act 1989 an emergency protection order may provide for medical or psychiatric examination (though not treatment) of the child.[12] While it is in force, however, an emergency protection order gives the applicant (normally the local authority) parental responsibility for the child,[13] which effectively confers the power to consent to medical treatment.

(5) Patients with mental disorder

(a) Treatment under the Mental Health Act 1983

6–066   Most patients who suffer from mental disorder are subject to the same rules with respect to consent to medical treatment as any other adult. Part IV of the Mental Health Act 1983 (sections 56 to 64), which deals with consent to treatment, applies only to patients liable to be detained under the Act,[14] and accordingly it does not apply to patients voluntarily admitted to hospital,[15]

---

[11] *ibid.* at 200. Parents are not free to make martyrs of their children before they have reached the age of full and legal discretion when they can make that choice for themselves: *Prince v Massachusetts* 321 U.S. 158, 166 (1944) (U.S. Supreme Court). On the administration of blood products to minors despite parental objection see *Re E. (a minor)(wardship: medical treatment)* [1993] 1 F.L.R. 386; *Re R. (A Minor)* (1993) 15 B.M.L.R. 72; *Re O. (A Minor)(Medical Treatment)* [1993] 4 Med. L.R. 272; (1993) 19 B.M.L.R 148; *Re S. (A Minor) (Medical Treatment)* [1993] 1 F.L.R. 376; (1992) 11 B.M.L.R 105; *Re S. (A Minor) (Consent to Medical Treatment)* [1994] 2 F.L.R. 1065; *Re L. (Medical Treatment: Gillick competency)* [1998] 2 F.L.R. 810; [1999] 2 F.C.R. 524. For an argument that the decision in *Re F. (Mental Patient: Sterilisation)* [1990] 2 A.C. 1, para. 6–092 provides a justification for routine medical treatment of children (*i.e.* "non-necessary" but medically desirable in the child's best interests) without parental consent: see Lavery [1990] J.S.W.L. 375. See also Busuttil and McCall Smith [1990] J.S.W.L. 385 for discussion of the problem of medical examination of children who are suspected victims of sexual abuse without parental consent.

[12] Children Act 1989, s.44.

[13] *ibid.*, s.44(4)(*c*).

[14] Mental Health Act 1983, s.56(1).

[15] With the exception of s.57 (requiring the patient's consent *and* a second opinion to surgical procedures for destroying brain tissue or the functioning of brain tissue) which is an additional safeguard for patients: Mental Health Act 1983, s.56(2).

to mentally disordered patients who live in the community,[16] to patients subject to guardianship,[17] nor to certain patients who are liable to be detained but who are specifically excluded from Part IV.[18] The Act is concerned only with treatment of the patient's mental disorder, and it cannot be used to authorise treatment for other medical conditions, even in circumstances where the patient lacks the capacity to consent to such treatment.[19] It cannot be used to detain an individual "against her will merely because her thinking process is unusual, even apparently bizarre and irrational, and contrary to the views of the overwhelming majority of the community at large."[20] Where the provisions of the Act do not apply, the power to give treatment depends upon the rules of the common law, which requires either a valid consent given by the patient or justification under the principle of necessity.[21] In *R v Bournewood Community and Mental Health NHS Trust, ex parte L*[22] the House of Lords held that in the case of patient admitted to hospital informally under section 131(1) of the Act, where the patient is incapable of consenting to the admission or treatment, the common law principle of necessity could justify both the detention and the treatment of the patient, in his best interests.[23]

The Mental Health Act 1983 does not assume that a patient with a mental disorder automatically lacks the capacity to consent to treatment under the   6–067

---

[16] *R. v Hallstrom, ex parte W. (No. 2)* [1986] Q.B. 1090. But a patient who is liable to be detained, does not cease to be so liable simply because she has been given leave of absence under s.17 of the Act: *Barker v Barking, Havering and Brentwood Community Healthcare NHS Trust* [1999] Lloyd's Rep. Med. 101; also reported as *R. v BHB Community Healthcare NHS Trust, ex parte Barker* [1999] 1 F.L.R. 106; (1999) 47 B.M.L.R. 112, CA.

[17] Mental Health Act 1983, s.8(5) providing that a patient received into guardianship ceases to be "liable to be detained."

[18] Mental Health Act 1983, s.56(1); in effect, patients liable to be detained for short periods only.

[19] *Re F. (Mental Patient: Sterilisation)* [1990] 2 A.C. 1; *T. v T.* [1988] Fam. 52; *St. George's Healthcare NHS Trust v S; R v Collins and Others, ex parte S* [1999] Fam. 26, CA.

[20] *St. George's Healthcare NHS Trust v S; R v Collins and Others, ex parte S* [1999] Fam. 26, 51.

[21] "It goes without saying that, unless clear statutory authority to the contrary exists, no one is to be detained in hospital or to undergo medical treatment or even to submit himself to a medical examination without his consent. This is as true of a mentally disordered person as of anyone else," *per* McCullough J. in *R. v Hallstrom, ex parte W. (No. 2)* [1986] Q.B. 1090, 1104; cited with approval by the Court of Appeal in *St. George's Healthcare NHS Trust v S; R v Collins and Others, ex parte S* [1999] Fam. 26, 51.

[22] [1999] 1 A.C. 458.

[23] See para. 6–078 *et seq.* Note, however, that a majority of their Lordships considered that a mental patient in an open, unlocked ward, who appeared to be compliant and made no attempt to leave, was not in fact detained, even though if he had attempted to leave he would have been prevented from doing so by the medical staff, who would then have taken steps to detain him compulsorily under the Mental Health Act 1983. *cf.* Lord Nolan and Lord Steyn, dissenting on this point. Lord Steyn said that the argument that the patient was free to leave was "a fairy tale." The health care professionals had detained him. They intentionally assumed control over him to such a degree (including sedating him with drugs, keeping him under continuous observation, preventing his carers from visiting, and resolving to apply for compulsory admission if he physically resisted) as to amount to a complete deprivation of his liberty. Of course, if the patient is not in fact detained, there was no need for any legal justification for his detention, a point which concerned Lord Nolan, though the hospital clearly would have to justify any treatment given to the patient.

Act, since both section 57 and section 58 provide for consent by the patient to some forms of treatment. But, by virtue of section 63 the consent of a patient is not required for any medical treatment given to him for the mental disorder from which he is suffering, not being treatment falling within section 57 or 58, if the treatment is given by or under the direction of the responsible medical officer.[24] This permits treatment without consent, or indeed notwithstanding the specific refusal of consent by a patient, but only in respect of the mental illness or disorder with which the patient has been classified.[25] In both *Re KB. (adult) (mental patient: medical treatment)*[26] and *B. v Croydon Health Authority*[27] the issue was whether force-feeding an anorexic patient was treatment falling within section 63 for which the patient's consent was not required.[28] In *Re KB.* the patient argued that feeding was not treatment of her mental disorder, it was for the physical symptoms. The feeding was to increase her weight and was not being given for her mental disorder. The hospital argued that K was suffering from an eating disorder and relieving the symptoms was just as much a part of the treatment as relieving the underlying cause. If the symptoms were exacerbated by the patient's refusal to eat and drink, the mental disorder became progressively more difficult to treat, and therefore the feeding by naso-gastric tube was an integral part of the treatment of the mental disorder itself. It was also argued that the treatment was necessary in order to make psychiatric treatment of the underlying cause possible at all. Ewbank J. accepted that the naso-gastric feeding did fall within section 63.

6–068   Similarly, in *B. v Croydon Health Authority* the Court of Appeal agreed that force-feeding an anorexic patient is medical treatment within section 63, since such treatment includes treatment administered to alleviate the symptoms of the disorder as well as treatment to remedy its underlying cause. B suffered from a psychopathic disorder which was incapable of treatment except by psycho-analytical psychotherapy. She argued that giving food might be a prerequisite to a treatment for mental disorder or it might be

---

[24] For the definition of "responsible medical officer" see s.34(1)

[25] *R. (on the application of B.) v Ashworth Hospital Authority* [2003] EWCA Civ 547; [2003] 1 W.L.R. 1886. Thus, if the patient is classified as suffering from mental illness, and that is the basis on which he is detained or remains liable to be detained, he cannot be treated under s.63 for an unrelated mental disorder, unless that disorder is exacerbating the mental illness, so that treatment of the disorder can also be regarded as treatment of the mental illness. Of course, if there is a re-classification of the basis on which the patient is detained, so that the mental disorder is then classified, the patient can then be compulsorily treated for that disorder under the Act. But if the mental disorder would not have satisfied the criteria for the patient's detention, he cannot be compulsorily treated for it merely because he happens to be detained for another condition, such as mental illness.

[26] (1994) 19 B.M.L.R. 144.

[27] [1995] Fam. 133, CA.

[28] It is assumed that anorexia is a mental illness falling within the terms of the Mental Health Act 1983, although in *B. v Croydon Health Authority* the patient suffered from a psychopathic disorder known as borderline personality disorder coupled with post-traumatic stress disorder. Symptoms included depression and a compulsion to self-harm stemming from an irrationally low self-regard. In *Riverside Mental Health Trust v Fox* [1994] 1 F.L.R. 614 the Court of Appeal considered that anorexia may be a mental disorder within the Mental Health Act 1983. See further Fennell (1995) 145 N.L.J. 319.

treatment for the consequences of the mental disorder, but it was not treatment for the disorder itself. Hoffmann L.J. considered that this was too atomistic. It required every individual element of the treatment being given to the patient to be directed to her mental condition. But the test applied to treatment as a whole. Section 145(1) of the Mental Health Act 1983 was included within the definition of medical treatment "nursing, care, habilitation and rehabilitation under medical supervision," and so a range of acts ancillary to the core treatment fell within the definition. His Lordship accepted that if there was *no* proposed treatment for B's psychopathic disorder, section 63 could not be invoked to justify feeding her by naso-gastric tube. Indeed, it would not be lawful to detain her at all.[29] But it did not follow that every act which formed part of that treatment within the wide definition in section 145(1) must in itself be likely to alleviate or prevent a deterioration of that disorder:

> "Nursing and care concurrent with the core treatment or as a necessary prerequisite to such treatment or to prevent the patient from causing harm to himself or to alleviate the consequences of the disorder are in my view capable of being ancillary to a treatment calculated to alleviate or prevent a deterioration of the psychopathic disorder."[30]

Notwithstanding the effect of section 63, some forms of treatment are considered to be so controversial that special safeguards are built into the Mental Health Act. Under section 58 the patient's refusal of consent to electro-convulsive therapy cannot be disregarded unless an independent doctor has certified in writing that the treatment should be given; and under section 57 even consent by the patient is not itself sufficient where the treatment consists of destroying brain tissue.   6–069

Section 57 (treatment requiring consent *and* a second opinion) provides that a patient cannot be given any form of medical treatment for mental disorder consisting of a surgical operation for destroying brain tissue or for destroying the functioning of brain tissue (and such other forms of treatment as may be specified in regulations by the Secretary of State[31]) unless he has consented to it, and it has been certified in writing by a registered medical practitioner (not being the responsible medical officer) and two other persons (not being registered medical practitioners) that the patient is capable of understanding the   6–070

---

[29] By virtue of s.3(2)(*b*) of the Mental Health Act 1983, which provides that a patient with a psychopathic disorder cannot be detained unless the proposed treatment is "likely to alleviate or prevent a deterioration in his condition."

[30] [1995] Fam. 133, 138–139.

[31] See the Mental Health (Hospital, Guardianship and Consent to Treatment) Regulations 1983 (S.I. 1983 No. 893) reg. 16(1) specifying the surgical implantation of hormones for the purpose of reducing the male sex drive. These provisions do not apply to a drug reducing sexual drive which is neither a hormone nor surgically implanted: *R. v Mental Health Act Commission, ex parte X.* (1988) 9 B.M.L.R. 77, D.C. Other forms of treatment to which s.57 should apply may be specified in a Code of Practice: see Mental Health Act 1983, s.118(2). No other forms of treatment have been specified in the Code: see Fennell (1990) 53 M.L.R. 499, 507.

nature, purpose and likely effects of the treatment in question and has consented to it.[32] It must also be certified by the registered medical practitioner that, having regard to the likelihood of the treatment alleviating or preventing a deterioration of the patient's condition, the treatment should be given. This provision means that competent patients can never be given such treatment without their consent, and the requirement for a second opinion is an additional safeguard.[33] On the face of it section 57 would appear to rule out these forms of surgery for patients who are incapable of consenting.[34]

6–071   Section 58 (treatment requiring consent *or* a second opinion) applies to such forms of treatment for mental disorder as may be specified in regulations made by the Secretary of State,[35] and to the administration of medicine to a patient by any means (not being treatment consisting of a surgical operation for destroying brain tissue or for destroying the functioning of brain tissue) at any time during a period for which he is liable to be detained, if three months or more have elapsed since the first occasion in that period when medicine was administered to him by any means for his mental disorder. Under section 58 a patient cannot be given treatment to which the section applies unless he has consented to it, and a registered medical practitioner has certified in writing that the patient is capable of understanding its nature, purpose and likely effects and has consented to it; or an independent registered medical practitioner has certified in writing that the patient is not capable of understanding the nature, purpose and likely effects of the treatment or has not consented to it, but that, having regard to the likelihood of the treatment alleviating or preventing a deterioration of the patient's condition, the treatment should be given.

6–072   A patient who has consented to any treatment for the purposes of sections 57 and 58 can withdraw his consent at any time before the completion of the treatment.[36] This power to withdraw consent is subject to section 62(2), which provides for the continuation of treatment where, in the view of the

---

[32] In these circumstances the team of one registered medical practitioner and two laypersons do not owe a private law duty of care to the patient in deciding whether to grant or withhold the certification that the patient is competent to, and has in fact, consented. Their duties are quasi-judicial, and fall within the field of administrative law. Thus, although a decision that the claimant's treatment fell within s.57 was erroneous, and the decision to refuse to issue a certificate under s.57(2) was *Wednesbury* unreasonable, a private law action for negligence would be struck out as disclosing no reasonable cause of action: *X. v A., B. and C. and the Mental Health Act Commission* (1991) 9 B.M.L.R. 91, QBD.

[33] The "second opinion" doctor must form his own independent opinion on the existence of the statutory criteria. He should not simply review the responsible medical officer's decision that the criteria are satisfied. At the very least he must act in good faith and with reasonable care in forming his judgment: *R. (on the application of W) v Broadmoor Hospital* [2001] EWCA Civ 1545; [2002] 1 W.L.R. 419 at [71] *per* Hale L.J.

[34] Given the wording of the section it seems doubtful that treatment would be justified under the common law principle of necessity, although the major premise of the decision of the House of Lords in *Re F. (Mental Patient: Sterilisation)* [1990] 2 A.C. 1 was that incompetent patients should not be "deprived" of treatment that would otherwise be available to a competent adult.

[35] See the Mental Health (Hospital, Guardianship and Consent to Treatment) Regulations 1983, (S.I. 1983 No. 893), reg. 16(2)(a) specifying electro-convulsive therapy.

[36] Mental Health Act 1983, s.60.

responsible medical officer, discontinuance of the treatment would cause serious suffering to the patient.

In the case of "urgent treatment" sections 57 and 58 do not apply to any treatment: 6–073

(a) which is immediately necessary to save the patient's life; or

(b) which (not being irreversible) is immediately necessary to prevent a serious deterioration of his condition; or

(c) which (not being irreversible or hazardous) is immediately necessary to alleviate serious suffering by the patient; or

(d) which (not being irreversible or hazardous) is immediately necessary and represents the minimum interference necessary to prevent the patient from behaving violently or being a danger to himself or to others.[37]

Where a patient has been received into guardianship, the guardian can require the patient to attend some specified place for the purpose of medical treatment,[38] but the guardian cannot require the patient to receive treatment nor can he consent to the giving of treatment to which the patient does not himself consent.[39] 6–074

In *R. (on the application of W) v Broadmoor Hospital*[40] the Court of Appeal held that challenges to a decision to administer treatment compulsorily under the Mental Health Act 1983 can be made by way of judicial review, an action in the tort of battery, proceedings for a declaration as to the lawfulness of the proposed treatment plan, and proceedings under section 7 of the Human Rights Act 1998 claiming that the hospital was proposing to act in a way that was incompatible with the patient's rights under the European Convention on Human Rights. But whatever procedure is used there must be a full merits review of the decision, with oral evidence and cross-examination, if necessary.[41] The "super-*Wednesbury*" approach[42] to 6–075

---

[37] Mental Health Act 1983, s.62. Treatment is irreversible if it has unfavourable irreversible physical or psychological consequences and hazardous if it entails significant physical hazard: s.62(3). S.62 merely removes the formal requirements for compliance with ss.57 and 58; it does not itself authorise treatment, which must be justified either under s.63, or at common law by the patient's consent or under the principle of necessity. See also National Assistance Act 1948, s.47, although it may be that this provision does not authorise medical treatment: Hoggett, *Mental Health Law*, 4th ed., 1996, pp. 94–95.

[38] Mental Health Act 1983, s.8(1)(*b*).

[39] *R. v Hallstrom, ex parte W. (No. 2)* [1986] Q.B. 1090, 1103; *T. v T.* [1988] Fam. 52, 57. Under the Mental Health Act 1959, s.34(1) a guardian exercised the powers of a father of a child under 14 years of age, which meant that he could consent to treatment on the patient's behalf. The powers of the guardian were amended by the Mental Health (Amendment) Act 1982, ss.8, 65(1), Sch. 3, para. 66. See generally Fisher [1988] J.S.W.L. 316.

[40] [2001] EWCA Civ 1545; [2002] 1 W.L.R. 419 at [24], [59] and [62].

[41] *ibid.* at [31], [53], [83]; *R. (on the application of N.) v Dr. M.* [2002] EWCA Civ 1789; [2003] 1 W.L.R. 562

[42] Adopted in *R. v Ministry of Defence, ex parte Smith* [1996] Q.B. 517 and *R. v Collins and Ashworth Health Authority, ex parte Brady* [2000] Lloyd's Rep. Med. 335.

judicial review was not appropriate to a case where the applicant's human rights were in issue.[43] The review will be a "proportionality" review,[44] but given that the intensity of the review depends on the subject matter in hand,[45] and compulsory medical treatment potentially engages Article 2 (the right to life), Article 3 (protection against torture or inhuman or degrading treatment) and Article 8 (the right to respect for private and family life) of the Convention, this effectively entails a full merits review, with the court reaching its own view as to whether the patient is competent to consent, and whether compulsory treatment is justified. In *Herczegfalvy v Austria*[46] the European Court of Human Rights, considering whether compulsory treatment could amount to a breach of Article 3, said:

> "While it is for the medical authorities to decide, on the basis of the recognisable rules of medical science, on the therapeutic methods to be used, if necessary by force, to preserve the physical and mental health of patients who are entirely incapable of deciding for themselves and for whom they are responsible, such patients nevertheless remain under the protection of Article 3, the requirements of which permit no derogation. The established principles of medicine are admittedly in principle decisive in such cases; as a general rule, a method which is a therapeutic necessity cannot be regarded as inhuman or degrading. The court must nevertheless satisfy itself that the medical necessity has been convincingly shown to exist."

Thus, the crucial test is whether the medical need for treatment "has been convincingly shown to exist." The Court applied the same test to alleged breaches of the applicant's rights under Article 8. In *R. (on the application of W) v Broadmoor Hospital* Hale L.J., commenting on *Herczegfalvy*, said that: "One can at least conclude from this that forcible measures inflicted upon an incapacitated patient which are *not* a medical necessity may indeed be inhuman or degrading. The same must apply to forcible measures inflicted upon a capacitated patient."[47] In other words, compulsory treatment which cannot be convincingly shown to be a medical necessity will amount to a breach of the patient's Convention rights, whether the patient is competent or not. But the fact that there is a responsible body of medical opinion against the proposed treatment is not decisive to determine that medical necessity has not been convincingly shown.[48] The existence of a competing

---

[43] Applying *Smith and Grady v UK* (1999) 29 E.H.R.R. 493 (E.C.H.R.).

[44] Applying *R. v Home Secretary, ex parte Daly* [2001] UKHL 26; [2001] 2 A.C. 532. Lord Steyn, at [27], said: ". . . the doctrine of proportionality may require the reviewing court to assess the balance which the decision maker has struck, not merely whether it is within a range of rational or reasonable decisions. Secondly, the proportionality test may go further than the traditional grounds of review in as much as it may require attention to be directed to the relative weight accorded to interests and considerations."

[45] *ibid.* at [28] *per* Lord Steyn.

[46] (1992) EHRR 437, 484 at [82].

[47] [2001] EWCA Civ 1545; [2002] 1 W.L.R. 419 at [79], original emphasis.

[48] *R. (on the application of N.) v Dr. M.* [2002] EWCA Civ 1789; [2003] 1 W.L.R. 562.

body of medical opinion is relevant to the question of whether treatment is in the patient's best interests or medically necessary, but it is no more than that.[49] The standard is a high one, and the answer to the question whether medical necessity has been convincingly shown depends upon a number of factors, including: "(a) how certain is it that the patient does suffer from a treatable mental disorder; (b) how serious a disorder is it; (c) how serious a risk is presented to others; (d) how likely is it that, if the patient does suffer from such a disorder, the proposed treatment will alleviate the condition; (e) how much alleviation is there likely to be; (f) how likely is it that the treatment will have adverse consequences for the patient; and (g) how severe may they be."[50]

(b) Treatment at common law

There is no power under the Mental Health Act 1983 to give treatment to a mentally disordered person who withholds his consent unless he is detained in hospital or has first been detained and been given leave of absence under section 17. Thus, in *R. v Hallstrom, ex parte W. (No. 2)*[51] McCullough J. said that there is no provision in the Act to the effect that "a patient whose mental disorder is of a nature or degree which makes it appropriate that he should receive treatment as a hospital out-patient, but whose condition does not warrant his detention for treatment in hospital, may be treated as an out-patient, without his consent, if two registered medical practitioners are of the view etc."[52] On the other hand, where a patient to whom the provisions of the Act do not apply lacks the capacity to consent to treatment (and hence the capacity to refuse consent to treatment) a doctor will be justified in providing treatment for the mental disorder which is in the patient's "best interests," following the decision of the House of Lords in *Re F. (Mental Patient: Sterilisation).*[53] This case was not concerned with the treatment of mental disorder, but the broad interpretation placed upon the common law principle of necessity by their Lordships extends to this situation.[54] This creates a potential conflict between the common law and the Mental Health Act 1983, since the Act is clearly concerned with restricting the circumstances in which treatment may be given compulsorily in order to

6–076

---

[49] *ibid.* at [27] to [29].

[50] *ibid.* at [19].

[51] [1986] Q.B. 1090, 1103.

[52] Although, strictly, this statement is still correct, see the decision of the Court of Appeal in *Barker v Barking, Havering and Brentwood Community Healthcare NHS Trust* [1999] Lloyd's Rep. Med. 101; also reported as *R. v BHB Community Healthcare NHS Trust, ex parte Barker* [1999] 1 F.L.R. 106; (1999) 47 B.M.L.R. 112, CA where it was held that a detained patient granted leave of absence for five days a week (which was to be increased to seven days a week) under s.17 of the Act was liable to have her detention renewed under s.20 of the Act. The "assessment" or monitoring of the patient subject to this regime was not to be interpreted narrowly, but could constitute "treatment" for the purposes of the Act.

[53] [1990] 2 A.C. 1; para. 6–078.

[54] See *R v Bournewood Community and Mental Health NHS Trust, ex parte L* [1999] 1 A.C. 458.

protect the patient's rights, whereas in *Re F. (Mental Patient: Sterilisation)* the House of Lords was more concerned with facilitating treatment for patients with mental incapacity, leaving the decision about the nature and purpose of treatment largely to the discretion of the medical profession.

6–077   The Mental Health Act 1983 deals with treatment for the patient's mental disorder. It does not authorise treatment for anything other than mental disorder, even where the patient's capacity to give a valid consent is affected by that disorder. It had been generally assumed (or, at least, no one had sought to question it) that doctors were acting lawfully in giving medical treatment to adults who lacked the capacity to consent. The basis for that assumption was not tested in the courts in this country until cases involving the highly controversial issues of abortion and sterilisation of mentally handicapped women arose. In the case of girls under the age of 18 it was clear that the court, in the exercise of the wardship jurisdiction, may authorise an abortion or sterilisation of a minor where it is in her best interests.[55] The wardship jurisdiction is not available, however, once the child reaches the age of majority. In *T. v T.*[56] the question was whether it would be lawful to perform an abortion and sterilisation on a 19 year-old woman with a serious mental handicap. Wood J. considered and rejected a number of possible justifications, concluding that the operation would be lawful if it could be justified under the principle of necessity. Where there was no-one in a position to give consent for the patient, and where the patient was suffering from such mental abnormality as never to be able to give such consent, a doctor would be justified in taking such steps as good medical practice demanded.[57] By this Wood J. envisaged "a situation where based upon good medical practice there are really no two views of what course is for the best".[58] This approach leaves the substantive decision as to what is justified to the medical profession, but it is more restricted in its scope than the *Bolam* test since it does not allow for treatment when there are competing but "responsible" medical opinions about what should be done in the patient's best interests.

6–078   In *Re F. (Mental Patient: Sterilisation)*[59] the patient was a woman of 36 years who suffered from a serious mental disability. She was a voluntary in-

---

[55] *Re B. (a minor)(wardship: sterilisation)* [1988] A.C. 199; *Re P. (a minor)* (1982) 80 L.G.R. 301; *Re D. (a minor)(wardship: sterilisation)* [1976] Fam. 185, where the decision went the other way on the facts; *cf.* the approach of the Supreme Court of Canada in *Re Eve* (1986) 31 D.L.R. (4th) 1, taking the view that the non-therapeutic sterilisation of a mentally handicapped minor could never be justified. The House of Lords were highly critical of this decision in *Re B. (a minor)*.

[56] [1988] Fam. 52; Fortin (1988) 51 M.L.R. 634. See also *Re X., The Times*, June 4, 1987, QBD.

[57] *ibid.* at 68. His Lordship distinguished patients with temporary incapacity, such as a person under an anaesthetic.

[58] *ibid.* at 63.

[59] [1990] 2 A.C. 1, CA and HL; Shaw (1990) 53 M.L.R. 91; Jones (1989) 5 P.N. 178. See further the Law Commission Consultation Paper No. 129, *Mentally Incapacitated Adults and Decision-Making: Medical Treatment and Research*, 1993; and the final Report, *Mental Incapacity*, Law Com. No. 231, 1995, HMSO. For comment on the Consultation Paper see Gunn (1994) 2 Med. L. Rev. 8 and Freeman (1994) 2 Med. L. Rev. 77; and for comment on the Report see Wilson (1996) 4 Med. L. Rev. 227.

patient at a mental hospital, and had formed a sexual relationship with a male patient. The psychiatric evidence was that F would not understand the meaning of pregnancy, labour or delivery, and would be unable to care for a baby if she had one. From a psychiatric point of view it would have been "disastrous for her to conceive a child." Other contraceptive methods were considered to be unreliable and/or to involve a risk of harm to her physical health. In these circumstances it was thought appropriate that F be sterilised. The Court of Appeal considered that the *Bolam* test (a practice accepted as proper by a responsible body of professional opinion) was an insufficiently stringent standard by which to measure necessity, though the test suggested by Wood J. in *T. v T.* was rejected as too strict because there "will always or usually be a minority view and this approach, if strictly applied, would often rule out all treatment. On the other hand, the existence of a significant minority view would constitute a serious contra-indication."[60] The court was clearly concerned that patients who lack the capacity to consent to medical treatment are not simply the equivalent of competent adults who are unable to give an assent. They are also incapable of refusing treatment, and therefore "other things being equal there must be greater caution in deciding whether to treat and, if so, how to treat."[61]

The House of Lords agreed that the principle of necessity provided the solution to the problem of patients who lack the capacity to consent, but considered that legal protection for patients was secondary to facilitating treatment. It was axiomatic, said Lord Bridge, that treatment which is necessary to preserve the life, health or well-being of the patient may lawfully be given without consent.[62] Lord Goff had no doubt that the common law recognised a principle of necessity which might justify action which would otherwise be unlawful, and Lord Brandon, without referring specifically to a general principle of necessity, said that the common law would be seriously defective if it failed to provide a solution to the problem created by an inability to consent to treatment.

6–079

Lord Brandon concluded that an operation or other treatment performed on adult patients who are incapable, for one reason or another, of consenting, would be lawful provided that it is in the best interests of the patient. It will be in their best interests "if, but only if, it is carried out in order either to save their lives or to ensure improvement or prevent deterioration in their physical or mental health."[63] This statement of the patient's best interests is extremely wide. Procedures designed to "ensure improvement or prevent

6–080

---

[60] [1990] 2 A.C. 1, 19, *per* Lord Donaldson M.R.

[61] *ibid. per* Lord Donaldson M.R. See also *per* Neill L.J. at 32: "I would define necessary in this context as that which the general body of medical opinion in the particular speciality would consider to be in the best interests of the patient in order to maintain the health and to secure the well-being of the patient. One cannot expect unanimity but it should be possible to say of an operation which is necessary in the relevant sense that it would be unreasonable in the opinion of most experts in the field not to make the operation available to the patient."

[62] *Re F. (Mental Patient: Sterilisation)* [1990] 2 A.C. 1, 52.

[63] *ibid.* at 55.

deterioration in . . . physical or mental health" would encompass virtually anything that a doctor might ever do to a patient.[64] It would, for example, provide a blanket common law justification for the treatment of mental illness or disorder for which statutory provision is considered necessary in the Mental Health Act 1983, which provides specific safeguards for the patient. His Lordship was clearly concerned not to place constraints on the defence which might otherwise deprive patients of medical care which they need and to which they are entitled.[65] Lord Brandon used the same argument to justify adopting the *Bolam*[66] test as the appropriate standard for measuring the patient's best interests:

> "If doctors were to be required, in deciding whether an operation or other treatment was in the best interests of adults incompetent to give consent, to apply some test more stringent than the *Bolam* test, the result would be that such adults would, in some circumstances at least, be deprived of the benefit of medical treatment which adults competent to give consent would enjoy. In my opinion it would be wrong for the law, in its concern to protect such adults, to produce such a result."[67]

6–081   The difficulty with applying the *Bolam* test to the defence of necessity was that there could well be more than one view, or indeed several views, as to what is in the best interests of the patient and, accordingly, as to what course of conduct in relation to incompetent patients is justified in law. When applied in the context of a negligence action the *Bolam* test effectively means that competing "responsible bodies of medical opinion" cannot be challenged. Following *a* responsible practice means that a defendant is not negligent, even where there are other, and possibly better, responsible practices. If this applied to treatment decisions about incapacitated adults it would leave decisions about medical treatment, even controversial treatment such as sterilisation, within the discretion of the medical profession.[68] The patient

---

[64] It clearly covers diagnostic as well as therapeutic procedures: *Re H. (Mental Patient)* [1993] 4 Med. L.R. 91; [1993] 1 F.L.R. 28; (1992) 9 B.M.L.R. 71.

[65] [1990] 2 A.C. 1, 55. See also, at 52, *per* Lord Bridge, who was worried that a "rigid criterion of necessity" would deprive many patients of treatment which it would be entirely beneficial for them to receive. Lord Goff, at 76, said that in the case of a mentally disordered person the permanent nature of the incapacity calls for a wider range of treatment than would be appropriate in the case of temporary incapacity to be covered by the defence, including routine medical or dental treatment, and even simple care such as dressing and undressing and putting to bed. Indeed, in *R v Bournewood Community and Mental Health NHS Trust, ex parte L* [1999] 1 A.C. 458 the House of Lords held that the principle of necessity could justify the detention and treatment of patients who are admitted to hospital as informal patients under s.131(1) of the Mental Health Act 1983, but lack the capacity to consent to treatment or care.

[66] *Bolam v Friern Hospital Management Committee* [1957] 2 All E.R. 118.

[67] *Re F. (Mental Patient: Sterilisation)* [1990] 2 A.C. 1, 68; see also *per* Lord Bridge at 52.

[68] See *Re W. (Mental Patient) (Sterilisation)* [1993] 1 F.L.R. 381, where Hollis J. held that sterilisation of a 20-year-old patient, having a mental age of seven, was in her best interests, notwithstanding that there was only a small risk of her becoming pregnant, since a responsible body of medical opinion was in favour of sterilisation.

would have a right to have non-negligent decisions made about her medical treatment, but no right to the "best" decision.

This concern led the Court of Appeal to emphasise in *Re S (Adult Patient:* **6–082** *Sterilisation)*[69] that where the question of appropriate medical treatment comes before a court for decision, while there may be a number of different options which might be lawful in any particular case (since there could be more than one responsible practice), logically there is only one best option, and the court must choose that option in making decisions in the patient's best interests rather than leaving the doctors to choose from the range of lawful options. The issue was whether a 29-year-old woman with severe learning difficulties could lawfully be sterilised despite her lack of capacity because her mother was concerned that she might get pregnant when she moved into a local authority home. The judge held that both contraception (by the insertion of an intra-uterine coil) or surgery were lawful options and had left the decision to the woman's mother in conjunction with the doctors. The Court of Appeal held that the insertion of the intra uterine device was in S's best interests as it was the least invasive option, was not irreversible, and left room for surgical procedures if it proved ineffective. The question for the judge, said Butler-Sloss P., was not whether the proposed treatment fell within the range of acceptable opinion among competent and responsible practitioners, but was it in the best interests of S? Once the judge was satisfied that the range of options was within the range of acceptable opinion among competent and responsible practitioners, the *Bolam* test was irrelevant to the judge's decision.[70] Thorpe L.J. explained the rationale for this:

"... in determining the welfare of the patient the *Bolam* test is applied only at the outset to ensure that the treatment proposed is recognised as proper by a responsible body of medical opinion skilled in delivering that particular treatment. That may be a necessary check in an exercise where it would be impossible to be over scrupulous ... In practice the dispute will generally require the court to choose between two or more possible treatments both or all of which comfortably pass the *Bolam* test ... One of the most important services provided by a consultant is to explain the available alternatives to the patient, particularly concentrating on those features of advantage and disadvantage most relevant to his needs and circumstances. In a developing relationship of confidence the consultant then guides the patient to make the

---

[69] [2001] Fam. 15. Also reported as *Re SL (Adult Patient) (Medical Treatment)* [2000] Lloyd's Rep. Med. 339; [2000] 2 F.L.R. 389; [2000] 2 F.C.R. 452.

[70] *ibid.* at 28 *per* Butler-Sloss P. See also *Re A (Medical Treatment: male sterilisation)* [2000] 1 F.L.R. 549; [2000] 1 F.C.R. 193, also reported as *R-B (A Patient) v Official Solicitor* [2000] Lloyd's Rep. Med. 87, where the Court of Appeal held that on an application for approval of sterilisation of a mentally incapacitated patient it is the judge, not the doctor, who decides whether it is in the patient's best interests. See further the Law Commission report, *Mental Incapacity*, Law Com. No. 231, (1995), para. 3.27: "It should be clear beyond any shadow of a doubt that acting in a person's best interests amounts to something more than not treating that person in a negligent manner."

choice that best suits his circumstances and personality. It is precisely because the patient is prevented by disability from that exchange that the judge must in certain circumstances either exercise the choice between alternative available treatments or perhaps refuse any form of treatment. In deciding what is best for the disabled patient the judge must have regard to the patient's welfare as the paramount consideration. That embraces issues far wider than the medical. Indeed it would be undesirable and probably impossible to set bounds to what is relevant to a welfare determination. In my opinion the *Bolam* case has no contribution to make to this second and determinative stage of the judicial decision."[71]

6–083   In *Simms v Simms*; *A. v A.*[72] two young patients were suffering from vCJD, an invariably fatal degenerative disease of the brain. It was proposed that they be subjected to experimental treatment which had a slight, but not non-existent, chance of improving their condition. There was a possibility of arresting the disease temporarily, and a possibility of prolonging their lives to some extent. An application was made for a declaration that the experimental treatment was in their best interests. Butler-Sloss P. observed: "I have to assess the best interests in the widest possible way to include the medical and non-medical benefits and disadvantages, the broader welfare issues of the two patients, their abilities, their future with or without treatment, the views of the families, and the impact of refusal of the applications. All of these matters have to be weighed up and balanced in order for the court to come to a decision in the exercise of its discretion."[73] On the evidence, the prospect of a slightly longer life was held to be a benefit worth having for each of the patients. There was sufficient possibility of unquantifiable benefit to hold that it would be in their best interests to have the treatment. The reality was that the patients had very little to lose in the treatment going ahead, and therefore it was a reasonable risk to take.

6–084   On the other hand, on an application to sterilise a male patient who lacks the capacity to consent, it will be extremely difficult to establish that the procedure is in the best interests of the patient. In *Re A (Medical Treatment:*

---

[71] *ibid.* at 30. For consideration of the courts' approach to the patient's best interests in cases of proposed sterilisation see: (1) where sterilisation was held not to be in the patient's best interests: *Re LC (medical treatment: sterilisation)* [1997] 2 F.L.R. 258; *Re S (medical treatment: adult sterilisation)* [1998] 1 F.L.R. 944; [1999] 1 F.C.R. 277—risk of pregnancy had to be identifiable rather than speculative; and (2) where sterilisation was held to be in the patient's best interests: *Re X (Adult Sterilisation)* [1998] 2 F.L.R. 1124; *Re ZM and OS (Sterilisation: Patient's Best Interests)* [2000] 1 F.L.R. 523; [2000] 1 F.C.R. 274 (where there were also other therapeutic benefits to the patient having an hysterectomy).

[72] [2002] EWHC 2734 (Fam); [2003] 1 All E.R. 669.

[73] *ibid.* at [60]. When considering the best interests of a patient the court's duty is "to assess the advantages and disadvantages of the various treatments and management options, the viability of each such option and the likely effect each would have on the patient's best interests and, I would add, his enjoyment of life. On the facts of the present case in particular, any likely benefit of treatment has to be balanced and considered in the light of any additional suffering the treatment option would entail": *per* Butler-Sloss P. in *An Hospital NHS Trust v S* [2003] EWHC 365 (Fam); [2003] Lloyd's Rep. Med. 137 at [47].

male sterilisation)[74] the Court of Appeal held that it was not in the best interests of a 28-year-old male Down's Syndrome patient to have a vasectomy. Although an assessment of his best interests was not limited to medical interests, and could include medical, emotional and other welfare interests,[75] neither the fact of the birth nor the possible disapproval of his conduct was likely to impinge on a mentally incapacitated man to a significant degree, other than in exceptional circumstances. The question of whether the interests of third parties could ever be taken into account in a case concerned with the best interests of an incapacitated patient was specifically left open.[76]

(c) Withdrawing treatment[77]

In the case of a permanently insensate patient (extreme persistent vegetative state) it cannot be said to be in the patient's best interests to continue to receive medication or nourishment which is futile, and therefore the justification for continuing treatment under *Re F. (Mental Patient: Sterilisation)* does not apply. Accordingly, it is not unlawful to terminate medical treatment or nourishment for such a patient, even though it is known, and indeed it is the intention, that the consequence will be that the patient will die.[78] Again, this is a matter to be determined on the basis of responsible medical opinion, so that provided the doctor's view that further treatment is futile is supported by a responsible body of professional opinion the decision to withdraw treatment will be lawful, despite the existence of a responsible body of professional opinion taking a contrary view.[79] The withdrawal of artificial nutrition and hydration in such cases does not constitute an act, by someone acting on behalf of the state, resulting in death. Rather a responsible decision by a

6–085

---

[74] [2000] 1 F.L.R. 549; [2000] 1 F.C.R. 193.

[75] *ibid.* at 555 *per* Butler-Sloss P.; *An Hospital NHS Trust v S* [2003] EWHC 365 (Fam); [2003] Lloyd's Rep. Med. 137 at [45] *per* Butler-Sloss P.

[76] *ibid.* at 556 and 558 *per* Butler-Sloss P. and Thorpe L.J. respectively. See generally on the "best interests" test, the Law Commission report, *Mental Incapacity*, Law Com. No. 231, (1995) paras 3.24 *et seq.* The Draft Mental Incapacity Bill, June 2003, cl. 4 now sets out some of the issues that have to be taken into account when deciding what is in a person's best interests.

[77] See the GMC Guidance, *Withholding and Withdrawing Life-prolonging Treatments: Good Practice in Decision-making*, August 2002, available at *www.gmc-uk.org/standards/whwd.htm*.

[78] *Airedale NHS Trust v Bland* [1993] A.C. 789; *Frenchay Healthcare NHS Trust v S.* [1994] 1 W.L.R. 601, CA. See also *Nancy B v Hôtel-Dieu de Québec* (1992) 86 D.L.R. (4th) 385 (Qué.S.C.); Dickens (1993) 38 McGill L.J. 1053; *Auckland Area Health Board v A.-G.* [1993] 1 N.Z.L.R. 235; [1993] 4 Med. L.R. 239 (N.Z.H.C.). For comment on *Bland* see Finnis (1993) 109 L.Q.R. 337; Hinchliffe and Andrews [1993] Fam. Law 137; Wells [1994] J.S.W.F.L. 65; Lord Goff (1995) 3 Med. L. Rev. 1. For a general discussion of withholding treatment from adults at common law see Gilmour (1993) 31 Osgoode Hall L.J. 473.

[79] Only Lord Mustill in *Airedale NHS Trust v Bland* [1993] A.C. 789, 898 expressed reservations about applying the *Bolam* test to "decisions on 'best interests' in a field dominated by the criminal law." In *Frenchay Healthcare NHS Trust v S.* [1994] 1 W.L.R. 601, 609 Sir Thomas Bingham M.R. commented that: "It is, I think, important that there should not be a belief that what the doctor says is in the patient's best interests *is* in the patient's best interests. For my part I would certainly reserve to the court the ultimate power and duty to review the doctor's decision in the light of all the facts" (original emphasis).

medical team based on the clinical judgment that it is no longer in the patient's best interests to continue treatment is an omission, and so cannot amount to an intentional deprivation of life by the state contrary to Article 2 of the European Convention on Human Rights.[80] The death of the patient in such circumstances results from the illness or injury from which he suffered. It does not constitute a "deprivation of life" and does not fall within the negative obligation to refrain from taking life intentionally.[81] Thus, Article 2 does not impose an absolute obligation to treat if the treatment would be futile.[82] Nor does the withdrawal of futile treatment constitute a breach of Article 3 which prohibits torture and inhuman or degrading treatment or punishment. As a general rule a measure which is a therapeutic necessity cannot be regarded as inhuman or degrading.[83] Moreover, Article 3 requires the victim to be aware of the inhuman and degrading treatment which he or she is experiencing, or at least to be in a state of physical or mental suffering. An insensate patient in a permanent vegetative state has no feelings and comprehension of the treatment, and therefore Article 3 cannot apply to such cases.[84]

6–086   The courts will now consider authorising the withdrawal of treatment in cases where the patient is not in a permanent vegetative state, though the legal basis for these decisions remains the patient's "best interests." In *Re D (Medical Treatment: Mentally Disabled Patient)*[85] the patient was unable to consent to or refuse kidney dialysis treatment due to mental disability. Sir Stephen Brown P. held that where a patient required kidney dialysis several times a week but, as a result of mental disability and drug and alcohol misuse, could not be relied upon to co-operate with the treatment except under general anaesthetic, which was dangerous and impracticable, the court could grant a declaration that it was lawful not to impose dialysis treatment. Despite lack of capacity to consent to or refuse treatment because of his mental disability, where the medical evidence supported the conclusion that treatment was not practicable, the court could grant such a declaration, obliging doctors to provide only such palliative care as the patient would accept. And in *South Buckinghamshire NHS Trust v R*[86] the same judge held that it would be in the best interests of a 23-year-old patient who existed in a "low awareness state" to withhold cardio-pulmonary resuscitation in the event of a cardiac arrest, and antibiotics in the event of him developing a potentially life-threatening infection.[87]

---

[80] *NHS Trust A v M; NHS Trust B v H* [2001] Fam. 348. See also *NHS Trust A v H* [2001] 2 F.L.R. 501; *Re G (Adult Incompetent: Withdrawal of Treatment)* (2002) 65 B.M.L.R. 6.

[81] *ibid.* at [30] per Butler-Sloss P.

[82] *ibid.* at [37].

[83] Provided the medical necessity has been convincingly shown to exist: *Herczegfalvy v Austria* (1992) 15 E.H.R.R. 437 at [82] (E.C.H.R.). Note also that for a breach of Article 3 the ill-treatment must attain a minimum level of severity: *T v UK* (1999) 7 B.H.R.C. 659 at [68] (E.C.H.R.).

[84] *NHS Trust A v M; NHS Trust B v H* [2001] Fam. 348 at [49] *per* Butler-Sloss P.

[85] [1998] 2 F.L.R. 22; [1998] 2 F.C.R. 178.

[86] [1996] 7 Med. L.R. 401.

[87] Applying *Re J.* [1991] Fam. 33, a case concerning a minor; see para. 6–061.

(d) Procedure

Re F. (Mental Patient: Sterilisation) raised a procedural problem. The **6–087** House of Lords concluded that there was no equivalent of the wardship jurisdiction by which the court could exercise a power to consent on behalf of an incompetent adult. The ancient *parens patriae* jurisdiction of the Crown to protect the persons and property of those unable to do so for them- selves was no longer available.[88] The court did not have jurisdiction to consent to medical treatment under Part VII of the Mental Health Act 1983, nor was there any residual inherent jurisdiction (in the absence of the *parens patriae* jurisdiction) to approve or disapprove of a proposed operation. Although it was not essential as a matter of law to obtain the approval of the court to a sterilisation operation on an incompetent adult,[89] nonetheless it would be good medical practice to obtain the "approval" of the court by means of an application for a declaration that the operation would be in the patient's best interests, and this is now the appropriate procedure.[90] Similarly, as a matter of practice, doctors should seek the guidance of the court, by an application for a declaration, in all cases before withholding life- prolonging treatment from a patient in a persistent vegetative state.[91] It is not necessary, however, to obtain the approval of the High Court prior to performing an abortion on a mentally handicapped adult provided that the requirements of the Abortion Act 1967 are satisfied and it is in the patient's best interests.[92] Nor is it necessary, as a matter of good medical practice, to

---

[88] [1990] 2 A.C. 1, 57–58. For the history of this jurisdiction see Hoggett, "The Royal Prerogative in Relation to the Mentally Disordered: Resurrection, Resuscitation or Rejection," in Freeman (ed.), *Medicine, Ethics and the Law*, 1988, p. 85.

[89] *cf.* the dissent of Lord Griffiths on this point: *ibid.* at 70.

[90] See the speech of Lord Brandon at [1990] 2 A.C. 1, 65; *Practice Direction (Declaratory Proceedings: Incapacitated Adults)* [2002] 1 W.L.R. 325; [2002] 1 All E.R. 794, and the Annex to that Practice Direction *Practice Note (Declaratory Proceedings: Medical and Welfare Decisions for Adults who lack Capacity)* [2001] 2 F.C.R. 569; *J. v C.* [1990] 3 All E.R. 735. Lord Goff suggested, [1990] 2 A.C. 1, 83, that if it became the invariable practice of the medical profession to seek a declaration before sterilising an incompetent adult there would be little practical difference between obtaining the court's approval under the *parens patriae* jurisdiction and obtaining a declaration. There is no power, however, to grant an interim declaration: *Riverside Mental Health Trust v Fox* [1994] 1 F.L.R. 614, CA; and therefore a declaration should not be made on an *ex parte* basis: *St. George's Healthcare NHS Trust v S; R v Collins and Others, ex parte S* [1999] Fam. 26, 60. A dispute between rival claimants as to the care of an adult patient incapable of expressing his wishes in respect of treatment or care is a justiciable issue for which the court's declaratory jurisdiction can be invoked, and a claimant who can demonstrate a genuine and legitimate interest in obtain- ing a decision will have standing to make an application: *Re S. (Hospital Patient: Court's Jurisdiction)* [1996] Fam. 1. See also *Re F (Adult Patient: Jurisdiction)* [2001] Fam. 38; [2000] Lloyd's Rep. Med. 381, where the Court of Appeal held that where an incapacitated adult did not fall within the guardianship provisions of the Mental Health Act 1983, a deci- sion as to where and with whom he lived was a justiciable issue and it was open to a court to grant a declaration to protect the adult's welfare.

[91] *Airedale NHS Trust v Bland* [1993] A.C. 789; *Frenchay Healthcare NHS Trust v S.* [1994] 1 W.L.R. 601; *Practice Direction (Declaratory Proceedings: Incapacitated Adults)* [2002] 1 W.L.R. 325, and Annex, *Practice Note (Declaratory Proceedings: Medical and Welfare Decisions for Adults who lack Capacity)* [2001] 2 F.C.R. 569.

[92] *Re S.G. (adult mental patient: abortion)* [1991] 2 F.L.R. 329; [1993] 4 Med. L.R. 75.

apply for a declaration as to the lawfulness of a proposed therapeutic operation which would have the incidental effect of sterilisation of a woman who by reason of mental disability cannot consent to the procedure, where the operation is necessary in order to ensure the improvement or prevent a deterioration in her health;[93] *a fortiori* where a proposed invasive diagnostic procedure (a CT brain scan) is agreed to be in the best interests of the patient, the procedure is lawful and it is not appropriate to grant a declaration to that effect simply as a "comfort" to the doctors or as protection against the risk of vexatious litigation in the future by the disgruntled patient.[94]

6–088   The Mental Incapacity Bill will change the legal basis upon which medical treatment is provided for incapacitated patients, whether the incapacity is permanent or temporary. The provisions of the Bill will not apply, however, to medical treatment for mental disorder where such treatment is governed by the Mental Health Act 1983, Part 4.[95] There will be a "general authority" which will make it lawful for any person to do an act when providing any form of care for another person (the patient), if the patient lacks, or the person reasonably believes that the patient lacks, capacity and in all the circumstances it is reasonable for the person to the act.[96] A new Court of Protection will have the power to make declarations as to whether a person has or lacks capacity to make decisions and declarations as to the lawfulness of an act or omission, or course of conduct, in relation to that person.[97] The court will also have the power to make decisions on behalf of the person lacking capacity and to appoint a deputy to make decisions on the patient's behalf.[98] This includes the power to give or refuse consent to the carrying out or continuation of treatment by a person providing health care for the patient.[99] It will also be possible for an adult who has capacity to grant a "lasting power of attorney" to another adult, conferring on the donee of the power authority to make decisions about the adult's personal welfare and property and affairs (or specified matters concerning personal welfare or property and affairs) which includes authority to make such decisions when the adult no longer has capacity.[1] A lasting power of attorney would have to

---

[93] *Re G.F. (medical treatment)* [1992] 1 F.L.R. 293; [1993] 4 Med. L.R. 77; though if a case falls near the boundary of what is therapeutically necessary or in the best interests of the patient, it should be referred to the court for a declaration of lawfulness: *Re S (Adult Patient: Sterilisation)* [2001] Fam. 15, 32 *per* Thorpe L.J. For the analogous position where the patient is a minor see: *Re E. (a minor)(medical treatment)* [1991] 2 F.L.R. 585; (1991) 7 B.M.L.R. 117. The Law Commission, *Mental Incapacity*, Law Com. No. 231, (1995), para. 6.4 has recommended that any treatment likely to render the patient permanently infertile should require court authorisation, unless it is to treat disease of the reproductive organs or relieve existing detrimental effects of menstruation.

[94] *Re H. (Mental Patient)* [1993] 4 Med. L.R. 91; [1993] 1 F.L.R. 28; (1992) 9 B.M.L.R. 71.

[95] Draft Mental Incapacity Bill, June 2003, cl. 27. See paras 6–066 to 6–075.

[96] *ibid.*, cl. 6. This is subject to cl. 4, providing that the act must be done in the patient's best interests, and cl. 7 which creates specific restrictions on the general authority. The general authority is also subject to cll. 23 to 25 on advance decisions made by the patient: see para. 6–008.

[97] *ibid.* cll. 14 and 15.

[98] *ibid.* cl. 16. The power to make decisions is again subject to cl. 4, the patient's best interests. The powers of deputies will be much more restricted than the powers of the court: cl. 20.

[99] *ibid.* cl. 17(1)(d).

[1] *ibid.* cl. 8(1).

be exercised in the best interests of the patient, and subject to any restrictions specified in the document itself. It would not authorise the donee of the power to use or threaten to use force to compel the patient to do something that the patient resisted, or to restrict the patient's liberty of movement, unless the patient lacked, or the donee reasonably believed that the patient lacked, capacity and the donee reasonably believed that it was necessary to do the act to avert a substantial risk of significant harm to the patient.[2] Subject to any restrictions in the instrument itself, the authority conferred by a lasting power of attorney to make decisions about personal welfare includes the giving or refusing of consent to the carrying out or continuation of treatment by a person providing health care, except where the patient has capacity to give or refuse consent to treatment, where there is an advance decision of the patient that applies, or in the case of life-sustaining treatment if there is no express provision in the lasting power of attorney.[3]

(6) Emergency (temporary incapacity)

It is generally agreed that in an emergency, where an otherwise competent   6–089
patient is unable to consent for some reason, doctors may lawfully proceed to treat the patient without consent. Doctors have been acting on this supposition for years, every time an unconscious patient is wheeled into the casualty department of a hospital, for example. Moreover, it would be absurd if the law did not provide for this situation. As Lord Bridge observed in *Re F. (Mental Patient: Sterilisation)*,[4] doctors and other health care professionals would otherwise face an intolerable dilemma: if they administer the treatment which they believe to be in the best interests of the patient they might face an action for trespass to the person, but if they withhold that treatment they could be in breach of a duty of care in negligence.

One possible justification that has been canvassed in relation to emergency   6–090
procedures is implied consent.[5] The argument is that the unconscious patient, although unable to consent, would very probably consent to emergency treatment if he were able to do so and so his consent can be implied. The patient's "consent" is clearly fictional in these circumstances and this has been regarded as an unsatisfactory approach, particularly as it invites confusion with situations in which the patient is capable of exercising a capacity to consent, refrains from giving an express consent, and yet can be taken to have impliedly consented, for example, by his conduct.

Another approach was suggested in *Wilson v Pringle*[6] where it was said that   6–091
a touching must be proved to be a "hostile touching" in order to constitute a

---

[2] *ibid*. cl. 10(1) and (2).
[3] *ibid*. cl. 10(3), (4) and (5).
[4] [1990] 2 A.C. 1, 52.
[5] See, *e.g.*, Skegg (1974) 90 L.Q.R. 512; Brazier, *Medicine Patients and the Law*, 2nd ed., 1992, p. 90; Mason, McCall Smith and Laurie, *Law and Medical Ethics*, 6th ed., 2002, para. 10.10; *Schweizer v Central Hospital* (1974) 53 D.L.R. (3d) 494, 507.
[6] [1987] Q.B. 237.

battery. The Court of Appeal took the view that a general exception to the tort of battery, which embraces all physical contact which is generally acceptable in the ordinary conduct of daily life provided "a solution to the old problem of what legal rule allows a casualty surgeon to perform an urgent operation on an unconscious patient who is brought into hospital . . . Hitherto it has been customary to say in such cases that consent is to be implied . . . It is better simply to say that the surgeon's action is acceptable in the ordinary conduct of everyday life."[7] This dictum was doubted by Wood J. in *T. v T.*,[8] who commented that operative treatments and some more serious medical treatments did not seem to fall within the phrase "the ordinary conduct of daily life." In *Re F. (Mental Patient: Sterilisation)*[9] Lord Goff, whose judgment in *Collins v Wilcock*[10] had been relied upon by the Court of Appeal in *Wilson v Pringle*, confirmed that medical treatment, even treatment for minor ailments, does not fall into the category of "physical contact which is generally acceptable in the ordinary conduct of everyday life." Treatment given without consent has to be justified on some other principle—lack of "hostility" is not sufficient.

6–092   The third possible basis for justifying emergency treatment without consent is the principle of necessity.[11] The discussion of the defence of necessity in *Re F. (Mental Patient: Sterilisation)*[12] proceeded on the assumption that it applied in any situation where an adult was incapable of giving a valid consent to medical treatment, whether the capacity was permanent or temporary. Thus, treatment of a temporarily incapacitated patient in an emergency will be lawful if it is in the best interests of the patient, that is if, but only if, it is carried out in order either to save his life or to ensure improvement or prevent deterioration in his physical or mental health. Again, this is measured by reference to the *Bolam* test. There are limits, however, to what may be done to the temporarily incapacitated patient. Lord Goff said that officious intervention cannot be justified; nor can intervention be justified when it is contrary to the known wishes of the assisted person, to the extent that he is capable of rationally forming such a wish.[13] Moreover, Lord Goff explicitly recognised that there was a difference between cases of permanent incapacity and temporary incapacity:

> "Where, for example, a surgeon performs an operation without his consent on a patient temporarily rendered unconscious in an accident, he should do no more than is reasonably required, in the best interests

---

[7] *ibid.* at 252.

[8] [1988] Fam. 52.

[9] [1990] 2 A.C. 1, 73. See further para. 6–005, above.

[10] [1984] 3 All E.R. 374.

[11] See Skegg (1974) 90 L.Q.R. 512, 514 commenting that the principle is too vague.

[12] [1990] 2 A.C. 1; see para. 6–078.

[13] Leaving open the possibility of arguing that a patient who "unreasonably" refuses consent to treatment can be categorised as "irrational", thereby lacking the capacity either to consent or withhold consent. Are all beliefs, values, fears, prejudices upon which we base decisions rational, and, if not, does that mean that we lack the capacity to make those decisions? See Brazier (1987) 7 L.S. 169, 175; and the discussion of tests for competence at paras 6–026 *et seq.*

of the patient, before he recovers consciousness. I can see no practical difficulty arising from this requirement, which derives from the fact that the patient is expected before long to regain consciousness and can then be consulted about longer term measures."[14]

In the Court of Appeal Neill L.J. also drew a clear distinction between permanent and temporary incapacity. In an emergency situation treatment should be confined to "such treatment as is necessary to meet the emergency and such as needs to be carried out at once and before the patient is likely to be in a position to make a decision for himself."[15]

The Canadian courts distinguish between procedures which it would have been unreasonable to postpone in the circumstances, as opposed to being merely convenient to perform immediately. In *Marshall v Curry*,[16] in the course of a hernia operation being performed under general anaesthetic, the surgeon discovered that his patient had a diseased testicle. It was held that he was justified in removing the testicle without first bringing the patient round to obtain his consent, because the organ could have become gangrenous and constituted a threat to the patient's life. The circumstances could not have been foreseen before the operation, and the doctor had acted in the best interests of his patient. The removal of the testicle was necessary because it would have been unreasonable to postpone the procedure. On the other hand, in *Murray v McMurchy*,[17] during the course of a Caesarean section, the doctor discovered fibroid tumours in the patient's uterus. He took the view that the tumours would be a danger if the patient were to become pregnant again, and so without reviving the patient from the general anaesthetic he performed a sterilisation operation. The doctor was held liable in battery, because it would not have been unreasonable to postpone the operation. There was no immediate threat to the patient's health; it was merely convenient to perform the operation without consent as she was already under general anaesthetic.[18]

6–093

In *Re F. (Mental Patient: Sterilisation)* Lord Goff apparently took the view that the Canadian cases were restricted to the situation where a surgeon, in the course of an operation, discovers some other condition which he believes requires immediate attention although he has not obtained the patient's consent for that. It is not clear why the cases should be limited in this way, since the distinction could apply just as well to the patient who is incapacitated prior to the operation as the patient who is incapacitated during the operation itself. Thus, it is arguable that the measure of what is "reasonably required" under Lord Goff's approach to the temporarily incapacitated patient could be whether it would have been unreasonable to postpone the

6–094

---

[14] [1990] 2 A.C. 1, 77.
[15] *Re F. (Mental Patient: Sterilisation)* [1990] 2 A.C. 1, 30, CA.
[16] [1933] 3 D.L.R. 260.
[17] [1949] 2 D.L.R. 442.
[18] See also *Parmley v Parmley and Yule* [1945] 4 D.L.R. 81, 89 (S.C.C.). For an English case with similar facts to *Murray v McMurchy* see *Devi v West Midlands Regional Health Authority* (1981, CA; unreported) para. 6–013.

operation or procedure, as opposed to merely convenient to perform it without consent.[19]

6–095   The medical profession appears to have assumed for many years that consent by a spouse or relative will suffice where an adult patient is incapable of consenting. While it may be "good medical practice" to consult relatives about a proposed treatment,[20] this has no effect in law.[21] If the procedure cannot be justified under the principle of necessity, the consent of a relative offers no protection, other than the practical observation that a patient may be less likely to litigate if the treatment had the approval of a relative.

(7) Refusals of consent

6–096   The refusal of a competent patient to consent to medical treatment is normally considered to be conclusive. The doctor must respect the patient's wishes, no matter how misguided he believes the patient to be, and no matter that he has only the patient's best interests in mind. The doctor who ignores the patient's refusal of consent risks a claim for battery.[22] On the other hand, a doctor must also consider the true scope of a refusal of consent: "Was it intended to apply in the circumstances which have arisen? Was it based upon assumptions which in the event have not been realised? A refusal is only effective within its true scope and is vitiated if it is based upon false assumptions."[23] Moreover, as Lord Donaldson M.R. pointed out in *Re T. (Adult: Refusal of Treatment)*[24] simply because adult patients have a right to choose it does not

---

[19] Whether this would prove, in practice, to be a more stringent test than the *Bolam* test depends upon expert evidence as to what was convenient and what was unreasonable. There is, in theory, a difference between whether it was unreasonable to postpone an operation and whether it was reasonable to proceed. Sometimes it may be reasonable to proceed (and therefore not negligent to do so) but also not unreasonable to postpone the operation until the patient could consent. In other words, the test is stricter than in negligence: see Skegg (1974) 90 L.Q.R. 512, 518. Note that since necessity is a defence the burden of proving that the treatment was necessary must lie with the defendant.

[20] See Lord Goff in *Re F. (Mental Patient: Sterilisation)* [1990] 2 A.C. 1, 78. See also the Draft Mental Incapacity Bill, June 2003, cl. 4(2)(d).

[21] *Re T. (Adult: Refusal of Treatment)* [1993] Fam. 95, 103, *per* Lord Donaldson M.R.; *Re S. (Hospital Patient: Court's Jurisdiction)* [1996] Fam. 1, 19, *per* Sir Thomas Bingham M.R.; Skegg, *Law, Ethics and Medicine*, O.U.P., 1988, p. 73; see also *Paton v British Pregnancy Advisory Service Trustees* [1979] Q.B. 276, where it was held that the putative father was not entitled to intervene to prevent the mother undergoing an abortion; *cf. Wilson v Pringle* [1987] Q.B. 237, 252 where Croom-Johnson L.J. seemed to assume that the "next of kin" could consent for an unconscious patient.

[22] "At common law a doctor cannot lawfully operate on adult patients of sound mind, or give them any other treatment involving the application of physical force however small . . . without their consent. If a doctor were to operate on such patients, or give them other treatment, without their consent, he would commit the actionable tort of trespass to the person," *per* Lord Brandon in *Re F. (Mental Patient: Sterilisation)* [1990] 2 A.C. 1, 55; "There is no doubt that a person of full age and capacity cannot be ordered to undergo a blood test against his will . . . [because] English law goes to great lengths to protect a person of full age and capacity from interference with his personal liberty," *per* Lord Reid in *S. v S.* [1972] A.C. 24, 43.

[23] *Re T. (Adult: Refusal of Treatment)* [1993] Fam. 95, 116.

[24] *ibid.* at 102.

follow that they have exercised the right. Doctors faced with a refusal of consent should give very careful consideration to the patient's capacity to decide at the time when the decision was made. A patient's capacity may be temporarily reduced, and the doctors should consider whether at the time the decision is made the patient has the capacity commensurate with the gravity of the decision which he purports to make. The more serious the decision, the greater the capacity required. In cases of doubt about the patient's capacity, said his Lordship, where the withholding of treatment would lead to serious damage to the patient's health or even death, that doubt should be resolved in favour of the preservation of life, since if the individual wants to override the public interest in preserving life, he must do so in clear terms. Staughton L.J. agreed that an apparent consent or refusal may not be a "true" consent or refusal. The patient's understanding and reasoning powers may be seriously reduced by drugs or other circumstances, although she is not actually unconscious.[25] Conversely, doctors should resist the temptation to conclude that the patient is not competent *simply because she has refused treatment*;[26] and, in any event, simply because a patient's capacity is reduced, it does not follow that he is unable effectively to refuse consent.[27] Most patients want their medical condition to improve, if at all possible, and where differences between patient and doctor arise this is likely to be the product of differing assessments of the risks and benefits of the proposed treatment. In some situations, however, the objectives of doctor and patient are at odds.

(a) Hunger strikes

In *Leigh v Gladstone*[28] it was held to be lawful for prison authorities to force-feed a prisoner on hunger strike. The decision was influenced by the fact that suicide, and attempted suicide, was a criminal offence at the time, although it is questionable whether the offence could be committed by omission. The case is now of doubtful authority, and the practice of force-feeding hunger strikers in British prisons has been discontinued.[29] In *Secretary of*

6–097

---

[25] *ibid.* at 122.

[26] "That his choice is contrary to what is to be expected of the vast majority of adults is only relevant if there are other reasons for doubting his capacity to decide. The nature of his choice or the terms in which it is expressed may then tip the balance," *ibid.* at 113, *per* Lord Donaldson M.R. The refusal to accept treatment is more likely to lead to a conclusion that the patient is incompetent in the case of minors: see *Re E. (a minor) (wardship: medical treatment)* [1993] 1 F.L.R. 386.

[27] See *Re C. (adult: refusal of treatment)* [1994] 1 W.L.R. 290; para. 6–029.

[28] (1909) 26 T.L.R. 139.

[29] See Zellick [1976] P.L. 153. See also *A.-G. of British Columbia v Astaforoff* [1984] 4 W.W.R. 385 where the court refused to order treatment of a prisoner on hunger strike; Somerville (1985) 63 Can. Bar Rev. 59. American courts have declined to regard a patient's refusal of life-sustaining medical treatment (including tubal feeding) as equivalent to an attempt to commit suicide: see *Bouvia v Superior Court* 225 Cal. Rptr 297 (1986) (Cal. C.A.); *Re Conroy* 486 A. 2d 1209 (1985) (New Jersey S.C.); *Thor v Superior Court* 855 P. 2d 375 (1993) (Cal. S.C.). The European Court of Human Rights has held that the forcible feeding of a prisoner on hunger strike does not violate Art. 3 of the European Convention on Human Rights: *X v Federal Republic of Germany* (1984) 7 E.H.R.R. 152.

State for the Home Department v Robb[30] Thorpe J. held that prison officials
and medical staff may abide by the decision of a prisoner of sound mind and
understanding who goes on hunger strike, and may lawfully abstain from
providing hydration and nutrition for so long as the prisoner retains the
capacity to refuse them. There was no countervailing state interest which
should prevail over the prisoner's right to self-determination. His Lordship
said that *Leigh v Gladstone* was "of no surviving application and can be con-
signed to the archives of legal history."

6–098   On the other hand, in *R. v Collins and Ashworth Hospital Authority, ex
parte Brady*[31] Kay J. held that where the prisoner lacks the relevant mental
capacity to make a competent decision, necessity may justify force-feeding.
Moreover, Kay J. questioned whether there may be circumstances in which
state or public interests might prevail over a self-determined hunger strike so
as to enable, even if not to require, intervention.[32] His Lordship noted the
incongruity of a law that imposes a common law duty to take reasonable
care to prevent a prisoner committing suicide or harming himself,[33] and a
rule by which the prison authorities have no power to intervene to prevent
a prisoner from starving himself to death. Thus, Kay J. observed that: "It
would be somewhat odd if there is a duty to prevent suicide by an act (for
example, the use of a knife left in a cell) but not even a power to intervene
to prevent self-destruction by starvation. I can see no moral justification for
the law indulging its fascination with the difference between acts and omissions in a context such as this and no logical need for it to do so."[34]

(b) Religious objections

6–099   Jehovah's Witnesses, who object on religious grounds to surgical interven-
tions which may involve the use of blood products, are entitled to decline
treatment. In the Canadian case of *Malette v Shulman*[35] a surgeon administered blood to an unconscious patient admitted into a casualty department
after a road accident. He was aware that she carried a card declaring that
she was a Jehovah's Witness and that she was not willing to accept blood in
any circumstances. Notwithstanding that the operation may well have saved

---

[30] [1995] Fam. 127. See also *Airedale NHS Trust v Bland* [1993] A.C. 789, 859 where Lord
Keith commented that the principle of the sanctity of life does not authorise the forcible
feeding of prisoners on hunger strike. However, *cf.* the approach taken to patients suffering
from anorexia nervosa in *Re KB. (adult) (mental patient: medical treatment)* (1994) 19
B.M.L.R. 144 and *B. v Croydon Health Authority* [1995] Fam. 133, above paras 6–031,
6–067.

[31] [2000] Lloyd's Rep. Med. 355.

[32] *ibid.* at [72]-[73].

[33] On which see *Orange v Chief Constable of West Yorkshire Police* [2001] EWCA Civ 611;
[2002] Q.B. 347; and *Reeves v Commissioner of Police for the Metropolis* [2000] 1 A.C.
360.

[34] [2000] Lloyd's Rep. Med. 355 at [71]. It seems unlikely that this distinction can rest on the
prisoner's mental state, since in *Reeves* it was accepted that the duty of care derives from the
fact that the prisoner is a known suicide risk, not from any particular mental state (whether
sane or insane).

[35] (1990) 67 D.L.R. (4th) 321 (Ont. C.A.).

the claimant's life, the defendant was held liable in battery. The claimant was entitled to make a decision to refuse blood prior to and in anticipation of the emergency that arose, and the doctor was obliged to comply with those advance instructions notwithstanding that he had not had an opportunity to dissuade her or explain the risks of refusing a transfusion:

> "The principles of self-determination and individual autonomy compel the conclusion that the patient may reject blood transfusions even if harmful consequences may result and even if the decision is generally regarded as foolhardy . . . To transfuse a Jehovah's Witness in the face of her explicit instructions to the contrary would, in my opinion, violate her right to control her own body and show disrespect for the religious values by which she has chosen to live her life."[36]

It was not for the doctor to second-guess the reasonableness of the decision or to pass judgment on the religious principles which motivated it.[37] In *Re T. (Adult: Refusal of Treatment)*[38] Butler-Sloss L.J. agreed with the principles set out in *Malette v Shulman*, observing that doctors who treat a Jehovah's Witness against his known wishes "do so at their peril."[39] On the other hand, this principle does not apply to Jehovah's Witnesses who object to the administration of blood products to their incompetent minor children, where the treatment is in the best interests of the child.[40] Arguably, the position of a person who has attempted suicide is analogous to the adult Jehovah's Witness. Provided the patient is competent to refuse consent to treatment a doctor is not entitled to intervene.[41]

---

[36] *ibid.* at 330, *per* Robins J.A. See also the quotation cited above para. 6–001, n. 1.

[37] Damages were assessed at $20,000 for mental distress. In *R. v Blaue* [1975] 1 W.L.R. 1411 the Court of Appeal touched upon this issue indirectly. The defendant had stabbed a young woman who subsequently refused a blood transfusion on religious grounds which would have saved her life. His appeal against a conviction for manslaughter on the ground that her unreasonable refusal of medical treatment broke the chain of causation between the attack and her death was dismissed. Lawton L.J. clearly considered that the woman's refusal to consent to a blood transfusion might be considered to be reasonable, although he accepted that there might be a difference between the criminal law and the civil law.

[38] [1993] Fam. 95.

[39] *ibid.* at 117. Though the force of this statement is diminished somewhat by Butler-Sloss L.J.'s comment that: "I do not believe an English court would give damages in those particular circumstances."

[40] See *Re E. (a minor)(wardship: medical treatment)* [1993] 1 F.L.R. 386; *Re R. (A Minor)* (1993) 15 B.M.L.R. 72; *Re O. (A Minor)(Medical Treatment)* [1993] 4 Med. L.R. 272; (1993) 19 B.M.L.R. 148; *Re S. (A Minor) (Medical Treatment)* [1993] 1 F.L.R. 376; (1992) 11 B.M.L.R 105; *Re S. (A Minor) (Consent to Medical Treatment)* [1994] 2 F.L.R. 1065; see also *B.(R.) v Children's Aid Society of Metropolitan Toronto* (1995) 122 D.L.R. (4th) 1 (S.C.C.); *cf. Walker v Region 2 Hospital Corp.* (1994) 110 D.L.R. (4th) 477 (N.B.C.A.) where the minor was considered to be competent.

[41] *cf.* Skegg, *Law, Ethics and Medicine*, O.U.P., 1988, pp. 110–112. In *Re F. (Mental Patient: Sterilisation)* [1990] 2 A.C. 1, 29–30 Neill L.J. appeared to leave open the possibility that there may be circumstances in which a doctor is entitled to give treatment in order to save the life of a patient who, having the capacity to make a choice, has refused treatment. Note, also, that in some circumstances a doctor may have a duty to exercise reasonable care prevent suicide attempts: see paras 4–110 to 4–123; but in these circumstances it may be that the patient would not be regarded as competent.

(c) Enforced Caesarian section

6–100   Some American courts have taken the view that it may be justifiable to compel a person to accept medical treatment where this is essential to protect the life or health of a third party, particularly in the case of pregnant women. Thus, a pregnant woman has been ordered to undergo a blood transfusion contrary to her religious beliefs where this was considered necessary to save the life of a foetus of 32 weeks,[42] and women have been compelled to undergo Caesarian deliveries in circumstances where there was a high risk of death both to the child and the mother from a natural birth,[43] and even more disturbingly where the mother was dying from cancer and the operation was clearly contrary to her medical interests.[44] The issue first arose in this country in *Re S. (Adult: Refusal of Medical Treatment)*,[45] a case where a mature woman of 30 refused, on religious grounds, to consent to a Caesarian section. She had been admitted to hospital with ruptured membranes, was in spontaneous labour and had continued in labour since admission. The baby could not be born alive and there was a serious risk to the mother's life without the operation. Sir Stephen Brown P. granted a declaration that it would be lawful to perform the operation and any necessary consequential treatment despite S's refusal of consent, because it was in the "vital interests" of the patient and her unborn child. This decision created a storm of controversy, apparently undermining the normal principle that there is no legal basis for overriding the decision of a competent patient to refuse surgical intervention, even if as a consequence of that decision she will suffer serious injury or die.[46] A foetus has no independent legal personality in law, and only acquires legal personality at birth.[47] Moreover, in *Re F. (In Utero)*[48] the Court of Appeal refused to make a foetus a ward of court because of the effect that this would have on the mother's individual liberty. How much greater, then, is the interference with individual liberty of a non-consensual Caesarian section?[49]

---

[42] *Raleigh Fitkin-Paul Morgan Memorial Hospital v Anderson* 201 A. 2d 537 (1964) (New Jersey S.C.).

[43] *Jefferson v Griffin Spalding County Hospital Authority* 274 S.E. 2d 457 (1981) (Georgia S.C.); *Re Madyun* 573 A. 2d 1259 (1986).

[44] *Re AC.* 533 A. 2d 611 (1988). This decision authorising intervention was reversed on appeal, though obviously this was far too late in the day for the mother: 573 A. 2d 1253 (1990) (District of Columbia C.A.).

[45] [1993] Fam. 123.

[46] See para. 6–006. This is subject to any statutory exceptions allowing for compulsory treatment, such as the Mental Health Act 1983.

[47] See *Paton v British Pregnancy Advisory Service Trustees* [1979] Q.B. 276; *C. v S.* [1988] Q.B 135, 140.

[48] [1988] Fam. 122; see Morgan [1988] J.S.W.L. 197; *cf. D. v Berkshire County Council* [1987] A.C. 317 allowing a local authority to proceed with care proceedings on an infant on the basis of the mother's behaviour during pregnancy (drug-addiction). In *Winnipeg Child and Family Services (Northwest Area) v G.* (1997) 152 D.L.R. (4th) 193 the Supreme Court of Canada came to the same conclusion as the Court of Appeal in *Re F. (In Utero)*.

[49] See Stern (1993) 56 M.L.R. 238; de Gama [1993] J.S.W.F.L. 147; Thomson (1994) 2 Med. L. Rev. 127; *cf.* Wells [1994] J.S.W.F.L. 65, 67–70. Moreover, when weighing the relative claims of mother and foetus it should be remembered that s.1(1)(b) of the Abortion Act 1967

Following *Re S. (Adult: Refusal of Medical Treatment)* there were a **6–101** number of instances in which the courts ordered pregnant women to undergo Caesarian sections, though on each occasion the woman was found to be incompetent.[50] This line of cases was brought to a halt, at least with respect to competent women, in two important Court of Appeal decisions. In *Re MB (Medical Treatment)*[51] the woman was found to be incompetent on the facts, because she had consented to the Caesarian section, but was refusing the anaesthetic because of an overwhelming needle phobia.[52] This meant that it was open to the court to conclude that a Caesarian section should be authorised, in her best interests. The Court of Appeal made it clear, however, that in the case of a competent pregnant woman the patient has an absolute right to refuse medical intervention. The fact that the baby may be injured or die as result of her refusal of surgery is irrelevant:

"... we are none the less sure that however desirable it may be for the mother to be delivered of a live and healthy baby, on this aspect of the appeal it is not a strictly relevant consideration. If therefore the competent mother refuses to have the medical intervention, the doctors may not lawfully do more than attempt to persuade her. If that persuasion is unsuccessful, there are no further steps towards medical intervention to be taken. We recognise that the effect of these conclusions is that there will be situations in which the child may die or may be seriously handicapped because the mother said no and the obstetrician was not able to take the necessary steps to avoid the death or handicap. The mother may indeed later regret the outcome, but the alternative would be an unwarranted invasion of the right of the woman to make the decision."[53]

(n.49 contd.) provides that a termination of a pregnancy is not unlawful if it is necessary to prevent grave permanent injury to the physical or mental health of the pregnant woman. In other words, the interests of the mother should prevail over those of the foetus.

[50] *Norfolk and Norwich Healthcare Trust v W* [1996] 2 F.L.R. 613; [1997] 1 F.C.R. 269; (1997) 34 B.M.L.R. 16—where Johnson J. held that the patient was incompetent because she was incapable of weighing up the considerations (she had arrived at hospital ready to deliver her baby but in a state of arrested labour and denying that she was pregnant); *Rochdale Healthcare NHS Trust v C* [1997] 1 F.C.R. 274—where the woman had previously had a Caesarean section and said that she would rather die than undergo the same procedure again. The patient was capable of comprehending and retaining information about the proposed treatment and of believing that information, but Johnson J. held that she was not competent because she was in the throes of labour with all the pain and emotional stress that that involved. A patient who in those circumstances appeared able to accept the inevitability of her own death was not capable of giving full consideration to the options available; *Tameside & Glossop Acute Services NHS Trust v CH* [1996] 1 F.L.R. 762; [1996] 1 F.C.R. 753—where a paranoid schizophrenic patient, who was detained under the Mental Health Act 1983, s.3, was found to be incompetent because she had a delusional belief that the medical staff wanted to harm both her and the baby. Wall J. held that the proposed Caesarean section fell within a broad interpretation of s.63 of the Mental Health Act 1983 because a successful pregnancy was a necessary part of the treatment for her psychiatric condition. But see now *St. George's Healthcare NHS Trust v S; R v Collins and Others, ex parte S* [1999] Fam. 26 on this point.

[51] [1997] 8 Med. L.R. 217; [1997] 2 F.L.R. 426.

[52] See para. 6–030 above. See also *Bolton Hospitals NHS Trust v O* [2002] EWHC 2871 (Fam); [2003] 1 F.L.R. 824.

[53] [1997] 8 Med. L.R. 217, 224; [1997] 2 F.L.R. 426, 438.

The court simply does not have jurisdiction to take the interests of the foetus into account when a competent woman refuses consent to medical intervention.[54]

6-102   In *St. George's Healthcare NHS Trust v S; R v Collins and Others, ex parte S*[55] the applicant was 36 weeks pregnant and was diagnosed as having preeclampsia. She was advised that she needed to rest and that labour would have to be induced, otherwise her life and that of the foetus were in danger. S wanted a natural delivery and rejected the advice. She was compulsorily admitted to a mental hospital under section 2 of the Mental Health Act 1983, and shortly afterwards transferred to a general hospital where she continued to refuse to consent to any medical or surgical intervention. The hospital made an emergency *ex parte* application to a judge who granted a declaration that it was lawful to treat S without her consent, the judge having been informed, incorrectly, that S had been in labour for 24 hours, that without intervention she and the baby would probably die, and that this was an immediately life-threatening situation. A Caesarian section was then performed, and a few days later S was returned to the mental hospital where the detention under the Mental Health Act 1983 was terminated. During her detention under the Act she was not given any treatment for a mental disorder or illness. Subsequently, S appealed against the declaration and applied for judicial review of the decision to apply for her compulsory admission to mental hospital. The case proceeded on the basis that S had been competent to make decisions about her medical treatment throughout. The Court of Appeal reaffirmed the view expressed in *Re MB (Medical Treatment)* that the court has no jurisdiction to order a competent woman to undergo medical treatment, even where the life of a viable foetus is at risk:

> "In our judgment while pregnancy increases the personal responsibilities of a woman it does not diminish her entitlement to decide whether or not to undergo medical treatment. Although human, and protected by the law in a number of different ways set out in the judgment in *Re MB (An Adult: Medical Treatment)* [1997] 2 F.C.R. 541, an unborn child is not a separate person from its mother. Its need for medical assistance does not prevail over her rights. She is entitled not to be forced to submit to an invasion of her body against her will, whether her own life or that of her unborn child depends on it. Her right is not reduced or diminished merely because her decision to exercise it may appear morally repugnant. The declaration in this case involved the removal of the baby from within the body of her mother under physical compulsion. Unless lawfully justified this constituted an infringement of the mother's autonomy. Of themselves the perceived needs of the foetus did not provide the necessary justification"[56]

---

[54] *ibid.* at 225–226; and 440–441 respectively.
[55] [1999] Fam. 26.
[56] *ibid.* at 50.

In addition, said the Court, the Mental Health Act 1983 did not provide a basis on which to detain a patient in order to perform a non-consensual Caesarian section. A patient may be perfectly rational (and outside the ambit of the Act) notwithstanding her eccentric thought process.[57] Thus, "a woman detained under the Act for mental disorder cannot be forced into medical procedures unconnected with her mental condition unless her capacity to consent to such treatment is diminished. When she retains her capacity her consent remains an essential prerequisite . . ."[58] It followed that there had been no lawful basis for the non-consensual Caesarian section performed on S, and that surgery amounted to a battery.

It is respectfully submitted that the decisions in *Re MB (Medical Treatment)* and *St. George's Healthcare NHS Trust v S* are correct and entirely in accordance with principle. There is no legal basis for overriding the decision of a competent patient to refuse surgical intervention, except under the Mental Health Act 1983 where the treatment *is for the patient's mental illness or disorder*. In so far as *Re S. (Adult: Refusal of Medical Treatment)* purported to authorise the compulsory treatment of a competent patient, it must be taken to have been overruled. Rights only take on significance if they can be exercised when it matters. There is little comfort in the assertion that competent patients have a right to refuse medical treatment, if they are only to be permitted to exercise the right when doctors, or the courts, agree with their judgment. The focus of attention in cases where a pregnant woman refuses medical intervention must now be the question of her mental capacity to make that decision. If she is found to be competent, then that is the end of the matter, no matter how tragic the potential outcome. If she is found not to be competent, the question then is whether the intervention can be justified by the principle of necessity in *her* best interests (not the interests of the foetus).[59]

6–103

(d) Statute

Certain statutory provisions allow for an element of compulsion where "patients" refuse consent. Most prominent of these is the Mental Health Act 1983 which authorises the compulsory admission to hospital of certain patients suffering from mental disorder for assessment or treatment.[60] The Public Health (Control of Disease) Act 1984 sections 35–38 provide for the

6–104

---

[57] *ibid.* at 51, citing Sir Thomas Bingham M.R. in *Re S.C. (Mental Patient: Habeas Corpus)* [1996] Q.B. 599, 603, and McCullough J. in *R. v Hallstrom, ex parte W. (No. 2)* [1986] Q.B. 1090, 1104 (see para. 6–066, n. 21, above).

[58] *ibid.* at 52.

[59] For the procedure to be followed when there is serious doubt about the patient's capacity to accept or decline treatment see: *St. George's Healthcare NHS Trust v S; R v Collins and Others, ex parte S* [1999] Fam. 26 at 63–64. See also *Practice Direction (Declaratory Proceedings: Incapacitated Adults)* [2002] 1 W.L.R. 325; [2002] 1 All E.R. 794, and the Annex to that Practice Direction *Practice Note (Declaratory Proceedings: Medical and Welfare Decisions for Adults who lack Capacity)* [2001] 2 F.C.R. 569.

[60] Mental Health Act 1983, ss.2–6; see para. 2–142. For detailed discussion see Hoggett, *Mental Health Law*, 4th ed., 1996, Chs 2–4.

compulsory medical examination, removal to hospital or detention in hospital of a person suffering from or carrying a notifiable disease, although there would appear to be no specific authorisation in the Act for compulsory medical treatment.[61] Finally, section 47 of the National Assistance Act 1948 allows for the removal to suitable accommodation of persons who are suffering from grave chronic disease or, being aged, infirm or physically incapacitated, are living in insanitary conditions and are not receiving proper care and attention.[62] This procedure overlaps to some extent with the procedures for compulsory admission to hospital under the Mental Health Act 1983, but again there is no express power to give medical treatment against the person's wishes.

2. NEGLIGENCE

6–105   Consent to medical treatment involves the exercise of a choice. The power to consent involves also the power to refuse consent, and it is argued that a person cannot make a real choice unless he has information about the options so as to be able to make a reasoned choice. Hence it is said that the consent must be an "informed consent." In law, the question of a patient's consent to medical treatment is inextricably linked to the tort of battery, but the courts have stipulated that a minimal level of information must be conveyed to the patient for this purpose. The failure to go into risks and implications of a proposed treatment is an issue to be considered under the doctor's duty of care in negligence, not battery.[63] It is thus a misnomer to speak of "informed consent," since a patient's right to the information which will enable him to make a meaningful choice about treatment options (including the option of no treatment) depends upon the nature of the doctor's duty to exercise reasonable care in performing his professional functions as a doctor. Although the doctor's duty to give the patient information only makes sense in the light of the patient's right to exercise a choice through the power to give or withhold consent,[64] the courts in this country have to a large extent separated these two issues, principally to curtail the use of actions for battery against medical practitioners.[65]

---

[61] See, however, s.13(1)(*a*). Notifiable diseases are cholera, plague, relapsing fever, smallpox and typhus: s.10. The Public Health (Infectious Diseases) Regulations 1988 (S.I. 1988 No. 1546) extend these provisions to, *inter alia*, AIDS, but not persons who are HIV positive. On preserving the anonymity of persons compulsorily removed to hospital under s.37 see: *Birmingham Post & Mail Ltd v Birmingham City Council* (1993) 17 B.M.L.R. 116.

[62] For discussion of this provision see Hoggett, *op. cit.* pp. 92–95; Counsell (1990) 140 N.L.J. 750.

[63] *Chatterton v Gerson* [1981] Q.B. 432, 443, para. 6–034.

[64] See the comments of Lord Scarman in *Sidaway v Bethlem Royal Hospital Governors* [1985] A.C. 871, 888.

[65] The evidence, such as it is, is that cases of informed consent are comparatively few and far between, and successful actions by claimants are even more rare: see Jones (1999) 7 Med. L. Rev. 103.

The duty of care in negligence applies to diagnosis, treatment and advice, and there is no doubt that part of this duty involves giving information to the patient about the diagnosis of his medical condition and the prognosis, in the light of the various treatment options that are available. This inevitably requires some assessment of the prospects that treatment will be successful, and, it should follow, the prospects that treatment may be unsuccessful, or may cause additional harm. The crucial question is how much or how little information must be disclosed to satisfy the doctor's duty of care, and by what standard this is to be judged.[66]

6–106

(1) The duty to disclose information

One aspect of the claimant's case in *Bolam v Friern Hospital Management Committee*[67] was that he had not been warned of the risks involved in electro-convulsive therapy before he received the treatment. In directing the jury, McNair J. applied the same test to the question of warning the patient as applied to treatment, namely whether the defendant fell below a proper standard of competent professional opinion in deciding whether to warn or not. In the early 1980s a series of cases sought to challenge this approach, which states, in effect, that a patient is entitled only to such information as a reasonable doctor deems appropriate. In *Chatterton v Gerson*[68] Bristow J. held that it was the doctor's duty "to explain what he intends to do, and its implications, in the way a careful and responsible doctor in similar circumstances would have done" applying the *Bolam* test. If there was a real risk of misfortune inherent in the procedure a doctor ought to warn of it. Hirst J. adopted the same approach in *Hills v Potter*[69] in which the claimant had an operation on her neck to alleviate a deformity of the neck (spasmodic torticollis), and was left paralysed from the neck down after the operation. There was an inherent risk of paralysis from the operation even if performed competently. Death occurred in one per cent to two per cent of cases, but the risks of death were no worse than in neurosurgery generally. Good results were obtained in some 70 per cent to 80 per cent of cases. Hirst J. held that the proper standard of disclosure was the medical standard, in accordance with the *Bolam* test and *Chatterton v Gerson*.[70]

6–107

---

[66] In considering what the test should be in law it is worth bearing in mind that in empirical studies there is a marked discrepancy between what patients want to know and what doctors think patients want to know. Doctors regularly underestimate the amount of information that patients would like to have: (1986) *Institute of Medical Ethics Bulletin*, Supplement No. 3.

[67] [1957] 2 All E.R. 118; see paras 3–007 to 3–008, 4–108 n. 44.

[68] [1981] Q.B. 432, 443, para 6–034.

[69] [1983] 3 All E.R. 716.

[70] See also *Sankey v Kensington and Chelsea and Westminster Area Health Authority* (1982, QBD; unreported), where the claimant sustained a stroke following a bilateral carotid arteriogram, performed with a view to identifying a lesion in the pituitary fossa. Tudor Evans J. held that "the question of warning has to be judged by competent responsible medical opinion"; *O'Malley-Williams v Board of Governors of the National Hospital for Nervous Diseases* (1975) 1 B.M.J. 635.

6–108   The issue of the appropriate standard of disclosure was finally considered by the House of Lords in *Sidaway v Bethlem Royal Hospital Governors*.[71] The claimant suffered from persistent pain in her neck and shoulders, and she was advised to have an operation on her spinal column to relieve the pain. The defendant surgeon warned the claimant of the possibility of disturbing a nerve root and the consequences of this, but he did not mention the possibility of damage to the spinal cord, although the operation would be within millimetres of the spinal cord. The overall risk of either of these events materialising was between one per cent and two per cent., although the risk of spinal cord damage was less than one per cent. The potential consequences of these risks ranged from mild to severe, with the most severe consequence of spinal cord damage being partial paralysis. During the course of the operation, which was not performed negligently, the claimant sustained damage to the spinal cord resulting in severe disability from partial paralysis. She alleged that the defendant had been negligent in failing to inform her about this risk, and that had she known the true position she would not have accepted the treatment. The trial judge, Skinner J., applied the *Bolam* test and concluded that the defendant had acted in accordance with a practice accepted as proper by a responsible body of medical opinion by not informing the claimant of the risk of damage to the spinal cord. The decision was upheld by the Court of Appeal,[72] and the House of Lords affirmed this finding, although there was some disparity in their Lordships' reasoning.

6–109   Lord Scarman, in a strong dissenting speech, pointed out that applying the *Bolam* test to the question of how much information a patient is entitled to be given leaves the matter almost entirely to the discretion of the medical profession, which places too much judicial reliance on medical judgment instead of seeing the problem from the patient's point of view:

> "If one considers the scope of the doctor's duty by beginning with the right of the patient to make his own decision whether he will or will not undergo the treatment proposed, the right to be informed of significant risk and the doctor's corresponding duty are easy to understand, for the proper implementation of the right requires that the doctor be under a duty to inform his patient of the material risks inherent in the treatment."[73]

Accordingly, his Lordship preferred a standard of disclosure based on the "reasonably prudent patient test," which was derived from the American case of *Canterbury v Spence*[74] and the decision of the Supreme Court of Canada in *Reibl v Hughes*.[75] Under this test a doctor must disclose all

---

[71] [1985] A.C. 871.
[72] [1984] Q.B. 493.
[73] [1985] A.C. 871, 888.
[74] 464 F. 2d 772 (1972) (U.S.C.A., District of Columbia).
[75] (1980) 114 D.L.R. (3d) 1.

material risks, and a risk is material "when a reasonable person, in what the physician knows or should know to be the patient's position, would be likely to attach significance to the risk or cluster of risks in deciding whether or not to forego the proposed therapy."[76] This requires the doctor to communicate the inherent and potential hazards of the proposed treatment, the alternatives to that treatment, if any, and the likely results if the patient remains untreated. The factors contributing significance to the dangerousness of a medical technique were said to be the incidence of injury and the degree of harm threatened. This standard of disclosure is subject to two exceptions. First, where there is a genuine emergency, *e.g.*, the patient is unconscious; and, secondly, where the information would be harmful to the patient, *e.g.*, where it might cause psychological damage,[77] or where the patient would become so emotionally distraught as to prevent a rational decision. This "therapeutic privilege" defence does not allow the doctor to remain silent about material risks simply because disclosure might prompt the patient to forego treatment that the doctor believes the patient needs in his best interests, otherwise the exception might become so wide as to undermine the requirement of disclosure.

Lord Diplock favoured applying the *Bolam* test. He pointed out that the only effect that mention of risks can have on the patient's mind will be in the direction of deterring the patient from undergoing the treatment which in the expert opinion of the doctor it is in the patient's interests to undergo: **6–110**

> "To decide what risks the existence of which a patient should be voluntarily warned and the terms in which such warning, if any, should be given, having regard to the effect that the warning may have, is as much an exercise of professional skill and judgment as any other part of the doctor's comprehensive duty of care to the individual patient, and expert medical evidence on this matter should be treated in just the same way. The *Bolam* test should be applied."[78]

Lord Bridge, with whom Lord Keith agreed, accepted that a conscious adult patient of sound mind is entitled to decide for himself whether or not he will submit to a particular course of treatment proposed by a doctor, particularly in the case of surgical treatment under general anaesthesia. His Lordship recognised "the logical force of the *Canterbury* doctrine" but regarded it as "quite impractical" for three reasons. First, it gives insufficient weight to the nature of the doctor-patient relationship. The doctor cannot educate the patient to his own standard of medical knowledge, and volunteering information about remote risks may lead to the risk assuming an undue significance **6–111**

---

[76] 464 F. 2d 772, 787 (1972).

[77] "Even if the risk be material, the doctor will not be liable if on a reasonable assessment of his patient's condition he takes the view that a warning would be detrimental to his patient's health," *per* Lord Scarman at [1985] A.C. 871, 889–890. For an unusual example of this see *Furniss v Fitchett* [1958] N.Z.L.R. 396.

[78] [1985] A.C. 871, 895.

for the patient. Secondly, it was "unrealistic" to confine the medical evidence to an explanation of primary medical facts and to deny the court evidence of medical opinion and practice on the particular question of disclosure. Thirdly, the objective *Canterbury* test of what a reasonable person in the patient's position would consider to be a significant risk was "so imprecise as to be almost meaningless."[79]

6–112   Lord Bridge realised that applying the *Bolam* test without qualification to the question of what risks inherent in a proposed treatment should be disclosed carried the danger of medical paternalism which might not be controlled by the courts.[80] Nonetheless, he continued:

> "I fully appreciate the force of this reasoning, but can only accept it subject to the important qualification that a decision what degree of disclosure of risks is best calculated to assist a particular patient to make a rational choice whether or not to undergo a particular treatment must primarily be a matter of clinical judgment. It would follow from this that the issue whether non-disclosure in a particular case should be condemned as a breach of the doctor's duty of care is an issue to be decided primarily on the basis of expert medical evidence, applying the *Bolam* test. But I do not see that this approach involves the necessity 'to hand over to the medical profession the entire question of the scope of the duty of disclosure, including the question whether there has been a breach of that duty'. Of course, if there is a conflict of evidence whether a responsible body of medical opinion approves of non-disclosure in a particular case, the judge will have to resolve that conflict. But even in a case where, as here, no expert witness in the relevant medical field condemns the non-disclosure as being in conflict with accepted and responsible medical practice, I am of opinion that the judge might in certain circumstances come to the conclusion that disclosure of a particular risk was so obviously necessary to an informed choice on the part of the patient that no reasonably prudent medical man would fail to make it. The kind of case I have in mind would be an operation involving a substantial risk of grave adverse consequences, as for example the 10 per cent risk of a stroke from the operation which was the subject of the Canadian case of *Reibl v Hughes* (1980) 114 D.L.R. (3d) 1. In such a

---

[79] *ibid.* at 899. His Lordship did not explain why a test based on what a reasonable doctor would consider should be disclosed is any more precise or meaningful. In the Court of Appeal [1984] Q.B. 493, 512, Sir John Donaldson M.R. rejected the American formulation of the duty by reference to a "prudent patient" test: "No doubt it is valid if the doctor happens to be treating that happy abstraction, the 'prudent patient,' but I suspect that he is a fairly rare bird and I have no doubt that his removal to the courts from his natural habitat, which would, I assume, be a seat or hand rail on the Clapham omnibus, would do nothing for patients or medicine, although it might do a great deal for lawyers and litigation."

[80] "To allow expert medical evidence to determine what risks are material and, hence, should be disclosed and, correlatively, what risks are not material is to hand over to the medical profession the entire question of the scope of the duty of disclosure, including the question whether there has been a breach of that duty," *per* Laskin C.J.C. in *Reibl v Hughes* (1980) 114 D.L.R. (3d) 1, 13 (S.C.C.), cited by Lord Bridge at [1985] A.C. 871, 899–900.

case, in the absence of some cogent reason why the patient should not be informed, a doctor, recognising and respecting his patient's right of decision, could hardly fail to appreciate the necessity for an appropriate warning."[81]

It is not entirely clear what test for information disclosure Lord Templeman adopted. In his Lordship's view a doctor has an obligation to provide information which is adequate to enable the patient to reach a balanced judgment about whether to submit to recommended treatment, subject to the doctor's obligation to say nothing which will be harmful to the patient.[82] The doctor, too, must make a balanced judgment: 6–113

"If the doctor making a balanced judgment advises the patient to submit to the operation, the patient is entitled to reject that advice for reasons which are rational or irrational or for no reason at all. The duty of the doctor in these circumstances, subject to his overriding duty to have regard to the best interests of the patient, is to provide the patient with information which will enable the patient to make a balanced judgment if the patient chooses to make a balanced judgment. A patient may make an unbalanced judgment because he is deprived of adequate information. A patient may also make an unbalanced judgment if he is provided with too much information and is made aware of possibilities which he is not capable of assessing because of his lack of medical training, his prejudices or his personality."[83]

His Lordship also considered that a patient who knows that a major operation may entail serious consequences cannot complain of lack of information unless he asks in vain for more information, or unless there is some danger which by its nature or magnitude or for some other reason is required to be separately taken into account by the patient in order to reach a balanced judgment in deciding whether or not to submit to the operation.[84] Thus, a doctor ought to draw the attention of a patient to a danger which may be special in kind or magnitude or special to the patient.[85] Lord Templeman emphasised that it is for the court to decide whether a doctor is in breach of his duty with respect to the disclosure of information to a patient, but if he conscientiously endeavoured to explain the arguments for and against the treatment the court would be slow to conclude that the doctor was negligent merely because he omitted some specific item of information.[86]

---

[81] [1985] A.C. 871, 900.

[82] *ibid.* at 904.

[83] *ibid.*

[84] *ibid.* at 902.

[85] *ibid.* at 903, citing the example of a 4% risk of death and 10% risk of stroke in *Reibl v Hughes* (1980) 114 D.L.R. (3d) 1.

[86] In *Pearce v United Bristol Healthcare NHS Trust* [1999] P.I.Q.R. P53, 58 Lord Woolf M.R. considered that although Lord Templeman's approach was not precisely that of the majority, it did not involve taking a different view from the majority.

6–114   Notwithstanding the diversity of the speeches in *Sidaway* it is submitted
that the majority of their Lordships adopted the *Bolam* test as the measure
of a doctor's duty to disclose information about the potential consequences
and risks of proposed medical treatment. This would seem to be the view of
most commentators,[87] and indeed the Court of Appeal has specifically
endorsed this interpretation on two occasions.[88] It has, however, been argued
that *Sidaway* represents an extension of *Bolam*. Professor Kennedy has suggested that the exception that Lord Bridge makes in the case of a non-
disclosure of a substantial risk of grave adverse consequences where a doctor
could hardly fail to appreciate the necessity for an appropriate warning
"cannot be very far from the reasonable or prudent patient test,"[89] whereas
Lord Diplock was in a minority of one. This interpretation appears to rest
upon the assumption, which was explicit in Lord Scarman's dissenting
speech,[90] that the *Bolam* test depends solely upon professional practice and
that it is never open to the court to condemn a common professional practice as negligent.

6–115   It is respectfully submitted that this view misstates the nature of the *Bolam*
test. The objective nature of the test for negligence means that it is always for
the court to determine, ultimately, what constitutes negligence on the basis of
the evidence presented. The practices of a profession may be good evidence
of "reasonable care" but cannot be conclusive.[91] Lord Bridge's "exception"
for the non-disclosure of a substantial risk of grave adverse consequences
where a doctor could hardly fail to appreciate the necessity for an appropriate warning is simply an instance of the "obvious folly" test where it would
be appropriate for a court to condemn a common practice as negligent.[92] This

---

[87] Brazier (1987) 7 L.S. 169, 182; Norrie (1985) 34 I.C.L.Q. 442, 450; Tan (1987) 7 L.S. 149,
161, n. 42; Dugdale and Stanton, *Professional Negligence*, 3rd ed., 1998, para. 17.30;
Jackson & Powell on Professional Negligence, 5th ed., 2002, para. 12.211.

[88] *Gold v Haringey Health Authority* [1988] Q.B. 481; *Blyth v Bloomsbury Health Authority*
(1987) reported at (1989) 5 P.N. 167, 171; [1993] 4 Med. L.R. 151; see also *Worster v City
and Hackney Health Authority*, The Times, June 22, 1987, *per* Garland J.; *Moyes v Lothian
Health Board* [1990] 1 Med. L.R. 463, 469.

[89] Kennedy, *Treat Me Right*, 1988, O.U.P., p. 201. See also Teff (1985) 101 L.Q.R. 432, 448
who considers that *Sidaway* represents a modest modification of *Bolam*, almost indistinguishable from *Bolam* in practice. Kennedy & Grubb, *Medical Law*, 3rd ed., 2000, p. 694
suggest that: "The majority in *Sidaway* opted for a duty of disclosure which, while rejecting
the *Bolam* test *simpliciter*, leaves the exact nature of the duty somewhat obscure." This is
because they identify the majority speeches in *Sidaway* as consisting of Lords Bridge, Keith
and Templeman. The import of Lord Templeman's speech is indeed, with respect, obscure,
and as Kennedy & Grubb point out may suffer from "a degree of internal inconsistency."

[90] See paras 3–020 to 3–021.

[91] See paras 3–022 to 3–036. See in particular *Bolitho v City and Hackney Health Authority*
[1998] A.C. 232.

[92] See para 3–030. Teff (1985) 101 L.Q.R. 432, 448 points out that in *Reibl v Hughes* (1980)
114 D.L.R. (3d) 1 the defendant had been found liable at first instance on a professional
judgment standard, and that it is difficult to envisage the example which Lord Bridge cites
from *Reibl v Hughes* satisfying the *Bolam* test, by which, presumably, he means that it is
unlikely that a body of reasonable medical practitioners would accept non-disclosure of such
a risk (see further Dugdale and Stanton, *Professional Negligence*, 3rd ed., 1998, para. 17.30,
n. 6 making the same point). The court would conclude that no *responsible* body of professional opinion could have failed to disclose that degree of risk: see the comment of Hirst J.
in *Hills v Potter* [1983] 3 All E.R. 716, 728 cited at para. 3–034.

point was clear in the judgment of Sir John Donaldson M.R. in the Court of Appeal, when his Lordship said that the definition of the duty of care is a matter for the law and the courts, and that the duty is fulfilled if the doctor acts in accordance with a practice *rightly* accepted as proper by a body of skilled and experienced medical men.[93] In an appropriate case, said his Lordship, a judge would be entitled to reject a unanimous medical view if he were satisfied that it was manifestly wrong. Moreover, this qualification was "analogous to that which has been asserted in the context of treating a trade practice as evidencing the proper standard of care . . . and would be equally infrequently relevant."[94] Similarly, when Lord Bridge said that the issue whether non-disclosure in a particular case should be held to be negligent "is an issue to be decided *primarily* on the basis of expert medical evidence, applying the *Bolam* test," (emphasis added) he was not suggesting that normally the *Bolam* test applied but in exceptional circumstances it could be dispensed with. Rather he was stating the effect of the *Bolam* test itself, which relies *primarily* on expert evidence as to responsible professional practice, but, exceptionally, the court may decline to accept that evidence as a measure of the proper standard in law. Thus, the majority in *Sidaway* consisted of Lords Bridge, Keith and Diplock, who all applied the *Bolam* test.[95]

In *Pearce v United Bristol Healthcare NHS Trust*[96] the claimant was preg-   **6–116**
nant and the delivery of her baby was overdue. She was examined by a doctor who indicated that medical intervention by inducing labour or by proceeding to a Caesarian section was not advisable. The doctor did not inform the claimant that non-intervention carried an increased risk that her baby would be stillborn. A week later the claimant suffered a stillbirth. The risks associated with inducing labour were such that the claimant would not have opted for induction, but she argued that had she known about the risks she would have considered a Caesarian section. The claimant relied on *Bolitho v City and Hackney Health Authority*[97] where Lord Browne-Wilkinson said:

> "where there are questions of assessment of the relative risks and benefits of adopting a particular medical practice, a reasonable view necessarily presupposes that the relative risks and benefits have been weighed by the experts in forming their opinions. But if, in a rare case, it can be demonstrated that the professional opinion is not capable of withstanding logical analysis, the judge is entitled to hold that the body of opinion is not reasonable or responsible."

---

[93] *Sidaway v Bethlem Royal Hospital Governors* [1984] Q.B. 493, 514, original emphasis.
[94] *ibid.* at 513, citing *Cavanagh v Ulster Weaving Co Ltd* [1960] A.C. 145; *Morris v West Hartlepool Steam Navigation Co Ltd* [1956] A.C. 552; see para. 3–023.
[95] A view accepted by Lord Woolf M.R. in *Pearce v United Bristol Healthcare NHS Trust* [1999] P.I.Q.R. P53, 57 where his Lordship said: ". . . Lord Diplock also gave a speech which adopted the same approach as that of Lord Bridge. That approach involved applying the *Bolam* test to the giving, or failure to give, advice."
[96] [1999] P.I.Q.R. P53.
[97] [1998] A.C. 232 at 243. See paras 3–028 *et seq.*

Lord Woolf, having considered *Bolitho*, said:

"In a case where it is being alleged that a plaintiff has been deprived of the opportunity to make a proper decision as to what course he or she should take in relation to treatment, it seems to me to be the law . . . that if there is a significant risk which would affect the judgment of the reasonable patient, then in the normal course it is the responsibility of a doctor to inform the patient of that significant risk, if the information is needed so that the patient can determine for him or herself as to what course he or she should adopt."[98]

This appears to combine a prudent patient standard with a reasonable doctor standard—a significant risk affecting the judgment of a reasonable patient would place the onus upon the doctor to disclose that significant risk by virtue of the *Bolam* test. In other words, no reasonable doctor would fail to disclose a risk regarded as significant by a reasonable patient. The circumstances in which this approach might assist a claimant would appear to be rather limited, however. The Court in *Pearce* considered that, although it was not possible to talk in terms of precise percentages when considering what constituted a significant risk, something in the region of a 10 per cent risk would clearly qualify (consistent with Lord Bridge's speech in *Sidaway*). But an increased risk of stillbirth from non-intervention of 0.1 per cent to 0.2 per cent did not fall into the category of significant risk.

(a) Canada

6–117   In Canada the Supreme Court has established a standard of disclosure based on the "reasonably prudent patient." In *Hopp v Lepp*[99] it was said that a surgeon should answer any specific questions posed by the patient as to the risks involved and should, without being questioned, disclose to him the nature of the proposed operation, its gravity, any material risks and any special or unusual risks attendant upon the performance of the operation. A risk which is a mere possibility, which ordinarily need not be disclosed, could be regarded as a material risk, requiring disclosure, if its occurrence carries serious consequences such as paralysis or death. Subsequently, in *Reibl v Hughes*[1] the Court explicitly rejected a professional medical standard for determining what are material risks and whether there has been a breach of the duty of disclosure:

"To allow expert medical evidence to determine what risks are material and, hence, should be disclosed and, correlatively, what risks are not

---

[98] [1999] P.I.Q.R. P53 at 59. Roch and Mummery L.J. agreed with Lord Woolf M.R.
[99] (1980) 112 D.L.R. (3d) 67, 81 (S.C.C.).
[1] (1980) 114 D.L.R. (3d) 1, 13 (S.C.C.).

material is to hand over to the medical profession the entire question of the scope of the duty of disclosure, including the question whether there has been a breach of that duty . . . The materiality of non-disclosure of certain risks to an informed decision is a matter for the trier of fact, a matter on which there would, in all likelihood, be medical evidence but also other evidence, including evidence from the patient or from members of his family."

For example, in *Meyer Estate v Rogers*[2] the Canadian Association of Radiologists had specifically recommended that patients should not be informed of the risks of an allergic reaction to contrast media during an intravenous pyelogram. Nonetheless, it was held that this risk was material, and that the Association's recommendation directly contravened the standard required by *Reibl v Hughes*.

In *Videto v Kennedy*[3] the Ontario Court of Appeal summarised the effect   **6–118** of *Hopp v Lepp* and *Reibl v Hughes* in the following terms:

(i)   The question of whether a risk is material and whether there has been a breach the duty of disclosure should not be determined solely by the standards of the profession. Professional standards are a factor to be considered;

(ii)   The duty of disclosure embraces what the surgeon knows or ought to know that the patient deems relevant to his decision whether or not to undergo the treatment. If the patient asks specific questions he is entitled to be given reasonable answers;

(iii)   A risk which is a mere possibility does not ordinarily have to be disclosed, but if its occurrence would have serious consequences it should be treated as a material risk;[4]

(iv)   The patient is entitled to be given an explanation of the nature of the operation and its gravity;

(v)   Subject to this, other inherent dangers such as the dangers of anaesthetic or the risks of infection do not have to be disclosed;[5]

(vi)   The scope of the duty and whether it has been breached must be decided in the circumstances of each case;[6]

---

[2] (1991) 78 D.L.R (4th) 307 (Ont. H.C.).

[3] (1981) 125 D.L.R. (3d) 127, 133–134 (Ont. C.A.).

[4] See, *e.g.*, *Lachambre v Nair* [1989] 2 W.W.R. 749; *Meyer Estate v Rogers* (1991) 78 D.L.R (4th) 307 (Ont. H.C.), where a risk of death of between 1 in 40,000 and 1 in 100,000 was held to be a material risk.

[5] See, *e.g.*, *Hajgato v London Health Association* (1982) 36 O.R. (2d) 669, 680. Note, however, that certain risks of infection, such as the risk of contracting hepatitis from blood products, may be an "unusual or special risk" which should be disclosed: *Kitchen v McMullen* (1989) 62 D.L.R. (4th) 481 (N.B.C.A.).

[6] For example, the patient may already know about the risks from a similar previous experience: *Goguen v Crowe* (1987) 40 C.C.L.T. 212, 226 (N.S.S.C.).

(vii)   The emotional condition of the patient may in certain cases justify the surgeon in withholding or generalising information which otherwise should be more specific;[7]

(viii) The question of whether a particular risk is a material risk and whether there has been a breach of the duty is a matter for the trier of fact.

6–119   In *White v Turner*[8] Linden J. explained that "material risks" are significant risks that pose a real threat to the patient's life, health or comfort. The court must balance the severity of the potential result and the likelihood of its occurring. Even if there is only a small chance of serious injury or death, the risk may be considered material.[9] On the other hand, if there is a significant

---

[7]   See, *e.g.*, *Hajgato v London Health Association* (1982) 36 O.R. (2d) 669, 680; although it has been held that there is no defence of therapeutic privilege in Canadian law on the ground that the defence undermines the very obligation to disclose material risks: *Meyer Estate v Rogers* (1991) 78 D.L.R (4th) 307 (Ont. H.C.); *sed quaere*. In *Pittman Estate v Bain* (1994) 112 D.L.R. (4th) 257, 399 (Ont. Ct., Gen. Div.) Lang J. accepted that there could be cases where a patient is unable or unwilling to accept bad news from a doctor: "In those circumstances, a physician is obliged to take reasonable precautions to ensure that the patient has communicated their desire not to be told, or that the patient's health is *so precarious* that such news will *undoubtedly* trigger an adverse reaction that will cause further unnecessary harm to the patient," (emphasis added).

[8]   (1981) 120 D.L.R. (3d) 269, 284–285 (Ont. H.C.); affirmed (1982) 12 D.L.R. (4th) 319 (Ont. C.A.).

[9]   Thus the risk of stroke, however minimal, is a material risk: *Forgie v Mason* (1986) 30 D.L.R. (4th) 548, 558 (N.B.C.A.). A doctor does not satisfy his duty to warn of the risk of stroke by warning of the risk of death and assuming that mentioning the more serious risk, death, comprehended the less serious risk, stroke, because a reasonable patient may be prepared to run the risk of death but not the risk of stroke: *Ferguson v Hamilton Civic Hospitals* (1983) 144 D.L.R. (3d) 214, 248; affirmed (1985) 18 D.L.R. (4th) 638 (Ont. C.A.). The risk of death is a material risk, even when it is extremely small. In *Meyer Estate v Rogers* (1991) 78 D.L.R (4th) 307 (Ont. H.C.) it was held that a risk of severe allergic reaction during an intravenous pyelogram of 1 in 2,000 and a risk of death of between 1 in 40,000 and 1 in 100,000 was a material risk. The risk of permanent loss or serious impairment of voice is a material risk in the context of the performance a carotid endarterectomy: *Casey v Provan* (1984) 11 D.L.R. (4th) 708 (Ont. H.C.). A small risk of perforation of the bowel during the course of laparoscopic sterilisation and during a bowel examination by sigmoidoscope has been held not to be a material risk: *Videto v Kennedy* (1981) 125 D.L.R. (3d) 127 (Ont. C.A.); *Gonda v Kerbel* (1982) 24 C.C.L.T. 222; *cf. Painter v Rae* [1998] 8 W.W.R. 717 (Man Q.B.) where the risk of injury to the bowel during a postpartum tubal ligation was small, but the gravity of the consequences rendered it a material risk; and *Berezowski-Aitken v McGregor* [1998] 8 W.W.R. 322 (Man Q.B.) where it was held that a failure to warn of the remote risk of bowel damage leading to infertility, following the performance of a dilatation and curettage ("D&C"), constituted a material risk because of the seriousness of the risk of infertility. In *Arndt v Smith* [1994] 8 W.W.R. 568 (B.C.S.C.) a mother was informed about the most common risks to her foetus of exposure to chickenpox (skin and muscle problems) but was not warned about the most serious, though more remote, risks (cortical atrophy and mental retardation). This was held to be negligent. The more remote risks were material risks, and non-disclosure was "classic medical paternalism." The decision was affirmed by the Supreme Court of Canada on the question of causation: (1997) 148 D.L.R. (4th) 48. In *Krangle v Brisco* (1997) 154 D.L.R. (4th) 707 (B.C.S.C.) the failure of a general practitioner to advise a 36 year old pregnant woman to undergo an amniocentesis test for Down's syndrome was held to be negligent. Note that where the risk is very small the claimant is likely to fail on causation: see para. 6–149.

chance of slight injury this may also be held to be material.[10] "Unusual or special risks" are risks that are extraordinary or uncommon, but they are known to occur occasionally. Though rare they should be described to a reasonable patient because of their unusual or special character. Thus, in the case of cosmetic surgery, where the operation can be described as elective, a doctor must be careful to make full disclosure of even remote risks of minor consequences since the patient may well decide that he would prefer to live with a blemish than to take the risk.[11]

In addition to the risks of treatment a doctor should explain the consequences of leaving the ailment untreated, and the alternative means of treatment and their risks.[12] Lack of negligence in the choice of treatment or the manner in which it is performed does not negate the doctor's duty to inform the patient of the risks of proceeding in one way as opposed to another.[13] So a patient should be informed of a known treatment which other doctors in the same specialty consider to be superior, even if the doctor does not agree.[14] In *Van Mol (Guardian ad Litem of) v Ashmore*[15] the British Columbia Court of Appeal held that a 16-year-old patient who was competent to consent should have been informed about the three surgical alternatives that were being considered to repair a narrowing of her aorta, and the risks and advantages of each of them. She should also have been informed that she could obtain a second opinion before deciding to proceed with the surgery.

6–120

---

[10] *Rawlings v Lindsey* (1982) 20 C.C.L.T. 301, where a 5% to 10% risk of nerve damage and resultant numbness to the face following wisdom tooth extraction was held to be a material risk; *cf. Diack v Bardsley* (1983) 25 C.C.L.T. 159 (B.C.S.C.) where the claimant failed on causation. The possibility of partial paraesthesia of the lower side of the face caused by a needle entering the inferior alveolar nerve during the routine administration of local anaesthetic prior to performing root canal work on the patient's teeth is too remote to constitute a material risk: *Schinz v Dickinson* [1985] 2 W.W.R. 673 (B.C.C.A.); *Mallette v Hagarty* [1994] 7 W.W.R. 402 (Alta. Q.B.), where Rowbotham J. pointed out that the risk of this form of damage was considerably greater where wisdom teeth were being extracted, as in *Rawlings v Lindsey*. See also *Carter v Higashi* [1994] 3 W.W.R. 319 (Alta. Q.B.), where the risk of fracturing the patient's jaw during extraction of wisdom teeth, put at one in 100,000, was held not to be a material risk; *Thibault v Fewer* [2002] 1 W.W.R. 204 (Man Q.B.)—a less than 1% risk of developing keratitis, which even if it occurred usually resolved without permanent complication, was not a material or unusual risk of a glycerol rhizotomy procedure.

[11] *White v Turner* (1981) 120 D.L.R. (3d) 269; affirmed (1982) 12 D.L.R. (4th) 319 (Ont. C.A.); *Petty v McKay* (1979) 10 C.C.L.T. 85 (B.C.S.C.); *Hankins v Papillon* (1980) 14 C.C.L.T. 198, 203 (Qué.S.C.); *Guertin v Kester* (1981) 20 C.C.L.T. 225 (B.C.S.C.); *MacDonald v Ross* (1983) 24 C.C.L.T. 242. Despite the different approach to the law in Canada, in a study of informed consent cases in the 10 years following *Reibl v Hughes* it was found that the claimant's action failed in 82% of cases: Robertson (1991) 70 Can. Bar Rev. 423.

[12] *Haughian v Paine* (1987) 37 D.L.R. (4th) 624, 639 (Sask. C.A.); *Schanczi v Singh* [1988] 2 W.W.R. 465 (Alta. Q.B.); *Seney v Crooks* (1998) 166 D.L.R. (4th) 337 (Alta. C.A.); *cf. Bucknam v Kostuik* (1983) 3 D.L.R. (4th) 99, 111 (Ont. H.C.), where Krever J. doubted whether a surgeon was under a duty to inform a patient of a less serious alternative procedure which in his own mind was an entirely unreasonable procedure to undertake, even though another school of thought believed the alternative procedure was appropriate for the patient's condition.

[13] *Seney v Crooks* (1998) 166 D.L.R. (4th) 337 (Alta. C.A.) at [54] *per* Conrad J.A.

[14] *ibid.* at [60].

[15] (1999) 168 D.L.R. (4th) 637 (B.C.C.A.).

Moreover, a general discussion of the risks with the patient's parents was not sufficient to discharge the surgeon's duty.

6–121   The clarity with which the doctor expresses a warning can, obviously, be crucial to a determination of negligence. In *Bryan v Hicks*[16] a surgeon gave a warning that there was a 1 to 2 per cent risk of "sympathetic pain" following surgery on a ganglion in the wrist. This was the defendant's standard way of telling patients about the risk of reflex sympathetic dystrophy. The British Columbia Court of Appeal held that this was not the same as a warning that there was a risk that the patient's arm could end up being useless. The total risk of reflex sympathetic dystrophy was 3 per cent of all cases, but of these, 95 per cent of patients were left with no symptoms after about a month. The rest (amounting to about three cases in 2,000) developed a severe, permanent form of the condition. It was held that this constituted a material risk, although medical opinion did not consider it necessary to disclose it. A reasonable person would want to know about the risk, particularly given the alternative forms of treatment available.

6–122   Where the patient has been given a full explanation of the risks involved in a procedure, and, having consented, during the course of the procedure withdraws that consent, the duty of disclosure is modified. The doctor is not under an obligation to repeat the full explanation in order to obtain consent to resume the procedure. The obligation is to disclose all facts that a patient would want to know, in the light of any material changes in circumstances since the former explanation, which could alter the assessment of costs or benefits of continuing the procedure.[17] A patient would want to know of any significant changes in the risks involved or in the need for continuation of the procedure which had become apparent during its course.

6–123   Non-disclosure of the treating doctor's own health status has been held not be negligent where the doctor's condition did not affect the treatment provided to the patient. In *Halkyard v Mathew*[18] a surgeon conducted an hysterectomy, following which the patient's bladder did not function properly. She underwent further surgery to correct the bladder problem, but died as a result of a pulmonary embolism shortly after the second operation. It was argued that she had not given informed consent to the hysterectomy because, although she was informed about the risks of the surgery, including bladder complications, the surgeon had not informed her that he had a history of epilepsy, for which he was taking medication. The defendant had not suffered a seizure during the operation, and the medication did not affect the surgeon's ability to carry out the operation. Lewis J. held that there was no duty to disclose to the patient the surgeon's personal medical history. It was the duty of the defendant's own physician to determine whether the defendant was fit to continue with surgery, and it was the duty of the hospital employing the surgeon to determine whether a doctor was fit to continue his practice in the hospital. Any doctor also has a personal responsibility to determine whether

---

[16] [1995] 10 W.W.R. 145 (B.C.C.A.).
[17] *Ciarlariello v Schacter* (1993) 100 D.L.R. (4th) 609 (S.C.C.).
[18] [1999] 5 W.W.R. 643 (Alta. Q.B.).

a physical or mental incapacity would preclude him from continuing to treat patients, but there was no link between the doctor's medical condition and the damage that occurred to the bladder during the operation.

(b) Australia

In Australia the High Court has rejected the *Bolam* test as an appropriate   **6–124** standard for the disclosure of information by the medical profession, effectively adopting the reasonably prudent patient standard. In *Rogers v Whitaker*[19] the claimant, who was aged 48, was almost totally blind in her right eye following an accident at the age of nine. Her left eye was normal. The defendant ophthalmic surgeon advised that an operation could improve the sight of the right eye. The claimant asked about the possible consequences of the operation, but did not specifically ask whether it could cause damage to the left eye. There was a one in 14,000 chance of sympathetic ophthalmia developing in the left eye, but the defendant did not mention this. If the claimant had known about this risk she would not have agreed to the surgery. Following the operation on the right eye, which was conducted with reasonable skill and care, sympathetic ophthalmia developed and she ultimately lost the sight in her left eye. The claimant had "incessantly" questioned the defendant as to the possible complications. She was, to the defendant's knowledge, keenly interested in the outcome of the procedure, including the danger of accidental interference with her "good" left eye. There was evidence from a body of reputable medical practitioners that, in the circumstances of this case, they would not have warned the claimant of the danger of sympathetic ophthalmia; there was also evidence from similarly reputable medical practitioners that they would have given such a warning. The New South Wales Court of Appeal held[20] that despite the evidence that a body of reputable medical practitioners would not have given a warning of the danger of sympathetic ophthalmia, the defendant had been negligent in failing to mention the risk in response to the claimant's general question about possible complications. The High Court of Australia upheld this decision, and an award of damages in excess of $800,000. The question, said the Court, was not whether the defendant's conduct accorded with the practice of the medical profession or some part of it, but whether it conformed to the standard of reasonable care demanded by the law. That was a question for the court, and the duty of deciding it could not be delegated to any profession or group in the community.[21] The nature of the matter to be

---

[19] (1992) 109 A.L.R. 625; [1993] 4 Med. L.R. 79 (H.C. of Aust.); Trindade (1993) 109 L.Q.R. 352; McDonald and Swanton (1993) 67 A.L.J. 145; McSherry (1993) 1 J. Law and Med. 5; Kerridge and Mitchell (1994) 1 J. Law and Med. 239; Jones (1994) 2 Tort L. Rev. 5; Malcolm (1994) 2 Tort L. Rev. 81.
[20] (1991) 23 N.S.W.L.R. 600; [1992] 3 Med. L.R. 331.
[21] Approving *F. v R.* (1983) 33 S.A.S.R. 189; *Battersby v Tottman* (1985) 37 S.A.S.R. 524; *Gover v South Australia* (1985) 39 S.A.S.R. 543; *Ellis v Wallsend District Hospital* (1989) 17 N.S.W.L.R 553; *E. v Australian Red Cross Society* (1991) 99 A.L.R. 601; [1991] 2 Med. L.R. 303; (1991) 105 A.L.R. 53 (Aus. Fed. C.A.). The High Court specifically disapproved

disclosed, the nature of the treatment, the desire of the patient for information, the temperament and health of the patient and the general surrounding
circumstances were all matters to be considered by a medical practitioner in
deciding whether to disclose or advise of some risk in a proposed procedure.
It followed that a doctor has a duty to warn a patient of a material risk inherent in the proposed treatment. A risk is material if, in the circumstances of
the particular case, a reasonable person in the patient's position, if warned
of the risk, would be likely to attach significance to it or if the medical practitioner is or should reasonably be aware that the particular patient, if
warned of the risk, would be likely to attach significance to it.[22]

6–125   The High Court rejected the "somewhat amorphous phrase 'informed
consent'" as apt to mislead, since it suggested a test of the validity of a
patient's consent, and consent was relevant to actions framed in trespass not
in negligence. Nonetheless the Court identified the central problem of such
cases in terms of the patient's ability to make a true choice about whether to
accept or reject proposed treatment. Except in cases of emergency or necessity, all medical treatment is preceded by the patient's choice to undergo it:

> "In legal terms, the patient's consent to the treatment may be valid once
> he or she is informed in broad terms of the nature of the procedure
> which is intended. But the choice is, in reality, meaningless unless it is
> made on the basis of relevant information and advice. Because the
> choice to be made calls for a decision by the patient on information
> known to the medical practitioner but not to the patient, it would be
> illogical to hold that the amount of information to be provided by the
> medical practitioner can be determined from the perspective of the prac-
> titioner alone or, for that matter, of the medical profession."[23]

There was a fundamental difference between, on the one hand, diagnosis and
treatment and, on the other hand, the provision of advice or information to
a patient. Whether a doctor carried out a particular treatment in accordance
with the appropriate standard of care was a question in the resolution of
which responsible professional opinion would have an influential role to
play. But whether the patient has been given all the relevant information to
choose between undergoing and not undergoing the treatment was a question of a different order. It was not a question the answer to which was
dependent upon medical standards or practices. Except where the defence of
therapeutic privilege might apply, no special medical skill was involved in
disclosing information, including the risks attending the proposed treatment.

(n.21 contd.) *Bolam v Friern Hospital Management Committee* [1957] 1 W.L.R. 582 and
Sidaway v Board of Governors of Bethlem Royal Hospital [1985] A.C. 871. In *Rosenberg
v Percival* [2001] H.C.A. 18; (2001) 178 A.L.R. 577 at [7], Gleeson C.J. commented that
Rogers v Whitaker makes it clear that professional practice and opinion was relevant, but
what the case denied was its *conclusiveness*.
[22] (1992) 109 A.L.R. 625, 634, *per* Mason C.J., Brennan, Dawson, Toohey, and McHugh JJ.;
Rosenberg v Percival [2001] H.C.A. 18; (2001) 178 A.L.R. 577 at [75] *per* Gummow J.
[23] *ibid.* at 633.

Rather, the skill was in communicating the relevant information to the patient in terms which were reasonably adequate for the purpose having regard to the patient's apprehended capacity to understand that information.[24] On the facts of *Rogers v Whitaker*, sympathetic ophthalmia was the only danger whereby both eyes might be rendered sightless. The defendant had acknowledged that, except for death under anaesthetic, it was the worst possible outcome for the claimant. The claimant had incessantly questioned the defendant as to possible complications, including the danger of accidental interference with her good eye, but she did not ask a specific question as to whether the operation on her right eye could affect her left eye. Remarkably, there was a body of professional opinion which considered that an inquiry by a patient should only have elicited a reply dealing with sympathetic ophthalmia if specifically directed to the possibility of the left eye being affected by the operation on the right eye. This view appears to require the claimant to be sufficiently knowledgeable about medical matters to be able to ask the precise question before the doctors consider it appropriate tell her about the dangers of sympathetic ophthalmia. The High Court described this state of affairs as "curious." The claimant may not have asked the right question, but she had made clear her concern about injury to her one good eye. The risk, although extremely small, was a material risk, because a reasonable person in the claimant's position would be likely to attach significance to the risk, and thus require a warning.[25] It was reasonable, said the Court, for a person with one good eye to be concerned about the possibility of injury to it from a procedure which was elective.

In *Rosenberg v Percival*[26] the claimant alleged that the defendant, a dentist, had failed to warn her in advance of the complications of a surgical procedure on the jaw. The trial judge held that the defendant had not failed to warn, and in any event the claimant would have proceeded with the procedure had she been informed of the risks, a view that was upheld by the High Court of Australia. Gummow J. said that in deciding whether a patient was "likely to attach significance to" a particular risk, the extent or severity   **6–126**

---

[24] *ibid.* at 632–633. In *Smith v Tunbridge Wells Health Authority* [1994] 5 Med. L.R. 334, Morland J., having been referred to *Rogers v Whitaker*, commented that "it is the decision in *Sidaway* and the test in *Bolam* which I must, and do apply, and not the Australian approach."

[25] In *F. v R.* (1983) 33 S.A.S.R. 189, 191 King C.J. said that a risk of harm or of the procedure failing might be so slight in relation to the consequences of not undergoing the proposed treatment that no reasonable person would be influenced by it. The duty to disclose would not extend to such a risk. On the other hand, a small risk of great harm might call for disclosure, although a greater risk of slight harm would not. The more drastic the proposed intervention the more necessary it would be to keep the patient fully informed of the risks and likely consequences. Major surgery calls for special care in this regard. The existence of reasonably available alternative methods of treatment was also an important factor. See also *Chappel v Hart* [1998] H.C.A. 55; (1998) 156 A.L.R. 517; [1999] Lloyd's Rep. Med. 223 (H.C. of Aust.), where the failure to disclose the risk of damage to the claimant's vocal cords in the course of an endoscopic division of the pharyngeal pouch was held to be negligent, applying *Rogers v Whitaker*.

[26] [2001] H.C.A. 18; (2001) 178 A.L.R. 577; Kumaralingham Amirthalingham (2001) 117 L.Q.R. 532.

of the potential injury is of great importance, as is the likelihood of the injury actually occurring. These issues should be considered together: "A slight risk of a serious harm might satisfy the test, while a greater risk of a small harm might not."[27] This should then be weighed against the patient's circumstances, including the patient's need for the operation and the existence of alternative treatments. A patient may be more likely to attach significance to a risk if the procedure is elective rather than life saving.[28] The second, or subjective, limb of the *Rogers* test recognises that the particular patient may not be reasonable. "Unreasonable" fears or concerns will be given full weight under the second limb if the doctor was or should have been aware of them. If the patient asked questions revealing the fear or concern then the doctor would clearly have been aware of them, but that was not the only means of satisfying the second limb, and the courts "should not be too quick to discard the second limb merely because it emerges that the patient did not ask certain kinds of questions."[29] Kirby J. identified a number of reasons, both of principle and policy, to support the strictness of the rule established by *Rogers v Whitaker*:

"(1)   Fundamentally, the rule is a recognition of individual autonomy that is to be viewed in the wider context of an emerging appreciation of basic human rights and human dignity. There is no reason to diminish the law's insistence, to the greatest extent possible, upon prior, informed agreement to invasive treatment, save for that which is required in an emergency or otherwise out of necessity;

(2)   While it may be desirable to instil a relationship between the healthcare professional and the patient, reality demands a recognition that sometimes (as in the present case) defects of communication demand the imposition of minimum legal obligations so that even those providers who are in a hurry, or who may have comparatively less skill or inclination for communication, are obliged to pause and provide warnings of the kind that *Rogers* mandates;

(3)   Such obligations have the added benefit of redressing, to some small degree, the risks of conflicts of interest and duty which a provider may sometimes face in favouring one healthcare procedure over another;

(4)   Also, to some extent, the legal obligation to provide warnings may sometimes help to redress the inherent inequality in power between the professional provider and a vulnerable patient; and

(5)   Even those who are dubious about obligations, such as those stated in decisions such as *Rogers*, commonly recognise the value of the symbolism which such legal holdings afford . . . In so far as

---

[27] *ibid.* at [77].
[28] *ibid.* at [78].
[29] *Ibid.* at [79].

the law can influence such practice, it should tend, as *Rogers* does, towards the provision of detailed warnings so that the ultimate choice, to undertake or refuse an invasive procedure, rests, and is seen to rest, on the patient rather than the healthcare provider. To the extent that this result is upheld, it seems likely that recriminations and litigation following disappointment after treatment will be diminished."[30]

The duty to disclose material risks is subject to the defence of therapeutic privilege, *i.e.* it is open to the doctor to prove that he or she reasonably believed that disclosure of a risk would be harmful to the patient. A good example of the application of this principle is the case of *Battersby v Tottman*[31] in which the Supreme Court of South Australia held that the defendant was not liable for failing to warn a patient about the risk of blindness associated with the use of a particular drug in high doses because the claimant was incapable by reason of her abnormal mental condition of using the information as the basis for calm or rational decision. She was likely to react hysterically and irrationally and to refuse treatment not on rational grounds or as a result of calm deliberation but as a result of distorted mental processes produced by her mental illness.[32] In *F. v R.*[33] King C.J. said that there may be circumstances where reasonable care for the patient may justify or even require an evasive or less than fully candid answer even to a direct request, and the doctor may reasonably judge that a patient has made an inquiry, not out of a desire for a frank answer, but out of a desire for reassurance.[34] Similarly, the doctor can withhold information where he judges on reasonable grounds that the patient's health, mental or physical, might be seriously harmed by the information, or when the doctor reasonably judges that a patient's temperament or emotional state is such that he would be unable to make the information a basis for a rational decision. In *Rogers v Whitaker* Gaudron J. was anxious to ensure that the defence of therapeutic privilege should not be used to create an exception so wide as to undermine the basic principle requiring disclosure. There was no basis for any defence of therapeutic privilege which was not based in medical emergency or in considerations of the patient's ability to receive, understand or properly evaluate the significance of the information that would ordinarily be required with respect to his or her condition or the treatment proposed.

6–127

---

[30] *ibid.* at [145].

[31] (1985) 37 S.A.S.R. 524 (S.C. of S. Aus.).

[32] *ibid.* at 527, *per* King C.J.; *cf.* the forthright dissent of Zelling J. at 534–535: "In my opinion it is no answer to the claimant's claim to say that the claimant might have had her treatment seriously affected or might have become suicidal if she had been told the truth. In my view no doctor is entitled to give a patient treatment which may blind her or seriously damage her eyesight without first discussing it with the patient and obtaining her consent to the treatment."

[33] (1983) 33 S.A.S.R. 189, 192, 193 (S.C. of S. Aus.); see Manderson (1988) 62 A.L.J. 430.

[34] Though this view has now to be considered in the light of the High Court's reaction to questioning by a patient in *Rogers v Whitaker*: see para. 6–144.

(c) New Zealand

6–128   In *Smith v Auckland Hospital Board*[35] the New Zealand Court of Appeal effectively applied a *Bolam* standard to the disclosure of information to a patient, even in response to a specific request for information by the patient. Barrowclough C.J. said that the court would, in most cases, require the assistance of expert medical evidence as to what is generally accepted medical or surgical practice.[36]

(d) Ireland

6–129   In *Walsh v Family Planning Services Ltd*[37] Finlay C.J. said that there is a clear obligation on a medical practitioner carrying out or arranging for the carrying out of an operation to inform the patient of "any possible harmful consequence arising form the operation, so as to permit the patient to give an informed consent."[38] The extent of this obligation varies with the elective nature of the surgery concerned. There could be instances where notwithstanding substantial medical risks of harmful consequences the carrying out of a particular surgical procedure was so necessary to maintain the life or health of the patient and the consequences of failing to carry it out were so clearly disadvantageous that limited discussion or warning of the possible harmful side-effects might be appropriate. But at the other end of the scale, to the extent to which the surgery was elective, the obligation to warn of possible harmful consequences may be more stringent and onerous. The test of negligence for failing to warn of risks was the same as that applied to allegations of negligence in treatment and diagnosis. But where a doctor sought to establish that the warning he gave complied with general practice, it may be, and certainly in relation to very clearly elective surgery such as a vasectomy, that the court might more readily come to the conclusion that the extent of the warning given or omitted contained inherent defects which ought to have been obvious to any person giving the matter due consideration than it could do in the case of complicated medical or surgical procedures.

(2) What must be disclosed voluntarily?

6–130   Although it is the *Bolam* test which sets the standard of disclosure for the medical profession it is nonetheless possible to identify some specific matters

---

[35] [1965] N.Z.L.R. 191 (N.Z.C.A.).
[36] *ibid.* at 198; see also *per* Turner J. at 205. Prior to changes introduced to New Zealand's system of no-fault accident compensation in 1992 it was uncertain whether the non-disclosure of risks of treatment fell within the definition of "medical misadventure" under that scheme. It is now clear that a negligent failure to obtain informed consent would be covered by the no-fault compensation scheme. See para. 1–028.
[37] [1992] 1 I.R. 496, (Supreme Court of Ireland).
[38] *ibid.* at 510.

that either do or do not fall within the doctor's duty. In practice it is easier to identify the information that need not be disclosed. There is no obligation to inform a patient about the risk of death from general anaesthetic,[39] nor about other everyday risks that exist in all surgery, such as bleeding, pain, scars from an incision, or the risk of infection in any surgical procedure, because everyone is expected to know about them.[40] The doctor is not under a duty to tell the patient that if he is negligent in performing an operation he will cause damage,[41] nor that he is inexperienced in performing the particular procedure,[42] nor his own health status where it does not affect his ability to undertake the treatment.[43]

There is no obligation to disclose information which the doctor believes will be medically harmful to the patient, or where the patient indicates that he does not want to know.[44] Under English law the notion of "therapeutic privilege"[45] is not part of a defence to a claim for non-disclosure, it is incorporated within the duty of disclosure itself applying *Sidaway v Bethlem Royal Hospital Governors*. This allows for different levels of disclosure to different patients, within the doctor's exercise of clinical judgment. It is a "defence" only in the sense that if the medical evidence indicates that the normal practice of the profession is to disclose a particular risk, it will be for the defendant to justify non-disclosure to the patient. The doctor may take the view that a patient would be confused, frightened or misled by detailed information which he would be unable to evaluate at a time when he is suffering from

6–131

---

[39] *Sidaway v Bethlem Royal Hospital Governors* [1984] Q.B. 493, 522, *per* Browne-Wilkinson L.J.: "It is of course obvious that the doctor is not under any duty give information as to the ordinary risks normally attendant on any operation"; *Sidaway v Bethlem Royal Hospital Governors* [1985] A.C. 871, 897, *per* Lord Bridge; *cf.* Lord Diplock *ibid.* at 894; *Considine v Camp Hill Hospital* (1982) 133 D.L.R. (3d) 11, 39 (N.S.S.C.). For consideration of consent to, and the disclosure of the risks of, anaesthesia see Nunn (1996) 2 Clinical Risk 74.

[40] *White v Turner* (1981) 120 D.L.R. (3d) 269, 285, *per* Linden J. (Ont. H.C.); affirmed (1982) 12 D.L.R. (4th) 319 (Ont. C.A.). A failure to mention statistics should not be a factor in deciding whether the duty to inform has been breached: *Reibl v Hughes* (1980) 114 D.L.R. (3d) 1, 13. In some circumstances certain infection risks, such as the risk of contracting AIDS from contaminated blood products, should be disclosed: see *H. v Royal Alexandra Hospital for Children* [1990] 1 Med. L.R. 297, 324 (N.S.W.S.C.), though the action failed on causation, since, given the balance of risk of infection compared with the risk to the patient, who was a haemophiliac, of not having the treatment the doctors would have gone ahead with the transfusions even if informed of the risk of infection, and the parents would also have given their consent.

[41] "The fundamental assumption is that he knows his job and will do it properly," *per* Bristow J. in *Chatterton v Gerson* [1981] Q.B. 432, 444; *Holmes v Board of Hospital Trustees of the City of London* (1977) 81 D.L.R. (3d) 67, 83 (Ont. H.C.); *MacDonald v Ross* (1983) 24 C.C.L.T. 242, 248.

[42] *Holmes v Board of Hospital Trustees of the City of London* (1977) 81 D.L.R. (3d) 67, 83 (Ont. H.C.).

[43] *Halkyard v Mathew* [1999] 5 W.W.R. 643 (Alta. Q.B.).

[44] *Sidaway v Bethlem Royal Hospital Governors* [1984] Q.B. 493, 521, *per* Browne-Wilkinson L.J. The doctor must identify the patient's "true wishes" and distinguish between patients who want information and patients who are only seeking reassurance: *per* Sir John Donaldson M.R. at 513. If the information would be harmful to the patient the doctor could be in breach of a duty of care by disclosing it: see *Furniss v Fitchett* [1958] N.Z.L.R. 396.

[45] In *Meyer Estate v Rogers* (1991) 78 D.L.R (4th) 307 (Ont. H.C.) it was held that there is no defence of therapeutic privilege in Canadian law.

stress, pain and anxiety.[46] There is an obvious danger in giving too wide an interpretation to this "exception" in that it could be used to undermine the patient's right to exercise a choice about whether to accept treatment. The mere fact that the doctor believes that if the patient were informed about the risks he would decline the treatment which the doctor believes to be in the patient's best interests would not justify withholding the information, otherwise whenever the proposed treatment was medically appropriate, doctors would have no obligation to give patients information about risks.

6–132   The doctor does not have a duty to make the patient understand; it is a duty to make a reasonable effort to communicate information to the patient.[47] It is not an answer, however, for the doctor to say that he does not have the time to give seminars in medicine or that the information is too complicated or technical for the patient to understand. The duty must be to give an explanation in terms which are reasonably comprehensible to a layman, although there can be no guarantee that the patient will in fact understand the information.[48] Where it is quite apparent to the doctor that the patient has not understood he may have to make further efforts. The Canadian courts, for example, have taken the view that where the patient has language difficulties the doctor is under a special duty to be sure that the patient has understood.[49] In *Lybert v Warrington Health Authority*[50] the Court of Appeal accepted that a doctor has a responsibility to take reasonable steps to ensure that the information given is understood. The claimant had been sterilised at the time of giving birth to her third child by Caesarian section but had not been warned before the operation of the risk that the procedure would fail to achieve sterility. The post-operative warning was inadequate because the timing and the conditions in which it was given were

---

[46] *Sidaway v Bethlem Royal Hospital Governors* [1985] A.C. 871, 902, *per* Lord Templeman; *Male v Hopmans* (1967) 64 D.L.R. (2d) 105, 113 (Ont. C.A.).

[47] See *Kelly v Hazlett* (1976) 75 D.L.R. (3d) 536, 565 (Ont. H.C.), *per* Morden J. stating that it is a duty to be reasonably satisfied that the patient is aware of the risks associated with the treatment of which he should be aware. See also *Stobie v Central Birmingham Health Authority* (1994) 22 B.M.L.R. 135, QBD, where the claimants misunderstood the defendant's advice about failure rates for vasectomy, despite the fact that he "did what he could" to ensure that the claimants did understand that there remained a risk of failure, put at about one in a thousand.

[48] See Brazier (1987) 7 L.S. 169, 177 commenting on the intrinsic difficulty of communicating medical information to patients. One study found that between two and five days after an operation 27% of patients did not know which organ had been operated on, and 44% were unaware of the basic facts relating to the operation, *e.g.*, that a gall bladder had been removed: Byrne, Napier and Cuschieri (1988) 296 B.M.J. 839. See also McMahon, Clark and Bailie (1987) 294 B.M.J. 355 on the provision of drug information to patients. See further Jones (1999) 7 Med. L. Rev. 103, 123–129 where the medical literature on "informed consent" is reviewed.

[49] *Reibl v Hughes* (1980) 114 D.L.R. (3d) 1, 34; *Schanczi v Singh* [1988] 2 W.W.R. 465, 474 (Alta. Q.B.); *Ciarlariello v Schacter* (1993) 100 D.L.R. (4th) 609, 622–623 (S.C.C.). See also the G.M.C. guidance, *Seeking patients' consent: the ethical considerations*, February 1999 [available at *www.gmc-uk.org*] para. 13 which states, amongst other things, that a doctor should "make arrangements, wherever possible, to meet particular language and communication needs, for example through translations, independent interpreters, signers, or the patient's representative."

[50] [1996] P.I.Q.R. P45; [1996] 7 Med. L.R. 71.

inappropriate, and the warning was not expressed in terms sufficient to impinge upon the claimant's thoughts. An emphatic and clear warning was required, with an assurance that it was being taken in.

In *Smith v Tunbridge Wells Health Authority*[51] the claimant underwent a   **6-133**
Wells operation (ivalon sponge rectopexy) to repair a rectal prolapse. The surgery was successful in effecting the repair, but due to nerve damage during the surgery the claimant, who was aged 28 at the time of the operation, was rendered impotent and suffered from bladder dysfunction. This is a recognised risk of the operation. Responsible medical opinion, including the defendant surgeon, regarded it as important to explain the particular risks to a patient such as the claimant, *i.e.* a young, sexually active married man suffering from a condition which was distressing, embarrassing and inconvenient, but which was not life-threatening. He had had the condition for eight years, and was not psychologically vulnerable or mentally unstable. This type of operation was normally performed on elderly women, and it was exceedingly rare on a sexually active man, partly because for anatomical reasons it is a more difficult operation in men. Morland J. held the defendants liable on the basis that the surgeon had failed to get across to the claimant the risks involved in the operation:

> "When recommending a particular type of surgery or treatment, the doctor, when warning of the risks, must take reasonable care to ensure that his explanation of the risks is intelligible to his particular patient. The doctor should use language, simple but not misleading, which the doctor perceives from what knowledge and acquaintanceship that he may have of the patient (which may be slight), will be understood by the patient so that the patient can make an informed decision as to whether or not to consent to the recommended surgery or treatment."[52]

The defendant had not been clear in his own mind as to how and to what extent he should explain the risks to the claimant, with the result that his explanation was confused, and the claimant misunderstood the message. If the claimant had been informed of the risk of impotence he would have refused the operation. The very fact of consent and the speed of consent were indicative, said his Lordship, that a clear warning of the risk of impotence was not communicated to the claimant.

The doctor will also have to take into account the patient's condition at   **6-134**
the time of explaining the risks, since if the patient is debilitated the information may not "get through." In *Smith v Salford Health Authority*[53] the claimant was informed of the risks to his health if he did not have corrective cervical surgery (an occipetal/cervical fusion), but he was not informed of the risks of paralysis or, indeed, death from the surgery itself. Moreover, even

---

[51] [1994] 5 Med. L.R. 334, QBD.
[52] *ibid.* at 339.
[53] [1994] 5 Med. L.R. 321, QBD. The action failed on causation. See also *Lybert v Warrington Health Authority* [1996] P.I.Q.R. P45; [1996] 7 Med. L.R. 71, CA, para. 6–131.

if these risks were mentioned, they were not mentioned in terms adequate to register upon the claimant, who at the time was suffering from a headache and the general adverse effects of a recent myelogram. All the experts were agreed that the risks should have been explained, as indeed was the defendant's usual practice, and therefore he had been negligent.

6–135   Similarly, in *McAllister v Lewisham and North Southwark Health Authority*[54] the claimant had a neurological deficit in her left leg which was identified as being attributable to a large arteriovascular malformation (avm), a congenital vascular deformity in the skull. The defendant neurosurgeon recommended an operation to remove the avm. He told the claimant that without the operation her leg would not improve and was likely to get worse in the not too distant future. He also said that there was a 20 per cent chance that the operation itself would make the leg worse, but he made no mention of any of the general risks of brain surgery (such as the possibility of epilepsy and the inevitable consequence that after surgery of this nature she would not be allowed to drive for at least twelve months), and did not inform her that there was any risk that the increased deficit could extend beyond the leg. In particular:

> "he did not get through to her that there was any risk of the arm becoming impaired, still less of any left-sided hemiplegia. Mr. Strong told me, reciting his general habit in the case of other operable brain conditions, that he thinks he would have mentioned some risk to the left side or arm. If he did so, I can only conclude that he did not do so in any way which was sufficient to enter the plaintiff's consciousness. In fact I rather doubt that he did . . ."[55]

The claimant was left with the impression that she really "had nothing to lose." This was simply untrue, since the risks associated with the operation were high; indeed the evidence indicated that many neurosurgeons would not even have attempted it in the claimant's circumstances. After the operation the claimant had increased weakness in her leg, and complete hemiplegia on her left side, involving her arm which was completely useless. Rougier J. held that to leave the claimant with the impression that there were really no two ways about the operation and that she had nothing to lose constituted negligence. *McAllister v Lewisham and North Southwark Health Authority* demonstrates that a highly selective approach to the disclosure of risk which is positively misleading is likely to result in a finding of negligence, whereas *Smith v Tunbridge Wells Health Authority* indicates that a genuine but ineffective attempt to explain the risks may also be culpable.

6–136   It is difficult to state precisely what must be disclosed since under the *Bolam* test this depends upon the practice of a responsible body of professional opinion at the time. One consequence of this is that patients will be

---

[54] [1994] 5 Med. L.R. 343, QBD.
[55] *ibid.* at 345, *per* Rougier J.

entitled to more information as professional attitudes to the question of information disclosure change (assuming, of course, that changes in practice will reflect the growing concern that consent should be "informed").[56] It must be remembered that non-disclosure is not necessarily negligent merely because some doctors would have disclosed a particular risk, if other responsible practitioners would not have told the patient about it.[57] It is implicit from Lord Bridge's speech in *Sidaway v Bethlem Royal Hospital Governors*,[58] however, that there must be some limits to the medical profession's discretion to withhold information. His Lordship cited *Reibl v Hughes*,[59] in which there was a 4 per cent risk of death and a 10 per cent risk of stroke in the context of an operation intended to remove the risk of stroke, as an example of a case where a court could reasonably conclude that the disclosure of the risk was so obviously necessary to an informed choice on the part of the patient that no reasonably prudent doctor would fail to make it, notwithstanding the practice of the profession. In such a case, where there was a substantial risk of grave adverse consequences, a doctor could hardly fail to appreciate the necessity for an appropriate warning.[60] In making this judgment there must inevitably be some degree of interrelationship between the chances of a successful outcome and the inherent risks of the procedure.[61] Similarly, there ought to be an interrelationship between the nature and severity of the potential risks and the purpose of the procedure. In the case of minor surgical operations the court could reasonably require doctors to disclose lower degrees of risk, whether measured by incidence or severity. Conversely, the more serious the patient's medical condition requiring treatment the greater the level of risk the doctor could reasonably omit to disclose:

---

[56] Compare, *e.g.*, *Gold v Haringey Health Authority* [1988] Q.B. 481, where it was said that in 1979 there was a responsible body of professional opinion that would not have given a warning about the risk of a sterilisation operation failing, with *Gowton v Wolverhampton Health Authority* [1994] 5 Med. L.R. 432, where the defendants' experts conceded that by 1986 there was no responsible body of opinion which would have omitted to give such a warning.

[57] See, *e.g.*, *Gold v Haringey Health Authority* [1988] Q.B. 481 where all the expert witnesses said that they would have disclosed the risk of a sterilisation operation failing to produce sterility, but that in 1979 there was a responsible body of professional opinion which would not have disclosed the risk; see also *Moyes v Lothian Health Board* [1990] 1 Med. L.R. 463. Where there is no independent expert evidence as to professional practice the court may treat the defendant's own usual practice as evidence of the appropriate standard: *Thake v Maurice* [1986] Q.B. 644.

[58] [1985] A.C. 871, 900.

[59] (1980) 114 D.L.R. (3d) 1.

[60] In *Smith v Tunbridge Wells Health Authority* [1994] 5 Med. L.R. 334, 339 Morland J. concluded that by 1988, although some surgeons may still not have been warning patients in a similar situation to the claimant of the risk of impotence associated with an operation to repair a rectal prolapse, "that omission was neither reasonable nor responsible." His Lordship may have been fortified in that view, however, by the fact that the defendant himself believed that the risk should have been disclosed.

[61] "An operation with a very high success rate and a very low risk of paralysis may, rationally, be accepted much more readily than one where the prospects of success were more circumscribed, though the risk of paralysis was still slight," *per* Kirby P. in *Ellis v Wallsend District Hospital* (1989) 17 N.S.W.L.R. 553, 561 (N.S.W.C.A.).

"Moreover, the materiality of any particular risk must in the ordinary case depend on the relationship between the object to be achieved by the operation and the nature of the risks involved. If there is a ½ per cent risk of total paralysis, that might well be a material risk in the context of an operation designed to get rid of a minor discomfort but not in the context of an operation required to avoid death. The decision as to the materiality of a risk does not depend simply on the difference between an elective operation and an essential operation: it depends on the balancing of benefits and risks."[62]

6–137   In *Newbury v Bath District Health Authority*[63] Ebsworth J. indicated that in a case of major spinal surgery the patient was entitled to be appraised of the nature and extent of the risks of neurological injury (put at 1 to 5 per cent by the surgeon who carried out the operation and at 1 to 2 per cent by the expert witnesses) and to make her own decision about taking them. There might also be circumstances where a patient was entitled to be told that a proposed operation was not in the mainstream of treatment: "That would, I think obviously, be so if it involved a method which was entirely new or even relatively untried. I accept that it would be so if the method had fallen out of use because it had been shown to be defective and was not accepted by a responsible body of opinion."[64]

6–138   The courts in this country have been reluctant to accept a distinction between elective and non-elective procedures. Sir John Donaldson M.R. has said that the distinction is meaningless to a patient, because all operations are elective: the patient always has a choice.[65] Whilst on one level this

---

[62] *Sidaway v Bethlem Royal Hospital Governors* [1984] Q.B. 493, 521–522, *per* Browne-Wilkinson L.J. See also *H. v Royal Alexandra Hospital for Children* [1990] 1 Med. L.R. 297, 324, (N.S.W.S.C.) *per* Badgery-Parker J.: "The greater the chance that the risk will eventuate, the more obviously will disclosure be necessary, even though the consequences of the happening of the risk may not be enormous. Conversely, where the possible consequence is disastrous, disclosure may be 'obviously necessary' even though the risk may be quantified as tiny." In *McAllister v Lewisham and North Southwark Health Authority* [1994] 5 Med. L.R. 343, QBD the defendant was held to have been negligent in failing to disclose the risks associated with the particular form of brain surgery he was recommending, despite the fact that the risks of leaving the condition untreated were high (a 2% per year cumulative risk of brain haemorrhage; and if an haemorrhage did occur the risk of death was 29% and the risk of morbidity in some form 23%). This was because the risks of surgery were also high (*e.g.* the defendants' own expert witness put the risk of some form of further sensory deficit at 100%); indeed the decision to undertake the operation at all was very much a minority view. In *Goorkani v Tayside Health Board* [1991] 3 Med. L.R. 33 Lord Cameron held that the defenders were negligent in failing to warn the pursuer of the risk of infertility from the use of the drug Chlorambucil, which was prescribed for a period of 18 months for the treatment of Behcet's disease, a relatively rare condition which can cause blindness. Infertility is a recognised side effect of long-term use of the drug. The claim failed on causation, because, had he known about it, the pursuer would probably have accepted the risk for the chance of saving his sight by continuing with the course of treatment (though see para. 6–162).

[63] (1998) 47 B.M.L.R. 138, QBD.

[64] *ibid.* at 150. Ebsworth J. considered, however, that the evidence in the case had not reached that state, despite the fact that the defendant surgeon had accepted that he was probably the only mainline surgeon using the method by 1991.

[65] *Sidaway v Bethlem Royal Hospital Governors* [1984] Q.B. 493, 514.

is patently true, the concept of an elective medical procedure does seek to distinguish those situations where the patient's condition is such that there is in reality very little choice (all the evidence points to the treatment being accepted, possibly in an emergency[66]) from those where the options are more evenly balanced and there is time for considered reflection. In Canada, for example, cosmetic surgery has been treated as elective, requiring a greater degree of information disclosure about inherent risks.[67] The point was made very clear by McCarthy J. in *Walsh v Family Planning Services Ltd*:

> "All surgery, in a sense, is elective although the election may have to be implied from the circumstances rather than determined as express . . . A patient's condition may be such as to demand surgical intervention as the only hope for survival. Such may be called non-elective surgery. The patient given the choice between enduring pain and having limb replacement surgery or fusion surgery may technically be electing as between the pain and the surgery but the election may be more apparent than real. An extreme of elective surgery would be what is purely cosmetic —simply to improve the natural appearance rather than to remedy the physical results of injury or disease. Even it may have an element of quasi-medical care because of the psychological reaction of the patient to personal appearance. A like argument may be advanced in respect of contraceptive surgery, male or female. Such surgery does not have a direct effect on the health or well being of the patient nor in prolongation of life; it may alleviate marital stress or other domestic pressure and in that sense be therapeutic. Essentially, however, it is for the improvement of the sex life of the couple concerned."[68]

O'Flaherty J. commented that where elective surgery which is not essential to health or bodily well-being is undertaken, if there is a risk—however exceptional or remote—of grave consequences involving severe pain stretching for an appreciable time into the future and involving the possibility of further operative procedures, the exercise of the duty of care owed by the defendant required that the possible consequences should be explained in the clearest language to the claimant.[69]

---

[66] See *Hills v Potter* [1983] 3 All E.R. 716, 718 where Hirst J. observed that it was common ground in that case that it was not an emergency procedure "but was 'elective' in character, so that it was for the plaintiff to choose whether or not to undergo it."

[67] *White v Turner* (1981) 120 D.L.R. (3d) 269 (Ont. H.C.); affirmed (1982) 12 D.L.R. (4th) 319 (Ont. C.A.); *cf. Gold v Haringey Health Authority* [1988] Q.B. 481, 489.

[68] [1992] 1 I.R. 496, 517–18 (Supreme Court of Ireland).

[69] *ibid.* at 535; see also *per* Egan J. at 537. In *Geoghegan v Harris* [2000] 3 I.R. 536 Kearns J. regarded *Walsh v Family Planning Services Ltd* as requiring the disclosure of any risk which carries the possibility of grave consequences, irrespective of its statistical frequency, in cases of elective surgery. Accordingly, it was held that there was an obligation to warn of a very remote risk of developing neuropathic pain in the patient's lower jaw following surgery for a dental implant, even though all the medical experts were of the view that no warning was necessary. The claim failed, however, on causation.

6–139   The English Court of Appeal has also rejected a distinction between advice given in a therapeutic context and advice given in a non-therapeutic context. In *Gold v Haringey Health Authority*[70] Schiemann J. attempted to avoid applying the *Bolam* test to the non-disclosure of the chance that a sterilisation operation might not render the claimant completely sterile, taking the view that in the context of a sterilisation for contraceptive purposes, as opposed to therapeutic purposes, there was no body of responsible professional opinion which would have omitted to give a warning. Alternatively, his Lordship held that the *Bolam* test did not apply in a non-therapeutic context, and accordingly the defendant was negligent despite the medical evidence to the effect that a responsible body of professional opinion would not have given a warning. The Court of Appeal reversed this finding. Lloyd L.J. said that:

> ". . . a distinction between advice given in a therapeutic context and advice given in a non-therapeutic context would be a departure from the principle on which the *Bolam* test is itself grounded. The principle does not depend on the context in which any act is performed, or any advice given. It depends on a man professing skill or competence in a field beyond that possessed by the man on the Clapham omnibus."[71]

The consequence of this appears to be that the *Bolam* test will be applied to the disclosure of information by doctors in all contexts, although it must remain arguable that even under the *Bolam* test a reasonable doctor should give patients more information about the inherent risks of a procedure which is "elective" (a term which would encompass "non-therapeutic") in the sense that it is not essential for the patient's well-being. It should also be remembered that the *Bolam* test itself does not require the court to accept uncritically all the evidence of every expert witness.[72] For example, in *McAllister v Lewisham and North Southwark Health Authority*[73] Rougier J. rejected the view of one expert witness for the defence that the defendant's level of disclosure was appropriate, first because the expert had assessed the risk of injury to the patient's arm as something in the region of 1 per cent., a view which was inconsistent with the evidence of other expert witnesses who had assessed the risk as at least 5 per cent or more. Secondly, the witness's view was inherently contradictory in that despite a 100 per cent risk of sensory deficit which might be serious, he made no criticism of the defendant's failure to mention this to

---

[70] [1988] Q.B. 481; Montgomery (1988) 51 M.L.R. 245.

[71] *ibid.* at 489–490. For criticism of a distinction between therapeutic and non-therapeutic sterilisation in a different context see *Re B. (a minor)* [1988] A.C. 199, 205, *per* Lord Hailsham and Lord Bridge respectively; *cf. Re E. (a minor)(medical treatment)* [1991] 2 F.L.R. 585; (1991) 7 B.M.L.R. 117, where Sir Stephen Brown P. said that there was a "clear distinction between an operation to be performed for a genuine therapeutic reason and one to achieve sterilisation."

[72] See *Bolitho v City and Hackney Health Authority* [1998] A.C. 232, para. 3–029. The court is entitled to reject expert evidence which is not capable of withstanding logical analysis.

[73] [1994] 5 Med. L.R. 343, QBD.

the claimant. Thus, there was no body of responsible professional opinion which would have supported the defendant's failure to disclose these risks.

Moreover, if the approach in *Pearce v United Bristol Healthcare NHS Trust*[74] comes to be accepted, then a reasonable doctor would disclose those risks which a reasonable patient would consider to be "significant." It is arguable that a reasonable patient would take into account not only the incidence and severity of any risk, should it materialise, but also the context in which the issue arises, so that procedures which are clearly "elective" as understood by a reasonable patient or, indeed, a reasonable doctor (notwithstanding Sir John Donaldson M.R.'s inability to attach any meaning to the term) are on a different footing from those where the patient really has little option. At its most obvious, an elective procedure such as cosmetic surgery to improve one's appearance should require significantly greater disclosure of the attendant risks than surgery to remove an appendix which is about to rupture, threatening the patient's life.

The General Medical Council now gives quite detailed advice as to what   **6–140** doctors should tell their patients. For example, paragraph 5 of the GMC document *Seeking patients' consent: the ethical considerations*[75] states that the information which patients want or ought to know, before deciding whether to consent to treatment or an investigation, may include:

- details of the diagnosis, and prognosis, and the likely prognosis if the condition is left untreated;

- uncertainties about the diagnosis including options for further investigation prior to treatment;

- options for treatment or management of the condition, including the option not to treat;

- the purpose of a proposed investigation or treatment; details of the procedures or therapies involved, including subsidiary treatment such as methods of pain relief; how the patient should prepare for the procedure; and details of what the patient might experience during or after the procedure including common and serious side effects;

- for each option, explanations of the likely benefits and the probabilities of success; and discussion of any serious or frequently occurring risks, and of any lifestyle changes which may be caused by, or necessitated by, the treatment;

- advice about whether a proposed treatment is experimental;

- how and when the patient's condition and any side effects will be monitored or re-assessed;

---

[74] [1999] P.I.Q.R. P53; para. 6–116.
[75] February 1999, available at *www.gmc-uk.org*.

- the name of the doctor who will have overall responsibility for the treatment and, where appropriate, names of the senior members of his or her team;

- whether doctors in training will be involved, and the extent to which students may be involved in an investigation or treatment;

- a reminder that patients can change their minds about a decision at any time;

- a reminder that patients have a right to seek a second opinion;

- where applicable, details of costs or charges which the patient may have to meet.

Paragraph 13 states, *inter alia*, that a doctor should explain the probabilities of success, or the risk of failure of, or harm associated with options for treatment, using accurate data. Although GMC guidance does not have the force of law, nonetheless it is strong evidence of what amounts to good medical practice and hence responsible medical practice within the context of the *Bolam* test. As the profession becomes more pro-active in setting standards, whether in the area of information disclosure or any other aspect of practice, it will become easier to argue that a failure to conform to those standards constitutes negligence, at least in the absence of very good, and logical, reasons for not complying with them.[76]

(3) Asking questions

6–141   If a patient is only entitled to have volunteered the information that a reasonable doctor considers to be appropriate in the light of the practices adopted by other responsible medical practitioners, it might be thought that he would be able to elicit more information by asking direct questions. In *Hatcher v Black*[77] the defendant doctor deliberately lied to a patient because he did not want her to worry, telling her that there was no risk to her voice in the procedure that was to be performed when he knew that there was some slight risk. Denning L.J., in an instruction to a jury, said that the law only condemns a doctor when he falls short of the accepted standards of the profession, and pointed out that none of the medical witnesses had criticised the defendant: "They did not condemn him; nor should we." In *Sidaway v Bethlem Royal Hospital Governors*, however, Lord Bridge commented that:

> "... when questioned specifically by a patient of apparently sound mind about risks involved in a particular treatment proposed, the doctor's

---

[76] See Jones (1999) 7 Med. L. Rev. 103 where this argument is developed in more detail.
[77] *The Times*, July 2, 1954.

duty must, in my opinion, be to answer both truthfully and as fully as the questioner requires."[78]

Both Lord Diplock and Lord Templeman appeared to support this proposition.[79] Lord Bridge's dictum seems to preclude the judicially sanctioned white lie of *Hatcher v Black*, but it is not entirely clear what his Lordship meant by the phrase "as fully as the questioner requires." In *Lee v South West Thames Regional Health Authority* Sir John Donaldson M.R. suggested that a doctor has a discretion about the manner in which an answer to a patient's question should be given:

> "This duty is subject to the exercise of clinical judgment as to the terms in which the information is given and the extent to which, in the patient's interests, information should be withheld."[80]

The nature of the doctor's duty in response to questioning was considered   **6–142**
by the Court of Appeal in *Blyth v Bloomsbury Health Authority*.[81] The claimant was given an injection of the contraceptive drug Depo-Provera. She claimed that she was not given an adequate warning of the potential side-effects of the drug. The trial judge rejected the claimant's evidence that she had asked a series of specific questions, though he did accept that she had asked for some information and advice. The Court of Appeal reversed the decision that the defendants had been negligent, on the basis that the medical experts who gave evidence would not have given the claimant any more information than in fact she received, although no one suggested that information was withheld because it might have been harmful to the claimant. Kerr L.J. referred to the dicta of Lord Bridge and Lord Diplock in *Sidaway* and commented:

> "The question of what a plaintiff should be told in answer to a general enquiry cannot be divorced from the *Bolam* test, any more than when no such enquiry is made. In both cases the answer must depend upon the circumstances, the nature of the enquiry, the nature of the information which is available, its reliability, relevance, the condition of the patient, and so forth. Any medical evidence directed to what would be the proper answer in the light of responsible medical opinion and

---

[78] [1985] A.C. 871, 898.
[79] "No doubt, if the patient in fact manifested this attitude [of wanting to be fully informed of inherent risks] by means of questioning, the doctor would tell him whatever it was the patient wanted to know . . .," *ibid.* at 895, *per* Lord Diplock. It is not clear whether this was simply Lord Diplock's expectation of what in fact would happen, or whether he considered that the doctor would be under a legal duty to inform his patient. Lord Templeman said that a patient would be entitled to complain of a lack of information if he asked in vain for more information: *ibid.* at 902.
[80] [1985] 2 All E.R. 385, 389.
[81] (1987) reported at (1989) 5 P.N. 167; [1993] 4 Med. L.R. 151. See Bowen-Simpkins (1995) 1 *AVMA Medical & Legal Journal* 80 for discussion of the side-effects of Depo-Provera.

CONSENT TO TREATMENT

practice—that is to say the *Bolam* test—must in my view equally be placed in the balance in cases where the patient makes some enquiry, in order to decide whether the response was negligent or not . . . Indeed I am not convinced that the *Bolam* test is irrelevant even in relation to the question of what answers are properly to be given to specific enquiries, or that Lord Diplock or Lord Bridge intended to hold otherwise. It seems to me that there may always be grey areas, with differences of opinion, as to what are the proper answers to be given to any enquiry, even a specific one, in the particular circumstances of any case."[82]

Neill L.J. agreed that the *Bolam* test should apply, adding that neither Lord Bridge nor Lord Diplock had laid down a rule of law to the effect that where a patient asks questions a doctor is under an obligation to put the patient in possession of all the information on the subject which may have been available to the doctor. This decision may seem surprising in the light of the dicta in *Sidaway*,[83] and may leave patients wondering just what they have to do in order to obtain full and truthful information.[84]

6–143 It is arguable that a doctor who did not answer questions truthfully could be held liable in negligence even where there is a practice within the profession not to make full disclosure, on the basis that disclosure was so obviously necessary to an informed choice on the part of the patient that no reasonably prudent doctor would fail to make it.[85] Alternatively, it is possible that a deliberate lie might constitute a misrepresentation, vitiating the claimant's consent for the purpose of trespass to the person.[86] The difficulty

---

[82] *ibid.* at 173 and 157 respectively.

[83] See, however, the comment of Kennedy & Grubb, *Medical Law*, 3rd ed., 2000, p. 723 that it may be possible to interpret *Blyth* as a case concerned with how much knowledge about risks a doctor must have (to be measured by the standards of a reasonably competent doctor), rather than a case concerning how much information a doctor must give (assuming that the doctor has the information) when questioned by the patient, an interpretation which might preserve intact the force of the comments made by Lords Bridge, Diplock and Templeman in *Sidaway*.

[84] Sir John Donaldson M.R. commented in *Sidaway v Bethlem Royal Hospital Governors* [1984] Q.B. 493, 513 that the doctor's duty of disclosure had to take account of the patient's "true wishes" because "it by no means follows that the expression of a wish for full information either generally or specifically represents the reality of the patient's state of mind." The patient might simply be seeking reassurance. Does the patient who asks questions have to convince the doctor that he wants a truthful answer? Can the doctor assume, unless there is evidence to the contrary, that the patient wants to be told lies?

[85] *Sidaway v Bethlem Royal Hospital Governors* [1985] A.C. 871, 900, *per* Lord Bridge; paras 6–112 and 6–115. See also the GMC guidance, *Seeking patients' consent: the ethical considerations*, February 1999, para 9: "You must respond honestly to any questions the patient raises and, as far as possible, answer as fully as the patient wishes. In some cases, a patient may ask about other treatments that are unproven or ineffective. Some patients may want to know whether any of the risks or benefits of treatment are affected by the choice of institution or doctor providing the care. You must answer such questions as fully, accurately and objectively as possible."

[86] See the comment of Lord Donaldson M.R. in *Re T. (Adult: Refusal of Treatment)* [1993] Fam. 95, 115; and paras 6–038 and 6–039. See Montgomery (1988) 51 M.L.R. 245, 248 criticising the decision in *Blyth v Bloomsbury Health Authority* (1987) reported at (1989) 5 P.N. 167; [1993] 4 Med. L.R. 151.

with this argument, however, is that a misrepresentation as to the inherent risks of the treatment may not be interpreted as going to the *nature* of the procedure such as to render the patient's consent invalid.

In both Australia and New Zealand the courts have accepted that medical **6–144** practitioners must have some discretion as to the terms in which they deal with patients' questions. In *F. v R*[87] King C.J. said that if the claimant had asked a direct question the doctor would have had a duty to give full and frank advice. An express and seriously intended request for information would normally place the doctor under an obligation to give a truthful and careful answer. In *Rogers v Whitaker*[88] the High Court of Australia expressly rejected the application of the *Bolam* test when the patient asks questions, because even if a patient asked a direct question about the possible risks or complications, the making of that inquiry would logically be of little or no significance; medical opinion would determine whether the risk should or should not be disclosed and the express desire of the patient for information or advice would not alter that opinion or its legal significance. This provided a strong reason for rejecting the *Bolam* test:

> "The fact that the various majority opinions in *Sidaway*, for example, suggest that, over and above the opinion of a respectable body of medical practitioners, the questions of a patient should truthfully be answered (subject to therapeutic privilege) indicates a shortcoming in the *Bolam* approach. The existence of the shortcoming suggests that an acceptable approach in point of principle should recognise and attach significance to the relevance of a patient's questions. Even if a court were satisfied that a reasonable person in the patient's position would be unlikely to attach significance to a particular risk, the fact that the patient asked questions revealing concern about the risk would make the doctor aware that *this patient* did in fact attach significance to the risk. Subject to the therapeutic privilege, the question would therefore require a truthful answer."[89]

On the other hand, in *F. v R*. King C.J. recognised that there might be circumstances where reasonable care for the patient would justify or even require an evasive or less than fully candid answer even to a direct request, and the doctor may reasonably judge that a patient is merely seeking reassurance.[90] The claimant in *Smith v Auckland Hospital Board*[91] asked whether there was any risk involved in aortography, in which a catheter was introduced into the femoral artery and guided into the aorta for the purpose of obtaining an X-ray. He was given a reassuring answer but was not told

---

[87] (1983) 33 S.A.S.R. 189, 196 (S.C. of S. Aus.); see also *per* Legoe J. at 199, *per* Bollen J. at 207.
[88] (1992) 109 A.L.R. 625; [1993] 4 Med. L.R. 79; *Chappel v Hart* [1998] H.C.A. 55; (1998) 156 A.L.R. 517; [1999] Lloyd's Rep. Med. 223 (H.C. of Aust.).
[89] *ibid.* at 630–631.
[90] (1983) 33 S.A.S.R. 189, 192
[91] [1965] N.Z.L.R. 191 (N.Z.C.A.).

about the known risk of complications, which did in fact materialise and led ultimately to the amputation of his leg below the knee. The New Zealand Court of Appeal held the defendant liable on the basis that all the medical evidence indicated the defendant's answer fell below the appropriate standard. The normal practice in response to such a question was to disclose the risk, and the defendant had departed from that practice.[92]

6–145   In Canada it may be that a stricter test applies to a doctor's response to questions. In *Hopp v Lepp*[93] Laskin C.J.C. said that where a patient asks specific questions, not by way merely of general inquiry, the questions must be answered, even if they invite answers to merely possible risks. It is a question of fact how specific the questions are. In Ireland it has been said that the strictness of the duty of disclosure is such that there is no room for the operation of an "inquisitive patient" test, because its requirements are subsumed within the broader disclosure rule: "Current Irish law requires that the patient be informed of any material risk, whether he inquires or not, regardless of its infrequency."[94]

3. CAUSATION

6–146   One of the objections to using the tort of battery as the mechanism for ensuring that doctors disclose information concerning the risks of proposed treatment has been said to be that in battery the claimant does not have to prove causation. Thus, in *Chatterton v Gerson* Bristow J. said that:

> "When the claim is based on negligence the plaintiff must prove not only the breach of duty to inform but that had the duty not been broken she would not have chosen to have the operation. Where the claim is based on trespass to the person, once it is shown that the consent is unreal, then what the plaintiff would have decided if she had been given the information which would have prevented vitiation of the reality of her consent is irrelevant."[95]

---

[92] "What is a proper answer will vary according to the circumstances of each case and it cannot always be said—especially when a patient is asking questions of his doctor—that the doctor is bound to give a full, complete and true answer. Much may depend on the effect of the answer on the health of the patient," *ibid.* at 198, *per* Barrowclough C.J.; see also Turner J. at 205 stating that a proper response must be measured by what other competent and experienced doctors would consider appropriate in the circumstances.

[93] (1980) 112 D.L.R. (3d) 67, 77 (S.C.C.); *Zimmer v Ringrose* (1981) 124 D.L.R. (3d) 214, 221 (Alta C.A.).

[94] *Geoghegan v Harris* [2000] 3 I.R. 536, 563 *per* Kearns J.

[95] [1981] Q.B. 432, 442–443; *cf. Koehler v Cook* (1975) 65 D.L.R. (3d) 766 (B.C.S.C.) where the defendant was held liable in trespass for non-disclosure of the risk of loss of smell, and Dryer J. went on to consider the causation issue, concluding that the claimant would have declined the operation to cure migraine headaches if she had known about the risk. This case must now be read in the light of *Reibl v Hughes* (1980) 114 D.L.R. (3d) 1.

This is considered to be unfair to defendants because the claimant could in theory succeed in an action where, even if the risks had been disclosed in advance of treatment, the claimant would nonetheless have agreed to proceed and would therefore have sustained the very same injuries as a result of the materialisation of an inherent risk of the treatment.[96] It was this problem that led Bristow J. to assert that "justice requires that in order to vitiate the reality of consent there must be a greater failure of communication between doctor and patient than that involved in a breach of duty if the claim is based on negligence."[97] It could be argued, however, that since consent to medical treatment is essentially concerned with the patient's right to exercise a choice about whether to accept or forego a particular treatment, the *reality* of that consent is intrinsically linked to the question of what the patient would have chosen to do had he been informed of the risks. If the information would not have altered his decision to accept treatment his consent was "real," whereas if disclosure of the risks would have caused him to change his mind about proceeding with the treatment his consent was not "real" and accordingly should be considered invalid. This approach would build the causation issue into the whole question of the reality of the patient's consent, and thus remove one of the objections to employing the tort of battery in this area. This argument does not appear to have been presented in any case where the problem has arisen, although the courts' clear hostility in this country to the use of actions in battery against doctors would probably lead to its rejection. On the other hand, where the defendant mistakenly fails to obtain the patient's consent, or exceeds the consent given, the present interpretation of "real consent" does not allow the defendant to plead that the patient would, in any event, have consented if he had known the situation.[98]

In battery the test of remoteness of damage is the directness of the damage.   **6–147**
The defendant is liable for all the consequences which are a direct result of the tortious act whether they are foreseeable or not. If no damage has been sustained the claimant is still entitled to nominal damages, because battery is actionable *per se*. Accordingly, in *Allan v New Mount Sinai Hospital*[99] the defendant anaesthetist was held liable for the claimant's rare and unforeseeable reaction to the mishap occasioned by the needle slipping out of the claimant's vein, even though he was not negligent and in negligence the damage would probably have been regarded as too remote.[1]

---

[96] In *Brushett v Cowan* (1987) 40 D.L.R. (4th) 488 the defendant was held liable in battery for performing a bone biopsy without the patient's consent, although a claim in negligence failed because a reasonable patient would have consented to the biopsy had she been informed about it. The decision on battery was reversed on the facts, without affecting this point: see (1990) 69 D.L.R. (4th) 743 (Newfd. C.A.).

[97] *Chatterton v Gerson* [1981] Q.B. 432, 442.

[98] See also Dugdale and Stanton, *Professional Negligence*, 3rd ed., 1998, para. 11.59 arguing that in any case where the claimant seeks substantial, as opposed to nominal, damages it should be open to the doctor to show that the damage would have been suffered irrespective of the failure to obtain consent.

[99] (1980) 109 D.L.R. (3d) 634 (Ont. H.C.); see para. 6–010.

[1] "In negligence, the damage that occurs must be within the risk created by the negligent conduct or else there is no responsibility for it because it is too remote. In battery, however,

6–148   Where the claimant brings an action in negligence for breach of the doctor's duty to provide information it is clear that he does have to establish causation by proving that had he been given a proper warning he would not have accepted the treatment.[2] Although this will normally depend upon evidence given by the claimant, and the court's assessment of the claimant's credibility, there is no rule of law that a claimant must give evidence personally about what would or would not have happened if she had been properly informed of the facts before making a decision.[3] In both *Chatterton v Gerson*[4] and *Hills v Potter*[5] the claimants failed to convince the court that even if they had been given a fuller explanation about the risks of the procedure they would have declined to undergo it. In each of these cases the court adopted a subjective test for causation: would *this* claimant have accepted the treatment if adequately informed?[6] In *Reibl v Hughes*,[7] on the other hand, the Supreme Court of Canada considered that a subjective test was too favourable to claimants, creating the risk of self-serving testimony from patients who, with the benefit of hindsight, would invariably claim that they would have declined treatment had they known about the risks.[8] In order to deal with this perceived problem the Court applied an objective test of causation: would a reasonable person in the claimant's position have declined the treatment? This makes it more difficult for the claimant to overcome the causation hurdle, because even where he can demonstrate that he would not have accepted treatment the action will fail if a reasonable person in his position would have gone ahead. The Court recognised that this could place a premium on the doctor's assessment of the desirability of the treatment being undertaken, but concluded that merely because the recommended treatment was, objectively, medically appropriate it did not necessarily follow that a reasonable person in the claimant's position would agree to it, because the test takes account of the patient's particular situation. Thus in *Reibl v*

(n.1 contd.) any and all damage is recoverable, if it results from the wrongful act, whether it is foreseeable or not. The limitation devices of foresight and remoteness are not applicable to intentional torts, as they are in negligence law," *ibid*. at 643, *per* Linden J.

[2] See *Bolam v Friern Hospital Management Committee* [1957] 2 All E.R. 118, 124. Thus, if the claimant already has the knowledge upon which he could base an informed decision about whether to accept treatment, the action will fail for lack of causation, even though he did not receive the information from his own doctor: *Davidson v Connaught Laboratories* (1980) 14 C.C.L.T. 251, 272 (Ont. H.C.).

[3] *Webb v Barclays Bank plc and Portsmouth Hospitals NHS Trust* [2001] EWCA Civ 1141; [2002] P.I.Q.R. P61; [2001] Lloyd's Rep. Med. 500 at [42].

[4] [1981] Q.B. 432, 445.

[5] [1983] 3 All E.R. 716, 728.

[6] Leonard J. also applied a subjective test in *Blyth v Bloomsbury Health Authority* (1985, QBD; unreported); rev'd on other grounds (1987) CA, reported at (1989) 5 P.N. 167; [1993] 4 Med. L.R. 151. See also *Moyes v Lothian Health Board* [1990] 1 Med. L.R. 463, 468.

[7] (1980) 114 D.L.R. (3d) 1, 15–17.

[8] *White v Turner* (1981) 120 D.L.R. (3d) 269, 286 (Ont. H.C.); affirmed (1982) 12 D.L.R. (4th) 319 (Ont. C.A.). Note that all testimony given by a claimant or defendant is potentially open to the criticism that it is self-serving. This is not necessarily a reason for adopting an objective test: *Ellis v Wallsend District Hospital* (1989) 17 N.S.W.L.R. 553, 581, *per* Samuels J.A. (N.S.W.C.A.). Moreover, all reasoning about causation which relies upon the "but for" test is necessarily hypothetical and depends upon the drawing of appropriate inferences from other facts: see para. 5–018.

Hughes the claimant's action succeeded because although without the operation he had a continuing risk of suffering a stroke, the operation itself carried a 10 per cent risk of stroke (which in fact materialised) and a 4 per cent risk of death, and the claimant said that if he had known about these risks he would have delayed the operation in order to earn his full pension benefits at work. There was, moreover, no emergency making the surgery imperative, and the claimant was also under the mistaken impression that the operation would cure his headaches.

More generally, however, the effect of the objective test applied to causa- **6–149** tion in Canada has been that even where claimants are successful in establishing a breach of the duty of disclosure, the action is much more likely to fail on causation than to succeed.[9] Most of the cases in which claimants have succeeded have involved procedures that could more readily be described as "elective" such as sterilisation[10] or cosmetic surgery,[11] where the balance of

---

[9] Robertson (1991) 70 Can. Bar Rev. 423, 428 points out that even where the claimant succeeds on breach of duty, in 56% of the cases decided in the 10 years following *Reibl v Hughes* the claimant failed to establish causation. See further Dugdale (1986) 2 P.N. 108–111; Jones (1999) 7 Med. L. Rev. 103, 121–123. Actions have failed on the grounds of causation in: *Bickford v Stiles* (1981) 128 D.L.R. (3d) 516 (N.B.S.C.), where the incidence of vocal cord paralysis from mediastinoscopy was 0.5% and the alternative possible diagnosis was cancer; *Considine v Camp Hill Hospital* (1982) 133 D.L.R. (3d) 11 (N.S.S.C.), where there was a risk of permanent incontinence of between 1% to 4% in the performance of a prostate operation; *Grey v Webster* (1984) 14 D.L.R. (4th) 706, where evidence of failure rates for tubal ligation ranged from 1 in 300–500, or 2 to 5 per 1,000; *Stamos v Davies* (1985) 21 D.L.R. (4th) 507, 521 (Ont. H.C.), where there was a risk of damage to the spleen during the performance of a lung biopsy, but provisional diagnosis was of a life-threatening disease with a high mortality rate; *Poole v Morgan* [1987] 3 W.W.R. 217, 263 (Alta. Q.B.), where there were risks inherent in laser treatment of the claimant's eye; *Arndt v Smith* [1994] 8 W.W.R. 568 (B.C.S.C.); affirmed (1997) 148 D.L.R. (4th) 48 (S.C.C.), where the fact that the parents did not want an ultrasound scan of the developing foetus indicated "less concern with risks in foresight than in hindsight"; *Petty v McKay* (1979) 10 C.C.L.T. 85 (B.C.S.C.); *Hajgato v London Health Association* (1982) 36 O.R. (2d) 669, 680; *Diack v Bardsley* (1983) 25 C.C.L.T. 159, 170 (B.C.S.C.), affirmed (1984) 31 C.C.L.T. 308 (B.C.C.A.); *Ferguson v Hamilton Civic Hospitals* (1983) 144 D.L.R. (3d) 214; affirmed (1985) 18 D.L.R. (4th) 638 (Ont. C.A.); *Bucknam v Kostuik* (1983) 3 D.L.R. (4th) 99 (Ont. H.C.); *Casey v Provan* (1984) 11 D.L.R. (4th) 708 (Ont. H.C.); *Kueper v McMullin* (1986) 30 D.L.R. (4th) 408 (N.B.C.A.); *Rocha v Harris* (1987) 36 D.L.R. 410 (B.C.C.A.); *Lachambre v Nair* [1989] 2 W.W.R. 749 (Sask. Q.B.); *Kitchen v McMullen* (1989) 62 D.L.R. (4th) 481 (N.B.C.A.); *Ciarlariello v Schacter* (1993) 100 D.L.R. (4th) 609, 623 (S.C.C.), where the statistical risk of a serious adverse reaction to angiography was far less than the risk of death from the non-treatment of a subarachnoid haemorrhage; *Meyer Estate v Rogers* (1991) 78 D.L.R (4th) 307 (Ont. H.C.), where there was a risk of severe allergic reaction during an intravenous pyelogram of 1 in 2,000 and a risk of death of between 1 in 40,000 and 1 in 100,000.

[10] *Dendaas v Yackel* (1980) 109 D.L.R. (3d) 455, para. 6–198; *Painter v Rae* [1998] 8 W.W.R. 717 (Man Q.B.) where there was a small but material risk of injury to the bowel during a postpartum tubal ligation. The claimant succeeded on causation since she had never undergone surgery before, was apprehensive about the anaesthetic, and she knew that there was an alternative, namely that her husband could have a vasectomy.

[11] *White v Turner* (1981) 120 D.L.R. (3d) 269 (Ont. H.C.); affirmed (1982) 12 D.L.R. (4th) 319 (Ont. C.A.), on breast reduction surgery; *Normand v Stranc* [1994] 10 W.W.R. 175 (Man. Q.B.), where the failure to inform the claimant of the risks of infection and scarring following breast reduction surgery was held to be negligent, though the action failed on causation; *Hollis v Dow Corning Corp.* (1993) 103 D.L.R. (4th) 520, 547 (B.C.C.A.), where it was held that a reasonable woman in the claimant's position would not have consented to

risks between the recommended treatment and the alternative treatments (or the alternative of foregoing any treatment) are more finely balanced, and the medical justification for proceeding is less overwhelming.[12] Similarly, it may be easier for a claimant to succeed on causation when the operation was designed to relieve chronic pain, where the claimant's discomfort is highly subjective, particularly where there were other treatment options which carried a lower, or no, risk.[13]

6–150   The objective test is open to the criticism that it represents a departure from the principle that the individual patient is entitled to make the decision about whether to accept or reject medical treatment, a principle which the doctor's duty of disclosure is intended to serve.[14] If the success of the claimant's action depends upon what a "reasonable" patient would have

---

(n.11 contd.) implantation of breast prostheses if warned of the possibility of rupture of the implants inside her body, particularly since the claimant did not require and had not actively sought out the surgery. [The Supreme Court of Canada subsequently held in *Hollis* that in products liability actions a subjective test of causation should apply: (1995) 129 D.L.R. (4th) 609, see para. 6–151]; *cf. Petty v McKay* (1979) 10 C.C.L.T. 85 (B.C.S.C.) where it was held that the claimant, an "exotic dancer," would have gone ahead with the operation (a modified abdominoplasty) even if the risks had been disclosed because she had a desire to attain a state of cosmetic perfection; *Cherewayko v Grafton* [1993] 3 W.W.R. 604 (Man. Q.B.), where the claimant would have proceeded with breast augmentation even if fully informed about the risks.

[12] See, *e.g., Rawlings v Lindsey* (1982) 20 C.C.L.T. 301, in which there was a failure to disclose a 5 to 10% risk of nerve damage and resultant numbness to the face following wisdom tooth extraction; the action succeeded on causation because the teeth were not giving any trouble at the time, they were merely superfluous; *cf. Diack v Bardsley* (1983) 25 C.C.L.T. 159 (B.C.S.C.) where the teeth were causing problems. In *Berezowski-Aitken v McGregor* [1998] 8 W.W.R. 322 (Man Q.B.) there was a negligent failure to warn of the remote risk of bowel damage, leading to infertility, during the performance of a dilatation and curettage (D&C). The claimant succeeded on causation because there was a reasonable alternative to the D&C, namely the conservative option of simply waiting.

[13] *Schanczi v Singh* [1988] 2 W.W.R. 465 (Alta. Q.B.), where the claimant contracted arachnoiditis (inflammation of one of the membranes sheathing the spinal cord) which was caused by the dye used in the diagnostic myelogram, followed by the surgery (a disectomy performed in the lumbar spine). The option of conservative treatment had not been explored; *Haughian v Paine* (1987) 37 D.L.R. (4th) 624 (Sask. C.A.), where there was a small risk (c. 1 in 500) of paralysis associated with a laminectomy and discotomy, but the alternative treatment, conservative management, carried no risk; *Forgie v Mason* (1986) 30 D.L.R. (4th) 548, 559 (N.B.C.A.); *cf. Thibault v Fewer* [2002] 1 W.W.R. 204 (Man Q.B.) in which the action failed on causation because the claimant had suffered with constant pain for 20 years and had continued to seek relief from it; she had elected to undergo surgical procedures in the past which carried a higher risk of complications than the procedure in question; the pain had been so bad that she had considered suicide on at least two occasions; and she also continued to take high doses of medication for the pain on a long-term basis, which itself carried serious risk of complications. See also the English case of *Newbury v Bath District Health Authority* (1998) 47 B.M.L.R. 138, QBD, where Ebsworth J. held that the claimant would have agreed to accept the risk of neurological damage from spinal surgery, put at between 1 and 5%, because she was "was desperate for relief from pain." The operations in the three English cases of *Sidaway v Bethlem Royal Hospital Governors* [1985] A.C. 871, *Chatterton v Gerson* [1981] Q.B. 432 and *Hills v Potter* [1983] 3 All E.R. 716 all involved treatment for chronic pain. Only in *Sidaway* did the claimant succeed on the causation issue.

[14] *Ellis v Wallsend District Hospital* (1989) 17 N.S.W.L.R. 553, 560, *per* Kirby P. (N.S.W.C.A.); *Rosenberg v Percival* [2001] H.C.A. 18; (2001) 178 A.L.R. 577 at [145] *per* Kirby J, quoted at para. 6–126 above.

done, then it can hardly be said that the patient can reject treatment "for reasons which are rational, or irrational, or for no reason."[15] Moreover, it is doubtful whether the objective test is, strictly speaking, a test of *causation* which, applying the general principles of the tort of negligence, is a question of whether *this* damage would have been suffered by *this* claimant but for the defendant's breach of duty.[16] What, for example, is the position where a reasonable patient in the claimant's position would have declined treatment, but nonetheless the evidence indicates that the claimant would not have declined treatment—does the action fail in these circumstances? What if, as with cosmetic surgery, for example, many reasonable people would refuse surgery when told about the risks but others, arguably equally reasonable, would accept it despite the risks?[17]

There have been occasional attempts to move away from the objective test in Canada. Thus, in *Buchan v Ortho Pharmaceutical (Canada) Ltd*[18] the Ontario Court of Appeal held that the objective test was "inappropriate" to the disclosure of information by a manufacturer in a products liability case, at least where the product was an oral contraceptive, because the selection of a method of preventing unwanted pregnancy in the case of a healthy woman was a matter, not of medical treatment, but of personal choice, and it was not unreasonable that notice of a serious potential hazard to users of oral contraceptives could influence her selection of another method of birth control. The court considered that a subjective test should be applied. This view was endorsed by the Supreme Court of Canada in *Hollis v Dow Corning Corp.*,[19] a case where the claimant suffered damage following the rupture of a silicone breast implant. Whilst the objective causation test was appropriate to the disclosure of information by doctors to patients, manufacturers were in a different category because they could be expected to act in a more self-interested manner. There was a greater likelihood that a manufacturer would overemphasise the value of a product, and underemphasise the risk, and it was therefore highly desirable from a policy perspective to hold manufacturers to a strict standard

6–151

---

[15] *Sidaway v Bethlem Royal Hospital Governors* [1985] A.C. 871, 904, *per* Lord Templeman. See also *per* T.A. Gresson J. in *Smith v Auckland Hospital Board* [1965] N.Z.L.R. 191, 219; *Lepp v Hopp* (1979) 98 D.L.R. (3d) 464, 470, *per* Prowse J.A.; affirmed (1980) 112 D.L.R. (3d) 67 (S.C.C.).

[16] See, *e.g.*, *McWilliams v Sir William Arroll & Co Ltd* [1962] 1 W.L.R. 295, para. 5–007; Nicholson (1990) 6 P.N. 83, 84–85.

[17] See *Hollis v Dow Corning Corp.* (1993) 103 D.L.R. (4th) 520, 525, *per* Southin J.A. A similar problem arises in the context of termination of pregnancy where it may be difficult to find any common or shared values, and there may be more than one reasonable choice. See *Mickle v Salvation Army Grace Hospital* (1998) 166 D.L.R. (4th) 743, 758–761, (Ont. Ct.), where alleged the negligence concerned non-disclosure of the risk that the foetus carried by a pregnant woman could be handicapped, and the causation issue, applying an objective test, depended not on whether the claimant would have had an abortion, but whether a reasonable woman in her circumstances would have had an abortion. On the facts, it was held that in a case involving relatively minor physical disabilities (asymmetrical limb development) a reasonable woman would not have chosen a termination of a planned pregnancy.

[18] (1986) 25 D.L.R. (4th) 658, 685–7 (Ont. C.A.).

[19] (1995) 129 D.L.R. (4th) 609; Black and Klimchuck (1996) 75 Can. Bar Rev. 355.

of warning consumers of the dangerous side-effects of their products, by applying a subjective causation test.[20]

6–152   In *Reynard v Carr*[21] it was held that, although ordinarily the claimant has the burden of proving that if properly informed he would not have elected for the treatment, where the want of information is due not just to non-disclosure of the risk, but to culpable ignorance of its very existence, the claimant did not have to prove that he would not have consented if the doctor had known of the risk and had explained the nature of the risk to him. In *Arndt v Smith*[22] the Supreme Court of Canada re-affirmed, by a 6–3 majority, that the proper test of causation in an action against a medical practitioner was that laid down in *Reibl v Hughes*, namely the "modified objective test" of whether a reasonable person, having the claimant's particular characteristics would have proceeded with the treatment had all material and special risks been disclosed.[23]

6–153   Where the defendant's breach of duty consists of a failure to advise the patient, not simply about the risks of the treatment undertaken, but of any alternative procedure and the risks associated with that, the claimant will have to prove both that she would have opted for the alternative procedure (applying the "modified objective test") and also that the alternative procedure would probably have produced a better outcome than the treatment she has actually undergone.[24]

---

[20] *ibid.* at 634, *per* La Forest J. The reference to the standard of warning is slightly puzzling in this context, given that the issue under consideration was the test to be applied to assessing causation. The explanation can be seen in La Forest J.'s citation (at 633), with approval, of the reasoning of Robins J.A. in *Buchan v Ortho Pharmaceuticals (Canada) Ltd* (1986) 25 D.L.R. (4th) 658, 687: "The suggestion that the determination of this causation issue other than by way of an objective test would place an undue burden on drug manufacturers is answered by noting that drug manufacturers are in a position to escape all liability by the simple expedient of providing a clear and forthright warning of the dangers inherent in the use of their products of which they know or ought to know. In my opinion, it is sound in principle and in policy to adopt an approach which facilitates meaningful consumer choice and promotes market-place honesty by encouraging full disclosure. This is preferable to invoking evidentiary burdens that serve to exonerate negligent manufacturers as well as manufacturers who would rather risk liability than provide information which might prejudicially affect their volume of sales." For discussion of the causation test to be applied to the actions of a "learned intermediary", when the manufacturer has been found to be in breach of a duty to warn, see paras 8–044 *et seq.*

[21] (1983) 30 C.C.L.T. 42 (B.C.S.C.). See also *Grey v Webster* (1984) 14 D.L.R. (4th) 706 (N.B.Q.B) where it was said that a subjective test should be applied to the disclosure of the risk that an operation (sterilisation) might not succeed in its purpose, whereas the objective test applied to the non-disclosure of the risk of additional harm being inflicted by the operation. Nonetheless, the action failed on causation; see para. 6–202, n. 55.

[22] (1997) 148 D.L.R. (4th) 48 (S.C.C.).

[23] The "reasonable person" must be "taken to possess the patient's reasonable beliefs, fears, desires and expectations", but "purely subjective fears *which are not related to the material risks* should not be taken into account in applying the modified objective test": *ibid.* at 54 and 55 *per* Cory J. (original emphasis). Thus, the honestly held, but idiosyncratic and unreasonable or irrational beliefs of patients are excluded from the equation: *ibid.* at 57. For criticism, see Honoré (1998) 114 L.Q.R. 52; Nelson and Caulfied (1998) 32 U.B.C.L. Rev. 353.

[24] *Seney v Crooks* (1998) 166 D.L.R. (4th) 337 (Alta. C.A.). Though note that Conrad J.A. suggested, at [99] and [101] that there was a good argument that once the claimant proves that she would have opted for the alternative treatment, the burden of proof should shift to the defendant to establish that it would not have made any difference.

The courts in this country have not considered whether an objective test **6–154** should be applied to cases of non-disclosure,[25] and have been content to apply the subjective test. It may be that there is little difference in practice between the two approaches, since even under the subjective test the court will not simply accept uncritically the claimant's evidence that he would have declined treatment. The court must weigh the claimant's evidence against objective criteria in order to assess its credibility, and if a hypothetical reasonable patient would have accepted the treatment, given the balance of risks involved, this will tend to undermine the claimant's credibility.[26] This point was made by Samuels J.A. in *Ellis v Wallsend District Hospital*,[27] in which the New South Wales Court of Appeal adopted a subjective test of causation. In assessing the evidence the court would have regard to evidence about the claimant's temperament, the course of any prior treatment for the same or a similar condition, and the nature of the relationship between patient and doctor, including pre-eminently the degree of trust that the patient placed in the doctor. Clearly, the greater the trust the greater the likelihood that the patient would have accepted the doctor's advice to undergo the treatment.[28] Finally, the extent to which the procedure was elective or imposed by circumstantial exigency, and the nature and degree of the risk involved will also be relevant.[29] All of these factors could be relevant to an objective test which takes into account the claimant's particular situation.

---

[25] Although see *Hills v Potter* [1983] 3 All E.R. 716 where Hirst J. concluded that the claimant's action failed on causation whether the test was subjective or objective.

[26] "I wholeheartedly accept that in retrospect she sincerely believes that she would have so declined. But, having regard to the evidence as to the gravity of her condition, I think it is more likely than not that she would have agreed to go ahead with the operation notwithstanding," *per* Hirst J. in *Hills v Potter* [1983] 3 All E.R. 716, 728. Similarly in *Chatterton v Gerson* [1981] Q.B. 432, 445 Bristow J. commented that: ". . . I would not have been satisfied that if properly informed Miss Chatterton would have chosen not to have it. The whole picture on the evidence is of a lady desperate for pain relief." In *Sidaway v Bethlem Royal Hospital Governors* [1985] A.C. 871 the trial judge, Skinner J., did conclude that the claimant would have declined treatment had she known about the risks.

[27] (1989) 17 N.S.W.L.R. 553 (N.S.W.C.A.); Nicholson (1990) 6 P.N. 83. It is clear that in Australia the test of causation is subjective: *Chappel v Hart* [1998] H.C.A. 55; (1998) 156 A.L.R. 517; [1999] Lloyd's Rep. Med. 223 (H.C. of Aust.); *Rosenberg v Percival* [2001] H.C.A. 18; (2001) 178 A.L.R. 577 at [24] and [87]. See also *Gover v State of South Australia* (1985) 39 S.A.S.R. 543, 566; *H. v Royal Alexandra Hospital for Children* [1990] 1 Med. L.R. 297, 324. In *Smith v Auckland Hospital Board* [1965] N.Z.L.R. 191 the New Zealand Court of Appeal apparently supported a subjective test of causation.

[28] In *Moyes v Lothian Health Board* [1990] 1 Med. LR 463, 468 the pursuer failed to establish that she would have declined diagnostic angiography had she been given a full warning of the risks, partly because in her evidence she had emphasised the trust that she had in the neurosurgeon's experience and judgment. The pursuer accepted that any general anaesthetic posed a risk, which she estimated (wrongly) was about 5%, when the total risk from the angiography and the anaesthetic was much lower than this. Given that she was prepared to accept a 5% risk it was difficult to conclude that she would have rejected the angiography procedure had she been informed of the much lower risk associated with it. Moreover, she appeared to have failed to take into account the risk of not having a potentially serious disease diagnosed if she had declined the angiography.

[29] (1989) 17 N.S.W.L.R. 553, 581, citing Robertson (1981) 97 L.Q.R. 102, 122.

6–155   In *Smith v Barking, Havering and Brentwood Health Authority*[30] the claimant had undergone an operation on her spine at the age of nine to drain a cyst in her spinal cord. This had been causing pain associated with mild quadriparesis. Following the operation the claimant's symptoms abated and she was able to live a normal life for nine years. When she was 18 she began to experience symptoms again. The defendant neurosurgeon considered that a further operation was advisable in the hope of arresting the progress of the condition. Without the operation the claimant's condition would have continued to deteriorate such that within three months she would have been in a wheelchair and within a further six months she would have been tetraplegic. The second operation carried a very real risk of an unsuccessful outcome. In about 50 per cent of cases there was some temporary arrest of the condition, and in the other 50 per cent there was some worsening of the condition. The operation was unsuccessful, and the claimant suffered immediate and permanent tetraplegia. It was common ground that the neurosurgeon should have warned the claimant about the risks involved, and that he had failed to do so. Hutchison J. said that the question to be asked was: if this claimant had been given the advice that she should have been given, would she have decided to undergo the operation or not? In other words, a subjective test of causation should apply, but this must be mediated by objective considerations:

> "However, there is a peculiar difficulty involved in this sort of case—not least for the plaintiff herself—in giving, after the adverse outcome is known, reliable answers as to what she would have decided before the operation had she been given proper advice as to the risks inherent in it. Accordingly, it would, in my judgment, be right in the ordinary case to give particular weight to the objective assessment. If everything points to the fact that a reasonable plaintiff, properly informed, would have assented to the operation, the assertion from the witness box, made after the adverse outcome is known, in a wholly artificial situation and in the knowledge that the outcome of the case depends upon the assertion being maintained, does not carry great weight unless there are extraneous or additional factors to substantiate it. By extraneous or additional factors I mean, and I am not doing more than giving examples, religious or some other firmly held convictions; particular social or domestic considerations justifying a decision not in accordance with what, objectively, seems the right one; assertions made in the immediate aftermath of the operation made in a context other than that of a possible claim for damages; in other words some particular factor which suggests that the plaintiff had grounds for not doing what a reasonable person in her situation might be expected to have done. Of course, the less confidently the judge reaches the conclusion as to what objectively the reasonable patient

---

[30]   (1988), [1994] 5 Med. L.R. 285.

might be expected to have decided, the more readily will he be persuaded by her subjective evidence."[31]

Hutchison J. concluded that there was nothing that differentiated the claimant from an ordinary reasonable patient. She would have agreed to have the operation because: (a) if nothing was done she would quite quickly become totally disabled; (b) the risk to which the operation exposed her, if unsuccessful, was not a risk of something worse than she was going to have to experience anyway, merely an earlier onset of the condition; (c) the operation held out the prospect of a postponement of the total disability for a significant period; (d) the claimant would have been influenced by the fact that the surgeon, whom she trusted, had concluded that the chances of success were such as to justify attempting the operation. The approach to causation adopted in *Smith v Barking, Havering and Brentwood Health Authority* suggests that it would probably be rare for a claimant to succeed on the subjective test but fail on the objective test.[32]

In *Chester v Afshar*[33] there was a dispute between the patient and the doctor   **6–156**
as to whether the claimant had been informed about the risk of developing cauda equina syndrome as a consequence of surgery on her spine to deal with back pain. The defendant estimated this risk at 0.9 per cent, and it was common ground that, acting in accordance with good medical practice, the defendant should have warned the claimant of this risk. The only question was whether she was in fact informed. The judge held that the claimant's version of events was probably correct, taking into account a number of factors: (1) the claimant was an intelligent and articulate woman whose work (as a journalist) was likely to have developed her abilities to absorb and retain information; (2) for the claimant it was a unique and extremely important event, whereas for the defendant it was one of many; (3) her description of the conversation had the ring of truth about it, and was unlikely to be the product of invention or reconstruction; (4) at an early stage after the operation she was complaining about not having been told about the risks; (5) before the consultation, the claimant was clearly averse to surgery, and anxious to avoid it if possible; (6) the operation was not a matter of urgency; (7) it was extremely improbable that if the claimant had been adequately informed about the risks she would have agreed to the surgery so soon after the consultation (three days later), which effectively prevented her from taking a second or even a third opinion. This was the position, said the judge, whether one applied the subjective test of what this individual claimant would have done, or whether one tested the claimant's subjective evidence against the objective criterion of what a reasonable patient in the claimant's position would have done. The Court of Appeal found the judge's reasoning on this issue "compelling".

In some instances the claimant will have been warned about some, but not   **6–157**
all, of the risks associated with the procedure. If the combined, total risk of

---

[31] *ibid.* at 289.
[32] This did occur in *Considine v Camp Hill Hospital* (1982) 133 D.L.R. (3d) 11 (N.S.S.C.).
[33] [2002] EWCA Civ 724; [2003] Q.B. 356.

adverse consequences would have led the claimant to refuse treatment, but he was warned about the specific risk which has materialised, does the action fail on causation on the basis that the claimant was aware of the specific risk and agreed to the procedure? In *Moyes v Lothian Health Board*[34] the pursuer suffered a stroke while undergoing an angiography, which had been recommended to diagnose the cause of a severe facial pain. This involved injecting a contrast medium into the cerebral blood vessels to render them opaque for the purpose of performing an X-ray. Angiography carries a degree of risk, even in a healthy patient, of about 0.2 per cent to 0.3 per cent of significant neurological symptoms being caused (which included the risk of stroke). If the procedure is carried out under general anaesthetic, there is the additional, though small, risk inherent in the anaesthetic procedure. Specific problems, such as hypersensitivity to the contrast medium may increase the risk. If the patient is known to be hypersensitive the risk of an allergic reaction can be reduced by the administration of premedication. With these precautions the additional risk of neurological complications due to a hypersensitive reaction is about 0.2 per cent to 0.3 per cent, effectively doubling the normal risk. The pursuer claimed that she should have been warned of the risk of stroke inherent in the angiography procedure, a risk which she claimed was increased by her alleged hypersensitivity and her history of migraine. The defender claimed that he did give a general warning about the risk of stroke, but did not warn her of any special risk associated with hypersensitivity or migraine. The medical evidence was that the pursuer's stroke was not caused by an hypersensitive reaction, but by an embolism which was one of the general risks of the procedure. The defender argued that even if it was proved that the pursuer had been hypersensitive it was irrelevant that she had not been warned about the added risk, since it was not this particular risk which had caused the stroke and there was therefore no causal connection between the failure to warn and the injury. The pursuer argued that even if the hypersensitivity did not cause the stroke, since it was one of the factors aggravating the risks she should have been told about it; if she had been told about the cumulative risks she would not have agreed to the angiography and therefore she would not have suffered the stroke (albeit that she was aware of the general risk of stroke associated with angiography). Lord Caplan accepted the pursuer's argument on this point:

> "The ordinary person who has to consider whether or not to have an operation is not interested in the exact pathological genesis of the various complications which can occur but rather in the nature and extent of the risk. The patient would want to know what chance there was of the operation going wrong and if it did what would happen. If we were to suppose a situation where an operation would give rise to a one per cent risk of serious complication in the ordinary case but where

---

[34] [1990] 1 Med. L.R. 463 (Court of Session, Outer House).

there could be four other special factors each adding a further one per cent to the risk, a patient to whom all five factors applied might have a five per cent risk rather than the one per cent risk of the average person. It is perfectly conceivable that a patient might be prepared to accept the risk of one in 100 but not be prepared to face up to a risk of one in 20. If a doctor contrary to established practice failed to warn the patient of the four special risks but did warn the patient of the standard risk and then the patient suffered complications caused physiologically by the standard risk factor rather [than] by one or other of the four special risk factors I do not think the doctor should escape the consequences of not having warned the patient of the added risks which that patient was exposed to. A patient might well with perfect reason consider that if there were five risk factors rather than one then the chance of one or other of these factors materialising was much greater. The coincidence that the damage which occurred was due to the particular factor in respect of which a warning was given does not alter the fact that the patient was not properly warned of the total risks inherent in the operation and thus could not make an informed decision as to whether or not to go through with it . . . If he had been given due warning he would not have risked suffering adverse complication from that particular operation and the fact that such complication occurred is causal connection enough to found a claim against the doctor."[35]

Thus, where there are cumulative risks some, but not all, of which the claimant has been informed about, and the claimant would have declined treatment had he known of the total risk, he does not have to prove that the specific risk which has materialised was the one about which he was not informed, *i.e.* a claimant could succeed on causation even though he was warned about the particular complication that has occurred.

It might be thought that if a claimant states frankly that she cannot now   **6–158** say what she would have done had she been informed of the risks, given that the risks have materialised and she is being asked to answer an hypothetical question in hindsight, the claim must fail on the basis that the claimant has failed to establish causation, on the balance of probabilities. There are two grounds for saying that this is not necessarily the case. First, where there is other evidence which the court can take into account in assessing what the claimant would have done, the proper inference may be that the claimant would have declined to proceed. In *McAllister v Lewisham and North Southwark Health Authority*[36] the claimant was not informed about the relatively high risks of serious consequences arising from a particular form of brain surgery. Nor, indeed, was she informed about the dangers of not having the operation, *i.e.* a cumulative two per cent per annum risk of suffering a brain haemorrhage, the consequences of which could be very

---

[35] *ibid.* at 467. The pursuer failed on causation for other reasons: see n. 28, above.
[36] [1994] 5 Med. L.R. 343, QBD.

serious. The claimant said that had she been informed of the risks she would have postponed the operation because she had just got a job which was important to her, and would not have wanted to risk losing it. Beyond that, she was unable to say what she would have done had she been given appropriate information, particularly since she now knew what the result would have been. The defendants argued that in these circumstances the judge had no basis on which to make a finding about whether the claimant would have proceeded or declined the operation after the initial period of postponement, but Rougier J. rejected this argument.[37] Looking at all the evidence his Lordship was able to conclude that she would probably have continued to decline the operation: she was a sensible person, and could make a rational judgment; the neurological deficit for which she had first consulted the doctor was not advancing rapidly; there was a slight chance of the progress of the deficit arresting itself spontaneously; her job, and the independence that it brought, would be just as precious as it had been before; and most importantly, given time to think, and given the fact that this was one of the most important decisions of her life, she would have taken a second opinion, and that second opinion would have been much more keenly aware of the dangers of operating and would not have been in favour of the operation. That would have tipped the balance of the claimant's mind.

6–159   The second, much more radical ground, applies where the claimant establishes, on the balance of probabilities, that she would have deferred the decision about whether to proceed. She may be unable in all honesty to say what she would ultimately have decided, given the hypothetical nature of the question, but according to the decision of the Court of Appeal in *Chester v Afshar*[38] that is irrelevant to the causation question. The claimant underwent spinal surgery for back pain and developed cauda equina syndrome, a recognised risk which she had not been informed about. She had had a consultation with the defendant on a Friday and underwent the surgery on the following Monday. The judge accepted that had she been warned of the risks the claimant would not have consented to the operation taking place on the Monday; she would have a sought a second or a third opinion. There was no urgency, and operating on the Monday did not allow time for a further opinion. The claimant did not argue that she would never at any time or under any circumstances have consented to surgery, and the judge found that it was impossible to say who she would have seen, what advice would have been given, and how she would have acted in response to that advice, although it was improbable that any surgery she might eventually have had would have been identical in circumstances to the operation she actually underwent. The Court of Appeal upheld the judge's conclusion that in these circumstances the claimant had established a sufficient causal link between

---

[37] "The fact that the plaintiff herself, fully conscious of the distortion to her thinking likely to be caused by hindsight, is reluctant to hypothesise, should not of itself preclude a judge from the attempt, provided there exists sufficient material upon which he can properly act," *ibid.* at 353.

[38] [2002] EWCA Civ 724; [2003] Q.B. 356.

the non-disclosure and the cauda equina syndrome. The defendant argued that the claimant must prove that, if she had been properly advised, she would never have undergone the surgery in question, either on the date on which it was performed or on any subsequent date. If the claimant would have undergone the procedure at some stage in the future then she would have faced the same inherent risks associated with it, and therefore the defendant's negligent failure to inform her of those risks would have been of no causative effect. The alternative view is that the materialisation of a small random risk inherent in a medical procedure producing injury to the claimant is the result of the particular time and circumstances in which the treatment was given (assuming that there is nothing which predisposes the particular patient to this risk), and therefore if treatment had been delayed to another occasion the probability is that the small inherent risk would not have materialised *on that occasion*, and thus the materialisation of the risk is causally linked to the negligent non-disclosure of risk. The defendant's argument seeks to define the claimant's damage as exposure to the risk itself, rather than the physical injury caused by the materialisation of the risk, but a willingness to expose oneself to the same potential risk in the future is not proof that the risk would probably have materialised, and therefore the defendant cannot say that his negligence made no difference. Just as a defendant is entitled to say that proof that he increased the risk of harm is not normally regarded[39] as proof that he caused the harm (bearing in mind that a careless breach of duty, by definition, involves exposing others to an unreasonable risk, and proof of breach is not treated as equivalent to proof of cause), so too a claimant can say that being willing to accept a risk in the future is not proof that damage would probably have occurred on a different occasion. Moreover, if the defendant's argument were correct and the claimant's loss consisted of being exposed to the risk of harm rather than the harm itself, this would also be true of those cases where the claimant can establish that she would never at any time have been willing to run the risk, and therefore the measure of damages should, logically, be determined by reference to the risk to which the claimant was exposed not the physical harm that has resulted from the materialisation of the risk. Of course, this is not how quantum is measured in such cases.

In holding that the defendant was responsible for the claimant's partial paralysis in *Chester v Afshar*, the Court of Appeal relied heavily on the reasoning of the majority of the High Court of Australia in *Chappel v Hart*.[40] The claimant in that case underwent surgery on her throat which carried an inherent risk of damage to her voice. She was not told about this risk, which materialised, despite the defendant exercising reasonable care in carrying out the operation, leaving the claimant with a weak voice. She said that if she had been warned of the risk she would have postponed the

6–160

---

[39] Except in situations where the principle in *Fairchild v Glenhaven Funeral Services Ltd* [2002] UKHL 22; [2003] 1 A.C. 32, para. 5–027 applies.
[40] [1998] H.C.A. 55; (1998) 156 A.L.R. 517; [1999] Lloyd's Rep. Med. 223; Cane (1999) 115 L.Q.R. 21.

surgery, and had it carried out by the most experienced surgeon with a reputation in the field. The defendant argued that there was no causal connection between the failure to warn and the injury because the surgery was inevitable at some point (the claimant's throat condition was gradually deteriorating) and carried the risk which eventuated. Thus, the claimant had not lost a real or valuable chance of the risk being diminished or avoided, and the injury resulted from a random risk that she was willing to accept. It was held that the failure to warn was the cause of the damage to the claimant's voice. The damage consisted of the physical injury resulting in the weak voice; it was not the loss of a chance or an opportunity to avoid that damage by going to a more experienced surgeon. Gaudron J said that:

> "Where there is a duty to inform it is, of course, necessary for a plaintiff to give evidence as to what would or would not have happened if the information in question had been provided. If that evidence is to the effect that the injured person would have acted to avoid or minimise the risk of injury, it is to apply sophistry rather than common sense to say that, although the risk of physical injury which came about called the duty of care into existence, breach of that duty did not cause or contribute to that injury, but simply resulted in the loss of an opportunity to pursue a different course of action."[41]

Kirby J. commented that the standard of disclosure in Australian law established by *Rogers v Whitaker*[42] was that the doctor has a duty to warn a patient of material risks, that is those risks to which a reasonable person in the patient's position would be likely attach significance, or if the medical practitioner is or should be reasonably aware that the particular patient, if warned of the risk, would be likely to attach significance to it. Though these standards may be onerous, they are established by law and when not complied with "it should occasion no surprise that legal consequences follow."[43]

6–161   The minority view in *Chappel v Hart* was that the defendant had not increased the risk to which the claimant was exposed. But as the Court of Appeal in *Chester v Afshar* pointed out, if it were only appropriate to focus on the risks of having the operation whenever it took place, the claimant could never succeed, even when she could show that she would never have had the operation, because the risks were always the same and the defendant did not increase them. But, said the Court, *McAllister v Lewisham and North Southwark Health Authority*[44] was rightly decided. The defendant changes the risk in a material way, because he "causes the patient to have an operation which she would not otherwise have had then and there and pos-

---

[41] *ibid.* at [9], cited by the Court of Appeal in *Chester v Afshar* [2002] EWCA Civ 724 at [31].
[42] (1992) 175 C.L.R. 479.
[43] [1998] H.C.A. 55 at [96].
[44] [1994] 5 Med. L.R. 343, QBD; para. 6–158.

sibly not at all. Logically, the correct comparison of risk is between having that operation on that occasion and not having it."[45] Moreover, the issue can be considered from the perspective of the nature of the defendant's duty. The Court of Appeal cited Lord Hoffmann's observation in *Environment Agency v Empress Car Co (Abertillery) Ltd*[46] that one cannot give a commonsense answer to a question of causation for the purpose of attributing responsibility under some rule without knowing the purpose and scope of the rule. The purpose of the rule requiring doctors to give information to their patients about risks was to enable the patient to exercise her right to choose whether or not to have the particular operation to which she is asked to give her consent. Thus:

> "The law is designed to require doctors properly to inform their patients of the risks attendant on their treatment and to answer questions put to them as to that treatment and its dangers, such answers to be judged in the context of good professional practice, which has tended to a greater degree of frankness over the years, with more respect being given to patient autonomy. The object is to enable the patient to decide whether or not to run the risks of having that operation at that time. If the doctor's failure to take that care results in her consenting to an operation to which she would not otherwise have given her consent, the purpose of that rule would be thwarted if he were not to be held responsible when the very risk about which he failed to warn her materialises and causes her an injury which she would not have suffered then and there."[47]

It followed that it would be unjust to hold that the effective cause of the claimant's injury was the random occurrence of the 1 to 2 per cent risk rather than the defendant's failure to bring that risk to her attention.

It is possible that even if the claimant fails to prove that if warned about **6–162** the risk of complications he would have declined the treatment, he may nonetheless be entitled to compensation for the shock and depression consequent upon discovering, without prior warning that a complication has occurred. In *Smith v Barking, Havering and Brentwood Health Authority*[48] an award of £3,000 general damages was made for the "shock and depression" caused on the claimant discovering, without any prior warning, that she had been rendered tetraplegic immediately following the operation. Similarly, in *Goorkani v Tayside Health Board*[49] it was held that had the pursuer known about the risk of becoming irreversibly infertile as a side-effect of drug therapy, he would still have taken the drug because the disease from which he was suffering, for which the drug was prescribed, could lead

---

[45] [2002] EWCA Civ 724 at [40].
[46] [1999] 2 A.C. 22 at 31.
[47] [2002] EWCA Civ 724 at [47].
[48] (1988), [1994] 5 Med. L.R. 285.
[49] [1991] 3 Med. L.R. 33 (Court of Session, Outer House).

to blindness. Nonetheless, damages of £2,500 were awarded for the "distress and anxiety" which arose from the pursuer's discovery of the risk of infertility associated with the treatment, and the fact that he was almost certainly infertile. Lord Cameron said that in assessing damages, it was proper to have regard to the concern which the pursuer had about his inability to father children, the frustration and disruption which ignorance about his infertility and the sudden shock of discovery brought to the marital relationship, and the "shock and anger" he experienced.[50] In both of these cases the defendants conceded that this head of damage was recoverable, although it may be doubtful whether in the absence of any physical injury for which the defendants are liable, there should be any award for "shock" or "distress" not amounting to a positive psychiatric illness, such as an anxiety neurosis or reactive depression.[51]

4. SPECIAL CASES

(1) Research

6–163   The fact that a person is the subject of medical research, as a participant in a drug trial for example, may change the nature of the legal requirements for consent.[52] Medical research is normally divided into two broad categories: therapeutic research; and non-therapeutic research. Therapeutic research is an activity which has a therapeutic intention, as well as a research intention, towards the subjects of the research. Thus, the subjects are also patients. Non-therapeutic research is an activity which does not have a therapeutic intention. This research is normally carried out on healthy volunteers, who are not patients. The legal principles applicable to these different categories of research may well differ, although there is a dearth of caselaw on the subject, and the most comprehensive statements of proper safeguards for research subjects are to be found in national and international ethical

---

[50] See further *Laferrière v Lawson* (1991) 78 D.L.R. (4th) 609 (S.C.C.) where the claimant was not informed that she had breast cancer and no follow-up treatment was arranged by the defendant. The claimant was held to be entitled to compensation for "psychological damage" attributable to her belief that had she known about the diagnosis earlier something could have been done to prevent the illness from becoming terminal. In *Snider v Henniger* (1992) 96 D.L.R. (4th) 367; [1993] 4 Med. L.R. 211 (B.C.S.C.) the defendant did not inform the claimant that, after a second suture in her cervix to stop bleeding following a miscarriage, there was a risk that if the suture broke down a hysterectomy would probably have to be performed. The evidence indicated that even if the claimant had been informed, the hysterectomy could not have been prevented. The claimant was nonetheless awarded damages for negligence on the ground that the failure to inform her about the risk exacerbated her post-hysterectomy stress and anxiety and adversely affected her recovery from the operation.

[51] Applying *McLoughlin v O'Brian* [1983] 1 A.C. 410, 431, *per* Lord Bridge; *Alcock v Chief Constable of the South Yorkshire Police* [1992] 1 A.C. 310, 409, *per* Lord Oliver; see para. 2–097.

[52] For consideration of the standard of care to be applied to the conduct of research see paras 3–052 to 3–061.

codes.[53] It is arguable that these codes of practice provide good evidence of appropriate standards of conduct and information disclosure, although with many, particularly the international codes, the statements of principle tend to be at too high a level of abstraction to be helpful in resolving a specific case.

(a) Therapeutic research

Therapeutic research involves medical treatment of the patient's illness   6–164
or disability, and on this basis it may be that there is little or no difference
in the requirements for an effective consent by the patient, or, indeed as to
the doctor's duty to disclose information about the risks of the procedure.
The patient's competence to consent for the purpose of the tort of battery

---

[53] Codes of practice for ethical biomedical research are now very common, both nationally and internationally. See: (1) World Medical Association, *Declaration of Helsinki* (1964, revised in 1975, 1983, 1989, 1996 and 2000, and clarified in 2002), available at *www.wma.net/e/ ethicsunit/helsinki.htm*; (2) Royal College of Physicians, *Guidelines on the Practice of Ethics Committees in Medical Research Involving Human Subjects*, 3rd ed., 1996; (3) Royal College of Physicians, *Research Involving Patients*, 1990; (4) the Council for International Organisations of Medical Sciences ("the CIOMS") *Guidelines for Biomedical Research Involving Human Subjects*, 1993, on which see J. Legemaate, "The CIOMS Guidelines for Biomedical Research Involving Human Subjects" (1994) 1 E.J.H.L. 161; (5) the International Conference on Harmonisation, *Guideline for Good Clinical Practice*, 1996, which replaced the guidance of the European Community Committee for Proprietary Medicinal Products, *Good Clinical Practice Guidelines*, 1991, and deals with the regulation of research involving pharmaceutical products (see Kennedy & Grubb, *Medical Law*, 3rd ed., 2000, Butterworths, p. 1712); (6) Council of Europe, *Convention on Human Rights and Biomedicine*, 1997 (for discussion of the background to the Convention see C. Byk, "The European Convention on Bioethics" (1993) 19 J. Med. Ethics 13); (7) Medical Research Council (M.R.C.), *Guidelines for Good Clinical Practice in Clinical Trials*, 1998; (8) M.R.C., *Good Research Practice*, 2000; (9) M.R.C., *Ethical Conduct of Research on the Mentally Incapacitated*, 1991; (10) the General Medical Council's guidance to the medical profession *Seeking patients' consent: the ethical considerations*, February 1999, para. 36, sets out guidance concerning the consent of participants in the research context; (11) G.M.C. guidance, *Research: The Role and Responsibilities of Doctors*, February 2002. See also The Law Commission consultation paper, *Mentally Incapacitated Adults and Decision-Making: Medical Treatment and Research*, Law Com. No. 129, 1993, and the Law Commission's final report, *Mental Incapacity*, Law Com. No. 231, HMSO, 1995. Most of these guidelines assume that a research project has been scrutinised and approved by an ethics committee of some kind. For discussion of the potential liability of research ethics committees see Brazier (1990) 6 P.N. 186; and more generally Kirk (1986) 2 P.N. 186; Teff (1987) 3 P.N. 182; Giesen (1995) 3 Med. L. Rev. 22; Mander (1996) 2 Med. Law Int. 149. Multi-Centre Research Ethics Committees were established in the NHS in 1997: NHS Executive, *Ethics Committee Review of Multi-centre Research*, HSG (97)23, on which see Stacey, "Ethical review of research in the NHS: the need for change" (1998) 32 J. of the R.C.P. of London 190. See also the draft Medicines for Human Use (Clinical Trials) Regulations 2003 which will implement Directive 2001/20/EC on good clinical practice in the conduct of clinical trials on medicinal products for human use. The draft regulations establish the UK Ethics Committees Authority which will be the body responsible for establishing, recognising and monitoring ethics committees in the UK. The committees will be responsible for giving opinions on the ethics of all clinical trials involving medicinal products. The regulations will also provide that a clinical trial may be conducted only if it has been authorised by the Licensing Authority (see Medicines Act 1968, s.6) and an ethics committee has given a favourable opinion. These Regulations will put ethics committees on a statutory footing for the first time in the United Kingdom. Member States are required to bring the provisions of the Directive fully into force by May 1, 2004. The draft regulations are available at *www.doh.gov.uk/clinicaltrialsconsult*.

would, presumably, be measured by the same criteria as are applied to any form of medical treatment, which depends upon his ability to understand the nature of the procedure.[54] Similarly, the voluntariness of the consent would be treated as a question of fact. Just as in a prison setting a court should be alive to the risk that what may appear, on the face of it, to be a real consent is not in fact so,[55] the court should also bear in mind that the stress of illness and the psychological pressures that a patient may experience in a "dependent" relationship with his doctor might affect the voluntariness of the patient's consent.[56] The patient may think, for example, that if he were to decline to participate then subsequently he would not be given the best available treatment or the most careful attention of the medical staff.[57] Thus, it is important that the patient is aware that he is free to decline to participate, and that this will not affect the treatment that he will receive.

6–165   The final issue concerns the question of how much information the patient must be given. It will be recalled that "once the patient is informed in broad terms of the nature of the procedure which is intended, and gives her consent, that consent is real."[58] If the treatment also has a research purpose the question is whether this alters the nature of the procedure, so that a failure to tell the patient that he is part of a research study would vitiate the consent. Alternatively, it might be argued that a failure to inform the patient constitutes fraud or misrepresentation, on the basis that it involves withholding information in bad faith.[59] Here, everything turns on the meaning that is to be given to the term "nature of the procedure," and, in the absence of authority in this country, the answer must be largely speculative. If the court placed the emphasis on the therapeutic nature of the procedure, the fact that it was also experimental or part of a research project might be regarded as collateral to the therapy, to which consent "in broad terms" had been obtained. On this view the doctor's research intention would be irrelevant to the validity of the patient's consent. On the other hand, it is arguable that

---

[54] See paras 6–026 to 6–032. Children of 16 or 17 years of age will be in the same position as adults by virtue of the Family Law Reform Act 1969, s.8(1). Children under 16 should have capacity if they have sufficient understanding, applying *Gillick v West Norfolk & Wisbech Area Health Authority* [1986] A.C. 112 . Query, however, whether a higher degree of understanding would be required for therapeutic research procedures than for simple "therapy," just as a high level of understanding is apparently required for contraceptive advice or treatment; see paras 6–048 to 6–049.

[55] *Freeman v Home Office* [1984] Q.B. 524, 557; see para. 6–024.

[56] In *Kaimowitz v Michigan Department of Mental Health* 42 U.S.L.W. 2063 (1973) it was held that an involuntarily detained mental patient could not give a valid consent to experimental psychosurgery because the process of institutionalisation undermined the voluntary nature of the consent.

[57] The *Declaration of Helsinki* para. 23 provides that when obtaining consent the physician should be particularly cautious if the subject is in a dependent relationship with the physician or may consent under duress. In such a case consent should be obtained by a doctor who is not engaged in the research and who is completely independent of this relationship. Para. 31 specifies that the refusal of the patient to participate in a study must never interfere with the patient-physician relationship.

[58] *Chatterton v Gerson* [1981] Q.B. 432, 443, para. 6–034.

[59] See paras 6–038 to 6–039.

the existence of the research intention does indeed change the nature of what is done, irrespective of any additional risk to which the patient may be exposed by virtue of the research aspect.[60] It is submitted that the latter approach is correct on principle, on the basis that no one, least of all patients who may be in a particularly vulnerable position, should be the subject of medical research without being aware of the circumstances and consenting to participate.

It has also been suggested that if the consent is to be valid the patient must   **6–166**
be informed of three further matters:

(1) that he may refuse to participate in the research project or may withdraw at any time from the research, and will suffer no adverse consequences in terms of the treatment he will then receive;

(2) that he may be a member of a control group in a trial which is intended to evaluate the effectiveness of a new therapy; and

(3) that the trial is a randomised controlled trial.[61]

The first matter relates to the question of the voluntariness of the consent: if the patient does not know that there is no compulsion to participate it may be arguable that his consent was involuntary. The second and third issues relate to the patient's knowledge of the treatment that he will receive. Although the patient will normally be unaware of which group he will be allocated to, he should be informed of the nature of the treatment which each group will receive, otherwise he cannot consent, even in broad terms, to the nature of the procedure.

Notwithstanding that participation in therapeutic medical research may   **6–167**
increase the inherent risks of injury to a patient, it is unlikely that the courts would regard non-disclosure of risks as vitiating the reality of consent, given the general approach that has been taken to the tort of battery and the non-disclosure of risks. Clearly, a doctor would owe at least the same duty of care to inform a patient about the risks of treatment as for any other form of

---

[60] Kennedy & Grubb, *Medical Law*, 3rd ed., 2000, p. 1710.

[61] *ibid.* Under a randomised controlled trial two or more groups of research subjects are given different treatments and the results are compared for any statistically significant difference in outcomes; subjects are allocated to the trial groups randomly in order to eliminate any bias in the selection of subjects for particular treatments. It has been found, however, that the majority of patients do not understand the process of randomisation when it is explained to them: see Simes *et al.* (1986) 293 B.M.J. 1065, 1067. Query whether patients should be informed that the doctor is receiving payment from a pharmaceutical company for enrolling patients in the trial. Earlier guidance from the General Medical Council did not require disclosure of this fact to the patient. The current GMC guidance *Research: The Role and Responsibilities of Doctors*, February 2002, states at para. 13: "You must always act in the participants' best interests when carrying out research. You must ensure that your judgement about the research is not influenced, or seen by others to be influenced, by financial, personal, political or other external interests at any stage of the process. You should always declare any conflicts that may arise to an appropriate person, authority or organisation, as well as to the participants." This paragraph does not, unequivocally, require disclosure of financial arrangements, unless this can be regarded as giving rise to a conflict of interest.

treatment, applying *Sidaway v Bethlem Royal Hospital Governors*.[62] The question is whether he would be under a duty to volunteer any additional information by virtue of a research intention.

6–168   In *Wilsher v Essex Area Health Authority*, Mustill L.J. observed that where the doctor embarks on a form of treatment which is still comparatively untried, with techniques and safeguards which are still in the course of development, then "if the decision to embark on the treatment at all was justifiable and was taken with the informed consent of the patient, the court should . . . be particularly careful not to impute negligence simply because something has gone wrong."[63] This leaves open the question of just how "informed" the patient should be, although, it may possibly be inferred that his Lordship contemplated a greater degree of disclosure than would be applied to the ordinary patient under *Sidaway*. It has been argued that *Sidaway* should not apply to therapeutic research because the reliance on what a responsible body of professional opinion would disclose is not relevant to the question of research, since the need for research is based on public policy, not professional opinion. What should be disclosed ought therefore to be a matter for the courts.[64] It could be said in reply that the patient's need for treatment is the consequence of his medical condition and any question of the potential benefits of research to the public is incidental.[65] Thus, the court could take the view that the risks entailed in the "research aspect" of the therapy have to be weighed in the balance by the doctor in deciding what information to give to the patient, just as with any other treatment, and accordingly that this is part and parcel of the doctor's clinical judgment, to which *Sidaway* should apply.

6–169   Moreover, the Court of Appeal has said that a distinction between advice given in a therapeutic and a non-therapeutic context was "elusive" and

---

[62] [1985] A.C. 871. In *Chadwick v Parsons* [1971] 2 Lloyd's Rep. 49, and 322, CA, the claimant agreed to undergo an experimental operation for the insertion of an electrical device into her skull in an attempt to alleviate her hearing problem. She was not given any warning of the potentially disastrous consequences, and liability was admitted.

[63] [1987] Q.B. 730, 749. In *R. v Mental Health Commission, ex parte W*, *The Times*, May 27, 1988, Stuart-Smith L.J. said that: "No doubt the consent has to be an informed consent in that he knows the nature and likely effect of the treatment. There can be no doubt that the applicant knew this. So too in this case, where the treatment was not routinely used for control of sexual urges and was not sold for this purpose, it was important that the applicant should realise that the use on him was a novel one and the full implications with use on young men had not been studied, since trials had only been involved with animals and older men."

[64] Kennedy & Grubb, *Medical Law*, 3rd ed., 2000, p. 1711. The authors also suggest that in addition to the information necessary for the purpose of avoiding liability in battery a doctor would be required, in law, to disclose: (i) material risks associated with the research; and (ii) material information necessary to enable the patient to make an "informed decision," *e.g.* any inconvenience associated with the fact that the patient is a research subject, such as additional hospital visits, additional tests, etc.

[65] The argument that a patient should not be informed that he is part of a research study because this would necessarily involve telling him other things about his condition which it would be better for him that he did not know is clearly without substance. If it is in the patient's interests not to be informed about his medical condition then this is an argument for excluding him from the study, not failing to inform him about it: see Kennedy, *Treat Me Right*, 1988, O.U.P., p. 223.

"wholly unwarranted and artificial."[66] This suggests that the test of negligence in any situation requiring the exercise of specialist skill, whether that of a doctor or a researcher, is the *Bolam* test and that therefore the standard of information disclosure is to be assessed by reference to what a reasonable doctor/researcher would have disclosed in the circumstances. Although the case was specifically concerned with the question of contraceptive advice, its implications may stretch to the question of research and, indeed, possibly to non-therapeutic research.

On the other hand, even if *Sidaway* were to be applied to cases of therapeutic research, it could be argued that a failure to inform the patient that he was part of a research project is a matter that so obviously should have been disclosed that no reasonable doctor would fail to disclose it, applying Lord Bridge's dictum.[67] Alternatively, it might be said that the measure of what is responsible professional opinion should be determined not by the expert evidence of what in fact happens, but by the requirements of an ethical code, such as the *Declaration of Helsinki*. The Declaration states that a research subject "must be adequately informed of the aims, methods, sources of funding, any possible conflicts of interest, institutional affiliations of the researcher, the anticipated benefits and potential risks of the study and the discomfort it may entail." He should be informed of the right to abstain from participation in the study or to withdraw consent to participate at any time without reprisal. The research subject should then give a free, informed consent, preferably in writing.[68]   **6–170**

The Canadian approach to this problem may be instructive. In *Zimmer v Ringrose*[69] the claimant was subjected to a novel and experimental method of sterilisation. At first instance the defendant was held liable because he had failed to inform the claimant that the technique had not been generally accepted by the medical profession, and had not informed her of the failure rate of up to 30 per cent MacDonald J. applied *Halushka v University of Saskatchewan*,[70] a case which was concerned with non-therapeutic research, holding the defendant liable in battery. The Alberta Court of Appeal reversed this decision, taking the view that the standard of disclosure required in *Halushka* was limited to non-therapeutic research: **6–171**

"In the case of a truly 'experimental' procedure, like the one conducted in *Halushka v University of Saskatchewan*, no therapeutic benefit is intended to accrue to the participant. The subject is simply part of a scientific investigation designed to enhance human knowledge. By contrast,

---

[66] *Gold v Haringey Health Authority* [1988] Q.B. 481; see para. 6–139.
[67] [1985] A.C. 871, 900; see paras 6–112 and 6–115.
[68] All at para. 22. However, this is qualified under para. 26 in the case of research on individuals from whom it is not possible to obtain consent. The Declaration states that the specific reasons for involving research subjects with a condition that renders them unable to give informed consent should be stated in the experimental protocol for consideration and approval of a research ethics committee.
[69] (1978) 89 D.L.R. (3d) 646 (Alta. S.C.).
[70] (1965) 53 D.L.R. (2d) 436.

the sterilization procedure performed by the appellant in this case was directed towards achieving a therapeutic end . . . [T]he silver nitrate method was experimental only in the sense that it represented an innovation in sterilisation techniques which were relatively untried . . . To hold that every new development in medical technology was 'experimental' in the sense outlined in *Halushka v University of Saskatchewan* would be to discourage advances in the field of medicine."[71]

6–172   Nonetheless, the defendant was found to have been negligent in failing to discuss alternative methods of sterilisation because the claimant was given no opportunity to measure the risks involved in the silver nitrate method against those involved in other forms of sterilisation. A reasonable practitioner would also have informed the claimant that the technique had not been approved by the medical profession, since he would realise that this information would be likely to influence the patient's decision whether to undergo the procedure.[72] Similarly, in *Coughlin v Kuntz*[73] the defendant was held liable for failing to disclose that the contemplated operation was novel, unique to the defendant, and under investigation by a professional body, and for failing to inform the claimant that other medical experts had specifically advised against neck surgery.

6–173   The lawfulness of medical treatment given to adults who lack the capacity to give a valid consent depends upon the principle of necessity. This is measured by the patient's "best interests," and a medical procedure will be in the patient's best interests "if, but only if, it is carried out in order either to save their lives, or to ensure improvement or prevent deterioration in their physical or mental health."[74] Given that the major premise of the decision in *Re F. (Mental Patient: Sterilisation)* was that incompetent patients should not be deprived of treatment that would be available to a competent adult the courts would probably take the view that therapeutic research on incompetent adults can be justified if the treatment is in the patient's best interests. The *Bolam*[75] test will be applied to determine the patient's best interests: if a responsible body of professional opinion considers that the procedure was in the patient's best interests it is irrelevant that others believed that the patient should not have been included in the research project. Moreover, the

---

[71] (1981) 124 D.L.R. 215, 222–223, *per* Prowse J.A. See also *Cryderman v Ringrose* [1977] 3 W.W.R. 109; affirmed [1978] 3 W.W.R. 481 (Alta. C.A.) in which the claimant agreed to be sterilised by the same defendant by the same experimental procedure. The claimant was not informed that the procedure was unreliable or that it might damage the uterus. The trial judge distinguished *Halushka v University of Saskatchewan* (1965) 53 D.L.R. (2d) 436 on the basis that *Halushka* was a case of "pure medical experimentation," where different considerations would apply.

[72] "When an experimental procedure is employed the common law requires a high degree of care and also disclosure to the patient of the fact that the treatment is new and risky," *per* Stevenson D.C.J. in *Cryderman v Ringrose* [1977] 3 W.W.R. 109, 118. The claim for nondisclosure in *Zimmer v Ringrose* failed on the ground that the claimant would have accepted the treatment in any event, although the action succeeded in respect of negligent after-care.

[73] (1987) 42 C.C.L.T. 142 (B.C.S.C.); affirmed [1990] 2 W.W.R. 737, 745 (B.C.C.A.).

[74] *Re F. (Mental Patient: Sterilisation)* [1990] 2 A.C. 1, 55, *per* Lord Brandon; see para. 6–080.

[75] *Bolam v Friern Hospital Management Committee* [1957] 2 All E.R. 118.

Bolam test "ought not to be allowed to inhibit medical progress. And it is clear that if one waited for the '*Bolam* test' to be complied with to its fullest extent, no innovative work such as the use of penicillin or performing heart transplant surgery would ever be attempted."[76] Thus, where there is no alternative treatment, and the disease from which the incapacitated patient is suffering is progressive and fatal it would be reasonable to "consider experimental treatment with unknown benefits and risks, but without significant risks of increased suffering to the patient, in cases where there is some chance of benefit to the patient. A patient who is not able to consent to pioneering treatment ought not to be deprived of the chance in circumstances where he would have been likely to consent if he had been competent."[77]

Therapeutic research on children who lack the relevant capacity will be lawful where parental consent has been obtained, provided the procedure can be said to be in the child's best interests. To the extent that doctors have a duty to disclose additional information to competent patients when the treatment forms part of a research project, the parents would be entitled to a comparable degree of disclosure.   **6–174**

Certain forms of research give rise to problems in the case of incompetent patients. In a randomised controlled trial, some patients may well receive a treatment which the doctor does not believe to be in their best interests medically. The consent of a competent patient to participate may be taken to waive the doctor's duty to act in the patient's best interests, but it is a matter of some doubt whether such a waiver can ever apply where the patient is incapable of consenting.[78]   **6–175**

(b) Non-therapeutic research

As with therapeutic research, the three central issues are the competence of the research subject to give a valid consent, the voluntariness of the consent, and the appropriate level of information disclosure. With adults, competence will be treated as a question of fact, namely whether the subject understands the nature of the procedure to which he is consenting. Children of 16 or 17 years would not be presumed to be competent by virtue of section 8(1) of the Family Law Reform Act 1969, since that section applies only to "surgical, medical or dental *treatment*,"[79] but presumably *Gillick v West Norfolk and Wisbech Area Health Authority*[80] would apply to determine the competence of children to consent to non-therapeutic research. Possibly a   **6–176**

---

[76] *Simms v Simms; A. v A.* [2002] EWHC 2734 (Fam); [2003] 1 All E.R. 669 at [48] *per* Butler-Sloss P., citing Lord Diplock in *Sidaway v Bethlem Royal Hospital Governors* [1985] A.C. 871, 893 (cited at para. 3–053).

[77] *ibid.* at [57] *per* Butler-Sloss P. On the evidence in *Simms v Simms* it could not be said that treatment was clearly futile, and therefore it satisfied the *Bolam* test.

[78] See Kennedy, *Treat Me Right*, 1988, O.U.P., Ch. 10 for extended discussion of the law on randomised controlled trials.

[79] See para. 6–046.

[80] [1986] A.C. 112.

higher degree of understanding would be required from a child than in the case of medical treatment,[81] and the greater the potential risk the greater the understanding that will be required. The voluntary nature of the consent will also be treated as a question of fact.[82]

6–177   The argument that the research subject should be fully informed is clearly much stronger in the case of non-therapeutic research. Withholding information about potential risks cannot be justified by reference to the research subject's medical condition or "best interests,"[83] and so it is arguable that non-therapeutic research subjects should be given full and complete information about the nature of the research and the inherent risks. In *Halushka v University of Saskatchewan*[84] the claimant was a student who volunteered, for a fee, to undergo an experimental test on a new anaesthetic. He was told that it was a safe test which had been conducted many times before and that there was nothing to worry about. This was untrue, since the anaesthetic had not previously been used or tested by the defendants. The claimant was not told that all anaesthetic agents involve a certain degree of risk, nor was he told that a catheter, which he knew would be inserted into a vein in his arm, would be advanced into his heart. The claimant suffered cardiac arrest, caused by the anaesthetic, and was unconscious for four days. The defendants were held liable in trespass to the person on the basis of a lack of consent, a finding upheld by the Saskatchewan Court of Appeal. Hall J.A. said that:

> "There can be no exceptions to the ordinary requirements of disclosure in the case of research as there may well be in ordinary medical practice. The researcher does not have to balance the probable effect of lack of treatment against the risk involved in the treatment itself. The example of risks being properly hidden from a patient when it is important that he should not worry can have no application in the field of research. The subject of medical experimentation is entitled to a full and frank disclosure of all the facts, probabilities and opinions which a reasonable man might be expected to consider before giving his consent."[85]

This statement specifies an objective test for disclosure, based upon the information that a "reasonable volunteer" would want to have. Arguably, in the case of non-therapeutic research the test should be subjective (what

---

[81] *cf.* the high level of understanding stipulated by Lord Scarman in *Gillick v West Norfolk and Wisbech Area Health Authority* [1986] A.C. 112, 189 before a child under 16 could be said to have sufficient capacity to consent to contraceptive advice or treatment: para. 6–049.

[82] Where large financial inducements are provided to students or the unemployed this may raise a question mark about the voluntariness of the consent: see, *e.g.*, *The Observer*, October 2, 1988, and *The Times*, October 6, 1986. In 1984 two student volunteers in drug trials died in separate incidents: *The Times*, May 30 1984, June 11 1984, and April 25, 1985.

[83] It has been suggested, however, that "informed consent" may bias the results of a clinical trial: Dahan *et al.* (1986) 293 B.M.J. 363; for criticism of this study see Launer (1986) 293 B.M.J. 627–628.

[84] (1965) 53 D.L.R. (2d) 436 (Sask. C.A.).

[85] *ibid.* at 443.

this volunteer would want to know) for the very reasons that Hall J.A. gives.

It is not clear whether a lack of information about risks, as opposed to the **6–178** "nature" of the research procedure, would be treated in this country as relating to the researcher's duty of care in negligence rather than battery. It will be recalled that in *Gold v Haringey Health Authority*[86] the Court of Appeal refused to draw a distinction between advice given in a therapeutic and a non-therapeutic context. The *Bolam* test did not, it was said, depend on the context in which advice was given, but on a man professing skill or competence in a field beyond that possessed by the man on the Clapham omnibus. Lloyd L.J. said that the *Bolam* test was not confined to a defendant exercising or professing the particular skill of medicine, and there was no basis for distinguishing between doctors and any other profession or calling requiring special skill, knowledge or experience. On this view a research subject would only be entitled to be informed about the risks that a reasonably competent researcher would disclose. It is submitted that such an approach should be rejected and that the reasoning in *Gold* should not be extended to non-therapeutic research. The healthy volunteer has an ethical claim to full information about the anticipated risks of the procedure, and this should be reflected in the law.

Even where a volunteer is fully informed about the risks involved in an **6–179** experimental procedure there may well be some limits to the risks which he can agree to accept, such that if the risks are too great an apparently valid consent might be ineffective.[87]

Where a potential research subject lacks the capacity to give a valid consent **6–180** the question arises whether it can ever be lawful for non-therapeutic research to be performed. By definition the research is not in the interests (whether these are categorised as "best interests" or merely "interests") of the research subject, and will normally carry some, albeit remote, risk of harm. On what legal basis could a proxy, whether it be a parent, the court or a doctor "authorise" a procedure that carried risk to the subject but was not intended to have any direct benefit for that person? In *Re F. (Mental Patient: Sterilisation)*[88] the House of Lords adopted a wide interpretation of the principle of necessity so as to facilitate the provision of medical treatment to permanently incapacitated adults. The rationale was that adults lacking the capacity to consent should not be in a worse position than competent adults, and should not be deprived of treatment that would be available to them if they were in a position to consent, provided that the treatment could be shown to be in their best interests. The same logic, that they should not be in a worse position than

---

[86] [1988] Q.B. 481, 489, *per* Lloyd L.J., para. 6–139.
[87] *cf. Attorney-General's Reference (No. 6 of 1980)* [1981] Q.B. 715, where it was held that public policy may dictate that a consent is not valid in law, *e.g.*, in the course of a prize fight. The report of an Institute of Medical Ethics working group recommended that non-therapeutic research procedures on children should not be carried out if they involve "greater than minimal risk": Nicholson, *Medical Research with Children*, 1986, O.U.P., p. 233. For discussion of the problems involved in quantifying acceptable levels of risk in the conduct of research see *ibid.*, Ch. 5.
[88] [1990] 2 A.C. 1, paras 6–079 to 6–080.

competent adults, would suggest that it would never be lawful to subject an incompetent adult to non-therapeutic research which carried any risk of harm, because otherwise the individual lacking capacity clearly is placed in a worse position than the competent adult who has the right and ability to refuse to participate. Moreover, their Lordships made it clear in *Re F. (Mental Patient: Sterilisation)* that the justification for providing treatment did not rest upon a proxy "consent" (which might give the proxy a limited power of choice or discretion) but on the principle of necessity, with the question of "necessity" to be determined, not by the needs of some other person or society in general, but by the best interests of the patient.

6–181   This problem was considered by the Law Commission in its report *Mental Incapacity*, where it was recommended that "research which is unlikely to benefit a participant, or whose benefit is likely to be long delayed, should be lawful in relation to a person without capacity to consent if (1) the research is into an incapacitating condition with which the participant is or may be affected and (2) certain statutory procedures are complied with."[89] The Commission recommend that there should be a statutory Mental Incapacity Research Committee, and a non-therapeutic research procedure should be lawful in relation to a person without capacity only if the Mental Incapacity Research Committee had approved the research. The Committee could approve the research if satisfied:

> "(1) that it is desirable to provide knowledge of the causes or treatment of, or of the care of people affected by, the incapacitating condition with which any participant is or may be affected,
> (2) that the object of the research cannot be effectively achieved without the participation of persons who are or may be without capacity to consent, and
> (3) that the research will not expose a participant to more than negligible risk, will not be unduly invasive or restrictive of a participant and will not unduly interfere with a participant's freedom of action or privacy."[90]

The Committee would approve research protocols, but it would not grant approval for the inclusion of specific research subjects. Thus, the Law Commission recommended that in addition to approval by the Mental Incapacity Research Committee, non-therapeutic research in relation to a person without capacity should require either court approval, the consent of an attorney or manager, a certificate from a doctor not involved in the research that the participation of the person is appropriate, or designation

---

[89] Law Com. No. 231, (1995), para. 6.31. Apparently, the majority of consultees argued that there is an ethical case for conducting non-therapeutic research on incompetent adults, which rested on the desirability of eradicating painful and distressing disabilities, where progress can be achieved without harming research subjects. See also the Law Commission's consultation paper, which preceded the final report, *Mentally Incapacitated Adults and Decision-Making: Medical Treatment and Research*, Law Com. No. 129, 1993.

[90] *ibid.* at para. 6.34.

of the research as not involving direct contact with the participants (such as covert observation or inspection of written records).[91] These recommendations have not yet been enacted.

A similar problem arises in the case of non-therapeutic research on children.   **6–182** How can a parent or indeed the court give a valid consent for research which by definition is not in the interests of the child, and may expose him to some risk, however small. The power of parents to exercise consent to medical treatment exists to protect the interests of children and must be exercised in their "best interests."[92] The view that non-therapeutic research on children is unlawful has been widely held by, *inter alia*, the Medical Research Council, the Medical Defence Union and the Medical Protection Society.[93] In more recent years, however, attitudes seem to have shifted and it has been argued that non-therapeutic research on children would be lawful in certain limited circumstances.[94] It remains to be seen how a court would respond to this question.

(c) Embryo research

The Human Fertilisation and Embryology Act 1990, section 11, provides   **6–183** for the regulation of research on human embryos by a statutory Licensing Authority which may grant licences for the purpose of approved research projects. There are restrictions on the type and purpose of research that may be conducted.[95] Under section 12 one of the conditions for the grant of a licence is that the provisions of Schedule 3 concerning consent must be complied with. The consent required is the consent of each person whose gametes are used for the creation of an *in vitro* embryo, and the consent must specify the purpose for which the embryo may be used, namely treatment services or for the purposes of a project of research.[96] Consent is also required for the storage of gametes or embryos, but in any event embryos may not be stored for more than five years and gametes may not be stored for more than ten years.[97] The consent must be in writing and may be varied or withdrawn, but not after the embryo has been used in research.[98] Before a person gives consent he must be given an opportunity to receive proper counselling about the implications and he must be "provided with such information as is proper," including his right to vary or withdraw consent.[99]

---

[91] *ibid.* at para. 6.37.
[92] *Gillick v West Norfolk and Wisbech Area Health Authority* [1986] A.C. 112, para. 6–057. The same test is applied to the courts' exercise of the wardship jurisdiction: para. 6–059.
[93] See Dworkin (1978) 53 Arch. Disease in Childhood 443.
[94] *ibid.*; Dworkin (1987) 13 Monash Univ. L.R. 189. For an extended discussion of this problem see Nicholson, *Medical Research with Children*, 1986, O.U.P.
[95] Human Fertilisation and Embryology Act 1990, s.3 and Sch. 2, para. 3. For consideration of what constitutes an embryo see *R. (on the application of Quintavalle) v Secretary of State for Health* [2003] UKHL 13; [2003] 2 W.L.R. 692.
[96] *ibid.*, Sch. 3, para. 6.
[97] *ibid.*, Sch. 3, para. 8, and s.14.
[98] *ibid.*, Sch. 3, para. 1, and para. 4.
[99] *ibid.*, Sch. 3, para. 3. See *Mrs U v Centre for Reproductive Medicine* [2002] EWCA Civ 565; [2002] Lloyd's Rep. Med. 259.

6–184   The Act does not confer any civil remedy for breach of the provisions concerning consent, although failure to comply with the consent requirements would be a breach of the licence conditions stipulated by section 12 and thus would be in contravention of section 3(1), constituting a criminal offence.[1] It might possibly be argued that a breach of the consent requirements should give rise to a tort of breach of statutory duty, although it could be replied that if Parliament had intended to grant a civil remedy for breach of the Act it could easily have made express provision to this effect.[2] Alternatively, it might be possible to argue that an action for psychiatric harm should be available, if, for example, a person's gametes or embryos were used for research purposes without his or her consent.[3] This is highly speculative, however, and would depend, *inter alia*, upon proving that the claimant had suffered from a genuine psychiatric illness as a consequence, not simply emotional distress or grief.

(2) Transplantation

6–185   The live donation of organs must be limited to regenerative tissue such as blood or bone marrow, or paired organs such as kidneys, where it is known that the donor can survive with a single organ. A donor could not give valid consent to the removal of an organ that would result in his death or serious disability.[4] The recipient of an organ transplant will be in the same position as any other patient receiving treatment with regard to consent and information disclosure, bearing in mind the degree of risk associated with the particular form of transplantation.[5] It is arguable, however, that a much stricter standard of information disclosure is required for the donor of the organ. His position is analogous to that of a volunteer for non-therapeutic research, since the operation is of no medical benefit to the donor, and carries the risk of harm to his health. On this basis, it is submitted that there should be a full and frank disclosure of risks.[6]

6–186   This view has some statutory support in Regulations made under the Human Organ Transplants Act 1989. Under section 1 of the Act, commer-

---

[1]   *ibid.*, s.41(2). It is a defence for the person charged to prove that he took all reasonable steps and exercised all due diligence to avoid committing the offence.

[2]   For discussion of the problems surrounding the inference of the tort when Parliament has not expressly dealt with the matter see *Clerk & Lindsell on Torts*, 18th ed., 2000, Ch. 11.

[3]   On psychiatric harm generally, see paras 2–096 *et seq.*

[4]   *Attorney-General's Reference (No. 6 of 1980)* [1981] Q.B. 715; *R. v Brown* [1994] 1 A.C. 212; see generally Dworkin (1970) 33 M.L.R. 353.

[5]   Where the patient is incapable of giving a valid consent, for example, in the case of a minor the question is whether the surgery is in the child's best interests: see *An Hospital NHS Trust v S* [2003] EWHC 365 (Fam); [2003] Lloyd's Rep. Med. 137. For a case involving the refusal of a parent to consent to a liver transplant for an 18 month old child see: *Re T. (a minor) (wardship: medical treatment)* [1997] 1 All E.R. 906, CA, para. 6–063; *cf. Re M. (A Child) (Refusal of Medical Treatment)* [1999] 2 F.L.R. 1097; [1999] 2 F.C.R. 577, where the court considered that heart transplant surgery should be authorised for a 15-year-old girl, in her best interests.

[6]   See Norrie (1985) 34 I.C.L.Q. 442, 452. If the doctor's negligence is the cause of the need for the transplantation he may be liable to the donor for the consequences of the donation: *Urbanski v Patel* (1978) 84 D.L.R. (3d) 650 (Man. Q.B.); para. 2–094.

cial dealings in human organs for transplantation are prohibited.[7] Section 2(1) prohibits the removal from a living person of an organ intended to be transplanted into another person, or the transplantation of an organ removed from a living person into another person, unless the donor is genetically related to the donee,[8] or the procedure satisfies the requirements of regulations made by the Secretary of State.[9] The Human Organ Transplants (Unrelated Persons) Regulations 1989[10] created the Unrelated Live Transplant Regulatory Authority. The Regulations provide that section 2(1) of the Act shall not apply where the doctor who has clinical responsibility for the donor has referred the matter to the Authority and the Authority is satisfied that no payment has been made or is to be made in contravention of section 1, and (except where the primary purpose of removal of an organ from a donor is the medical treatment of that donor) that the following conditions are satisfied:

(a) the doctor has given the donor an explanation of the nature of the medical procedure for, and the risk involved in, the removal of the organ;

(b) the donor understands the nature of the medical procedure and the risks, and consents to the removal of the organ;

(c) the donor's consent was not obtained by coercion or the offer of an inducement;

(d) the donor understands that he is entitled to withdraw his consent, but has not done so;

(e) the donor and recipient have been interviewed by a suitably qualified person, who has reported to the Authority on the conditions (a) to (d) and has included an account of any difficulties of communication with the donor or the recipient and an explanation of how the difficulties were overcome.

These statutory requirements for disclosure of the risks involved in transplantation apply only to non-related live donations, but it is submitted that a similar level of disclosure would be required at common law for all live organ donors.   **6–187**

The position of donors who are incapable of giving a valid consent is unclear. It would appear to be analogous to non-therapeutic research on children and incompetent adults. On one view, this would mean that organs can   **6–188**

---

[7] "Organ" means any part of a human body consisting of a structured arrangement of tissues which, if wholly removed, cannot be replicated by the body: s.7(2). Thus, blood products and bone marrow, which do replicate, are not within the Act.

[8] "Genetically related" is defined in s.2(2). For the tests to be used to establish genetic relationship see the Human Organ Transplants (Establishment of Relationship) Regulations 1998 (S.I. 1998 No. 1428).

[9] Human Organ Transplants Act 1989, s.2(3).

[10] S.I. 1989 No. 2480.

never be taken from such donors, since donation clearly creates risk to the donor, especially where it involves surgical intervention, and a parent cannot consent to procedures which are contrary to the interests of the child.[11] Some American courts have adopted an extended interpretation of an incompetent donor's "best interests" to include the psychological benefits that would accrue to the donor in order to justify donation between siblings.[12] On the other hand, nine Canadian provinces have enacted legislation based on the Uniform Tissue Gift Act, which prohibits minors and mentally incompetent adults from making live donations of non-regenerative tissue.[13] Donation of regenerative tissue such as blood, bone marrow, or skin by minors is left to the common law.

6–189   There are no English cases dealing with organ donation from an incompetent donor, although in *Re F. (Mental Patient: Sterilisation)* Neill L.J. did touch upon the point:

> "There are, however, some operations where the intervention of a court is most desirable if not essential. In this category I would place operations for sterilisation and organ transplant operations where the incapacitated patient is to be the donor. The performance of these operations should be subject to outside scrutiny. The lawfulness of the operation will depend of course on the question of whether it is necessary or not, but in my view it should become standard practice for the approval of the court to be obtained before an operation of this exceptional kind is carried out."[14]

His Lordship clearly contemplated that organ donation from incompetent donors could be lawful, subject to the supervision of the court,[15] depending upon whether it was "necessary or not." This rather begs the question, however, since the operation may well be necessary from the recipient's point of view, but it might be extremely difficult to claim that it was *necessary* for the incompetent donor's welfare that he should give up one of his organs.

---

[11] See para. 6–057; Norrie (1985) 34 I.C.L.Q. 442, 453. The Draft Mental Incapacity Bill, June 2003, will not affect the position, since cl. 28 prevents a decision being made through the Incapacity Bill procedures on behalf of a person under the Human Organ Transplants Act 1989.

[12] *Strunk v Strunk* 445 S.W. 2d 145 (1969) (Kentucky App.); *Hart v Brown* 289 A. 2d 386 (1972) (Conn.); *Little v Little* 576 S.W. 2d 493 (1979) (Texas C.A.); Dickens (1981) 97 L.Q.R. 462, 476–477; cf. *Re Richardson* 284 So. 2d 388 (1973) (Louisiana C.A.); *Re Pescinski* 226 N.E. 2d 180 (1975) (Wisconsin S.C.); *Curran v Bosze* 566 N.E. 2d 1319 (1990) (Ill. S.C.); see Robertson (1976) 76 Columbia Law Rev. 48 discussing the principle of "substituted judgment" under which the decision-maker attempts to make the judgment about donation on behalf of the incompetent donor which the donor would have made if competent.

[13] Picard, *Legal Liability of Doctors and Hospitals in Canada*, 3rd ed. 1996, pp. 95–96; although a few provinces do permit the *inter vivos* donation of non-regenerative tissue by minors aged 16 or over.

[14] [1990] 2 A.C. 1, 33.

[15] A view which had been taken in *Hart v Brown* 289 A. 2d 386, 391 (1972).

The argument is somewhat easier to mount in the case of regenerative   **6–190**
tissue, at least where it can be said that there is some benefit to the donor. In
Re Y (Mental Patient: Bone Marrow Donation)[16] the claimant, who was
aged 36, needed a bone marrow transplant for the treatment of non-
Hodgkin's lymphoma. There was a strong likelihood that her condition
would progress to acute myeloid leukaemia within three months. Her sister
(the defendant), aged 25, was a suitable donor, but was severely mentally and
physically handicapped, and incapable of consenting. She had lived in residential accommodation since the age of 10. Her family kept in touch with
her through visits, but the relationship between the sisters was not particularly strong. The claimant's own ill-health had reduced her ability to visit her
sister. The relationship with her mother, who visited regularly, was close, but
the mother was herself now in bad health. The claimant sought an order that
two preliminary blood tests and a bone marrow harvesting operation under
general anaesthetic could lawfully be performed on the defendant, on the
basis that they were in the defendant's best interests. Connell J. granted the
order. His Lordship acknowledged that any benefits to the claimant were
only relevant in so far as they had a positive effect on the interests of the
defendant. The "substituted judgment" approach, whereby the court considers what decision the defendant would have come to had she been capable
of consenting, was not relevant. Connell J. accepted that the defendant benefited from the visits of her family. If the claimant died it would have an
adverse effect on the mother, who was already in ill-health, and she would
then probably be more restricted in her ability to visit the defendant by
having to look after the claimant's daughter, her only grandchild. The defendant would then be harmed by the reduction in or loss of contact with her
mother. On the basis of the medical evidence, the physical risks of the procedure were less than 1 in 10,000 from the general anaesthetic (which was
the same risk as for any healthy patient undergoing a general anaesthetic),
and the defendant had previously had surgery under a general anaesthetic.
Thus, although there were no medical benefits to the defendant, the procedure was to her "emotional, psychological and social benefit." Connell J.
was careful to limit the ambit of his decision to a case involving regenerative
tissue:

"It is doubtful that this case would act as a useful precedent in cases
where the surgery involved is more intrusive than in this case, where the
evidence shows that the bone marrow harvested is speedily regenerated
and that a healthy individual can donate as much as two pints with no
long term consequences at all. Thus, the bone marrow donated by the
defendant will cause her no loss and she will suffer no real long term
risk."[17]

---

[16] [1997] Fam. 110.
[17] *ibid.* at 116.

In principle, however, although the medical risks involved in the donation of bone marrow are probably less than those involved in the donation of a kidney, there is little to distinguish the two situations. It is a difference of degree rather than of kind, so that if the balance of advantage in weighing the "emotional, psychological and social benefit" against the medical risk to the incompetent donor comes down in favour of the donation, there would seem to be no difficulty in law in the court granting a declaration that the procedure would be lawful. It is clear that, in such cases, the court must be involved in determining the best interests of the incompetent donor.[18]

6–191   Cadaver donations are governed by the Human Tissue Act 1961, which provides that authorisation for removal of organs for transplantation purposes may be given by the person "lawfully in possession" of the body in certain circumstances. There is considerable doubt as to whether there is any sanction for non-compliance with the requirements of the Act. In particular it is a matter of conjecture whether the unauthorised removal of tissue from a corpse would give rise to an action in tort by the relatives of the deceased person. The legal position remains unclear, although the problems that can arise were highlighted by the "retained organs" scandal, which was not concerned with organs for transplantation but with organs and tissue retained for research purposes.[19] Although the retention of organs was particularly distressing to the families of the deceased, particularly in the case of parents

---

[18] See *Practice Direction (Declaratory Proceedings: Incapacitated Adults)* [2002] 1 W.L.R. 325; [2002] 1 All E.R. 794, and in particular the Annex to that Practice Direction *Practice Note (Declaratory Proceedings: Medical and Welfare Decisions for Adults who lack Capacity)* [2001] 2 F.C.R. 569. The Law Commission report, *Mental Incapacity*, Law Com. No. 231, (1995), para. 6.6 recommended that any treatment or procedure to facilitate the donation of non-regenerative tissue or bone marrow by a person without capacity should require court authorisation. Although it seems inconceivable that doctors could proceed without first obtaining a declaration from the court, strictly speaking, a declaration does not render lawful what was otherwise unlawful, it simply declares what the law is. Thus, until the statutory scheme recommended by the Law Commission for dealing with incompetent patients is enacted, the doctors would not be acting *unlawfully* (though extremely unwisely) if they proceeded without a declaration in circumstances where the court would have granted a declaration.

[19] The retention of organs and human tissue following post-mortem without the consent of relatives was found to be a widespread practice after the issue first came to light in the course of the Bristol Inquiry and subsequently at Alder Hey Children's Hospital in Liverpool. See the *Public Inquiry into children's heart surgery at Bristol Royal Infirmary*, 2001 and *The Royal Liverpool Children's Inquiry Report*, 2001 respectively, (available at *www.bristol-inquiry.org.uk* and *www.rlcinquiry.org.uk*). The Department of Health has issued a number of documents offering guidance on the issue, pending legislation to modernise the Human Tissue Act 1961. See Department of Health, *Consent to Organ and Tissue Retention at Post-mortem Examination and Disposal of Human Materials*, 2000, (*www.doh.gov.uk/orgretentionconsent/index.htm*); *Interim guidance on post-mortem examination to the NHS*, March 2000 (*www.doh.gov.uk/publications/pointh.html*); *The removal, retention and use of human organs and tissue from post-mortem examination: advice from the Chief Medical Officer*, January 2001 (*www.doh.gov.uk/orgretentionadvice*). The most recent guidance from the Department of Health was published in April 2003: *Removal, retention and use of human organs and tissue* (*www.doh.gov.uk/tissue*). See also NHS Central Office for Research Ethics Committees, (COREC), *The use of human organs and tissue, An interim statement*, April 2003, (*www.doh.gov.uk/tissue/interimstatement.pdf*). See further Ellis [2001] J.P.I.L. 264; Austin (2002) 8 Clinical Risk 185. For discussion of the ethics of organ retention see Harris (2003) 22 L.S. 527 and Brazier (2003) 22 L.S. 550.

of young children, the legal basis for any claim that the relatives might have had is somewhat tenuous. The general principle of English law is that there is no property in a corpse,[20] and therefore no general proprietary right to control what happens to a corpse or body parts. In the absence of an intention to cause harm[21] on the part of the persons removing the organs a claim would probably have to be based in negligence for any provable psychiatric harm.[22] The current structure of English law on the recovery of damages for negligently inflicted psychiatric harm is such that this type of claim would be very difficult to establish, given that members of the family would not qualify as "primary" victims and would therefore have to satisfy all the requirements of claims by a "secondary" victim.[23]

(3) Omission to warn about risk of sterilisation failing[24]

It is well-known within the medical profession that there is a risk that a sterilisation operation will fail to render the patient sterile. The risk can vary with the procedure used and the time at which it is carried out.[25] The existence of this small, but quantifiable, failure rate can make it difficult to prove that there has been negligence in the performance of the operation itself. This has led to a number of cases in which claimants have alleged that the surgeon was negligent in failing to inform them about the failure rate, although, with rare exceptions, these actions have been spectacularly unsuccessful. Following the decision of the House of Lords in *McFarlane v Tayside Health Board*[26] that

6–192

---

[20] *R. v Kelly* [1998] 3 All E.R. 741, 749; *Dobson v North Tyneside Health Authority* [1997] 1 W.L.R. 596. See further Grubb, (1998) 3 Med. Law Int. 299; Skegg (1992) 32 Med. Sci. Law 311.

[21] Which, theoretically at least, could give rise to a claim under the principle of *Wilkinson v Downton* [1897] 2 Q.B. 57, though in practice this would be difficult to prove.

[22] See Kennedy, *Treat Me Right*, 1988, O.U.P., Ch. 11, arguing that an action for psychiatric harm might be held to lie; and Norrie (1985) 34 I.C.L.Q. 442, 463–464 identifying Scottish cases which raised the possibility of claims for psychiatric harm following unauthorised post-mortems, and thus, by analogy, following unauthorised removal of organs for transplantation. It is doubtful, however, whether in the absence of any physical injury for which the defendants were liable, there can be any award for "shock" or "distress" not amounting to a positive psychiatric illness (such as an anxiety neurosis or reactive depression): *McLoughlin v O'Brian* [1983] 1 A.C. 410, 431, *per* Lord Bridge; *Alcock v Chief Constable of the South Yorkshire Police* [1992] 1 A.C. 310, 409, *per* Lord Oliver; para. 2–097.

[23] See paras 2–096 *et seq*. Claims were brought by the relatives of deceased children in respect of the psychiatric distress caused by the removal and retention of organs at the Alder Hey Children's Hospital, but the actions were settled in January 2003 for approximately £5,000 per child: *The Guardian*, February 1 and 27, 2003.

[24] For guidance issued by the Royal College of Obstetricians and Gynaecologists on both male and female sterilisation procedures, which includes guidance on the information that patients should be given, see RCOG, *Male and Female Sterilisation*, 1999, available at *www.rcog.org.uk* (good practice; guidelines).

[25] See, *e.g.*, *Eyre v Measday* [1986] 1 All E.R. 488, 490–491; *Gold v Haringey Health Authority* [1988] Q.B. 481, 484; *Videto v Kennedy* (1980) 125 D.L.R. (3d) 612, 618 (Ont. H.C.). The Royal College of Obstetricians and Gynaecologists estimates the risk to be 1 in 200 for female sterilisation and 1 in 2000 for male sterilisation: RCOG, *Male and Female Sterilisation*, 1999.

[26] [2000] 2 A.C. 59. See paras 2–039 *et seq*.

no duty of care is owed in respect of the cost of raising a healthy child these cases are likely to have even less significance, though where the child is born with disabilities it remains possible to claim in respect of the financial costs associated with the disability (even though the child's disabilities are unrelated to the defendant's duty[27]), and the mother may also have a claim in respect of her losses.[28]

6–193   The early cases appear to have been pleaded solely in negligence, relying on the *Bolam* test, with the result that if a responsible body of medical opinion would not have advised the claimant of the risk that the operation might not succeed in its objective the action failed.[29] There have been several attempts by claimants to circumvent this problem. In *Eyre v Measday*[30] the claimant entered into a contract with the defendant surgeon to be sterilised. The defendant had emphasised that a sterilisation operation was irreversible, but he did not inform the claimant that there was a less than one per cent risk of pregnancy occurring following such a procedure. The claimant argued that the defendant was in breach of a contractual term that she would be rendered irreversibly sterile, and/or a collateral warranty to that effect which induced her to enter the contract. It was held that the contract was to perform a sterilisation operation, it was not a contract to render the claimant sterile, and there was neither an express nor an implied warranty that the procedure would be an unqualified success. In *Thake v Maurice*[31] the Court of Appeal reached a similar conclusion that, on an objective interpretation, the defendant had not given a contractual guarantee that a vasectomy operation would render the male claimant irreversibly sterile, relying on the observation that medicine is not an exact science and results are to some extent unpredictable. The contractual approach is not entirely ruled out by these decisions; it is simply that it will be extremely difficult to prove that the defendant did in fact guarantee to achieve complete sterility.[32]

6–194   The defendant was, nonetheless, held liable for negligence in *Thake v Maurice*. He had failed to give his usual warning that there was a slight risk that the male claimant might become fertile again. There was no independent evidence called by either party as to the general practice of the profession with regard to warnings at the time of the operation in 1975. The Court of Appeal held that in these circumstances the claimants were entitled to rely on the defendant's own evidence (which was that he considered a warning to be necessary) as indicative of the appropriate standard of care, and that

---

[27] That is, it was not because of a foreseeable risk of the child being born with disabilities that the defendant was under a duty to warn about the sterilisation failure rate. See paras 2–045 and 2–046.

[28] See paras 9–082 *et seq.*

[29] *Waters v Park, The Times,* July 15, 1961; *Williams v St. Helens and District Hospital Management Committee* (1977, QBD; unreported), where the defendant's omission to warn of a risk of failure of 1 in 300 was held not to be negligent where the evidence was that some gynaecologists gave a warning while others did not.

[30] [1986] 1 All E.R. 488; see para. 2–010.

[31] [1986] Q.B. 644; see para. 2–011.

[32] In *Thake v Maurice* both Pain J. and Kerr L.J. took the view that the claimant had established this on the evidence. Neill and Nourse L.JJ. came to a different conclusion.

accordingly the defendant was negligent by inadvertently failing to give his usual warning.[33]

Where the claimant has not had the operation performed privately the contractual guarantee argument is clearly not available. In *Worster v City and Hackney Health Authority*[34] the claimant argued that, having signed a consent form which included the words ". . . and we understand that this means we can have no more children," the surgeon was liable for a negligent misrepresentation under the principle of *Hedley Byrne & Co Ltd v Heller & Partners Ltd.*[35] The fact that the defendant did not inform her of the risk of the operation failing, it was suggested, combined with the wording of the consent form constituted a representation that sterilisation was certain. Garland J. rejected this contention. *Hedley Byrne* did not avail the claimant since that case was concerned with establishing that a duty of care existed when giving gratuitous advice. Once the duty is established the nature of the duty is governed by the *Bolam* test, and in the application that test the action failed.[36]

6–195

The third attempt to avoid the implications of the *Bolam* test occurred in *Gold v Haringey Health Authority.*[37] The claimant underwent a sterilisation operation the day after the birth of her third child which failed to render her sterile, and she subsequently had a fourth child. She alleged that the defendants were negligent in failing to warn her of the risks of failure. The evidence was that the failure rate for female sterilisation was in the range 20 to 60 per 10,000, with operations carried out post-partum at the higher end of the range. The failure rate for vasectomy was five per 10,000.[38] The trial

6–196

---

[33] The defendant had been prevented from leading evidence from expert witnesses by a procedural error. If there had been some evidence that responsible practitioners did not give a warning, the defendant would have escaped liability, notwithstanding that he had inadvertently failed to follow his own usual practice and that he regarded a warning as necessary. See *Moyes v Lothian Health Board* [1990] 1 Med. L.R. 463, 470; and *Gascoine v Ian Sheridan & Co* [1994] 5 Med. L.R. 437, 458, where Mitchell J., commenting on a case of alleged negligent treatment said that: "If on some hit-and-miss basis they treated correctly (or correctly in the opinion of a respected reasonably competent body of thinking in 1978) then liability in negligence could not be established."

[34] *The Times*, June 22, 1987.

[35] [1964] A.C. 465.

[36] A claim for negligent misrepresentation was also rejected by the Court of Appeal in *Gold v Haringey Health Authority* [1988] Q.B. 481, 492. The claimant was not entitled to rely on the word "irreversible" as a representation that the operation would succeed, applying *Eyre v Measday* [1986] 1 All E.R. 488. Advice that a sterilisation operation is irreversible, and that there is a risk of the operation failing to achieve sterility, are two different things: *McLennan v Newcastle Health Authority* [1992] 3 Med. L.R. 215, 216. In *Danns v Department of Health* [1998] P.I.Q.R. P226 the Court of Appeal held that the failure of the Department to publish information in the media about the risks of late re-canalisation following a vasectomy (put at 2,000 to 1) did not give rise to a private law action for breach of the Ministry of Health Act 1919, s.2. The claimants had to show that a decision not to publish information about the known risks to members of the public (the risks had been notified to doctors) was a decision that the Department could not rationally have taken (applying well-known principles of public law). This was not the case on the facts.

[37] [1988] Q.B. 481.

[38] Though see the comment of Roger Clements in (1993) 4 *AVMA Medical & Legal Journal* (No. 2) p. 19, stating that the failure rates for male and female sterilisation are very similar, and that the claimant's expert evidence in *Gold* was not challenged. But see also *McLennan*

judge, Schiemann J., found that the defendants did not explain the risk of the operation failing to render the claimant sterile, and did not counsel her and her husband about the possibility of vasectomy, or explain the relative failure rates of the two operations. The medical experts were unanimous that although they themselves would have warned of the risk of failure, nonetheless a substantial body of responsible doctors would not have given any such warning in 1979. Thus, applying the *Bolam* test the claimant's action would fail. Schiemann J. drew a distinction, however, between advice given in a therapeutic context and advice given in a contraceptive context. In a therapeutic context there was a body of responsible medical opinion which would not have given a warning, but in a contraceptive context there was no such body of medical opinion. Moreover, even if there had been such a body of opinion, the defendants were still negligent because the *Bolam* test did not apply to advice given in a non-therapeutic context.

6–197   This decision was reversed by the Court of Appeal. Lloyd L.J. was unconvinced by the distinction between therapeutic and non-therapeutic advice, finding it "elusive." The distinction between advice given in a therapeutic context and advice given in a non-therapeutic context was rejected as a departure from the *Bolam* test.[39] Accordingly, the defendant was not liable because there was a responsible body of medical opinion which would not have given any warning in 1979.[40] The exercise of reasonable care may require a doctor to take reasonable steps to ensure that information about the risks of a sterilisation operation failing to achieve sterility is understood, which may require an emphatic and clear warning, with some assurance that it was being taken in by the patient.[41]

(n.38 contd.) *v Newcastle Health Authority* [1992] 3 Med. L.R. 215, QBD, where the claimant was told that vasectomy had a smaller failure rate than female sterilisation by tubal ligation; and the advice from the Royal College of Obstetricians and Gynaecologists about the different failure rates for male and female sterilisation, cited above, n. 25.

[39] [1988] Q.B. 481, 489–490, *per* Lloyd L.J. (see the quotation at para. 6–139). His Lordship continued: "The fact (if it be the fact) that giving contraceptive advice involves a different sort of skill and competence from carrying out a surgical operation does not mean that the *Bolam* test ceases to be applicable . . . To dissect a doctor's advice into that given in a therapeutic context and that given in a contraceptive context would be to go against the whole thrust of the decision of the majority of the House of Lords in [*Sidaway*]."

[40] In *Gowton v Wolverhampton Health Authority* [1994] 5 Med. L.R. 432 it was accepted by the defendants' experts that by 1986 it would have been negligence to fail to warn of the risk of recanalisation following a vasectomy operation, a risk put at one in two to three thousand; and in *Newell and Newell v Goldenberg* [1995] 6 Med. L.R. 371 Mantell J. acknowledged that there were some doctors who, in September 1985, would not have given a warning against the risk of late recanalisation following a vasectomy, but concluded that commonsense and prudence indicated that such a warning ought to have been given, and such doctors could not be considered to be acting reasonably or responsibly.

[41] In *Lybert v Warrington Health Authority* [1996] P.I.Q.R. P45; [1996] 7 Med. L.R. 71 the Court of Appeal held that the warning was inadequate because the timing and the conditions in which it was given were not appropriate, and the warning was not expressed with sufficient force to have been brought home to the claimant; *cf. Stobie v Central Birmingham Health Authority* (1994) 22 B.M.L.R. 135, QBD, where the claimants misunderstood the defendant's advice about failure rates for vasectomy. The defendant was not liable since he had done what he could to ensure that the claimants did understand that there remained a risk of failure.

The decision in *Gold* may be contrasted with *Dendaas v Yackel*[42] where **6–198** the defendant was held negligent for failing to discuss the relative failure rates of two different methods of female sterilisation (tubal ligation and the "abdominal method"). Bouck J. said that: "An average, prudent or reasonable woman who wished to be assured of sterility would probably have elected to follow the abdominal technique rather than the tubal ligation procedure since fear of future pregnancy was the overriding and dominant factor in such a choice."[43] The Supreme Court of South Australia distinguished *Dendaas v Yackel* in *F. v R.*[44] on the basis that in that case there were two medically acceptable sterilisation procedures available, each having some risk of failure. In *F. v R.* the only operations having a lower failure rate were medically unacceptable merely for sterilisation purposes. The claimant's husband had asked specifically about the desirability of his having a vasectomy, and the defendant had said that there was no sense in him being operated on when his wife was being sterilised, since the tubal ligation would be performed at same time as a Caesarian section. It was held that the non-disclosure of an overall failure rate for tubal ligation between 0.5 per cent and 1 per cent did not amount to negligence, particularly since in the defendant's hands the odds against failure were very much longer. The statistical risk referred to all tubal ligations wherever done and whatever the circumstances. The defendant was experienced and competent. She was entitled to expect that the operation done by her in a modern hospital would be successful. On the other hand, had there been an alternative procedure with even less chance of failure, the defendant would have been under a duty to offer more information, including the statistical rate of failure of the alternative procedure.[45]

Of course, sterilisation operations may carry other risks, in addition to the **6–199** risk that the procedure may not succeed in achieving sterility. In *Walsh v Family Planning Services Ltd*[46] the Supreme Court of Ireland held that, notwithstanding medical evidence to the contrary from some of the witnesses, there was an obligation to warn a patient about to undergo a vasectomy that very rarely, for no known reason, some patients experience pain for some years after the operation. McCarthy J. said that:

> "In determining whether or not to have an operation in which sexual capacity is concerned, it seems to me that to supply the patient with the material facts is so obviously necessary to an informed choice on the part of the patient that no reasonably prudent medical doctor would fail to make it. What then is material? Apart from the success ratio of the operation, what could be more material than sexual capacity after the

---

[42] (1980) 109 D.L.R. (3d) 455 (B.C.S.C.).
[43] *ibid.* at 462. The medical evidence of the failure rate for tubal ligation varied between 3 in 1,000 and 17 per 1,000.
[44] (1983) 33 S.A.S.R. 189.
[45] *ibid.* at 207, *per* Bollen J.
[46] [1992] 1 I.R. 496.

operation and its immediate sequelae? Whatever about temporary or protracted pain or discomfort, the only information given to the plaintiff and his wife on the score of sexual capacity, upon which they placed so much emphasis, was that contained in the brief paragraph headed 'Does it affect your sex-life? No.' This is not a question merely determining that a particular outcome is so rare as not to warrant such disclosure that might upset a patient but, rather, that those concerned, and this includes the authors of the information sheet, if they knew of such a risk, however remote, had a duty to inform those so critically concerned with that risk. Remote percentages of risk lose their significance to those unfortunate enough to be 100 per cent involved."[47]

Accordingly, the defendants were in breach of their duty for failing to identify the risk of impotence, whether it be functional, due to pain and discomfort, or mechanical, due to some other cause.

6–200   Even if the claimant succeeds in proving that the defendant was negligent in failing to disclose the risk that the operation would not produce sterility, the claimant must still establish causation. Most patients who consider sterilisation for contraceptive purposes would probably undergo the operation even if informed about the remote risk of the procedure failing to achieve sterility, and it would be highly unlikely that they would continue with other contraceptive methods "just in case" the sterilisation had failed,[48] although in *Gowton v Wolverhampton Health Authority*[49] the claimants managed to persuade the trial judge that this is what would have happened had they been warned of the risk of a vasectomy operation not producing complete sterility. The couple were determined not to have any further children, and were very fearful of the prospect of a fifth pregnancy. Had she known of the risk of recanalisation following her husband's sterilisation operation it was probable that the female claimant would have continued to take the contraceptive pill, and this would have been sufficient to make it improbable that she would become pregnant. On the other hand, in *Newell and Newell v Goldenberg*[50] Mantell J. did not accept the claimants' contention that had they known about the risk of late recanalisation following a vasectomy, the female claimant would also have undergone sterilisation, reducing the overall risk of pregnancy almost to vanishing point. This was rejected as unpersuasive, despite the claimants' evidence that they were desperate to avoid a further pregnancy, because they had engaged in sexual intercourse

---

[47] *ibid.* at 520–21. In *Geoghegan v Harris* [2000] 3 I.R. 536, 549 Kearns J., commenting on the last two sentences of this quotation, said: "However, the attractiveness of the observation should not occlude the possibility that at times a risk may become so remote, in relation at any rate to the less than most serious consequences, that a reasonable man may not regard it as material or significant. While such cases may be few in number, they do suggest that an absolute requirement of disclosure in every case is unduly onerous, and perhaps in the end counter-productive if it needlessly deters patients from undergoing operations which are in their best interests to have."

[48] *Grey v Webster* (1984) 14 D.L.R. (4th) 706, 715 (N.B.Q.B).

[49] [1994] 5 Med. L.R. 432.

[50] [1995] 6 Med. L.R. 371.

between January and November 1992 and in the period between the vasectomy and the second sterile sperm sample using only condoms for protection. There was also evidence from experts that no patient who had been informed of the risk of late failure of vasectomy had declined the operation for that reason or sought additional contraceptive measures. Thus, had the claimants been advised about the failure rate, they would probably have been content to accept the risk without taking any additional precautions. The defendant was held liable, however, for the "anxiety and distress" suffered by the claimants on finding that the female claimant was pregnant, *i.e.* the distress attributable to the fact the male claimant suspected his wife of having an extra-marital affair, since he believed that he could not possibly be the child's father. That could have been avoided had the defendant given a warning about the risk of late recanalisation.[51]

In *Gold v Haringey Health Authority*[52] the causation point rested on the argument that if the comparative failure rates had been discussed the male claimant would have had a vasectomy, and thus there would have been no difficulty in showing that the claimant would not have proceeded with the operation. In *Thake v Maurice*,[53] on the other hand, the argument was not that if the claimants had known of the risk of recanalisation the male claimant would not have had the vasectomy operation, since on the evidence the failure rate was lower than for female sterilisation. Rather, it was that if they had realised that this was a possibility, the female claimant would have appreciated that she was pregnant earlier in the pregnancy than in fact she did and would have had an abortion at an early stage. The defendant's claim that this risk was unforeseeable and therefore too remote was rejected by the Court of Appeal.

6–201

Nonetheless, causation will remain a problem in most cases of failure to warn about the risk of the sterilisation not being effective,[54] unless the claimant can point to a medically acceptable alternative procedure which carried a lower failure rate,[55] or is in a position to adopt the argument in *Thake v Maurice* that because she was not informed about the remote risk that the sterilisation might be ineffective she did not realise that she might

6–202

---

[51] Damages were agreed at £500. The law report does not indicate the basis of this agreement, though claims in respect of "anxiety and distress" are not usually maintainable in the tort of negligence unless there is also a genuine psychiatric illness. See para. 2–097. The action was brought in both contract and tort.

[52] [1988] Q.B. 481.

[53] [1986] Q.B. 644.

[54] See, *e.g.*, *Zimmer v Ringrose* (1981) 124 D.L.R. (3d) 215 (Alta. C.A.) where despite the fact that the defendant was held negligent in failing to disclose that his method of sterilisation was experimental, and had not been approved by the profession, the action for non-disclosure failed because a reasonable patient in the claimant's position would have accepted the treatment. The decisive factor in her case was that she wanted to avoid having to go into hospital to be sterilised when she had a young baby at home to look after.

[55] In *Grey v Webster* (1984) 14 D.L.R. (4th) 706 (N.B.Q.B) the claimant said that if she had known about the failure rate for tubal ligation she would have undergone a hysterectomy to ensure sterility. The medical evidence, however, indicated that hysterectomy was not a medically acceptable procedure merely for sterilisation purposes, and the action failed on causation.

be pregnant until it was too late safely to have an abortion. Where, on the other hand, the defendant knows that the sterilisation procedure has failed to render the claimant sterile, but fails to inform the claimant of that fact to give her the opportunity to take alternative contraceptive measures, there will be no difficulty in establishing both negligence and causation.[56] Conversely, where the claimant knows that she is not sterile following a sterilisation operation, but proceeds to have sexual intercourse without taking alternative contraceptive measures, this will break the causal link between the negligence (whether this be in the performance of the surgery or the failure to warn of the risks) and the subsequent birth of a child.[57]

---

[56] *Cryderman v Ringrose* [1977] 3 W.W.R. 109; affirmed [1978] 3 W.W.R. 481 (Alta. C.A.). Note that where the sterilisation operation itself has been performed negligently (see para. 4–077), there will be no difficulty in proving causation. The claimant's refusal to undergo an abortion when she discovers that she is pregnant does not amount to a *novus actus interveniens*: see *Emeh v Kensington and Chelsea Area Health Authority* [1985] Q.B. 1012, para. 5–090.

[57] *Sabri-Tabrizi v Lothian Health Board*, 1998 S.C. 373.

CHAPTER 7

LIABILITY OF HOSPITALS AND CONTRIBUTION

In theory there are two grounds upon which a hospital authority[1] may be held responsible for injury to patients. The first, and by far the most common, is by virtue of an employer's vicarious liability for the torts of an employee committed during the course of employment. Although in the past hospital authorities had an effective immunity from liability for the negligence of professional staff, for over fifty years now hospitals have been in the same position as other employers with respect to vicarious liability. The only lingering uncertainty concerns precisely which staff are considered to be employees. The second, and in some respects more speculative, ground is the concept of direct liability, by which a hospital is held liable not for the tort of an employee but for breach of its own duty owed directly to the patient. This may be the result of some organisational error, where, for example, there is an inadequate system for co-ordinating the work of staff which has put patients at risk. Alternatively, it may be that a hospital owes a primary, non-delegable duty to patients. Breach of such a duty renders the hospital liable to the patient whether it is occasioned by the conduct of an employee or of someone who is not an employee, such as an independent contractor. Thus, there can be some overlap between vicarious liability and a non-delegable duty. These two forms of liability are conceptually quite distinct, though in reality the purpose of imposing a non-delegable duty is simply to establish the responsibility of an "employer" for the negligence of independent contractors. This Chapter considers both the vicarious liability of a hospital authority and its potential direct liability to patients and others. It then discusses the rules on contribution between tortfeasors, which though not frequently an issue in medical negligence litigation, can be relevant in this context. The Chapter concludes with a brief section on NHS Indemnity, the practical consequences of which can occasionally render the precise legal position of a defendant irrelevant.

7-001

---

[1] The organisation of the NHS seems to change on a regular basis, no matter what the political orientation of the government of the day. One consequence is that the body legally responsible for the consequences of harm to patients and others changes from time to time (previously "health authorities", now NHS Trusts and Primary Care Trusts, though in some circumstances the NHS Litigation Authority). The term "hospital authority" is used in this Chapter in a generic sense to refer to the body responsible in law for damage arising out of the provision of health care.

1. VICARIOUS LIABILITY

7–002   An employer is vicariously liable for torts committed by his employees acting in the course of their employment.[2] Vicarious liability arises from the employer-employee relationship, it does not depend upon any personal fault by the employer. Liability is imposed on the employer, not for a breach of the employer's duty to the claimant, but for the employee's breach of a duty owed by the employee to the claimant. This can be distinguished from the situation in which the employee's act results in the breach of a primary duty owed by the employer to the claimant.

7–003   At one time it was thought that hospital authorities were not vicariously liable for the negligence of their "professional" staff, whether doctors or nurses, in the performance of their professional duties. This stemmed from the ruling of the Court of Appeal in *Hillyer v Governors of St. Bartholomews Hospital*,[3] which was based to some extent on the view that when acting on a professional judgment doctors exercised a discretion which the hospital authority could not control, and in the absence of control they were not employees.[4] The authority's responsibility was limited to exercising reasonable care in the selection of competent staff (which was a primary duty) and to vicarious liability for the performance of "purely ministerial or administrative duties, such as . . . attendance of nurses in the wards, the summoning of medical aid in cases of emergency, the supply of proper food and the like."[5]

7–004   The "control test" is no longer considered adequate as a determinant of the employer-employee relationship in modern economic conditions, where employers often do not have the technical expertise to supervise and control the manner in which skilled employees perform their work.[6] The current approach to identifying the employer-employee relationship is that there is no single test: the question depends upon weighing a number of possibly conflicting factors in order to decide whether the work is performed under a contract of service or a contract for services.[7]

---

[2] See generally *Clerk & Lindsell on Torts*, 18th ed., 2000, Ch. 5.

[3] [1909] 2 K.B. 820; see also *Evans v Liverpool Corporation* [1906] 1 K.B. 160 which was followed by the Court of Appeal in *Hillyer*; *Hall v Lees* [1904] 2 K.B. 603, where a nursing association undertook to supply competent nurses, not to nurse the patient, and so were not liable for a nurse's negligence. In *Gold v Essex County Council* [1942] 2 K.B. 293, 301 Lord Greene M.R. said that in *Hall v Lees* the contract was a special one "and the case has nothing to do with hospitals or nursing homes."

[4] In *Cassidy v Ministry of Health* [1951] 2 K.B. 343, 361 Denning L.J. suggested that the decision in *Hillyer* was attributable "to a desire to relieve the charitable hospitals from liabilities which they could not afford"; see also the comments of Lord Cooper in *MacDonald v Board of Management for Glasgow Western Hospitals* 1954 S.C. 453, 476. Lord Denning returned to this theme, but this time as a champion of financially beleaguered NHS hospitals, on a number of occasions: see paras 3–110 n. 68, and 4–119.

[5] [1909] 2 K.B. 820, 829. *Hillyer* was followed in *Strangeways-Lesmere v Clayton* [1936] 2 K.B. 11; *Dryden v Surrey County Council* [1936] 2 All E.R. 535; and *Marshall v Lindsey County Council* [1935] 1 K.B. 516, CA. The House of Lords in *Lindsey County Council v Marshall* [1937] A.C. 97 did not consider whether *Hillyer* was correctly decided.

[6] A point made more than fifty years ago by Kahn-Freund (1951) 14 M.L.R. 504.

[7] *Ready Mixed Concrete (South East) Ltd v Minister of Pensions and National Insurance*

The move away from the consequences of *Hillyer* began in *Gold v Essex*   7–005
County Council,[8] where the Court of Appeal refused to accept the distinction between purely administrative duties and professional duties, holding
the hospital authority vicariously liable for the negligence of a qualified
radiographer employed under a contract of service. Lord Greene M.R.
approached the question in terms of the obligation to the patient undertaken
by a hospital. It was not a duty simply to provide suitable equipment and
facilities, and to take reasonable care in selecting competent staff. It was a
duty to treat the patient with the apparatus provided, and this could not be
avoided by employing someone to discharge the duty, irrespective of whether
the procedure involved the use of skill. MacKinnon and Goddard L.JJ.
simply took the view that since the radiographer was employed under a contract of service, and was therefore an employee, the hospital authority were
vicariously liable for his negligence. The position of the hospital in the case
of negligence by a doctor was left unresolved. Goddard L.J. considered that
the hospital would be responsible for the negligence of doctors on the permanent staff, provided they were employed under a contract of service,
although visiting surgeons and physicians were not employed under a contract of service, but rather a contract for services.[9] This was applied by
Hilbery J. in *Collins v Hertfordshire County Council*,[10] holding a hospital
authority vicariously liable for the negligence of a resident junior house
surgeon (employed on a temporary, but full-time basis). On the other hand,
the authority was not responsible for the conduct of a visiting surgeon,
although he had been engaged on similar written terms (but part-time) to the
resident junior houseman.[11]

In *Cassidy v Ministry of Health*[12] the Court of Appeal confirmed that a   7–006
hospital authority will be held vicariously liable for the negligence of all
staff, nurses and doctors alike, employed under a contract of service as part
of the permanent staff of the hospital. Denning L.J. was clear that a hospital is in the same position as any other employer with respect to the torts of
employees:

(n.7 contd.) [1968] 2 Q.B. 497; *Market Investigations Ltd v Minister of Social Security*
   [1969] 2 Q.B. 173; *O'Kelly v Trusthouse Forte plc* [1983] I.R.L.R. 367.
[8] [1942] 2 K.B. 293.
[9] *ibid.* at 313 and 310. See also Lord Greene M.R. *ibid.* at 302 commenting that with consultants the nature of the work and their relationship with the hospital is such that the hospital does not undertake responsibility for their negligence. His Lordship expressly left open
   the position of a resident house surgeon.
[10] [1947] 1 K.B. 598, 614–620.
[11] *ibid.* at 619. In *Cassidy v Ministry of Health* [1951] 2 K.B. 343, 352 Somervell L.J. described
   the relationship between the visiting surgeon and the hospital in *Collins* as "obscure."
[12] [1951] 2 K.B. 343. The same view has been taken in Scotland: *MacDonald v Board of
   Management for Glasgow Western Hospitals* 1954 S.C. 453; *Fox v Glasgow South Western
   Hospitals* 1955 S.L.T. 337; Ireland: *O'Donovan v Cork County Council* [1967] I.R. 173;
   Australia: *Samios v Repatriation Commission* [1960] W.A.R. 219; and in Canada: *Fleming
   v Sisters of St. Joseph* [1938] S.C.R. 172; *Fraser v Vancouver General Hospital* (1951) 3
   W.W.R. 337, 340, 347 (B.C.C.A.), affirmed [1952] 3 D.L.R. 785 (S.C.C.); *Martel v Hotel-
   Dieu St.-Vallier* (1969) 14 D.L.R. (3d) 445 (S.C.C.); *Toronto General Hospital v Aynsley*
   (1971) 25 D.L.R. (3d) 241 (S.C.C.).

"In my opinion authorities who run a hospital, be they local authorities, government boards, or any other corporation, are in law under the self-same duty as the humblest doctor; whenever they accept a patient for treatment, they must use reasonable care and skill to cure him of his ailment. The hospital authorities cannot, of course, do it by themselves: they have no ears to listen through the stethoscope, and no hands to hold the surgeon's knife. They must do it by the staff they employ; and if their staff are negligent in giving the treatment, they are just as liable for that negligence as is anyone else who employs others to do his duties for him."[13]

The position of a consultant surgeon or physician who is not an employee of the hospital was, however, expressly distinguished by Somervell and Singleton L.JJ.[14] Somervell L.J. suggested that a patient who is treated by a consultant is in much the same position as a private patient who has arranged to be operated upon by a specific doctor. Denning L.J. went further than the majority, taking the view that a hospital is under a non-delegable duty to treat patients, a duty which cannot be discharged by delegating its performance to a consultant under a contract for services. If this is correct the basis on which a consultant is engaged, whether as an employee or an independent contractor is, in practice, irrelevant: the hospital will be liable for his negligence.[15]

7–007   Subsequently, in *Roe v Minister of Health*[16] the Court of Appeal considered the question of a hospital authority's responsibility in respect of a part-time anaesthetist, and concluded that there would be vicarious liability, although on the facts there had been no negligence. Denning L.J. repeated the view he had expressed in *Cassidy v Ministry of Health*, apparently conflating the question of vicarious and primary liability:

"... the hospital authorities are responsible for the whole of their staff, not only for the nurses and doctors, but also for the anaesthetists and the surgeons. It does not matter whether they are permanent or temporary, resident or visiting, whole-time or part-time. The hospital authorities are responsible for all of them. The reason is because, even if they are not servants, they are the agents of the hospital to give the treatment. The only exception is the case of consultants or anaesthetists selected and employed by the patient himself."[17]

Morris L.J., relying on the judgment of Lord Greene M.R. in *Gold v Essex County Council*, said that the question depended upon what the hospital had undertaken to provide, and that this was a question of fact in each case. On the

---

[13] *ibid*. at 360.
[14] *ibid*. at 351 and 358 respectively.
[15] See paras 7–026 to 7–027. There is, however, a possible difference between vicarious liability for employees and liability under a non-delegable duty for the acts of independent contractors, in that the employer is not liable for the "collateral negligence" of an independent contractor; see para. 7–033.
[16] [1954] 2 Q.B. 66.
[17] *ibid*. at 82.

facts the anaesthetists in *Roe* "were members of the 'organisation' of the hospital: they were members of the staff engaged by the hospital to do what the hospital itself was undertaking to do."[18] On this basis the principle of *respondeat superior* applied. It would seem that both Lord Greene M.R. and Morris L.J. considered that the hospital's "undertaking" was the basis for imposing *vicarious* liability, not as giving rise to a non-delegable duty. Under a non-delegable duty the hospital would be responsible for the conduct of a consultant (unless the consultant was privately engaged by the patient) but the consultant was specifically excluded from the hospital's responsibility by Lord Greene.

The cumulative effect of these cases is that a hospital authority will be vicariously liable for the negligence of all full-time or part-time employees.[19] It is possible that visiting consultants do not fall into the category of employees,[20] although in *Razzel v Snowball*[21] Denning L.J. said that since the introduction of the National Health Service the term "consultant" does not denote a particular relationship between a doctor and a hospital. Rather, it is simply a title denoting his place in the hierarchy of the hospital staff: "He is a senior member of the staff but nevertheless just as much a member of the staff as the house surgeon."[22] This view has not had to be tested in the courts since in practice, whatever the legal niceties may be, hospital authorities within the NHS do not argue the point that a consultant is not an employee when engaged on NHS work. Consultants clearly fall within the terms of HC (89)34 which introduced "NHS indemnity," on the assumption that they are members of staff for whom the hospital authority or NHS Trust will be vicariously liable.[23] This is also true of staff supplied to the hospital by outside agencies. It is arguable that an agency nurse, for example, remains the employee of the agency and does not become an employee of the hospital authority for the purpose of vicarious liability.[24] The hospital authority will accept responsibility for the negligence of agency staff, however, under the

7–008

---

[18] *ibid.* at 91.

[19] *Gold v Essex County Council* [1942] 2 K.B. 293 (radiographer); *Collins v Hertfordshire County Council* [1947] 1 K.B. 598 (resident house surgeon and pharmacist); *Cassidy v Ministry of Health* [1951] 2 K.B. 343 (assistant medical officer); *MacDonald v Board of Management for Glasgow Western Hospitals* 1954 S.C. 453 (resident medical officer); *Roe v Minister of Health* [1954] 2 Q.B. 66 (anaesthetist); *Fox v Glasgow South Western Hospitals* 1955 S.L.T. 337 (nurses). An employer will be vicariously liable for injury to an employee caused by the negligence of an occupational medical officer: *Stokes v Guest, Keen and Nettlefold (Bolts and Nuts) Ltd* [1968] 1 W.L.R. 1776, para. 4–008.

[20] This was the view of Hilbery J. in *Collins v Hertfordshire County Council* [1947] 1 K.B. 598, 619–620; see also *MacDonald v Board of Management for Glasgow Western Hospitals* 1954 S.C. 453, 478, 485; *Higgins v North West Metropolitan Hospital Board* [1954] 1 W.L.R. 411, 417.

[21] [1954] 1 W.L.R. 1382.

[22] *ibid.* at 1386.

[23] See paras 7–052 to 7–053.

[24] For the effect of transferring employees between employers see *Mersey Docks and Harbour Board v Coggins & Griffith (Liverpool) Ltd* [1947] A.C. 1; *Bhoomidas v Port of Singapore Authority* [1978] 1 W.L.R. 189; *Gibb v United Steel Companies Ltd* [1957] 1 W.L.R. 668; *Morris v Breaveglen Ltd* [1993] I.C.R. 766; *Nelhams v Sandells Maintenance Ltd* [1996] P.I.Q.R. P52. Note, however, that staff supplied by an employment agency may not be employees of the agency: see *Ironmonger v Movefield Ltd* [1988] I.R.L.R. 461.

terms of NHS indemnity.[25] The fact that NHS hospital authorities accept vicarious responsibility for consultants and agency staff removes much of the practical import of the arguments about whether a hospital is under a non-delegable duty to patients.

7–009   Surgeons do not normally employ the nurses in the operating theatre or on the ward and will not be responsible for their negligence in carrying out the instructions that have been given with regard to the patient's treatment.[26] Nursing staff remain the employees of the hospital, and if the hospital is not liable for the conduct of a nurse who is acting under the instructions of the surgeon or doctor the reason is "not that *pro hac vice* she ceases to be the servant of the hospital, but that she is not guilty of negligence if she carries out the orders of the surgeon, however negligent those orders may be."[27]

General practice

7–010   General practitioners are not employees,[28] and so a claim for negligence against a general practitioner (or a general dental practitioner) would have to be pursued against the individual doctor.[29] General practitioners will be vicariously liable for the negligence of their employees, such as nurses or receptionists.[30] The position of a locum tenens is unclear. It seems likely that a deputising doctor would not be considered to be an employee, but would be categorised as an independent contractor.[31] It is doubtful whether a general practitioner would be under a non-delegable duty with respect to the

---

[25] See HC (89)34, para. 8 and Annex A para. 18. The Circular was updated by H.S.G. (96)48 and *NHS Indemnity—Arrangements for Clinical Negligence Claims in the NHS*, NHS Executive, 1996 (see Appendix 1).

[26] *Perionowsky v Freeman* (1866) 4 F. & F. 977; *Morris v Winsbury-White* [1937] 4 All E.R. 494, 498.

[27] *Gold v Essex County Council* [1942] 2 K.B. 293, 299, *per* Lord Greene M.R.; *Johnston v Wellesley Hospital* (1970) 17 D.L.R. (3d) 139, 152 (Ont. H.C.). Note, however, that a nurse does not necessarily act with reasonable care by mechanically following a doctor's orders. If the instruction was obviously incorrect the nurse would have a duty to seek confirmation from the doctor: *per* Goddard L.J. at [1942] 2 K.B. 293, 313; see para. 4–065.

[28] In *Wadi v Cornwall and Isles of Scilly Family Practitioner Committee* [1985] I.C.R. 492 the Employment Appeal Tribunal held that the relationship between general practitioners and a Family Health Service Authority was not contractual but statutory; and in *Roy v Kensington and Chelsea and Westminster Family Practitioner Committee* [1992] 1 A.C. 624 the House of Lords doubted, without deciding, whether the relationship between a general practitioner and the NHS was contractual in nature. There were "contractual echoes in the relationship." Nonetheless, a general practitioner has private law rights against the health authority, arising from the legislation (the National Health Service Act 1977 and the National Health Service (General Medical Services) Regulations 1992 (S.I. 1992 No. 635), as frequently amended).

[29] The National Health Service Act 1977, s.43C, inserted by the Health Act 1999, s.9, gives the Secretary of State the power to make professional indemnity cover mandatory for any of the professions providing services under Pt II of the 1977 Act (i.e. general practitioners, dentists, pharmacists and optometrists). See further the Medical Practitioners and Dentists (Professional Negligence Insurance) Bill 2003 which would require approved indemnity cover for all medical and dental practitioners.

[30] See, *e.g.*, *Lobley v Nunn* (1985, C.A.; unreported), where an action against a receptionist failed on the facts; *Hancke v Hooper* (1835) 7 C. & P. 81, where a surgeon was held liable for the negligence of an apprentice.

[31] This was the conclusion of Osler J. in *Rothwell v Raes* (1988) 54 D.L.R. (4th) 193, 262

negligence of a locum. Staff directly employed by a health authority or Primary Care Trust (*e.g.* as a public health doctor or a district nurse) clearly are employees for whose negligence the employer is vicariously liable. Primary Care Trusts are now eligible to participate in the Clinical Negligence Scheme for Trusts,[32] and guidance issued by the NHS Litigation Authority as to who is eligible for indemnity cover under the scheme renders much of the debate about who is an employee redundant.[33]

Private Treatment

Where a patient has received treatment privately he could sue the hospi-   **7–011**
tal or clinic, who will be vicariously liable for the negligence of their employees, but, in practice, the doctor may not be employed by the hospital or clinic. Unless the hospital has held the doctor out to the patient as an employee,[34] they will not be liable for his negligence and the patient will have to sue the doctor individually. This may depend upon the construction placed on the contract between the hospital and patient. On the other hand, it is arguable that where the patient's contract is with the hospital then the hospital undertakes a non-delegable duty, at least where the contract is to provide treatment as opposed to merely providing facilities for treatment to be given by an independent doctor. This view derives some support from an observation by Morris L.J. in *Roe v Minister of Health*:

> "While the requisite standard of care does not vary according as to whether treatment is gratuitous or on payment, the existence of arrangements entitling the plaintiffs to expect certain treatment might

---

(n.31 contd.) (Ont. H.C.) who emphasised the independence of the locum's professional judgment. The locum's freedom of action as a medical practitioner was not circumscribed in any way, other than financial. The National Health Service (General Medical Services) Regulations 1992 (S.I. 1992 No. 635), as frequently amended, provide that under a general practitioner's terms of service a doctor is responsible for the acts and omissions of a deputy, except where the deputy is included in the medical list of a Primary Care Trust, in which case the deputy alone is responsible for his own acts and omissions and the acts and omissions of any person employed by the deputy or acting on his behalf: see Sch. 2, para. 20. Although this regulates the general practitioner's position under the terms of service with a health authority or Primary Care Trust, it is not necessarily conclusive in law *vis-à-vis* the patient.

[32] See para. 7–058.

[33] See *The NHSLA's Risk Pooling Schemes: Who is indemnified?*, November 2002 [available at *www.nhsla.com* under "Events"], which quotes a CNST guideline: "NHS Indemnity covers the actions of staff in the course of their NHS employment. It also covers people in certain other categories whenever the NHS body owes a duty of care to the person harmed, including, for example, locums, medical academic staff with honorary contracts, students, those conducting clinical trials, charitable volunteers and people undergoing further professional education, training and examinations. This includes staff working on income generation projects. GPs or dentists who are directly employed [by Health Authorities], *e.g.* as Public Health doctors (including port medical officers and medical inspectors of immigrants at UK air/sea ports), are covered." The term "employment" also includes formal secondment to a Primary Care Trust from a partner organisation.

[34] See, *e.g.*, *Rogers v Night Riders* [1983] R.T.R. 324, CA, where a minicab hire firm were held to be under a non-delegable duty with regard to the safety of vehicles, although the vehicle drivers were independent contractors.

be a relevant factor when considering the extent of the obligation assumed by the hospital."[35]

7–012   Where a doctor who is not employed by the hospital has been engaged directly by the patient the hospital will not be liable for the doctor's negligence, and the patient's claim will be against the doctor personally. This applies both to vicarious liability and non-delegable duties.[36] If staff employed by the hospital, such as nurses, are involved in assisting the doctor to provide treatment, then the hospital is potentially vicariously liable for their negligence in the usual way, whether the hospital is private or NHS

Acts in the course of employment

7–013   The vicarious liability of an employer is limited to the torts of an employee who is acting in the course of his employment. This is treated as a question of fact in each case. Provided that the employee is still engaged on the tasks he was employed to do, albeit he is doing it in a wrongful and unauthorised manner, he will be acting in the course of employment. This aspect of vicarious liability does not appear to have created problems in the context of medical negligence actions. In theory a surgeon who performed an operation beyond the sphere of his experience could be considered to be acting outside the scope of employment, but this is a question of degree, and the circumstances would probably have to be quite extreme before this would become a live issue.[37] Liability will not necessarily be limited to acts in the course of providing treatment itself, so, for example, the hospital may be responsible for negligence which leads to the patient falling out of bed.[38]

7–014   The traditional test for what constitutes the "course of employment" is whether the employee's conduct was a wrongful and unauthorised mode of doing some act authorised by the employer.[39] Although this test has not generally been a problem in the context of medical negligence claims, there are certain situations, particularly where the employee's conduct is an intentional wrong, where there is a tendency to blur the distinction between the employee's duty and the employer's duty to the claimant. Intentional wrongs are comparatively rare in the health care setting but they can occur,[40] and an

---

[35] [1954] 2 Q.B. 66, 89.
[36] See Denning L.J. in *Cassidy v Ministry of Health* [1951] 2 K.B. 343, 362 and *Roe v Minister of Health* [1954] 2 Q.B. 66, 82; *Johnston v Wellesley Hospital* (1970) 17 D.L.R. (3d) 139, 152–153 (Ont. H.C.); *Crits v Sylvester* (1956) 1 D.L.R. (2d) 504, 508 (Ont. C.A.); affirmed (1956) 5 D.L.R. (2d) 601 (S.C.C.), holding that a hospital authority is not liable if a doctor employed by the patient, not the hospital, fails to use the equipment available; the hospital is not required to oversee the use of appliances by a privately engaged doctor.
[37] HC(89)34, Annex A, para. 12 stated that "actions in the course of NHS employment" should be interpreted liberally.
[38] *Smith v Lewisham Group Hospital Management Committee*, *The Times*, June 21, 1955; *Beatty v Sisters of Misericorde of Alberta* [1935] 1 W.W.R. 651.
[39] See *Clerk & Lindsell on Torts*, 18th ed., 2000, para. 5.24, citing *Salmond & Heuston on the Law of Torts*, (21st ed., 1996) p. 443.
[40] The Beverley Allitt case would be one example. See Appleyard (1994) 308 B.M.J. 287;

issue may then arise as to whether the NHS Trust employing the individual would be vicariously liable. In *Lister v Hesley Hall Ltd*[41] the warden of a boarding house attached to a school for children with emotional and behavioural difficulties systematically sexually abused the claimants who were resident in the boarding house. The question was whether the warden's employers were vicariously liable for the sexual abuse (a claim that there had been negligence by the school in appointing and supervising the warden having been abandoned). The traditional test for the course of employment does not provide a ready solution to cases involving intentional conduct. Indeed, as a general rule the more egregious the conduct, the less likely it is that the test will be satisfied, because it becomes difficult to categorise it as merely an "unauthorised mode" of performing an "authorised" act. The warden was responsible for the care of the children, and the abuse could hardly be called an unauthorised mode of doing some act authorised by the employers. It was the very antithesis of what he was authorised to do. Nonetheless, the House of Lords unanimously held the school to be vicariously liable for the warden's conduct, placing some emphasis on the fact that the school had undertaken the care and safekeeping of the boys. Lord Steyn said that the question was:

> "whether the warden's torts were so closely connected with his employment that it would be fair and just to hold the employers vicariously liable. On the facts of the case the answer is yes. After all, the sexual abuse was inextricably interwoven with the carrying out by the warden of his duties . . ."[42]

Lord Clyde said that the sufficiency of the connection could be gauged by asking whether the wrongful acts could be seen as ways of carrying out the work which the employer had authorised. There had to be some greater connection between the tortious act of the employee and the circumstances of his employment than the mere opportunity to commit the act which has been provided by the access to the premises which his employment has permitted.[43] Thus, as Lord Millett pointed out, the fact that the employment provided access to the premises would not be sufficient, because the same would have been true of a groundsman or the school porter. It was the employee's position as warden and the close contact with the boys which that work involved which created a sufficient connection between the acts of abuse and the work he had been employed to do. His general duty was to look after the claimants. The fact that he performed that function in a way which was an

---

(n.40 contd.) Dyer (1993) 306 B.M.J. 1431. Another would be the doctor who uses the opportunity of examining patients as a means of committing sexual assaults. See *R v Tabassum* [2000] Lloyd's Rep. Med. 404, CA, although the defendant in that case was not a doctor.

[41] [2001] UKHL 22; [2002] 1 A.C. 215; Feldthusen (2001) 9 Tort L. Rev. 173.
[42] *ibid.* at [28].
[43] *ibid.* at [45].

abuse of his position and a negation of his duty did not sever the connection with his employment.[44]

7–015   The approach in *Lister* attaches significance to the nature of the relationship between the claimant and the employer rather than that between the claimant and the employee, though it remains true that there must be a tort committed by an employee of the defendant. In *Balfron Trustees Ltd v Peterson*[45] Laddie J. suggested that the problem with the phrase "course of employment" as a yardstick was that the courts' conception of vicarious liability has changed and expanded over the years. Although in theory it directs attention to the nature of the relationship between the employer and the employee, in practice the expression is used "to cover the situation where the employee's activities were not, in fact, within the terms of his employment, but were to be treated as if they were." But it is not the precise terms of the employment which determines whether there is vicarious liability: "Rather it is whether there is vicarious liability which determines whether the wrongful act is *to be regarded* as having been committed in the course of the employee's employment."[46] Thus, the crucial question is not the relationship between employer and employee, but the relationship between the employer and the victim of the employee's tort, combined with a normative judgment as to whether the employer *ought* to be held liable in the circumstances. This, as Laddie J. observed, is at the heart of *Lister*:

> "All of these passages emphasise the necessity of identifying the duty or responsibility of the employer to the victim. If such a duty or responsibility exists, the employer cannot avoid liability because it was delegated to an employee who failed to comply with his employer's instructions. Even though the employee's acts are so heinous that they could not reasonably be said to form part of his obligations vis-à-vis his employer, they are treated as within the scope of his employment vis-à-vis the victim, since he was employed to discharge the employer's duty to the victim. If this analysis is right, then the first issue to be determined is whether or not the employer owed a duty to the victim/claimant . . . Whether or not a duty of care of the employer to the victim is involved, there must be some form of responsibility towards the victim. Once there is, the employer cannot escape his obligations by delegating to an employee."[47]

Although this analysis conflates the traditional distinction between vicarious liability (in which the employer is held liable for the employee's tort) and primary liability (where the conduct of another person, whether employee or independent contractor, constitutes a breach of the employer's own duty to the claimant) it is respectfully submitted that Laddie J.'s understanding of

---

[44] *ibid.* at [82].
[45] [2001] I.R.L.R. 758.
[46] *ibid.* at [23], emphasis added.
[47] *ibid.* at [33].

Lister is correct. The consequence is that, particularly in cases involving deliberate wrongdoing by employees, one should look to the nature of the relationship between the employer and the claimant, rather than that between the employee and claimant.

2. DIRECT LIABILITY

The concept of the direct liability of a hospital authority is used in two dis-   **7–016**
tinct ways. First, where the authority is itself at fault in the manner in which it has performed its functions, although it may not be possible to identify any particular employee who was negligent. This may be categorised as a form of organisational failure. Second, direct liability is also used to describe the imposition of a non-delegable duty, for the purpose of establishing the authority's responsibility for the negligence of an independent contractor. As a general rule a person is not liable for the torts of an independent contractor, unless he authorised or ratified the tort,[48] or unless he has himself been negligent in selecting an incompetent contractor, or employing an inade-quate number of employees for the job,[49] or he has interfered with the manner in which the work was performed so causing the damage.[50] If an employer discovers that the contractor's work is being done in a foreseeably dangerous fashion he may be liable if he condones the negligence.[51] In each of these instances the employer is personally at fault. There are, however, a number of circumstances in which a person may be liable for the negligence of an independent contractor without fault on his part. Here the employer is said to be under a non-delegable duty, which means that he may delegate the performance of the duty to another, but not the responsibility for the manner in which the duty is performed. If the contractor is negligent it is the employer's primary duty to the claimant that is broken.[52] In this situation there is no "personal" fault by the employer, and the concept of non-delegable duty simply means that the employer is liable for non-performance of the duty: it is no defence to show that he delegated the performance to another person, whether his employee or not, whom he reasonably believed to be competent to perform it.[53] The circumstances in which a non-delega-ble duty will be imposed are relatively fixed, but there is no guiding princi-ple which determines precisely how and when such a duty arises.[54]

---

[48] *Ellis v Sheffield Gas Consumers Co* (1853) 2 E. & B. 767.
[49] *Pinn v Rew* (1916) 32 T.L.R. 451.
[50] *McLoughlin v Pryor* (1842) 4 M. & G. 48.
[51] *D. & F. Estates Ltd v Church Commissioners for England* [1989] A.C. 177, 209.
[52] Sometimes referred to as a duty to see that care is taken, as opposed to a duty to exercise reasonable care: *cf. The Pass of Ballater* [1942] P. 112, 117; and *Stennett v Hancock* [1939] 2 All E.R. 578.
[53] *McDermid v Nash Dredging and Reclamation Co Ltd* [1987] A.C. 906, 919, *per* Lord Brandon.
[54] For discussion see McKendrick (1990) 53 M.L.R. 770.

(1) Organisational Errors

7–017   The notion that a hospital authority may be directly liable for negligence in the organisation of its services is not new. Actions have in the past been formulated in this way in order to overcome the argument that the hospital were not vicariously liable for the negligence of their professional staff. Thus, in *Vancouver General Hospital v McDaniel*[55] the claimant went into a hospital for infectious diseases for the treatment of diphtheria, and contracted smallpox. She claimed that the defendants were negligent in the system of infection control that they adopted, namely the juxtaposition of smallpox patients to the claimant, and the attendance on the claimant by nurses who also nursed smallpox patients. Lord Alness observed that the claimant had not alleged negligence on the part of an employee of the hospital:

> "The complaint is that the technique was adopted by the appellants, not that it failed in its execution. In other words, the case made against the appellant is one, not of vicarious, but of direct responsibility."[56]

7–018   This type of direct liability may take a number of forms. A hospital will be under a primary liability if it fails to provide suitable medical facilities or equipment,[57] or if it has been negligent in selecting incompetent staff.[58] A hospital also owes a duty to establish adequate procedures to safeguard patients from cross-infection,[59] and from the risk of errors in the administration of drugs.[60] In *Bull v Devon Area Health Authority*[61] the health authority were held liable for instituting an unreliable system for calling expert assistance to an obstetric emergency. It was unclear as to precisely why the communication system had broken down, but the inference was that

---

[55] (1934) 152 L.T. 56.

[56] *ibid.* at 57.

[57] *Vuchar v Trustees of Toronto General Hospital* [1937] 1 D.L.R. 298, 321 (Ont. C.A.), a case which applied *Hillyer v Governors of St. Bartholemews Hospital* [1909] 2 K.B. 820; *Denton v South West Thames Regional Health Authority* (1980, QBD; unreported) on failing to have a system to check the safety of equipment.

[58] *Wilsher v Essex Area Health Authority* [1987] Q.B. 730, 775, *per* Glidewell L.J. This was the limit of the hospital's duty in *Hillyer v Governors of St. Bartholemews Hospital* [1909] 2 K.B. 820.

[59] *Vancouver General Hospital v McDaniel* (1934) 152 L.T. 56; *Lindsey County Council v Marshall* [1937] A.C. 97.

[60] *Collins v Hertfordshire County Council* [1947] 1 K.B. 598, where a hospital failed to bring to the attention of an unqualified junior medical officer the requirements of their routine procedures for having a written prescription signed by a qualified person. Hilbery J. commented, at 614, that: "If they had had a proper system in operation, this solution could not have arrived at the theatre, let alone arrived at the body of the unfortunate patient." There may also be an obligation to have a system for informing patients about the side-effects of drugs: see the discussion of *Blyth v Bloomsbury Health Authority* (1987), (1989) 5 P.N. 167; [1993] 4 Med. L.R. 151, CA, by Montgomery (1987) 137 N.L.J. 703.

[61] (1989), [1993] 4 Med. L.R. 117 CA; para. 4–101. See also *Robertson v Nottingham Health Authority* [1997] 8 Med. L.R. 1, 13, CA—systems of communication between staff are "essentially management as opposed to clinical matters"; para. 7–027. For discussion of the duty with regard to hospital casualty departments see para. 4–005.

either there had been negligence in the operation of the system, or it was inadequate to cope with even minor hitches which it should have been possible to anticipate. This illustrates the point that a safety system may be either poorly designed or poorly implemented. Moreover, the stronger the evidence that the system is adequate to cope with all eventualities, the more compelling will be the inference that there must have been some negligence on the part of the hospital staff in implementing the procedure, for which the hospital authority will be vicariously liable.[62] The failure to enforce its own rules and regulations can amount to negligence on the part of the hospital.[63]

A hospital authority may be negligent by providing an inadequate number   **7–019**
of staff to care safely for the patients,[64] or in permitting an inexperienced doctor to administer anaesthetics without proper supervision.[65] Similarly, employing too many inexperienced staff can amount to negligence by the hospital. In *Wilsher v Essex Area Health Authority* Browne-Wilkinson V.-C. said that:

> "In my judgment, a health authority which so conducts its hospital that it fails to provide doctors of sufficient skill and experience to give the treatment offered at the hospital may be directly liable in negligence to the patient. Although we were told in argument that no case has ever been decided on this ground and that it is not the practice to formulate claims in this way, I can see no reason why, in principle, the health authority should not be so liable if its organisation is at fault."[66]

---

[62] See Nathan, *Medical Negligence*, 1957, p. 102; *Voller v Portsmouth Corp* (1947) 203 L.T.J. 264. In practice it may be impossible to identify whether the system was inadequate or whether individuals have been careless in implementing it: see, *e.g.*, *Cassidy v Ministry of Health* [1951] 2 K.B. 343, 359, *per* Singleton L.J. This has the effect of blurring the distinction between the hospital's primary liability for organisational errors and vicarious liability.

[63] *Bergen v Sturgeon General Hospital* (1984) 28 C.C.L.T. 155 (Alta. Q.B.), on inconsistency between the hospital's policy on the keeping of accurate notes and records and what happened in practice; *Bernier v Sisters of Service* [1948] 2 D.L.R. 468 (Alta. S.C.).

[64] *Laidlaw v Lions Gate Hospital* (1969) 8 D.L.R. (3d) 730 (B.C.S.C.), where the hospital had provided a sufficient number of nurses per patient, but had failed to correct a lackadaisical attitude which had arisen among the nurses as to how many should be present in the post-anaesthesia recovery room; *Krujelis v Esdale* (1971) 25 D.L.R. (3d) 557 (B.C.S.C.), where the hospital was held vicariously liable for the negligence of nurses, when three out of five on duty in the post-anaesthesia recovery room went for their coffee-break together. Employing insufficient staff may mean that existing staff have to work excessive hours. If this results in harm to an employee's health the health authority may be liable in its capacity as an employer: see *Johnstone v Bloomsbury Health Authority* [1992] Q.B. 333.

[65] *Jones v Manchester Corporation* [1952] Q.B. 852; *cf. Hinfey v Salford Health Authority* [1993] 4 Med. L.R. 143, where it was held that the defendants were not negligent to permit an allegedly inexperienced obstetrician deliver a baby unsupervised.

[66] [1987] Q.B. 730, 778 citing *McDermid v Nash Dredging and Reclamation Co Ltd* [1987] A.C. 906 a case in which the House of Lords subsequently applied the principle that an employer's duty with respect to the safety of employees is non-delegable. Glidewell L.J. agreed, *ibid.* at 775, "that there seems to be no reason in principle why, in a suitable case different on its facts from this, a hospital management committee should not be held directly liable in negligence for failing to provide sufficient qualified and competent medical staff."

An individual patient could face considerable difficulty, however, in proving negligence on this basis, a point that Browne-Wilkinson V.-C. acknowledged:

> "To what extent should the authority be held liable if (*e.g.* in the use of junior housemen) it is only adopting a practice hallowed by tradition? Should the authority be liable if it demonstrates that, due to the financial stringency under which it operates, it cannot afford to fill the posts with those possessing the necessary experience? But, in my judgment, the law should not be distorted by making findings of personal fault against individual doctors who are, in truth, not at fault in order to avoid such questions."[67]

7–020   In *Bull v Devon Area Health Authority*[68] Slade L.J. considered that an allegation about inadequate levels of staffing would have to be judged according to professional standards at the time, applying the *Bolam* test,[69] and Dillon L.J. simply commented that the level of staffing should be "reasonably sufficient for the foreseeable requirements of the patient." Mustill L.J. had some reservations, however, about the argument that the hospital authority could not be expected to do more than their best, allocating their limited resources as favourably as possible. Although public medicine might not be precisely analogous to other public services, there was a danger in assuming that it was *sui generis*, and that it was necessarily a complete answer to say that even if the system in any hospital was unsatisfactory, it was no more unsatisfactory than those in force elsewhere.[70] Similarly, in *Re HIV Haemophiliac Litigation*[71] Ralph Gibson L.J. said that although it was difficult to prove negligence when the defendant was required to exercise discretion and form judgments on the allocation of public resources, that was not sufficient to make it clear that there could be no claim in negligence.

7–021   An action in negligence against a hospital authority which alleges that the claimant sustained injury through an inadequate provision of resources, whether it be staff, equipment, or funds for drugs, would have to prove that the lack of resources was a consequence of negligence in the *organisation* of the hospital itself.[72] It is not sufficient simply to point to the lack of

---

[67] *ibid.*

[68] (1989), [1993] 4 Med. L.R. 117, CA.

[69] On the differences in the standards of care that can be expected at different hospitals see: *Koerber v Trustees of the Kitchener-Waterloo Hospital* (1987) 62 O.R. (2d) 613 (Ont. H.C.); *Bateman v Doiron* (1993) 18 C.C.L.T. (2d) 1 (N.B.C.A.), para. 4–101, n. 21.

[70] See para. 4–101. See also *Knight v Home Office* [1990] 3 All E.R. 237, 243, para. 4–099 where Pill J. said that the lack of resources to provide a better staff/patient ratio was not necessarily a complete defence. Lack of funds would not justify a failure to provide *any* medical facilities for prisoners in a large prison.

[71] (1990), [1996] P.I.Q.R. P220; see also *Brown v Alberta* [1994] 2 W.W.R. 283 (Alta. Q.B.).

[72] In *Wilsher v Essex Area Health Authority* [1987] Q.B. 730, 778 Browne-Wilkinson V.-C. said: ". . . I can see no reason why, in principle, the health authority should not be so liable *if its organisation is at fault*" (emphasis added). See Montgomery (1987) 137 N.L.J. 703, 705 who comments that: "To hold health authorities liable for inadequate systems would provide a mechanism whereby managers can be made accountable for the effects which their activities have on patient care."

resources, since this may well be a consequence of resource allocation decisions over which the hospital has no control. Moreover, challenges on public law grounds to decisions about resource allocation made by the Secretary of State or individual health authorities have been notably unsuccessful.

By virtue of section 3 of the National Health Service Act 1977 the   7–022
Secretary of State has a duty to provide throughout England and Wales, to such extent as he considers necessary to meet all reasonable requirements, *inter alia*, hospital accommodation; medical, dental, nursing and ambulance services; services for the diagnosis and treatment of illness; facilities for the prevention of illness, the care and after-care of persons suffering from illness and facilities for the care of expectant and nursing mothers and young children.[73] In *R. v Secretary of State for Social Services, ex parte Hincks*[74] four patients, who had been waiting for orthopaedic operations for some years, sought to challenge a decision to postpone the expansion of a local hospital due to the cost, relying on section 3. The application for judicial review failed. Lord Denning M.R. said that additional words had to be implied into section 3(1) which should read: "to such extent as he considers necessary to meet all reasonable requirements *such as can be provided within the resources available.*" Bridge L.J. commented that there must be some limitation on the resources available to finance the health service and that limitation must be determined in the light of the current government economic policy. That was an implication which must be read into section 3(1).

This approach has been followed in two cases where parents sought to   7–023
require a hospital to provide the facilities and staff necessary to perform heart surgery on two young children. Both applications for judicial review were unsuccessful. In *R. v Central Birmingham Health Authority, ex parte Walker*[75] Sir John Donaldson M.R. said that:

> "It is not for this court, or indeed for any court, to substitute its own judgment for the judgment of those who are responsible for the allocation of resources. This court could only intervene where it was satisfied that there was a *prima facie* case, not only of failing to allocate resources in the way in which others would think that resources should be allocated, but a failure to allocate resources to an extent which was *Wednesbury* unreasonable . . . [T]he jurisdiction does exist. But it has to be used extremely sparingly."

---

[73] See also National Health Service Act 1977, ss.4 and 5: provision of special hospitals for mental health, and provision of other services, including school medical services, contraceptive services, a microbiological service, and the conduct of research. For a general discussion of the issues raised in paras 7–019 to 7–024 see Newdick (1993) 1 Med. L. Rev. 53; and Newdick, *Who Should We Treat?*, Clarendon Press, 1995. On judicial review in the NHS see Schwehr [1994] J.P.I.L. 192.

[74] (1979) 123 S.J. 436; affirmed (1980) 1 B.M.L.R. 93, CA.

[75] (1987) 3 B.M.L.R. 32, 35–36; *The Times*, November 26, 1987, CA.

Subsequently, in *R. v Central Birmingham Health Authority, ex parte Collier*[76] Stephen Brown L.J. considered that this would be the position even if the medical evidence were to establish that there was immediate danger to the child's health. Ralph Gibson L.J. commented that the courts have no role as a general investigator of social policy and of the allocation of resources. Rather, the court's jurisdiction was limited to dealing with breaches of duty under law, including decisions made by public authorities which are shown to be unreasonable.

7–024   These cases make it clear that an action which alleges that the failure to provide adequate resources constitutes negligence would be unlikely to succeed. Decisions about the allocation of resources are made under statutory powers which confer a broad discretion upon the Secretary of State and health authorities. A claim that such a decision has been taken negligently must first establish that the discretion was exercised *ultra vires* the statutory power, applying public law principles,[77] but the courts are apparently reluctant to make such a finding in the context of health resources. Where, however, it can be proved that the health authority has failed to establish any policy about the allocation of resources for a particular treatment or has adopted a blanket policy which is applied rigidly, without reference to the circumstances of the particular case, it is more likely that the authority will be held to have acted *ultra vires*.[78]

7–025   It is arguable that where the decision challenged by an applicant for judicial review engages the applicant's rights under the European Convention on Human Rights, the court should undertake a full "merits review" of that decision, and not limit itself to considering whether the decision fell within the range of reasonable decisions that a reasonable public authority could take (as would be required under a *Wednesbury* review). This seems to be the effect of the decision of the Court of Appeal in *R. (on the application of W) v Broadmoor Hospital*,[79] although the standard of review is dependent upon the context in which the decision has been

---

[76] (1988, CA.; unreported). See also *R. v Cambridge Health Authority, ex parte B.* [1995] 1 W.L.R. 898; [1995] 2 All E.R. 129, CA.

[77] See *Anns v Merton London Borough Council* [1978] A.C. 728, 754; *Dorset Yacht Co Ltd v Home Office* [1970] A.C. 1004, 1067; *X. (minors) v Bedfordshire County Council* [1995] 2 A.C. 633, 736–737, though Lord Browne-Wilkinson said that it was not a question of whether the decision was *ultra vires*, but whether it was outside the ambit of the public authority's discretion. See further para. 8–015 for discussion of the distinction between policy and operational decisions.

[78] See *R. v North Derbyshire Health Authority, ex parte Fisher* [1997] 8 Med. L.R. 327—failure of a health authority to establish a policy for the provision of a drug (beta-interferon) for the treatment of multiple sclerosis in accordance with guidance issued by the Department of Health; and *North West Lancashire Health Authority v A, D and G* [2000] 1 W.L.R. 977; [1999] Lloyd's Rep. Med. 399—a policy to accord cases of transsexualism lower priority in the allocation of funding than other medical conditions, and refuse treatment save in exceptional cases, was not irrational, but such a policy must have genuine regard for individual clinical needs and recognise the possibility of exceptional cases. Each request for treatment should be considered on its individual merits.

[79] [2001] EWCA Civ 1545; [2002] 1 W.L.R. 419 at [24], [59] and [62]. See the discussion at para. 6–075.

taken.[80] But in *North West Lancashire Health Authority v A, D and G*[81] the Court of Appeal was critical of the applicants' resort to arguments about human rights. The suggestion that the failure to provide medical treatment as part of a general policy of setting priorities for health care constituted a breach of Article 3 of the Convention (prohibiting torture and inhuman or degrading treatment) trivialised that Article and the important values that it protects. And though Article 8 (the right to respect for private and family life) could be engaged in such a case, the jurisprudence on Article 8 did not suggest that there was a positive obligation on states to provide medical treatment.

(2) Non-delegable Duty

There are two grounds for suggesting that a hospital authority owes a non-delegable duty to patients in the hospital. The first stems to a large extent from *Cassidy v Ministry of Health*[82] where Denning L.J. asserted that hospital authorities were under a primary, non-delegable duty to patients, at least where the doctor or surgeon, whether a consultant or not, was employed and paid, not by the patient but by the hospital authorities. It was irrelevant whether the contract under which he was employed was a contract of service or a contract for services; the hospital authorities were liable for his negligence in treating the patient:

7–026

> "... the hospital authorities accepted the plaintiff as a patient for treatment, and it was their duty to treat him with reasonable care. They selected, employed, and paid all the surgeons and nurses who looked after him. He had no say in their selection at all. If those surgeons and nurses did not treat him with proper care and skill, then the hospital authorities must answer for it, for it means that they themselves did not perform their duty to him. I decline to enter into the question whether any of the surgeons were employed only under a contract for services, as distinct from a contract of service. The evidence is meagre enough in all conscience on that point. But the liability of the hospital authorities should not, and does not, depend on nice considerations of that sort. The plaintiff knew nothing of the terms on which they employed their staff: all he knew was that he was treated in the hospital by people whom the hospital authorities appointed; and the hospital authorities must be answerable for the way in which he was treated."[83]

---

[80] See *R. v Secretary of State for the Home Department, ex parte Daly* [2001] UKHL 26; [2001] A.C. 532.
[81] [2000] 1 W.L.R. 977; [1999] Lloyd's Rep. Med. 399.
[82] [1951] 2 K.B. 343, 362–365.
[83] *ibid.* at 365.

7–027   His Lordship repeated this view in both *Roe v Minister of Health*[84] and in *Jones v Manchester Corp.*[85] The authority of this proposition remained uncertain, since the majority of the Court of Appeal in both *Cassidy* and *Roe* proceeded on the basis that the doctors concerned were employees for whom the health authority would be vicariously liable.[86] But in *X. (minors) v Bedfordshire County Council* Lord Browne-Wilkinson appeared to confirm Lord Denning's approach when he said that: "It is established that those conducting a hospital are under a direct duty of care to those admitted as patients to the hospital (I express no view as to the extent of that duty). They are liable for the negligent acts of a member of the hospital staff which constitute a breach of that duty, whether or not the member of staff is himself in breach of a separate duty of care owed by him to the plaintiff."[87] This view was applied in *Robertson v Nottingham Health Authority*,[88] where the Court of Appeal held that a hospital has a "non-delegable duty" to establish a proper system of care, just as much as it has a duty to engage competent staff and a duty to provide proper and safe equipment and safe premises: "A health authority owes its patient a duty to provide her with a reasonable regime of care at its hospital."[89] A reasonable regime of care meant "a regime of a standard that can reasonably be expected of a hospital of the size and type in question—in the present case a large teaching centre of excellence."[90] The problem in *Robertson* concerned a breakdown in communications between staff. As in *Bull v Devon Area Health Authority*,[91] the Court of Appeal held that a hospital authority owes a duty to a patient to provide her with a reasonable regime of a standard that can reasonably be expected of a hospital of the size and type in question. If there was an effective system in place, then the hospital would be vicariously liable for the negligence of any member of staff who did not take reasonable care to see that that the system worked efficiently; whereas if there was no effective system in place, the hospital would be directly liable in negligence for the lacuna. Thus,

"if a patient is injured by reason of a negligent breakdown in the systems for communicating material information to the clinicians responsible for her care, she is not to be denied redress merely because no identifiable person or persons are to blame for deficiencies in setting

---

[84] [1954] 2 Q.B. 66, 82.
[85] [1952] Q.B. 852, 869.
[86] *Jackson & Powell on Professional Negligence*, 5th ed., 2002, para. 12.155. See further the comments of Lord Jauncey in *Esso Petroleum Co Ltd v Hall Russell and Co Ltd* [1989] A.C. 643, 686–687.
[87] [1995] 2 A.C. 633, 740, citing *Gold v Essex County Council* [1942] 2 K.B. 293, 301, *per* Lord Greene; *Cassidy v Ministry of Health* [1951] 2 K.B. 343, *per* Denning L.J.; *Roe v Minister of Health* [1954] 2 Q.B. 66; *Wilsons & Clyde Coal Co Ltd v English* [1938] A.C. 57; and *McDermid v Nash Dredging and Reclamation Co Ltd* [1987] A.C. 906.
[88] [1997] 8 Med. L.R. 1, CA.
[89] *ibid.* at 13, citing *Gold v Essex County Council* [1942] 2 K.B. 293, *Roe v Minister of Health* [1954] 2 Q.B. 66, and *Cassidy v Ministry of Health* [1951] 2 K.B. 343.
[90] *ibid.*
[91] (1989), [1993] 4 Med. L.R. 117, CA.

up and monitoring the effectiveness of the relevant communication systems. She is entitled to say, like the successful plaintiff in *Bull*: 'You, the health authority were responsible for my care: you are responsible if there is a breakdown, reasonably attributable to improper practice, in the systems used at your hospital for communicating material information to the clinicians responsible for my care: and I was injured as a result of this negligence.'"[92]

The application of the principle of a non-delegable duty can be seen in the county court decision of *M. v Calderdale & Kirklees Health Authority*.[93] The claimant was sent by her general practitioner to a private clinic for a termination of pregnancy which was carried out negligently, with the result that she subsequently gave birth to a healthy child. The defendants argued that the limit of their duty was to exercise reasonable care to select a competent private clinic. That view was rejected (though on the facts, it was arguable that they had failed even in that respect—the defendants had no idea whether the clinic had insurance, no up to date information about the competence of staff at the clinic, and could not produce the contract with the clinic). The judge held that the NHS is under a non-delegable duty and therefore was responsible for the negligence of the clinic.[94] The health authority had a duty to bring about the effective provision of services, either by providing the services themselves or securing others to provide them on their behalf. The claimant had "never left the care of" the health authority. She had not had an opportunity to divert from the route of treatment arranged on her behalf, and should not be in a worse position than a patient who remained "in-house". Thus, her rights and remedies should be the same. **7–028**

The view that the liability of a hospital to a patient is based on a personal non-delegable duty has been approved, *obiter*, on two occasions by the High Court of Australia.[95] In *Ellis v Wallsend District Hospital*,[96] the one Australian case which has had to decide the issue, the New South Wales Court of Appeal was divided as to whether a non-delegable duty arose on the facts. The majority (Samuels and Meagher JJ.A.) distinguished between a hospital which functions merely as a provider of facilities pursuant to an arrangement between the doctor and the hospital, and a hospital which functions as a place **7–029**

---

[92] [1997] 8 Med. L.R. 1, 13. See also *Collins v Mid-Western Health Board* [2000] 2 I.R. 154 (Supreme Court of Ireland), discussed at para. 3–103, a case concerning a systems failure in the admission of a patient to hospital.

[93] [1998] Lloyd's Rep. Med. 157 (Huddersfield County Court).

[94] Again, applying *Gold v Essex County Council* [1942] 2 K.B. 293 and the dictum of Denning L.J. in *Cassidy v Ministry of Health* [1951] 2 K.B. 343, 365. See, however, *A (A Child) v Ministry of Defence* [2003] EWHC 849 (QB); *The Times*, May 16, 2003 at [53] where Bell J. was critical of the decision in *M v Calderdale & Kirklees Health Authority*, suggesting that it had gone much further than anything said in *Gold* or *Cassidy*.

[95] *Commonwealth v Introvigne* (1982) 56 A.L.J.R. 749, 755; *Kondis v State Transport Authority* (1984) 55 A.L.R. 225, 234. The possibility of establishing a personal non-delegable duty owed by a hospital to a patient was accepted by the New South Wales Court of Appeal in *Albrighton v Royal Prince Alfred Hospital* [1980] 2 N.S.W.L.R. 542, 561–562, although this would depend upon the facts proved. See further Whippy (1989) 63 A.L.J. 182.

[96] (1989) 17 N.S.W.L.R. 553, CA; Nicholson (1990) 6 P.N. 83.

where a person in need of treatment goes to obtain treatment.[97] In the latter case a non-delegable duty could arise,[98] but such a duty "does not extend to treatment which is performed by a doctor pursuant to a direct engagement with the patient, and not on behalf of the hospital."[99] The basis for establishing a non-delegable duty lies in the nature of the relationship between the patient and the hospital. Where the patient goes directly to the hospital for advice and treatment, the hospital, by accepting the patient, undertakes to make available all the therapeutic skill and devices which it is reasonably able to deploy:

> "If the hospital's response is to open the door and admit the patient to the benefits of the medical and surgical cornucopia within it remains responsible to ensure that whatever treatment or advice the horn disgorges is given with proper care; its duty cannot be divested by delegation."[1]

7–030   The patient had been treated by a doctor who was an "honorary medical officer" with privileges at the hospital. She had approached the doctor herself and he had arranged for her admission to the hospital and performed the surgery. In these circumstances a non-delegable duty did not arise. The hospital was merely a provider of the facilities for the treatment. Kirby P., dissenting, took the view that the hospital was not a "mere venue" for the performance of private medical procedures, it was an integrated institution and an honorary medical officer was part of it.[2] In his Honour's opinion the hospital was vicariously liable for all its staff, whether the position was "honorary" or not, and directly liable by virtue of a non-delegable duty.

7–031   The courts in Australia have accepted that a hospital may come under a non-delegable duty to its patients, albeit that there is a difference of opinion as to precisely when the duty arises. On the other hand, in *Yepremian v Scarborough General Hospital*[3] the majority of a five judge Ontario Court of Appeal held that in Canada a hospital does not undertake a non-delegable duty to a patient, whether he presents himself directly at the door of the hospital or not.[4]

---

[97] Relying on the judgment of Houlden J.A. in *Yepremian v Scarborough General Hospital* (1980) 110 D.L.R. (3d) 513, 581 (Ont. C.A.).

[98] Thus, accounting for the dicta in *Albrighton v Royal Prince Alfred Hospital* [1980] 2 N.S.W.L.R. 542, 561–562, which was a case where the patient had gone directly to the hospital for treatment.

[99] (1989) 17 N.S.W.L.R. 553, 604. Denning L.J. would have agreed that where the patient himself selects and employs the doctor or surgeon, the hospital authorities are not liable for his negligence, because he is not employed by them: *Cassidy v Ministry of Health* [1951] 2 K.B. 343, 362.

[1] *ibid.* at 605, *per* Samuels J.A.

[2] "He was integrated into the discipline and direction of the hospital. What he did in his rooms was his affair. But when he came into the hospital, he was part of the hospital. When working on its premises he was part of its integrated medical team": *ibid.* at 566.

[3] (1980) 110 D.L.R. (3d) 513 (Ont. C.A.). The action was settled before an appeal to the Supreme Court of Canada was heard: (1981) 120 D.L.R. (3d) 341.

[4] *cf. Aynsley v Toronto General Hospital* (1969) 7 D.L.R. (3d) 193, 209 (Ont. C.A.); affirmed

The second ground for suggesting that under the NHS a hospital author- 7–032
ity is under a non-delegable duty to provide medical services to the patient
derives from the statutory obligation placed on a health authority under the
National Health Service Act 1977, through the duty placed on the Secretary
of State. In *Razzel v Snowball*[5] the Court of Appeal held that the duty placed
on the Minister of Health by section 3(1)(*c*) of the National Health Service
Act 1946 was not limited to merely providing competent specialists, but
extended to providing treatment by means of their services. The effect of this
particular ruling was that the defendant doctor was to be regarded as carrying out the Minister's duty and therefore he was entitled to claim the benefit
of a one year period of limitation that applied to acts done in pursuance or
execution of any Act of Parliament or any public duty under section 21 of
the Limitation Act 1939. It is arguable that the consequence of this is that
the equivalent provision in section 3(1) of the National Health Service Act
1977 creates a non-delegable statutory duty to provide treatment services
which is not discharged by the appointment of competent staff, whether as
an employee or an independent contractor, such as a consultant.[6] This argument has not been tested in the courts, and it remains to be seen how the
proposition would be received if advanced by a claimant.[7]

Even where a non-delegable duty is established the employer is not liable 7–033
for acts of collateral negligence by an independent contractor. This is negligence which is not committed in the performance of the very work which
has been delegated, although in practice it can be very difficult to distinguish
between collateral acts and acts which are simply a manner of performing
the delegated work.[8] The distinction was accepted by Denning L.J. in
Cassidy v Ministry of Health,[9] but was said to be unimportant in that case

---

(n.4 contd.) (1971) 25 D.L.R. (3d) 241 (S.C.C.) where Aylesworth J.A. said that a hospital
was liable for the negligence of a doctor even if he had been employed under a contract for
services. This suggests that the hospital was under a non-delegable duty, since the negligence
would have been that of an independent contractor. This was a case of private medicine,
however, and a contractual relationship between the hospital and the patient may well create
a non-delegable duty.

[5] [1954] 1 W.L.R. 1382; see also *Higgins v North West Metropolitan Hospital Board* [1954]
1 W.L.R. 411.

[6] Dugdale and Stanton, *Professional Negligence*, 3rd ed., 1998, para. 22.20, who state that
"it is undoubtedly the case that the effect of basing this duty on statute is to ensure that it is
non-delegable in its nature."

[7] One unusual feature of the case was that it was the claimant who argued that the Minister's
duty was merely to provide the specialists and not the treatment, whereas it was the defendant who was claiming that he was performing the Minister's non-delegable duty. In
Yepremian v Scarborough General Hospital (1980) 110 D.L.R. (3d) 513, 565 Blair J.A. considered that the liability of hospitals in the United Kingdom "now rests on a clear statutory
foundation," relying on *Razzel v Snowball* [1954] 1 W.L.R. 1382. There is authority for the
view that where a statute imposes an "absolute" duty, responsibility for its performance
cannot be delegated: *Smith v Cammell Laird & Co Ltd* [1940] A.C. 242; *The Pass of Ballater*
[1942] P. 112. Whether a duty is "absolute" depends upon the construction of the statute,
but it can apply to a duty to use "due diligence": *Riverstone Meat Co Pty Ltd v Lancashire
Shipping Co Ltd* [1961] A.C. 807.

[8] See *Padbury v Holliday & Greenwood Ltd* (1912) 28 T.L.R. 494; *Holliday v National
Telephone Co* [1899] 2 Q.B. 392.

[9] [1951] 2 K.B. 343, 365.

"because we are not concerned with any collateral or casual acts of negligence by the staff, but negligence in the treatment itself which it was the employer's duty to provide." There is no comparable restriction on an employer's vicarious liability, provided the employee's negligence occurred in the course of employment.

7–034   The underlying justification for imposing a non-delegable duty on hospital authorities rests on patient expectations. Patients know nothing about the terms upon which the hospital engages its staff. They go to hospital for treatment and if they suffer injury in the course of that treatment their entitlement to damages should not turn upon whether the negligence was inflicted by an employed nurse or an agency nurse, a house surgeon or a visiting consultant.[10] In *Yepremian v Scarborough General Hospital*[11] Arnup J.A. was critical of the notion of non-delegable duties because it seemed to be a case of saying: "In all the circumstances, the hospital *ought* to be liable." This, however, is the very point, and it is as true of the principle of vicarious liability, and indeed most tort duties.

7–035   The policy that has been adopted with regard to negligent treatment given in NHS hospitals of, in effect, ignoring the distinction between employees and independent contractors provided that the claimant's injury was caused in the course of receiving NHS treatment, has rendered much (but not all[12]) of the argument about non-delegable duties redundant. The hospital authority will accept vicarious liability for the negligence of consultants and agency staff irrespective of whether they are engaged under a contract of service or a contract for services. Moreover, even with private medical treatment, in practice it will rarely matter to the claimant whether the hospital owes a non-delegable duty since if the doctor is proved to have been negligent the patient will have a claim against him, and if he is not an employee but an independent contractor he will normally have insured against liability through a medical defence organisation. If the doctor is not negligent there would not in any event have been an action against the hospital for breach of its non-delegable duty. The issue becomes of practical importance to the claimant if the doctor has no, or limited, insurance cover,[13] or where the claimant has chosen to sue only the hospital and not the doctor.[14] The effect of imposing a non-delegable duty on a hospital is to make the hospital a guarantor of the independent contractor's solvency, or rather to place the risk of the contractor's insolvency or lack of insurance cover on the hospital

---

[10] See Whippy (1989) 63 A.L.J. 182, 201. This point has been made by McKendrick (1990) 53 M.L.R. 770 in the wider context of employers' vicarious liability. Given the elusiveness of the distinction between a contract of service and a contract for services, and the difficulty that the courts have in identifying it, there is no obvious reason why an employer's responsibility should hang on this particular issue.

[11] (1980) 110 D.L.R. (3d) 513, 532 (Ont. C.A.).

[12] See paras 7–027 to 7–028.

[13] As was the case in *Ellis v Wallsend District Hospital* (1989) 17 N.S.W.L.R. 553, 569.

[14] As occurred in *Yepremian v Scarborough General Hospital* (1980) 110 D.L.R. (3d) 513 (Ont. C.A.).

rather than the claimant. If the contractor is negligent the hospital will have either a contractual claim for indemnity or a right to contribution under the Civil Liability (Contribution) Act 1978.

The question of whether a hospital owes a non-delegable duty to its 7–036 patients does have potential practical significance where patients are sent overseas, at NHS expense, to have treatment (as has occurred over the last two years). If a patient is injured as a result of the negligence of the treating hospital, she will want to be able to sue the health authority or NHS Trust that referred her in this country. The existence of a non-delegable duty would make that course much simpler to pursue. The practical importance of this is illustrated by *A. v Ministry of Defence.*[15] The claimant suffered serious brain damage during the course of his birth in 1998 in a German obstetric unit as a result of negligence by a German doctor. A's father was in the Army, and his mother was provided with obstetric services on the basis of arrangements entered into by the Ministry of Defence (MoD) to provide health care for members of the armed forces and their families while posted to Germany. Until 1996 secondary healthcare was provided in Germany in British military hospitals staffed by Army and RAF doctors and nurses or civilian health professionals employed by the MoD, for whose negligence the MoD was vicariously liable. During the mid-1990s arrangements for medical care for service personnel and their families were changed. As part of that change, the MoD subcontracted to Guy's and St Thomas Hospital NHS Trust (GST) the procurement of secondary hospital care in five German hospitals. A was born in one of these hospitals. Negligence by the German doctor was admitted. The question for Bell J. was whether A could sue the MoD or GST in England under English law, or whether he would have to bring a claim in Germany under German law. The answer to that issue depended upon the nature of the duty undertaken by the MoD and GST to the claimant, who were clearly not vicariously liable for the doctor's negligence. Had either the MoD or GST undertaken a non-delegable duty to ensure that medical treatment in the German hospital was provided with reasonable care and skill, or was it limited to exercising reasonable care in the selection of appropriate German providers of hospital care and the supervision of standards in those hospitals? Bell J. concluded that the defendants' responsibility was limited to exercising reasonable care in selecting and supervising standards in the German hospitals. They had not undertaken a non-delegable duty for the provision of healthcare to Army personnel and their families in Germany, and therefore were not responsible for the doctor's negligence.

Bell J. identified the rationale for imposing a non-delegable duty on hos- 7–037 pitals in the relationship between the parties which gives rise to a special responsibility—the hospital undertakes the care, supervision and control of patients who are in special need of care, and has assumed responsibility in circumstances where the claimant could reasonably expect that reasonable

---

[15] [2003] EWHC 849 (QB); *The Times*, May 16, 2003.

care will be exercised.[16] On the facts of *A. v Ministry of Defence*, the MoD was generally responsible for the well-being of service personnel, civilian employees, and their dependants, while residing in another country, and encouraged the feeling that "the Army will look after you". But the MoD had informed service personnel of the changed arrangements for the provision of health care, and there was no justification for any assumption by A's parents that the Army itself was continuing to provide hospital care. The MoD was under a duty to provide access to an appropriate regime of healthcare in Germany. It had not assumed responsibility for treating service personnel or their dependants and had not accepted them as patients for the purposes of hospital care. It had assumed an obligation to provide access to an appropriate system of hospital care provided by a third party. This was a duty, said Bell J., to exercise reasonable care in selecting and putting into action appropriate providers, and it discharged that duty by contracting with GST to procure German hospitals and to manage their contracts. Similarly, when it came to the legal position of GST, it was never envisaged that GST would itself provide medical services directly to service personnel or their families in Germany. GST's duty of care had to be seen in the context of what GST was contracted to do. It did not contract to treat British patients in German hospitals. It did not contract to manage the German hospitals, as opposed to managing its contracts with the German hospitals. It followed that there was no basis for a non-delegable duty on GST to ensure that reasonable care and skill were used in hospital treatment in Germany. The duty was to exercise reasonable care in the selection of German hospitals to provide particular forms of treatment and to manage the contract with the hospital in such a manner as would avoid an unsafe hospital regime.[17]

7–038   There is a world of difference, of course, between the position of military personnel and their families posted abroad, who are (or should be) aware of the arrangements put in place for their medical treatment while abroad, and the position of a NHS patient who is referred to a NHS hospital for treatment, and is then invited to have that treatment abroad at the NHS's expense

---

[16] See the judgment of Mason J. in *Kondis v State Transport Authority* (1984) 55 A.L.R. 225, cited by Bell J. *ibid.* at [59], and the judge's comment at [69] that: "in so far as those features lead in the Australian cases to a duty to ensure the safety of the claimant, they go further than the English cases." *Sed quaere*, in light of Lord Browne-Wilkinson's dictum in *X. (minors) v Bedfordshire County Council* and the Court of Appeal's judgment in *Robertson v Nottingham Health Authority*, para. 7–027, above. Indeed, Bell J. acknowledged, at [68], that: "What Lord Greene M.R. said in *Gold*, has great force, to my mind, but his wider personal, non-delegable duty still depends upon the hospital's acceptance of the patient for treatment, or advice, by itself." In *Gold v Essex County Council* [1942] 2 K.B. 293, 304 Lord Greene had said: "It is clear therefore, that the powers of the defendants include the power of treating patients . . . If they exercise that power, the obligation which they undertake is an obligation to treat, and they are liable if the persons employed by them to perform the obligation on their behalf act without due care. I am unable to see how a body invested with such a power and to all appearance exercising it can be said to be assuming no greater obligation than to provide a skilled person and proper appliances."

[17] "Even the Australian cases require acceptance of the claimant as the hospital's own patient for treatment, before the duty to ensure safe care arises": [2003] EWHC 849 at [69] *per* Bell J.

as part of a scheme for reducing NHS waiting lists or waiting times. The NHS, unlike the MoD, is in the business of providing health care to its patients. Those patients go to a NHS hospital with a view to receiving treatment at that or another NHS facility. The hospital has undertaken a responsibility to provide treatment to the patient (as Lord Greene in *Gold* and Denning L.J. in *Cassidy* indicated). It would be unfortunate, to say the least, if the consequence of referring patients abroad for treatment in order to meet particular political or financial objectives in the NHS were that injured patients would have to undertake the litigation process abroad, against the hospital that actually carried out the treatment, with all the practical and financial impediments that this would create for a claimant. The simple solution in this situation is that the NHS hospital should be regarded as having undertaken to provide treatment to the patient and should be under a nondelegable duty to see that care is taken. The standard required to discharge this duty is still a negligence standard. The NHS is not subject to strict liability. To cover the risk of negligently inflicted injury in the course of treatment, the NHS hospital should simply obtain an indemnity from the overseas provider of treatment against their liability to patients for breach of this nondelegable duty, as part of the contract with that hospital to provide the treatment services.

3. JOINT LIABILITY AND CONTRIBUTION

Where two or more tortfeasors[18] are liable for the same damage[19] they will be entitled to claim contribution from each other under the Civil Liability (Contribution) Act 1978.[20] The Act allows for the apportionment of damages[21] between the respective defendants, it does not operate as a   **7–039**

---

[18] Where the alleged defendant does not owe a duty of care to the claimant then clearly there can be no claim for contribution. Thus, a defendant sued in respect of damage to a child cannot seek contribution from the child's mother in respect of her alleged pre-natal negligence, which may have contributed to the child's damage, because the mother does not owe a duty of care to the foetus that she carries: *Preston v Chow* (2002) 211 D.L.R. (4th) 758 (Man. C.A.). The Congenital Disabilities (Civil Liability) Act 1976, s.1(1) specifically excludes the child's mother as a potential defendant, except where the injury is attributable to her negligent driving of a motor vehicle: *ibid.* s.2.

[19] See para. 7–047 for discussion of this term. Note that where the court is in a position to apportion the causal contribution made by each defendant's tortious conduct, as in *Holtby v Brigham & Cowan (Hull) Ltd* [2000] 3 All E.R. 421, the Civil Liability (Contribution) Act 1978 does not come into play, because each defendant is liable to the claimant only to the extent of his contribution to the damage. The claimant cannot sue one defendant for the full extent of his loss, leaving that defendant to obtain contribution from other defendants under the Act. The claimant is effectively forced to sue each and every defendant for that part of the damage caused by each defendant. See para. 5–042. See also Weir [2001] C.L.J. 237, 239 for critical comment.

[20] See Dugdale (1979) 42 M.L.R. 182.

[21] The apportionment can include a payment reasonably made under a settlement agreement in respect of the defendant's liability to meet the claimant's costs: *BICC Ltd v Cumbrian Industrial Ltd* [2001] EWCA Civ 1621; [2002] Lloyd's Rep. P.N. 526.

defence to the claimant's claim. Similarly, judgment against one defendant is not a bar to a subsequent action against other defendants.[22] If the first judgment remains unsatisfied the claimant can sue the other tortfeasors, subject to a possible penalty in costs.[23] Where the claimant does not sue all the persons responsible for the damage a defendant may join the others in third party proceedings.[24]

7–040   Although the Act specifically preserves the claimant's right to bring later proceedings against another defendant, in some circumstances the settlement of his action against one defendant may preclude a subsequent action against another defendant. In *Jameson v Central Electricity Generating Board*[25] the House of Lords held that where a claimant enters into a settlement with a concurrent tortfeasor,[26] D1, which is expressed to be in "full and final settlement" of the claim, he cannot then claim against a second concurrent tortfeasor, D2, in respect of the same damage. It follows that if D2 is not liable to the claimant there can be no claim for contribution under the Act by D2 against D1. Whether the agreement can be said to have "satisfied" the claim for damages depends on the wording of the settlement. If it is not expressed to be in full and final satisfaction, or if the claimant specifically reserves the right to maintain a claim against other concurrent tortfeasors, it will not have the effect of extinguishing those claims. In *Jameson* itself, J contracted mesothelioma from exposure to asbestos at work. He brought an action against his former employers (D1), and settled the claim for substantially less than its full value. After his death, his widow brought an action for loss of dependancy under the Fatal Accidents Act 1976 against the Central Electricity Generating Board (D2), the occupiers of the premises where he had been exposed to asbestos. The claim against D2 was worth substantially more than the sum for which J had settled his claim against D1. Both defendants were in breach of a duty to J, in respect of the same damage (the mesothelioma) and under the Civil Liability (Contribution) Act 1978, section 1(3), the employers, D1, would have been liable to make contribution to D2, notwithstanding the settlement. Their Lordships held, however, that the settlement by a claimant of an action against one concurrent tortfeasor could have the effect of barring a further claim against another concurrent tortfeasor. In these circumstances the Act becomes irrelevant because D2 then has no liability to C, and therefore no need to seek contribution from D1. The solution to this potential problem for claimants is expressly to reserve the right to claim

---

[22] Civil Liability (Contribution) Act 1978, s.3.
[23] *ibid.*, s.4.
[24] CPR Part 20.
[25] [2000] 1 A.C. 455.
[26] As opposed to a joint tortfeasor. The defendants are "joint tortfeasors" where they have participated in some common enterprise, where a person has authorised another to commit a tort, and where an employer is vicariously liable for the torts of his employees. Where, however, their independent actions coincide to produce the same damage they are "several concurrent tortfeasors" (*e.g.*, the negligence of two drivers causes a road accident which injures a third party).

against other potential defendants when accepting a settlement from one defendant.[27]

In *Rawlinson v North Essex Health Authority*[28] Mitchell J. applied   **7–041**
Jameson v Central Electricity Generating Board to a medical negligence action. In 1995 the claimant had settled his action for negligence against a pharmaceutical company in respect of damage attributable to the use of the drug myodil in the performance of a myelogram. In 1997 the claimant issued proceedings against the health authority alleging negligent treatment in respect of the manner in which the myodil was used and of a failure to aspirate. This was similar to the allegation of negligence that was made against the pharmaceutical company, in that it was alleged that aspiration of the myodil would have eliminated or substantially reduced the risk of the claimant contracting arachnoiditis. The claimant accepted that the settlement had been in full and final satisfaction of any claim or cause of action that he may have had against the pharmaceutical company in respect of the use of myodil. Mitchell J. held that the settlement barred a subsequent claim against the hospital. The loss on which the claimant relied was identical to that which had been the subject of the settlement. The question was not whether the claimant has received the full value of his claim, but whether the sum he received in settlement of it was intended to be in full satisfaction of the tort.

Subsequently, in *Heaton v Axa Equity & Law Assurance Society plc*[29] the   **7–042**
House of Lords explained that the decision in *Jameson* was based on the proposition that where the claimant has entered into an agreement with D1 under which he accepts a sum as full compensation for the damage suffered, an action by the claimant against D2 cannot proceed because if the compensation is in full satisfaction of the damage sustained it reflects the claimant's full loss and thereby extinguishes it.[30] It is not that the agreement between the claimant and D1 was intended to confer some benefit on D2, but that the claimant no longer has any loss which requires compensation. Conversely, as Lord Bingham pointed out: "While it is just that [the claimant] should be precluded from recovering substantial damages against [D2] in a case where he has accepted a sum representing the full measure of his estimated loss, it is unjust that [the claimant] should be so precluded where he has not."[31] The primary focus in deciding whether the claimant has received full compensation for his loss will be the terms of the settlement agreement, but even so, said Lord Bingham, a number of factors have to be taken into account: (1) The release of one concurrent tortfeasor does not have the effect in law of releasing another concurrent tortfeasor; (2) An agreement made between the

---

[27] Although D1 may be reluctant to agree to such a reservation because it leaves open the possibility of a contribution claim under the Act from D2 if the claimant brings a further action against D2. The better option might be for the claimant to agree to indemnify D1 against any potential liability to make contribution that D1 has.

[28] [2000] Lloyd's Rep. Med. 54.

[29] [2002] UKHL 15; [2002] 2 A.C. 329.

[30] *ibid. per* Lord Mackay at [41] and Lord Rodger at [80].

[31] *ibid.* at [5].

claimant and D1 will not affect the claimant's rights against D2 unless either: (a) the claimant agrees to forgo or waive rights which he would otherwise enjoy against D2, in which case his agreement is enforceable by D1; or (b) the agreement falls within the limited class of contracts which either at common law or by virtue of the Contracts (Rights of Third Parties) Act 1999 is enforceable by D2 as a third party; (3) The use of clear and comprehensive language to preclude the pursuit of claims and cross-claims as between the claimant and D1 has little bearing on the question whether the agreement represents the full measure of the claimant's loss. The more inadequate the compensation agreed to be paid by D1, the greater the need for D1 to protect himself against any possibility of further action by the claimant to obtain a full measure of redress; (4) An express reservation by the claimant of his right to sue D2 will fortify the inference that the claimant is not treating the sum recovered from D1 as representing the full measure of his loss, but the absence of such a reservation is of less significance, since there is no need for the claimant to reserve a right to do that which he is ordinarily fully entitled to do without any such reservation; (5) If D1, on compromising the claimant's action, wishes to protect himself against any claim against him by D2 for contribution, he can achieve that end either (a) by obtaining an enforceable undertaking by the claimant not to pursue any claim against D2 relating to the subject matter of the compromise, or (b) by obtaining an indemnity from the claimant against any liability to which D1 may become subject relating to the subject matter of the compromise.[32]

7–043   The Civil Liability (Contribution) Act applies to any type of action; the defendants' liability need not be based on breach of the same obligation. So a defendant who is in breach of contract may seek contribution from a defendant who is in breach of a duty of care in tort, provided that both contributed to the claimant's damage.[33]

7–044   A settlement of the claimant's action before judgment by one defendant does not remove his right to seek contribution from another defendant, irrespective of whether he is or ever was liable in respect of the damage, provided, however, "that he would have been liable assuming that the factual basis of the claim against him could be established."[34] Thus, settlement of a doubtful claim does not prejudice the defendant's claim to contribution provided the doubts concern issues of fact. Where the settlement is based on uncertainty about the law the defendant may have to prove that he was liable to the claimant in order to maintain the claim for contribution.[35] In these

---

[32] *ibid*. at [9].
[33] Civil Liability (Contribution) Act 1978, s.6(1). But a defendant's liability to make contribution to another defendant under the Act depends upon his being liable to the claimant. If by virtue of a contract between the claimant and D1, D1 is not liable to the claimant, D2 cannot claim contribution from D1: *Co-operative Retail Services Ltd v Taylor Young Partnership* [2002] UKHL 17; [2002] 1 W.L.R. 1419, where architects and consulting engineers, who were allegedly negligent in respect of a fire, were not entitled to claim contribution from the main contractor or an electrical sub-contractor, even though their share of responsibility for the loss was comparatively minor.
[34] *ibid*., ss.1(2) and 1(4).
[35] Dugdale (1979) 42 M.L.R. 182, 184.

circumstances he may have to submit to judgment in order to protect his right to contribution.

Where a defendant has ceased to be liable to the claimant he is nonethe-   7–045
less still subject to a claim for contribution by another defendant, unless he ceased to be liable to the claimant by virtue of the expiry of a limitation period which extinguished the claimant's right of action against him.[36] Most limitation periods, including those applying to actions for personal injuries, do not extinguish the claimant's right of action but merely bar his remedy. Thus, the fact that a defendant would not be liable to the claimant because the claimant's limitation period has expired against him does not prevent another defendant bringing a contribution claim against him.[37] If the claimant has sued the defendant to judgment, section 1(5) of the Civil Liability (Contribution) Act 1978 provides that the judgment is conclusive in contribution proceedings "as to any issue determined by that judgment" in favour of the person from whom contribution is sought. There is a potential conflict here between subsection 1(3) and subsection 1(5), since if the claimant's action failed because it was statute barred by the Limitation Act 1980 then subsection 1(5) appears to preclude a contribution claim by another defendant. This provision was intended to apply to a determination of the issue on the merits, not on a procedural point.[38]

The Act does not affect an express or implied contractual or other right to   7–046
indemnity, or an express contractual provision regulating or excluding contribution.[39] Thus, a defendant who is liable to make a contribution under the Act may recover this sum from another defendant under an indemnity clause.[40]

---

[36] Civil Liability (Contribution) Act 1978, s.1(3).

[37] Similarly, where a defendant (D1) has settled the claimant's (C's) action against him he may still be liable to make a contribution to another defendant (D2): *Logan v Uttlesford District Council* (1984) 136 N.L.J. 541; *Jameson v Central Electricity Generating Board* [1997] 4 All E.R. 38, CA. This point was not appealed to the House of Lords in *Jameson* but was assumed to be correct by Lord Hope: [2000] 1 A.C. 455, 471. This is subject to the proviso that D2 remains liable to C. In the light of the decision of the House of Lords in *Jameson v Central Electricity Generating Board*, if D1's settlement extinguishes D2's liability to C, D2 will have no need to claim contribution from D1. The limitation period for contribution proceedings under the Civil Liability (Contribution) Act 1978 is two years from the date of judgment or compromise: Limitation Act 1980, s.10.

[38] *Clerk & Lindsell on Tort*, 18th ed., 2000, para. 4–118. See, however, *Nottingham Health Authority v Nottingham City Council* [1988] 1 W.L.R. 903, 906 where, without reference to subsection 1(5), Balcombe L.J. assumed that a defendant who was held not liable due to a successful limitation plea would still be liable to make contribution; and *R.A. Lister & Co Ltd v E.G. Thomson (Shipping) Ltd* (No. 2) [1987] 3 All E.R. 1032, 1039–1040, holding that a stay in proceedings or dismissal of an action for want of prosecution, which are procedural not substantive issues, do not fall within subs.1(5) and so do not preclude contribution proceedings.

[39] Civil Liability (Contribution) Act 1978, s.7(3).

[40] *Sims v Foster Wheeler Ltd* [1966] 1 W.L.R. 769. An employer has no right to indemnity from an employee under the contract of employment if the employer has himself contributed to the damage or if he bears some part of the responsibility, where, for example, a more senior employee's negligence has contributed to the damage: *Jones v Manchester Corporation* [1952] Q.B. 852, 865, *per* Singleton L.J. Clearly, this rule does not apply to a claim for contribution under the Civil Liability (Contribution) Act 1978.

The "same damage"

7–047   A claim for contribution can only be brought against a person liable in respect of the "same damage." This phrase has given rise to some difficulties of interpretation. In *Eastgate Group Ltd v Lindsey Morden Group Inc*[41] the Court of Appeal held that a claim against a person in breach of contract falls to be reduced by a payment made by a person liable for breach of a professional duty. The normal rule is that any actual diminution of a claimant's loss should be brought into account in assessing his claim for damages. The fact that the claimant might recover different sums by way of *damages* from D1 and D2 did not mean that D1 and D2 were not liable for the same *damage.*

7–048   There are a number of situations where the claims have been found not to be in respect of the same damage. In *Royal Brompton Hospital NHS Trust v Hammond*[42] a distinction was drawn between the damage caused by primary claims and secondary claims. A secondary claim arises from the loss or devaluation of a primary claim, for example where a solicitor handling a personal injuries claim is negligent, resulting in the loss of the claim against the original tortfeasor. The claim against the negligent solicitor is not for the same damage as the original action of the client against the tortfeasor. Thus, a claim against an architect for negligence resulting in a weakening of the client's claim for breach of contract against the main contractor under a building contract was not for the same damage as the client's claim against the main contractor for delay in performing the contract. The architect's negligence had not led to any delay in performing the contract. Similarly, where D1 and D2 are liable to different parties the claim is not in respect of the same damage.[43]

7–049   In *Rahman v Arearose Ltd*[44] the claimant was seriously assaulted by two black youths, causing an injury to his right eye. His employers were held liable in negligence for failing to take reasonable care to reduce the risk of such assaults. Subsequently, as a result of the negligence of a surgeon, the claimant was rendered blind in the right eye. In addition to the physical injuries, the claimant developed severe psychiatric consequences, including post traumatic stress disorder, a severe depressive disorder, a specific phobia of Afro-Caribbean people, and an enduring personality change. The psychiatric evidence indicated that the post traumatic stress disorder was due to the loss of the eye; the phobia was due to the assault and subsequent events; and the personality change was due to the synergistic interaction between the depression and the post traumatic stress disorder. One of the issues for the Court of Appeal was whether there could be an apportionment of respon-

---

[41] [2001] EWCA Civ 1446; [2002] 1 W.L.R. 642; distinguishing *Howkins & Harrison (a firm) v Tyler* [2001] P.N.L.R. 27; [2001] Lloyd's Rep. P.N. 1, CA.

[42] [2002] UKHL 14; [2002] 1 W.L.R. 1397.

[43] *Birse Construction v Haiste Ltd* [1996] 1 W.L.R. 675, CA, where D2 was liable to D1 (in respect of a claim by the claimant) but could not claim contribution from D3, even though D1 could have claimed contribution from D3 on the basis that D3 was liable to the claimant.

[44] [2001] Q.B. 351.

sibility between the claimant's employers and the hospital in respect of the claimant's psychiatric condition. Laws L.J. pointed out that tortfeasors are concurrent when their wrongful acts or omissions cause a single indivisible injury. Each tortfeasor is then liable in full to compensate the claimant for the whole of the damage: "The characteristic of such torts is the *logical* impossibility of apportioning the damage among the different tortfeasors."[45] The expression the "same damage" in the 1978 Act meant (and meant only) the kind of single indivisible injury as arises at common law in a case of concurrent torts.[46] The clearest example of concurrent torts was: "one where the injury in question would not have occurred but for both torts: where, if only one had been committed, the injury would not have occurred at all . . . [For example] two assailants, not acting in concert, shoot a man who dies in consequence; but the expert evidence is that either shot on its own, while causing grave injuries, would not have been fatal. The death is entirely and only the result of both shots."[47] In this situation, both defendants are fully liable for the death. A second example of concurrent tortfeasors was where each of two causes was necessary to produce the damage, *e.g.* where two persons independently shoot at a person at the same time, with both shots being fatal. Again, both are fully liable for the death. But where each tortfeasor caused some part of the damage, but neither caused the whole, and some part of the damage (but not all) would therefore have occurred if only one tort had been committed, but on the evidence it is impossible to identify with precision what part of the damage has been caused by which defendant, the defendants are not concurrent tortfeasors. Laws L.J. said that it would plainly be unjust to proceed on the footing that a defendant is responsible for the whole of the claimant's damage when, demonstrably, he is not. Once the case is categorised as one of concurrent torts then the rule is that each tortfeasor is liable for the whole of the damage in question. But where the court knows that the initial stage of the damage was caused by A (and not B) and that the latter stage was caused by B (and not A), it is not obliged to proceed contrary to the true facts on the assumption that each has caused the whole of the damage. The difficulty of apportioning responsibility between A and B was not a reason to hold both liable for the whole. Thus, on the facts of *Rahman v Arearose Ltd* it was not a case of concurrent torts. The respective torts were causes of distinct aspects of the claimant's overall psychiatric condition, neither caused the whole of it, and therefore the Civil Liability (Contribution) Act 1978 did not apply.[48]

Apportionment

Section 2(1) provides that the amount of contribution shall be "such as   7–050
may be found by the court to be just and equitable having regard to the

---

[45] *ibid.* at [17], original emphasis.
[46] *ibid.* at [18].
[47] *ibid.* at [19].
[48] For criticism of this decision see Weir [2001] C.L.J. 237.

extent of that person's responsibility for the damage in question." This wording is similar to that of section 1 of the Law Reform (Contributory Negligence) Act 1945 and it is not surprising that the courts should take a similar approach to apportioning responsibility under the two statutes.[49] The court's discretion is limited by section 2(3) which provides that where the claimant's damages would be subject to any limitation (imposed by statute or agreement) or any reduction because of contributory negligence the contribution award should not exceed this amount. In other words a defendant cannot be required to pay more by way of contribution than he would have been liable to pay to the claimant. There is no rule of law that a party who has been merely negligent cannot be required to make contribution to a party found guilty of fraud,[50] although the discrepancy in their conduct will clearly be relevant when assessing the amount of contribution, even to the extent of assessing a nil contribution.[51] But the personal innocence of an employer held vicariously liable for the fraud of an employee is not a relevant consideration when determining apportionment between the employer and another defendant.[52] The correct approach is to determine the respective responsibilities of the defendants who are personally responsible, and the employer is then vicariously responsible for the employee's contribution.

7–051   The effect of NHS Indemnity and the arrangements for pooling claims brought against the NHS (considered below) is that, in practice, contribution claims under the Civil Liability (Contribution) Act 1978 tend to be limited to actions arising out of private medicine,[53] disputes between general practitioners and hospitals, and disputes between general practitioners and pharmacists.[54] Of course, it is always open to any defendants to seek to agree their respective responsibilities without recourse to the legislation.

---

[49] See, e.g., *J (A Child) v Wilkins* [2001] P.I.Q.R. P179. The claimant was a two-year-old child who was held on her mother's knee in the front passenger seat of a car being driven by her aunt. The defendant negligently collided with the car, causing serious injuries to the claimant which could have been wholly avoided if she had been restrained in an approved child seat. The defendant joined the claimant's mother and aunt as CPR Pt 20 defendants. The Court of Appeal upheld the judge's assessment that liability should be apportioned 75% to the defendant and 25% to the mother and aunt, applying the well-known approach adopted in *Froom v Butcher* [1976] Q.B. 286 to the assessment of contributory negligence in cases involving a failure to wear a seat belt.

[50] For example, in *Downs v Chappell* [1996] 3 All E.R. 344, 363 a negligent defendant was required to contribute equally with a fraudulent defendant on the basis that the negligence had a greater causative impact.

[51] *K v P (J, third party)* [1993] Ch. 140, where it was held that the common law maxim *ex turpi causa non oritur actio* did not apply as a defence to a claim for contribution under the 1978 Act.

[52] *Dubai Aluminium Co Ltd v Salaam* [2002] UKHL 48; [2002] 3 W.L.R. 1913; [2003] 1 All E.R. 97.

[53] *Trustees of London Clinic v Edgar* (2000, QBD; unreported) is an example of a contribution claim between the private clinic responsible for the negligence of the nursing staff and the consultant surgeon.

[54] See, *e.g., Dwyer v Roderick, The Times,* November 12, 1983, CA, where a general practitioner negligently prescribed too high a dosage of a drug, and the pharmacist negligently failed to spot the error in the prescription. On appeal, liability was apportioned 45% to the general practitioner and 55% to the pharmacist; *Prendergast v Sam and Dee Ltd* [1989]

NHS Indemnity

Although the contribution legislation has been used in medical negligence litigation,[55] its significance was greatly reduced in actions against NHS hospital doctors in 1954 when Circular HM (54)32 was introduced. This established a private arrangement between doctors' defence organisations and the Department of Health by which payment to the claimant was apportioned between the defendants by agreement amongst themselves in each case, or in the absence of agreement in equal shares. This provided a formal, though not legally binding, mechanism which would reduce defendants' costs and at the same time present a united front to the claimant in the conduct of the litigation. The arrangement was replaced from January 1, 1990 with the introduction of "NHS indemnity" under which health authorities assumed responsibility for claims of medical negligence and ceased to require their medical and dental staff to subscribe to a defence organisation.[56] NHS indemnity was introduced as a result of substantial increases in the subscription rates of the medical defence organisations in the 1980s, and the growing pressure to relate subscription rates to the doctor's specialty, with high risk specialties paying a higher rate. It was considered that this could lead to distortion in pay and recruitment to the medical profession.

7-052

Since NHS indemnity was first introduced the administrative structure of the NHS has changed considerably. Health authorities no longer manage NHS hospitals (all NHS hospitals are now NHS Trusts) and Primary Care Trusts are in the process of replacing health authorities as the bodies responsible for commissioning (and in some instances providing) general medical services in primary care. Moreover, a special health authority, the NHS Litigation Authority now manages all claims for clinical negligence against NHS employees, and administers risk pooling schemes for clinical negligence, the first of which was established in 1995 (the Clinical Negligence Scheme for Trusts (CNST)). Thus, the question of who is covered by NHS indemnity tends to resolve into the issue of who is covered by CNST.

7-053

(n.54 contd.) 1 Med. L.R. 36, CA, where liability was apportioned 25% to the doctor who negligently wrote a prescription which could be misread, 75% to the pharmacist who misread the prescription and supplied the patient with the wrong drug.

[55] See, *e.g.*, *Jones v Manchester Corporation* [1952] Q.B. 852 where the issue concerned the respective responsibilities of a junior and inexperienced anaesthetist whose negligence resulted in the death of a patient, and the hospital authority which failed to provide appropriate supervision. The Court of Appeal, taking the view that the hospital should bear the brunt of the responsibility, allocated 80% to the hospital and 20% to the doctor; *Collins v Hertfordshire County Council* [1947] 1 K.B. 598, 623–625.

[56] See *Claims of Medical Negligence Against NHS Hospital and Community Doctors and Dentists*, HC(89)34, HC(89)(FP) 22. This was updated by HSG (96)48 and *NHS Indemnity—Arrangements for Clinical Negligence Claims in the NHS*, NHS Executive, 1996 (see Appendix 1). On the original Health Circular see Brazier (1990) 6 P.N. 88; Tingle (1991) 141 N.L.J. 630. The NHS was unusual as an employer, in requiring doctors employed in NHS hospitals to subscribe to a medical defence organisation (the Medical Defence Union, the Medical Protection Society, or the Medical and Dental Defence Union of Scotland) as part of the term of the contract of employment. Although that requirement has been removed, most doctors are members of a defence organisation which will provide indemnity in respect of private work and legal representation for disciplinary matters.

7–054   NHS indemnity applies to hospital authority responsibilities, namely a hospital's vicarious liability for the negligence of staff acting in the course of their employment, including consultants and staff provided by external agencies, irrespective of the precise legal relationship between these individuals and the hospital (*i.e.* whether or not they are in law employees or contractors).[57] HSG (96)48 and the accompanying documentation[58] updated the guidance given in HC(89)34 and takes the view that in addition to staff acting in the course of their NHS employment, NHS indemnity covers locum doctors, medical academic staff with honorary contracts, students, researchers conducting clinical trials, charitable volunteers and people undergoing professional education, training and examinations, "whenever a NHS body owes a duty of care to the person harmed". Any work which is outside the scope of a hospital doctor's employment (*e.g.*, reports for insurance companies or locum work for a general practitioner) is not covered, and the doctor will have to rely on subscription to a defence organisation for indemnity. A "Good Samaritan" act of assisting at an accident, although apparently excluded from coverage under the Guidance, appears now to fall within the coverage of CNST.[59]

7–055   NHS indemnity does not apply to general practitioners except where the general practitioner has a contract of employment (*e.g.* as a clinical assistant at a hospital or as a public health doctor) with a Primary Care Trust or NHS Trust and the treatment is being given under that contract. If a hospital is essentially providing only hotel services and the patient remains in the general practitioner's care, the hospital authority will not be responsible, and the claim will be dealt with by the general practitioner's defence organisation. Where a case involves a claim against both a NHS Trust and a general practitioner the possibility of a contribution claim exists, but the guidance emphasises that, as previously, NHS defendants should seek to reach agreement out of court as to the proportion of their respective liabilities, and to co-operate fully in the formulation of the defence. Primary Care Trusts are now eligible for membership of CNST but guidance from the NHS Litigation Authority makes it clear that the scheme only covers employees. Indemnity does not apply to independent contractors, whether providing NHS care or private treatment, unless the contractor is working as a direct agent of the Primary Care Trust.[60]

7–056   NHS indemnity does not apply to private hospitals or private work performed by a consultant in a NHS hospital. But where junior medical staff

---

[57] Of course, this does not resolve the legal issues, but simply specifies how hospital authorities are to deal with them in practice. NHS indemnity did not change the law as to whose conduct a hospital authority is responsible for, and theoretically it would still be open to take a vicarious liability point in a particular case involving, say, agency staff who are probably not employees. This is not done in practice, and, indeed, health authorities did not take the vicarious liability point for agency staff and consultants before 1990.

[58] *NHS Indemnity—Arrangements for Clinical Negligence Claims in the NHS*, NHS Executive, 1996 (see Appendix 1).

[59] See *The NHSLA's Risk Pooling Schemes: Who is indemnified?*, November 2002 [available at *www.nhsla.com* under "Events"] which states: "'Good Samaritan' acts: are covered unless prohibited by the employer, notwithstanding the statement implying the contrary in the CNST guideline."

[60] *ibid.* Though see para. 7–010, n. 33, above.

are involved in the care of private patients in NHS hospitals, they would normally be doing so as part of their contract with the hospital authority or NHS Trust. To the extent that NHS employees participate in the treatment, the hospital will be vicariously liable for their negligence.

In November 1995 the NHS Litigation Authority, a special health author- 7–057
ity, was established with the responsibility for administering schemes set up under section 21 of the NHS and Community Care Act 1990 permitting NHS bodies to pool the costs of injury, loss or damage to property and liabilities to third parties arising out of their NHS activities.[61] The NHS Litigation Authority is also responsible for determining standards of risk management and claims handling for members of the scheme (and NHS bodies generally) and managing the handling of claims. The Authority administers two principal[62] schemes: (i) the Clinical Negligence Scheme for Trusts (CNST); and (ii) the Existing Liabilities Scheme (ELS)

CNST covers liabilities for clinical negligence where the adverse event 7–058
occurred on or after April 1, 1995.[63] The scheme applies to England only.[64]
Clinical negligence liability is defined as:

"any liability in tort owed by a member to a third party in respect of or consequent upon personal injury or loss arising out of or in connection with any breach of a duty of care owed by that body to any person in connection with the diagnosis of any illness, or the care or treatment of any patient, in consequence of any act or omission to act on the part of a person employed or engaged by a member in connection with any relevant function of that member"[65]

---

[61] *NHS Litigation Authority Framework Document*, NHS Executive, 1996, amended December 2002 [available at *www.nhsla.com/docs/framework.doc*].

[62] The NHS Litigation Authority also has responsibility for miscellaneous residual medical negligence liabilities of certain special health authorities and the Regional Health Authorities (which were abolished from April 1, 1996). The Ex-Regional Health Authorities Scheme covers the liabilities of the hospitals and other services formerly managed at a regional level, prior to the abolition of Regional Health Authorities. The Authority also administers two other risk pooling schemes in respect of non-clinical claims.

[63] See the NHS (Clinical Negligence Scheme) Regulations 1996 (S.I. 1996 No. 251) which came into force on March 1, 1996; as amended by NHS (Clinical Negligence Scheme) (Amendment) Regulations 1997 (S.I. 1997 No. 527); NHS (Clinical Negligence Scheme) (Amendment) Regulations 1999 (S.I. 1999 No. 1274); NHS (Clinical Negligence Scheme) (Amendment) Regulations 2000 (S.I. 2000 No. 2341); NHS (Clinical Negligence Scheme) Amendment Regulations 2002 (S.I. 2002 No. 1073). See further Hickey (1995) 1 Clinical Risk 43; Pincombe (1995) 1 Clinical Risk 132; Fenn and Dingwall (1995) 310 B.M.J. 756.

[64] The functions of the Secretary of State under s.126(4) of the National Health Service Act 1977 and s.21 of the National Health Service and Community Care Act 1990 were transferred to the National Assembly for Wales under the National Assembly for Wales (Transfer of Functions) Order 1999 (S.I. 1999 No. 672) art. 2 and Sch. 1, as amended by s.66(5) of the Health Act 1999.

[65] NHS (Clinical Negligence Scheme) Regulations 1996 (S.I. 1996 No. 251), reg. 4. Similar wording, with appropriate amendments, applies to the Existing Liabilities Scheme: NHS (Existing Liabilities Scheme) Regulations 1996 (S.I. 1996 No. 686), regs.4 and 3. There is no reference to claims arising from failures to obtain consent, which give rise to actions in trespass to the person rather than negligence, which technically do not involve breach of a duty of care. This is probably an oversight and the NHS Litigation Authority will not take the point.

The scheme is funded by contributions from the NHS Trusts and Primary Care Trusts who are members of the scheme. It is not an insurance fund, but a "pay as you go" scheme which only collects enough money each year in contributions to cover the actual costs which fall into that year, plus a small margin to form a contingency reserve and cover administrative expenses. There are discounts on the Trust's contributions for putting into place appropriate risk management standards. CNST operates on a "claims paid" basis, which means that it will cover a NHS Trust if the Trust is a member of the scheme continuously at the date of the adverse event which subsequently gives rise to the claim and the date of settlement. The object is to permit NHS Trusts and Primary Care Trusts to spread the cost of claims. From April 2002 the NHS Litigation Authority took over from NHS Trusts the handling and management of all clinical negligence claims against NHS Trusts in England, although the NHS Trust remains the legally responsible defendant.[66]

7–059   The Existing Liabilities Scheme covers incidents of clinical negligence which occurred before April 1, 1995.[67] It is funded by the Secretary of State, through the NHS Litigation Authority. From April 1 2000, the NHS Litigation Authority assumed responsibility for recording, handling and accounting for payments under the scheme, although legal responsibility remained with the NHS Trusts and Health Authorities. From the same date, health organisations no longer make, or account for, any part of the payment, and the NHS Litigation Authority now undertakes all the administration arrangements.

---

[66] Prior to this change there were complicated rules about the levels of "excess", which ranged from £10,000 to £500,000, that had to be met by the individual NHS Trust before it could claim indemnity from CNST. These excess levels were abolished from April 1, 2002, so that the whole cost of indemnity is now met from the CNST.

[67] NHS (Existing Liabilities Scheme) Regulations 1996 (S.I. 1996 No. 686); as amended by NHS (Existing Liabilities Scheme) (Amendment) Regulations 1997 (S.I. 1997 No. 526); NHS (Existing Liabilities Scheme) (Amendment) Regulations 1999 (S.I. 1999 No. 1275).

CHAPTER 8

DEFECTIVE PRODUCTS

It was the tragedy of thalidomide that first brought to public attention the   8–001
problems confronting the victims of defective drugs in obtaining compensation for their injuries. This provided the stimulus for tighter control of drug
marketing by the Medicines Act 1968, and ultimately led to the setting up
of the Pearson Commission to look into the system of compensation for personal injuries. Actions in respect of defective drugs are probably the most
common form of medical product liability claims, but they are not the only
product which could give rise to litigation in a health care setting. Claims
have been made in respect of defective heart valves,[1] intra-uterine devices,[2]
contaminated blood products,[3] human growth hormone,[4] breast implants,[5]
and tampons,[6] and it would not be difficult to think of other products which
could provoke litigation if defective.[7]

---

[1] *Sunday Times*, March 10, 1985 reporting on deaths linked to a faulty valve, the Bjork-Shiley
valve, manufactured in the US by a subsidiary of Pfizer; [1990] 32 Law Soc. Gaz. 7. See also
the Medical Devices Regulations 1994, S.I. 1994 No. 3017 (as amended by S.I. 2000 No.
1315), specifying safety requirements for medical devices; the Active Implantable Medical
Devices Regulations 1992, S.I. 1992 No. 3146, (as amended by S.I. 1995 No. 1671), specifying minimum requirements for active implantable medical devices.
[2] Claims against A.H. Robins, the American pharmaceutical company that marketed the
Dalkon Shield, led to that company going into voluntary liquidation with an estimated liability of $US 2.5 billion. See Ferrell (1988) 62 A.L.J. 92.
[3] *A. v National Blood Authority* [2001] 3 All E.R. 289; *Re HIV Haemophiliac Litigation*
(1990), [1996] P.I.Q.R. P220; *Brown v Alberta* [1994] 2 W.W.R. 283 (Alta. Q.B.). See also
H. v Royal Alexandra Hospital for Children [1990] 1 Med. L.R. 297 (N.S.W.S.C.); *E. v
Australian Red Cross Society* (1991) 99 A.L.R. 601; [1991] 2 Med. L.R. 303 (Fed. Court of
Aust.); (1991) 105 A.L.R. 53 (Aust. Fed. C.A.); *P.Q. v Australian Red Cross Society* [1992]
1 V.R. 19 (Vict.S.C.); *Pittman Estate v Bain* (1994) 112 D.L.R. (4th) 257 (Ont. Ct., Gen.
Div.); *Kitchen v McMullin* (1989) 62 D.L.R. (4th) 481 (N.B.C.A.). On defective blood bags
see (1995) 311 B.M.J. 145.
[4] *The Creutzfeldt-Jakob Disease Litigation, Plaintiffs v United Kingdom Medical Research
Council* (1996) 54 B.M.L.R. 8; [1996] 7 Med. L.R. 309; para. 3–057.
[5] *Foster v Biosil* (2000) 59 B.M.L.R. 178; *Hollis v Dow Corning Corp* (1995) 129 D.L.R.
(4th) 609 (S.C.C.); *Bendall v McGhan Medical Corp.* (1993) 106 D.L.R. (4th) 339, a case
dealing with the procedural issue of whether a class action should be instituted in Ontario.
See Balen (2002) 8 Clinical Risk 177.
[6] *Worsley v Tambrands Ltd* [2000] P.I.Q.R. P95; *Thompson v Johnson and Johnson Pty Ltd*
[1992] 3 Med. L.R. 148; [1991] 2 V.R. 449 (S.C. of Victoria, App. Div.); see (1990) 301
B.M.J. 257.
[7] For example: heart pacemakers; limb joints (a patient was reported to be suing Depuy
International in respect of an allegedly faulty hip replacement which the company had manufactured: *The Times*, September 12, 1995.); donated organs (see *Sumners v Mid-Downs*

8–002   The same legal principles apply whatever the product in question, although drug injuries do appear to create their own special problems. All drugs have some inherent risk. They are designed to interfere with the body's chemistry, and some patients will have idiosyncratic reactions. Many drugs cannot be made completely safe for their intended or ordinary use even when they are properly manufactured and are not impure. Notwithstanding the medically recognisable risk of harm that they present, the marketing of such drugs may be justified by their utility.[8] Thus, it can be difficult to come to a judgment about what is a "defective" drug, since the risk of side-effects for a minority of patients may be acceptable in view of the benefits for the majority of patients.[9] Where, on the other hand, an alternative, safe, option is available a product which carries inherent risk may be categorised as defective.[10]

8–003   A further problem stems from the difficulty of proving causation. This arises at two levels. First, it must be shown that the drug in question is capable of causing the type of harm from which the claimant is suffering. This will depend upon scientific evidence, which may be difficult to obtain and may be equivocal in its conclusions.[11] Where, for example, there is a substantial delay

---

(n.7 contd.) *Health Authority and South East Thames Health Authority* discussed at (1989) 298 B.M.J. 1544); contaminated or defective donated sperm (*ter Neuzen v Korn* (1995) 127 D.L.R. (4th) 577 (S.C.C.)). In *A. v National Blood Authority* [2001] 3 All E.R. 289 it was held that human blood amounted to a "product," for the purposes of the Consumer Protection Act 1987 and it would seem to follow that other bodily fluids or organs would also fall within the terms of the Act. In any event, so far as the tort of negligence is concerned liability turns on the foreseeability of the risk of harm from contamination, rather than categorisation as a "product" or otherwise.

[8] *Buchan v Ortho Pharmaceutical (Canada) Ltd* (1986) 25 D.L.R. (4th) 658, 668, (Ont. C.A.). Surprisingly, perhaps, there is no reported case in this country in which a court has had to make a finding of liability against a drug manufacturer. Claims have been made in respect of, *inter alia*, Thalidomide, Opren, Debendox, Myodil, pertussis vaccine, neomycin, and benzodiazepine, but the actions have, to date, either settled or failed for want of proof of causation: see *Davies v Eli Lilly & Co* (1987) 137 N.L.J. 1183 and Dyer (1988) 296 B.M.J. 109 on the Opren settlement; Orme (1985) 291 B.M.J. 918 on Debendox; and *The Times*, August 1, 1995 on the Myodil settlement. The group actions in the benzodiazepine litigation gave rise to numerous procedural difficulties and were eventually struck out as an abuse of process, and for want of prosecution: see *A.B. v John Wyeth & Brother Ltd and Roche Products Ltd* [1992] 3 Med. L.R. 190; [1992] P.I.Q.R. P437; [1992] 1 W.L.R. 169, CA; *A.B. v John Wyeth & Brother Ltd* [1993] 4 Med. L.R. 1; *A.B. v John Wyeth & Brother Ltd* [1994] P.I.Q.R. P109; [1994] 5 Med. L.R. 149, CA; *A.B. v John Wyeth & Brother Ltd* [1997] P.I.Q.R. P385; [1997] 8 Med. L.R. 57. For discussion of some of the difficulties still faced by claimants suing in respect of drug injuries 30 years after the Thalidomide disaster see Ferguson [1992] J.R. 226; and in respect of claims arising from the side-effects of the contraceptive pill, see Ferguson (1995) 145 N.L.J. 846. See further Bowen-Simpkins (1995) 1 *AVMA Medical & Legal Journal* 80 for discussion of the side-effects of Depo-Provera.

[9] This is the logic of the limited no-fault compensation available under the Vaccine Damage Payments Act 1979 for individuals who suffer vaccine damage, since they bear the brunt of the cost of a scheme that is intended to benefit the population at large. Despite significant increases in recent years the sums available are still comparatively small in relation to the harm suffered, and there may still be problems in proving causation: see *Loveday v Renton* [1990] 1 Med. L.R. 117. For discussion of the Act see Dworkin [1978–79] J.S.W.L. 330; and para. 1–037.

[10] *Nicholson v John Deere Ltd* (1986) 34 D.L.R. (4th) 542, 549, *per* Smith J., (Ont. H.C.): "A manufacturer does not have the right to manufacture an inherently dangerous article when a method exists of manufacturing the same article without risk of harm. No amount of or degree of specificity of warning will exonerate him from liability if he does."

[11] Or may even demonstrate that the drug does not have the adverse effects which are alleged:

in the injuries becoming manifest, as can be the case with teratogenic injuries,[12] and/or where the adverse reactions constitute an addition to the background risk so that it is extremely difficult, if not impossible, to distinguish drug injuries from other, often unknown, causes, the difficulties of proving causation may be insurmountable.[13] Secondly, even where it is accepted that the drug is capable of causing the type of injury concerned, the claimant must still prove that *his* injury was attributable to the drug in question and not some other factor, such as the illness for which he was being treated, or an unforeseen interaction between a number of drugs taken at the same time. Where generic drugs or drugs from different manufacturers have been used over a number of years, there may be difficulties simply in identifying a defendant.[14]

Donoghue v Stevenson[15] established that, in addition to any liability in contract, there could also be liability in the tort of negligence for defective products, but, in spite of some cases which suggested that in certain circumstances a high standard of care would be required, the action has remained fault-based. The English courts have not followed the American example where strict liability in tort was established.[16] In the 1970s a number of law reform bodies recommended that strict liability for defective products should be introduced, and now, following a European Community initiative, the United Kingdom has a form of strict liability by virtue of the Consumer Protection Act 1987. Thus, liability for damage caused by defective products is a combination of liability in contract, the tort of negligence and under Part I of the Consumer Protection Act 1987.

8–004

1. CONTRACT

The ultimate consumer of a product will rarely be in a contractual relationship with the manufacturer, and this is particularly true of medicinal products.

8–005

(n.11 contd.) see Goldberg (1996) 4 Med. L. Rev. 32, discussing the distorting effect of litigation on the scientific evidence in cases where it was alleged that the drug Debendox caused birth defects.

[12] See, *e.g.*, *Sindell v Abbott Laboratories* 607 P. 2d 924, (1980) below, para. 8–061.

[13] *Kay v Ayrshire and Arran Health Board* [1987] 2 All E.R. 417, where the claimant failed to prove that an overdose of penicillin could cause deafness; *Loveday v Renton* [1990] 1 Med. L.R. 117, where the claimant failed to prove, on a balance of probabilities, that pertussis vaccine could cause brain damage in young children, although it was "possible" that there was a causal link; see also *Rothwell v Raes* (1988) 54 D.L.R. (4th) 193; affirmed (1990) 76 D.L.R. (4th) 280 (Ont. C.A.) on the pertussis vaccine and causation; *cf.* the more robust approach of the Supreme Court of Ireland to the question of the causal link between a defective batch of pertussis vaccine and brain damage in children in *Best v Wellcome Foundation Ltd* [1994] 5 Med. L.R. 81; [1993] 3 I.R. 421; (1992) 17 B.M.L.R 11; *D. and R. v Schering Chemicals Ltd* (1982, QBD; unreported). See also the *Royal Commission on Civil Liability and Compensation for Personal Injury*, Cmnd. 7054 (1978), Vol. I, para. 1364.

[14] See, *e.g.*, *Mann v Wellcome Foundation Ltd* (1989, QBD; unreported); *cf.* the approach adopted to this type of problem by the California Court of Appeal in *Sindell v Abbott Laboratories* 607 P. 2d 924, (1980), para. 8–061, below.

[15] [1932] A.C. 562.

[16] See *Restatement, Torts* (2d), § 402A.

However, a defective product sold by a retailer may give rise to an action for breach of contract, which through the contractual chain of supply may be traced back to the manufacturer in the form of indemnity claims. The contractual action is limited, by the doctrine of privity of contract, to the purchaser of the product and it is of no value to, for example, a member of the purchaser's family injured by the product. This is the major drawback of the claim in contract.

8–006   Where a contractual remedy is available it will often be more advantageous to the claimant than a claim in tort. A purchaser of goods will have the benefit of implied terms as to the satisfactory quality and fitness for purpose of the goods,[17] which in the case of "consumer" transactions cannot be excluded.[18] Liability is strict, in the sense that it does not have to be shown that the defect was attributable to the vendor's fault, and the exercise of reasonable care is not a defence. Moreover, the contractual action is available for products which are defective in quality, though not dangerous, if the defect is such as to constitute a breach of warranty. This type of claim is not available in the tort of negligence.

8–007   Thus, non-prescription products sold by retail pharmacists over the counter may be the subject of a contractual action if the purchaser sustains injury, as would drugs supplied on private (*i.e.* non-NHS) prescription. Products supplied under NHS prescriptions, on the other hand, are not supplied under a contract between the pharmacist and the consumer, but by virtue of the of the patient's statutory right to demand the product on payment of the prescription charge and the Minister's statutory obligation to supply it.[19] The result is that, in practice, contractual claims arising from defective drugs are likely to be extremely rare.

8–008   A retailer sued in contract by the purchaser of defective goods will normally have a contractual claim for indemnity against his own vendor (wholesaler or distributor), and so on, up the contractual chain to the manufacturer who produced the defective goods, subject to any valid exemption clauses. In this way, in theory at least, liability will rest with the person responsible for the defect. This contractual chain may break down if, for example, one link is missing, having gone into liquidation or is simply untraceable through lack of records.[20] The doctrine of privity of contract then prevents any further claims along the contractual chain.[21] From the

---

[17] Sale of Goods Act 1979, s.14; Supply of Goods and Services Act 1982, ss.4 and 9, as amended by the Sale and Supply of Goods Act 1994. Note that what is satisfactory quality or fit for its purpose will be a matter of degree in the case of drugs which may have known side-effects; it does include, however, the packaging and instructions for use, so that if the instructions are wrong or misleading the goods are not of satisfactory quality or fit for their purpose: *Wormell v R.H.M. Agriculture (East) Ltd* [1986] 1 All E.R. 769.

[18] Unfair Contract Terms Act 1977, s.6.

[19] *Pfizer Corp v Ministry of Health* [1965] A.C. 512; *Appleby v Sleep* [1968] 2 All E.R. 265, 269.

[20] As occurred in *Lambert v Lewis* [1982] A.C. 225.

[21] There may be a claim, however, under the Civil Liability (Contribution) Act 1978. In addition, it has been held that economic loss suffered by a distributor in a chain of supply which consists of a liability to pay damages to the ultimate consumer for physical injuries, or to

claimant purchaser's point of view this will be irrelevant, unless it is the retailer who is no longer available to be sued, in which case the purchaser's contractual claim will be useless. This will leave the purchaser in the same position as all other claimants injured by a defective product, having to rely on a claim in tort for negligence or under the Consumer Protection Act 1987.

2. TORT

(1) Manufacturers' duty

In *Donoghue v Stevenson*[22] the House of Lords held that the manufactur-   8-009
ers of a defective product owed a duty of care in negligence to the ultimate consumer of the product, notwithstanding the absence of any contractual relationship between the consumer and the manufacturer.[23] In the course of his speech Lord Atkin expressed the duty in these terms:

> "A manufacturer of products which he sells in such a form as to show that he intends them to reach the ultimate consumer in the form in which they left him, with no reasonable possibility of intermediate examination, and with the knowledge that the absence of reasonable care in the preparation or putting up of the products will result in injury to the consumer's life or property, owes a duty to the consumer to take that reasonable care."[24]

Lord Thankerton said that the defendant brought himself into a direct relationship with the consumer by placing his product upon the market in a form which precluded interference with or examination of the product by any intermediate handler, with the result that the consumer was entitled to rely on the exercise of reasonable care by the manufacturer to secure that the product should not be harmful.

(n.21 contd.) indemnify a distributor lower in the chain for his liability to the consumer for physical injuries, may be recoverable from the manufacturer under the principle of *Donoghue v Stevenson* [1932] A.C. 562: see *Lambert v Lewis* [1982] A.C. 225, 277–278; *Virgo Steamship Co S.A. v Skaarup Shipping Corp* [1988] 1 Lloyd's Rep. 352.

[22] [1932] A.C. 562.

[23] So removing the so-called "privity of contract" fallacy, which argued that the claimant was seeking to take the benefit of a contract (between manufacturer and wholesaler or retailer) to which he was not a party, attributed to *Winterbottom v Wright* (1842) 10 M. & W. 109. For discussion of the privity of contract fallacy see *Dutton v Bognor Regis Urban District Council* [1972] 1 Q.B. 373, 392–393.

[24] [1932] A.C. 562, 599. This duty applies to personal injuries and physical damage to other property, including economic loss consequential on the physical damage, applying the usual principles of the tort of negligence. Pure economic loss, which includes physical damage to the product itself, is not recoverable: *Murphy v Brentwood District Council* [1991] 1 A.C. 398; *Muirhead v Industrial Tank Specialities Ltd* [1986] Q.B. 507.

8–010   The manufacturer's duty has been given a broad interpretation. "Product" includes almost any item capable of causing damage, such as underpants,[25] motor cars,[26] hair dye,[27] lifts,[28] and chemicals.[29] Similarly, "ultimate consumer" means anyone foreseeably harmed by the defective product. This includes the user of the product, such as a donee, a member of the purchaser's family, including a foetus *in utero*,[30] or an employee of the purchaser,[31] someone who handles the product, such as a storeman or a shopkeeper,[32] and a by-stander.[33]

8–011   The range of potential defendants has also been extended to include not only manufacturers, but also repairers,[34] and assemblers.[35] A supplier of goods, such as a retailer or wholesaler, may be liable if the circumstances are such that he ought reasonably to have inspected the goods or tested them.[36] Distributors who obtain goods from suppliers of doubtful reputation ought to test them,[37] and *a fortiori* when the manufacturers' instructions state that the product should be tested.[38] The duty does not arise in all cases of supply, only where the circumstances indicate that an inspection or test is reasonably required. Clearly, if the dangerous defect was in fact known to the supplier he ought, at least, to give a warning to the recipient.

8–012   An issue that arises in the context of pharmaceutical products is the possible liability of statutory regulatory agencies. Under the Medicines Act 1968 the manufacture and distribution of medicines in this country is regulated by a Licensing Authority, which consists of Health Ministers and Agriculture Ministers.[39] The Licensing Authority is advised by the Medicines Commission, and specialist committees set up under section 4 of the Act, including the Committee on the Safety of Medicines (CSM) which assesses product licence applications. Product licences are granted only when the Licensing Authority is satisfied as to the safety, efficacy and quality of the product.[40]

8–013   The effect is that pharmaceutical products distributed in the United

---

25 *Grant v Australian Knitting Mills Ltd* [1936] A.C. 85.
26 *Herschtal v Stewart & Arden Ltd* [1940] 1 K.B. 155.
27 *Watson v Buckley, Osborne Garrett & Co Ltd* [1940] 1 All E.R. 174.
28 *Haseldine v Daw & Son Ltd* [1941] 2 K.B. 343.
29 *Vacwell Engineering Co Ltd v B.D.H. Chemicals Ltd* [1971] 1 Q.B. 88.
30 Congenital Disabilities (Civil Liability) Act, 1976; see paras 2–080 to 2–088.
31 *Davie v New Merton Board Mills Ltd* [1959] A.C. 604.
32 *Barnett v H. and J. Packer & Co Ltd* [1940] 3 All E.R. 575.
33 *Stennett v Hancock* [1939] 2 All E.R. 578.
34 *Stennett v Hancock* [1939] 2 All E.R. 578; *Haseldine v Daw & Son Ltd* [1941] 2 K.B. 343, 379.
35 *Howard v Furness Houlder Argentine Lines Ltd* [1936] 2 All E.R. 781.
36 *Andrews v Hopkinson* [1957] 1 Q.B. 229; *cf. Hurley v Dyke* [1979] R.T.R. 265. See also *Good-Wear Treaders Ltd v D. & B. Holdings Ltd* (1979) 98 D.L.R. (3d) 59, holding that a supplier owes a duty not to supply a product to a purchaser whom he knows intends to misuse the product, thereby endangering the safety of third parties.
37 *Watson v Buckley, Osborne Garrett & Co* [1940] 1 All E.R. 174.
38 *Kubach v Hollands* [1937] 3 All E.R. 907.
39 Medicines Act 1968, ss.1, 6. The Act applies to "medicinal products" which means a substance or article (but not an instrument, apparatus or appliance) used for a medicinal purpose: see s.130 for a detailed definition. For discussion of the effectiveness of the regulatory scheme established by the Medicines Act see Teff (1984) 47 M.L.R. 303.
40 *ibid.*, ss.19–20. See the Medicines (Applications for Grant of Product Licences—Products for Human Use) Regulations 1993, S.I. 1993 No. 2538. On April 1, 2003 two Department of Health agencies, the Medicines Control Agency and the Medical Devices Agency, were

Kingdom will have been scrutinised for safety by an independent statutory body. If the product is found to have a design defect it is arguable that the licensing authority should be responsible along with the manufacturer, for allowing a defective product to be marketed. The Medicines Act 1968 does not confer any general civil right of action for breach of its terms, nor does it grant any immunities from any action that would otherwise be available.[41] It is not certain, however, that the Licensing Authority would be held to owe a duty of care to members of the public in granting a licence.

Whilst the regulatory agencies have been sued, until recently[42] the issue has been considered by the courts only in the course of interlocutory proceedings.[43] In *Department of Health and Social Security v Kinnear*[44] claims were brought against the DHSS in respect of injuries alleged to have been caused by reaction to whooping cough vaccine. The DHSS adopted a policy of promoting immunization against whooping cough in the bona fide exercise of a statutory discretion under the National Health Service Act 1946, section 26. Stuart-Smith J. held that since the policy was within the limits of the discretion it could not give rise to a cause of action.[45] Even allegations of negligence on the part of the department's servants, *e.g.* in failing to submit relevant reports to the persons taking the policy decisions prior to and leading up to the formulation of the policy, could not found a cause of action against the department. | 8–014

On the other hand, claims that the DHSS had given negligent or misleading advice to health authorities regarding the circumstances in which inoculations should be performed, and the factors to be applied in determining whether particular individuals should be inoculated, were not struck out as disclosing no reasonable cause of action. It was at least arguable that the | 8–015

(n.40 contd.) merged into a new executive agency of the Department of Health, the Medicines and Healthcare Products Regulatory Agency ("MHRA"—see *www.mhra.gov.uk*). This puts the regulation of medicines and medical devices under the remit of a single agency. See further the draft Medicines for Human Use (Clinical Trials) Regulations 2003 (available at *www.doh. gov.uk/clinicaltrialsconsult*) which will implement the European Clinical Trials Directive, 2001/20/EC, which lays down standards for the manufacture, import and labelling of investigational medicinal products. The Directive requires member states to set up inspection systems for good manufacturing practice and good clinical practice. It also provides for safety monitoring of patients/volunteers in trials, and sets out procedures for reporting and recording adverse drug reactions and events. The draft regulations provide, *inter alia*, that a clinical trial may be conducted only if it has been authorised by the licensing authority and an ethics committee has approved it.

[41] Medicines Act 1968, s.133(2).

[42] See para. 8–019. See also *The Creutzfeldt-Jakob Disease Litigation, Plaintiffs v United Kingdom Medical Research Council* (1996) 54 B.M.L.R. 8; [1996] 7 Med. L.R. 309; discussed at paras 3–057 *et seq.* The action in this case was not against a regulatory agency as such, but against the Medical Research Council and the Department of Health, who had sponsored the research/treatment programme of injecting children with human growth hormone.

[43] For example, in the Opren litigation: *Davies v Eli Lilly & Co* [1987] 3 All E.R. 94 (the report deals only with the issue of costs); and in connection with the contamination of blood products with HIV: *Re HIV Haemophiliac Litigation* (1990), [1996] P.I.Q.R. P220; *Brown v Alberta* [1994] 2 W.W.R. 283 (Alta. Q.B.).

[44] *The Times*, July 7, 1984.

[45] Applying *Anns v Merton London Borough Council* [1978] A.C. 728, 754; *Dorset Yacht Co Ltd v Home Office* [1970] A.C. 1004, 1067. See also *Bonthrone v Secretary of State for Scotland* 1987 S.L.T. 34; *Ross v Secretary of State for Scotland* [1990] 1 Med. L.R. 235. In *Danns v Department of Health* [1998] P.I.Q.R. P226, the Court of Appeal held that the

alleged negligent advice fell within the operational category, in which negligence in the performance of a statutory power could give rise to a duty of care, adopting the operational/policy dichotomy used by Lord Wilberforce in *Anns v Merton London Borough Council*.[46] In *Re HIV Haemophiliac Litigation*[47] the Court of Appeal had to consider whether haemophiliacs who had been infected with the HIV virus as a result of receiving contaminated blood products, had a *prima facie* case in negligence against, *inter alia*, the Department of Health, the Licensing Authority under the Medicines Act 1968 and the CSM, in the course of proceedings for discovery of documents. Ralph Gibson L.J. commented that although it was difficult to prove negligence when the defendant was required to exercise discretion and form judgments on the allocation of public resources, that was not sufficient to make it clear that there could be no claim in negligence. This interlocutory decision appears simply to assume, without deciding the issue, that a duty of care could exist.[48]

8–016   In a number of cases it has been held that certain regulatory authorities do not owe a duty of care to members of the public when performing their statutory functions.[49] Most, though not all,[50] of these cases were concerned with pure economic loss, rather than personal injuries and thus may not be

---

(n.40 contd.) failure of the Department of Health to publish information in the media about the risks of late re-canalisation following a vasectomy (put at 2,000 to 1) did not give rise to a private law action for breach of the Ministry of Health Act 1919, s.2.

[46] [1978] A.C. 728. Similarly, in *Rothwell v Raes* (1988) 54 D.L.R. (4th) 193, 346 (Ont. H.C.) it was held that the Ontario Ministry of Health did owe a duty of care with regard to the implementation of a policy decision to establish a system for pertussis vaccination, although the Ministry had not been negligent on the facts. The trial judge relied on *City of Kamloops v Neilsen* (1984) 10 D.L.R. (4th) 641, in which the Supreme Court of Canada had adopted Lord Wilberforce's operational/policy dichotomy. *Anns v Merton London Borough Council* has been overruled by the House of Lords in *Murphy v Brentwood District Council* [1991] 1 A.C. 398 on the question of the *type of loss* which may be recoverable for acts of negligence. The distinction between operational and policy decisions, which was relied on by Lord Diplock in *Home Office v Dorset Yacht Co Ltd* [1970] A.C. 1004, has continued to be used by the courts as a basis for determining negligence in the performance of statutory powers. In *X. (minors) v Bedfordshire County Council* [1995] 2 A.C. 633, 736–737, Lord Browne-Wilkinson suggested that the public law doctrine of *ultra vires* was not a suitable test; rather, where it is sought to make a public body liable at common law for negligence in the exercise of a discretion the first requirement is to show that the decision was outside the ambit of the discretion altogether, but where the factors relevant to the exercise of the discretion include matters of policy the court cannot adjudicate on such policy matters, and thus a common law duty of care in relation to the taking of decisions involving policy matters cannot exist.

[47] (1990), [1996] P.I.Q.R. P220.

[48] See also *Brown v Alberta* [1994] 2 W.W.R. 283 (Alta. Q.B.) where, on similar facts, the court refused to strike out the claimant's claims against the Crown as disclosing no reasonable cause of action, on the ground that claims should not be struck out unless it could be said that the actions were doomed to fail on the facts, which would not be the case unless the issue was beyond doubt, clear and unambiguous. The pleadings raised issues of general importance which should be tried on the facts. It was alleged that the Crown had failed to pass regulations and adopt policies relating to the collection and distribution of blood products, and had failed to provide funding for the implementation of blood testing.

[49] See *Yuen Kun-yeu v A.-G. of Hong Kong* [1988] A.C. 175; *Davis v Radcliffe* [1990] 2 All E.R. 536; *Rowling v Takaro Properties Ltd* [1988] A.C. 473; *Minories Finance Ltd v Arthur Young* [1989] 2 All E.R. 105; *Mills v Winchester Diocesan Board of Finance* [1989] 2 All E.R. 317; *Murphy v Brentwood District Council* [1991] 1 A.C. 398; *X. (minors) v Bedfordshire County Council* [1995] 2 A.C. 633.

[50] *cf. Hill v Chief Constable of West Yorkshire* [1989] 1 A.C. 53.

directly applicable to actions against the Licensing Authority, the Medicines Commission or the CSM. Various other factors have been taken into account, however, in denying the existence of a duty of care, some of which would be relevant in this context. All deal with liability for the conduct of third parties, where the question will frequently be: what degree of control did the defendant have over the third party's conduct? The mere fact that the regulatory body could register or de-register the third party and thus had some control over whether he could continue the operations which caused the claimant's loss is not a ground for imposing a duty of care.[51] It has been said that the imposition of a duty of care might lead to a conflict of duties, in which the regulatory agency adopts an unusually conservative or defensive approach to its functions because of the fear of liability, a practice which may not be in the public interest.[52] Where the claimant would have an alternative remedy, even against another defendant,[53] or where the claimant is merely a member of a large unascertained class of potential claimants the courts may deny the existence of a duty of care.[54]

In *Yuen Kun-yeu v A.-G. of Hong Kong*[55] the Privy Council took the view   8–017
that since the statutory framework which established the particular regulatory system did not provide for compensation, it would be "strange" for the courts to superimpose a common law duty of care. Similarly, in *Murphy v Brentwood District Council*[56] Lord Oliver pointed to the absence of any specific provision in the legislation creating a private law right of action for breach of statutory duty, as one reason for not imposing a duty of care on the local authority in exercising its statutory powers to ensure that new buildings comply with building regulations. Section 133(2) of the Medicines Act 1968 expressly provides that the Act does not confer a civil right of action, and a court could adopt the reasoning of the Privy Council in *Yuen Kun-yeu* in order to deny the existence of a duty of care.

In response it might be argued that most of these cases have been con-   8–018
cerned with actions for pure economic loss, and that different considerations apply where a statutory body can be said to owe a statutory duty to the public with regard to public health and safety, as is clearly the position under the Medicines Act 1968.[57] This was, in theory at least, the rationale for the

---

[51] *Yuen Kun-yeu v A.-G. of Hong Kong* [1988] A.C. 175; *Davis v Radcliffe* [1990] 2 All E.R. 536.
[52] *Yuen Kun-yeu v A.-G. of Hong Kong* [1988] A.C. 175, 198; *Rowling v Takaro Properties Ltd* [1988] A.C. 473, 502; *Hill v Chief Constable of West Yorkshire* [1989] 1 A.C. 53, 63; *X. (minors) v Bedfordshire County Council* [1995] 2 A.C. 633, 750. On the risk of "defensive licensing" of pharmaceutical products see Teff (1984) 47 M.L.R. 303, 310–311.
[53] *La Banque Financière de la Cité SA v Westgate Insurance Co Ltd* [1988] 2 Lloyd's Rep. 513, 563; *Simaan General Contracting Co v Pilkington Glass Ltd (No. 2)* [1988] 1 All E.R. 791, 804–806.
[54] *Hill v Chief Constable of West Yorkshire* [1989] 1 A.C. 53, 62.
[55] [1988] A.C. 175, 195.
[56] [1991] 1 A.C. 398, 490.
[57] Thus, where a regulatory agency has been established with the specific objective of protecting the public from dangerous practices then, arguably, it should be easier to find a duty of care owed to individual members of the public injured or killed as a result of the agency's negligent failure to regulate. For example, in *Swanson v The Queen in Right of Canada*

decision in *Anns*, since the local authority's duty was said to arise where there was a present or imminent danger to the health or safety of the occupants of the premises. This interpretation of the nature of the claimants' loss in *Anns* was finally shown to be mistaken in *Murphy v Brentwood District Council*,[58] where the damage to the claimant's house was categorised as economic loss. Counsel for the local authority in *Murphy* had conceded, however, that the local authority would owe a duty of care with respect to any personal injuries sustained as a result of the defendants' negligent failure adequately to perform their statutory powers, although this concession was not necessarily approved.[59] Moreover, in *X. (minors) v Bedfordshire County Council*[60] the House of Lords concluded that a social services authority should not owe a duty of care in negligence in respect of the manner in which it performed its statutory child protection functions, whether by wrongly taking a child into care whereby the child suffered psychiatric damage or by negligently failing to take steps to protect children at risk of abuse or neglect. Lord Browne-Wilkinson said that "the courts should proceed with great care before holding liable in negligence those who have been charged by Parliament with the task of protecting society from the wrongdoings of others."[61]

8–019   In *Smith v Secretary of State for Health*[62] it was alleged that the Committee on the Safety of Medicines (the CSM) had been negligent in delaying a public announcement warning of the risk that asprin could cause serious harm to children. The claimant was a six-year-old child who contracted chicken pox in May 1986. She was given asprin for relief of symptoms, in accordance with recommended doses for children. She developed Reye's syndrome, and sustained a seriously disabling injury. Less than a month later the Department of Health issued a general public warning advising that children under 12 should not be given asprin in any form, and required pharmacists to remove all junior asprin from their shelves. This was as a result of advice from the CSM, that in some cases asprin had been linked to children developing this condition. The CSM had been monitoring the potential problem before it concluded at a meeting in March 1986 that the evidence of a causal link between asprin and Reye's syndrome in children was overwhelming. It recommended that a general warning on the use of asprin in children should be given without delay. Shortly after that meeting

---

(n.57 contd.) (1991) 80 D.L.R. (4th) 741 (Fed. C.A.) it was held that an agency with responsibility for regulating the safety of commercial airlines was liable for negligently permitting an airline to continue unsafe practices, having issued warnings to the airline but failed to take any further enforcement proceedings to require compliance with safety standards.

[58] [1991] 1 A.C. 398; having been radically undermined in *D. & F. Estates Ltd v Church Commissioners for England* [1989] A.C. 177.

[59] Lord Mackay (*ibid.* at 457) and Lord Keith (*ibid.* at 463) reserved their opinions on whether any duty would be owed at all, and Lord Bridge (*ibid.* at 479) was prepared to assume, but was by no means satisfied that the assumption was correct, that the local authority's potential liability in tort was co-extensive with that of the negligent builder.

[60] [1995] 2 A.C. 633.

[61] *ibid.* at 751.

[62] [2002] Lloyd's Rep. Med. 333.

the Department of Health held a meeting in April 1986 with representatives of the asprin industry where it became apparent that the manufacturers would probably be willing to withdraw paediatric asprin from sale voluntarily. It was judged that this would be a much more effective means of dealing with the problem than invoking the statutory mechanisms under the Medicines Act 1968. The Department therefore decided to postpone the CSM recommendation to publish an immediate warning. Following further meetings with the industry, the manufacturers agreed to the voluntary withdrawal from sale of paediatric asprin and to participate in a campaign of public education. The CSM met again at the end of May and the Department made a public announcement on June 10th, 1986. The claimant argued that the decision to delay a public announcement after the meeting of the CSM in March 1986 was negligent.

Causation was not seriously contested. Morland J. found that had the warnings about the danger been prominently publicised in the media before the claimant became unwell, her mother would have become of aware of them and would not have given asprin. The defendants accepted that the administration of asprin was a contributing cause of the claimant's Reye's syndrome. Thus, the two substantive issues were whether the decision to postpone the publication of the warning was negligent and whether the defendants owed a duty of care to a member of the public in reaching a decision about such a warning in its role as regulator. Morland J. found for the defendants on both issues. First, on the question of breach of duty, although there was a real risk of grave or fatal injury to two or three children created by the delay in issuing the warning, this had to be balanced against the "undoubted benefit of a coherent co-ordinated comprehensive campaign including the withdrawal of paediatric asprin with the full weight of the Department of Health, the CSM and the industry behind it thus giving a clear definitive unambiguous message to both professionals and the general public."[63] Without a postponement of the warning there was a risk that the positive co-operation of the industry, and the benefits to the campaign that that created, might be lost. In the circumstances, his Lordship concluded that the postponement was reasonably justifiable, and therefore the defendants had not been negligent.

8–020

With regard to the duty of care, Morland J. held that it could not be said that the Secretary of State or the CSM could never owe a duty of care to an individual member of the public from a failure to exercise or an improper exercise of statutory powers and duties. For example, decisions that were irrational or reached in bad faith could give rise to a duty.[64] Moreover, there was "no blanket immunity from a common law suit if the special circumstances demand a remedy."[65] But where the CSM was making discretionary or policy decisions its conduct was not justiciable in private law, and it would

8–021

---

[63] *ibid.* at [106].
[64] *ibid.* at [95]. His Lordship gave the examples of a decision to delay an announcement for political reasons or a decision to delay a meeting to avoid a clash with a sporting event.
[65] *ibid.*

be contrary to the public interest to allow those decisions to form the basis of a duty of care. Although there could be a narrow line between discretionary/policy decisions and operational decisions, the decision to postpone the CSM's final recommendation until the May meeting and the decision to advise against an interim warning were clearly on the discretionary/policy side of the line. So were a number of other decisions that the CSM had to make in relation to the warnings, such as the upper age limit of children; the mode of issuing the warning (whether by a general media warning or a warning to doctors only); whether to delay the warning until the pharmaceutical industry had agreed fully to co-operate; whether or not paediatric aspirin should be withdrawn; and the details of labelling.[66] It followed that no common law duty was owed by the CSM or the Secretary of State in respect of these decisions because they were matters of discretion or policy and so not justiciable.

(2) Intermediate inspection

8-022   The manufacturer's duty applies to products which are intended to "reach the ultimate consumer in the form in which they left him, with no reasonable possibility of intermediate examination."[67] The article need not reach the ultimate consumer in a sealed package for the duty to apply. It is sufficient if it was subject to the same defect as it had when it left the manufacturer, and the consumer used it as it was intended to be used.[68] The mere opportunity for inspection of the product after it has left the hands of the manufacturer will not excuse the defendant.[69] Lord Atkin's term "reasonable possibility" of intermediate inspection has been interpreted to mean "reasonable probability" of intermediate inspection.[70] Thus, the manufacturer is liable if he has no reason to contemplate that an intermediate examination will occur, whether by a third party or the consumer. The question is whether a reasonable person would anticipate an examination before use which would avoid injury to the user.[71]

8-023   Where the manufacturer has given a warning, for example, to test a product before use, this may be sufficient to discharge his duty.[72] The effect

---

[66] *ibid.* at [91] to [94].
[67] *Donoghue v Stevenson* [1932] A.C. 562, 599, *per* Lord Atkin.
[68] *Grant v Australian Knitting Mills Ltd* [1936] A.C. 85.
[69] *Herschtal v Stewart & Arden Ltd* [1940] 1 K.B. 155; *Griffiths v Arch Engineering Co Ltd* [1968] 3 All E.R. 217.
[70] *Paine v Colne Valley Electricity Supply Co Ltd* [1938] 4 All E.R. 803, 808–9; *Buckner v Ashby and Horner Ltd* [1941] 2 K.B. 321, 333; *Haseldine v Daw & Son Ltd* [1941] 2 K.B. 343, 376.
[71] *Gallagher v N. McDowell Ltd* [1961] N.I. 26, 42. In *Aswan Engineering Establishment Co v Lupdine Ltd* [1987] 1 All E.R. 135, 153–4 Lloyd L.J. said that there is no independent requirement for the claimant to show that there was no reasonable possibility of intermediate examination. Rather, this is merely a factor, usually an important factor, which the court must consider when determining whether the damage was reasonably foreseeable.
[72] See further paras 8–034 to 8–040. In *Holmes v Ashford* [1950] 2 All E.R. 76 the manufacturers of a hair dye were held not liable when a hairdresser disregarded an instruction to test

of the warning will depend upon its terms. For example, the suggestion that the product be tested before use creates a reasonable probability of intermediate inspection, whereas a warning against using the product in certain circumstances (*e.g.* contra-indications for use of a drug) limits what can be regarded as ordinary use. Ignoring the warning might constitute a misuse of the product. It is clear that the warning need not necessarily be addressed to the ultimate consumer. A warning to an intermediary, such as a prescribing doctor or pharmacist, may be sufficient.[73]

The question of intermediate examination is closely related to the concepts of causation and contributory negligence. It has been held that there is no liability if the claimant knew of the danger and ignored it,[74] nor if a third party knew of the danger, and, being under a duty to remove the product from circulation, failed to do so.[75] These cases can be explained in terms of causation rather than intermediate examination. The defendant's negligence was not the cause of the damage because the intervening conduct of the claimant or the third party broke the chain of causation.[76]   **8–024**

It is arguable, however, that a defendant who has created a dangerous situation should not be excused merely because someone else, whether an intermediary or the claimant, has failed to remove the danger. If both have been at fault then both should be held responsible. In the case of a negligent intermediary this could be achieved by apportioning liability between the manufacturer and the intermediary under the Civil Liability (Contribution) Act 1978. If it is the claimant who has failed to use a reasonable opportunity to examine the goods, then it is a case of contributory negligence, for which damages can be apportioned.[77] Knowledge of the danger will be irrelevant, however, if there were no practical steps that the claimant could take to avoid it.[78] In *Rimmer v Liverpool City Council* the Court of Appeal said that an opportunity for inspection by the claimant will not exonerate the defendant unless the claimant "was free to remove or avoid the danger in the sense that it was reasonable to expect him to do so, and unreasonable for him to run the risk of being injured by the danger."[79] The circumstances in which a   **8–025**

(n.72 contd.) the product before using it on a customer; *Kubach v Hollands* [1937] 3 All E.R. 907 the manufacturer of a chemical was held not liable to a schoolgirl injured in an explosion, having warned the retailer to examine and test the chemical before use. The retailer did not test the chemical or warn the teacher who purchased it that it should be tested.

[73] See paras 8–035 to 8–038, below.

[74] *Farr v Butters Bros & Co* [1932] 2 K.B. 606.

[75] *Taylor v Rover Co Ltd* [1966] 1 W.L.R. 1491.

[76] *Grant v Australian Knitting Mills Ltd* [1936] A.C. 85, 105.

[77] See, *e.g.*, *McCain Foods Ltd v Grand Falls Industries Ltd* (1991) 80 D.L.R. (4th) 252 (N.B.C.A.).

[78] *Denny v Supplies and Transport Co Ltd* [1950] 2 K.B. 374.

[79] [1985] Q.B. 1, 14. In *Targett v Torfaen Borough Council* [1992] 3 All E.R. 27, 37 Sir Donald Nicholls V.-C. said that: "Knowledge of the existence of a danger does not always enable a person to avoid the danger. In simple cases it does. In other cases, especially where buildings are concerned, it would be absurdly unrealistic to suggest that a person can always take steps to avoid a danger once he knows of its existence, and that if he does not do so he is the author of his own misfortune."

patient could be said to have a realistic opportunity for intermediate inspection of a medicinal product must be rare indeed.

8–026   If the consumer misuses the product in an unforeseeable fashion the defendant will not be liable. This is not because of contributory negligence or causation, but because the manufacturer is responsible only for dangers arising from a product's contemplated use. If misused, the product cannot be said to be "defective", so there is no breach of duty.[80] On the other hand, where the misuse is foreseeable there will at least be an obligation to give a warning not to use the product in this manner, and in some instances there may be a duty not to supply a product which it is known will be misused.[81]

(3) What is "defective"?

8–027   Defects may arise in the manufacture or design of the product, or in its presentation with inadequate warnings or instructions for use. The standard of care required is the usual standard in all actions for negligence: reasonable care in all the circumstances of the case.

(a) Manufacturing defects

8–028   Examples of manufacturing defects include construction faults, contamination of the product, errors in mixing compounds, and faulty packaging which cause the product to deteriorate. Manufacturers are almost invariably held liable for this type of error,[82] although they may escape responsibility where the defect could have been identified by intermediate inspection. Since the product fails to conform to the manufacturer's own design specification it is easier for the claimant to prove negligence. In *Best v Wellcome Foundation Ltd*[83] the defendants were held liable for brain damage to the claimant caused by the administration of a defective batch of pertussis vaccine. The batch was excessively high in both potency and toxicity, and had failed the "mouse weight gain test" by a considerable margin, but was nonetheless released for use without further testing. Given that the manufacturers were aware of the possibility of serious reaction in small children to the vaccine by way of brain damage, however rare:

> "they owed a duty to exercise a high degree of care in regard to the testing, before issue of such a vaccine where they knew, or must have known, that it would be injected into children on a general or universal basis, at a very young age, and with the recommendation of the medical profession and of national health authorities."[84]

---

[80] *Aswan Engineering Establishment Co v Lupdine Ltd* [1987] 1 All E.R. 135, 154.
[81] See, *e.g.*, *Good-Wear Treaders Ltd v D. & B. Holdings Ltd* (1979) 98 D.L.R. (3d) 59.
[82] See para. 8–057.
[83] [1994] 5 Med. L.R. 81; [1993] 3 I.R. 421; (1992) 17 B.M.L.R 11 (Supreme Court of Ireland).
[84] *ibid.* at 98, *per* Finlay C.J.

The defect must have arisen while under the defendant's control; intermeddling by a third party at a later stage will exculpate the manufacturer, unless the intermeddling ought reasonably to have been foreseen and guarded against.[85] For example, the manufacturer is not liable if the product has been stored improperly by a retailer causing it to deteriorate, or (in the context of an allegation of a failure to warn) if consumer information leaflets have been removed from the package after it left the manufacturer's control.

(b) Design defects

Where the product has a design defect it conforms to the manufacturer's   8–029
specification but causes injury from ordinary use in a manner that was not anticipated at the time of design or manufacture. The product is intrinsically unsafe. Manufacturers undoubtedly have a duty to exercise reasonable care in the design of a new product,[86] which includes an obligation to be careful in conducting the research which goes into the design.[87] The courts are generally reluctant, however, to impose liability for negligent design. One of the difficulties is that the defect may not have been apparent before the product was marketed. For liability in negligence the defect must have been foreseeable at the time of design and manufacture: if the risk was unforeseeable in the light of the scientific and technical knowledge at the time there is no negligence.[88] Whilst a manufacturer is under a duty to keep abreast of medical and scientific discoveries,[89] the courts are wary of making judgments with the benefit of hindsight.[90]

---

[85] See also the Consumer Protection Act 1987, s.4(1)(*d*) which provides a defence where the defect arose after the supply by the defendant.

[86] *Hindustan Steam Shipping Co Ltd v Siemens Bros & Co Ltd* [1955] 1 Lloyd's Rep. 167.

[87] *Vacwell Engineering Co Ltd v B.D.H. Chemicals Ltd* [1971] 1 Q.B. 88, 99, *per* Rees J.: ". . . it was the duty of BDH to have established and maintained a system under which adequate investigation and research into the scientific literature took place in order to discover, *inter alia*, what hazards were known before a new, or little known, chemical was marketed"; see also at 109.

[88] For an example of this in the context of a medical product liability action see *Mann v Wellcome Foundation Ltd* (1989, QBD; unreported), where it was held that the risk of deafness from the application of neomycin spray to burns was unforeseeable in the light of the medical and scientific knowledge. Unforeseeable reactions may also be held to be too remote a consequence of the breach of duty: see *Sheridan v Boots Co Ltd* (1980, QBD; unreported) in which the claimant contracted Stevens-Johnson syndrome as a side-effect of an anti-inflammatory drug, which was known to cause gastric ulcers. The injury was held to be too remote, because Stevens-Johnson syndrome was not damage of the same type as gastric disturbance. See further para. 5–103.

[89] *Stokes v Guest, Keen & Nettlefold (Bolts & Nuts) Ltd* [1968] 1 W.L.R. 1776, 1783; *Cartwright v G.K.N. Sankey Ltd* [1972] 2 Lloyd's Rep. 242, 259; *Bolam v Friern Hospital Management Committee* [1957] 2 All E.R. 118, 122.

[90] See, *e.g.*, the comments of Mustill J. in *Thompson v Smiths Shiprepairers (North Shields) Ltd* [1984] Q.B. 405, 422 on the question of the time at which employers became negligent in failing to take precautions against hearing loss, given the knowledge within the industry: "One must be careful, when considering documents culled for the purpose of a trial, and studied by reference to a single isolated issue, not to forget that they once formed part of a flood of print on numerous aspects of industrial life, in which many items were bound to be overlooked. However conscientious the employer, he cannot read every textbook and periodical, attend every exhibition and conference, on every technical issue which might arise in

8–030   On the other hand, manufacturers cannot automatically rely on the innovative nature of their product, claiming that they were engaged on a "venture
into the unknown" where the risks were unforeseeable because they were
operating at the frontiers of human knowledge. In *Independent Broadcasting Authority v E.M.I. Electronics Ltd and B.I.C.C. Construction Ltd*[91]
the House of Lords held that the designers of a new type of television mast
were negligent, even though it was the first such mast to be constructed anywhere in the world. Lord Edmund-Davies said that, although judgment with
hindsight has to be avoided, the designers had a duty to identify and think
through the problems presented by their lack of empirical knowledge so that
the dimensions of the venture into the unknown could be adequately
assessed:

> "And it is no answer to say . . . 'it wasn't obvious because it hadn't been
> considered'. The learned trial judge held that it should have been, and
> in my judgment he was right in saying so."[92]

The graver the danger, the greater the need for special care, and in some
instances the risks may be so great or their elimination may be so difficult to
ensure with reasonable certainty that the only reasonable course is to
abandon the project altogether. "The law requires even pioneers to be
prudent."[93]

8–031   The difficulty with medicinal products, and particularly drugs, is that most
if not all are recognised as carrying some degree of risk, from side-effects,
allergic reactions, or other unforeseen consequences. The question of what
is safe is inevitably a relative concept, particularly in this field. It is a question of whether a reasonable person would consider the relative risk acceptable given the objective desired in using the product, and the risks associated
with alternative treatments or non-treatment. The risks that would be
acceptable in producing a new analgesic would be far less than the risks
attached to a new drug for the treatment of, say, cancer or AIDS. Provided
that the risk-benefit ratio is acceptable, and provided the manufacturer has
taken all reasonable care to eliminate risks (*e.g.* by proper scientific research,
including volunteer and clinical trials, and full reference to published literature) it is not negligent to market the drug. Where the reaction is rare, but
severe, it will be unlikely that studies will reveal this before marketing.[94] On
the other hand, where a manufacturer had sold 20 million bottles of corn
solvent to the public, it was said that one aspect of the danger to the public

---

(n.90 contd.) the course of his business; nor can he necessarily be expected to grasp the
importance of every single item which he comes across." *Mann v Wellcome Foundation Ltd*
(1989, QBD; unreported) provides a similar example in the context of product liability; *cf.*
also the "development risks" defence under the Consumer Protection Act 1987, s.4(1)(*e*),
para. 8–102, below.

[91] (1980) 14 Build. L.R. 1.
[92] *ibid.* at 31.
[93] *ibid.* at 28, *per* Lord Edmund-Davies.
[94] See, *e.g.*, Newdick (1985) 101 L.Q.R. 405, 418–9.

arose from the wide variation in tolerance by different individuals of the kerotolytic substance when applied to the skin as distinct from corns. Accordingly:

> "one must have in contemplation pretty well the whole scope of human variation in that vast market. There was a duty on the defendants to give some warning and to secure the bottle in some better way . . ."[95]

The difficulty of proving negligence will be even greater where the claimant has sustained injury while taking part in a programme of research, whether in the form of pre-clinical or clinical trials. Adverse reactions are more likely to be regarded as unforeseeable and so unavoidable with the exercise of reasonable care. A claimant would probably have to establish negligence in the conduct of the research.[96]   8–032

(c) Marketing defects

It is not necessarily enough for a manufacturer simply to produce an article that has a "safe" design and conforms to its design specification. There is an obligation to supply adequate information to the consumer to allow him to use the product safely. At its simplest this involves informing the consumer how the product should be used, and where necessary warning against improper and potentially dangerous misuse. A warning may allow the user to avoid the danger altogether. Moreover, some products have an inherent and irreducible element of risk in their use, and a warning may give the user the opportunity to make an informed decision whether to expose himself to that risk. This is more likely to be the position in the case of drugs.   8–033

(4) Warnings

An adequate warning may be sufficient to discharge the manufacturer's duty of care, as may a warning that in its existing condition a product is unsafe.[97] The explicitness of the warning will vary with the danger likely to be encountered in the ordinary use of the product,[98] although where a   8–034

---

[95] *Devilez v Boots Pure Drug Co Ltd* (1962) 106 S.J. 552, *per* Elwes J.

[96] See para. 3–052. An *ex gratia* payment of compensation may be available to a healthy volunteer or a patient who sustains injury during the course of a drug trial: see para. 3–061, n. 40.

[97] *Kubach v Hollands* [1937] 3 All E.R. 907; *Holmes v Ashford* [1950] 2 All E.R. 76. See the example of Goddard L.J. in *Haseldine v Daw & Son Ltd* [1941] 2 K.B. 343, 380. In *Hurley v Dyke* [1979] R.T.R. 265 the House of Lords apparently accepted that a warning that a second hand car was sold "as seen and with all its faults" might have been sufficient to fulfil the defendant's duty even if he had known of a specific defect but had failed to advise the purchaser of the danger; *cf. Andrews v Hopkinson* [1957] 1 Q.B. 229.

[98] *Lambert v Lastoplex Chemical Co* (1971) 25 D.L.R. (3d) 121 (S.C.C.). There is no duty to warn of an obvious danger which is known to the ultimate consumer: *Deshane v Deere & Co* (1993) 106 D.L.R. (4th) 385 (Ont. C.A.).

method exists of manufacturing the same product without risk of harm then no amount of or degree of specificity of warning will exonerate the manufacturer of an inherently dangerous article.[99]

8–035   It is not necessary that the warning be addressed directly to the consumer where a product is intended to be used under the supervision of experts. A warning given to the expert will normally be sufficient to discharge the manufacturer's duty of care.[1] In the case of prescription products the prescribing doctor is clearly in the position of an intermediary. In *Buchan v Ortho Pharmaceuticals (Canada) Ltd* Robins J.A. commented that:

> ". . . the manufacturer of drugs, like the manufacturer of other products, has a duty to provide consumers with adequate warning of the potentially harmful side-effects that the manufacturer knows or has reason to know may be produced by the drug . . . In the case of prescription drugs, the duty of manufacturers to warn consumers is discharged if the manufacturer provides prescribing physicians, rather than consumers, with adequate warning of the potential danger."[2]

8–036   Prescription drugs are available only on prescription and the prescribing doctor is in a position to take into account the propensities of the drug and the susceptibilities of the patient. He has a duty to inform himself of the benefits and potential dangers of the drug he is prescribing, and he has to exercise an independent judgment as a medical expert based on his knowledge of the patient and the drug.[3] The duty to supply full information to the medical profession about prescription drugs is greater than the doctor's duty to give information to a patient, since the manufacturer's disclosure does not intrude upon the practice of medicine or the doctor-patient relationship, and doctors need the information so that they can properly assess the situation.[4]

---

[99] *Nicholson v John Deere Ltd* (1986) 34 D.L.R. (4th) 542, 549 (Ont. H.C.); see also *Good-Wear Treaders Ltd v D. & B. Holdings Ltd* (1979) 98 D.L.R. (3d) 59, where it was held that a warning may be inadequate where the manufacturer knows that the product will be used in a dangerous manner.

[1] *Holmes v Ashford* [1950] 2 All E.R. 76; *Kubach v Hollands* [1937] 3 All E.R. 907.

[2] (1986) 25 D.L.R. (4th) 658, 669 (Ont. C.A.). See also *H. v Royal Alexandra Hospital for Children* [1990] 1 Med. L.R. 297 (N.S.W.S.C.) on warnings about the risks of infection with HIV from blood products.

[3] Under the Medicines Act 1968, s.96 products cannot be promoted to doctors unless the doctor has been supplied with a data sheet about the product in prescribed form: see Medicines (Data Sheet) Regulations 1972 (S.I. 1972 No. 2076) (as amended by S.I. 1979 No. 1760; S.I. 1981 No. 1633; S.I. 1989 No. 1183; S.I. 1994 No. 3142; and S.I. 1996 No. 2420) reg. 2(1)(b) and Sch. 2 para. 5. The data sheet must inform the doctor of the contra-indications, any warnings that should be given and the necessary precautions for safe administration. The information that has to be given to patients in product leaflets is governed by regulations made under the Medicines Act 1968: Medicines (Leaflets) Regulations 1977 (S.I. 1977 No. 1055) (as amended by S.I. 1992 No. 3274; S.I. 1994 No. 104; and S.I. 1994 No. 3144). See also the Medicines (Labelling) Regulations 1976 (S.I. 1976 No. 1726), as frequently amended (see, *inter alia*, S.I. 1992 No. 3273; S.I. 1994 No. 104; S.I. 1994 No. 3144; S.I. 1996 No. 2194; and especially the Medicines (Codification Amendments Etc.) Regulations 2002 S.I. 2002 No. 236). Despite all the regulation it would seem that many doctors are inadequately informed about the drugs they prescribe: see Teff (1984) 47 M.L.R. 303, 314–315.

[4] *Davidson v Connaught Laboratories* (1980) 14 C.C.L.T. 251, 276 (Ont. H.C.)—manufacturer

This principle is known as the "learned intermediary rule."[5] Generally, it applies where a product is highly technical in nature and is intended to be used only under the supervision of experts, or where the nature of the product is such that the consumer will not realistically receive a direct warning from the manufacturer before using the product.[6] Thus, the rule was held to apply to silicone breast implants by the Supreme Court of Canada in *Hollis v Dow Corning Corp.*,[7] since direct warnings to the consumer are not feasible, given the need for intervention by a surgeon. The rule presumes that the intermediary is fully apprised of the risks associated with the use of the product, and therefore the manufacturer can only discharge its duty to the consumer when the intermediary's knowledge approximates to that of the manufacturer: "To allow manufacturers to claim the benefit of the rule where they have not fully warned the physician would undermine the policy rationale for the duty to warn, which is to ensure that the consumer is fully informed of all risks."[8] Accordingly, the onus on the manufacturer to be forthcoming with information to the medical profession was "extremely high", as information about unexplained ruptures of the implants became available to the defendants, even if they did not consider the developments to be conclusive. They had to take into account the seriousness of the risk posed by the potential rupture of the implants.

8–037

The "learned intermediary rule" has been held to be inapplicable to the manufacturers of oral contraceptives in some jurisdictions in the United States of America, where it has been held that, to be effective, a warning must reach the consumer/patient.[9] The rationale for this approach is that in the case of the contraceptive pill there is heightened participation of patients in the decision to use the drug; there may be substantial risks associated with its use; it is feasible for the manufacturer to give warnings direct to the user; there is frequently limited participation by the physician in the decision to take the pill; and there is a real possibility that patients may not be fully informed by their doctors. This view was followed *obiter* by the Ontario

8–038

(n.4 contd.) of a rabies vaccine held negligent in failing to supply information to doctors about the risks associated with the vaccine. The action failed for lack of causation: see para. 8–041. There is, of course, no guarantee that the doctor will pass on the information to the patient, since he may take the view that the patient would be unduly alarmed, or the risk may be so small that a reasonable doctor would not consider it appropriate to mention it: see *Sidaway v Bethlem Royal Hospital Governors* [1985] A.C. 871, paras 6–108 *et seq.*

[5] For discussion and criticism of the learned intermediary rule see Ferguson (1992) 12 O.J.L.S. 59; Peppin (1991) 70 Can. Bar Rev. 473.

[6] *Hollis v Dow Corning Corp* (1995) 129 D.L.R. (4th) 609, 623 (S.C.C.).

[7] *ibid.* at 624.

[8] *ibid.* at 623 *per* La Forest J. For comment on *Hollis* see Black and Klimchuck (1996) 75 Can. Bar Rev. 355.

[9] *MacDonald v Ortho Pharmaceutical Corp* 475 N.E. 2d 65 (1985) (Mass.); *Odgers v Ortho Pharmaceutical Corp* 609 F. Supp. 867 (1985) (D.C. Mich.); *Stephens v G. D. Searle & Co* 602 F. Supp. 379 (1985) (Mich.); *Lukaszewicz v Ortho Pharmaceutical Corp.* 510 F. Supp. 961 (1981) (Wis.), holding that the manufacturer of oral contraceptives has a duty to provide the consumer with written warnings conveying reasonable notice of the nature, gravity, and likelihood of known or knowable side-effects, and advising the consumer to seek fuller explanation from the prescribing physician.

Court of Appeal in *Buchan v Ortho Pharmaceuticals (Canada) Ltd*,[10] where it was said that manufacturers of oral contraceptives should be obliged to warn the ultimate consumer as well as prescribing physicians about the risks associated with the pill.

What is an "adequate" warning?

8–039   An adequate warning should be communicated clearly and understandably in a manner calculated to inform the user of the nature of the risk and the extent of the danger; it should be in terms commensurate with the gravity of the potential hazard, and it should not be neutralised or negated by collateral efforts on the part of the manufacturer.[11] For example, promotional literature which seeks to minimise any suggestion of risk or promote the drug as "completely safe" would tend to negate the effectiveness of a warning.[12] The location and prominence of a warning may be a significant factor.[13] In *Buchan v Ortho Pharmaceuticals (Canada) Ltd* Robins J.A. said that:

> "Whether a particular warning is adequate will depend on what is reasonable in the circumstances. But the fact that a drug is ordinarily safe and effective and the danger may be rare or involve only a small percentage of users does not necessarily relieve the manufacturer of the duty to warn. While a low probability of injury or a small class of endangered users are factors to be taken into account in determining what is reasonable, these factors must be balanced against such considerations as the nature of the drug, the necessity for taking it, and the magnitude of the increased danger to the individual consumer. Similarly where medical evidence exists which tends to show a serious danger inherent in the use of a drug, the manufacturer is not entitled to ignore or discount that information in its warning solely because it finds it to be unconvincing; the manufacturer is obliged to be forthright and to tell the whole story. The extent of the warning and the steps to be taken to bring the warning home to physicians should be commensurate with the potential danger—the graver the danger, the higher the duty."[14]

---

[10] (1986) 25 D.L.R. (4th) 658, 688–689 (Ont. C.A.).

[11] *Buchan v Ortho Pharmaceuticals (Canada) Ltd* (1986) 25 D.L.R. (4th) 658, 667.

[12] On misleading advertising campaigns by pharmaceutical companies see *The Times*, March 25, 1985, p. 8, which also suggested that regulation of advertising by the DHSS was ineffective; see also Teff (1984) 47 M.L.R. 303, 314. For the provisions regulating the contents of drug advertisements to doctors see the Medicines (Advertising) Regulations 1994, S.I. 1994 No. 1932 (as amended by S.I. 1994 No. 3144; S.I. 1996 No. 1552; S.I. 1999 No. 267; and S.I. 2002 No. 236).

[13] *Lambert v Lastoplex Chemical Co* (1971) 25 D.L.R. (3d) 121 (S.C.C.).

[14] (1986) 25 D.L.R. (4th) 658, 678–9 (Ont. C.A.). See also *Rothwell v Raes* (1988) 54 D.L.R. (4th) 193, 341–342 (Ont. H.C.) on inadequate warnings by the manufacturers of pertussis vaccine to the medical profession. The action failed on the ground that the vaccine did not cause the claimant's injuries (affirmed (1990) 76 D.L.R. (4th) 280).

The defendant manufacturers in that case were held liable in negligence   8–040
on the basis of a failure to give sufficient information to the medical profession about the risks of oral contraceptives. The fact that the manufacturers
were aware that warnings had been circulated to the profession by the
Canadian Food and Drugs Directorate on the instructions of the relevant
Minister did not relieve them of their legal duty to warn the profession.[15]
Thus, the duty to warn doctors cannot be delegated. The manufacturer
cannot justify a failure to warn on the ground that doctors were in a position to learn about the risks inherent in the product from other sources. In
Davidson v Connaught Laboratories Linden J. observed that:

> "A drug company cannot rely upon doctors to read all the scientific lit-
> erature outlining the specific dangers involved in the many drugs they
> have to administer each day . . . They have little time for deep research
> into the medical literature. They rely on the drug companies to supply
> them with the necessary data."[16]

In *Buchan* a significant factor in the conclusion that the defendants had negligently failed to give adequate warning to consumers was the fact that the
defendants' associated companies in other countries (including the United
Kingdom) had given a much more comprehensive warning. Where there
have been developments in the state of the manufacturer's knowledge there
is an obligation to keep the medical community advised of those developments. Thus, in *Hollis v Dow Corning Corp.*[17] the manufacturers of breast
implants became aware of the fact that an implant could rupture for a variety
of reasons, including normal use, and that the life expectancy of implants
was unpredictable, before the claimant received her implant in October
1983, but did not update their warning to surgeons until 1985. The statistical risk of rupture was less than 0.1 per cent, though the consequences for
the patient were serious. The manufacturers were held liable for failing to
pass on this new information to doctors. It was not an obligation to issue a
new warning each time a rupture occurred, but it was not expecting too

---

[15] "The report of the advisory committee cannot be considered determinative of the nature and
extent of the legal duty imposed on drug manufacturers to warn the medical profession. The
duty to warn of a risk so grave as stroke . . . arose long before the report . . . The report did
not release Ortho from its common law duty, limit its ability to discharge the duty, or fix a
standard of disclosure to the medical profession": (1986) 25 D.L.R. (4th) 658, 680–1, *per*
Robins J.A.; *Thompson v Johnson and Johnson Pty Ltd* [1992] 3 Med. L.R. 148; [1991] 2
V.R. 449 (S.C. of Victoria, App. Div.)—manufacturers of tampons held not liable for failing
to warn users of the risk of toxic shock syndrome at the time when the claimant's injury
occurred, given the significant differences between the situation in North America and that
in Australia, the different attitudes of the health authorities, and the fact that at the time
there had been no case of toxic shock syndrome associated with the use of tampons in
Australia despite extensive use over a considerable period of time.
[16] (1980) 14 C.C.L.T. 251, 276 (Ont. H.C.). In the UK doctors' other sources of drug information, in addition to the manufacturers, include the *British National Formulary*, produced
jointly by the BMA and the British Pharmaceutical Society, *MIMS* (the *Monthly Index of
Medical Specialities*), and *Prescribers' Journal*.
[17] (1993) 103 D.L.R. (4th) 520 (B.C.C.A.); affirmed (1995) 129 D.L.R. (4th) 609 (S.C.C.).

much to require the manufacturers to issue updated information to the medical community on a yearly basis, or sooner if the circumstances warranted it.[18]

(5) Failure to warn and causation

8–041   Where the alleged negligence consists of a failure to warn either the consumer or an intermediary, such as a prescribing doctor, about the side-effects or contra-indications of a drug, for example, the claimant still has to prove that had the warning been given he would not have taken the drug. In other words he must demonstrate that the negligent omission caused or contributed to the damage. In the case of prescription drugs or medical devices the causation issue is complicated by the effect of the "learned intermediary rule." Strictly, the claimant would have to prove not only that she would have declined the treatment or procedure had she been informed about the risks, but also that the intermediary, who will usually be the doctor, would have acted differently had a suitable warning been given. Thus, in *Davidson v Connaught Laboratories*[19] the manufacturer of a rabies vaccine was found to have given an inadequate warning to doctors in its literature accompanying the vaccine. The manufacturer did not mention myelitis or neuritis; nor the possibility of paralysis or death; nor were there any figures relating to the risks, nor any source material. The defendants had known of these dangers for a long time. The manufacturer was held not liable, however, because:

(i)   the information would not have changed the doctors' decision to recommend use of the vaccine, because of the grave danger associated with rabies (it is normally fatal); and,

(ii)   the claimant had been given full information about the risks, in any event, by another doctor.[20]

Accordingly, there are two causation issues that arise in these cases: (1) what would the doctor have done had the manufacturer complied with its duty to provide appropriate information; and (2) what would the claimant have

---

[18] *ibid.* at 544, *per* Prowse J.A.: "A manufacturer should not be too coy about revealing the risks associated with its product and then expect to avoid liability by placing the full burden of those risks on either the medical community or the patient." In the Supreme Court of Canada, La Forest J. indicated that in the case of medical products "the standard of care to be met by manufacturers in ensuring that consumers are properly warned is necessarily high. Medical products are often designed for bodily ingestion or implantation, and the risks created by their improper use are obviously substantial": (1995) 129 D.L.R. (4th) 609, 619.

[19] (1980) 14 C.C.L.T. 251 (Ont. H.C.).

[20] See also *H. v Royal Alexandra Hospital for Children* [1990] 1 Med. L.R. 297 (N.S.W.S.C.), where it was held that the failure of the manufacturers of blood products in 1983 to warn doctors of the risk that the products could transmit HIV was negligent, but that such a warning would have had no effect on the decision of the doctors to use the products for the treatment of a haemophiliac with a joint bleed, given the perception of the relative risks of treatment and non-treatment.

done had the doctor passed on the relevant information about the associated risks?

In principle, since determining causation is essentially a factual enquiry,[21] the test in both cases should be subjective. In other words, it depends on whether *this* patient would have taken the drug in question or accepted the use of the relevant medical device;[22] and where causation depends upon what the prescribing doctor would have done had he been given an adequate warning by the manufacturer, the test should also be subjective to *that* doctor and should not be determined by what a reasonable doctor would have done in the circumstances. Thus, in *The Creutzfeldt-Jakob Disease Litigation, Straddlers Group A. and C. v Secretary of State for Health*,[23] the causation question depended on whether clinicians treating patients with human growth hormone would have stopped the treatment had they been informed about the small risk of transmitting to the patient the agent that causes CJD. Morland J. held that this issue was to be determined simply on the balance of probabilities as to how the treating clinicians would have responded to the information, though the evidence was that the clinicians probably would have halted the treatment programme. On the other hand, it is at least arguable that where the causation question depends upon the hypothetical conduct of an independent third party, the analysis should proceed on the basis of the loss of a chance of avoiding the harm.[24] As between the defendant manufacturer and the injured patient, the treating doctor would seem to be "an independent third party." This point has not yet been tested in the English courts.

8–042

By contrast, the Canadian courts take a different approach to these issues. The normal rule in Canada for the non-disclosure of risks associated with medical treatment is that the test is objective, *i.e.* the action fails if a reasonable patient in the claimant's position would have proceeded had she been informed about the risks.[25] In *Hollis v Dow Corning Corp.*[26] a majority of the Supreme Court of Canada held that in the context of a product liability claim the test of causation should be subjective not objective. Although a different, subjective, test of causation in cases of failure to warn where the action was against a manufacturer (as opposed to the objective reasonable patient test when the action was against a doctor or hospital) might seem anomalous, the justification, said La Forest J., was to be found in the different circumstances in which the relevant duties arise. The duty of the doctor was to give the best medical advice to a particular patient in a specific context. The manufacturer, on the other hand, could be expected to act in a more self-interested manner: "In the case of a manufacturer, therefore, there

8–043

---

[21] Notwithstanding that this enquiry is sometimes infused with policy questions: see paras 5–014, 5–023, 5–027 *et seq*.

[22] See paras 6–146 *et seq*. in the context of actions against health professionals in respect of non-disclosure of the risks of treatment.

[23] (1998) 54 B.M.L.R. 104.

[24] See *Allied Maples Group Ltd v Simmons & Simmons* [1995] 4 All E.R. 907, para. 5–060.

[25] *Reibl v Hughes* (1980) 114 D.L.R. (3d) 1 (S.C.C.). See para. 6–148.

[26] (1995) 129 D.L.R. (4th) 609 (S.C.C.).

is a greater likelihood that the value of a product will be overemphasised and the risk underemphasised. It is, therefore, highly desirable from a policy perspective to hold the manufacturer to a strict standard of warning consumers of the dangerous side-effects to these products."[27]

8–044   Moreover, for similar policy reasons the Canadian courts have taken a highly relaxed view of the first causation issue in a case involving a learned intermediary, namely what would the intermediary have done had the manufacturer complied with its duty to provide a warning to the intermediary? In *Buchan v Ortho Pharmaceuticals (Canada) Ltd*[28] the Ontario Court of Appeal held that it ought not to be incumbent on a claimant to prove as part of her case what her doctor might or might not have done had he been adequately warned. One could assume that a doctor would not ignore a proper warning or fail to disclose a material risk or otherwise act negligently. Moreover, even if the evidence indicated that the doctor was negligent, the manufacturer would not be shielded from liability if the negligence was a foreseeable consequence of the manufacturer's breach of duty to warn. This was said to be a rebuttable presumption. In *Hollis v Dow Corning Corp.*,[29] however, the Supreme Court of Canada went a step further and held that, in effect, what the intermediary would have done in a hypothetical situation was irrelevant to the causation issue. The claimant was in a position of great informational inequality with respect to both the manufacturer and the doctor, and the defendant's argument would require her to prove a hypothetical situation relating to her doctor's conduct, a hypothetical situation that had been brought about by the defendant's own failure to perform its duty. Justice dictated that she should not be penalised for the fact that had the manufacturer actually met its duty to warn, the doctor might still have been at fault and failed to pass on the information.[30] La Forest J., giving the majority judgment, explained the basis for this conclusion:

> "Simply put, I do not think a manufacturer should be able to escape liability for failing to give a warning it was under a duty to give, by simply presenting evidence tending to establish that even if the doctor had been given the warning, he or she would not have passed it on to the patient, let alone putting an onus on the claimant to do so. Adopting such a rule would, in some cases, run the risk of leaving the claimant with no compensation for her injuries ... As I see it, the claimant's claim against the manufacturer should be dealt with in accordance with the following rationale. The ultimate duty of the manufacturer is to warn the claimant adequately. For practical reasons, the law permits it to acquit itself of that duty by warning an informed intermediary. Having failed to warn the intermediary, the manufacturer has failed in its duty to warn the claimant who ultimately suffered injury by using the

---

[27] *ibid.* at [46].
[28] (1986) 25 D.L.R. (4th) 658, 682 and 686–688.
[29] (1995) 129 D.L.R. (4th) 609 (S.C.C.).
[30] *ibid.* at [55] and [57] *per* La Forest J.

product. The fact that the manufacturer would have been absolved had it followed the route of informing the claimant through the learned intermediary should not absolve it of its duty to the claimant because of the possibility, even the probability, that the learned intermediary would not have advised her had the manufacturer issued it. The learned intermediary rule provides a means by which the manufacturer can discharge its duty to give adequate information of the risks to the claimant by informing the intermediary, but if it fails to do so it cannot raise as a defence that the intermediary could have ignored this information."[31]

This reverses the effect of the decision in *Davidson v Connaught Laboratories* to the extent that causation rested on what the doctor would have done, and appears to convert what the Ontario Court of Appeal in *Buchan v Ortho Pharmaceuticals (Canada) Ltd* regarded as a rebuttable presumption into an irrebuttable presumption. It would seem that the second basis for the decision in *Davidson*, namely that the claimant had already received full information from another source, remains intact, since if the claimant was aware of the risk (from whatever source) but nonetheless chose to proceed with the treatment this must be clear evidence of what she subjectively would have done had the manufacturer complied with its duty to warn.[32] 8–045

It is unlikely that an English court would take so generous a view of the causation issue in relation to the actions of a learned intermediary, and that the test will continue to be subjective (*i.e.* what would this intermediary have done?). Whether that should be resolved on an "all or nothing" basis, on the balance of probabilities, or on the basis of a lost chance, with the question turning on whether there was substantial chance (which might be less than 50 per cent) of the intermediary passing on the warning, remains to be seen. 8–046

Another alternative would be to ask whether the negligence made a material contribution to the damage. This involves a departure from the "but for" test, without resorting to the lost chance analysis. In *Walker Estate v York-Finch General Hospital*[33] the Canadian Red Cross Society was held to have been negligent in the manner in which it screened potential blood donors for HIV, in that it had asked potential donors about their general health instead of asking about symptom specific conditions and risks. Whether a properly conducted screening method would have elicited the relevant information and enabled the defendants to screen out high risk donors depended upon how the potential donors would have reacted to more specific questioning. The Supreme Court of Canada held that the claimant could not rely on the presumptive causation test established in *Hollis* because *Walker* did not involve the "learned intermediary" rule.[34] This left the question of what 8–047

---

[31] *ibid.* at [60] and [61].
[32] Note also that establishing what subjectively the claimant would have done in an hypothetical situation often involves testing the credibility of her subjective assertions against objective criteria. See para. 6–155.
[33] (2001) 198 D.L.R. (4th) 193 (S.C.C.).
[34] *ibid.* at [86].

approach should be taken to establishing causation where the causal link depended on the actions of a third party. It was held that the correct approach was not to apply the "but for" test, but to ask whether the negligence constituted a material contribution to the damage:

> "In cases of negligent donor screening it may be difficult or impossible to prove hypothetically what the donor would have done had he or she been properly screened by the C.R.C.S. The added element of donor conduct in these cases means that the but-for test could operate unfairly, highlighting the possibility of leaving legitimate plaintiffs uncompensated. Thus, the question in cases of negligent donor screening should not be whether the C.R.C.S.'s conduct was a necessary condition for the plaintiff's injuries using the 'but-for' test, but whether that conduct was a sufficient condition. The proper test for causation in cases of negligent donor screening is whether the defendant's negligence 'materially contributed' to the occurrence of the injury."[35]

8–048   It would certainly be open to an English court to adopt this approach, applying *Bonnington Castings Ltd v Wardlaw*[36] and *Fairchild v Glenhaven Funeral Services Ltd*,[37] though their Lordships in *Fairchild* were careful to limit the application of this more relaxed causation test. Although there is nothing in principle to prevent it, it is not clear that the *Fairchild* principle would be applied to circumstances where the causal uncertainty rests on the hypothetical conduct of individuals, as opposed to scientific uncertainty about the causal mechanism of a disease. The decision of the Court of Appeal in *Allied Maples Group Ltd v Simmons & Simmons*[38] would suggest that where the causal outcome depends upon the hypothetical actions of an independent third party the correct approach is to assess the chances that, in the absence of negligence by the defendant, the third party would have acted in way which would have avoided the claimant's damage, with damages being assessed on the basis of the value of the lost chance.

(6) Continuing duty

8–049   Negligence depends upon foreseeability of injury. If at the time that a product was put onto the market the defect was unknown the manufacturer was not negligent. If a danger becomes apparent (or ought to have been discovered) it will be negligent to continue to produce the same unmodified product, or at least to do so without attaching a warning.[39]

---

[35] *ibid.* at [88].
[36] [1956] A.C. 613.
[37] [2002] UKHL 22; [2003] 1 A.C. 32. See the discussion at paras 5–027 *et seq.*
[38] [1995] 4 All E.R. 907.
[39] *Wright v Dunlop Rubber Co Ltd* (1972) 13 K.I.R. 255, 272.

In addition, the manufacturer is under a continuing duty in respect of products already in circulation which are now known to be defective. The manufacturer must take reasonable steps either to warn users of the danger or recall the defective products.[40] Moreover, where a product has not been recalled and there is strong evidence to suggest that problems in the manufacture of the product have been concealed to avoid the commercial repercussions that a recall would entail, the court will more readily infer that a defect was due to negligence in the manufacturing process.[41]

8–050

In *Buchan v Ortho Pharmaceuticals (Canada) Ltd*[42] the Ontario Court of Appeal applied the principle of a continuing duty to the manufacturer of oral contraceptives with respect to warnings of side-effects to be given to doctors who prescribed the drug. Robins J.A. expressed the proposition in these terms:

8–051

"A manufacturer of prescription drugs occupies the position of an expert in the field; this requires that it be under a continuing duty to keep abreast of scientific developments pertaining to its product through research, adverse reaction reports, scientific literature and other available methods. When additional dangerous or potentially dangerous side-effects from the drug's use are discovered, the manufacturer must make all reasonable efforts to communicate the information to prescribing physicians. Unless doctors have current, accurate and complete information about a drug's risks, their ability to exercise the fully informed medical judgment necessary for the proper performance of their vital role in prescribing drugs for patients may be reduced or impaired."[43]

A new drug which produces a high incidence of adverse reactions (c. 1 in 300) should be spotted in pre-clinical or clinical trials. Less common reactions may only become apparent when the drug is in widespread use. It is almost inevitable, then, that some drug injuries will only be identified after the product has been marketed. The exercise of reasonable care clearly requires that manufacturers have an effective system for monitoring adverse

8–052

---

[40] *Rivtow Marine Ltd v Washington Iron Works* (1973) 40 D.L.R. (3d) 530, 536 (S.C.C.); *Buchan v Ortho Pharmaceuticals (Canada) Ltd* (1986) 25 D.L.R. (4th) 658, 667 (Ont. C.A.); *Hollis v Dow Corning Corp* (1995) 129 D.L.R. (4th) 609, 618 (S.C.C.); *Hobbs (Farms) Ltd v Baxenden Chemical Co Ltd* [1992] 1 Lloyd's Rep. 54, 65, *per* Sir Michael Ogden Q.C.: ". . . a manufacturer's duty of care does not end when the goods are sold. A manufacturer who realises that omitting to warn past customers about something which might result in injury to them must take reasonable steps to attempt to warn them, however lacking in negligence he may have been at the time the goods were sold." The continuing duty to warn only applies to dangerous defects. Thus, a manufacturer's knowledge that an engine was likely to fail much sooner than indicated in the manual did not give rise to a duty to warn users to have the engine checked more frequently so as to avoid the risk of damage to the engine itself, which is a form of economic loss: *Hamble Fisheries Ltd v Gardner & Sons Ltd, The "Rebecca Elaine"* [1999] 2 Lloyd's Rep. 1, CA.

[41] *Carroll v Fearon* [1998] P.I.Q.R. P416, CA.

[42] (1986) 25 D.L.R. (4th) 658.

[43] *ibid.* at 678.

reactions and for the recall of defective products, both for manufacturing defects (to identify faulty batches, for example) and for design defects, which may involve removing the product from the market altogether.[44] In a suitable case an appropriate warning may be sufficient to satisfy the manufacturer's duty. In this country it is a condition of the grant of a product licence for pharmaceutical products that such a procedure exists,[45] but nonetheless there might be negligence in implementing the recall procedure.[46]

(7) Common practice

8–053   Where a manufacturer has complied with the standards normally adopted within the industry, this will usually be taken as good evidence that he has acted with reasonable care, just as a departure from common practice may be evidence of negligence.[47] Neither, however, is necessarily conclusive of the issue. In the case of pharmaceutical products manufacturers must comply with the statutory requirements of the Medicines Act 1968. Compliance will not be conclusive, but it will undoubtedly constitute strong evidence of the exercise of reasonable care. If an independent body, such as the CSM, has reached the same view as the manufacturer on the safety of a product or the adequacy of warnings this will inevitably influence the court's assessment of whether there has been negligence, assuming that the same information was available to both the CSM and the manufacturer, and assuming, of course, that the CSM has not been negligent.[48] In *Thompson v Johnson and Johnson Pty Ltd*[49] it was said that the attitude, advice and response of the Australian Department of Health and the

---

[44] The "yellow card scheme," in which doctors submit reports on adverse reactions to the CSM, is not particularly effective in identifying adverse reactions: see Teff (1984) 47 M.L.R. 303, 315. The anti-arthritis drug, Opren, was not suspended by the Licensing Authority under the Medicines Act 1968 until after more than 3,500 reports of adverse reactions, including 61 fatalities: Teff, *op. cit.*, at p. 304, n. 5. See further *The Lancet*, November 5, 1988, p. 1059, 1060 on the withdrawal of "Merital" (nomifensine), suggesting that undue reliance on the yellow card scheme may result in insufficient emphasis on other preventive measures. The CSM put pressure on the manufacturers to withdraw the drug following a sharp increase in reports under the scheme in 1985, but there had been suspicions about adverse reactions since 1979. See also *The Lancet*, January 31, 1987, p. 287, reporting the withdrawal of "Dorbanex" (danthron).

[45] Medicines (Standard Provisions for Licences and Certificates) Regulations 1971 (S.I. 1971 No. 972) Sch. 1 para. 6, as amended.

[46] See, *e.g.*, *Nicholson v John Deere Ltd* (1986) 34 D.L.R. (4th) 542. The defendants "had a duty to devise a programme that left nothing to chance," *per* Smith J. at 549. The defendants' efforts to warn were deficient in that they were doomed to failure with respect to the vast majority of users; *McCain Foods Ltd v Grand Falls Industries Ltd* (1991) 80 D.L.R. (4th) 252.

[47] See paras 3–017 to 3–043.

[48] See *Buchan v Ortho Pharmaceuticals (Canada) Ltd* (1986) 25 D.L.R. (4th) 658, 672–3, where the issue was raised, but not decided, whether compliance by the manufacturer with the requirements of the Canadian Food and Drug Directorate as to the warnings to be given directly to the users of oral contraceptives absolved them from liability. The trial judge had held that the statement required by the FDD "amounted to no warning at all."

[49] [1992] 3 Med. L.R. 148, 171–172; [1991] 2 V.R. 449 (S.C. of Victoria, App. Div.).

Public Health Advisory Committee of the National Health and Medical Research Council to a reported case of toxic shock syndrome caused by tampons was a significant factor to take into account when considering whether the manufacturers had been negligent in failing to give warnings of the risk to the public:

"Whether or not the N.H.M.R.C. recommended that a warning be given was not determinative of the question of reasonable care, for to accept that proposition would permit the respondents to abrogate the duty of reasonable care owed by them. It is not the response of such a body which determines whether a person in the position of the respondent is or is not negligent. That is for the courts to decide. However, it is a relevant fact to be taken into account when determining whether reasonable care has been exercised."

In *Budden v B.P. Oil Ltd and Shell Oil Ltd*[50] it was alleged that children **8–054** had sustained injuries attributable to inhaling petrol fumes containing lead, and they brought an action against the oil companies. The levels of lead in petrol complied with statutory regulations, and these levels had been set by the Secretary of State, having received expert advice. The Court of Appeal took the view that in these circumstances the decision about lead levels must be presumed to be in the public interest, and accordingly the manufacturers or suppliers of petrol could not be said to be negligent if the limit to which they adhered was one which they were entitled reasonably to believe to be consistent with the public interest. It could not be said that "a reasonable person, with the knowledge which the oil companies had or should have had, objectively weighing all relevant considerations, had failed in his duty owed to the children in complying with the requirements prescribed by the Secretary of State and approved, impliedly, by Parliament, after the investigation which had been made of the very matters which were relevant for the companies' decisions."[51]

The grant of product licences under the Medicines Act 1968 does not **8–055** depend upon express approval by Parliament, but nonetheless the logic of *Budden v B.P. Oil Ltd and Shell Oil Ltd* could well be applied to pharmaceutical products licensed by the Licensing Authority.[52] On the other hand, in *Best v Wellcome Foundation Ltd*[53] a manufacturer of pertussis vaccine was held to have been negligent in releasing a batch of the vaccine which tests had shown to have a high level of potency, which it was known could

---

[50] [1980] J.P.L. 586.

[51] *ibid*. at 587. The court was worried that if it were to make a finding of negligence there would be a constitutional anomaly, because the court would effectively be declaring a decision of Parliament to be unlawful: "The authority of Parliament must prevail."

[52] *cf*. also Consumer Protection Act 1987, s.4(1)(*a*), para. 8–095, below, providing a defence to strict liability under that Act where the defect was attributable to compliance with any statutory requirement or a European Community obligation. For further discussion see Newdick (1992) 47 Food and Drug L.J. 41.

[53] [1993] 3 I.R. 421; [1994] 5 Med. L.R. 81; (1992) 17 B.M.L.R 11 (Supreme Court of Ireland).

be linked with high levels of toxicity, although the relevant regulations laid down only minimum not maximum levels of potency. The batch had also failed the "mouse weight gain test," a test routinely carried out, but not mandatory under the regulations. Finlay C.J. considered that, in the circumstances, compliance with minimum criteria was inadequate:

> "Merely to comply, in my view, with mandatory or minimum requirements imposed by national health authorities in the area in which the vaccine was manufactured, or merely to rely on one particular point of view in a debated question concerning the risks involved, would not necessarily, in any given case, constitute a sufficient degree of care to discharge the legal duty of a manufacturer of vaccine in these circumstances."[54]

Moreover, where a manufacturer has failed to comply with the provisions of the Medicines Act 1968 concerning testing the safety of a pharmaceutical product this must put the onus on the defendant to justify its conduct, although breach of the Act or regulations made under the Act is not negligence *per se*.[55]

(8) Proof

8–056   The burden of proving negligence rests with the claimant. In *Donoghue v Stevenson*[56] Lord Macmillan said that there was no presumption of negligence nor any justification for applying the maxim *res ipsa loquitur* in such a case. Where, however, a defect has arisen in the course of construction it will be virtually impossible for a claimant to show by affirmative evidence what went wrong. In *Grant v Australian Knitting Mills Ltd*[57] this difficulty was recognised. Lord Wright said that:

> "[The manufacturing] process was intended to be foolproof. If excess sulphites were left in the garment, that could only be because someone was at fault. The appellant is not required to lay his finger on the exact person in all the chain who was responsible or to specify what he did wrong. Negligence is found as a matter of inference from the existence of the defects taken in connection with all the known circumstances."[58]

8–057   The effect of this is that in cases of manufacturing defects the claimant will normally establish negligence by proving the existence of the defect, and

---

[54] [1994] 5 Med. L.R. 81, 98.
[55] Medicines Act 1968, s.133(2).
[56] [1932] A.C. 562.
[57] [1936] A.C. 85.
[58] *ibid.* at 101.

that this was probably not a result of events that occurred after the product left the manufacturer's possession.[59] The possibility of intermediate deterioration or tampering with the product will be taken into account in terms of the degree of likelihood that the defect was present when it left the manufacturer.[60] It is irrelevant whether the inference of negligence is called *res ipsa loquitur* or not, because in some instances it amounts in practice to a form of strict liability. The greater the danger the greater the precautions that will be required to discharge a duty of care.[61] The defendant may rebut the inference by proving how the defect occurred and showing that this was not due to lack of care on his part, but this may be difficult. Ironically, the stronger the evidence that his manufacturing system was "foolproof," the stronger is the inference that the defect arose as a result of carelessness by one of his employees, for whose negligence he will be held vicariously liable.[62]

The claimant will have greater difficulty in proving negligence where the product is defective in design rather than manufacture. It is easier to demonstrate that a product is defective if it does not meet the manufacturer's own standards because something has gone wrong during manufacture. Where, however, a product performs as it was designed and intended there is no obvious standard against which to compare it.[63] The design may have been the result of a conscious compromise between cost and safety, or between efficacy and safety.[64] In the case of a drug, if the risk was a known risk it may be treated as an unavoidable side-effect which was acceptable because of the otherwise beneficial effects of the drug, either for the claimant or other users. Side-effects are simply part of the cost-benefit analysis undertaken when considering whether a drug has a safe design. 8–058

On the other hand, if a particular risk was unforeseeable it is not possible to take reasonable precautions against it by amending the design. This is especially true of products such as drugs, where, despite extensive pre-marketing research, it may not be possible to predict all the potential reactions that may occur in a large population. In addition to the problem of proving causation, this will make it difficult to prove that the manufacturer was negligent because at the time when the product was marketed the risk 8–059

---

[59] *Mason v Williams & Williams Ltd* [1955] 1 W.L.R. 549. In *Carroll v Fearon* [1998] P.I.Q.R. P416, 422 the Court of Appeal commented that: "once it was established that the tyre disintegrated because of an identified fault in the course of its manufacture the judge had to decide whether this fault was the result of negligence at Dunlop's factory. He did not have to identify any individual or group of employees or the acts or omissions which resulted in [the defect]. If the manufacturing process had worked as intended this defect should not have been present."

[60] See, *e.g.*, *Evans v Triplex Safety Glass Co Ltd* [1936] 1 All E.R. 283.

[61] *Wright v Dunlop Rubber Co Ltd* (1972) 13 K.I.R. 255, 273–4.

[62] *Grant v Australian Knitting Mills Ltd* [1936] A.C. 85; *Hill v James Crowe (Cases) Ltd* [1978] 1 All E.R. 812, 816, criticising *Daniels v White & Sons Ltd* [1938] 4 All E.R. 258 where carbolic acid used in washing bottles contaminated lemonade, and the defendants were held not liable on proving the effectiveness of the system.

[63] Unless specifically governed by statute; see, *e.g.*, Consumer Protection Act 1987, s.11.

[64] "Most, if not all, drugs cannot be effective unless they are also powerful enough to be potentially harmful": Teff (1984) 47 M.L.R. 303, 309.

was unknown.[65] Thus, although design defects can be negligent, the courts are more reluctant to hold defendants liable in such cases.[66]

(9) Causation in fact

8–060   In addition to any questions of causation which may arise from intermediate examination, the claimant has to prove that the defective product in fact caused the injury of which he complains, applying the usual principles of causation. This will tend to be more difficult with defective drugs.[67] There may be difficulty in isolating drug-induced harm from the background incidence of such injuries. Merely proving an increased risk of injury does not in itself establish causation. The question is whether one can a infer a causal link. In *Best v Wellcome Foundation Ltd*[68] the Supreme Court of Ireland was prepared to make an assumption that if there was a temporal connection between the child's first convulsion and the administration of the pertussis vaccine manufactured by the defendants then causation was established. It was accepted in this case that there was a possibility that pertussis vaccine could, in rare cases, cause brain damage. The only alternative explanation was that the claimant had suffered from "infantile spasms, cause unknown," which, as O'Flaherty J. pointed out, was a description rather than a diagnosis of the claimant's condition. *McGhee v National Coal Board*[69] was never a complete solution to the problem of separating drug-induced injuries from the background incidence of such harm. There, it was known that excess exposure to brick dust could cause dermatitis; the only question was whether on the particular facts it was the negligent period of exposure that had caused the claimant's dermatitis. Where it is not known whether a drug can cause a particular reaction this approach cannot assist the claimant.[70] Nor does it solve the problem of multiple potential defendants in cases of generic prescribing, where it may be impossible for a claimant to say which manufacturer was responsible for the drug he took, especially if it was taken over a long period of time.[71]

---

[65] *Mann v Wellcome Foundation Ltd* (1989, QBD; unreported). See also Newdick (1985) 101 L.Q.R. 405; and on the thalidomide tragedy see Teff and Munro, *Thalidomide: The Legal Aftermath*, 1976.

[66] Newdick (1987) 103 L.Q.R. 288, 300–4.

[67] See Newdick (1985) 101 L.Q.R. 405, 420; Stapleton (1985) 5 O.J.L.S. 248, 250 discussing the difficulties of proving causation with certain types of disease; and *Kay v Ayrshire and Arran Health Board* [1987] 2 All E.R. 417; *Loveday v Renton* [1990] 1 Med. L.R. 117; *Rothwell v Raes* (1988) 54 D.L.R. (4th) 193; affirmed (1990) 76 D.L.R. (4th) 280 (Ont. C.A.); *cf. Best v Wellcome Foundation Ltd* [1994] 5 Med. L.R. 81; [1993] 3 I.R. 421; (1992) 17 B.M.L.R 11. See generally paras 5–015 *et seq*.

[68] [1994] 5 Med. L.R. 81; [1993] 3 I.R. 421; (1992) 17 B.M.L.R 11.

[69] [1972] 3 All E.R. 1008; see para. 5–022.

[70] As, *e.g.*, in *Loveday v Renton* [1990] 1 Med. L.R. 117, and *Rothwell v Raes* (1988) 54 D.L.R. (4th) 193; affirmed (1990) 76 D.L.R. (4th) 280 (Ont. C.A.). Though *cf.* the more robust approach of the Supreme Court of Ireland to this issue in *Best v Wellcome Foundation Ltd* [1994] 5 Med. L.R. 81; [1993] 3 I.R. 421; (1992) 17 B.M.L.R 11.

[71] For an example of this type of problem see *Mann v Wellcome Foundation Ltd* (1989, QBD; unreported).

This issue was addressed by the California Court of Appeal in *Sindell v*   8–061
Abbott Laboratories,[72] where, due to the very long delay in the teratogenic
effects of the drug DES (diethylstilboestrol) becoming apparent, it was
impossible for the claimant to identify the particular manufacturers of the
drug taken by her mother during pregnancy. The court reversed the burden
of proof, requiring the manufacturers to show that their product was not
used, and in the absence of proof, damages were apportioned between the
various defendants on the basis of their market share of sales of the drug.[73]

It seemed unlikely that this was an approach that would be followed by the   8–062
English courts, though the decision of the House of Lords in *Fairchild v
Glenhaven Funeral Services Ltd*[74] does now open up this possibility. In
Fairchild, according to the scientific evidence, the overwhelming probability
was that the claimants' mesothelioma was caused by occupational exposure
to asbestos fibres, but because mesothelioma is not a cumulative condition,
and can be caused by a few or even one asbestos fibre, it was impossible to
say which of a number of exposures during a working life caused the
claimants' disease. This made it impossible to identify which of a number of
defendants (employers and/or occupiers) was responsible for the mesothelioma. Their Lordships held that in the special circumstances of the case, there
should be a relaxation of the normal rule that a claimant must prove that but
for the defendant's breach of duty he would not have suffered the damage.
Although this involved potential injustice by imposing liability on a defendant who had not been proved to have caused the claimants' damage, that
had to be weighed against the injustice to the claimants of being denied a
claim because they were unable to pin responsibility on a specific defendant,
in circumstances where the defendants were in breach of duty and the very
high probability was that the illness was caused by the breach of at least one
of the defendants. Thus, in the particular circumstances of the case, a defendant's breach of duty which materially increased the risk of the claimant
contracting mesothelioma should be treated *as if* it had materially contributed to the disease.[75] Although their Lordships were careful in seeking to limit
the application of this principle,[76] the analogy with *Sindell v Abbott
Laboratories* is self-evident. If a noxious agent (a "defective" drug) can be
proved to be the cause of a claimant's damage, but it is impossible for the claimant to prove which of a number of defendants manufactured the particular
drug that that he took, it would be no less unjust to the claimant to deny him
a remedy against the manufacturers than it would have been to deny the claimants in *Fairchild* a remedy. The only real difference between the two cases
is that in *Sindell* the defendants were held liable for a proportion of the
damage only, based on their market share, rather than each defendant being

---

[72] 607 P. 2d 924 (1980).
[73] For discussion of this case see Newdick (1985) 101 L.Q.R. 405, 427–429; Teff (1982) 31
I.C.L.Q. 840; and see further *Hymowitz v Eli Lilly & Co* 73 N.Y. 2d 487 (1989) applying
Sindell even where the defendants could prove that the claimant had not used their product.
[74] [2002] UKHL 22; [2003] 1 A.C. 32. See the discussion at paras 5–027 *et seq*.
[75] Applying *Bonnington Castings Ltd v Wardlaw* [1956] A.C. 613.
[76] See the discussion at paras 5–031 to 5–037.

held fully responsible for the claimant's loss. This leaves it up to the defendants to sort out their respective shares of responsibility through contribution proceedings under the Civil Liability (Contribution) Act 1978.[77]

3. CONSUMER PROTECTION ACT 1987

8–063   Although in cases of manufacturing defects the liability of manufacturers in negligence amounts, in effect, to a form of strict liability, the action for negligence remains essentially fault-based and subject to all the vagaries associated with such actions. Some claimants simply fall through the compensation net due to an inability to prove negligence, particularly if the risk of injury was unforeseeable. Iatrogenic and teratogenic drug injuries are often in this category, and it was one of the most prominent and poignant examples of drug injuries, the thalidomide tragedy, which prompted calls for reform. Both the Law Commission and the Pearson Commission recommended the introduction of strict liability for defective products.[78] The Strasbourg Convention on Products Liability in regard to Personal Injury and Death 1977, and two draft European Community Directives, led finally to the European Community Directive on Liability for Defective Products 1985,[79] which required member states to implement its terms within three years. This was done by Part I of the Consumer Protection Act 1987 which came into force on March 1, 1988 and applies to damage caused by products which were put into circulation by the producer after that date.[80] Section 1(1) states that Part I of the Act "shall have effect for the purpose of making such provision as is necessary in order to comply with the product liability Directive and shall be construed accordingly." In the light of section 1(1), it is arguable that where there is a conflict between the Act and the Directive then the Directive should prevail. Indeed, in *A v The National Blood Authority*[81] Burton J. considered that in view of section 1(1) and the decision of the European Court of Justice in *Commission of the European Communities v UK*,[82] the Act had to be interpreted consistently with the Directive and therefore it was simpler to "go straight to the fount" and apply the wording of the Directive.

---

[77] See paras 7–039 *et seq*. Note that Stapleton (2002) 10 Torts L.J. 276, 286 suggests that the claimants in *Fairchild* recovered for their full loss by default, because the litigants (and the court) ignored the possibility of apportionment. A decision that the claimant was only entitled to proportionate damages from each defendant would put the onus on the claimant to sue all the relevant defendants, and it would also place the risk of a defendant being insolvent or uninsured on the claimant, rather than the other defendants.

[78] Law Com. No. 82, Cmnd. 6831, 1977; *Royal Commission on Civil Liability and Compensation for Personal Injury*, Cmnd. 7054 (1978), Vol. I, Ch. 22.

[79] Dir. 1985 No. 374.

[80] Consumer Protection Act 1987, s.50(7); S.I. 1987 No. 1680.

[81] [2001] 3 All E.R. 289, 297.

[82] (C300/95) [1997] All E.R. (EC) 481; [1997] 3 C.M.L.R. 923.

In theory the Act introduces a regime of strict liability for injuries inflicted 8–064
by defective products, but the very concept of a product which is "defective"
involves resorting to much the same approach as when deciding whether
there has been negligence, particularly where it is alleged that a product is
defective in design.[83] This is even more apparent with the development risks
defence, which would seem to exclude liability for unforeseeable design
defects. Moreover, the problem of proving causation remains intractable.
Given that liability in negligence for most construction defects comes close
to strict liability, since negligence tends to be inferred from the defect itself,
it was considered unlikely that the Consumer Protection Act would produce
a marked change from the action in negligence apart from the reversal of the
burden of proof in one area.[84] Indeed, it has been doubted whether the
victims of thalidomide, who provoked the initial cry for reform, would be in
any better position under the Act than in the tort of negligence. Now, the
decision of Burton J. in *A. v The National Blood Authority*[85] to interpret the
Product Liability Directive as creating a regime of truly strict liability will
require a reassessment of the effect of the legislation. Burton J. concluded
that the purpose of the Product Liability Directive had been to remove the
need for a claimant to prove that the defendant had been negligent, and
therefore the defendants' argument that they had exercised all reasonable
care to avoid transmitting the Hepatitis C virus through blood products was
irrelevant. His Lordship made the not unreasonable observation that if both
the Directive and the Act were to were to be interpreted as simply a variant
of negligence there would have been no point to enacting the legislation.
Similarly, in *Abouzaid v Mothercare (UK) Ltd*[86] the Court of Appeal had no
difficulty with the notion that a product could be defective within the
meaning of the Act, even though the defendant was not liable in negligence
at common law because the risk of injury, although identifiable (and therefore not entirely unforeseeable), was very small.

The Act has not replaced the common law, it is an additional remedy.[87] If 8–065
for any reason the Act does not apply (if, for example, the special limitation
periods under the Act have expired, or the product which caused the damage
was put into circulation before the Act came into force on March 1, 1988)
a claim for negligence may still be available.[88]

---

[83] Clark (1985) 48 M.L.R. 325; Stapleton (1986) 6 O.J.L.S. 392.
[84] See Stapleton (1986) 6 O.J.L.S. 392; Newdick (1987) 103 L.Q.R. 288; Newdick [1988]
C.L.J. 455; Stoppa (1992) 12 L.S. 210.
[85] [2001] 3 All E.R. 289; see para. 8–079.
[86] [2000] All E.R. (D) 246; *The Times*, February 20, 2001.
[87] Consumer Protection Act 1987, s.2(6).
[88] Pt II of the Consumer Protection Act 1987 lays down general requirements for the safety of
certain consumer goods and gives the Secretary of State power to make specific safety regulations (see, *e.g.*, the Medical Devices Regulations 1994, S.I. 1994 No. 3017, as amended by S.I.
2000 No. 1315, and the Active Implantable Medical Devices Regulations 1992, S.I. 1992 No.
3146, as amended by S.I. 1995 No. 1671). Breach of these regulations is a criminal offence,
and by s.41 and individual injured by an infringement of a safety regulation (but not the general
safety requirement) can bring an action for breach of statutory duty. Pt II replaces earlier legislation containing similar provisions (Consumer Safety Act 1978, which itself replaced the
Consumer Protection Act 1961). This right of action appears not to have been widely used.

(1) Claimants

8–066   Section 2(1) provides that "where any damage is caused wholly or partly by a defect in a product, every person to whom subsection 2 below applies shall be liable for the damage." This section confers a right of action on *any* person who suffers damage as a result of a defective product.[89] There is no need to establish that the claimant was foreseeable as likely to be affected by the defect, nor that the defendant was negligent. Proof that the product was "defective" and that the defect caused the damage puts the onus on the defendant to establish one of the specific defences.

(2) Defendants

8–067   Section 2 imposes liability on four categories of defendant: (i) the producer of the product; (ii) anyone who holds himself out as the producer; (iii) an importer; and (iv) in certain circumstances, the supplier.[90] This creates the possibility of suing multiple defendants under the Act for a single injury.

8–068   (i) A "producer" is the manufacturer of the product, or the person who won or abstracted a substance which has not been manufactured, or the processor where the "essential characteristics" of a product are attributable to an industrial or other process.[91] "Producer" also includes the manufacturer of a component part.[92] The component manufacturer will be liable together with the manufacturer of the finished product if the damage caused by the finished product is attributable to a defect in the component. On the other hand, it would seem that the component manufacturer is not liable for damage caused by the finished product if the component was not defective. This is the position where the defect in the finished product was wholly attributable to the design of that product, because section 4(1)(*f*) provides a specific defence for the component manufacturer. The Act does not deal with the position of the component manufacturer where the defect in the finished product is a construction defect or the result of a defective component supplied by another manufacturer, but under the Directive a person is liable only for products which he has supplied, and the component manufacturer does not supply the finished product.

8–069   The definition of producer is wide enough to encompass, not only a large pharmaceutical company, but also the individual pharmacist or doctor who mixes small amounts of product to produce a compound or mixture, or the doctor who modifies an appliance, or uses an additive in an intravenous solution.

8–070   (ii) A person holds himself out as the producer of the product "by putting his name on the product or using a trade mark or other distinguishing mark

---

[89] Including ante-natal injuries: Consumer Protection Act 1987, s.6(3).
[90] *ibid.*, ss.2(2), 2(3).
[91] *ibid.*, s.1(2). "Essential characteristics" are not defined by the legislation.
[92] This is by virtue of the definition of "product" in s.1(2).

in relation to the product."[93] Whereas a retail supplier will not normally be liable, retailers who adopt the practice of putting their own brand name on goods produced by others will be liable for defects in those goods. This is now a common practice with large retail chain stores in the United Kingdom. Supermarkets and retail chemists who supply non-prescription medicines under their own brand name will be treated as the producer. However, it is not thought that simply attaching a name and address to a product, which pharmacists and dispensing doctors are required to do by law, constitutes holding oneself out as the producer.

(iii) The importer of a product is liable if he imported it from a place   8–071
outside the European Community into a member State in the course of any business of his, to supply it to another.[94] The importer from another member State into the United Kingdom is not liable under this subsection. So the importer of a defective product from Japan is liable for damage caused by the defect, but not the importer of a product from France. If the Japanese product had first been imported to France and then imported to the United Kingdom, the French importer would be liable, but not the U.K. importer.

(iv) The supplier of goods, whether a retailer or intermediate distributor,   8–072
is not normally liable under the Act. A supplier will be liable, however, if he fails, within a reasonable period of receiving a request from the person who suffered the damage, to identify either the producer, "own-brander," or importer, or the person who supplied the product to him.[95] The supplier is not liable under section 2(3) merely because he cannot identify who provided the component parts or raw materials in a finished product supplied to him,[96] rather it is the producer or supplier of the finished product that he must identify. The claimant's request must be made within a reasonable period after the damage occurs, and at a time when it is not reasonably practical for the claimant to identify them. This section is intended to give claimants an identifiable defendant and puts the onus on suppliers, such as retail pharmacists and dispensing general practitioners, to keep accurate records of their own sources of supply. This may be a particular problem for pharmacists dispensing generic drugs. If the supplier complies with the request he is not liable under the Act, even if the claimant cannot pursue a remedy against the identified defendants, e.g., because they are in liquidation. The liability of suppliers in the tort of negligence is potentially wider than this.

(3) Products

"Product" means any "goods or electricity" and includes a product which   8–073
is comprised in another product whether as a component part or raw

---

[93] Consumer Protection Act 1987, s.2(2)(b); the "own-brander".
[94] ibid., s.2(2)(c).
[95] ibid., s.2(3); on the meaning of "supply" see s.46.
[96] ibid., s.1(3).

material.[97] There was some doubt as to whether human organs or bodily fluids, such as blood, should be treated as "products" under the Act, though this doubt has now been resolved in favour of treating them as products to which the Act does apply.[98]

8–074   Agricultural produce and game were excluded unless it had undergone an industrial process,[99] although there is no definition of an "industrial process." The processor was only liable as a producer if the "essential characteristics" of the product were attributable to an industrial or other process.[1] This requirement does not apply to other potential defendants in respect of processed products, the "own-brander," the importer or the supplier. Nor was it necessary that the defect in the product was the result of the industrial process itself. For example, food that was contaminated prior to processing could give rise to liability under the Act, once processed, whereas the same contaminated food sold to consumers unprocessed was not within the Act. This could be a relevant distinction with some forms of herbal remedy. The exception for agricultural products was removed by EU Directive 99/34 which extends the 1985 Product Liability Directive to agricultural produce, but only in respect of products put into the market after December 4th 2000.[2]

(4) Defects

8–075   Liability under the Consumer Protection Act 1987 is strict, not absolute. The claimant does not succeed simply by showing that the product caused damage; he must prove that the damage was caused by a defect in the product. By section 3(1) a product has a defect "if the safety of the product is not such as persons generally are entitled to expect." Safety includes safety with respect to component parts, and with respect to property damage as well as personal injury. The crucial question is: what are persons generally entitled to expect by way of safety? The answer, almost inevitably, must be: it all depends on the circumstances of the case.[3]

8–076   They are entitled to expect that food and drink will not be contaminated with decomposed snails or acid, that clothes and hair dye will not contain

---

[97] *ibid.*, s.1(2). "Goods" includes substances, growing crops and things comprised in land by virtue of being attached to it, and any ship, aircraft or vehicle: s.45.

[98] *A. v National Blood Authority* [2001] 3 All E.R. 289; the Pearson Commission recommended that organs and blood should be subject to a strict liability regime: Cmnd. 7054, (1978), Vol. I, para. 1276. See Lee and Morgan, *Human Fertilisation & Embryology*, 2000, p. 261, discussing whether embryos or gametes could be regarded as "products." See also Stern (1994) 2 Med. L. Rev. 261, 262. In *E. v Australian Red Cross Society* (1991) 99 A.L.R. 601; [1991] 2 Med. L.R. 303, 326 (Fed. Court of Aust.) Wilcox J. considered, without resolving, the question of whether blood could amount to "goods."

[99] Consumer Protection Act 1987, s.2(4). Agricultural produce means "any produce of the soil, of stock-farming or of fisheries": s.1(2).

[1] *ibid.*, s.1(2).

[2] See O'Rourke (1999) 149 N.L.J. 1106.

[3] In *Abouzaid v Mothercare (UK) Ltd* [2000] All E.R. (D) 246 at [40] Chadwick L.J. said that the question of whether the safety of a product was such as persons generally were entitled to expect is a question of fact.

skin irritants, that motor cars will not have defective steering, that danger-ous chemicals will be adequately labelled, and so on. But they are not nec-essarily entitled to expect that drugs will have no adverse side-effects, that all motor cars will be as safe as modern technology can make them, nor that hot drinks will not burn skin if the drink is spilled.[4] The seriousness of the potential injury is a factor relevant to what persons are entitled to expect.[5] Safety, like risk, is a relative concept, and this is just as true in determining what is "defective" as it is in deciding whether a manufacturer has been neg-ligent. It is a question of degree, in which levels of safety are traded off against both cost and the usefulness of the product, although this is more likely to be an intuitive judgment than a strict cost-benefit analysis.[6]

Section 3(2) provides that in determining what persons generally are enti-tled to expect "all the circumstances shall be taken into account," including: 8–077

"(a) the manner in which, and purposes for which, the product has been marketed, its get-up, the use of any mark in relation to the product and any instructions for, or warnings with respect to, doing or refraining from doing anything with or in relation to the product;

(b) what might reasonably be expected to be done with or in relation to the product; and

(c) the time when the product was supplied by its producer to another; and nothing in this section shall require a defect to be inferred from the fact alone that the safety of a product which is supplied after that time is greater than the safety of the product in question."

In *Richardson v LRC Products Ltd*[7] it was held that, though the natural   8–078 expectation of consumers would be that a condom would not fail, this was not something that persons generally were entitled to expect, particularly since the defendants did not claim that their product would be 100 per cent effective. Thus, the fact that a condom had failed did not prove that it was defective under section 3(1).[8] It is not clear why a condom which is proved

---

[4] *B v McDonald's Restaurants Ltd* [2002] EWHC 490, QB.
[5] *Abouzaid v Mothercare (UK) Ltd* [2000] All E.R. (D) 246 at [27] where Pill L.J. considered that the seriousness of an injury to the eye would affect the expectations of members of the public, whereas expectations would be lower if the worst that could happen was the risk of striking a hand with an elasticated strap.
[6] See Clark (1985) 48 M.L.R. 325. In *G. v Fry Surgical International Ltd* (1992) 3 *AVMA Medical & Legal Journal* (No. 4) p. 12 an action under the Consumer Protection Act 1987 against the importers of a pair of arthroscopy scissors which fractured during the course of an operation, leaving a fragment in the claimant's knee, was settled by the defendants on the basis that the scissors were defective.
[7] [2000] P.I.Q.R. P164; [2000] Lloyd's Rep. Med. 280.
[8] In *Foster v Biosil* (2000) 59 B.M.L.R. 178 (County Court) it was held that in a claim in respect of allegedly defective silicone breast implants, which ruptured and leaked silicone, the claimant must prove both that the implant was defective under s.3 and the cause of the defect, applying *Richardson v LRC Products Ltd*. The claimant had to prove that there was

to have failed as a result of a rupture is not defective. In *Richardson* Kennedy J. stated that:

> "Naturally enough the users' expectation is that a condom will not fail. There are no claims made by the defendants that one will never fail and no-one has ever supposed that any method of contraception intended to defeat nature will be 100 per cent effective. This must particularly be so in the case of a condom where the product is required to a degree at least to be, in the jargon, 'user friendly'."[9]

With respect, this fails to address the statutory test as to what is defective. The suggestion that the fact that the manufacturer has not claimed that his products will never fail should be taken into account in assessing what is defective is misplaced. Few, if any, manufacturers would make such an inflated claim, but that tells us nothing about whether any particular product is defective.[10] Most failures of condoms are probably due to consumer misuse and lack of skill in using the condom may be a risk that consumers must accept, but it is entirely unclear why consumers must accept that some condoms will fail through manufacturing defects, simply because the manufacturers have never claimed that their products are 100 per cent safe. What if, instead of pregnancy, the consequence of the failure was that one of the parties transmitted HIV to the other. Would the consumer expectation test suggest that the condom was not defective in these circumstances?

8–079   In contrast, in *A v National Blood Authority*[11] Burton J. held that consumers are entitled to expect that blood products would be 100 per cent safe, and therefore the supplier of blood infected with the virus Hepatitis C had supplied a product which was defective. The claimants were infected with the Hepatitis C virus through blood transfusions which had used blood from infected donors. Although the risk of infection with Hepatitis C in this manner was known, at the time when the claimants were infected it was impossible to avoid, either because the virus had not been discovered or because there was no test for the virus in blood products. The defendants accepted that liability under Article 6 of the European Union Product Liability Directive 1985 was strict, in the sense that it did not depend on the proof of fault by the claimant.

(n.8 contd.) a defect in the product, not merely that the product failed in circumstances which were unsafe and contrary to what persons generally are entitled to expect. This she failed to do, on the balance of probabilities, in the face of evidence from the manufacturer that there had been no other implant from the particular batch which had been reported as defective, and statistics showing that failures were very rare. On the other hand, as Balen (2002) 8 Clinical Risk 177, 184 comments: "To give protection to consumers it should be sufficient to demonstrate that a product was not as safe as expected (as per the wording of the Act and Directive) without having to identify the precise cause of the defect." See also Freeman [2001] J.P.I.L. 26.

9   [2000] Lloyd's Rep. Med. 280, 285.

10   For example, in *Grant v Australian Knitting Mills Ltd* [1936] A.C. 85, 95 it was said that 4,737,600 garments had been manufactured by a similar process, without any complaint from consumers, before the product in question was worn by the claimant. That, however, did not prevent the Privy Council from holding the defendants liable in negligence.

11   [2001] 3 All E.R. 289.

Nonetheless, they argued that in determining whether the blood was defective under Article 6 (which corresponds to section 3 of the 1987 Act) the fact that the risk was unavoidable should be taken into account. Blood was an inherently risky product, and therefore the infected blood should not be regarded as a non-standard product, that is a product which fell below the levels of safety to be expected in a standard product, where the harmful (non-standard) characteristic had caused the claimants' damage. The blood supplied by the defendants was provided as a service to society, and the defendants had no alternative but to supply it to hospitals.

In a robust judgment, Burton J. held that blood infected with Hepatitis C   8–080
virus was defective under the Product Liability Directive. Article 6 states that a product is defective if it does not provide a level of safety which a person is entitled to expect, irrespective of whether that lack of safety could have been avoided by the manufacturer. The argument that the public were only entitled to expect that level of safety which could have been achieved by the exercise of reasonable precautions was rejected. The consumer had an expectation, and was entitled to expect, that blood used in transfusions would be 100 per cent safe and would not be infected with Hepatitis C. The Directive was intended to eliminate proof of fault or negligence in order to make it easier for claimants to prove their case. Not only does a consumer not have to prove that the producer did not take reasonable steps, or all reasonable steps, to comply with his duty, but also he does not have to show that the producer did not take all legitimately expectable steps either. The infected blood products were non-standard products because they were different from the norm which the producer intended for use by the public.[12] The fact that the risk of viral infection is inherent in blood, as a natural product, was irrelevant. Moreover, the question of whether the defendants could have avoided the damage to the claimants was not one of the circumstances to be taken into account within Article 6. It was not a relevant circumstance since it was beyond the purpose of the Directive and had it been intended, would have been included as a derogation from it. Also excluded from consideration were the impracticability, cost or difficulty of identifying the potentially harmful agent and taking preventive measures, and the potential social benefits of the product. As Burton J. commented:

> "This is obviously a tough decision for any common lawyer to make. But I am entirely clear that this was the purpose of the Directive, and that without the exclusion of such matters (subject only to the limited defence of Article 7(e) [the 'development risks' defence]) it would not only be toothless but pointless."[13]

---

[12] 99 out of 100 bags of blood were not infected and would cause no injury, but the defendants' argument, rejected by Burton J., was that all of the bags of blood were standard because they all carried the *risk* of infection, in the sense that, without a test, it was possible that any individual bag carried the virus.

[13] [2001] 3 All E.R. 289 at [69]. For comment on *A v The National Blood Authority* see Howells and Mildred (2002) 65 M.L.R. 95; Hodges (2001) 117 L.Q.R. 528; Goldberg (2002) 10 Med. L. Rev. 165; Brown (2001) 7 Clinical Risk 144; Melville Williams [2001] J.P.I.L. 238.

In other words, if the Directive and the 1987 Act are interpreted in such a manner as to be little different from the law of negligence, there was no point to the legislation. This strengthened Burton J.'s conclusion that, on the wording of the Directive, it was clear that a true form of strict liability had been enacted.

8–081   Similarly, in *Abouzaid v Mothercare (UK) Ltd*[14] Chadwick L.J. said that the question under section 2(1) of the Act is how was the damage caused; it is not was the cause of the damage foreseeable. The question of whether the manufacturer might have been expected to discover the defect, given the state of scientific and technical knowledge at the time, though relevant to the defence under section 4(1)(*e*), was not relevant to the issue to be addressed under section 3, which is what degree of safety are persons generally entitled to expect?[15] Thus, Chadwick L.J. observed:

> "in the context of the test to be applied under sections 2(1) and 3(1) it is irrelevant whether the hazard which causes the damage has come, or ought reasonably to have come, to the attention of the producer before the accident occurs. To hold otherwise is, to my mind, to seek to reintroduce concepts familiar in the context of a claim in negligence at common law into a statutory regime which has been enacted in order to give effect to the Product Liability Directive . . ."[16]

8–082   The types of defect which can arise fall into the same categories as are found with the tort of negligence, namely defects in the manufacture, design, or the presentation of the product with inadequate warnings or instructions for use. "Consumer expectations" are treated as a measure of defectiveness, but medicinal products almost invariably carry some risk of adverse reactions, even if in only a small minority of consumers. Thus, although the decision in *A v National Blood Authority* indicates that consumers are entitled to expect that blood used for transfusion will not be contaminated with a dangerous virus, it is arguably still the case that they are not necessarily entitled to expect that other medical products will be entirely risk-free. The risks have to be weighed against the anticipated benefits, and indeed against the "costs" of not using the product, such as the harm associated with the disease, and the risks and anticipated benefits of alternative treatments. This process is familiar from the assessment of what constitutes negligence. Similarly, consumer expectations may be limited by any warnings or contraindications given by the manufacturer, either directly to the consumer or to an intermediary such as the prescribing physician. It does not make sense, however, to speak of warnings against dangers which were unknown or unforeseeable by the producer, and once the question of foreseeability arises the concept of reasonable care is reintroduced.[17] A warning contained in a

---

[14] [2000] All E.R. (D) 246 at [38], CA.
[15] *ibid.* at [43].
[16] *ibid.* at [44].
[17] Clark (1987) 50 M.L.R. 614, 617. Notwithstanding the introduction of strict product liability

legible and unambiguous leaflet will normally suffice. A manufacturer cannot be expected to cater for lost leaflets or consumers who choose not to replace a lost leaflet.[18]

Misuse of the product by the consumer will be taken into account. If the product is used in a way which could not reasonably be expected then, as with negligence, it cannot be considered defective. Presumably, foreseeable misuse will make the product defective, subject to a possible defence of contributory negligence.   8–083

Section 3(2)(c) takes account of the time at which the product was supplied by the producer (not when supplied to the consumer) in assessing whether it was defective. The product may have deteriorated since it left the producer's hands, as a result of the passage of time, or repeated use, or misuse or mishandling. A product which has deteriorated in this way is not necessarily defective, though it is not necessarily safe either. It will depend upon the nature of the product, how much time has elapsed, how much use it has had, and so on. Keeping and using drugs after their expiry date may be an example of contributory negligence, but it may also indicate that the drugs were not even defective if the consumer was not entitled to expect that they would not deteriorate. But the mere passage of time, during which period a danger in a product has become apparent, does not mean that consumer expectations have changed. The question of what consumers can reasonably expect does not depend on whether a manufacturer could reasonably have been expected to be aware of the hazard at the time. The product is to be judged by the expectations of the public at large, as determined by the court, and the passage of time does not necessarily alter public expectations as to the safety of a product.[19]   8–084

The proviso to section 3(2) states that the defectiveness of a product is not to be inferred simply from the fact that products which are supplied at a later date are safer than the product in question. In negligence, of course, carelessness is measured by reference to the knowledge and standards applicable at the time of the accident, ignoring subsequent improvements,[20] and the proviso appears to apply a similar standard. This must go to the question of proof, however, rather than creating a rule of law, otherwise all unforeseeable defects would be excluded from the ambit of the   8–085

(n.17 contd.) in the United States, defective design cases and cases of failure to warn are treated as equivalent to actions in negligence: see *Feldman v Lederle Laboratories* 479 A. 2d 374 (1984); *Brown v Superior Court* 751 P. 2d 470 (1988). On the other hand, a product which could have been rendered "safe" by an appropriate warning can nonetheless be held to be defective even though the producer was unaware of the danger associated with its design because there had been no previous reports of accidents with the product: *Abouzaid v Mothercare (U.K.) Ltd* [2000] All E.R. (D) 246, CA.

[18] *Worsley v Tambrands Ltd* [2000] P.I.Q.R. P95.

[19] *Abouzaid v Mothercare (U.K.) Ltd* [2000] All E.R. (D) 246 at [43] and [25] *per* Chadwick and Pill L.JJ. respectively.

[20] *Roe v Minister of Health* [1954] 2 Q.B. 66, para. 3–071, but the duty does at least extend beyond the date of putting the product into circulation, requiring a manufacturer to warn about any subsequently discovered dangers or in an appropriate case to recall the product; see para. 8–050.

Act, as in negligence. Presumably, a case such as *Roe v Minister of Health*[21] is just the type of situation which ought to be covered by strict liability, since persons generally are entitled to expect that anaesthetics will not be contaminated with paralysing agents.[22] Once an improved product becomes available this may be relevant to whether the old product is defective if the supply of the old product is *continued*, as in negligence, but this begs the question of what is meant by "improved". A new drug may have fewer side-effects, but be less effective, or it may be more effective, but have more side-effects. At what point can it be said that the drug is "improved"? This is all a matter of degree, and also depends upon knowledge about the new product, which it may take some time to acquire through clinical use.[23]

8–086   Moreover, it would appear that there is no equivalent under the Act of a "continuing duty" parallel to that in the tort of negligence, requiring the manufacturer to recall products which were not known to be defective at the time of supply, where it has subsequently been discovered that the product does create an unacceptable risk of harm. Although the supply of similar products after the date of knowledge could result in the conclusion that they are defective, there is nothing in section 3 to indicate how a product that was "safe" at the time of supply can subsequently become defective, unless it can be said that some obligation to recall products forms part of consumer expectations. Indeed, there is a specific defence where the defendant can show that the defect did not exist in the product when he supplied it to another.[24]

8–087   The Act does not mention the cost of the product as a factor in determining defectiveness. Where the defect is a construction defect or a failure to warn or provide adequate instructions for use then cost is probably irrelevant, but it may well be a significant feature where it is claimed that the product is defective in design.[25] In *A v National Blood Authority*[26] Burton J. held that the impracticability and the cost or difficulty of identifying the potentially harmful agent and taking suitable precautions, were to be ignored when considering whether blood products contaminated with the Hepatitis C virus were defective.

8–088   Once it is established that the product was defective liability is strict, in the sense that it is not a defence for the producer to show that he exercised reasonable care. It is arguable, however, that, notwithstanding *A v National Blood Authority*, many of the factors taken into account in deciding whether

---

[21] [1954] 2 Q.B. 66.

[22] See, however, the development risks defence, paras 8–102 to 8–109, below.

[23] Drugs which are supplied as part of a clinical trial probably do fall within the ambit of the Act, but the fact the product is still under research would have a bearing on whether it could be said to be defective. Moreover, the development risks defence would apply, effectively excluding the manufacturer's responsibility for unforeseeable reactions: para. 8–102. See further paras 3–056 *et seq.*

[24] See para. 8–098.

[25] See Stapleton (1986) 6 O.J.L.S. 392, 404; Newdick (1987) 103 L.Q.R. 288, 300–4.

[26] [2001] 3 All E.R. 289.

a manufacturer has discharged a duty of care in negligence are relevant to the decision-making process about whether a product is defective under the Act.

(5) Types of loss

The Act is designed to protect consumer expectations in the safety of products, and therefore there is no liability in respect of pure economic loss, damage to commercial property or damage to the product itself, even if the product is potentially dangerous. For the purpose of liability under section 2, damage means "death or personal injury or any loss of or damage to any property (including land)."[27] Loss of or damage to the product itself is specifically excluded, as is loss of or damage to a product caused by a defective component product which had been supplied with the product.[28]

8–089

By section 5(3) property damage claims are limited to property which is: (a) ordinarily intended for private use, occupation and consumption; and (b) intended by the person suffering the loss or damage mainly for his own private use, occupation or consumption. This excludes damage to business property. Actions in respect of property damage (but not personal injury) below £275 are also excluded.[29]

8–090

(6) Causation

The claimant has the burden of proving that the product was defective and that the damage was caused "wholly or partly" by the defect.[30] The difficulty of proving factual causation in some instances is just as great as in the tort of negligence, although there is no requirement to prove that the damage was of a foreseeable type, as in negligence. In *A v The National Blood Authority*[31] Burton J. held that a claim based on loss of a chance is not appropriate in the context of an action for breach of section 3 of the Act. Both the Act, and the European Union Product Liability Directive 1985, impose strict liability. The question is whether the product was defective, and if so what damage was caused by that defect. It is not what damage was caused by any conduct, whether wrongful or otherwise, or breach of duty. Thus, questions of what would or might have happened in hypothetical circumstances are not relevant.

8–091

The Act makes it clear that the producer remains liable where the damage is caused partly by the defect and partly by some other event. The other event may be entirely innocent or it may be the "faulty" conduct of a third

8–092

---

[27] Consumer Protection Act 1987, s.5(1).
[28] *ibid.*, s.5(2).
[29] *ibid.*, s.5(4).
[30] *ibid.*, s.2(1).
[31] [2001] 3 All E.R. 289.

party, for example, the failure of a third party to examine or test the product or heed warnings in the manufacturer's instructions for use. It will be recalled that so far as the tort of negligence is concerned the failure to take advantage of a reasonable opportunity for intermediate inspection may be treated as breaking the chain of causation. It is arguable that this is not the position under the Act, because the damage is "partly" caused by the defective product and "partly" by the failure of the intermediate examination.[32] The manufacturer and the third party will be jointly and severally liable, and their respective responsibilities can be apportioned under the Civil Liability (Contribution) Act 1978. On the other hand, it is possible that where the manufacturer has good grounds for contemplating that an intermediate inspection will occur or that an intermediary will follow instructions then the product will not be categorised as defective. Section 3(2) provides that instructions, warnings, and "what might reasonably be expected to be done with or in relation to the product" can be taken into account in determining what is defective. Thus, the effects of intermediate examination may simply have been shifted from the causation stage of the inquiry to the earlier point of deciding whether the product was unsafe in all the circumstances. If the product is categorised as defective, then the omission of an intermediate examination should not defeat the action on grounds of causation.

8–093   Logically, the same approach should apply to "faulty" conduct by the claimant. If he misuses the product in an unforeseeable fashion or disregards a warning the conclusion may simply be that the product was not defective. If it is found to be defective, the claimant's conduct should be treated as contributory negligence.

(7) Defences

8–094   Once the claimant proves that the product was defective and caused the damage the onus shifts to the defendant to establish one of the specific defences provided in section 4. One potential defence is expressly prohibited. By section 7 liability cannot be "limited or excluded by any contract term, by any notice or by any other provision." This prevents the manufacturer excluding liability under the Act to the injured consumer.[33] It does not, however, affect possible exclusion or limitation clauses in the contracts which constitute the chain of supply from manufacturer to distributor to retailer. Such clauses would not necessarily be caught by the Unfair Contract Terms Act 1977.[34]

---

[32] Brazier and Murphy, *Street on Torts*, 10th ed., 1999, p. 356.

[33] An exclusion of liability for personal injuries caused by negligence will be invalid by virtue of the Unfair Contract Terms Act 1977, s.2(1).

[34] See *Thompson v T. Lohan (Plant Hire) Ltd* [1987] 1 W.L.R. 649; *cf. Phillips Products Ltd v Hyland* [1987] 1 W.L.R. 659. Of course, exclusion clauses in the chain of supply are irrelevant to the consumer's action.

(a) Miscellaneous defences[35]

It is a defence for the defendant to show[36] that:

(i) The defect was attributable to compliance with any statutory require-   8–095
ment or European Community obligation.[37] Compliance with regulations
made under the Medicines Act 1968 should not be an automatic defence, but
this may be good evidence that the product conformed to what persons generally are entitled to expect by way of safety, as in the case of negligence.

(ii) He never supplied the product to another.[38] In *Veedfald v Arhus*   8–096
Amtskommune,[39] a fluid used for flushing kidneys prior to transplantation
was defective so that a kidney donated by the claimant's brother for transplantation to the claimant was damaged and could not be used. The fluid
was manufactured at a laboratory owned and managed by the defendant for
use at another hospital owned and managed by the defendant, a public body
which was a non-profit making organisation. The defendant argued that the
product had not been put into circulation. The European Court of Justice
held that the fact that it had not left the defendant's premises did not mean
that it had not been put into circulation. A defective product was put into
circulation when it was used during the provision of a specific medical
service, consisting of preparing a human organ for transplantation, and the
damage caused to the organ resulted from that preparatory treatment
(applying Article 7(a) of Council Directive 85/374/EEC).

(iii) The only supply by him was otherwise than in the course of a busi-   8–097
ness, and if he is a producer, "own-brander" or importer that this is by virtue
only of things done by him otherwise than with a view to profit.[40] Thus, free
samples would not be within the defence, since they are distributed with a
view, ultimately, to profit. In the *Veedfald* case[41] the defendant also argued
that the product had not been manufactured for an "economic purpose"
(within the meaning of Article 7(c) of Council Directive 85/374/EEC) as the
laboratory and hospital were entirely publicly funded. Again, the European
Court of Justice rejected the defendant's argument. The exemption from
liability where an activity has no economic or business purpose does not
extend to the case of a defective product which has been manufactured and
used in the course of a specific medical service which is financed entirely from
public funds and for which the patient is not required to pay directly.

(iv) The defect did not exist in the product when he supplied it to another.[42]   8–098
If the defendant is a supplier, as opposed to a producer, an "own-brander" or

---

[35] Note that special rules in respect of limitation periods apply to claims brought under the
Consumer Protection Act 1987: see para. 10–088.
[36] This clearly places the burden of proof upon the defendant. The defendant must plead the
defence: *Abouzaid v Mothercare (U.K.) Ltd* [2000] All E.R. (D) 246 at [10], CA.
[37] Consumer Protection Act 1987, s.4(1)(*a*).
[38] *ibid.*, s.4(1)(*b*), *e.g.*, if it was stolen from him.
[39] Case C-203/99, (2001) 66 B.M.L.R. 1; Bright (2002) 8 Clinical Risk 67.
[40] Consumer Protection Act 1987, s.4(1)(*c*).
[41] (2001) 66 B.M.L.R. 1.
[42] Consumer Protection Act 1987, ss.4(1)(*d*) and 4(2)(*a*).

an importer, it is a defence to show that the defect did not exist, not when *he* supplied it, but when it was last supplied by the producer, "own-brander" or importer.[43]

8–099   (v) A component manufacturer is not liable for a defect in the finished product which was wholly attributable to the design of the finished product (*e.g.*, where the component product is normally safe in its contemplated use but is misused in the design of the finished product); nor where the defect is due to the compliance by the component manufacturer with instructions given by the manufacturer of the finished product.[44]

8–100   (vi) Contributory negligence is a partial defence.[45] Of course, misuse of the product by the claimant may be relevant to the question of whether the product was defective at all, or whether an otherwise defective product caused the claimant's damage. Conceptually these are distinct issues—if the product was defective, and if it was a cause, even a partial cause, of the damage the defendant is liable, and the claimant's fault is relevant only to apportionment of the damages. In practice, however, it may be difficult to separate these questions.

8–101   In theory problems could arise as to the basis of apportionment of damages since the claimant is at fault and the defendant in breach of a strict duty which may not involve any negligence on his part. In such circumstances what is the "claimant's share in the responsibility for the damage"?[46] This is not likely to be a major obstacle, however, because the courts have considerable experience of apportionment in other areas where the defendant may have been in breach of a strict statutory duty (*e.g.*, employers' liability) and the claimant has been negligent.

(b) The "development risks" defence

8–102   Under section 4(1)(*e*) of the Consumer Protection Act 1987 it is a defence to prove that:

> "the state of scientific and technical knowledge at the relevant time was not such that a producer of products of the same description as the product in question might be expected to have discovered the defect if it had existed in his products while they were under his control."

The "relevant time" is the time when the defendant supplied the product to another, in effect, when it was put into circulation.[47]

8–103   This so-called development risks defence was one of the most controversial aspects of both the European Community Directive and the Consumer Protection Act 1987. Its effect is to excuse a defendant who can show that

---

[43] *ibid.*, s.4(2)(*b*).
[44] *ibid.*, s.4(1)(*f*).
[45] *ibid.*, s.6(4).
[46] Law Reform (Contributory Negligence) Act 1945, s.1(1); see paras 4–137 to 4–143.
[47] Consumer Protection Act 1987, s.4(2)(*a*).

the defect was unknown and unforeseeable when he put the product into circulation, the justification being that if defendants were held responsible for unknown and unknowable risks this might deter the development of new products which might be beneficial to the public at large. The objection to the defence is that it represents a policy of allowing individual consumers to bear these development risks should they materialise, when the possibility of loss spreading through insurance and the price mechanism was readily available. It amounts to a retreat into negligence theory at precisely the point that strict liability is most useful.[48]

Both the Law Commission and the Pearson Commission recommended that this defence should not be available. Pearson, for example, commented that it would "leave a gap in the compensation cover, through which, for example, the victims of another thalidomide disaster might easily slip."[49] Indeed, the pharmaceutical industry could be one of the principal beneficiaries of this defence. There is a public policy argument in favour of the development and marketing of new drugs which are intended to save life and reduce pain and suffering, even where the drugs carry risks to the public. The central issue, however, is who should carry the burden of these development risks. If it is in the public interest then maybe the public should bear the risks, either through strict liability and the market mechanism or through a no-fault compensation scheme.[50]   **8–104**

The wording of the defence invites comparison with the scientific and technical knowledge of a hypothetical producer of "products of the same description as the product in question." This is a subjective test of knowledge, by reference to the knowledge of the industry concerned, not general scientific and technical knowledge. The Act seemed to differ significantly from the Directive on this point. Article 7(e) of the Directive confers the defence where "the state of scientific and technical knowledge at the time when he put the product into circulation was not such as to enable the existence of the defect to be discovered." This version of the defence appeared to be narrower than section 4(1)(e) of the Act, since it is easier to prove that no producer of similar products could have discovered the defect, than to prove that no one, considering the state of scientific and technical knowledge, could have discovered the defect.[51] Thus, it had been argued that section 4(1)(e) effectively excused a defendant when he had not been negligent in failing to discover the defect, and amounted to little more than a reversal of the burden of proving negligence.[52] The discrepancy between   **8–105**

---

[48] Although see Stapleton (1986) 6 O.J.L.S. 392, 408–13 arguing that even without a development risks defence the same considerations have to be taken into account in a scheme which bases liability on defectiveness; Stoppa (1992) 12 L.S. 210.

[49] *Royal Commission on Civil Liability and Compensation for Personal Injury*, Cmnd. 7054 (1978), Vol. I, para. 1259.

[50] On no-fault compensation for drug injuries see Fleming (1982) 30 Am. J. Comp. Law 297.

[51] Crossick (1988) 138 N.L.J. 223; *cf.* Newdick [1988] C.L.J. 455, 459–60 who argues that the Directive is ambiguous and that s.4(1)(e) is the correct interpretation of the ambiguity.

[52] Newdick [1988] C.L.J. 455, 460, 475. See also Newdick (1985) 101 L.Q.R. 405, 406 commenting that: "... a state of the art defence would be sufficient to undermine the entire policy of a scheme of strict liability so far as it applied to drug damage."

Article 7(e) and section 4(1)(e) was referred to the European Commission on the basis that the Act did not fully implement the Directive, and the Commission took the issue to the European Court of Justice. The Court concluded, however, that there was no conflict between Article 7(e) and section 4(1)(e). The UK courts would be able to achieve the purpose of Article 7(e) in interpreting section 4(1)(e).[53] Moreover, section 1(1) states that Part I of the Act "shall have effect for the purpose of making such provision as is necessary in order to comply with the product liability Directive and shall be construed accordingly," and thus it is arguable that if there is any discrepancy between the Act and the Directive a domestic court should interpret provisions in the Act in accordance with the Directive. Indeed, in *A v The National Blood Authority*[54] Burton J. simply applied the provisions of the Directive, as directly applicable in English law, effectively bypassing any potential conflict with the Consumer Protection Act 1987.

8–106   A major problem in applying section 4(1)(e) is the interpretation of the words "scientific and technical knowledge." It is not clear when "information" becomes "knowledge." This could be when it is accepted as scientific fact; or when it is published in a scientific journal as a hypothesis; or when a researcher in a laboratory considers it to be a remote possibility. Where there are conflicting views within the scientific community, then which view must the manufacturer follow? How discoverable must the defect be? With the expenditure of moderate or reasonable or extensive resources? Indeed, is cost a relevant consideration at all? If the defect could have been discovered from existing information but the appropriate intellectual "connections" have not been made by researchers, is this "knowledge" from which the defect might be expected to have been discovered?[55]

8–107   In *Abouzaid v Mothercare (UK) Ltd*[56] the claimant was struck in the eye by an elasticated strap used to attach an accessory to a child's pushchair. The Court of Appeal rejected the defendants' argument that the absence of any accident records for similar types of accident meant that they did not have the relevant scientific or technical knowledge, within the meaning of section 4(1)(e). Pill L.J. said that the defence contemplated scientific and technical advances which throw additional light, for example, on the propensities of materials and allow defects to be discovered.[57] Chadwick L.J. said that the question of whether the defendants could have discovered the defect in 1990 before the accident to the claimant occurred had nothing to do with the state

---

[53] *Commission of the European Communities v UK* (C300/95) [1997] All E.R. (EC) 481; for discussion of this case and its implications for the development risks defence see C. Hodges (1998) 61 M.L.R. 560 and M. Mildred and G. Howells (1998) 61 M.L.R. 570.

[54] [2001] 3 All E.R. 289, 297.

[55] In *Independent Broadcasting Authority v EMI Electronics Ltd and B.I.C.C. Construction Ltd* (1980) 14 Build. L.R. 1, 36 Lord Fraser commented that: "The error arose not from difficulty of calculation but from the omission of what seems to me to have been a simple piece of reasoning about known facts"; *cf.* where the primary information has not been discovered. For discussion of what is meant by "knowledge" in the context of development risks see Newdick (1991) 20 Anglo-Am. L.R. 127.

[56] [2000] All E.R. (D) 246.

[57] *ibid.* at [29].

of scientific or technical knowledge at that time. There was a simple, practical test which could have been carried out. No advance in scientific or technical knowledge was required to enable the test to be carried out, and the only reason that it had not been carried out before 1990 was that defendants had not thought of doing so. Thus, the defence under section 4(1)(e) was "simply not engaged in the present case."[58]

In *Commission of the European Communities v UK*[59] the European Court of Justice indicated that for the defence to be overcome the relevant knowledge must have been accessible at the time when the product was put into circulation. In *A v The National Blood Authority*[60] Burton J. held that the defence in Article 7(e) of the European Union Product Liability Directive (on which section 4(1)(e) of the 1987 Act is based) does not apply where the existence of a generic defect was known, or should have been known, in the light of accessible information. Burton J. concluded that a risk ceases to be a development risk and becomes a known risk, not if and when the producer in question has the requisite knowledge, but if and when such knowledge is accessible anywhere in the world "outside Manchuria."[61] The reference to Manchuria was meant to deal with the situation where the relevant knowledge was available, but only to scientists in an unknown research laboratory in an inaccessible part of the world. In such circumstances it would not be treated as "accessible" knowledge. But once the existence of the defect was known, there was a risk of that defect materialising in any particular product, and it was immaterial that the known risk was unavoidable in the particular product. In those circumstances a producer continued to produce and supply the product at its own risk. It would be inconsistent with the purpose of the Directive if a producer, in the case of a known risk, continued to supply products simply because he was unable to identify in which of his products that defect would occur, or, where he was obliged to supply or continued to supply without accepting the responsibility for any injuries resulting. The purpose of Article 7(e) was to avoid discouraging innovation and to exclude development risks, hence it protected a producer in respect of the unknown. The effect was not that non-standard products (*i.e.* products which were different from the norm which the producer intended for use by the public) were excluded from falling within Article 7(e), since they could qualify where the problem was not known. However, once the problem was known, by virtue of accessible information, then a non-standard product would no longer qualify for protection under Article 7(e). Thus, in the case of contaminated blood products, where the risk was known but the there were no means of avoiding the risk, Article 7(e) provided no defence.

8–108

---

[58] *ibid.* at [46]. Note also that if the defendants' argument were accepted it would mean that the first victim of a defective product would have considerable difficulty in establishing liability.

[59] (C300/95) [1997] All E.R. (EC) 481.

[60] [2001] 3 All E.R. 289.

[61] *ibid.* at [76].

8–109   At one time it was unclear whether the defence applied to manufacturing defects. On the face of it the defence is concerned with the producer's knowledge of the possibility that the defect might exist, and excuses him from liability if he could not have known about the risk. Thus, it appears to be concerned with design defects rather than construction defects. However, it was arguable that the defence might also apply to construction defects which it is known can occur but the state of technical knowledge is such that it is impossible to devise a quality control system that would detect all defective items in the production line.[62] In *Richardson v LRC Products Ltd*[63] Ian Kennedy J. took a narrow view of the development risks defence. It did not apply unless the evidence showed that "there was a defect of whose possible existence the leading edge of available scientific knowledge was ignorant." The test was not what the defendants knew but what they could have known if they had consulted those who might be expected to know the state of research and all available literature sources. The defence did not apply in the case of "a defect of a known character merely because there is no test which is able to reveal its existence in every case".[64] This indicates that the defence does not apply to construction defects, a view which is supported by the decision of Burton J. in *A v The National Blood Authority*.[65]

---

[62] See Newdick [1988] C.L.J. 455, 469–73.
[63] [2000] P.I.Q.R. P164; [2000] Lloyd's Rep. Med. 280.
[64] *ibid.* at 285.
[65] [2001] 3 All E.R. 289.

CHAPTER 9

DAMAGES

Most actions against medical practitioners are claims in respect of personal   9–001
injuries or death, and the consequential financial loss, and there is no difference in the principles applied to the assessment of damages in medical negligence cases from other actions for personal injuries. Injunctive relief is
rarely relevant, with the possible exception of actions for breach of confidence. Accordingly, this Chapter concentrates largely on the principles
adopted by the courts in the assessment of damages for personal injuries and
death, though the final section deals with damages for breach of confidence.[1]

1. GENERAL PRINCIPLES

(1)   Types of damages

The fundamental principle applied to the assessment of an award of damages   9–002
in tort is that the claimant should be fully compensated. He is entitled to be
restored to the position that he would have been in had the tort not been committed, in so far as this can be done by the payment of money.[2] In contract the
claimant is entitled to be placed in the position he would have been in had the
contract been performed, but in practice this is unlikely to produce a different

---

[1] It is not possible to give more than an outline of the law on damages for personal injuries
here. For detailed discussion see Kemp & Kemp, *The Quantum of Damages*; *McGregor on
Damages*, 16th ed., 1997, Chs 33 and 34. Strictly speaking, claims in respect of certain financial losses arising out of "wrongful conception" or "wrongful birth" may not be categorised
as actions for personal injuries but they are nonetheless included in this chapter. It is arguable that such claims, at least in respect of the costs associated with raising a child, constitute pure economic loss, but in practice the courts have not drawn a sharp distinction
between these categories of loss in such cases: see *Greenfield v Irwin* [2001] EWCA Civ 113;
[2001] 1 W.L.R. 1279, applying *McFarlane v Tayside Health Board* [2000] 2 A.C. 59, HL.
[2] *Livingstone v Rawyards Coal Co* (1880) 5 App. Cas.25, 39. In torts actionable *per se*, such
as trespass to the person, a claimant could be awarded nominal damages where it is clear
that a tort has been committed but the claimant has suffered no loss. Similarly, in contract
nominal damages may be awarded where there has been a breach of contract but no loss. In
the tort of negligence damage is the gist of the action, and some substantive damage must be
proved for the action lie. These distinctions will rarely, if ever, be relevant to claims in respect
of personal injuries.

measure of damages in contract and tort in an action for personal injuries. In the case of non-pecuniary loss the principle of restoring the claimant to his pre-accident position is inappropriate. No amount of money can restore a lost limb or take away the claimant's experience of pain. Here the principle applied by the courts is that damages for non-pecuniary loss should be "fair" or "reasonable." This is patently unhelpful, because it simply begs the question of what is a fair or reasonable sum. The award is inevitably an arbitrary one. In practice, the courts adopt a tariff or "going rate" for specific types of injury in an attempt to achieve some degree of consistency between claimants with similar injuries and to provide a basis for the settlement of claims.

9–003   Inexact or unliquidated losses are compensated by an award of "general damages." In an action for personal injuries this includes the non-pecuniary losses which are compensated under the heads of pain and suffering, and loss of amenity. It also includes prospective pecuniary losses such as future loss of earnings and medical expenses. "Special damages" are the losses that are capable of being calculated with reasonable accuracy, and will normally consist of accrued pecuniary losses, such as loss of earnings and other expenses incurred from the date of the injury to the date of assessment. These distinctions are important for pleading and procedural purposes and for the purpose of determining the appropriate rate of interest, since different rates apply to special damages and general damages for non-pecuniary loss, and no interest will be awarded in respect of future pecuniary loss.[3] Although the court will assess damages under these broad heads, the court should also have regard to the appropriateness of the total award in order to avoid any overlapping of the different heads of damage, though it is doubtful whether there can be any overlap between pecuniary and non-pecuniary losses.[4]

9–004   Where damages are at large, that is where the award is not limited to the pecuniary loss that can be specifically proved,[5] the court may take into account the manner in which the tort was committed in assessing damages. If it was such as to injure the claimant's proper feelings of dignity and pride then aggravated damages may be awarded.[6] Aggravated damages are compensatory, but they are higher than would normally be the case to reflect the greater injury to the claimant.[7] In *Kralj v McGrath*[8] Woolf J. held that aggra-

---

[3] CPR 16PD para. 4.3 provides that a claimant in an action for personal injuries must attach to or serve with his particulars of claim a medical report about the personal injuries which he alleges in his claim. There must also be a schedule of details of any past and future expenses and losses which he claims: CPR 16PD para. 4.2. On the payment of interest see para. 9–025.

[4] *Lim Poh Choo v Camden and Islington Area Health Authority* [1980] A.C. 174, 191, 192; see also *Royal Commission on Civil Liability and Compensation for Personal Injury*, Cmnd. 7054 (1978), Vol. I, para. 759.

[5] *Rookes v Barnard* [1964] A.C. 1129, 1221. This includes loss of reputation, injured feelings, pain and suffering or loss of amenity: *Broome v Cassell & Co Ltd* [1972] A.C. 1027, 1073.

[6] *Jolliffe v Willmett & Co* [1971] 1 All E.R. 478—an "insolent and high-handed trespass" by a private investigator.

[7] The Law Commission has recommended that aggravated damages should be renamed "damages for mental distress" and that it should be made clear that such awards are compensatory. They are not intended to punish the defendant: Law Com. No. 247, *Aggravated, Exemplary and Restitutionary Damages*, 1997.

[8] [1986] 1 All E.R. 54.

vated damages should not be awarded in an action for negligence against a doctor, notwithstanding that the medical evidence indicated that the claimant's treatment had been "horrific." If, on the other hand, the particular treatment increased the claimant's pain and suffering this should be reflected in a higher award under this head. This approach was approved by the Court of Appeal in *A.B. v South West Water Services Ltd.*[9] Thus, in a case of personal injuries the measure of compensatory damages should include all the injuries that have been suffered, physically, psychologically and mentally, and to the extent that these effects have been exacerbated by distress and anxiety caused by the defendant's conduct, this will be reflected in the ordinary measure of compensatory damages. On the other hand, mere indignation and anger aroused by the defendant's conduct is not a proper subject for compensation, since it is neither pain nor suffering.[10]

In *Appleton v Garrett*[11] the defendant dentist had carried out large-scale, unnecessary treatment in order to increase his income. He deliberately, and in bad faith, withheld from the claimants the information that the treatment was unnecessary because he knew that they would not have consented to the treatment had they known the true position. The defendant was held liable in trespass to the person, and the Dyson J. took the view that there was contumelious conduct or motive on the part of the defendant, having deliberately caused pain and damage to his patients, taken advantage of their young age, and abused his position of trust. He had "wilfully damaged teeth on a massive scale". Dyson J. distinguished *A.B. v South West Water Services Ltd* on the basis that, first, the tort in that case was a negligently committed nuisance, whereas in *Appleton v Garrett* it was a case of trespass to the person. In *A.B. v South West Water* the Court of Appeal appeared to have accepted that indignation aroused by a defendant's conduct can increase the claimant's damages in defamation cases because "injury to the plaintiff's feelings and self-esteem is an important part of the damage for which compensation is awarded." There was no reason in principle, said Dyson J., why awards of aggravated damages should not be made for feelings of anger or indignation in other causes of action such as trespass to the person, where injury to feelings is an important part of the damage for which compensation is awarded: "To say that the law permits recovery of aggravated damages where the relevant conduct has caused injury to feelings, insult, indignity, humiliation and a heightened sense of injury or grievance, but not where it has caused anger or indignation, is very difficult to justify in terms of principle or common sense."[12] The observations of the Court of Appeal should be understood as being restricted to cases where injury to a claimant's feelings and self-esteem were not an important part of the damage for which compensation is awarded. Secondly, and in any event, in addition to feelings of anger and indignation, all the claimants had suffered mental distress and

9–005

[9] [1993] Q.B. 507.
[10] *ibid.* at 528, 532.
[11] [1996] P.I.Q.R. P1.
[12] *ibid.* at 7.

injury to their feelings, as well as a heightened sense of injury or grievance, when they learned that the treatment they had undergone was unnecessary. Assessing the aggravated damages on a "moderate basis" Dyson J. held that they should be assessed at 15 per cent of the sum awarded in each case for general damages for pain, suffering and loss of amenity.

9–006   It is submitted that, as a matter of principle, there is no reason why doctors should be specifically excluded from the ambit of aggravated damages, which are compensatory not punitive, although in practice it will be unlikely that mere negligence would be sufficient for such an award. In *Broome v Cassell & Co Ltd*[13] Lord Reid said that the commission of a tort in a malicious, insulting or oppressive manner may aggravate the claimant's injury. It is arguable that some forms of treatment could be regarded as oppressive or insulting: sterilisation of a competent adult without consent, for example.[14] In *Barbara v Home Office*[15] a remand prisoner was forcibly injected with a tranquillising drug by prison officers, and the defendants admitted liability for trespass to the person. The claimant was awarded £100 general damages and £500 aggravated damages, but a claim for exemplary damages was rejected. Mere negligence, it was said, did not justify an award of exemplary damages simply because it resulted in a trespass to the person which from the claimant's point of view could be regarded as oppressive.

9–007   Aggravated damages should be distinguished from exemplary damages. Exemplary damages are punitive in nature and are awarded in addition to compensatory damages in order to teach the defendant that "tort does not pay." English common law limits the circumstances in which exemplary damages may awarded to two categories of case, namely: (i) oppressive, arbitrary or unconstitutional action by servants of the government; and (ii) where the defendant's conduct has been calculated by him to make a profit for himself which may well exceed the compensation available.[16] In *A.B. v South West Water Services Ltd*[17] the Court of Appeal held that, in addition to these restrictions, exemplary damages should only be available in torts which were

---

[13] [1972] A.C. 1027, 1085.
[14] See para. 6–013. In *Devi v West Midlands Regional Health Authority* (1981, CA; unreported) compensatory damages of £4,000 were awarded in a case of non-consensual sterilisation, without any reference to aggravated damages. In *Muir v The Queen in right of Alberta* (1996) 132 D.L.R. (4th) 695 (Alberta Q.B.) the court awarded very substantial aggravated damages (of $125,000 in addition to $250,000 for pain and suffering) in respect of the claimant's unlawful sterilisation following her wrongful detention at the age of 10 in an institution for "mental defectives" (for which a further $250,000 compensatory award was made).
[15] (1984) 134 N.L.J. 888. A similar allegation failed on the facts in *Freeman v Home Office* [1984] Q.B. 524.
[16] *Rookes v Barnard* [1964] A.C. 1129; *Broome v Cassell & Co Ltd* [1972] A.C. 1027. What is required is knowledge by the defendant that what he proposes to do is against the law or a reckless disregard for whether it is legal or illegal. Carelessness alone, however extreme, is not enough: *John v Mirror Group Newspapers Ltd* [1997] Q.B. 586, 618 *per* Sir Thomas Bingham M.R. An attempt by the defendant to conceal the commission of a tort with the object of limiting the amount of damages payable to the claimant, though reprehensible, does not fall into the second category: *A.B. v South West Water Services Ltd* [1993] Q.B. 507, 526.
[17] [1993] Q.B. 507.

recognised before the decision in *Rookes v Barnard* as establishing a claim for exemplary damages. This effectively excluded such awards in actions for negligence, including medical negligence, although they are a feature in malpractice claims against doctors in some American and Commonwealth jurisdictions.[18] In *Kuddus v Chief Constable of Leicestershire Constabulary*,[19] however, the House of Lords held that this "cause of action" test was not good law (overruling *A.B. v South West Water* on this point). The question to be considered was the nature of the defendant's conduct and whether it fitted into Lord Devlin's categories in *Rookes v Barnard*, not the basis of the cause of action. Although the issue did not arise for decision in *Kuddus*, Lord Nicholls even suggested that the restrictions inherent in Lord Devlin's categories ought to be reconsidered.[20] With regard to the second category, the "key", said his Lordship, should be outrageous conduct on the part of the defendant. There was no obvious reason why, if exemplary damages were to be available "the profit motive should suffice but a malicious motive should not."[21] The Law Commission has recommended that the power to award exemplary damages should be retained, while being put on a more rational basis, with the test laid down in *Rookes v Barnard* being abolished.[22] This would open up the possibility of such awards in clinical negligence actions, though only in respect of conscious wrongdoing by a defendant which is outrageous, or where his disregard of the claimant's rights is contumelious. Clearly, this would be a rare case, although the facts of *Appleton v Garrett* might be thought to fall into such a category.

In *A v Bottrill*[23] the Privy Council considered the extent of the jurisdiction to award exemplary damages in New Zealand for negligent conduct. The case arose out of the "wholesale misreading of cervical smears" by the defendant pathologist. The defendant's false reporting rate was 50 per cent or higher. The majority of the Privy Council (in an opinion delivered by Lord Nicholls) considered that the rationale for exemplary damages was to punish

9–008

---

[18] See, e.g., *Backwell v AAA* [1997] 1 V.R. 182 (Vict. C.A.), where having inseminated the claimant with semen from a donor of an incompatible blood type, the defendant doctor persuaded the claimant to have a termination of the resulting pregnancy, contrary to her beliefs, by making false threats that if she had a miscarriage her identity might be revealed in the ensuing publicity, that this might force the donor insemination program to close, and that it might be difficult for the claimant to receive donor insemination in the future. See also the discussion by Lord Nicholls in *A v Bottrill* [2002] UKPC 44; [2003] 1 A.C. 449 at [41] to [49].

[19] [2001] UKHL 29; [2002] 2 A.C. 122.

[20] *ibid.* at [66]: "Whatever may have been the position 40 years ago, I am respectfully inclined to doubt the soundness of this distinction today. National and international companies can exercise enormous power. So do some individuals. I am not sure it would be right to draw a hard-and-fast line which would always exclude such companies and persons from the reach of exemplary damages. Indeed, the validity of the dividing line drawn by Lord Devlin when formulating his first category is somewhat undermined by his second category, where the defendants are not confined to, and normally would not be, government officials or the like."

[21] *ibid.* at [67].

[22] Law Com. No. 247, *Aggravated, Exemplary and Restitutionary Damages*, 1997, para. 5.41: "there appears to be no sound reason why outrageously wrongful conduct should not attract a punitive award even if it is not committed by a servant of the government."

[23] [2002] UKPC 44; [2003] 1 A.C. 449; Manning (2003) 119 L.Q.R. 24.

the defendant for his outrageous conduct, to mark the court's disapproval of such conduct and to deter him from repeating it.[24] Thus, in principle a court's jurisdiction to award exemplary damages should extend to all cases of tortious wrongdoing where the defendant's conduct satisfied the criterion of outrageousness, because otherwise some types of outrageous conduct would fall within the jurisdiction and others would not.[25] Cases satisfying the test of outrageousness would usually involve intentional wrongdoing with, additionally, an element of flagrancy or cynicism or oppression; something additional, rendering the wrongdoing or the manner or circumstances in which it was committed particularly appalling. These were the features rendering the defendant's conduct outrageous. Overwhelmingly, in cases of negligence, an award of exemplary damages would be appropriate only where the defendant's wrongdoing was intentional or consciously reckless.[26] There could be rare cases, however, where "the defendant departed so far and so flagrantly from the dictates of ordinary or professional precepts of prudence, or standards of care, that his conduct satisfies this test even though he was not consciously reckless."[27] The ultimate touchstone was the outrageous conduct of the defendant which called for punishment. Thus, under the common law of New Zealand the court's jurisdiction to award exemplary damages in cases of negligence was not confined to cases where the defendant intended to cause the harm or was consciously reckless as to the risks involved.[28] The different views on exemplary damages evident in the House of Lords in *Kuddus v Chief Constable of Leicestershire Constabulary* and the difference of opinion in the Privy Council in *A v Bottrill*[29] suggest that there is an ongoing debate at the highest judicial level as to the future role of exemplary damages. Lord Nicholls, for example, would seem to favour the Law Commission's position that the restrictive test laid down in *Rookes v Barnard* should be abolished.[30] It had already established in New Zealand that exemplary damages could be available in an action for negligence.[31] The

---

[24] Citing Lord Devlin in *Rookes v Barnard* [1964] A.C. 1129, 1228.

[25] [2002] UKPC 44; [2003] 1 A.C. 449 at [22].

[26] *ibid.* at [24].

[27] *ibid.* at [26].

[28] *ibid.* at [63]. Though cases where it was appropriate to make an award of exemplary damages in the absence of intentional wrongdoing or conscious recklessness would be "exceptional and rare indeed." *ibid.* at [64].

[29] Lord Hutton and Lord Millett dissented on the basis that exemplary damages should only be awarded in cases where the defendant was subjectively aware of the risk to which his conduct exposed the claimant and deliberately or recklessly took that risk. *ibid.* at [73].

[30] His Lordship commented in *A v Bottrill* [2002] UKPC 44 at [41] that: "Their Lordships also consider that past experience, as expressed in observations or decisions of the higher courts in New Zealand and elsewhere in the common law world, supports the broader approach. Leaving aside England, still toiling in the chains of *Rookes v Barnard* [1964] A.C. 1129, courts in common law countries have remained true to the underlying rationale of the exemplary damages jurisdiction."

[31] New Zealand, of course, has a no-fault accident compensation scheme for persons who suffer personal injury by accident, and someone who qualifies for compensation under the statutory scheme has no claim for damages at common law for personal injuries arising out of the accident. This bar to action does not, however, preclude a claim for exemplary damages: *Donselaar v Donselaar* [1982] 1 N.Z.L.R. 97 (N.Z.C.A.).

significance of *A v Bottrill* for English law lies in the marker it lays down for potential future developments.

(2) Lump sum awards

The claimant can only bring one action in respect of a single tort. He cannot bring a second action based on the same facts simply because the damage turns out to be more extensive than was first anticipated.[32] Damages are normally assessed once-and-for-all and will be awarded in the form of a lump sum, both for accrued and prospective losses. The court currently has no power to require a defendant to make periodical payments nor to review the award at a later date if the estimate of the claimant's loss turns out to be either too low or too high.[33] A limited exception may apply where there is evidence of a change of circumstances after the trial of an action, but before an appeal. In these circumstances the Court of Appeal may admit the new evidence to mitigate the consequences of the lump sum system.[34] As a general

9–009

---

[32] *Fetter v Beale* (1701) 1 Ld Raym. 339, 692; *Bristow v Grout*, *The Times*, November 9, 1987, CA; *cf. Brunsden v Humphrey* (1884) 14 QBD 141 where the claimant was held to be entitled to bring two separate actions in respect of damage to property and personal injuries arising out of the same events, because they are two distinct rights. There cannot be two actions, however, for two separate forms of personal injury arising from a single negligent act, even where one of the injuries only comes to light after damages for the first injury have been recovered: see *Bristow v Grout*, *The Times*, November 9, 1987. In *Talbot v Berkshire County Council* [1994] Q.B. 290 Stuart-Smith L.J. said that *Brunsden v Humphrey* might have been decided differently if *Henderson v Henderson* (1843) 3 Hare 100, applying the doctrine of *res judicata*, had been cited. In *Crawford v Dally and Royal Marsden Hospital* [1995] 6 Med. L.R. 343, QBD, the claimant issued a counterclaim to an action for payment of fees in respect of private medical treatment, alleging negligence in the treatment, but limited to the further medical expenses arising out of the treatment. A subsequent claim in respect of the serious personal injury allegedly caused by the original treatment was barred by the principle of *res judicata*, applying *Talbot*. The rule can produce real injustice, however, as in *Wain v F. Sherwood and Sons Transport Ltd* [1999] P.I.Q.R. P159 where the Court of Appeal held that it applied even where the claimant had not advanced an earlier claim due the negligence of his lawyer, but due to the advocate's immunity from suit (subsequently abolished) the claimant had no redress for that negligence. In *Johnson v Gore Wood & Co (a firm)* [2002] 2 A.C. 1 the House of Lords held that *Henderson* should not be rigidly applied. The court should take a broad, merits-based approach which takes account of all the facts of the case and focuses on whether, in bringing a claim or raising a defence in later proceedings, a party is misusing or abusing the process of the court. See *Toth v Ledger* [2002] P.I.Q.R. P1, CA, where a claim for bereavement damages under the Fatal Accidents Act 1976 was settled, but the claimant was entitled to continue with his common law claim for psychiatric damage. For comment on *Johnson v Gore Wood* see Watt (2001) 20 C.J.Q. 90.

[33] *Fournier v Canadian National Railway* [1927] A.C. 167, 169; *British Transport Commission v Gourley* [1956] A.C. 185, 212; *Burke v Tower Hamlets Health Authority*, *The Times*, August 10, 1989. In *Wells v Wells* [1999] 1 A.C. 345, 384 Lord Steyn said that the court ought to be given the power, of its own motion, to make an award of periodical payments in appropriate cases, but this power could only be introduced by Parliament.

[34] *Mulholland v Mitchell* [1971] A.C. 666; *Lim Poh Choo v Camden and Islington Area Health Authority* [1980] A.C. 174. In *Lim* Lord Scarman described this exception as "an unsatisfactory makeshift, and of dubious value in any case where the new facts are themselves in issue." The Court may permit a party to argue a point that was not raised at trial where there has been a change in the law in the interim: see *e.g. McCamley v Cammell Laird Shipbuilders Ltd* [1990] 1 All E.R. 854, 864. CPR r. 52.11 is less stringent than RSC, Ord. 59, which it replaced, because the former reference to "special grounds" for admitting new evidence is

rule, however, once the time limit for an appeal has expired an appeal out of time on the basis of changed circumstances will not be permitted.[35]

9–010   When assessing damages the court will make an estimate of the chances that a particular event will or would have happened, and reflect those chances in the amount of damages awarded, irrespective of whether the chance was more or less than even.[36] The question is whether the chance is substantial. If it is a mere possibility or speculative it must be ignored, although the question of whether the chance is substantial or speculative should be decided without regard to legal niceties, but on a consideration of all the facts in proper perspective.[37]

9–011   The rule that damages may only be awarded as a lump sum causes particular problems in cases of serious personal injuries, especially where the medical prognosis is uncertain, because the court has to assess damages based on assumptions about what will happen to the claimant in the future which may well turn out to be incorrect. The claimant's condition may become worse than could have been anticipated at the trial or it may improve. He may live longer than the predicted life expectancy and the damages may be inadequate or he may die sooner, with the result that the damages will not be used for their intended purpose and will result in a windfall for the beneficiaries of his estate. As Lord Scarman commented in *Lim Poh Choo v Camden and Islington Area Health Authority*:

> "Knowledge of the future being denied to mankind, so much of the award as is attributed to future loss and suffering will almost surely be wrong. There is really only one certainty: the future will prove the award to be either too high or too low."[38]

9–012   In March 2002 the Lord Chancellor's Department issued a consultation paper on the question of whether the courts should be given the power to order periodical payments for future loss and care costs in personal injury cases.[39] The responses to that paper indicated that there was widespread support for promoting the use of periodical payments to compensate for future loss and care costs, and the majority of respondents agreed that the courts should have the power to order periodical payments without consent.[40] The government stated that it would introduce legislation on the

---

(n.34 contd.) omitted, but the principle remains that fresh evidence will not normally be received: *Briody v St Helens and Knowsley Area Health Authority* [2001] EWCA Civ 1010; [2002] Q.B. 856 *per* Judge L.J. at [47]. The principles of *Ladd v Marshall* [1954] 1 W.L.R. 1489 continue to apply under the Civil Procedure Rules: *ibid.* at [50] *per* Judge L.J.

[35]   The time limits for filing a notice of appeal are very short. See CPR, r. 52.4. The grounds for granting an extension of time in which to appeal are set out in CPR, r. 3.9, on which see *Sayers v Clarke Walker (a firm)* [2002] EWCA Civ 645; [2002] 1 W.L.R. 3095.

[36]   *Mallett v McMonagle* [1970] A.C. 166, 176, *per* Lord Diplock.

[37]   *Davies v Taylor* [1974] A.C. 207, 212, *per* Lord Reid.

[38]   [1980] A.C. 174, 183.

[39]   LCD, *Damages for Future Loss*, CP 01/02 [available at *www.lcd.gov.uk/consult/general/periodpay.htm*].

[40]   LCD, *Responses to Consultation on Damages for Future Loss*, CP (R) 01/02, November 2002.

matter. Clause 92 of the Courts Bill will amend the Damages Act 1996 to provide that a court awarding damages for future pecuniary loss in respect of personal injury may order that the damages are wholly or partly to take the form of periodical payments, and that a court awarding other damages in respect of personal injury may, if the parties consent, order that the damages are wholly or partly to take the form of periodical payments. When enacted this provision will constitute a radical change to the common law's approach to the assessment of future losses, and should go some way towards removing the uncertainties involved in calculating future loss claims.

There are currently three mechanisms by which some of the problems caused by awarding damages only in the form of a lump sum can be ameliorated, though not removed entirely. These are: the possibility of claiming provisional damages; separate trials on liability and quantum; and the possibility of the parties agreeing to the compensation being paid in the form of a structured settlement.   9–013

(a) Provisional damages

Section 32A of the Supreme Court Act 1981 introduced a procedure for the award of provisional damages in cases where there is a "chance" that as a result of the tort the claimant will develop some serious disease or suffer some serious deterioration in his condition. In such cases the claimant may be awarded provisional damages assessed on the basis that the disease or deterioration will not occur. If the event subsequently materialises the claimant can then make an application for further damages in order to compensate for the loss that has now occurred. This procedure should produce assessments of damages which more accurately reflect the loss that the claimant has sustained, since he will not be compensated for a risk that may never materialise, and moreover, if the risk does materialise the claimant will receive fuller compensation, instead of damages heavily discounted under the lump sum system on the basis that there is only a small risk that the loss may occur.   9–014

Under CPR Part 41 a claim for provisional damages must be pleaded by the claimant,[41] and when making an order the court must specify the disease or type of deterioration which will entitle the claimant to make a further application for damages, and the period of time within which the second application should be made.[42] The claimant must apply for further damages   9–015

---

[41] See CPR, r. 16.4(1)(d). The information that must be included in the particulars of claim is specified in CPR 16PD para. 4.4.

[42] CPR, Part 41, r. 2(2). The claimant may make more than one application to extend the period within which the application for further damages must be made: r. 2(3). The court may also order that there should be no limit of time within which the application must be made, where there is no medical or other scientific evidence upon which any limit could sensibly be based: *Thurman v Wiltshire and Bath Health Authority* [1997] P.I.Q.R. Q115, where the order concerned the recurrence of cancer secondary to cancer of the cervix; *A v National Blood Authority* [2001] 3 All E.R. 289 at [211], where Burton J. ordered that the duration of the period within which claimants in the "Hepatitis C litigation" could make an application should be the life of each claimant.

within the specified period, giving the defendant 28 days' notice of intention to apply, and only one application for further damages can be made.[43]

9–016   Provisional damages are not appropriate in all, or even most, cases.[44] Since the disease or type of injury for which the claimant is entitled to seek further damages must be specified when the claimant applies for provisional damages, the procedure does not cover a general deterioration in the claimant's condition, nor an unforeseen complication. The term "chance" can cover a wide range between something that is *de minimis* and something that is a probability, but it must be measurable rather than fanciful. Provided the chance is measurable it can fall within the procedure for provisional damages, however slim the chance may be.[45] "Serious deterioration" in the claimant's condition means "something beyond ordinary deterioration" and this is a question of fact depending on the circumstances of the case, including the effect of the deterioration on the claimant.[46]

9–017   "Chance" cases must be distinguished from cases where the medical evidence can forecast with a reasonable degree of certainty that the claimant's condition will deteriorate causing a reasonably probable degree of disability. A typical example of this situation occurs where it is possible to predict that over the years arthritis is likely to develop in a damaged joint. Here damages should be assessed on the single lump sum basis, discounting the award for the chance that arthritis will not occur. In *Willson v Ministry of Defence*[47] it was held that the development of arthritis to the point at which surgery is required, or which requires the claimant to change his employment, did not fall within the definition of serious deterioration, rather it was "simply an aspect of a progression of this particular disease." Similarly, the chance that due to a disabling injury the claimant may sustain a further injury, even if that injury could be severe, did not call for provisional damages. The risk of a serious injury was not to be equated with a serious deterioration in the claimant's physical condition.

9–018   Provisional damages are limited to cases where there is a clear-cut event, or events,[48] which will trigger an entitlement to further compensation, *i.e.* cases where there would be little room for later dispute whether or not the contemplated deterioration had actually occurred.[49] The claimant still has to

---

[43] CPR, Part 41, r. 3. Though if there is more than one event or trigger identified in the order, there can be an application in respect of each trigger event that occurs: *A v National Blood Authority* [2001] 3 All E.R. 289 at [211].

[44] An award of provisional damages is discretionary. The court will weigh up the possibility of doing justice by a once-and-for-all assessment against the possibility of doing better justice by reserving the claimant's right to return at a future date: *Willson v Ministry of Defence* [1991] 1 All E.R. 638, 645. Lewis (1997) 60 M.L.R. 230, 237 describes provisional damages as a "backwater of personal injury litigation" because they are so rarely used.

[45] *Willson v Ministry of Defence* [1991] 1 All E.R. 638, 642, *per* Scott Baker J.

[46] *ibid.*

[47] *ibid.* at 642 and 643.

[48] In *A v National Blood Authority* [2001] 3 All E.R. 289 at [211] Burton J. specified five possible "triggers", any one of which would entitle a claimant to make an application for further damages.

[49] *Willson v Ministry of Defence* [1991] 1 All E.R. 638 at 644; *Patterson v Ministry of Defence* [1987] C.L.Y. 1194. Thus, they are appropriate for cases with "a clear and severable risk

establish causation, of course, when making the application for further damages, *i.e.* that the damage of which he now complains is causally linked to the defendant's tort. But where a defendant had agreed to "an award of immediate damages on a full liability basis" and also agreed that "damages which may fall to be assessed in the future under the terms of the Order [for provisional damages], shall also fall to be assessed on the same basis as the immediate award" the effect was that it was not open to the defendant to argue that it was not his breach of duty which caused the damage.[50] Thus, defendants must be careful about the terms of any agreement when settling orders for provisional damages.

It was previously the case that where a claimant had received an award of provisional damages to reflect the chance that his condition might deteriorate, but the claimant subsequently died as a result of that deterioration, his dependants could not bring an action for their loss of financial dependency under the Fatal Accidents Act 1976 (because a claim under that Act requires that the deceased had a subsisting claim against the defendant at the time of death). There was no mechanism for granting a declaration, as part of the claim for provisional damages, that the claimant's surviving dependants should be entitled to claim under the Fatal Accidents Act 1976 if he should subsequently die.[51] Now, section 3 of the Damages Act 1996 provides that an award of provisional damages to a claimant shall not operate as a bar to an action in respect of that person's death under the Fatal Accidents Act 1976 where the claimant subsequently dies as a result of the act or omission which gave rise to the cause of action for which the damages were awarded. If the deceased had received any damages in respect of pecuniary loss which, in the event, falls after his death, this must be taken into account in assessing the loss of dependency claim under the Fatal Accidents Act.

9–019

In *Molinari v Ministry of Defence*[52] the claimant was suffering from leukaemia, and the question arose whether provisional damages should be awarded on the basis of the risk of a relapse in his medical condition, in circumstances where there was a substantial chance that if a relapse were to occur the claimant would die. The procedure for awarding provisional damages appears to assume that a deterioration in the claimant's condition could only result in an increase in the global damages recoverable by him;

9–020

(n.49 contd.) rather than a continuing deterioration, as is the typical osteoarthritic picture": *ibid.* at 644; *Allott v Central Electricity Generating Board* (1988, QBD; unreported). The fact that there is disagreement in the medical evidence, however, about the risk of the claimant contracting cancer in the future does not preclude the court from making an award of provisional damages: *Hurditch v Sheffield Health Authority* [1989] 2 All E.R. 869.

[50] *Green v Vickers Defence Systems Ltd* [2002] EWCA Civ 904; *The Times*, July 1, 2002. Provided that the claimant established that he had developed a condition specified in the Order, it was irrelevant that he could not prove which of several defendants had exposed him to the relevant asbestos. The specific point on which the defendants were seeking to rely in this case (concerning the development of mesothelioma after exposure to asbestos by multiple defendants) is no longer open, following the ruling of the House of Lords in *Fairchild v Glenhaven Funeral Services Ltd* [2002] UKHL 22; [2003] 1 A.C. 32, paras 5–027 et seq.

[51] *Middleton v Elliott Turbomachinery Ltd*, *The Independent*, November 16, 1990 CA.

[52] [1994] P.I.Q.R. Q33, QBD.

but this may not be the case where the deterioration leads to death. In an extreme case, said the judge, where there was a risk of a deterioration leading to a decrease in the loss, the proper course might be for the court to refuse to award provisional damages on the ground that the potential injustice to the defendants far outweighed the potential injustice to the claimant of a traditional award. On the facts, however, it was held that provisional damages should be awarded, since any injustice to the defendants of making a provisional award was more than outweighed by the potential injustice to the claimant of making a lump-sum award on the traditional basis.

9–021   In *A v The National Blood Authority and Others (Hepatitis C Litigation)*[53] Burton J. considered that it was not clear that the undergoing of treatment in the future, and the consequential damage that might ensue, fell within the court's jurisdiction to make an order for provisional damages under section 32A of the Supreme Court Act 1981. But in any event, the court's wide case-management powers under the Civil Procedure Rules were such that the court could make an order under CPR r. 3.1(2) for the separate trial of any issue of damages arising out of future treatment, and adjourn the trial of such issue generally. This effectively creates an alternative procedure akin to that for provisional damages, but without the specific restrictions that section 32A and CPR Part 41 impose.

(b) Split trial and interim payments

9–022   The Civil Procedure Rules provide for separate trials on liability and damages, so that the assessment of damages can be made at a later date when the medical prognosis is more certain.[54] The court may at any stage of the proceedings, and of its own motion, direct a separate trial of any issue. This procedure is of value where the claimant's medical condition is unstable and needs time to settle, and it may be particularly useful in the case of young children where it may be very difficult to assess the extent of the long-term disability when the child is still developing. The procedure can be combined with the power to seek an interim payment to meet the claimant's immediate needs, which is then deducted from the final award.[55] An interim payment can be obtained where the defendant has admitted liability, or the claimant has obtained judgment for damages to be assessed, or if the claim went to trial, the claimant would obtain judgment for a substantial amount of money against the defendant from whom he is seeking the interim payment, provided that (in a claim for personal injuries) the defendant is insured against liability to the claimant, or is a public authority.[56]

---

[53] [2002] Lloyd's Rep. Med. 487.
[54] CPR, Pt 3, r. 3.1(2)(i).
[55] CPR, Pt 25, rr. 25.6 to 25.9 and PD25. On the court's exercise of discretion as to whether to order an interim payment and the effect on the ultimate assessment of quantum see *Campbell v Mylchreest* [1999] P.I.Q.R. Q17, CA.
[56] CPR, Pt 25, r. 25.7. See John (1992) 3 *AVMA Medical & Legal Journal* (No. 1) p. 10 on the advantages of split trials.

(c) Structured settlements

A structured settlement allows the claimant to take the award of damages in the form of periodic payments. This is a private arrangement between the claimant and the defendant's liability insurer under which the normal lump sum damages award can be varied or "structured" over a period of time.[57] The settlement may include a lump sum element plus periodic payments intended to meet the claimant's future losses. The payments can be for a fixed period or until the claimant's death, and they can be index-linked. The payments are financed by the purchase of an annuity by the liability insurer with the money, or part of it, that would have been paid to the claimant as a lump sum. The annuity is held by the insurer on behalf of the claimant and the payments are not taxable as income in the claimant's hands.[58] Moreover, the insurer is not liable to tax on the annuity either. The result is that for large awards, where the tax liability on the income generated by investment of the lump sum damages would be high, the value of the arrangement to both claimant and insurer is substantially greater than the traditional lump sum award.[59] The possibility of index-linking also addresses the problem of inflation eroding the value of the award, though it cannot eliminate this problem entirely when certain costs (such as the cost of care) may increase at a higher rate than the chosen index.

9–023

Structured settlements are advantageous to some claimants who have sustained serious personal injury and who will have a substantial claim for future pecuniary loss.[60] They do not, however, constitute the form of periodic payments recommended by the Pearson Commission in order to remove some of the uncertainties in assessing future pecuniary losses.[61] They depend

9–024

---

[57] For a statutory definition of a structured settlement see the Damages Act 1996, s.5; on the Damages Act 1996 see Lewis (1997) 60 M.L.R. 230, 235. See further Law Commission Report, *Structured Settlements and Interim and Provisional Damages*, Law Com. No. 224, (1994); Ashcroft [1995] J.P.I.L. 3; Redmond-Cooper [1995] J.P.I.L. 12. For a detailed analysis of this subject see R. Lewis, *Structured Settlements: The Law and Practice*, Sweet & Maxwell, (1993) and the Report of the Master of the Rolls' Working Party, *Structured Settlements*, August 2002.

[58] See the Income and Corporation Taxes Act 1988, ss.329AA, 329AB, added by the Finance Act 1996, s.150. Such payments are treated as income, however, for the purpose of entitlement to income support: *Beattie v Secretary of State for Social Security* [2001] Lloyd's Rep. Med. 297, CA. But see now the Social Security Amendment (Personal Injury Payments) Regulations 2002, S.I. 2002 No. 2442, considered at para. 9–035 below.

[59] The sum awarded under a structured settlement should be smaller than with a straightforward payment of a lump sum, since there are tax savings which result in the same benefits accruing to the claimant: *Kelly v Dawes*, *The Times*, September 27, 1990. The discount tends to range between eight and 15%, though it can be higher or lower than this: see *Grimsley v Grimsley and Meade* (1991; unreported) discussed by Lewis (1993) 143 N.L.J. 772.

[60] Of course, there are also advantages for defendants. For a helpful discussion of structured settlements in the context of medical negligence claims see: Lewis (1993) 56 M.L.R. 844; and R. Lewis, *Structured Settlements: The Law and Practice*, Sweet & Maxwell, (1993), Ch. 16. There are significant differences in structured settlements in the context of NHS clinical negligence claims because there is no liability insurer involved, and it is possible to structure a settlement without purchasing an annuity from a life insurer.

[61] *Royal Commission on Civil Liability and Compensation for Personal Injury*, Cmnd. 7054 (1978), Vol. I, para. 573; *cf.* Law Com. No. 56, HC 373, 1973, para. 28 rejecting the introduction of periodical payments.

upon agreement between the parties; the court currently has no power to order a defendant to accept this form of settlement[62] (although this will change when the Damages Act 1996 is amended by the Courts Bill, clause 92). It is still necessary to estimate what the lump sum award would be, applying the normal principles, before setting up a structured settled settlement, if only to advise the client whether the arrangement is appropriate in the circumstances. The periodic payments are only varied over time in accordance with the terms agreed at the outset; they cannot take account of unanticipated events which affect the claimant's future pecuniary expenditure (though, again, this may change in the future).

(3) Interest

9–025 Where damages for personal injuries or death exceeding £200 are awarded the court must award interest unless there are special reasons for not doing so.[63] In the case of special damages for accrued pecuniary loss interest will normally be awarded at half the special investment rate on money paid into court, running from the date of the accident to the date of trial, the reasoning being that part of the loss will have occurred immediately after the tort and part immediately before the assessment.[64] Interest at half the rate is a compromise. If, however, there are special circumstances which would make it unfair to apply this rule it may be possible to obtain interest at the full rate on certain items of special damage which have been incurred shortly after the accident.[65] Where the defendant has failed to beat a CPR Part 36 offer, interest may be awarded at an enhanced rate.[66] No deduction is made to allow for the receipt of social security benefits by the

[62] *Burke v Tower Hamlets Health Authority, The Times*, August 10, 1989; Damages Act 1996, s.2. The refusal of a public body to agree to a structured settlement is not amenable to judicial review: *R (on the application of Hopley) v Liverpool Health Authority* [2002] EWHC 1723; [2002] Lloyd's Rep. Med. 494; [2003] P.I.Q.R. P143, where Pitchford J. held that the Health Authority, though a public body, was exercising a private law function when settling a claim for medical negligence. The process did not involve any public law duty owed to the claimant. In any event, the decision to refuse to enter into a "with profits" structured settlement (as opposed to an RPI linked structured settlement, backed by index-linked government securities) was not *Wednesbury* unreasonable, having regard to the potential financial implications for the NHS. See Lewis (2003) 19 P.N. 297.
[63] Supreme Court Act 1981, s.35A; County Courts Act 1984, s.69. A claim for interest must be specifically pleaded: CPR Part 16.4. The interest is not taxed as income: Income and Corporation Taxes Act 1988, s.329.
[64] *Jefford v Gee* [1970] 2 Q.B. 130, 146; *Cookson v Knowles* [1979] A.C. 556. In the case of a split trial in a personal injuries action, where liability is agreed or determined first with damages to be assessed later, interest on the damages awarded under s.17 of the Judgments Act 1838 will run from the date of judgment on damages and not from the date of judgment on liability: *Thomas v Bunn* [1991] 1 All E.R. 193, HL.
[65] *Ichard v Frangoulis* [1977] 1 W.L.R. 556. Private medical fees are one possible example: see *Dexter v Courtalds Ltd* [1984] 1 All E.R. 70, 73. In the "generality of personal injury cases," however, the principles laid down in *Jefford v Gee* [1970] 2 Q.B. 130 should be applied: *ibid.* at 74, *per* Lawton L.J. A claim for the full rate of interest must be pleaded.
[66] For discussion of the principles to be applied to the assessment of this enhanced rate, see *Petrotrade Inc. v Texaco Ltd* [2001] 4 All E.R. 853, CA.

claimant.[67] Interest is not awarded on future pecuniary loss, such as prospective loss of earnings or medical expenses, because the loss has not yet accrued.[68]

Interest on damages for non-pecuniary loss (pain and suffering and loss of amenity) is awarded at a modest rate, currently 2 per cent, for the period from the date of service of the claim form to the date of trial.[69] This low rate is attributable to the fact that a large proportion of nominal interest rates is represented by inflation, and inflation is taken into account when the court assesses the damages for non-pecuniary loss by a general uprating of the tariffs or bands applied to different types of injury.[70] Interest at 2 per cent represents an approximate real rate of return for the claimant not having the use of his money.[71] The fact that interest runs from the date of service of the claim form provides a very good reason for both issuing and serving a claim form early, even where negotiations are proceeding, since interest can amount to a substantial sum (notwithstanding the low interest rate) where the award of damages for non-pecuniary loss is likely to be high and the delay between initiating a claim and trial is likely to be lengthy, which may well be the case in a medical negligence action. Moreover, where the claimant has delayed in bringing a claim to trial the judge has a discretion to disallow interest on pre-trial damages.[72] Prompt issue and service of the claim form also avoids problems with limitation periods and the time-limits for service.

9–026

(4) Mitigation of damage

The claimant is under a duty to mitigate the damage caused by the defendant's tort, although he commits no wrong against the defendant if he fails

9–027

---

[67] *Wisely v John Fulton (Plumbers) Ltd* [2000] 1 W.L.R. 820—thus, recoverable social security benefits should not be deducted from damages for loss of earnings when calculating interest; see also *Davies v Inman* [1999] P.I.Q.R. Q26, CA—claimant entitled to interest on his loss of earnings even though his employer continued to pay him, the claimant having undertaken to repay the employer from any damages he received.

[68] *Cookson v Knowles* [1979] A.C. 556; *Joyce v Yeomans* [1981] 1 W.L.R. 549.

[69] *Birkett v Hayes* [1982] 2 All E.R. 710; [1982] 1 W.L.R. 816; *Wright v British Railways Board* [1983] 2 A.C. 773. Personal injury cases seem to be in a special category, since interest on damages for non-pecuniary loss will not be awarded in actions for deceit or false imprisonment: *Saunders v Edwards* [1987] 2 All E.R. 651; *Holtham v Commissioner of Police of the Metropolis, The Times*, November 28, 1987.

[70] It is arguable that this low rate should not apply to damages for bereavement under the Fatal Accidents Act 1976, s.1A (see para. 9–106), because the amount of the award is fixed by statute and does not increase when tariffs are uprated: see *Prior v Bernard Hastie & Co* [1987] C.L.Y. 1219; *Sharman v Sheppard* [1989] C.L.Y. 1190.

[71] It was arguable that the rate should be increased to 3% in the light of the decision of the House of Lords in *Wells v Wells* [1999] 1 A.C. 345—see the comments of Lord Lloyd on *Wright v British Railways Board* at 371–372; *Burns v Davies* [1999] Lloyd's Rep. Med. 215, 217 where Connell J. applied a rate of 3%; *cf. Lawrence v Chief Constable of Staffordshire* [2000] P.I.Q.R. Q349, where the Court of Appeal said that there was no reason to depart from the 2% rate, a view which is more in tune with current low levels of general interest rates.

[72] *Birkett v Hayes* [1982] 2 All E.R. 710, 717; [1982] 1 W.L.R. 816; *Spittle v Bunney* [1988] 1 W.L.R. 847; [1988] 3 All E.R. 1031; *Corbett v Barking Havering and Brentwood Health Authority* [1991] 2 Q.B. 408; *Read v Harries* [1995] P.I.Q.R. Q34.

to do so.[73] If he has lost his job as a result of the injury he should seek alternative employment, if he is capable of working. If he takes a lower paid job he can only recover from the defendant the difference between his previous earnings and his present earnings. The claimant should also seek medical attention which will improve his medical condition, although he will not be required to undergo a medical procedure where there is a substantial risk of further injury or the outcome is uncertain. The test is whether in all the circumstances, including particularly the medical advice received, the claimant acted reasonably in refusing the treatment.[74] Where the medical advice is conflicting, or the treatment involves some risk and the doctors prefer to leave the final decision to the claimant, a refusal of treatment will be considered to be reasonable.[75] The burden of proving that the claimant acted unreasonably in failing to mitigate the loss is the defendant's.[76]

9–028   If the claimant has acted unreasonably in refusing medical treatment a question arises as to how damages should be assessed where the treatment cannot guarantee an improvement in the claimant's condition. In *Janiak v Ippolito*[77] the mitigating operation which the claimant had unreasonably refused to undergo had a 70 per cent chance of success. The Supreme Court of Canada held that, rather than assuming (on the basis of the balance of probabilities) that the operation would succeed, the 30 per cent chance of

---

[73] *Darbishire v Warran* [1963] 1 W.L.R. 1067, 1075.

[74] *Selvanayagam v University of West Indies* [1983] 1 All E.R. 824, 827; [1983] 1 W.L.R. 585, PC; *Marcroft v Scruttons Ltd* [1954] 1 Lloyd's Rep. 395; *McAuley v London Transport Executive* [1957] 2 Lloyd's Rep. 500; *cf.* the more subjective approach of the Australian courts in *Glavonjic v Foster* [1979] V.R. 536 and *Karabotsos v Plastex Industries Pty Ltd* [1981] V.R. 675 where the test was said to be whether a reasonable man in the claimant's particular circumstances and subject to the various factors that affected the claimant, would have refused the treatment; see further Hudson (1983) 3 L.S. 50. In *Marcroft v Scruttons Ltd* [1954] 1 Lloyd's Rep. 395 the Court of Appeal clearly had some sympathy for the claimant's subjective response to the recommended treatment, which was electro-convulsive therapy, but nonetheless applied an objective test.

[75] *Savage v T. Wallis Ltd* [1966] 1 Lloyd's Rep. 357; *McAuley v London Tranpsort Executive* [1957] 2 Lloyd's Rep. 500, 505; *Selvanayagam v University of West Indies* [1983] 1 All E.R. 824; [1983] 1 W.L.R. 585. There is no obligation upon a claimant who has become pregnant following a negligently performed sterilisation operation to undergo an abortion to mitigate the loss: *Emeh v Kensington and Chelsea Area Health Authority* [1985] Q.B. 1012; *McFarlane v Tayside Health Board* [2000] 2 A.C. 59 at 81, 105, 112–113; para. 5–090 to 5–092. See also *Richardson v LRC Products Ltd* [2000] P.I.Q.R. P164, 173; [2000] Lloyd's Rep. Med. 280, 286—a claimant's failure to seek advice about the "morning after pill" to avoid conception following the discovery that a condom had "failed" during sexual intercourse could amount to a failure to mitigate the damage or an intervening cause.

[76] *Steele v Robert George & Co (1937) Ltd* [1942] A.C. 497; *Richardson v Redpath, Brown & Co Ltd* [1944] A.C. 62, HL. A dictum to the contrary effect in *Selvanayagam v University of West Indies* [1983] 1 All E.R. 824; [1983] 1 W.L.R. 585 would seem to be incorrect (see McGregor (1983) 46 M.L.R. 758; Kemp (1983) 99 L.Q.R. 497) a view which has now been accepted by the Privy Council: *Geest plc v Lansiquot* [2002] UKPC 48; [2002] 1 W.L.R. 3111; [2002] Lloyd's Rep. Med. 482 at [14]. If the defendant intends to contend that a claimant has failed to act reasonably to mitigate his damage, notice must be clearly given to the claimant long enough before the hearing to enable the claimant to prepare to meet it: *ibid.* at [16].

[77] (1985) 16 D.L.R. (4th) 1 (S.C.C.); affirming (1981) 126 D.L.R. (3d) 623 (Ont. C.A.). The same principles apply to the claimant's refusal to take medical tests: *Engel v Kamppelle Holdings Ltd* [1993] 2 W.W.R. 373 (S.C.C.).

the operation failing to alleviate the claimant's condition should be taken into account in assessing damages for prospective loss of earnings. It is unclear how the English courts would approach this problem because, although an action for the loss of a less than 50 per cent chance of a successful medical outcome is unlikely to be accepted,[78] the courts have no difficulty in taking into account even small chances of future events when assessing damages. It is suggested that the chance of the treatment failing to achieve its purpose should be taken into account, particularly since it may well be this factor which persuades the claimant to refuse the treatment and notwithstanding that objectively the refusal is considered to be unreasonable.[79]

Where the claimant is unable, through impecuniosity, to mitigate the damage, the defendant is liable for the full loss.[80] This should be distinguished from the situation where the damage itself is the product of the claimant's impecuniosity, when it may be treated as too remote. In practice this distinction is not easy to draw, although it will rarely be relevant in a claim for medical negligence since the court would probably treat impecuniosity in the context of personal injuries as a question of mitigation rather than remoteness.[81]

9–029

2. PERSONAL INJURIES: PECUNIARY LOSSES

A claimant who sustains personal injuries will normally suffer two distinct types of loss, pecuniary and non-pecuniary loss. Pecuniary loss is the damage that is capable of being directly calculated in monetary terms, whether accrued or prospective. It includes, for example, loss of earnings and pension rights, medical expenses, travelling expenses, the cost of special equipment and the cost of employing someone to carry out domestic duties which the claimant is no longer able to perform. Following *Jefford v Gee*[82] damages in

9–030

---

[78] See paras 5–050 *et seq.*
[79] In *McAuley v London Tranpsort Executive* [1957] 2 Lloyd's Rep. 500, 505, Jenkins L.J. said that: "damages ought to be assessed as they would properly have been assessable if [the claimant] had, in fact, undergone the operation and secured the degree of recovery to be expected from it." This permits the defendant to benefit from an assumption that a particular event would have occurred as a certainty, whereas claimants normally have their future losses discounted for the chance that particular events might not have occurred, *e.g.* that they might not have continued working until retirement age. It is not clear why defendants should be in better position than claimants in this respect. Thus, where the claimant has reasonably refused to undergo an operation in the short term, but might choose to accept treatment in the future, there will be a discount of the award of damages which reflects the chance both that the claimant might have the treatment and that it might be successful; it should not be assumed in the defendant's favour that there will be an operation and that it would be successful: *Thomas v Bath District Health Authority* [1995] P.I.Q.R. Q19, CA.
[80] *Clippens Oil Co v Edinburgh & District Water Trustees* [1907] A.C. 291, 303; *Dodd Properties (Kent) Ltd v Canterbury City Council* [1980] 1 All E.R. 928, 935, 941; [1980] 1 W.L.R. 433.
[81] See para. 5–117.
[82] [1970] 2 Q.B. 130.

a personal injuries action must be particularised under at least three broad heads for the purpose of calculating interest, namely special damages, prospective pecuniary loss, and non-pecuniary damages, though in practice distinct items of loss are particularised in much greater detail. Care should be taken when identifying these items of loss to avoid overlap or duplication in the total assessment.

(1) Medical and other expenses

9–031   The claimant is entitled to recover his medical and other expenses (such as additional housing and travel costs) which are reasonably incurred.[83] Accrued expenses will be awarded as part of the special damages, whereas future medical expenses will be estimated by the multiplier method and awarded as general damages.[84] The possibility of avoiding medical expenses, or part of them, by taking advantage of NHS facilities is disregarded.[85] Thus, the claimant can insist on damages to cover the cost of private medical treatment at the defendant's expense, although the court does not exercise any control over how the claimant uses the award (except where he is a minor or of unsound mind). If it seems likely that the claimant will be unable to receive privately all the treatment or care that he needs, and will eventually have to enter a publicly-funded facility, a deduction from the award for future medical expenses will be made to allow for this.[86] Indeed, if, on the balance of probabilities, private medical treatment is not going to be used, *for whatever reason*, the claimant is not entitled to claim for an expense which he is not going to incur.[87] Where the claimant has in fact used NHS facilities for medical treatment he cannot recover what he would have paid had he received private treatment.[88] Any saving to the claimant which is attributable to his maintenance wholly or partly at public expense in a hospital, nursing home or other institution will be set off against any income he has lost as a

---

[83] He is not entitled to the cost of an operation which he would have had to undergo in any event: *Cutler v Vauxhall Motors Ltd* [1971] 1 Q.B. 418.

[84] For discussion of the "multiplier method" in the context of future loss of earnings see para. 9–041 *et seq*. When dealing with future nursing care or domestic assistance the multiplier may be higher than for the loss of earnings claim because the period during which nursing care is needed may well exceed the claimant's pre-accident working life expectancy. For the approach to be applied to assessing the life expectancy of a seriously disabled child see: *The Royal Victoria Infirmary & Associated Hospitals NHS Trust v B (A Child)* [2002] EWCA Civ 348; [2002] Lloyd's Rep. Med. 282; [2002] P.I.Q.R. Q137. See also Strauss and Shavelle, "Life expectancy: what lawyers need to know" (1999) 5 *AVMA Medical & Legal Journal* 25; and Hermer and Pickering [2002] J.P.I.L. 377 on the approach to multipliers in cases involving very serious injuries.

[85] Law Reform (Personal Injuries) Act 1948, s.2(4). The Pearson Commission recommended repeal of this provision: *Royal Commission on Civil Liability and Compensation for Personal Injury*, Cmnd. 7054 (1978), Vol. I, para. 342.

[86] *Lim Poh Choo v Camden and Islington Area Health Authority* [1980] A.C. 174; *Housecroft v Burnett* [1986] 1 All E.R. 332, 342.

[87] *Woodrup v Nicol* [1993] P.I.Q.R. Q104, 114 CA, *per* Russell L.J., citing *Harris v Brights Asphalt Contractors* [1953] 1 Q.B. 617 and *Cunningham v Harrison* [1973] Q.B. 942, 957.

[88] *Harris v Brights Asphalt Contractors Ltd* [1953] 1 Q.B. 617, 635; *Lim Poh Choo v Camden and Islington Area Health Authority* [1980] A.C. 174, 188.

result of his injuries.[89] A similar rule applies to claimants who make savings in domestic expenditure while being looked after in a private institution.[90]

If the claimant has to live in a special institution, such as a nursing home,   9–032
or receive attendance or care at home, he is entitled to the cost of that, provided that it is reasonably necessary.[91] Where there is a choice as to where the claimant is cared for it is not necessarily a question of which option is the cheapest. Thus, a claimant who needs constant nursing care may be entitled to be cared for at home rather than in an institution, even if this is more expensive, provided it is reasonable in the circumstances.[92] Where the cost of care at home is substantially greater than that of care in an institution the burden of proving that it is reasonable to incur this expense is the claimant's. The claimant can recover the cost of adapting accommodation to his special needs resulting from his disability, subject to a deduction for the added capital value of the property which would be recoverable on a sale.[93] If it is not possible to adapt existing accommodation damages will be awarded in respect of the purchase of special accommodation, but they will be assessed, not on the basis of the capital cost of the property, but by reference to the additional annual cost over the claimant's lifetime of providing that accommodation, as compared with ordinary accommodation. This is because the award is intended to compensate for the claimant's loss, it should not enhance the capital value of the claimant's estate after death.[94]

Where the claimant receives services, such as accommodation, provided by   9–033
a local authority then the claimant may or may not be liable to pay for those services depending upon the statutory basis upon which they have been provided. In some, but not all, instances the authority is entitled to make a reasonable charge for those services. If the authority is entitled to charge, or may become entitled to charge in the future, then the claimant will want to seek an indemnity from the defendant to cover that potential cost. In *Avon County Council v Hooper*[95] the costs of maintaining the patient in a residential home were wholly met by the local authority in discharge of its duties under the National Assistance Act 1948, section 29 and the National Health Service Act 1977, Schedule 8 to provide for the welfare of disabled persons and the care of persons suffering from illness. The settlement of the patient's claim for medical negligence against the health authority included a provision to cover

---

[89] Administration of Justice Act 1982, s.5.
[90] *Lim Poh Choo v Camden and Islington Area Health Authority* [1980] A.C. 174.
[91] *Shearman v Folland* [1950] 2 K.B. 43. See Browne and Gardiner [2002] J.P.I.L. 369.
[92] *Rialas v Mitchell, The Times*, July 17, 1984.
[93] *Roberts v Johnstone* [1989] Q.B. 878.
[94] *ibid.* at 893. Damages "are notionally intended to be such as will exhaust the fund, contemporaneously with the termination of the plaintiff's life expectancy." The Court of Appeal applied a rate of 2% of the capital value as the annual cost. This is then multiplied by the appropriate multiplier for the claimant's life expectancy. It was arguable that this rate should have been increased to 3% in the light of the decision of the House of Lords in *Wells v Wells* [1999] 1 A.C. 345, 380–381 *per* Lord Lloyd; though now the rate should, presumably, be 2.5% which is the rate of return prescribed by the Damages (Personal Injury) Order 2001, S.I. 2001 No. 2301, for the calculation of future pecuniary loss. See para. 9–047.
[95] [1997] 1 W.L.R. 1605; [1997] 1 All E.R. 532.

the cost of keeping the patient at the home from the date of the agreed order approving the settlement, and an indemnity to the patient (and his estate) against any liability to the local authority for the cost of his care at the home prior to that date. Following the patient's death, the local authority commenced an action against the patient's estate to recover the cost of the provision of services to him prior to the settlement, under section 17 of the Health and Social Services and Social Security Adjudications Act 1983. The health authority were added as second defendants on the basis of the indemnity. The Court of Appeal held that since the patient had a right to be indemnified by the health authority against any liability to pay for the cost of services provided to him, he had the "means" to pay for them (within the meaning of section 17(3) of the 1983 Act) and therefore the local authority acted reasonably in seeking to exercise the power under section 17(1) of the 1983 Act to charge for services it provided. The local authority was entitled to recover the cost of providing those services, notwithstanding that the services had been provided in the past. Thus, the health authority were liable to meet the costs by virtue of the indemnity.[96]

9–034   The basis on which the services are provided to the claimant is important when the claimant seeks an indemnity from the defendant in respect of the risk of being required to meet the cost of those services. Thus, in *Thrul v Ray*[97] the accommodation being provided to the claimant was expressly excluded from the effects of section 17(1) and (3) of the 1983 Act (by the proviso to section 17(2)), and since the claimant could not be required by the local authority to meet the cost of the accommodation, it was held that therefore she was not entitled to an indemnity from the defendants against the risk that she might in future be required to meet that cost. In any event, on the facts, even if there were such a liability, it did not arise because of the accident, because the evidence was that the claimant would have been in such a home in any event. Similarly, in *Firth v Geo. Ackroyd Junior Ltd*[98] it was held that any award of damages for personal injury has to be disregarded in assessing the claimant's ability to pay the costs of his accommodation and care provided by the local authority under the National Assistance Act 1948, section 22, by virtue of the National Assistance (Assessment of Resources) Regulations 1992, regulation 31 and Schedule 4. Therefore, the damages recoverable by the claimant from the defendant did not include anything in respect of the cost of accommodation and care provided by the local authority. The claimant was not entitled to a declaration that the defen-

---

[96] The claim was limited by the Limitation Act 1980, s.9 to those services provided within six years of the local authority commencing the action to recover the cost.

[97] [2000] P.I.Q.R. Q44.

[98] [2001] P.I.Q.R. Q27; [2000] Lloyd's Rep. Med. 312. See also *Bell v Todd and South Tyneside Metropolitan Borough Council* [2002] Lloyd's Rep. Med. 12; *Ryan and Liverpool City Council v Liverpool Health Authority* [2002] Lloyd's Rep. Med. 23; *Beattie v Secretary of State for Social Security* [2001] EWCA Civ 498; [2001] 1 W.L.R. 1404—a child was not entitled to income support because payments from a structured settlement were payments received under an annuity which were a category of capital to be treated as income under the Income Support (General) Regulations 1987, reg. 41(2).

dant should indemnify him if at some point in the future he should become liable to pay for the accommodation and care, because this contravened the lump sum principle that damages must be assessed once and for all. Nor was the claimant entitled to damages for the risk that at some point in the future he might become liable to pay for the accommodation and care if there was a change in the law. That risk was not real or substantial—it was purely speculative.

These cases illustrate the importance of the inter-relationship between large   9–035
awards of damages for personal injuries and the claimant's entitlement to means-tested benefits, a relationship which can be extremely complex.[99] That complexity was, in part, caused by different rules for the treatment of capital and income in assessing the claimant's means, depending on the type of benefit and the source of the claimant's resources. The rules have now been simplified in relation to some means-tested benefits and in relation to the provision of accommodation and care by a local authority under the National Assistance Act 1948. The Social Security Amendment (Personal Injury Payments) Regulations 2002[1] amends the regulations[2] governing entitlement to certain means-tested benefits (council tax benefit, housing benefit, income support and jobseeker's allowance) so that where an agreement or court order provides for payments to be made, wholly or partly, by way of periodical payments to a claimant in consequence of any personal injury then any such periodical payments received by the claimant are treated as income (except where the principal regulations treat the payment as capital). However, the regulations then deem that, in some circumstances, the following payments of income, *inter alia*, are to be disregarded for the purposes of assessing a person's entitlement to the benefits: (1) a payment from a trust whose funds are derived from a payment made in consequence of any personal injury to the claimant; (2) a payment under an annuity purchased (i) pursuant to any agreement or court order to make payments to the claimant, or (ii) from funds derived from a payment made, in consequence of any personal injury to the claimant; and (3) a payment received by virtue of any agreement or court order to make payments to the claimant in consequence of any personal injury to the claimant. The effect is that these payments are entirely disregarded when used for items other than every day living expenses (which covers food, clothes, fuel, rent or rates), and the first £20 of the payment is disregarded when used for such expenses. The National Assistance (Assessment of Resources) (Amendment) (No. 2) (England) Regulations 2002[3] amend the National Assistance (Assessment of Resources) Regulations 1992[4] in a similar fashion, so that in assessing a resident's liability to pay for

---

[99] See the discussion in the Report of the Master of the Rolls' Working Party, *Structured Settlements*, August 2002, paras 80–85.

[1] S.I. 2002 No. 2442.

[2] Council Tax Benefit (General) Regulations 1992, S.I. 1992 No. 1814; Housing Benefit (General) Regulations 1987 S.I. 1987 No. 1971; Income Support (General) Regulations 1987 S.I. 1987 No. 1967; Jobseeker's Allowance Regulations 1996 S.I. 1996 No. 207.

[3] S.I. 2002 No. 2531.

[4] S.I. 1992 No. 2977. The amendments apply to England only.

accommodation provided under the National Assistance Act 1948 such payments of income are to be disregarded when intended and used for any item that was not taken into account when the standard rate for the accommodation was fixed; otherwise £20 of such income is disregarded.

9–036   Where a claimant suffers from a major disability as a result of his injuries the items of additional expense can be numerous. They may include the cost of adapting a car; the extra costs of running a household such as higher costs attributable to having to run larger accommodation or accommodation adapted to the claimant's disability; additional laundry bills; the cost of clothes which may wear out more frequently; the expense of maintaining a car[5] or house[6] which the claimant will no longer be able to do for himself; the cost of special equipment such as wheelchairs, and nursing or medical appliances; physiotherapy and other forms of rehabilitative therapy; the additional costs of going on holiday; and, where the claimant is incapable of managing his own affairs, the cost of administration of the damages fund by the Court of Protection.[7] The claimant is entitled to travelling expenses incurred in obtaining medical treatment, and also the travelling expenses attributable to relatives' visits to claimant, provided the visits are of benefit to the claimant in mitigating the damage (but not where the sole justification is the claimant's comfort or pleasure).[8]

9–037   Where a non-earner, such as a housewife, is injured then, clearly, she cannot claim for the earnings that she would have lost had she been in paid employment. But a housewife who is deprived of her ability to look after her family suffers a real loss, even though other members of the family now perform the tasks that she used to do, and she is entitled to compensation for this loss.[9] For the future this loss is estimated on the basis of the cost employing domestic help, irrespective of whether a housekeeper will be employed. Past loss, on the other hand, is compensated as an addition to the award of general damages if a housekeeper has not been employed.[10] A claimant is also entitled to damages for care which, as a result of the defendant's negligence, he is no longer able to give to a relative, spouse or partner living as part of the same household, where that care goes beyond the ordinary interaction of members of a household. To the extent that another member

---

[5] There is potentially a degree of overlap in the award of damages if the claimant receives a large sum for loss of earnings from which he may have purchased and run a car in any event. If he is claiming the cost of specially adapted transport there will clearly be an element of overlap which should be taken into account.

[6] See Snell, "Damages for DIY and Gardening" [2002] J.P.I.L. 385.

[7] *Jones v Jones* [1985] Q.B. 704; *Rialas v Mitchell, The Times,* July 17, 1984.

[8] *Hunt v Severs* [1994] 2 A.C. 350, 356–357. This curious head of damage stems from a dictum of Diplock J. in *Kirkham v Boughey* [1958] 2 Q.B. 338, 343, and now appears to be well-established, although strictly speaking it is not the claimant's loss. The expenses are normally agreed, as *e.g.* in *Donnelly v Joyce* [1974] Q.B. 454 and *Thomas v Wignall* [1987] Q.B. 1098.

[9] *Daly v General Steam Navigation Co Ltd* [1981] 1 W.L.R. 120.

[10] This approach is criticised as illogical by Burrows, *Remedies for Torts and Breach of Contract*, 2nd ed., Butterworths, 1994, pp. 195–196; and the Law Commission in its report *Damages for Personal Injury: Medical, Nursing and Other Expenses; Collateral Benefits,* Law Com. No. 262, 1999.

of the family has mitigated the loss by providing additional care, the claimant would hold the damages on trust for that member of the family.[11]

In many instances a third person, such as a relative or friend, bears part   9–038
of the cost of the claimant's injury, either in the form of direct financial payments or by providing gratuitous services, such as nursing assistance. A spouse or relative may give up paid employment to look after the claimant, but the third party has no direct claim in tort against the defendant. The claimant can recover this cost, however, from the defendant, irrespective of whether he is under any legal or moral obligation to reimburse the third party. In *Donnelly v Joyce*[12] the Court of Appeal held that this expense was the claimant's loss, and consisted of the need for nursing services or special equipment, not the expenditure of the money itself. The question of who provided the service or purchased equipment, or whether the claimant was under an obligation to repay, were said to be irrelevant to the defendant's liability. The measure of the loss is the "proper and reasonable cost" of supplying the claimant's needs. In the case of a relative who has given up paid employment this will be at least the relative's loss of earnings, subject to a ceiling of the commercial rate for supplying those services to the claimant.[13] It would seem that, normally, the full commercial rate should not be applied unless the relative has given up paid employment, the assumption being that where relatives look after the claimant out of love or a sense of duty the commercial rate is inappropriate.[14] In *Hunt v Severs*[15] the House of Lords accepted that the basis of the claimant's claim consisted of his need for services, but disapproved the suggestion that the question of what source the claimant's needs have been met from was irrelevant to the assessment of damages. The underlying rationale of the law is to enable the voluntary carer to receive proper recompense for his or her services, and thus the injured claimant who recovers damages under this head should hold them on trust for

---

[11] *Lowe v Guise* [2002] EWCA Civ 197; [2002] Q.B. 1369, CA—claimant who looked after his disabled brother full-time was no longer able to do so after sustaining injuries caused by the defendant's negligence.

[12] [1974] Q.B. 454, approved by the Pearson Commission: *Royal Commission on Civil Liability and Compensation for Personal Injury*, Cmnd. 7054 (1978), Vol. I, paras 343–351; *cf.* Burrows, *Remedies for Torts and Breach of Contract*, 2nd ed., Butterworths, 1994, pp. 193–194.

[13] *Housecroft v Burnett* [1986] 1 All E.R. 332. In *Croke v Wiseman* [1981] 3 All E.R. 852; [1982] 1 W.L.R. 71 the claimant's mother had given up her employment to look after him. Her loss of earnings included loss of pension rights in the job she had given up. An award under this head can be made even though the carer has not lost wages of her own in order to look after the claimant: *Mills v British Rail Engineering Ltd* [1992] P.I.Q.R. Q130, CA.

[14] *McCamley v Cammell Laird Shipbuilders Ltd* [1990] 1 All E.R. 854, 857 CA; see *Almond v Leeds Western Health Authority* [1990] 1 Med. L.R. 370, where half the commercial rate was awarded for past care; *cf. Van Gervan v Fenton* (1992) 109 A.L.R. 283, where the High Court of Australia held that the reasonable value of a carer's services should be the market cost. In practice the loss will usually be assessed on the basis of the carer's net loss of earnings, even where the commercial rate is higher and the carer is providing 24 hour a day care and had previously been employed for five days a week for eight hours a day: *Fitzgerald v Ford* [1996] P.I.Q.R. Q72, CA; *Evans v Pontypridd Roofing Ltd* [2001] EWCA Civ 1657; [2002] P.I.Q.R. Q61.

[15] [1994] 2 A.C. 350; Reed [1994] J.P.I.L. 139, 215.

the voluntary carer.[16] It followed that where the services are provided by the defendant tortfeasor the claimant cannot recover the cost of the services by way of damages.[17] There can be no claim for gratuitous services provided by a spouse to the claimant's business as a result of the injury. This is in a different category from caring services.[18]

9–039   Where the claimant's injuries lead to the break up of his marriage the financial consequences of the divorce are not recoverable, either on the basis that the loss is too remote or on the ground of public policy.[19] On the other hand, loss of marriage prospects may be the subject of an award of general damages for pain and suffering.[20]

(2) Loss of Earnings

9–040   Loss of earnings will be calculated over two periods: the loss up to the date of assessment and the prospective loss, for which the multiplier method is used. Where the claimant's working life expectancy has been reduced the prospective loss of earnings will have to be further divided into the period during which the claimant is expected to survive, and the period during which he would have been employed but is not now expected to survive (the "lost years"), because the basis of the calculation is different in these periods. Calculating the loss of earnings up to the date of assessment is usually a reasonably precise exercise, intended to measure the claimant's actual loss over the period that he has been unable to work. This is the net loss, after deducting the claimant's income tax[21] and national insurance contributions,[22] and

---

[16] Approving *Cunningham v Harrison* [1973] Q.B. 942, 952. For criticism of this approach see Matthews (1994) 13 C.J.Q. 302; Kemp (1994) 110 L.Q.R. 524; Hoyano (1995) 3 Tort L. Rev. 63; Reed (1995) 15 O.J.L.S. 133; Matthews and Lunney (1995) 58 M.L.R. 395. The Australian High Court has declined to follow *Hunt v Severs*, preferring instead the approach of the Court of Appeal in *Donelly v Joyce*, while taking a more robust view of the practical realities in such cases, including the insurance position: see *Kars v Kars* (1996) 141 A.L.R. 37; Luntz (1997) 113 L.Q.R. 201; Vines (1997) 5 Tort L. Rev. 93; Degeling (1997) 71 A.L.J. 882. The court must take steps to see that the terms of the trust are fulfilled: *ATH v MS* [2002] EWCA Civ 792; [2002] 3 W.L.R. 1179 at [30]. For discussion on the nature of the *Hunt v Severs* trust and the implications for claimants and their advisers see Watson and Barrie (2003) 19 P.N. 320.

[17] Overruling *Donnelly v Joyce* on this point. The Law Commission has recommended legislation to reverse this effect of *Hunt v Severs*, though approving much of the reasoning in the case: *Damages for Personal Injury: Medical, Nursing and Other Expenses; Collateral Benefits*, Law Com. No. 262, 1999. See also *Hayden v Hayden* [1992] 1 W.L.R. 986, where the Court of Appeal held that in a claim under the Fatal Accidents Act 1976 the gratuitous services of the tortfeasor could be taken into account as reducing the claimant's loss and were not a "benefit" accruing as a result of the death which, under s.4, would have to be disregarded.

[18] *Hardwick v Hudson* [1999] 3 All E.R. 426, CA.

[19] *Pritchard v J.H. Cobden Ltd* [1988] Fam. 22, CA, disapproving *Jones v Jones* [1985] Q.B. 704. Subsequently in *Pritchard v J.H. Cobden Ltd* [1987] 2 F.L.R. 56 the same court held that the legal costs of the divorce *were* recoverable from the tortfeasor on the particular facts of the case.

[20] See para. 9–075.

[21] *British Transport Commission v Gourley* [1956] A.C. 185. For criticism of this principle see Bishop and Kay (1987) 104 L.Q.R. 211.

[22] *Cooper v Firth Brown Ltd* [1963] 1 W.L.R. 418.

the claimant's contributions to a compulsory pension scheme.[23] Any loss of pension rights resulting from the contributions not having been paid is calculated separately.[24] All forms of earnings are included, such as perquisites.[25] If the claimant's rate of pay would have changed during this period, then this is taken into account.[26] The accrued loss of earnings to the date of trial form part of the special damages. The claimant must give credit for the expenses he would have incurred had he been at work, for example, the cost of travel to and from work should be deducted.

(a) Prospective loss of earnings

Calculating the claimant's future loss of earnings can cause real problems   9–041
because the court will have to prophesy both what will happen to the claimant in the future and what would have happened if he had not been injured, in order to estimate the difference. This involves considering the claimant's life expectancy, his earnings, the chance that he may have increased his earnings through promotion or reduced them through redundancy or illness, and what financial benefits he will now receive. The starting point is to work out the claimant's net annual loss of earnings, as at the date of assessment, not the date of injury.[27] The net annual loss is known as the "multiplicand." This will be adjusted to take account of the claimant's individual prospects of a future increase in income (for example, through a promotion[28]), but no allowance will be made for a general rise in real average earnings. This sum is then multiplied by a "multiplier" which is based on the number of years that the loss is likely to continue. The multiplier is discounted, however, to take account of the uncertainty of the prediction (*e.g.* the claimant might have lost his job in any event through redundancy or illness in the future), and the fact that the claimant receives the money immediately as a capital sum, instead of in instalments over the rest of his working life.[29] The claimant is then expected to invest the award of damages and use both the income and part of the capital over the expected period of the loss, so that at the end of that period the whole award will be exhausted (although part of his living expenses may have included provision for retirement). Thus, the claimant is compensated on an annuity basis.

In some cases where the claimant's prospects of having improved earnings   9–042
in the future have been fairly speculative the courts have resorted to a "loss

---

[23] *Dews v National Coal Board* [1988] A.C. 1.

[24] *Auty v National Coal Board* [1985] 1 All E.R. 930; [1985] 1 W.L.R. 784.

[25] *Kennedy v Bryan, The Times*, May 3, 1984—company car.

[26] *Cookson v Knowles* [1979] A.C. 556, 569, a Fatal Accidents Act case.

[27] *Cookson v Knowles* [1979] A.C. 556.

[28] *Roach v Yates* [1938] 1 K.B. 256; *Robertson v Lestrange* [1985] 1 All E.R. 950.

[29] No reduction is made for the fact that the claimant does not have to "earn" the money. For discussion of the multiplier to be applied to future loss of earnings where there was a chance that a young woman in employment would have given up that employment to have children see *Hughes v McKeown* [1985] 3 All E.R. 284; [1985] 1 W.L.R. 963 and *Housecroft v Burnett* [1986] 1 All E.R. 332, 345 stating that this chance should be ignored; *cf.* the alternative approach in *Moriarty v McCarthy* [1978] 2 All E.R. 213.

of chance" approach to the assessment, based on the likely actions of third parties, rather than adopting the more traditional multiplier method (which, of course, is also concerned with assessing the chances that something might or might not have happened).[30] In *Herring v Ministry of Defence*[31] Potter L.J. suggested that the loss of chance approach might be suitable where the chance to be assessed was the chance that the career of a claimant would take a particular course leading to significantly higher overall earnings than those which it was otherwise reasonable to take as the baseline for calculation. But in a case where the career model adopted by the judge had been chosen because it was itself the appropriate baseline, and/or was one of a number of alternatives likely to give more or less similar results, then it was neither necessary nor appropriate to adopt the loss of chance approach in respect of the possibility that the particular career may not, after all, be followed. Rather the multiplier method was appropriate, with the multiplier or multiplicand within the career model being adjusted to the circumstances of the particular claimant. The starting point was to form a view as to the most likely future working career ("the career model") of the claimant had he not been injured. If at the time of the accident, the claimant was in an established job in which he was likely to have remained but for the accident, the working assumption is that he would have done so and the conventional multiplier/multiplicand method of calculation is adopted, taking into account any reasonable prospects of promotion or movement to a better paid field of work. If a job change is unlikely significantly to affect the level of future earnings, it should be ignored in the multiplicand/multiplier exercise, except that it will generally be appropriate to make a discount in the multiplier in respect of contingencies or "the vicissitudes of life."[32] The discount for the general vicissitudes of future illness or unemployment should be around 10 per cent.[33] A higher discount by virtue of additional future contingencies would only be justified if there were tangible reasons relating to the personality or likely future circumstances of the claimant going beyond the purely speculative.[34]

9–043   Where there is no, or an uncertain, pre-accident record of the claimant's earnings the claim for prospective loss of earnings can be more speculative, and the court may decide not to use the multiplier method and may simply

---

[30] See *Doyle v Wallace* [1998] P.I.Q.R. Q146, CA; *Langford v Hebran* [2001] EWCA Civ 361; [2001] P.I.Q.R. Q160. This approach applies *Allied Maples Group Ltd v Simmons & Simmons* [1995] 4 All E.R. 907; [1995] 1 W.L.R. 1602; para. 5–060, which is more usually relevant to questions of causation rather than the assessment of quantum.

[31] [2003] EWCA Civ 528; *The Times*, April 11, 2003 at [25] and [26].

[32] *ibid.* at [23] *per* Potter L.J.

[33] *ibid.* at [38] *per* Potter L.J.: "The Tables in the Notes to the Ogden Tables make plain that on an 'average' basis the discount appropriate to be allowed for the possibility that illness and unemployment will interrupt a claimant's earning career is a small one as compared with levels which have been traditionally applied. In my view that is a matter which should be borne in mind by judges when considering the level of discount to be made for contingencies generally." The trial judge in *Herring v Ministry of Defence* had applied a 25% discount for general contingencies. Note that In *De Sales v Ingrilli* [2002] H.C.A. 52; (2002) 193 A.L.R. 130 the High Court of Australia held that a 5% deduction for general contingencies or general vicissitudes was appropriate.

[34] *ibid.* at [31].

award a lump sum for loss of earning capacity.[35] This will often be the position where young children suffer serious injury. Such an award is not "calculated" arithmetically but is largely impressionistic, and the sum will often be discounted quite heavily to allow for its inherent uncertainty. Where possible, however, the court will attempt to make an assessment of the loss of earnings using the multiplier method, even if that involves relying on national average earnings figures to establish the multiplicand.[36]

In the past the multipliers used rested on the assumption that a person who invested a capital sum would receive a return of approximately 4.5 per cent after the effects of tax and inflation had been taken into account.[37] It had long been argued that that assumption was unrealistic, with the result that the multipliers were too low and claimants were being under compensated.[38] The problem is greater in periods of high inflation, but the courts refused to make any allowance for future inflation eroding the value of an award.[39] Protection against inflation was to be sought by careful investment, the assumption being that some capital appreciation of the money invested will offset increases in the cost of living.[40] In *Lim Poh Choo v Camden and Islington Area Health Authority*[41] it was accepted, however, that in an exceptional case some allowance might be made if, on the particular facts, an award which ignored inflation would not result in fair compensation, although Lord Scarman commented that claimants who receive a lump sum award "are entitled to no better protection against inflation than others who have to rely on capital for their support."[42] His Lordship added that

9–044

---

[35] See para. 9–052.

[36] In *Herring v Ministry of Defence* [2003] EWCA Civ 528; *The Times*, April 11, 2003, at [24], Potter L.J. commented: "In the situation of a young claimant who has not yet been in employment at the time of injury but is still in education or has otherwise not embarked on his career, or (as in this case) one who has taken time out from employment in order to acquire a further qualification for a desired change of direction, it may or may not be appropriate to select a specific career model in his chosen field. In this connection the court will have regard to the claimant's previous performance, expressed intentions and ambitions, the opportunities reasonably open to him and any steps he has already taken to pursue a particular path. In many cases it will not be possible to identify a specific career model and it may be necessary simply to resort to national average earnings figures for persons of the claimant's ability and qualifications in his likely field(s) of activity. In other cases, however, it may be possible with confidence to select a career model appropriate to be used as the multiplicand for calculating loss."

[37] *Cookson v Knowles* [1979] A.C. 556, 577, *per* Lord Fraser; *Auty v National Coal Board* [1985] 1 All E.R. 930; [1985] 1 W.L.R. 784; *Robertson v Lestrange* [1985] 1 All E.R. 950.

[38] See Kemp (1985) 101 L.Q.R. 556; Luckett and Craner [1994] J.P.I.L. 139; *Read v Harries* [1995] P.I.Q.R. Q25, 28, *per* Morland J.

[39] See *Taylor v O'Connor* [1971] A.C. 115; *Mitchell v Mulholland (No. 2)* [1972] 1 Q.B. 65; *Cookson v Knowles* [1979] A.C. 556; *Lim Poh Choo v Camden and Islington Area Health Authority* [1980] A.C. 174.

[40] *Taylor v O'Connor* [1971] A.C. 115, 143, *per* Lord Pearson.

[41] [1980] A.C. 174.

[42] This view is inconsistent with the basic principle in assessing tort damages of restoring the claimant to his pre-accident position, because if he would have had better protection from inflation if he were in employment then he is worse off as a result of the tort by now being forced to rely on investment income. This point was acknowledged by Lords Lloyd and Hutton in *Wells v Wells*; *Thomas v Brighton Health Authority*; *Page v Sheerness Steel Co Ltd* [1999] 1 A.C. 345, hereafter "*Wells v Wells*".

attempts to take inflation into account sought a perfection in the assessment of damages which was beyond the inherent limitations of the system.

9–045   This approach to calculating the multiplier was challenged in *Wells v Wells*,[43] on the basis that the advent of index-linked government securities provided a much fairer solution to the problem of protecting claimants from the effects of inflation. The advantage of index-linked government securities from the claimant's perspective is that they are virtually a risk free investment and the return can be calculated with some precision. The same sum invested in equities might produce a much higher return, but might equally produce a significantly lower return. Shares are an inherently volatile investment, particularly in the short-term. That volatility creates a serious risk because a claimant has to sell part of the investment at regular intervals to meet his income needs. If the claimant has to sell in a period when the stock market is depressed, he will have to realise a larger part of the underlying investment to produce the same sum, and as Lord Lloyd observed, "the depleted fund may never recover." What is prudent for an ordinary investor (*i.e.* investing in a spread of equities and more secure bonds and gilts), said Lord Lloyd, is not necessarily prudent for a claimant, because an ordinary investor may be able to take a long term view and "ride out" falls in the market until the value of equities has recovered, whereas "what the prudent plaintiff needs is an investment which will bring him the income he requires without the risks inherent in the equity market." The House of Lords held that the claimants were entitled to be compensated on the assumption that they would invest in index-linked government securities, a view which had been recommended by the Law Commission.[44]

9–046   Claimants are not required to invest in index-linked government securities. Except for claimants who fall within the jurisdiction of the Court of Protection, the courts do not exercise a supervisory role, and a claimant is normally free to spend the damages award as he sees fit. But in *assessing* the level of compensation, the calculation is not to be made on the assumption that he is obliged to invest in equities. Since the average return on index-linked government securities in 1998 was approximately 3 per cent (as opposed to the assumed return of 4.5 per cent upon which the traditional approach was based) their Lordships in *Wells v Wells* indicated that, as a matter of guidance rather than precedent,[45] the appropriate discount rate should be 3 per cent. This would require a larger initial lump sum, which is reflected in a higher multiplier. The consequence of this change is that for seriously injured claimants awards of damages in respect of future pecuniary losses have increased significantly. The rationale of investing in index-linked government securities is reflected in the "Ogden Tables", originally produced in 1984 by a joint working party of lawyers and actuaries. The Ogden Tables are regularly relied upon when valuing claims, and though

---

[43] [1999] 1 A.C. 345. See Goldrein (1998) 148 N.L.J. 1149.
[44] *Structured Settlements and Interim and Provisional Damages*, Law Com. No. 224, 1994, paras 2.25–2.28.
[45] Different economic circumstances might justify a change to the guide figure in the future.

they have not been formally adopted by the courts, the practice was endorsed in *Wells v Wells*.[46]

The Damages Act 1996, section 1 permits the Lord Chancellor to give   9–047
general guidance on rates of return, though leaving discretion to the courts to apply different rates where appropriate. The Damages (Personal Injury) Order 2001[47] prescribes 2.5 per cent as the rate of return that the courts should apply to calculations of future pecuniary loss (reflecting the fall in general interest rates since the decision in *Wells v Wells*). Section 1(2) of the Damages Act 1996 permits the court to adopt a different rate in special circumstances, but the Court of Appeal has made it clear such cases will be rare.[48]

A similar problem arises in connection with the effect of taxation. The   9–048
award of damages in a personal injuries action is not itself liable to tax,[49] but the income produced by investing the award is taxable. Where the claimant receives a very large award it is possible that the income generated will be subject to higher rate tax, with the effect that the combined fund of capital and income from which the claimant must meet his annual loss may be inadequate. In *Hodgson v Trapp*[50] the House of Lords held that it was not permissible, having selected a multiplier on the conventional basis, then to increase the multiplier to take account of the effects of higher rates of tax. Lord Oliver reiterated that the process of assessing future pecuniary loss cannot, by its nature, be a precise science. Future taxation was just as uncertain as future inflation, and so predicting what might happen to future political, economic or fiscal policies required not the services of an actuary or an accountant, but those of a prophet. There was no justification for singling out taxation for special treatment when it was merely one of the many imponderables that have to be taken into account in the conventional method of assessing damages.[51]

As in *Lim Poh Choo*, their Lordships accepted that there might be very   9–049
exceptional cases where special allowance might have to be made for inflation and taxation,[52] although Lord Oliver observed that it was difficult to

---

[46] Again, a view supported by the Law Commission, *Structured Settlements and Interim and Provisional Damages*, Law Com. No. 224, 1994, para. 2.15.

[47] S.I. 2001 No. 2301.

[48] *Warriner v Warriner* [2002] EWCA Civ 81; [2002] 1 W.L.R. 1703, CA—the 2.5% rate will only be departed from if the case falls into a category that the Lord Chancellor had not considered when recommending the rate and/or had special features shown not to have been taken into account by him.

[49] Income and Corporation Taxes Act 1988, s.329.

[50] [1989] A.C. 807, overruling *Thomas v Wignall* [1987] Q.B. 1098.

[51] *ibid.* at 835.

[52] A point which was accepted in *Wells v Wells* [1999] 1 A.C. 345—see the speech of Lord Steyn. See *Van Oudenhoven v Griffin Inns Ltd* [2000] 1 W.L.R. 1413, CA, where an argument that higher rates of taxation in Holland justified either a higher multiplier or a reduced discount rate was rejected on the facts. In any event, said the Court of Appeal, where it was argued that the incidence of foreign taxation made the case exceptional, the court would also take into account corresponding advantages in the country concerned, such as a lower cost of living or lower indirect taxation, or the possibility of a higher rate of return on investments.

envisage circumstances in which something so inherently uncertain could be proved to the satisfaction of the court. Possibly it could tip the balance in favour of the selection of a higher multiplier as part of the assessment of all the uncertain factors that have to be taken into account, but it would not be proper to make a specific addition to the multiplier on account of this one factor. Moreover, when considering the effect of higher rate tax on the damages award the court must be careful to look only at the damages awarded for future loss (whether for prospective loss of earnings or the cost of future care) to which the multiplier method is appropriate. Only the income from that fund would be relevant to the question of higher rate taxation. If, for example, the claimant chose to invest the damages awarded for non-pecuniary loss in order to supplement his income, and this put him into a higher tax bracket, that would not be a reason for increasing the award for loss of future earnings and future care.

(b) The lost years

9–050   Where the claimant's life expectancy has been reduced by his injuries this may well have reduced the period during which he would have been earning in the future. In *Oliver v Ashman*[53] the Court of Appeal held that the losses incurred in these "lost years" (the period between his expected date of death and the date that he would have stopped working but for the tort) were not recoverable, on the basis that a claimant cannot suffer a loss during a period when he will be dead. This rule created a problem for claimants with dependants because of the interrelationship with the Fatal Accidents Act. Normally, where the victim of a tort dies as a result of his injuries his dependants have a claim against the tortfeasor for their financial loss under the Fatal Accidents Act 1976. Such a claim is only available, however, where at the date of the death the victim would have had a right of action against the tortfeasor. If, while still alive the deceased had obtained a judgment against the tortfeasor or settled his claim, then on his death there is no subsisting right of action and the dependants have no claim under the Act. Thus, *Oliver v Ashman* penalised the claimant's dependants, since their dependency in the lost years would generally have been met from the claimant's earnings during that period. It was this consideration which led the House of Lords to overrule *Oliver v Ashman* in *Pickett v British Rail Engineering Ltd*.[54] Damages for prospective loss of earnings will be awarded for the whole of the claimant's pre-accident life expectancy, subject to a deduction for the money that the claimant would have spent on his own (not his dependants') living expenses during the lost years. His own living expenses will not be incurred and therefore they are not a real loss.[55]

---

[53] [1962] 2 Q.B. 210.

[54] [1980] A.C. 136.

[55] See *Harris v Empress Motors Ltd* [1983] 3 All E.R. 561; [1984] 1 W.L.R. 212 and *Phipps v Brooks Dry Cleaning Services Ltd* [1996] P.I.Q.R. Q100 on the calculation of the living expenses; *White v London Transport Executive* [1982] Q.B. 489; *Adsett v West* [1983] Q.B. 826; *Wilson v Stag* (1986) 136 N.L.J. 47; Evans and Stanton (1984) 134 N.L.J. 515, 553; Kelly [2000] J.P.I.L. 137.

Although the objective of *Pickett v British Rail Engineering Ltd* was, in 9–051
effect, to protect the interests of dependants, there is no way of ensuring that
the claimant does in fact use the damages to make provision for his dependants.
Moreover, the claimant is entitled to an award covering the lost years even
where he has no dependants. Where the claimant has an established pattern of
earnings it will be easier to make an appropriate calculation. In the case of a
young single person the award is likely to be modest to reflect the high degree
of speculation involved.[56] Exceptionally a young child may have a claim for loss
of earnings in the lost years,[57] but though in principle the loss is recoverable the
speculative nature of the loss will often result in an assessment of nil damages.[58]

(c) Loss of earning capacity

Where a person suffers a permanent disability which affects his ability to 9–052
earn in the future at the same rate as he earned before the injury, then he may
or may not suffer a loss of earnings. The loss may be total if he is unable to
work at all, or partial if he is able to take a less remunerative job. In some
instances, although the injuries have affected the claimant's ability to earn, he
suffers no loss of earnings because his employer continues to employ him at
the same rate of pay. In these circumstances the claimant is entitled to
damages for his loss of earning capacity if there is a real risk (as opposed to
a fanciful or speculative risk) that he could lose his existing employment in
the future, because his capacity to find a job with equivalent remuneration
has been reduced, and he is now at a disadvantage in the labour market.[59] If
the court makes a separate assessment for loss of earning capacity and loss of
future earnings, care must be taken to avoid any duplication in the award.[60]

It has been said that there is no real difference between damages for loss 9–053
of earning capacity and damages for future loss of earnings.[61] A reduction

---

[56] *Harris v Empress Motors Ltd* [1983] 3 All E.R. 561; [1984] 1 W.L.R. 212; *Adsett v West*
[1983] Q.B. 826. It may be that where the lost years claim is highly speculative, it is better
simply to make a small adjustment to the multiplier (adding 1 or _) as applied to the full
multiplicand, rather than attempting to speculate on notional earnings and notional living
expenses: *Housecroft v Burnett* [1986] 1 All E.R. 332, 345, *per* O'Connor L.J.
[57] *Gammell v Wilson* [1982] A.C. 27, 78.
[58] *Croke v Wiseman* [1981] 3 All E.R. 852; [1982] 1 W.L.R. 71; *Connolly v Camden and
Islington Area Health Authority* [1981] 3 All E.R. 250.
[59] *Smith v Manchester Corp* (1974) 17 K.I.R. 1; *Moeliker v Reyrolle & Co Ltd* [1977] 1 All
E.R. 9; Ritchie [1994] J.P.I.L. 103. This is a two stage test: (1) was there a substantial or real
risk that the claimant would lose his present job at some time before the end of his working
life? and (2) if so, what is the present value of that future risk? A risk can be real even though
it is unlikely, and substantial does not mean that it is likely to happen on the balance of probabilities: *Robson v Liverpool City Council* [1993] P.I.Q.R. Q78, CA. It is good practice to
plead expressly a claim for *Smith v Manchester* damages, but where sufficient facts about
the claimant's medical condition are pleaded to make it clear that, in the eyes of most potential employers, the claimant's value as an employee has been reduced, that will be sufficient:
Thorn v Powergen plc [1997] P.I.Q.R. Q71, CA.
[60] *Clarke v Rotax Aircraft Equipment Ltd* [1975] 1 W.L.R. 1054.
[61] *Foster v Tyne and Wear County Council* [1986] 1 All E.R. 567, 571–572; *Tait v Pearson*
[1996] P.I.Q.R. Q92; *Royal Commission on Civil Liability and Compensation for Personal
Injury*, Cmnd. 7054 (1978), Vol. I, para. 338.

in the claimant's present earning capacity is ultimately likely to have some impact on the level of his future earnings. In practice, however, awards for loss of earning capacity are more impressionistic and less susceptible to the multiplier method of calculation, though in an appropriate case the multiplier method can be used.[62] The assessment is particularly speculative in the case of children where there may be little or no evidence about what the child may eventually do for a living.[63] The solution is to award only moderate sums in this situation, although there is no tariff or conventional award for loss of earning capacity and each case must be considered on its own facts.[64] In *Foster v Tyne and Wear County Council*,[65] for example, an award of £35,000 to an adult claimant under this head was upheld by the Court of Appeal. Where an assessment of loss of earning capacity is made in respect of a claimant's contribution to the profits of a business in which he is a partner, the loss should be assessed on the basis of the claimant's actual contribution to the running of the business, not the internal arrangements in the accounts agreed with the Inland Revenue for tax purposes.[66]

(3) Deductions[67]

9–054   A person who suffers personal injury may receive financial support from a number of sources other than tort damages.[68] The most common source is social security benefits, but others include sick pay, pensions, private insurance and charitable donations. The compensatory principle applied to the assessment of tort damages should mean that, in theory, any receipt of financial assistance from another source is deducted in full from the award of

[62] *Dhaliwal v Personal Representatives of Hunt (Deceased)* [1995] P.I.Q.R. Q56, 59; *Tait v Pearson* [1996] P.I.Q.R. Q92. For an argument that the courts should adopt a formulaic approach to assessing the loss, rather than an "impressionistic" approach see Chippindall [2001] J.P.I.L. 37.

[63] See *S. v Distillers Co (Biochemicals) Ltd* [1970] 1 W.L.R. 114; *Joyce v Yeomans* [1981] 1 W.L.R. 549; *Croke v Wiseman* [1981] 3 All E.R. 852; [1982] 1 W.L.R. 71; *Mitchell v Liverpool Area Health Authority*, The Times, June 17, 1985. In *Cronin v Redbridge London Borough Council*, The Times, May 20, 1987 the Court of Appeal complained that this was an exercise in unsatisfactory guesswork. See Denyer [1992] Fam. Law 207 and Denyer [1997] J.P.I.L. 244 on the calculation of loss of earnings for injured children.

[64] *Page v Enfield and Haringey Area Health Authority*, The Times, November 7, 1986. The court may be willing to use the multiplier method for assessment of loss of earnings of even a young child, based on a multiplicand of the national average wage: see *Croke v Wiseman* [1981] 3 All E.R. 852; [1982] 1 W.L.R. 71; *Moser v Enfield and Haringey Area Health Authority* (1983) 133 N.L.J. 105. In *Aboul-Hosn v Trustees of the Italian Hospital* (1987) 137 N.L.J. 1164 an 18 year-old with four "A" Levels and a place at university was held to have a good prospect of earning £18,000 per annum, plus a company car.

[65] [1986] 1 All E.R. 567.

[66] *Ward v Newalls Insulation Co Ltd* [1998] 2 All E.R. 690; [1998] 1 W.L.R. 1722, CA, where the claimant, W, contributed 50% with his other partner, E, but for tax purposes it was declared that there were four partners, W, E and their respective spouses.

[67] See generally, Lewis, R., *Deducting Benefits from Damages for Personal Injury*, OUP, 1999.

[68] The Pearson Commission found that the tort system provided about 25% of the total compensation paid out to the victims of personal injury: *Royal Commission on Civil Liability and Compensation for Personal Injury*, Cmnd. 7054 (1978), Vol. I, para. 44.

damages, since they reduce the claimant's loss. There are, however, a number of competing policy factors which may justify non-deduction.[69]

(a) Social security benefits

In principle, benefits paid by the state in the form of social security should   **9–055**
be deducted from damages awards on the basis that damages are meant to be compensatory and the claimant should not be in a better financial position than he would have been but for the tort. By 1988, although there were statutory exceptions, the common law had essentially reached the position that most social security benefits should be fully deducted. The Social Security Act 1989, however, introduced a scheme for recoupment by the state from tortfeasors of certain social security benefits paid to claimants.[70] This system was significantly amended by the Social Security (Recovery of Benefits) Act 1997, but the pre-1989 rules remain potentially relevant to any case which is not covered by the 1997 Act.[71]

Under the old rules the extent of deduction of benefits depended to a large   **9–056**
extent upon whether the case was governed by statute or the common law. By section 2(1) of the Law Reform (Personal Injuries) Act 1948[72] half the value of certain benefits was deducted from the damages for loss of earnings, up to five years after the accident.[73] Where the matter was free from statutory regulation the courts had increasingly taken the view that benefits should be fully deducted in order to avoid double recovery by the claimant.[74] Most benefits have been held to be fully deductible, including attendance allowance and mobility allowance,[75] statutory sick pay,[76] unemployment benefit,[77]

---

[69] For an analysis of the policy issues see Lewis, R., *Deducting Benefits from Damages for Personal Injury*, OUP, 1999, pp. 15–47, also at Lewis (1998) 18 L.S. 15; Law Commission Consultation Paper No. 147, *Damages for Personal Injury: Collateral Benefits*, 1997; Law Commission Report, *Damages for Personal Injury: Medical, Nursing and Other Expenses; Collateral Benefits*, Law Com. No. 262, 1999.

[70] The recoupment provisions of the Social Security Act 1989 were subsequently incorporated into Pt IV of the Social Security Administration Act 1992.

[71] Over time the names of some benefits have changed, and some have been abolished or replaced by new benefits. Where the rules on deductions are governed by a statutory provision then changes to the benefits will have to be reflected in the legislation in order for those rules to apply; but where the common law applies the courts will look to the nature of the benefit in assessing whether the principle of deductibility applies. For example, the renaming of supplementary benefit as income support makes no difference to the common law principle of deductibility.

[72] This provision was repealed by the Social Security (Recovery of Benefits) Act 1997, Sch. 3, para. 1.

[73] But after five years these benefits were not deducted at all: *Jackman v Corbett* [1988] Q.B. 154; *Almond v Leeds Western Health Authority* [1990] 1 Med. L.R. 370.

[74] *Hodgson v Trapp* [1989] A.C. 807, 823, *per* Lord Bridge. The Pearson Commission also recommended that there should be no overlap between tort damages and social security payments: *Royal Commission on Civil Liability and Compensation for Personal Injury*, Cmnd. 7054 (1978), Vol. I, para. 482.

[75] *Hodgson v Trapp* [1989] A.C. 807, overruling *Bowker v Rose* (1978) 122 S.J. 147.

[76] *Palfrey v Greater London Council* [1985] I.C.R. 437.

[77] *Nabi v British Leyland (UK) Ltd* [1980] 1 All E.R. 667; *Westwood v Secretary of State for Employment* [1985] A.C. 20.

reduced earnings allowance,[78] past receipts of income support and family credit,[79] and, in a claim for the cost of maintaining a child following a failed sterilisation operation, child benefit.[80] State retirement pension may be an exception to the principle of full deductibility.[81]

Recoupment of benefits

9–057   Under the "recoupment" rules the amount of any "relevant benefit" paid or likely to be paid to or for the claimant in respect of the accident, injury or disease was disregarded in assessing damages in respect of an accident, injury or disease.[82] In other words, the benefit was *not* deducted in calculating damages payable by the defendant. The person paying compensation (the "compensator") in respect of an accident, injury or disease suffered by the "victim" was not allowed to make the payment until the Secretary of State had furnished him with a certificate of the total benefit. The compensator then deducted from the payment a sum equal to the gross amount of any relevant benefits paid or likely to be paid to or for the victim during the "relevant period" in respect of that accident, injury or disease. That deduction was then paid to the Secretary of State. Even where the damages were reduced to take account of the claimant's contributory negligence the whole of the "relevant benefits" had to be deducted. The "relevant period" was five years from the date of the accident or injury, or in the case of a disease five years from the first claim for a relevant benefit consequent upon the disease, but a payment of compensation in final discharge of the claim before the end of the five years brought the "relevant period" to an end. After the relevant period the recoupment provisions did not apply, but under the legislation the relevant benefits were still to be disregarded in assessing damages and so were not deducted. This produced double recovery in any case where the claimant's entitlement to relevant benefits continued after the settlement of the damages claim (indirectly encouraging early settlement) and in any case where the entitlement to benefit exceeded five years (which would tend to be the more serious cases).

9–058   On the other hand, the recoupment rules could work hardship for claimants. Certain compensation payments were exempted, most notably

---

[78] *Flanagan v Watts Blake Bearne & Co plc* [1992] P.I.Q.R. Q144.

[79] *Lincoln v Hayman* [1982] 2 All E.R. 819; [1982] 1 W.L.R. 488; *Gaskill v Preston* [1981] 3 All E.R. 427. Supplementary benefit and family income supplement were replaced by income support and family credit respectively by the Social Security Act 1986, ss.20–22. The possibility of future receipts of these benefits should be ignored because an award of damages for prospective loss of earnings will probably remove the claimant's entitlement to the benefit: *Gaskill v Preston*, above.

[80] *Emeh v Kensington and Chelsea Area Health Authority* [1985] Q.B. 1012, 1022; *cf. Rand v East Dorset Health Authority (No. 2)* [2001] P.I.Q.R. Q1; [2000] Lloyd's Rep. Med. 377 where the claim was limited to the costs of raising a disabled child, deducting the ordinary costs of raising a healthy child, and the defendants conceded that child benefit was not deductible because that was not paid by reason of the child's disability.

[81] *Hewson v Downs* [1970] 1 Q.B. 73. It is doubtful, however, whether this decision can survive the reasoning in *Hodgson v Trapp* [1989] A.C. 807.

[82] Social Security Administration Act 1992, s.81(5).

"small payments" (payments under £2,500). Under the recoupment rules any relevant benefit could be recouped against the whole award of damages. Thus, a claimant's non-pecuniary losses could be set against benefits received, with the result that in some cases claimants received no damages at all. In many instances, insurers would make an offer of settlement under £2,500 which the claimant would effectively be forced to accept because a higher settlement would mean that all the damages would be recouped. This meant that the claimant did not receive an award of damages that reflected his true loss under normal tort rules, and the Secretary of State did not recoup any social security benefits either, with a resulting windfall to insurers. Moreover, once the level of benefits reached the point at which they equalled or exceeded the damages, that was the limit of the compensator's liability to repay to the Secretary of State the benefits paid as a result of the accident/disease.

Another problem could arise where the claimant was unemployed and in receipt of benefits prior to the accident, and the benefits became "recoupable" by virtue of the accident, even though there was no loss of earnings claim against the defendant because the claimant was unemployed with little prospect of obtaining employment.[83] This effectively allowed the compensator to set off the social security benefits (which the claimant would probably have received in any event) against any damages for non-pecuniary loss. The solution devised by the courts to this situation was for the claimant to claim as part of the special damages the loss of "non-recoupable benefit" to which the claimant had been entitled prior to the accident.[84]

9-059

Recovery of benefits

The Social Security (Recovery of Benefits) Act 1997[85] made important changes to this system. Benefits are no longer "recouped" they are "recovered" from the compensator. Any "recoverable benefits" paid to the victim of an accident, injury or disease in respect of the accident, injury or disease in the "relevant period" are recoverable from the compensator. The two most significant changes were that: (1) only certain specified benefits are recoverable against specified heads of damages; and (2) the compensator is liable to pay to the Secretary of State an amount equal to the total amount

9-060

---

[83] *Hassall v Secretary of State for Social Security* [1995] 3 All E.R. 909; [1995] 1 W.L.R. 812, CA.

[84] *ibid.*; *Neal v Bingle* [1998] Q.B. 466, CA, a decision on the construction of s.81(5) of the Social Security Administration Act 1992. This problem does not arise under the system of recovery of benefits introduced by the Social Security (Recovery of Benefits) Act 1997 where there is no loss of earnings claim, because benefits received in respect of loss of income can only be recovered against loss of earnings. If there is no loss of earnings there can be no deduction under that head.

[85] The Act applies retrospectively to all settlements made or judgments given on or after October 6, 1997: s.2. The Act is discussed in detail by Dismore [1998] J.P.I.L. 14. For the procedure on appeals see the Social Security (Recovery of Benefits) Act 1997, ss.10–14 [as amended by the Social Security Act 1998, Sch. 7], and the Social Security and Child Support (Decisions and Appeals) Regulations 1999, S.I. 1999 No. 991.

of the recoverable benefits, which can exceed the amount that would have been payable as compensation.[86]

9–061   Schedule 2 of the 1997 Act sets out the heads of damages against which the specified benefits can be recovered. There has been an attempt to relate the benefits to the nature of the loss for which the damages have been awarded. Thus, the following benefits can be recovered only against that part of the award of compensation relating *loss of earnings* during the relevant period: disablement pension; incapacity benefit; income support; invalidity pension and allowance; jobseeker's allowance; reduced earnings allowance; severe disablement allowance; sickness benefit; statutory sick pay;[87] unemployability supplement; and unemployment benefit. The following benefits are recoverable only against the compensation for the *cost of care* incurred during the relevant period: attendance allowance; care component of disability living allowance; and disablement pension increase. Where care is provided gratuitously the claimant is normally entitled to recover as special damages the reasonable value of that care, the damages being held on trust for the person providing the care.[88] The compensator is entitled to offset the benefits reimbursed to the Secretary of State under this heading against his liability to the claimant in respect of the damages for gratuitous care.[89] Finally, the following benefits are recoverable only against the compensation for *loss of mobility* during the relevant period: mobility allowance;[90] mobility component of disability living allowance.

9–062   In the absence of agreement between the parties, the court has to specify the amount of the damages attributable to "earnings lost during the relevant period", the "cost of care incurred during the relevant period" and "loss of mobility during the relevant period."[91] The first two heads are normally calculated separately, but compensation for loss of mobility could include pecuniary losses (*e.g.* walking aids, adaptations to vehicles, etc.) and non-pecuniary loss (*e.g.* loss of amenity from the inability to get around as easily). The intention behind the amendments, however, was that benefits should not be deducted from awards for non-pecuniary loss.

9–063   If the amount of recoverable benefit is greater than the amount deductible from the compensation payment, the compensator is liable to repay the additional amount to the Secretary of State. For example, say the claimant has losses of £12,000 in respect of lost earnings, and £10,000 in respect of pain and suffering, and has received £15,000 in Incapacity Benefit and £5,000 in respect of Disability Living Allowance (care component) as result of the injuries he received. The claimant's compensation for loss of earnings will be reduced to nil, because the Incapacity Benefit is a benefit listed against loss of earnings and can be set off against the lost earnings element. Neither the

---

[86] Social Security (Recovery of Benefits) Act 1997, s.6.
[87] Only 80% of payments of statutory sick pay paid between April 6, 1991 and April 5, 1994 is recoverable, and none is recoverable from April 6, 1994.
[88] See *Hunt v Severs* [1994] 2 A.C. 350, para. 9–038.
[89] *Griffiths v British Coal Corporation* [2001] EWCA Civ 336; [2001] 1 W.L.R. 1493.
[90] Which ceased to be paid from April 6, 1992.
[91] Social Security (Recovery of Benefits) Act 1997, s.15.

balance of £3,000 Incapacity Benefit (£15,000 minus £12,000) nor the £5,000 Disability Living Allowance (care component) can be deducted from the compensation for pain and suffering. The claimant therefore receives £10,000 for pain and suffering. The compensator is liable to pay £20,000 of recoverable benefit to the Secretary of State. Thus, the compensator pays in total £30,000, of which the claimant receives £10,000 and the Secretary of State £20,000. This exceeds the total compensation (£22,000 for loss of earnings and pain and suffering) that would have been payable to the claimant in the absence of social security benefits.

The 1997 Act provides that certain compensation payments are exempted 9–064 payments.[92] Although the Act provides for small payments to be exempted no figure has been prescribed in Regulations, and it would seem that a figure will not be prescribed because the small payments limit was used by insurers to drive down offers of settlement under the old recoupment system.

The listed benefits continue to be disregarded under the compensation 9–065 recovery scheme when assessing damages,[93] and there is no recovery of benefits paid after the date of settlement or after five years, whichever is the sooner,[94] thus retaining the advantage of early settlement for claimants, and the element of overcompensation for those claimants who continue to receive benefits in respect of the accident after settlement. This overcompensation is also reflected in the assessment of interest on damages since in *Wisely v John Fulton (Plumbers) Ltd*; *Wadey v Surrey County Council*[95] the House of Lords held that by virtue of section 17 receipt of benefit is to be disregarded when calculating interest. Thus, a claimant is entitled to interest on past loss of earnings, without bringing into account the fact that some of that loss of earnings was met by receipt of benefits. Where, however, the claimant has received recoverable benefits which exceed the damages payable under a particular head of damages, such as loss of earnings, with the result that the defendant is required to reimburse the Secretary of State for benefits paid to the claimant which exceed the damages for which the defendant would otherwise have been liable, the defendant is entitled to

---

[92] Social Security (Recovery of Benefits) Act 1997, Sch. 1; and Social Security (Recovery of Benefits) Regulations 1997, reg. 2 (S.I. 1997 No. 2205). These include, *inter alia*: small payments; awards under the criminal injuries compensation scheme; payments under the Powers of Criminal Courts Act 1973, s.35; payments made in respect of Fatal Accidents Act 1976 claims; payments under the Vaccine Damage Payments Act 1979; payments under accident insurance policies entered into by the victim before the accident; any redundancy payments taken into account in assessing damages; payments from certain trusts; contractual sums paid by an employer to his employee in respect of a period of incapacity for work; and, so much of the payment as is referable to costs.

[93] Social Security (Recovery of Benefits) Act 1997, s.17. Thus, where a defendant makes a payment into court setting out the gross figure for compensation, and identifying the recoverable benefits payable to the Secretary of State, and the claimant accepts the payment into court, but the amount of recoverable benefit is subsequently reduced to nil following an appeal, the claimant is entitled to the gross amount of the payment into court. The defendant cannot amend the notice of payment into court in order to delete any reference to the recoverable benefits: *Hilton International Hotels (UK) Ltd v Smith* [2001] P.I.Q.R. P197, QBD.

[94] *ibid.*, s.3.

[95] [2000] 1 W.L.R. 820; [2000] 2 All E.R. 545.

offset his liability to pay the claimant interest on that head of damages against the "excess" benefits repaid to the Secretary of State.[96]

9–066   There has to be a causal link between the claimant's entitlement to the relevant benefits and the accident, injury or disease which gives rise to the claim for compensation, for recovery of benefits to apply.[97] The causal link does not have to be a "but for" cause. Provided that the accident, injury or disease was *a* cause of the payment of benefit then the benefit has been paid "in respect of" the accident, injury or disease. Where the claimant was in receipt of benefits before the accident and continues to receive the same benefits after the accident, the benefit may be attributable to the accident.[98] The causation issue not infrequently gives rise to disputes between the Secretary of State and defendants and their insurers. Where, for example, benefit has been paid to the claimant as a result of incapacity for work arising out of an accident for a period of, say, three years, but the medical evidence in the civil action indicates that the claimant was unfit for work for only six months, the Secretary of State will often have issued a certificate of recoverable benefits to cover the three year period. The defendant will dispute the total amount of the recoverable benefit stated on the certificate, but although the amount can be reviewed by the Secretary of State,[99] in practice this will commonly lead to an appeal to a medical appeal tribunal which can only take place after the claim has been finally disposed of and the recoverable benefits paid to the Secretary of State.[1] If the tribunal concludes that the accident, injury or disease was not actually the cause of the disablement in respect of which benefit (such as disablement benefit following an industrial accident) has been paid, or that the accident, injury or disease did not cause the claimant to be incapable of work (where benefits have been paid in respect of that incapacity) the benefits are not recoverable.[2] In other words, if benefit has been mistakenly paid to the claimant and included in the certificate of recoverable benefits, it is open to the compensator to appeal the certificate on the grounds of lack of causation.

9–067   The recovery of benefits only applies to actions for personal injuries. So where the claim is based on the financial losses resulting from a negligent

---

[96] *Griffiths v British Coal Corporation* [2001] EWCA Civ 336; [2001] 1 W.L.R. 1493.

[97] This is the effect of Social Security (Recovery of Benefits) Act 1997, s.1(1)(*b*).

[98] *Hassall v Secretary of State for Social Security* [1995] 3 All E.R. 909; [1995] 1 W.L.R. 812, CA—income support paid to the claimant who was unemployed at the date of the accident and already in receipt of income support was paid "in respect of" the accident. So where a claimant accepts a sum from the defendant in respect of loss of earnings over a shorter period than the certificate of relevant benefit covers, the benefit is nonetheless recoverable provided that it was paid in consequence of the accident, injury or disease giving rise to the claim for compensation. The fact that the claimant reluctantly accepted a "reduced" payment into court because he was under financial pressure is irrelevant where the benefit he has received is all related to the injuries he sustained in the accident: *Re R. (Social Security Claimant)* [1993] P.I.Q.R. P254 (a decision under the old "recoupment" rules).

[99] Social Security (Recovery of Benefits) Act 1997, s.10.

[1] *ibid*, s.11.

[2] See the decisions of the tribunal of Social Security Commissioners *R(CR) 1/02* and *R(CR) 2/02*. See Axon [2001] J.P.I.L. 411.

misrepresentation, not personal injury suffered by the claimants, any benefits paid to the claimants are not recoverable under the 1997 Act.[3]

The justification for the recovery of social security benefits is relatively   9–068
simple to state. The pre-1989 method of deducting benefits meets the compensation principle by reflecting the claimant's actual loss. It ignores,
however, the consequences for the defendant, or more realistically his insurers, which is that the damages are reduced and he is better off by an amount
equivalent to the benefits paid by the State and funded by the taxpayer.
Recovery merely puts the loss where it belongs, with the defendant's insurers rather than the taxpayer, reducing public expenditure and contributing
to economic efficiency by internalising this cost to the activity generating the
risk of injury. Whatever the logic of this proposition (and it is by no means
clear that those who effectively have to pay the insurance premiums which
fund the tort system are a significantly different group from taxpayers[4]) it
clearly makes no sense in relation to medical negligence claims which are met
from NHS funds, also provided by the taxpayer. Recovery in this context
simply means shifting taxpayers' money from one government department
to another government department, while adding to administrative costs,
although it would seem that the unit cost of administering the system is low.[5]

Non-recoverable benefits

Benefits which are not subject to the statutory regime of recovery are dealt   9–069
with on the basis of common law rules, which prior to the introduction of
recoupment in 1989, had effectively reached the point of full deductibility.
Thus, in assessing loss of earnings any housing benefit received by the claimant as a result of the tort should be deducted.[6]

(b) Other collateral benefits

Where the claimant has received compensation or pecuniary benefits from   9–070
a source other than social security, the question of deduction depends upon
the nature of the benefit and the source. *Prima facie*, the recoverable loss is
the net loss, and so financial gains accruing to the claimant which he would
not have received but for the accident should be taken into account in mitigation of his loss.[7] There are, however, two well-established exceptions to

---

[3] *Rand v East Dorset Health Authority (No. 2)* [2001] P.I.Q.R. Q1; [2000] Lloyd's Rep. Med.
377; see para. 9–092 below.
[4] See the comments of Lord Bridge in *Hodgson v Trapp* [1989] A.C. 807 at 823 on the significant overlap between those groups that effectively fund the tort system and taxpayers. Nor
is it clear that the taxpayer should benefit from the recovery of contributory benefits, which
are paid for wholly by employees' and employers' national insurance contributions, and are
arguably analogous to private insurance purchased by the claimant; see paras 9–070 to
9–071.
[5] Dismore [1998] J.P.I.L. 14, 33 suggested that this was, on average, £10 per case.
[6] *Clenshaw v Tanner* [2002] EWCA Civ 1848; [2002] All E.R. (D) 412 (Nov).
[7] *Hussain v New Taplow Paper Mills Ltd* [1988] A.C. 514, 527, *per* Lord Bridge. A tax rebate
under the PAYE system due to the fact that the claimant is not earning is deductible from the

this. First, the proceeds of a personal accident insurance policy taken out by the claimant are ignored, on the basis that otherwise the claimant's foresight and thrift would benefit the defendant rather than himself.[8] Secondly, gratuitous payments to the claimant from charitable motives are not deducted, again on the basis that the donor intended to benefit the claimant, not the defendant.[9]

9–071   In *Parry v Cleaver*[10] the House of Lords held, by a bare majority, that an occupational disability pension should not be deducted from lost earnings, whether the pension was contributory or non-contributory. The majority of their Lordships took the view that the nature of a pension makes it analogous to private insurance effected by the claimant.[11] On the other hand, occupational sick pay will be deducted if it is paid as a term of the claimant's contract of employment, and this is the case whether or not the employer has taken out a policy of insurance to cover the contractual commitment to pay sick pay, and irrespective of the fact that the entitlement to sick pay applies to long-term incapacity for work.[12] It has been argued, however, that where there is some direct or indirect link between the benefits received by the claimant and wages foregone, as part of the overall wage structure, for example, then the position is closer to *Parry v Cleaver* in the sense that the claimant has "purchased" the benefits himself.[13] There would seem to be little in logic to justify the different approaches to occupational sick pay and occupational

---

(n.3 contd.) loss of earnings: *Hartley v Sandholme Iron Co Ltd* [1975] Q.B. 600. Savings attributable to the fact that the claimant is being maintained in a public or private institution should be deducted from the loss of earnings claim: Administration of Justice Act 1982, s.5; *Lim Poh Choo v Camden and Islington Area Health Authority* [1980] A.C. 174. Any savings from expenses which are no longer being incurred, such as travelling expenses to and from work, should be deducted.

[8] *Bradburn v Great Western Railway Co* (1874) L.R. 10 Ex. 1; *Parry v Cleaver* [1970] A.C. 1, 14, *per* Lord Reid.

[9] *Redpath v Belfast and County Down Railway* [1947] N.I. 167; *Parry v Cleaver* [1970] A.C. 1, 14; *Hussain v New Taplow Paper Mills Ltd* [1988] A.C. 514, 527.

[10] [1970] A.C. 1.

[11] Lord Morris, dissenting, pointed out that in reality there is no difference between receipt of sick pay and receipt of a pension. The true loss of earnings in each case is the difference between what the claimant received prior to his injury and what he now receives by virtue of his contract of employment. Nor is it an answer to say that he "earned" his pension entitlement by his own efforts, since if he obtains alternative employment the claimant must account for his new earnings in mitigation of his lost earnings, notwithstanding that these receipts are "earned." In *Smoker v London Fire and Civil Defence Authority* [1991] 2 A.C. 502 the House of Lords affirmed that *Parry v Cleaver* was correctly decided, on the basis that pension benefits constitute deferred remuneration in respect of the claimant's past work, and the tortfeasor cannot appropriate the fruit of the claimant's past service. Where, however, the injury leads to a reduction of the claimant's retirement pension under his occupational pension scheme, because he is prevented from making full contributions, then disability pension payments which will be received after the claimant would have retired should be taken into account as mitigating the loss of pension: *Parry v Cleaver* [1970] A.C. 1, 20–21, *per* Lord Reid.

[12] *Hussain v New Taplow Paper Mills Ltd* [1988] A.C. 514, HL, distinguishing *Parry v Cleaver* [1970] A.C. 1. Lord Bridge commented, at 530, that sick pay is "a partial substitute for earnings and . . . the very antithesis of a pension, which is payable only after employment ceases."

[13] Anderson (1987) 50 M.L.R. 963, 970. This argument is open to the objection that all "benefits" under a contract of employment form part of the wage or salary structure, which the employee "purchases" by working under the terms of the contract.

pensions, though in practice everything turns upon how the payment is characterised: if it is a "pension" it is not deducted, if it is "sick pay" it is deducted.

In *Longden v British Coal Corp*[14] the claimant was unable to work following an accident at work. He was awarded an incapacity pension under his occupational pension scheme which he would continue to receive after his normal retirement age of 60, though it was lower than the pension he would have received had he continued to work to age 60. The defendants sought to deduct the incapacity pension that would be received to age 60 from the claim in respect of loss of pension rights from age 60 (the disability pension payable *after* age 60 was clearly deductible from the sum claimed in respect of lost retirement pension). The House of Lords held that (with the exception of a lump sum received on accepting the disability pension) such payments received before the normal retirement age did not have to be brought into account. Lord Hope said that the claimant could not reasonably be expected to set aside the sums received as incapacity pension during the period when he is unable to earn wages because of his disability in order to make good his loss of pension after his normal retirement age. It would be "unjust if the plaintiff's claim for loss of pension after his normal retirement age were to be extinguished by capitalising sums paid to him before that age as an incapacity pension to assist him during his disability."[15]

9–072

Where the claimant is under a contractual obligation to repay to his employer any payments of sick pay if he is successful in an action for damages, then sick pay should not be deducted from the award.[16] Similarly, gratuitous payments of sick pay should not be deducted since they are analogous to charitable payments, although where the employer is also the tortfeasor it would seem that the payments should be deducted.[17] If the claimant is made redundant as a result of his injuries, in the sense that his disability makes him a more likely candidate for redundancy, any redundancy payment

9–073

---

[14] [1998] A.C. 653.

[15] *ibid.* at 669.

[16] *Browning v War Office* [1963] 1 Q.B. 750, 759, 770; see also *Dennis v London Passenger Transport Board* [1948] 1 All E.R. 779 where the claimant was under a moral but not a legal obligation to repay. The sum to be repaid to the employer will normally be net of income tax and national insurance contributions: *Franklin v British Railways Board* [1994] P.I.Q.R. P1.

[17] *Hussain v New Taplow Paper Mills Ltd* [1987] 1 All E.R. 417, 428, CA, *per* Lloyd L.J., approved by the House of Lords in *Hunt v Severs* [1994] 2 A.C. 350, 358; *Williams v BOC Gases Ltd* [2000] P.I.Q.R. Q253, CA; *cf. McCamley v Cammell Laird Shipbuilders Ltd* [1990] 1 All E.R. 854 where the Court of Appeal held that the proceeds of an ordinary personal accident policy taken out by an employer for the benefit of employees should not be deducted from the award of damages made against the employer, although the claimant made no contribution to the premiums, and, indeed, was unaware of the existence of the policy prior to his accident. The money was payable as a lump sum regardless of fault, with the sum quantified in advance (by reference to a formula in the policy) when it could not have been foreseen what damages might have to be paid if an accident occurred. This was analogous to an act of benevolence by the employer; it was not a method of meeting the employers' liability for sick pay (as in *Hussain v New Taplow Paper Mills Ltd* [1988] A.C. 514); nor was it equivalent to an *ex gratia* payment by the tortfeasor where the accident had already occurred.

should be deducted.[18] But if he would have been redundant regardless of the accident the payment will not be deducted,[19] although this will clearly be factor in calculating the loss of earnings attributable to the tort since it is known that the claimant would not have continued in that employment. A compensation payment from a statutory compensation scheme for workers who developed an industrial disease (pneumoconiosis) is fully deductible from damages awarded in respect of the same illness.[20] There was no reason why the normal principle against over-compensation should not apply.

3. PERSONAL INJURIES: NON-PECUNIARY LOSSES

9–074   Non-pecuniary losses consist of the pain and suffering caused by the injury itself, and the loss of amenity which is consequent upon any disability attributable to the injury. Here restoring the claimant to his pre-accident position is clearly impossible, and the guiding principle is said to be that the award should be fair or reasonable.

(1) Pain and Suffering

9–075   The claimant is entitled to damages for actual and prospective pain and suffering caused by the injury, by a neurosis resulting from the injury, or attributable to any necessary medical treatment for the injury. This includes any discomfort, humiliation, or disfigurement suffered by the claimant. A person who suffers mental anguish because he is aware that his life expectancy has been reduced can recover for that anguish.[21] Similarly, a person who is physically or mentally incapacitated by his injuries and is capable of appreciating the condition to which he has been reduced is entitled to be compensated for the anguish that this creates.[22] On the other hand, if the claimant is permanently unconscious or for some other reason is incapable of subjectively experiencing pain, there will be no award for pain and suffering.[23] If the claimant's marriage prospects have been affected the award will include an element to compensate for the loss of comfort and companionship which marriage might have brought, although disregarding the economic aspect of loss of marriage prospects.[24]

---

[18] *Colledge v Bass Mitchells & Butlers Ltd* [1988] 1 All E.R. 536.
[19] *ibid.* at 540.
[20] *Ballantine v Newalls Insultation Co Ltd* [2001] I.C.R. 25; [2000] P.I.Q.R. Q327, CA.
[21] Administration of Justice Act 1982, s.1(1)(*b*). He is not entitled to claim merely for the fact that his life expectancy has been reduced: *ibid.*, s.1(1)(*a*), abolishing the claim for loss of expectation of life.
[22] *H. West & Son Ltd v Shephard* [1964] A.C. 326.
[23] *Wise v Kay* [1962] 1 Q.B. 638.
[24] *Moriarty v McCarthy* [1978] 2 All E.R. 213; *Hughes v McKeown* [1985] 3 All E.R. 284; [1985] 1 W.L.R. 963; *Morgan v Gwent Health Authority*, *The Independent*, December 14,

A claimant who sustains psychiatric harm in the form of a recognised   9–076
psychiatric illness is entitled to be compensated for that illness, but not for
mere sorrow or grief.[25] If, however, the claimant's mental distress or grief at
the death of a loved one exacerbates the pain and suffering which the claimant sustained in the same incident, preventing the claimant from making a
recovery as quickly as would otherwise have occurred, this will be reflected
in the award of damages for pain and suffering. In *Kralj v McGrath*[26] the
claimant suffered physical injuries due to the defendant doctor's negligent
treatment in the course of delivering a baby. She also suffered shock as a
result of being told about the baby's injuries and seeing the child for the eight
weeks that it survived. No award was made for the claimant's grief at the
death of the child, but allowance was made for the fact that her experience
of her own injuries was more drastic than it would otherwise have been
because of the grief which she suffered at the same time in relation to the
death of the child. Conversely, if the child had been healthy this would probably have reduced the impact of the claimant's injuries, because she would
have had the joy of motherhood to console her. In a number of cases awards
have included an element for a reactive depression suffered by a patient following negligent medical treatment.[27]

---

25 *Hinz v Berry* [1970] 2 Q.B. 40, 42; *McLoughlin v O'Brian* [1983] 1 A.C. 410, 431, *per* Lord
  Bridge; *Alcock v Chief Constable of the South Yorkshire Police* [1992] 1 A.C. 310, 409, *per*
  Lord Oliver.

(n.24 contd.) 1987 CA—breakup of the claimant's engagement as a result of a negligently
administered blood transfusion which would have caused serious complications to a foetus
conceived with her fiancé. The chances that the claimant would find a husband with whom
there would be no complications if she conceived were 17%.

26 [1986] 1 All E.R. 54; see also *Bagley v North Hertfordshire Health Authority* (1986) 136
  N.L.J. 1014 and *cf. Kerby v Redbridge Health Authority* [1993] 4 Med. L.R. 178; [1994]
  P.I.Q.R. Q1 on the assessment of damages following a stillbirth. This can include the
  mother's loss of earnings in having to undergo another pregnancy to complete her planned
  family: *Kralj v McGrath* [1986] 1 All E.R. 54; and damages for "the rigours of an additional
  pregnancy" that she will have to undergo: *Kerby v Redbridge Health Authority* above. See
  also *Phillips v Salford Health Authority* (1991) 2 *AVMA Medical & Legal Journal* (No. 2)
  p. 14 on the assessment of damages following the death of a nine-month old child as result
  of injuries sustained during birth. See further Burrows, *Remedies for Torts and Breach of
  Contract*, 2nd ed., Butterworths, 1994, p. 206.

27 *Biles v Barking Health Authority* [1988] C.L.Y. 1103 (discussed by Puxon and Buchan
  (1988) 138 N.L.J. 80)—clinical depression and sexual disfunction following unnecessary
  sterilisation and probable permanent sterility; *Ackers v Wigan Area Health Authority* [1991]
  2 Med. L.R. 232—severe depression after an operation under general anaesthetic where the
  claimant was awake; *Phelan v East Cumbria Health Authority* [1991] 2 Med. L.R. 419—
  £15,000 in respect of "awareness" during surgery under general anaesthetic; *Grieve v
  Salford Health Authority* [1991] 2 Med. L.R. 295 reactive depression following a stillbirth;
  Kerby v Redbridge Health Authority [1993] 4 Med. L.R. 178; [1994] P.I.Q.R. Q1—depression following the death of one twin, three days after the birth; *Wheatley v Cunningham*
  [1992] P.I.Q.R. Q100—loss of a child in early pregnancy by miscarriage (not a medical negligence case); *G. v North Tees Health Authority* [1989] F.C.R. 53—general damages of
  £5,000 each to a six-year-old child and mother, where the child was wrongly identified as a
  victim of sexual abuse as a result of a mix up with a vaginal swab, and the mother had
  become depressed and suicidal, until the error was discovered; *Smith v Barking, Havering
  and Brentwood Health Authority* (1988), [1994] 5 Med. L.R. 285, where general damages
  of £3,000 were awarded to a patient for shock and depression caused by discovering,
  without any prior warning of the risk, that she had been rendered tetraplegic following an

(2) Loss of Faculty and Amenity

9–077   The injury itself represents loss of faculty whereas the consequences of the injury on the claimant's activities represents loss of amenity. This includes *inter alia* loss of job satisfaction,[28] loss of leisure activities and hobbies, and loss of family life. It is rare for the courts to distinguish between these separate heads of damage since normally a single global award is made to cover all the claimant's non-pecuniary losses. An award of damages will be made for loss of amenity even where the claimant is permanently unconscious and is unable to appreciate his condition.[29] This treats loss of amenity as an "objective" loss which the fact of unconsciousness does not change.[30]

9–078   The courts operate a "tariff" system with a view to obtaining some degree of uniformity between claimants with comparable injuries, and to facilitate the settlement of claims. The tariff is not precisely fixed. There is a band or range of figures for particular injuries which allows the court to take account of subjective factors which may exacerbate, or reduce, the impact of a particular injury on the claimant. The Law Commission Report on *Damages for Personal Injury: Non-Pecuniary Loss*[31] suggested that awards for non-pecuniary loss were too low, at least in serious cases. In *Heil v Rankin*[32] a specially constituted five judge Court of Appeal accepted the thrust of the Law Commission's proposals, whilst not accepting that there should be an "across the board" increase in awards for non-pecuniary loss. The Court held that there should be a tapered increase in awards, with an increase of about a third for the most serious injuries, but no increase at all for awards

---

(n.27 contd.) operation. The claimant would have progressed to this condition within six to nine months in any event, and the claim in respect of an omission to disclose the risk failed on causation; *Goorkani v Tayside Health Board* [1991] 3 Med. L.R. 33—£2,500 awarded for the "distress and anxiety" which arose from the pursuer's discovery of the risk of infertility associated with drug therapy and the fact that he was almost certainly infertile. Query, however, whether in the absence of any physical injury for which the defendants were liable, there should be any award for "shock" or "distress" not amounting to a positive psychiatric illness: *McLoughlin v O'Brian* [1983] 1 A.C. 410, 431, *per* Lord Bridge; *Alcock v Chief Constable of the South Yorkshire Police* [1992] 1 A.C. 310, 409, *per* Lord Oliver; para. 2–097.

[28] *Champion v London Fire and Civil Defence Authority*, *The Times*, July 5, 1990.

[29] *Wise v Kay* [1962] 1 Q.B. 638; *H. West & Son Ltd v Shephard* [1964] A.C. 326; *Lim Poh Choo v Camden and Islington Area Health Authority* [1980] A.C. 174.

[30] In *H. West & Son Ltd v Shephard* [1964] A.C. 326, 341 Lord Reid, dissenting, commented that: ". . . there is something unreal in saying that a man who knows and feels nothing should get the same as a man who has to live with and put up with his disabilities, merely because they have sustained comparable physical injuries. It is no more possible to compensate an unconscious man than it is to compensate a dead man." The Pearson Commission recommended that damages for non-pecuniary loss should not be recoverable in cases of permanent unconsciousness: *Royal Commission on Civil Liability and Compensation for Personal Injury*, Cmnd. 7054 (1978), Vol. I, para. 397–398. In *Lim Poh Choo v Camden and Islington Area Health Authority* [1980] A.C. 174 the House of Lords were unwilling to reverse *H. West & Son Ltd v Shephard*, preferring to leave the issue to legislation.

[31] Law Com. No. 257, 1999. See also Law Com. No. 225, *Personal Injury Compensation: How Much is Enough?*, 1994, making the same point. For cogent criticism of awards of damages for pain and suffering and loss of amenity in general, and of the Law Commission's approach in particular, see Lewis (2001) 64 M.L.R. 100.

[32] [2001] Q.B. 272; Lewis (2001) 64 M.L.R. 100.

which were currently assessed at under £10,000. The bracket for the most serious injuries should start at £150,000 rising to £200,000 for the very worst cases, with £175,000 being appropriate for an "average" case of tetraplegia. These figures will, in future, increase in line with the retail prices index, although the Court accepted that part of the argument for the tapered increase that they applied was that, over time, the retail prices index does not fully reflect the general increase in prosperity. The public might reasonably expect that such awards bear some relationship to levels of income and wealth in society, particularly since assessing the level of damages was essentially a "jury function."

4. WRONGFUL BIRTH

Claims for wrongful birth refer to actions by parents in respect of their losses arising out of the birth of a child which it is alleged would not have been born but for the defendant's negligence. The act of negligence may arise prior to conception, as for example with a failed sterilisation operation,[33] an omission to warn about the risks of a sterilisation operation failing to achieve its purpose,[34] or negligent genetic counselling about the risks of having a child with a congenital disability.[35] Some commentators have categorised these actions as claims for "wrongful conception" to distinguish them from the situation where the negligence occurs after conception, a category of case labelled as "wrongful birth", which essentially consists of failing to offer a pregnant woman the opportunity to have a lawful termination of pregnancy or to carry out the termination carefully. Thus, "wrongful birth" would cover negligence in the performance an abortion operation,[36] failing to detect that the claimant was pregnant in circumstances where, if the pregnancy had been diagnosed earlier, the mother would have had an abortion,[37] and a failure to advise a mother known to be pregnant of the risk that the foetus may be born with serious disabilities thus depriving her of the opportunity to have an abortion under the Abortion Act 1967.[38] Although the distinction between "wrongful conception" and "wrongful birth" may be descriptively accurate, the courts have concluded that conceptually there is no real distinction between them, at least for the purpose of identifying the defendant's duty of care.[39]

9–079

In the context of assessing damages, the factual differences between the circumstances of each type of case will give rise to some distinctions of

9–080

---

[33] See para. 4–077.
[34] See paras 6–192 *et seq.*
[35] *Anderson v Forth Valley Health Board*, 1998 SLT 588; (1997) 44 B.M.L.R. 108 (Court of Session, Outer House).
[36] See para. 4–041.
[37] *Allen v Bloomsbury Health Authority* [1993] 1 All E.R. 651.
[38] *McKay v Essex Area Health Authority* [1982] Q.B. 1166; para. 2–084; *Salih v Enfield Health Authority* [1990] 1 Med. L.R. 333, QBD.
[39] See para. 2–038.

significance, particularly in the light of the decision of the House of Lords *McFarlane v Tayside Health Board*[40] that the parents are not entitled to recover the financial cost of raising a healthy child. So, the typical "wrongful conception" case, a failed sterilisation, is likely to result in the birth of a healthy child (though as a matter of random chance, the child could be disabled) though an allegation of negligent genetic counselling will probably be focused on the fact that the parents have a disabled child, or at least a child with the congenital condition which they sought to avoid. On the other hand, the typical "wrongful birth" case, the failure through appropriate testing to identify the fact that the foetus has or is at risk of having a serious disability, will result in the birth of a disabled child, though the negligent performance of an abortion which fails to terminate the pregnancy or the negligent failure to detect the pregnancy early enough for a lawful abortion could result in the birth of healthy child. Thus, the distinction between "wrongful conception" and "wrongful birth" is not analytically useful in this context. Rather, it is the factual context of the negligent act or omission that is important to the assessment of the parents' loss (was the child wanted or unwanted? is it healthy or disabled?), not whether it was prior or subsequent to the conception.

9–081   Until the decision of the House of Lords in *McFarlane v Tayside Health Board*, the assessment of damages in wrongful birth cases had not given rise to particular problems. The general principles of compensation in tort actions were applied, although the nature of the loss—whether economic or personal injuries—had not been seriously addressed.[41] After some initial hesitation about awarding damages for the financial consequences of a wrongful birth, at least where the child was healthy,[42] the Court of Appeal came to the conclusion in *Emeh v Kensington and Chelsea and Westminster Area Health Authority*[43] that since a sterilisation operation is lawful, and the avoidance of pregnancy and birth was the object of the operation undergone by the claimant, the compensatable loss extended to any reasonably foreseeable financial loss directly caused by the unexpected pregnancy. Moreover, there were no good policy reasons for denying the claim for the financial loss, regardless of whether the child was healthy or disabled. However, the view that parents could recover for the financial cost of raising an unwanted healthy child was rejected by the House of Lords in *McFarlane v Tayside Health Board*.[44] Their Lordships distinguished the parents' claim for the financial consequences of the existence of a healthy child (which was not recoverable) from the mother's claim in respect of the pregnancy itself, and any adverse consequences for her of the pregnancy (for which damages

---

[40] [2000] 2 A.C. 59. See para. 2–039.

[41] See *Allen v Bloomsbury Health Authority* [1993] 1 All E.R. 651, 658, *per* Brooke J.

[42] *Udale v Bloomsbury Area Health Authority* [1983] 2 All E.R. 522, Jupp J.; *cf.* the decision of Pain J. in *Thake v Maurice* [1986] Q.B. 644.

[43] [1985] Q.B. 1012, preferring the view of Pain J. in *Thake v Maurice* [1986] Q.B. 644.

[44] [2000] 2 A.C. 59. See para. 2–039. It follows that some of the cases which pre-date *McFarlane* have to be treated with caution, and those which are concerned exclusively with the assessment of loss in respect of the cost of raising a healthy child are no longer relevant.

remained recoverable).[45] Subsequently, the Court of Appeal held that *McFarlane* did not have the effect of precluding the parents' claim for financial loss in respect of a disabled child;[46] nor indeed for the financial loss associated with raising a healthy child where the mother is herself disabled.[47] Thus, in broad terms, there are two aspects to the assessment of damages in these cases: (a) the mother's claim; and (b) the parents' claim where the child or a parent is disabled.

(1) The healthy child—the mother's claim

Although their Lordships were in general agreement in *McFarlane* that the 9–082 mother had a claim for damages, they were not unanimous in their views as to which losses were compensatable. Lord Slynn considered that Mrs McFarlane was entitled to general damages for the pain, discomfort and inconvenience of the unwanted pregnancy and birth, and to special damages consisting of: (1) any extra medical expenses, (2) clothes for herself, (3) equipment on the birth of the baby, and (4) "in principle" compensation for loss of earnings due to the pregnancy and birth. Lord Steyn agreed that Mrs McFarlane had suffered personal injury as a consequence of the birth and was entitled to damages for that, including loss of earnings during the later stages of pregnancy. Lord Hope characterised the unwanted conception as a harmful event to the mother—it was the very thing that she had been told would not happen after the vasectomy. Objections to her claim on moral or religious grounds must be rejected since this was an area of family life where freedom of choice may properly be exercised. The claim for solatium and financial loss attributable to the pregnancy did not terminate at the birth— she might have suffered physical or emotional problems after the birth or sustained a loss of income due to the effects upon her of the pregnancy, applying the normal rules of remoteness of damage. But Lord Hope excluded the costs of the child's layette as being part of the child's rearing costs. Lord Clyde agreed that the mother was entitled to general damages by way of solatium, but excluded the costs of rearing the child, including the layette and any loss of earnings by the mother "as a result of the birth of the child" (though this appears not to exclude loss of earnings during the pregnancy). Lord Millett would have excluded the mother's claim for the pain and distress of the pregnancy and delivery: they were the "price of parenthood" and the fact that this particular price was paid by the mother alone was irrelevant. On the other hand, his Lordship would have awarded general damages

---

[45] This is the "distinction between damage attributable to the effects of pregnancy and confinement and alleged damage attributable to the existence of the healthy child that is born": *Greenfield v Irwin* [2001] EWCA Civ 113; [2001] 1 W.L.R. 1279 at [52] *per* Laws L.J.

[46] *Parkinson v St. James and Seacroft University Hospital NHS Trust* [2001] EWCA Civ 530; [2002] Q.B. 266; *Groom v Selby* [2001] EWCA Civ 1522; [2002] P.I.Q.R. P201; [2002] Lloyd's Rep. Med. 1; see para. 2–043.

[47] *Rees v Darlington Memorial Hospital NHS Trust* [2002] EWCA Civ 88; [2002] 2 All E.R. 177; para. 2–048.

to both Mr and Mrs McFarlane for the fact that their autonomy has been breached because they had lost the freedom to limit the size of their family. This should be a conventional sum, not exceeding £5,000. The expense of the child's layette was not recoverable.[48] Lord Millett's views were clearly in the minority in respect of what the mother was entitled to claim.

9–083   Logically, in any case where, but for the defendant's negligence, the mother would not have become pregnant (such as a failed sterilisation or pre-conception negligent genetic counselling) she should be entitled to damages for the pain and suffering associated with the pregnancy and birth itself, which she would otherwise have avoided, and, in the case of a failed sterilisation the pain and suffering attributable to a further sterilisation operation. In the case of post-conception negligence (which may consist of simply failing to identify that the mother is pregnant or of a failure in the screening process for foetal abnormality) the mother would not be entitled to damages for the pregnancy itself, though insofar as she has continued with the pregnancy after the date at which she would have opted for a termination there may be additional losses, such as the inconvenience and distress associated with the later stages of pregnancy, the pain and suffering of the birth itself, and possibly loss of earnings.[49] Against this may be offset the inconvenience, pain and suffering associated with the termination of the pregnancy which she did not undergo.[50] There should be no offset, however, against the award for the pain and distress suffered by the mother during the pregnancy and birth on account of the happiness that a healthy child will bring after the birth.[51]

9–084   With regard to pecuniary losses, in the case of a failed sterilisation the mother is entitled to the cost of a second sterilisation operation.[52] Any claim in respect of the mother's loss of earnings must be limited to losses during the pregnancy and, presumably, in respect of a period after the birth when it would not be reasonable to expect her to return to work.[53] She is not entitled to loss of earnings attributable to giving up work simply to look after the child, since this is regarded as part of the cost of raising a healthy child.[54] If, however, the mother sustains injury in the course of the pregnancy, or develops a condition, such as post-natal depression, which is causally linked to the pregnancy, which prevents her from returning to work then she should

---

[48] Unless, as a result of the incorrect information, the McFarlanes had disposed of equipment previously purchased for other children which they would have kept had they known that they would have another child. This was "a direct and foreseeable consequence of the information they were given being wrong."

[49] In *Scuriaga v Powell* (1979) 123 S.J. 406; affirmed (1980, CA; unreported) the award included a sum for diminution of the claimant's marriage prospects following a failed abortion operation.

[50] *Thake v Maurice* [1986] Q.B. 644, 682; *Allen v Bloomsbury Health Authority* [1993] 1 All E.R. 651, 657.

[51] *ibid.*, at 682.

[52] As had been conceded in *Emeh v Kensington and Chelsea Area Health Authority* [1985] Q.B. 1012.

[53] There would be some logic in linking this period to the statutory provisions on a woman's right to maternity leave.

[54] *Groom v Selby* [2001] EWCA Civ 1522; [2002] P.I.Q.R. P201; [2002] Lloyd's Rep. Med. 1.

be entitled to loss of earnings under the normal principles applied to any personal injuries action.

(2) The disabled child

Where the child is disabled there are three aspects to the assessment of the damages: (1) the mother's claim in respect of losses flowing from the pregnancy or its continuation, which includes pecuniary losses and general damages in respect of pain and suffering and loss of amenity; (2) the parents' claim for general damages arising from the shock of discovering that the child is disabled; and (3) the parents' claim in respect of the financial loss flowing from the child's disability.

9–085

(a) The mother's claim where the child is disabled

The mother will clearly be entitled to damages in respect of the pregnancy on a similar basis as if the child were born healthy, including general damages for pain and suffering,[55] and special damages for any additional medical expenses or clothing, and loss of earnings during the pregnancy, where the negligence resulted in the pregnancy itself.[56] Where the child was wanted, and the negligence consisted of a failure to diagnose the child's disabilities during the pregnancy thereby depriving the mother of an opportunity of having an abortion, the damages must be limited to the consequences of the failure to terminate the pregnancy, rather than the pregnancy itself, though in reality it is probable that any loss of earnings would be towards the end of the pregnancy and therefore that loss is related to the continuation of the pregnancy. General damages will cover the inconvenience of the pregnancy and childbirth and the shock of the mother's realisation that she had given birth to a disabled child.[57]

9–086

Against the general damages should be offset the pain and suffering associated with a termination of the pregnancy which the mother did not undergo.[58] If as a consequence of the birth of the disabled child the mother chooses not to have a further child that she would otherwise have had there may be an additional offset in respect of the further pregnancy that she will not now experience.[59] In addition, if the evidence establishes that had the mother had a termination of the pregnancy she would have subsequently

9–087

---

[55] Which includes both the physical and psychological effects of the pregnancy: *Taylor v Shropshire Health Authority* [2000] Lloyd's Rep. Med. 96, a failed sterilisation case decided before *McFarlane*; *Rand v East Dorset Health Authority* [2000] Lloyd's Rep. Med. 181.

[56] *Hardman v Amin* [2000] Lloyd's Rep. Med. 498; *Lee v Taunton and Somerset NHS Trust* [2001] 1 F.L.R. 419, QBD.

[57] *Hardman v Amin* [2000] Lloyd's Rep. Med. 498; *Lee v Taunton and Somerset NHS Trust* [2001] 1 F.L.R. 419. The assumption is that the shock of discovering that the child is disabled at the birth, rather than at the time of the scan during the pregnancy, is more traumatic for the mother: *Rand v East Dorset Health Authority* [2000] Lloyd's Rep. Med. 181, 200.

[58] *Rand v East Dorset Health Authority* [2000] Lloyd's Rep. Med. 181.

[59] *Salih v Enfield Health Authority* [1991] 3 All E.R. 400, CA.

become pregnant again in an attempt to have a healthy child, there should be an offset in relation to the loss and expense of that hypothetical future pregnancy and childbirth. Such a set-off may reduce the claim under this head to nil.[60] On the other hand, in *Rand v East Dorset Health Authority*[61] Newman J. awarded *additional* general damages in respect of a further pregnancy to a mother who claimed that she went on to have a third child, after the birth of the disabled child, in order to "prove" to herself and her family that she was able to have a healthy child.[62]

(b) General damages to the parents

9–088   Before *McFarlane* precluded claims in respect of the costs of raising a healthy child, it was the standard practice to offset the parents' claim for general damages in respect of loss of amenity for the time and trouble involved in raising the child against the parents' happiness and joy in having the child. That offset was not applied in the case of a disabled child, however, thereby recognising the additional stress, anxiety and burdens involved in bringing up a disabled child.[63] This head of loss has continued to be recognised in cases involving disabled children. In *Rand v East Dorset Health Authority*[64] Newman J. awarded general damages of £30,000 to the mother and £5,000 to the father for loss of amenity, namely the real and physical experience of looking after a disabled child with all its consequences for their private life.[65] The argument that this involved an award of general damages for pain and suffering and loss of amenity as a consequence of economic loss rather than personal injury to the parents was rejected. Similarly, in

---

[60] *Hardman v Amin* [2000] Lloyd's Rep. Med. 498 at 501. In *Lee v Taunton and Somerset NHS Trust* [2001] 1 F.L.R. 419, 429 Toulson J. commented that: ". . . in attempting to draw a balance sheet which shows a true and fair view of the injured party's loss, credit items can only be taken into account which are commensurable with the debits claimed. You can offset apples against apples, and pears against pears, but not apples against pears."

[61] [2000] Lloyd's Rep. Med. 181, 200.

[62] The causal link between the defendant's negligence in failing to inform the parents of the results of routine pregnancy scan which disclosed the risk that the mother was carrying a Down's Syndrome baby, and the further pregnancy, is somewhat tenuous in this case. The mother's evidence was that she wanted to prove that she could have another healthy baby and wanted her first child to have a "normal" brother or sister. Arguably, this would still have been the case even if the defendant's had not been in breach of duty and the mother had had an abortion.

[63] *Emeh v Kensington and Chelsea Area Health Authority* [1985] Q.B. 1012, 1028–1029; *Allen v Bloomsbury Health Authority* [1993] 1 All E.R. 651, 657.

[64] [2000] Lloyd's Rep. Med. 181.

[65] "The defendant is not liable for the disability but liable for having failed to protect the claimants from the consequences of the disability. The burdens are consequential upon the failure of the defendant to take reasonable steps to protect the claimants from having to suffer the burdens. It is obvious that the birth of a disabled child will dramatically affect the quality of life of both parents and it is to be inferred that a reason why they would have terminated the pregnancy was to avoid such a loss of amenity in their lives. As the law stands they cannot recover for any distress which causes no injury, but the loss of amenity caused by being required to expend time caring for a disabled child is a real and physical consequence. I have no doubt that it has sometimes led to exhaustion. In my judgment the law can recognise a claim for a continuing loss of amenity where a breach of duty has caused physical consequences giving rise to the loss of amenity." *ibid.* at 201, *per* Newman J.

McLelland v Greater Glasgow Health Board[66] an award of £5,000 to the father was upheld on appeal. This was compensation for the shock and distress of discovering, soon after the birth, and contrary to the expectation that the defendants had created, that the child was affected by Down's Syndrome. It also reflected the "stress and wear and tear" of bringing up a child with the Syndrome.[67] Lord Prosser rejected the defendants' argument that the father was a "secondary victim" (a categorisation derived from claims in respect of psychiatric damage[68]). Nor was the distinction between ordinary emotional reactions and a positive psychiatric illness drawn in cases involving pure psychiatric damage relevant in the context of this type of claim.[69]

(c) Financial loss arising from the child's disability

In addition to the mother's claim to financial loss stemming from the pregnancy or the continuation of the pregnancy, and general damages to both the mother and father in respect of the shock of discovering that the child is disabled and the "wear and tear" of raising a disabled child, the parents are entitled to recover the costs of caring for the child associated with the disability. In *Hardman v Amin*[70] the defendant conceded that the mother was entitled to claim for her loss of earnings due to having to give up work to look after her disabled child. On the other hand, in the case of a healthy child a mother is not entitled to claim her lost earnings when she gives up work to look after the child, since that is treated as part of the child-rearing costs.[71] Since the basis of the claim in respect of the disability is limited to the additional costs attributable to the child's disability,[72] it would seem that there should be some deduction from the award in respect a disabled child of those child-rearing costs that would have been incurred in any event, if the child had been healthy, *i.e.* the basic maintenance costs.[73] Thus, if the mother would have given up work to look after her child if it had been born healthy it is difficult to see how she could recover for the identical loss simply because the child is disabled. A further issue in *Hardman v Amin* was whether the mother was entitled to

9–089

---

66 2001 S.L.T. 446, Court of Session, Extra Div.
67 See also *Allen v Bloomsbury Health Authority* [1993] 1 All E.R. 651, 657–8 where Brooke J. described this as "general damages for the burden of bringing up a handicapped child" and stressed that "this head of damages is different in kind from the typical claim for anxiety and stress associated with and flowing from an injured person's own personal injuries." For other examples see *Taylor v Shropshire Health Authority* [2000] Lloyd's Rep. Med. 96; *Hardman v Amin* [2000] Lloyd's Rep. Med. 498.
68 See para. 2–109.
69 *cf. Jackson & Powell on Professional Negligence*, 5th ed., (2002), para. 12–289, n. 35, suggesting that an award for mental distress falling short of mental illness would not have been made in England and Wales; though see the comment of Brooke J. in *Allen v Bloomsbury Health Authority* [1993] 1 All E.R. 651, 657–8, cited at n. 67 above.
70 [2000] Lloyd's Rep. Med. 498 at 508.
71 *Greenfield v Irwin* [2001] EWCA Civ 113; [2001] 1 W.L.R. 1279; Grubb (2001) 9 Med. L. Rev. 54.
72 Applying *Parkinson v St. James and Seacroft University Hospital NHS Trust* [2001] EWCA Civ 530; [2002] Q.B. 266.
73 See *McLelland v Greater Glasgow Health Board* 2001 S.L.T. 446, Extra Div.

recover for the cost of gratuitous services provided to the disabled child, following *Housecroft v Burnett*[74] (provided that there was no overlap between the loss of earnings and the cost of care[75]). The defendant argued that the mother could not claim the cost of gratuitous services to the child, because the claim was for economic loss by the mother, not for physical injury sustained by the child. This approach was rejected by Henriques J. Compensation for the mother's time spent caring for the child was to be assessed on the basis of *Housecroft v Burnett*, for which the measure of damages should be the "commercial cost" of the care, less 25 per cent.[76] Alternatively, if the claim for the loss calculated in accordance with *Housecroft v Burnett* was wrong, Henriques J. held that the mother was entitled to damages for the loss of amenity consisting of the stress, anxiety and disruption of her life resulting from the obligation to bring up a disabled child.[77]

9–090   In *Salih v Enfield Health Authority*[78] the Court of Appeal held that where the parents decide not to have further children because of the problems they face in bringing up a handicapped child, this would produce a saving in expenditure which would otherwise have been incurred and this saving must be brought into account in assessing the cost of providing for the handicapped child. Logically, this approach appears to be correct and there is nothing in *McFarlane* which would suggest that *Salih* is wrong. It would seem to be somewhat rough justice, however, if parents who had wanted to have, say, two children, decide that the emotional and financial cost of raising their one disabled child is such that they will not have a second child, and are then told that the financial saving they will make in not having the second child will reduce the defendants' liability to contribute to the cost of their child's disability.[79]

9–091   In principle any other benefits or savings arising out the defendants' negligence should be brought into account in reducing the parents' financial loss. For example, before *McFarlane* it had been accepted that child benefit must be deducted from the cost of maintaining the child.[80] Child benefit is not a "relevant benefit" for the purpose of the recovery of social security benefits under

---

[74] [1986] 1 All E.R. 332.

[75] In *Fish v Wilcox* (1993) 13 B.M.L.R. 134; [1994] 5 Med. L.R. 230, CA, it was held that an award of damages in respect of the birth of a handicapped child should not include an amount in respect of the mother's lost earnings *in addition* to a sum for the services she was rendering in caring for the child. She cannot make a profit by being compensated for doing two jobs.

[76] [2000] Lloyd's Rep. Med. 498 at 509.

[77] *ibid.* at 510: "To retreat to a position where claimants who sustain stress or psychological damage without compensation in circumstances such as this would not only be insensitive but would constitute a failure to compensate in manifestly meritorious circumstances." See also *Taylor v Shropshire Health Authority* [2000] Lloyd's Rep. Med. 96 where, before the decision in *McFarlane*, it had been held that in addition to general damages for the physical and psychological effects of the pregnancy, the mother was entitled to damages for the additional burden of bringing up a disabled child.

[78] [1991] 3 All E.R. 400.

[79] *cf. McLelland v Greater Glasgow Health Board* 2001 S.L.T. 446, declining to follow *Salih* on this point.

[80] *Emeh v Kensington and Chelsea Area Health Authority* [1985] Q.B. 1012.

the Social Security (Recovery of Benefits) Act 1997,[81] and therefore the principle of full deductibility from the assessment of the damages applied. But now that the compensatable financial loss is limited to the costs attributable to the child's disability, rather than the full costs of raising the child, it would seem that receipts of child benefit should not be deducted. In *Rand v East Dorset Health Authority (No. 2)*[82] the defendants conceded, rightly it is submitted, that child benefit was not deductible because it was not paid by reason of the child's disability. Child benefit is a contribution to the cost of raising every child, healthy or disabled, and it would be wrong to offset a benefit that was not linked to the basis of the defendants' liability, namely the child's disability.

In *Rand*, Newman J. also held that recovery of benefits under the Social Security (Recovery of Benefits) Act 1997 did not apply to a claim made by parents against a health authority in respect of the additional cost of raising a disabled child, where the negligence consisted of failing to inform the parents of the risk that the child would be born disabled thereby denying the parents the option of having a termination of the pregnancy. That was a claim for financial loss resulting from negligent misrepresentation not personal injury suffered by the claimants. But the 1997 Act only applies to actions for personal injuries. Accordingly, recovery of benefits does not apply. That means that the common law rules on deduction of benefits applies, which in most instances means that the full value of benefits paid in consequence of the tort should be deducted. However, receipt of invalid care allowance by the parents of the child should not be deducted because that is awarded in respect of the care of the child, whereas the parents were compensated by the defendants, not for caring for the child, but for their reasonable expenditure in connection with the child's disability.[83] Moreover, any benefits paid to the child in respect of her disabilities do not reduce the loss to the parents, since the benefits were for the child who was not compensated by the defendants, and therefore they should not be deducted from the damages award.[84]   9–092

Three further issues in relation to the assessment of the financial loss associated with the child's disability have arisen: 9–093

(i) Can the costs of raising the disabled child extend beyond age 18?

The costs associated with the child's disability beyond the age of 18 are recoverable.[85] This is because the normal principles of foreseeability apply   9–094

---

[81] See para. 9–060 *et seq.*

[82] [2001] P.I.Q.R. Q1; [2000] Lloyd's Rep. Med. 377

[83] *ibid.* It is not clear how this view sits with the approach of Henriques J. in *Hardman v Amin* where it was held that the mother was entitled to recover the cost of gratuitous services provided to the disabled child: see para. 9–089.

[84] *ibid.* These benefits were Disability Living Allowance, and from age 18, Income Support and Severe Disablement Allowance.

[85] *Rand v East Dorset Health Authority* [2000] Lloyd's Rep. Med. 181; *Nunnerley v Warrington Health Authority* [2000] P.I.Q.R. Q69, QBD. Although *Nunnerley* predates *McFarlane* leave to appeal on the question of whether damages should be limited to the date of the child's 18th birthday was subsequently refused, *sub nom. Gaynor N v Warrington Health Authority*, unreported, March 9th 2000, CA.

to the assessment of the loss, and in any event it cannot be said that the parents' responsibility towards a disabled child ends at the child's 18th birthday.[86]

(ii) Can the loss exceed what the parents could afford to spend?

9–095   The claim for the economic loss attributable to the child's disability is not limited to the amounts which a claimant would have been able to contribute to such costs in the absence of an award of damages to meet them. An argument to limit damages in this way had been accepted in *Rand v East Dorset Health Authority*.[87] Newman J. considered that this followed from the categorisation of the loss as economic loss. But in *Hardman v Amin*[88] Henriques J. rejected this view, accepting the claimant's argument that categorisation of a claim as one for economic loss identified the criteria to be satisfied before a duty and its scope are established, but has nothing to do with the quantification of damages once a breach of duty is shown to have resulted in loss of a type which the defendant was under a duty to avoid.[89] As Henriques J. commented the effect of the defendant's argument would be that "The poorer the claimant, the less she will be able to spend on her disabled child. Indeed, it might deny the claim of the poorest parent unable to buy in any care or equipment." The measure of the loss was the reasonable needs of the disabled child, and was not limited by reference to what the claimant would, but for the award, have been able to afford to spend on care. In *Lee v Taunton and Somerset NHS Trust* Toulson J. agreed with Henriques J. on this point.[90] Similarly, in *Roberts v Bro Taf Health Authority*[91] Turner J. considered that the approach adopted by Henriques J. in *Hardman* was correct:

---

[86] As Hale L.J. commented in *Gaynor N v Warrington Health Authority*, unreported, March 9th 2000, CA, "the argument that damages should be limited up to the age of eighteen was based on a very narrow view of what might or might not be the responsibilities of parents towards children, particularly those children who sadly suffer a disability. There is a great deal in family law to indicate that liabilities not only towards those children, but also to the parent who is looking after those children (should there have been a marriage as there was in this case), may indeed endure long beyond the age of eighteen. But in any event I would have thought that there is no basis for departing from the normal principles of reasonable foreseeability of the loss in question in this case."

[87] [2000] Lloyd's Rep. Med. 181, 194: "The claimants may only recover such losses as they have in fact sustained, or will probably sustain, in the future. Their own means, as opposed to Katy's needs, are determinative of this issue. In my judgment, this must follow as a matter of law from the categorisation of the claim as a claim for pure economic loss."

[88] [2000] Lloyd's Rep. Med. 498 at 506–508.

[89] See also *Taylor v Shropshire Health Authority* [2000] Lloyd's Rep. Med. 96 at 103; *Anderson v Forth Valley Health Board* (1997) 44 B.M.L.R. 108 at 139.

[90] [2001] 1 F.L.R. 419, 433: "I do not see why the quantification of her loss under this head should be affected by her means. Her need exists, whether she has the means to meet it or not. It is quantifiable. It was caused by the defendants' negligence. In principle she should therefore be entitled to recover the cost of it. It would be invidious if two mothers in Mrs Lee's situation, each having the same needs, differed in their ability to recover the cost of meeting those needs, because one possessed independent means and the other did not."

[91] [2002] Lloyd's Rep. Med. 182.

"It would be inconsistent with the *rationale* [of *Parkinson*] that the *needs* of the family in connection with extra expenditure should be rationed by the economic circumstances in which the family found itself."[92]

Moreover, as Turner J. pointed out, in this type of case the mother also has a claim to substantial damages in respect of the pregnancy itself. If she were to expend this sum on providing care for the child then the claim in respect of that care becomes "self-funding at the defendants' expense."[93] In other words the mother would become richer in any event and so can afford the care for the child, and therefore the defendants have to pay for that care.[94]

(iii) Does section 2(4) of the Law Reform (Personal Injury) Act 1948 apply?

There is some uncertainty as to how the financial loss attributable to the child's disability should be categorised. In principle, it would appear to be a claim for pure economic loss. There are statements in *McFarlane* to the effect that the costs of raising a healthy child constitutes pure economic loss,[95] and in most actions since *McFarlane* the claim in respect of the costs of raising a disabled child has been characterised as one for pure economic loss. The issue is significant in the context of a number of statutory provisions where the legislation makes the outcome turn upon whether the claimant's action is one for personal injuries.   9–096

In *Hardman v Amin*[96] the defendant argued that the claimant had not suffered personal injuries, and therefore section 2(4) of the Law Reform (Personal Injuries) Act 1948, which requires the court to disregard the possibility that the claimant can avoid expenses by taking advantage of facilities under the NHS, did not apply. The consequence, said the defendant, was that the claimant must mitigate her loss by taking advantage of facilities under the NHS. Henriques J. considered *Walkin v South Manchester Health Authority*,[97] where, in the context of the Limitation Act 1980, the Court of Appeal treated a wrongful conception claim as an action for personal injuries, and at the comments of their Lordships in *McFarlane*, and held that the claim was an action for personal injuries: "It would be an anomaly for a   9–097

---

[92] *ibid.* at [15], original emphasis.
[93] *ibid.* at [16].
[94] See further Whitfield (2002) 18 P.N. 234, 246.
[95] *McFarlane v Tayside Health Board* [2000] 2 A.C. 59 at 75 *per* Lord Slynn: "It is to be remembered on this part of the case that your Lordships are concerned only with liability for economic loss"; at 79 *per* Lord Steyn: "the father's part of the claim for the cost of bringing up the unwanted child is undoubtedly a claim for pure economic loss. Realistically, despite the pregnancy and child birth, the mother's part of the claim is also for pure economic loss." See also *per* Lord Hope at 89; *per* Lord Clyde at 102; and *per* Lord Millett at 109. Note, however, that not all of their Lordships considered that the categorisation of the loss as pure economic loss or consequential economic loss was determinative of the outcome.
[96] [2000] Lloyd's Rep. Med. 498.
[97] [1995] 4 All E.R. 132; [1995] 1 W.L.R. 1543; see para. 10–010.

wrongful conception claim to be an action for damages for personal injuries whilst a wrongful birth case was not."[98] The continuation of a pregnancy which should not have been continued could amount to a personal injury. While the logic of treating the unnecessary continuation of a pregnancy as personal injury to the mother is obvious, it is not so clear that the financial costs of raising a disabled child are part and parcel of that injury, so as to be treated as consequential loss. Indeed, their Lordships in *McFarlane* drew a distinction between the mother's claim in respect of her losses during and shortly after the pregnancy and the parents' claim in respect of the costs of raising the child, the latter being treated as pure economic loss; and in *Rand v East Dorset Health Authority (No. 2)*[99] Newman J. held that recovery of benefits under the Social Security (Recovery of Benefits) Act 1997 did not apply because the parents' claim for the cost of raising a disabled child was not an action for personal injuries. If the mother's loss and the parents' loss are distinct claims, it would seem that the costs of raising a disabled child should not be covered by section 2(4) of the Law Reform (Personal Injuries) Act 1948.[1] That is not the end of the matter, of course, since the defendant would have to demonstrate that the parents had failed to mitigate their loss by not taking advantage of facilities for free treatment for the child under the NHS, and that is a question of whether they acted unreasonably in insisting on private medical care.

(3) The disabled parent

9–098   In *Rees v Darlington Memorial Hospital NHS Trust*[2] a majority of the Court of Appeal accepted that, in principle, a mother who was herself disabled who, as a consequence of the defendant's negligence, gave birth to a healthy child was entitled to bring an action in respect of the additional costs of raising the child attributable to the mother's disability. The Court did not consider the basis on which an award of damages would be calculated in such a case. Logically, the same principles as are applied to the *mother's claim* in relation to the birth of a healthy child or a disabled child would apply, including the assessment of general damages (though in *Rees*, it had been conceded in argument that the claim was limited to the additional costs of bringing up the child attributable to the mother's disability). Calculation

---

[98] [2000] Lloyd's Rep. Med. 498 at 501. Note that for the purpose of the Limitation Act 1980 it makes sense to have a single commencement point for the running of the limitation period, and *Walkin* can be seen as an attempt by the Court of Appeal to prevent claimants opting for either the longer six year period in cases not involving personal injuries (but without a discretion to extend to the period) or the three year period plus a discretion to disapply the primary limitation period in cases involving personal injuries, depending upon whichever option suited the circumstances of the claimant's case. Moreover, it remains to be seen whether *Walkin* can survive the reasoning in *McFarlane*. See para. 10–011.

[99] [2001] P.I.Q.R. Q1; [2000] Lloyd's Rep. Med. 377; see para. 9–092 above.

[1] See *Lee v Taunton and Somerset NHS Trust* [2001] 1 F.L.R. 419, 431 *per* Toulson J. suggesting, provisionally, that s.2(4) did not apply to the financial costs of raising a disabled child.

[2] [2002] EWCA Civ 88; [2002] 2 All E.R. 177; para. 2–048.

of the financial costs attributable to the parent's disability would be more problematic, however, and could be complicated by the presence of another, able-bodied, carer such as a father. If the claim is that the mother is entitled to the costs of paying for someone else to look after the child, it could be argued that the father is in a position to provide that care. Nor could it be said that the father would suffer a loss by reason of having to give up work to look after the child, since this is no different from the position of a mother who gives up work to look after a healthy child, for which she cannot recover her lost earnings.[3] Moreover, the disabled mother must not be so disabled that she is prevented entirely from caring for the child, because in that situation she will have no claim at all.[4]

(4) Loss of fertility

In the wrongful birth cases the claimant is complaining that the defendants have failed to prevent the birth of a child. But the converse situation can also arise: the negligence can interfere with a claimant's fertility, giving rise to a claim for damages for that loss. The question then may be to what lengths is the claimant allowed go, at the defendant's expense, in an effort to redress the loss. In *Briody v St. Helen's & Knowsley Health Authority*[5] as a result of the defendant's negligence the claimant underwent a sub-total hysterectomy, which left her ovaries intact, but rendered her sterile. Ebsworth J. held that she was not entitled to the cost of a surrogacy arrangement as part of her loss. It was contrary to public policy to award damages to enable a party to enter into a contract which under English law was unenforceable.[6] Moreover, the chances of a successful conception were so low as to make it unreasonable to require the defendant to fund the treatment. Ebsworth J. did not exclude the possibility that, on different facts (for example, a younger claimant with a higher prospect of success using her eggs; and an arrangement that fell within English law, *i.e.* non-commercial), the costs of surrogacy might be a recoverable head of damage where the claimant's fertility had been affected by the defendant's negligence. This decision was upheld by the Court of Appeal.[7] The facts had changed slightly by the time of the appeal, in that the claimant had successfully had her own eggs artificially fertilised by her partner's sperm, and the frozen embryos were in storage. However, the prospects of a successful pregnancy arising form the use of the embryos were extremely small (put at one per cent by one expert witness and much less than one per cent by another), so "vanishingly small" that it was not reasonable to expect the defendants to pay the expense of such a slim

9–099

---

[3] *Greenfield v Irwin* [2001] EWCA Civ 113; [2001] 1 W.L.R. 1279.
[4] *AD v East Kent Community NHS Trust* [2002] EWCA Civ 1872; [2003] 3 All E.R. 1167, para. 2–050.
[5] [2000] P.I.Q.R. Q165; [2000] Lloyd's Rep. Med. 127.
[6] See the Surrogacy Arrangements Act 1985.
[7] *Briody v St Helens and Knowsley Area Health Authority (Claim for Damages and Costs)* [2001] EWCA Civ 1010; [2002] Q.B. 856.

chance.[8] An alternative proposal to use donor eggs was more likely to succeed, but it would not restore the claimant to her position before the negligent act. Neither the child nor the pregnancy would be hers, and it could be compared to adoption, the costs of which it would not be reasonable to expect the defendants to meet. The Court did not rule out the possibility, on appropriate facts, that damages in respect of the costs of surrogacy might be recoverable, though Hale L.J. expressed the tentative view that this might be a step too far.

5. DEATH

9–100 At common law a person's death extinguished any cause of action that may have existed against him and any cause of action that the deceased may have had against another. Moreover, a person's death did not confer any common law right of action on another person against the person who had caused the death, which meant that the dependants of someone killed by another's negligence had no action in respect of their loss of financial support by the deceased. Both of these rules have been changed by legislation: the Law Reform (Miscellaneous Provisions) Act 1934 and the Fatal Accidents Act 1976 (consolidating previous Fatal Accidents Acts) respectively.[9]

(1) Survival of actions

9–101 The Law Reform (Miscellaneous Provisions) Act 1934, section 1(1) provides that on the death of any person all causes of action (except defamation) subsisting against or vested in him survive against, or, as the case may be, for the benefit of, his estate. The Act does not create a cause of action, it merely allows for the survival of existing actions, except that where, as a result of an act or omission by the deceased, damage has been suffered which would have given rise to a cause of action had he not died before or at the same time as the damage suffered, section 1(4) deems that the cause of action shall subsist as if he had died after the damage was sustained.

9–102 An action brought by the estate of a deceased claimant is dealt with on the same basis as for a living claimant, and the measure of damages will generally be the same. The estate can recover any expenses incurred or any loss of earnings attributable to the tort up to the date of death, but not after the death.[10] Similarly, pain and suffering and loss of amenity up to the date of

---

[8] *ibid.* at [22] *per* Hale L.J.

[9] See generally the Law Commission Report, *Claims for Wrongful Death*, Law Com. No. 263, 1999.

[10] Claims in respect of loss of earnings in the "lost years" do not survive for the benefit of the estate: Law Reform (Miscellaneous Provisions) Act 1934, s.1(2)(*a*) (as amended by the Administration of Justice Act 1982, s.4(2)), reversing the effect of *Gammell v Wilson* [1982]

death are recoverable.[11] Where the death was caused by the act or omission which gives rise to the cause of action, damages are calculated without reference to any loss or gain consequent upon the death, except that a sum in respect of funeral expenses may be included.[12] Thus, gains to the estate, such as the proceeds of a life insurance policy, and losses, such as the loss of a life interest under a trust, are ignored.

(2) Fatal Accidents

The Fatal Accidents Act 1976 section 1(1) confers upon the dependants of   9–103
a deceased person a cause of action in respect of their loss of financial dependency, provided that the deceased would have had an action in tort in respect of the injuries that caused his death.[13] The dependants have a cause of action in their own right in respect of financial loss[14] irrespective of any claim that might be made on behalf of the deceased's estate under the Law Reform (Miscellaneous Provisions) Act 1934. The dependants' action is derivative, in that it can be maintained only if the defendant would have been liable to the deceased, and it is subject to any defences, such as contributory negligence or *volenti non fit injuria*, that the defendant could have raised against the deceased.[15] If for any reason the deceased could not himself have maintained an action at the moment of his death, if, for example, he has sued the defendant to a judgment or settled the claim while still alive, the dependants have no claim.[16]

(n.10 contd.) A.C. 136. Thus, lost years claims are only available to living claimants, or where the death occurred before January 1, 1983.

[11] In *Hicks v Chief Constable of South Yorkshire Police* [1992] 2 All E.R. 65 however, the House of Lords held that damages for pain and suffering in the few minutes between an injury and death are not recoverable under the Law Reform (Miscellaneous Provisions) Act 1934.

[12] Law Reform (Miscellaneous Provisions) Act 1934, s.1(2)(c).

[13] Fatal Accidents Act 1976, s.2(3) provides that: "Not more than one action shall lie for and in respect of the same subject matter of complaint." In *Cachia v Faluyi* [2001] EWCA Civ 998; [2001] 1 W.L.R. 1966 the Court of Appeal held that the word "action" should be interpreted to mean "served process." Thus, where a writ had been issued in a Fatal Accidents Act claim on behalf of three young children, but never served, there was nothing to prevent a further writ being issued and served provided the children's claims were not barred by a limitation period. This was because s.2(3) was a "procedural quirk" which did not have any legitimate aim, and therefore an interpretation which restricted the children's right to claim would be in breach of Article 6 of the European Convention on Human Rights, by restricting access to the courts.

[14] There can be no award under the Act in respect of a claimant's emotional dependency: *Thomas v Kwik Save Stores Ltd*, *The Times*, 27 June 2000, CA. The only exception is entitlement to damages for bereavement (para. 9–106), but this is a fixed statutory sum and does not depend on proof of damage in the form of grief or psychiatric harm.

[15] An apportionment will be made where the death was caused partly by the negligence of the dependant: *Mulholland v McRae* [1961] N.I. 135; but this does not affect the claims of other dependants: *Dodds v Dodds* [1978] Q.B. 543.

[16] The House of Lords assumed that this was the position in *Pickett v British Rail Engineering Ltd* [1980] A.C. 136. Where the deceased's action was statute-barred under the Limitation Act 1980 the dependants can request the court to exercise its discretion to allow the action to proceed under s.33: see para. 10–081.

9–104   The class of dependants who can bring a claim under the Fatal Accidents Act 1976 is exhaustively defined in section 1 to include: a spouse, former spouse or "cohabitee"[17] of the deceased; any parent or other ascendant, any child or other descendant, or any person treated by the deceased as his parent or as his child; and any person who is, or is the issue of, a brother, sister, uncle or aunt of the deceased. A relationship by marriage is treated as a relationship by blood, and a relationship by half-blood as a relationship of the whole blood. The stepchild of any person is treated as his child, and an illegitimate person is treated as the legitimate child of his mother and reputed father. An action will normally be instituted by the personal representative of the deceased person's estate on behalf of the dependants, but if an action is not commenced within six months any dependant can sue on behalf of all the dependants.[18]

9–105   An award of damages under the Fatal Accidents Act may consist of either damages for bereavement or damages for the dependant's actual and prospective pecuniary loss. If the dependants have in fact incurred funeral expenses they are entitled to be reimbursed.[19]

(a) Bereavement

9–106   Damages for bereavement were introduced by the Administration of Justice Act 1982, section 3, creating a new section 1A of the Fatal Accidents Act 1976. This is a fixed sum of £10,000 for deaths after March 31, 2002[20] awarded to the spouse of the deceased or the parents of a deceased unmarried minor child (though only the mother in the case of an illegitimate child).[21] Where both parents of a child claim damages for bereavement the

---

[17] *i.e.*, a person who was living as the husband or wife of the deceased in the same household immediately before the date of the death, and had been so living for at least two years: Fatal Accidents Act 1976, s.1(3)(*b*). On the meaning of "living in the same household" see *Pounder v London Underground Ltd* [1995] P.I.Q.R. P217. A divorced woman who remarries, but who subsequently returns to live with her first husband, is capable of being a dependant, as a former wife, and does not have to satisfy the residence requirements of s.1(3)(*b*): *Shepherd v Post Office, The Times*, June 15, 1995, CA.

[18] Fatal Accidents Act 1976, s.2.

[19] *ibid.*, s.3(5).

[20] Damages for Bereavement (Variation of Sum) (England and Wales) Order 2002, S.I. 2002 No. 644. The sum had previously been increased from £3,500 to £7,500 for causes of action accruing on or after April 1, 1991 by the Damages for Bereavement (Variation of Sum)(England and Wales) Order 1990 (S.I. 1990 No. 2575).

[21] Damages for bereavement will not be awarded to the parents of a stillborn child, although a mother will be entitled to general damages for the loss of satisfaction of bringing her pregnancy to a successful conclusion, and where appropriate, for being unable to complete her planned family: *Bagley v North Hertfordshire Health Authority* (1986) 136 N.L.J. 1014. Damages under these heads should be not less than the statutory sum awarded for bereavement; *cf. Kerby v Redbridge Health Authority* [1993] 4 Med. L.R. 178; [1994] P.I.Q.R. Q1, where Ognall J. held that there should be no award for the "dashed hopes" of bringing a pregnancy to a successful conclusion, because this was either the same as bereavement, or an award for grief, sorrow or distress attendant on the loss of a loved one, which is not actionable in negligence (applying *McLoughlin v O'Brian* [1983] 1 A.C. 410, 431; see para. 2–097). His Lordship also doubted whether distress associated with fact that the claimant is unable to achieve her planned size of family is a head of damage recognised by law. This

award will be divided equally between them. The award does not require proof of any financial dependency, and there is no inquiry into the extent of the claimant's grief; the award is a conventional sum which may be increased by regulations but not by the courts. A claim for bereavement damages will not survive for the benefit of the spouse's or parent's estate. Where young children are killed damages for bereavement plus funeral expenses will commonly be the only sum payable by the defendant.

(b) Loss of dependency

Damages for loss of financial dependency upon the deceased will be awarded in proportion to the injury resulting from the death to the dependants respectively.[22] This is determined by the multiplier method. The purpose of the award is to provide the dependants with a capital sum which, with prudent management, will be sufficient to provide material benefits of the same standard and duration as would have been provided for them out of the deceased's earnings had he lived.[23] The starting point is the amount of the deceased's wages, less an amount for his own personal and living expenses. This provides a basic figure for estimating the dependency.[24] The length of the dependency must then be estimated.[25] This involves consideration of the deceased's pre-accident life expectancy, discounted for the contingency that he might not have lived or continued working for that long in any event. The multiplier must then be modified to take account of the dependant's future prospects. With dependent children the dependency would not normally extend beyond the end of their full time education.[26] A dependent spouse's life expectancy will be taken into account in determining the multiplier, and where the dependant has died, before the trial, damages will be awarded only for the period of survival after the deceased's death.[27] The multiplier should be calculated from the date of the deceased's death rather than from the date of assessment, as occurs when calculating the prospective pecuniary loss of living claimants, because the multiplier

9–107

(n.21 contd.) latter issue did not arise on the facts in *Kerby*, since the claimant was willing and able to attempt further pregnancies, and on this basis she was entitled to damages for "the rigours of an additional pregnancy" that the she would now have to undergo to achieve her planned size of family (assessed at £1,500).

[22] Fatal Accidents Act 1976, s.3(1).

[23] *Mallett v McMonagle* [1970] A.C. 166, 174, *per* Lord Diplock.

[24] *Davies v Powell Duffryn Associated Collieries Ltd* [1942] A.C. 601, 617. The multiplicand will be based upon what the deceased would have been earning at the date of assessment not the date of death: *Cookson v Knowles* [1979] A.C. 556, 573, 575.

[25] For discussion of the factors to be taken into account in arriving at an appropriate multiplier see *Corbett v Barking Havering and Brentwood Health Authority* [1991] 2 Q.B. 408, 421–423, *per* Purchas L.J.

[26] Where there is a chance that a child will proceed to higher education, this chance should be reflected in the multiplier and should not be discounted completely: *Corbett v Barking Havering and Brentwood Health Authority* [1991] 2 Q.B. 408, CA, applying *Davies v Taylor* [1974] A.C. 207.

[27] *Whittome v Coates* [1965] 1 W.L.R. 1285, where the dependant's reduced life expectancy was taken into account; *Williamson v John I. Thornycroft & Co Ltd* [1940] 2 K.B. 658, where the dependant died.

method is appropriate for periods of uncertainty in the assessment and the uncertainty runs from the date of death.[28] This does not mean, however, that where something has happened in the period between the death and the date of assessment which makes the calculation more certain that the event should be ignored. The court will not speculate when it knows. Thus, where there is a long delay between the date of the death and the trial, and it is known that the dependant has survived for that period, this may result in a higher multiplier being applied to the calculation of the dependency because the discount to be applied to allow for the uncertainty of the dependant's survival should be lower.[29]

9–108   In assessing damages payable to a widow in respect of the death of her husband, the prospects of remarriage or, indeed, the fact of remarriage is not taken into account.[30] This rule relieves the court from having to make what were regarded as distasteful assessments of a widow's prospects of remarriage, although it departs from the compensatory principle of assessing damages, particularly where the widow has in fact remarried and is being supported by her new husband. On the other hand, the prospects of remarriage of a widower, a former spouse and a "cohabitee" are taken into account, and even a widow's prospects of remarriage may have to be considered in relation to her children's claim for loss of dependency.[31] Section 3(4) of the Fatal Accidents Act provides that when assessing the dependency of a "cohabitee" the fact that the dependant had no enforceable right to financial support by the deceased as a result of their living together should be taken into account. This will be reflected in a lower multiplier.

---

[28] *Cookson v Knowles* [1979] A.C. 556; *Graham v Dodds* [1983] 2 All E.R. 953. It is arguable that this results in under-compensation in respect of losses between the date of death and the date of trial because the actuarial tables used for the calculation were adjusted to reflect a discount for early receipt of the damages, but there is no such early receipt in respect of pre-trial losses. The Law Commission Report, *Claims for Wrongful Death*, Law Com. No. 263 (1999) recommended changes to the Ogden tables to deal with this problem, and these changes were introduced to the 4th edition. In *White v ESAB Group (UK) Ltd* [2002] P.I.Q.R. Q76 Nelson J. accepted that the Law Commission's arguments were correct, but concluded that he was nonetheless bound by the decisions of the House of Lords in *Cookson v Knowles* and *Graham v Dodds*. *Wells v Wells* [1999] 1 A.C. 345, said his Lordship, did not provide a basis for distinguishing those cases. On the determination of the appropriate multiplier see Kemp and Hogg [2000] J.P.I.L. 142.
[29] *Corbett v Barking Havering and Brentwood Health Authority* [1991] 2 Q.B. 408. This does not put a premium on delay in bringing the claim because the claimant may be penalised by the court refusing to award interest on all or part of the award: *ibid.*
[30] Fatal Accidents Act 1976, s.3(3). In *Owen v Martin* [1992] P.I.Q.R. Q151 the Court of Appeal held that in assessing the spouse's dependency the court should take account of the possibility that a married couple might divorce, since what has to be valued is the dependant's expectation of continuing dependency on the deceased had he or she lived; *D and D v Donald* [2001] P.I.Q.R. Q44, QBD; *cf. Wheatley v Cunningham* [1992] P.I.Q.R. Q100, QBD, where it was held that mere statistics as to the prevailing divorce rate should not to be taken into account where the evidence was that the claimant and the deceased were happily married.
[31] *Thompson v Price* [1973] Q.B. 838. *cf. De Sales v Ingrilli* [2002] H.C.A. 52; (2002) 193 A.L.R. 130 at [46], [161], [169] where a majority of the High Court of Australia held that normally, no deduction should be made on account of the contingency that a surviving partner (whether widow or widower) will remarry, whether as a separate deduction, or as an item added to the deduction for the vicissitudes of life.

The dependant must establish a pecuniary loss resulting from the death, **9–109** but need not prove that he had received a pecuniary advantage from the deceased before the death. A reasonable expectation of pecuniary benefit had the deceased lived is sufficient.[32] This will usually arise where parents had some expectation of financial support from a child. With young children, however, the prospect of any pecuniary benefit will normally be too speculative.[33] The benefit lost must be the product of the relationship between the dependant and the deceased, not, for example, as a consequence of a contractual obligation.[34] Where the deceased's earnings were obtained from "moonlighting", whereby he did not disclose his earnings while drawing social security benefits at the full rate, his widow was not entitled to claim for loss of dependency under the Fatal Accidents Act.[35] Such a claim was contrary to public policy because: (1) it assumed that someone who had committed fraud in the past would continue to do so in the future, ignoring the possibilities of repentance or detection; and (2) it treated the proceeds of illegally concealed earnings as a valid head of damages. To support a claim for loss of dependency under section 3(1) the deceased's income must have been honestly earned or received;[36] although if the earnings are from a lawful source, collateral illegality (such as the failure to pay tax or national insurance contributions) will not prevent recovery in respect of lost earnings.[37] Conversely, the loss of social security benefits on the death of a spouse can constitute loss of financial dependency, though this will depend upon the type of benefit lost.[38]

The pecuniary advantage lost as a result of the death must be capable of **9–110** being calculated in monetary terms, but need not be merely financial. It includes gratuitous services rendered by a member of the family, such as a

---

[32] *Taff Vale Railway Co v Jenkins* [1913] A.C. 1; *Kandalla v British European Airways* [1981] Q.B. 158; *Singh v Aitken* [1998] P.I.Q.R. Q37 (County Court), where the expected benefit consisted of a share of the damages that the deceased would have received from a previous tortfeasor had he not died as a result of the defendants' negligence. In *Davies v Taylor* [1974] A.C. 207 the claimant widow had left her husband five weeks before he was killed in a road accident. The House of Lords held that she did not have to prove that it was more probable than not that there would have been a reconciliation, merely that there was a substantial, as opposed to speculative, chance that she would have returned to him and thereby benefited from his survival. Lord Reid said that if the chance was substantial it must be evaluated, but if it was a mere possibility it must be ignored. On the facts the chance of a reconciliation was speculative.

[33] *Barnett v Cohen* [1921] 2 K.B. 461.

[34] *Malyon v Plummer* [1964] 1 Q.B. 330.

[35] *Hunter v Butler* [1996] R.T.R. 396, CA.

[36] *ibid.*, per Waite L.J.

[37] *Newman v Folkes and Dunlop Tyres Ltd* [2002] P.I.Q.R. Q13, QBD, which was not a Fatal Accidents Act case. Garland J. explained that the difference between *Newman* and *Hunter v Butler* was that in *Hunter v Butler* the claimant was equally guilty with her deceased husband of a fraud on the social security system. In *Hewison v Meridian Shipping PTE* [2002] EWCA Civ 1821; [2003] P.I.Q.R. P252 the Court of Appeal held that where the claimant's future employment had depended on a continuing deceit of his employers that he did not have epilepsy, the deceit was essential to the claim for loss of future earnings. The claim was based substantially on an unlawful act, so that public policy could exclude the claim.

[38] *Cox v Hockenhull* [2000] 1 W.L.R. 750; [1999] 3 All E.R. 577, CA.

wife or mother.[39] This will be assessed not merely on the basis of the physical tasks that a mother would perform, and so damages are not necessarily limited to the cost of hiring a housekeeper but take into account the whole of a good mother's care of her family.[40] Conversely, where the deceased mother was unreliable and may not have been available to provide steady parental support had she lived, the dependent child's award should be discounted to allow for the real possibility that the mother would not have stayed with her family.[41] Where the court assesses the loss of a mother's services on the basis of the commercial cost of hiring a nanny to look after a child, the award will be reduced to take account of the fact that, as the child gets older and becomes more independent, he will be less in need of the services of a nanny.[42]

(c) Deductions

9–111   Any benefits which have accrued, or will or may accrue, to any person from the deceased's estate or otherwise as a result of his death are disregarded.[43] Thus, any insurance money, pension,[44] social security benefits[45] or inheritance from the deceased's estate (including any damages awarded to the estate under a Law Reform (Miscellaneous Provisions) Act 1934

---

[39] *Regan v Williamson* [1976] 1 W.L.R. 305. The fact that those services are now being provided gratuitously by another member of the family does not affect the dependant's claim to compensation: *Hay v Hughes* [1975] 1 All E.R. 257, where it was held that dependant children were entitled to the cost of future care following the death of their parents even though they had been, and would continue to be, cared for by their grandmother.

[40] *Hay v Hughes* [1975] 1 All E.R. 257; *Mehmet v Perry* [1977] 2 All E.R. 529, where a father gave up his job to look after the children and damages were assessed as his loss of earnings; *Cresswell v Eaton* [1991] 1 W.L.R. 1113; [1991] 1 All E.R. 484. See also *K. v JMP Co Ltd* [1976] Q.B. 85 in relation to claims by three illegitimate children in respect of their father's death. Part of the award to the children included an element for their mother's financial loss, because this affected her ability to provide for the children. For consideration of the principles involved in assessing the value of a mother's lost services see: Exall [2003] J.P.I.L. 51; Leech (1994) 144 N.L.J. 1438.

[41] *Stanley v Saddique* [1992] Q.B. 1. In these circumstances the multiplier method of assessment will be inappropriate, and damages should be assessed on the basis of a jury award.

[42] *Spittle v Bunney* [1988] 1 W.L.R. 847; [1988] 3 All E.R. 1031; see also *Corbett v Barking Havering and Brentwood Health Authority* [1991] 2 Q.B. 408, 419 where Purchas L.J. said that the method of establishing an infant dependant's loss of its mother's services by taking the net wages of a notional nanny as the basis for the multiplicand was a crude and approximate instrument, acceptable only because there is no better means of approaching this almost unquantifiable aspect of dependency. For the effect of adoption on a child's claim for loss of dependency see *Watson v Willmott* [1991] 1 Q.B. 140.

[43] Fatal Accidents Act 1976, s.4, as substituted by the Administration of Justice Act 1982, s.3. On the relationship between establishing the loss under s.3(1) and disregarding benefits accruing from the death see: *Wood v Bentall Simplex Ltd* [1992] P.I.Q.R. P332; *Cape Distribution Ltd v O'Loughlin* [2001] P.I.Q.R. Q73.

[44] *Pidduck v Eastern Scottish Omnibuses Ltd* [1990] 1 W.L.R. 993; [1990] 2 All E.R. 69, C.A., where it was held that a widow's allowance payable to the claimant from the deceased's pension scheme on his death should be disregarded by virtue of s.4 in calculating her loss of dependency.

[45] Damages awarded under the Fatal Accidents Act 1976 are specifically excluded from the rules on recovery of social security benefits: Social Security (Recovery of Benefits) Regulations 1997, reg. 2(2)(a), S.I. 1997 No. 2205.

claim[46]) are ignored in calculating the financial loss. "Benefits" are not restricted to direct pecuniary benefits, and so in assessing a child's loss of dependency following the death of his mother the fact that he will have a better home and receive a higher standard of motherly services from his stepmother than he would have received from his natural mother, had she lived, is to be disregarded by virtue of section 4.[47] On the other hand, in *Hayden v Hayden*[48] the Court of Appeal held that gratuitous services provided by the tortfeasor could be taken into account as reducing the dependant's loss. The defendant was the father of the infant claimant who was claiming in respect of the loss of her mother's services following a fatal car accident. The defendant had given up work to look after the claimant. It was held that the father's services were not a benefit which had accrued to the claimant as a result of the death and so did not fall to be disregarded under section 4. Rather they could be taken into account as diminishing the claimant's loss under section 3(1). This appears to be inconsistent with the approach taken in *Stanley v Saddique*, or alternatively with the view adopted in *Hay v Hughes*[49] that gratuitous services provided by the dependant's grandmother should be disregarded on the basis that the services did not result from the death but from the generosity of the grandmother. Nonetheless, the approach adopted in *Hayden v Hayden* would seem to be consistent with that applied by the House of Lords to the question of gratuitous services provided to a claimant by the tortfeasor in non-fatal accident cases.[50] In *R. v Criminal Injuries Compensation Board, ex parte K (Minors)*[51] the Divisional Court said that *Hayden v Hayden* did not establish any general principles of law applicable to the valuation of claims by children. It was a case where the father who took on additional parental responsibilities was also the tortfeasor, and there was no third party who stepped in to look after the orphaned child, as had occurred in *Stanley v Saddique* and *Hay v Hughes*. Where, as in *ex parte K* itself, a third party provides replacement services, insofar as those services were a benefit they must be disregarded when assessing damages. Thus, it could not be said that the children had suffered no loss, because to say this would involve taking into account something which section 4 said the court should not take into account.[52]

---

46 Since a claim for loss of earnings in the lost years does not survive for the benefit of the estate (Law Reform (Miscellaneous Provisions) Act 1934, s.1(2)(a)) the Law Reform Act damages will be limited to any pecuniary loss, including loss of earnings, prior to the death, and an award for pain and suffering and loss of amenity during the period in which the deceased survived. Before the amendment of s.4 of the Fatal Accidents Act 1976 in 1982, Law Reform Act damages passing to a dependant under the estate would have been deducted from the dependency claim.

47 *Stanley v Saddique* [1992] Q.B. 1.

48 [1992] 1 W.L.R. 986.

49 [1975] 1 All E.R. 257.

50 See *Hunt v Severs* [1994] 2 A.C. 350, para. 9–038. See further Kemp (1993) 109 L.Q.R. 173.

51 [2000] P.I.Q.R. Q32.

52 See further *L (A Child) v Barry May Haulage* [2002] P.I.Q.R. Q35, QBD; and *ATH v MS* [2002] EWCA Civ 792; [2002] 3 W.L.R. 1179 where the Court of Appeal held that children whose divorced mother was killed in an accident were entitled to compensation for loss of

6. DAMAGES FOR BREACH OF CONFIDENCE

9–112   Although there is no doubt that a legal duty of confidence exists between doctor and patient, the remedies available for the enforcement of that duty are somewhat limited in the particular context of the doctor/patient relationship. If the patient becomes aware that a doctor is about to make an unauthorised disclosure of confidential information then he is entitled to an injunction to restrain the disclosure, and in a case such as *W. v Egdell*[53] the return of any medical reports disclosed to third parties. But if the breach of confidence has already taken place an injunction may be pointless, and the patient may well seek damages for the disclosure itself.

9–113   There is considerable doubt, however, about the availability of damages as a remedy for a past breach of confidence which is not based on a breach of contract.[54] Claims brought by patients in the NHS would not be founded on contract. Moreover, even where the claim is based in contract it is doubtful that damages would be awarded for the mental distress occasioned by the disclosure of personal information. The general rule is that damages will not be awarded in contract for the mental distress, injury to feelings or annoyance resulting from a breach of contract,[55] unless the contract was itself a contract to provide peace of mind or freedom from distress.[56] This was the view taken by Scott J. in *W. v Egdell*. If W's claim had succeeded he would not have been entitled to damages in contract for shock and distress (except for nominal damages for the breach), and, his Lordship concluded, there was no reason why equity should not follow the law on this point.[57]

9–114   In *Cornelius v De Taranto*[58] the defendant passed a medico-legal report that had been commissioned and paid for by the claimant to a psychiatrist and a NHS hospital, in breach of contract and in breach of confidence. The report, for which the claimant had paid £630, contained information about the claimant's medical history and private life, which she had tried, unsuc-

---

(n.52 contd.) her services, and the services now provided by their father (who had previously contributed nothing to their welfare) were to be disregarded by virtue of s.4. The damages can only be awarded on the basis that they are used to reimburse the voluntary carer for the services. They are held on an enforceable trust for the carer (*ibid.* at [30]). On the other hand, a father has parental responsibilities to provide care and support for his children. It seems odd, to say the least, that a father who has been avoiding his legal duties to his children should then be paid for providing the very services it was his responsibility in law to provide.

[53] [1990] Ch. 359; see para. 2–187.

[54] See the Law Commission Report No. 110, *Breach of Confidence*, 1981, Cmnd. 8388, paras 4.75 to 4.77. See, however, Capper (1994) 14 L.S. 313, arguing that in an appropriate case equitable compensation or damages under Lord Cairns' Act (the Chancery Amendment Act 1858) should be available for breach of an equitable duty of confidentiality.

[55] *Addis v Gramophone Co Ltd* [1909] A.C. 488; *Bliss v South East Thames Regional Health Authority* [1987] I.C.R. 700, 717–18. Similarly, in the absence of physical injury, there is no liability in tort for mental distress falling short of psychiatric illness: *Hinz v Berry* [1970] 2 Q.B. 40, 42; *McLoughlin v O'Brian* [1983] 1 A.C. 410, 431; see para. 2–097.

[56] *Jarvis v Swan Tours Ltd* [1973] Q.B. 233; *Heywood v Wellers* [1976] Q.B. 446.

[57] [1990] Ch. 359, 398. This point was not considered by the Court of Appeal in *W. v Egdell* [1990] Ch. 359, in view of the result on liability.

[58] [2001] EWCA Civ 1511; (2001) 68 B.M.L.R. 62.

cessfully, to retrieve from the NHS. Morland J. referred to Article 8 of the European Convention on Human Rights, which provides for the right to respect for private and family life, and pointed out that it would be a "hollow protection" of that right if in a case involving breach of confidence in which details of the confider's private and family life were disclosed to others, the only remedy that English law allowed was nominal damages.[59] An injunction or order for delivery up of all copies of the report would have been of little use in this case, because the damage had already been done. In his Lordship's view, to refuse recovery of damages for mental distress caused by breach of confidence, when no other substantial remedy was available, would illustrate that something was wrong with the law.[60] Although Morland J. appreciated that awarding damages for mental distress caused by breach of a duty of confidence was contrary to the view expressed by Scott J. in *W. v Egdell*, nonetheless he concluded that he should award damages for injured feelings: "Although it is a novel instance of such a remedy, it is in accord with the movement of current thinking."[61] Even so, damages for the mental distress sustained should be modest, said his Lordship. They were assessed at £3,000.[62]

The result for the patient is less than satisfactory. There are now conflicting first instance decisions on the point, and if the views of Scott J. in *W. v Egdell* are applied a past breach of confidence will give rise to a claim for damages only if the patient can establish substantive damage which flowed from the breach, and possibly this would only apply to contractual breaches of confidence.[63] The Law Commission has recommended that the action for breach of confidence should take the form of a statutory tort and that damages for mental distress caused by a past breach should be available,[64] but this recommendation has not been implemented.

9–115

---

[59] *ibid* at [65].

[60] *ibid* at [69].

[61] *ibid* at [77].

[62] The Court of Appeal upheld Morland J.'s finding on liability on the basis that there had been no express consent to the report being sent to the claimant's general practitioner and a consultant psychiatrist. But the question damages for mental distress was not discussed in the Court of Appeal.

[63] Though if the breach of confidence leads to foreseeable physical harm to the patient this may amount to a breach of the doctor's duty of care to his patient: see *Furniss v Fitchett* [1958] N.Z.L.R. 396, where the facts were somewhat unusual.

[64] Law Commission Report No. 110, *Breach of Confidence*, Cmnd. 8388 (1981), paras 6.5 and 6.114.

CHAPTER 10

PROCEDURE

10–001 Although there are some important practical differences, such as finding suitable expert witnesses and interpreting medical records, in many other respects the conduct of medical negligence claims is no different from any other action in respect of personal injuries, which are now governed by the Civil Procedure Rules. This Chapter deals with some of the most important procedural issues that can arise in the conduct medical negligence litigation, in particular periods of limitation, the related question of dismissal for want of prosecution, and disclosure. A section on patients' rights of access to their medical records is included in this Chapter because of its relevance to disclosure, although the import of these rights is clearly much wider than the conduct of litigation. The Chapter concludes with a brief new section on expert witnesses.

10–002 This is not a book on how to sue health professionals or the NHS. This Chapter cannot hope to provide a comprehensive guide to all the procedural issues that arise in the conduct of medical negligence litigation, and it does not attempt to do so. Rather it focuses on some of the more substantial issues that are likely to arise.[1] It should also be borne in mind that since the last edition of this book was published the system of civil litigation has changed radically, with the introduction of the Civil Procedure Rules as a result of the Woolf reforms. One consequence of the new system is that, on matters of procedure related to the old Rules of the Supreme Court, decisions in the cases that predated the introduction of the CPR can no longer be regarded as authoritative. Indeed, Lord Woolf has said that: "The whole purpose of making the CPR a self-contained code was to send the message which now generally applies. Earlier authorities are no longer generally of any relevance once the CPR applies."[2] On the other hand, there are sometimes common issues of principle involved, even when considering matters of procedure, and though clearly not binding the decisions in earlier cases may be persuasive. This caveat is limited, of course, to decisions on the old RSC, so, for example, in relation to questions of limitation governed by the Limitation Act 1980 there has not been a wholesale change. Another significant development in the conduct of civil litigation arising out the Woolf

---

[1] For detailed guidance please refer to the "White Book", *Civil Procedure*, Vol. 1, 2003, Sweet & Maxwell.

[2] *Biguzzi v Rank Leisure plc* [1999] 1 W.L.R. 1926, 1934, CA.

reforms has been the development of pre-action protocols, and in this particular context the *Pre-Action Protocol for the Resolution of Clinical Disputes*.[3] The general aims of the Protocol are to maintain/restore the patient/healthcare provider relationship and to resolve as many disputes as possible without litigation. There are a number of specific objectives, including (amongst others) greater openness between the parties when something has gone wrong with a patient's treatment to encourage early communication of the perceived problem; sufficient disclosure of information to encourage early resolution of a dispute; to ensure that relevant medical records are provided on request to patients or their representatives; where resolution is not achievable to lay the ground for litigation to proceed on a reasonable timetable at a reasonable and proportionate cost; to discourage the prolonged pursuit of unmeritorious claims and the prolonged defence of meritorious claims; and to ensure that the parties are aware of the options available to pursue and resolve disputes. The Protocol outlines a timed sequence of steps for patients and healthcare providers, and their advisers, which reflect good practice in the conduct disputes.

1. LIMITATION

Periods of limitation, within which the claimant must commence his action   **10–003**
or find it barred, are entirely the creation of statute, now mostly consolidated in the Limitation Act 1980. The basic rule governing an action in tort is that a claim cannot be brought more than six years from the date on which the cause of action accrued.[4] In torts actionable *per se*, such as trespass to the person, the cause of action normally accrues at the date of the defendant's wrong, whereas with torts actionable only on proof of damage, such as negligence, the action accrues when damage occurs. This will usually be at the same time as the defendant's act or omission, but not necessarily so. In contract the limitation period is also six years from the accrual of the action,[5] which normally occurs at the date of the breach of contract.

The rationale for limitation periods is that they protect defendants from   **10–004**
stale claims, they encourage claimants to proceed without unreasonable delay, and they provide finality so that a person can feel confident after a certain period of time that potential claims against him are closed and he can arrange his affairs accordingly.[6] On the other hand, claimants should not be penalised for failing to institute proceedings at a time when they were

---

[3] See Appendix 2, and *Civil Procedure*, Vol. 1, 2003, Sweet & Maxwell, C3–001. For discussion of some of the benefits and disadvantages of the Pre-Action Protocol and of the Woolf reforms generally see: (1998) 4 Clinical Risk (No. 5) and (2001) 7 Clinical Risk, (No. 1 and No. 2).

[4] Limitation Act 1980, s.2.

[5] *ibid.*, s.5.

[6] *Report of the Committee on Limitation of Actions in Cases of Personal Injury* (1962), Cmnd. 1829, para. 17; *Birkett v James* [1978] A.C. 297, 331.

unaware that they had sustained any damage or that it was attributable to the defendant, or were simply not in a position to institute proceedings. The difficulty is to reach a reasonable balance between the interests of claimants and those of defendants. This has been achieved by grafting onto the basic limitation periods special rules for cases of personal injuries, claimants under a disability, latent damage, and fraud or concealment of the cause of action by the defendant. In broad terms, the effect of these special statutory provisions is to postpone the operation of the limitation period whilst the claimant is unaware of facts conferring a right of action, though ignorance of the law does not prevent time from running. Medical negligence actions are usually, though not exclusively,[7] concerned with claims for personal injuries or death, and this section will concentrate largely on the special rules applying to this form of action.[8]

10–005   The Law Commission has recommended reform of the law on limitation periods to introduce a single, core limitation regime, applying, as far as possible, to all claims for a remedy for a wrong, claims for the enforcement of a right and claims for restitution.[9] The core regime would consist of a primary limitation period of three years starting from the date on which the claimant knows, or ought reasonably to know: (a) the facts which give rise to the cause of action; (b) the identity of the defendant; and (c) if the claimant has suffered injury, loss or damage or the defendant has received a benefit, that the injury, loss, damage or benefit was significant. There would be a longstop limitation period of 10 years, starting from the date of the accrual of the cause of action or (for claims in tort where damage is an essential element of the cause of action, or claims for breach of statutory duty) from the date of the act or omission which gave rise to the cause of action. This core regime would apply to the majority of tort claims, but would be modified in the case of claims in respect of personal injuries. For personal injuries (and claims under the Law Reform (Miscellaneous Provisions) Act 1934 and the Fatal Accidents Act 1976 arising out of personal injury to the deceased person) the court would have a discretion to disapply the primary limitation period (as under the current law), with no longstop limitation period. This would apply to all personal injury actions, whatever the cause of action, except that for claims under the Consumer Protection Act 1987 the longstop would be an absolute bar and would run from a different starting date. The core regime would also apply to claims by a subsequent owner of damaged property and claims for contribution or an indemnity.

---

[7] Any action which gives rise to a claim for pure economic loss will be subject to the ordinary six year period of limitation, unless it can be said to cause latent damage; see para. 10–090. On the possible claims in respect of economic loss which could be made against a medical practitioner see paras 2–035 to 2–037, 2–038 *et seq.*, 2–057, 2–071 to 2–072, 2–157 to 2–159.

[8] For a more detailed discussion see: M.A. Jones, *Limitation Periods in Personal Injury Actions*, Blackstone Press, 1995.

[9] Law. Com. No. 270, *Limitation of Actions*, 2001. The government has indicated that it accepts, in principle, the proposals in the Law Commission report: Lord Chancellor's Department press release of July 16, 2002.

(1)   Personal Injuries and Death

Limitation of action in cases involving personal injuries or death is gov-   **10–006**
erned, as a general rule,[10] by the provisions of the Limitation Act 1980, sections 11–14 and 33. The basic scheme provides for a three year limitation
period which runs from either (a) the date on which the cause of action
accrued, or (b) if later, the date of knowledge of the existence of a cause of
action.[11] This is subject to the court's discretion to allow the action to
proceed notwithstanding the expiry of the three year period.[12]

The three year period applies to "any action for damages for negligence,   **10–007**
nuisance or breach of duty . . . where the damages claimed by the plaintiff
. . . consist of or include damages in respect of personal injuries to the plaintiff or any other person."[13] This expressly includes breach of a contractual
duty. In *Letang v Cooper*[14] the Court of Appeal held that the wording also
applied to an action for trespass to the person, and this was subsequently
held to be the position even where the trespass was intentional.[15] In
Stubbings v Webb,[16] however, the House of Lords concluded that section
11(1) of the Limitation Act 1980, which was in identical terms to and bore
the same meaning as section 2(1) of the Law Reform (Limitation of Actions)
Act 1954, had been intended by Parliament to be limited to personal injury
resulting from accidents caused by negligence, nuisance or breach of a duty
of care. Injuries arising from deliberate assault, including indecent assault
and rape, are subject to the six year limitation period of section 2 of the
Limitation Act 1980, under which there is no discretionary power to allow
the action to proceed once the six year period has elapsed.[17] *Letang v Cooper*

---

[10] The Limitation Act 1980 does not apply where a period of limitation is prescribed by other
legislation: s.39. Special rules apply to accidents occurring in the course of international
travel (Carriage by Air Act 1961, ss.1(1), 5(1), Sch. Art. 29; International Transport
Conventions Act 1983; Merchant Shipping Act 1979, Sch. 3; Carriage of Passengers by Road
Act 1974, s.1(1), Art. 22), and nuclear incidents (Nuclear Installations Act 1965, s.15). See
also Consumer Protection Act 1987, Sch 1, in respect of claims under that Act, amending
the Limitation Act 1980, below, para. 10–088.

[11] Limitation Act 1980, s.11(3) and (4). The date of accrual will often be the same as the date
of the claimant's knowledge; see para. 10–014. The fact that the Limitation Act 1980 is a
consolidating statute means that earlier caselaw on the interpretation of its provisions
remains authoritative. The present scheme covering personal injuries was introduced by the
Limitation Act 1975, adding new sections 2A-2D to the Limitation Act 1939.

[12] *ibid.*, s.33; see paras 10–057 *et seq.*

[13] *ibid.*, s.11(1).

[14] [1965] 1 Q.B. 232.

[15] *Long v Hepworth* [1968] 1 W.L.R. 1299.

[16] [1993] A.C. 498.

[17] Subject to the effect of s.28 postponing the *commencement* of the limitation period during the
claimant's minority or unsoundness of mind; see para. 10–084. On the other hand, a daughter's allegation that her mother had been negligent in failing to protect her from sexual abuse
by her father during her minority falls within s.11 rather than s.2: *S. v W.* [1995] 1 F.L.R.
862; [1995] P.I.Q.R. P470, CA. Where a claim is brought against an employer, as being vicariously liable for the deliberate abuse by an employee of children in the care of the employer,
in the absence of some provable allegation of systemic negligence by the employer, s.11 does
not apply and the claim is subject to a six year limitation period: *KR v Bryn Alyn Community
(Holdings) Ltd (in liquidation)* [2003] EWCA Civ 85; [2003] 1 F.C.R. 385.

was correctly decided in so far as it held that negligent driving is a cause of action falling within section 2(1) of the 1954 Act, but it was wrong to the extent that it suggested that the words "breach of duty" had the effect of including within the section all actions in which damages for personal injuries are claimed. There is a distinction between breach of a duty of care not to cause personal injury, and an obligation not to infringe any legal right of another person. It followed that cases of "deliberate assault" such as rape or indecent assault are not actions for breach of duty within the meaning of section 11(1).[18]

10–008   The decision in *Stubbings v Webb* has important implications in the field of medical malpractice litigation. It is clear from the approach to *Letang v Cooper* that a claimant will not be able to avoid the application of the three year period in an ordinary case of negligence simply by pleading that the facts also give rise to a cause of action in trespass to the person (which is what the claimant was attempting to do in that case). But this does not necessarily mean that where a defendant has committed what by any measure is a trespass to the person as a result of his *carelessness* the action can be regarded as arising from breach of a duty of care, and therefore subject to the three year limitation period. Thus, a surgeon who operates on a competent patient without having obtained the patient's consent is liable in battery. Sometimes this may be the result of a conscious decision by the doctor to proceed without full consent, but more commonly it is the result of a careless mix-up, and the surgeon performs the wrong operation or operates on the wrong limb or even the wrong patient. In these circumstances the doctor is liable in trespass to the person, notwithstanding that the battery is the product of carelessness. Battery is an intentional tort, but in this situation the surgeon has the relevant intention (the direct application of force to the patient's body) and he is simply mistaken as to whether he has the defence of consent. In *Letang v Cooper* the defendant did not intend to inflict any injury at all, it was simply a case of negligent driving which the claimant wanted to categorise as a battery for the purpose of the Limitation Act. On the other hand, it might be argued that the Tucker Committee,[19] while expressly excluding actions for trespass to the person from the recommendation for a shorter limitation period, specifically included a reference to "such actions as claims for negligence against doctors." It is not clear why this specific reference to doctors was included, since claims for medical *negligence* would have been covered by the general words "negligence, nuisance or breach of duty" incorporated into section 2(1) of the Law Reform (Limitation of Actions) Act 1954, and if the Committee intended to limit their remarks about claims against doctors to the tort of negligence it could

---

[18] *cf. Mason v Mason* [1997] 1 V.R. 325 where the Court of Appeal of Victoria declined to follow the House of Lords' interpretation. The European Court of Human Rights has held that the operation of the Limitation Act 1980 in this manner does not contravene the European Convention on Human Rights: *Stubbings v UK* [1997] 1 F.L.R. 105; Mullis (1997) 9 C.F.L.Q. 291.

[19] *Report of the Committee on the Limitation of Actions*, 1949, Cmnd. 7740. This report preceded amendments to the law in the Law Reform (Limitation of Actions) Act 1954.

be said that the comment was superfluous. Possibly, the Committee wanted all malpractice claims against doctors to be covered by the three year limitation period, but this would appear not to be the position in the light of the House of Lords' interpretation of the legislation in *Stubbings v Webb*, and despite the emphasis that Lord Griffiths placed on the fact that the trespass in that case was "deliberate." Accordingly, a patient who alleges that a doctor has undertaken a procedure involving bodily contact without a valid consent must bring the action for trespass to the person within six years, without any possibility of the court's discretion to allow the action to proceed under section 33 being available.[20] On the other hand, a psychiatrist or psychologist who enters into an improper relationship with a patient commits a breach of a duty of care in negligence, not "wilful conduct calculated to cause the claimant injury", and therefore the three year limitation period specified by section 11 applies, not the six year period created by section 2 (which would be the case following *Stubbings v Webb* if the conduct was intentional).[21]

"Personal injuries" includes any disease and any impairment of a person's physical or mental condition.[22] Where the breach of duty does not itself cause the personal injuries, but deprives the claimant of a chance of receiving compensation for the injuries the three year period does not apply. For example, a solicitor's negligence which results in his client's claim for personal injuries becoming statute-barred gives rise to a claim for financial loss which is subject to the ordinary six year limitation period under section 2 (tort) or section 5 (contract) of the Limitation Act,[23] although this is now subject to specific provisions on latent damage. So where a patient suffers purely financial loss due to a doctor's negligence (*e.g.* giving up work following a negligent misdiagnosis[24]) the six year period will apply.

The question of the nature of the loss where a claim is made in respect of the costs of raising a child following negligence on the part of medical

10–009

10–010

---

[20] See *Dobbie v Medway Health Authority* [1994] 4 All E.R. 450, 458–459; [1994] 5 Med. L.R. 160, 166, CA, where Sir Thomas Bingham M.R. made it clear that following *Stubbings v Webb* an allegation of lack of consent to medical treatment is subject to s.2 of the Limitation Act 1980. This would not be the case, however, where the patient died and an action was brought by the dependants under the Fatal Accidents Act 1976, since the action is governed by s.12 of the Limitation Act 1980 (see para. 10–080) which applies a three year limitation period running from the date of death or the date of the dependants' knowledge, subject to the court's discretionary power to override the primary limitation period under s.33. On the other hand, a claim on behalf of the estate under the Law Reform (Miscellaneous Provisions) Act 1934 is governed by s.11(5) of the Limitation Act (see para. 10–082), with the result that *Stubbings v Webb* applies s.2, and the limitation period will be six years from the date of the battery.

[21] *Bowler v Walker* [1996] P.I.Q.R. P22, CA.

[22] Limitation Act 1980, s.38(1).

[23] See, *e.g.*, *Ackbar v Green & Co Ltd* [1975] 1 Q.B. 582, where insurance brokers who failed to obtain insurance against the risk of personal injury were subject to the six year period, although the claim materialised when the claimant sustained personal injury. Croom-Johnson J. gave the example of a claim against a solicitor.

[24] See *Hedley Byrne & Co Ltd v Heller & Partners Ltd* [1964] A.C. 465, 517, *per* Lord Devlin, para. 2–036; see also *Stevens v Bermondsey and Southwark Group Hospital Management Committee* (1963) 107 S.J. 478, para. 2–035.

staff is problematic. In *Pattison v Hobbs*[25] the Court of Appeal held that the financial loss resulting from the birth of a healthy child following a negligently performed sterilisation operation did not involve a claim for personal injuries, and therefore section 2 applied. The significance of this is that within the six year period the claimant has an absolute right to bring an action, but if the claim is for personal injuries there is no absolute right after three years, and the claimant must rely on the court exercising its discretion to allow his claim to proceed. Thus, it was arguable that in some "wrongful birth" cases, where the action had not been commenced within three years, it might be preferable for the claimant to forego the claim for personal injuries (*e.g.* the pain and suffering of pregnancy or of a repeat sterilisation operation), since the bulk of the damages reflect the financial costs of rearing the child.[26] In *Walkin v South Manchester Health Authority*,[27] however, the Court of Appeal held that a claim for the economic loss attributable to the birth of a child following a failed sterilisation operation fell within section 11, as a claim for "damages in respect of personal injuries." The unwanted conception was a personal injury because the physical change to the claimant's body was an unwanted condition which she had sought to avoid by being sterilised. Auld L.J. observed that: "Post-natal economic loss may be unassociated with 'physical injury' in the sense that it stems from the cost of rearing a child rather than any disability in pregnancy or birth, but it is not unassociated with the cause of both, namely the unwanted pregnancy giving rise to the birth of a child. In my view, claims in such circumstances for pre-natal pain and suffering and post-natal economic costs arise out of the same cause of action."[28] Although the claim for the costs of raising the child depended on the birth of the child, rather than the pregnancy, the birth was not an intervening event: it was caused by the personal injury, namely the unwanted pregnancy. *Pattison v Hobbs*, said Auld L.J., was a decision of a two-judge Court of Appeal which turned on a point of pleading. The question

---

[25] *The Times*, November 11, 1985. In *Allen v Bloomsbury Health Authority* [1993] 1 All E.R. 651, 658; [1992] P.I.Q.R. Q50, a case of a negligent failure to diagnose that the claimant was pregnant, where the claimant would have had a termination if she had known about the pregnancy early enough, Brooke J. said: "I realise that if Parliament does not intervene this is likely to mean that different limitation periods may apply to the two types of claim, since it is hard to see how section 11 of the Limitation Act 1980 would apply to a claim limited to the financial costs associated with the upbringing of the unwanted child since this would be, on the facts of a case like the present, a straightforward *Hedley Byrne & Co Ltd v Heller & Partners Ltd* type of claim for foreseeable economic loss caused by negligent advice or misstatement."

[26] See para. 9–079 *et seq.* See, however, the comments of Nicholls L.J. in *Howe v David Brown Tractors (Retail) Ltd (Rustons Engineering Co Ltd, third party)* [1991] 4 All E.R. 30, 41, pointing out that in an ordinary claim for personal injuries which includes a claim for the financial loss resulting from the physical injury, such as loss of future earnings, "the claim for financial loss is as much a claim for 'damages in respect of personal injuries' as is the claim for damages in respect of the physical injury itself. The plaintiff could not step outside the three-year limitation period prescribed by s.11 by abandoning any claim for damages in respect of the physical injury and claiming only damages in respect of his loss of earnings."

[27] [1995] 1 W.L.R. 1543; *Saxby v Morgan* [1997] P.I.Q.R. P531; [1997] 8 Med. L.R. 293, CA.

[28] *ibid.* at 1549.

whether an action was for damages in respect if personal injuries was a matter of substance, not pleading.[29]

This issue has been complicated by the ruling of the House of Lords in **10–011** *McFarlane v Tayside Health Board*[30] that no duty of care is owed to the parents in respect of the financial cost of bringing up a healthy child following negligent advice about, or the negligent performance of, a sterilisation operation. Subsequently, in *Parkinson v St. James and Seacroft University Hospital NHS Trust*[31] the Court of Appeal held that the parents of a disabled child born following a negligently performed sterilisation operation were entitled to the additional costs of raising that child, *i.e.* the additional costs attributable to the disability itself. Thus, such claims are in any event limited to cases involving a disabled child. But the decision in *McFarlane* has cast some doubt on the status of *Walkin*, because their Lordships drew a clear distinction between the *mother's* claim in respect of the pain, suffering and consequential losses associated with the pregnancy, and the *parents'* claim in respect of the financial costs of raising the child, apparently categorising the parents' claim as one for pure economic loss.[32] Certainly, in *Greenfield v Irwin*,[33] the Court of Appeal treated *McFarlane* as deciding that the nature of the parents' claim for the costs of childrearing was purely economic, a view which led Laws L.J. to comment[34] that if the Court of Appeal's reasoning in *Walkin* was at variance with *McFarlane* then it was impliedly disapproved by *McFarlane*. In the one case which has, so far, had to consider this issue in the limitation context, Leveson J. held that he was bound by the Court of Appeal's decision in *Walkin*.[35] It was clear that the mother's claim was a claim for personal injuries. The question was whether the claim which was made for the costs incurred in looking after a disabled child also represented part of the claim in respect of personal injuries or was a separate claim for economic loss, based on the tort of negligent misrepresentation.[36]

---

[29] See also *Bennett v Greenland Houchen & Co (a firm)* [1998] P.N.L.R. 458 in which the claimant brought an action against the defendant firm of solicitors in respect of financial loss alleged to have been caused by the defendants' negligence, but also alleged that he suffered clinical depression arising out of the defendants' negligent handling of his case against his former employers. The Court of Appeal applied *Walkin*, holding that it was an action which included a claim for personal injuries, and therefore subject to a three year limitation period. Similarly, where a former client sues a solicitor for financial loss arising from negligence in the handling of her divorce ancillary relief claim and includes a claim for "anxiety and stress" the three year limitation period applies: *Oates v Harte Reade & Co (A Firm)* [1999] 1 F.L.R. 1221; and a claim against the owner of a motor vehicle for permitting a driver to use the vehicle without insurance (under the principle of *Monk v Warbey* [1935] 1 K.B. 75), which on the face of it seems to be a claim for financial loss, nonetheless falls within s.11 rather than s.2: *Norman v Aziz* [2000] P.I.Q.R. P72, CA.

[30] [2000] 2 A.C. 59. See paras 2–039 *et seq.*

[31] [2001] EWCA Civ. 530; [2002] Q.B. 266; see para. 2–043.

[32] This was the approach of Lord Slynn and Lord Hope. Lord Steyn and Lord Millett refused to treat the distinction between economic loss and physical damage as relevant to the outcome in *McFarlane*, Lord Millett suggesting that the distinction between pure or consequential was "technical and artificial if not actually suspect."

[33] [2001] EWCA Civ. 113; [2001] 1 W.L.R. 1279.

[34] *ibid.* at [53].

[35] *Godfrey v Gloucestershire Royal Infirmary NHS Trust* [2003] EWHC 549 (QB).

[36] *ibid.* at [21].

Leveson J. did not regard Laws L.J.'s observation in *Greenfield v Irwin* "as appellate encouragement to reach the conclusion that *Walkin* is no longer good law." The question posed by Auld L.J. in *Walkin* was whether the claim in respect of the childrearing costs was an action for damages "consisting of or including damages in respect of personal injuries. That is or at least could be different from the question whether the claim for the cost of upbringing of a child is pure or consequential economic loss."[37] It followed that section 11 of the Act applied, which meant that the limitation period was three years from the date of the claimant's knowledge, but with the discretionary power to disapply the limitation period.

10–012   In computing the three year period the date on which the accident occurred is ignored.[38] If the court office is closed for the whole of the last day of the period, it is extended until the next day on which the court office is open.[39] As a general rule, once the period has started to run it cannot be suspended; only the issue of the claim form stops time running. The parties may agree, expressly or impliedly, to extend the time, but the mere fact that negotiations towards a settlement were in progress when the three year period expired will not constitute such an agreement, unless the defendant's conduct is such that he is estopped from relying on the defence.[40] For these purposes it is only safe to rely on an express admission of liability or an express statement that the defendant will not take the limitation point.

(2) Commencement of the Three Year Period

10–013   Time begins to run from either the date on which the cause of action accrued or the date of the claimant's knowledge, if later.

(a) Accrual of the cause of action

10–014   A cause of action is simply a factual situation entitling a person to a remedy.[41] In negligence the action accrues when damage occurs, which is usually but not always at the same time as the defendant's breach of duty. The action will accrue even though the damage is undiscoverable.[42] In the case of minor or trivial harm it will be a question of fact whether the claimant has sustained "damage" sufficient for the cause of action to accrue. If it falls within the principle *de minimis non curat lex* it will be ignored, but not

---

[37] *ibid.* at [35].
[38] *Marren v Dawson Bentley & Co Ltd* [1961] 2 Q.B. 135.
[39] *Pritam Kaur v Russell & Sons Ltd* [1973] Q.B. 336.
[40] *Deerness v John Keeble & Son Ltd* [1983] 2 Lloyd's Rep. 260, where the House of Lords declined to infer such an agreement from continuing negotiations and an interim payment; *K. Lokumal & Sons (London) Ltd v Lotte Shipping Co Pte. Ltd* [1985] 2 Lloyd's Rep. 28; *cf. Hare v Personal Representatives of Mohammed Yunis Malik* (1980) 124 S.J. 328, CA, in the context of a failure to serve the claim form within the period allowed by what is now CPR r. 7.5.
[41] *Letang v Cooper* [1965] 1 Q.B. 232, 242–3, *per* Diplock L.J.
[42] *Cartledge v Jopling & Sons Ltd* [1963] A.C. 758.

otherwise.[43] In cases of progressive damage resulting from a *continuing* breach of duty a fresh cause of action arises so long as the wrongful act continues (as *e.g.* in industrial deafness cases). The claimant is entitled to claim for so much of the damage as was caused in the three years immediately preceding the issue of the claim form. He may be able to claim for earlier damage if the court exercises its discretion under section 33 of the Limitation Act 1980, provided that the earlier damage was attributable to the defendant's breach of duty.[44] If, as a question of fact, the subsequent deterioration of the claimant's condition is attributable to events which occurred more than three years before the issue of the claim form the claim is out of time.

In simple contract the cause of action accrues at the date of breach of contract, although it is possible that where there is an omission to perform a contractual duty this may constitute a "continuing breach of contract" up to the point at which it is no longer possible to perform the duty, with the cause of action accruing at that date.[45] Thus, an omission to give a warning to avoid certain activities which might be dangerous to the patient during the course of treatment could give rise to a continuing duty to give the appropriate advice.   **10–015**

There is a practical advantage to the claimant in issuing the claim form within three years of the accrual of the cause action, since no question of having to establish the precise date of knowledge will then arise. But if more than three years have elapsed since the date of accrual of the action, the primary limitation period will not necessarily have expired. Time does not run unless and until the claimant acquires the relevant "knowledge," which can occur at the date of accrual or later, but never before the action has accrued.   **10–016**

(b) Date of Knowledge

By section 14(1) references to a person's date of knowledge are references to the date on which he first had knowledge of the following facts: **10–017**

"(a) that the injury in question was significant; and

(b) that the injury was attributable in whole or in part to the act or omission which is alleged to constitute negligence, nuisance or breach of duty; and

(c) the identity of the defendant; and

---

[43] *ibid.* Asymptomatic, minor physiological damage may be sufficient to give rise to a cause of action: see *Church v Ministry of Defence* (1984) 134 N.L.J. 623; *Sykes v Ministry of Defence, The Times,* March 23, 1984; *Patterson v Ministry of Defence* [1987] C.L.Y. 1194.

[44] See, *e.g., Thompson v Smiths Shiprepairers (North Shields) Ltd* [1984] Q.B. 405. If the earlier damage cannot be attributed to the defendant's breach of duty, nonetheless the award of damages for the later, actionable damage may be proportionately greater because additional harm to a person who has an existing disability may have more catastrophic consequences than the initial injury: *Paris v Stepney Borough Council* [1951] A.C. 367; *Berry v Stone Manganese & Marine Ltd* [1972] 1 Lloyd's Rep. 182, 196.

[45] *Midland Bank Trust Co Ltd v Hett, Stubbs & Kemp* [1979] Ch 384; *cf. Bell v Peter Browne & Co* [1990] 2 Q.B. 495, CA.

(d)   if it is alleged that the act or omission was that of a person other than the defendant, the identity of that person and the additional facts supporting the bringing of an action against the defendant ..."

These provisions are conjunctive: if the claimant does not have the knowledge specified in any of these paragraphs then he does not have "knowledge" for the purpose of starting the limitation period running (though paragraph (d) only applies in certain circumstances). On the other hand, section 14(1) is also exhaustive: no knowledge of any further facts is required.[46]

10–018   The word "knowledge" has troubled the courts on a number of occasions, since the state of mind which might induce an individual to undertake proceedings may range from "suspicion," through "belief", to "knowledge" as a certainty, and yet a claimant may not know for certain whether, for example, the defendant's conduct caused his injuries until after the case has been tried and a ruling been given by the court. In *Halford v Brookes*[47] Lord Donaldson M.R. said that the word knowledge:

"has to be construed in the context of the purpose of the section, which is to determine a period within which a plaintiff can be required to start any proceedings. In this context 'knowledge' clearly does not mean 'know for certain and beyond possibility of contradiction.' It does, however, mean 'know with sufficient confidence to justify embarking on the preliminaries to the issue of the writ, such as submitting a claim to the proposed defendant, taking legal and other advice and collecting evidence.' Suspicion, particularly if it is vague and unsupported, will indeed not be enough, but reasonable belief will normally suffice. It is probably only in an exceptional case such as *Davis v Ministry of Defence* that it will not, because there is some other countervailing factor."

In *Nash v Eli Lilly & Co.*,[48] in which the claimants claimed that they had suffered adverse reactions to the drug Opren, the Court of Appeal held that "knowledge" is a condition of mind which imports a degree of certainty:

"and . . . the degree of certainty which is appropriate for this purpose is that which, for the particular plaintiff, may reasonably be regarded as sufficient to justify embarking upon the preliminaries to the making of a claim for compensation such as the taking of legal or other advice."

---

[46] *Dobbie v Medway Health Authority* [1994] 4 All E.R. 450, 462; [1994] 5 Med. L.R. 160, 168, *per* Steyn L.J. Where a defendant applies to strike out an action *in limine* on the ground that the date of the claimant's knowledge of the relevant facts was more than three years before the issue of the claim form, the court should not grant the application unless the issue is clear and obvious and the contrary unarguable: *Davis v Ministry of Defence*, The Times, August 7, 1985, CA, *per* May L.J.

[47] [1991] 3 All E.R. 559, 573–574; [1991] 1 W.L.R. 428.

[48] [1993] 1 W.L.R. 782, 792; [1992] 3 Med. L.R. 353, 365, CA.

This is a two stage process involving: (i) the nature of the information received, the extent to which the claimant pays attention to the information as affecting him, and his capacity to understand it; and (ii) evaluation of the information that has been received and understood, *e.g.* it may be regarded as unreliable or uncertain. Therefore the court must assess the intelligence of the claimant, consider and assess his assertions as to how he regarded such information as he had, and determine whether he had knowledge of the facts by reason of his understanding of the information.[49]

In *North Essex District Health Authority v Spargo*[50] Brooke L.J. set out a number of propositions, taken from previous authorities, about the meaning of the word "knowledge" for the purpose of section 14: **10–019**

"(1) The knowledge required to satisfy section 14(1)(b) is a broad knowledge of the essence of the causally relevant act or omission to which the injury is attributable;

(2) 'Attributable' in this context means 'capable of being attributed to' in the sense of being a real possibility;

(3) A plaintiff has requisite knowledge when she knows enough to make it reasonable for her to begin to investigate whether or not she has a case against the defendant. Another way of putting this is to say that she will have such knowledge if she so firmly believes that her condition is capable of being attributed to an act or omission which she can identify (in broad terms) that she goes to a solicitor to seek advice about making a claim for compensation;

(4) On the other hand she will not have the requisite knowledge if she thinks she knows the acts or omissions she should investigate but in fact is barking up the wrong tree; or if her knowledge of what the defendant did or did not do is so vague or general that she cannot fairly be expected to know what she should investigate; or if her state of mind is such that she thinks her condition is capable of being attributed to the act or omission alleged to constitute negligence, but she is not sure about this, and would need to check it with an expert before she could be properly said to know that it was."

In an area of the law where judicial comment is quite frequent, and not always consistent, Brooke L.J.'s statement has been treated as particularly authoritative. Thus, it has been said that the *Spargo* principles were intended not simply as guidelines, but as binding rules.[51]

The third principle is concerned with the degree of the claimant's "belief", and appears to treat any claimant who goes to a solicitor as having the **10–020**

[49] *ibid.* See also *Skitt v Khan and Wakefield Health Authority* [1997] 8 Med. L.R. 105, CA.
[50] [1997] P.I.Q.R. P235, 242; [1997] 8 Med. L.R. 125, 129–130
[51] *Griffin, Lawson and Williams v Clwyd Health Authority* [2001] EWCA Civ 818; [2001] P.I.Q.R. P420; *Corbin v Penfold Metallising Company Ltd* [2000] Lloyds Rep. Med. 247, 249, CA: the Court "intended to lay down, not merely guidelines, but authoritative statements of how s.14 should be interpreted."

requisite degree of knowledge. What, though, if the claimant is simply unsure, and is seeking advice? It cannot be suggested that simply by going to a solicitor the claimant necessarily has knowledge of all the relevant *facts*, *e.g.* as to the identity of the defendant. In *Sniezek v Bundy (Letchworth) Ltd*[52] the Court of Appeal said that, applying the third *Spargo* principle, there was a distinction to be drawn between a claimant who has a firm belief that he has a significant injury, attributable to his working conditions (especially a belief that takes him to a solicitor for advice about a claim), a belief that he retains whatever contrary advice he receives, and a claimant who believes that he may have, or even probably has, a significant injury which is attributable to his working conditions, but is not sure and feels it necessary to have expert advice on those questions. The former has knowledge of significant injury and attribution for the purposes of section 14, but the latter does not.

10–021   In *O'Driscoll v Dudley Health Authority*[53] Stuart-Smith L.J. said that the fourth *Spargo* principle "must be read as postulating a situation antithetical to that covered by the third principle; *i.e.* the fourth principle postulates a state of mind short of a firm belief which takes a potential claimant to a solicitor." The reference in principle (4) to "the need to check with an expert" was a reference to the need for an expert's opinion before even the claimant can be said to know that the attributability of her condition to a particular "act or omission" was a real possibility:

> "That is not the same investigation as is referred to in the first limb of principle three; this latter is an investigation into whether the plaintiff 'has a case against the defendant'—what Brooke L.J. later in his judgment called 'enquiry whether the identified injury was indeed probably caused by the identified omission and whether the omission (identified initially in broad terms) amounted to actionable negligence'—an investigation which must be carried out whilst the limitation clock is ticking."[54]

10–022   In *Ali v Courtaulds Textiles Ltd*[55] the question was whether the claimant knew that deafness in a man in his sixties was caused by the ageing process or by noise at work. The claimant knew he was deaf. He knew that exposure to noise could cause deafness. He also knew that the ageing process could cause deafness. But, said the Court of Appeal, he could not know whether his deafness had been caused by ageing or noise until he received an expert's report to that effect. The judge had held that the mere fact that he sought that advice by going to a solicitor fixed him with constructive knowl-

---

[52] [2000] P.I.Q.R. P213, 224.
[53] [1998] Lloyd's Rep. Med. 210, 221. See also *Roberts v Winbow* [1999] P.I.Q.R. P77; [1999] Lloyd's Rep. Med. 31, CA, for discussion of the distinction between Brooke L.J.'s principles (3) and (4).
[54] *ibid*. at pp. 221–222.
[55] [1999] Lloyd's Rep. Med. 301, CA. See also *Harrild v Ministry of Defence* [2001] Lloyd's Rep. Med. 117, QBD.

edge. That conclusion flew in the face of the proviso to section 14(3).[56] Knowledge as to whether his deafness was noise-induced or age-induced was ascertainable only with the help of expert medical advice, and he had taken all reasonable steps to obtain that advice once he became aware that deafness could be noise-induced. Thus, the case fell within the third category of principle 4 of Brooke L.J.'s categories in *Spargo*, i.e. he thought that his condition was capable of being attributed to the act or omission alleged to constitute negligence, but he was not sure about this, and needed to check it with an expert before he could properly be said to know that it was.[57]

(i) Significant injury

An injury is significant if the person whose date of knowledge is in question would reasonably have considered it sufficiently serious to justify his instituting proceedings for damages against a defendant who did not dispute liability and was able to satisfy a judgment.[58] This is a combined subjective/objective test:

10–023

> "Taking *that* plaintiff, with *that* plaintiff's intelligence, would he have been reasonable in considering the injury not sufficiently serious to justify instituting proceedings for damages?"[59]

It is a question of what a reasonable man of the claimant's age, with his background, his intelligence and his disabilities would reasonably have known.[60] However, "significant injury" refers to the gravity of the damage and its monetary value, not to the claimant's evaluation of its cause, nature or usualness.[61] Other personal reasons that the claimant may have had for not commencing proceedings are irrelevant, even if they are objectively reasonable.[62] The claimant's subjective reasons and beliefs may, however, be

---

[56] Which deals with constructive knowledge. See para. 10–048.

[57] The defendants' case on limitation was not assisted by its argument on causation: "At the same time as the defendants allege that that the claimant 'knew that his deafness was attributable to exposure to noise' they were relying on their own expert's report that, subject to further tests, there was nothing in the pattern of his pure tone audiometry to suggest noise exposure as a cause of the deafness, and that the 'genuine conductive loss' originated from childhood otitis media . . ." *per* Henry L.J. [1999] Lloyd's Rep. Med. 301 at 303.

[58] Limitation Act 1980, s.14(2).

[59] *McCafferty v Metropolitan Police District Receiver* [1977] 1 W.L.R. 1073, 1081, *per* Geoffrey Lane L.J. See also *Denman v Essex Area Health Authority* (1984) 134 N.L.J. 264, where the claimant was not aware that his injury (the breakdown of a repair effected by a bone graft operation in 1972, following an accident in 1973 for which the defendants were responsible) was "significant" until he was informed about it by a consultant surgeon in 1979.

[60] *Davis v City and Hackney Health Authority* [1991] 2 Med. L.R. 366.

[61] *Dobbie v Medway Health Authority* [1994] 4 All E.R. 450, 457; [1994] 5 Med. L.R. 160, 165, *per* Sir Thomas Bingham M.R., though his Lordship added that time does not run, even if the claimant is aware of the injury, if he would reasonably have accepted it as a fact of life or not worth bothering about.

[62] *Miller v London Electrical Manufacturing Co Ltd* [1976] 2 Lloyd's Rep. 284, where the injury turned out to be more serious than the claimant initially thought; *Buck v English*

relevant to the court's exercise of discretion under section 33. There may be some difficulty in determining when a claimant first knew that his injury was significant where the injury consists of psychological damage, particularly where the claimant put the relevant events to the back of his mind, or tried to block or suppress the events. This is a highly fact-sensitive question.[63]

10–024   Where an injury initially appears to be trivial but subsequently turns out to be serious, time does not run until the claimant knows that the injury is in fact serious. However, section 14(2) appears to make most injuries significant in monetary terms, since it may not take much to justify instituting proceedings against a solvent defendant who admits liability. Thus, where the injury, though minor, is sufficiently serious to institute proceedings, and the claimant subsequently discovers a far more serious injury caused by the same accident, time will run from the date of the first injury known to be significant. An action in respect of the second injury commenced more than three years after knowledge of the first injury will be barred,[64] though the claimant's appreciation of the seriousness of an injury may depend upon the medical advice which he receives.[65] If the initial injury is minor but there is a medically recognised risk of deterioration in the future, knowledge of the risk is probably enough to start time running, provided the risk itself is sufficiently serious. The claimant should not wait for the risk to materialise.[66] On the other hand, where an existing injury or disability has allegedly been exacerbated by the defendant's negligence, the relevant knowledge for the purpose of section 14 is the claimant's knowledge of the exacerbation, not his knowledge of the original injury.[67]

---

[63] *KR v Bryn Alyn Community (Holdings) Ltd (in liquidation)* [2003] EWCA Civ 85; [2003] 1 F.C.R. 385.

(n.62 contd.) *Electric Co Ltd* [1977] 1 W.L.R. 806, where the claimant was still working and did not want to "sponge" on his employer by bringing an action; *McCafferty v Metropolitan Police District Receiver* [1977] 1 W.L.R. 1073, where the claimant wanted to preserve good relations with his employer; *Farmer v National Coal Board, The Times,* April 27, 1985, CA, where the claimant believed that the only potential defendant was not worth suing because he had no resources.

[64] *Bristow v Grout, The Times,* November 3, 1986; *Roberts v Winbow* [1999] P.I.Q.R. P77; [1999] Lloyd's Rep. Med. 31, CA; see also *Miller v London Electrical Manufacturing Co Ltd* [1976] 2 Lloyd's Rep. 284, 287, and the comments of Butler-Sloss L.J. on *Miller* in *Harding v Peoples' Dispensary for Sick Animals* [1994] P.I.Q.R. P270, 273.

[65] In *Harding v Peoples' Dispensary for Sick Animals* [1994] P.I.Q.R. P270 the claimant sustained a back injury in 1988 which resulted in her being off work for seven weeks. The Court of Appeal held that she did not acquire knowledge that the injury was significant until 1990 when it became apparent that the injury was considerably more serious than had initially been appreciated. She had undergone an inconclusive X-ray, and her general practitioner did not suggest that there were any serious symptoms. She was led to the view that the injury would resolve itself in due course, and thus was entitled to view her injury as not being significant, even though it was painful, "because the issue was whether it was of sufficient significance to institute proceedings, not whether it was of discomfort or pain to her in circumstances in which it would not occur to any reasonable person to bring proceedings."

[66] Symptomless, minor physiological damage may be actionable, particularly where it carries a slight risk of future damage, and/or gives rise to anxiety in the claimant: *Church v Ministry of Defence* (1984) 134 N.L.J. 623; *Sykes v Ministry of Defence, The Times,* March 23, 1984. An award of provisional damages may be appropriate in such a case: see *Patterson v Ministry of Defence* [1987] C.L.Y. 1194.

[67] *McManus v Mannings Maine Ltd* [2001] EWCA Civ 1668.

In *Nash v Eli Lilly & Co.*[68] the claimants alleged that they had suffered   **10–025**
side-effects from the use of the prescription drug Opren. Since many drugs
carry a risk of unwanted side-effects which a patient may be prepared to tolerate, given the benefits that the drug confers in treating the ailment, the issue
arose as to the point at which it could be said that they had suffered "significant injury." The Court of Appeal accepted that there was a valid distinction between an expected, or accepted, side-effect, which would not
constitute "significant injury", and an injurious or unacceptable consequence. Time would not begin to run until the claimants had knowledge that
the side-effects were injurious or unacceptable. However, in *Briggs v Pitt-
Payne & Lias*[69] the Court of Appeal held that the question of balancing side-
effects against the overall beneficial effects of a drug was "simply not
relevant" to the question of whether the claimant is aware that he is suffering from "significant injury."

(ii) Causation

The claimant must have knowledge that the injury was attributable in   **10–026**
whole or in part to the "act or omission which is alleged to constitute negligence." This refers to the claimant's knowledge of *factual* causation.[70] The
claimant's ignorance of causation in law is irrelevant. Once the claimant has
the broad knowledge that his injuries are attributable to the defendant's acts
or omissions he has sufficient knowledge for the purpose of section 14(1)(b),
even if he does not know the specific acts or omissions and is not in a position to draft a fully particularised statement of claim.[71] Moreover, a claimant
will be taken to know that his injury was "attributable" to the defendant's
act or omission if he knew that it was "capable of being so attributed."[72] It
has been said that reasonable belief or suspicion are not sufficient to constitute knowledge.[73] In *Stephen v Riverside Health Authority*[74] it was held that
even a deep-rooted suspicion or conviction on the part of the claimant that
an incompetently conducted X-ray had caused her symptoms did not
amount to knowledge, when she had been assured by several highly qualified doctors that the dose of radiation she had received was not high and
could not have caused the symptoms. It was not until she was informed by

---

[68] [1993] 1 W.L.R. 782; [1992] 3 Med. L.R. 353, CA.
[69] [1999] Lloyd's Rep. Med. 1.
[70] *Dobbie v Medway Health Authority* [1994] 4 All E.R. 450, 462; [1994] 5 Med. L.R. 160,
168, *per* Steyn L.J. See, *e.g.*, *Marston v British Railways Board* [1976] I.C.R. 124.
[71] *Wilkinson v Ancliff (BLT) Ltd* [1986] 1 W.L.R. 1352; [1986] 3 All E.R. 427, 438, CA;
Hayward v Sharrard (1998) 56 B.M.L.R. 155, 165, CA.
[72] *ibid.* "Capable of being so attributed" means attributable as a real, not a fanciful, possibility, but it does not have to be a *probable* cause of the injury. "One is dealing here with knowledge, actual or imputed, and not with proof of liability": *Guidera v NEI Projects (India)*
(1990, CA; unreported) *per* Sir David Croom-Johnson. "To 'attribute' means 'to reckon as
a consequence of'": *Halford v Brookes* [1991] 3 All E.R. 559, 573, *per* Lord Donaldson
M.R.
[73] *Wilkinson v Ancliff (BLT) Ltd* [1986] 3 All E.R. 427, 438.
[74] [1990] 1 Med. L.R. 261.

a medical expert that the symptoms were indicative of a radiation dosage high enough to increase the risk of cancer that the claimant acquired knowledge for the purpose of section 14, notwithstanding that an earlier, protective claim form had been issued in 1980.

10–027   Similarly, in *Scuriaga v Powell*[75] the defendant performed an unsuccessful abortion on the claimant, but the doctor told the claimant that the operation had failed because she had a physical defect. She did not know that the failure to terminate the pregnancy was due to the doctor's negligence until she received a consultant's report more than three years after the failed operation. It was held that time did not begin to run until the claimant discovered that the failure was due to the doctor's conduct of the operation.

10–028   The distinction between "belief" and "knowledge" may be particularly difficult to draw in the case of a claimant who initially has a firm belief that his injuries are due to the default of the defendant, but on making appropriate inquiries is informed by expert opinion that he is mistaken. If, subsequently, his initial belief is confirmed by further expert opinion, at what point did he acquire "knowledge", thereby setting the limitation period running? In *Davis v Ministry of Defence*[76] the Court of Appeal held that the claimant's strong belief that his dermatitis had been caused by his working conditions and that he had a good claim for damages against the defendants did not amount to "knowledge" where his medical and legal advisers took a different view of the cause of the dermatitis, stating that it was constitutional. The claimant accepted this advice until, following a subsequent severe attack of dermatitis, he received different expert advice that it was indeed attributable to his working conditions. May L.J. said that the words "act or omission which is alleged to constitute negligence, nuisance or breach of duty" of section 14(1)(b) could be affirmed compendiously described as the defendants' failure to provide the claimant with safe working conditions. Thus, the question that had to be asked was when did the claimant first know that his dermatitis was attributable in whole or in part to his employers' failure to provide safe working conditions? On the facts, he did not acquire knowledge until he received expert advice which confirmed his suspicions. Commenting on this case in *Nash v Eli Lilly & Co.*,[77] however, the Court of Appeal said that:

> "The decision does, however, appear to regard as arguable the contention that, if a claimant is shown to have had knowledge, as we understand the meaning of that word in this context, that his injury is attributable to the act or omission of the defendant, the subsequent obtaining of expert advice for the purpose of legal proceedings which says that the injury is not so attributable, could retrospectively cause him never to have had such knowledge. We do not accept that that contention is arguable. It seems to us to be in conflict with the words of the statute."

---

[75] (1979) 123 S.J. 406; affirmed (1980, CA; unreported).
[76] *The Times*, August 7, 1985.
[77] [1993] 1 W.L.R. 782, 795; [1992] 3 Med. L.R. 353, 366, CA.

On the other hand, the Court explained:

> ". . . whether a claimant has knowledge depends both upon the information he has received and upon what he makes of it. If it appears that a claimant, while believing that his injury is attributable to the act or omission of the defendant, realises that his belief requires expert confirmation before he acquires such a degree of certainty of belief as amounts to knowledge, then he will not have knowledge until that confirmation is obtained."[78]

In other words, if the claimant has acquired "knowledge" he cannot subsequently lose it simply because he receives expert advice which tends to undermine his belief. But the claimant's state of mind may not be such as to be categorised as "knowledge," even where he holds a strong "belief" that his injuries are attributable to the default of the defendant. Everything would seem to hang upon the degree of conviction with which the claimant holds his belief, and whether he appreciated that he required expert confirmation.[79]

In *North Essex District Health Authority v Spargo*[80] Brooke L.J. said that: **10–029** "The test is a subjective one: what did the plaintiff herself know? It is not an objective one: what would have been the reasonable layman's state of mind in the absence of expert confirmation?" The implication is that where the claimant is convinced in her own mind that there is a causal link, even though objectively that belief is not reasonable in the absence of confirmation from an expert, she nonetheless has the requisite knowledge and it is not open to argue that her knowledge runs from the date of confirmation of that belief by an expert. Of course, this rather begs the question of what the claimant "knew". The strength of her conviction or belief is not itself evidence that she "knew", because her belief may have been mistaken. Brooke L.J.'s approach appears to imply that an irrational and wholly unfounded (in the sense of there being no objective supporting evidence) belief, if held with sufficient conviction, could constitute "knowledge" if subsequently there is discovered objective evidence supporting the belief. But in some cases the claimant may have a firm belief, even a conviction, that his injuries were

---

[78] *ibid.*

[79] Thus, in circumstances where the claimant has a strong belief, issues proceedings against the defendant and then receives negative expert advice leading him to discontinue the action, that belief will probably be treated as knowledge for the purpose of s.14. He could not then claim that he only acquired knowledge on receipt of further expert advice confirming his original belief. On this approach, *Stephen v Riverside Health Authority* [1990] 1 Med. L.R. 261, para. 10–026, and *Davis v Ministry of Defence*, where protective claim forms had been issued, would appear to have been wrongly decided on their facts. In *Sniezek v Bundy (Letchworth) Ltd* [2000] P.I.Q.R. P213, 219, CA, Bell J. said that *Davis* had not survived *Nash*. Nor will the claimant be able to invoke the court's discretion under s.33 of the Limitation Act 1980 to disapply the primary limitation period, since having issued proceedings within the primary limitation period the claimant cannot rely on s.33 following the ruling of the House of Lords in *Walkley v Precision Forgings Ltd* [1979] 1 W.L.R. 606; see para. 10–058.

[80] [1997] P.I.Q.R. P235; [1997] 8 Med. L.R. 125 at 131.

caused in a particular way, but it subsequently turns out that he was mistaken and his injuries were caused by other acts or omissions of the defendant. In these circumstances he was "barking up the wrong tree" and on the wording of section 14(1)(b) he does not have the required knowledge until he discovers his mistake, notwithstanding the possibility that a claim form has already been issued.[81]

10–030   Even issuing a claim form should not be treated as *conclusive* evidence that the claimant had the relevant knowledge.[82] In *Sniezek v Bundy (Letchworth) Ltd*[83] Judge L.J. said that *Nash v Eli Lilly & Co* was not authority for the proposition that time automatically starts to run against a claimant who has taken legal advice. There was nothing in the Limitation Act to suggest that any special consequences must or should be deemed to arise from his doing so. The question remains the individual's state of knowledge of the relevant facts, rather than his adviser's opinion about the prospects of success in legal proceedings. But once time starts to run, it is not postponed even if the claimant sensibly thinks, on the basis of legal and medical advice, that he should not proceed to litigation.[84]

10–031   There has been some difficulty in identifying precisely what a patient must know about his medical treatment for the purpose of section 14(1)(b). Can it be said that a claimant's knowledge that his injury was attributable to his "medical treatment" is knowledge in "broad terms",[85] that it was attributable to an act or omission which is alleged to constitute negligence where he cannot identify, let alone particularise, the relevant acts or omissions? It is strongly arguable that knowledge that an injury was caused by, say, an operation is not necessarily knowledge for the purpose of section 14, given that injury following an operation may arise without negligence as an unavoidable complication of the procedure, or the operation may simply have been unsuccessful in preventing the claimant's medical condition from deteriorating as a consequence of the original disease or injury which was being treated.[86] Moreover,

---

[81]   *Rowbottom v Royal Masonic Hospital* [2002] EWCA Civ 87; [2002] Lloyd's Rep. Med. 173; [2003] P.I.Q.R. P1, where the claimant believed that complications arising from a wound infection following surgery for a hip replacement, leading eventually to amputation of his leg, were due to the failure of a drain inserted into his leg. He believed that he had been given prophylactic antibiotics. He did not acquire knowledge that he had not been given prophylactic antibiotics until he received confirmation from a medical expert that it was reasonable to assume that if there was no record of antibiotics having been given then he probably had not received any. See also *Driscoll-Varley v Parkside Health Authority* [1991] 2 Med. L.R. 346, and the comments of Hoffmann L.J. on this case in *Broadley v Guy Clapham & Co* [1994] 4 All E.R. 439, 449, para. 10–034; *Khan v Ainslie* [1993] 4 Med. L.R. 319; *North Essex District Health Authority v Spargo* [1997] P.I.Q.R. P235; [1997] 8 Med. L.R. 125, 130 *per* Brooke L.J.; *Baig v City & Hackney Health Authority* [1994] 5 Med. L.R. 221, 224; para. 10–043.

[82]   See *Whitfield v North Durham Health Authority* [1995] 6 Med. L.R. 32, 37 where the Court of Appeal held that it was wrong to treat the issue of a protective claim form as determinative, by itself, of the question of knowledge under s.14; nor was there anything in the decision in *Nash* that constrained the judge to reach this conclusion.

[83]   [2000] P.I.Q.R. P213 at 229.

[84]   *ibid.* at 230, *per* Judge L.J.

[85]   Applying *Wilkinson v Ancliff (BLT) Ltd* [1986] 3 All E.R. 427, 438, CA.

[86]   See, *e.g.*, *Harrington v Essex Area Health Authority, The Times*, November 14, 1984, where

most people would not regard *successful* medical treatment as constituting an *injury*, so that if a patient is informed that surgery was successful she would not even consider that she had been injured, let alone address her mind to the question of which acts or omissions had caused the "injury." Thus, the minimum knowledge that a claimant would require is knowledge that "something has gone wrong" with the treatment in order to distinguish those injuries which were unavoidable consequences of the procedure and those which are attributable to the "act or omission which is alleged to constitute negligence." This, indeed, has been the approach taken in a number of cases

In *Bentley v Bristol and Weston Health Authority*[87] Hirst J. held that a   **10–032** claimant's knowledge that an injury which she had suffered was attributable in whole or in part to an operation did not arise until she became aware of some act or omission which could have affected the safety of the operation. Broad knowledge that the injury was caused by the operation *per se* did not set the limitation period running, since the operation is not the act or omission which is itself alleged to constitute negligence. The crucial issue was knowledge of the act or omission alleged to constitute negligence, namely some conduct or failure which could affect the safety of the operation:

> "... the performance of a surgical operation (*i.e.* an act invasive to the plaintiff's body to which the plaintiff has consented) is not the act or omission which is itself alleged to constitute negligence. The act or omission which *is* alleged to constitute negligence in operation cases is some conduct or failure which can affect the safety of the operation. Knowledge of such act or omission will frequently depend on information derived by the plaintiff from expert opinion ..."[88]

In *Nash v Eli Lilly & Co.*[89] Hidden J. adopted the approach of Hirst J. in *Bentley v Bristol and Weston Health Authority*, commenting that there must

---

(n.86 contd.) it was held that knowledge by the claimant that he had contracted an infection in the operating theatre, was not knowledge that the infection was attributable to an act or omission constituting negligence, since an infection can be contracted without negligence on the part of anyone.

[87] [1991] 2 Med. L.R. 359.

[88] *ibid.* at 364 (original emphasis); *cf. Hendy v Milton Keynes Health Authority* [1992] 3 Med. L.R. 114; [1992] P.I.Q.R. 281 where Blofeld J. concluded that, while a claimant's date of knowledge that an injury was attributable in whole or in part to an operation could well have depended on the date when she had received an expert's report, in a less complicated case the date of knowledge arose when she appreciated in general terms that her problems were attributable to the operation, even if the precise terms of what had gone wrong were not known.

[89] [1991] 2 Med. L.R. 169. See also *Driscoll-Varley v Parkside Health Authority* [1991] 2 Med. L.R. 346 where Hidden J. held that the test to be applied in s.14(1)(b) was not "was there some negligence in the treatment at St Mary's Hospital which cannot be properly identified but which must have happened?" The Act refers to knowledge that the injury was attributable to "the act or omission which is alleged to constitute negligence" and thus the relevant knowledge was of an act or omission alleged in the claimant's statement of claim to constitute negligence, namely premature mobilization following a fractured leg. An awareness that the leg was not healing properly and a belief that this was attributable to post-operative care was not "knowledge."

be a degree of specificity, not a mere global or catch-all character about the act or omission which is alleged to constitute negligence. Attributing the injury to vague and generalised conduct such as "the operation at the hospital" was not enough. The claimant must know some specific fact in relation to the conduct of the operation. Moreover, the fact of which the claimant must have knowledge is the fact which is the basis of the allegation of negligence upon which the action is founded. That did not mean, however, that the claimant must have knowledge of every act or omission set out in the statement of claim, which in *Nash* amounted to 60 pages of pleadings. The crucial issue in that case, which dealt with a number of late claims in the Opren litigation, was the definition of the relevant acts or omissions of the defendants. Hidden J. held that these consisted of exposing the claimants to a drug which was unsafe in that it was capable of causing persistent photo-sensitivity and/or in failing to take reasonable steps to protect the claimants from such a condition. The Court of Appeal accepted that this was the appropriate degree of "specificity" with which the defendants' act or omission must be identifiable by the claimant:

> "It was not, in our judgment, the intention of Parliament to require for the purposes of section 11 and section 14 of the Act proof of knowledge of the terms in which it will be alleged that the act or omission of the defendants constituted negligence or breach of duty. What is required is knowledge of the essence of the act or omission to which the injury is attributable."[90]

10–033   In *Broadley v Guy Clapham & Co*,[91] however, the Court of Appeal held that the approach adopted by Hirst J. in *Bentley* was inconsistent with the proviso to section 14(1)(b) that "knowledge that any acts or omissions did or did not, as a matter of law, involve negligence . . . or breach of duty is irrelevant."[92] *Bentley* required knowledge on the claimant's part of all matters necessary to establish negligence or breach of duty, and this was too high a test. The claimant in *Broadley* underwent an operation to remove a foreign body from her knee and for at least seven months after the operation she needed two sticks in order to walk. It was held that by then she must have considered that something was significantly wrong and that she was suffering from something other than a direct and inevitable consequence of the operation. She had constructive knowledge of a potential cause of action because a reasonable person in her position would have sought further medical assistance or made further enquiries of the doctor. The claimant argued that she did not have knowledge until she knew of: "some act or omission which could adversely affect the safety of the operation or proper recovery from the operation, such as unreasonable interference with the nerve or failure reasonably to safeguard it from damage, or failure properly

---

[90] *Nash v Eli Lilly & Co* [1993] 1 W.L.R. 782, 799; [1992] 3 Med. L.R. 353, 368, CA.
[91] [1994] 4 All E.R. 439; [1993] 4 Med. L.R. 328, CA.
[92] See para. 10–046.

to investigate and/or repair the nerve lesion in time." In response to this Leggatt L.J. commented that:

> "The use of the words 'unreasonable', 'reasonably' and 'properly' would only be justified if section 14(1)(b) required knowledge that the injury was attributable to negligence. It is plain from the concluding words of section 14(1) that 'knowledge that any acts or omissions did or did not, as a matter of law, involve negligence' is irrelevant. In my judgment the only function of the words 'which is alleged to constitute negligence . . .' is to point to the relevant act or omission to which the injury was attributable."[93]

Accordingly, the decision in *Bentley* was wrong, since it required a too detailed knowledge on the part of the claimant. Mrs Bentley knew that her injuries were attributable to damage caused in the sciatic nerve in the course of a hip replacement operation, and she knew soon afterwards that one way in which nerves can be damaged in the course of an operation is when they are retracted to keep them out of the way while the surgeon is working on the hip joint. What she did not know was that the retraction in her case might have been *excessive*. In holding that until then she did not have sufficient knowledge for the purposes of section 14(1) Hirst J. was requiring knowledge that the surgeon had fallen short of some standard of care, and this was not required by the Act.[94] *Driscoll-Varley v Parkside Health Authority*[95] was different, said Hoffmann L.J., because there the claimant was "barking up the wrong tree." The claimant thought that the complications from which she suffered had been caused by the way the operation on her leg had been done, and only later did she discover that the real cause was not the operation but the subsequent removal of her leg from traction. Thus, *Driscoll-Varley* was concerned with identification of the act which caused the injury and not with appreciation of whether the act was capable of being attributable to negligence or fault.[96] Balcombe L.J. referred to four heads under which the required knowledge for the purpose of section 14 could be considered:

> "(1) Broad knowledge. Carrying out the operation to her knee in such a way that something went wrong, namely that it caused foot drop (an injury to her foot) . . .

10–034

---

[93] [1994] 4 All E.R. 439, 447; [1993] 4 Med. L.R. 328, 333. See also *per* Hoffmann L.J. at 448 and 333 respectively: ". . . the words 'which is alleged to constitute negligence, nuisance or breach of duty' serve to *identify* the facts of which the plaintiff must have knowledge without implying that he should know that they constitute a breach of a rule, whether of law or some other code of behaviour. s. 14(1)(b) requires that one should look at the way the plaintiff puts his case, distil what he is complaining about and ask whether he had in broad terms knowledge of the facts on which that complaint is based."

[94] *ibid.* at 449 and 333 respectively, *per* Hoffmann L.J.

[95] [1991] 2 Med. L.R. 346.

[96] See also *Khan v Ainslie* [1993] 4 Med. L.R. 319; *Baig v City and Hackney Health Authority* [1994] 5 Med. L.R. 221, 224; para. 10–043.

(2)   Specific knowledge. Carrying out the operation in such a way as to damage a nerve thereby causing foot drop (an injury to her foot) ...

(3)   Qualitative knowledge. Carrying out the operation in such a way as unreasonably to cause injury to a nerve (unreasonably to expose a nerve to a risk of injury).

(4)   Detailed knowledge (which I take to be knowledge sufficiently detailed to enable the plaintiff's advisers to draft a statement of claim)."[97]

Qualitative or detailed knowledge went beyond the standard necessary for the purposes of section 14, said his Lordship.

10–035   In *Dobbie v Medway Health Authority*[98] the claimant issued a claim form in 1989 in respect of the removal of her breast during the course of a breast biopsy operation performed in 1973. Although the surgeon believed a lump in the breast to be malignant, subsequent pathological examination revealed that it was benign. The claimant was told by medical staff that the breast had been removed to be safe rather than sorry; that the hospital did not have facilities for testing breast lumps while the patient was under anaesthetic; and that she should be grateful that she did not have cancer. She subsequently suffered severe psychological problems attributable to the loss of her breast. It was argued that since the claimant had been told at the time that she had received the appropriate treatment, she did not know that she should not have had her breast removed until either she received an expert's report to this effect in 1990, or at the earliest in 1988 when she heard about a successful claim in a similar case. Otton J. held that in 1973 the claimant had broad knowledge of sufficient facts to conclude that her breast had been unnecessarily removed, that something had gone wrong, and that this was attributable to the defendants' negligence and/or that her breast had been removed without her consent.[99] She may not have had sufficient knowledge to enable counsel to draft a fully particularised statement of claim, but she knew that her injuries were capable of being attributable to what could compendiously be called the defendants' fault. This was sufficient knowledge to set time running against her in both negligence and trespass to the person. This decision was upheld by the Court of Appeal, except that Sir Thomas Bingham M.R. suggested that the judge had been wrong to refer to the breast being "unnecessarily" removed, to something going wrong and to the health authority's negligence. These matters were irrelevant under section 14. It could not plausibly be suggested that the words "act or omission" import any requirement that the act or omission should be actionable or tortious, since that would stultify the closing words of subsection 14(1) and would flout the recommendation[1] on which the legislation was founded:

---

[97] [1994] 4 All E.R. 439, 446–447; [1993] 4 Med. L.R. 328, 332.

[98] [1994] 4 All E.R. 450; [1994] 5 Med. L.R. 160, CA. Leave to appeal refused: [1994] 1 W.L.R. 1553.

[99] [1992] 3 Med. L.R. 217, QBD.

[1] *i.e.* the Law Reform Committee's Twentieth Report, *Interim Report on Limitation of Actions in Personal Injury Claims*, (1974) Cmnd. 5630.

"... it is customary in discussing tortious liability to refer to acts and omissions, and I do not think the meaning of section 14(1)(b) would be any different had the reference been to conduct. Time starts to run against the claimant when he knows that the personal injury on which he founds his claim is capable of being attributed to something done or not done by the defendant whom he wishes to sue. This condition is not satisfied where a man knows that he has a disabling cough or shortness of breath but does not know that his injured condition has anything to do with his working conditions. It is satisfied when he knows that his injured condition is capable of being attributed to his working conditions, even though he has no inkling that his employer may have been at fault."[2]

The claimant argued that the word "injury" should be interpreted in a way   10–036
which distinguished between the normal or expected consequences of successful medical treatment and the consequences of faulty treatment. The man in the street, it was suggested, would not regard himself as "injured" by a successful operation. He would only regard himself as injured if he suffered consequences other than those normally attributed to the treatment. Beldam L.J. rejected this argument because it could not be reconciled with the definition of personal injuries in section 38(1):

"The interpretation of 'personal injuries' in section 38(1), though plainly not exhaustive, does indicate that 'injury' cannot be qualified by the addition of words implying its source or aetiology. Nor is there any need to import the perception of the reasonable patient."[3]

The implication of refusing to draw a distinction between successful and unsuccessful surgery, however, would seem to be that everyone who undergoes a surgical operation is, by definition, "injured" and knows that he has suffered injury immediately. The fact that the patient does not know that the surgery has gone wrong would be irrelevant to the running of the limitation period. This conclusion seems so bizarre that the proposition must be open to serious question. Consider, for example, a patient who has an appendix removed. She would not consider, and reasonably so, that she had suffered any injury at the hands of the doctor. Appendectomy is a potentially life-saving procedure. The pain and suffering involved in the surgery, and the resultant scar, though clearly "caused" by the surgeon's knife would not normally be thought of as an "injury" when the operation is undertaken on reasonable grounds. If, however, the operation was totally unnecessary on the clinical signs, then a patient would reasonably consider that she had been damaged by having to undergo a needless operation. If

---

[2] [1994] 4 All E.R. 450, 456; [1994] 5 Med. L.R. 160, 164.
[3] *ibid.* at 461 and 167 respectively. The Limitation Act 1980, s.38(1) provides that "'personal injuries' includes any disease and any impairment of a person's physical or mental condition, and 'injury' and cognate expressions shall be construed accordingly."

the fact that the operation was unnecessary only became apparent much later, the patient only acquired knowledge that she had suffered an *injury* at that time. It is the decision to undertake the operation itself, rather than the performance of the operation (which may have been technically perfect) that is the gist or the "essence" of her complaint.[4] But the decision to perform the operation can only be characterised as an "injury" if the decision was mistaken, and therefore the claimant can only acquire knowledge that she has suffered an injury when she learns that the decision was mistaken. She need not know that it was a careless or negligent mistake, but she has to know that there *was* a mistake, *i.e.* that there was an error or that "something had gone wrong," before she can have knowledge that she has even suffered an injury.

10–037   It is clear that in *Dobbie* the Court of Appeal was concerned not to reach a position where the claimant could effectively postpone the running of the limitation period by asserting that she did not know that she had a cause of action in law.[5] With great respect, this interpretation appears to confuse the question of whether the claimant knew that the facts would give her a cause of action in law, which is excluded by the proviso, with the question of the claimant being able to identify the relevant act or omission of the defendant as a cause of her injuries. Knowledge that the defendant's acts or omissions have or have not caused the claimant's injuries is knowledge about a *fact*, not about the law. The question is *which facts* must the claimant have knowledge of, given that section 14(1)(b) clearly does *not* state that it is sufficient to know that the injury was attributable to the defendant's *conduct* (notwithstanding Sir Thomas Bingham M.R.'s statement to the contrary). Although in most cases reference to the defendant's conduct would not make any difference, in some cases the wording is crucial. The subsection focuses attention on the specific conduct of the defendant which it is subsequently alleged by the claimant constitutes negligence, nuisance or breach of duty. The claimant need not be aware that this conduct would in law give rise to an action for damages, but she must have *some* knowledge of the relevant acts

---

[4] See, *e.g.*, *Gascoine v Ian Sheridan & Co* [1994] 5 Med. L.R. 437, a case where judgment was delivered (three months) after, but without reference to, the Court of Appeal's decision in *Dobbie*. Mitchell J., at 442, defined the "act" alleged to constitute negligence to which the claimant's injury was attributable as neither the manner of administering the treatment (external pelvic irradiation) nor the dosage, but the decision to treat her with external pelvic irradiation at all, thereby exposing her unnecessarily to the inherent risks of that procedure. The validity of the decision to treat was an "act" quite independent from the "act" constituting the conduct of the treatment. Although the claimant knew that she was ill, she did not acquire knowledge for the purpose of s.14 until she became aware not only that the immediate cause of her injuries was irradiation, but also that it was the decision to treat unnecessarily which caused the injuries.

[5] ". . . in so far as it has been suggested the judgments in some cases imply that the plaintiff must have some indication of fault or error in his treatment before he is aware that he has suffered injury, such a requirement is inconsistent with the clear words of section 14," *per* Beldam L.J. at [1994] 4 All E.R. 450, 462. Steyn L.J. said, at 463, that: "Stripped to its essentials counsel's argument is simply an attempt to argue that the injured party must know that he has a possible cause of action. That is not a requirement of section 14(1)." See also the comment of Hoffmann L.J. in *Broadley v Guy Clapham & Co* [1994] 4 All E.R. 439, 448, cited above, n. 93.

or omissions.[6] In an ordinary road traffic or work accident this is relatively straightforward. In a medical negligence action, however, because, as is frequently stressed when considering whether a defendant is in breach of duty, the fact that "injury" has occurred following surgical intervention cannot itself indicate that there has even been an error, let alone negligence, the claimant needs more than simply knowledge that the injury was attributable to the operation.

This point has been made clear by the Court of Appeal in *Hallam-Eames*   10–038
v Merrett,[7] which was concerned with the interpretation of the analogous provision in section 14A of the Limitation Act 1980 in respect of claims for economic loss. Hoffmann LJ said that:

> "If all that was necessary was that a plaintiff should have known that the damage was attributable to an act or omission of the defendant, the statute would have said so. Instead, it speaks of the damage being attributable to 'the act or omission which is alleged to constitute negligence.' In other words, the act or omission of which the plaintiff must have knowledge must be that which is causally relevant for the purposes of an allegation of negligence. There may be many acts, omissions or states which can be said to have a causal connection with a given occurrence, but when we make causal statements in ordinary speech, we select on common sense principles the one which is relevant for our purpose . . ."[8]

The words "which is alleged to constitute negligence" served to identify the facts of which the claimant must have knowledge. It was not sufficient for the claimant to know merely that the relevant damage had been caused by *an* act or omission of the defendant. Commenting on *Dobbie*, Hoffmann L.J. said that Mrs Dobbie had to know more than that her breast had been removed. She had to know that a healthy breast had been removed. That was the essence of what she was complaining about. Nor did this require knowledge of fault or negligence:

> "The plaintiff does not have to know that he has a cause of action or that the defendant's acts can be characterised in law as negligent or as falling short of some standard of professional or other behaviour . . . He must have known the facts which can fairly be described as constituting the negligence of which he complains. It may be that knowledge of such facts will also serve to bring home to him the fact that the defendant has

---

[6] In *Baig v City and Hackney Health Authority* [1994] 5 Med. L.R. 221, 224, Rougier J. commented that the words of s.14(1)(b) "admit of no interpretation other than" that the knowledge required is "knowledge, at any rate in general outline, of just what it was that the defendant had either done or failed to do which had caused the damage." Rougier J. did not refer to *Dobbie*, although his Lordship's judgment was given a month after the Court of Appeal's decision.

[7] [1996] 7 Med. L.R. 122.

[8] *ibid.* at 125–126.

been negligent or at fault. But that in itself is not a reason for saying that he need not have known them."[9]

10–039   This approach now seems to be accepted in cases of medical negligence. In *Forbes v Wandsworth Health Authority*[10] a claimant who was unaware of the acts or omissions of the defendants constituting negligence did not have the relevant knowledge, notwithstanding that it might mean that he would not acquire knowledge until he also knew of the negligence. He had no cause to suspect that anything had gone wrong, other than that the operation had not been a success. Accordingly, he had no reason to believe that the amputation of his leg was due to an act or omission of the defendants until he received an expert's report 10 years after the operation.[11]

10–040   The point is at its most obvious where the alleged negligence consists of an omission to treat. The claimant must know more than mere fact that he has not been treated. In *Smith v West Lancashire Health Authority*[12] the claimant had been told that the initial treatment had not worked and that there was nothing further that could be done. He presumed that he had received proper treatment, but in fact the operation had been performed too late to achieve full recovery. Russell L.J. said that the alleged negligence consisted of the omission to operate promptly, together with the failure properly to diagnose his condition. The reality was that the claimant did not know that there had been an omission to operate at all until he received advice to that effect from his own expert witness:

> "True, he knew that he had not had an operation on or about November 12, 1981, but that knowledge cannot, in my judgment, be knowledge of an omission 'which is alleged to constitute negligence'. One cannot know of an omission without knowing what it is that is omitted. In this case, that was an operation to reduce the fracture dislocations, as opposed to conservative treatment. Simply to tell the plaintiff that the first course of treatment had not worked, is not the same as imbuing the plaintiff with the knowledge of an omission to operate."[13]

---

[9] *ibid.* at 126. See also *Ostick v Wandsworth Health Authority* [1995] 6 Med. L.R. 338 (Mayor's and City of London Court) where it was held that it was not sufficient that the claimant knew she had received an injury that had not healed. It was necessary to know that there was a causal link between the treatment or lack of treatment and the subsequent physical disability, i.e. the fact that the injury had not healed.

[10] [1997] Q.B. 402.

[11] Although the Court of Appeal did consider that he had constructive knowledge when, following an unsuccessful heart by-pass operation, he had his leg amputated. See para. 10–049.

[12] [1995] P.I.Q.R. P514, CA.

[13] *ibid.* at 517. See also *Parry v Clwyd Health Authority* [1997] P.I.Q.R. P1; [1997] 8 Med. L.R. 243; *Hind v York Health Authority* [1998] P.I.Q.R. P235; [1997] 8 Med. L.R. 377— a claimant who was repeatedly assured by medical staff that her incontinence was a natural consequence of the birth process, had nothing to do with any medical intervention, and in time would correct itself, did not have knowledge of the causally relevant omission, namely the failure to repair a tear immediately after the birth. Similarly, in *James v East Dorset Health Authority* (1999) 59 B.M.L.R. 196 the Court of Appeal held that a patient whose condition had deteriorated following an operation and who inferred that it had not been a

Similarly, in *Bates v Leicester Health Authority*[14] it was held that the claimant's knowledge that his disability was caused by the duration of his mother's labour when he was born was not sufficient to give him knowledge of the omission alleged to constitute negligence, *i.e.* the doctors' failure to intervene in a protracted labour. The claimant had to know that the failure to intervene was avoidable, as opposed to knowing that the failure to intervene was negligent, which is irrelevant. Moreover, in determining a claimant's knowledge the court must take into account any advice she has received, because "until someone or some incident directly challenges the advice, you continue reasonably to assume it was correct."[15]

10–041

In *Broadley*, Hoffmann L.J. said that section 14(1)(b) required that "one should look at the way the plaintiff puts his case, distil what he is complaining about and ask whether he had in broad terms knowledge of the facts on which that complaint is based." In the context of complications arising from medical treatment the claimant's "complaint" is not that there has been a complication which is attributable to treatment as such, since he can have no complaint about that *per se*, but that the complication was attributable *to the act or omission of defendant which is now alleged to constitute negligence*. That knowledge cannot be derived from the knowledge that the defendant performed the operation, but only from the knowledge, in broad terms, that "something has gone wrong affecting the safety of the operation."[16] This is why many of the cases, including several Court of Appeal decisions, refer to the claimant having to have knowledge of some error by the defendant before section 14(1)(b) is satisfied, despite Beldam L.J.'s suggestion that this is inconsistent with the clear words of the subsection. For example, in both *Davis v Ministry of Defence*[17] and *Wilkinson v Ancliff (BLT) Ltd*[18] the Court of Appeal considered that an employee had to know that his injuries were attributable to the defendant's failure to

10–042

---

[14] (n.13 contd.) success, nonetheless did not acquire knowledge within section 14 when there was nothing to alert him to the fact that he had suffered an injury during the operation. A claimant must know that he has suffered an injury before he can have knowledge that it was a significant injury. Sedley L.J. commented, at 201, that: "I do not believe that in enacting s.14 Parliament intended to reward those alert to assume that every misfortune is someone else's fault and to place at a disadvantage those who do not assume the worst when there is nothing to alert them to it."

[14] [1998] Lloyd's Rep. Med. 93.

[15] *Oakes v Hopcroft* [2000] Lloyd's Rep. Med. 394, at [33] *per* Lord Woolf C.J. As Clarke L.J. commented, at [49]: "It is not easy to identify what a claimant must know about an omission in order to have knowledge that her loss is capable of being attributed to it." Thus, where a claim was brought in respect of allegedly negligent medical advice as a result of which the claimant settled an action against a third party for much less than the true value of the claim, the question was whether she was aware of "the essence of the omission which had caused the original settlement to be too low, *i.e.* that there had been a misdiagnosis; not ... whether that misdiagnosis had been negligent but simply whether there had been a misdiagnosis": *ibid.* at [41] *per* Waller L.J. *Oakes v Hopcroft* is a decision on the virtually identically worded provisions in s.14A concerned with latent damage.

[16] Note that even in *Broadley v Guy Clapham & Co* [1994] 4 All E.R. 439, 446, Balcombe L.J. appeared to accept that "broad knowledge" was required, and that this involved knowledge "that something went wrong." See para. 10–034.

[17] *The Times*, August 7, 1985.

[18] [1986] 3 All E.R. 427, 438, CA.

provide *safe* working conditions.[19] Similarly, in *Nash v Eli Lilly & Co.*[20] the Court of Appeal accepted that the relevant acts or omissions of the defendants consisted of exposing the claimants to a drug which was *unsafe*. Knowledge that their symptoms were simply attributable to taking a drug could not constitute knowledge by the claimants of any relevant act or omission on the part of the defendant manufacturers. The reference to "safety" clearly requires that the claimant know more than simply that the defendant's *conduct* caused the injury. It is submitted that she must either know, or have constructive knowledge, that "something has gone wrong" sufficiently to consider investigating the circumstances. In any event, where the claimant is informed at the time by the medical staff involved that nothing has gone wrong, and that her treatment was consistent with good medical practice, she does not know that she has suffered an injury because there is no basis for challenging either the performance of the treatment itself or the decision to proceed with the treatment. When Mrs Dobbie was informed that she was lucky to be alive, she was not simply being advised that the surgery to remove her breast had been technically competent, she was being advised that the decision to remove her breast was not an error or a mistake. On that information, she did not know that she had suffered an injury.[21]

10–043   Moreover, the cases where the claimant mistakenly believed that his injuries were attributable to a particular aspect of his treatment in which it has been held that this did not constitute knowledge for the purpose of section 14, also indicate that knowledge that an injury was attributable simply to "the treatment" or "the defendant's conduct" is not sufficient. In *Khan v Ainslie*[22] the claimant initially believed, incorrectly, that eye drops put into his eye for the purpose of a test in 1983 were the cause of the loss of sight in his left eye. He was not aware, until he received an expert's report in 1989, that the problems with his eye were attributable to the omission to refer him for immediate treatment. Despite the fact that the claimant clearly believed that his eye problems were attributable to the defendants' conduct, it was held that the relevant date was 1989 when the report was obtained, because until that stage the claimant had no knowledge of the attributability of his disability to delay, and was ignorant of the link to the act or omission on which he now relied as being negligent. Similarly, in *Baig v City & Hackney Health Authority*[23] Rougier J. commented that though a sufficiently firm conviction will suffice for the purpose of knowledge, the conviction must be

---

[19] See also *Farmer v National Coal Board, The Times*, April 27, 1985, CA, where Griffiths L.J. said that if the claimant is told that the cause of an injury has been the *faulty operation* of a complicated process by an employer, that was sufficient knowledge of an act or omission to start time running.

[20] [1993] 1 W.L.R. 782, 799.

[21] *cf. Scuriaga v Powell* (1979) 123 S.J. 406; affirmed (1980, CA; unreported) para. 10–027 above, where the defendant lied to the claimant about the reason for the failure of the operation.

[22] [1993] 4 Med. L.R. 319.

[23] [1994] 5 Med. L.R. 221, QBD.

right, in the sense that it accords with the way in which the case is ultimately advanced in reliance on specialist opinion:

> "It seems to me to be a travesty of language to hold that somebody who approaches his case in a wholly erroneous belief—however strong—as to the cause of his injury could ever have the requisite knowledge. On the contrary, he has the reverse."[24]

Thus, contrasting these cases with *Dobbie*, the claimant may be in a better position for limitation purposes to adopt a belief which turns out to be incorrect than to have no belief at all about her medical treatment.

(iii) Defendant's identity

This will not normally be a problem in cases of medical negligence, although the claimant may not know which individual in a team caused the injury.[25] This is irrelevant, however, since where the claimant knows that the injuries were caused by one or other of two defendants, but not both, and does not know which defendant is responsible the claimant would be expected to sue both in the alternative.[26]   **10–044**

(iv) Vicarious liability

Section 14(1)(d) refers to the circumstances required to establish an employer's vicarious liability for the torts of employees committed in the course of employment, though the wording is wide enough to cover liability for the conduct of independent contractors where the defendant is under a relevant "non-delegable" duty. The precise identity of the employee is irrelevant if the claimant is aware that the damage was caused by one or more of the defendant's employees acting in the course of employment.[27] The claimant does not have to know that on the facts the defendant would be held vicariously liable in law.   **10–045**

(v) Ignorance of the law

It is the claimant's knowledge of *facts* that governs the commencement date. Section 14(1) specifically provides that the claimant's ignorance that,   **10–046**

---

[24] *ibid.* at 224. See also *Driscoll-Varley v Parkside Health Authority* [1991] 2 Med. L.R. 346, and the comments of Hoffmann L.J. on this case in *Broadley v Guy Clapham & Co* [1994] 4 All E.R. 439, 449, para. 10–034.

[25] As, *e.g.*, in *Cassidy v Ministry of Health* [1951] 2 K.B. 343. For the problems a claimant may encounter in identifying a corporate defendant see: *Simpson v Norwest Holst Southern Ltd* [1980] 1 W.L.R. 968; [1980] 2 All E.R. 471.

[26] *Halford v Brookes* [1991] 3 All E.R. 559, 574, *per* Lord Donaldson M.R.

[27] Since, where the defendant is responsible in law for all the staff who played some role in the claimant's treatment, it is unnecessary for the claimant to identify the particular employee who was at fault in order to establish vicarious liability: *Cassidy v Ministry of Health* [1951] 2 K.B. 343.

as a matter of law, the facts would give him a cause of action is irrelevant.[28] This is the case even where the claimant has received incorrect advice about the legal position, whether from a lawyer or not.[29] Care has to be taken, however, to distinguish clearly between ignorance of facts which would be relevant to the potential success of the claim and ignorance of the law. For example, in *Jones v Liverpool Health Authority*[30] Glidewell L.J. said that if a claimant is informed by a medical expert that he probably does not have a valid claim, and years later he is advised by another medical expert, on the same facts, that he probably does have a valid claim, he cannot claim that he did not have knowledge until he received the later opinion. With respect, this rather assumes that it is the function of medical experts to advise about the law, which, clearly, it is not. If the first expert advised that in his opinion there was no causal connection between the relevant acts or omissions and the claimant's injury, then the advice concerns a fact, notwithstanding that the conclusion would also be that no claim in law would be sustainable because the injury could not be attributed to the defendant's acts or omissions. If this was the only information that the claimant had then he would only acquire the relevant knowledge when informed by the second expert that there was a causal connection.

10–047   Although ignorance of the law is irrelevant to the question of the claimant's knowledge for the purpose of section 14, it is relevant to the court's exercise of discretion under section 33.[31]

(c) Constructive knowledge

10–048   A person's knowledge includes constructive knowledge, which by virtue of section 14(3) means:

> "knowledge which he might reasonably have been expected to acquire—
>
> (a)   from facts observable or ascertainable by him; or
> (b)   from facts ascertainable by him with the help of medical or other appropriate expert advice which it is reasonable for him to seek;
>
> but a person shall not be fixed under this subsection with knowledge of a fact ascertainable only with the help of expert advice so long as he has

---

[28] The nature of the claimant's ignorance of the law is also irrelevant. So it does not matter whether the claimant's ignorance relates to whether there has been a breach of duty by the defendant or whether the defendant owed the claimant a duty of care: *Bowie v Southorns* [2002] EWHC 1389; [2003] P.N.L.R. 135.

[29] See *Farmer v National Coal Board, The Times*, April 27, 1985, CA, where erroneous legal advice by a union official that the claimant's action had no chance of success did not prevent time running against the claimant, since from facts ascertainable by her she could reasonably have acquired the necessary knowledge.

[30] [1996] P.I.Q.R. P251, 266.

[31] Limitation Act 1980, s.33(3)(a) and (e); *Brooks v Coates (UK) Ltd* [1984] 1 All E.R. 702, 713; *Coad v Cornwall and Isles of Scilly Health Authority* [1997] 1 W.L.R. 189, CA.

taken all reasonable steps to obtain (and, where appropriate, to act on) that advice."

As with actual knowledge, mere suspicion does not amount to knowledge.[32] It has been said that constructive knowledge is a combination of a subjective and an objective test. The claimant is fixed with knowledge which *he* might reasonably have been expected to acquire from facts observable or ascertainable by *him*. Was it reasonable for this particular claimant, taking into account his circumstances, character and intelligence, to have acquired knowledge from facts observable or ascertainable by him or through consulting an expert?[33]

In *Forbes v Wandsworth Health Authority*[34] the Court of Appeal had   **10–049** some difficulty in seeing how the individual character and intelligence of the claimant in a personal injury case could be relevant to the question of constructive knowledge (doubting the view expressed by Purchas L.J. in *Nash v Eli Lilly & Co*). The claimant had his leg amputated in 1982 following an unsuccessful heart by-pass operation. He did not consult a solicitor until 1991, and obtained a report from a vascular surgeon in 1992 indicating that delay in treating him after the first operation had caused the damage that resulted in the amputation. The Court of Appeal held that, although the claimant had no actual knowledge, he did have constructive knowledge. He expected the operation to be successful and it was not, and a reasonable man would have sought advice reasonably promptly. He should have sought expert medical advice some 12 to 18 months after he came out of hospital, by which time he would have had time to overcome his shock at losing his leg and take stock of his disability and its consequences. On the question of whether it was reasonable for the claimant to take expert advice, Stuart-Smith L.J. said that two alternative courses of conduct may both be perfectly reasonable. Accepting the situation, and saying 'It was just one of those things. The doctors probably did their best' may be reasonable, just as taking a second opinion as to whether there was any lack of care may be reasonable. But a claimant who takes the first option is making a choice. A reasonable man in the claimant's position, who knew that the operation had been unsuccessful, and that he had suffered a major injury which would seriously affect his enjoyment of life in the future would take advice reasonably promptly:

---

[32] *Wilkinson v Ancliff (BLT) Ltd* [1986] 3 All E.R. 427; *Stephen v Riverside Health Authority* [1990] 1 Med. L.R. 261. Similarly, the claimant's "firm belief" that his injury was attributable to the defendant's act or omission is not knowledge that it was so attributable where his medical and legal advisers take the view that it could not be so attributed, but rather was constitutional: see *Davis v Ministry of Defence, The Times*, August 7, 1985, CA.

[33] *Nash v Eli Lilly & Co* [1993] 1 W.L.R. 782, 799; [1992] 3 Med. L.R. 353, 368, CA. "It boils down to this, that the test is objective but it is applied to the particular plaintiff in the particular circumstances in which he found himself, so to that extent it does involve a subjective element," *per* Buckley J. in *Colegrove v Smyth* [1994] 5 Med. L.R. 111, 114, applying *McCafferty v Metropolitan Police District Receiver* [1977] 1 W.L.R. 1073, CA.

[34] [1997] Q.B. 402.

"It does not seem to me that the fact that a plaintiff is more trusting, incurious, indolent, resigned or uncomplaining by nature can be a relevant characteristic, since this too undermines any objective approach."[35]

In *O'Driscoll v Dudley Health Authority*[36] Otton L.J. commented that it was not easy to reconcile *Nash* and *Forbes* on this point:

"Applying the *Forbes* test a person who is too incurious, indolent, resigned or uncomplaining to do anything about it would be unreasonable if he allowed a potential claim to lapse through effluxion of time. I would see no reason to exclude a person who is too trusting. It would not be unreasonable to expect him to take reasonable steps to obtain advice, if only to verify whether his trust was not misplaced."[37]

The problem with this is that it may be very difficult for even a reasonable person to know whether he is being "too trusting" particularly if there is nothing to put him on notice that he should make enquiries. For example, if a patient is informed after surgery that the injury he sustained in the course of the operation was an inherent risk of the treatment, is he entitled to accept that statement at face value? At what point must the patient question what he is told in order to verify whether his trust is misplaced?[38]

10–050   In *Smith v Leicester Health Authority*[39] the Court of Appeal regarded *Nash* and *Forbes* as conflicting decisions, and concluded that the claimant's individual characteristics, which might distinguish her from the reasonable woman should be disregarded. Constructive knowledge involves an objective test which does not take account of the claimant's individual characteristics (such as her forbearance, or unwillingness to criticise) but does take account of her individual circumstances, such as what she has been told by medical staff. The claimant in *Smith* was told and accepted that the cyst which rendered her tetraplegic was congenital, and that the operation in question had saved her life. She had no reason to suppose that the earlier diagnoses were wrong. In the case of an omission what the claimant has to know is that there was a lost opportunity to prevent the injury:

"If the decision in *Forbes* is being read as saying that every time a patient has an operation and, following the operation is significantly disabled,

---

[35] *ibid.* at 414. See also *Slevin v Southampton and South West Hampshire Health Authority* [1997] 8 Med. L.R. 175, QBD applying *Forbes*: the claimant knew that she should have been delivered by Caesarian section and that if she had been she would not have suffered her injury; she knew that her injury occurred at the hands of the defendant in the course of a breech delivery; this was sufficient to give her constructive knowledge that the injury was attributable to the act or omission alleged to constitute negligence.

[36] [1998] Lloyd's Rep. Med. 210, 217.

[37] *ibid.* at 218.

[38] See the comment of Lord Woolf C.J. in *Oakes v Hopcroft* [2000] Lloyd's Rep. Med. 394 at [33]: "until someone or some incident directly challenges the advice, you continue reasonably to assume it was correct."

[39] [1998] Lloyd's Rep. Med. 77.

the patient has some 12 to 18 months to decide consciously or unconsciously whether to investigate a possible claim against those who operated, then in our view the decision in *Forbes* is being misinterpreted and misapplied. The question posed by s.14(3) with respect to the seeking of medical or other appropriate expert advice is the simple one whether it was reasonable for the plaintiff to seek such advice. Whether it was reasonable for the plaintiff to seek such advice depends on the facts and circumstances of each case, but excluding the character traits of the individual plaintiff."[40]

The courts have not resolved the apparent conflict between *Forbes* and *Nash* on the subjective/objective test for constructive knowledge, but have reached the compromise position that "the claimant's situation is obviously relevant but other more personal characteristics are not."[41]

A failure to seek legal advice will give rise to constructive knowledge of **10–051** the facts which would have been discovered after the date at which it would have been reasonable to seek such advice;[42] and where the claimant refused further tests to assist diagnosis and discharged himself from hospital when he knew that the diagnosis was provisional, he acted unreasonably and had constructive knowledge of the diagnosis that the tests would probably have revealed.[43] A reasonable man obeys the law, and therefore a claimant who did not seek advice because he was concerned that this might lead to his own illegal conduct being referred to the police was fixed with constructive knowledge of facts which the expert would have ascertained.[44]

Where the question is whether it was reasonable for the claimant to seek **10–052** expert advice, even applying an objective test it would seem that his personal circumstances should be taken into account, so that it may well be reasonable for a claimant who is seriously ill or dying not to seek legal advice,[45]

---

[40] *ibid.* at 87.

[41] *Adams v Bracknell Forest Borough Council* [2003] EWCA Civ 706; *The Times*, May 14, 2003 at [27] *per* Tuckey L.J. In *Fenech v East London and City Health Authority* [2000] Lloyds Rep. Med. 35; [2000] P.N.L.R. 205, CA, Simon Brown L.J. said (at p. 38) that, without resolving the difference of view expressed in *Forbes* and *Nash* as to whether s.14(3) is objective or subjective, in taking into account the circumstances and character of the claimant "some degree of objectivity at least must be required in determining when it is reasonable for someone to seek advice—otherwise the provision could never apply save only where a person acts out of character."

[42] *Hills v Potter* [1983] 3 All E.R. 716, 728.

[43] *Denford v Redbridge and Waltham Forest Health Authority* [1996] 7 Med. L.R. 376.

[44] *Coban v Allen* [1997] 8 Med. L.R. 316, CA, where the claimant did not pursue his action because of his illegal immigration status. This was a decision on the latent damage provisions contained in s.14A(10) of the Limitation Act 1980, which is in identical terms to s.14(3).

[45] *Newton v Cammell Laird & Co (Shipbuilders and Engineers) Ltd* [1969] 1 W.L.R. 415. In *Davis v City and Hackney Health Authority* [1991] 2 Med. L.R. 366 it was held that it was appropriate to look at the difficulties faced by the particular claimant, including any physical disability from which he suffered, the fact that his parents, on whom he had been largely dependent, had discouraged him from seeking to pursue a claim arising from injuries sustained at the time of his birth, and the fact that the prospect of seeing a solicitor alone intimidated him. See also *Bates v Leicester Health Authority* [1998] Lloyd's Rep. Med. 93 where the claimant had significant communication difficulties and relied heavily on his mother who was forcefully dismissive of his chances of a claim and therefore he acted reasonably in not pursuing the matter sooner.

though this is a question of degree.[46] Similarly, it may be reasonable for a claimant to delay seeking legal advice where she was still receiving treatment and did not wish to sour relations with the doctors who were treating her.[47] Some account will be taken of the limited resources available to the claimant by way of advice, where, *e.g.*, his solicitors could only seek expert advice to the extent that they were authorised to do so by the Legal Aid Board.[48] Constructive knowledge does not include the knowledge of a child's parents during the child's minority.[49] Moreover, an ordinary person of average intelligence and average understanding of medical matters is not expected to infer from the fact that a child is born with cerebral palsy that there was a real possibility that an act or omission of the medical staff was the cause of the injury.[50]

10–053 The proviso to section 14(3) prevents a claimant from being fixed with constructive knowledge where an expert has failed to discover or disclose a relevant fact that ought to have been revealed.[51] It will only apply, however,

---

[46] So in *Forbes v Wandsworth Health Authority* [1997] Q.B. 402 the Court of Appeal took the view that where a claimant has had his leg amputated following heart bypass surgery he should have sought expert medical advice some 12 to 18 months after he came out of hospital, by which time he would have had time to overcome his shock at losing his leg and take stock of his disability and its consequences.

[47] *Ostick v Wandsworth Health Authority* [1995] 6 Med. L.R. 338 — the claimant was justified in waiting to see if her treatment was successful before seeking legal advice; *Driscoll-Varley v Parkside Health Authority* [1991] 2 Med. L.R. 346, 357 where the claimant had been warned by her solicitors that commencing litigation against the hospital might alienate the surgeon. It was not unreasonable to fail to take the matter further at an earlier stage, given her concern not to antagonise the consultant who had the continued care of her and in whom she had confidence.

[48] *Khan v Ainslie* [1993] 4 Med. L.R. 319. On the other hand, in *Skitt v Khan and Wakefield Health Authority* [1997] 8 Med. L.R. 105 the Court of Appeal held that though lack of funds to obtain an expert's report could be a factor, that has to be weighed against the seriousness of the injury and its consequences for the claimant in deciding whether objectively it was reasonable to seek expert medical advice. On the facts it was understandable that the claimant did not seek such advice, but it was not reasonable.

[49] *Parry v Clwyd Health Authority* [1997] P.I.Q.R. P1; [1997] 8 Med. L.R. 243; *Appleby v Walsall Health Authority* [1999] Lloyd's Rep. Med. 154; *cf. O'Driscoll v Dudley Health Authority* [1998] Lloyd's Rep. Med. 210, 220, where Sir Christopher Slade treated the parents' actual knowledge as imputed to the child, so that her actual knowledge commenced at age 18.

[50] *ibid.* See also *De Martell v Merton and Sutton Health Authority* [1995] 6 Med. L.R. 234 where it was held that the claimant had acted reasonably in not inquiring into the circumstances of his birth, because his mother had become pregnant by her uncle and was reluctant to talk about it.

[51] See, *e.g.*, *Marston v British Railways Board* [1976] I.C.R. 124, where the expert dealt only with the hardness of a metal hammer, not its defective condition; see also *Stephen v Riverside Health Authority* [1990] 1 Med. L.R. 261, where the claimant had been assured by a "chorus of highly qualified experts" that her symptoms could not have been caused by the dose of radiation that she had received; *Davis v Ministry of Defence, The Times,* August 7, 1985, CA, para. 10–062. In *Baig v City and Hackney Health Authority* [1994] 5 Med. L.R. 221, 225, Rougier J. suggested that it would be inappropriate to impute the necessary knowledge to the claimant by reason of an expert's report which was "puzzling and ambiguous in its terms." In *Hepworth v Kerr* [1995] 6 Med. L.R. 135 the claimant suffered paraplegia following an operation under general anaesthetic and, despite a suggestion in the medical notes that his condition might have been attributable to the operation, he was assured on several occasions, by the neurosurgeon who subsequently treated him for the paralysis, that the operation had not caused his condition. A report by the neurosurgeon to

to facts which are "ascertainable *only* with the help of expert advice." Where the claimant himself could have discovered the information then he is fixed with any knowledge that the expert acting on his behalf ought to have acquired,[52] provided that it was information which the claimant could reasonably be expected to acquire.[53]

Particular problems arise when the claimant's "expert" is a lawyer. First, by virtue of the proviso to section 14(1), where a claimant receives erroneous advice about the law (*e.g.* that the facts do not disclose a cause of action) this is irrelevant and does not prevent time running.[54] Secondly, where legal "advice" consists of a failure to discover relevant facts, or a failure to suggest a line of enquiry that would have revealed the facts, then in theory the proviso to section 14(3) applies, and the claimant is not fixed with constructive knowledge.[55] But in *Leadbitter v Hodge Finance Ltd*[56] a very narrow view was taken of the facts which are ascertainable *only* with the help of expert advice. In that case an accident victim was expected to be capable of obtaining a police report, making inquiries of the fire brigade and local residents, and interviewing potential witnesses. This raises a question as to precisely what facts would be treated as ascertainable only with legal assistance. For example, would a patient be expected to seek and obtain his own medical records?

      10–054

Thirdly, it is possible that section 14(3)(b) does not apply to *any* form of legal advice. In *Fowell v National Coal Board*[57] the Court of Appeal doubted, without deciding the point, that a party's solicitor was an "expert" within the meaning of the subsection, which was directed to experts in the sense of expert witnesses.[58] If correct, this would mean that a claimant is not

      10–055

(n.51 contd.) the claimant's solicitors came to the same conclusion. The defendants argued that the claimant had constructive knowledge because a competent solicitor should have realised that the neurosurgeon was the wrong expert and had not indicated that he had read the hospital medical notes. This argument was rejected by Latham J. To require the claimant or his solicitor to question whether the expert had obtained sufficient information from the notes or to question whether or not he was the appropriate expert was "asking for a startling degree of scepticism." Some solicitors might have been sceptical, but that did not mean that it was something that any reasonably competent solicitor would have done.

[52] *Leadbitter v Hodge Finance Ltd* [1982] 2 All E.R. 167, 174–175; *Halford v Brookes* [1991] 3 All E.R. 559, 565. This includes any knowledge about facts that his solicitors ought to have acquired: *Henderson v Temple Pier Co Ltd* [1998] 1 W.L.R. 1540.

[53] In *Fowell v National Coal Board*, *The Times*, May 28, 1986, Parker L.J. said that the missing facts (namely that workmen were not employed by the defendant but by an independent contractor) were ascertainable by the claimant, because he could have simply written to the National Coal Board, but this was knowledge which he could not himself have been reasonably expected to acquire; *cf.* the investigative skills expected of the claimant in *Leadbitter v Hodge Finance Ltd* [1982] 2 All E.R. 167, para. 10–054.

[54] *Farmer v National Coal Board*, *The Times*, April 27, 1985, CA.

[55] See *Central Asbestos Co Ltd v Dodd* [1973] A.C. 518, 555–556, *per* Lord Salmon commenting on the effect of the earlier legislation, the Limitation Act 1963, and distinguishing between legal advice which leaves the claimant in ignorance of material facts, and legal advice that on the facts he has no remedy in law.

[56] [1982] 2 All E.R. 167, 174–175.

[57] *The Times*, May 28, 1986; *Khan v Ainslie* [1993] 4 Med. L.R. 319, 325.

[58] *cf.* s.33(3)(f): in exercising its discretion to allow the action to proceed the court will consider the steps taken by the claimant to obtain expert advice, including legal advice.

constructively fixed with the knowledge of his solicitor *by virtue of section 14(3)*.[59] It would seem, however, that under the general law of agency a claimant is fixed with the knowledge that his solicitor actually has,[60] and in *Simpson v Norwest Holst Southern Ltd*[61] it appears to have been assumed by the Court of Appeal that a claimant will also be fixed with knowledge which his solicitor ought reasonably to have acquired.[62] Presumably this would be the position even where the claimant could not reasonably have acquired the knowledge himself. Thus, a claimant who has no actual or constructive knowledge may be caught by his solicitor's constructive knowledge and will be unable to rely on the proviso to section 14(3)(b). In this situation time will run against the claimant and he may have to apply to the court to allow the action to proceed under section 33.

10–056   In *Nash v Eli Lilly & Co.*,[63] on the other hand, Hidden J. observed that the discussion of this question in *Fowell* was *obiter* and that there was no binding authority as to whether facts ascertainable by a claimant with the help of legal advice fall within the terms of section 14(3)(b). His Lordship doubted whether ordinarily they do, but could envisage circumstances where they might. If, for example, the identification of a potential defendant turned upon the construction of legislation (*e.g.* the Committee on the Safety of Medicines and the Licensing Authority under the Medicines Act 1968). Moreover, Hidden J. came to the conclusion that a claimant may be fixed with constructive knowledge of facts that his solicitor knows or ought reasonably to have known, because this falls within section 14(3)(a) as a fact "ascertainable by him."[64] Thus, "ascertainable" would include facts ascertainable by the claimant personally and by others (including lawyers and doctors) ascertaining facts for him. On this interpretation it is not clear why there is any need for subsection 14(3)(b), which would appear to be subsumed within subsection 14(3)(a). This view would also seem to restore the application of the proviso to legal advice, at least if legal advice can be said to be "expert advice."[65]

---

[59] *Fowell v National Coal Board* was cited on this point by Russell L.J. in *Halford v Brookes* [1991] 3 All E.R. 559, 565, with apparent approval.

[60] *Khan v Ainslie* [1993] 4 Med. L.R. 319, 325, *per* Waterhouse J.: "There are, of course, reasons why [s.14(3)] could and should be interpreted narrowly, on the basis that 'him' simply means a plaintiff and not his legal adviser. But my impression is that the balance of the argument is in favour of including the agent of the plaintiff within the scope of 'him'." On the other hand, for the purpose of the exercise of discretion under s.33 there is no rule that anything done by the lawyers must be visited on the client: *Das v Ganju* [1999] P.I.Q.R. P260, 268; [1999] Lloyd's Rep. Med. 198, 204, CA; *Corbin v Penfold Metallising Company Ltd* [2000] Lloyds Rep. Med. 247, 251, CA; *Steeds v Peverel Management Services Ltd* [2001] EWCA Civ 419; *The Times*, May 16, 2001, CA.

[61] [1980] 2 All E.R. 471, 476; [1980] 1 W.L.R. 968.

[62] See the discussion in *Fowell v National Coal Board*, *The Times*, May 28, 1986, where Parker L.J. specifically left this point open.

[63] [1991] 2 Med. L.R. 169.

[64] A view supported, *obiter*, by Buckley J. in *Colegrove v Smyth* [1994] 5 Med. L.R. 111. See also the comments of Waterhouse J. in *Khan v Ainslie* [1993] 4 Med. L.R. 319, 325, cited above, n. 60.

[65] The Court of Appeal could "see no reason to depart from" Hidden J.'s general approach to this issue, merely commenting that: "where constructive knowledge is under consideration

(3) Court's discretion

A claimant has an indefeasible right to bring an action within the primary three year limitation period. Where that period has expired the claimant may still be able to proceed if he can persuade the court to exercise its discretion under section 33 in his favour.

10–057

(a) Availability of the Discretion

In *Firman v Ellis*[66] the Court of Appeal said that the court's discretion under section 33 was unfettered. It was not restricted to a residual category of exceptional cases. This view was approved by the House of Lords in *Thompson v Brown Construction (Ebbw Vale) Ltd*,[67] subject, however, to the ruling in *Walkley v Precision Forgings Ltd*.[68] In *Walkley* the House of Lords distinguished between a claimant who had not issued any proceedings within the primary three year limitation period, who could invoke section 33, and a claimant who had issued a claim form within the limitation period but who had not proceeded with the action, who could not. A second claim form issued out of time would be statute-barred. In *Chappell v Cooper*[69] the Court of Appeal held that *Walkley* would apply, whatever the reason had been that the claimant had not proceeded with the first action: whether because he or his solicitors had failed to serve the claim form in time;[70] or because the action had been dismissed for want of prosecution; or, for good or bad reasons, the action had been discontinued by the claimant.[71]

10–058

The reasoning behind this distinction is that section 33(1) directs the court to have regard to the degree to which the operation of the primary limitation period has prejudiced the claimant, but where the claimant has issued a claim form in time and then for some reason the action has not been pursued he has not been prejudiced by the effect of sections 11 or 12 but by his own dilatoriness. This argument could be applied, however, with as much force to some claimants who have not issued proceedings within the primary limitation

10–059

(n.65 contd.) through the channel of a solicitor, this can only be relevant where it is established that the plaintiff ought reasonably to have consulted a solicitor at all. Thus, it is for the defendant to establish not only that a solicitor whom the plaintiff might consult would have the necessary knowledge but also that it was reasonable to expect the plaintiff to consult him." See *Nash v Eli Lilly & Co* [1993] 1 W.L.R. 782, 800; [1992] 3 Med. L.R. 353, 369, CA.

[66] [1978] Q.B. 886.

[67] [1981] 2 All E.R. 296; [1981] 1 W.L.R. 744; see also *Donovan v Gwentoys Ltd* [1990] 1 W.L.R. 472; [1990] 1 All E.R. 1018, 1023, *per* Lord Griffiths.

[68] [1979] 1 W.L.R. 606.

[69] [1980] 1 W.L.R. 958; [1980] 2 All E.R. 463.

[70] See *Deerness v John Keeble & Son Ltd* [1983] 2 Lloyd's Rep. 260, H.L.

[71] This has implications for negligence claims against solicitors. For example, practitioners who issue the claim form in time but carelessly fail to serve it within the four months allowed by CPR r. 7.5(2) are in a worse position than those who carelessly allow the primary limitation period to expire, since in the latter, but not the former, case the client has the option of making a section 33 application. If successful, this reduces the chances of the client making a claim in negligence against the solicitor; see Jones (1985) 1 P.N. 159.

period who are prejudiced by their own dilatoriness, but they are at least permitted to argue that the discretion should be exercised. *Walkley v Precision Forgings Ltd* creates an arbitrary and unjustifiable distinction between categories of claimant who are permitted to seek the benefit of section 33.[72] In *Whitfield v North Durham Health Authority*[73] the Court of Appeal held that where the claimant has issued an earlier claim form within the limitation period against one defendant (but due to the negligence of the claimant's solicitors has failed to issue a claim form against a second defendant), its consideration as to whether it is equitable to exercise the discretion to permit an action against the second defendant to proceed, should take into account the fact that the claimant was not caught by the effect of *Walkley v Precision Forgings Ltd* as a result of the failings of his solicitors. The claimant had gained a fortuitous advantage, and this was a highly relevant, though not conclusive, consideration. This appears to take the anomalies of *Walkley* one stage further by introducing the notion of "constructive *Walkley*", *i.e.* the claimant falls within the terms of *Walkley* (albeit as a matter of discretion) if, but for the negligence of his solicitors, he would have fallen within the rule.

10–060   One exception to the rule in *Walkley* is where the claimant has been induced to discontinue the action by a misrepresentation or other improper conduct by the defendant. The defendant is then estopped from relying on sections 11 or 12, and it is not a matter of judicial discretion under section 33. However, this exception will be construed narrowly, and does not arise merely from an admission of liability and the making of an interim payment by the defendant.[74] In the absence of an unequivocal agreement by the defendant to waive reliance upon the Limitation Act it will be difficult to establish that the circumstances are exceptional.[75]

10–061   A second exception occurs where the first claim form, although issued in time, is technically invalid, and a second claim form is subsequently issued outside the three year period. In these circumstances the claimant is not caught by *Walkley* and can invoke the court's discretion.[76] This only serves

---

[72] See Davies (1982) 98 L.Q.R. 249, 260–265; Morgan (1982) 1 C.J.Q. 109; Jones (1985) 1 P.N. 159, 160; Patten [2003] J.P.I.L. 127.

[73] [1995] 6 Med. L.R. 32, 38.

[74] See *Deerness v John Keeble & Son Ltd* [1983] 2 Lloyd's Rep. 260, where there had been no dispute on liability and the interim payment had not been made on a "without prejudice" basis. A claim form had been issued within the three year period but not served, and a second claim form issued out of time was held statute-barred by the House of Lords. An interim payment does not constitute an admission of liability, and, moreover, an admission of liability does not reset the "limitation clock." See also *Forward v Hendricks* [1997] 2 All E.R. 395.

[75] Note, however, that where the claimant's "error" consists of a failure to serve the claim form within the period permitted by CPR r. 7.5 the court has a discretion to extend the time for service of the claim form under CPR r. 7.6; see para. 10–098.

[76] *White v Glass, The Times*, February 18, 1989, CA; *Wilson v Banner Scaffolding Ltd, The Times*, June 22, 1982; *Re Workvale Ltd (No. 2)* [1992] 1 W.L.R. 416, CA; *McEvoy v A.A. Welding and Fabrication Ltd* [1998] P.I.Q.R. P226, CA—first claim form invalid because defendants were in liquidation and the claimant had not obtained the appropriate leave to proceed against a party in liquidation. It was irrelevant that the claim form could have been retrospectively validated. Provided the claimant's advisers reasonably believed that the first claim form was a nullity, and then proceeded to issue a second claim form outside the

to emphasise the completely arbitrary effect of the rule in *Walkley*. Similarly, and perhaps more obviously, *Walkley* does not apply where the second claim is against a different defendant in respect of a different cause of action.[77]

A third apparent "exception" is where, although earlier proceedings have been commenced and discontinued, it can be said that the claimant did not *know* that his injury was capable of being attributed to the defendant's act or omission until much later, notwithstanding his firm belief that it was so attributable. In these circumstances *Walkley* is irrelevant, since the "second" claim form will be within the *primary* limitation period. In *Stephen v Riverside Health Authority*[78] a first, protective, claim form had been issued in March 1980 within three years of the incident, and a second claim form was issued in February 1988. The claimant did not acquire knowledge, within the meaning section 14, of the causal link between her injury and the defendants' negligence until February 1985 because she had been assured by several experts that her symptoms could not have been caused by the dose of radiation that she had received. Similarly, in *Davis v Ministry of Defence*[79] the claimant's first medical and legal advisers had concluded that his dermatitis could not be attributed to the alleged negligence, but was constitutional. The Court of Appeal held that the claimant's contrary belief was not the same as knowledge for the purpose of section 14(1)(b), and until the claimant acquired the relevant knowledge the three year period did not start to run. Thus, no question of the exercise of the discretion arose; the limitation period had simply not commenced, despite a previous claim form. In *Nash v Eli Lilly & Co*,[80] however, the Court of Appeal said that a claimant who has acquired "knowledge" cannot subsequently lose it by obtaining an adverse expert report stating that his injury is not attributable to the defendant's acts or omissions. This will be particularly true where the claimant has issued a previous claim form:

10–062

"... we have difficulty in perceiving how in any case where a claimant has sought advice and taken proceedings, it can rightly be held that the claimant had not then had relevant knowledge."

Thus, where the claimant has issued proceedings but discontinued the action following receipt of negative expert advice he may be unable to claim that he only acquired knowledge on receipt of further, favourable expert advice, confirming his initial belief.[81] This tends to suggest that both *Stephen v*

(n.76 contd.) limitation period, *Walkley* did not apply; *Piggott v Aulton* [2003] EWCA Civ 24; [2003] P.I.Q.R. P371—service of proceedings on the estate of a deceased person where no personal representative had been appointed, without the leave of the court, were invalid. In subsequent proceedings issued outside the limitation period, the claimant could invoke s.33.

[77] *Shapland v Palmer* [1999] 1 W.L.R. 2068, CA—first action against D1, employers of D2, as vicariously liable for D2's negligence; second action against D2 personally.

[78] [1990] 1 Med. L.R. 261.

[79] *The Times*, August 7, 1985.

[80] [1993] 1 W.L.R. 782, 795–796; [1992] 3 Med. L.R. 353, 366.

[81] See, however, para. 10–018.

Riverside Health Authority and *Davis v Ministry of Defence* are wrongly decided on their facts. On the other hand, it remains the case that mere suspicion on the claimant's part does not amount to knowledge, and it is arguable that even issuing a claim form should not be treated as *conclusive* evidence that the claimant had the relevant knowledge.[82] And where the claimant was "barking up the wrong tree", the fact that previous proceedings have been issued cannot be conclusive as to the question of his knowledge of the relevant acts or omissions.[83]

(b) Exercise of the Discretion

10–063   Once it has been determined that the claimant is entitled to invoke section 33 the court's discretion is completely unfettered.[84] Section 33(1) provides that the court may direct that the three year period specified by sections 11 and 12 shall not apply if it would be equitable to allow the action to proceed, having regard to the degree to which (a) those sections prejudice the claimant, and (b) the decision to allow the action to proceed would prejudice the defendant.[85] The court has to balance the degree of prejudice to the claimant caused by the operation of the primary limitation period against the prejudice to the defendant if the action were to be allowed to proceed. The stronger the claimant's case is on the merits the greater the prejudice to him, and conversely, the weaker his case the less he is prejudiced.[86] On the other hand, if the defendant has a good case on the merits there is probably less prejudice to him in allowing the action to proceed, although in *Thompson v Brown Construction (Ebbw Vale) Ltd*[87] Lord Diplock said that it was still

---

[82] See para. 10–028, and *Whitfield v North Durham Health Authority* [1995] 6 Med. L.R. 32, 37, CA.

[83] *Rowbottom v Royal Masonic Hospital* [2002] EWCA Civ 87; [2002] Lloyd's Rep. Med. 173.

[84] *Thompson v Brown Construction (Ebbw Vale) Ltd* [1981] 2 All E.R. 296; [1981] 1 W.L.R. 744; *Donovan v Gwentoys Ltd* [1990] 1 W.L.R. 472; [1990] 1 All E.R. 1018, 1023.

[85] The word "equitable" is not a term of art, it is simply another way of saying "fair and just" as between the parties: *Ward v Foss, The Times*, November 29, 1993, CA, *per* Hobhouse L.J. Where the claimant has been untruthful and sought to mislead the court on key issues, it is unlikely that the court will consider it equitable to disapply the limitation period: *Long v Tolchard* [2001] P.I.Q.R. P18, CA; *cf. Davis v Jacobs and Camden & Islington Health Authority and Novartis Pharmaceuticals (UK) Ltd* [1999] Lloyd's Rep. Med. 72, 87–88, where it was alleged that as a result of the defendants' negligence the claimant's personality was substantially altered by the drugs he was prescribed as part of a clinical trial.

[86] "Plainly it is more prejudicial to a plaintiff to be deprived of a cause of action when it is almost bound to succeed . . . than one that looks highly speculative. Equally, although it is always prejudicial to a defendant to be deprived of a defence under the Limitation Act, it may be less inequitable or unfair where the plaintiff has a strong case and more unfair where he has a weak one. But where, as here, the limitation issue is tried and determined before the merits of the claim, the court cannot and should not attempt to determine the merits on affidavit evidence. All that can be done and should be done is for the judge to take an overall view of the prospects of success . . ." *per* Stuart-Smith L.J. in *Dale v British Coal Corp* [1992] P.I.Q.R. P373, 380, CA; *Forbes v Wandsworth Health Authority* [1997] Q.B. 402, 418: "The court can, of course, only take a broad view of the matter at this stage."

[87] [1981] 2 All E.R. 296, 301; [1981] 1 W.L.R. 744.

highly prejudicial to a defendant to allow the action to proceed even where he has a good defence on the merits.

It has been argued, and indeed apparently accepted in some cases, that the prejudice to the defendant is at its greatest when he has no defence on the merits since he has been deprived of a cast-iron (limitation) defence. This is not an attractive argument, however, since it undermines the whole rationale of giving the court a discretion to override the primary limitation period.[88] "Prejudice" to the defendant must mean more than simply the removal of the limitation defence. Why, it might be asked, should the court be concerned with the cogency of the evidence and its effect on the defendant's ability to establish a defence on the merits when the prejudice to the defendant is greater if he has no such defence? This point was acknowledged by Leggatt L.J. in *Hartley v Birmingham City District Council*:

10–064

> "The defendants' approach produces the bizarre, if logical, result that the prejudice to the defendants is greatest when they have no defence to the merits of the claim, because not disapplying the limitation provision affords them a defence on liability which they would not otherwise have had. But a decision not [sic. query delete the "not"] to allow the action to proceed would cause the defendants to suffer no injustice whatever in being required to meet a claim of which they had had prompt notice and which they had had every opportunity of preparing themselves to meet. Equity need not be concerned to afford adventitious protection to a tortfeasor who has not been deprived of any opportunity to defend himself."[89]

Parker L.J. suggested that in nearly all cases the prejudice to the claimant by the operation of the limitation period and the prejudice to the defendant if the limitation period is disapplied will be equal and opposite. The stronger the claimant's case against the defendant the greater the prejudice to him from the operation of the limitation period and the greater the prejudice to the defendant if the provision is disapplied. Similarly, the weaker the claimant's case the less he will be prejudiced by the operation of the limitation period and the less the defendant is prejudiced if the provision is disapplied. This led his Lordship to the conclusion that the loss of the defence *as such* was of little importance. What was of paramount importance was the effect of the delay on the defendant's ability to defend.[90] Thus, where there was a short delay after the expiry of the primary limitation period, which was not caused by the claimant's fault but was entirely the fault of his solicitors, and the delay did not affect the defendant's ability to defend the action on the merits, the court was justified in exercising the discretion in favour of the claimant under section 33 even though he would have a cast-iron action against his solicitors if the action were not allowed to proceed.

---

[88] See Jones (1985) 1 P.N. 159, 162.
[89] [1992] 2 All E.R. 213, 226; [1992] 1 W.L.R. 968.
[90] *ibid.* at 224.

10–065   In *Ward v Foss*[91] Hobhouse L.J. considered the "paradox" postulated by Parker L.J. in *Hartley v Birmingham City Council* but concluded that the paradox does not exist:

> "The prejudice to the plaintiff is indeed the prejudice which would result from being de-barred from pursuing his action. But the prejudice to the defendant is not the prejudice of meeting a liability but of having to defend, or otherwise deal with, a stale claim. This prejudice to the defendant may well be no less, indeed it may be greater, where the claim is unmeritorious. I agree with Parker L.J. and Leggatt L.J. when they stressed the importance of the 'effect of the delay upon the defendant's ability to defend' and whether the defendant is still 'properly equipped to meet' the claim notwithstanding the delay that has occurred."

But it was not inequitable, said his Lordship, that a defendant should meet his liabilities in accordance with the laws of this country, nor did a requirement that he should meet his legal liabilities show, without more, that he would suffer relevant prejudice within the meaning of section 33:

> "For the purposes of section 33, if a defendant is to say that he is prejudiced, he must show something more than merely that he is going to be required to meet his legal liabilities. The prejudice must arise from some other additional element—some change of his position which would not have occurred if the action had been brought within time—some belief by the defendant that he was not going to be troubled with the claim—some alteration in his financial position or some failure to make provision for the claim—the loss of relevant evidence—some difficulty in having a fair trial after the lapse of time. No list can be exhaustive and the statute requires the court to have regard to all the circumstances of the case. But it must be some factor over and on top of the legal liability of the defendant which creates the prejudice."[92]

It is respectfully submitted that the approach of Hobhouse L.J. is correct. In the same case Simon Brown L.J. said that section 33 was concerned with prejudice to the defendant *caused by the delay*. This was plain both from the express terms of section 33 and on the authorities. It would seem, then, that whereas from the claimant's perspective the inability to continue the action as a result of the operation of the Limitation Act does constitute prejudice, loss of the limitation defence in itself cannot constitute relevant prejudice to the defendant, and in exercising the discretion conferred by section 33 the court should

---

[91] *The Times*, November 29, 1993, CA.

[92] *ibid*. See also *McEvoy v A.A. Welding and Fabrication Ltd* [1998] P.I.Q.R. P226, 273 where Pill L.J. commented that: "An important feature of the present case is *the lack of prejudice to the defendants* by reason of the fact that they have, subject to their limitation defence, admitted liability.' (emphasis added). In *Shapland v Palmer* [1999] 1 W.L.R. 2068, CA the only prejudice to the defendant was being deprived of the limitation defence, and accordingly the Court exercised the discretion in the claimant's favour.

balance the prejudice to the claimant of *losing the right to bring an action* with the prejudice to the defendant of having to face a *late claim*, not the prejudice of having to face a claim at all after the expiry of the primary limitation period.

It cannot always be said, however, that where the ability of a defendant to **10–066** defend on the merits has not been affected by the delay, the benefit of the limitation defence must be regarded as a "windfall." In *Nash v Eli Lilly & Co.*[93] the Court of Appeal held that there may be significant and relevant prejudice to a defendant even if it is shown that the claimant's claim is a poor case lacking in merit, since by disapplying the primary limitation period the defendants are put to the expense of defending a poor case, which may well cost far more to defend than the case would be held to be worth. Allowing the action to proceed may simply enable a dilatory claimant to claim from the defendants a sum in settlement which reflects the risk in costs to the defendants rather than the fair value of the claim.

When considering the degree of prejudice to the parties the court is **10–067** required by section 33(3) to "have regard to all the circumstances of the case, and in particular to:

(a) the length of and reasons for the delay on the part of the plaintiff;

(b) the extent to which, having regard to the delay, the evidence . . . is likely to be less cogent . . .;

(c) the conduct of the defendant after the cause of action arose, including the extent (if any) to which he responded to requests reasonably made by the plaintiff for information or inspection for the purpose of ascertaining facts which were or might be relevant to the plaintiff's cause of action against the defendant;

(d) the duration of any disability of the plaintiff arising after the date of the accrual of the cause of action;

(e) the extent to which the plaintiff acted promptly and reasonably once he knew whether or not the act or omission of the defendant, to which the injury was attributable, might be capable at that time of giving rise to an action for damages;

(f) the steps, if any, taken by the plaintiff to obtain medical, legal or other expert advice and the nature of any such advice he may have received."

It has been stressed by both the Court of Appeal and the House of Lords that the court should consider *all* the circumstances of the case, not simply the issues identified by section 33(3).[94] Provided this has been done, the Court

---

[93] [1993] 1 W.L.R. 782, 804, 808; [1992] 3 Med. L.R. 353, 371, 373.
[94] *Taylor v Taylor, The Times*, April 14, 1984, CA; *Donovan v Gwentoys Ltd* [1990] 1 W.L.R. 472; [1990] 1 All E.R. 1018; *KR v Bryn Alyn Community (Holdings) Ltd (in liquidation)* [2003] EWCA Civ 85; [2003] 1 F.C.R. 385 at [74].

of Appeal will be reluctant to interfere with the trial judge's exercise of discretion,[95] though it has been said that the fact that the judge did not specifically have regard to the degrees of prejudice to the claimant and the defendant respectively, but went straight to the circumstances mentioned in paragraphs (a) to (f) of section 33(3) does not necessarily mean that the judgment is flawed. The prejudice to each side may be "obvious" and not have to be expressly considered.[96]

(i) Length of and reasons for delay

10–068   "Delay" in subsection 33(3)(a) and (b) refers to the period between the expiry of the primary limitation period and the issue of the claim form, not the period between the accrual of the action or the claimant's "knowledge" and the issue of the claim form.[97] However, in *Donovan v Gwentoys Ltd*[98] the House of Lords, whilst agreeing with this interpretation of section 33(3), held that in weighing the degree of prejudice to the defendant the court was entitled to take into account the whole period of delay, including that within the primary limitation period, as part of all the circumstances of the case. The delay which their Lordships had in mind appears to be the delay between the commencement of the limitation period and notification to the defendant of the claim, rather than the issue of the claim form, the object being to bar "thoroughly stale claims." Lord Griffiths said that:

> ". . . it must always be relevant to consider when the defendant first had notification of the claim and thus the opportunity he will have to meet the claim at the trial if he is not to be permitted to rely on his limitation defence."[99]

Thus, there will be a distinction between cases where the defendant was notified of the claim fairly promptly, and so had an opportunity to give it full consideration, but the limitation period has expired through an oversight by the claimant's solicitors,[1] and cases such as *Donovan v Gwentoys Ltd*, where

---

[95] *Conry v Simpson* [1983] 3 All E.R. 369; *Bradley v Hanseatic Shipping Co Ltd* [1986] 2 Lloyd's Rep. 34. The court will overturn a judge's exercise of discretion only if it can be shown that he has "gone very wrong indeed," *per* Lawton L.J. at 38.

[96] *Yates v Thakeham Tiles Ltd* [1995] P.I.Q.R. P135, 139, *per* Nourse L.J., CA. But where a judge is minded to grant a long "extension" he should take meticulous care in giving reasons for doing so: *KR v Bryn Alyn Community (Holdings) Ltd (in liquidation)* [2003] EWCA Civ 85; [2003] 1 F.C.R. 385 at [74].

[97] *Thompson v Brown Construction (Ebbw Vale) Ltd* [1981] 2 All E.R. 296, 301; [1981] 1 W.L.R. 744; *Eastman v London County Bus Services Ltd*, *The Times*, November 23, 1985, CA.

[98] [1990] 1 All E.R. 1018; [1990] 1 W.L.R. 472.

[99] *ibid.* at 1024. His Lordship added that to the extent that *Eastman v London County Bus Services Ltd*, *The Times*, November 23, 1985, appears to cast doubt on this proposition, it should not be followed.

[1] As occurred in *Thompson v Brown Construction (Ebbw Vale) Ltd* [1981] 2 All E.R. 296; [1981] 1 W.L.R. 744; see also *Simpson v Norwest Holst Southern Ltd* [1980] 2 All E.R. 471, 478; [1980] 1 W.L.R. 968 where the claim was only 14 days out of time and the defendants

the defendant first heard of the claim some five years after the accident and was not in a position to investigate it until six years after the events.[2] In *Ward v Foss*[3] there was a delay of over four years after the expiry of primary limitation period, but there had been prompt notification of the claims and within two years of the accident the defendant's solicitors had been instructed to negotiate a settlement, which implied an appropriate degree of investigation. The early notification of the claim made the case more like *Thompson v Brown Construction (Ebbw Vale) Ltd* than *Donovan v Gwentoys Ltd*. In contrast, Stuart-Smith L.J. pointed out in *Dale v British Coal Corp*[4] that where the existence of a claim and sufficient particulars of it are given so late that it is virtually impossible for the defendants to investigate it a defendant will be gravely prejudiced if section 11 is disapplied, because he is almost powerless to defend the case on its merits. Such a case would require exceptional circumstances to outweigh that prejudice, and to bring the scales down in favour of the claimant.

A short delay probably causes little prejudice to the defendant,[5] indeed, a very short delay (of one day) causes no prejudice at all, particularly where the defendant was notified about the claim at an early stage.[6] It has been suggested that a delay of five or six years could raise a rebuttable presumption of prejudice,[7] though the Court of Appeal has indicated that a presumption of prejudice is not justified because it would "impermissibly cut down the wide discretion" in section 33 cases,[8] though as a general proposition the

10–069

(n.1 contd.) had had an early opportunity of investigating the claim and getting their evidence together. In *Godfrey v Gloucestershire Royal Infirmary NHS Trust* [2003] EWHC 549 (QB) Leveson J. commented, at [38], that since the claimant's complaint about the management of her pregnancy had been put into writing very quickly, giving the defendants the opportunity to obtain information from the medical staff almost contemporaneously with events, and they were put on notice that proceedings were being contemplated, it could not be "suggested that the claim has come out of the blue many years after the events."

2 [1990] 1 All E.R. 1018, 1024; [1990] 1 W.L.R. 472, *per* Lord Griffiths; *cf.* the position where the claimant is under a disability; the defendant may be seriously prejudiced in his ability to produce evidence, but this is irrelevant: see para. 10–084, and *Bull v Devon Area Health Authority* (1989), [1993] 4 Med. L.R. 117, CA.

3 *The Times*, November 29, 1993, CA.

4 [1992] P.I.Q.R. P373, 385, CA.

5 *Firman v Ellis* [1978] Q.B. 886; *Simpson v Norwest Holst Southern Ltd* [1980] 2 All E.R. 471, 478; [1980] 1 W.L.R. 968; *Atha v ATV Network* (1983, QBD; unreported); *Grenville v Waltham Forest Health Authority* (1992, CA; unreported); *cf. Davis v Soltenpar* (1983) 133 N.L.J. 720 where the claim form was 24 days late, the defendant's case was "wholly without merit" but the discretion was not exercised in the claimant's favour.

6 *Hartley v Birmingham City District Council* [1992] 2 All E.R. 213; [1992] 1 W.L.R. 968. See also *Hendy v Milton Keynes Health Authority* [1992] 3 Med. L.R. 114; [1992] P.I.Q.R. P281, where there was a delay of nine days, but no effect on the cogency of the evidence, and no prejudice to the defendants.

7 *Buck v English Electric Co Ltd* [1977] 1 W.L.R. 806, where there was a nine year delay, but the defendants were not seriously prejudiced because in that period they had dealt with many similar claims and evidence was available; *Pilmore v Northern Trawlers Ltd* [1986] 1 Lloyd's Rep. 552, another case involving a nine year delay; *cf. Cornish v Kearley* (1983) 133 N.L.J. 870, where there was a three year delay, but the reasons for the delay were reasonable, the cogency of the evidence was affected but not greatly, and, in the circumstances, it was not unreasonable for the claimant to have delayed taking legal advice.

8 *KR v Bryn Alyn Community (Holdings) Ltd (in liquidation)* [2003] EWCA Civ 85; [2003] 1 F.C.R. 385 at [79].

longer the delay the more likely it is that the balance of prejudice will swing against disapplying the primary limitation period.[9] The length of the delay is probably of less significance than the reasons for the delay and the effect on the cogency of the evidence. Reasons for the delay will vary considerably, and whereas the claimant's subjective beliefs may be irrelevant to the question of his knowledge under section 14 they are relevant to the court's exercise of discretion.[10] The claimant may have been unaware of his legal rights;[11] or the injury may not have seemed so serious at first;[12] or he may have felt that he was "sponging" if he sued and may have wanted to maintain good relations with the defendant;[13] or the claimant may have been in a debilitated physical and mental state throughout the relevant period;[14] or the defendant may have contributed to the delay by withholding information from the claimant.[15] Generally, where the claimant's conduct has not been personally blameworthy this will carry considerable weight in persuading the court to exercise the discretion in his favour.[16]

(ii) Cogency of the evidence

10–070 Usually it is the effect of the delay on the cogency of the evidence which is most significant. If documents have been destroyed or witnesses have disappeared this is a different situation from cases where there is little real dispute about the facts, since the defendant's ability to defend the case has clearly been prejudiced.[17] The defendant is not required to adduce evi-

---

[9] *ibid.* at [80].

[10] *Buck v English Electric Co Ltd* [1977] 1 W.L.R. 806; *McCafferty v Metropolitan Police District Receiver* [1977] 1 W.L.R. 1073; *Coad v Cornwall & Isles of Scilly Health Authority* [1997] 1 W.L.R. 189.

[11] *Brooks v Coates (UK) Ltd* [1984] 1 All E.R. 702, 713, where the delay was 15 years, but the claimant's ignorance was not unreasonable; *Coad v Cornwall & Isles of Scilly Health Authority* [1997] 1 W.L.R. 189; *cf. Dobbie v Medway Health Authority* [1994] 4 All E.R. 450; [1994] 5 Med. L.R. 160, CA, where there was a gap of 16 years between the claimant's operation and the issue of the claim form. The Court of Appeal held that the delay was too great, despite the fact that the claimant had been unaware of her right to bring an action.

[12] *McCafferty v Metropolitan Police District Receiver* [1977] 1 W.L.R. 1073.

[13] *Buck v English Electric Co Ltd* [1977] 1 W.L.R. 806; *McCafferty v Metropolitan Police District Receiver* [1977] 1 W.L.R. 1073. A patient's natural reluctance to upset the doctor/patient relationship by engaging in litigation will be relevant here.

[14] *Mills v Dyer-Fare* (1987, QBD; unreported); *Birnie v Oxfordshire Health Authority* (1982) 2 *The Lancet* 281, QBD; *Pearse v Barnet Health Authority* [1998] P.I.Q.R. P39; *Godfrey v Gloucestershire Royal Infirmary NHS Trust* [2003] EWHC 549 (QB) at [41], where the claimant had to "cope with a severely disabled baby which will have imposed its own emotional physical and financial constraints on the single minded pursuit of this litigation."

[15] *Drury v Grimsby Health Authority* [1997] 8 Med. L.R. 38.

[16] *Brooks v Coates (UK) Ltd* [1984] 1 All E.R. 702; *Bates v Leicester Health Authority* [1998] Lloyd's Rep. Med. 93, 102; *cf. Davies v British Insulated Callenders Cables Ltd* (1977) 121 S.J. 203, where the claimant had no good reason for the delay and the discretion was not exercised in his favour; and where the claimant offers no explanation for the delay she is unlikely to persuade the court to disapply the primary limitation period: *Berry v Calderdale Health Authority* [1998] Lloyd's Rep. Med. 179, CA.

[17] "In my judgment where the existence of a claim and sufficient particulars of it are given so late that it is virtually impossible for the defendants to investigate it, either because witnesses cannot be traced, memories will inevitably have faded or vital documents are lost, a defendant

dence of specific prejudice as a result of delay, since the court is entitled to draw an inference that there has been prejudice caused by delay as a result of impairment of witnesses recollections.[18] Cases which are based on allegations about failures in systems of work are likely to be better documented than "one off" accidents.[19] Similarly, where the defendants have had to investigate and prepare to meet another case on liability arising out of the same facts, the cogency of the evidence may not be affected by the delay.[20] Cases of medical negligence should be reasonably well documented in the medical records;[21] although this is not always the case. In *Forbes v Wandsworth Health Authority*[22] the Court of Appeal declined to exercise the discretion under section 33 in the claimant's favour having regard to the prejudice to the defendants after a long delay, caused by an inability now to locate medical records and witnesses, fading memories, the difficulty that experts would have in dealing with the appropriate standards of practice of 14 years earlier, and the fact that the claimant's case

---

(n.17 contd.) is gravely prejudiced if section 11 of the Act is disapplied, because he is almost powerless to defend the case on its merits. In such a case it will require exceptional circumstances to outweigh the prejudice and to bring the scales down in favour of the plaintiff," *per* Stuart-Smith L.J. in *Dale v British Coal Corp* [1992] P.I.Q.R. P373, 385, CA; *Hattam v National Coal Board* (1978) 122 S.J. 777; *cf. Brooks v Coates (UK) Ltd* [1984] 1 All E.R. 702, 713–714. On the other hand, where there is a long limitation period, as in the case of minors, delay after expiry of the limitation period may have no real effect on the cogency of the evidence, since the delay during the primary limitation period may have done all the damage to the cogency of the evidence that is going to occur: see *Doughty v North Staffordshire Health Authority* [1992] 3 Med. L.R. 81, 85, *per* Henry J.; *Colegrove v Smyth* [1994] 5 Med. L.R. 111, 118, *per* Buckley J.

[18] *Price v United Engineering Steels Ltd* [1998] P.I.Q.R. P407.

[19] See, *e.g.*, *Cotton v General Electric Co Ltd* (1979) 129 N.L.J. 73; *Pilmore v Northern Trawlers Ltd* [1986] 1 Lloyd's Rep. 552; *Buck v English Electric Co Ltd* [1977] 1 W.L.R. 806, where the evidence was no less cogent due to the delay because the defendants had dealt with a number of similar claims.

[20] *Bowers v Harrow Health Authority* [1995] 6 Med. L.R. 16—claim brought by a mother in respect of her psychological injury where the defendants had already investigated the case on liability brought by the estate of a young child.

[21] See, *e.g.*, *Bentley v Bristol and Weston Health Authority* [1991] 2 Med. L.R. 359; *Farthing v North East Essex Health Authority* [1998] Lloyd's Rep. Med. 37, CA; *Smith v Leicester Health Authority* [1998] Lloyd's Rep. Med. 77, CA, where the case on liability turned almost entirely on X-rays taken in 1954 and 1955 which did not come to light until 1995; *Godfrey v Gloucestershire Royal Infirmary NHS Trust* [2003] EWHC 549 (QB) at [40]. In *Pearse v Barnet Health Authority* [1998] P.I.Q.R. P39 it was held that there was no prejudice to the defendants from a delay between 1991 and 1994 in dealing with a case based on events in 1970 which would inevitably turn on the (virtually complete) medical records; see also *Ward v Foss, The Times,* November 29, 1993, CA; *cf. Bull v Devon Area Health Authority* (1987, QBD; unreported); affirmed [1993] 4 Med. L.R. 117, CA. In *Hills v Potter* [1983] 3 All E.R. 716, 728 Hirst J. said that if the defendant's evidence was accepted then he had suffered no prejudice as a result of the delay. Since the defendant's evidence was accepted, and particularly having regard to the gravity of the claimant's injuries, it was proper to disapply the limitation bar. But see *KR v Bryn Alyn Community (Holdings) Ltd (in liquidation)* [2003] EWCA Civ 85; [2003] 1 F.C.R. 385 at [74] where the Court of Appeal said that where a judge determines the s.33 issue along with the substantive issues in the case, he should take care not to determine the substantive issues, including liability, causation and quantum, before determining the issue of limitation and, in particular, the effect of delay on the cogency of the evidence: "To rely on his findings on those issues to assess the cogency of the evidence for the purpose of the limitation exercise would put the cart before the horse."

[22] [1997] Q.B. 402.

was supported by scanty evidence and had only modest prospects of success.

10–071   In *Nash v Eli Lilly & Co*[23] Hidden J. said that it was not simply a matter of assessing the effect of delay on the cogency of the *defendant's* evidence when assessing prejudice to the defendant, because a lack of cogency in the claimant's evidence due to delay may be used to the advantage of the claimant, for example, in an attempt to explain away or mitigate the effects of omissions or contradictions in that evidence. This approach was rejected, however, by the Court of Appeal.[24] There was no basis in subsection 33(3) for the concept that lack of cogency in the claimant's case could inure to the benefit of the claimant's case and thereby prejudice the defendant. This was logically unsustainable because it depended upon an assumption that the trial judge would not be able properly to assess the evidence led on behalf of the claimant. On the other hand, in *Hammond v West Lancashire Health Authority*[25] the defendants had destroyed the claimant's X-rays because they did not consider them to be part of the patient's medical record (*sic.*). They claimed to have suffered prejudice. The Court of Appeal considered that the prejudice, if anything, was to the claimant and upheld the judge's decision to disapply the limitation period.

(iii) Conduct of the defendant

10–072   Section 33(3)(c) refers specifically to the extent to which the defendant responded to reasonable requests for information or inspection for the purpose of ascertaining facts which were or might be relevant to the claimant's cause of action. A potential defendant does not have a duty to volunteer information but he should not obstruct the claimant in obtaining information.[26] This includes the conduct of the defendant's solicitors and his insurers. The defendant's conduct is relevant even where he has made an honest mistake in giving misleading information.[27]

(iv) Duration of the disability

10–073   If the claimant is under a disability at the date at which the cause of action accrued, the commencement of the limitation period is postponed until he

---

[23] [1991] 2 Med. L.R. 169.
[24] [1993] 1 W.L.R. 782, 807.
[25] [1998] Lloyd's Rep. Med. 146.
[26] *Thompson v Brown Construction (Ebbw Vale) Ltd* [1981] 2 All E.R. 296, 302; [1981] 1 W.L.R. 744. A serious delay in providing the claimant's medical records may be a relevant consideration: *Mills v Dyer-Fare* (1987, QBD; unreported); *Atkinson v Oxfordshire Health Authority* [1993] 4 Med. L.R. 18, QBD, where a failure to tell the claimant or his mother what had happened during the course of an operation meant that to a large extent the delay was of the defendants' own making.
[27] *Marston v British Railways Board* [1976] I.C.R. 124; *a fortiori* where the defendant has deliberately misled the claimant: see, *e.g.*, *Scuriaga v Powell* (1979) 123 S.J. 406, para. 10–027, a case where the defendant's conduct prevented the claimant from acquiring knowledge of the relevant facts under s.14.

ceases to be under a disability,[28] but supervening disability does not stop time running. It will be taken into account, however, in the exercise of the discretion. Since minority can never supervene, section 33(3)(d) applies only to supervening mental incapacity. Although there are some cases in which the claimant's physical disability has been considered to be relevant under this paragraph,[29] it is submitted that the better view is that section 33(3)(d) is restricted to supervening mental incapacity which is of sufficient degree to satisfy the requirements of section 38(2), *i.e.* the claimant must be "of unsound mind."[30] The claimant's physical disabilities can be considered under section 33(3)(a), as part of the reasons for the delay, or as part of "all the circumstances of the case."[31]

(v) Extent to which claimant acted promptly

Clearly, the date at which the claimant became aware of the existence of **10–074** a cause of action is not necessarily the same as the date of his "knowledge" for the purpose of section 14, and may well be later.[32] If the claimant has acted promptly and reasonably once he became aware of the cause of action it is not to be counted against him that his lawyers have been dilatory and allowed the primary limitation period to expire.[33] In *Yates v Thakeham Tiles Ltd*[34] the claimant consulted solicitors after the expiry of the primary limitation period, and the solicitors did not notify the defendants of a potential claim until a year later. The Court of Appeal held that this was proper where the solicitors were obtaining all the relevant information to support the claim, such as advice from counsel, and obtaining legal aid. On the other hand, if the claimant has a potential claim against

---

[28] Limitation Act 1980, s.28; see para. 10–084.
[29] *Wood v SFK (UK) Ltd* (1982, QBD; unreported); *Hart v British Leyland Cars Ltd* (1983, QBD; unreported); *Pilmore v Northern Trawlers Ltd* [1986] 1 Lloyd's Rep. 552, 554; *Bater v Newbold* (1991, CA; unreported).
[30] See *Cornish v Kearley and Tonge Ltd* (1983) 133 N.L.J. 870; *Yates v Thakeham Tiles Ltd* [1995] P.I.Q.R. P135, CA; *Thomas v Plaistow* [1997] P.I.Q.R. P540, CA.
[31] *Pearse v Barnet Health Authority* [1998] P.I.Q.R. P39. The fact that the claimant's physical disabilities have been mistakenly considered under section 33(3)(d) does not detract from the exercise of the overall discretion: *Yates v Thakeham Tiles Ltd* [1995] P.I.Q.R. P135. Moreover, to the extent that the claimant suffers psychological damage falling short of unsoundness of mind, her psychological condition can be taken into account under section 33(3)(a) as part of the reasons for the delay: *Jones v City and Hackney Health Authority* (1993, QBD; unreported).
[32] *Eastman v London County Bus Services Ltd, The Times,* November 23, 1985, CA.
[33] *Thompson v Brown Construction (Ebbw Vale) Ltd* [1981] 2 All E.R. 296, 303; [1981] 1 W.L.R. 744; *Das v Ganju* [1999] P.I.Q.R. P260; [1999] Lloyd's Rep. Med. 198, CA; *Corbin v Penfold Metallising Company Ltd* [2000] Lloyds Rep. Med. 247, 251 CA; *Steeds v Peverel Management Services Ltd* [2001] EWCA Civ. 419; *The Times,* May 16, 2001, CA; s.33(3)(e) is concerned only with the conduct of the claimant, not his advisers: *Davis v Jacobs and Camden & Islington Health Authority and Novartis Pharmaceuticals (UK) Ltd* [1999] Lloyd's Rep. Med. 72, 86, *per* Brooke L.J.; *cf.* constructive knowledge under s.14(3) where the claimant is fixed with the knowledge about facts that his lawyers ought reasonably to have discovered: *Henderson v Temple Pier Co Ltd* [1998] 1 W.L.R. 1540; *Hayward v Sharrard* (1998) 56 B.M.L.R. 155.
[34] [1995] P.I.Q.R. P135, CA.

his solicitors as a result of delay, this may reduce the degree of prejudice suffered by the claimant.

(vi) Steps taken to obtain expert advice

10–075   This includes legal advice and whether it was favourable or unfavourable.[35] Thus, while erroneous legal advice will not prevent time running under the three year limitation period, it is relevant to the exercise of discretion.

(vii) Other factors: availability of an alternative remedy

10–076   The availability of an alternative remedy (e.g. against the claimant's negligent solicitors) is a "highly relevant consideration," but it is not conclusive against the exercise of the discretion in the claimant's favour. Even where the claimant would have a cast iron case against his solicitors he will suffer some prejudice, even if only minor, in having to find and instruct new solicitors, additional delay, and a possible personal liability for costs up to the date of the court's refusal of the application.[36] The fact that the claimant would have a cast iron case against his solicitors is not necessarily a reason to use the occasion to teach the solicitors a lesson, particularly where the delay after the expiry of the limitation period was short and had caused the defendants no material prejudice.[37] Where there is any real dispute about the solicitors' liability in negligence then the chances of the claimant having an alternative remedy should be largely disregarded.[38]

10–077   Where the claimant has already changed solicitors there is less prejudice to him if the discretion is not exercised, even in the case of a short delay,[39] and a fortiori where the claimant has already commenced proceedings against his

---

[35] Jones v G.D. Searle & Co Ltd [1978] 3 All E.R. 654. The claimant can be required to disclose the nature of the advice he received. See also Halford v Brookes [1991] 3 All E.R. 559, where the delay was attributable to the claimant being advised that her only civil remedy was against the Criminal Injuries Compensation Board. As soon as she was advised that there was another remedy she acted promptly in issuing a claim form.

[36] Thompson v Brown Construction (Ebbw Vale) Ltd [1981] 2 All E.R. 296, 301–302; [1981] 1 W.L.R. 744. He might prefer to sue the real tortfeasor, said Lord Diplock, rather than his former solicitors. Query, however, why the claimant's preferences should have any bearing on the balance of prejudice between claimant and defendant. See also Ramsden v Lee [1992] 2 All E.R. 204, 212, a case where the defendant had been notified of the claim within a month of the accident, and there was no dispute on liability; there had been two interim payments, but the claim form was issued six months out of time. The Court of Appeal held that the judge had exercised his discretion correctly in allowing the action to proceed. Part of the prejudice to the claimant consists of being forced to change from bringing an action against a tortfeasor, who may know little or nothing of the weak points of the claimant's case, to bringing an action against his solicitor, who will know a great deal about his case: Hartley v Birmingham City District Council [1992] 2 All E.R. 213, 224; [1992] 1 W.L.R. 968, CA.

[37] Steeds v Peverel Management Services Ltd [2001] EWCA Civ 419; The Times, May 16, 2001, CA.

[38] Firman v Ellis [1978] Q.B. 886, 916, per Geoffrey Lane L.J., who added that it was undesirable that there should be any detailed enquiry into the question of the solicitors' negligence; Das v Ganju [1999] P.I.Q.R. P260 270; [1999] Lloyd's Rep. Med. 198, 205, CA; see generally Jones (1985) 1 P.N. 159; Steiner (1990) 6 P.N. 183.

[39] Straw v Hicks (1983, CA; unreported).

former solicitors.[40] In *Conry v Simpson*,[41] however, the Court of Appeal refused to interfere with the trial judge's exercise of discretion in favour of the claimant, although the claim form had been issued three years and ten months out of time and an action against the former solicitors had been commenced. Stephenson L.J. commented that it is very seldom that a remedy against a solicitor can be as satisfactory as a remedy against the original tortfeasor. On the other hand, in *Donovan v Gwentoys Ltd*[42] Lord Griffiths said that the claimant would suffer "only the slightest prejudice" if she were required to pursue her remedy against her solicitors, although in that case there was severe prejudice to the defendant caused by the delay in notification of a claim.

Other factors may also be relevant to the court's exercise of discretion. It   **10–078** is legitimate to take into account the insurance position of both defendant and claimant, as part of all the circumstances of the case.[43] The court will not apply different principles to multi-party litigation, however, from the principles applied to ordinary, single claimant actions when exercising the discretion. The merits of each case must be considered individually.[44] It has been suggested that the fact that a medical negligence action is a claim for professional negligence may be an additional factor in the defendant's favour when the court considers the exercise of discretion, because such actions have more serious consequences for defendants and should be prosecuted without delay.[45] In *Biss v Lambeth Health Authority*[46] the Court of Appeal held, in the somewhat analogous context of an application to strike out an action for want of prosecution, that there was prejudice to the defendants in the worry that professional staff would suffer with the action hanging over them like the "sword of Damocles," although it would be exceptional to treat the "mere sword of Damocles, hanging for an unnecessary period" as a sufficient reason in itself to strike out.[47] In *Dobbie v Medway Health Authority*,[48] a

---

[40] *Mills v Ritchie* (1984, QBD; unreported).

[41] [1983] 3 All E.R. 369.

[42] [1990] 1 W.L.R. 472; [1990] 1 All E.R. 1018; *cf. Ramsden v Lee* [1992] 2 All E.R. 204 where, having been notified of the claim at an early stage and admitted liability, the only prejudice to the defendant was the loss of the "windfall" limitation defence.

[43] *Firman v Ellis* [1978] Q.B. 886, 916; *Liff v Peasley* [1980] 1 W.L.R. 781, 789. Since it is legitimate, when considering prejudice to the claimant, to take into account the fact that the claimant will have a claim against his solicitors, it is also legitimate to take into account the fact that the defendant is insured and that if he is deprived of his fortuitous limitation defence he will have a claim on his insurers: *Hartley v Birmingham City District Council* [1992] 2 All E.R. 213, 224; [1992] 1 W.L.R. 968, CA. In *Kelly v Bastible* [1997] 8 Med. L.R. 15 the Court of Appeal held that the fact that the defendant is insured was one of the factors that could be placed in the scales when weighing prejudice to the parties under s.33, but if, treating the defendant and insurer as a composite unit, the delay had seriously prejudiced their ability to defend the action, and if the court would not have allowed the action to proceed had the defendant not been insured, the weight to be given to the mere fact that the defendant was insured should be nil.

[44] *Nash v Eli Lilly & Co* [1991] 2 Med. L.R. 169; affirmed [1993] 1 W.L.R. 782, 810; [1992] 3 Med. L.R. 353, 373, CA.

[45] *Jackson & Powell on Professional Negligence*, 5th ed., 2002, para. 5.069.

[46] [1978] 1 W.L.R. 382.

[47] *Department of Transport v Chris Smaller (Transport) Ltd* [1989] A.C. 1197, 1209–1210, *per* Lord Griffiths.

[48] [1992] 3 Med. L.R. 217.

case in which there was a 13 year delay after the expiry of the primary limitation period, Otton J. applied this reasoning to the exercise of discretion under section 33:

> "There must come a time when the Sword of Damocles must be removed from above the head of a professional man and he can either continue with his professional work or retire from it with the knowledge that his conduct (whatever it may be) will not continue to haunt him. That time has surely come in this case. Likewise for the hospital and the health authority."[49]

This was a "potent factor" which tipped the balance substantially in favour of the defendants. In the Court of Appeal, however, Beldam L.J. disagreed with the decision to take into account the Sword of Damocles argument, commenting that he could not see how such a consideration could apply to a doctor who does not know that any action is contemplated against him.[50] It would seem that the issue could only be relevant where the doctor had had a claim intimated but there had been a long delay in issuing the claim form.[51]

10–079   The financial consequences for the defendant of the delay itself is a relevant consideration (as opposed to the "mere" fact that removal of the limitation defence may result in the defendant being required to pay damages). Thus, in *Smith v Leicester Health Authority*[52] the judge took into account the defendants' changed financial arrangements, which meant that the defendants would have to bear some £100,000 more than if the action had been brought before January 1990. But in balancing the prejudice between the parties the judge did not refer at all to the financial loss that the claimant would suffer if section 11 was not disapplied (she had succeeded on liability). The Court of Appeal considered the fact that the claimant's financial loss, if the action was statute barred, was likely to have been ten times greater than the additional financial prejudice to the defendants was an important factor in exercising the discretion in her favour. On the other hand, the court must also consider the question of proportionality in the exercise of the discretion under section 33. Thus, "courts should be slow to exercise their discretion in favour of a claimant in the absence of cogent medical evidence showing a serious effect on the claimant's health or enjoyment of life or employability. The likely amount of an award is an important factor to consider, especially if . . . they are likely to take a considerable time to try."[53]

---

[49] *ibid.* at 224.

[50] [1994] 4 All E.R. 451, 462; [1994] 5 Med. L.R. 160, 167.

[51] In *Birnie v Oxfordshire Area Health Authority* (1982) 2 *The Lancet* 281, QBD, Glidewell J. considered that it was a relevant point in the case of an individual defendant doctor that he had had the claim hanging over him since it was first intimated to him; and also that he was not insured. See further *Slevin v Southampton and South West Hampshire Health Authority* [1997] 8 Med. L.R. 175, 181 and *Sims v Dartford and Gravesham Health Authority* [1996] 7 Med. L.R. 381 on the "sword of Damocles" point.

[52] [1998] Lloyd's Rep. Med. 77.

[53] *Robinson v St. Helens MBC* [2002] EWCA Civ 1099; [2003] P.I.Q.R. P128 at [33].

(4) Death

(a) Fatal Accidents Act 1976

In an action for loss of dependency under the Fatal Accidents Act 1976, if **10–080** the death occurred before the expiry of the deceased's three year limitation period, then a new three year period commences in favour of the dependants. This period runs from the date of death or the date of the dependants' "knowledge," whichever is later.[54] If there is more than one dependant and their dates of knowledge are different, time runs separately against each of them.[55] If the Fatal Accidents action is not commenced within three years of the death or the date of knowledge of the dependants the action is barred.[56] The court may "disapply" the provisions of section 12, however, by virtue of its discretion under section 33, in which case the guidelines of section 33(3) have effect as if references to the claimant (usually the personal representative) included references to the dependants.

If the deceased's three year limitation period had expired before he died **10–081** then in theory he could not have maintained an action at the date of his death and the dependants' action is barred by section 12(1). For this purpose no account is taken of the possibility that the deceased might have made a successful application to override the fixed period under section 33. However, section 33 applies to the Fatal Accidents Act and the court can exercise its discretion and direct that section 12(1) of the Limitation Act 1980 and section 1(1) of the Fatal Accidents Act 1976 shall not apply. In exercising its discretion the court must have regard to the length of and reasons for the delay on the part of the deceased.[57] The court may disapply section 12 only where the reason why the deceased could no longer maintain an action was because of the time limit in section 11.[58] If he could no longer maintain an action for any other reason the court has no discretion to allow the dependants' action to proceed.

(b) Law Reform (Miscellaneous Provisions) Act 1934

The position in the case of an action on behalf of the estate of a deceased **10–082** person under the Law Reform (Miscellaneous Provisions) Act 1934 is similar to that which applies to Fatal Accident Act claims. If the deceased died before the expiry of his three year limitation period, a new three year period commences which runs from either the date of death or the date of the personal representative's knowledge, whichever is later.[59] If there is more than one personal representative and their dates of knowledge are different, time

---

[54] Limitation Act 1980, s.12. "Knowledge" is defined in s.14; see para. 10–017.
[55] *ibid.*, s.13(1).
[56] *ibid.*, s.12(2).
[57] Limitation Act 1980, s.33(4).
[58] *ibid.*, s.33(2).
[59] *ibid.*, s.11(5).

runs from the earliest date.[60] If this period expires the personal representative may invoke section 33 requesting the court to exercise its discretion to override the effect of section 11(5).

10–083   Where the deceased died after the expiry of his three year limitation period an action by his personal representative is barred by section 11(3), but the court can exercise its discretion under section 33 in favour of the personal representative, again having regard to the length of and the reasons for the delay by the deceased.

(5) Persons under a Disability

10–084   A person is under a disability while he is an infant or of unsound mind.[61] An infant is a person under the age of 18,[62] and a person is of unsound mind if, by reason of mental disorder within the meaning of the Mental Health Act 1983, he is incapable of managing and administering his property and affairs.[63] If a person to whom a right of action accrues is under a disability at the date when the action accrued, time does not run until he ceases to be under a disability or dies, whichever occurs first.[64] Thus, an infant has an indefeasible right to bring an action for personal injuries at any time before the age of 21,[65] and a person of unsound mind has three years from the date he becomes sane. The fact that a defendant may suffer prejudice from a long delay is immaterial.[66] There is, of course, nothing to stop a person under a

---

[60] *ibid.*, s.11(7); *cf.* the position with dependants under the Fatal Accidents Act, where time runs separately against each dependant: s.13(1).

[61] *ibid.*, s.38(2).

[62] Family Law Reform Act 1969, s.1.

[63] Limitation Act 1980, s.38(3). For discussion of the circumstances in which a person is incapable of managing and administering his property and affairs see *Masterman-Lister v Jewell and Home Counties Dairies* [2002] EWHC 417 (Q.B.); [2002] Lloyd's Rep. Med. 239; affirmed [2002] EWCA Civ 1889; [2003] P.I.Q.R. P310. Under the Mental Health Act 1983, s.1(2) mental disorder is defined as "mental illness, arrested or incomplete development of the mind, psychopathic disorder, and any other disorder or disability of mind." Mental illness does not necessarily mean that the claimant was incapable of managing his affairs, and if he is capable of managing his affairs s.28 does not apply: *Dawson v Scott-Brown* (1988, CA; unreported).

[64] Limitation Act 1980, s.28(1) and (6). This assumes, of course, that the claimant has the relevant "knowledge" under s.14. If not, then time will not run until he acquires knowledge. If the person under a disability dies the primary limitation period starts to run, and there can be no further extension under s.28, even if the person to whom the cause of action accrues is himself under a disability: s.28(3).

[65] *Tolley v Morris* [1979] 1 W.L.R. 592.

[66] If Parliament had intended prejudice to be a material consideration under s.28, it would have said so, as it did elsewhere in the Limitation Act 1980: *Headford v Bristol and District Health Authority* [1995] P.I.Q.R. P180, 184; [1995] 6 Med. L.R. 1, 4, *per* Rose L.J., CA. If the Law Commission's proposals to amend the Limitation Act are implemented the rules applying to claimants under a disability would change significantly (Law. Com. No. 270, *Limitation of Actions*, July 2001). During the claimant's minority the initial limitation period would not run. However, the 10-year longstop period would run during minority, though it would not bar an action before the claimant reached the age of 21. Adult disability (including supervening disability) would suspend the initial limitation period, but would not affect the longstop limitation period. Where the claimant under a disability had suffered personal injury (to which the longstop would not apply) and was in the care of a responsible

disability bringing an action while still under the disability. If the accident itself caused immediate unsoundness of mind time will not begin to run.[67]

If the claimant was not under a disability when the action accrued, super- **10–085** vening unsoundness of mind will not prevent time running.[68] This applies even where the supervening disability arose before the claimant's date of knowledge under section 14.[69] The apparent harshness of this rule may be mitigated by the court's exercise of discretion under section 33(3)(d).

(6) Deliberate Concealment

Where any fact relevant to the claimant's right of action has been deliber- **10–086** ately concealed from him by the defendant, the limitation period does not begin to run until the claimant has discovered the concealment or could with reasonable diligence have discovered it.[70] This provision is not limited to fraud in a technical sense, but includes the deliberate commission of a breach of duty in circumstances in which it is unlikely to be discovered for some time.[71] This includes the commission of a wrong knowingly or recklessly, but mere negligence is not sufficient. In a novel interpretation of section 32, the Court of Appeal held that concealment was deliberate if the defendant had intentionally committed an act or omission which involved a breach of duty in circumstances in which it was unlikely to be discovered for some time, even though the defendant had no knowledge or intention of concealment.[72]

[n.66 contd.] adult ten years after the later of (a) the act or omission that gave rise to the claim and (b) the onset of disability, the primary limitation period would run from the date the responsible adult knew or ought to have known the relevant facts (unless the responsible adult was a defendant to the claim). The longstop would not apply, however, where the defendant had dishonestly concealed relevant facts. In the case of a claim in respect of personal injuries, the court would retain a discretion to disapply the primary limitation period. Thus, in the case of permanent disability there would be no open-ended right to bring a claim for personal injuries, but the claimant's entitlement to sue would be subject to the court's discretion.

[67] *Kirby v Leather* [1965] 2 Q.B. 367, CA. This applies if the unsoundness of mind arises at any time before the end of the day on which the accident occurred; *Boot v Boot* (1991, CA; unreported); *Turner v W.H. Malcolm Ltd* (1992) 15 B.M.L.R. 40, CA. As Glidewell L.J. observed, at 48, in this case "Parliament has in effect provided that there is no limitation period for a plaintiff who is under a permanent disability."

[68] *Purnell v Roche* [1927] 2 Ch 142. Hence where it is alleged that the accident which is the subject of the litigation caused the unsoundness of mind it may be crucial to know whether this was immediate or whether there was a period of time during which the claimant was not under a disability: see, *e.g.*, *Boot v Boot* (1991, CA; unreported).

[69] Except that in a case of latent damage which does not involve a claim for personal injuries, where the claimant was under a disability at the "starting date" (as defined in s.14A(5) of the Limitation Act 1980) the limitation period is extended to three years from the date when the claimant ceased to be under a disability or died (whichever occurred first), subject to the overall longstop specified in s.14B of 15 years from the date of breach of duty: Limitation Act 1980, s.28A.

[70] Limitation Act 1980, s.32(1). "Defendant" includes the defendant's agent and any person through whom the defendant claims and his agent.

[71] *ibid.*, s.32(2).

[72] *Cave v Robinson Jarvis & Rolf (a firm)* [2001] EWCA Civ 245; [2002] 1 W.L.R. 581, applying the earlier Court of Appeal decision in *Brocklesby v Armitage & Guest (Note)* [2002] 1 W.L.R. 598.

This interpretation meant that a defendant must simply intend the act or omission which resulted in a breach of duty; she did not have to intend to commit a breach of duty. The result was that many instances of "ordinary negligence" by professionals fell with section 32 (since professionals normally intend to act in performing their job), apparently rendering many other provisions of the Limitation Act redundant. The House of Lords reversed this ruling in *Cave v Robinson Jarvis & Rolf (a firm).*[73] Lord Millett said that concealment and non-disclosure, though different concepts, both required knowledge of the fact which is to be kept secret, and a man could "not sensibly be said either to conceal or to fail to disclose something of which he is ignorant." Accordingly, his Lordship concluded that:

> "section 32 deprives a defendant of a limitation defence in two situations: (i) where he takes active steps to conceal his own breach of duty after he has become aware of it; and (ii) where he is guilty of deliberate wrongdoing and conceals or fails to disclose it in circumstances where it is unlikely to be discovered for some time. But it does not deprive a defendant of a limitation defence where he is charged with negligence if, being unaware of his error or that he has failed to take proper care, there has been nothing for him to disclose."[74]

10–087   In most cases of "deliberate concealment" in an action involving personal injuries the claimant will simply not have the knowledge required under section 14 of the Limitation Act 1980 to start the limitation period running.[75] Deliberate concealment under section 32 might possibly be relevant where the claim for medical negligence is not categorised as an action for personal injuries, since the limitation period runs from the date of accrual of the cause of action not the claimant's date of knowledge, unless the damage is latent. In *Sheldon v R.H.M. Outhwaite (Underwriting Agencies) Ltd*[76] the Court of Appeal held that deliberate concealment of a cause of action which occurs after the cause of action has accrued does not suspend or postpone the running of the limitation period until discovery of the concealment, because the wording of section 32(1)(b) did not have the effect of interrupting a limitation period that had already started to run. The Latent

---

[73] [2002] UKHL 18; [2003] 1 A.C. 384.

[74] *ibid.* at [25]. The non-disclosure to the claimant of a medical report prepared by the defendant for the claimant's employers does not amount to deliberate concealment: *Dawson v Scott-Brown* (1988, CA; unreported). On the other hand, a failure by a firm of solicitors to inform the claimant of an offer of £100 compensation by potential defendants, because that might have revealed their own earlier negligence, was held to be deliberate concealment: *Kitchen v Royal Air Force Association* [1958] 1 W.L.R. 563, CA (a decision under the Limitation Act 1939).

[75] See *Scuriaga v Powell* (1979) 123 S.J. 406; affirmed (1980, CA: unreported), para. 10–027. Claims under the Fatal Accidents Act 1976 are specifically excluded from the provisions of s.32: Limitation Act 1980, s.12(3).

[76] [1994] 4 All E.R. 481; [1994] 3 W.L.R. 999, CA, Staughton L.J. dissenting. See, however, *Kitchen v Royal Air Force Association* [1958] 1 W.L.R. 563, a case where subsequent concealment appears to have been treated as precluding reliance on the limitation period.

Damage Act 1986 was intended to fill any unjust lacuna in which claimants in non-personal injury actions could lose their cause of action before they knew of its existence. This decision effectively permitted a defendant to reap the fruits of his own unconscionable conduct (subject to the latent damage provisions), and, as Sir Thomas Bingham M.R. acknowledged, deprived the subsection of much practical substance. By a bare majority the House of Lords reversed the decision of the Court of Appeal.[77] Section 32(1)(b) operated to postpone the running of the limitation period in every case where there was deliberate concealment by the defendant of facts relevant to the claimant's cause of action, regardless of whether the concealment was contemporaneous with or subsequent to the accrual of the cause of action. Thus, subsequent concealment has the effect of bringing section 32 into play, thereby excluding sections 2 and 5, and the claimant has a full six years from the date of discovery of the concealment in which to bring the action.

(7) Defective Products

Special rules in respect of limitation periods apply to claims brought under the Consumer Protection Act 1987.[78] The claimant has three years within which to bring an action, running from either the date on which the action accrued (*i.e.* when the damage occurred) or, if later, the date of his 'knowledge'.[79] Knowledge is defined in similar terms to that for ordinary personal injuries claims, to include the fact that the damage was significant, that it was caused by the defect and the identity of the defendant.[80] The claimant's ignorance that as a matter of law the product was defective is irrelevant and does not prevent time running.   **10–088**

---

[77] [1996] 1 A.C. 102. In *Westlake v Bracknell District Council* (1987) 282 E.G. 868 it was held that an assurance to the claimant by the defendant that there was "nothing to worry about" when the claimant raised a query about facts which could indicate that the defendant has been negligent might constitute deliberate concealment, or, alternatively, the defendant would be estopped from raising the limitation defence. But if the claimant is aware of the relevant *facts* during the period preceding the concealment, the subsequent acts of the defendant cannot conceal those facts from the claimant: *Sheldon v R.H.M. Outhwaite (Underwriting Agencies) Ltd* [1996] 1 A.C. 102, 144; *Ezekiel v Lehrer* [2002] EWCA Civ 16; [2002] Lloyd's Rep. P.N. 260. In *Markes v Coodes* [1997] P.N.L.R. 252, QBD it was held that a solicitor's failure to inform a client of a possible claim in negligence by the client against the solicitor, or at least to advise the client to seek independent legal advice, amounted to deliberate concealment within s.32(1)(b). But query this, notwithstanding the solicitor's professional duty to inform a client to seek alternative legal advice when the solicitor becomes aware that something has gone wrong in the handling of the client's affairs: see the Law Society's *Guide to the Professional Conduct of Solicitors*, para. 29.09. If the failure to inform a client that something has gone wrong could constitute deliberate concealment where there is a professional duty to provide such information, this could have major implications for the medical profession if the Chief Medical Officer's recommendation that there should be a statutory "duty of candour" imposed on health professionals in the NHS ever becomes law: see *Making Amends*, Department of Health, June 2003, recommendation 12 (available at *www.doh.gov.uk/makingamends/cmoreport.htm*).

[78] Consumer Protection Act 1987, Sch. 1, amending the Limitation Act 1980.

[79] Limitation Act 1980, s.11A(4).

[80] *ibid.*, s.14(1A); *cf.* s.14(1).

10–089   These rules apply both to personal injuries and property damage claims brought under the Consumer Protection Act 1987. In the case of personal injuries, however, the court has a discretion under the Limitation Act 1980, section 33 to override the three year limit and allow the action to proceed. But these limitation periods are subject to an overall longstop which expires 10 years after the product was put into circulation by the defendant.[81] The longstop is an absolute bar, even in cases where there has been deliberate concealment or the claimant was under a disability, and the court has no discretion to override this limit in personal injuries cases, even where the damage had not occurred by the end of the ten year period. A claimant caught by the longstop (a situation which could arise with certain types of drug injury) will have to sue in negligence in order to invoke the court's discretion, since other forms of action are not subject to this longstop. The longstop does not apply, however, to the substitution of a new party in an existing action where that action was commenced within the limitation period, but the application to substitute the new party is made after the expiry of the longstop. In those circumstances, section 35 of the Limitation Act 1980 gives the court a discretion to substitute the new party.[82]

(8) Latent Damage

10–090   The vast majority of medical negligence actions involve claims in respect of personal injuries, but in some circumstances a doctor's negligence may cause purely financial loss.[83] In this situation the ordinary six year limitation period under section 2 (tort) or section 5 (contract) of the Limitation Act 1980 would normally apply. Where, however, the claimant is unaware that he has sustained any damage or loss he may be able to rely on an extended limitation period applicable to cases of latent damage. If, for example, as a result of a negligent diagnosis the doctor wrongly advised the patient that he was medically unfit to carry out a particular type of work and the patient took a lower paid job, he would have suffered a continuing loss of earnings. If more than six years later the patient discovered the error he might be faced with the argument that the six year limitation period has already expired.[84]

---

[81] *ibid.*, s.11A(3).

[82] *Horne-Roberts v Smithkline Beecham plc* [2001] EWCA Civ 2006; [2002] 1 W.L.R. 1662, where the claimant initially sued Merck believing that they were the manufacturers of a particular batch of the MMR vaccine, but it subsequently came to light that Smithkline were the manufacturers of that batch. For discussion of s.35 of the Limitation Act 1980 see paras 10–094 and 10–095.

[83] See paras 2–035 to 2–053, 2–157 to 2–159.

[84] This example could raise problems, however, as to precisely when the cause of action accrued, since it involves a continuing loss. In cases of negligent professional (usually legal) advice the courts have tended to the view that the claimant sustains damage when he acts in reliance on the advice by entering into the particular transaction, not when the subsequent financial loss occurs, the damage consisting of a contingent liability to future loss for which the claimant could have sued immediately: see *Forster v Oughtred & Co* [1982] 1 W.L.R. 86; *D.W. Moore & Co Ltd v Ferrier* [1988] 1 W.L.R. 267; *Bell v Peter Browne & Co* [1990] 2 Q.B. 495; *Byrne v Hall, Pain & Foster* [1999] 1 W.L.R. 1849; *cf. Midland Bank Trust Co*

The Latent Damage Act 1986 introduced a special extension of the ordinary six year limitation period in tort[85] in cases of latent damage (other than personal injuries). The claimant has three years from the date on which he discovered or ought reasonably to have discovered significant damage, subject to an overall "longstop" which bars all claims brought more than 15 years from the date of the defendant's negligence.[86] The limitation period is six years from the date on which the action accrued or three years from the "starting date," whichever expires later.[87] The starting date is the earliest date on which the claimant (or any person in whom the cause of action was vested before him) first had both a right to bring the action, and knowledge of (a) the material facts about the damage, (b) that the damage was caused by the defendant's negligence, (c) the identity of the defendant, and (d) if the negligence was that of a person other than the defendant, the identity of that person and the facts supporting an action against the defendant.[88] Material facts are such facts about the damage as would lead a reasonable person who had suffered such damage to consider it sufficiently serious to justify instituting proceedings for damages against a defendant who did not dispute liability and was able to satisfy a judgment.[89] As with the scheme for personal injuries the claimant's ignorance that, as a matter of law, he has a cause

10–091

(n.84 contd.) *Ltd v Hett, Stubbs & Kemp* [1979] Ch 384. In *Hopkins v Mackenzie* [1995] P.I.Q.R. P43; [1995] 6 Med. L.R. 26, CA, it was held that where, as a result of a solicitor's negligence, the claimant's action for personal injuries was struck out for want of prosecution the action against the solicitor accrued, and therefore the limitation period began, when the action was struck out, not when it became probable or even inevitable that the action would be struck out. This view was criticised, however, in *Khan v R.M. Falvey & Co* [2002] EWCA Civ 400; [2002] P.N.L.R. 623, CA, on the basis that it was inconsistent with the approach of the House of Lords in *Nykredit Mortgage Bank plc v Edward Erdman Group Ltd (No. 2)* [1997] 1 W.L.R. 1627, HL, where some of the difficulties involved in deciding precisely when a claimant has suffered financial loss as a result of relying on negligent advice by a professional person were considered. Thus, in *Khan v R.M. Falvey & Co* it was held that an action against a firm of solicitors in respect of actions which had been struck out for want of prosecution accrued before the claims had been struck out, because the value of the actions had been affected by the solicitors' negligence before they were actually struck out. "There is a fine distinction . . . between a situation where no actual loss is suffered, notwithstanding a risk of potential loss, and one where there is an actual loss which can only be measured by assessing the present value of future risks" *per* Sir Anthony Evans in *Havenlodge Ltd v Graeme John & Partners* [2001] Lloyd's Rep. P.N. 223 at [17].
85 The provisions do not apply to claims in contract: *Iron Trade Mutual Insurance Co Ltd v J.K. Buckenham Ltd* [1990] 1 All E.R. 808; *Société Commerciale de Réassurance v ERAS (International) Ltd (Note)* [1992] 2 All E.R. 82. Where, however, the defendant owes concurrent duties in contract and tort the claimant is entitled to pursue the action which will give him a practical advantage on the question of limitation: *Henderson v Merrett Syndicates Ltd* [1995] 2 A.C. 145, 191 *per* Lord Goff.
86 Latent Damage Act 1986, s.1, inserting new ss.14A and 14B into the Limitation Act 1980.
87 Limitation Act 1980, s.14A(3) and (4).
88 *ibid.*, s.14A(5), (6) and (8). It is clear that the courts' approach to s.14A closely mirrors that taken to the analogous provisions in s.14: see *Spencer-Ward v Humberts* [1995] 06 E.G. 148, CA; *Hallam-Eames v Merrett* [1996] 7 Med. L.R. 122, CA; *Oakes v Hopcroft* [2000] Lloyd's Rep. Med. 394. For discussion of the meaning of knowledge under s.14, see paras 10–017 *et seq.*
89 *ibid.*, s.14A(7). See *Horbury v Craig Hall & Rutley* (1991) 7 P.N. 206; *Hamlin v Edwin Evans* (1996) 80 B.L.R. 85, CA—negligent house survey report gives rise to one single cause of action accruing when damage was suffered for the first time, and later, more serious, damage is not relevant.

of action does not prevent time running,[90] and the claimant will be fixed with constructive knowledge, including the knowledge of experts.[91]

10–092   Section 14B provides that an action for damages for negligence (other than for personal injuries) shall not be brought more than 15 years from the date of the act or omission which is alleged to constitute negligence. This overrides section 14A, and it is irrelevant that the cause of action may not yet have accrued (*i.e.* no damage has occurred) or that the starting date has not yet occurred (*i.e.* the damage is still latent).[92]

(9) Contribution Proceedings

10–093   In contribution proceedings the limitation period is two years from the date of judgment or settlement, even if the claimant's claim against the defendant would be statute-barred.[93]

(10) New claims in pending actions

10–094   As a general rule, new claims which are outside a relevant limitation period cannot be brought by addition to or amendment of existing proceedings since this would have the effect of depriving a defendant of an otherwise valid limitation defence.[94] Section 35 of the Limitation Act 1980 allows for limited exceptions to this rule, in combination with CPR r. 17.4 and r. 19.5, which deal with amendments to statements of case and the addition or substitution of new parties after the end of a relevant limitation period respectively. A new claim made in the course of any action is deemed to be a separate action and to have been commenced, in the case of a CPR Part 20 claim, on the date on which that claim was commenced, and in the case of any other new claim, on the same date as the original claim.[95] A "new claim" is any claim by way of set-off or counter-claim, any claim involving the addition or substitution of a new cause of action or a

---

[90] *ibid.*, s.14A(9).

[91] *ibid.*, s.14A(10). The claimant will not be fixed with knowledge of a fact ascertainable only with the help of expert advice so long as he has taken all reasonable steps to obtain, and where appropriate act on, that advice: *ibid.*

[92] The provisions in s.32 concerning deliberate concealment are not, however, subject to the longstop. ss.14A and 14B do not apply to actions commenced or claims barred before they came into force on September 18, 1986.

[93] Limitation Act 1980, s.10. Where, however, the expiry of the claimant's limitation period extinguishes the claimant's right of action against the defendant the right to contribution is lost: Civil Liability (Contribution) Act 1978, s.1(3). Most limitation periods do not extinguish the claimant's right, but merely bar his remedy. An exception is the ten year longstop applied to claims for defective products under the Limitation Act 1980, s.11A(3) which does bar the claimant's right of action. See further para. 7–045.

[94] If the limitation period has not expired at the date when the application to amend is heard the court has an unrestricted discretion to allow the amendments: CPR r. 19.2; *Welsh Development Agency v Redpath Dorman Long Ltd* [1994] 4 All E.R. 10, 17; [1994] 1 W.L.R. 1409, CA. For criticism of this decision see James (1995) 14 C.J.Q. 42.

[95] Limitation Act 1980, s.35(1).

new party, and a claim made in or by way of a Part 20 claim.[96] By section 35(3) of the Limitation Act 1980 the court cannot allow a new claim, other than an original set-off or counter-claim,[97] to be made in a pending action after the expiry of a limitation period which would affect a new action to enforce that claim. The court has no discretion to allow amendments to add or substitute a new cause of action or a new party to an existing claim, except in three situations: first, where the court exercises its discretion under section 33 to disapply the provisions of sections 11 or 12 in a personal injuries action;[98] second, in the case of a claim involving a new party, if the relevant limitation period was current when the proceedings were started and the addition or substitution of the new party is necessary;[99] and third, where the claim involves the addition or substitution of a new claim, if the new claim arises out of the same or substantially the same facts in respect of which the party applying for permission has already claimed a remedy in the proceedings.[1]

The addition or substitution of a new party will be "necessary" only if the **10–095** court is satisfied that: (a) the new party is to be substituted for a party who was named in the claim form in mistake for the new party; (b) the claim cannot properly be carried on by or against the original party unless the new

---

[96] *ibid.*, s.35(2) and (1)(a). The Civil Procedure Rules replaced the term "third party proceedings" with "Part 20 claim". The old terminology is still to be found in the Limitation Act 1980. "Third party proceedings" means any proceedings brought in the course of any action by any party to the action against a person not previously a party to the action, other than proceedings brought by joining any such person as a defendant to any claim already made in the original action by the party bringing the action: *ibid.*, s.35(2). Thus, a claim for contribution between existing defendants to an action does not constitute third party proceedings (because "third party proceedings" involve bringing somebody in who is not already a party to the action), and they are deemed by s.35(1)(b) to have been commenced on the same date as the original action: *Kennett v Brown* [1988] 2 All E.R. 600; [1988] 1 W.L.R. 582.

[97] A claim is an original set-off or an original counterclaim if it is a claim made by way of set-off or by way of counterclaim by a party who has not previously made any claim in the action: Limitation Act 1980, s.35(3). Thus, a defendant sued within the limitation period may claim once in respect of a set-off or counterclaim even though they are not pleaded until after the limitation period has expired.

[98] Limitation Act 1980, s.35(3); CPR r. 19.5(4). The s.33 application must be made before, or at the same time as, the application for leave to amend, because the effect of making the amendment to add a new party or a new claim is that the amendment relates back to date of issue of the claim form, thereby defeating the limitation defence: *Welsh Development Agency v Redpath Dorman Long Ltd* [1994] 4 All E.R. 10, CA, overruling *Kennett v Brown* [1988] 2 All E.R. 600; [1988] 1 W.L.R. 582 on this point. See also *Howe v David Brown Tractors (Retail) Ltd (Rustons Engineering Co Ltd, third party)* [1991] 4 All E.R. 30, where *Kennett v Brown* had been distinguished. For criticism of the effects of *Welsh Development Agency v Redpath Dorman Long Ltd* see James (1995) 14 C.J.Q. 42.

[99] Limitation Act 1980, s.35(5)(b); CPR r. 19.5(2).

[1] Limitation Act 1980, s.35(5)(a); CPR r. 17.4(2). A statement of case can be amended after the expiry of the limitation period to add a new claim which is founded on the defendant's version of the facts rather than those in the claimant's existing claim: *Goode v Martin* [2001] EWCA Civ 1899; [2002] 1 W.L.R. 1828. The court may also allow an amendment to a statement of case to correct a mistake as to the name of a party, but only where the mistake was genuine and not one which would cause reasonable doubt as to the identity of the party: CPR r. 17.4(3). Similarly, an amendment to alter the capacity in which a party claims may be permitted if the new capacity is one which that party had when the proceedings started or has since acquired: CPR r. 17.4(4)

party is added or substituted as claimant or defendant;[2] or (c) the original party has died or had a bankruptcy order made against him and his interest or liability has passed to the new party.[3] Section 35(5) permits a claim involving a new cause of action to be added if the new cause of action arises out of the same facts or substantially the same facts as are already in issue on any claim previously made in the original action. The question of what constitutes "the same or substantially the same facts" has been said to be "substantially a matter of impression."[4] In *Sayer v Kingston & Esher Health Authority*[5] it was held that where the claimant had pleaded negligence in the performance of a Caesarian section operation, and subsequently sought to include allegations in respect of events leading up to the operation and the post-operative treatment, the amendments arose out of substantially the same facts as were already in issue. Mann L.J. commented that the facts were the "facts relating to the birth of the plaintiff's second child" and it was unreal to compartmentalise that single event into a number of discrete parts. Similarly, in *Grewal v National Hospital for Nervous Diseases*[6] the claimant sought to add an allegation of trespass to the person in a medical negligence action, on the basis that the defendants had exceeded the consent given by the claimant by performing a laminectomy on the spine when all that had been consented to was a biopsy. Dunn L.J. said that, although the legal issue was a different one, the question was whether the cause of action arose out of the same or substantially the same facts. That involved a consideration of the evidence which would be likely to be led in support of the new cause of action. Since it would be necessary to lead substantially the same evidence

---

[2] See, e.g., *Merrett v Babb* [2001] EWCA Civ. 214; [2001] QB 1174; [2001] Lloyd's Rep. P.N. 468, where a claim was mistakenly brought by one co-owner of property against a valuer in respect of a negligent valuation for the whole of the financial loss attributable to the negligence. The Court of Appeal held that the other co-owner could be added as a claimant, even though by that time the limitation period had expired.

[3] Limitation Act 1980, s.35(6); CPR r. 19.5(3). CPR r. 17.4(3) requires that the mistake as to the name of a party be genuine, but CPR r. 19.5(3)(a) states simply that a new party may be substituted for a party who was named in the claim form by mistake. However, in *International Distillers and Vinters Ltd v J.F. Hillebrand (UK) Ltd, The Times,* January 25, 2000, QBD it was held that it would be unlikely for an application for substitution of a new party under CPR r. 19.5(3)(a) to succeed unless the original mistake was genuine. For discussion of the meaning of a mistake in identity see *The Al Tawwab* [1991] 1 Lloyd's Rep. 201, 205–206; *Evans Construction Co Ltd v Charrington & Co Ltd and Bass Holdings Ltd* [1983] QB 810; *The Hibernian Dance Club v Murray* [1997] P.I.Q.R. P46, CA; *Horne-Roberts v Smithkline Beecham plc* [2001] EWCA Civ 2006; [2002] 1 W.L.R. 1662. The provision is not limited to the correction of mere "misnomers", but relates to the "identity" of the intended defendant by reference to a description which is specific to the particular case, *e.g.* "the landlord", "the employers", "the manufacturer of the product".

[4] *Welsh Development Agency v Redpath Dorman Long Ltd* [1994] 4 All E.R. 10, 19, CA. In the case of a fatal accident, a claim on behalf of the deceased's dependants under the Fatal Accidents Act 1976 will usually arise out of the same facts or substantially the same facts as a claim on behalf of the estate under the Law Reform (Miscellaneous Provisions) Act 1934: *Booker v Associated British Ports* [1995] P.I.Q.R. P375, CA.

[5] (1989, CA; unreported); *Booker v Associated British Ports* [1995] P.I.Q.R. P375, CA—the facts in issue in a Fatal Accidents Act claim were substantially the same facts as were already in issue in the claim being conducted on behalf of the deceased employee's estate under the Law Reform (Miscellaneous Provisions) Act 1934.

[6] (1982) 132 N.L.J. 1149, CA.

as would have been necessary to support the statement of claim as originally pleaded, the claim in trespass arose out of substantially the same facts. It was artificial to distinguish between what had happened in the ward, as opposed to what had happened in the operating theatre.[7] Where the court has jurisdiction to permit an amendment after the relevant period of limitation has expired it must still exercise a discretion as to whether to allow the amendment.[8]

(11) Burden of proof

The defendant must plead the limitation period in his defence if he seeks to rely on it,[9] though he is not obliged to take the point and the court will not do so if the defendant omits it.[10] There is some uncertainty concerning who has the burden of proof as to whether the action is or is not statute barred. Logically, if limitation is considered to be a defence, the burden of proving that the claim is out of time should rest with the defendant. This view has been adopted on more than one occasion.[11] On the other hand, the Court of Appeal has also stated that the burden of proof lies with the claimant.[12] In *Fowell v*

10–096

---

[7] See further, on this issue: *Dornan v J.W. Ellis & Co Ltd* [1962] 1 Q.B. 583; *Hay v London Brick Co Ltd* [1989] 2 Lloyd's Rep. 7; *Adam v Hemming* (1991, CA; unreported); *Sion v Hampstead Health Authority* [1994] 5 Med. L.R. 170.

[8] Under the old Rules of the Supreme Court the test was whether it was "just to do so", which was a matter of balancing the prejudice to the claimant and the prejudice to the defendant. See *Hancock Shipping Co Ltd v Kawasaki Heavy Industries Ltd, The Casper Trader* [1992] 1 W.L.R. 102; [1992] 3 All E.R. 132. The court was not required to treat a claimant seeking permission to amend in the same way as a claimant seeking the court's exercise of discretion under s.33 of the Limitation Act 1980: *Adam v Hemming* (1991, CA; unreported) *per* Ralph Gibson L.J. The exercise of the discretion is now subject to the overriding objective "to deal with cases justly": CPR r. 1.1.

[9] CPR 16PD.13.1. If the defendant considers that he has a good limitation defence his proper course is either to plead the defence and seek a trial of the defence as a preliminary issue, or, in a very clear case, to apply to strike out the claim on the ground that it is frivolous and vexatious and an abuse of the process of the court, but he cannot seek to strike out the claim on the ground that it discloses no reasonable cause of action: *Ronex Properties Ltd v John Laing Construction Ltd* [1983] Q.B. 398. Given the availability of the discretion under s.33 of the Limitation Act 1980, it will rarely be possible, in a personal injuries action, to say that the case is "very clear." The claimant may, but is not required to, stay silent about the limitation issue in the statement of claim, leaving the defendant to raise it as a matter of defence. The claimant may, however, simply plead that the action is not statute-barred: see *Driscoll-Varley v Parkside Health Authority* [1991] 2 Med. L.R. 346, 358. Wherever it is feasible a judge should decide the limitation point by a preliminary hearing by reference to the pleadings and written witness statements and the extent and content of disclosure: *KR v Bryn Alyn Community (Holdings) Ltd (in liquidation)* [2003] EWCA Civ 85; [2003] 1 F.C.R. 385 at [74].

[10] See *Kennett v Brown* [1988] 2 All E.R. 600; [1988] 1 W.L.R. 582.

[11] *Darley Main Colliery Co v Mitchell* (1886) 11 App. Cas.127, 135; *O'Connor v Isaacs* [1956] 2 Q.B. 288, 364; *The Pendrecht* [1980] 2 Lloyd's Rep. 56, 60.

[12] See *Cartledge v Jopling & Sons Ltd* [1962] 1 Q.B. 189; *London Congregational Union Inc. v Harriss & Harriss* [1988] 1 All E.R. 15; *Crocker v British Coal Corp* (1996) 29 B.M.L.R. 159, QBD; see also *Nash v Eli Lilly & Co* [1991] 2 Med. L.R. 169, QBD, where it was said that the preliminary burden of establishing that a case falls within the limitation period rests with the claimant, but thereafter, in relation to the question of a claimant's constructive knowledge, the burden falls upon the defendant; see also *Driscoll-Varley v Parkside Health Authority* [1991] 2 Med. L.R. 346, 357, to the same effect.

National Coal Board,[13] a case involving personal injuries, Parker L.J. said that as limitation is a matter of defence, it must be for the person setting up limitation to assert and prove that the claim is time barred, which, in the first instance, requires no more than proof that the three-year period has elapsed. If this period has elapsed but the claimant wishes to argue that the date of knowledge was later, it is for him to assert and give evidence that he first had knowledge of the relevant facts under section 14(1) of the Act on a date later than the accrual of the cause of action. If, however, the defendant wishes to displace this by asserting an earlier date of knowledge, it was for him to do so.

10–097   Where the claimant makes an application under section 33 to disapply the primary limitation period the burden of proving that it is just and equitable to allow the action to proceed is the claimant's.[14] The burden is heavy one, because "it is an exceptional indulgence to a claimant, to be granted only where equity between the parties demands it."[15]

(12) Issuing the Claim Form

10–098   Issuing the claim form has the effect of stopping the limitation period from running. Once the claim form has been issued it must normally be served on the defendant within four months of the date of issue.[16] Although there may be practical obstacles, such as the need to remove a Legal Aid restriction, there is generally little point in delaying service of the claim form, particularly since interest on general damages runs from the date of service,[17] and the Civil Procedure Rules are based on the premise that proceedings will be conducted with reasonable dispatch. The court has a power to extend the time for serving the claim form for periods of up to four months at a time,[18] but once the period permitted for service has expired the court can only extend the time for service in limited circumstances. CPR r. 7.6(3) provides that: "If the claimant applies for an order to extend the time for service of the claim form after the end of the period specified by rule 7.5 or by an order made under this rule, the court may make such an order only if—(a) the court has been unable to serve the claim form; or (b) the claimant has taken all reasonable steps to serve the claim form but has been unable to do so; and (c) in either case, the claimant has acted promptly in making the application."[19]

---

[13]   *The Times*, May 28, 1986. See also *Nash v Eli Lilly & Co* [1993] 1 W.L.R. 782, 796; [1992] 3 Med. L.R. 353, 367, CA.

[14]   *Thompson v Brown Construction (Ebbw Vale) Ltd* [1981] 2 All E.R. 296, 303; [1981] 1 W.L.R. 744.

[15]   *KR v Bryn Alyn Community (Holdings) Ltd (in liquidation)* [2003] EWCA Civ 85; [2003] 1 F.C.R. 385 at [74].

[16]   CPR r. 7.5(2). See Lord, "Service of Claim Forms" [2002] J.P.I.L. 292.

[17]   See para. 9–026.

[18]   CPR r. 7.6. The application must be supported by evidence: CPR r. 7.6(4)(a). On the court's discretion to extend the time for service of the particulars of claim see: *Totty v Snowden*; *Hewitt v Wirral and West Cheshire Community NHS Trust* [2001] EWCA Civ 1415; [2002] 1 W.L.R. 1384; [2001] 4 All E.R. 577.

[19]   On the meaning of "all reasonable steps to serve the claim form" see *Nanglegan v Royal Free Hampstead NHS Trust* [2001] EWCA Civ 127; [2001] 3 All E.R. 793.

In *Cranfield v Bridgegrove Ltd*[20] the Court of Appeal held that CPR r.   10–099
7.6(3)(a) is not confined to cases where the court has attempted to serve the
claim form or has applied its mind to the question of whether or not to serve.
It applies to all cases where the court has failed to serve the claim form, so
the court has jurisdiction to extend the time for service where it has failed to
serve through mere neglect. In most cases where the real cause of the failure
to serve in time was court neglect it would be appropriate to grant an extension of time if the claimant had acted promptly in applying for an extension.
There were some cases where, though court neglect had contributed to the
failure to serve in time, the real cause had been the claimant or his legal representatives. In these cases the court will often refuse an extension of time,
but each case depends on its own facts.

If the claimant cannot bring his case within CPR r. 7.6(3) he cannot rely   10–100
on the court's general discretion under CPR r. 3.1(2)(a) (to extend or shorten
the time for compliance with any rule), since this is specifically excluded by
the plain wording of r. 7.6(3);[21] nor can he rely on CPR r. 6.8 (allowing the
court to authorise an alternative method of service) retrospectively, because
r. 6.8 is prospective, and cannot be applied after the event to cure an error
already made in effective service;[22] nor by relying on CPR r. 3.9 (relief from
sanctions for failing to comply with any rule).[23] The court does have discretion, however, under CPR r. 6.9 (the power of the court to dispense with
service) which can be exercised retrospectively in "an appropriate case."[24]
The power to dispense with service retrospectively will only be exercised in
exceptional circumstances, and not where there has not been any attempt to
serve in accordance with the methods specified in CPR r. 6.2 (category 1
cases). But if there has been an attempt using one of the permitted methods
which has been "ineffective" under r. 6.7, but the claim form has in fact been
received by the defendant or his representative before expiry of the period
for service, then there is a discretion to dispense with service under r. 6.9 (category 2 cases).[25] The court will also take account of other relevant circumstances, such as the explanation for late service, whether any criticism could
be made of the claimant or his advisers in their conduct of the proceedings
and any possible prejudice to the defendant on dispensing with service of the
claim form.[26] Subsequently, in *Wilkey v British Broadcasting Corp*,[27] the

---

[20] [2003] EWCA Civ 656; [2003] 3 All E.R. 129.
[21] *Vinos v Marks & Spencer plc* [2001] 3 All E.R. 784, CA.
[22] *Nanglegan v Royal Free Hampstead NHS Trust* [2001] EWCA Civ 127; [2001] 3 All E.R.
793 at [31] *per* May L.J.
[23] *Infantino v MacLean* [2001] 3 All E.R. 802, QBD.
[24] *Anderton v Clwyd County Council* [2002] EWCA Civ 933; [2002] 1 W.L.R. 3174 As to
what constitutes an "appropriate case" see [57] to [58].
[25] This allowed the court to avoid the effect of *Godwin v Swindon Borough Council* [2001]
EWCA Civ 1478; [2002] 1 W.L.R. 997 (confirmed in *Anderton v Clwyd County Council*)
which held that CPR r. 6.7(1), which stipulates that where the method of service is first class
post, the day of service is deemed to be the second day after posting (excluding Saturday and
Sunday), created an irrebuttable presumption. The fact that the defendant actually received
the claim form the following day, and within the four month period, is irrelevant.
[26] *Anderton v Clwyd County Council* [2002] EWCA Civ 933; [2002] 1 W.L.R. 3174 at [59].
[27] [2002] EWCA Civ 1561; [2003] 1 W.L.R. 1.

Court of Appeal held that there would be a presumption in favour of exercising the discretion to dispense with service under r. 6.9 only in category 2 cases that arose before the decision of the Court of Appeal in *Anderton v Clwyd County Council* (which was handed down on July 3, 2002). The presumption would apply unless the defendant could establish either that he would suffer prejudice or there was some other good reason why the power should not be exercised. But in category 2 cases arising after *Anderton* the power to dispense with service would not ordinarily be exercised in the claimant's favour. The objective is to provide for certainty in the application of deemed dates of service provided for in CPR r. 6.7. It would seem, however, that although the discretion to dispense with service under r. 6.9 is confined to "truly exceptional cases", it is not necessarily limited to cases where there has been an attempt to serve the claim form using one of "the permitted methods" nor indeed is it restricted to post-*Anderton* cases.[28]

2. DISMISSAL FOR WANT OF PROSECUTION

10–101   Limitation periods are meant to encourage claimants to issue proceedings promptly, and in effect they penalise delay prior to the commencement of the action. Delay can occur, however, after the action has been started. Under the old Rules of the Supreme Court a complex set of rules determined when it was appropriate for the court to strike out actions for want of prosecution on the part of claimants. There were two grounds for exercising this power: (i) intentional and contumelious default in complying with a peremptory order of the court, *e.g.*, disobedience of a peremptory order of the court or conduct amounting to an abuse of the process of the court; and (ii) inordinate and inexcusable delay on the part of the claimant or his lawyers which gave rise to a substantial risk that a fair trial would not be possible, or was likely to cause or had caused serious prejudice to the defendant or a third party.[29] Under the Civil Procedure Rules the court retains the power to strike out claims both under its inherent jurisdiction and under express provision in the Rules, but it is clear that the principles under which this power was previously exercised have changed.[30] In *Biguzzi v Rank Leisure plc*[31] Lord Woolf M.R. said that: "The whole purpose of making the CPR a self-contained code was to send the message which now generally applies. Earlier

---

[28] See *Cranfield v Bridgegrove Ltd* [2003] EWCA Civ 656; [2003] 3 All E.R. 129, where, at [32], the Court of Appeal said: "In our view it is not appropriate to attempt to provide an exhaustive guide to the circumstances in which it is proper to dispense with service of a claim form retrospectively under r. 6.9, whether in pre-*Anderton* cases, or in post-*Anderton* cases."

[29] *Allen v Sir Alfred McAlpine & Sons Ltd* [1968] 2 Q.B. 229; *Birkett v James* [1978] A.C. 297, 318. The old rules were discussed in the second edition of this book at paras 10–078 to 10–085.

[30] For a helpful discussion of the principles to be applied to applications to strike out claims for delay under the Civil Procedure Rules see Petts [2001] J.P.I.L. 78.

[31] [1999] 1 W.L.R. 1926, 1934, CA.

authorities are no longer generally of any relevance once the CPR applies."
His Lordship endorsed the decision of a judge to apply the Civil Procedure
Rules although the parties had previously been conducting the litigation
under a different regime:

> "The fact that they were acting under a different regime does not mean
> that the judge is constrained to make the same sort of decision as would
> be made under the previous regime. The courts have learnt, in conse-
> quence of the periods of excessive delay which took place before April
> 1999, that the ability of the courts to control delay was unduly
> restricted by such decisions as *Birkett v James* [1978] A.C. 297. In more
> recent decisions the courts sought to introduce a degree of flexibility
> into the situation because otherwise the approach which was being
> adopted by litigants generally of disregarding time limits for taking
> certain actions under the rules would continue. Under the CPR the posi-
> tion is fundamentally different. As rule 1.1 makes clear the CPR are: 'a
> new procedural code with the overriding objective of enabling the court
> to deal with cases justly.'"[32]

CPR r. 3.4(2)(b) gives the court the power to strike out a statement of case   **10–102**
if it is an abuse of the court's process or is otherwise likely to obstruct the
just disposal of the proceedings and r. 3.4(2)(c) confers the same power
where there has been a failure to comply with a rule, practice direction or
court order. CPR r. 3.1(2)(m) also provides that the court may take any step
or make any other order for the purpose of managing the case and further-
ing the overriding objective of the Civil Procedure Rules (which is that the
court should deal with cases justly: CPR r. 1.1). In *Axa Insurance Co Ltd v
Swire Fraser Ltd*[33] Tuckey L.J. said: "Rule. 3.4(2)(c) confers a wide discretion on the court and does not require proof of prejudice. It obviously enables
the court to strike out in cases of deliberate default or repeated failure to
comply with the rules and orders of the court without resort to the court's
inherent jurisdiction, although no doubt the court still has an inherent power
to strike out for abuse of its process." Thus, the court had an unqualified discretion in CPR r. 3.4(2)(c) to strike out for failure to comply with a rule, practice direction or court order and it was no longer necessary to consider
prejudice in the *Birkett v James* sense. Prejudice to the defendant was still relevant as part of a general inquiry as to what is just, but there was no longer
any need to seek out prejudice or ascribe it to a particular period or particular periods of delay.[34] The decision of the Court of Appeal in *Biguzzi* was not
to be interpreted as treating delay or the failure to comply with the rules more
leniently than under the old rules. It was simply that the new rules permitted
the courts to adopt a more flexible approach. On the facts of *Axa Insurance*
it was not just or proportionate to strike out the whole claim, having regard

---

[32] *ibid.* at 1932.
[33] [2001] C.P. Rep. 17; *The Times*, January 19, 2000, CA at [20].
[34] *ibid.* at [19].

to its history, but the claimant's allegations against the defendants were restricted and the claimants were penalised in costs.

10–103 It does not follow, of course, that under the Civil Procedure Rules the issues that were relevant to the question of striking out a claim for want of prosecution are no longer relevant. It is simply that the technicalities that surrounded the application of some the principles can be dispensed with. In *Nasser v The United Bank of Kuwait*[35] Sir Christopher Slade said that: "I am, however, sure that in saying this [in *Biguzzi*], Lord Woolf M.R. was not intending to suggest that the factors regarded by the court in *Birkett v James* as crucial, namely the length of the relevant delay, the culpability for it, the resulting prejudice to the defendant and the prospects of a fair trial are no longer relevant considerations when the court has to deal with an application for dismissal for want of prosecution." In *Annodeus Ltd v Gibson*[36] Neuberger J. identified some of the factors relevant to the determination of a strike out for want of prosecution, namely: the length of the delay; any excuses for the delay; the extent to which the claimant had complied with the rules and any orders of the court; the prejudice to the defendant; the effect on the trial; the effect on other litigants; the extent if any to which the defendant had contributed to the delay; the conduct of the claimant and the defendant with regard to the litigation; any other relevant factors.[37]

10–104 In *Purefuture Ltd v Simmons & Simmons*[38] Clarke L.J. agreed with the following propositions in relation to an application to strike out for want of prosecution:

(1) The central issue is whether it would be fair or just to allow the action to go to trial. In deciding this question the court must consider its alternative powers so that a decision may, but need not necessarily be, the same as would have obtained under the old rules.

(2) Although the court no longer needs to consider prejudice in the *Birkett v James* sense, prejudice remains relevant to the issue of what is just.

(3) In many cases there will be alternatives that will allow the case to be dealt with justly without taking the draconian step of striking out.

(4) In coming to its decision the court should consider:

---

[35] [2001] EWCA Civ 1454 at [27].

[36] *The Times*, March 3, 2000, ChD.

[37] See, however, the comment of Jonathan Parker L.J. in *Audergon v La Baguette Ltd* [2002] EWCA Civ 10; [2002] C.P. Rep. 27 at [107] on Neuberger J.'s list: "I do respectfully doubt the value of adopting a judicially-created checklist which does not appear in the rule itself. Inherent in such an approach, as it seems to me, is the danger that a body of satellite authority may be built up, rather as it was under the old rules in relation to the dismissal of an action for want of prosecution, leading in effect to the rewriting of the relevant rule through the medium of judicial decision."

[38] [2001] C.P. Rep. 30, CA at [54] to [57].

(a) the overriding objective in Part 1 CPR;

(b) the flexibility to deal with this type of claim as given by the court's new case management powers;

(c) the rules which allow striking out (in an appropriate case) are to be interpreted in accordance with the overriding objective; and

(d) no single one of the available range of powers is inherently more appropriate than any other so that the court should consider all its relevant powers.

(5) Whether the prejudice is so serious that it would be unjust to the defendant to require the case to be tried.

3. ACCESS TO HEALTH RECORDS

Although it has long been recognised that a doctor owes a duty of confidence   **10–105**
with respect to information concerning the patient arising out of the
doctor/patient relationship, so that a patient can restrain the unauthorised
disclosure of his medical records to third parties, the courts have been reluctant to establish a common law right for the patient to demand access to his
own medical records.[39] Patients have statutory rights of access to their
records, now principally through the Data Protection Act 1998, the Access
to Health Records Act 1990 and the Access to Medical Reports Act 1988.
This legislation is essentially concerned with the right of patients to know
what is contained in their medical records and to permit the correction of
inaccurate records, but it may also be relevant in the context of litigation as
one means of discovering what went wrong with the patient's treatment.

(1) Data Protection Act 1998

The Data Protection Act 1984 gave individuals a right of access to infor-   **10–106**
mation, including medical records, held about them in computerised form
for the first time. Subsequently, the Access to Health Records Act 1990
granted patients a right of access to non-electronic health records. The Data
Protection Act 1998 replaced the 1984 Act and most of the 1990 Act, bringing electronic and non-electronic records under the same statutory regime.
The only part of the Access to Health Records Act 1990 still in force relates
to access to a patient's medical records after his death.

The Data Protection Act 1998 (which came into force on March 1, 2000)   **10–107**
gives an individual a right of access to information held about him. Section
1(1) provides that "data" means information which: (a) is being processed

---

[39] See, however, paras 10–135 to 10–139.

by means of equipment operating automatically in response to instructions given for that purpose; (b) is recorded with the intention that it should be processed by means of such equipment; (c) is recorded as part of a relevant filing system or with the intention that it should form part of a relevant filing system; or (d) does not fall within (a), (b) or (c) but forms part of an accessible record as defined by section 68. Section 68 defines an "accessible record" as, *inter alia*, a health record, which means any record which (a) consists of information relating to the physical or mental health of an individual, and (b) has been made by or on behalf of a health professional in connection with the care of that individual. "Health professional" is widely defined in section 69. "Personal data" means data which relate to a living individual who can be identified from that data or from that data and other information in the possession of, or likely to come into the possession of, the data controller, and includes any expression of opinion about the individual and any indication of the intentions of the data controller or any other person in respect of that individual. Information as to the physical or mental health or condition of the data subject is "sensitive personal data."[40] "Data controller" means a person who determines the purposes for which and the manner in which any personal data are processed; and "data processor" means any person, other than an employee of the data controller, who processes the data on behalf of the data controller. "Data subject" means an individual who is the subject of personal data.

10–108   Section 7(1) of the Act confers a right of access to personal data by the data subject. A request to supply the information must be in writing and the data controller may charge a fee (subject to a maximum fee).[41] The data controller is not obliged to comply with the request for access where he cannot comply with the request without disclosing information relating to another individual[42] who can be identified from the information unless: (a) the other individual consents; or (b) it is reasonable in all the circumstances to comply with the request without the consent of the other individual.[43] Where information can be communicated without disclosing the identity of the other individual (*e.g.* by omitting names or other identifying particulars) the exception in section 7(4) does not apply.[44] In the case of information as to the physical or mental health or condition of the data subject, section 7(4) is modified by the addition of another sub-paragraph, so that (in addition to the situations in (a) and (b) above) where the data controller cannot comply with the request without disclosing information relating to another individual who can be identified from the information, he is not obliged to comply with that request unless the information is contained in a health record and the other individual is a health professional who has compiled

---

[40] Data Protection Act 1998, s.2.
[41] *ibid*. s.7(2).
[42] This includes a reference to information identifying that individual as the source of the information sought by the request: *ibid*. s.7(5).
[43] *ibid*. s.7(4). As to when it may be reasonable to comply without consent see s.7(6).
[44] *ibid*. s.7(5).

or contributed to the health record or has been involved in the care of the data subject in his capacity as a health professional.[45] The data controller is not excused from supplying so much of information sought by the request as can be communicated without disclosing the identity of the other individual concerned, whether by omitting names or identifying particulars or otherwise.[46]

A data subject has a right to prevent processing likely to cause damage or distress. Under section 10 an individual can give written notice to a data controller to cease, or not to begin, processing personal data of which he is the data subject on the ground that it is likely to cause substantial damage or substantial distress to him or another person, and that the damage would be unwarranted. This right does not apply if: (1) the data subject has given his consent to the processing; (2) the processing is necessary for the performance of a contract to which the data subject is a party or for the taking of steps at the request of the data subject with a view to entering into a contract; (3) the processing is necessary for compliance with any legal obligation to which the data controller is subject, other than a contractual obligation; or (4) the processing is necessary to protect the vital interests of the data subject. The Secretary of State may prescribe other cases to which section 10(1) does not apply.

10–109

Remedies

If the court is satisfied that the data controller has failed to comply with the request for access to information, in contravention of the Act, the court can order him to comply with the request.[47] This provision is modified, however, in relation to personal data consisting of information as to the physical or mental health or condition of the data subject to permit any other person to whom serious harm to his physical or mental health or condition would be likely to be caused by compliance with the request, in contravention of the Act, to request that the court order the data controller not to comply with the request.[48] This permits the court to rule one way or the other on the question of whether disclosure of the information to the data subject is potentially dangerous to another person (an issue that is most likely to arise in the context of psychiatric patients).

10–110

An individual is entitled to compensation for any damage by reason of any contravention by the data controller of any requirements of the Act.[49] An individual is also entitled to compensation for any distress if he also suffers damage by reason of the contravention, or the contravention relates to processing

10–111

---

[45] Data Protection (Subject Access Modification) (Health) Order 2000, S.I. 2000, No. 413, art. 8(a).
[46] Data Protection Act 1998, s.7(5).
[47] *ibid.* s.7(9).
[48] Data Protection (Subject Access Modification) (Health) Order 2000, S.I. 2000, No. 413, art. 8(b).
[49] Data Protection Act 1998, s.13(1).

personal data for "special purposes."[50] Special purposes are the purposes of journalism, artistic or literary purposes.[51] This means that, effectively, in the context of health records there is no compensation for distress if there is no damage, unless health records are processed for special purposes.[52] It is a defence for a defendant against whom compensation is sought to prove that he exercised reasonable care to comply with the requirements of the Act.[53] An individual may apply to a court for rectification, blocking, erasure or destruction, of inaccurate data, including an expression of opinion which is based on inaccurate data.[54] A similar order can be made where the data subject has suffered damage by reason of contravention of the Act entitling him to compensation under section 13 where there is a substantial risk of further contravention of the Act in respect of that data.[55]

Exemptions

10–112   The Secretary of State has power to exempt from the subject information provisions, or modify those provisions, in relation to personal data consisting of information as to the physical or mental health or condition of the data subject.[56] The Data Protection (Subject Access Modification) (Health) Order 2000[57] exempts from the subject information provisions of the Act personal data processed by a court consisting of information supplied in a report or other evidence given to the court in proceedings involving children where the relevant rules of court permit information to be withheld by the court in whole or in part from the data subject.[58] Article 5 provides that the access provisions under section 7 of the Data Protection Act do not apply where access "would be likely to cause serious harm to the physical or mental health of the data subject or any other person." A data controller who is not a health professional must not withhold information to which the Order applies on this ground unless he first consults the person who appears to be the appropriate health professional on the question whether or not the exemption applies with respect to the information.[59]

---

[50] *ibid*. s.13(2).

[51] *ibid*. s.3.

[52] *e.g.* journalism, where the newspaper is in breach of s.10, there could be a claim for distress alone if it is "substantial" distress, though there is a "public interest" defence for data processed for "special purposes": s.32.

[53] Data Protection Act 1998, s.12(3).

[54] *ibid*., s.14(1).

[55] *ibid*., s.14(4).

[56] *ibid*., s.30.

[57] S.I. 2000, No. 413.

[58] *ibid*. art. 4.

[59] *ibid*. art. 5(2). This provision does not apply if the data controller has consulted the appropriate health professional before receiving the request for access, and obtained in writing from that health professional an opinion that the exemption in art. 5(1) applies with respect to all the information which is the subject of the request: art. 7(1). That opinion must have been obtained within six months prior to the request for information, or if it was obtained within six months and it is reasonable in all the circumstances to re-consult the appropriate health professional the data controller must consult the health professional: art. 7(2).

Conversely, a data controller who is not a health professional must not **10–113**
communicate information as to the physical or mental health or condition
of the data subject in response to a request unless he has first consulted the
person who appears to be the appropriate health professional on the question whether or not the exemption in article 5(1) applies,[60] though this does
not apply where the request relates to information which the data controller is satisfied has previously been seen by the data subject or is already
within the knowledge of the data subject,[61] nor where the data controller has
consulted the appropriate health professional prior to receiving the request
and obtained in writing from that health professional an opinion that the
exemption on article 5(1) does not apply with respect to all the information
which is the subject of the request.[62]

Where the data subject is a child and the application for access is made by **10–114**
a person having parental responsibility, or the data subject is incapable of
managing his own affairs and the application for access is made by a person
appointed by the court to manage his affairs, then the data is exempt from
access under section 7 to the extent to which it would involve disclosure of
information (a) provided by the data subject in the expectation that it would
not be disclosed to the person making the request; (b) obtained as a result of
any examination or investigation to which the data subject consented in the
expectation that the information would not be so disclosed; or (c) which the
data subject has expressly indicated should not be so disclosed.[63]

(2) Access to Health Records Act 1990

The Data Protection Act 1998 repealed almost the whole of the Access to **10–115**
Health Records Act 1990 which previously conferred a right of access to
non-computerised records. The one exception relates to applications for
access to health records where the patient has died, and therefore the 1990
Act is now exclusively concerned with access where the patient has died. By
section 1(1) a "health record" means a record which (a) consists of information (including an expression of opinion) relating to the physical or mental
health of an individual who can be identified from that information, or from
that and other information in the possession of the holder of the record; and
(b) has been made by or on behalf of a health professional[64] in connection
with the care of that individual. Under section 3(1)(f) of the Access to Health
Records Act 1990, where the patient has died, an application for access to a
health record may be made to the holder of the record by the patient's personal representative and any person who may have a claim arising out of the
patient's death. The holder of the record, within a maximum period of 40
days, must give access to the record by allowing the applicant to inspect the

---

[60] *ibid.* art. 6(1).
[61] *ibid.* art. 6(2).
[62] *ibid.* art. 7(3).
[63] *ibid.* art. 5(3).
[64] For the definition of "health professional" see Access to Health Records Act 1990, s.2(1).

record (or an extract), or if the applicant so requires by supplying him with a copy of the record or extract.[65] Where any information is expressed in terms which are not intelligible without explanation, an explanation of those terms must be provided.[66]

10–116   The right of access is not absolute; there are a number of exceptions. On an application after the patient has died by the patient's personal representative or any person who may have a claim arising out of the patient's death, access shall not be given if the record includes a note, made at the patient's request, that he did not wish access to be given on such an application.[67] Section 5(4) excludes access in the case of an application made by someone other than the patient (or on the patient's authority) to any part of the record which, in the opinion of the record holder, would disclose information provided by the patient in the expectation that it would not be disclosed to the applicant, or information obtained as a result of any examination or investigation to which the patient consented in the expectation that the information would not be disclosed. In addition, access does not have to be given to any part of the record which, in the opinion of the holder of the record, would disclose information which is not relevant to any claim which may arise out of the patient's death.[68]

10–117   Section 5(1) contains two significant restrictions on the right of access. Where, in the opinion of the holder of the record, access to any part of a health record would disclose: (i) information likely to cause serious harm to the physical or mental health of the patient or of any other individual; or (ii) information relating to or provided by an individual, other than the patient, who could be identified from that information (unless the individual concerned consents or the individual is a health professional who has been involved in the care of the patient[69]), access shall not be given. Furthermore, section 5(1)(b) excludes any part of a health record which was made before the commencement of the Act, namely November 1, 1991,[70] except, and to the extent that, in the opinion of the holder of the record, the giving of access is necessary in order to make intelligible any part of the record to which access is required to be given.[71]

10–118   A person who considers that any information contained in a health record to which he has been given access is inaccurate may apply to the holder of the record to have the record corrected.[72] The holder of the record must either make the necessary correction, or, if he is not satisfied that the information is inaccurate, make a note in the record of the matters which the applicant considers to be inaccurate, and in either case, supply the applicant with a copy of the correction or note. There is no remedy in damages,

---

[65] Access to Health Records Act 1990, s.3(2) and 3(5).
[66] *ibid.*, s.3(3).
[67] *ibid.*, s.4(3).
[68] *ibid.*, s.5(4).
[69] *ibid.*, s.5(2).
[70] *ibid.*, s.12(2).
[71] *ibid.*, s.5(2).
[72] *ibid.*, s.6(1). "Inaccurate" means incorrect, misleading or incomplete: *ibid.*, s.6(3).

however, in respect of damage or distress suffered as a result of inaccuracy in the health record. The only remedy available under the Act is an application to the court for an order requiring the holder of a health record to comply with any requirement of the Act.[73] For the purpose of determining this issue the court may require the record to be available for its own inspection, but shall not require the record to be disclosed to the applicant or his representatives whether by disclosure or otherwise.[74]

The Act clearly contemplates applications for access to health records in advance of litigation, and to this extent it may supplement the provisions of section 33(2) of the Supreme Court Act 1981 for pre-action disclosure.[75] It cannot entirely replace this procedure, however, because there are several drawbacks. First, a "health record" is defined as information relating to the physical or mental health of an individual who can be identified from that information, and has been made by or on behalf of a health professional *in connection with the care of that individual.* It is doubtful whether this would apply to all the documents (an accident report, for example) that might be relevant to the conduct of litigation, and which are subject to disclosure under the procedure for pre-action disclosure. Secondly, the Access to Health Records Act applies only to health records made after November 1, 1991, except to the extent that access is necessary to an earlier record to make intelligible access to a record made after that date. No such restriction applies to the procedure for pre-action disclosure. Thirdly, information may be withheld if, in the opinion of the holder of the record, it is likely to cause serious harm to the physical or mental health of the patient or of any other individual, or if the information would, in effect, break another person's confidence. Again, no such restriction applies to disclosure under the Supreme Court Act 1981, although an order may direct that disclosure be limited to the applicant's legal advisers or his legal and medical advisers. Finally, it would seem inappropriate to allow the holder of the record, who may be a potential defendant, to determine which information is or is not relevant to any claim which may arise out of the patient's death, as is possible under section 5(4), although, admittedly, under section 33(2) of the Supreme Court Act the documents sought by the applicant must be "relevant to an issue arising or likely to arise out of that claim."

10–119

The Access to Health Records Act 1990 may have at least one advantage over the Supreme Court Act 1981 in respect of pre-action disclosure against a party who is not likely to be a party to the proceedings. It is not possible to obtain an order for pre-action disclosure against someone who is not likely to be a party to proceedings, although disclosure against third parties is possible once an action has been commenced. Where, however, a third party holds documents which constitute a "health record" within the meaning of section 1(1) the claimant will be able to make an application for access to that record under the 1990 Act.

10–120

---

[73] *ibid.*, s.8(1).
[74] *ibid.*, s.8(4).
[75] See paras 10–125 to 10–131.

(3) Access to Medical Reports Act 1988

10–121   The Access to Medical Reports Act 1988, section 1, grants an individual a right of access to any medical report relating to the individual which is to be, or in the previous six months has been, supplied by a medical practitioner, who is or has been responsible for the clinical care of the individual, for employment or insurance purposes. The Act does not apply to a report prepared by a doctor who had not previously been responsible for the individual's clinical care, *e.g.*, a doctor instructed by employers or prospective employers on an ad hoc basis. The individual must consent to any application to a medical practitioner for a medical report on the individual for employment or insurance purposes, and when giving consent he can state that he wishes to have access to the report before it is supplied. Access means making the report or a copy of it available for the individual's inspection or supplying him with a copy.[76] Where an individual has been given access to a report it should not be supplied to the applicant unless the individual consents, and the individual may request the doctor to amend any part of the report which he considers to be incorrect or misleading.[77]

10–122   Under section 7 there are exceptions to the right of access where disclosure would be likely to cause serious harm to the physical or mental health of the individual or others, or would be likely to reveal information about another person, or to reveal the identity of another person who has supplied information to the practitioner about the individual, (unless that person consents, or the person is a health professional who has been involved in the care of the individual and the information relates to or has been provided by him in that capacity). Where the exceptions apply to a part but not the whole of a medical report the individual's right of access applies to the remainder, and where the exceptions apply to the whole report, the doctor must not supply the report unless the individual consents.

10–123   There is no remedy in damages for a failure to comply with the terms of the Act, but where a person has failed or is likely to fail to comply with any requirement of the Act an individual may apply to the court for an order that he comply with that requirement.

4. DISCLOSURE

10–124   In the past the adversarial nature of civil proceedings was regarded as justification for allowing the parties to a civil action to conceal the nature of their case from each other. This was particularly true of actions for medical negligence. The modern approach, however, is to conduct litigation with "cards on the table" so that the parties can assess the relative strengths and weaknesses of their respective cases and where appropriate, settle the action.

---

[76] Access to Medical Reports Act 1988, s.4(4). The doctor may charge a reasonable fee for supplying a copy.
[77] *ibid.*, s.5(1) and (2).

A more open approach also helps the parties narrow the issues in dispute. This approach has been significantly improved by the Woolf reforms and the new regime of civil litigation introduced by the Civil Procedure Rules. Access to a patient's medical records in order to identify whether a claim has any prospects of success should no longer present the hurdle that it once did.

(1) Pre-Action Disclosure

(a) Against a potential defendant

Access to a patient's medical records is essential to enable his legal and medical advisers to determine whether an action for negligence has any prospect of success. Section 33(2) of the Supreme Court Act 1981 and CPR r. 31.16 provide a procedure by which a potential claimant may apply for disclosure of relevant documents from a potential defendant before proceedings have started.[78] As Lord Denning M.R. has observed, one of the objects of the provision is to enable the claimant to find out whether or not he has a good cause of action before he issues proceedings.[79] It is designed to facilitate settlements and to avoid fruitless actions.[80] Before considering an application to court, the claimant should make a written request for voluntary disclosure in accordance with the *Pre-Action Protocol for the Resolution of Clinical Disputes*, Annex B, *A Protocol for Obtaining Hospital Medical Records*, which includes standard forms to facilitate the process.[81] This procedure, and the more open climate to litigation, means that applications to court should rarely be required in medical negligence litigation.

10–125

Claimants' solicitors should not accept disclosure of the medical records to a nominated medical expert, but should insist on disclosure to themselves in order to organise the records into chronological order, check them against the claimant's statement, identify missing documents, and identify the relevant issues for consideration and/or clarification by the medical experts and/or counsel. Orders under section 33(2) of the Supreme Court Act 1981 can exclude production to the patient himself but not to his legal advisers, and if a NHS Trust persists in seeking to limit disclosure to a medical expert an application will have to be made. It is now rare for NHS defendants to refuse voluntary disclosure, provided that it is made clear in the letter of request that there is some basis for the request and that it is not purely speculative.[82]

10–126

---

[78] This procedure was formerly limited to actions involving claims in respect of personal injuries or death. That restriction was removed by the Civil Procedure (Modification of Enactments) Order 1998, S.I. 1998 No. 2940, art. 5.

[79] *Dunning v Board of Governors of the United Liverpool Hospitals* [1973] 2 All E.R. 454, 457; *Shaw v Vauxhall Motors Ltd* [1974] 1 W.L.R. 1035, 1039.

[80] *Lee v South West Thames Regional Health Authority* [1985] 2 All E.R. 385, 387.

[81] See Appendix 2, p. 873. The courts always did encourage voluntary disclosure, even under the old Rules of the Supreme Court. See the comments of Lord Denning M.R. in *Shaw v Vauxhall Motors Ltd* [1974] 1 W.L.R. 1035, 1039.

[82] Note, however, that a patient who makes a request to see his health records under the Data Protection Act 1998 does not have to give any reason or justification for the request. In *Hall v Wandsworth Health Authority* (1985) 129 S.J. 188 Tudor Price J. said that a period of six

10–127   The Supreme Court Act 1981 permits a person who has not issued a claim form to make an application for disclosure of documents from a person who is likely to be a party to the proceedings. Section 33(2) provides that:

> "On an application, in accordance with rules of court, of a person who appears to the High Court to be likely to be a party to subsequent proceedings in that court the High Court shall, in such circumstances as may be specified in the rules, have power to order a person who appears to the court to be likely to be a party to the proceedings and to be likely to have or to have had in his possession, custody or power any documents which are relevant to an issue arising or likely to arise out of that claim—
>
> (a)   to disclose whether those documents are in his possession, custody or power; and
>
> (b)   to produce such of those documents as are in his possession, custody or power to the applicant or, on such conditions as may be specified in the order -
>
>   (i)   to the applicant's legal advisers; or
>
>   (ii)   to the applicant's legal advisers and any medical or other professional adviser of the applicant; or
>
>   (iii)   if the applicant has no legal adviser, to any medical or other professional adviser of the applicant."[83]

Applications under section 33(2) of the Supreme Court Act 1981 must be supported by evidence. An order may be made only where the respondent is likely to be a party to subsequent proceedings; the applicant is also likely to be a party to those proceedings; if proceedings had started the respondent's duty by way of standard disclosure under CPR r. 31.6 would extend to the documents or classes of documents of which the applicant seeks disclosure;[84] and disclosure before proceedings have started is desirable in order to dispose fairly of the anticipated proceedings, assist the dispute to be resolved without proceedings, or save costs.[85] An order must specify the documents

---

(n.82 contd.) weeks for the health authority to comply with a request for voluntary disclosure was a reasonable period: "If in a particular case for a particular reason it is insufficient the defendants . . . should request more time, preferably with an explanation . . . [I]f there is a prompt answer and a promise of discovery is given at an early stage there will be no need for plaintiffs to threaten or issue section 33 proceedings."

[83] See also Supreme Court Act 1981, s.33(1) which provides that the court may make an order providing for the inspection, photographing, preservation, custody and detention of property, the taking of samples of property and the carrying out of any experiment on or with any property which may become the subject matter of subsequent proceedings in the High Court.

[84] Pre-action disclosure can only take place when the issues in dispute have been sufficiently identified and can only extend to those documents which are liable to be disclosed at the stage in proceedings when the general obligation of disclosure arises. This is a matter for the discretion of the judge: *Bermuda International Securities Ltd v KPMG (A Firm)* [2001] EWCA Civ 269; [2001] Lloyd's Rep. P.N. 392, CA.

[85] CPR r. 31.16(3). For discussion of the meaning of the word "likely" in this context see:

or the classes of documents which the respondent must disclose and require him to specify any of the documents which are no longer in his control or in respect of which he claims a right or duty to withhold inspection.[86] In a medical negligence action there should be little difficulty in establishing the relevance of the medical records to a potential claim.

In dealing with applications for pre-action disclosure the court has to ask itself two questions, the first jurisdictional, the second as to the exercise of discretion.[87] The jurisdictional question is resolved by considering whether there is a real prospect of the order being fair to the parties if litigation was commenced, or of assisting the parties to avoid litigation, or of saving costs in any event.[88] The words "likely to be a party to proceedings" mean likely to be involved if proceedings are issued, and "likely" means no more than "might well." The prospective claimant does not have show that he has a "reasonable basis" for making the claim against the prospective defendant.[89] The procedure is not simply about providing evidence for a claimant to bring an action. When the claimant obtains disclosure this may well indicate that there is truly no basis for an allegation of negligence, and it is in the public interest that litigation which has no prospect of success should not be initiated.[90]

10–128

(i) Relevance of a possible limitation defence

In *Harris v Newcastle Health Authority*[91] the defendants declined the claimant's request for pre-action disclosure on the ground that the action was statute-barred, the events giving rise to the claim having occurred over 20 years before. Both the district registrar and, on appeal, the judge refused the claimant's application because the strength of the limitation defence was such that the action was doomed to fail. In the Court of Appeal Kerr L.J. said that if it was plain beyond doubt that a defence of limitation would be raised and would succeed, then the court was entitled to take that matter into

10–129

---

86 (n.85 contd.) *Medisys plc v Arthur Andersen (A Firm)* [2002] P.N.L.R. 538; [2002] Lloyd's Rep. P.N. 323, QBD. See also *Burns v Shuttleworth Ltd* [1999] 1 W.L.R. 1449, CA concerning the interpretation of the words "in which a claim for personal injuries is likely to be made" which were in the differently worded RSC Ord 24, r 7A.

86 CPR r. 31.16(4).

87 *Black v Sumitomo Corp* [2001] EWCA Civ 1819; [2002] 1 W.L.R. 1562; *Harris v Newcastle Health Authority* [1989] 2 All E.R. 273, 278, *per* Mann L.J.

88 *ibid.*

89 *ibid.* Under the old RSC it was said that the court would not permit "fishing expeditions": *Shaw v Vauxhall Motors Ltd* [1974] 1 W.L.R. 1035, 1040, *per* Buckley L.J. But that did not mean that the applicant had to prove that he had a good cause of action: "One of the objects of the section is to enable a plaintiff to find out—before he starts proceedings—whether he has a good cause of action or not. This object would be defeated if he had to show—in advance—that he had already got a good cause of action before he saw the documents," *per* Lord Denning M.R. in *Dunning v Board of Governors of the United Liverpool Hospitals* [1973] 2 All E.R. 454, 457; see also *Shaw v Vauxhall Motors Ltd* [1974] 1 W.L.R. 1035, 1039.

90 60% of legally aided clinical negligence litigation is not pursued beyond the initial investigation: see para. 1–011.

91 [1989] 2 All E.R. 273.

account. However, a claimant in a personal injuries action can always make an application to override the limitation period under section 33 of the Limitation Act 1980, and that must also be taken into account before it can be said that the action is clearly bound to be defeated by the limitation defence. Kerr L.J. accepted that in the normal run of cases:

> "... even where a defence of limitation has a strong prospect of success, like here, it is very difficult for a court, on limited material, before pleadings and discovery, to conclude at that stage that the situation is such that the proposed action is bound to fail and therefore frivolous, vexatious or otherwise ill-founded. So in general I would accept . . . that issues relevant to limitation should not enter into consideration on applications for pre-trial discovery."[92]

Accordingly, since it was likely that proceedings would be instituted regardless of the outcome of the application for disclosure, and since it could not be said that the proceedings were doomed to failure because pre-trial disclosure might reveal facts which would be relevant to the success or otherwise of the limitation defence, the court would exercise its discretion to order disclosure of the hospital records.

(ii) To whom must disclosure be made?

10–130   Under sections 33(2) and 34(2) of the Supreme Court Act 1981 the court can order disclosure to the applicant's legal advisers, plus any medical or other professional adviser of the applicant, or if the applicant has no legal adviser, to any medical or other professional adviser. This permits the court to order that disclosure exclude the patient himself (though not the patient's legal adviser). In *Davies v Eli Lilly & Co.*[93] the Court of Appeal held that in exceptional circumstances the court would permit a person who is neither a party's legal adviser, nor an employee of a legal adviser, nor a professional expert to undertake the inspection of documents if the person's assistance was essential in the interests of justice and the court was satisfied that there would be no breach of the duty of confidentiality.[94] Accordingly inspection by a "scientific co-ordinator" in the Opren litigation was authorised, even though the defendants objected on the ground that he was a journalist who had been critical of the pharmaceutical industry. This decision concerned inspection of documents after an action had been commenced, but there is no reason in principle why it should not also apply to pre-trial disclosure provided that the person qualifies as a "professional adviser."

---

[92] *ibid.* at 277. Sir John Megaw said, at 279, that ". . . it cannot be said with any certainty that on discovery facts would not emerge which would be relevant to the issue of limitation."
[93] [1987] 1 W.L.R. 428.
[94] This was under the provisions of the old RSC Ord 24, r 9.

(iii) Costs

The general rule is that the court will award the person against whom the   **10–131**
order is sought his costs of the application and of complying with any order
made on the application.[95] But the court has a discretion to make a different
order, having regard to all the circumstances, including the extent to which it
was reasonable to oppose the application and whether the parties have complied with any relevant per-action protocols.[96] Under the old Rules of the
Supreme Court, where the defendant had no reasonable excuse for failing to
comply with a written request for disclosure of documents before an application for disclosure was made, he could be ordered to pay the applicant's
costs.[97] In view of the greater emphasis now placed on patients' entitlement
to see their medical records, and the Department of Health's policy on the
disclosure of records, which is reflected in the *Pre-Action Protocol for the
Resolution of Clinical Disputes*, there is generally no good reason for a NHS
Trust to refuse a voluntary request for the for disclosure of medical records.

(iv) Congenital disabilities

The Congenital Disabilities (Civil Liability) Act 1976 confers a right of   **10–132**
action on a child who is born alive and disabled in respect of the disability, if
it is caused by an occurrence which affected either parent's ability to have a
normal healthy child, or affected the mother during pregnancy, or affected the
mother or child in the course of its birth, causing disabilities which would not
otherwise have been present.[98] It is possible for a father, though generally not
the mother, to be a defendant to an action brought under the Act by a child.
Sections 27–29 of the Human Fertilisation and Embryology Act 1990 deal
with the status of the "parents" of children born as a consequence of in vitro
fertilisation or artificial insemination, with the consequence that a child's
mother or father may, in law, not be the same person as his genetic mother or
father. Under section 35(1) of that Act, where for the purpose of instituting
proceedings under the Congenital Disabilities (Civil Liability) Act 1976 it is
necessary to identify a person who would or might be the parent of a child but
for sections 27–29 of the Human Fertilisation and Embryology Act 1990, the
court may on the application of the child make an order requiring the Human
Fertilisation and Embryology Authority to disclose any information contained
in the register kept in pursuance of section 31 identifying that person. The
court must satisfied that the interests of justice require it to make the order.[99]

---

[95] CPR r. 48.1(2).
[96] CPR r. 48.1(3). See *Bermuda International Securities Ltd v KPMG (A Firm)* [2001] EWCA
    Civ 269; [2001] Lloyd's Rep. P.N. 392, CA.
[97] *Hall v Wandsworth Health Authority* (1985) 129 S.J. 188; see also *Jacobs v Wessex Regional
    Health Authority* [1984] C.L.Y. 2618, where the claimant's solicitors had pointed out in cor-
    respondence with the defendants that an application would result in needless public expense,
    since the claimant was legally aided. The defendants were ordered to pay the claimant's costs.
[98] See paras 2–079 *et seq.*
[99] Human Fertilisation and Embryology Act 1990, ss.35(3) and 34(2).

(b) Against third parties

10–133   An order for pre-action disclosure can only be made under section 33(2) of the Supreme Court Act 1981 against a person who is "likely to be a party to the proceedings." Thus, if the claimant needs disclosure of documents from some other person, then, in the absence of voluntary disclosure, he will normally have to issue the claim form and apply for disclosure against the other person under section 34 of the Supreme Court Act 1981. Voluntary disclosure, however, should be regarded as the norm. In *Walker v Eli Lilly & Co.*[1] Hirst J. stated that health authorities and doctors who are not likely to be defendants should respond readily and promptly to requests for disclosure to avoid unnecessary expense and delay. This point is reinforced by the Data Protection Act 1998 (and the Access to Health Records Act 1990 in relation to requests following the death of a patient) which gives patients a right of access to their health records irrespective of the possibility of litigation. These statutes may be of some value in seeking disclosure against a doctor or health authority who is not a potential defendant, but there are some restrictions on its effectiveness for this purpose.[2] Moreover, the *Protocol for Obtaining Hospital Medical Records* (Annex B to the *Pre-Action Protocol for the Resolution of Clinical Disputes*), applies equally to third parties as it does to potential defendants. The protocol is approved by the Department of Health, whose policy is that patients are entitled to see their records.

10–134   A further possibility to consider when seeking disclosure from a third party is the court's inherent power to order a person to disclose information under the principle in *Norwich Pharmacal Co v Commissioners of Customs and Excise.*[3] Where a person through no fault of his own, and whether voluntarily or not, "has got mixed up in the tortious acts of others so as to facilitate their wrongdoing he may incur no personal liability but he comes under a duty to assist the person who has been wronged by giving him full information and disclosing the identity of the wrongdoers."[4] This allows a potential claimant to examine third party documents to identify a wrongdoer and establish a cause of action, including "fishing" for the names of wrongdoers.[5] The principle applies even though without the information sought the claimant cannot ascertain whether an unidentified third party has in fact committed a tort against him; nor is it necessary that the tort committed against him be criminal in nature.[6] Disclosure under the *Norwich Pharmacal* principle is only available, however, where the third party has been involved in the wrongdoing in some way. It will not be

---

[1] (1986) 136 N.L.J. 608.
[2] See para 10–119.
[3] [1974] A.C. 133.
[4] *ibid.* at 175, *per* Lord Reid.
[5] *Loose v Williamson* [1978] 1 W.L.R. 639.
[6] *P v T Ltd* [1997] 1 W.L.R. 1309.

ordered against a "mere witness."[7] For the purpose of disclosure under *Norwich Pharmacal* there is no requirement that the person against whom the proceedings had been brought should be a wrongdoer. It is sufficient if he has become involved in the wrongdoing. If he was involved it is irrelevant that he was innocent and in ignorance of the wrongdoing by the person whose identity was sought by the applicant. Nor is there a requirement that disclosure be for the purpose of enabling civil proceedings being brought against the wrongdoer.[8]

(c) A common law duty of disclosure?

It is possible that the courts could develop a common law duty requiring   **10–135** doctors to inform patients about what has happened in the course of a treatment or procedure that has gone wrong. Sir John Donaldson M.R. has expressed strong views on this issue. In *Lee v South West Thames Regional Health Authority*, his Lordship referred to the doctor's duty to answer the patient's questions about proposed treatment following *Sidaway v Bethlem Royal Hospital Governors*,[9] and commented:

> "Why, we ask ourselves, is the position any different if the patient asks what treatment he has in fact had? Let us suppose that a blood transfusion is in contemplation. The patient asks what is involved. He is told that a quantity of blood from a donor will be introduced into his system. He may ask about the risk of AIDS and so forth and will be entitled to straight answers. He consents. Suppose that, by accident, he is given a quantity of air as well as blood and suffers serious ill effects. Is he not entitled to ask what treatment he in fact received, and is the doctor and hospital authority not obliged to tell him, 'in the event you did not only get a blood transfusion. You also got an air transfusion'? Why is the duty different before the treatment from what it is afterwards?
>
> If the duty is the same, then if the patient is refused information to which he is entitled, it must be for consideration whether he could not

---

[7] *Ricci v Chow* [1987] 1 W.L.R. 1658; *AXA Equity & Law Life Assurance Society plc v National Westminster Bank plc* [1998] C.L.C. 1177, CA. An employee or agent of a corporation which is party to the proceedings is not to be regarded as a mere witness and can be required to give disclosure on behalf of the corporation: *Harrington v North London Polytechnic* [1984] 3 All E.R. 666.

[8] *Ashworth Hospital Authority v MGN Ltd* [2002] UKHL 29; [2002] 1 W.L.R. 2033, where a newspaper was ordered to disclose the name of an intermediary, who had received from an employee of Ashworth Hospital, details of the medical records of a patient at the hospital. The hospital wanted to discover the name of the employee in order to dismiss him, rather than to bring civil proceedings against him. For consideration of the order for costs on a *Norwich Pharmacal* application see *Totalise plc v Motley Fool Ltd* [2001] EWCA Civ 1897; [2002] 1 W.L.R. 1233. As a general rule costs should be recovered from the wrongdoer rather than the innocent party. In a normal case the applicant for a *Norwich Pharmacal* order should be ordered to pay the costs of the party making the disclosure, including the costs of the disclosure. *Norwich Pharmacal* applications are akin to proceedings for pre-action disclosure, where costs are governed by CPR r. 48.2.

[9] [1985] A.C. 871.

bring an action for breach of contract claiming specific performance of the duty to inform. In other words, whether the patient could not bring an action for discovery, albeit on a novel basis."[10]

10–136   Subsequently, in *Naylor v Preston Area Health Authority*[11] his Lordship returned to this theme, suggesting that in professional negligence cases, and in particular in medical negligence cases, there is a duty of candour resting on the professional man:

> "In this context I was disturbed to be told during the argument of the present appeals that the view was held in some quarters that whilst the duty of candid disclosure, [referred to in *Lee v South West Thames Regional Health Authority*], might give rise to a contractual implied term and so benefit private fee-paying patients, it did not translate into a legal or equitable right for the benefit of national health service patients. This I would entirely repudiate. In my judgment, still admittedly and regretfully *obiter*, it is but one aspect of the general duty of care, arising out of the patient/medical practitioner or hospital authority relationship and gives rise to rights both in contract and in tort. It is also in my judgment, not obiter, a factor to be taken into account when exercising the jurisdiction under Ord. 38 with which we are concerned."

The legal basis for this "duty of candour" remains unclear, particularly since in the tort of negligence, at least, the claimant would have to prove that breach of the duty caused him damage, and the circumstances in which non-disclosure will cause further harm to the claimant will be rare.[12] A breach of contract, on the other hand, is actionable *per se*, and, indeed, might give rise to a claim for specific performance of the duty. These differences between contract and tort lend some substance to the view that private patients would stand in a better position than NHS patients in this respect. Whatever the

---

[10] [1985] 2 All E.R. 385, 389–390. Mustill L.J. agreed with this statement. The difficulty of obtaining information from medical staff when something has gone wrong was illustrated in *Bayliss v Blagg* (1954) 1 B.M.J. 709, in which there had been a long delay by the hospital staff in telling parents about a deterioration in their child's medical condition, and the court concluded that there had been a deliberate attempt by the hospital to conceal and misrepresent to the family the condition of the child. Stable J. observed: "I would like to know if this is the system under our State medical service. The parent has a right to know—this isn't Russia." Counsel for the *defendants* replied: "One can't get facts from hospitals. They are grossly impertinent when you ask."

[11] [1987] 2 All E.R. 353, 360.

[12] See *Stamos v Davies* (1985) 21 D.L.R. (4th) 507, 522, paras 4–036 to 4–038; Robertson (1987) 25 Alberta L. Rev. 215. Sir John Donaldson M.R. has said that in *Lee* he was "flying a kite": (1985) 53 Medico-Legal J. 148, 157. There are circumstances where a doctor may come under a duty to pass on to a patient information about the state of his health, even though the doctor was not negligent in causing the condition: see *Pittman Estate v Bain* (1994) 112 D.L.R. (4th) 257 (Ont. Ct., Gen. Div.), para. 4–040, where a general practitioner was held negligent for failing to inform a patient that he had received a blood transfusion that was potentially contaminated with HIV. If the patient had known about his HIV status there were steps that he could have taken to extend his life expectancy.

legal position, it is now clear that doctors have an ethical duty to inform patients, or their relatives, when something has gone wrong with their treatment.[13]

In *McInerney v MacDonald*[14] the New Brunswick Court of Appeal held that patients do have a contractual right of access to their medical records, even when the records in the hands of the treating doctor have not been created by the doctor herself. On appeal, the Supreme Court of Canada was not convinced by arguments based on contract.[15] Nonetheless, it was held that patients are entitled to have access to their records, on the basis that the doctor-patient relationship is a fiduciary relationship and that certain equitable duties arise between doctor and patient. Medical records consist of information that is highly private and personal, information that goes to the personal integrity and autonomy of the patient. The trust-like "beneficial interest" of the patient in the information indicated that as a general rule the patient should have a right of access to it and the doctor should have a corresponding obligation to provide it. This principle also applied when the information was conveyed to another doctor who then becomes subject to the duty to afford the patient access to that information. La Forest J. pointed out that:

10–137

". . . one of the duties arising from the doctor-patient relationship is the duty of the doctor to act with utmost good faith and loyalty. If the patient is denied access to his or her records, it may not be possible for the patient to establish that this duty has been fulfilled. As I see it, it is important that the patient have access to the records for the very purposes for which it is sought to withhold the documents, namely, to ensure the proper functioning of the doctor-patient relationship and to protect the well-being of the patient. If there has been improper conduct in the doctor's dealings with his or her patient, it ought to be revealed. The purpose of keeping the documents secret is to promote

---

[13] See General Medical Council guidance, *Good Medical Practice*, May 2001, available at *www.gmc-uk.org*: "22. If a patient under your care has suffered harm, through misadventure or for any other reason, you should act immediately to put matters right, if that is possible. You must explain fully and promptly to the patient what has happened and the likely long- and short-term effects. When appropriate you should offer an apology. If the patient is an adult who lacks capacity, the explanation should be given to a person with responsibility for the patient, or the patient's partner, close relative or a friend who has been involved in the care of the patient, unless you have reason to believe the patient would have objected to the disclosure. In the case of children the situation should be explained honestly to those with parental responsibility and to the child, if the child has the maturity to understand the issues. 23. If a child under your care has died you must explain, to the best of your knowledge, the reasons for, and the circumstances of, the death to those with parental responsibility. Similarly, if an adult patient has died, you should provide this information to the patient's partner, close relative or a friend who has been involved in the care of the patient, unless you have reason to believe that the patient would have objected." The Department of Health consultation paper *Making Amends*, June 2003, has recommended that there should be a statutory "duty of candour" imposed on health professionals in the NHS to inform patients when something has gone wrong with their treatment.

[14] [1991] 2 Med. L.R. 267; (1990) 66 D.L.R. (4th) 736.

[15] (1992) 93 D.L.R. (4th) 415 (S.C.C.).

the proper functioning of the relationship, not to facilitate improper conduct."[16]

The equitable nature of the remedy gives the court discretion to refuse access to the records where non-disclosure is appropriate, if, for example, it is in the patient's best interests to deny access, the onus being on the doctor to justify an exception to the general rule of access.[17]

10–138   In *R. v Mid-Glamorgan Family Health Services Authority, ex parte Martin*[18] Popplewell J. took the view that, since in *Sidaway v Bethlem Royal Hospital Governors* both the Court of Appeal and the House of Lords had rejected the notion that the doctor-patient relationship was fiduciary in nature, the basis on which the Supreme Court proceeded in *McInerney v MacDonald* could not be accepted in English law.[19] The applicant sought to know why, in 1969, he had been committed under the Mental Health Act 1959 and what the basis of his treatment had been. A consultant psychiatrist considered that the records contained information that it would be detrimental for the claimant to see, and the health authority claimed an absolute right, as owners of the records, to control access to them. They had offered to give conditional disclosure, to a medical expert nominated by the applicant. Popplewell J. drew a distinction between the information conveyed by a patient for the benefit of the doctor's consideration and the conclusion which the doctor comes to, based on that information:

---

[16] *ibid.* at 425–426. See Dickens (1994) 73 Can. Bar Rev. 234. In *Parslow v Masters* [1993] 6 W.W.R. 273 (Sask. Q.B.) it was held that the claimant was entitled to see a medical report and the doctor's entire medical file concerning her where the report was prepared for the purposes of an insurance company, on the basis that the physician-patient relationship is a fiduciary relationship. Although the insurer paid for the report the insured disclosed private information about herself to enable the doctor to prepare the report, and this created the doctor-patient relationship.

[17] It is clear that the denial of access to information was to be regarded as exceptional, where for example there was real potential for harm to the patient or a third party. Paternalistic assumptions about the patient's "best interests" were inappropriate, since non-disclosure itself could affect the patient's well-being; and, moreover, the patient's well-being had to be balanced with the patient's right to self-determination: "In short, patients should have access to their medical records in all but a small number of circumstances. In the ordinary case, these records should be disclosed upon the request of the patient unless there is a *significant likelihood of a substantial adverse effect* on the physical, mental or emotional health of the patient or harm to a third party," *per* La Forest J., at (1992) 93 D.L.R. (4th) 415, 430, emphasis added.

[18] [1993] P.I.Q.R. P426; [1994] 5 Med. L.R. 383.

[19] See *Sidaway v Bethlem Royal Hospital Governors* [1984] Q.B. 493, 515 and 518–519, *per* Dunn and Browne-Wilkinson L.JJ. respectively, and *per* Lord Scarman in the House of Lords: [1985] A.C. 871, 884. In *Breen v Williams* (1996) 138 A.L.R. 259 the High Court of Australia held that property in medical records remains that of the doctor, and there was no implied contractual right to access to the record. Declining the invitation to apply *McInerny*, it was held that the doctor-patient relationship is not fiduciary in character, but based on the doctor's contractual or tortious duty to exercise reasonable care. It was not permissible to use the law of fiduciary obligations to provide relief which would have the effect of imposing a novel positive obligation on a doctor to maintain and furnish medical records to a patient. For discussion of this case see Nolan (1997) 113 L.Q.R. 220.

"The opinion of the doctor is wholly the property of the doctor. It does not seem to me that the fact that the patient provides the original information entitles the him subject to exceptions, to see the conclusions of the doctors based on that information . . ."[20]

Accordingly, there was no right at common law to the access of any medical records which predated the coming into force of the Access to Health Records Act 1990. Indeed, the existence of this legislation, together with the Data Protection Act 1984 and the Access to Medical Reports Act 1988, supported the view that there was no common law right of access, said his Lordship, since this legislation would have been unnecessary if the right had existed at common law.[21] Moreover, Article 8 of the European Convention for the Protection of Human Rights and Fundamental Freedoms, providing for a right to respect for private and family life, did not assist the applicant's argument for access. Although his Lordship commented that the logic behind Lord Donaldson M.R.'s observations in *Lee v South West Thames Regional Health Authority* and *Naylor v Preston Area Health Authority* could scarcely be doubted, even so there might be:

"a difference between the doctor generally explaining what has happened and the patient being provided with the detailed written records which it was never intended for his eyes to see. Thus a doctor may be perfectly willing to give factual information but be disinclined to allow the patient to see opinions for instance expressed about the reliability or otherwise or the sanity or otherwise of that patient."[22]

On appeal, the Court of Appeal accepted that a doctor, and likewise a **10–139** health authority, as the owner of the patient's medical records, might deny him access to them if it was in the patient's best interests to do so, for example if disclosure would be detrimental to his health.[23] In the light of the health authority's offer, that was a complete answer to the case. But, whereas Popplewell J. considered that the issue was whether, at common law, a patient had an unconditional right of access to his medical records, Nourse L.J. preferred to state the issue in terms of whether a doctor or health authority, as

---

[20] [1993] P.I.Q.R. P426, 438.

[21] If the existence of legislation on a subject demonstrated that there was no equivalent common law right prior to the passage of the legislation the Court of Appeal could not have concluded in *Burton v Islington Health Authority* [1993] Q.B. 204 that a duty of care in negligence could be owed to a child born injured as a consequence of the defendant's negligence where the injuries were inflicted while the child was *in utero*, following the passage of the Congenital Disabilities (Civil Liability) Act 1976.

[22] [1993] P.I.Q.R. P426, 437. It is not clear, however, why the doctor's willingness or disinclination to provide information to the patient should be relevant to the question of whether the patient has a legal *right* to information. Note that a failure to tell the patient that something has gone wrong with treatment may be relevant when the court considers an application to disapply the three-year primary limitation period under the Limitation Act 1980, s.33: see *Atkinson v Oxfordshire Health Authority* [1993] 4 Med. L.R. 18, QBD.

[23] [1995] 1 All E.R. 356; [1995] 1 W.L.R. 110; Grubb (1994) 2 Med. L. Rev. 354; Feenan (1996) 59 M.L.R. 101.

owner of the patient's medical records, was entitled to deny him access to them on the ground that their disclosure would be detrimental to him. A public body was in no different position from that of a private doctor whose relationship with his patient was governed by contract. There was no absolute right to deal with medical records in any way that a health authority chose. The doctor's duty, like the authority's, was to act at all times in the best interests of the patient. This involves a duty to keep the records confidential, and to hand them on to the patient's next doctor or make them available to the patient's legal advisers if they are reasonably required for the purpose of legal proceedings in which he is involved:

> "The respondents' position seems to be that no practical difficulty could arise in such circumstances, but that they would act voluntarily and not because they were under a legal duty to do so. If it ever became necessary for the legal position to be tested, it is inconceivable that this extreme position would be vindicated."[24]

Evans L.J. said that there was no good reason for doubting that a right of access to medical records does exist, or that it was qualified where disclosure would harm the physical or mental health of the patient:

> "The record is made for two purposes which are relevant here: first, to provide part of the medical history of the patient, for the benefit of the same doctor or his successors in the future; and secondly, to provides a record of diagnosis and treatment in case of future inquiry or dispute. These purposes would be frustrated if there was no duty to disclose the records to medical advisers or to the patient himself, or his legal advisers, if they were required in connection with a later claim. Nor can the duty to disclose for medical purposes be limited, in my judgment, to future medical advisers. There could well be a case where the patient called for them in order to be able to give them to a future doctor as yet unidentified, e.g. in case of accident whilst travelling abroad."[25]

(2) Post-Action Disclosure

(a) Between the parties to the action

10–140   Once a claim has been commenced the normal rules on disclosure between the parties apply.[26] CPR r. 31.6 provides for standard disclosure, which requires a party to the action to disclose only the documents[27] on which he relies, the documents which adversely affect his own or another party's case

---

[24] *ibid.* at 363–364, *per* Nourse L.J.
[25] *ibid.* at 365.
[26] See the Civil Procedure Rules, Part 31.
[27] "Document" means anything in which information of any description is recorded: CPR r. 31.4.

or support another party's case, and the documents which he is required to disclose by a relevant practice direction.[28] The duty of disclosure is limited to documents which are or have been in a party's control,[29] but the duty of disclosure continues throughout the proceedings.[30] The Court may also make an order for specific disclosure or specific inspection of documents, under CPR r. 31.12.

(b) Against third parties

Once an action has been commenced a person who is not a party to the action may be ordered to disclose documents under section 34(2) of the Supreme Court Act 1981 and CPR r. 31.17. Section 34(2) is expressed in almost identical terms to section 33(2), except that the court has the power to order disclosure and production of documents by a person who is not a party to the proceedings. An application must be supported by evidence. The court may make an order for disclosure only where the documents are likely to support the case of the applicant or adversely affect the case of one of the other parties to the proceedings, and disclosure is necessary in order to dispose fairly of the claim or to save costs.[31]   **10–141**

The jurisdiction to make an order against a non-party must be exercised   **10–142**
with caution.[32] Before making an order, the court must be satisfied that the requirements of CPR r. 31.17(3) were satisfied and that the documents did in fact exist. The non-party, who has no access to the pleadings or the evidence, should not be left to determine whether the documents satisfy r. 31.17(3). Thus the court must be satisfied that (i) there were documents falling within the specified classes and (ii) that those documents were, not might be, documents the disclosure of which would support the applicant's case or adversely affect the case of another party to the proceedings.[33]

There is, of course, nothing to stop voluntary disclosure. In *Walker v Eli*   **10–143**
Lilly & Co[34] the claimant applied under section 34(2) for disclosure of her hospital medical records from a health authority which was not a party to the proceedings. The authority was reluctant to disclose the records voluntarily. Hirst J. said that where no special consideration of confidentiality is invoked, the court will "almost certainly" order disclosure if an application should become necessary, and so health authorities and medical practitioners should respond readily and promptly to any requests for disclosure in such cases, so that unnecessary expense and delay can be avoided. The health authority had been anxious that any documents disclosed might subsequently be used against them. His Lordship pointed out, however, that there is an implied undertaking by a party seeking disclosure in legal proceedings

---

[28] CPR r. 31.10 sets out the procedure for standard disclosure.
[29] CPR r. 31.8.
[30] CPR r. 31.11.
[31] CPR r. 31.17(3).
[32] *Re Howglen Ltd* [2001] 1 All E.R. 376, 382.
[33] *ibid.* at 382–383.
[34] (1986) 136 N.L.J. 608.

that documents so obtained will be used only for the purpose of those proceedings and for no other purpose. Where it is the defendant seeking disclosure of the claimant's medical records from a third party, the usual practice would be for the claimant to consent to production of the relevant documents to the defendant's medical advisers. If the claimant unreasonably withholds consent then rather than making an application under section 34 the defendant can apply for a stay of the proceedings until the claimant does consent. This is quicker and cheaper than a section 34 application.[35]

(3) Privilege

10–144   There is no obligation to produce for inspection a privileged document, although it should normally be disclosed as in the party's possession if it is relevant to the action.[36] The claim for privilege should be made in the party's list of documents, with a statement of the grounds on which privilege is claimed.[37] The ground of privilege which will most commonly be relevant to medical negligence actions is legal professional privilege, though public interest immunity may, on rare occasions, apply.[38]

(a) Legal Professional Privilege

10–145   Legal professional privilege can take two forms. First, confidential communications between a solicitor acting in his professional capacity and his client for the purpose of obtaining legal advice and assistance are privileged, whether or not in contemplation of litigation. This will be construed broadly. Where information is passed by the solicitor or client to the other as part of a continuing process aimed at keeping both informed so that advice may be sought and given, privilege will attach.[39] Legal advice is not limited to advice

---

[35] *Dunn v British Coal Corp* [1993] P.I.Q.R. P275, 280, where the Court of Appeal held that if the claimant claims that he has suffered an injury causing permanent loss of earnings and loss of earning capacity, he must prove that the loss of future earnings or earning capacity was caused by the accident. The onus is upon him, and therefore he has to prove that he was in normal health. Accordingly, all his medical records should be disclosed to the defendant, not merely those relating to the injury which is the subject of the litigation. If they would reveal an unrelated but embarrassing condition, disclosure should be limited to the defendant's medical advisers, except in so far as it is necessary to refer to matters relevant to the litigation. Where, however, the application is made under s.34 of the Supreme Court Act 1981 or s.53 of the County Courts Act 1984 disclosure will not be limited to the defendant's medical advisers, but will extend to legal advisers: *Hipwood v Gloucester Health Authority* [1995] P.I.Q.R. P447; [1995] 6 Med. L.R. 187, CA.

[36] CPR r. 31.3.

[37] CPR r. 31.19(3)(4).

[38] Privilege also applies to documents which will expose a party to criminal proceedings or a penalty: Civil Evidence Act 1968, s.14; and to communications conducted on a "without prejudice" basis for the purpose of settling a dispute. "Without prejudice" privilege applies to the substance of the communication rather than the form, so that a document marked "without prejudice" may not be privileged if its purpose is not to reach a compromise, and, conversely privilege may attach even where the words are not used: *Buckinghamshire County Council v Moran* [1990] Ch. 623; *South Shropshire District Council v Amos* [1986] 1 W.L.R. 1271.

[39] *Balabel v Air India* [1988] Ch. 317, CA.

about the law, but can include advice about what should prudently and sensibly be done in the relevant legal context. Privilege does not extend, however, to all communications between solicitor and client on matters within the ordinary business of a solicitor.[40] Once it is established that it applies, legal professional privilege is absolute. No exceptions are permitted whereby the court balances the conflict of interest between the solicitor's client in maintaining the privilege against the damage to someone else, or indeed the public interest, if the evidence is not made available.[41] In *General Mediterranean Holdings SA v Patel*[42] Toulson, J. held that the Civil Procedure Act 1997 did not delegate power to restrict the right to legal confidentiality and therefore the Civil Procedure Rules could not abrogate a "fundamental substantive right" to legal professional privilege. The only circumstance in which the right to legal confidentiality could be questioned was where a client attempted to use the solicitor and client relationship for illegal purposes. And in *Linstead v East Sussex, Brighton and Hove Health Authority*[43] Forbes J. held that the same principle applied to the second category of legal professional privilege, which applies to a witness statement prepared in the course of litigation, where the sole or dominant purpose for which it came into existence was for obtaining legal advice in relation to contemplated proceedings. The coming into force of the Civil Procedure Rules, with the overriding objective of dealing with cases justly, and the Human Rights Act 1998 had not changed the rules on legal professional privilege, which remained absolute if it was not waived or abrogated. Legal professional privilege was not subject to any balancing exercise of weighting competing public interests.

The second form of legal professional privilege applies to communication between a solicitor and a third party, either directly or through an agent, which arise after litigation is contemplated or commenced and the   **10–146**

---

[40] *ibid.*; see, *e.g.*, *Conlon v Conlons Ltd* [1952] 2 All E.R. 462. Privilege applies to communications between an "in-house" salaried lawyer and his employer: *Alfred Crompton Amusement Machines Ltd v Commissioners of Customs and Excise (No. 2)* [1974] A.C. 405; and to communications with counsel: *Curtis v Beaney* [1911] P. 181.

[41] *R. v Derby Magistrates Court, ex parte B* [1996] A.C. 487. The rule applies even if it may prejudice a defendant's defence to a charge of murder. Lord Taylor C.J. said, at p. 507, that: "The principle which runs through all these cases, and the many other cases which were cited, is that a man must be able to consult his lawyer in confidence, since otherwise he might hold back half the truth. The client must be sure that what he tells his lawyer in confidence will never be revealed without his consent. Legal professional privilege is thus much more than an ordinary rule of evidence, limited in its application to the facts of a particular case. It is a fundamental condition on which the administration of justice as a whole rests." In *Paragon Finance plc v Freshfields (a firm)* [1999] 1 W.L.R. 1183, CA Lord Bingham C.J. said that *R. v Derby Magistrates Court, ex parte B* made it plain that in the context of legal professional privilege there was no balance to be drawn between the requirements of fairness and justice against any legitimate interest a claimant might have in maintaining the confidentiality of a confidential relationship, though his Lordship did exclude cases "where client and legal adviser have abused their confidential relationship to facilitate crime or fraud." In this situation the privilege probably does not arise, rather than criminal activity constituting an exception.

[42] [2000] 1 W.L.R. 272.

[43] [2001] P.I.Q.R. P356.

communication is made with a view to that litigation. Such communication is privileged if its purpose is to obtain or give advice on the litigation, or obtain evidence to be used in it.[44] Where documents have a dual purpose, the test is whether the dominant purpose of the document was for legal advice in contemplation of litigation. Thus, an accident report will not be privileged unless the sole or dominant purpose for which it was prepared was for submission to a legal adviser for advice in the light of anticipated or existing proceedings.[45] Accident reports are often prepared as a matter of course in order to find out the cause of the accident and avoid future occurrences. In this situation it will be difficult for the report to satisfy the dominant purpose test. The court will look to the substance of the matter. Defendants will be unable to claim privilege by dressing up reports to appear as though the dominant or sole purpose was the collection of evidence in contemplation of litigation, if in reality the report had a dual purpose.[46]

10–147   The dominant purpose of a document is not necessarily to be determined by the intention of the person who created the document, and so privilege could attach to a letter written by a party to his insurers to inform them about circumstances giving rise to a claim on an indemnity policy which subsequently led to litigation, even though it was the insurers, rather than the party, who wanted the document for the purpose of obtaining legal advice.[47] It is not necessary for a decision to have been made to instruct solicitors before it can be said that proceedings are contemplated. The test is that if litigation is reasonably in prospect, documents brought into existence for the purpose of enabling solicitors to advise whether a claim should be made or

---

[44] *Anderson v Bank of British Columbia* (1876) 2 Ch D 644. In wardship proceedings the court has power, in an appropriate case, to override the legal professional privilege attaching to documents, where it is necessary to achieve the best interests of the child: *Re A. (minors: disclosure of material)* (1991) 7 B.M.L.R. 129; *Re D. and M. (minors)* (1993) 18 B.M.L.R. 71, CA. In *Re L (Police Investigation: Privilege)* [1997] A.C. 16 the House of Lords held that though communications between solicitor and client were absolutely privileged, communications between a solicitor and a third party in contemplation of litigation were not absolute, at least in the context of non-adversarial proceedings brought under the Children Act 1989, where the child's welfare was the paramount consideration.

[45] *Waugh v British Railways Board* [1980] A.C. 521. The time for determining the purpose of a document is when it was brought into being. Thus, the mere fact that litigation was reasonably in prospect and that the documents are subsequently used to obtain legal advice does not necessarily mean that the documents will be privileged where, at the time they were brought into being, there was another dominant purpose: *Alfred Crompton Amusement Machines Ltd v Commissioners of Customs and Excise (No. 2)* [1974] A.C. 405.

[46] *Lask v Gloucester Health Authority* (1985) 2 P.N. 96, 100; [1991] 2 Med. L.R. 379, 383, *per* O'Connor L.J.: "Once the second purpose is shown to be a purpose of the document, it seems to me that it is impossible to say that the judge was wrong to say that it was an equal purpose because by itself I would have thought that the prevention of similar accidents must be, in a hospital of all places, at least of equal importance as the provision of material for the solicitor." The prevention of future accidents was expressly stated to be a purpose of hospital accident reports in the NHS Circular HM (55)66; *cf. McAvan v London Transport Executive* (1983) 133 N.L.J. 1101.

[47] *Guiness Peat Properties v Fitzroy Robinson Partnership* [1987] 1 W.L.R. 1027.

resisted are privileged, provided that this was their dominant purpose when they were created.[48]

The privilege is the client's not the solicitor's,[49] and can be waived by the client. A client can expressly waive his legal professional privilege by electing to disclose communications which the privilege would entitle him not to disclose, though where the disclosure is partial, an issue as to the scope of the waiver may arise. There is no rule that a party who waives privilege in relation to one communication is taken to waive privilege in relation to all communications, but he may not waive privilege in such a partial and selective manner that unfairness or misunderstanding may result.[50] When a former client sues a solicitor the claimant impliedly waives any right to legal professional privilege in relation to any communication between them so far as necessary for the just determination of his claim. But the implied waiver does not apply to communications to which the solicitor was not privy, and the solicitors are not entitled to disclosure of communications between their former client and their new solicitors, instructed for the purpose of continuing the transaction that the defendant solicitors had originally been instructed to deal with.[51]

10–148

Where there has been inadvertent disclosure and inspection of a privileged document the question of whether the party making the inadvertent disclosure has waived privilege depends upon whether the recipient realised that he had been permitted to see the privileged document only by reason of an obvious mistake. Where it would have been evident to a reasonable person with the qualities of the recipient that there had been a mistake, the court may restrain by injunction the recipient from using the document in the proceedings, even though the mistake was not in fact evident to the recipient.[52] The onus is on the party seeking the injunction to satisfy the court that the mistake was obvious and that the recipient ought to have realised this. But in any event, a party who has inspected a privileged document which has been inadvertently passed to him may only use it or its contents with the permission of the court.[53]

10–149

In *Clough v Tameside & Glossop Health Authority*[54] Bracewell J. held that where a report or statement which would otherwise be privileged is referred to in an expert witness report produced on behalf of a party and

10–150

---

[48] *ibid.* Internal documents supplied by employees of a bank were not covered by legal professional privilege, notwithstanding the fact that the documents were used as raw material by a committee created to obtain legal advice regarding the inquiry into the collapse of BCCI: *Three Rivers D.C. v Bank of England (Disclosure) (No. 3)* [2003] EWCA Civ 474; [2003] 3 W.L.R. 667.

[49] *Goddard v Nationwide Building Society* [1987] Q.B. 670.

[50] *Paragon Finance plc v Freshfields (a firm)* [1999] 1 W.L.R. 1183, CA.

[51] *ibid.*

[52] See *Pizzey v Ford Motor Company Ltd* [1994] P.I.Q.R. P15, CA; *Goddard v Nationwide Building Society* [1987] Q.B. 670, CA; *Guiness Peat Properties v Fitzroy Robinson Partnership* [1987] 1 W.L.R. 1027, CA; *Derby & Co Ltd v Weldon (No. 8)* [1991] 1 W.L.R. 73, CA.

[53] CPR r. 31.20.

[54] [1998] 1 W.L.R. 1478.

844   PROCEDURE

disclosed to the other party, with the intention of relying on that expert report, service of the report waived privilege in respect of the statement or document. The duties of an expert witness included the duty to state the facts or assumptions upon which the opinion was based. An essential element in the process was for a party to know and to be able to test in evidence the information supplied to experts in order to ascertain whether the opinion is based on a sound factual basis or on disputed matters or hypothetical facts yet to be determined by the court. Thus, the court would exercise its discretion to order production of the document.[55] However, in *R. v Davies*[56] the Court of Appeal doubted whether passing reference in an expert's report to another document would necessarily amount to a waiver of privilege in that document by the client. The Civil Procedure Rules now provide that an expert's report must state the substance of all material instructions, whether written or oral, on the basis of which the report was written;[57] and that the instructions are not privileged from disclosure, but the court will not order disclosure of any specific document or permit any questioning in court, other than by the party who instructed the expert, unless it is satisfied that there are reasonable grounds to consider the statement of instructions to be inaccurate or incomplete.[58] Moreover, an expert instructed within the terms of CPR Part 35 owes an overriding duty to the court,[59] so it could be argued that the expert may have to disclose otherwise privileged information.[60] On the other hand, privilege protects the client's interests and if it exists must be protected unless the client waives the privilege. Thus, it is arguable that it cannot be part of a witness's duty to the court to override the client's privilege without the client's consent. Moreover, given that privilege is a matter of substantive law, indeed a fundamental right, it is difficult to see how rules of procedure can abrogate the client's privilege.[61]

10–151   For example, in *Carlson v Townsend*,[62] in accordance with the Personal Injuries Pre-Action Protocol, the claimant supplied a list of three potential experts to the defendant, who objected to one of the names on the list. The claimant instructed one of the other two experts to provide a report, but did

---

[55] This was a decision under the old RSC Ord. 24, r.10(1).
[56] [2002] EWCA Crim 85.
[57] CPR r. 35.10(3).
[58] CPR r. 35.10(4).
[59] CPR r. 35.3. For the purpose of the CPR an "expert witness" is an expert who has been instructed to give or prepare evidence for the purpose of court proceedings: CPR r. 35.2.
[60] See the very helpful discussion of this issue in Chippindall [2003] J.P.I.L. 61. Chippindall points out that para. (4) of the *Code of Guidance on Expert Evidence*, which is now part of the Practice Direction to CPR Part 35, states that: "Although the point has yet to be definitively decided, the power to order disclosure may in certain circumstances extend to the instructions or advice that were privileged when they were given." One implication of this is that privilege may not apply to an expert's report provided in an advisory capacity (*i.e.* an expert's report not falling within the definition in CPR r. 35.2 [see n. 59, above]), where the expert subsequently provides a report to which Part 35 applies. However, this argument would involve accepting that the CPR can change the substantive law of privilege.
[61] See *General Mediterranean Holdings SA v Patel* [2000] 1 W.L.R. 272 and *Linstead v East Sussex, Brighton and Hove Health Authority* [2001] P.I.Q.R. P356, above, para. 10–145.
[62] [2001] EWCA Civ 511; [2001] 1 W.L.R. 2415.

not disclose that report. The claimant then instructed another expert who was not on the agreed list and appended a copy of that report to the particulars of claim. The defendant claimed that the originally selected expert was jointly instructed and therefore he was entitled to see a copy of that report. The Court of Appeal held that there had been joint selection of the expert, but not joint instruction. The claimant had not waived privilege in the first report by agreeing to joint selection in accordance with the Protocol, and therefore was entitled to refuse to disclose the report. Nor did the failure to disclose the report constitute non-compliance with the Pre-Action Protocol, because disclosure was voluntary under the Protocol. On the other hand, the instruction of the second expert without giving the defendant the opportunity to object did amount to non-compliance. The claimant would have to obtain the court's permission to call the second expert to give evidence and the defendant would be permitted to call her own expert witness (which would not have been the case had the first expert been jointly instructed).[63]

Since privilege is the client's, it cannot normally be relied upon by a third party. In *Lee v South West Thames Regional Health Authority*,[64] however, the Court of Appeal held that a memorandum prepared by a third party at the request of a potential defendant for the purpose of enabling the potential defendant to obtain legal advice was privileged, and the third party would not be required to disclose the memorandum to the claimant on an application for pre-action disclosure under section 33(2) of the Supreme Court Act 1981, even though the third party was not at the time that the memorandum was prepared a potential defendant and was in effect sheltering under another potential defendant's privilege. The infant claimant was taken to hospital for treatment of burns. He developed respiratory problems and was put on a ventilator, and then he was transferred from a hospital under the responsibility of Hillingdon Area Health Authority to another hospital under North East Thames Area Health Authority. The transfer was carried out by the ambulance service provided by South West Thames Regional Health Authority. The claimant sustained brain damage, either in hospital or in transit. Hillingdon, for the purpose of obtaining legal advice, requested and obtained a report by the ambulance crew from South West Thames. Subsequently, South West Thames refused to allow the claimant to inspect the memorandum on the ground that it was privileged. It was held that a defendant should be free to seek evidence without being obliged to disclose the results of his researches to his opponent, and that since Hillingdon had not waived their claim to privilege, and it would

10–152

---

[63] See also In *Nicholson v Halton General Hospital NHS Trust* [1999] P.I.Q.R. P310 where the Court of Appeal held that a claimant was entitled to maintain the right of confidentiality between a treating doctor and patient, and it was for the claimant to waive that right. The court would not compel him to waive the right, but in an appropriate case it could order that the action be stayed until he consented to waive the right of confidentiality (to enable the defendant to have access to relevant information in the claimant's medical records). In *Kapadia v London Borough of Lambeth* (2000) 57 B.M.L.R. 170, the Court of Appeal held that a claimant who consents to a medical examination requested by the defendant also consents to the disclosure of the report resulting from that examination to the defendant. He cannot insist on seeing the report first or vetoing its disclosure.

[64] [1985] 2 All E.R. 385.

be impossible in the circumstances for matters to be arranged so that the document could be used against one defendant (South West Thames) and not the other (Hillingdon), inspection should not be ordered.[65]

(b) Public interest immunity

10–153   Documents do not have to be disclosed where disclosure would damage the public interest.[66] This immunity does not depend upon a party objecting to disclosure, but should and can be raised by the court if necessary. The proper approach where there is a question of public interest immunity is to weigh the two public interests, that of the nation or public service in non-disclosure and that of justice in the production of the documents. The court will consider the importance of the documents in the litigation, and whether their absence will result in a denial of justice to one or other of the parties.[67] In *Campell v Tameside Metropolitan Borough Council*[68] Ackner L.J. said that there is a heavy burden on the party seeking to justify non-disclosure of relevant documents. The confidential nature of the communication is not of itself a sufficient ground if disclosure would assist the court to ascertain facts relevant to the action:

> "The private promise of confidentiality must yield to the general public interest, that in the administration of justice truth will out, unless by reason of the character of the information or the relationship of the recipient of the information to the informant a more important public interest is served by protecting the information or identity of the informant from disclosure in a court of law."[69]

The Court of Appeal held that confidential psychiatric reports held by an education authority on a pupil were not protected by public interest immu-

---

[65] Sir John Donaldson M.R. said that the Court had reached this conclusion "with undisguised reluctance, because we think that there is something seriously wrong with the law if Marlon's mother cannot find out what exactly caused this brain damage": *ibid*. at 389. This prompted his Lordship's comments about a doctor's common law duty to inform patients when something has gone wrong with the treatment: see paras 10–135 to 10–136.

[66] Supreme Court Act 1981, s.35(1); *Conway v Rimmer* [1968] A.C. 910; *Burmah Oil Co Ltd v Bank of England* [1980] A.C. 1090; *D. v NSPCC* [1978] A.C. 171; *Air Canada v Secretary of State for Trade (No. 2)* [1983] 2 A.C. 394. CPR r. 31.19(1) provides that a person may apply without notice for an order permitting him to withhold disclosure of a document on the ground that disclosure would damage the public interest. CPR r. 31.19(8) provides that Part 31 of the CPR does not affect any rule of law permitting a document to be withheld from disclosure or inspection on the ground that disclosure or inspection would damage the public interest.

[67] Though the strength of the claimant's case is not a relevant consideration: *D. v NSPCC* [1978] A.C. 171, 216, *per* Lord Diplock; *Sharpe Estate v Northwestern General Hospital* (1991) 76 D.L.R. (4th) 535, 540 (Ont. Ct. Gen Div.).

[68] [1982] Q.B. 1065.

[69] *ibid*. at 1075, citing Lord Diplock in *D. v NSPCC* [1978] A.C. 171, 218. It may be that in an appropriate case it would be possible for the court to order production of only part of a document which was otherwise subject to the immunity: *Goodwill v The Chief Constable of Lancashire Constabulary* [1993] P.I.Q.R. P187, 193, *per* Evans L.J.

nity in an action for negligence against the authority brought by a teacher who had been assaulted by the boy. Lord Denning M.R. commented that he could see no "difference between this case and the ordinary case against a hospital authority for negligence. The reports of nurses and doctors are, of course, confidential; but they must always be disclosed . . ."[70] Once the court has engaged in the balancing exercise by weighing the public interest in preserving the immunity against the public interest that all relevant information which might assist a court to adjudicate should be before the court and concluded that public interest immunity applies, there is no further discretion. The material to which the immunity applies must be excluded from the case.[71]

Public interest immunity will rarely be relevant to medical negligence litigation. The issue was raised in *Re HIV Haemophiliac Litigation*[72] in which haemophiliacs and their families who had been infected with HIV as a result of treatment with contaminated blood products imported from the United States were suing, *inter alia*, the Department of Health, the licensing authority under the Medicines Act 1968, and the national Blood Products Laboratory. The Department of Health claimed public interest immunity in respect of certain documents on the basis that they related to the formulation of policy by ministers or were briefings for ministers about whether a policy of self-sufficiency in blood products should be established, the resources necessary for such a policy, and the role and organisation of the Blood Products Laboratory and the National Blood Transfusion Service. The claimants conceded that public interest immunity arose, but argued that the public interest in the fair trial of the proceedings outweighed the public interest in preserving the immunity. The Court of Appeal accepted the claimants' argument that it was very likely that the documents contained material which would give substantial support to their contentions in the action and that without them the claimants might be deprived of the means of proper presentation of their case.[73]

10–154

In *Australian Red Cross Society v B.C.*[74] the Supreme Court of Victoria ordered the defendants to disclose the identity of a blood donor to the claimant on the basis that the public interest in the administration of justice outweighed the public interest in preserving the privacy and confidentiality of blood donors. Although not treated as a ground for the decision the court noted that legislation in Victoria made it an offence for a blood donor to make a false statement when supplying information to the defendants in the prescribed form, and this represented a deliberate public policy that information given to the Red Cross by donors would not necessarily be kept in confidence, since it could be the subject of criminal

10–155

---

[70] *ibid.* at 1074.
[71] *Powell v Chief Constable of North Wales Constabulary, The Times*, February 11, 2000, CA.
[72] [1996] P.I.Q.R. P220.
[73] Applying the test of Lord Fraser in *Air Canada v Secretary of State for Trade (No. 2)* [1983] 2 A.C. 394.
[74] [1992] 3 Med. L.R. 273 (S.C. of Vict., App. Div.).

prosecution.[75] In *Sharpe Estate v Northwestern General Hospital*[76] the claimant, a haemophiliac, was seeking access to Canadian Red Cross records in an attempt to identify whether any of the donors from whom he had received blood was HIV positive at the time of the donation. Without this evidence his action against the Red Cross Society was bound to fail on causation. There were about 1,250 donors from whom the blood and blood products came. Again the argument was that without confidentiality the supply of donated blood would be reduced. There was no evidence that donors demanded or expected confidentiality of their records, though it was the perception of the Red Cross that this was the case. It was held that the interests of the claimant should take precedence. Given that, following the introduction of HIV testing of blood donors, cases such as the claimant's were now unlikely to occur, the small possibility of the undesirable effects of disclosure on the donors was "insignificant when measured against the overwhelming need of society to have all legitimate tools available in the search for truth in the trial process."[77]

10–156   In *A.B. v Glasgow and West of Scotland Blood Transfusion Service*,[78] on the other hand, it was held that a material risk of a national deficiency in the supply of blood for transfusion was sufficient public interest to override petitioner's claim to know the identity of a blood donor for the purpose of bringing an action in negligence against the donor. The existence of such a material risk was assumed, however, on the basis that the claim to public interest immunity was made by a Minister of the Crown. Lord Morison indicated that the position would have been different in the absence of a ministerial objection to disclosure, in that the court would assess the merits of the defendants' objection on the available evidence, in order to determine whether the petitioner's interest should prevail over the objection.[79]

---

[75] This point was central to the decision of the New South Wales Court of Appeal in *P.D. v Australian Red Cross Society (New South Wales Division)* (1993) 30 N.S.W.L.R. 376. The defendants had undertaken a survey which purported to show that a substantial number of donors would not donate blood again if they knew that their name and information about them could be made available to a person who developed an infection after a transfusion of the donor's blood. The court acknowledged that any significant diminution in the level of blood donations would be a serious matter. The process of balancing the public interest in the proper administration of justice, and non-disclosure in the public interest of preserving an adequate blood supply did not have to take place, however, because since 1985 the Red Cross had been under a statutory obligation to obtain a certificate from donors relating to their medical suitability before accepting a donation. A person who signed a certificate containing a statement which, to that person's knowledge, was false or misleading was to have committed a criminal offence. The certificates could not be withheld from the police or from the legal advisers of intending claimants or the courts. Legislation also authorised the courts to order the Red Cross to disclose information enabling a blood donor who had given HIV contaminated blood to be identified and traced. In these circumstances the blanket public interest immunity claimed by the Red Cross could not be supported.

[76] (1991) 76 D.L.R. (4th) 535 (Ont. Ct. Gen Div.), affirming (1990) 74 D.L.R. (4th) 43.

[77] *ibid*. at 540, *per* Haley J.

[78] (1989), 1993 S.L.T. 36; 15 B.M.L.R. 91 (Court of Session, Outer House).

[79] See further Grubb and Pearl (1991) 141 N.L.J. 897 and 938. Public interest immunity might also be raised with respect to the disclosure of raw data in research projects, on the ground that patients and doctors might be unwilling to participate in research if they thought that confidential information would have to be disclosed in the course of litigation. On the other

Moreover, his Lordship suggested that the risk to the blood supply was perhaps a little overstated, commenting that:

> "It is not immediately apparent to me why [donors acting from altruistic motives] would be deterred from pursuing these motives by an apprehension that they might be unjustifiably sued. If on the other hand there are any persons who give blood without due regard to their responsibilities, the public interest would plainly be served if they were discouraged from doing so."

5. THE ROLE OF EXPERTS

The duties and responsibilities of expert witnesses were summarised with particular clarity by Cresswell J. in *National Justice Compania Naviera SA v Prudential Assurance Company Ltd, "The Ikarian Reefer"*.[80] Those principles have been expanded upon in the CPR Part 35, and in particular the Practice Direction that supplements CPR Part 35 and more recently the *Code of Guidance on Expert Evidence*.[81] In the context of medical negligence litigation expert evidence on both liability and causation will normally be crucial to the outcome of the case. Cases can be won or lost on the quality of the expert evidence.   10–157

CPR Part 35 was regarded as a significant plank in the Woolf reforms, and lays down detailed rules for managing the use of expert witnesses, in an attempt to reduce cost and delay in litigation. Expert evidence should be restricted to that which is reasonably required to resolve the proceedings.[82] Experts have an overriding duty to the court. The expert's duty is to help the court on matters within his expertise,[83] and this duty overrides any obligation to the person who instructed him or by whom he is paid.[84] Expert evidence should generally be given in the form of a written report.[85] An expert's report must state the substance of all material instructions, whether written or oral, on the basis of which the report was written.[86] The instructions are not privileged from disclosure, but the court will not order disclosure of any specific document or permit any questioning in court, other than by the party   10–158

(n.79 contd.) hand, confidentiality could be protected by maintaining anonymity of the research subjects, if possible.

[80] [1993] 2 Lloyd's Rep. 68, 81–82, QBD; affirmed [1995] 1 Lloyd's Rep. 496. See para. 3–156.

[81] See the "White Book", *Civil Procedure*, Volume 1, 2003, Sweet & Maxwell, 35PD and 35.16. The Code of Guidance is also extracted at (2002) 8 Clinical Risk 60.

[82] CPR r. 35.1.

[83] CPR r. 35.3(1).

[84] CPR r. 35.3(2). Where a party's expert witness completely disregards the CPR and orders of the court, he may be barred from giving evidence on behalf of that party, even though this may result in the party losing his case: *Stevens v Gullis* [2000] 1 All E.R. 527, CA.

[85] CPR r. 35.5(1).

[86] CPR r. 35.10(3).

who instructed the expert, unless it is satisfied that there are reasonable grounds to consider the statement of instructions to be inaccurate or incomplete.[87]

10–159   A party may put written questions about an expert's report to an expert instructed by another party or a single joint expert appointed under CPR r. 35.7,[88] but written questions may only be put once, within 28 days of service of the expert's report and for the purpose of clarification only, unless the court gives permission or the other party agrees.[89] Answers to these questions are then treated as part of the expert's report. If the expert does not answer a written question the court may order that the party who instructed the expert may not rely on the evidence of that expert and/or that the party may not recover the fees and expenses of that expert from any other party.[90]

Single joint experts

10–160   The court has the power to direct that evidence be given by a single joint expert.[91] If the parties cannot agree who should act as the expert the court may select from a list prepared or identified by the instructing parties or direct that the expert be selected in such other manner as the court may direct.[92] This creates the possibility that one of the parties may not be happy with a report of the single joint expert. In *Daniels v Walker*[93] the defendant was unhappy with the report obtained from a jointly instructed expert. He wanted to obtain his own expert's report, and permission for that expert to interview the claimant. The Court of Appeal held that where the parties agree a joint expert, the fact of agreement does not preclude a party from obtaining a report from a different expert, or if appropriate from relying on the evidence of another expert. The joint instruction of an expert was the first step, but if having obtained the joint expert's report a party, for reasons which were not fanciful, wanted to obtain further information before deciding whether to challenge part or the whole of the joint report, they should normally be allowed to obtain that evidence. But if the claim for damages was modest, the court might refuse the instruction of a second expert and merely permit the dissatisfied party to put questions to the expert who had already prepared the report, to ensure proportionality in the conduct of the litigation.

10–161   In *Peet v Mid-Kent Healthcare NHS Trust*[94] the claimant's parents wanted to have a conference with jointly instructed experts in the absence of any representative of the defendants, who objected. The Court of Appeal held that

---

[87] CPR r. 35.10(4).
[88] CPR r. 35.6(1).
[89] CPR r. 35.6(2). For discussion of the meaning of "clarification" see *Mutch v Allen* [2001] EWCA Civ 76 [2001] P.I.Q.R. P26.
[90] CPR r. 35.6(4).
[91] CPR r. 35.7(1).
[92] CPR r. 35.7(3).
[93] [2000] 1 W.L.R. 1382.
[94] [2001] EWCA Civ 1703; [2002] 1 W.L.R. 210.

to have an experts' conference, including lawyers, without a representative of the defendants was inconsistent with the concept of a single joint expert. There was nothing wrong, subject to both sides being present, with having a discussion with joint experts in order for the lawyers to understand and test the views of each individual expert, but the idea that one side should be able to test the views of an expert in the absence of the other party was not permissible. Thus, a party cannot have unilateral access to a joint expert without the consent of the other jointly instructing party.

In practice it will be very rare to have a single joint expert dealing with   **10–162** liability or causation in medical negligence cases. Given the nature of the *Bolam* test and the differences of professional opinion that often arise on causation, a single expert would effectively be determining the outcome of the case. Thus, in *Oxley v Penwarden*[95] the Court of Appeal took the view that in clinical negligence claims the parties should have an opportunity of investigating causation through an expert of their own choice:

> "It is inevitable in a case of this class that parties will find the greatest difficulty in agreeing on the appointment of a single expert. That burden would then be cast upon the court and would, in turn, lead to the judge selecting an expert, if there be more than one school of thought on this issue, from one particular school of thought and that would effectively decide an essential question in the case without opportunity for challenge."[96]

Again, in *Simms v Birmingham Health Authority*[97] the Court of Appeal confirmed that the parties in a complex clinical negligence claim should be able to plead their own case on breach of duty and causation fully, with the assistance of their own expert evidence.

On the other hand, a single joint expert is now expected on issues of   **10–163** quantum. In *Peet v Mid-Kent Healthcare NHS Trust* Lord Woolf indicated that:

> "The starting point is: unless there is reason for not having a single expert, there should be only a single expert. If there is no reason which justifies more evidence than that from a single expert on any particular topic, then again in the normal way the report prepared by the single expert should be the evidence in the case on the issues covered by that expert's report. In the normal way, therefore, there should be no need for that report to be amplified or tested by cross-examination. If it needs amplification, or if it should be subject to cross-examination, the court has a discretion to allow that to happen. The court may permit that to happen either prior to the hearing or at the hearing. But the assumption should be that the single joint expert's report is the evidence. Any

---

[95] [2001] Lloyd's Rep. Med. 347, CA.
[96] *ibid.* at [8] *per* Mantell L.J.
[97] [2001] Lloyd's Rep. Med. 382.

amplification or any cross-examination should be restricted as far as possible. Equally, where parties agree that there should be a single joint expert, and a single joint expert produces a report, it is possible for the court still to permit a party to instruct his or her own expert and for that expert to be called at the hearing. However, there must be good reason for that course to be adopted. Normally, where the issue is of the sort that is covered by non-medical evidence, as in this case, the court should be slow to allow a second expert to be instructed."[98]

Meetings of Experts

10–164   The court may, at any stage, direct a discussion between experts for the purpose of requiring the experts to: (a) identify and discuss the expert issues in the proceedings; and (b) where possible, reach an agreed opinion on those issues.[99] This is now standard practice in medical negligence cases. The court may also direct that following a discussion between experts they must prepare a statement for the court showing: (a) those issues on which they agree; and (b) those issues on which they disagree and a summary of their reasons for disagreeing.[1] In *H, H and R v Lambeth, Southwark & Lewisham Health Authority, West Kent Health Authority and Bexley & Greenwich Health Authority*[2] the claimant objected to an order that the expert witnesses of both sides meet, because it was said that without lawyers present at the meeting, her expert might waver under pressure from experts for the defence (given that it was a small area of medical specialisation, where everybody knew everybody else, and the defendant was a particularly eminent practitioner). This, said the claimant, would be unfair. The Court of Appeal held that a meeting to narrow the medical issues before trial was valuable in meeting the overriding objective of the Civil Procedure Rules, by permitting active case management.[3] CPR r. 1.4 required the court to further the overriding objective by actively managing cases. This included identifying issues at an early stage and encouraging the parties to co-operate with one another. The power in CPR r. 35.12 to order a meeting of experts was designed to further this objective. Even if both parties objected the court could make such an order. The general approach should be that a meeting should usually occur where there has been an exchange of experts reports. Some very good reason for not having a meeting would have to be shown.[4] CPR r. 35.12(4) provides that the content of such discussions would not be referred to at trial, unless by agreement between the parties, and where the experts reach

---

[98] [2001] EWCA Civ 1703; [2002] 1 W.L.R. 210 at [28].
[99] CPR r. 35.12(1).
[1] CPR r. 35.12(3).
[2] [2001] EWCA Civ 1455; [2002] P.I.Q.R. P152.
[3] See CPR r. 1.4(2), which sets out the objectives of case management, including, amongst others, identifying the issues at an early stage, deciding promptly which issues need full investigation at trial and disposing summarily of the others, and helping the parties to settle the whole or part of the case.
[4] [2001] EWCA Civ 1455; [2002] P.I.Q.R. P152 at [17] and [18] *per* Tuckey L.J.

agreement on an issue it is not binding, unless the parties agree. This gave the claimant some protection. The Court of Appeal also refused an order permitting the parties' lawyers to be present at the meeting.[5] The lawyers could draw up the agenda. The meeting could be recorded so that if anything improper occurred, or there was any misunderstanding of the legal issues, it would be apparent.

Although the content of the discussion between the experts cannot be referred to at trial unless the parties agree,[6] there is nothing to prevent cross-examination of an expert at trial on an issue discussed at the experts' meeting. So if the expert conceded a point in discussion, he is likely to concede it again in the witness box. Any agreement between the experts at the discussion does not bind the parties unless the parties expressly agree to be bound by the agreement,[7] although this rule does not affect the admissibility of the experts' joint statement.

10–165

---

[5] See the view expressed in the *Code of Guidance on Expert Evidence*, para. 27: "Lawyers will not normally be present at such discussions. If lawyers do attend they should not normally intervene save to answer questions put to them by the experts or to advise them on the law."

[6] CPR r. 35.12(4).

[7] CPR r. 35.12(5).

NHS INDEMNITY

ARRANGEMENTS FOR CLINICAL NEGLIGENCE CLAIMS IN THE NHS

Executive summary

Introduction

This is a summary of the main points contained within *NHS Indemnity Arrangements for clinical negligence claims in the NHS,* issued under cover of HSG 96/48. The booklet includes a Q&A section covering the applicability of NHS indemnity to common situations and an annex on sponsored trials. It covers NHS indemnity for clinical negligence but not for any other liability such as product liability, employers liability or liability for NHS trust board members.

Clinical Negligence

Clinical negligence is defined as "a breach of duty of care by members of the health care professions employed by NHS bodies or by others consequent on decisions or judgements made by members of those professions acting in their professional capacity in the course of their employment, and which are admitted as negligent by the employer or are determined as such through the legal process".

The term health care professional includes hospital doctors, dentists, nurses, midwives, health visitors, pharmacy practitioners, registered ophthalmic or dispensing opticians (working in a hospital setting), members of professions allied to medicine and dentistry, ambulance personnel, laboratory staff and relevant technicians.

Main Principles

NHS bodies are vicariously liable for the negligent acts and omissions of their employees and should have arrangements for meeting this liability.

NHS Indemnity applies where

   (a) the negligent health care professional was:

      (i) working under a contract of employment and the negligence occurred in the course of that employment;

      (ii) not working under a contract of employment but was contracted to an NHS body to provide services to persons to whom that NHS body owed a duty of care.

      (iii) neither of the above but otherwise owed a duty of care to the persons injured.

   (b) persons, not employed under a contract of employment and who may or may not be a health care professional, who owe a duty of care to the persons injured. These include locums; medical academic staff with honorary contracts; students; those conducting clinical trials; charitable volunteers; persons undergoing further professional education, training and examinations; students and staff working on income generation projects.

Where these principles apply, NHS bodies should accept full financial liability where negligent harm has occurred, and not seek to recover their costs from the health care professional involved.

Who is Not Covered

NHS Indemnity does not apply to family health service practitioners working under contracts for services, eg GPs (including fundholders), general dental practitioners, family dentists, pharmacists or optometrists; other self employed health care professionals eg independent midwives; employees of FHS practices; employees of private hospitals; local education authorities; voluntary agencies. Exceptions to the normal cover arrangements are set out in the main document.

Circumstances Covered

NHS Indemnity covers negligent harm caused to patients or healthy volunteers in the following circumstances: whenever they are receiving an established treatment, whether or not in accordance with an agreed guideline or protocol; whenever they are receiving a novel or unusual treatment which, in the judgement of the health care professional, is appropriate for that particular patient; whenever they are subjects as patients or healthy volunteers of clinical research aimed at benefitting patients now or in the future.

Expenses Met

Where negligence is alleged, NHS bodies are responsible for meeting: the legal and administrative costs of defending the claim or, if appropriate, of reaching a settlement; the plaintiff's costs, as agreed by the two parties or as awarded by the court; the damages awarded either as a one-off payment or as a structured settlement.

NHS Indemnity

Clinical Negligence—Definition

1.   Clinical negligence is defined as:

> "A breach of duty of care by members of the health care professions employed by NHS bodies or by others consequent on decisions or judgements made by members of those professions acting in their professional capacity in the course of employment, and which are admitted as negligent by the employer or are determined as such through the legal process." *

2.   In this definition "breach of duty of care" has its legal meaning. NHS bodies will need to take legal advice in individual cases, but the general position will be that the following must all apply before liability for negligence exists:

2.1   There must have been a duty of care owed to the person treated by the relevant professional(s);

2.2   The standard of care appropriate to such duty must not have been attained and therefore the duty breached, whether by action or inaction, advice given or failure to advise;

2.3   Such a breach must be demonstrated to have caused the injury and therefore the resulting loss complained about by the patient;

2.4   Any loss sustained as a result of the injury and complained about by the person treated must be of a kind that the courts recognize and for which they allow compensation; and

2.5   The injury and resulting loss complained about by the person treated must have been reasonably foreseeable as a possible consequence of the breach.

3   This booklet is concerned with NHS indemnity for clinical negligence and does not cover indemnity for any other liability such as product liability, employers liability or liability for NHS trust board members.

---

* The NHS (Clinical Negligence Scheme) Regulations 1996, which established the Clinical Negligence Scheme for Trusts,' defines clinical negligence in terms of '. . . a liability in tort owed by a member to a third party in respect of or consequent upon personal injury or loss arising out of or in connection with any breach of a duty of care owed by that body to any person in connection with the diagnosis of any illness, or the care or treatment of any patient, in consequence of any act or omission to act on the part of a person employed or engaged by a member in connection with any relevant function of that member'.

Other Terms

4.   Throughout this guidance:

4.1   The terms "an NHS body" and "NHS bodies" include Health Authorities, Special Health Authorities and NHS Trusts but excludes all GP practices whether fundholding or not, general dental practices, pharmacies and opticians' practices

4.2   The term "health care professional" includes:

Doctors, dentists, nurses, midwives, health visitors, hospital pharmacy practitioners, registered ophthalmic or registered dispensing opticians working in a hospital setting, members of professions supplementary to medicine and dentistry, ambulance personnel, laboratory staff and relevant technicians.

Principles

5.   NHS bodies are legally liable for the negligent acts and omissions of their employees (the principle of vicarious liability), and should have arrangements for meeting this liability. NHS Indemnity applies where:

5.1   the negligent health care professional was working under a contract of employment (as opposed to a contract for services) and the negligence occurred in the course of that employment; or

5.2   the negligent health care professional, although not working under a contract of employment, was contracted to an NHS body to provide services to persons to whom that NHS body owed a duty of care.

6.   Where the principles outlined in paragraph 5 apply, NHS bodies should accept full financial liability where negligent harm has occurred. They should not seek to recover their costs either in part or in full from the health care professional concerned or from any indemnities they may have. NHS bodies may carry this risk entirely or spread it through membership of the Clinical Negligence Scheme for Trusts (CNST—see EL(95)40).

Who is Covered

7.   NHS Indemnity covers the actions of staff in the course of their NHS employment. It also covers people in certain other categories whenever the NHS body owes a duty of care to the person harmed, including, for example, locums, medical academic staff

with honorary contracts, students, those conducting clinical trials, charitable volunteers and people undergoing further professional education, training and examinations. This includes staff working on income generation projects. GPs or dentists who are directly employed by Health Authorities, eg as Public Health doctors (including port medical officers and medical inspectors of immigrants at UK air/sea ports), are covered.

8.   Examples of the applicability of NHS Indemnity to common situations are set out in question and answer format in Annex A.

Who is not Covered

9.   NHS Indemnity does not apply to general medical and dental practitioners working under contracts for services. General practitioners, including GP fundholders, are responsible for making their own indemnity arrangements, as are other self-employed health care professionals such as independent midwives. Neither does NHS Indemnity apply to employees of general practices, whether fundholding or not, or to employees of private hospitals (even when treating NHS patients) local education authorities or voluntary agencies.

10.   Examples of circumstances in which independent practitioners or staff who normally work for private employers are covered by NHS Indemnity are given in Annex A. The NHS Executive advises independent practitioners to check their own indemnity position.

11.   Examples of circumstances in which NHS employees are not covered by NHS Indemnity are also given in Annex A.

Circumstances Covered

12.   NHS bodies owe a duty of care to healthy volunteers or patients treated or undergoing tests which they administer. NHS Indemnity covers negligent harm caused to these people in the following circumstances:

12.1 whenever they are receiving an established treatment, whether or not in accordance with an agreed guideline or protocol;

12.2 whenever they are receiving a novel or unusual treatment which in the clinical judgement of the health care professional is appropriate for the particular patient;

12.3 whenever they are subjects of clinical research aimed at benefiting patients now or in the future, whether as patients or as healthy volunteers. (Special arrangements, including the availability of no-fault indemnity apply where research is sponsored by pharmaceutical companies. See Annex B.)

Expenses Met

13. Where negligence is alleged NHS bodies are responsible for meeting:

    13.1 the legal and administrative costs of defending the claim and if appropriate, of reaching a settlement, including the cost of any mediation;

    13.2 where appropriate, plaintiff's costs, either as agreed between the parties or as awarded by a court of law;

    13.3 the damages agreed or awarded, whether as a one-off payment or a structured settlement.

Claims Management Principles

14. NHS bodies should take the essential decisions on the handling of claims of clinical negligence against their staff, using professional defence organizations or others as their agents and advisers as appropriate.

Financial Support Arrangements

15. Details of the Clinical Negligence Scheme for Trusts (CNST) were announced in EL(95)40 on 29 March 1995.

16. All financial arrangements in respect of clinical negligence costs for NHS bodies have been reviewed and guidance on transitional arrangements (for funding clinical accidents which happened before 1 April 1995), was issued on 27 November 1995 under cover of FDL(95)56. FDL(96)36 provided further guidance on a number of detailed questions.

ANNEX A

Questions and Answers on NHS Indemnity

Below are replies to some of the questions most commonly asked about NHS Indemnity.

1. Who is covered by NHS Indemnity?

NHS bodies are liable at law for the negligent acts and omissions of their staff in the course of their NHS employment: Under NHS Indemnity, NHS bodies take direct responsibility for costs and damages arising from clinical negligence where they (as employers) are vicariously liable for the acts and omissions of their health care professional staff.

2. Would health care professionals opting to work under contracts for services rather than as employees of the NHS be covered?

Where an NHS body is responsible for *providing* care to patients NHS Indemnity will apply whether the health care professional involved is an employee or not. For example a doctor working under a contract for services with an NHS Trust would be covered because the Trust has responsibility for the care of its patients. A consultant undertaking contracted NHS work in a private hospital would also be covered.

3. Does this include clinical academics and research workers?

NHS bodies are vicariously liable for the work done by university medical staff and other research workers (eg employees of the MRC) under their honorary contracts, but not for pre-clinical or other work in the university.

4. Are GP practices covered?

GPs, whether fundholders or not [and who are not employed by Health Authorities as public health doctors], are independent practitioners and therefore they and their employed staff are not covered by NHS indemnity.

5. Is a hospital doctor doing a GP locum covered?

This would not be the responsibility of the NHS body since it would be outside the contract of employment. The hospital doctor and the general practitioners concerned should ensure that there is appropriate professional liability cover.

6. Is a GP seeing a patient in hospital covered?

A GP providing medical care to patients in hospital under a contractual arrangement, eg where the GP was employed as a clinical assistant, will be covered by NHS Indemnity, as will a GP who provides services in NHS hospitals under staff fund contracts (known as "bed funds"). Where there is no such contractual arrangement, and the NHS body provides facilities for patient(s) who continue to be the clinical responsibility of the GP, the GP would be responsible and professional liability cover would be appropriate. However, junior medical staff, nurses or members of the professions supplementary to medicine involved in the care of a GP's patients in NHS hospitals under their contract of employment would be covered.

7. Are GP trainees working in general practice covered?

In general practice the responsibility for training and for paying the salary of a GP trainee rests with the trainer. While the trainee is receiving a salary in general practice it is advisable that both the trainee and the trainer, and indeed other members of the practice, should have appropriate professional liability cover as NHS indemnity will not apply.

8. Are NHS employees working under contracts with GP fundholders covered?

If their employing NHS body has agreed a contract to provide services to a GP fundholding practice's patients, NHS employees will be working under the terms of their contracts of employment and NHS Indemnity will cover them. If NHS employees themselves contract with GP fundholders (or any other independent body) to do work outside their NHS contract of employment they should ensure that they have separate indemnity cover.

9. Is academic General Practice covered?

The Department has no plans to extend NHS Indemnity to academic departments of general practice. In respect of general medical services, Health Authorities' payments of fees and allowances include an element for expenses, of which medical defence subscriptions are a part.

10. Is private work in NHS hospitals covered by NHS Indemnity?

NHS bodies will not be responsible for a health care professional's private practice, even in an NHS hospital. However, where junior medical staff, nurses or members of professions supplementary to medicine are involved in the care of private patients in NHS hospitals, they would normally be doing so as part of their NHS contract, and would therefore be covered. It remains advisable that health professionals who might be involved in work outside the scope of his or her NHS employment should have professional liability cover.

11. Is Category 2 work covered?

Category 2 work (eg reports for insurance companies) is by definition not undertaken for the employing NHS body and is therefore not covered by NHS Indemnity. Unless the work is carried out on behalf of the employing NHS body, professional liability cover would be needed.

12. Are disciplinary proceedings of statutory bodies covered?

NHS bodies are not financially responsible for the defence of staff involved in disciplinary proceedings conducted by statutory bodies such as the GMC (doctors), UKCC (nurses and midwives), GDC (dentists) CPSM (professions supplementary to medicine) and RPSGB (pharmacists). It is the responsibility of the practitioner concerned to take out professional liability cover against such an eventuality.

13. Are clinical trials covered?

In the case of negligent harm, health care professionals undertaking clinical trials or studies on volunteers, whether healthy or patients, in the course of their NHS employment are covered by NHS Indemnity. Similarly, for a trial not involving medicines, the NHS body would take financial responsibility unless the trial were covered by such other indemnity as may have been agreed between the NHS body and those responsible for the trial. In any case, NHS bodies should ensure that they are informed of clinical trials in which their staff are taking part in their NHS employment and that these trials have the required Research Ethics Committee approval. For non-negligent harm, see question 16 below.

14. Is harm resulting from a fault in the drug/equipment covered?

Where harm is caused due to a fault in the manufacture of a drug or piece of equipment then, under the terms of the Consumer Protection Act 1987, it is no defence for the producer to show that he exercised reasonable care. Under normal circumstances, therefore, NHS indemnity would not apply unless there was a question whether the health care professional either knew or should reasonably have known that the drug/equipment was faulty but continued to use it. Strict liability could apply if the drug/equipment had been manufactured by an NHS body itself, for example a prototype as part of a research programme.

15. Are Local Research Ethics Committees (LRECs) covered?

Under the Department's guidelines an LREC is appointed by the Health Authority to provide independent advice to NHS bodies within its area on the ethics of research proposals. The Health Authority should take financial responsibility for members' acts and omissions in the course of performance of their duties as LREC members.

16. Is there liability for non-negligent harm?

Apart from liability for defective products, legal liability does not arise where a person is harmed but no one has acted negligently. An example of this would be unexpected side-effects of drugs during clinical trials. In exceptional circumstances (and within the delegated limit of £50,000) NHS bodies may consider whether an ex-gratia payment could be offered. NHS bodies may not offer advance indemnities or take out commercial insurance for non-negligent harm.

17. What arrangements can non-NHS bodies make for non-negligent harm?

Arrangements will depend on the status of the non-NHS body. Arrangements for clinical trials sponsored by the pharmaceutical industry are set out in Annex B. Other independent sector sponsors of clinical research involving NHS patients (eg universities and medical research charities) may also make arrangements to indemnify research subjects for non-negligent harm. Public sector research funding bodies such as the Medical Research Council (MRC) may not offer advance indemnities nor take out commercial insurance for non-negligent harm. The MRC offers the assurance that it will give sympathetic consideration to claims in respect of non-negligent harm arising from an MRC funded trial. NHS bodies should not make ex-gratia payments for non-negligent harm where research is sponsored by a non-NHS body.

18. Would health care professionals be covered if they were working other than in accordance with the duties of their post?

Health care professionals would be covered by NHS Indemnity for actions in the course of NHS employment, and this should be interpreted liberally. For work not covered in this way health care professionals may have a civil, or even, in extreme circumstances, criminal liability for their actions.

19. Are health care professionals attending accident victims ("Good Samaritan" acts) covered?

"Good Samaritan" acts are not part of the health care professional's work for the employing body. Medical defence organizations are willing to provide low-cost cover against the (unusual) event of anyone performing such an act being sued for negligence. Ambulance services can, with the agreement of staff, include an additional term in the individual employee contracts to the effect that the member of staff is expected to provide assistance in any emergency outside of duty hours where it is appropriate to do so.

20. Are NHS staff in public health medicine or in community health services doing work for local authorities covered? Are occupational physicians covered?

Staff working in public health medicine, clinical medical officers or therapists carrying out local authority functions under their NHS contract would be acting in the course of their NHS employment. They will therefore be covered by NHS Indemnity. The same principle applies to occupational physicians employed by NHS bodies.

21. Are NHS staff working for other agencies, eg the Prison Service, covered?

In general, NHS bodies are not financially responsible for the acts of NHS staff when they are working on an individual contractual basis for other agencies. (Conversely, they are responsible where, for example, a Ministry of Defence doctor works in an NHS hospital.) Either the non-NHS body commissioning the work would be responsible, or the health care professional should have separate indemnity cover. However, NHS Indemnity should cover work for which the NHS body pays the health care professional a fee, such as domiciliary visits, and family planning services.

22. Are former NHS staff covered?

NHS Indemnity will cover staff who have subsequently left the Service (eg on retirement) provided the liability arose in respect of acts or omissions in the course of their NHS employment, regardless of when the claim was notified. NHS bodies may seek the co-operation of former staff in providing statements in the defence of a case.

23. Are NHS staff offering services to voluntary bodies such as the Red Cross or hospices covered?

The NHS body would be responsible for the actions of its staff only if it were contractually responsible for the clinical staffing of the voluntary body. If not, the staff concerned may wish to ensure that they have separate indemnity cover.

24. Do NHS bodies provide cover for locums?

NHS bodies take financial responsibility for the acts and omissions of a locum health care professional, whether "internal" or provided by an external agency, doing the work of a colleague who would be covered.

25. What are the arrangements for staff employed by one trust working in another.

This depends on the contractual arrangements. If the work is being done as part of a formal agreement between the trusts, then the staff involved will be acting within their normal NHS duties and, unless the agreement states otherwise, the employing trust will be liable. The NHS Executive does not recommend the use of ad hoc arrangements, eg a doctor, in one trust asking a doctor in another to provide an informal second opinion, unless there is an agreement between the trusts as to which of them will accept liability for the "visiting" doctor in such circumstances.

26. Are private sector rotations for hospital staff covered?

The medical staff of independent hospitals are responsible for their own professional liability cover, subject to the requirements of the hospital managers. If NHS staff in the training grades work in independent hospitals as part of their NHS training, they would be covered by NHS Indemnity, provided that such work was covered by an NHS contract of employment.

27. Are voluntary workers covered?

Where volunteers work in NHS bodies, they are covered by NHS Indemnity. NHS managers should be aware of all voluntary activity going on in their organizations and should wherever possible confirm volunteers' indemnity position in writing.

28. Are students covered?

NHS Indemnity applies where students are working under the supervision of NHS employees. This should be made clear in the agreement between the NHS body and the student's educational body. This will apply to students of all the health care professions and to school students on, for example, work experience placements. Students working in NHS premises, under supervision of medical academic staff employed by universities holding honorary contracts, are also covered. Students who spend time in a primary care setting will only be covered if this is part of an NHS contract. Potential students making preliminary visits and school placements should be adequately supervised and should not become involved in any clinical work. Therefore, no clinical negligence should arise on their part.

In the unlikely event of a school making a negligent choice of work placement for a pupil to work in the NHS, then the school, and not NHS indemnity, should pick up the legal responsibility for the actions of that pupil. The contractual arrangement between the NHS and the school should make this clear.

29. Are health care professionals undergoing on-the-job training covered?

Where an NHS body's staff are providing on-the-job training (eg refresher or skills updating courses) for health care professionals, the trainees are covered by NHS Indemnity whether they are normally employed by the NHS or not.

30. Are Independent midwives covered?

Independent midwives are self-employed practitioners. In common with all other health care professionals working outside the NHS, they are responsible for making their own indemnity arrangements.

31. Are overseas doctors who have come to the UK temporarily, perhaps to demonstrate a new technique, covered?

The NHS body which has invited the overseas doctor will owe a duty of care to the patients on whom the technique is demonstrated and so NHS indemnity will apply. NHS bodies, therefore, need to make sure that they are kept informed of any such demonstration visits which are proposed and of the nature of the technique to be demonstrated. Where visiting clinicians are not formally registered as students, or are not employees, an honorary contract should be arranged.

32. Are staff who are qualified in another member state of the European Union covered?

Staff qualified in another member state of the European Union, and who are undertaking an adaptation period in accordance with EEC directive 89/48EEC and the European Communities (Recognition of Professional Qualifications) Regulations 1991 which implements EEC Directive 89/48/EEC and EEC Directive 92/51/EEC, must be treated in a manner consistent with their qualified status in another member state, and should be covered.

ANNEX B

Indemnity for Clinical Studies Sponsored by Pharmaceutical companies

Section One

1. Clinical research involving the administration of drugs to patients or non-patient human volunteers is frequently undertaken under the auspices of Health Authorities or NHS Trusts.

2. When the study is sponsored by a pharmaceutical company, issues of liability and indemnity may arise in case of injury associated with administration of the drug or other aspects of the conduct of the trial.

3. When the study is not sponsored by a company but has been independently organised by clinicians, the NHS body will carry full legal liability for claims in negligence arising from harm to subjects in the study.

4. The guidance in Section 2 and the Appendix has three purposes:

    • to ensure that NHS bodies enter into appropriate agreements which will provide indemnity against claims and proceedings arising from company-sponsored clinical studies;

    • to ensure that NHS bodies, where appropriate, use a standard form of agreement (Appendix) which has been drawn up in consultation with the Association of the British Pharmaceutical Industry (ABPI);

    • to advise Local Research Ethics Committees (LRECs) of the standard form of agreement.

Section Two

1. A wide variety of clinical studies involving experimental or investigational use of drugs is carried out within NHS bodies. This includes studies in patients (clinical trials) and studies in healthy human volunteers. They may involve administration of a totally new (unlicensed) drug (active substance or 'NAS') or the administration of an established (licensed) drug by a novel route, for a new therapeutic indication, or in a novel formulation or combination.

2. Detailed guidance on the design, conduct, and ethical implications of clinical studies is given in:

    HSG(91)5: Local Research Ethics Committees (with accompanying booklet). NHS Executive: 1991;

    Guidelines for Medical Experiments in non-Patient Human Volunteers ABPI:1988, amended 1990;

    Research Involving Patients, Royal College of Physicians of London: 1990;

    Guidelines in the Practice of Ethics Committees in Medical Research, 2nd edition; Royal College of Physicians of London: 1990;

    Clinical Trial Compensation Guidelines ABPI: 1991

3. The Medicines Act 1968 provides the regulatory framework for clinical studies involving administration of drugs to patients. Drugs which are used in a sponsored* clinical study in patients will be the subject of either a product licence (PL), a clinical trial certificate (CTC), or clinical trial exemption (CTh) which is held by the company as appropriate. A non-sponsored study conducted independently by a practitioner must be notified to the Licensing Authority under the Doctors and Dentists Exemption (DDX) scheme. Studies in healthy volunteers are not subject to regulation under the Medicines Act and do not require a CTC, Cm, or DDX. Further particulars of these arrangements are provided in Medicines Act leaflet $M_1 11\ 30$: *A guide to the provisions affecting doctors and dentists (DHSS: 1985).*

4. Participants in a clinical study may suffer adverse effects due to the drug or clinical procedures. The appendix to this annex is a model form of agreement between the company sponsoring a study and the NHS body involved, which indemnifies the authority or trust against claims and proceedings arising from the study.

---

* A sponsored study may be defined as one carried out under arrangements made by or on behalf of the company who manufactured the product, the company responsible for its composition, or the company selling or supplying the product.

The model agreement has been drawn up in consultation with the Association of the British Pharmaceutical Industry (ABPI).

5. This form of indemnity will not normally apply to clinical studies which are not directly sponsored by the company providing the product for research, but have been independently organised by clinicians. In this case, the NHS body will normally carry full legal liability for any claims in negligence arising from harm to subjects in the study.

6. The NHS body will also carry full legal liability for any claims in negligence (or compensation under the indemnity will be abated) where there has been significant non-adherence to the agreed protocol or there has been negligence on the part of an NHS employee, for example, by failing to deal adequately with an adverse drug reaction.

7. The form of indemnity may not be readily accepted by sponsoring companies outside the UK or who are not members of the ABPI. NHS bodies should, as part of their risk management, consider the value of indemnities which are offered and consider whether companies should have alternative arrangements in place.

8. Several health authorities and trusts have independently developed forms of indemnity agreement. However, difficulties have arisen when different authorities have required varying terms of indemnity and this has, on occasion, impeded the progress of clinical research within the NHS. Particular difficulties may arise in large multi-centre trials involving many NHS bodies when it is clearly desirable to have standardised terms of indemnity to provide equal protection to all participants in the study.

9. Responsibility for deciding whether a particular company-sponsored research proposal should proceed within the NHS rests with the Health Authority or Trust within which the research would take place, after consideration of ethical, clinical, managerial, financial, resource, and legal liability issues. The NHS body is responsible for securing an appropriate indemnity agreement and should maintain a register of all clinical studies undertaken under its auspices with an indication whether it is a company-sponsored study and, if so, with confirmation that an indemnity agreement is in place. If for any reason it is considered that the model form of indemnity is not appropriate or that amendments are required, the NHS body involved should seek legal advice on the form or amendments proposed.

10. Even when the model form of indemnity is agreed, the NHS body should satisfy itself that the company sponsoring the study is substantial and reputable and has appropriate arrangements in place (for example insurance cover) to support the indemnity. The NHS

body will carry full liability for any claims in negligence if the indemnity is not honoured and there is not supporting insurance.

11. Where a clinical study includes patients or subjects within several NHS bodies, for example in a multi-centre clinical trial, it is necessary for each Authority or Trust to complete an appropriate indemnity agreement with the sponsoring company.

12. Where independent practitioners, such as general medical practitioners, are engaged in clinical studies, Health Authorities should seek to ensure that such studies are the subject of an appropriate indemnity agreement. It is good practice for the GP to notify the Health Authority of his participation in any clinical study.

13. Clinical investigators should ensure that details of any proposed research study are lodged with the appropriate NHS body and should not commence company-sponsored research unless an indemnity agreement is in place.

14. Local Research Ethics Committees (LRECs) provide independent advice to NHS and other bodies and to clinical researchers on the ethics of proposed research projects that involve human subjects [HSG(91)5]. Clinical investigators should not commence any research project involving patients or human volunteers without LREC agreement. Acceptance of the ABPI guidelines and the terms of the model indemnity agreement should normally be a condition of LREC approval of any pharmaceutical company sponsored project.

ANNEX B: APPENDIX

Form of Indemnity for Clinical Studies

To: [Name and address of sponsoring company] ("the Sponsor")
From: [Name and address of Health Authority/Health Board/NHS Trust] ("the Authority")
Re: Clinical Study No [ ] with [name of product]

1. It is proposed that the Authority should agree to participate in the above sponsored study ("the Study") involving [patients of the Authority] [non-patient volunteers] ("the Subjects") to be conducted by [name of investigator(s)] ("the Investigator") in accordance with the protocol annexed, as amended from time to time with the agreement of the Sponsor and the Investigator ("the Protocol"). The Sponsor confirms that it is a term of its agreement with the Investigator that the Investigator shall obtain all necessary

approvals of the applicable Local Research Ethics Committee and shall resolve with the Authority any issues of a revenue nature.

2. The Authority agrees to participate by allowing the Study to be undertaken on its premises utilising such facilities, personnel and equipment as the Investigator may reasonably need for the purpose of the Study.

3. In consideration of such participation by the Authority, and subject to paragraph 4 below, the Sponsor indemnifies and holds harmless the Authority and its employees and agents against all claims and proceedings (to include any settlements or ex-gratia payments made with the consent of the parties hereto and reasonable legal and expert costs and expenses) made or brought (whether successfully or otherwise):

   (a) by or on behalf of Subjects taking part in the Study (or their dependants) against the Authority or any of its employees or agents for personal injury (including death) to Subjects arising out of or relating to the administration of the product(s) under investigation or any clinical intervention or procedure provided for or required by the Protocol to which the Subjects would not have been exposed but for their participation in the Study.

   (b) by the Authority, its employees or agents or by or on behalf of a Subject for a declaration concerning the treatment of a Subject who has suffered such personal injury.

4. The above indemnity by the Sponsor shall not apply to any such claim or proceeding:

   4.1 to the extent that such personal injury (including death) is caused by the negligent or wrongful acts or omissions or breach of statutory duty of the Authority, its employees or agents;

   4.2 to the extent that such personal injury (including death) is caused by the failure of the Authority, its employees, or agents to conduct the Study in accordance with the Protocol;

   4.3 unless as soon as reasonably practicable following receipt of notice of such claim or proceeding, the Authority shall have notified the Sponsor in writing of it and shall, upon the Sponsor's request, and at the Sponsor's cost, have permitted the Sponsor to have full care and control of the claim or proceeding using legal representation of its own choosing;

   4.4 if the Authority, its employees, or agents shall have made any admission in respect of such claim or proceeding or taken any action relating to such claim or proceeding prejudicial to the defence of it without the written consent of the Sponsor such consent not to be unreasonably withheld provided that this condition shall not be treated as breached by any statement properly made by the Authority, its employees or agents in connection with the operation of the Authority's internal complaint procedures, accident reporting procedures or disciplinary procedures or where such statement is required by law.

5. The Sponsor shall keep the Authority and its legal advisers fully informed of the progress of any such claim or proceeding, will consult fully with the Authority on the nature of any defence to be advanced and will not settle any such claim or proceeding without the written approval of the Authority (such approval not to be unreasonably withheld).

6. Without prejudice to the provisions of paragraph 4.3 above, the Authority will use its reasonable endeavours to inform the Sponsor promptly of any circumstances reasonably thought likely to give rise to any such claim or proceeding of which it is directly aware and shall keep the Sponsor reasonably informed of developments in relation to any such claim or proceeding even where the Authority decides not to make a claim under this indemnity. Likewise, the Sponsor shall use its reasonable endeavours to inform the Authority of any such circumstances and shall keep the Authority reasonably informed of developments in relation to any such claim or proceeding made or brought against the Sponsor alone.

7. The Authority and the Sponsor will each give to the other such help as may reasonably be required for the efficient conduct and prompt handling of any claim or proceeding by or on behalf of Subjects (or their dependants) or concerning such a declaration as is referred to in paragraph 3(b) above.

8. Without prejudice to the foregoing if injury is suffered by a Subject while participating in the Study, the Sponsor agrees to operate in good faith the Guidelines published in 1991 by The Association of the British Pharmaceutical Industry and entitled "Clinical Trial Compensation Guidelines" (where the Subject is a patient) and the Guidelines published in 1988 by the same Association and entitled "Guidelines for Medical Experiments in non-patient Human Volunteers" (where the Subject is not a patient) and shall request the Investigator to make clear to the Subjects that the Study is being conducted subject to the applicable Association Guidelines.

9. For the purpose of this indemnity, the expression "agents" shall be deemed to include without limitation any nurse or other health professional providing services to the Authority under a contract for services or otherwise and any person carrying out work for the Authority under such a contract connected with such of the

Authority's facilities and equipment as are made available for the Study under paragraph 2 above.

10. This indemnity shall be governed by and construed in accordance with English/Scottish* law.

SIGNED on behalf of the Health Authority/
Health Board/NHS Trust   ....

Chief Executive/
District General Manager

SIGNED on behalf of the Company   ....

Dated ....

* Delete as appropriate

Note: © NHS Litigation Authority. This version of the guidance on NHS Indemnity is taken from the NHS Litigation Authority's website (*www.nhsla.com*) with permission.

Appendix 2

PRE-ACTION PROTOCOL FOR THE RESOLUTION OF CLINICAL DISPUTES

Clinical Disputes Forum Executive summary

1. The Clinical Disputes Forum is a multi-disciplinary body which was formed in 1997, as a result of Lord Woolf's 'Access to Justice' inquiry. One of the aims of the Forum is to find less adversarial and more cost-effective ways of resolving disputes about healthcare and medical treatment. The names and addresses of the Chairman and Secretary of the Forum can be found at Annex E.

2. This protocol is the Forum's first major initiative. It has been drawn up carefully, including extensive consultations with most of the key stakeholders in the medico-legal system.

3. The protocol—

   • encourages a climate of openness when something has 'gone wrong' with a patient's treatment or the patient is dissatisfied with that treatment and/or the outcome. This reflects the new and developing requirements for clinical governance within healthcare;

   • provides **general guidance** on how this more open culture might be achieved when disputes arise;

   • recommends **a timed sequence** of steps for patients and healthcare providers, and their advisers, to follow when a dispute arises. This should facilitate and speed up exchanging relevant information and increase the prospects that disputes can be resolved without resort to legal action.

4. This protocol has been prepared by a working party of the Clinical Disputes Forum. It has the support of the Lord Chancellor's Department, the Department of Health and NHS Executive, the Law Society, the Legal Aid Board and many other key organisations.

1. WHY THIS PROTOCOL?

Mistrust in healthcare disputes

1.1 The number of complaints and claims against hospitals, GPs, dentists and private healthcare providers is growing as patients become more prepared to question the treatment they are given, to seek explanations of what happened, and to seek appropriate redress. Patients may require further treatment, an apology, assurances about future action, or compensation. These trends are unlikely to change. The Patients' Charter encourages patients to have high expectations, and a revised NHS Complaints Procedure was implemented in 1996. The civil justice reforms and new Rules of Court should make litigation quicker, more user friendly and less expensive.

1.2 It is clearly in the interests of patients, healthcare professionals and providers that patients' concerns, complaints and claims arising from their treatment are resolved as quickly, efficiently and professionally as possible. A climate of mistrust and lack of openness can seriously damage the patient/clinician relationship, unnecessarily prolong disputes (especially litigation), and reduce the resources available for treating patients. It may also cause additional work for, and lower the morale of, healthcare professionals.

1.3 At present there is often mistrust by both sides. This can mean that patients fail to raise their concerns with the healthcare provider as early as possible. Sometimes patients may pursue a complaint or claim which has little merit, due to a lack of sufficient information and understanding. It can also mean that patients become reluctant, once advice has been taken on a potential claim, to disclose sufficient information to enable the provider to investigate that claim efficiently and, where appropriate, resolve it.

1.4 On the side of the healthcare provider this mistrust can be shown in a reluctance to be honest with patients, a failure to provide prompt clear explanations, especially of adverse outcomes (whether or not there may have been negligence) and a tendency to 'close ranks' once a claim is made.

What needs to change

1.5 If that mistrust is to be removed, and a more co-operative culture is to develop:

- healthcare professionals and providers need to adopt a constructive approach to complaints and claims. They should accept that concerned patients are entitled to an explanation and an apology, if warranted, and to appropriate redress in the event of negligence. An overly defensive approach is not in the long-term interest of their main goal: patient care;
- patients should recognise that unintended and/or unfortunate consequences of medical treatment can only be rectified if they are brought to the attention of the healthcare provider as soon as possible.

1.6 A protocol which sets out 'ground rules' for the handling of disputes at their early stages should, if it is to be subscribed to, and followed—

- encourage greater openness between the parties;
- encourage parties to find the most appropriate way of resolving the particular dispute;
- reduce delay and costs;
- reduce the need for litigation.

Why this Protocol now?

1.7 Lord Woolf in his Access to Justice Report in July 1996, concluded that major causes of costs and delay in medical negligence litigation occur at the pre-action stage. He recommended that patients and their advisers, and healthcare providers, should work more closely together to try to resolve disputes co-operatively, rather than proceed to litigation. He specifically recommended a pre-action protocol for medical negligence cases.

1.8 A fuller summary of Lord Woolf's recommendations is at Annex D.

Where the Protocol fits in

1.9 Protocols serve the needs of litigation and pre-litigation practice, especially—

- predictability in the time needed for steps pre-proceedings;
- standardisation of relevant information, including records and documents to be disclosed.

1.10 Building upon Lord Woolf's recommendations, the Lord Chancellor's Department is now promoting the adoption of protocols in specific areas, including medical negligence.

1.11 It is recognised that contexts differ significantly. For example: patients tend to have an ongoing relationship with a GP, more so than with a hospital; clinical staff in the National Health Service are often employees, while those in the private sector may be contractors; providing records quickly may be relatively easy for GPs and dentists, but can be a complicated procedure in a large multi-department hospital. The protocol which follows is intended to be sufficiently broadly based, and flexible, to apply to all aspects of the health service: primary and secondary; public and private sectors.

Enforcement of the Protocol and sanctions

1.12 The civil justice reforms will be implemented in April 1999. One new set of Court Rules and procedures is replacing the existing rules for both the High Court and county courts. This and the personal injury protocol are being published with the Rules, practice directions and key court forms. The courts will be able to treat the standards set in protocols as the normal reasonable approach to pre-action conduct.

1.13 If proceedings are issued it will be for the court to decide whether non-compliance with a protocol should merit sanctions. Guidance on the court's likely approach will be given from time to time in practice directions.

1.14 If the court has to consider the question of compliance after proceedings have begun it will not be concerned with minor infringements, e.g. failure by a short period to provide relevant information. One minor breach will not entitle the 'innocent' party to abandon following the protocol. The court will look at the effect of non-compliance on the other party when deciding whether to impose sanctions.

2. THE AIMS OF THE PROTOCOL

2.1 The *general* aims of the protocol are—

* to maintain/restore the patient/healthcare provider relationship;
* to resolve as many disputes as possible without litigation.

2.2 The *specific* objectives are—

Openness
* to encourage early communication of the perceived problem between patients and healthcare providers;
* to encourage patients to voice any concerns or dissatisfaction with their treatment as soon as practicable;
* to encourage healthcare providers to develop systems of early reporting and investigation for serious adverse treatment outcomes and to provide full and prompt explanations to dissatisfied patients;
* to ensure that sufficient information is disclosed by both parties to enable each to understand the other's perspective and case, and to encourage early resolution;

Timeliness
* to provide an early opportunity for healthcare providers to identify cases where an investigation is required and to carry out that investigation promptly;
* to encourage primary and private healthcare providers to

involve their defence organisations or insurers at an early stage;

- to ensure that all relevant medical records are provided to patients or their appointed representatives on request, to a realistic timetable by any healthcare provider;
- to ensure that relevant records which are not in healthcare providers' possession are made available to them by patients and their advisers at an appropriate stage;
- where a resolution is not achievable to lay the ground to enable litigation to proceed on a reasonable timetable, at a reasonable and proportionate cost and to limit the matters in contention;
- to discourage the prolonged pursuit of unmeritorious claims and the prolonged defence of meritorious claims.

Awareness of Options

- to ensure that patients and healthcare providers are made aware of the available options to pursue and resolve disputes and what each might involve.

2.3 This protocol does not attempt to be prescriptive about a number of related clinical governance issues which will have a bearing on healthcare providers' ability to meet the standards within the protocol. Good clinical governance requires the following to be considered—

(a) **Clinical risk management:** the protocol does not provide any detailed guidance to healthcare providers on clinical risk management or the adoption of risk management systems and procedures. This must be a matter for the NHS Executive, the National Health Service Litigation Authority, individual trusts and providers, including GPs, dentists and the private sector. However, effective co-ordinated, focused clinical risk management strategies and procedures can help in managing risk and in the early identification and investigation of adverse outcomes.

(b) **Adverse outcome reporting:** the protocol does not provide any detailed guidance on which adverse outcomes should trigger an investigation. However, healthcare providers should have in place procedures for such investigations, including recording of statements of key witnesses. These procedures should also cover when and how to inform patients that an adverse outcome has occurred.

(c) **The professional's duty to report:** the protocol does not recommend changes to the codes of conduct of professionals in healthcare, or attempt to impose a specific duty on those professionals to report known adverse outcomes or untoward incidents. Lord Woolf in his final report suggested that the professional bodies might consider this. The General Medical Council is preparing guidance to doctors about their duty to report adverse incidents and to co-operate with inquiries.

3. THE PROTOCOL

3.1 This protocol is not a comprehensive code governing all the steps in clinical disputes. Rather it attempts to set out **a code of good practice** which parties should follow when litigation might be a possibility.

3.2 The **commitments** section of the protocol summarises the guiding principles which healthcare providers and patients and their advisers are invited to endorse when dealing with patient dissatisfaction with treatment and its outcome, and with potential complaints and claims.

3.3 The **steps** section sets out in a more prescriptive form, a recommended sequence of actions to be followed if litigation is a prospect.

Good practice commitments

3.4 **Healthcare providers** should—

(i)   ensure that **key staff**, including claims and litigation managers, are appropriately trained and have some knowledge of healthcare law, and of complaints procedures and civil litigation practice and procedure;

(ii) develop an approach to **clinical governance** that ensures that clinical practice is delivered to commonly accepted standards and that this is routinely monitored through a system of clinical audit and clinical risk management (particularly adverse outcome investigation);

(iii) set up **adverse outcome reporting systems** in all specialties to record and investigate unexpected serious adverse outcomes as soon as possible. Such systems can enable evidence to be gathered quickly, which makes it easier to provide an accurate explanation of what happened and to defend or settle any subsequent claims;

(iv) use the results of **adverse incidents and complaints positively** as a guide to how to improve services to patients in the future;

(v)   ensure **that patients receive clear and comprehensible infor-**

mation in an accessible form about how to raise their concerns or complaints;

(vi) establish **efficient and effective systems of recording and storing patient records**, notes, diagnostic reports and X-rays, and to retain these in accordance with Department of Health guidance (currently for a minimum of eight years in the case of adults, and all obstetric and paediatric notes for children until they reach the age of 25);

(vii) **advise patients** of a serious adverse outcome and provide on request to the patient or the patient's representative an oral or written explanation of what happened, information on further steps open to the patient, including where appropriate an offer of future treatment to rectify the problem, an apology, changes in procedure which will benefit patients and/or compensation.

3.5 **Patients and their advisers** should—

(i) **report any concerns and dissatisfaction** to the healthcare provider as soon as is reasonable to enable that provider to offer clinical advice where possible, to advise the patient if anything has gone wrong and take appropriate action;

(ii) consider the **full range of options** available following an adverse outcome with which a patient is dissatisfied, including a request for an explanation, a meeting, a complaint, and other appropriate dispute resolution methods (including mediation) and negotiation, not only litigation;

(iii) **inform the healthcare provider when the patient is satisfied** that the matter has been concluded: legal advisers should notify the provider when they are no longer acting for the patient, particularly if proceedings have not started.

Protocol steps

3.6 The steps of this protocol which follow have been kept deliberately simple. An illustration of the likely sequence of events in a number of healthcare situations is at Annex A.

Obtaining the health records

3.7 Any request for records by the **patient** or their adviser should—

- **provide sufficient information** to alert the healthcare provider where an adverse outcome has been serious or had serious consequences;
- be as **specific as possible** about the records which are required.

3.8 Requests for copies of the patient's clinical records should be made using the Law Society and Department of Health approved **standard forms** (enclosed at Annex B), adapted as necessary.

3.9 The copy records should be provided **within 40 days** of the request and for a cost not exceeding the charges permissible under the Access to Health Records Act 1990 (currently a maximum of £10 plus photocopying and postage).

3.10 In the rare circumstances that the healthcare provider is in difficulty in complying with the request within 40 days, the **problem should be explained** quickly and details given of what is being done to resolve it.

3.11 It will not be practicable for healthcare providers to investigate in detail each case when records are requested. But healthcare providers should **adopt a policy on which cases will be investigated** (see paragraph 3.5 on clinical governance and adverse outcome reporting).

3.12 If the healthcare provider fails to provide the health records within 40 days, the patient or their adviser can then apply to the court for an **order for pre-action disclosure.** The new Civil Procedure Rules should make pre-action applications to the court easier. The court will also have the power to impose costs sanctions for unreasonable delay in providing records.

3.13 If either the patient or the healthcare provider considers **additional health records are required from a third party**, in the first instance these should be requested by or through the patient. Third party healthcare providers are expected to co-operate. The Civil Procedure Rules will enable patients and healthcare providers to apply to the court for pre-action disclosure by third parties.

Letter of claim

3.14 Annex C1 to this protocol provides **a template for the recommended contents of a letter of claim**: the level of detail will need to be varied to suit the particular circumstances.

3.15 If, following the receipt and analysis of the records, and the receipt of any further advice (including from experts if necessary—see Section 4), the patient/adviser decides that there are grounds for a claim, they should then send, as soon as practicable, to the healthcare provider/potential defendant, a **letter of claim.**

3.16 This letter should contain a **clear summary of the facts** on which the claim is based, including the alleged adverse outcome, and the **main allegations of negligence**. It should also describe the **patient's injuries**, and present condition and prognosis. The **financial loss** incurred by the plaintiff should be outlined with an indication of the heads of damage to be claimed and the scale of the loss, unless this is impracticable.

3.17 In more complex cases a **chronology** of the relevant events should be provided, particularly if the patient has been treated by a number of different healthcare providers.

3.18 The letter of claim **should refer to any relevant documents**, including health records, and if possible enclose copies of any of those which will not already be in the potential defendant's possession, e.g. any relevant general practitioner records if the plaintiff's claim is against a hospital.

3.19 Sufficient information must be given to enable the healthcare provider defendant to **commence investigations** and to put an initial valuation on the claim.

3.20 Letters of claim are **not** intended to have the same formal status as a **pleading**, nor should any sanctions necessarily apply if the letter of claim and any subsequent statement of claim in the proceedings differ.

3.21 Proceedings should not be issued until after three months from the letter of claim, unless there is a limitation problem and/or the patient's position needs to be protected by early issue.

3.22 The patient or their adviser may want to make an **offer to settle** the claim at this early stage by putting forward an amount of compensation which would be satisfactory (possibly including any costs incurred to date). If an offer to settle is made, generally this should be supported by a medical report which deals with the injuries, condition and prognosis, and by a schedule of loss and supporting documentation. The level of detail necessary will depend on the value of the claim. Medical reports may not be necessary where there is no significant continuing injury, and a detailed schedule may not be necessary in a low value case. The Civil Procedure Rules are expected to set out the legal and procedural requirements for making offers to settle.

The response

3.23 Attached at Annex C2 is a template for the suggested contents of the **letter of response.**

3.24 The healthcare provider should **acknowledge** the letter of claim **within 14 days of receipt** and should identify who will be dealing with the matter.

3.25 The healthcare provider should, **within three months** of the letter of claim, provide a **reasoned answer—**

- if the **claim is admitted** the healthcare provider should say so in clear terms;
- if only **part of the claim is admitted** the healthcare provider should make clear which issues of breach of duty and/or causation are admitted and which are denied and why;
- if it is intended that any **admissions will be binding;**
- if the claim is denied, this should include specific comments on the allegations of negligence, and if a synopsis or chronology of relevant events has been provided and is disputed, the healthcare provider's version of those events;
- where additional documents are relied upon, e.g. an internal protocol, copies should be provided.

3.26 If the patient has made an offer to settle, the healthcare provider should **respond to that offer** in the response letter, preferably with reasons. The provider may make its own offer to settle at this stage, either as a counter-offer to the patient's, or of its own accord, but should accompany any offer by any supporting medical evidence, and/or by any other evidence in relation to the value of the claim which is in the healthcare provider's possession.

3.27 If the parties reach agreement on liability, but time is needed to resolve the value of the claim, they should aim to agree a reasonable period.

4. EXPERTS

4.1 In clinical negligence disputes **expert opinions** may be needed—

- on breach of duty and causation;
- on the patient's condition and prognosis;
- to assist in valuing aspects of the claim.

4.2 The civil justice reforms and the new **Civil Procedure Rules** will encourage economy in the use of experts and a **less adversarial expert culture**. It is recognised that in clinical negligence disputes, the parties and their advisers will require flexibility in their approach to expert evidence. Decisions on whether experts might be instructed jointly, and on whether reports might be disclosed sequentially or by exchange, should rest with the parties and their advisers. Sharing expert evidence may be appropriate on issues relating to the value of the claim. However, this protocol does not attempt to be prescriptive on issues in relation to expert evidence.

4.3 Obtaining expert evidence will often be an expensive step and may take time, especially in specialised areas of medicine where there are limited numbers of suitable experts. Patients and healthcare providers, and their advisers, will therefore need to consider carefully how best to obtain any necessary expert help quickly and cost-effectively. Assistance with locating a suitable expert is available from a number of sources.

5. ALTERNATIVE APPROACHES TO SETTLING DISPUTES

5.1 It would not be practicable for this protocol to address in any detail how a patient or their adviser, or healthcare provider, might decide which method to adopt to resolve the particular problem. But, the courts increasingly expect parties to try to settle their differences by agreement before issuing proceedings.

5.2 Most disputes are resolved by **discussion and negotiation.** Parties should bear in mind that carefully planned face-to-face meetings may be particularly helpful in exploring further treatment for the patient, in reaching understandings about what happened, and on both parties' positions, in narrowing the issues in dispute and, if the timing is right, in helping to settle the whole matter.

5.3 Summarised below are some other alternatives for resolving disputes

- The revised **NHS Complaints Procedure,** which was implemented in April 1996, is designed to provide patients with an explanation of what happened and an apology if appropriate. It is not designed to provide compensation for cases of negligence. However, patients might choose to use the procedure if their only, or main, goal is to obtain an explanation, or to obtain more information to help them decide what other action might be appropriate.
- **Mediation** may be appropriate in some cases: this is a form of facilitated negotiation assisted by an independent neutral party. It is expected that the new Civil Procedure Rules will give the court the power to stay proceedings for one month for settlement discussions or mediation.
- Other methods of resolving disputes include **arbitration, determination by an expert, and early neutral evaluation** by a medical or legal expert. The Legal Services Commission has published a booklet on "**Alternatives to Court**", LSC August 2001, CLS information leaflet number 23, which lists a number of organisations that provide alternative dispute resolution services.

ANNEX A

Illustrative flowchart

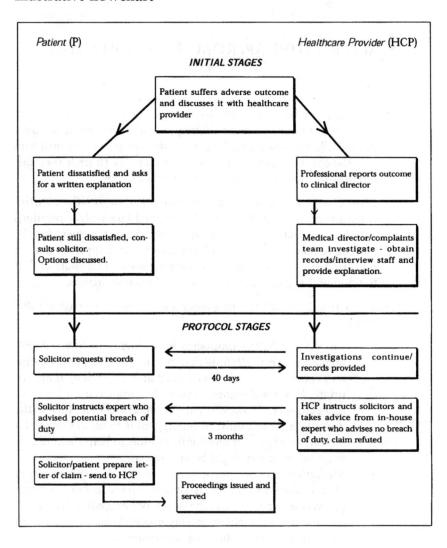

ANNEX B

Medical negligence and personal injury claims

APPLICATION ON BEHALF OF A PATIENT FOR HOSPITAL MEDICAL RECORDS FOR USE WHEN COURT PROCEEDINGS ARE CONTEMPLATED

Purpose of the forms

This application form and response forms have been prepared by a working party of the Law Society's Civil Litigation Committee and approved by the Department of Health for use in NHS and Trust hospitals. The purpose of the forms is to standardise and streamline the disclosure of medical records to a patient's solicitors, who are investigating pursuing a personal injury claim against a third party, or a medical negligence claim against the hospital to which the application is addressed and/or other hospitals or general practitioners.

Use of the forms

Use of the forms is entirely voluntary and does not prejudice any party's right under the Access to Health Records Act 1990, the Data Protection Act 1984, or ss.33 and 34 of the Supreme Court Act 1981. However, it is Department of Health policy that patients be permitted to see what has been written about them, and that healthcare providers should make arrangements to allow patients to see all their records, not only those covered by the Access to Health Records Act 1990. The aim of the forms is to save time and costs for all concerned for the benefit of the patient and the hospital and in the interests of justice. Use of the forms should make it unnecessary in most cases for there to be exchanges of letters or other enquiries. If there is any unusual matter not covered by the form, the patient's solicitor may write a separate letter at the outset.

Charges for records

The Access to Health Records Act 1990 prescribes a maximum fee of £10. Photocopying and postage costs can be charged in addition. No other charges may be made. The NHS Executive guidance makes it clear to healthcare providers that 'it is a perfectly proper use' of the 1990 Act to request records in that framework for the purpose of potential or actual litigation, whether against a third party or against the hospital or trust. The 1990 Act does not permit differential rates of charges to be levied if the application is made by the patient, or by a solicitor on his or her behalf, or whether the response to the application is made by the healthcare provider directly (the medical records manager or a claims manager) or by a solicitor.

The NHS Executive guidance recommends that the same practice should be followed with regard to charges when the records are provided under a voluntary agreement as under the 1990 Act, except that in those circumstances the £10 access fee will not be appropriate.

The NHS Executive also advises—

- that the cost of photocopying may include 'the cost of staff time in making copies' and the costs of running the copier (but not costs of locating and sifting records);

- that the common practice of setting a standard rate for an application or charging an administration fee is not acceptable because there will be cases when this fails to comply with the 1990 Act.

Records: what might be included

X-rays and test results form part of the patient's records. Additional charges for copying X-rays are permissible. If there are large numbers of X-rays, the records officer should check with the patient/solicitor before arranging copying.

Reports on an 'adverse incident' and reports on the patient made for risk management and audit purposes may form part of the records and be disclosable: the exception will be any specific record or report made solely or mainly in connection with an actual or potential claim.

Records: quality standards

When copying records healthcare providers should ensure—

1. All documents are legible, and complete, if necessary by photocopying at less than 100% size.

2. Documents larger than A4 in the original, e.g. ITU charts, should be reproduced in A3, or reduced to A4 where this retains readability.

3. Documents are only copied on one side of paper, unless the original is two sided.

4. Documents should not be unnecessarily shuffled or bound and holes should not be made in the copied papers.

Enquiries/further information

Any enquiries about the forms should be made initially to the solicitors making the request. Comments on the use and content of the forms should be made to the Secretary, Civil Litigation Committee, The Law Society, 113 Chancery Lane, London WC2A 1PL, telephone 0171 320 5739, or to the NHS Management Executive, Quarry House, Quarry Hill, Leeds LS2 7UE.
The Law Society
May 1998

APPLICATION ON BEHALF OF A PATIENT FOR HOSPITAL MEDICAL RECORDS FOR USE WHEN COURT PROCEEDINGS ARE CONTEMPLATED

This should be completed as fully as possible

Insert
Hospital
Name
and
Address

TO: Medical Records Officer

Hospital

1 (a)	Full name of patient (including previous surnames)	
(b)	Address now	
(c)	Address at start of treatment	
(d)	Date of birth (and death, if applicable)	
(e)	Hospital ref. no if available	
(f)	N.I. number, if available	
2	This application is made because the patient is considering	
(a)	a claim against your hospital as detailed in para 7 overleaf	YES/NO
(b)	pursuing an action against some one else	YES/NO

PRE-ACTION PROTOCOL FOR THE RESOLUTION OF CLINICAL DISPUTES

3	Department(s) where treatment was received	
4	Name(s) of consultant(s) at your hospital in charge of the treatment	
5	Whether treatment at your hospital was private or NHS, wholly or in part	
6	A description of the treatment received, with approximate dates	
7	If the answer to Q2(a) is "Yes" details of	
	(a) the likely nature of the claim,	
	(b) grounds for the claim,	
	(c) approximate dates of the events involved	
8	If the answer to Q2(b) is "Yes" insert	
	(a) the names of the proposed defendants	
	(b) whether legal proceedings yet begun	YES/NO
	(c) if appropriate, details of the claim and action number	
9	We confirm we will pay reasonable copying charges	
10	We request prior details of	
	(a) photocopying and administration charges for medical records	YES/NO
	(b) number of and cost of copying x-ray and scan films	YES/NO

11	Any other relevant information, particular requirements, or any particular documents not required (e.g. copies of computerised records)	
	Signature of Solicitor	
	Name	
	Address	
	Ref.	
	Telephone Number	
	Fax number	

Signature of patient	*Please print name beneath each signature. Signature by child over 12 but under 18 years also requires signature by parent.*
Signature of parent or next friend if appropriate	
Signature of personal representative where patient has died	

FIRST RESPONSE TO APPLICATION FOR HOSPITAL RECORDS

NAME OF PATIENT Our ref. Your ref.		
1	Date of receipt of patient's application	
2	We intend that copy medical records will be dispatched within 6 weeks of that date	YES/NO
3	We require pre-payment of photocopying charges	YES/NO
4	If estimate of photocopying charges requested or pre-payment required the amount will be	£/notified to you
5	The cost of x-ray and scan films will be	£/notified to you
6	If there is any problem, we shall write to you within those 6 weeks	YES/NO
7	Any other information	
	Please address further correspondence to	
	Signed	
	Direct telephone number	
	Direct fax number	
	Dated	

SECOND RESPONSE ENCLOSING PATIENT'S HOSPITAL MEDICAL RECORDS

Address   Our Ref.
                                             Your Ref.

	NAME OF PATIENT:	
1	We confirm that the enclosed copy medical records are all those within the control of the hospital, relevant to the application which you have made to the best of our knowledge and belief, subject to paras 2–5 below	YES/NO
2	Details of any other documents which have not yet been located	
3	Date by when it is expected that these will be supplied	
4	Details of any records which we are not producing	
5	The reasons for not doing so	
6	An invoice for copying and administration charges is attached	YES/NO
	Signed	
	Date	

ANNEX C

Templates for letters of claim and response

C1 LETTER OF CLAIM
Essential Contents

1. Client's name, address, date of birth, etc.

2. Dates of allegedly negligent treatment

3. Events giving rise to the claim:
   - an outline of what happened, including details of other relevant treatments to the client by other healthcare providers.

4. Allegation of negligence and causal link with injuries:
   - an outline of the allegations or a more detailed list in a complex case;
   - an outline of the causal link between allegations and the injuries complained of.

5. The Client's injuries, condition and future prognosis

6. Request for clinical records (if not previously provided)
   - use the Law Society form if appropriate or adapt;
   - specify the records require;
   - if other records are held by other providers, and may be relevant, say so;
   - state what investigations have been carried out to date, e.g. information from client and witnesses, any complaint and the outcome, if any clinical records have been seen or experts advice obtained.

7. The likely value of the claim
   - an outline of the main heads of damage, or, in straightforward cases, the details of loss.

Optional information
   - What investigations have been carried out
   - An offer to settle without supporting evidence
   - Suggestions for obtaining expert evidence
   - Suggestions for meetings, negotiations, discussion or mediation

Possible enclosures
   - Chronology
   - Clinical records request form and client's authorisation
   - Expert report(s)
   - Schedules of loss and supporting evidence

C2 LETTER OF RESPONSE
Essential Contents

1. Provide **requested records** and invoice for copying:
   - explain if records are incomplete or extensive records are held and ask for further instructions;
   - request additional records from third parties.

2. **Comments on events and/or chronology:**
   - if events are disputed or the healthcare provider has further information or documents on which they wish to rely, these should be provided, e.g. internal protocol;
   - details of any further information needed from the patient or a third party should be provided.

3. **If breach of duty and causation are accepted:**
   - suggestions might be made for resolving the claim and/or requests for further information;
   - a response should be made to any offer to settle.

4. **If breach of duty and/or causation are denied:**
   - a bare denial will not be sufficient. If the healthcare provider has other explanations for what happened, these should be given at least in outline;
   - suggestions might be made for the next steps, e.g. further investigations, obtaining expert evidence, meetings/negotiations or mediation, or an invitation to issue proceedings.

Optional Matters
- An offer to settle if the patient has not made one, or a counter offer to the patient's with supporting evidence

Possible enclosures:
- Clinical records
- Annotated chronology
- Expert reports

ANNEX D

Lord Woolf's recommendations

1.   Lord Woolf in his Access to Justice Report in July 1996, following a detailed review of the problems of medical negligence claims, identified that one of the major sources of costs and delay is at the pre-litigation stage because—

     (a)   Inadequate incident reporting and record keeping in hospitals, and mobility of staff, make it difficult to establish facts, often several years after the event.

     (b)   Claimants must incur the cost of an expert in order to establish whether they have a viable claim.

     (c)   There is often a long delay before a claim is made.

     (d)   Defendants do not have sufficient resources to carry out a full investigation of every incident, and do not consider it worthwhile to start an investigation as soon as they receive a request for records, because many cases do not proceed beyond that stage.

     (e)   Patients often give the defendant little or no notice of a firm intention to pursue a claim. Consequently, many incidents are not investigated by the defendants until after proceedings have started.

     (f)   Doctors and other clinical staff are traditionally reluctant to admit negligence or apologise to, or negotiate with, claimants for fear of damage to their professional reputations or career prospects.

2.   Lord Woolf acknowledged that under the present arrangements healthcare providers, faced with possible medical negligence claims, have a number of practical problems to contend with—

     (a)   Difficulties of finding patients' records and tracing former staff, which can be exacerbated by late notification and by the health care provider's own failure to identify adverse incidents.

     (b)   The healthcare provider may have only treated the patient for a limited time or for a specific complaint: the patient's previous history may be relevant but the records may be in the possession of one of several other healthcare providers.

     (c)   The large number of potential claims which do not proceed beyond the stage of a request for medical records, or an explanation; and that it is difficult for healthcare providers to investigate fully every case whenever a patient asks to see the records.

ANNEX E

How to contact the forum

The Clinical Disputes Forum

Chairman

Dr Alastair Scotland
Medical Director and Chief Officer
National Clinical Assessment Authority
9th Floor, Market Towers
London
SW8 5NQ
Telephone: 020 7273 0850

Secretary

Sarah Leigh
c/o Margaret Dangoor
3 Clydesdale Gardens
Richmond
Surrey
TW10 5EG
Telephone: 020 8408 1012

GLOSSARY OF MEDICAL TERMS

Abdominoplasty: plastic surgery on the abdomen.

Abduction: movement away from the mid-line.

Acceleration injury: diffuse shearing injury to the brain substance.

Acute myeloid leukaemia: a form of leukaemia in which the type of blood cell that proliferates abnormally originates in the blood forming (myeloid) tissue of the bone marrow. Can involve any of the cells produced by the marrow. Myeloid leukaemia may be acute or chronic, depending on the rate of progression of the disease.

Adduction: movement towards the mid-line.

Adrenaline: hormone secreted by the adrenal gland, having effects on the circulation, muscles and sugar metabolism.

Agnosia: inability to recognise familiar complex auditory, visual or tactile stimuli, despite intact sensory input to the brain.

Agraphia: inability to express thoughts in writing.

AIDS: acquired immune deficiency syndrome; an illness (often if not always fatal) in which opportunistic infections or malignant tumours develop as a result of the severe loss of cellular immunity, which is itself caused by earlier infection with a retrovirus, HIV, transmitted in sexual fluids and blood.

Akinesia: inability to start a movement.

Alexia: loss of power to grasp meaning of written or printed words and sentences.

Amenorrhoea: absence or suppression of menstrual discharge.

Amnesia: disorders of memory, literally without (a) memory (mnesis). May be an imprinting deficit for new material, or a memory retrieval deficit for old material.

Amniocentesis: the process whereby a needle is inserted in the sac which surrounds the fetus in the uterus (the amnion) and some of the contained amniotic fluid is withdrawn. The procedure as a great potential for antenatal diagnosis.

Aneurism: swelling in the wall of an artery.

Angiography: X-ray of the blood vessels.

Ankylosis: obliteration of a joint by fusion, either bony or fibrous.

Anosmia: loss of sense of smell. May also affect the perceived taste of liquid and solid foodstuffs.

Anoxia: deficiency in oxygen supply to the brain, if profound, causes permanent brain damage.

Anterior colporrhaphy: stitching of the vagina in order to reduce laxity in a case of prolapse of the bladder.

Anterior spinal artery syndrome: spinal stroke, caused by interruption of the flow of blood to the spine

Anterograde amnesia: loss of memory for events occurring subsequent to amnesia-causing trauma; patient is unable to acquire or learn new information.

Anticonvulsant: a drug used to reduce the incidence of epileptic fits, for example valproate (Epilim), carbamazepine (Tegretol), phenytoin (Epanutin).

Aorta: the major artery of the body from which all other systemic arteries derive; it originates in the left ventricle of the heart and ends by dividing into the common iliac arteries which are destined to supply blood to the legs.

Aortography: radiographic examination of the aorta, usually by insertion of a catheter into the femoral artery.

Aortoplasty: operation to repair aorta.

Aphasia: absence of the capacity for language comprehension, or expression, in the absence of any defect in the voice, sight or hearing.

Aphonia: inability to make sounds.

Apnoea: suspension or cessation of breathing.

Aplastic anaemia: anaemia (lack of haemoglobin) caused by poor or absent production of blood cells in the bone marrow.

Appendicectomy: surgical removal of the appendix.

Apraxia: loss of ability to carry out skilled voluntary movements, in the absence of limb paralysis.

Arachnoid mater: a water-tight meningeal membrane forming the outer boundary of the subarachnoid space that contains cerebrospinal fluid.

Arachnoiditis: an inflammatory response of the arachnoid, one of three coverings, or meninges, that envelop the brain and spinal cord, which may result from infection, including syphilis and tubercular meningitis, or trauma (including that resulting from surgery, lumbar puncture, and spinal anaesthesia).

Arteriography: X-ray examination of an artery that has been outlined by the injection of a radio-opaque contrast medium.

Arteriovascular malformation: variation in the normal physical structure of the arteriovascular system.

Arteriovenous fistula: an abnormal communication between an artery and a vein.

Arthoplasty: surgical remodelling of a diseased joint.

Arthrodesis: surgical fusion of a joint.

Arthroplasy: surgical reconstitution or replacement of a joint.

Arthroscopy: inspection by means of an arthroscope of the cavity of a joint.

Artificial insemination: introduction of semen into the vagina by means of an instrument in order to achieve conception.

Aseptic necrosis: the death of cells in an organ or tissue caused by disease, physical or chemical injury or interference with the blood supply, in aseptic conditions (*i.e.* the absence of bacteria, fungi, viruses or other organisms that could cause disease).

Aspiration: sucking out fluid (*e.g.* from a joint or cavity) through a hollow needle.

Astereognosis: inability to recognise objects by touching them alone.

Ataxia: loss of coordination and precision of movement of torso, head or limbs due to a defect in the cerebellum, vestibular or proprioceptive system.

Atrophy: a state of wasting due to some interference with tissue nutrition.

Attention: the active selection of information, with concurrent inhibition of other, competing information.

Audiometry: the assessment and quantification of hearing function.

Avascular necrosis: death of tissue through deprivation of blood supply; refers particularly to bones – *e.g.* head of femur following fracture of neck of femur.

Babinski reflex: extension of the great toe on scratching the sole, indicating an upper motor neurone lesion.

Basal ganglia: clusters of nerve cells (grey matter), deep in each cerebral hemisphere, relaying motor and sensory impulses.

Behcet's disease: a rare, chronic inflammatory disorder, the cause of which is unknown; symptoms include recurrent ulcers in the mouth and on the genitals, and eye inflammation. The disorder may also cause various types of skin lesions, arthritis, bowel inflammation, meningitis, and cranial nerve palsies. Behcet's disease may involve all organs and affect the central nervous system, causing memory loss and impaired speech, balance, and movement.

Benzodiazepine: a group of pharmacologically active compounds used as minor tranquillizers and hypnotics.

Bilateral carotid arteriogram: a picture of the arteries on either side of the neck which supply blood to the head. The examination of the arteries is effected by means of radiology after injection of a radio-opaque material.

Bilirubin encephalopathy: see *kernicterus*

Biopsy: sample of tissue taken from the living body for microscopic examination.

Bitemporal hemianopia: loss of the outer halves of both visual fields.

Bi-valve: removal of a plaster cast by cutting along each side of its length, permitting replacement if required.

Bradykinesia: slowness in movement.

Brachial palsy: a condition characterised by a weak, numb or paralysed arm. Often caused by injury to the brachial plexus of nerves which arise from the neck to supply the arm (e.g. as a result of a road traffic accident).

Brachial plexus: a network of nerves arising from the spine at the base of the neck, from which arise the nerves supplying the arm, forearm and hand, and part of the shoulder.

Brain stem: posterior part of the brain comprising the midbrain, pons and medulla containing vital centres, ascending and descending tracts, nuclei of cranial nerves and the reticular formation.

Broca's area: an area for speech in the dominant, frontal lobe of the brain.

Bulbar: concerning the medulla.

Burr-hole: hole drilled in the skull.

Bursa: a cyst-like sac between a bony prominence and the skin, *e.g.* prepatellar bursa, inflammation in which constitutes "housemaid's knee".

Callus: the cement-like new bone formation which produces union of the fragments of a fracture.

Capsulotomy: an incision into the capsule of the eye lens.

Cardiac: pertaining to the heart.

Carotid endarterectomy: operation on the carotid artery (in the neck) to remove debris blocking the artery and hence reduce the risk of a stroke.

Carpal tunnel: the channel in the wrist through which the median nerve passes.

Cataract: opacity in the lens of the eye, resulting in blurred vision.

Catheter: a tube for insertion into a narrow opening so that fluids may be introduced or removed.

Cauda equina syndrome: impairment of the nerves in the cauda equina (the bundle of spinal nerve roots that arise from the lower end of the spinal cord), resulting in low back pain, unilateral or usually bilateral sciatica, saddle sensory disturbances, bladder and bowel dysfunction, and variable lower extremity motor and sensory loss.

Caudal block: a type of epidural anaesthesia which is particularly suitable for operations on the anus, the vagina and the urethra.

Central nervous system (CNS): comprising the spinal cord and brain, the latter containing the cerebrum, cerebellum, mid-brain, pons and medulla. Excludes peripheral nerves that run outside the spinal cord.

Cephalic: pertaining to the head.

Cerebral: pertaining to the brain.

Cerebral palsy: any of various non-progressive forms of paralysis caused by damage to motor areas of the brain before or during birth, manifested in early childhood by weakness and imperfect control of the affected muscles.

Cerebral thrombosis: clotting in a blood vessel in the brain.

Cervical: pertaining to the neck.

Cervical laminectomy: an operation to remove a prolapsed spinal disc from the neck.

Chondral: pertaining to the cartilage.

Crohn's disease: inflammation of the bowel.

Chronic adhesive arachnoiditis: inflammation of the lining of the brain and spinal cord.

Circumflex artery: an artery of curved or winding form, or which bends around others; example—the circumflex iliac artery.

Cirrhosis: a condition in which the liver responds to injury or death of some of its cells by producing interlacing strands of fibrous tissue between which are nodules of regenerating cells.

Claudication: lameness, applied particularly to pain in the calf muscles resulting from defective blood supply owing to arterial disease.

Cognition: mental functions of attention, memory, thinking, perception, and intellectual activity.

Colon: main part of the large intestine.

Colostomy: the operation of making an artificial opening into the colon (the greater portion of the large intestine) through the abdominal wall.

Coma: absence of awareness of self and environment even when the subject is externally stimulated. Defined on the Glasgow Coma Scale as a score of eight or less.

Comminuted: a type of fracture of a bone in which there are more than two fragments.

Concussion: a reversible disturbance of consciousness following head trauma.

Confabulation: filling in gaps in memory with invented and often improbable stories or facts which the patient accepts as true.

Congenital disabilities: a disabling condition recognised at birth or believed to have been present since birth, whether inherited or caused by an environmental factor.

Consciousness: state of awareness of the self and the environment, the opposite of coma.

Contusion: bruising of neural tissue.

Cord prolapse: downward displacement of the umbilical cord.

Corneal reflex: normal blinking on touching the cornea of the eye.

Corpus callosum: a large bank of nerve fibres connecting the two cerebral hemispheres.

Cortex: the outer layer of a structure, *e.g.* the "shell" of a bone; the surface layer (grey matter) of the cerebral and cerebellar hemispheres of the brain.

Cortical atrophy: thinning of cortical tissue.

Costal: pertaining to the ribs.

Cranial nerves: the nerves of the brain, twelve on each side, arising directly from the brain and the brain stem.

Craniectomy: opening in the skull where the bone is not replaced.

Craniotomy: opening in the skull where the bone is replaced.

Crepitus: a creaking or grating, found in osteo-arthritic joints; also in recent fractures and with inflammation of tendons and their sheaths (tenosynovitis).

Creutzfeldt-Jakob Disease: a rare, degenerative, fatal brain disorder, which causes rapid, progressive dementia and associated neuromuscular disturbances.

Cryoprecipitate: a component of blood used to aid coagulation.

Curettage: scraping of the internal surface of an organ or body cavity by means of a spoon-shaped instrument.

CSF: cerebrospinal fluid, which covers the surface of the brain and spinal cord and circulates inside the ventricles of the brain.

CT (Computed Tomography): a scan which uses a finely collimated moving X-ray beam and a computer to construct pictures of a part of the body, which show internal structure as though the organ examined had been sliced open.

Cyanosis: blueness from deficient oxygenation of the blood.

Cytology: the study of the structure and function of cells.

Deceleration injury: *see* Acceleration injury.

Deep vein thrombosis: a blood clot (thrombus) that develops in a deep vein, usually in the leg; this can happen if the vein is damaged or if the flow of blood slows down or stops

Degeneration: death of tissue.

Dementia: deterioration of intellect, involving a diffuse reduction in cognitive functions, and changes in personality.

Demyelination: loss of the myelin that sheathes nerve fibres.

Denial: a defence mechanism whereby unacceptable ideas or facts are not perceived or allowed into full conscious awareness.

Depo-Provera: injectible contraceptive hormone.

Dermatitis: inflammation of the skin caused by an external agent.

Diabetes insipidus: passage of uncontrolled amounts of dilute urine.

Diabetes mellitus: passage of uncontrolled amounts of urine containing too high a concentration of glucose.

Diffuse injury: pattern of brain injury following rapid acceleration or deceleration of the head, as in some falls or road traffic accidents.

Dilatation and Curettage (D and C): scraping the inside of the womb; this procedure is often performed in cases of excessive bleeding.

Diphtheria: an acute contagious infection caused by the bacterium Corynebacterium diphtheriae.

Diplopia: double vision.

Disarticulation: amputation through a joint.

Disc, intervertebral: fibro-cartilaginous "cushion" between two vertebrae.

Discotomy: surgical incision into a spinal disc.

Disorientation: a state of mental confusion with respect to time, place, identity of self, or other persons or objects.

Distal: farthest point from the centre (opposite to proximal).

Dominant hemisphere: the cerebral hemisphere or side of the brain controlling speech. The left hemisphere in most people.

Dorsal spine: that part of the spine to which the ribs are connected; known also as the "thoracic" spine.

Dorsiflexion: movement of a joint in a backward direction.

Dorsum: back or top, *e.g.* back of hand, top of foot;

Duodenal ulcer: an ulcer in the duodenum caused by the action of acid and pepsin on the lining of the duodenum.

Dupuytren's contracture: thickened fibrous tissue in the palm of the hand causing contracture of the fingers.

Dura mater: outer layer of the meninges that are the membranous coverings of the brain. Closely applied to the inner surface of the skull and spinal canal in the vertebrae.

Dys-: prefix meaning difficult, defective, painful, e.g. dyspnoea, meaning shortness of breath.

Dyscrasia: an abnormal state of the body or part of the body, especially one due to abnormal development or metabolism.

Dysarthria: disturbance of speech articulation. Pronunciation, intonation and metre of spoken word defective.

Dyslexia: a reading disability.

Dysphagia: disturbance of swallowing.

Dysphasia: disturbance of communication. Receptive component in which the written or spoken word is not perceived correctly. Expressive component in which the patient cannot find the correct word to express themselves.

Dysplasia: malformation, abnormal development of tissue.

-ectomy: suffix meaning surgical excision—e.g. patellectomy, removal of the patella.

EEG: (electroencephalography) recording the amplified spontaneous electrical activity of the brain from surface electrodes.

Effusion: extravasation of fluid in a joint (or any cavity), *e.g.* "water on the knee" (*i.e.* synovitis).

Electrocardiogram (ECG): a tracing which represents the passage of the nervous electrical discharge through the muscle of the heart. The technique involves recording from the leads placed on the limbs and on specified parts of the chest wall. Its main use is to follow the progress of a myocardial infarction (ischaemic death of portions of heart muscle) or to assist in the diagnosis in the event of uncertainty: indigestion is, for example, notorious for mimicking cardiac disease.

Electroconvulsive therapy (ECT): an accepted treatment for particularly, depressive psychosis. It consists of the passage of an electric current through the frontal lobes of the brain.

ELISA test: enzyme linked immunosorbent assay test; an initial screening test for detecting HIV antibodies.

EMG: (electromyography) recording of muscle and nerve electrical activity.

Embolism: blockage of a blood vessel by a clot which has migrated.

Emphysema, surgical: collection of air in the tissues through puncture of the lung by a fractured rib.

Encephalopathy: brain damage due, to various (*e.g.* toxic) causes.

Encephalitis: inflammation of the brain. A potentially fatal viral or bacterial disease that damages the brain and brainstem bilaterally.

Endocartis: inflammation of the lining of the heart cavity and valves.

Endometriosis: the presence of membranous material of the kind lining the womb at other sites within the cavity of the pelvis.

ENT: ear, nose and throat.

Enuresis: urinary incontinence during the night.

Epidural: an injection of anaesthetic into the epidural space of the spine, used especially to control pain during childbirth by producing a loss of sensation below the waist without affecting consciousness.

Epilepsy: an episodic disturbance of brain activity following abnormal spontaneous electrical discharges within the brain, leading to a fit.

Epiphyseal line: the cartilaginous plate near the end of a bone at which the bone grows in length.

Epiphysis: the end of a bone during the period of growth.

Erythema: superficial blush or redness of the skin, *e.g.* as from a very slight burn or scald.

Erythrocyte: red blood corpuscle.

Eschar: crust of dead skin.

ESR: erythrocyte sedimentation rate. A laboratory test upon the blood to detect the presence of an inflammatory process in the body.

Evoked response: (or potential) an electrical response recorded in some part of the nervous system (*e.g.* visual cortex); evoked or elicited by stimulation elsewhere (*e.g.* eyes—visual evoked responses).

Extension: moving a joint into the straight position (opposite to flexion).

Extensor plantar response: *see* Babinski.

External: outer side, syn, lateral (opposite to medial).

Factor VIII: a protein found in blood which aids coagulation. Deficiency of this factor results in haemophilia A. Produced from plasma by fractionation.

Fascia: a fibrous membrane.

Fibro-cartilaginous embolism (FCE): a rare occurrence whereby emboli locate themselves in the arteries and/or veins supplying the cervical cord causing loss of blood supply to the spinal cord, and resulting in paralysis or death. An embolus consists of material, such as a blood clot, fat, air, amniotic fluid or a foreign body that is carried from one point in the blood circulation to lodge at another.

Flaccidity: loss of normal tone in muscles leaving them abnormally limp.

Flexion: moving a joint into the bent position (opposite to extension).

Flexor plantar response: the normal downward movement of the big toe when the sole is scratched.

Flexor spasm: painful contraction of muscles in spastic limbs.

Focal injury: injury to a circumscribed area of brain.

Foetal hypoxia Hypoxia of the foetus (see Hypoxia).

Fossa: anatomical term for a depression or furrow.

Fractionation: a biochemical process of separating out certain blood components, such as factor VIII, from plasma.

Frontal: at the front of the brain, or the skull.

Frontal lobes: the brain's anterior portions lying above the eyes.

Gangrene: total death of a structure through deprivation of blood supply.

Genu: the knee joint.

Gestational diabetes: glucose intolerance of variable degree with onset or first recognition during pregnancy, which affects about 4% of all pregnant women.

Glasgow Corna Scale (GCS): numerical scale from three (total unresponsiveness) to 15 (normal consciousness).

Glaucoma: a condition in which loss of vision is caused by an abnormally high pressure in the eye.

Gliosis: scar tissue replacement of damaged brain tissue.

Gluteal: pertaining to the buttock.

Grand mal epilepsy: epilepsy involving loss of consciousness and generalised convulsions, often associated with urinary incontinence and tongue biting during the fits.

Grey matter: neural tissue largely comprising nerve cell bodies and dendrites constituting the cerebral cortex, the brain nuclei, and central columns of the spinal cord.

Gyri: convolutions on the cortical surface of the brain, representing folds of the cerebral cortex.

Haemarthrosis: effusion of blood in a joint.

Haematoma: an accumulation of blood within the tissues which clots to form a solid swelling.

Haemophilus Influenza type b: a bacterial infection which can cause meningitis, epiglottitis, pneumonia, septic arthritis, infection of tissues under the skin, infected lining of the heart, pus in the lungs, and infection of bone. Despite its name, it is not related to influenza. It is the leading cause of acute bacterial meningitis in infants and children under five.

Heamorrhage: blood that has escaped from a blood vessel. An extradural haemorrhage becomes an extradural haematoma when the blood begins to clot.

Hallux: the great toe.

Hemianopia: loss of half of the visual field. If vision is lost on the same side in both eyes, the hemianopia is termed homonymous.

Hemiparesis: unilateral motor weakness, affecting face, arm, and or leg.

Hepatitis: infection of the liver. Hepatitis A, known as infective hepatitis, is spread by ingestion through faecal transmission, and is thus very common in institutions. Hepatitis B, or serum hepatitis, spreads from blood or blood products to blood; it requires either to be injected or to be applied to open breaches in the skin—thus, drug addicts, haemophiliacs and the like are particularly at risk. The third principle variant of the disease is known as hepatitis non-A, non-B and is diagnosed by exclusion of the other recognisable types.

Heterotopic ossification: (calcification) the formation of extraneous bone in muscle tissue, causing painful and often severely restricted movement.

HIV: human Immuno-deficiency virus; this is the virus which causes aids.

Hodgkin's disease: a malignant disease of lymphatic tissues.

Human growth hormone: a hormone essential for bone and organ growth in youth; too little causes dwarfism, too much causes gigantism.

Hydrocephalus: accumulation of excessive cerebrospinal fluid in the ventricles of the brain.

Hyper-: prefix meaning increase above the normal.

Hypercarbia: abnormally high concentration of carbon dioxide in the blood.

Hyperphagia: pathological over-eating.

Hypo-: prefix meaning decrease below the normal; anatomical term for below.

Hypoglycaemia: a deficiency of glucose in the blood stream causing muscular weakness and lack of co-ordination, mental confusion and sweating.

Hypotension: low blood pressure.

Hypoxia: the condition of the body when it is supplied with insufficient oxygen for its needs

Hysterectomy: excision of the uterus.

Hysterosalpingogram: radiogram of the Fallopian tubes.

Hysterosalpinogram: radiogram of the interior of the womb and the Fallopian tubes following injection of a radio-opaque fluid.

Iatrogenic: induced unintentionally by a physician through his diagnosis, manner or treatment; of or pertaining to the induction of (mental or bodily) disorders, symptoms. etc., in this way.

Ictal: a symptom or sign during an epileptic fit, causally related to the fit.

Idiopathic: of unknown cause.

Illeum: the lower half of the small intestine.

Illium: the main bone of the pelvis.

Induration: hardening of a tissue.

Infarct: a wedge shaped area of non-viable tissue, produced by loss of the blood supply.

Inguinal: pertaining to the groin.

Intelligence: those aspects of cognitive function which are measured by an intelligence test; may reflect the ability to learn from experience, think in abstract terms, and deal effectively with one's environment.

Intercostal: between the ribs.

Intracranial hypertension: high tissue pressure inside the skull, not high blood pressure.

Intercranial shunt: a passage within the skull connecting two anatomical channels and diverting blood from one to the other.

Intramedullary nail: a device used to align and stabilise fractures of the long bones, such as the tibia or femur.

Intraventricular haemorrhage: a collection of blood within the ventricular system, commonly associated with intracerebral haematoma or subarachnoid haemorrhage.

Intravenous pyelogram: a succession of X-ray films of the urinary tract following the injection into a vein of a radio-opaque substance, used to test kidney function.

Intubation: the introduction of a tube into part of the body for the purpose of diagnosis or treatment.

Ipsilateral: on the same side.

IQ (Intelligence Quotient): a statistically derived average of verbal, non-verbal and general ability from one or many test performances which comprise a standardised intelligence test (*e.g. see* WAIS). An individual, performance is compared to the average for a particular age group.

Ischaemia: a reduced or insufficient amount of blood being supplied to a region of the brain or body.

-itis: suffix meaning inflammation, *e.g.* osteitis, inflammation of a bone.

Ivalon sponge rectopexy (Wells operation): a surgical procedure to correct, a rectal prolapse.

Keloid: a scar which is thickened and deep pink in colour.

Kernicterus (bilirubin encephalopathy): damage to the brain of a neonate by an excess of bilirubin (bile pigment) in the blood.

Kyphosis: posterior convexity of the spine.

Laceration: tearing of tissue.

Laminectomy: excision of one or more of the posterior arches of the vertebrae (each arch being formed by the junction of two laminae), especially as a method of access to the spinal canal.

Laparoscopy: visual examination of the interior of the peritoneal cavity by means of a laparoscope inserted into it through the abdominal wall or vagina.

Laparotomy: a cutting through the abdominal walls into the cavity of the abdomen.

Lateral: outer side, or external (opposite to medial).

Lesion: a structural change in a tissue caused by disease or injury.

Leucocyte: white blood corpuscle.

Leukaemia: any of a group of malignant diseases in which the blood-forming organs produce increased numbers of white blood cells (leucocytes).

Lipoma: a common benign tumour composed of well-differentiated fat cells.

Lipping: ridge of adventitious bone at joint edges in arthritis (syn. osteophytic formation).

Lobectomy: excision of diseased or traumatised lobe of the brain.

Logynon: an oral contraceptive pill.

Long term memory: the relatively permanent component of memory, one's previously acquired knowledge, as opposed to the more fluid short term memory.

Lordosis: anterior convexity of spine.

Lumbar: the "small of the back, *i.e.* situated between the dorsal (thoracic) and sacral levels.

Lumen: the cavity of a tubular structure.

Macro-: prefix meaning abnormally large size.

Malar: pertaining to the cheek.

Mallet finger: inability actively to straighten the terminal joint of a finger.

Mandible: the lower jaw.

Marsupiliasation: an operative technique for curing a cyst.

Mastectomy: surgical removal of a breast.

Mastoidectomy: an operation to clear out infection in the bony protuberance behind the ear.

Maxilla: the upper jaw and cheek bones.

Measles: a highly infectious viral disease, mainly affecting children.

Medial: inner side, or internal (opposite to lateral).

Mediastinoscopy: procedure to view the organs of the mediastinum. The mediastinum is in the central chest and contains the heart, windpipe (trachea) and gullet (oesophagus).

Medullary cavity: the soft interior of a bone.

Memory: the process through which we retain learned knowledge, in a form that can be recalled later.

Memory span: the number of items (digits, words) that are correctly recalled after a single presentation.

Meningitis: inflammation of the membranes of the brain or spinal cord.

Meniscus: the semilunar cartilage of the knee.

Mesothelioma: a cancer of the pleura (the linings of the inner chest wall and outside surface of the lungs) which is associated with asbestos inhalation.

Micro-: prefix meaning abnormally small size.

Migraine: hemicranial headache due to a disturbance in the normal calibre of the cranial blood vessels. May be precipitated by trauma, and has a number of clinical variants.

Minoxidil: a drug for the treatment of high blood pressure.

Motor: pertaining to movement (applied particularly to muscle action).

MRI: (Magnetic Resonance Image) a scan which uses signals emitted from water in tissue placed in a strong magnetic field and a computer to construct pictures that are presented as apparent slices through the body in any plane. Can detect subtle tissue abnormalities.

Mumps: a common viral infection, mainly affecting children between the ages of 5 and 15.

Myalgic encephalomyelitis: also referred to as chronic fatigue syndrome; a neurological disease which affects the brain at a physical, mental and emotional level. The first symptoms are similar to flu, but they do not resolve and may become worse. Symptoms include poor memory and concentration, sleep disorders, mood swings, extreme fatigue, muscle pain and stomach pains. Myalgic encephalomyelitis is still not generally accepted as a "disease" because there is no accepted test for it and the same condition may result from a number of different causative factors.

Myelination: formation of fatty substance around nerve fibres or axons, important for nerve impulse conduction, the white matter of the brain and spinal cord.

Myelo-: prefix meaning pertaining to the spinal cord.

Myelography: radiography of; the spinal cord after injection of a contrast medium (radio opaque liquid) into the subarachnoid space.

Myeloid leukaemia: a virulent species of white cell cancer.

Myo-: prefix meaning pertaining to muscle.

Myocardial infarction: death of part of the heart, following interruption of its blood supply.

Myodil: a contrast medium injected into the back to improve X-ray images of the spine.

Myopericarditis: inflammation of the muscular wall of the heart and of the enveloping pericardium.

Necrosis: death of tissue, end stage of infarction.

Neomycin: an anti-bacterial drug.

Neural function: the electrical and chemical activity of nerve cells and fibres.

Non-Hodgkin's lymphoma: any malignant tumour of lymph nodes, excluding Hodgkin's disease.

Nystagmus: rhythmic involuntary oscillatory movement of the eyes.

Obtundation: reduction in alertness accompanied by a lowered awareness of the environment, slower psychological responses to stimulation, and increased hours of sleep, often with drowsiness in between.

Occipital lobes: the brain's posterior portions.

Oculo-vestibular reflex: eye movement reflex that is elicited in comatose patients with an intact brain stem, by initiating convection currents in the vestibular apparatus by syringing ice cold water into the external auditory meatus.

Oculomotor: concerned with eye movement.

Oedema: accumulation of fluid in tissues, usually following tissue damage.

Olfactory: pertaining to the sense of smell.

Oligo-: prefix meaning few or lack of.

Oophorectomy: surgical removal of an ovary.

Opren: a drug for the treatment of arthritis.

Orthopaedic: relating to the muscular-skeletal system.

Osteitis: inflammation of bone.

Osteomyelitis: inflammation of the bone marrow due to infection.

Osteophyte: ridge of adventitious bone at joint edges in arthritis (syn. "lipping").

Osteoporosis: loss of mineral salts from bones, the result of lack of use owing to injury or disease, reducing the mechanical strength of the bone.

Osteotomy: dissection of the bones (*anat.*); cutting of a bone in order to correct a deformity (*surg.*).

Outcome: function at a specified interval after an insult or therapeutic intervention.

Ovarian cyst: a fluid-filled sac in the ovary.

Paget's Disease: a disease which affects chiefly the elderly and is often symptomless, being characterised by the localized alteration of tissue in one or more bones (most often in the spine, skull or pelvis), which becomes thickened and may undergo fracture or bending.

Paired associate learning: the learning of stimulus-response pairs. When the first member of a pair (stimulus) is presented, the patient must give the second member (response).

Palmar flexion: moving the wrist in the direction that the palm faces (syn. flexion).

Para-: prefix meaning by the side of, near, through, abnormality.

Paresis: incomplete paralysis.

Parietal lobes: area of brain midway between the front and back of the head.

Patent ductus arteriosis: the ductus arteriosis is a blood vessel adjacent to the heart which allows blood to bypass the lungs while a foetus is in the womb. At birth it should close. If it remains patent it can result in a "blue baby" and require an operation to tie it off.

Pelvic thrombosis: Thrombosis in the pelvis (see Thrombosis).

Peptic ulcer: a breach of the lining (mucosa) of the digestive tract produced by diges-
tion of the mucosa by pepsin and acid.

Periarthritis: inflammation round a joint, due to infection or injury, causing pain and
restricted movement.

Perinatal asphyxial damage: damage attributable to suffocation producing oxygen
deprivation, in the perinatal period (the period from about three months before
to one month after birth).

Peritoneum: the double serous membrane which lines the cavity of the abdomen.

Peritonitis: inflammation of the peritoneum, or of some part of it.

Pertussis: whooping-cough.

Petit mal epilepsy: a form of epilepsy involving a momentary alteration in consciousness.

Phenytoin: anticonvulsant drug (trade name: Epanutin).

Pia mater: inner layer of the meninges that are the membranous coverings of the brain.
Closely applied to the surface of the brain and the spinal cord.

Pituitary fossa: the bony cavity at the base of the skull where the pituitary gland (which
has an important influence on growth and bodily functions) is situated.

Plantar flexion: flexing the foot, pointing the toes downwards.

-plegia: suffix meaning paralysis.

Plasticity: the modifiability of a substrate, enabling functional change.

Pneumoconiosis: a disease of the lungs; this condition is often manifested by miners
who have been exposed to coal dust.

Pneumohorax: air in the pleural cavity, *e.g.* from puncture of the lung by a fractured
rib—and causing collapse of the lung.

Poly-: prefix meaning much or many.

Porencephaly: cavities in the brain substance due to tissue loss after severe brain
damage.

Post traumatic amnesia: absence of memory for events surrounding the insult. May
occur despite apparently normal levels of arousal.

Post traumatic stress disorder: the development of characteristic symptoms following a psychologically distressing event or situation of an exceptionally threatening or catastrophic nature. The characteristic symptoms include persistent
re-experiencing of the traumatic event; persistent avoidance of stimuli associated
with the trauma and "psychic numbing"; and persistent symptoms of anxiety or
increased arousal.

Pre-eclampsia: a condition that can affect women at an advanced stage of pregnancy,
marked by high blood pressure, swelling of the ankles, and protein in the urine;
can develop into the more serious condition of eclampsia, involving convulsions.

Prefrontal: the most anterior portion of the frontal lobe.

Primacy effect: (in memory) the tendency for initial words in a list to be recalled more
readily than those from the middle or end of the list.

Proactive Interference: the interference of earlier learning with the learning and recall
of new material.

Prolapse: extrusion or protrusion, of a structure.

Pronation: twisting the forearm, the elbow being fixed, to bring the palm of hand
facing downwards (opposite to supination).

Proximal: nearest the centre (opposite to distal).

Psychomotor epilepsy: a form of epileptic seizure in which the individual loses contact
with the environment but appears conscious and performs some routine, repetitive act, or engages in more complex activity.

Psychosocial: areas of psychological and social functioning, which may include family
status, emotional adjustment, interpersonal skills and adjustment employment or
other activity, financial status, and acceptance of disability.

Ptosis: drooping of the eyelid.

Puerperal Fever: infection of the vagina and uterus consequent on childbirth.

Pulmonary: pertaining to the lung.

Quadriplegia: paralysis of all four limbs.

Rabies: an acute virus disease of the central nervous system that can affect all warm-blooded animals; usually transmitted to people by a bite from an infected dog.

Reaction time: the time between the presentation of a stimulus and the occurrence of a response.

Recency effect: (in memory) the tendency for the last few words on a list to be recalled more readily than words elsewhere from the list.

Recognition: the correct association of an item with a category.

Reduction: restoration to a normal position, *e.g.* of a fractured bone or a dislocated joint.

Reflex sympathetic dystrophy: a chronic condition characterised by severe burning pain, pathological changes in bone and skin, excessive sweating, tissue swelling, and extreme sensitivity to touch. The syndrome is a nerve disorder that occurs at the site of an injury (most often to the arms or legs), but it can occur without apparent injury.

Reflux oesophagitis: inflammation of the oesophagus due to frequent regurgitation of acid and peptic juices from the stomach.

Repex: an automatic response to a stimulus.

Rena: pertaining to the kidney.

Retinoplasty of prematurity: see retrolental fibroplasia.

Retrieval: locating and reproducing information from memory.

Retro-: prefix meaning behind or backward.

Retroactive interference: the interference in recall of something earlier learned by something subsequently learned.

Retrobulbar bleed: bleeding which occurs behind the eyeball.

Retrograde amnesia: loss of memory for information acquired prior to the event that causes amnesia.

Retrolental fibroplasia: the abnormal proliferation of fibrous tissue immediately behind the lens of the eye, leading to blindness. It was formerly seen in, newborn premature infants due to overadministration of oxygen.

Reye's syndrome: involves brain damage (encephalopathy) and liver damage of an unknown cause. It is associated with the use of aspirin in children to treat chickenpox or influenza.

Rigidity: increased tone in limb or trunk.

Rocky Mountain Spotted Fever: a disease of rodents and other small animals in the USA caused by the micro-organism Rickettsia rickettsii, transmitted to people by ticks.

Romberg's sign: pathological increase of body sway when the patient stands erect with toes and heels touching and eyes closed; unsteadiness occurs if test positive. A test of balance and proprioception.

Rotational injury: diffuse shearing injury to brain substance magnified by rotatory forces.

Rubella: german measles.

Saggital split osteostomy: a surgical procedure performed on the jaw with the object of bringing forward the lower mandible.

Sclerosis: increased density, *e.g.* of a bone, owing to disease or injury.

Scoliosis: lateral (*i.e.* sideways) curvature of the spine.

Sensory: pertaining to sensation.

Septicaemia: destruction of tissues due to absorption of disease-causing bacteria or their toxins, from the blood stream. Sometimes used to refer simply to blood poisoning.

Sequestrum: a fragment of dead bone.

Short *term memory*: the component of the memory system that has limited capacity and will maintain information for only a brief time.

Shoulder dystocia: difficult delivery arising from the shoulders of the foetus failing to negotiate the inlet of the pelvis.

Sigmoidoscope: a speculum for examining the lower bowel and for assisting in minor operations therein.

Sinus: a track leading from an infected focus, *e.g.* in a bone—to an opening on the surface of the skin.

Slough: tissue, usually skin, dead from infection.

Smallpox: an acute infectious virus disease causing high fever and a rash that scars the skin, generally transmitted by direct contact with an infected person.

Sodium valproate: anticonvulsant drug (trade name: Epilim).

Somatosensory area: regions in the parietal lobes of the brain which register sensory experiences such as heat, cold, pain and touch.

Spasmodic torticollis: a rheumatic seizure of the muscles of the neck in which it is so twisted as to keep the head turned to one side; also known as wryneck.

Spina bifida: a developmental defect in which the newborn baby has part of the spinal cord and its coverings exposed through a gap in the backbone; symptoms can include paralysis of the legs, incontinence and mental retardation from the commonly associated brain defect hydrocephalus.

Spleen: a large ovoid organ on the left side of the body, below and behind the stomach, which forms a major part of the reticuloendothelial system.

Spondylolisthesis: a forward shift of one vertebra upon another, due to a defect of the joints that normally bind them together; may be congenital or develop after injury.

Spondylosis: degenerative changes in the spine.

Status epilepticus: epileptic fits following each other in continuous rapid succession.

Stevens-Johnson syndrome: an illness characterised by a severe widespread rash and mouth ulcers, often caused by an allergic reaction to a drug.

Stupor: unconscious state, but arousable.

Subarachnoid haemorrhage: bleeding into the subarachnoid space surrounding the brain, causing severe headache with stiffness of the neck.

Subclavian vein: part of a major vein of the upper extremities or forelimbs that passes beneath the clavicle and is continuous with the axillary vein.

Subcortical: beneath the cortex.

Subdural haemorrhage: bleeding, usually due to trauma, between the dura mater and the brain.

Sulci: grooves on the surface of the brain separating cerebral gyri or convolutions.

Supination: twisting the forearm, the elbow being flexed, to bring palm of hand facing upwards (opposite to pronation).

Suxamethonium: a muscle relaxant drug.

Sympathetic ophthalmia: an auto-immune disease in which a penetrating injury to one eye produces inflammation in the fellow, non-injured eye, usually associated with loss of uveal tissue or uveal prolapse.

Syndrome: characteristic collection of signs and symptoms.

Synovitis: inflammation of the lining membrane of a joint.

Syphilis: a chronic venereal disease, caused by the bacterium Treponema pallidum, resulting in the formation of lesions throughout the body.

Tachycardia: racing of the heart; increased pulse rate.

Tegretol: anticonvulsant drug.

Temporal lobes: the portions of the brain behind the eyes.

Teratogenic: pertaining to teratogenesis—any substance, agent or process that induces the formation of developmental abnormalities in a foetus.

Test battery: a collection of tests used to appraise individual abilities.

Tetanus: an acute, infectious disease affecting the nervous system, caused by the bacterium Clostridium tetani.

Thalidomide: a drug formerly used as a sedative, which if taken in the first three months of pregnancy could cause foetal abnormalities.

Therapeutia: pertaining to treatment, the application of a remedy.

Thorax, thoracic: the chest, pertaining to the chest.

Thrombosis: clotting (thrombus) in a blood vessel or in the heart.

Tissue: anatomically a complex of similar cells and fibres forming a structure within an organ of the body.

Toxic shock syndrome: a rare type of blood poisoning caused by the common bacteria Staphylococcus aureus, which normally live harmlessly on the skin and in the nose, armpit, groin or vagina of one in every three people. Half the reported cases of toxic shock syndrome are associated with women using tampons; half result from localised infections.

Tracheotomy: operative opening into the trachea (windpipe) to bypass laryngeal or pharyngeal obstruction to the airway.

Traction: method by which fractures are re-aligned by applying linear force at right angles to the displacement of the bone fragments.

Tinnitus: ringing in the ears.

Tone: the tension present in a muscle at rest.

Tubal ligation: the tying off of the fallopian tubes; sterilisation procedure.

Tuberculosis: an infectious disease caused by the bacillus Mycobacterium tuberculosis, characterised by the formation of nodular lesions (tubercles) in the tissues.

Upper respiratory tract infection: infection of the upper respiratory tract (the nose, nasal cavity, larynx, trachea, and some of the sinuses and air cells). Upper respiratory tract infections include the common cold, influenza, laryngitis, pharyngitis, sinusitis, tonsillitis, and croup (in children).

Ureteric damage: damage to the ureter.

Valgus: outward deviation, *e.g.* genu valgum knock-knee (the tibia deviates outwards from the knee).

Varicosity: dilatation of veins.

Varus: inward deviation, *e.g.* genu varum bow-leg (the tibia deviates inwards from the knee).

Vasectomy: sterilisation of the male by division of each vas deferens which connects each testis to the urethra; the operation can be carried out under local anaesthesia and on an out-patient basis.

Vegetative state: a condition after severe brain injury, involving a return of wakefulness accompanied by an apparent total lack of cognitive function and awareness of the environment.

Vena Cava: either of the two main veins, conveying venous (blue) blood from the other veins to the heart.

Ventricles: interconnected cavities in the brain containing CSF, comprising the two lateral ventricles, and the third and fourth ventricles.

Ventricular dilatation: an increase in the size of the lateral ventricles of the brain.

Vertigo: unpleasant sensation of abnormal rotation.

Vestibular: concerned with the inner ear labyrinth and its cerebral connections, particularly in the brainstem.

Visual fields: area perceived by each eye.

Wechsler Adult Intelligent Scale (WAIS): a set of 11 tests designed to assess general intellectual ability in adults. Latest revision published in 1981, known as the WAIS-R.

Wells operation: See *ivalon sponge rectopexy.*

Whiplash injury: injury to cervical structures when the head moves violently in one direction and then bounding back in the reverse direction, as when occupants in a vehicle without head restraints are struck from behind.

White matter: the part of the brain and spinal cord that contains myelinated fibres.

Whooping cough: an acute contagious disease, primarily affecting children, due to infection of the mucous membranes lining the air passages by the bacterium Haemophilus pertussis.

Xanth-: prefix meaning yellow.

INDEX

THOMSON

SWEET & MAXWELL ™

Thank you for purchasing **Medical Negligence**, 3rd edition.

Supplements to your main work

Medical Negligence is supplemented regularly in order to keep your main work up-to-date with ongoing developments.

In order to receive your updating supplements to **Medical Negligence** automatically on publication <u>you need to register</u>. Supplements will be invoiced on publication. You can cancel your request at any time.

How to register

Either complete and return this freepost card, or, if you have purchased your copy of **Medical Negligence** from a bookshop or other supplier, please ask your supplier to ensure that you are registered to receive your supplements.

Yes, please send me updating supplements to **Medical Negligence** on publication, unless countermanded.

Name

Organisation

Address

Postcode

Telephone

Email

S&M account number (if known)

Signed

LEGAL BUSINESS UNIT

SWEET & MAXWELL LTD

FREEPOST LON 12091

LONDON

NW3 4YS

UNITED KINGDOM